Why Do You Need This New Edition?

6 good reasons why you should buy this new Concise Seventh Edition of *The American People*!

1. More concise than ever, the new edition consists of twenty-eight chapters, down from thirty-one in the previous edition. That means your textbook delivers information more efficiently, which enables you to learn more efficiently.

2. This edition is tied more closely to the innovative website, MyHistoryLab, which helps you save time and improve results as you study history. Improved MyHistoryLab icons appear in the textbook, alerting you to important connections between the textbook and MyHistoryLab resources.

3. Each chapter now includes a *Recovering the Past* feature, many of which are completely new. These features demonstrate how historians analyze primary sources such as documents, diaries, artwork, and political cartoons.

4. Several chapters have been extensively revised and restructured to improve the historical narrative, making the presentation more streamlined and chronological, and better linking the discussion to the overarching themes of the text.

5. The Seventh Edition features a stronger international theme, which is woven into the main narrative of the text, emphasizing how American history intersects with the world.

6. To facilitate study and review, a list of key terms now appears at the end of each chapter, and a comprehensive glossary has been added as an appendix to the text.

PEARSON

THE AMERICAN PEOPLE

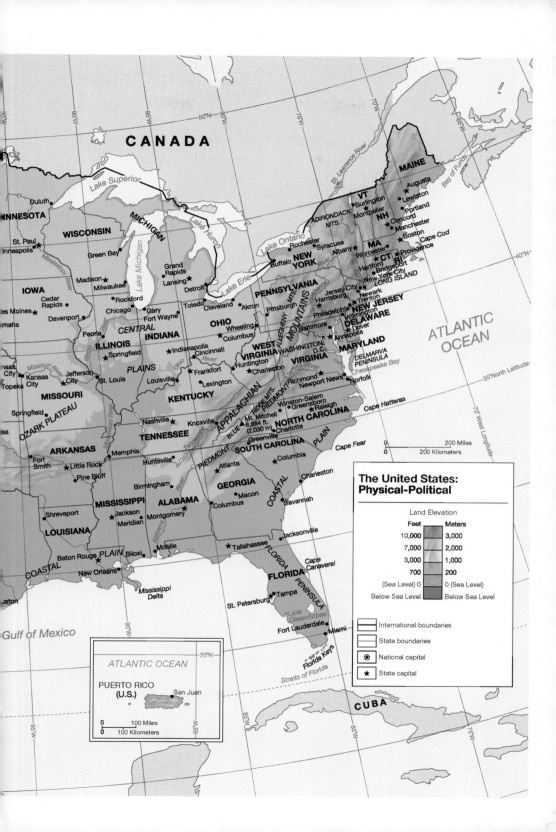

THE AMERICAN PEOPLE

Creating a Nation and a Society

Concise Seventh Edition

Combined Volume

GARY B. NASH
University of California, Los Angeles
GENERAL EDITOR

JULIE ROY JEFFREY
Goucher College
GENERAL EDITOR

John R. Howe
University of Minnesota

Allan M. Winkler
Miami University

Allen F. Davis
Temple University

Charlene Mires
Rutgers University—Camden

Peter J. Frederick
Wabash College

Carla Gardina Pestana
Miami University

Prentice Hall
Boston   Columbus   Indianapolis   New York   San Francisco   Upper Saddle River
Amsterdam   Cape Town   Dubai   London   Madrid   Milan   Munich   Paris   Montréal   Toronto
Delhi   Mexico City   São Paulo   Sydney   Hong Kong   Seoul   Singapore   Taipei   Tokyo

Editorial Director: *Craig Campanella*
Executive Editor: *Ed Parsons*
Editorial Assistant: *Alex Rabinowitz*
Supplements Editor: *Emsal Hasan*
Senior Manufacturing and Operations Manager for Arts & Sciences: *Nick Sklitsis*
Operations Specialist: *Christina Amato*
Director of Marketing: *Brandy Dawson*
Senior Marketing Manager: *Maureen E. Prado Roberts*
Marketing Assistant: *Marissa C. O'Brien*
Senior Managing Editor: *Ann Marie McCarthy*
Senior Project Manager: *Denise Forlow*
Director of Media and Assessment: *Brian Hyland*

Media Project Manager: *Tina Rudowski*
Digital Media Editor: *Andrea Messineo*
Senior Art Director: *Maria Lange*
Cover Design: *Red Kite Project*
Cover Image: *"Mike Evans, a welder, at the rip tracks at Proviso yard of the C & NW RR, Chicago, Ill.", 1943, Jack Delano, photographer, Library of Congress Prints and Photographs Division*
AV Project Manager: *Mirella Signoretto*
Full-Service Production, Interior Design, and Composition: *PreMediaGlobal*
Manager, Visual Research: *Beth Brenzel*
Printer/Binder: *Courier/Kendallville*
Cover Printer: *Lehigh-Phoenix Color/ Hagerstown*

For permission to use copyrighted material, grateful acknowledgment is made to the following copyright holders on p. C-1, which are hereby made part of this copyright page.

Library of Congress Cataloging-in-Publication Data

The American people : creating a nation and a society / Gary B. Nash . . . [et al.]. — Concise 7th ed.
   p. cm.
   Includes index.
   ISBN-13: 978-0-205-80553-2 (concise), ISBN-10: 0-205-80553-1 (concise)
   ISBN-13: 978-0-205-80539-6 (v. 1), ISBN-10: 0-205-80539-6 (v. 1)
   ISBN-13: 978-0-205-80538-9 (v. 2), ISBN-10: 0-205-80538-8 (v. 2)
  1. United States—History—Textbooks.   I. Nash, Gary B.
   E178.1.A49355 2010
   973—dc22

2010035740

10 9 8 7 6 5 4 3 2

Prentice Hall
is an imprint of

Combined Volume	Volume 1
ISBN 10: 0-205-80553-1	ISBN 10: 0-205-80539-6
ISBN 13: 978-0-205-80553-2	ISBN 13: 978-0-205-80539-6
Examination Copy	Volume 2
ISBN 10: 0-205-01453-4	ISBN 10: 0-205-80538-8
ISBN 13: 978-0-205-01453-8	ISBN 13: 978-0-205-80538-9

www.pearsonhighered.com

BRIEF CONTENTS

CONTENTS

FEATURES

RECOVERING *the* PAST

MAPS

PREFACE

The Yoruba people of West Africa have an old saying: "However far the stream flows, it never forgets its source." Why, we wonder, do ancient societies such as the Yoruba find history so important, while modern American students question its relevance? This book aims to end such skepticism about the usefulness of history.

As the twenty-first century progresses, history is of central importance in preparing us to exercise our rights and responsibilities as a free people within an ethnically and culturally diverse society caught up in an interdependent global system. Studying history cannot make good citizens, but without knowledge of history, we cannot understand the choices before us and think wisely about them. Lacking a collective memory of the past, we lapse into a kind of amnesia, unaware of the human condition and the long struggles of men and women everywhere to deal with the problems of their day and to create a better society. Unfurnished with historical knowledge, we deprive ourselves of knowing about the wide range of approaches people have taken to political, economic, and social life, to solving problems, and to surmounting the obstacles in their way.

History has a deeper, even more fundamental importance: the cultivation of the private person whose self-knowledge and self-respect provide the foundation for a life of dignity and fulfillment. Historical memory is the key to self-identity: to seeing one's place in the long stream of time, in the story of humankind.

When we study our own history, we see a rich and extraordinarily complex human story. This country, whose written history began with a convergence of Native Americans, Europeans, and Africans, has always been a nation of diverse peoples—a magnificent mosaic of cultures, religions, and skin shades. This book explores how American society assumed its present shape and developed its present forms of government; how as a nation we have conducted our foreign affairs and managed our economy; how science, technology, religion, and reform have changed our lives; how as individuals and in groups we have lived, worked, loved, married, raised families, voted, argued, protested, and struggled to fulfill our dreams and the noble ideals of the American experiment.

Several ways of making the past understandable distinguish this book from traditional textbooks. The coverage of public events such as presidential elections, diplomatic treaties, and economic legislation is integrated with the private human stories that pervade them. Within a chronological framework, we have woven together our history as a nation, as a people, and as a society. When, for example, national political events are discussed, we analyze their impact on social and economic life at the state and local levels. Wars are described not only as they unfolded on the battlefield and in the salons of diplomats, but also on the home front where they have been history's greatest motor of social change. The interaction of ordinary and extraordinary Americans runs as a theme throughout this book.

Above all, we have tried to show the "humanness" of our history as it is revealed in people's everyday lives. Throughout these pages, we have often used the words of unnoticed Americans to capture the authentic human voices of those who participated in and responded to epic events such as war, slavery, industrialization, and reform movements.

New to This Edition

This Edition represents a major revision and reorganization of the Concise Sixth Edition of *The American People*.

We believe that its reorganization will facilitate student learning and accommodate itself more easily to the usual length of the college semester. The book is now divided into four parts and contains seven chapters in each section. In Volume One, part one covers the period to 1815, while part two carries the narrative through Reconstruction for a total of fourteen chapters. Since many surveys begin with Reconstruction, part three of the Volume Two repeats that chapter and contains seven additional chapters, ending with an analysis of the 1920s. The final part of the book spans the period from the Great Depression and New Deal to the recent past. Volume Two contains fifteen chapters.

We have retained the balance of political, social, and economic history, as well as the emphasis on the interpretive connections and the "humanness" of history—the presentation of history as revealed through the lives of ordinary as well as extraordinary Americans and the interplay of social and political factors. This edition also continues the format and more compact size of the previous concise editions. The four-color design enhances the value of the maps and graphs and gives the book a vibrant appearance. This makes the book accessible, easy to read, and convenient for students to carry to and from class.

Each chapter has a clear structure, beginning with a chapter outline and then a personal story, called "American Stories," recalling the experience of an ordinary or lesser-known American. Chapter 3, for example, is introduced with an account of the life of Anthony Johnson, who came to Virginia as a slave and along with his wife, Mary, managed to gain his freedom. This brief anecdote introduces the overarching themes and major concepts of the chapter, in this case the tri-racial character of American society, the gradual tightening of racial slavery, and the instability of late seventeenth century colonial life. In addition, American Stories launches the chapter by engaging the student with a human account, suggesting that history was shaped by ordinary as well as extraordinary people. Following the personal story—and easily identifiable by its visual separation from the anecdote and the body of the chapter—is a brief chapter overview that links the American story and its themes to the text.

For this reorganization we have added to one of the most popular features of *The American People*: the two-page feature entitled *Recovering the Past*. Every chapter now includes this feature. The "RTPs," as the authors affectionately call them, introduce students to the fascinating variety of evidence—ranging from novels, political cartoons, and diaries, to houses and popular music—that historians have learned to employ in reconstructing the past. Each RTP gives basic information about the source and its use by historians and then raises questions—called "Reflecting on the Past"—for students to consider as they study the example reproduced for their inspection.

In this edition, we have strengthened the international framework so students will think across international boundaries and understand the ways in which our history intersects with the world. Rather than developing a separate discussion of global events, we have woven an international narrative into our analysis of the American past. Many maps underscore the international dimension of the text.

Our extensive changes to the Seventh Edition include:

- *Chapter 1's* opening American Stories recounts the experiences of three women, one from each continent, that would meet in the Atlantic encounter.
- *Chapter 2* contains a new Recovering the Past. Using the famous images of John White from Roanoke colony, the feature discusses how these representations of Native Americans were disseminated and how they shaped European perceptions.
- *Chapter 4* now features a Recovering the Past that explores how household inventories can be used as evidence of changes in American society.
- *Chapter 5*, now entitled "Bursting the Bonds of Empire," considers the period from the French and Indian War until the coming of the American Revolution. Discussion of Tom Paine's *Common Sense* and the first steps toward creating independent political entities are treated in this chapter.
- *Chapter 6* combines material from the last edition's chapters 6 and 7, moving from the Revolutionary War to the ratification of the Federal Constitution. The experience of ordinary people has been foregrounded throughout the chapter.
- *Chapter 7* addresses the history of the early Republic, from Washington's election through the end of the War of 1812 in 1815. Like the new chapter 6, it incorporates the experiences of people into the discussion

of political contests and governmental policies. The Recovering the Past in this chapter covers foreign visitors to the early United States.

- *Chapter 8* now features a Recovering the Past that explores family paintings.
- *Chapter 9* has incorporated a discussion of the Missouri Compromise that occurred in an earlier chapter in the last edition. The chapter also contains a new Recovering the Past, which explores folktales as a way of understanding the slaves' perspective.
- *Chapter 10* now features a Recovering the Past that uses slave narratives to understand some of the dynamics of reform.
- *Chapter 12* now includes a Recovering the Past on Senate speeches during the tense 1850s.
- *Chapter 16* has been reorganized to include both the expansion of industry and the national politics of the late nineteenth century. New to this edition is a Recovering the Past featuring a Congressional hearing on the relations between labor and capitol.
- *Chapter 17*, re-titled "The New Metropolis," provides extensive new coverage of the growth of cities in the late nineteenth century. The chapter opens with a new American Story featuring a journalist's travels to Chicago and cities in the West, and a new Recovering the Past that looks at world's fairs as evidence of trends in urban planning.
- *Chapter 20* places new emphasis on the Great Migration of African Americans from the South during and after World War I.
- *Chapter 21* includes a new Recovering the Past for this edition, focusing on advertising as a source for understanding American culture. Revisions in this chapter provide new information about immigration restriction and clarify the cause-and-effect relationships between modernity and reactions to it.
- *Chapter 22* now includes more material on English economist John Maynard Keynes and his views on the factors causing the Great Depression.
- *Chapter 23* underwent extensive reorganization in its coverage of World War II. It now begins with foreign policy and military affairs, then moves to the home front, and concludes with issues of women and minorities.
- *Chapter 28*, the final chapter in the book, is likewise very different. It takes the two final chapters from the previous edition and boils down the narrative into a crisper and more coherent account of the recent past, rather than simply adding one event after another.

Our aim has been to write a balanced and vivid history of the development of the American nation and its society. We have also tried to provide the support materials necessary to make teaching and learning enjoyable and rewarding. The reader will be the judge of our success. We welcome your comments.

Goals and Themes of the Book

Our primary goal is to provide students with a rich, balanced, and thought-provoking treatment of the American past. By this, we mean a history that treats the lives and experiences of Americans of all national origins and cultural backgrounds, at all class levels of society, and in all regions of the country. It also means a history that seeks connections between the many factors—political, economic, technological, social, religious, intellectual, and biological—that have molded and remolded American society over four centuries. And, finally, it means a history that encourages students to think about how they share an inherited and complex past filled with both notable achievements and thorny problems.

The only history befitting a democratic nation is one that inspires students to initiate a frank and informed dialogue with their past. Historians continually revise their understanding of what happened in the past. Historians reinterpret history because they find new evidence on old topics, add new voices, and are inspired by new sensibilities to ask questions about the past that did not interest earlier historians. Therefore, we hope to promote class discussions and inquiry organized around four recurring themes we see as basic to the American historical experience:

1. **The Peopling of America** What diverse peoples have come together to form this nation? How have their experiences shaped our larger national history? What tensions did they face in America? What contributions have they made?

2. **Democratic Dreams** How has our political system—and how have the principles that sustain it—developed over time? What changes and continuities have helped shape American values? How has the nation coped with the needs and demands of diverse groups in the quest for a better society?

3. **Economic, Religious, and Cultural Change** In what ways have economic, technological, and environmental developments affected the America people? How have religious shifts affected the nation? How have reform movements shaped the character of American life?

4. **America and the World** How have global events and trends shaped the United States? How has America's relationship with other nations and people evolved? What impact has America had on the rest of the world?

In writing a history that revolves around these themes, we have tried to convey two dynamics that operate in all societies. First, as we observe people continuously adjusting to new developments, such as industrialization, urbanization, and internationalism, over which they seemingly have little control, we realize that people are not paralyzed by history but rather are the fundamental creators of it. People retain the ability, individually and collectively, to shape the world in which they live and thus in considerable degree to control their own lives.

Second, we emphasize the connections that always exist among social, political, economic, and cultural events. Just as our individual lives are never neatly parceled into separate spheres of activity, the life of a society is made up of a complicated and often messy mixture of forces, events, and accidental occurrences. In this text, political, economic, technological, and cultural factors are intertwined like strands in a rope as ordinary and extraordinary American people seek to fulfill their dreams.

Acknowledgments

Over the years, as new editions of this text were being developed, many of our colleagues read and critiqued the various drafts of the manuscript. For their thoughtful evaluations and constructive suggestions, the authors wish to express their gratitude to the following reviewers:

Richard H. Abbott, Eastern Michigan University; John Alexander, University of Cincinnati; Kenneth G. Alfers, Mountain View College; Terry Alford, Northern Virginia Community College; Donna Alvah, St. Lawrence University; Gregg Andrews, Southwest Texas State University; Robert Asher, University of Connecticut at Storrs; Patrick Ashwood, Hawkeye Community College; Arthur H. Auten, University of Hartford; Harry Baker, University of Arkansas at Little Rock; L. Diane Barnes, Youngstown State University; Michael Batinski, Southern Illinois University; Gary Bell, Sam Houston State University; Virginia Bellows, Tulsa Junior College; Spencer Bennett, Siena Heights College; Edward Blum, San Diego State University; Pamela Bobo, Tennessee State University; Jackie R. Booker, Western Connecticut State University; Linda J. Borish, Western Michigan University; Steven Boyd, University of Texas San Antonio; James Bradford, Texas A&M University; Thomas A. Britten, Briar Cliff College; Neal Brooks, Essex Community College; Jeffrey P. Brown, New Mexico State University; Sheri Bartlett Browne, Tennessee State University; Dickson D. Bruce, Jr., University of California, Irvine; David Brundage, University of California, Santa Cruz; Steven J. Bucklin, University of South Dakota; Colin Calloway, Dartmouth University; D'Ann Campbell, Indiana University; Joan Cashin, Ohio State University; Jane Censer, George Mason University; Vincent A. Clark, Johnson County Community College; Neil Clough, North Seattle Community College; Stacy A. Cordery, Monmouth College; Matthew Ware Coulter, Collin County Community College; A. Glenn Crothers, Indiana University Southeast; David Culbert, Louisiana State University; Jolane Culhane, Western New Mexico University; Mark T. Dalhouse, Northeast Missouri State University; Amy Darty, University of Central Florida; Bruce Dierenfield, Canisius College; John Dittmer, DePauw University; Gordon Dodds, Portland State University; Richard Donley, Eastern Washington University; Dennis B. Downey, Millersville University; Robert Downtain, Tarrant County Community College; Robert C. Duncan, Western Oklahoma State College; Keith Edgerton, Montana State University at Billings; Trace Etienne-Gray, Southwest Texas State University; Robert Farrar, Spokane Falls Community College; Bernard Friedman, Indiana University–Purdue University at Indianapolis; Kathryn H. Fuller, Virginia Commonwealth University; Timothy Garvin, California State University, Long Beach; Bruce Glasrud, California State University, Hayward; Brian Gordon, St. Louis Community College; Barbara Green, Wright State University; Richard Griswold del Castillo, San Diego State University; Carol Gruber, William Paterson College; Gretchen Grufman, Dominican University; Donald F. Hall, Ivy Tech Community College; Stephen A. Harmon, Pittsburgh State University; Thomas D. Hamm, Earlham College; Colonel William L. Harris, The Citadel Military College; Robert Haws, University of Mississippi; Jerrold Hirsch, Northeast Missouri State University; Frederick Hoxie, University of Illinois; John S. Hughes, University of Texas; Link Hullar, Kingwood College; Carol Sue Humphrey, Oklahoma Baptist University; Donald M. Jacobs, Northeastern University; Delores Janiewski, University of Idaho; David Johnson, Portland State University; Richard Kern, University of Findlay; Charles Killinger, University of Central Florida; Robert J. Kolesar, John Carroll University; Holly Heinsohn Kropp, The Victoria College; Monte Lewis, Cisco Junior College; Xaio-bing Li, University of Central Oklahoma; William Link, University of North Carolina at Greensboro; Patricia M. Lisella, Iona College; Jeff Livingston, California State University, Chico; Ronald Lora, University of Toledo; Paul K. Longmore, San Francisco State University; Rita Loos, Framingham State College; George M. Lubick, Northern Arizona University; Suzanne Marshall, Jacksonville State University; John C. Massman, St. Cloud State University; Vernon Mattson, University of Nevada at Las Vegas; Joanne Maypole, Front Range Community College; Delove Nason McBroome, Humboldt State University; Arthur McCoole, Cuyamaca College; John McCormick, Delaware County Community College; George W. McDaniel, St. Ambrose University; David H. McGee, Central Virginia Community College; Sylvia McGrath, Stephen F. Austin University; James E. McMillan, Denison University; Kenneth Millen-Penn, Fairmont State University; Otis L. Miller, Belleville Area College; Walter Miszczenko, Boise State University; Norma Mitchell, Troy State University; Gerald F. Moran, University of Michigan at Dearborn; William G. Morris, Midland College; Marian Morton, John Carroll University; Ting Ni, St. Mary's University; Roger Nichols, University of Arizona; Elizabeth Neumeyer, Kellogg Community College; Jill M. Nussel, Indiana University-Purdue University Fort Wayne; Paul Palmer, Texas A&M University; Albert Parker, Riverside City College; Judith Parsons, Sul Ross State University; Carla Pestana, Ohio State University; Neva Peters, Tarrant County Community College; James Prickett, Santa Monica Community College; Noel Pugash, University of New Mexico; Juan Gomez-Quiñones, University of California, Los Angeles; George Rable, Anderson College; Joseph P. Reidy, Howard University; Leonard Riforgiato, Pennsylvania State University; Randy Roberts, Purdue University; Mary Robertson, Armstrong State University; David Robson, John Carroll University; Robert G. Rockwell, Mt. San Jacinto College; David E. Ruth, Pennsylvania State University; Judd Sage, Northern Virginia Community College; A. J. Scopino, Jr., Central Connecticut State University; Sylvia Sebesta, San Antonio College; Phil Schaeffer, Olympic College; Herbert Shapiro, University of Cincinnati; David R. Shibley, Santa Monica Community College; Ellen Shockro, Pasadena City College; Nancy Shoemaker, University of Connecticut; Bradley Skelcher, Delaware State University; Kathryn Kish Sklar, State University of New York at

Binghamton; James Smith, Virginia State University; John Snetsinger, California Polytechnic State University at San Luis Obispo; Jo Snider, Southwest Texas State University; Randi Storch, State University of New York at Cortland; Stephen Strausberg, University of Arkansas; Katherine Scott Sturdevant, Pikes Peak Community College; Nan M. Sumner-Mack, Hawaii Community College; Cynthia Taylor, Santa Rosa Junior College; Thomas Tefft, Citrus College; John A. Trickel, Richland College; Irma Valdivia, Rio Hondo College; Donna Van Raaphorst, Cuyahoga Community College; Morris Vogel, Temple University; Michael Wade, Appalachian State University; Jackie Walker, James Madison University; E. Sue Wamsley, University of Akron; Paul B. Weinstein, University of Akron-Wayne College; Joan Welker, Prince George's Community College; Michael Welsh, University of Northern Colorado; Andrew Wiese, San Diego State University; Seth Wigderson, University of Maine at Augusta; Kenneth H. Williams, Alcorn State University; Nelson E. Woodard, California State University, Fullerton; Mitch Yamasaki, Chaminade University; and Charles Zappia, San Diego Mesa College.

Gary B. Nash

Julie Roy Jeffrey

Supplements for Qualified College Adopters	Supplements for Students
PEARSON **myhistòrylab** **MyHistoryLab** (www.myhistorylab.com) **Save Time. Improve Results.** MyHistoryLab is a dynamic website that provides a wealth of resources geared to meet the diverse teaching and learning needs of today's instructors and students. MyHistoryLab's many accessible tools will encourage students to read their text and help them improve their grade in their course.	**PEARSON** **myhistòrylab** **MyHistoryLab** (www.myhistorylab.com) **Save Time. Improve Results.** MyHistoryLab is a dynamic website that provides a wealth of resources geared to meet the diverse teaching and learning needs of today's instructors and students. MyHistoryLab's many accessible tools will encourage you to read your text and help you improve your grade in your course.
Instructor's Resource Manual with Test Bank Available at the Instructor's Resource Center, at **www.pearsonhighered. com/irc**, the *Instructor's Resource Manual with Test Bank* contains chapter outlines, summaries, key points and vital concepts, and information on audio-visual resources that can be used in developing and preparing lecture presentations. The Test Bank includes multiple choice questions and essay questions, and is text specific.	**CourseSmart** www.coursemart.com CourseSmart eTextbooks offer the same content as the printed text in a convenient online format—with highlighting, online search, and printing capabilities. You save 60% over the list price of the traditional book.
PowerPoint Presentation Available at the Instructor's Resource Center, at **www.pearsonhighered.com/irc**, the PowerPoints contain chapter outlines and full-color images of maps and arts. They are text specific and available for download.	**Library of American Biography Series** www. pearsonhighered.com/educator/series/Library-of-American-Biography/10493.page Pearson's renowned series of biographies spotlighting figures who had a significant impact on American history. Included in the series are Edmund Morgan's *The Puritan Dilemma: The Story of John Winthrop*, B. Davis Edmund's *Tecumseh and the Quest for Indian Leadership*, J. William T. Young's, *Eleanor Roosevelt: A Personal and Public Life*, and John R. M. Wilson's *Jackie Robinson and the American Dilemma*.
MyTest Available at **www.pearsonmytest.com**, MyTest is a powerful assessment generation program that helps instructors easily create and print quizzes and exams. Questions and tests can be authored online, allowing instructors ultimate flexibility and the ability to efficiently manage assessments anytime, anywhere! Instructors can easily access existing questions and edit, create, and store using simple drag-and-drop and Word-like controls.	**Penguin Valuepacks** www.pearsonhighered.com/ penguin A variety of Penguin-Putnam texts is available at discounted prices when bundled with *The American People, Concise*, 7/e. Texts include Benjamin Franklin's *Autobiography and Other Writings*, Nathaniel Hawthorne's *The Scarlet Letter*, Thomas Jefferson's *Notes on the State of Virginia*, and George Orwell's *1984*.
Retrieving the American Past Available through the Pearson Custom Library (**www.pearsoncustom.com**, **keyword search | rtap**), the Retrieving the American Past (RTAP) program lets you create a textbook or reader that meets your needs and the needs of your course. RTAP gives you the freedom and flexibility to add chapters from several best-selling Pearson textbooks, in addition to *The American People, Concise*, 7/e, and/or 100 topical reading units written by the History Department of the Ohio State University, all under one cover. Choose the content you want to teach in depth, in the sequence you want, at the price you want your students to pay.	***A Short Guide to Writing About History, 7/e*** Written by Richard Marius, late of Harvard University, and Melvin E. Page, Eastern Tennessee State University, this engaging and practical text helps students get beyond merely compiling dates and facts. Covering both brief essays and the documented resource paper, the text explores the writing and researching processes, identifies different modes of historical writing, including argument, and concludes with guidelines for improving style. **ISBN-10: 0205673708; ISBN-13: 9780205673704**
	Longman American History Atlas This full-color historical atlas designed especially for college students is a valuable reference tool and visual guide to American history. This atlas includes maps covering the scope of American history from the lives of the Native Americans to the 1990s. Produced by a renowned cartographic firm and a team of respected historians, the *Longman American History Atlas* will enhance any American history survey course. **ISBN-10: 0321004868; ISBN-13: 9780321004864**
	Study Card for American History This timeline of major events in American social, political, and cultural history distills course information to the basics, helping you quickly master the fundamentals and prepare for exams. **ISBN-10: 0321292324; ISBN-13: 9780321292322**

MyHistoryLab (www.myhistorylab.com)

Save TIME. Improve Results. MyHistoryLab is a dynamic website that provides a wealth of resources geared to meet the diverse teaching and learning needs of today's instructors and students. MyHistoryLab's many accessible tools will encourage students to read their text and help them improve their grade in their course.

Here are some of the features that will help you and your students save time and improve results:

- Pearson eText—Just like the printed text, students can highlight and add their own notes. Students save time and improve results by having access to their book online.

- Gradebook—Students can follow their own progress and instructors can monitor the work of the entire class. Automated grading of quizzes and assignments helps both instructors and students save time and monitor their results throughout the course.

- History Bookshelf—Students may read, download, or print 100 of the most commonly assigned history works like Homer's *The Iliad* or Machiavelli's *The Prince.*

- MySearchLab—This website provides students access to a number of reliable sources for online research, as well as clear guidance on the research and writing process.

New Read/View/See/Watch/Hear/Study and Review Icons integrated in the text lead to Web-based expansions on topics, allowing instructors and students access to extra information, videos, and simulations. The icons are not exhaustive; many more resources are available than those highlighted in the book, but the icons do draw attention to some of the most high-interest material available at www.myhistorylab.com.

Read the Document

Expands on chapter content, providing students with primary and secondary source material on compelling topics such as *Brown v. Board of Education of Topeka, Kansas* and Engel, Address by a Haymarket Anarchist.

View the Image

Primary and secondary source material, including photographs, fine art, and artifacts, provide students with a visual perspective on history.

See the Map

Atlas and interactive maps, such as The War of 1812 and Utopian Communities before the Civil War, present both a broad overview and a detailed examination of historical developments.

Watch the Video

Author videos highlight topics ranging from Columbus to Lincoln to Obama, engaging students on both historical and contemporary topics. Also included are archival videos, such as footage of Ellis Island immigrants in 1903 and the Kennedy-Nixon debate.

Hear the Audio

Each chapter has an audio file for students to listen to, providing topics and support for a variety of learning styles. Songs such as *Battle Hymn of the Republic* and *The Star Spangled Banner* enrich students' experience of social and cultural history.

Study and Review

Each chapter provides information on practice quizzes, tests, downloadable flashcards, and other study resources available to students online.

ABOUT THE AUTHORS

Gary B. Nash received his Ph.D. from Princeton University. He is currently Director of the National Center for History in the Schools at the University of California, Los Angeles, where he teaches colonial and revolutionary American history. Among the books Nash has authored are *Quakers and Politics: Pennsylvania, 1681–1726* (1968); *Red, White, and Black: The Peoples of Early America* (1974, 1982, 1992, 2000); *The Urban Crucible: Social Change, Political Consciousness, and the Origins of the American Revolution* (1979); *Forging Freedom: The Formation of Philadelphia's Black Community, 1720–1840* (1988); *First City: Philadelphia and the Forging of Historical Memory* (2002); *The Unknown American Revolution: The Unruly Birth of Democracy and the Struggle to Create America* (2005); *Friends of Liberty: Tadeusz Kosciousko, Thomas Jefferson, and Agrippa Hull: A Tale of Three Patriots, Two Revolutionaries, and a Tragic Betrayal of Freedom in the New Nation* (2008); and *Liberty Bell* (2010). A former president of the Organization of American Historians, his scholarship is especially concerned with the role of common people in the making of history. He wrote the original Part One of this book.

Julie Roy Jeffrey earned her Ph.D. in history from Rice University. Since then she has taught at Goucher College. Honored as an outstanding teacher, Jeffrey has been involved in faculty development activities and curriculum evaluation. She was Fulbright Chair in American Studies at the University of Southern Denmark, 1999–2000, and John Adams Chair of American History at the University of Utrecht, The Netherlands, 2006. Jeffrey's major publications include *Education for Children of the Poor* (1978); *Frontier Women: The Trans-Mississippi West, 1840–1880* (1979, 1997); *Converting the West: A Biography of Narcissa Whitman* (1991); *The Great Silent Army of Abolitionism: Ordinary Women in the Antislavery Movement* (1998); and *Abolitionists Remember* (2008). She collaborated with Peter Frederick on *American History Firsthand* (Volumes 1 and 2, 2002, 2007). She is the author of many articles on the lives and perceptions of nineteenth-century women. Her research continues to focus on abolitionism as well as on history and film. She wrote Part Two in collaboration with Peter Frederick.

John R. Howe received his Ph.D. from Yale University. At the University of Minnesota, he has taught the U.S. history survey and courses on the American revolutionary era and the early republic. His major publications include *The Changing Political Thought of John Adams* (1966), *From the Revolution*

Through the Age of Jackson (1973), *The Role of Ideology in the American Revolution* (1977), and *Language and Political Meaning in Revolutionary America* (2003). His present research deals with the social politics of verbal discourse in late eighteenth- and early nineteenth-century Boston. He has received a Woodrow Wilson Graduate Fellowship, a John Simon Guggenheim Fellowship, and a Research Fellowship from the Charles Warren Center for Studies in American History. Howe wrote the original Part Two of this book.

Peter J. Frederick received his Ph.D. in history from the University of California, Berkeley. His career of innovative teaching began at California State University, Hayward, in the 1960s and continued at Wabash College (1970–2004) and Carleton College (1992–1994). He also served as distinguished Professor of American History and Culture at Heritage University on the Yakama Nation reservation in Washington between 2004 and 2006. Recognized nationally as a distinguished teacher and for his many articles and workshops on teaching and learning, Frederick was awarded the Eugene Asher Award for Excellence in Teaching by the AHA in 2000. He has also written several articles on life-writing and a book, *Knights of the Golden Rule: The Intellectual as Christian Social Reformer in the 1890s*. With Julie Jeffrey, he recently published *American History Firsthand*. He coordinated and edited all the Recovering the Past sections and with Julie Roy Jeffrey coauthored the original Parts Three and Four.

Allen F. Davis earned his Ph.D. from the University of Wisconsin. A former president of the American Studies Association, he is a professor emeritus at Temple University and editor of *Conflict and Consensus in American History* (9th ed., 1997). He is the author of *Spearheads for Reform: The Social Settlements and the Progressive Movement* (1967); *American Heroine: The Life and Legend of Jane Addams* (1973); and *Postcards from Vermont: A Social History* (2002). He is coauthor of *Still Philadelphia* (1983); *Philadelphia Stories* (1987); and *One Hundred Years at Hull-House* (1990). Davis wrote the original Part Five of this book.

Allan M. Winkler received his Ph.D. from Yale University. He has taught at Yale and the University of Oregon, and he is now Distinguished Professor of History at Miami University of Ohio. An award-winning teacher, he has also published extensively about the recent past. His books include *The Politics of Propaganda: The Office of War Information, 1942–1945* (1978); *Home Front U.S.A.: America During World War II* (1986, 2000); *Life Under a Cloud: American Anxiety About the Atom* (1993, 1999); *The Cold War: A History in Documents* (2000); *Franklin D. Roosevelt and the Making of Modern America* (2006); and, most recently, *"To Everything There Is a Season" Pete Seeger and the Power of Song* (2009). His research centers on the connections between public policy and popular mood in modern American history. Winkler is responsible for Part Four of this book.

Charlene Mires earned her Ph.D. in history at Temple University. At Rutgers University-Camden, she teaches courses in public history, urban history, and material culture. She is the author of *Independence Hall in American Memory* (2002) and serves as Director of the Mid-Atlantic Regional Center for the Humanities. A former journalist, she was a co-recipient of the Pulitzer Prize for general local news reporting with other staff members of the *Fort Wayne* (Indiana) *News-Sentinel*. She is responsible for revisions to Part Three of *The American People*.

Carla Gardina Pestana received her Ph.D. from the University of California at Los Angeles. She taught at the Ohio State University, where she served as a Lilly Teaching Fellow and launched an innovative on-demand publishing project. Currently, she holds the W. E. Smith Professorship in History at Miami University. Most recently, she published *Protestant Empire: Religion and the Making of the British Atlantic World* (2010). Other publications include *Liberty of Conscience and the Growth of Religious Diversity in Early America* (1986), *Quakers and Baptists in Colonial Massachusetts* (1991), and *The English Atlantic in an Age of Revolution, 1640–1661* (2004). She is also the co-editor, with Sharon V. Salinger, of *Inequality in Early America* (1999). In 2009 she was awarded a Guggenheim Fellowship. She is responsible for revisions to Part One of *The American People*.

1

Ancient America and Africa

American Stories

Three Women's Lives Highlight the Convergence of Three Continents

In what historians call the "early modern period" of world history—roughly the fifteenth to seventeenth century, when peoples from different regions of the world came into close contact with each other—three women played key roles in the convergence and clash of societies from Europe, Africa, and the Americas. Their lives highlight some of this chapter's major themes, which developed in an era when the people of three continents began to encounter each other and the shape of the modern world began to take form.

    Born in 1451, Isabella of Castile was a banner-bearer for *reconquista*—the centuries-long Christian crusade to expel the **Muslim** rulers who had controlled Spain for centuries. When the queen of Castile married Ferdinand, the king of Aragon, in 1469, the union of their kingdoms forged a stronger Christian Spain now prepared to realize a new religious and military vision. Eleven years later, after ending hostilities with Portugal, Isabella and Ferdinand began consolidating their power. By expelling Muslims and Jews, the royal couple pressed to enforce Catholic religious conformity. Isabella's religious zeal also led her to sponsor four voyages of Christopher Columbus as a means of extending Spanish power across the Atlantic. The first was commissioned in 1492, only a few months after what the Spanish considered a "just and holy war" against infidels culminated in the surrender of Moorish Granada, the last stronghold of Islam in Christian Europe. Sympathizing with Isabella's fervent piety and desire to convert the people of distant lands to Christianity, after 1493 Columbus signed his letters "Christopher Columbus, Christ Bearer."

    On the other side of the Atlantic resided an Aztec woman of influence, also called Isabella by the Spanish, who symbolized the mixing of her people with the Spanish. Her real name was Tecuichpotzin, which meant "little royal maiden" in Nahuatl, the Aztec language. The first-born child of the Aztec ruler Moctezuma II and Teotlalco, his wife, she entered the world in 1509—before the Aztecs had seen a

Chapter Outline

The Peoples of America Before Columbus

Africa on the Eve of Contact

Europe on the Eve of Invading the Americas

Conclusion: The Approach of a New Global Age

single Spaniard. But when she was 11, Tecuichpotzin witnessed the arrival of the conquistadors under Cortés. When her father was near death, he asked the conqueror to take custody of his daughter, hoping for an accommodation between the conquering Spanish and the conquered Aztecs. But Tecuichpotzin was reclaimed by her people and soon was married to her father's brother, who became the Aztec ruler in 1520. After he died of smallpox within two months, the last Aztec emperor claimed the young girl as his wife.

But then in 1521, the Spanish siege of Tenochtitlán, the Aztec island capital in Lake Texcoco, overturned the mighty Aztec Empire and soon brought Tecuichpotzin into the life of the victorious Spanish. In 1526, she learned that her husband had been tortured and hanged for plotting an insurrection against Cortés. Still only 19, she entered the household of Cortés, living among his other Indian mistresses. Pregnant with his child, she was married off to a Spanish officer. Another marriage followed, and in all she bore seven children, all descendants of Moctezuma II. All became large landowners and figures of importance. Tecuichpotzin was in this way a pioneer of *mestizaje*—the mixing of races—and thus one of the leading Aztec women who launched the creation of a new society in Mexico.

On the west coast of Africa was another powerful woman. Njinga was born around 1582 and so named because she entered the world with the umbilical cord (her name meant "to twist or turn") wrapped around her neck, which was believed to foretell a haughty character. She assumed the throne of Ndongo (present-day Angola) in 1624, leading a fierce resistance to the Portuguese slave trade and the Portuguese attempts to control Angola. By that time the Portuguese had been active in the region for a century, having converted the Kongolese king Afonso I to Catholicism in the 1530s. Her people were trapped in incessant wars in order to supply slaves to their Portuguese trading partners. Determined to resist the trade, Njinga fought a series of wars. A heroic figure in Angolan history, Queen Njinga's fierce battle cry was, according to legend, heard for miles around.

In opening this book, the stories of Queen Isabella of Castile, Aztec princess Tecuichpotzin, and Angola's Queen Njinga set the scene for the intermingling of Europeans, Africans, and Native Americans. As this historic convergence approached, how did the complex histories of each of these three regions set the stage for the future encounters in the Atlantic world?

In this chapter, we will examine the complexities of West African societies, delve into the societies of some of the peoples of North and South America, and study Western Europeans of the late fifteenth century. In drawing comparisons and contrasts, we better equip ourselves to see three worlds meet as a new global age began.

The Peoples of America Before Columbus

Thousands of years before the European exploratory voyages in the 1490s, the history of humankind in North America began. American history starts with some basic questions: Who were the first inhabitants of the Americas? Where did they come from? How did they live? How had the societies they formed changed over the millennia that preceded European arrival? To what extent can their history be reconstructed?

Migration to the Americas

Almost all the evidence suggesting answers to these questions comes from ancient sites of early life in North America. Archaeologists have unearthed skeletal remains, pots, tools, ornaments, and other objects to set a tentative date for the arrival of humans in America of about 35,000 B.C.E.—about the same time that humans began to settle Japan and Scandinavia.

Paleoanthropologists—scientists who study ancient peoples—generally agree that the first inhabitants of the Americas were nomadic bands from Siberia hunting big-game animals. These sojourners began to migrate across a land bridge connecting northeastern Asia with Alaska. Geologists conclude that this land bridge, perhaps 600 miles wide, existed most recently between 25,000 and 14,000 years ago. Ice-free passage through Canada was possible only briefly at the beginning and end of this period, however. Scholars debate the exact timing, but the main migration occurred between 11,000 and 14,000 years ago, if not earlier. Some new archaeological finds suggest multiple migrations, by both sea and land, from several regions of Asia and even from Europe. Nearly every Native American society has its own story about its origins in the Americas.

Hunters, Farmers, and Environmental Factors

Once on the North American continent, these early wanderers began trekking southward and then eastward, following vegetation and game. Over centuries, they reached the tip of South America. American history has traditionally emphasized the "westward movement" of people, but for thousands of years before Columbus's arrival, the frontier moved southward and eastward. Thus did people from the "Old World" discover the "New World" thousands of years before Columbus.

Archaeologists have excavated ancient sites of early life in the Americas, tentatively reconstructing the dispersion of these first Americans over an immense land mass. As centuries passed and population increased, the earliest inhabitants evolved separate cultures, adjusting to various environments in distinct ways. Europeans who rediscovered the New World

◉ View the Image
Clovis Points
at **www.myhistorylab.com**

thousands of years later would lump together the myriad societies they found. By the late 1400s, the "Indians" of the Americas were enormously diverse in the size and complexity of their societies, the languages they spoke, and their forms of social organization.

Native American history passed through several phases. The Beringian period of initial migration ended about 14,000 years ago. During the Paleo-Indian era, 14,000 to 10,000 years ago, big-game hunters flaked hard stones into spear points and chose "kill sites" where they slew herds of Pleistocene mammals. Overhunting and a shift of climate deprived these huge beasts of their grazing environment, bringing them to the brink of extinction. People were forced to kill new sources of food such as turkeys, ducks, and guinea pigs. During the Archaic era, from about 10,000 to 2,500 years ago, great geological changes brought further adaptations. As the massive Ice Age glaciers slowly retreated, a warming trend turned vast grassland areas from Utah to the highlands of Central America into desert. The Pleistocene mammals were weakened by more arid conditions, but human populations ably adapted as they learned to exploit new sources of food, especially plants.

About 9,000 to 7,000 years ago, a technological breakthrough occurred, probably independently in widely separated parts of the world. As humans learned how to plant, cultivate, and harvest—what historians call the **agricultural revolution**—they gained control over once ungovernable natural forces. Agriculture slowly brought dramatic changes in human societies everywhere.

As Native Americans learned to domesticate plant life, they began the long process of transforming their relationship to the physical world. Dating the advent of agriculture in the Americas is difficult, but archaeologists estimate it at about 5000 B.C.E. People already practiced agriculture in southwestern Asia and in Africa, and it spread to Europe at about the time people in the Tehuacán valley of central Mexico first planted maize and squash. Over the millennia, humans progressed to systematic clearing and planting of fields, and settled village life began to replace nomadic existence. Increases in food supply triggered other major changes. As more ample food fueled population growth, large groups split off to form separate societies. Greater social and political complexity developed. Men cleared the land and hunted; women tended crops. Many societies empowered religious figures, trusting them to ward off hostile forces.

Everywhere in the Americas, regional trading networks formed. Along routes carrying commodities such as salt for food preservation, obsidian rock for projectile points, and copper for jewelry also traveled technology, religious ideas, and agricultural practices. By the end of the Archaic period, about 500 B.C.E., hundreds of independent kin-based groups exploited the resources of their particular area and traded with other groups.

Mesoamerican Empires

Of the large-scale societies developing in the Americas during the millennia prior to contact with Europeans the most impressive were in Mesoamerica—the middle region bridging the great land masses of South and North America. The Valley of Mexico, now dominated by Mexico City, became the center of the largest societies that emerged in the centuries before the Spanish arrived. In less than two centuries, the Aztecs, successor to the earlier Olmec and Toltec civilizations, built a mighty empire rivaling any known in Europe, Asia, or Africa by subjugating smaller tribes. By the time of Columbus's first voyage in 1492, the Aztecs controlled most of central Mexico, an estimated population of 10 to 20 million. Exacting tribute from conquered peoples, the Aztecs built a great capital in Tenochtitlán ("Place of the Prickly Pear Cactus"), a canal-ribbed city island in the great lake of Texcoco. Boasting a population of perhaps 150,000, it was one of the world's greatest cities on the eve of the Columbian voyages. Aztec society was as stratified as any in Europe, and the supreme ruler's authority was as extensive as that of any European or African king. Every Aztec was born into one of four classes: nobility, free commoners, serfs, and slaves.

When they arrived in 1519, Spaniards could hardly believe the grandeur they saw. The immense Aztec capital covered about 10 square miles and boasted some 40 towers. They had found their way to the most

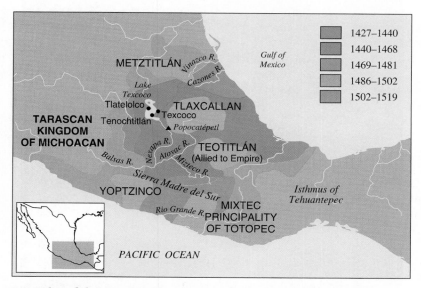

Expansion of the Aztec Empire, 1427–1519 In the century before Europeans breached the Atlantic to find the Americas, the Aztecs' rise to power brought 10 to 20 million people under their sway. How does this compare to empires in other regions of the Atlantic world at this time?

advanced civilization in the Americas, where through skilled hydraulic engineering the Aztecs cultivated *chinampas*, or "floating gardens," around their capital city in which a wide variety of flowers and vegetables grew. The Spaniards were unprepared for encountering such an advanced civilization built by what they considered savage people.

Regional North American Cultures

The regions north of Mesoamerica were never populated by societies of the size and complexity of the Aztecs, though some felt their influence.

⊙ See the Map

Pre-Columbian Societies of the Americas

at **www.myhistorylab.com**

Throughout North America in the last epoch of the **pre-Columbian** (or post-Archaic) era, many distinct societies thrived. In the southwestern region of North America, for example, Hohokam and Anasazi societies (the ancestors of the present-day Hopi and Zuni) had developed a sedentary village life thousands of years before the Spanish arrived there in the 1540s.

By about 1200 C.E., "Pueblo" people, as the Spanish later called them, constructed planned villages composed of large, terraced, multistoried buildings, each with many rooms and often located on defensive sites that would afford the Anasazi protection from their enemies. By the time the Spanish

An Anasazi Village The ruins of Pueblo Bonita in Chaco Canyon, New Mexico, mark the center of Anasazi culture in the twelfth century C.E. What do you notice about the layout of the town, which was in the San Juan River basin and may have contained 1,000 people?

arrived, the indigenous Pueblo people were using irrigation canals, dams, and hillside terracing to water their maize fields. In its agricultural techniques, skill in ceramics, use of woven textiles for clothing, and village life, Pueblo society resembled peasant communities in many parts of Europe and Asia.

Far to the north, on the Pacific coast of the Northwest, native Tlingit, Kwakiutl, Salish, and Haida people lived in villages of several hundred people. They subsisted on salmon and other spawning fish and lived in plank houses displaying elaborately carved red cedar pillars, guarded by gigantic carved totem poles. Reaching this region much later than most other parts of the hemisphere, European explorers were amazed at the architectural and artistic skills of the Northwest indigenous people. These native people defined their place in the cosmos with ceremonial face masks, which often represented animals, birds, and fish—reminders of magical ancestral spirits that inhabited what they understood as the four interconnected zones of the cosmos: the Sky World, the Undersea World, the Mortal World, and the Spirit World.

North and east, Native Americans had lived since at least 9000 B.C.E. From the Great Plains of the midcontinent to the Atlantic tidewater region, four main language groups had emerged: Algonquian, Iroquoian, Muskhogean, and Siouan. As in other tribal societies, agricultural revolution gradually transformed life, as people adopted semifixed settlements and developed trading networks that linked together societies occupying a vast region.

Among the most impressive of these societies were the Mound Builders of the Mississippi and Ohio valleys. When European settlers first crossed the Appalachian Mountains a century and a half after arriving on the continent, they were astounded to find hundreds of ceremonial mounds and gigantic sculptured earthworks. Believing "Indians" to be forest primitives, they reasoned that these must be the remains of some ancient, non-native civilization that had found its way to North America.

Archaeologists now conclude that the Mound Builders were the ancestors of the Creek, Choctaw, and Natchez tribes. Their societies, evolving slowly over the centuries, had developed considerable complexity by the advent of Christianity in Europe. In southern Ohio alone, about 10,000 mounds, used as burial sites, have been pinpointed, and archaeologists have excavated another 1,000 earth-walled enclosures, including one enormous fortification with a circumference of about 3½ miles enclosing 100 acres, or the equivalent of 50 modern city blocks. From the mounded tombs, archaeologists have recovered a great variety of items that have been traced to widely separated parts of the continent, showing that the Mound Builders participated in a vast trading network linking together hundreds of villages.

The mound-building societies of the Ohio valley declined many centuries before Europeans arrived, perhaps attacked by other tribes or damaged by severe climatic changes that undermined agriculture. By about 600 C.E., another mound-building agricultural society arose in the Mississippi valley. Its center, the city of Cahokia, with at least 20,000

View the Image
Reconstructed View of Cahokia
at www.myhistorylab.com

(and possibly as many as 40,000) inhabitants, stood near present-day St. Louis. Great ceremonial plazas, flanked by a temple that rose in four terraces to a height of 100 feet, marked this first metropolis in America. It served as an urban center of a far-flung Mississippi culture that encompassed hundreds of villages from Wisconsin to Louisiana and from Oklahoma to Tennessee. Before the mound-building cultures mysteriously declined, their influence was already transforming the woodland societies along the Atlantic.

In the far north, people lived by the sea and supplemented their diet with maple sugar and a few foodstuffs. Farther south, in what was to become New England, were smaller communities occupying fairly local areas and joined together only by occasional trade. In the mid-Atlantic area were various groups who added limited agriculture to their skill in using natural plants for food, medicine, dyes, and flavoring. Most eastern woodland residents lived in waterside villages. They often migrated seasonally between inland and coastal sites or situated themselves astride two ecological zones. In the Northeast, their birchbark canoes, light enough to be carried by a single man, helped them trade and communicate over immense territories.

The Southeast region housed densely populated, rich and complex cultures that traced their ancestry back at least 8,000 years. Belonging to several language groups, some of them joined in loose confederacies.

Mississippian Culture Shrine Figures Carved from marble seven to eight hundred years ago, these shrine figures, male and female, were found in a tomb in northwestern Georgia. Such artifacts give us insight into the ancient cultures of a region. What do you think can be learned from these Indian carvings, known to us only as part of a South Appalachian Mississippi culture? *(Lynn Johnson/Aurora & Quanta Productions)*

Called "Mississippian" societies by archaeologists, Southeast peoples created elaborate pottery and baskets and conducted long-distance trade. These cultures also were influenced by burial mound techniques, some of which involved earthmoving on a vast scale. A global warming trend helped agriculture flourish in this region, leading in some cases, as with the Natchez, to the development of highly stratified societies. After the "Little Ice Age," which occurred for several centuries from about 1300, the Southeast peoples abandoned their mounded urban centers and devolved into less populous, less stratified, and less centralized societies.

The Iroquois

Far to the north of the declining southeastern mound-building societies, between what would become French and English zones of settlement, five tribes comprised what Europeans later called the League of the Iroquois: the Mohawk, Oneida, Onondaga, Cayuga, and Senecas. The Iroquois Confederation began as a vast extension of the kinship group that characterized the northeastern woodland pattern of family settlement. It embraced perhaps 10,000 people by the sixteenth century.

Read the Document

Iroquois Creation Story

at **www.myhistorylab.com**

Not long before Europeans began coming ashore in eastern North America, the loosely organized and strife-ridden Iroquois created a more cohesive political confederacy. As a result, villages gained stability, population increased, and the Iroquois developed political mechanisms for solving internal problems and presenting a more unified front to outsiders. They would be prepared to launch a coordinated Iroquois policy when dealing with the European newcomers later.

In the palisaded villages of Iroquoia, work, land use, hunting, and even living arrangements in longhouses were communal. While there might be individual farming or hunting efforts, it was understood that the bounty was to be divided among all. One historian has called this "upside-down capitalism," where the goal was not to pile up material possessions but to reach the happy situation where individuals could give what they had to others. This Iroquois societal structure would stand in contrast to that of the arriving Europeans, as would Iroquois gender roles, political structure, and familial customs.

Read the Document

Dekanawida Myth and the Achievement of Iroquois Unity

at **www.myhistorylab.com**

Contrasting Worldviews

Having evolved in complete isolation from each other, European and Indian cultures exhibited widely different values. Colonizing Europeans called themselves "civilized" and typically described the people they met in the Americas as "savage," "heathen," or "barbarian." Lurking behind the confrontation that took place when Europeans and Native Americans met were conflicts over humans' relationship to the environment, the meaning of property, and personal identity.

Europeans and Native Americans conceptualized their relationship to nature in starkly different ways. Regarding the earth as filled with resources for humans to exploit for their own benefit, Europeans separated the secular and sacred parts of life, and they placed their own relationship to the natural environment mostly in the secular sphere. Native Americans, however, did not distinguish between the secular and sacred. For them, every aspect of the natural world was sacred, and all were linked together.

View the **Image**

Conquistadores Torturing
Native Amerindians
at **www.myhistorylab.com**

Europeans believed that land, as a privately held commodity, was a resource to be exploited. They took for granted property lines, inheritance of land, and courts to settle the resulting land disputes. Property was the basis not only of sustenance but also of independence, wealth, status, social structure, political rights, and identity. Native Americans also had concepts of property and boundaries. But they believed that land should be held in common. Communal ownership sharply limited social stratification and increased a sense of sharing in most Native American communities.

There were exceptions. The Aztec and Inca empires in present-day Mexico and Peru were highly developed, populous, and stratified. So, in North America, were a few tribes such as the Natchez. But on the eastern and western coasts of the continent and in the Southwest—the regions of contact in the sixteenth and seventeenth centuries—lived people whose values differed strikingly.

European colonizers found the **matrilineal** organization of many tribal societies contrary to the European male-dominated hierarchy. Family membership among the Iroquois, for example, was determined through the female line. When a son or grandson married, he moved from his female-headed household to one headed by the matriarch of his wife's family.

Native American women's relationship to politics and the exercise of power differed markedly from that of European women. For example, women were almost entirely excluded from European politics. But in Native American villages, again to take the Iroquois example, designated men sat in a circle to deliberate and make decisions, while senior women of the village stood behind them, lobbying and instructing. Village chiefs, who were male, were chosen by the elder women of their clans. If they moved too far from the will of the women who appointed them, these chiefs were removed.

The role of women in the tribal economy reinforced male-female power-sharing. Men hunted, fished, and cleared land, but women controlled the raising and distribution of crops, supplying probably three-quarters of their family's nutritional needs. When the men were away hunting, women directed village life. Europeans perceived such sexual equality as a mark of "savagery."

In economic relations, Europeans and Indians differed in ways that sometimes led to misunderstanding and conflict. Over vast stretches of the continent, Indians had built trading networks, making it easy for them to incorporate new European goods into their cultures. Indian peoples saw trade as a way to preserve reciprocity between individuals and communities, while Europeans viewed it mostly as an economic transaction.

The English noted a final damning defect in Native American religious beliefs. Europeans built their religious life around a single deity, written scriptures, a trained clergy, and churches with structured ceremonies. Native Americans were polytheistic, and their religious leaders used medicinal plants and chants to communicate with the spiritual world. For Europeans, the Indians' beliefs were pagan and devilish. European interpretations of Native culture affected their interactions, as well as the assessments of these societies that they recorded for posterity.

Africa on the Eve of Contact

Half a century before Columbus reached the Americas, a Portuguese sea captain made the first European landing on the west coast of sub-Saharan Africa. If he had been able to travel the length and breadth of the immense continent, he would have encountered a rich variety of African states, peoples, and cultures. During the period of early contact, Africa, like pre-Columbian America, hosted diverse cultures with complex histories.

The Kingdoms of Central and West Africa

The region of West Africa, to which Islam was spreading by the tenth century, embraced widely varied ecological zones—including vast desert, grasslands, and tropical forests. Africa experienced an agricultural revolution similar to that which had occurred elsewhere. Most people tilled the soil, using sophisticated agricultural techniques and livestock management. About 450 B.C.E. the Nok, in present-day Nigeria, developed a method of iron production long before Europeans did so. Over many centuries, more efficient iron implements for cultivating and harvesting increased agricultural productivity, in turn spurring population growth, greater specialization of tasks, and thus greater efficiency and additional technical improvements.

Cultural and political development in West Africa proceeded at varying rates, depending on ecological conditions. Regions blessed by good soil, adequate rainfall, and an abundance of minerals, as in coastal West Africa, engaged in interregional trade. Trade, in turn, brought population growth and cultural development. Where deserts were inhospitable or forests impenetrable, social systems remained small and changed slowly. The Sahara Desert had been depopulated by climate changes that brought higher temperatures and lower rainfall. Sahara people moved southward in search of more productive land, eventually settling in the fertile rain forests of the Niger River basin, where they built some of Africa's greatest empires.

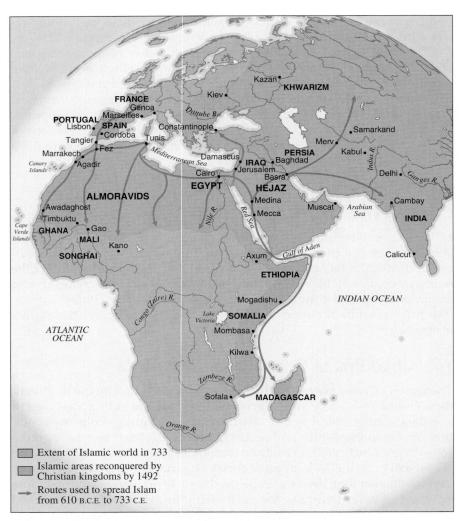

Spread of Islam in Africa, c. 1500 c.e. This map shows the extensive reach of Islam in Africa by 1500. On most of the North African Mediterranean coast and in the powerful Mali and Songhai kingdoms, the Muslim faith predominated. Do you think enslaved Africans who had converted to Islam practiced their faith after arriving in the American colonies? How would they do so on slave plantations?

The Ghana Empire   The first of these empires, Ghana, developed between the fifth and eleventh centuries. It occupied an immense territory between the Sahara and the Gulf of Guinea and stretched from the Atlantic Ocean to the Niger River. Though mostly a land of small villages, Ghana became a major empire noted for its extensive urban settlement, sculpture and metalwork, long-distance commerce, and complex political and military structure. With wealth built primarily on trade rather than military conquest, by the late 900s,

Ghana controlled more than 100,000 square miles of land and hundreds of thousands of people. Gold was so plentiful that a pound of it was traded for a pound of salt.

A thriving caravan trade with Arab peoples, fueled by gold, brought extensive Muslim influence by the eleventh century. Gold made Kumbi-Saleh, Ghana's capital, the busiest and wealthiest marketplace in West Africa. By Europe's Middle Ages, two-thirds of the gold circulating in the Christian Mediterranean region was coming from Ghana. Arab merchants came to live in the empire, often serving in government positions. They brought their number and writing systems as well as their Islamic religion.

Islam had spread rapidly in Arabia after its founder Muhammad began preaching in 610 C.E. Rising to global eminence after several centuries, Islam dominated Egypt by the tenth century, and was spreading southward from Mediterranean North Africa across the Sahara Desert into northern Sudan. There it took hold especially in the trading centers. In time, Islam encompassed much of the Eastern Hemisphere and became the main intermediary for exchanging goods, ideas, and technologies across a huge part of the world. In the Ghanaian empire, rulers adapted Arabic script but clung to their traditional religion. Many Ghanaians, especially in the cities, converted to Islam, however. By 1050, Kumbi-Saleh boasted 12 Muslim mosques.

The Mali Empire   An invasion of North African Muslim warriors beginning in the eleventh century eventually destroyed the kingdom of Ghana. The Islamic kingdom of Mali, dominated by Malinke, or Mandingo, people, rose to replace it. Through effective agricultural production and control of the gold trade, Mali flourished. Under Mansa Musa, a devout Muslim who assumed the throne in 1307, Mali came to control territory three times as great as the kingdom of Ghana. Famed for his 3,500-mile pilgrimage across the Sahara and through Cairo all the way to Mecca in 1324, Mansa Musa's image on maps of the world for centuries thereafter testified to his importance in advertising the treasures of western Africa. Muslim scholars and artisans who returned to Mali with Mansa Musa were instrumental in establishing Timbuktu, at the center of the Mali Empire, as a city of great importance. Noted for its extensive wealth, Timbuktu also had an Islamic university with a distinguished faculty.

The Songhai Empire   After Mansa Musa died in 1332, power in West Africa began to shift to the Songhai, centered on the middle Niger River. A mixture of farmers, traders, fishermen, and warriors, the Songhai declared independence from Mali in 1435 and began a slow ascendancy. By the time Portuguese traders in the late 1400s were establishing firm commercial links with the Kongo, far to the south, the Songhai Empire was at its peak under the rule of Sonni Ali (1464–1492) and Muhammad Ture (1493–1528).

Yet Songhai, too, collapsed, as some tribes that were resentful of Muslim kings began to break away. The most dangerous threat came from Morocco, in North Africa, whose rulers coveted Songhai's sources of salt and gold—two critical commodities in the African trade. Equipped with guns procured in the Middle East, Morocco's ruler conquered Timbuktu and Gao in 1591. The North Africans remained in loose control of western Sudan for more than a century, as the last great trading empire of West Africa faded. These empires slowly devolved into smaller states. Local conflicts made it easier for European slave traders to convince tribal leaders to send out warrior parties to capture people who could be sold as slaves.

The Kingdoms of Kongo and Benin   Farther south along the Atlantic coast and in Central Africa lay the vast kingdom of Kongo. In 1482 the Portuguese ship captain Diego Cao anchored in the mouth of the mighty Kongo River, the first European to encounter these people. Kongo's royal capital, Mbanza, was a trade center for a kingdom of several million people; Mbanza also became a center of trade with the Portuguese, who by the 1490s were sending Catholic missionaries to the court of King Mani-Kongo. Mani-Kongo's son was baptized Afonso I, and under Afonso's rule, in the early 1500s, a flourishing trade in slaves with the Portuguese began.

The kingdom of Benin, which would become important in the English slave trade, formed in about 1000 C.E. west of the Niger Delta. When Europeans

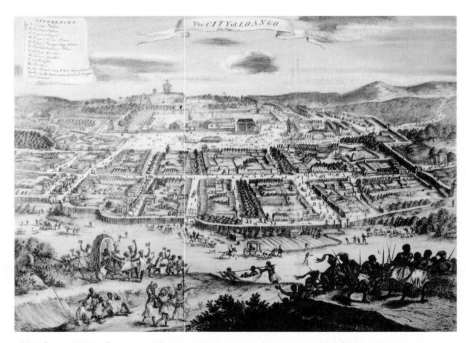

The African City of Loango The city of Loango, at the mouth of the Kongo River on the west coast of Africa, was larger at the time of this drawing in the mid-eighteenth century than all but a few seaports in the British colonies in North America. How does it compare to the Anasazi village ruins shown earlier? *(The Granger Collection, New York)*

reached Benin City hundreds of years later, they found a walled city with broad streets and hundreds of buildings. Thousands of slaves procured in the interior passed through Benin City on their way for exchange with the Portuguese, and later the English, at coastal Calabar, where one of the main slave forts stood.

African Slavery

The idea that slavery was a legitimate social condition in past societies offends modern values, and it is difficult for many Americans to understand why Africans would sell fellow Africans to European traders. But no people identified themselves as Africans four centuries ago; rather, they thought of themselves as Ibos or Mandingos, or Kongolese, or residents of Mali or Songhai. Moreover, slavery was not new for Africans or any other people in the fourteenth century. It had flourished in ancient Rome and Greece, in large parts of eastern Europe, in southwestern Asia, and in the Mediterranean world generally.

Slavery had existed in Africa for centuries. Unlike New World slavery, it had nothing to do with skin color. Like other peoples, Africans understood slavery as a condition of servitude or as a punishment for crimes. Slaveholding was a mark of wealth. African societies for centuries conducted an overland slave trade that carried captured people from West Africa across the vast Sahara Desert to Christian Roman Europe and the Islamic Middle East. The peoples of West Africa held a conception of slavery very different from that which would develop in colonies in the Americas. Slaves in Africa were entitled to certain rights including education, marriage, and parenthood. The enslaved served as soldiers, administrators, sometimes as royal advisors, and even occasionally as royal consorts. The status of slave was not necessarily lifelong and did not automatically pass on to the female slave's children.

The African Ethos

Those who eventually became African Americans made up at least two-thirds of all the immigrants who crossed the ocean to the Western Hemisphere in the three centuries after Europeans began colonizing there. They came from a rich diversity of African peoples and cultures, but most of them shared certain ways of life that differentiated them from Europeans.

As in Europe, the family was the basic unit of social organization. By maintaining intimate family connections, enslaved Africans developed an important defense against the cruelties of slavery. Europeans were patriarchal, putting the father and husband at the center of family life. For Africans, property rights and inheritance were often matrilineal, descending through the mother, a tradition that carried over into slavery. In Africa, identity was defined by family relationships, and individualism was an alien concept.

Africans brought a complex religious heritage to the Americas, which no amount of desolation or physical abuse could wipe out. Widespread across Africa was a belief in a supreme Creator of the cosmos and in a pantheon of lesser deities associated with natural forces that could intervene in human affairs and were therefore elaborately honored. West Africans, like most North American Indians, held that spirit imbued natural objects, and hence they exercised care in these objects' treatment. They also believed in an invisible "other world" inhabited by the souls of the dead that could be known through communications that spiritually gifted persons could interpret.

Africans honored ancestors, whom they believed mediated between the Creator and the living. Relatives held elaborate funeral rites to ensure the proper entrance into the spiritual world. The more ancient an ancestor, the greater that person's power to affect the living. Deep family loyalty and regard for family lineage flowed naturally into this belief system. Spirit possession, in which powerful supernatural forces spoke to men and women through priests and other religious figures, was another widespread practice. While their beliefs differed from those of Europeans, Africans shared some common ground that contributed to a hybrid African Christianity. Extensive contact with the Portuguese had allowed Christianity to graft itself onto African religious beliefs in the kingdom of Kongo and several small kingdoms by the seventeenth century.

Social organization in much of West Africa by the time Europeans arrived was as elaborate as in fifteenth-century Europe. At the top of society stood the king, supported by nobles and priests, usually elderly men. Beneath them were the great mass of people, mostly cultivators of the soil. In urban centers, craftsmen, traders, teachers, and artists lived beneath the ruling families. At the bottom of society toiled slaves.

Europe on the Eve of Invading the Americas

In the ninth century, about the time that the Mound Builders of the Mississippi valley were constructing their urban center at Cahokia and the kingdom of Ghana was rising in West Africa, western Europe was an economic and cultural backwater. The center of political power and economic vitality in the Old World had shifted eastward to Christian Byzantium, which controlled Asia Minor, the Balkans, and parts of Italy. The other dynamic culture of this age, Islam, had spread through the Middle East, spilled across North Africa, and penetrated Spain and West Africa south of the Sahara.

Within a few centuries, an epic revitalization of western Europe occurred, creating the conditions that enabled its leading maritime nations to extend their oceanic frontiers. By the late fifteenth century, a 400-year epoch of militant overseas European expansion was under way. Not until the second half of the twentieth century was this process of Europeanization reversed.

The Rebirth of Europe

The rebirth of western Europe, which began around 1000 C.E., owed much to a revival of long-distance trade from Italian ports on the Mediterranean and to the rediscovery of ancient knowledge that these contacts permitted. The once mighty cities of the Roman Empire had stagnated for centuries, but now Venice, Genoa, and other Italian ports began trading with peoples facing the Adriatic, the Baltic, and the North seas. These new contacts brought wealth and power to the Italian commercial cities, which gradually evolved into merchant-dominated city–states that freed themselves from the rule of feudal lords in control of the surrounding countryside. In the thirteenth and fourteenth centuries, kings began to assert their political authority, unify their realms, and curb the power of the other great feudal lords.

A Procession in Venice Venice's vibrant life along the Grand Canal is apparent in this painting of a procession making its way across the Rialto Bridge toward a balcony. Warehouses and handsome mansions flank the canal. In what ways does this painting reflect the class structure of Venice?

The **Black Death** (bubonic plague) first devastated China in the early 1330s, wiping out nearly one-third of the population, and then moved eastward following trade routes to India and the Middle East. By the time it reached western Europe and North Africa in 1348, famine and malnutrition had reduced the resistance of millions. Over the next quarter century, some 30 million Europeans died, producing economic disruption. Plague defied class distinction, promoting the unification of old realms into early modern states. Ironically, feudal landlords treated their peasant workers better for a time because their labor, tremendously reduced by the plague, became more valuable.

England, although a minor and relatively weak country within western Europe at this time, adopted significant new practices with implications for the future during this era. First, it developed a distinctive political system. In 1215, the English aristocracy curbed the powers of the king when they forced him to accept the **Magna Carta**. A parliament composed of elective and hereditary members eventually gained the

•◦•─[Read the **Document**

Magna Carta, 1215
at **www.myhistorylab.com**

right to pass money bills and therefore act as a check on the Crown. During the sixteenth century, the Crown and Parliament worked together toward a more unified state. Second, England witnessed economic changes of great significance during the sixteenth century. To practice more profitable agriculture, landowners began to "enclose" (consolidate) their estates. Peasant farmers, thrown off their plots, became wage laborers. The formation of this wage-earning class was the crucial first step toward industrial development.

Continental Europe lagged behind England in two respects. First, it was far less affected by the move to "enclose" agricultural land since continental aristocrats regarded the maximization of profit as unworthy of gentlemen. Second, continental rulers were less successful in engaging the interests of their nobles, who never shared governance with their king, as did English aristocrats. In France, a noble faction assassinated Henry III in 1589, and the nobles remained disruptive for nearly another century. In Spain, the final conquest of the Muslims and expulsion of the Jews, both in 1492, strengthened the monarchy's hold, but regional cultures and leaders remained strong. The continental monarchs would thus warmly embrace doctrines of royal absolutism developed in the sixteenth century.

The New Monarchies and the Expansionist Impulse

In the second half of the fifteenth century, ambitious monarchs coming to power in France, England, and Spain sought social and political stability in their kingdoms. They created armies and bureaucracies to quell internal conflict and to raise taxes. In these countries and in Portugal as well, economic revival and the reversal of more than a century of population decline and civil disorder nourished the impulse to expand. This impulse was also fed

Religious Wars Portuguese troops storm Tangiers in Morocco in 1471 as part of the ongoing struggle between Christianity and Islam in the mid-fifteenth century Mediterranean world. Why would such an image be produced?

by **Renaissance** culture. The Renaissance (Rebirth) encouraged innovation, freedom of thought, and an emphasis on human abilities. Beginning in Italy and spreading northward through Europe, the Renaissance peaked in the late fifteenth century.

The exploratory urge had two initial objectives: first, to circumvent overland Muslim traders by finding an eastward oceanic route to Asia; second, to tap the African gold trade at its source, avoiding intermediaries in North Africa. Since 1291, when Marco Polo returned to Venice with tales of

RECOVERING *the* PAST

Archaeological Artifacts

The recovery of the past before extensive written records existed is the domain of archaeology. Virtually our entire knowledge of native societies in North America before the arrival of European colonizers is drawn from the work of archaeologists who have excavated the ancient living sites of the first Americans. Many Native Americans today strongly oppose this rummaging in the ancient ancestral places; they particularly object to the unearthing of burial sites. But the modern search for knowledge about the past goes on.

Archaeological data have allowed us to overcome the stereotypical view of Native Americans as a primitive people whose culture was static for thousands of years before Europeans arrived in North America. This earlier view allowed historians to argue that the tremendous loss of Native American population and land accompanying the initial settlement and westward migration of white Americans was more or less inevitable.

When two cultures, one dynamic and forward-looking and the other static and backward, confronted each other, historians frequently maintained, the more advanced, "civilized" culture almost always prevailed.

Much of the elaborate early history of people in the Americas is unrecoverable. But many fragments of this long human history are being recaptured through archaeological research. Particularly important are studies that reveal how Indian societies were changing during the few centuries immediately preceding the European arrival in the New World. These studies allow us to interpret more accurately the seventeenth-century interaction of Native Americans and Europeans because they provide an understanding of Native American values, social and political organization, material culture, and religion as they existed when the two cultures first met.

One such investigation has been carried out over the last century at the confluence of the Mississippi and Missouri rivers near modern-day East St. Louis, Illinois. Archaeologists have found there the center of a vast Mississippi culture that began about 600 C.E., reached its peak about 300 years before Columbus's voyages, and then declined through a combination of drought, dwindling food supplies, and internal tensions. Cahokia is the name given to the urban center of a civilization that at its height dominated an area as large as New York State. At the center of Cahokia stood one of the largest earth constructions built by ancient humans anywhere on the planet. Its base covering 16 acres, this gigantic earthen temple, containing 22 million cubic feet of hand-moved earth, rises in four terraces to a height of 100 feet, as tall as a modern 10-story office building. The central plaza, like those of the Aztecs and Mayans, was oriented exactly on a north–south axis in order to chart the movement of celestial bodies. The drawing shown on page 21 indicates some of the scores of smaller geometric burial mounds near this major temple. Notice the outlying farms, a sure sign of the settled (as opposed to nomadic) existence of the people who flourished 10 centuries ago in this region. How does this depiction of ancient Cahokia change your image of Native American life before the arrival of Europeans?

By recovering artifacts from Cahokia burial mounds, archaeologists have pieced together a picture, still tentative, of a highly elaborate civilization along the Mississippi bottomlands. Cahokian manufacturers mass-produced salt, knives, and stone hoe blades for both local consumption and

Eastern treasures, Europeans had bartered with the Orient via a long eastward overland route. Eventually, Europe's mariners found they could voyage to Cathay (China) by both eastward and westward water routes.

Prince Henry the Navigator, for whom trade was secondary to the conquest of the Muslim world, led a poor country of only 1 million inhabitants

A reconstructed view of Cahokia, the largest town in North America before European arrival, painted by William R. Iseminger. The millions of cubic feet of earth used to construct the ceremonial and burial mounds must have required the labor of tens of thousands of workers over a long period of time. How does this relate to the population density of their communities? *(William Iseminger, "Reconstruction of Central Cahokia Mounds," c. 1150 c.e. Courtesy of Cahokia Mounds State Historic Site)*

export. Cahokian artisans made sophisticated pottery, ornamental jewelry, metalwork, and tools. They used copper and furs from the Lake Superior region, black obsidian stone from the Rocky Mountains, and seashells from the Gulf of Mexico, demonstrating that the people at Cahokia were involved in long-distance trade. In fact, Cahokia was a crucial crossroads of trade and water travel in the heartland of North America.

Some graves uncovered at Cahokia contain large caches of finely tooled objects, while other burial mounds contain skeletons unaccompanied by any artifacts. From this evidence archaeologists conclude that this was a more stratified society than those encountered by the first settlers along the Atlantic seaboard. Anthropologists believe that some of the mystery still remains concerning the fate and cultural diffusion of these early Americans of the Mississippi culture.

REFLECTING ON THE PAST: What other conclusions about Cahokian culture can you draw from figures such as these? Are there archaeological sites in your area that contain evidence of Native American civilization?

into the unknown. In the 1420s, Henry began dispatching Portuguese mariners to probe the Atlantic "sea of darkness." Important improvements in navigational instruments, mapmaking, and ship design aided his intrepid sailors.

Portuguese captains operated at sea on three ancient **Ptolemaic principles**: that the earth was round, that distances on its surface could be measured by degrees, and that navigators could "fix" their position at sea on a map by measuring the position of the stars. The invention in the 1450s of the quadrant, which allowed a precise measurement of star altitude necessary for determining latitude, represented a leap forward in navigation. A lateen-rigged caravel, adapted from a Moorish ship design, was equally important. Its triangular sails permitted ships to sail into the wind, allowing them to travel southward along the African coast and return northward against prevailing winds. By the 1430s, Prince Henry's captains had traveled to Madeira, the Canary Islands, and the more distant Azores. These islands soon developed as the first European-controlled agricultural plantations.

From islands off the West African coast, Portuguese sea captains pushed farther south, navigating down the west coast of Africa by 1460. While carrying their Christian faith to new lands, they began a profitable trade in ivory, slaves, and especially gold and were poised to capitalize on the connection between Europe and Africa. They did not yet know that a stupendous land mass, to become known as the Americas, lay far across the Atlantic Ocean.

Conclusion
The Approach of a New Global Age

All the forces that have made the world of the past 500 years "modern" began to come into play by the late fifteenth century. As the stories about three important women of this era demonstrate, deep transformations were under way in West Africa, in western Europe, and in the Americas. West African empires had reached new heights, some had been deeply influenced by the Islamic faith, and many had become experienced in transregional trade. Muslim scholars, merchants, and long-distance travelers were becoming the principal mediators in the interregional exchange of goods, ideas, and technical innovations. Meanwhile, the Renaissance, initiated in Italy, worked its way northward, bringing new energy and ambition to a weakened and disease-ridden Europe. Advances in maritime technology also allowed Europeans to make contact with the peoples of West Africa and develop the first slave-based plantation societies in tropical islands off the West African coast. In the Americas, large empires in Mexico and Peru were growing more populous and consolidating their power, while in North America the opposite was occurring—a decay of powerful mound-building societies and a long-range move toward decentralized tribal societies. The scene was set for the great leap of Europeans across the Atlantic, where the convergence between the peoples of Africa, the Americas, and Europe would occur.

TIME*line*

35,000 B.C.E.	First humans cross Bering Land Bridge to reach the Americas
500 B.C.E.– 1000 C.E.	Post-Archaic era in North America
600 C.E.–1100	Rise of mound-building center at Cahokia
632–750	Islamic conquest of North Africa spreads Muslim faith
1000	Kingdom of Benin develops
1000–1500	Kingdoms of Ghana, Mali, Songhai, Kongo in Africa
1200s	Pueblo societies develop village life in southwestern North America
1300s	Rise of Aztec society in Valley of Mexico
1300–1450	Italian Renaissance
1324	Mansa Musa's pilgrimage to Mecca expands Muslim influence in West Africa
1420s	Portuguese sailors explore west coast of Africa
1469	Marriage of Castile's Isabella and Aragon's Ferdinand creates Spain

✓•—Study and Review at **www.myhistorylab.com**

Questions for Review and Reflection

1. To what do you attribute the remarkable diversity of cultures in the Americas in the centuries prior to contact with Europeans? What are the most marked examples of that diversity?

2. What were the major features of western African society and culture prior to contact with European traders?

3. What were the causes and major consequences of the revitalization of western Europe in the period after 1000 C.E.?

4. Africa, Europe, and the Americas at the start of the "early modern period" are often treated as dramatically different in every way, yet commonalities existed. What were the most striking of these common features?

5. Why did western Europeans expand out of their geographical confines to explore, conquer, and colonize the Americas? What factors were *not* present in Africa or the Americas to foster expansion into the Atlantic basin from those areas?

Key Terms

Agricultural Revolution 4

Black Death 18

Magna Carta 18

Matrilineal 10

Muslim 1

Pre-Columbian 6

Prince Henry 20

Ptolemaic principles 21

Renaissance 19

2

Europeans and Africans Reach the Americas

American Stories

Old World Sojourners Mingle with New World Inhabitants

Just 15 years after conquistadors led by Hernán Cortés toppled the Aztec Empire in Mexico, Spanish horsemen, searching for Indians to capture as slaves, happened upon some 600 of them in northwestern Mexico. Traveling with the natives were an African and three Spaniards, all dressed in native garb. The horsemen were "thunderstruck to see me so strangely dressed and in the company of Indians," noted Alvar Núñez Cabeza de Vaca, one of the three Spaniards accompanying the Indians. "They went on staring at me for a long space of time, so astonished that they could neither speak to me nor manage to ask me anything."

De Vaca, his two Spanish companions, and the African had been lost for eight years and were presumed dead. They had been part of the 1528 expedition that intended to plant a permanent Spanish settlement in what the Spanish called La Florida. Establishing themselves near the swamplands of Tampa Bay, the Spanish adventurers encountered starvation, disease, a leadership crisis, and hostile Native Americans. Captured by the Apalachee, who enslaved them, de Vaca and his companions soon adopted Native American ways, adapted to a new environment, and convinced the Indians that they possessed magical healing power. The African, a slave of one of the captured Spaniards and known as Estevan (sometimes called Estanvanico or Esteban), became an accomplished linguist, healer, guide, and negotiator. When they fled their captors, the four fugitives plunged into the wilderness and headed west. Paddling crude boats across the Gulf of Mexico, they shipwrecked on the Texas coast and took refuge among merciful Indians.

Such forays into a rugged and uncharted territory cast the Spanish and African adventurers into unaccustomed roles and sorely tested their ability to survive among the indigenous people, who generally opposed their intrusion into their homelands. De Vaca, a conquistador experienced in enslaving Native Americans, had become a slave himself before their escape westward. Estevan's status as the slave of a Spanish conquistador all but dissolved in the process of becoming a Native American slave and then a refugee from enslavement. In his journal, de Vaca described Estevan as "a black," "a Moor," and "an Arabian." But these were only words describing his skin color (dark), his religion (Islam), and his geographical homeland (Morocco). What mattered in this strange and often hostile land was not Estevan's blackness or even his slave status. What counted, in this time before the idea of racial categories, were his linguistic abilities, his fortitude, and his cleverness as a go-between. Estevan was an Atlantic creole—a man who originated on one land bordering the Atlantic but was remade in the process of the cultural, linguistic, and social braiding that was occurring throughout the sixteenth-century Atlantic world.

For five years, Estevan, his master Andrés Dorantes, de Vaca, and another Spaniard traveled west, covering about 2,500 miles. Often following Native American guides, the four travelers came to be regarded as holy men, possessing the power to heal. Reaching present-day New Mexico, they found Native Americans who, according to de Vaca, described them as "four great doctors, one of them black, the other three white, who gave blessings [and] healed the sick." On one occasion, the natives gave Estevan a sacred gourd rattle. Then, in 1536, the foursome stumbled upon the Spanish expedition in northern Mexico. Three years later, after joining a new Spanish expedition, Estevan blazed a trail for Francisco Vásquez de Coronado's *entrada* of 1540. In what would later be called Arizona, Estevan was selected to forge ahead into Zuñi country with Native American guides in search of the fabled seven gold-filled cities of Cibola. His gift for acquiring native languages and his long experience with peoples of the vast territory north of New Spain made him the logical choice. But on this trip, Estevan met his death at the hands of Zuñi warriors, perhaps angry at his consorting with Zuñi women.

The voyages of Christopher Columbus from 1492 to 1504 brought together people like Estevan and de Vaca from three previously unconnected continents. Together, they made a new world, their lives intersecting, their cultures interacting. Since the Spanish were the first to breach the Atlantic barrier, how did their experience pave the way for later European involvement? Consider the epoch-making voyages of Columbus, the arrival of Spanish conquistadors, their remarkable conquest of vast territories in Mesoamerica and the southern regions of North America, and the momentous effect on plants, animals, and germs as they traveled across the Atlantic. The phenomenal exploits of Hernán Cortés and Francisco Pizarro, and the

Watch the Video
So Why Did Columbus Sail Across the Atlantic Anyway?
at **www.myhistorylab.com**

discovery of immense quantities of silver, attracted the attention of other Europeans—first the French, then the Dutch and English. Latecomers in the race to exploit the treasures of the Americas, the English finally appeared on the scene in the Americas a century after the Columbian voyages.

Breaching the Atlantic

When Ferdinand and Isabella married in 1469 to unite the independent states of Aragon and Castile, they launched Spain into its golden age, beginning with the four voyages of Christopher Columbus to the Americas between 1492 and 1504. Meanwhile, the Portuguese extended their influence along the west coast of Africa and all the way to East Asia. In a short period, contact between peoples in different parts of the world increased markedly, shrinking the globe. Then came the great leap across the Atlantic Ocean, triggering global changes of unimaginable significance. Western Europeans were on the verge of exerting a greater global influence than the people of any single region had ever done before.

The Columbian Voyages

Christopher Columbus, an Italian sailor, led the way for Spain. Celebrated for hundreds of years as a heroic discoverer and now often attacked as a ruthless exploiter of Indian peoples and lands, Columbus is best understood in the context of his times—an age of great brutality and violence. Columbus's urge to explore was nourished by ideas and questions about the geographic limits of his world, and he was inspired by the reconquest of Moorish Spain.

•••—Read the **Document**

From the Journal of Christopher Columbus (1492)

at **www.myhistorylab.com**

Like many sailors, Columbus had listened to sea tales about lands to the west. He may have heard Icelandic sagas about the Norse voyages to Newfoundland five centuries before. Other ideas circulated that the Atlantic Ocean stretched to India and eastern Asia. Could one reach the Indies by sailing west rather than by sailing east around Africa, as the Portuguese were attempting? Columbus hungered to know.

For nearly 10 years, Columbus tried unsuccessfully to secure financial backing and royal sanction in Portugal for exploratory voyages. Many mocked his modest estimates of the distance westward from Europe to Japan. Finally, in 1492, Queen Isabella commissioned him, and he sailed with three tiny ships and a crew of about 90 men. In the fifth week at sea—longer than any European sailors had been out of the sight of land—mutinous rumblings swept through the crews. But on the seventieth day, long after Columbus had calculated he would reach Japan, a lookout sighted land. On October 12, 1492, the sailors clambered ashore on a tiny island in the Bahamas, which Columbus named San Salvador (Holy Savior).

Believing he had reached Asia, Columbus explored the island-speckled Caribbean for 10 weeks. After landing on a heavily populated island that he named Hispaniola (today, Haiti and the Dominican Republic) and on Cuba, he set sail for Spain with cinnamon, coconuts, a bit of gold, and several kidnapped natives. Homeward bound, he documented what he believed were his Asian discoveries: hospitable people, fertile soils, magnificent harbors, and gold-filled rivers. When he landed, his report was quickly distributed throughout Europe.

◉─[View the **Image**
Columbus Landing at Hispaniola—Woodcut
at **www.myhistorylab.com**

Columbus's report brought him financing between 1494 and 1504 for three much larger expeditions. The second voyage, carrying over 1,200 Spanish in 17 ships, initiated the first extended contact between Europeans and Native Americans. In an ominous display of what was to come, Columbus's men captured some 1,600 Taínos on Hispaniola and carried 550 of

◉─[Watch the **Video**
The "Achievement" of Columbus
at **www.myhistorylab.com**

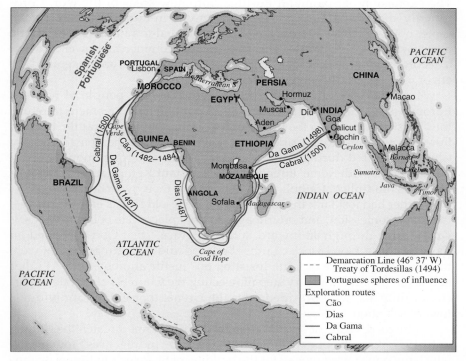

Portuguese Voyages of Exploration The four voyages by Portuguese sea captains between 1482 and 1500 show how those who sailed southward and eastward opened up distant parts of the world to Europeans in the same era when Columbus was sailing westward to the Americas. Did Columbus share his Atlantic Ocean experiences with the Portuguese sea captains who reached the Indian Ocean? If so, how? What did Columbus learn from the Indian Ocean voyagers that helped him in his Atlantic Ocean voyages?

them back to Spain as slaves in 1495. Although his discoveries seemed less significant than the Portuguese exploits, Columbus had led Spain to the threshold of a mighty empire. He died in 1506, to the end believing that he had found the water route to Asia.

While Spain began to project its power westward across the Atlantic, the Portuguese extended their influence in other directions—southward toward West Africa and then eastward to East Asia. In 1497, Vasco da Gama became the first European to sail around the Cape of Africa, allowing the Portuguese to trade in the Indian Ocean; they reached modern Indonesia and south China by 1513. By forcing trade concessions in the islands and coastal states of the East Indies, the Portuguese unlocked the fabulous Asian treasure houses that, since Marco Polo's time, had whetted European appetites. By 1500, they had captured control of the African gold trade monopolized for centuries by North African Muslims.

Religious Conflict During the Era of Reconnaissance

The expansion of Spain and Portugal into new areas of the world profoundly affected patterns of economic activity in Europe. Its commercial center now shifted away from the ports of the Mediterranean to the Atlantic ports facing the New World. This fast-growing commercial power also had a deeply religious aspect since it occurred in the midst of, and magnified, an era of religious conflict and reformation.

Shortly after Columbus's Atlantic voyages, the people of western Europe were torn by religious schisms. A continental movement to return the Christian Church to the purity of early Christianity was at the heart of Europe's religious strife. Criticism of the worldliness of the Roman Catholic Church mounted during the Renaissance. Then a German monk, **Martin Luther**, broke with Rome, initiating the **Protestant Reformation**. As Protestant sects multiplied, Catholics began to reform their own church.

Luther had lost faith in the power of the age-old rituals of the Church— the Mass, confession, and pilgrimages to holy places. He believed that salvation came through an inward faith, or "grace," that God conferred on those he chose. Good works, Luther believed, did not earn grace, but were the external evidence of faith. Insisting on "justification by faith," Luther had taken the revolutionary step of rejecting the Church's elaborate hierarchy of officials, who presided over the rituals that guided individuals toward salvation.

Luther's doctrine of "justification by faith" did not threaten the Church until 1517, when he openly attacked the sale of "indulgences" for sins, by which the pope raised money for the building of St. Peter's in Rome. By purchasing indulgences, individuals had been told, they could reduce their time (or that of a deceased relative) in purgatory. Printing, invented less than 70 years before, allowed the rapid circulation of Luther's protest. The printed word and the ability to read it were to become revolutionary weapons.

Luther's cry for reform soon inspired Germans of all classes. He denounced five of the seven sacraments of the Church, calling for a return to baptism and communion alone. He attacked the upper clergy for luxurious living and urged priests—who were nominally celibate but often involved in sexual relationships—to marry respectably. He railed against the "detestable tyranny of the clergy over the laity" and called for a priesthood of all believers. He urged people to seek faith by reading the Bible, which he translated into German and made widely available for the first time. Most provocatively, he called on the German princes to assume control over religion in their states, directly challenging the authority of Rome.

The basic issue dividing Catholics and Protestants thus centered on the source of religious authority. To Catholics, religious authority resided in the organized Church, headed by the pope. To Protestants, the Bible was the sole authority, and access to God's word or God's grace did not require the mediation of the Church.

Building on Luther's redefinition of Christianity, John Calvin, a Frenchman, brought new intensity and meaning to the Protestant Reformation. By Calvin's doctrine, God had saved a few souls before Creation and damned the rest. Humans could not alter this predestination, but those who were good Christians must struggle to understand and accept God's saving grace if he chose to impart it. Without mediation of ritual or priest but by "straightwalking," the godly were to behave as befitting God's elect, the "saints."

Calvin proposed reformed Christian communities structured around the elect few. To remake the corrupt world and follow God's will, communities of "saints" must control the state. Elected bodies of ministers and dedicated laymen, called presbyteries, were to govern the church, directing the affairs of society so that all, whether saved or damned, would work for God's ends.

Calvinism, a fine-tuned system of self-discipline and social control, was first put into practice in the 1550s in the city–state of Geneva, between France and Switzerland. Here Calvin established his model Christian community. A council of 12 elders drove nonbelievers from the city, disciplined daily life, and stripped the churches of every appeal to the senses. Religious reformers from all over Europe flocked to the community, and Geneva soon became the continental center of Reformed Christianity. Calvin's radical program converted large numbers of people to Protestantism throughout Europe. Like Lutheranism, it recruited most successfully among merchants, landowners, lawyers, nobles, master artisans, and shopkeepers.

The most important monarch to break with Catholicism was Henry VIII of England. When the pope refused him permission to divorce and remarry, Henry declared himself head of the Church of England. Although it retained many Catholic features, the Church of England moved further in a Protestant direction under Henry's son Edward. But when Mary, Henry's older Catholic daughter, became queen, she vowed to reinstate her mother's religion by suppressing Protestantism. Her policy created Protestant martyrs. Many people were relieved when she died in 1558, bringing Henry's younger Protestant daughter, Elizabeth, to the throne. During her long rule, the flinty Elizabeth steered England's church along a middle course between the radicalism of Geneva and the Catholicism of Rome.

Some of the countries most affected by the Reformation—England, Holland, and France—were slow to colonize the New World, so Protestant-ism did not gain as early a foothold in the Americas as Catholicism, which remained the official church of both Spain and Portugal. Thus, Catholicism swept across the Atlantic almost unchallenged during the century after 1492.

The Spanish Conquest of America

From 1492 to 1518, Spanish and Portuguese explorers made Europe aware of the Americas. Only modest attempts at settlement were made, mostly by the Spanish on the Caribbean islands. For three decades after 1518, the Spanish conquered vast tracts of the Americas. In some of the bloodiest chapters in recorded history, the Spanish nearly exterminated the native Caribbean people, toppled and plundered the great Aztec and Inca em-pires in Mexico and Peru, discovered fabulous silver mines, and built an important oceanic trade. These conquests had immense consequences for global history.

Portugal, meanwhile, concentrated mostly on building an eastward oceanic trade to Asia. In 1493, the pope had demarcated Spanish and Portu-guese spheres in the Atlantic. Drawing a north–south line 100 leagues (about 300 miles) west of the Azores, the pope confined Portugal to the east-ern side. One year later, in the **Treaty of Tordesillas**, Portugal obtained Spanish agreement to move the line 270 leagues farther west. A large part of South America, as yet undiscovered by Europeans, bulged east of the new demarcation line and therefore fell within the Portuguese sphere. In time, Portugal would develop this region, Brazil, into one of the most profitable areas of the Americas. These lines were some of the most significant ever drawn on a map.

Caribbean Experiments

Columbus's second Atlantic expedition in 1493 established the first Spanish colony in the New World on the island of Hispaniola (or Santo Domingo). The inhabitants, the Taíno, were the first New World indigenous people to encounter Europeans, and the meeting provided a preview of what would soon occur elsewhere in the Americas: subjugation, disease, and eventually immense ecological alterations to the island.

Columbus arrived with 17 ships and about 1,200 men. He was seeking gold, and when he found none, he visited Cuba and then returned to Spain with six Taíno captives. What he left behind—seeds and cuttings for prop-agating European crops, livestock, and weeds—would prove to be the agents of great ecological change. Once the Spanish saw that the island was teeming with as many as 3 million Taíno, they used military force to subdue them and turn them into a captive labor force. Similar conquests brought the people of Puerto Rico under Spanish control in 1508 and the people of Cuba in 1511. Spanish diseases soon touched off a biological holocaust that killed most of the island's population within a single generation. Some Taíno women married Spanish men and produced the first *mestizo* society in the Americas, but by 1550, the Taíno no longer existed as a distinct people.

Spanish immigration to the Caribbean islands was under way by 1510, closely followed by the importation of enslaved Africans, who were put to work on the first sugar plantations created in the Americas. Over the course of the sixteenth century, about a quarter of a million Spaniards—most of them young, single men—emigrated to the Americas. But the islands dotting the Caribbean did not reach their potential as cash-crop economies until much later. For now, they served as laboratories for larger experiments in Mexico and South America. The Spaniards launched invasions of the Mesoamerican mainland from these islands, while they fortified ports such as San Juan, Puerto Rico, and Havana, Cuba.

The Conquistadors' Onslaught at Tenochtitlán

Within a single generation of Columbus's death in 1506, Spanish conquistadors explored, claimed, and conquered most of South America except Brazil, as well as the southern parts of North America from present-day Florida to California. Led by audacious explorers and soldiers, and usually accompanied by enslaved Africans, they established Spanish authority and Catholicism over an area that dwarfed their homeland in size and population. "We came here," explained one Spanish foot soldier, "to serve God and the king, and also to get rich."

In two bold and bloody strokes, the Spanish overwhelmed the ancient civilizations of the Aztec and Inca. In 1519, Hernando Cortés, along with 550 soldiers, marched over rugged mountains to attack Tenochtitlán (now Mexico City), the capital of Moctezuma II's empire. Following two years of sparring between the Spaniards and the Aztecs, Cortés's assault succeeded and Tenochtitlán fell. The Spanish use of horses and firearms provided an important advantage, as did a murderous smallpox epidemic in 1520 that felled thousands of Aztecs. Cortés also benefited from the support of local peoples willing to rise up against Aztec tyranny. From the Valley of Mexico, the Spanish extended their dominion over the Maya of the Yucatán, Honduras, and Guatemala in the next few decades.

In the second conquest, Francisco Pizarro, marching from Panama through the jungles of Ecuador and into the towering mountains of Peru with a mere 168 men, toppled the Inca Empire. Like the Aztec, the populous Inca lived in a highly organized social system. They had also been weakened by internal violence and smallpox. This debility facilitated Pizarro's success in capturing their capital at Cuzco in 1533, and soon other gold- and silver-rich cities. Further expeditions into Chile, New Granada (Colombia), Argentina, and Bolivia in the 1530s and 1540s brought under Spanish control an empire larger than any in the Western world since the fall of Rome.

By 1550, Spain had overwhelmed the major centers of native population in the Americas. Spanish ships carried gold, silver, dyewoods, and sugar east across the Atlantic and transported African slaves, colonizers, and finished goods west. In a brief half century, Spain had exploited the advances in geographic knowledge and maritime technology of its Portuguese rivals and brought into harsh but profitable contact with each other the people of three continents. For nearly a century after Columbus's voyages, Spain enjoyed almost unchallenged dominion over the fabulous hemisphere newly revealed to Europeans. Greedy buccaneers snapped at the heels of homeward-bound Spanish treasure fleets, but such harassment was only a nuisance. France tried to contest Spanish or Portuguese control by planting small settlements in Brazil and Florida in the mid-sixteenth century, but these were quickly wiped out. England remained island-bound until the 1580s. Until the seventeenth century, only Portugal, which staked out important claims in Brazil in the 1520s, challenged Spanish rule in the Americas.

The Great Dying

Spanish conquest of major areas of the Americas triggered a biological epidemic, setting in motion one of the most dramatic population declines in history. The population of the Americas on the eve of European arrival had grown to an estimated 50 to 70 million. In central Mexico, the highlands of Peru, and certain Caribbean islands, population density exceeded that of most of Europe. Though far fewer than the peoples of the Americas, the European colonizers had one extraordinary advantage: Over the centuries, Europeans had built up immunities to nearly every lethal microbe that infects humans on an epidemic scale. Such biological defenses did not eliminate disease altogether, but they limited their deadly power. Geographic isolation had kept these diseases from the peoples of the Americas. So, too, did their lack of large domesticated animals, which were major disease carriers. The inhabitants of the Americas were defenseless against the infections the Europeans and their animals carried.

⊙ See the **Map**
Native American Population Loss, 1500–1700
at **www.myhistorylab.com**

The results were catastrophic. Hispaniola, with a population of about 1 million when Columbus arrived, had only a few thousand survivors by 1530. Of some 15 million inhabitants in central Mexico before Cortés's arrival, nearly half perished within 15 years. Demographic disaster also struck the populous Inca peoples of the Peruvian Andes, speeding ahead of Pizarro's conquistadors. Smallpox "spread over the people as great destruction," an old man told a Spanish priest in the 1520s. "There was great havoc. Very many died of it. They could not stir, they could not change position, nor lie on one side, nor face down, nor on their backs. And if they stirred, much did they cry out. . . . And very many starved; there was death from hunger, [for] none could take care of [the sick]." Such terrifying sickness convinced many natives that their gods had failed and left them ready to acknowledge the greater power of the Spaniards' God.

In most areas where Europeans intruded in the hemisphere for the next three centuries, the catastrophe repeated itself. Every European and African contributed to the spread of disease that typically eliminated, within a few generations, at least two-thirds of the native population. Moving in the other direction, syphilis and yaws, apparently not known in Europe until about 1500, were afflictions of the Americas that created misery in the Old World as they traveled eastward. The devastation they caused was never remotely on the scale of the smallpox epidemics.

The enslavement and brutal treatment of the native people intensified the lethal effects of European diseases. Having conquered the Inca and Aztec, the Spanish enslaved thousands of native people and assigned them work regimens that weakened them further. Some priests waged lifelong campaigns to reduce the exploitation of the Indians, but they had only limited power to control their colonizing compatriots.

The Columbian Exchange

Much more than lethal microbes crossed the Atlantic with the Spaniards as they conquered the Caribbean islands and then large parts of Central and South America. With them came animal and plant life that altered ecosystems and transformed the landscape. Most significant were the herd animals of the Europeans. Cattle, sheep, goats, and pigs caused the greatest transformation, flourishing as they grazed in the vast grasslands of the Americas safe from the large carnivores that attacked them in the Old World. Cattle reproduced so rapidly that feral livestock swarmed across the countryside, often increasing tenfold in three or four years. In time they ate themselves out of their new environment, stripping away plant life, which soon led to topsoil erosion and eventually to desertification.

View the **Image**

Cattle Arrive in the New World

at **www.myhistorylab.com**

Pigs were even harder on the environment. Reproducing at staggering rates, they tore into the manioc tubers and sweet potatoes in the Greater Antilles where Columbus first introduced eight of them in 1493. They devoured guavas and pineapples, ravaged lizards and baby birds, and stripped the land clean. Similar swine explosions occurred on the mainland of Mexico and Central America, where along with cattle they devastated the grasslands.

While Spaniards intentionally brought the flora and fauna that they prized most to the Americas, unwelcome passengers also accompanied them. Among the most destructive were weeds, their seeds hidden in sacks of fruit and vegetable seed. Once they took root, weeds spread rapidly. Rats and rabbits, which reproduced as fast as pigs, were also pesky stowaways on ships bound across the Atlantic. Rats especially decimated native small animals, spread diseases, and added a new dimension to the human struggle for life.

The "Columbian Exchange" had its eastbound dimension as well, one that mainly advantaged European, African, and eventually Asian recipients. Table foods from the Americas such as pumpkins, pineapples, squash, peanuts, beans, tomatoes, guinea pigs, and turkeys enriched the European diet. Llamas and alpacas produced wool for warmth. Over time, the most important food transfers to Europe proved to be maize and potatoes. The potato, with its fundamental advantage over Old World grains, slowly spread from its point of introduction in northern Spain northward and

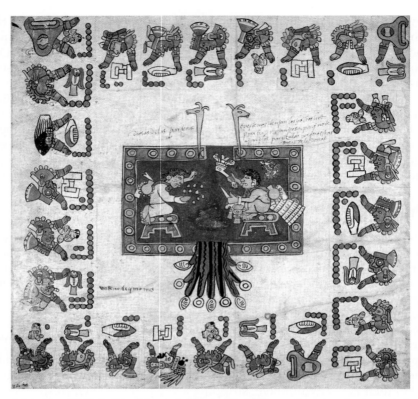

Aztec Corn Myth In this pictograph of an ancient Aztec myth, maize plays a central role; the first female spreads kernels of maize, or corn, while her male counterpart divines the future. Can you decipher the border figures?

eastward through Europe. Farmers on the northern European plain learned slowly that by substituting potatoes for rye—the only grain that would thrive in short and often rainy summers—they could quadruple their yield in calories per acre. The transition to the New World potato allowed for population growth and strengthened Europe's diet. Likewise, maize (to be renamed corn) could be cultivated in mountain valleys in Spain, Greece, and the Balkans, where it became the staple grain. Maize also reached Africa and China as early as the 1550s; the New World sweet potato also made its entry into China.

New World Plants
at **www.myhistorylab.com**

Silver, Sugar, and Their Consequences

The small amount of gold that Columbus brought home raised hopes that this metal, which along with silver formed the standard of wealth in Europe, might be found in abundance in the Americas. Though some gold was gleaned from the Caribbean islands and later from Colombia, Brazil, and

Peru, it would take three centuries before anyone would discover gold in windfall quantities in North America. Silver proved abundant—so plentiful, in fact, that when bonanza strikes were made in Peru (in the area today known as Bolivia) in 1545 and in Mexico in the 1550s, much of Spain's New World enterprise focused on its extraction.

Native people, along with some African slaves, provided the first labor supply for the mines. The Spaniards permitted the highly organized Native American societies to maintain control of their own communities but exacted from them labor drafts for mining. At Potosí, in Bolivia, 58,000 workers labored at elevations of up to 13,000 feet to dig the precious metal from a fabulous "mountain of silver." The town's population reached 120,000 by 1570, making it larger than any in Spain at the time. Thousands of other workers toiled in Mexican mines. By 1660, they had extracted more than 7 million pounds of silver from the Americas, tripling the European supply.

The flood of American bullion into Europe triggered profound changes. It financed further conquests and settlements in Spain's American empire, spurred long-distance trading in East Asian silks and spices, and capitalized agricultural development in the New World of sugar, coffee, cacao, and indigo. The bland diet of Europeans gradually changed as sugar and spices, previously luxury articles, became accessible to ordinary people.

The enormous increase of silver circulating in Europe after the mid-sixteenth century caused a **"price revolution."** The supply of silver increased faster than the demand for goods and services that Europeans could produce, so the value of silver coins declined. Put differently, prices rose, doubling in many parts of Europe between 1550 and 1600 and rising another 50 percent in the next half century. Farmers got more for their produce, and merchants thrived on the increased circulation of goods. The vast majority of the people, however, suffered when wages did not keep up with rising prices.

Overall, the price revolution brought a major redistribution of wealth and increased the number of people in western Europe living at the margins of society. It thus built up the pressure to immigrate to the Americas. At the same time, rising prices stimulated commercial development. Colonial expansion fed commercial expansion at home and intensified changes in modes of production under way in the sixteenth century.

While the Spaniards organized their overseas empire around the extraction of silver from the highlands of Mexico and Peru, the Portuguese staked their American future on sugar production in Brazil. Spanish colonial agriculture supplied the huge mining centers, but the Portuguese, using cultivation techniques developed earlier on their Atlantic islands, produced sugar for export markets.

Whereas Spanish mining operations rested primarily on the backs of the native labor force, Portuguese sugar planters scattered the indigenous people and replaced them with platoons of African slaves. By 1570, this regimented workforce produced nearly 6 million pounds of sugar annually;

by the 1630s, output reached 32 million pounds per year. The sweet "drug food" revolutionized the tastes of millions of Europeans and stimulated the transport of millions of African slaves across the Atlantic.

From Brazil, sugar production jumped to the Caribbean. Here, in the early seventeenth century, England, Holland, and France challenged Spain and Portugal. Once into the West Indies, Spain's enemies stood at the gates of the Hispanic New World empire. Through contraband trading with Spanish settlements, piratical attacks on Spanish treasure fleets, and outright seizure of Spanish-controlled islands, the Dutch, French, and English in the seventeenth century gradually sapped imperial Spain's strength.

Spain's Northern Frontier

Silver-rich Mexico and Peru were the crown jewels of Spain's New World empire, with the islands and coastal fringes of the Caribbean representing lesser, yet valuable, gemstones. Distinctly third in importance to Spain were the northern borderlands of New Spain—the present-day Sun Belt of the United States. Yet the early Spanish influence in Florida, the Gulf region, Texas, New Mexico, Arizona, and California indelibly marked the history of the United States. Spanish control of the southern fringes of North America began in the early 1500s and did not end for three centuries. Far outlasting the Spaniards' rule were the plants and animals they introduced to North America, ranging from sheep, cattle, and horses to weeds that crowded out native plants.

Spanish explorers began charting southeastern North America in the early sixteenth century. These overland journeys of exploration and conquest were called entradas, Spanish for "entrance." First came Juan Ponce de León's expeditions to Florida in 1515 and 1521 and a short-lived settlement in South Carolina in 1526. The Spanish made several attempts to bring the entire Gulf of Mexico region under their control. From 1539 to 1542, Hernán de Soto, a veteran of Pizarro's army, led a military expedition deep into the homelands of the Creek and Choctaw and explored from Tampa Bay to Arkansas. De Soto's expedition could not provide what the Spanish most wanted—gold. Pillaging Indian villages and seizing food supplies, de Soto's men cut a brutal swath, and disease followed in their wake. The Spanish unknowingly paved the way for later English-speaking conquerors by spreading lethal microbes that devastated Indian societies and broke up the great chiefdoms of the Southeast.

In 1559, Spaniards again marched northward from Mexico in an attempt to establish their authority in the lower Gulf region. Everywhere they went, they enslaved Native Americans to carry provisions. In 1565, they sought to secure Florida. Building a fort at St. Augustine, they evicted their French rivals 40 miles to the north. St. Augustine became the center of Spain's northeastern frontier, and Florida remained Spanish for more than two centuries. Especially active there were Franciscan friars, who

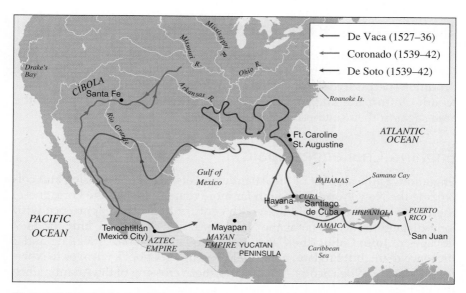

The Spanish *Entradas* in North America The *entradas* of the Spanish conquistadors were motivated by gold fever as well as the desire to claim vast territories across the lower tier of North America for the Spanish. Why were early Spanish activities concentrated in the southern portions of the continent?

worked to gather the local tribes into mission villages and convert them to Catholicism.

The Southwest became a more important region of early Spanish activity in North America. Francisco Vásquez de Coronado explored the region from 1540 to 1542. He never found the fabulous Seven Cities of Cibola, reported by earlier Spanish explorers, but he opened much of Arizona, New Mexico, and Colorado to eventual Spanish control, happened upon the Grand Canyon, and probed as far north as the Great Plains.

Like Florida and the Gulf region, the Southwest had no golden cities. In New Mexico, however, Franciscans tried to harvest souls. A half century after Coronado's exploratory intrusions, Juan de Oñate led 400 Spanish soldiers and 10 Franciscan friars up the Rio Grande in 1598. They found some 60,000 Pueblo gathered in scores of settled towns where they practiced centuries-old agriculture. For the next 80 years, the Franciscans tried to graft Catholicism onto Pueblo culture by building churches on the edges of ancient native villages. As long as the priests were content to overlay Indian culture with a Catholic veneer, they encountered little resistance. The Pueblo gained Spanish military protection from their Apache enemies and valued access to mission livestock and grain during years of drought. So, outwardly, they professed the Christian faith, while secretly adhering to their traditional religion.

England Looks West

By the time England awoke to the promise of the New World, Spain and Portugal were firmly entrenched there. But by the late sixteenth century, the conditions necessary to propel England overseas had ripened. In the late sixteenth century, the English, as well as the Dutch and French, entered the arena against their southern European rivals.

England Challenges Spain

England was the slowest of the Atlantic powers to begin exploring and colonizing the New World. Although far more numerous than the Portuguese, the English before the mid-sixteenth century had little experience with long-distance trade. As far as the New World was concerned, only the 1497 voyages of **John Cabot** (the Genoa-born Giovanni Caboto) gave England a presence there. But England never followed up on Cabot's voyages to Newfoundland and Nova Scotia—the first northern crossing of the Atlantic since the Vikings.

At first, England's interest in the far side of the Atlantic centered primarily on fish. This high-protein food, basic to the European diet, was the gold of the North Atlantic. Early explorers found the waters off Newfoundland and Nova Scotia teeming with fish—not only the ordinary cod but also the delectable salmon. In the 1520s, it was the fishermen of Portugal, Spain, and France, more than those of England, who made annual spring trips to the offshore fisheries. Not until the end of the century would the French and English drive Spanish and Portuguese fishermen from the Newfoundland banks.

Exploratory voyages along the eastern coast of North America hardly interested the English. Between 1524 and 1535, Jacques Cartier and Giovanni da Verrazano sailed for France across the Atlantic. They sought straits so that India-bound ships could sail around the northern land mass (still thought to be an island). The two navigators encountered many Indian peoples, charted the coastline from the St. Lawrence

•••—Read the Document

Jacques Cartier: First Contact with the Indians (1534)

at **www.myhistorylab.com**

River to the Carolinas, and realized that the northern latitudes of North America were suitable for settlement. The French were not yet interested in settlements, so their discoveries had no immediate value.

Changes in the late sixteenth century, however, propelled the English overseas. The rising production of woolen cloth, a mainstay of the English economy, had sent merchants scurrying for new markets after 1550. Their success in establishing trading companies in Russia, Scandinavia, the Middle East, and India vastly widened England's commercial orbit and raised hopes for developing still other spheres. Meanwhile, population growth and rising prices depressed the economic conditions of ordinary people and made them look across the ocean for new opportunities.

The cautious policy of Queen Elizabeth I, who ruled from 1558 to 1603, did not initially include promoting overseas colonies. She favored Protestantism, partly as a vehicle of national independence. Ambitious and talented, she had to contend with Philip II, the fervently Catholic king of Spain. Regarding Elizabeth as a Protestant heretic, Philip plotted incessantly against her. The pope added to Catholic–Protestant tensions in England by excommunicating Elizabeth in 1571 and absolving her Catholic subjects from paying her allegiance—in effect, inciting them to overthrow her.

The smoldering conflict between Catholic Spain and Protestant England broke into flames in 1587. Two decades before, Philip II had sent 20,000 Spanish soldiers into his Netherlands provinces to suppress Protestantism. Then, in 1572, he facilitated the massacre of thousands of French Protestants. By the 1580s, Elizabeth was providing covert aid to the Protestant Dutch revolt against Catholic rule. Philip vowed to crush the rebellion and decided as well to attack England to wipe out this emerging center of Protestant power.

Elizabeth fed the flames of the international Catholic–Protestant conflict in 1585 by sending 6,000 English troops to aid the Dutch Protestants. A year later, Francis Drake, who had been raiding Spanish shipping on the coasts of Mexico and Peru, bombarded Spanish St. Augustine in Florida for two days, looted the city, and touched off an epidemic that the Florida Indians attributed to the "English God that made them die so fast." Two years later, infuriated by English piracy and support of Protestant rebels in the Netherlands, Philip dispatched a **Spanish armada** of 130 ships to conquer Elizabeth's England. For two weeks in the summer of 1588, a sea battle raged off the English coast. A motley collection of smaller English ships, with Drake in the lead, defeated the armada, sinking many of the lumbering Spanish galleons and then retiring as the legendary "Protestant wind" blew the crippled armada into the North Sea.

The Spanish defeat prevented a crushing Catholic victory in Europe and brought a temporary stalemate to the religious wars. It also solidified Protestantism in England and brewed a fierce nationalistic spirit there. Shakespeare's love of "this other Eden, this demi-paradise" summed up popular sentiment; and with Spanish naval power checked, both the English and the Dutch found the seas more open to their maritime and commercial interests.

The Westward Fever

In the last decades of the sixteenth century, the idea of overseas expansion captured the imagination of important elements of English society. Urging them on was clergyman and author **Richard Hakluyt**. In the 1580s and 1590s, he advertised the advantages of colonizing across the Atlantic. For nobles at court, colonies offered new baronies, fiefdoms, and estates. For merchants, the New World promised exotic produce to sell at home and a new outlet for English cloth. For militant Protestant clergy, there awaited a continent of heathen to be saved from devilish savagery and Spanish Catholicism. For the commoner, opportunity meant bounteous land, almost for the taking. Hakluyt's writings trumpeted that the time was ripe for England to break the Iberian monopoly on New World riches.

England first attempted colonizing, however, in Ireland. In the 1560s and 1570s, the English gradually extended control over the island through

RECOVERING *the* PAST

Representations of Native America

Beginning in the late sixteenth century, when Europeans envisioned Native North America, they thought of images produced by an English painter and a Belgian engraver. These depictions of Native life, based on experiences in the failed colony of Roanoke, became iconic representations of Native Americans.

Roanoke, now popularly known as the "Lost Colony," was founded by Elizabethan courtier Sir Walter Raleigh. With the blessings of the Queen, Ralegh sent expeditions and eventually settlers to the North American mainland north of Spanish-held Florida. Among the participants in a 1585 expedition were two men assigned to collect information about the local peoples: Thomas Harriot (1560–1623) and John White (1540s?–1593?). Harriot learned the language, while White produced a series of paintings of the Algonquian peoples of the Carolina region. While Harriot's *A Briefe and True Report of the New Found Land of Virginia, directed to the Investors, Farmers and Wellwishers of the project of Colonizing and Planting There* (1588) stands as an influential early English text on America, White's images far outstrip Harriot's words in importance.

White painted his watercolors after he had returned to England. We do not know the intended recipient of the 75 stunningly beautiful paintings, but White probably produced them for Raleigh himself, Elizabeth I, or another wealthy patron. The originals apparently survived intact until the late eighteenth century, when they were water damaged in a fire. This ordeal washed out White's vibrant colors, and what survives today is only a pale reflection of the originals. Fortunately, others had produced fairly accurate copies over the centuries prior to this mishap, so versions of the images survive.

White's paintings are remarkable for their detail, for the variety of activities they portray, and for the way in which he captured individuals rather than relying on a generic Native person. The village "Secoton" captures many activities, depicting a friendly, busy village scene. White's depiction of Pomeiock Noblewoman and Daughter (see page 45) revels his attention to detail and to individual characteristics. Notice that the girl carries an Elizabethan doll, which is the only sign in all White's images that Europeans were present at the time that he encountered them. Scholars have suggested that the doll was meant to indicate that the girl would grow up to be English in her dress, manner, and even religion.

John White's representations of Native Americans were widely disseminated in his lifetime not in their original form, but in a revised version produced by the engraver Théodore de Bry. The Protestant de Bry had fled his native Liege as a refugee from the religious wars, settling eventually in Frankfurt am Main. In the late 1580s he was in London, and there he reproduced many of White's paintings as copperplate engravings for the second edition of Harriot's book on Roanoke, *A Briefe and True Report of the New Found Land of Virginia* (1590). With this publication, White's vision of Native America first reached a broad audience. Taking artistic liberties, de Bry made alterations that suggested that the Indians were even more like Europeans than White had indicated.

The illustrated reissue of *A Briefe and True Report* attracted great attention. It appeared as the first volume of a series of European travel accounts gathered by de Bry and advertised as *The Grand Voyages to America*. De Bry issued translations in three other European languages, making White's images available across much of western Europe. When John Smith published his *Generall Historie of Virginia, New England, and the Summer Isles* in 1624, the first lengthy eyewitness account of early English settlement in North America, it used many of de Bry's engravings, copied from John White's watercolors. See the illustration from *Generall Historie* reproduced in Chapter 3. Today few illustrated books mentioning the Indians of early North America appear without at least one White/de Bry image.

The depictions of the Algonquian peoples in the *Briefe and True Report* served manifold purposes. On the most basic level, White's visual representations offered evidence that he, Harriot, and others had indeed ventured to America—they supported the truth of the claims Harriot made about having experienced the New World firsthand. Depictions of prosperous and healthy people upheld Harriot's

English viewers of this watercolor of an Indian town on the bank of the Pamlico River (in present-day Beaufort County, North Carolina) might see that though they called them "savages," the Eastern Woodlands natives tilled their maize fields (shown on the right), enjoyed dancing (lower right), and buried their chiefs (see tomb in lower left) in ways familiar to Europeans. At the upper right is a small, elevated watchman's hut.

argument that the land was fertile with a pleasant climate; this evidence, it was hoped, would encourage prospective colonists and investors. The images further suggested that the Native peoples had achieved a level of social and technological organization that would make them open to the sorts of improvements that the English thought they had to offer. Indians who used tools, practiced agriculture, prepared their food rather than consuming it raw, adorned their bodies, and organized their communal life into villages ought to be easily educated in English ways. This vision of the people around Roanoke was in contrast to depictions of the Inuit living far to the north—people whom White may have encountered and drawn on Martin Forbisher's 1577 expedition to Baffin island. The English thought the Inuit displayed fewer marks of an organized society and doubted therefore that they could be brought to accept English civility. White's Natives, especially as revised by de Bry and glossed by Harriot, appeared not only non-threatening but also likely prospects to join in English trade and alliances.

By the time White's watercolors were revised and reproduced throughout Europe, White himself had returned to Roanoke to relieve the colony. He had been appointed governor of a colonial settlement there in 1587, but he proved less able as a leader than as an artist and ethnographer. His tenure as governor was plagued with difficulty, and he returned to England after less than a year to seek help for the struggling settlement. War between England and Spain (culminating in the famous attempted invasion of England by the Spanish Armada in 1588) prevented White from returning to the colony until 1590. When he finally got there, it was to discover the settlement abandoned. Among those missing were White's daughter Elinor and his granddaughter Virginia Dare, first American-born child of English parents. As his paintings introduced Europe to the people of the Carolina region, his own family was either killed or taken in by those very people. Their fate remains unknown.

REFLECTING ON THE PAST Look at the illustration and imagine that you saw it in England as you prepared to cross the Atlantic among a group of colonists. Having never lived outside the small village where you had been born, how do you see the Native Americans? How will you prepare yourself for encounters with them?

brutal military conquest. Ireland became a turbulent frontier for thousands of career-hungry younger sons of gentry families as well as landless commoners. Some leaders of England's initial New World colonization got their training in subjugating Ireland.

The first English attempts at transatlantic settlement were small, feeble, and ill-fated. Whereas the Spanish encountered unheard-of wealth and scored epic victories over ancient and populous civilizations, the English at first met only failure in relatively thinly settled lands. With the Spanish settled in the south, English settlement efforts centered on the temperate middle zone of the central North American coast. England began—unsuccessfully—to mount small settlements, first in Newfoundland in 1583. Others, organized by Walter Raleigh, planted a settlement from 1585 to 1588 at Roanoke Island, off the North Carolina coast. Small and poorly financed, the colony apparently failed to maintain peaceful relations with the local natives. By the time a relief expedition arrived in 1591, the colonists had vanished. A tiny colony in Guiana, off the South American coast, failed in 1604 and 1609. Another group, set down in Maine in 1607, lasted only a year. Although they would flourish in time, even the colonies founded in Virginia in 1607 and in Bermuda in 1612 floundered badly for several decades.

English merchants, sometimes supported by gentry investors, undertook these first tentative efforts, risking capital in the hope of realizing profits similar to those from their other overseas commercial ventures. The Spanish and Portuguese colonizing efforts were sanctioned, capitalized, and coordinated by the Crown. By contrast, English colonies had their queen's blessing, but were private ventures without royal subsidies or naval protection.

English colonization could not succeed until these first merchant adventurers solicited the wealth and support of the prospering middle class. This support grew steadily in the first half of the seventeenth century. Even then investors were drawn far more to the quick profits promised in West Indian tobacco production than to the uncertainties of mixed farming, lumbering, and fishing on the North American mainland. In the 1620s and 1630s, most of the English capital invested overseas went into establishing tobacco colonies in tiny Caribbean islands.

•••┤Read the Document

Thomas Hariot, "On Tobacco"
at **www.myhistorylab.com**

Apart from considerable financing, the vital element in launching a colony was suitable colonists. The changing agricultural system, combined with population growth and the unrelenting increase in prices caused by the influx of silver, produced a surplus of unskilled labor, squeezed many small producers, and spread poverty and crime. Pushed in response to these conditions, about 80,000 streamed out of England between 1600 and 1640, at the same time that dreams of opportunity and adventure pulled them westward. In the next 20 years, another 80,000 departed.

Beginning in 1618, the renewed European religious wars between Protestants and Catholics devastated the continental market for English woolen cloth, bringing more unemployment. Probably half the households in England lived on the edge of poverty. Religious persecution and political considerations intensified the pressure to emigrate from England in the early seventeenth century. For the first time in their history, large numbers of English people were abandoning their island homeland. The largest number went to the West Indies, about one-third migrated to the North American mainland, and fewer went to the plantations in northern Ireland.

Anticipating North America

The early English settlers in North America were far from uninformed about the indigenous people of the New World. Beginning with Columbus's first descriptions, published in several European cities in 1493 and 1494, reports and promotional accounts circulated among the participants in early voyages of discovery, trade, and settlement. This literature became the basis for anticipating the world that had been discovered beyond the setting sun.

Colonists who read or listened to these accounts got a dual image of the native people. Some accounts depicted Indians as a gentle people who eagerly received Europeans. Verrazano, the first European to touch the eastern edge of North America, wrote optimistically about the native people in 1524. The natives, he related, "came toward us joyfully uttering loud cries of wonderment, and showing us the safest place to beach the boat."

This positive image of the Native Americans reflected both the friendly reception that Europeans often actually received and the European vision of the New World as an earthly paradise where war-torn, impoverished, and persecuted people could build a new life. The strong desire to trade with the native people also encouraged a favorable view because only a friendly Indian could become a suitable partner in commercial exchange.

Early North American travel literature also portrayed a counterimage of a savage, hostile Indian. As early as 1502, Sebastian Cabot had paraded in England three Eskimos he had kidnapped on an Arctic voyage, describing them as flesh-eating savages and "brute

View the Image
How the Savages Roast Their Enemies (1575)
at **www.myhistorylab.com**

beasts." Many other accounts portrayed the New World natives as "half men," who lived, as Amerigo Vespucci put it, without "law, religion, rulers, immortality of the soul, and private property."

The English had another reason for believing that all would not be peace and friendship when they came ashore. For years they had read accounts of the Spanish experience in the Caribbean, Mexico, and Peru—and the story was not pretty. Many books described the wholesale violence that occurred when Spaniard met Mayan, Aztec, or Inca. Accounts of Spanish cruelty, even genocide, were useful to Protestant pamphleteers, who labeled the Catholic Spaniards "hell-hounds and wolves." Immigrants embarking for North America wondered whether similar violent confrontations awaited them.

For Englishmen, rooted in a tradition of private property ownership, the fact that Indians possessed the land necessary for settlement presented moral, legal, and practical problems. In the 1580s, George Peckham, an early promoter of colonization, admitted that the English doubted their right to take the land of others. English right to American soil could be justified by denying the legitimacy of Native American possession of it.

Manhattan before colonists first arrived This image shows Manhattan as it would have appeared before the first colonists arrived, when it was home to the Lenape people. What do you think would have been the first aspect of this landscape that the newly-arrived Europeans (who were Dutch) would have altered?

In English law, possession of land was ensured by "improving" it—fencing, cultivating according to European agricultural practices. Because Native Americans did not fence and till land, their land was defined as waste land, free for the taking. Colonial charters limited English expansion to land not already directly occupied by another "Christian prince." This policy dismissed both Spanish claims to lands they had not actually settled and Indian claims to land they did not use in an "appropriate manner."

Defining the Native Americans as incapable of owning land unless they used it in a European fashion did not give the English arriving in the Americas the power to dispossess the Indians of their soil. It did arm them with a justification for doing so when their numbers became sufficient. Few settlers arriving in North America doubted that their technological superiority would allow them to overwhelm the indigenous people.

African Bondage

For almost four centuries after Columbus's voyages, European colonizers, in the largest forced migration in history, transported Africans from their homelands and used their labor to produce wealth. Estimates vary widely,

Pomeiock Noblewoman and Daughter John White, governor of the second expedition to Virginia in 1587, rendered the first pictorial records of native life in the Americas. This watercolor of a tattooed noblewoman of Pomeiock shows her right arm resting in a chain of pearls or copper beads. Her young daughter holds a prized English doll in an Elizabethan dress. If you had been an early English viewer of this image, what would have struck you most forcibly about it?

but at least 9.6 million Africans were brought to the Americas, and millions more perished on the long, terrible journey.

Once the transatlantic African slave trade began, locales for producing desired commodities such as sugar, coffee, rice, and tobacco moved from the Old World to the Americas. As the first transoceanic European colonial empires were established, Europe's orientation shifted from the Mediterranean Sea to the Atlantic Ocean. African forced labor was an essential part of the immense Atlantic-basin system of trade and the success of the overseas colonies of European nations.

While the economic importance of enslaved Africans can hardly be overstated, it is equally important to understand the cultural interchange that occurred. From 1519 to the early nineteenth century, African newcomers probably outnumbered Europeans two or three to one. As a result, African slavery became the context in which European life would evolve in many parts of the Americas. At the same time, the slave trade etched lines of communication for the movement of crops, agricultural techniques, diseases, and medical knowledge among Africa, Europe, and the Americas.

North America remained a fringe area for slave traders until the early eighteenth century. Yet those slaves who came to the American colonies, about 10,000 in the seventeenth century and 350,000 in the eighteenth century, profoundly affected North American society. In a prolonged period of labor scarcity, they were indispensable to colonial economic development. Meanwhile, their African customs mixed continuously with those of their European masters. Moreover, the racial relations that grew out of slavery so deeply marked society that race has continued to be one of this nation's most difficult problems.

The Slave Trade

The African slave trade began as an attempt to fill a labor shortage in the Mediterranean world. As early as the eighth century, Arab and Moorish traders had driven slaves across Saharan caravan trails to Mediterranean ports.

•••⎡Read the Document

Alexander Falconbridge,
The African Slave Trade (1788)
at **www.myhistorylab.com**

Seven centuries later, Portuguese merchants became the first Europeans to trade these slaves. Portuguese ship captains exploring the west coast of Africa tapped into a slave-trading network that had operated for many generations.

More than anything else, sugar transformed the African slave trade. By the sixteenth century, the center of production was Portugal's Atlantic island of Madeira, the first European colony organized around slave labor. From it, sugar cultivation spread to Portuguese Brazil and Spanish Santo Domingo. By the seventeenth century, with Europeans developing a taste for sugar almost as insatiable as their craving for tobacco, they vied fiercely for Caribbean islands and West African coastal trading forts. African kingdoms, eager for European trade goods, fought each other to supply the "black gold" to white ship captains. Some Africans became slaves as punishment for crimes, but far more were war captives. This trend increased as the European demand for slaves led African rulers highly desirous of a part in the trade to wage wars to acquire additional slaves to trade.

European nations competed for West African trading rights. In the seventeenth century, when about 1 million Africans were brought to the New World, the Dutch replaced the Portuguese as the major supplier. Not until the 1690s, when they began their century-long rise to maritime greatness, did the English challenge the Dutch. By 1740, the British were the foremost European slave traders.

In the eighteenth century, European traders carried at least 6 million Africans to the Americas. By then an Englishman called slavery the "strength and the sinews of this western world."

The slave trade's horrors were almost unimaginable. The suffering began in the African interior, as slaves were kidnapped and marched to the coast. En route, many attempted suicide or died from exhaustion or hunger. Upon arrival, slaves were confined in fortified enclosures on the beach and inspected for sale to the captain of a waiting slave ship. European traders often branded the African slaves. The next trauma came with the ferrying of slaves in large canoes to the ships anchored in the harbor. "The Negroes

◉⎡Watch the Video

The Slave Trade
at **www.myhistorylab.com**

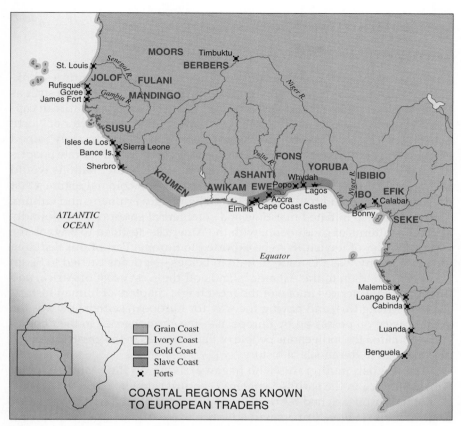

West African Slaving Forts Europeans fought lustily for control of slaving forts on the West African coast, and many forts changed hands several times during the long period of the Atlantic slave trade. Why do you think that European trading activity focused on coastal West Africa? Why not trade in the interior or in other regions of the continent?

are so loath to leave their own country," wrote one Englishman, "that they have often leaped out of the canoes, boat and ship, into the sea, and kept under the water till they were drowned."

•●•—Read the **Document**
Olaudah Equiano, The Middle Passage (1788)
at **www.myhistorylab.com**

Conditions aboard the slave ships were miserable, even though the traders' goal was to deliver alive as many slaves as possible. Manacled slaves below decks were crowded together like corpses in coffins. Many writers who experienced the slave ship remarked on "the loathsomeness of the stench." Slavers brutally flogged the many people who tried to kill themselves by starvation; they also applied hot coals to their lips. If this did not suffice, they force-fed them with a mouth wrench.

The Atlantic passage usually took four to eight weeks, and one of every seven captives died en route. Many others arrived deranged or dying. In all, the relocation of any African may have averaged about six months from the time of capture to the time of arrival at the plantation of a colonial buyer. Ahead lay endless bondage.

Conclusion

Converging Worlds

The Iberian voyages of the late fifteenth and early sixteenth centuries, linking Europe and Africa with the Americas, brought together people such as the Spanish conquistador Alvar Núñez Cabeza de Vaca, the Moroccan captive Estevan, and chiefs of Creek villages in the southeastern sector of North America. Here were the beginnings of networks that ultimately joined every region of the globe and linked the destinies of widely disparate peoples living on many parts of the immense Atlantic basin. Other nations would follow Spain, but it was the Spanish who first erected colonial regimes that drew upon homeland traditions of law, religion, government, and culture. The Spanish also initiated maritime and commercial enterprises profoundly affecting patterns of production, with the Americas destined to become the great producer of foodstuffs to be exported to Europe. Part of this fledgling global economy was the trade in human beings—Africans carried to Spain and Portugal, then to the Atlantic islands off the west coast of Africa, and finally to the Americas in one of the most tragic chapters of human history. Accompanying this, and paving the way for European settlement, was the greatest weapon possessed by Europeans—the germs carried in their bodies that decimated the indigenous people of the Americas in the greatest biological holocaust in the annals of history.

The English immigrants who began arriving on the eastern edge of North America in the early seventeenth century came late to a New World that other Europeans had been colonizing for more than a century. The first English arrivals were but a small advance wave of the large, varied, and determined fragment of English society that would flock to the western Atlantic during the next few generations. Like Spanish, Portuguese, and French colonizers before them, they would establish new societies in the newfound lands in contact with the people of two other cultures—one made up of ancient inhabitants of the lands they were settling and the other composed of those brought across the Atlantic against their will. With this background, English latecomers to the Atlantic arena would have richly diverse founding experiences as they battled with French, Dutch, and Spanish contenders for control of North America.

TIME*line* ▬▬▬▬

1440s Portuguese use enslaved Africans after kidnapping or trading them on Africa's western coast

1460s Using African labor, sugar plantations in Portuguese Madeira become major exporters

1492 Christopher Columbus lands on Caribbean islands

Spanish expel Moors (Muslims) and Jews

1493–1504	Columbus makes three additional voyages to the Americas
1493	Spain plants first colony in Americas on Hispaniola
1494	Treaty of Tordesillas
1497–1585	French and English explore northern part of the Americas
1498	Vasco da Gama reaches India after sailing around Africa
Early 1500s	First Africans reach the Americas with Spanish
1508–1511	Spanish conquistadors subjugate native people on Puerto Rico and Cuba
1517	Luther attacks Catholicism and begins Protestant Reformation
1521	Cortés conquers the Aztec
1528	Spain plants first settlement on Florida coast
1528–1536	Cabeza de Vaca entrada across southern region of North America
1530s	Calvin calls for religious reform
1533	Pizarro conquers the Inca
1540–1542	Coronado explores the Southwest
1558	Elizabeth I crowned queen of England
1585	English plant settlement on Roanoke Island
1588	English defeat the Spanish Armada
1590	Roanoke settlement fails

✓•–|Study and **Review** at **www.myhistorylab.com**

Questions for Review and Reflection

1. How did religious changes in Europe affect European expansion into the Americas?

2. What was the Columbian Exchange, and what impact did it have on Europe and the Americas?

3. Why was England slow to become involved in exploration and colonization? How did the late arrival of the English affect their history in the New World?

4. What were the causes and consequences of the African slave trade with the European colonies in the Americas?

5. What was the impact of the collision of cultures that occurred in the Americas in the early colonial period?

Key Terms

Calvinism 29

John Cabot 38

Martin Luther 28

Price revolution 35

Protestant Reformation 28

Richard Hakluyt 39

Spanish Armada 39

Treaty of Tordesillas 30

3

Colonizing a Continent in the Seventeenth Century

American Stories

An African on the Virginia Frontier

Anthony Johnson, an African, arrived in Virginia in 1621 with only the name Antonio. Caught as a young man in the Portuguese slave-trading net, he had passed from one trader to another until he reached Virginia. There he was purchased by Richard Bennett and sent to work at Warrasquoke, Bennett's tobacco plantation on the James River. In the next year, Antonio was brought face-to-face with the world of triracial contact and conflict that would shape the remainder of his life. On March 22, 1622, the Powhatan tribes of tidewater Virginia fell on the colonizers in a determined attempt to drive them from the land. Of the 57 people on the Bennett plantation, only Antonio and four others survived.

Antonio—his name anglicized to Anthony—labored on the Bennett plantation for some 20 years, slave in fact if not in law, for legally defined bondage had not yet fully taken hold in the Virginia colony. During this time, he married Mary, another African trapped in servitude, and fathered four children. In the 1640s, Anthony and Mary Johnson gained their freedom after half a lifetime of servitude. Probably at this point they chose a surname, Johnson, to signify their new status. Already past middle age, the Johnsons began carving out a niche for themselves on Virginia's eastern shore. By 1650, they owned 250 acres, a small herd of cattle, and two black servants. In a world in which racial boundaries were not yet firmly marked, the Johnsons had entered the scramble of small planters for economic security.

By schooling themselves in the workings of the English legal process, carefully cultivating white patronage, and working industriously on the land, the Johnsons gained their freedom, acquired property, established a family, warded off contentious neighbors, and hammered out a decent existence. But by the 1660s, the lines of racial slavery tightened, closing in on Virginia's free blacks.

In 1664, convinced that ill winds were blowing away the chances for their children and grandchildren in Virginia, the Johnsons began selling their land to white neighbors. The following spring, most of the clan moved north to Maryland, where they rented land and again took up farming and cattle raising. Five years later, Anthony Johnson died, leaving his wife and four children. His fears of the growing racial prejudice in Virginia proved well founded when a jury of white men in Virginia declared that because Johnson "was a Negroe and by consequence an alien," the 50 acres he had deeded to his son Richard before moving to Maryland should be awarded to a local white planter.

Johnson's children and grandchildren, born in America, could not duplicate the modest success of the African-born patriarch. By the late seventeenth century, people of color faced much greater difficulties in extricating themselves from slavery. When they did, they found themselves forced to the margins of society. Anthony's sons never rose higher than the level of tenant farmer or small freeholder. John Johnson moved farther north into Delaware in the 1680s, following a period of great conflict with Native Americans in the Chesapeake region. Members of his family married local Native Americans and became part of a triracial community that survives to the present day. Richard Johnson stayed behind in Virginia. When he died in 1689, just after a series of colonial insurrections connected with the overthrow of James II in England, he had little to leave his own four sons. They became tenant farmers and hired servants, laboring on plantations owned by whites. By now, slave ships were pouring Africans into Virginia and Maryland to replace white indentured servants, the backbone of the labor force for four generations. To be black had at first been a handicap. Now it became a fatal disability, an indelible mark of degradation and bondage.

Anthony and Mary Johnson's story is one of thousands detailing the experiences of seventeenth-century immigrants who arrived in North America. Their story is not that of those European immigrants who sought both spiritual and economic renewal in the New World. But their lives became intertwined with those who were trying to escape European war, despotism, material want, and religious conflict. How did the Johnsons, like free immigrants and indentured servants from Europe, learn to cope with new environments, new social situations, and new mixings of people who before had lived on different continents? Mastering the North American environment involved several processes that would echo down the corridors of American history. Prominent among them were the molding of an African labor force and the gradual subjugation of Native American tribes that contested white expansion. Both occurrences, taking place during the lifetimes of Anthony and Mary Johnson and their children, involved a high level of violence. Why did European expansion allow some to pursue democratic dreams while others faced growing inequality and servitude?

The manner of settlement and the character of immigrant life would shape six areas of early colonization: the Chesapeake Bay, southern New England, the French and Dutch area from the St. Lawrence River to the Hudson River, the Carolinas, Pennsylvania, and the Spanish toeholds on the northern boundaries of their empire. Comparing these colonies will show how the colonizers' backgrounds, ideologies, modes of settlement, and uses of labor—free, slave, and indentured—produced distinctly different societies in North America in the seventeenth century. These regional societies would change over the course of the century, experiencing internal strain, a series of Native American wars, a destructive witchcraft craze, and upheaval sparked by England's attempts to reorganize its overseas colonies.

The Chesapeake Tobacco Coast

In 1607, a group of merchants established England's first permanent colony in North America at Jamestown, Virginia. For the first generation, its permanence was anything but assured. Even into the second and third generation

View the Image

Mural of Jamestown Settlement along the waters that flowed into the huge Chesapeake Bay, the English colonizers were plagued with internal discord and violent clashes with the native peoples.

at **www.myhistorylab.com**

Jamestown, Sot Weed, and Indentured Servants

Under a charter from James I, the Virginia Company of London sold shares of stock and used the pooled capital to finance overseas expeditions. They expected to find gold, a rewarding trade with Native Americans, and a water route to China. But investors and settlers got a rude shock. Dysentery, malaria, and malnutrition carried off most of the first colonists. More than 900 settlers arrived between 1607 and 1609; only 60 survived. There were no profits.

One-third of the first immigrants were gold-seeking adventurers, which meant the colony had six times the population of gentry back home in England. Many others were unskilled servants, some with criminal backgrounds, who (according to John Smith, the colony's first strong leader) "never did know what a day's work was." Both types adapted poorly, and Smith got few of the blacksmiths, carpenters, and farmers he wanted.

The colony was also hampered by the common assumption that Englishmen could exploit the Native Americans, as Cortés and Pizarro had done in Mexico and Peru. The English found that the 24,000 local Powhatan Indians were not densely settled and could not be easily subjugated. Unlike Spain, England had sent neither an army of conquistadors nor an army of priests to subdue the natives. Instead, relations with the small groups that the able Powhatan had united in a confederacy were bitter almost from the beginning. The Powhatan brought supplies of maize to the sick and starving Jamestown colony during the first autumn. Entering a seven year drought that would prove the worst in 8 centuries, the Powhatan could ill afford to supply the hungry intruders indefinitely. John Smith, whose military experience in eastern Europe had schooled him in war, raided Native American food supplies and tried to cow the local tribes. In response, the Powhatan withdrew from trade with the English. Many settlers died in the "starving times" of the first years.

●●● Read the Document
Captain John Smith,
The Starving Time *(1624)*
at **www.myhistorylab.com**

Still, the Virginia Company of London poured in more money and settlers, many enticed with promises of free land after seven years of labor. In 1618, the company even offered 50 acres of land outright to anyone journeying to Virginia. To people on the margins of English society, the promise of land in America seemed irresistible. More than 9,000 crossed the Atlantic between 1610 and 1622. Yet only 2,000 remained alive at the end of that period.

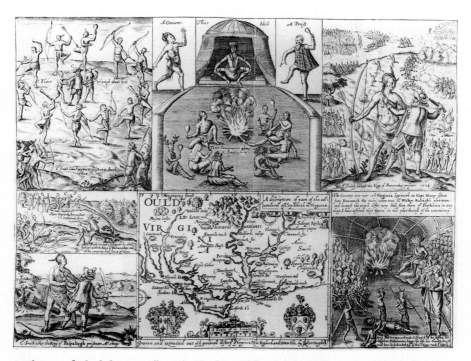

A History of Virginia A small caption in the middle of this set of panels reads, "A description of part of the adventures of Cap: Smith in Virginia." The images were rendered by Robert Vaughan, an English engraver, and were published in *The General Historie of Virginia* (1624), by Captain John Smith. In the lower right panel, an oversized Pocahontas (at the right) begs for the life of Smith, whose head is on a block, ready to be severed by an Indian executioner. What effect would this engraving have on readers of John Smith's history in England?

Besides the offer of free land, a crucial factor in the migration was the discovery that tobacco grew splendidly in Chesapeake soil. Francis Drake's boatload of the "jovial weed" (so named for its intoxicating effect), procured in the West Indies in 1586, popularized it among the upper class. Drake launched an addiction that continues to this day.

Even James I's denunciation of smoking as "loathsome to the eye, hateful to the nose, harmful to the brain, and dangerous to the lungs" failed to halt the smoking craze. The "sot weed" became Virginia's salvation. Planters shipped the first crop in 1617, and cultivation spread rapidly. By 1624, Virginia exported 200,000 pounds of the "stinking weed"; by 1638, though the price had plummeted, the crop exceeded 3 million pounds. Tobacco became to Virginia in the 1620s what sugar was to Brazil and silver to Mexico and Peru.

Because tobacco required intensive care, Virginia's planters had to find a reliable supply of cheap labor. They initially recruited mostly English laborers to be indentured servants, who willingly sold years of their working lives in exchange for free passage to America. About four of every five seventeenth-century immigrants to Virginia and, later, Maryland, were indentured. About three-quarters of them were male, mostly between 15 and 24 years old, and nearly all came from the lower rungs of the social ladder at home.

Only about 1 in 20 indentured servants realized the dream of freedom and land. If malarial fever or dysentery did not quickly kill them, they often succumbed to brutal work routines. Even by the middle of the seventeenth century, about half died during the first few years of "seasoning." Masters bought and sold servants as property, gambled for them, and worked them to death, for there was little motive for keeping them alive beyond their term of service. When servants neared the end of their contract, masters found ways to add time and were backed by courts that they controlled.

Contrary to English custom, masters often put women servants to work at the hoe. Sexual abuse was common, and servant women paid dearly for illegitimate pregnancies. The courts fined them heavily and ordered them to serve an extra year or two to repay the time lost during pregnancy and childbirth. They also deprived mothers of their illegitimate children, indenturing them out at an early age. Many servant women accepted the purchase of their indenture by any man who suggested marriage as the best release from this hard life.

Expansion and Indian War

As tobacco production caused Virginia's population to increase, violence mounted between white colonizers and the Powhatan tribes. In 1614, the sporadic hostility of the early years ended temporarily with the arranged marriage of Powhatan's daughter, the fabled Pocahontas, to planter John Rolfe. Meanwhile, the profitable cultivation of tobacco—first introduced by Rolfe himself—continued to create an intense demand for land.

In 1617, when Powhatan retired, leadership of the Chesapeake confederacy fell to Opechancanough. This proud and talented leader began preparing an all-out attack on his English enemies. The English murder of a Powhatan war captain and religious prophet triggered a fierce assault in 1622 that wiped out more than one-quarter of the white population and much of the colony's physical infrastructure.

This devastating attack bankrupted the Virginia Company. The king annulled its charter in 1624 and established a royal government, allowing the elected legislative body established in 1619, the House of Burgesses, to continue lawmaking in concert with the royal governor and his council.

The assault of 1622 fortified the determination of the surviving planters to pursue a ruthless new policy. John Smith, writing from England two years later, noted the grim satisfaction that had followed the attack. Many, he reported, believed that "now we have just cause to destroy them by all means possible." The Virginians conducted annual military expeditions against native villages. The colonial population grew after 1630, and tobacco quickly exhausted the soil and intensified the settlers' ambition for Indian land. The planters encroached on Indian territories, provoking war in 1644. The Chesapeake tribes, Virginians came to believe, were merely obstacles to be removed from the path of English settlement.

View the **Image**

John Smith Threatening Opechancanough

at **www.myhistorylab.com**

Proprietary Maryland

By the time Virginia had achieved commercial success in the 1630s, another colony on the Chesapeake took root. The founder aimed for profit and to create both a refuge for Catholics and a New World version of England's manor-dotted countryside.

George Calvert, an English nobleman, designed and promoted the new colony. Closely connected to England's royal family, he had received a huge grant of land in Newfoundland in 1628, just three years after James I had made him Lord Baltimore. In 1632, Charles I, James's son, granted him a more hospitable domain of 10 million acres, which Calvert named Terra Maria, or Maryland, to honor the king's Catholic wife, Henrietta Maria.

Catholics were an oppressed minority in England, and Calvert planned his colony as a haven for them. But knowing that he needed more than a small band of Catholic settlers, the proprietor invited others, too. Protestants, who jumped at the offer of free land with only a modest yearly fee to the Calverts, quickly overwhelmed Catholics, never a majority in his colony.

Lord Baltimore died in 1632, leaving his 26-year-old son, Cecilius, to carry out his plans. The charter guaranteed the proprietor control over all branches of government, but young Calvert learned that his colonists would not be satisfied with fewer liberties than they enjoyed at home or could find in other colonies.

Arriving in 1634, immigrants ignored Calvert's plans for 6,000-acre manors for his relatives and 3,000-acre manors for lesser aristocrats, each to be worked by serflike tenants. The settlers took up land, imported as many indentured servants as they could afford, maintained generally peaceful relations with local Indian tribes, grew tobacco on scattered riverfront plantations like their Virginia neighbors, and governed themselves as much as possible.

RECOVERING *the* PAST

Houses

Homesteading is central to our national experience. For 300 years after the founding of the first colonies, most Americans were involved in taming and settling the land. On every frontier, families faced the tasks of clearing the fields, beginning farming operations, and building shelter for themselves and their livestock. The kinds of structures they built depended on available materials, their resources and aspirations, and their notions of a "fair dwelling." The plan of a house and the materials used in its construction reveal much about the needs, resources, priorities, and values of the people who built it.

By examining archaeological remains of early ordinary structures and by studying houses that are still standing, historians are reaching new understandings of the social life of pioneering societies. Since the 1960s, archaeologists and architectural historians have been studying seventeenth-century housing in the Chesapeake Bay and New England regions. They have discovered a familiar sequence of house types from temporary shanties and lean-tos to rough cabins and simple frame houses to larger and more substantial dwellings of brick and finished timber. This hovel-to-house-to-home pattern existed on every frontier as sodbusters, gold miners, planters, and cattle raisers secured their hold on the land and then struggled to move from subsistence to success.

What is unusual in the findings of the Chesapeake researchers is the discovery that the second phase in the sequence—the use of temporary, rough-built structures—lasted for more than a century. Whereas many New Englanders had rebuilt and extended their temporary clapboard houses into timber-framed, substantial dwellings by the 1680s, Chesapeake settlers continued to construct small, rickety buildings that had to be repaired continually or abandoned altogether every 10 to 15 years.

The house on the opposite page is a typical reconstructed tobacco planter's house. Unlike New England structures, the chimney of the Chesapeake house is not built of brick but of mud and wood, and there is no window glass, only small shutters. The exterior is rough, unfinished planking. The placement of doors and windows and the overall dimensions indicate that this house has only one room downstairs and a loft above.

Historians have puzzled over this contrast between the architecture of the two regions. Part of the explanation may lie in the different climatic conditions and different immigration patterns of New England and the Chesapeake. In the southern region, disease killed thousands of settlers in the early decades. The imbalance of men and women produced a stunted and unstable family life, hardly conducive to an emphasis on constructing fine homes. In New England, good health prevailed almost from the beginning, and the family was at the heart of society. It made more sense, in this environment, to make a substantial investment in larger and more permanent houses.

Archaeological evidence combined with data recovered from land, tax, and court records, however, suggests another reason for the impermanence of housing in the Chesapeake region. Living in a labor-intensive tobacco world, it is argued, planters large and small economized on everything

Although Maryland grew slowly at first—in 1650 it had a population of only 600—it developed rapidly in the second half of the seventeenth century. By 1700, its population of 33,000 was half that of Virginia.

Daily Life on the Chesapeake

Most immigrants found Chesapeake life dismal. Only a minority could marry and rear a family. Marriage had to be deferred until the indenture

Reconstructed Chesapeake planter's house, typical of such simply built and unpainted structures in the seventeenth century.

possible in order to buy as many indentured servants and slaves as they could. Better to live in a shanty and have 10 slaves than to have a handsome dwelling and nobody to cultivate the fields. As late as 1775, the author of the text *American Husbandry* calculated that in setting up a tobacco plantation, five times as much ought to be spent on purchasing 20 black field hands as on the "house, offices, and tobacco-house."

Only after the Chesapeake region had emerged from its prolonged era of mortality and gender imbalance and a mixed economy of tobacco, grain, and cattle had replaced the tobacco monoculture did the rebuilding of the region begin. Excavated house sites indicate that this occurred after 1720. New research reveals that the phases of home building and the social and economic history of a society were closely interwoven.

REFLECTING ON THE PAST **What do houses today reveal about the resources, economic livelihood, priorities, and values of contemporary Americans? Do class and regional differences in house design continue?**

was completed, and there were three times more men than women. Marriages were fragile. Either husband or wife was likely to die of disease within about seven years. The vulnerability of pregnant women to malaria frequently terminated marriages, and death claimed half the children. Few children had two living parents while growing up. Grandparents were almost unknown. In a society so numerically dominated by men, widows were prized and often remarried quickly. Such conditions produced complex families full of stepchildren and stepparents, half-sisters and half-brothers.

Plagued by horrendous mortality, the Chesapeake remained, for most of the seventeenth century, a land of immigrants rather than of settled families. Churches and schools took root very slowly. The large number of indentured servants further destabilized community life. Strangers in a household, they served their time and moved on, or died, replaced by other strangers purchased fresh from England.

The region's architecture reflected the difficult conditions. Life was too uncertain, the tobacco economy too volatile, and the desire to invest every available shilling in field labor too great for men to build grandly. Even by the early eighteenth century, most Chesapeake families lived in a crude house without interior partitions. Eating, dressing, working, and loving all took place with hardly a semblance of privacy. For nearly two centuries, most ordinary Virginians and Marylanders were "pigg'd lovingly together," as one planter put it. Even prosperous planters did not begin constructing fully framed, substantial homesteads until a century after the colony was founded.

The crudity of life also showed in the household possessions of the Chesapeake colonists. Struggling farmers and tenants were likely to own only a straw mattress, a simple chest, and the tools for food preparation and eating. Most ordinary settlers owned no chairs, dressers, plates, or silverware. To be near the top of Chesapeake society meant having three or four rooms, sleeping more comfortably, sitting on chairs rather than squatting on the floor, and owning chamber pots, candlesticks, bed linen, a chest of drawers, and a desk. Only a few boasted such luxuries as clocks, books, punch bowls, wine glasses, and imported furniture. Four generations elapsed in the Chesapeake before the frontier quality of life slowly gave way to more refined living.

Bacon's Rebellion Engulfs Virginia

In 1675 and 1676, the Chesapeake colonies became locked in a struggle involving both an external war between the native and white populations and a civil war among the colonizers. This deeply tangled conflict was called **Bacon's Rebellion**, after the headstrong Cambridge-educated planter Nathaniel Bacon, who had arrived in Virginia at age 28.

Bacon and many other ambitious young planters detested the Indian policy of Virginia's royal governor, Sir William Berkeley. In 1646, after the second native attack on the Virginians, the Powhatan tribes had been granted exclusive rights to territory beyond the limits of white settlement. Stable relations suited the established planters, some of whom traded profitably with the natives, but became obnoxious to new settlers. Nor did harmonious conditions please the white ex–indentured servants who hoped for cheap frontier land.

Land hunger and dissatisfaction with declining tobacco prices, rising taxes, and lack of opportunity erupted into violence in the summer of 1675. A group of frontiersmen used an incident with a local tribe as an excuse to attack the Susquehannock, whose rich land they coveted. Governor Berkeley denounced the attack, but few supported his position. The badly outnumbered Susquehannock prepared for war as rumors swept the colony that they were offering large sums to gain western native allies or that New England tribes would support them.

Thirsting for revenge, the Susquehannock attacked during the winter of 1675–1676 and killed 36 Virginians. That spring, hot-blooded Bacon decided to take matters into his own hands. Leading hundreds of runaway servants and some slaves, he attacked friendly and hostile Native Americans alike. Governor Berkeley refused to sanction these attacks and declared Bacon a rebel, sending 300 militiamen to drag him to Jamestown for trial. Bacon recruited more followers, including prominent planters. Skirmishes against natives thus turned into civil war. During the summer of 1676, Bacon's and Berkeley's troops maneuvered, while Bacon's men continued their forays against local tribes. Then Bacon boldly captured and razed Jamestown, obliging Berkeley to flee across Chesapeake Bay.

Virginians at all levels had chafed under Berkeley's rule. High taxes, an increase in the governor's powers at the expense of local officials, and the monopoly that Berkeley and his friends held on the Native American trade were especially unpopular. This opposition surfaced in the summer of 1676 as Berkeley's and Bacon's troops pursued each other through the wilderness. Berkeley tried to rally public support by holding new assembly elections and extending the vote to all freemen, but the new assembly turned on the governor, passing laws to make government more responsive to the common people and to end rapacious officeholding. It also legalized enslaving Native Americans.

Time was on the governor's side, however. Having crushed the Native Americans, Bacon's followers began drifting home to tend their crops. Meanwhile, 1,100 royal troops were dispatched from England. By the time they arrived in January 1677, Bacon had died of swamp fever and most of his followers had melted away. Berkeley hanged 23 rebel leaders without benefit of trial.

Royal investigators afterwards reported that Bacon's followers "seem[ed] to wish and aim at an utter extirpation of the Indians." This hatred of Native Americans, along with hopes of land ownership, became a permanent feature of Virginia life. Even a royal governor could not restrain such men. A generation later, in 1711, the legislature spurned the governor's plea for quieting the frontier with educational missions and regulated trade, instead voting military appropriations of £20,000 "for extirpating all Indians without distinction of Friends or Enemys." The remnants of the once populous Powhatan Confederacy lost their last struggle. They perished, moved west, or submitted to a life on the margins of white society.

After Bacon's Rebellion, an emerging planter aristocracy annulled most of the reforms of 1676. By making new land available, the war relieved much of the social tension among white Virginians. Equally important, Virginians with capital to invest were turning from the impoverished rural villages of England to the villages of West Africa to supply their labor needs. This shift halted the influx of poor white servants who, once free, had formed a discontented mass at the bottom of Chesapeake society. Settlers of different ranks united in the common pursuit of a prosperous slave-based economy.

Bacon's Rebellion caused rumblings outside Virginia. Many of his followers fled to North Carolina, joining disgruntled farmers there in briefly seizing power. In Maryland, Protestant settlers chafed under high taxes, quitrents owed to the proprietor, and corrupt or Catholic officeholders. Declining tobacco prices and a fear of Indian attacks increased their touchiness. A month after Bacon razed Jamestown, insurgent small planters tried to seize the Maryland government. Two leaders were hanged for the attempt.

In all three southern colonies, the volatility of late-seventeenth-century life owed much to the region's peculiar social development. Where family formation was retarded by imbalanced gender ratios and fearsome mortality, and where geographic mobility was high, little social cohesion or attachment to community could grow. Missing in the southern colonies were the stabilizing power of mature local institutions, a vision of a larger purpose, and the presence of experienced and responsive political leaders.

The Southern Transition to Slave Labor

English colonists on the mainland of North America at first regarded Native Americans as the obvious source of labor. But European diseases ravaged native societies, and native people, more at home in the environment than the white colonizers, were difficult to subjugate. Indentured white labor proved the best way to meet the demand during most of the seventeenth century.

A few Africans entered the Chesapeake colonies within the first decade to labor in the tobacco fields alongside white servants. As late as 1671, when some 30,000 slaves toiled in English Barbados, fewer than 3,000 served in Virginia. They were still outnumbered there at least three to one by white indentured servants.

Only in the last quarter of the seventeenth century did southern field labor begin to shift to a black slave majority. This shift was due, first, to the rising commercial power of England, which swelled participation in the African slave trade and allowed southern planters to purchase slaves more readily and cheaply than before. Second, the supply of white servants from England began drying up. Third, Bacon's Rebellion, involving rebellious former servants seeking land, led white planters to seek a more pliable labor force. By the 1730s, the number of white indentured servants had dwindled to insignificance. Blacks tilled and harvested Chesapeake tobacco and Carolina rice, and slave labor became the priority in starting a plantation.

In enslaving Africans, English colonists in North America emulated their countrymen in Barbados, Jamaica, and the Leeward Islands, who had already used brutal repression to mold Africans into a sugar- and tobacco-producing slave labor force. Human bondage would later become the subject of intense debate, but in the seventeenth century, all but a few whites accepted it without question.

The System of Bondage

The first Africans in the American colonies probably came as bound servants. They served their term, and if (like Anthony and Mary Johnson) they survived, they gained freedom. Then they could own land, hire out their labor, and move as they pleased. Their children, like those of white indentured servants, were born free.

Gradually, seventeenth-century Chesapeake planters began to draw tighter lines around the activities of black servants. By the 1640s, Virginia forbade blacks, free or bound, to carry firearms. In the 1660s, marriages between white women and black servants were banned as "shameful matches." By the end of the century, when incoming Africans increased from a trickle to a torrent, even the few free blacks found themselves pushed to the margins of society. Slavery, which had existed for centuries in many societies as the lowest social status, was becoming a caste reserved for those with black skin. White society was turning the black servant into chattel.

In this dehumanization of Africans, which the English largely copied from their colonial rivals, the key step was instituting hereditary lifetime service. Once servitude ended only with death, all other privileges quickly vanished. When a mother's slave condition legally passed to her newborn (not the case in slavery in Africa), slavery became self-perpetuating.

Slavery became not only a system of forced labor but also a pattern of human relationships legitimated by law. By the early eighteenth century, most provincial legislatures limited black rights. Borrowed largely from England's Caribbean colonies, "Black Codes" forced Africans into an ever narrower world. Slaves could not testify in court, engage in commercial activity, hold property, participate in politics, congregate, travel without permission, or legally marry or be parents. Nearly stripped of human status, they became defined as property, and gradually all legal restraints on masters' treatment of them disappeared.

Eliminating slave rights did not eliminate resistance. With every African in chains a potential rebel, the rapid increase in the slave population brought demands for strict control and justifications for brutality. "The planters," wrote one Englishman in Jamaica, "do not want to be told that their Negroes are human creatures. If they believe them to be of human kind, they cannot regard them as no better than dogs or horses."

American slavery involved one of the great paradoxes of modern history. Many European immigrants saw the Americas as a liberating arena. Yet the opportunity to exploit its resources led to a historic process by which masses of people were wrenched from their homelands and forced into a system of slavery that could be maintained only by increasing intimidation and brutality.

Massachusetts and Its Offspring

While some English settlers in the reign of James I (1603–1625) scrambled for wealth on the Chesapeake, others looked to the wilds of North America as a place to build a tabernacle to God. The society they fashioned aimed at unity of purpose and utter dedication to reforming the corrupt world. American Puritanism would powerfully affect the nation's history by nurturing a belief in America's special mission in the world. It also attempted to banish diversity on a continent where the arrival of streams of immigrants from around the globe was destined to become a primary historical phenomenon.

Puritanism in England

England had been officially Protestant since 1558. Some people in the late sixteenth century, however, thought the Church of England was still riddled with Catholic vestiges. They wished to purify the Church of England, and so were dubbed "**Puritans**."

Puritans wanted not only to improve the church, moving it in a reformed Protestant direction; they also sought to reshape society.

They wanted to preserve the ideal of community in a time of rapid social change, and they upheld the belief that people were bound together by reciprocal rights and responsibilities. Symptoms of the "degeneracy of the times" included the defiling of the Sabbath by maypole dancing, card playing, fiddling, and bowling. Puritans vowed to reverse the march of disorder by imposing a new discipline. Their plan included a social ethic stressing work as a primary way of serving God. This emphasis on work made the religious quest of every member of society equally worthy. The "work ethic" would banish idleness and impart discipline throughout the community. Puritans also organized themselves into religious congregations in which each member hoped for personal salvation but also supported all others in their quest. Further, Puritans assumed responsibility for controlling "unconverted" people around them.

The relationship of Puritan reformers to the established church and the monarch had always been a troubled one, but when Charles I succeeded to the throne in 1625, the situation worsened. Determined to strengthen the monarchy and stifle dissent, he harassed Puritans, removing dozens of ministers from their pulpits and threatening many others. In 1628, he summoned a new Parliament and, one year later, adjourned this venerable body (which was the Puritans' main instrument of reform) when it would not accede to royal demands.

By 1629, as the king began ruling without Parliament, discontented subjects turned their eyes to northern Ireland, Holland, the Caribbean, and, especially, North America. They were convinced that God intended them to carry their religious and social reforms beyond the reach of persecuting authorities. A declining economy added to their discouragement about England. Many Puritans decided that they should transport a fragment of English society to some distant shore and there complete the Protestant Reformation.

Plymouth Plantation

Puritans were not the first Europeans to reach northeastern North America. Fishermen of various European nations had dried their Newfoundland catches on the coast of Cape Cod and Maine since the early 1500s. They frequently encountered the Algonquian-speaking people. A short-lived attempt at settlement in Maine had also been made in 1607. Seven years later, the aging Chesapeake war dog John Smith coined the name "New England."

No permanent settlement took root, however, until a small group arrived in Plymouth in 1620. Unlike the Puritans who followed, these humble Protestant farmers did not expect to convert a sinful world. Rather, they wanted to be left alone to realize their radical vision of a pure and primitive life. Instead of reforming the Church of England, they were separatists who left it. After James I threatened to "harry them out of the land," they fled first to Amsterdam in 1608, then to Leyden, Holland, and finally, in 1620, to North America.

Arriving at Cape Cod in November 1620, the Pilgrims were weakened by a stormy nine-week voyage and were ill-prepared for the harsh winter ahead. By the following spring, half the *Mayflower* passengers were dead, including 13 of the 18 married women.

[View the Image
Mayflower Replica at
Plymouth, Massachusetts
*at **www.myhistorylab.com***

The survivors, led by the staunch William Bradford, settled at Plymouth. Squabbles soon erupted with local Native Americans, whom Bradford considered "savage and brutish men." For two generations the settlers tilled the soil, fished, and tried to keep intact their religious vision. But with the much larger Puritan migration that began in 1630, the separatist villages around Cape Cod Bay became a backwater of the thriving, populous Massachusetts Bay Colony, which absorbed them in 1691.

Creating a Godly Society in the Wilderness   Migrants to New England hoped to solve their economic woes while pursuing their vision for a godly society. A disproportionate number of clergymen joined the migration, providing ample staffing for the churches the colonists quickly established. The settlement of New England offered an opportunity for a dissident minority within the established Church of England to create an alternative society and church order in the colonies. Governor John Winthrop and other early leaders were conscious that in pursuing their vision, they opened

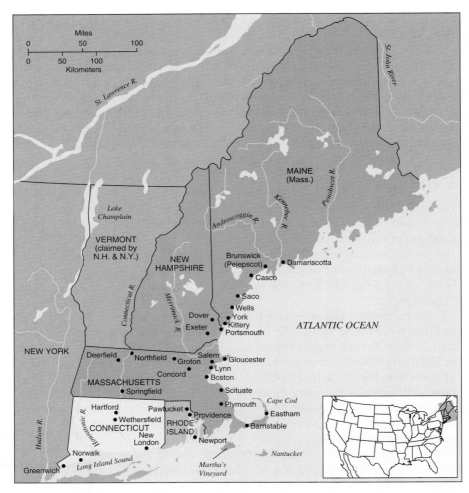

Early New England Maine and New Hampshire became the frontier to which New England settlers migrated when their towns and farmlands became too crowded. Why would settlers have tended to spread out along the coasts and rivers?

themselves and their efforts to the judgment of hostile observers. As he reminded the first settlers, "we shall be as a city upon a hill [and] the eyes of all people are upon us."

As in Plymouth and Virginia, the first winter tested the strongest souls. More than 200 of the first 700 settlers perished, and 100 others, disillusioned and sickened by the forbidding climate, soon returned to England. Still, colonists kept coming, settling along the rivers that emptied into Massachusetts Bay. A few years later, they pushed south into what became Connecticut and Rhode Island, as well as northward along the rocky coast.

Motivated by their militant work ethic and sense of mission, and led by men experienced in local government, law, and exhortation, these settlers thrived. The early leaders of Virginia were soldiers of fortune or roughneck adventurers with predatory instincts, men who had no families or had left them at home; ordinary Chesapeake settlers were mostly young men with little stake in English society who sold their labor to cross the Atlantic. But the early leaders in Massachusetts were university-trained ministers and experienced members of the lesser gentry, all men with a compulsion to fulfill God's mandates in New England. Most ordinary settlers came as free men and women in families. **Artisans** and farmers from the middle ranks of English society, they established tight-knit communities in which, from the outset, the brutal exploitation of labor rampant in the Chesapeake had no place.

Relying mostly on free labor, New Englanders built an economy based on agriculture, fishing, timbering, and trading for beaver furs with local Native Americans. Even before leaving England, the directors of the Massachusetts Bay Company transformed their commercial charter into a rudimentary government. In North America, they laid the foundations of self-government. Free male church members annually elected a governor and deputies from each town. The latter formed one house of a colonial legislature, the General Court. The other house was composed of the governor's assistants, later to be called councillors. Consent of both houses was required to pass laws. The Puritans founded Harvard College, which opened its doors in 1636 to train clergymen, established the first printing press in the English colonies, and launched an innovative attempt in 1642 to create a tax-supported school system, open to all wanting an education.

•**{**•**}**Read the Document
The Cambridge Agreement (1629)
at **www.myhistorylab.com**

Serious tensions within the community arose almost immediately. In 1633, Salem's minister, Roger Williams, began to voice disturbing opinions. He argued that the Massachusetts Puritans were not truly pure because they would not completely separate from the polluted Church of England (which most Puritans still hoped to reform). Williams denounced mandatory worship and contended that government officials should confine themselves to civil affairs and not interfere with religious matters. "Coerced religion," he warned, "on good days produces hypocrites, on bad days rivers of blood." Today honored as an early advocate for the separation of church and state, in 1633, Williams seemed to strike at the heart of the Bible commonwealth, whose leaders regarded civil and religious affairs as inseparable. Williams also charged the Puritans with illegally intruding on Native American land.

For two years, Puritan leaders could not quiet the determined young Williams. Finally, warned by Winthrop that he was about to be deported to England, Williams fled southward through winter snow with a small band of followers to found Providence in what would become Rhode Island. Even as they were driving Williams out, the Puritan authorities confronted another threat: Anne Hutchinson, a devout woman of extraordinary talent and intellect who arrived in 1634 with her husband and seven children. Quickly gaining respect among Boston's women as a midwife and spiritual counselor, she began to discuss religion and suggested that the "holy spirit" was absent in the preaching of some ministers. Before long Hutchinson was leading a movement labeled **antinomianism**, which stressed the mystical nature of God's free gift of grace while discounting the efforts the individual could make to gain salvation.

By 1636, Boston was dividing into two camps: those drawn to the theological views of a gifted though untrained woman without official standing and those who supported the leadership that thought she needed to be suppressed. Hutchinson offended many of the male leaders of the colony because she boldly stepped outside the subordinate position expected of women.

Determined to remove this thorn from their sides, the clergy and magistrates put Hutchinson on trial in 1637, convicting her of sedition and contempt in a civil trial and banishing her from the colony "as a woman not fit for our society." Six months later, the Boston church excommunicated her for preaching 82 erroneous theological opinions. In the last month of her eighth pregnancy, Hutchinson, with a band of supporters, followed Roger Williams's route to Rhode Island. Battles over the messages of Williams and Hutchinson demonstrated just how difficult it was to create a godly society that would suit the range of views that had been contained within the Puritan movement in England. Other, more minor differences contributed to the founding of two more colonies out of Massachusetts. By 1636, groups of Puritans had swarmed not only to Rhode Island but also to Hartford and New Haven in what became Connecticut.

New Englanders and Indians

Though the charter of the Massachusetts Bay Company spoke of converting "the natives to the knowledge and obedience of the only true God and Saviour of mankind and the Christian faith," the instructions that Winthrop carried from England reveal suspicions about the native inhabitants. According to Winthrop's orders, all men were to receive training in the use of firearms, a reversal of the sixteenth-century English policy of disarming the citizenry in order to quell public disorders. New England magistrates prohibited Native Americans from entering towns and threatened to deport any colonist selling arms to a native or instructing one in their use.

Only sporadic conflict with local tribes occurred at first since, in 1616, visiting English fishermen had triggered a ferocious outbreak of respiratory viruses and smallpox that wiped out three-quarters of some 125,000 Native Americans. Five years later, an Englishman exploring the area described walking through a forest where human skeletons covered the ground. The Puritans believed that God had intervened on their side, especially when smallpox returned in 1633, killing thousands more natives and allowing new settlers to find land. Many surviving natives welcomed the settlers because they now had surplus land and through trade hoped to gain English protection against enemies to the north.

The pressure for new land, however, soon reached into areas untouched by disease. Land hunger mingled with the sense of mission made an explosive mix. Native Americans represented a mocking challenge to the building of a religious commonwealth. Puritans believed that God would blame them for not civilizing and Christianizing the natives and would punish them with his wrath, so they tried to make the "savages" of New England strictly accountable to their ordinances. They succeeded with the smaller, disease-ravaged tribes of eastern Massachusetts, but control over the stronger Pequot required a bloody war in 1637. Victory ensured English domination over all the tribes of southern New England except the powerful Wampanoag and Narragansett of Rhode Island and removed the last obstacle to expansion into the Connecticut River valley. Missionary work, led by John Eliot, began among the remnant tribes in the 1640s. After a decade, about 1,000 Indians had been settled in four "praying villages," learning to live according to English ways.

The Web of Village Life

Unlike the dispersed Chesapeake tobacco planters, New Englanders established small, tightly settled villages that were vital centers of life. Most were "open field" agricultural communities with narrow strip fields radiating out from the town. Farmers grazed their cattle on common meadowland and cut firewood on common woodland. Some towns employed the "closed field" system of self-contained farms. Both systems re-created common English patterns of agriculture with families living close together in towns built around a common, with a meetinghouse and tavern. These small, communal villages kept families in close touch.

Settlers practiced community watchfulness, in which each person was responsible not only for his or her own transgressions, but also for those of his or her neighbors. To achieve godliness and communal unity, Puritans prohibited single men and women from living by themselves, beyond patriarchal authority. As Thomas Hooker put it, "every natural man and woman is born full of sin, as full as a toad of poison." Many Virginia planters counted the absence of restraint as a blessing. Most New Englanders feared it as the Devil.

Every community member gathered twice a week in the meetinghouse, a plain wooden structure at the center of each village. No man stood higher than the minister, the spiritual leader in these small, family-based, community-oriented settlements. The unique mixture of strict authority and incipient democracy, of hierarchy and equality, can be seen in the way the Massachusetts town distributed land and devised local government. After receiving a grant, townsmen met to parcel out land. They awarded individual grants according to the size of a man's household, his wealth, and his usefulness to the church and town, perpetuating existing differences in wealth and status. Yet some towns wrote language into their covenants that to the modern ear has an almost socialistic ring. Puritans believed that the community's welfare transcended individual ambitions and that unity demanded limits on the accumulation of wealth. Every family should have enough land to sustain it, and prospering men were expected to use their wealth for such community projects as repairing the meetinghouse, or aiding a widowed neighbor.

Having felt the sting of centralized power in church and state, Puritans emphasized local exercise of authority. Until 1684, only male church members could vote. These voters elected selectmen who allocated land, passed local taxes, and settled disputes. Once a year, all townsmen gathered for the town meeting where they selected officers for the next year and decided matters large and small. The appointment of many men to minor offices bred the tradition of local government.

The predominance of families lent cohesiveness to Puritan village life. Strengthening this family orientation was the remarkably healthy environment. Whereas the germs carried by English colonizers devastated neighboring Native American societies, the effect on the newcomers of a new environment was the opposite. The low density of settlement prevented infectious diseases from spreading, and the isolation of inland villages from Atlantic commerce, along which diseases as well as cargo flowed, minimized biological hazards.

The result was a spectacular natural increase in the population and a life span unknown in Europe. At a time when the population of western Europe was barely growing—deaths almost equaled births—the population of New England, discounting new immigrants, doubled every 27 years. The difference was not a higher birthrate. New England women typically bore about seven children during the course of a marriage, but this barely exceeded the European norm. The crucial factor was that chances for survival after birth were far greater than in England because of the healthier climate and better diet. In most of Europe, where life expectancy was less than 40 years, only half the babies born lived long enough to produce children themselves. In New England, nearly 90 percent of the infants born in the seventeenth century survived to marriageable age, and life expectancy exceeded 60 years—longer than for the American population as a whole at any time until the early twentieth century. About 25,000 people immigrated to New England in the seventeenth century, but by 1700 they had produced a population of 100,000. By contrast, some 75,000 immigrants to the Chesapeake colonies had yielded a population of only about 70,000 by the end of the century.

Women played a vital role in this society. Women not only served as wife, mother, and housekeeper; they also kept a vegetable garden, salted and smoked meats, preserved vegetables and dairy products, spun yarn, wove cloth, and made clothes.

The presence of women and a stable family life strongly affected New England's regional architecture. As communities formed, early economic gains were converted into more substantial housing rather than being invested in bound labor. Chesapeake colonists did the opposite,

The Mason Children Three of Arthur and Joanna Mason's five children were captured in this 1670 painting. The 9-year-old boy on the left holds a silver-headed walking stick, signifying his status as male heir. His 6-year-old sister in the middle holds a yellow fan and red and yellow ribbons. The 4-year-old sister to the right holds a rose, a common symbol of innocence associated with childhood. What you notice about the attire of the children and the manner in which the artist portrayed their faces?
(The Freake-Gibbs Painter, (American), active 1670. David, Joanna and Abigail Mason, 1670, Oil on canvas, 39-1/2″ × 42-1/2″; Frame: 42-3/4″ × 45-1/2″ × 1-1/2″. Fine Arts Museum of San Francisco, Gift of Mr. and Mrs. John D. Rockefeller 3rd to The Fine Arts Museum of San Francisco, 1979.7.3)

thereby retarding family formation and rendering the economy unstable. In New England, well-constructed one-room houses with sleeping lofts quickly replaced early "wigwams, huts, and hovels." Families added parlors and lean-to kitchens as soon as they could. Within a half century, New England immigrants accomplished a general rebuilding of their living structures. The Chesapeake lagged far behind.

A final binding element in Puritan communities was the stress on literacy and education, which eventually became a hallmark of American society. Placing religion at the center of their lives, Puritans emphasized the ability to read catechisms, psalm books, and especially the Bible. In literacy and education, Puritans saw guarantees for preserving their central values.

Though eager to be left alone, migrants could not escape events in England. In 1642, King Charles I pushed England into revolution by violating the country's customary constitution and attempting to reshape the religion of both Scotland and England. By 1649, the ensuing civil wars climaxed with the trial and beheading of the king. Thereafter, during the so-called Commonwealth period (1649–1660), the reform of religion and society was underway in England. Meanwhile, migration to New England abruptly ceased.

In the context of civil war at home, colonial leaders established the **Confederation of New England** in 1643. Through it they intended to coordinate government among the various settlements (Rhode Island excluded) and to provide more effective defense against the French, Dutch, and Native Americans. This first American attempt at federalism functioned fitfully for a generation and then dissolved.

Although the settlers fashioned stable communities, developed the economy, and constructed effective government, their leaders complained that the founding vision of Massachusetts Bay was faltering. If social diversity increased and the religious zeal of the founding generation waned, that was only to be expected. One second-generation Bay colonist put the matter bluntly. His minister had noticed his absence in church and found him later that day at the docks, unloading a boatload of cod. "Why were you not in church this morning?" asked the clergyman. Back came the reply: "My father came here for religion, but I came for fish."

King Philip's War in New England

For religious leaders concerned about declining piety, continued difficulties with Native Americans of southern New England signaled new signs of God's displeasure. Following the Pequot War of 1637, the Wampanoag and Narragansett tried to keep their distance from colonists who coveted their territories. As colonists quarreled over provincial boundaries, they gradually reduced the natives' land base.

By the 1670s, when New England's population had grown to about 50,000, the Wampanoag leader was Metacomet (called King Philip by the English). The son of Massasoit, a chief who had allied with the first Plymouth settlers in 1620, Metacomet had watched his older brother preside over the deteriorating position of his people after their father's death in 1661. Becoming chief in his turn, Metacomet faced one humiliating challenge after another, including in 1671, when Plymouth forced him to surrender a large stock of guns and accept his people's subjection to English law.

Metacomet began organizing a resistance movement fed by the rising anger of the young Wampanoag men. Younger Native Americans refused to imitate their fathers, who had acquiesced to the colonizers' encroachments. For the young men, revitalization of their ancient culture through war became as important a goal as defeating the enemy. Rather than submit further, they attempted a pan-Indian offensive against an ever-stronger intruder that would become known as **King Philip's War**.

In 1675, Puritans executed three Wampanoag for murdering John Sassamon, providing the spark for an insurrection. That summer, the Wampanoag unleashed daring hit-and-run attacks on villages in the Plymouth colony. By autumn, many New England tribes, including the powerful Narragansett, had joined Metacomet. Towns all along the frontier reeled under their attacks. By November, native warriors had devastated the entire upper Connecticut River Valley, and by March 1676, they were less than 20 miles from Boston and Providence. As assumptions about English military superiority faded, New England officials passed America's first draft laws. Widespread draft evasion and friction among the colonies hampered a counteroffensive.

Metacomet's offensive faltered in the spring of 1676, sapped by food shortages, disease, and the refusal of the Mohawk to join the New England tribes. Metacomet fell in battle. The head of this "hell-hound, fiend, serpent, caitiff and dog," as one colonial leader branded him, was displayed in Plymouth for 25 years.

Several thousand colonists and perhaps twice as many Native Americans lay dead. Of some 90 Puritan towns, 52 had been attacked and 13 completely destroyed; 1,200 homes lay in ruins and 8,000 cattle were dead. The estimated cost of the war exceeded the value of all personal property in New England. Not for 40 years would the frontier advance beyond the line it had reached in 1675. The devastation to Native Americans was even more extensive. An entire generation of young men had been nearly annihilated. Many of the survivors, including Metacomet's wife and son, were sold into slavery in the West Indies. Among the towns destroyed were several inhabited by "praying" Indians who had converted to Christianity. Suspected by their fellow Christians as well as by their native brethren, these people had been caught between the warring sides.

Slavery in New England

The Wampanoag captives sold as slaves in the West Indies continued New England's involvement in the dirty business of slavery. New England's crops were not labor-intensive, so coerced labor never became the foundation of its field workforce. Slavery did take root in the cities, though, where slaves worked as artisans and domestic servants. Northern colonial economies also became enmeshed in the Atlantic commercial network, which depended on slavery and the slave trade. New England's merchants eagerly pursued profits in the trade as early as the 1640s. By 1750, half the merchant fleet of Newport, Rhode Island, reaped profits from carrying human cargo. In New York and Philadelphia, building and outfitting slave vessels proved profitable.

New England's seaports became centers for distilling rum—the "hot, hellish and terrible liquor" made from West Indian sugar. Rum became one of the principal commodities traded for slaves on the African coast. As the number of slaves in the Caribbean multiplied—from about 50,000 in 1650 to 500,000 in 1750—New England's large fishing fleet found important markets for its cod. Wheat from the mid-Atlantic colonies and barrel staves and hoops from North Carolina also serviced the slave-based West Indies economy. In short, every North American colony participated in the business of slavery.

From the St. Lawrence to the Hudson

The New Englanders were not the only European settlers in the northern region, for both France and Holland created colonies there. While English settlers founded Jamestown, the French were settling Canada. As the planters at Plymouth were settling in on Cape Cod in the 1620s, the Dutch established an outpost on the Hudson River.

France's America

Henry IV, the first strong French king in half a century, sent Samuel de Champlain to explore deep into the territory even before the English had obtained a foothold on the Chesapeake. Champlain established a small settlement in Acadia (later Nova Scotia) in 1604 and another in Quebec in 1608. French trading with Indians for furs had already begun in Newfoundland, and his settlers hoped to keep making these easy profits. But the holders of the fur monopoly in France did not encourage immigration to the colony, fearing to reduce the forests from which the furs were harvested. New France remained lightly populated.

In 1609–1610, Champlain allied with the Algonquian Indians of the St. Lawrence region in attacking their Iroquois enemies to the south. Enmity between the two eventually drove the Iroquois to trade furs for European goods with the Dutch on the Hudson River; when the Iroquois exhausted the furs of their own territory, they turned north and west, determined to seize resource-rich forests from the Huron, French allies in the Great Lakes region.

When the Iroquois descended on them in the 1640s, the Huron were already decimated by epidemics that spread among them as Jesuit priests entered their villages. In the "beaver wars" of the 1640s and 1650s, the Iroquois used Dutch guns to attack Huron parties carrying beaver pelts to the French. By midcentury, Iroquois attacks had scattered the Huron, all but ending the French fur trade and reducing the Jesuit influence to a few villages of Christianized Huron.

The bitterness bred in these years colored future colonial warfare, driving the Iroquois to ally with the English against the French. At midcentury, however, these tensions did little to hamper the English, who vastly outnumbered the approximately 400 French settlers.

England Challenges the Dutch

By 1650, the Chesapeake and New England regions each contained about 50,000 settlers. Between them lay the mid-Atlantic area controlled by the Dutch, who planted **New Netherland** at the mouth of the Hudson River in 1624. In the next four decades they extended their control to the Connecticut and Delaware river valleys. South of the Chesapeake lay a vast territory where only the Spanish, from their mission frontier in Florida, challenged the power of Native American tribes.

Although for generations they had been the Protestant bulwarks in a mostly Catholic Europe, England and Holland became bitter commercial rivals in the mid-seventeenth century. By the time the English arrived in New England, the Dutch had become the mightiest carriers of seaborne commerce in western Europe. The Dutch had also muscled in on Spanish and Portuguese transatlantic commerce, trading illegally with Iberian colonists who gladly violated their government's commercial policies to obtain cloth and slaves more cheaply. By 1650, the Dutch had temporarily overwhelmed the Portuguese in Brazil, and soon their vast trading empire reached southeast and east Asia.

In North America, the Dutch West India Company's New Netherland colony was small, profitable, and multicultural. Agents fanned out from Fort Orange (Albany) and New Amsterdam (New York City) into the Hudson, Connecticut, and Delaware river valleys, establishing a lucrative fur trade with local tribes by hooking into the sophisticated trading network of the **Iroquois Confederacy**, which stretched to the Great Lakes. The Iroquois welcomed the Dutch, who were few in number, did not have voracious appetites for land, and willingly exchanged desirable goods for the pelts of animals plentiful in the vast Iroquois territory. At Albany, the center of the Dutch Iroquois trade, relations remained peaceful and profitable for several generations.

Although the Dutch never settled more than 10,000 people in their mid-Atlantic colonies, their commercial and naval powers were impressive. The Virginians learned this in 1667 when brazen Dutch raiders captured 20 tobacco ships on the James River and confiscated virtually the entire tobacco crop for that year. By 1650, England was ready to challenge Dutch maritime supremacy. War broke out three times between 1652 and 1675, as the two Protestant nations competed to control the emerging worldwide capitalist economy. In the second and third wars, New Netherland became an easy target for the English. They captured it in 1664 and then, after it fell to the Dutch in 1673, recaptured it almost immediately. By 1675, the Dutch had been permanently dislodged from the North American mainland. But they remained mighty commercial competitors of the English around the world.

New Netherland now became New York, so named because Charles II gave it (along with the former Dutch colonies on the Delaware River) to his brother the duke of York, later James II. Under English rule, the Dutch colonists remained ethnically distinct for several generations, clinging to their language, their Dutch Reformed Calvinist churches, and their architecture. In time, however, English immigrants overwhelmed the Dutch, and gradual intermarriage among the Dutch, the French Huguenots, and the English diluted ethnic loyalties. New York retained its polyglot, religiously tolerant character, and its people never allowed religious concerns or utopian plans to interfere with the pragmatic conduct of business.

Proprietary Carolina: A Restoration Reward

In 1663, three years after he was restored to his father's throne, England's Charles II granted a vast territory named Carolina to a group who supported him during his exile. Its boundaries extended from Virginia to central Florida and westward to the Pacific. Within this potential empire, eight London-based proprietors, including several involved in Barbados sugar plantations, gained governmental powers and semifeudal land rights. The system of governance planned for Carolina had both feudal and modern features. To lure settlers, the proprietors promised religious freedom and free land. The generous land offer included a scheme for a semimedieval government in which they, their deputies, and a few noblemen would monopolize political power. Reacting to a generation of revolutionary turbulence in England, its founders designed Carolina as a model of social and political stability in which a hereditary aristocracy would check boisterous small landholders.

Carolina realities bore faint resemblance to their plan. Rugged sugar and tobacco planters streamed in from economically depressed Barbados and Virginia and claimed their 150 acres of free land, as well as additional acreage for each family member or servant they brought. They ignored proprietary regulations about settling in compact rectangular patterns and reserving two-fifths of every county for appointed nobility. In government, they also did as they pleased. Meeting in assembly for the first time in 1670, they refused to accept the proprietors' Fundamental Constitutions of 1667 and disregarded orders from the proprietors' governor. Most of the settlers already knew how to run a slave society from having lived in Barbados, and they shaped local government from that experience.

The Indian Debacle

Carolina was the most elaborately planned colony in English history, yet the least successful in achieving the harmony the proprietors had intended. Mindful of the violence that had plagued other settlements, they projected a well-regulated Native American trade in deerskins, run exclusively by their appointed agents. Aggressive settlers from the West Indies and the Chesapeake flouted these plans. To the consternation of the London

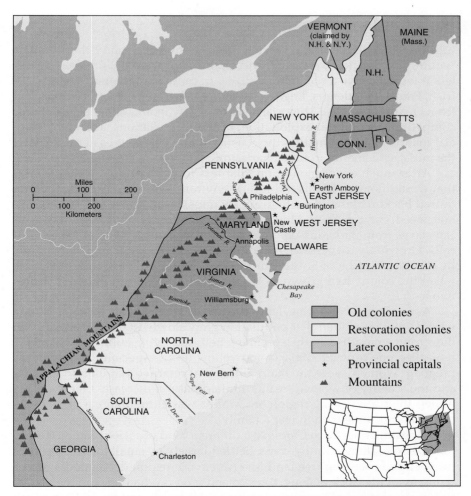

Restoration Colonies: New York, the Jerseys, Pennsylvania, and the Carolinas With the addition of the Restoration colonies (founded from the 1660s to the 1680s), England claimed the entire seaboard between Spanish Florida and French Canada. Why would settlements have clung fairly close to the coast even as late as 1700?

proprietors, capturing Indians for sale in New England and the West Indies became the cornerstone of commerce in Carolina in the early years, plunging the colony into a series of wars. Planters and merchants selected a tribe, armed it, and rewarded it handsomely for bringing in enemy captives. But even strong tribes found that after they had used English guns to enslave their weaker neighbors, they themselves were scheduled for elimination. The colonists claimed that "thinning the barbarous Indian natives" was needed to make room for white settlement, and the "thinning" was so thorough that by the early eighteenth century the two main tribes of the coastal plain, the Westo and the Savannah, were nearly extinct.

Early Carolina Society

Carolina's fertile land and warm climate convinced many that it was a "country so delicious, pleasant, and fruitful that were it cultivated doubtless it would prove a second Paradize." In came Barbadians, Swiss, Scots, Irish, French Huguenots, English, and migrants from northern colonies. Far from creating paradise, they clashed abrasively in an atmosphere of fierce competition, ecological exploitation, brutal race relations, and stunted social institutions. Decimating the coastal Indians made it easier to expand the initial settlements around Charleston.

After much experimentation, planters found a profitable staple crop that would flourish in this forbidding environment: rice. Its cultivation required backbreaking labor to drain swamps, build dams and levees, and hoe, weed, cut, thresh, and husk the crop. Many early settlers brought African slaves from Barbados, so their early reliance on slave labor came naturally. On widely dispersed plantations, black labor came to predominate. In 1680, four-fifths of South Carolina's population was white. By 1720, when the colony had grown to 18,000, black slaves outnumbered whites two to one.

As in Virginia and Maryland, the low-lying areas of coastal Carolina were so disease-ridden that population grew slowly in the early years. "In the spring a paradise, in the summer a hell, and in the autumn a hospital," remarked one traveler. Malaria and yellow fever, especially dangerous to pregnant women, were the main killers that retarded population growth, and the scarcity of women further limited natural increase. Like the West Indies, the rice-growing region of Carolina was at first more a place to accumulate a fortune than to rear a family.

In healthier northern Carolina, a different kind of society emerged amid pine barrens along a sandy coast. Settled largely by small tobacco farmers from Virginia seeking free land, the Albemarle region developed a mixed economy of livestock grazing, tobacco and food production, and the extraction of naval stores of lumber, turpentine, resin, pitch, and tar. In 1701, North and South Carolina became separate colonies, but their distinctiveness had already emerged. Slavery took root only slowly in North Carolina. Still 85 percent white in 1720, North Carolina had the potential for sustained growth: a healthier climate and settlement by families rather than slave-owning single men. But in North as well as South Carolina, settlement patterns, ethnic and religious diversity, and a lack of shared assumptions about social and religious goals inhibited the growth of a strong colony-wide identity.

The Quakers' Peaceable Kingdom

Of all the utopian dreams imposed on the North American landscape in the seventeenth century, the most remarkable was the **Quakers'**. During the English civil wars, the Society of Friends, as the Quakers called themselves, had sprung up as one of the many radical sects searching for a more just society and a purer religion. Their visionary ideas and defiance of civil authority cost them dearly in fines, brutal punishment, and imprisonment. After Charles II and Parliament stifled radical dissent in the 1660s, the Quakers sent many converts across the Atlantic. More than any other colony, the society they founded in Pennsylvania foreshadowed the religious and ethnic pluralism of the future United States.

The Early Friends

Born during the years of civil war and Commonwealth rule in England, the Quakers embraced a religious message that focused the individual believer on the "inward light," a redemptive spark in every human soul. They rejected the Calvinist view—common among many Protestants at the time—that God had elected only a few for salvation. Quakers believed instead that anyone could be saved. Early Quakers felt called to witness to their new faith, preaching to anyone who would listen. Other Protestants regarded them as dangerous fanatics, for the Quakers' doctrine of the "light within" took precedence even over Scripture and elevated all laypeople to the position of the clergy.

Garbing themselves in plain black cloth and practicing civil disobedience, the Quakers also threatened social hierarchy and order. They refused to observe the customary marks of deference, believing that God made no social distinctions. They used the familiar "thee" and "thou" instead of the formal and deferential "you," resisted taxes supporting the Church of England once it was reestablished in 1660, and refused to sign witnesses' oaths on the Bible, regarding this as profane. Most shocking, they renounced the use of force in human affairs and therefore refused to perform militia service.

Quakers also affronted traditional views when they insisted on the spiritual equality of the sexes and the right of women to participate in church matters on an equal, if usually separate, footing with men. Quaker women preached and established separate women's meetings. Among Quakers who fanned out from England to preach the doctrine of the inward light, 26 of the first 59 to cross the Atlantic were women. All but four of them were unmarried or without their husbands and therefore living, traveling, and ministering outside male authority.

Intensely committed at first to converting the world, Quakers ranged westward to North America and the Caribbean in the 1650s and 1660s. Nearly everywhere they faced jeers, prison, mutilation, and deportation. In Massachusetts, the authorities hanged four Quakers on Boston Common between 1658 and 1660. Among them was Mary Dyer, an old woman who had followed Anne Hutchinson a quarter century before.

Early Quaker Designs

By the 1670s, English Quakers were looking for a place in the New World to carry out their millennial dreams and escape severe repression. They found a leader in William Penn. His decision to identify with this persecuted sect was

●❖─[Read the **Document**

William Penn, Description of Pennsylvania *(1681)*

at **www.myhistorylab.com**

surprising, for he was the son of Admiral Sir William Penn, who had captured Jamaica from Spain in 1654. In 1666, the 23-year-old Penn was converted to Quakerism and thereafter devoted himself to the Friends' cause.

In 1674, Penn joined other Friends in establishing a North American colony, West Jersey. They had bought the land from one of the proprietors of New Jersey, itself a new English colony recently carved out of the former New Netherland. For West Jersey, Penn helped fashion a constitution extraordinarily liberal for its time; it allowed virtually all free males to vote for legislators and local officials. Settlers were guaranteed freedom of religion and trial by jury. As Penn and the other trustees of the colony explained, "We lay a foundation for [later] ages to understand their liberty as men and Christians, that they may not be brought in bondage, but by their own consent; for we put the power in the people."

The last phrase, summing up the document, shocked men of property and power. Most regarded "the people" as ignorant, dangerous, and certain to bring society to a state of anarchy if allowed to rule themselves. Nowhere in the English world had ordinary men, especially those who did not own land, enjoyed such extensive privileges. Nowhere had a popularly elected legislature received such broad authority.

West Jersey sputtered at first. Only 1,500 immigrants arrived in the first five years, and for several decades the colony was caught up in legal tangles. The center of Quaker hopes lay across the Delaware River, where in 1681, Charles II granted William Penn a territory almost as large as England, paying off a debt to Penn's father. Charles II also benefited by getting the pesky Quakers out of England. Thus Penn came into possession of the last unassigned segment of the eastern coast of North America, and one of the most fertile.

Pacifism in a Militant World: Quakers and Indians

On the day Penn received his royal charter for Pennsylvania, he wrote a friend, "My God that has given it to me will, I believe, bless and make it the seed of a nation." The nation that Penn envisioned was unique among colonizing schemes. Penn intended to make his colony an asylum for the persecuted and a refuge from arbitrary state power. Puritans had strived for social homogeneity and religious uniformity. Chesapeake and Carolina settlers exploited their lands and bondspeople. Penn dreamed of inviting to his forested colony people of all religions and ethnic backgrounds, offering them peaceful coexistence. His government would neither assert authority over citizens' consciences nor demand military service of them. Quakers began streaming into Pennsylvania in 1682, quickly absorbing earlier settlers. They participated in the government by electing representatives who initiated laws. Primarily farmers, they avidly acquired land, which Penn sold at reasonable rates.

Even before arriving, Penn laid the foundation for peaceful relations with the Delaware tribe inhabiting his colony. "The king of the Country

PENNS TREATY with the INDIANS, made 1681 without an Oath, and never broken. The foundation of Religious and Civil LIBERTY, in the U.S. of AMERICA.

Concluding a Treaty with the Indians Edward Hicks painted Penn's Treaty with the Indians in the nineteenth century. It is a romanticized version of the Treaty of Shackamaxon (1682) by which the Lenape chiefs ceded the site of Philadelphia to Penn. Hicks implied that the Lenape held Penn in high regard for his fair treatment of them. What evidence of Quaker pacifism do you find in this painting? *(1980.62.11 [2796]/PA Gift of Edgar William and Bernice Chrysler Garbisch, Penn's Treaty with the Indians, c. 1840/1844, © 2000 Board of Trustees, National Gallery of Art, Washington, D.C.)*

where I live, hath given me a great Province," he wrote to the Delaware chiefs, "but I desire to enjoy it with your Love and Consent, that we may always live together as Neighbors and friends." In this single statement Penn dissociated himself from the entire history of European colonization in the New World and from the widely held negative view of Native Americans. Recognizing them as the rightful owners of the land included in his grant, Penn pledged not to sell one acre until he had first purchased it from local chiefs. He also promised to strictly regulate the Indian trade and to ban alcohol sales.

Comparing Pennsylvania and South Carolina, both established after 1660, shows the power of pacifism. A quarter century after initial settlement, Pennsylvania had a population of about 20,000 whites. Meanwhile, Penn's policy had so impressed Native American tribes that Indian refugees began migrating into Pennsylvania from all sides. During the same 25 years, South Carolina had grown to only about 4,000 whites, while becoming a cauldron of violence. In the meantime, the native population was being seriously depleted by the slave trade and attendant warfare.

As long as the Quaker philosophy of pacifism and friendly relations with the local Native Americans held sway, interracial relations in the Delaware River Valley contrasted sharply with those in other parts of North America. Ironically, the Quaker policies attracted thousands of land-hungry immigrants to the colony (especially in the eighteenth century) whose disdain for Native Americans undermined Quaker trust and friendship. Driven from their homelands by hunger and war, Germans and Scots–Irish flooded in, swelling the population to 31,000 by 1720. Neither shared Quaker idealism about racial harmony. They pressed inland and, sometimes encouraged by the land agents of Penn's heirs, encroached on the lands of the local tribes. By the mid-eighteenth century, white immigrants were spilling blood with the natives who had also sought sanctuary in Pennsylvania.

Building the Peaceable Kingdom

Although Pennsylvania came closer to matching its founder's goals than any other European colony, Penn's dreams never completely materialized. Unconvinced that they should settle in compact villages, which Penn believed necessary for his "holy experiment," settlers instead created open country networks without any particular centers or boundaries.

Still, because Quaker farmers prized family life and immigrated almost entirely in kinship groups, a sense of common endeavor persisted and helped Quakers maintain their distinctive identity. So did other practices such as allowing marriage only within their society, carefully providing land for their offspring, and guarding against too great a population increase (which would cause too rapid a division of farms) by limiting the size of their families.

Settled by religiously dedicated farming families, Pennsylvania boomed. Its countryside became a rich grainland. By 1700, the port capital of Philadelphia overtook New York City in population, and a half century later, it was the largest city in the colonies, bustling with artisans, mariners, merchants, and professionals.

The Limits of Perfectionism

Despite commercial success and peace with Native Americans, not all was harmonious in early Pennsylvania. Politics were often turbulent, in part because of the state's weak leadership. Penn was a much-loved proprietor, but he returned to England in 1684, revisiting his colony again only briefly in 1700. His absence left a leadership vacuum.

A more important cause of disunity resided in the Quaker attitude toward authority. In England, balking at authority was almost a daily part of Quaker life. But in Pennsylvania, the lack of persecution eliminated a crucial binding element from Quaker society. The factionalism that developed among them demonstrated that people never unify so well as when under attack. Rather than looking inward and banding together, they looked outward to an environment filled with opportunity. Their squabbling filled Penn with dismay.

Meanwhile, Quaker industriousness and frugality helped produce great material success. After a generation, social radicalism and religious evangelicalism faded. As in other colonies, settlers discovered the door to prosperity wide open, and in they surged. Pennsylvania, it is said, was the first community since the Roman Empire to allow people of different national origins and religious persuasions to live together under the same government on terms of near equality. Their relations may not always have been friendly, but few attempts were made to discriminate against dissenting groups. Pennsylvanians thereby laid the foundations for the pluralism that was to become the hallmark of American society.

New Spain's Northern Frontier

Spain's outposts in Florida and New Mexico, preceding all English settlements on the eastern seaboard, fell into disarray between 1680 and the early eighteenth century just as the English colonies sank deeper roots. Trying to secure a vast northern frontier with only small numbers of settlers, the Spanish relied on forced Native American labor. This reliance proved to be their undoing in Florida and New Mexico.

Popé's Revolt

During the 1670s, when the Franciscans developed a new zeal to root out traditional Native American religious ceremonies, the Pueblo people turned on the Spanish intruders. The Spanish exacted tribute labor from the Pueblo, who at the same time suffered the ravaging effects of European diseases. Both of these hardships contributed to Pueblo alienation, but an assault on their religion pushed the natives to the edge. Launching a campaign to restrict native religious ceremonies in the 1670s, the Spanish friars seized **kivas** (underground ceremonial religious chambers), forbade native dances, and destroyed priestly masks and prayer sticks. In August 1680, Popé, a spiritual leader, responded, organizing about two dozen Pueblo villages scattered over several hundred miles to rise up in fury. They burned Spanish ranches and government buildings, systematically destroyed churches, lay waste to fields, and killed half of the friars.

Spanish settlers, soldiers, and friars streamed back to El Paso, abandoning their northern frontier in the Southwest for more than a decade. Only in 1694 did a new Spanish governor, the intrepid Diego de Vargas, regain Santa Fe and gradually subdue most of the Pueblo. Learning from Popé's rebellion, the Spanish declared a cultural truce, easing their demands for labor tribute and tolerating certain Pueblo rituals in return for nominal acceptance of Christianity. Periodic tension and animosity continued, but the

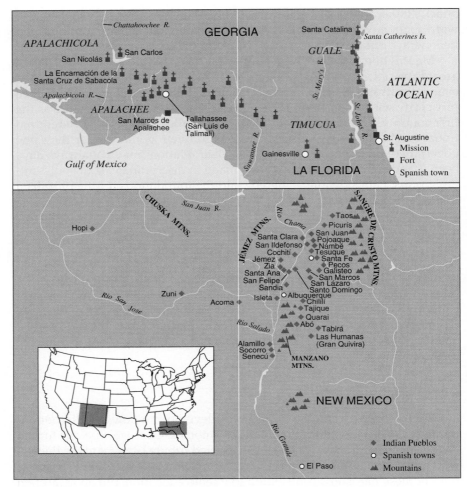

Spanish Missions in New Mexico and Florida in the Late Seventeenth Century
The extensive Spanish missionary activity in Florida and New Mexico had no English parallel.
What do you conclude from the preponderance of missions over Spanish towns?

Pueblo came to terms with the Spanish because of their need for defense against their old enemies, the Navajo, Ute, and Apache.

Decline of Florida's Missions

Franciscan missions consolidated New Spain's grip of the southeast corner of North America. Yet few Spanish settlers could be persuaded to colonize Florida. In addition, the Florida Indians and their Franciscan spiritual shepherds were devastated by disease. English settlers in neighboring South Carolina were eager to use Native American allies to attack the Spanish Indian villages and sell the captives into slavery. The attacks of Carolinians in the early 1680s destroyed a number of Spanish missions. When England and Spain went to war in 1701—called **Queen Anne's War** in the colonies— the Carolinians attacked Florida. The Spanish mission frontier was devastated, and only St. Augustine remained as a Spanish stronghold. Without a sufficient Spanish population, Spain's hold on Florida faltered. Unlike in New Mexico, no Spanish reconquest ensued. From this time onward, English and French traders, offering more attractive trade goods, would have the main influence over Florida Indians.

An Era of Instability

A dozen years after King Philip's War in New England and Bacon's Rebellion in Virginia, a series of insurrections and a devastating witchcraft incident convulsed colonial society. The Revolution of 1688 triggered these rebellions. Known thereafter to English Protestants as the **Glorious Revolution**, it limited the power of the monarch and assured that only a Protestant would sit on the English throne. In the colonies, it signified a struggle for social and political dominance, as did the Salem witchcraft trials in Massachusetts.

Organizing the Empire

From the beginning of colonization, the English assumed that overseas settlements existed to promote the national interest. Mercantilist theory held that colonies served as outlets for English manufactured goods, provided foodstuffs and raw materials, stimulated trade (and hence promoted a larger merchant navy), and filled royal coffers by exporting commodities such as sugar and tobacco on which duties were paid. In return, colonists received English military protection and guaranteed markets.

Beginning with small steps in 1621, when the king ordered tobacco exports sent to England only, the Crown slowly began to regulate its colonies. In 1651, Parliament passed acts guiding colonial affairs, including a navigation act requiring that English or colonial ships carry all goods entering England, Ireland, and the colonies, no matter where those goods originated. In 1660, after the monarchy was restored, a more comprehensive navigation act listed colonial products (tobacco, sugar, indigo, dyewoods, and cotton) that could be shipped only to England or other English colonies. Like its predecessor, the act took dead aim at Dutch domination of Atlantic commerce, while increasing England's revenues by imposing duties on the articles. Later **navigation acts** added other enumerated articles. Regulation bore lightly on the colonists because the laws lacked enforcement.

After 1675, international competition and war led England to impose greater imperial control. That year marked the establishment of the Lords of Trade, a committee of the king's Privy Council empowered to make and enforce decisions regulating the colonies. They aimed to create more uniform colonial governments that would do the Crown's will. Although movement toward imperial centralization often sputtered, the trend was unmistakable, especially to colonists who felt the sting of royal customs agents sent to enforce the navigation acts. England was becoming the shipper of the world, and its state-regulated policy of economic nationalism was essential to achieving commercial greatness.

The Glorious Revolution in North America

When Charles II died in 1685, his brother, the duke of York, became James II. This set in motion a chain of events that nearly led to civil war. In contrast to the vast majority of his subjects, James professed the Catholic faith. Protestant England recoiled when he issued the Declaration of Indulgence, granting liberty of worship to all, appointed Catholics to high government posts, and demanded that Oxford and Cambridge open their doors to Catholic students. In 1687, the king dismissed a resistant Parliament. When his wife bore a son in 1688, a Catholic succession loomed.

Convinced that James aimed at absolute power, Protestant leaders in 1688 invited a Dutch prince, William of Orange, to seize the throne with his wife, Mary, who was one of James's Protestant daughters from an earlier marriage. James fled rather than fight. It was a bloodless victory for Protestantism, for parliamentary power, and for the limitation of kingly prerogatives.

The response of New Englanders to these events stemmed from their previous experience with royal authority and their fear of "papists." New England had become a prime target for efforts to reorganize the empire and crack down on smuggling. Charles II annulled the Massachusetts charter in 1684, and two years later James II appointed Sir Edmund Andros, a crusty professional soldier and former governor of New York, to rule over the newly created **Dominion of New England**. Soon the Dominion gathered under one government all the English colonies from Maine to New Jersey. Puritans now had to swallow the bitter fact that they were subjects of London bureaucrats who cared more about shaping a disciplined empire than about New England's special religious vision.

At first, New Englanders accepted Andros, though coolly. But he soon earned their hatred by imposing taxes without legislative consent, ending trial by jury, abolishing the General Court of Massachusetts (which had met annually since 1630), muzzling Boston's town meeting, and questioning land titles. He also converted a Boston meetinghouse into a Church of England chapel, held services there on Christmas Day—a gesture that to Puritans stank of popery—and insisted on religious toleration.

When news reached Boston in April 1689 that William of Orange had landed in England, Bostonians streamed into the streets. They imprisoned Andros and overwhelmed the fort in Boston harbor, which held most of the governor's small contingent of red-coated royal troops. Boston's ministers, along with merchants and former magistrates, led the rebellion. For three years, an interim government ruled Massachusetts while the Bay colonists awaited a new charter.

Although Bostonians had dramatically rejected royal authority and the "bloody Devotees of Rome," no internal revolution occurred. Social conservatives like Boston minister Samuel Willard abhorred the popular spirit he saw unloosed as Bostonians took to the streets. Tensions that existed in the society manifested themselves not in further political conflict but in a new way—fears over witchcraft.

In New York, the Glorious Revolution was similarly bloodless at first but far more disruptive. Royal government melted away on news of James's ouster. Displacing the governor's "popishly affected dogs and rogues," German-born militia captain Jacob Leisler established an interim government and ruled with an elected Committee of Safety for 13 months until a governor appointed by William and Mary arrived.

Leisler's government enjoyed popularity among small landowners and urban laboring people who had resented the English seizing their colony in 1664 and crowding them out of the society they had built. Most of the upper echelon, however, had adjusted to English rule and many incoming English merchants had married into Dutch families.

The Glorious Revolution ignited this smoldering social conflict. Leisler shared Dutch hostility toward New York's English elite, and his sympathy for the common people, mostly Dutch, earned him the hatred of the city's oligarchy. Leisler freed imprisoned debtors, planned a town-meeting system of government for New York City, and replaced merchants with artisans in important offices. By the autumn of 1689, Leislerian mobs were attacking the property of some of New York's wealthiest merchants. Two merchants, refusing to recognize Leisler's authority, were jailed.

Leisler's opponents were horrified at the power of the "rabble." They believed that ordinary people had no right to rebel against authority or to exercise political power. When a new English governor arrived in 1691, the anti-Leislerians embraced him and charged Leisler and seven of his assistants with treason for assuming the government without royal instructions.

In the ensuing trial, Leisler and Jacob Milbourne, his son-in-law and chief lieutenant, were convicted of treason by an all-English jury and hanged. Leisler's popularity among the artisans of the city was evident when his wealthy opponents could find no carpenter in the city who would make a ladder for the scaffold. After his execution, peace gradually returned to New York, but for years provincial and city politics reflected the deep rift between Leislerians and anti-Leislerians.

The Glorious Revolution also focused dissatisfactions in several southern colonies. Because a Catholic proprietor ruled Maryland, the Protestant majority seized power in July 1689 on word of the Glorious Revolution, using it for their own purposes. They vowed to cleanse Maryland of popery and to reform a corrupt customs service, cut taxes and fees, and extend the rights of the representative assembly. Militant Protestants held power until the arrival of Maryland's first royal governor in 1692.

The Glorious Revolution brought lasting political changes to several colonies. The Dominion of New England collapsed. Connecticut and Rhode Island regained the right to elect their governors, but Massachusetts (now including Plymouth) and New Hampshire became royal colonies with governors appointed by the king. In Massachusetts, a new royal charter in 1691 eliminated Church membership as a voting requirement. The Maryland proprietorship was abolished (to be restored in 1715 when the Calverts became Protestant), and Catholics were barred from office. Everywhere Protestant Englishmen celebrated their liberties.

The Social Basis of Politics

The colonial insurrections associated with the Glorious Revolution revealed social and political tensions that accompanied the transplanting of English society to the North American wilderness. Colonial societies could be fluid, unruly, and competitive, lacking the stable political systems and leadership class thought necessary for social order.

The emerging colonial elite tried to foster stability by upholding a stratified Old World–style society where children were subordinate to parents, women to men, servants to masters, and the poor to the rich. Hence leaders tried to maintain social gradations. Churchgoers did not file into church on Sundays and occupy the pews randomly; seats were assigned according to customary yardsticks of respectability: age, parentage, social position, wealth, and occupation. In Virginia, lower-class people were hauled before courts for horse racing because this sport was legally reserved for men of social distinction.

These social distinctions proved difficult to maintain. Regardless of previous rank, settlers rubbed elbows so frequently and faced such raw conditions together that those without pedigrees often saw little reason to defer to men of superior rank. "In Virginia," explained John Smith, "a plain soldier that can use a pickaxe and spade is better than five knights." Colonists everywhere gave respect not to those who claimed it by birth but to those who earned it by deed. A colonial elite gradually formed, but it had no basis, as in Europe, in legally defined and hereditary social rank. Planters and merchants, accumulating large estates, aped the English gentry. Yet their place was rarely secure as new competitors nipped at their heels.

Amid such social flux, the elite never commanded general allegiance to the ideal of a fixed social structure. Men who led rebellion might be a society's traditional leaders, as was the case in New England during the Glorious Revolution. Then some worried about the power they had unleashed. In other instances, as with Nathaniel Bacon in Virginia and Jacob Leisler in New York, ambitious men might appeal to the discontented to rise up against the constituted authorities. When such men gained power, usually only briefly, the leaders of these uprisings linked themselves with a tradition of English struggle against tyranny and oligarchical power. They tried not to appear to be breaking with English tradition, even as they exploited the discontent of the ordinary people, who composed most of their societies.

Witchcraft in Salem

The tragic events of the Salem witch hunts arose in the period of uncertainty following the Glorious Revolution. In Massachusetts, deposing Governor Andros left the colony in political limbo for three years, and this lapse allowed what might have been a brief outbreak of witchcraft fear in the little community of Salem to escalate into a bitter and bloody battle. The provincial government, caught in transition, reacted only belatedly.

On a winter's day in 1692, 9-year-old Betty Parris and her 11-year-old cousin Abigail Williams began to play at magic in the kitchen of a small house in Salem Village, Massachusetts. They enlisted the aid of Tituba, the slave of Betty's father, Samuel Parris, the minister of the small community. Probably fearful of what they had done, the girls soon became seized with fits and began making wild gestures and speeches. Soon other girls and young women in the village were behaving strangely. Village elders extracted confessions that they were being tormented by Tituba and two other women, both social outcasts.

What began as young girls' play turned into a ghastly rending of a farm community capped by the deaths of 20 villagers accused of witchcraft. In the seventeenth century, people took literally the biblical injunction, "Thou shalt not suffer a witch to live." For centuries throughout western Europe, people had believed that witches followed Satan's bidding and did evil to anyone he designated. Communities accused and sentenced women to death for witchcraft far more often than men. In Massachusetts, more than 100 people, mostly older women, had been accused of witchcraft before 1692, and more than a dozen had been hanged.

◉ View the Image

A Further Account of the Tryals of the New England Witches at **www.myhistorylab.com**

In Salem, the initial accusations against three older women quickly multiplied. Within weeks, dozens had been charged. Formal prosecution of the accused witches could not proceed because neither the new royal charter issued in 1691 nor the royal governor to rule the colony had yet arrived. For three months, while charges spread, local authorities could only jail the accused without trial. When Governor William Phips arrived from England in May 1692, he ordered a special court to try the accused. By then, events had careened out of control.

All through the summer, the court listened to testimony. By September it had condemned about two dozen villagers. The authorities hanged 19 of them on a barren "Witches Hill" outside the town and crushed 80-year-old Giles Corey to death under heavy stones. The trials rolled on into 1693, but by then, colonial leaders, including many of the clergy, recognized that a feverish fear of one's neighbors, rather than witchcraft itself, had possessed Salem Village.

Many factors contributed to the hysteria. Among them were generational differences between older Puritan colonists and the sometimes less religiously motivated younger generation, old family animosities, population growth and pressures on the available farmland, and tensions between agricultural Salem Village and the nearby commercial center called Salem Town. A new Indian war on the Massachusetts–Maine frontier caused panic. Probably nobody will ever fully understand the exact mingling of causes, but the fact that most of the individuals charged with witchcraft were women underscores the relatively weak position of women in colonial society. The relentless spread of witchcraft accusations suggests the anxiety of this tumultuous era of war, economic disruption, and political tension, and the erosion of the early generation's utopian vision.

Conclusion
The Achievement of New Societies

Nearly 200,000 immigrants who had left their European homelands reached North America in the seventeenth century. Coming from a variety of social backgrounds and spurred by different motives, they represented the initial peopling of distinctive societies that matured in the colonies of England, France, Holland, and Spain. For three generations, northern North America served as a social laboratory for religious and social visionaries, political theorists, fortune seekers, social outcasts, and, most of all, ordinary men and women seeking a better life than they had known in Europe.

By the end of the seventeenth century, 12 English colonies on the eastern edge of North America (and several others in the West Indies) had secured footholds in the hemisphere and erected the basic scaffolding of colonial life. So had Spanish and French colonies lying north, south, and west of the English. The coastal Native American tribes were reeling from disease and a series of wars that secured the English colonists' land base along 1,000 miles of coastal plain. Though never controlling the powerful tribes of the interior, the colonists had established a profitable trade with them. English settlers had overcome a scarcity of labor by copying the other European colonists, who had linked the west coast of Africa to the New World through the ghastly trade in human flesh. Finally, the English colonists had engaged in insurrections against what they viewed as arbitrary and tainted governments imposed by England.

The embryo of British America carried into the eighteenth century contained peculiarly mixed features. Disease, stunted family life, and the harsh work regimen imposed by the planters who commanded the labor of the vast majority ended the dreams of most who came to the southern colonies. Yet population inched upward, and the bone and sinew of a workable economy formed. In the northern colonies, to which the fewest immigrants came, life was more secure. Organized around family and community, favored by a healthier climate, and motivated by religion and social vision, the Puritan and Quaker societies thrived.

Still physically isolated from Europe, the colonists developed a large measure of self-reliance. Slowly, they began to identify themselves as the permanent inhabitants of a new land rather than as transplanted English,

Dutch, or Scots–Irish. Viewing land and labor as the indispensable elements of a fruitful economy, they learned to exploit without apologies the land of one people and the labor of another. Although utopian visions of life in North America still preoccupied some, most colonists moved into the eighteenth century eager to exploit the unpredictable opportunity that this New World represented for them. A maturing colonial society would continue to grow through voluntary and forced migration as well as natural increase; it would be increasingly caught up in wider wars as well as expanding commercial networks; and it would continue to explore the religious and political options that life in the New World afforded. A New World in much more than a geographic sense, America was remade by the people of three cultures who inhabited it. And, while doing so, people like Anthony and Mary Johnson (whom we met at the beginning of the chapter) were remaking themselves.

⊙ See the **Map**
The Colonies to 1740
at **www.myhistorylab.com**

TIME*line*

1607	Jamestown settled
1616–1621	Native American population in New England decimated by European diseases
1619	First Africans arrive in Jamestown
1620	Pilgrims land at Plymouth
1622	Powhatan tribes attack Virginia settlements
1624	Dutch colonize mouth of Hudson River
1630	Puritan immigration to Massachusetts Bay
1632	Maryland grant to Lord Baltimore (George Calvert)
1636	Anne Hutchinson exiled to Rhode Island
1637	New England wages war against the Pequot people
1642–1649	English civil war ends great migration to New England
1650–1670	Judicial and legislative decisions in Chesapeake colonies solidify racial lines
1651	Parliament passes first navigation act
1660	Restoration of King Charles II in England
1663	Carolina charter granted to eight proprietors
1664	English capture New Netherland and rename it New York
	Royal grant of the Jersey lands to proprietors
1673–1685	French expand into Mississippi valley
1675–1677	King Philip's War in New England
1676	Bacon's Rebellion in Virginia
1680	Popé's revolt in New Mexico

1681	William Penn receives Pennsylvania grant
1688	Glorious Revolution in England, followed by accession of William and Mary
1689	Overthrow of Governor Andros in New England
	Leisler's Rebellion in New York
1690s	Transition from white indentured servitude to black slave labor begins in Chesapeake region
1692	Witchcraft hysteria in Salem

✔•⎡Study and Review at **www.myhistorylab.com**

Questions for Review and Reflection

1. What factors most shaped the development of the colonial Chesapeake region in the seventeenth century?

2. Early Massachusetts was organized around shared religious goals, yet it was riven by strife. How do you explain the tensions within this colony?

3. Seventeenth-century North America included a wide variety of colonial endeavors. What were the main regional divisions and distinguishing features of each area?

4. What were the causes and consequences of King Philip's War and Bacon's Rebellion? In what ways were the two conflicts similar or different?

5. What were the effects of the Glorious Revolution on the colonies and the empire?

6. Despite differences between colonial regions, it appears that prejudicial attitudes toward Africans and Native Americans were a common thread running through all colonial societies. Do you agree, and if so, do you see any exceptions to this rule?

Key Terms

Antinomianism 66

Artisan 65

Bacon's Rebellion 58

Confederation of New England 70

Dominion of New England 84

Glorious Revolution 83

Iroquois Confederacy 73

King Philip's War 71

Kivas 81

Navigation Acts 83

New Netherland 73

Puritans 62

Quakers 76

Queen Anne's War 83

4

The Maturing of Colonial Society

American Stories

A Struggling Farm Woman Finds True Religious Commitment

In 1758, 37-year-old Hannah Cook Heaton stood trial for her refusal to attend her local Congregationalist church. A resident of North New Haven, Connecticut, Hannah was required by law to attend Sunday worship services—a law derived from the belief that religious uniformity was a social good. Hannah did not object to churchgoing; in fact, she was a fervent Christian. She had been a member of Isaac Stiles's church—indeed, he had performed her marriage to Theophilus Heaton, Jr., in 1743. But later in that decade, after she had been caught up in the enthusiasm of the Great Awakening, a series of religious revivals that rocked New England in the 1740s, Hannah ceased to attend Sunday worship. Thereafter, finding that her minister's preaching left her cold and dissatisfied, Heaton quit the church, arguing that Stiles had never himself undergone conversion and was therefore a "blind guide" leading his flock astray.

Hannah's decision to leave the village church was prompted by the preaching of men she believed were imbued with the spirit. Hearing touring evangelists George Whitefield, James Davenport, and Gilbert Tennant sparked a profound conversion experience. As she later recorded in her diary, she "thought I see Jesus with the eyes of my soul." This religious transformation led her to join a small congregation headed by Benjamin Beach, a lay preacher. Uneducated and unlicensed, he was precisely the kind of man whom Harvard- and Yale-trained ministers regarded as a threat to well-ordered New England communities. Yet many like Hannah Heaton found him spiritually gifted, and so they separated themselves from the established church to meet regularly at Beach's home for worship and prayer.

Because she abandoned the established church for this community of believers, who called themselves Separatists, Hannah was pressured by both members of Stiles's church and local officials. Finally brought to trial, she remained defiant. Heaton told the magistrate at her trial that "there was a day a-coming when justice would be done . . . there is a dreadful day a-coming upon them that have no Christ." Declaring that she "talked sass," the justice convicted her of breaking the law and fined her twelve shillings.

To Hannah's dismay and despite her efforts, her husband never shared her commitment to the dissenters. He remained a member of Stiles's church, urged Hannah to rejoin it, and, against Hannah's wishes, paid her fine in the trial of 1758. Resenting his wife's involvement with the Separatists, he hid her spectacles so she could not read her Bible or write in her diary, threw her diary in the mud, and refused to provide her with a horse to ride to meetings. Hannah worried about his immortal soul, disheartened that even on his deathbed she could not persuade him to repent and seek after the Lord.

Hannah Cook Heaton was in many ways a typical colonial woman, married to a farmer and the mother of numerous children. Her life would be virtually unknown to us except that she kept a diary of her spiritual experiences, in which she revealed how she was dramatically reshaped by the Great Awakening. As was the case for many eighteenth-century colonists, revivalism fundamentally changed her experience, affecting her marriage and other intimate relationships. Her identity as a Separatist brought her briefly into public prominence, as one of the few members of her movement to be prosecuted in court in Connecticut in the 1750s. How did her religious convictions motivate her to defy various authorities in her life, including her husband, her minister, and the local magistrate?

The religious revivals that transformed Hannah Heaton's life were just one of the forces affecting colonial life during the eighteenth century. Between 1680 and 1750, a virtual population explosion occurred in the English colonies, swelling the number of settlers from 150,000 in 1680 to more than 1 million at midcentury. Such growth staggered English policymakers, who uneasily watched the population gap between England and its American colonies closing rapidly. A high marriage rate, large families, lower mortality than in Europe, and heavy immigration accounted for much of the population boom.

How did population growth and economic development gradually transform eighteenth-century British America? Three variations of colonial society emerged, which shared important characteristics but also exhibited distinctive features: the farming society of the North, the plantation society of the South, and the urban society of the seaboard commercial towns. Diversity generally increased in the eighteenth century as incoming streams of immigrants, mostly from Germany, Ireland, France, and especially from Africa, added new pieces to the emerging American mosaic.

Until the late seventeenth century, the Spanish, French, and English settlements in North America were largely isolated from each other. But when a long period of war erupted in Europe between these colonizing nations, North America and the Caribbean became important theaters of international conflict that would reach a climax in the second half of the eighteenth century.

As colonial society matured, local economies forged links with the Atlantic basin trade network. Colonists such as Hannah Heaton experienced a deep awakening that established evangelical religion as a hallmark of American society. How did the popularity of revival connect to the changing exercise of political power? From increasingly powerful legislative assemblies and local instruments of governance emerged seasoned leaders, a tradition of local autonomy, and a widespread belief in a political ideology stressing the liberties that freeborn Englishmen should enjoy. What was the process whereby raw frontier settlements developed into mature provincial societies?

The North: A Land of Family Farms

Although New England by the eighteenth century offered fewer opportunities for new immigrants, the mid-Atlantic colonies swarmed with waves of new arrivals from the Rhineland and Ireland. About 90,000 Germans flocked in during the eighteenth century, many fleeing "God's three arrows": famine, war, and pestilence. They settled where promoters promised cheap and fertile land, low taxes, and freedom from military duty. Coming mostly in families, they turned much of the mid-Atlantic hinterland into a German-speaking region. Even more Protestant Scots–Irish arrived. Mostly poor farmers, they streamed into the same backcountry areas where Germans were settling, especially New York and Pennsylvania.

Northern Agricultural Society

In the mid-eighteenth-century northern colonies, especially New England, tight-knit farming families organized in communities of several thousand people dotted the landscape. New Englanders staked their future on a mixed economy. They cleared forests for timber used in barrels, ships, houses, and barns. They plumbed the offshore waters for fish that fed both local populations and the ballooning slave population of the West Indies. And they cultivated and grazed as much of the thin-soiled, rocky hills and bottomlands as they could recover from the forest.

The farmers of the middle colonies—Pennsylvania, Delaware, New Jersey, and New York—drove their wooden plows through much richer soils than New Englanders. They enjoyed the additional advantage of settling land already cleared by Native Americans who had relied more on agriculture than New England tribes. Thus favored, mid-Atlantic farm families produced modest surpluses of corn, wheat, beef, and pork. By the mid-eighteenth century, New York and Philadelphia ships were carrying these foodstuffs not only to the Caribbean, always a primary market, but also to England, Spain, Portugal, and even New England, strengthening ties within the Atlantic basin.

In the North, the broad ownership of land distinguished farming society from every other agricultural region of the Western world. Although differences in circumstances and ability led gradually toward greater social stratification, in most communities, few were truly rich or abjectly poor. Except for indentured servants, most men lived to purchase or inherit a farm of at least 50 acres. With their family labor, they earned a decent existence and provided a small inheritance for each of their children. Settlers valued land highly, for **freehold tenure** ordinarily guaranteed both economic independence and political rights.

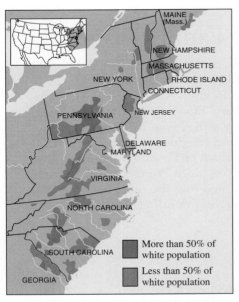 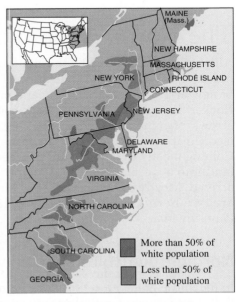

German Settlement Areas, 1775 (Left) Scots–Irish Settlement Areas, 1775 (Right) Most German and Scots–Irish immigrants in the 1700s were farmers, and they quickly moved into the interior. Why do you think they did so?

By the eighteenth century, with widespread property ownership, a rising population pressed against a limited land supply, especially in New England. Family farms could not be divided and subdivided indefinitely, for it took at least 50 acres to support a family. In Concord, Massachusetts, for example, the founders had worked farms averaging about 250 acres. A century later, in the 1730s, the average farm had shrunk by two-thirds, as farm owners struggled to provide an inheritance for the three or four sons that the average marriage produced.

Decreasing soil fertility compounded the problem. When land had been plentiful, farmers planted crops in the same field for three years and then let it lie fallow until it regained its strength. On the smaller farms of the eighteenth century, farmers reduced fallowing to only a year or two, limiting crop yields and forcing farmers to plow marginal land or shift to livestock production.

The diminishing size and productivity of family farms drove out many New Englanders. In Concord, one of every four adult males left town every decade from the 1740s on. In many towns, out-migration was even greater, with some drifting to New York and Pennsylvania and others going to western Massachusetts, New Hampshire, Maine, and Nova Scotia. Still others sought opportunities as artisans in the coastal towns or took to the sea.

Northern farming was far less intense than in the South. The growing season was shorter, and cereal crops required incessant labor only during spring planting and autumn harvesting. This seasonal rhythm led many northern cultivators to fill out their calendars with work as shoemakers, carpenters, and weavers.

Unfree Labor

Though the shorter growing seasons curbed the demand for labor in the North, slaves and indentured servants still made up much of the incoming human tide after 1713. They became a regular part of the commerce linking Europe, Africa, and North America.

Read the **Document**
Virginia Law on Indentured Servitude (1705)
at **www.myhistorylab.com**

Despite official attempts to reduce the "tight packing" of indentured immigrants, shipboard conditions for both slaves and servants worsened in the eighteenth century. Crammed between decks in stifling air, they suffered from smallpox and fevers, rotten food, impure water, cold, and lice. The shipboard mortality rate of about 15 percent in the colonial era made this the most unhealthy of all times to seek American shores.

Indentured servants, especially males, often found the labor system harsh. Every servant's goal was to secure a foothold on the ladder of opportunity. Many died before finishing their time; others won freedom only to toil for years as poor day laborers or tenant farmers. The chief beneficiaries of the system of bound white labor were the masters.

The number of enslaved Africans in the northern colonies grew in the eighteenth century, but not nearly as fast as the indentured labor force. Slaves made up less than 10 percent of the population in all northern colonies.

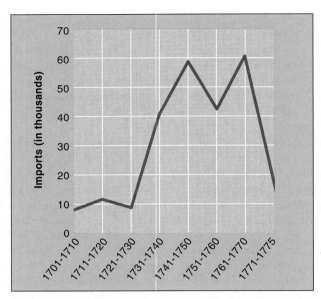

Slaves Imported to North America, 1701–1775 Overwhelmingly, Africans transported to the American colonies arrived from the 1730s to the 1770s. Given these importation statistics, how would you explain the fact that the African population swelled to about 500,000 by the outbreak of the American Revolution? *(Source:* R. C. Simmons, *The American Colonies: From Settlement to Independence, 1976.)*

Since in the North the typical slave labored alone or with only a few others while living in the same house as the master, slaves there adapted to European ways relatively quickly.

Northern slaves typically worked as artisans, farmhands, or personal servants. Slavery grew fastest in the northern ports. Artisans invested profitably in slaves; ship captains purchased them for maritime labor; and an emerging urban elite of merchants, lawyers, and landlords displayed its wealth with slave coachmen and personal servants. By the beginning of the eighteenth century, more than 40 percent of New York City households owned slaves. In Philadelphia, slaveholding increased sharply in the eighteenth century. Struggling white artisans resented slave workers for undercutting their wages, and the whites feared black arsonists and rebels. Yet high labor demand outweighed these reservations, and the advantage of purchasing lifelong servants for just two years' worth of a free white laborer's wages was obvious.

Changing Values

Boston weather on April 29, 1695, began warm and sunny, noted the devout merchant Samuel Sewall in his diary. But by afternoon, lightning and hailstones "as big as pistol and musket bullets" pummeled the town. Sewall dined that evening with Cotton Mather, a prominent clergyman. Mather wondered why "more ministers' houses than others proportionately had been smitten with lightning." The words were hardly out of his mouth before hailstones began to shatter the windows. Sewall and Mather fell to their knees in prayer "after this awful Providence." They concluded that God was angry with them as leaders of a people whose piety was giving way to worldliness. Massachusetts was becoming "sermon-proof," explained one dejected minister.

Throughout the North, the expansive environment and the Protestant emphasis on self-discipline and hard work were breeding qualities that would become hallmarks of American culture: ambitiousness, individualism, and materialism. One colonist remarked, "Every man expects one day or another to be upon a footing with his wealthiest neighbor." Commitment to religion, family, and community did not disappear, as Hannah Heaton's story demonstrates, but acquisitiveness was becoming more acceptable.

A slender almanac, written by the twelfth child of a poor Boston candle-maker, captured the new outlook with wit and charm. Born in 1706, Benjamin Franklin climbed the ladder of success spectacularly. Running away from a harsh apprenticeship to an older brother when he was 16, he abandoned a declining Boston for a rising Philadelphia. By 23, he had learned the printer's trade and was publishing the *Pennsylvania Gazette*. Three years later, he began *Poor Richard's Almanack*, which, next to the Bible, was the most widely read book in the colonies. Franklin filled it with quips, adages, and home-spun philosophy: "The sleeping fox gathers no poultry." "Lost time is never found again." Franklin caught the spirit of the rising secularism of the eighteenth century. He embodied the growing utilitarian doctrine that good is whatever is useful. For Franklin, the community was best served through individual self-improvement.

Women and the Family in the Northern Colonies

In 1662, Elnathan Chauncy, a Massachusetts schoolboy, copied into his writing book that the soul "consists of two portions, inferior and superior; the superior is masculine and eternal; the feminine inferior and mortal." Generations on both sides of the Atlantic had taught such ideas as part of a larger conception of God's design that assigned degrees of status and stations in life to all individuals. In that world, women were subordinate, taught from infancy to be modest, patient, and compliant. Regarded by men as weak of mind, they existed for and through men, subject first to their fathers and then to their husbands.

Colonial women usually accepted these narrowly circumscribed roles, and few openly complained that their work was generally limited to house-wifery and midwifery. Women were excluded from the early public schools, laws transferred to their husbands any property or income they brought into a marriage, they had no legal voice in politics, and (except in Quaker meetinghouses) they could not speak in their churches. In her role as wife and mother, the eighteenth-century northern woman differed somewhat from her English counterpart. One in 10 European women did not marry. Colonial men outnumbered women for the first century, so a spinster was almost unheard of, and widows remarried with astounding speed. *Woman* and *wife* thus became nearly synonymous. Whereas English women married in their mid-twenties, American women typically took husbands a few years earlier, increasing their childbearing years. Hence, the average colonial family included five children (two others typically died in infancy), whereas the English family had fewer than three.

Another change concerned property rights. As in England, single women and widows in the colonies could make contracts, hold and convey property, represent themselves in court, and conduct business. Colonial legislatures and courts, however, gave wives more control over property brought into marriage or left at their husband's death. They also enjoyed broader rights to act for and with their husbands in business transactions.

Women had limited career choices and rights but broad responsibilities. The work spaces and daily routines of husband and wife overlapped and intersected far more than today. "Deputy husbands" and "yoke mates" were revealing terms used by New Englanders to describe eighteenth-century wives.

Despite conventional talk of inferiority, women within their families and neighborhoods nevertheless shaped the world around them. Older women molded the behavior of young women, aided the needy, and subtly affected menfolk, who held formal authority. Women outnumbered men in church life and, like Hannah Heaton, promoted religion within their families, working for church buildings in outlying areas, to seat and unseat ministers, and to influence morals. Periodically, they appeared as visionaries and mystics.

Until the late eighteenth century, the "obstetrick art" was almost entirely in their hands. Midwives counseled pregnant women, delivered babies, supervised postpartum recovery, and participated in infant baptism and burial ceremonies. Because colonial women were pregnant or nursing infants for about half the years between the ages of 20 and 40 and because childbirth was dangerous, the circle of female friends and relatives attending childbirth created strong networks of mutual assistance.

The father-dominated family of New England gradually declined in the eighteenth century, replaced by the mother-centered family, in which affectionate parents encouraged self-expression and independence in their children. This "modern" approach, on the rise in Europe as well, brought the colonists closer to the methods of parenthood found among the coastal Native Americans, who initially had been disparaged for their lax approach to rearing their young.

The Plantation South

Between 1680 and 1750, the southern white tidewater settlements changed from a frontier society with high immigration, a surplus of males, and an unstable social organization to a settled society composed mostly of native-born families. As a mature southern culture took form on the coastal plains that stretched from the ocean to the piedmont, after 1715 Scots–Irish and German immigrants flooded into the backcountry of Virginia, the Carolinas, and the new colony of Georgia. The fast-growing slave population accounted for much more of the population growth than in the North. Virginia, with a population of nearly 340,000 by 1760, remained by far the largest colony in North America.

●●●─[Read the **Document**

Establishing the Colony of Georgia (1733)

at **www.myhistorylab.com**

Southern Economic Change

The southern colonies developed two different coastal economies. Rapidly expanding tobacco production in seventeenth-century Virginia and Maryland sent exports to 25 million pounds annually during the 1680s. Two decades of war then drove up transportation costs, depressing the tobacco market until about 1715.

During this period the Upper South underwent a profound social transformation. First, African slaves replaced European indentured servants so rapidly that by 1730 the unfree labor force was overwhelmingly black. Second, planters responded to the depressed tobacco market by diversifying their crops. They shifted some fields to grain, hemp, and flax; increased their herds of cattle and swine; and became more self-sufficient by developing local industries to produce iron, leather, and textiles. By the 1720s, when a profitable tobacco trade with France created a new period of prosperity, the economy was much more diverse and resilient. Third, the population structure changed rapidly. African slaves grew from about 7 percent to more than 40 percent of the region's population between 1690 and 1750, and the drastic imbalance between white men and women disappeared. Families rather than single men now predominated. The earlier frontier society of white immigrants, mostly living short, unrewarding lives as indentured servants, grew into an eighteenth-century plantation society of native-born freeholder families.

Notwithstanding the influx of Africans, slave owning was far from universal. As late as 1750, a majority of families owned no slaves at all. Not more than one-tenth of slaveholders held more than 20 slaves. Nonetheless, the common goal was the large plantation where slaves made the earth yield up profits to support an aristocratic life for their masters. The plantation economy of the Lower South in the eighteenth century rested on rice and indigo. Rice exports surpassed 1.5 million pounds per year by 1710 and reached 80 million pounds by the eve of the Revolution. Indigo,

Slaves on an Indigo Plantation Indigo production, mostly the work of enslaved Africans in South Carolina, was dirty, smelly, and debilitating. This eighteenth-century engraving shows each step, from the plant at lower right to tending vats of boiling water. What do you notice about the figure at the top right?

a smelly blue dye obtained from plants for use in textiles, became a staple crop in the 1740s after Eliza Lucas Pinckney, a wealthy South Carolina planter's wife, experimented successfully with its cultivation. Within a generation, indigo production had spread into Georgia, ranking among the leading colonial exports.

The expansion of rice production, exported to the West Indies and Europe, transformed the swampy coastal lowlands around Charleston, where planters imported thousands of slaves after 1720. By 1740, slaves comprised nearly 90 percent of the region's inhabitants. White population declined as wealthy planters entrusted their estates to resident overseers. Wintering in cosmopolitan Charleston, they spent summers in Newport, Rhode Island. At midcentury, a shocked New England visitor described it as a society "divided into opulent and lordly planters, poor and spiritless peasants, and vile slaves."

Southern Plantation Society

Planters who acquired the best land and accumulated enough capital to invest heavily in slaves created a gentry lifestyle that set them apart from ordinary farmers. By the eighteenth century, the development of the northern colonies had produced prosperous farmers worth several thousand pounds. But such wealth paled alongside the estates of men who counted their slaves by the hundreds, their acres by the thousands, and their fortunes by the tens of thousands of pounds.

Ritual display of wealth marked southern gentry life. Racing thoroughbred horses and gambling became common sport for young gentlemen, who had often been educated in England. Planters built stately brick Georgian mansions, filled with imported furniture. The emerging Chesapeake planter elite controlled the county courts, officered the local militia, ruled the parish vestries of the Anglican Church, made law in their legislative assemblies, and passed to their sons the mantle of political and social leadership. Learning how to manage and discipline slaves was as important as lessons with tutors. Bred to command, southern planters' sons developed a self-confidence and authority that propelled many of them into leadership roles during the American Revolution.

For all their airs, these southern squires were essentially agrarian businessmen. They spent their days haggling over credit, land, slaves, and tenant leases; scheduling planting and harvesting; conferring with overseers; and disciplining slaves. Tobacco cultivation (unlike that of wheat and corn) claimed the planter's year-round attention. A planter's reputation rested on the quality of his crop.

Planters' wives also shouldered many responsibilities. They superintended cloth production and the processing and preparation of food while ruling over households crowded with children, slaves, and visitors. An aristocratic veneer gave the luster of gentility to plantations from Maryland to North Carolina, but in fact these were large working farms, often completely isolated from one another.

Throughout the plantation South, the courthouse became a central male gathering place. All classes came to settle debts, dispute over land, sue and be sued. When court was over, a multitude lingered on, drinking, gossiping, and staging horse races, cockfights, wrestling matches, footraces, and fiddling contests—all considered tests of male prowess.

The church, almost always Anglican in the South before 1750, also became a center of community gathering. A visiting northerner described the animated socializing before worship: men "giving and receiving letters of business, reading advertisements, consulting about the price of tobacco and grain, and settling either the lineage, age, or qualities of favourite horses." Then people filed into church, with lesser planters entering first and standing attentively until the wealthy gentry, "in a body" took their pews at the front. After church, socializing continued with young people strolling together and older ones extending invitations to Sunday dinner. New England's pious Sabbath was little in evidence.

The Backcountry

While the southern gentry prospered along the coasts, settlers poured into the upland backcountry. As late as 1730, only hunters and Indian fur traders had known this area, the vast expanse of hilly red clay and fertile limestone soils from Pennsylvania to Georgia. Over the next four decades, it attracted some 250,000 inhabitants, nearly half the southern white population.

Thousands of land-hungry Germans and Scots–Irish filled the valleys along the eastern side of the Appalachians. They squatted on land they did not own, lived tensely among Indians, and created a subsistence society. Their enclaves remained isolated for several generations, which helped these pioneers cling fiercely to folkways they had brought across the Atlantic. Crude backcountry life appalled visitors from the more refined seaboard. "Through the licentiousness of the people," wrote one itinerant minister, "many hundreds live in concubinage—swopping their wives as cattle and living in a state of nature more irregularly and unchastely than the Indians."

This crudeness was actually a reflection of the poverty of frontier life and the lack of schools, churches, and towns. Most families plunged into the backcountry with only a few household possessions, tools, animals, and the clothes on their backs. They lived in log cabins and planted their crops between the tree stumps. Women labored in the fields alongside their menfolk. "She is a very civil woman," noted an observer of a southern frontierswoman, "and shows nothing of ruggedness or immodesty in her carriage; yet she will carry a gun in the woods and kill deer and turkeys, shoot down wild cattle, catch and tie hogs, knock down beeves with an ax, and perform the most manful exercises as well as most men in those parts." Marriage and family life were more informal in the backcountry. With vast areas unattended by ministers and with courthouses out of reach, most couples married or "took up" with each other until an itinerant clergyman on horseback appeared to bless marriages and baptize children. For a generation, everyone endured a poor diet, endless work, and meager rewards.

By the 1760s, the southern backcountry had begun to emerge from the frontier stage. Small marketing towns became centers of craft activity, church life, and local government. Farms began producing surpluses for shipment east. Density of settlement increased, creating a social life known for harvest festivals, log-rolling contests, horse races, wedding celebrations, dances, and prodigious drinking bouts. Class distinctions remained narrow compared with the older seaboard settlements.

Enslaved Africans in the Southern Colonies

From the late seventeenth century, the slave population grew rapidly—from about 15,000 in 1690 to 80,000 in 1730 and 325,000 in 1760. In the entire period from 1700 to 1775, more than 350,000 African slaves entered the British North American colonies. Ninety percent of these people went to southern colonies.

The basic struggle for Africans toiling on plantations 5,000 miles from their homes was to create strategies for living as satisfactorily as possible despite horrifying treatment. The master hoped to convert the slave into a mindless drudge who obeyed every command and worked efficiently for his profit. But attempts to cow slaves rarely succeeded completely. Masters could set the external boundaries of existence for their slaves, controlling physical location, work roles, diet, and shelter. They were less able to dictate how slaves established friendships, fell in love, formed kin groups, reared children, worshiped their gods, buried their dead, and organized their leisure time. At first, cultural differences divided slaves, who often came from many areas in Africa. In time, however, with the common experience of laboring in the South, a shared African American culture emerged.

Although slave codes severely restricted the lives of slaves, the possibility for family life increased as the southern colonies matured. Larger plantations employed dozens and even hundreds of slaves, and the growth of roads and market towns permitted them greater opportunities to forge relationships beyond their own plantation. By the 1740s, a growing proportion of Chesapeake slaves were American-born, established families, and lived in plantation outbuildings where after sundown they could fashion personal lives.

In South Carolina, slaves drew on agricultural skills they had practiced in Africa and made rice the keystone of the coastal economy by the early eighteenth century. Their numbers increased rapidly, from about 4,000 in 1708 to 90,000 by 1760. Working mostly on large plantations in swampy lowlands, they endured the worst conditions on the continent. But they also outnumbered whites three to one by 1760 and hence could maintain more of their African culture than slaves in the Chesapeake region. Many spoke Gullah, a "pidgin" mixing several African languages, gave African names to their children, and kept alive African religious customs.

Resistance and Rebellion

Enslaved Africans not only adapted to bondage but also resisted in ways that constantly reminded their masters that slavery's price was eternal vigilance. Slaveowners interpreted rebelliousness as evidence of the "barbarous, wild savage natures of Africans," as a South Carolina law of 1712 phrased it. But from the African point of view, resistance was essential to maintaining meaning and dignity in a life of degrading toil.

"Saltwater" Africans, fresh from their homelands, frequently fought slavery fiercely. "They often die before they can be conquered," said one white planter. Commonly, initial resistance took the form of fleeing—to renegade frontier settlements, to interior Native American tribes (which sometimes offered refuge), or to Spanish Florida. Rebellions, such as those in New York City in 1712 and at Stono, South Carolina, in 1739, mostly involved newly arrived slaves. There was no North American parallel, however, for the massive slave uprisings of the West Indies and Brazil.

The relatively small rebellions that did occur (or were feared) led to atrocious repression. Near Charleston in 1739, officials tortured and hanged 50 black rebels; their decapitated heads, impaled on posts, warned other potential insurrectionists. In New York City a year later, rumors of a planned insurrection caused the hanging of 18 slaves and 4 white allies and the burning of 13 other slaves.

Black Religion and Family

The balance of power was always massively stacked against the slaves. Only the most desperate challenged the system directly. As slaves struggled to find meaning and worth in their existence, religion and family became especially important.

Africans brought to the New World a complex religious heritage that no desolation or physical abuse could crush. Coming from cultures where the division between sacred and secular activities was less marked than in Europe, slaves made religion central to their existence. Most slaves died strangers to Christianity until the mid-eighteenth century. Then they began to blend African religious practices with the faith of the master class, using this hybrid religion both to light the spark of resistance and to find comfort from oppression.

The religious revival that began in the 1720s in the northern colonies and spread southward made important contributions to African American religion. Evangelicalism stressed personal rebirth; it encouraged an intense emotional experience, which slaves often expressed in music and bodily motion. The dancing, shouting, rhythmic clapping, and singing that came to characterize slaves' religious expression represented a creative mingling of West African and Christian religious practice.

Besides religion, the slaves' greatest refuge lay in their families. In West Africa, all social relations were centered in kinship, which included dead ancestors. Torn from their native societies, slaves placed great importance on rebuilding extended kin groups. Most English colonies prohibited slave marriages. But in practice, slaves and masters struck a bargain. Slaves desperately wanted families, and masters found that slaves with families would work harder and be less inclined to escape or rebel.

Slaves fashioned a family life only with difficulty, however. The general practice of importing three male slaves for every two females stunted family formation. Female slaves, much in demand, married in their late teens, but males usually had to wait until their mid- to late twenties. But as natural increase swelled the slave population in the eighteenth century, the gender ratio became more even.

Slave marriages were rarely secure. They were often severed by the sale of either husband or wife, especially when a deceased planter's estate was divided among his heirs or his slaves were sold to his creditors to satisfy debts. Children usually stayed with their mothers until about age 8; then they were frequently torn from their families through sale, often to small planters needing only a hand or two. Few slaves escaped separation from family members at some time during their lives.

White male exploitation of black women represented another assault on family life. How many black women were coerced or lured with favors into sexual relations with white masters and overseers cannot be known, but the sizable mulatto (mixed-race) population at the end of the eighteenth century indicates that the number was large.

In some interracial relationships, the coercion was subtle. In some cases, black women sought the liaison to gain advantages for themselves or their children. These unions nonetheless threatened both the slave community and the white plantation ideal. They bridged the supposedly unbridgeable gap between slave and free society and produced children who did not fit into the separate racial categories that planters attempted to enforce.

Despite such obstacles, slaves fashioned intimate ties as husband and wife, parent and child. If monogamous relationships did not last as long as in white society, much of the explanation lies in slave life: the shorter life span of African Americans, the shattering of marriage through sale of one or both partners, and the call of freedom that impelled some slaves to run away.

Whereas slave men struggled to preserve their family role, many black women assumed a position in the family that differed from that of white women. Plantation mistresses usually worked hard in helping manage estates, but nonetheless the ideal grew that they should remain in the house guarding white virtue and setting standards for white culture. In contrast, the black woman remained indispensable to both the work of the plantation and the functioning of the slave quarters. She toiled in the fields and slave cabins alike. Paradoxically, black women's constant labor made them more equal to men than was the case of women in white society.

Above all, slavery was a set of power relationships designed to extract the maximum labor from its victims. Hence, it regularly involved cruelties that filled life with tribulation. Still, slaves in North America toiled in less physically exhausting circumstances than slaves on sugar and coffee plantations and were better clothed, fed, and treated than Africans in the West Indies, Brazil, and other parts of the hemisphere. They were comparatively successful in establishing families. Slave family life in the American colonies brimmed with uncertainty and sorrow, but was nonetheless the greatest monument to slaves' will to endure captivity.

Contending for a Continent

By 1750, when English colonists numbered about 1.2 million, only a small fraction of them, along with their African slaves, lived farther than 100 miles from the Atlantic Ocean. Growing rapidly, the English colonies were beginning to press against the French and Spanish settlements in the rich river valleys of the Ohio and Mississippi and beyond. France posed the greatest threat to English colonists in the interior of North America, while the Spanish presented another challenge on their southern flank.

France's Inland Empire

In 1661, France's Louis XIV, determined to make his country the most powerful in Europe, looked with keen interest to North America and the Caribbean islands. New France's timber would build the royal navy, its fish would feed the growing mass of slaves in the French West Indies, and its fur trade, if greatly expanded, would fill the royal coffers. From the French Caribbean islands came precious sugar.

New France grew in population, economic strength, and ambition in the late seventeenth century. In 1673, Louis Joliet and Father Jacques Marquette, a Jesuit priest, explored an immense territory watered by the Mississippi and Missouri rivers. A decade later, military engineers and priests began building forts and missions in the Great Lakes region and the Mississippi valley. In the first half of the eighteenth century, the French were able to develop a system of forts, trading posts, and agricultural villages throughout the heart of the continent, threatening to pin the British to the seaboard. Their success was partly due to their dealings with the Native Americans. The two entered into alliances that ensured that the natives kept sovereignty over their land. The Indians still contended with French diseases and French-promoted intertribal wars.

Because France's interior empire was organized primarily as a military, trading, and missionizing operation, male French settlers arrived with few French women. French men and Native American women produced mixed-race offspring (called *metissage*). These relations formed the basis of a mingling of French and Native American economic, political, and social interests in the vast interior which had no British equivalent.

The French presence in the continent's vast heartland, thinly dotted with small farming communities, created a shield against the expansive British. The French population grew to about 70,000 by 1750, and almost all French settlements in the North American interior were mixed-race, or *meti*, communities—a sharp contrast to the English colonies. They demonstrated how European settlers and Indian peoples could coexist.

In 1718, French pioneers of the interior and those along the Gulf of Mexico were inundated when France settled New Orleans at great cost by transporting almost 7,000 whites and 5,000 African slaves to the mouth of the Mississippi River. Disease rapidly whittled down these numbers, and an attack by the powerful Natchez in 1729 discouraged further French immigration. Most of the survivors settled around the little town of New Orleans and on long, narrow plantations stretching back from the Mississippi River. While its economy and society resembled early Charleston, South Carolina, New Orleans was run and financed by royal government and knew nothing of representative political institutions such as elections, assemblies, newspapers, or taxes.

Slaves, with skills as rice growers, indigo processors, metal workers, river navigators, herbalists, and cattle keepers, became the backbone of the

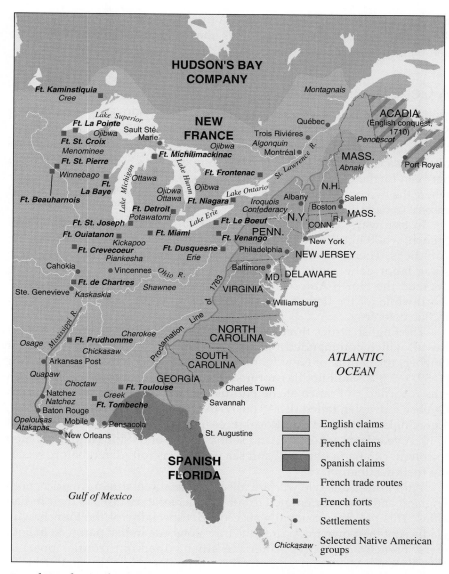

HUDSON'S BAY COMPANY

Ft. Kaminstiquia
Cree

Montagnais

Lake Superior
Ft. La Pointe
Ojibwa Sault Sté.
Ft. St. Croix   Marie
Menominee
Ft. St. Pierre

NEW FRANCE

Québec

ACADIA
(English conquest, 1710)
Penobscot

Ft. Michilimackinac

Trois Riviéres
Ojibwa
Algonquin
Montréal

MASS.
Abnaki

Port Royal

Winnebago Ottawa
Ft.
La Baye
Ft. Beauharnois

Ft. Frontenac

Ojibwa Ojibwa *Lake Ontario*
Ottawa
Ft. Detroit Ft. Niagara
Potawatomi   *Lake Erie*

Iroquois
Confederacy

Albany

N.H.

Salem

Boston

MASS.

Ft. St. Joseph

Ft. Le Boeuf **N.Y.** CONN. R.I.

Ft. Ouiatanon Ft. Miami
Kickapoo
Ft. Crevecoeur Ft. Dusquesne
Piankesha   Erie

Ft. Venango

PENN.

Philadelphia

New York

NEW JERSEY

Cahokia Vincennes *Ohio R.*

Baltimore

MD **DELAWARE**

Ft. de Chartres Shawnee
Ste. Geneviève Kaskaskia

1763

VIRGINIA

Williamsburg

Osage Ft. Prudhomme
Chickasaw
Arkansas Post
Quapaw

Cherokee

Proclamation Line of

NORTH CAROLINA

ATLANTIC OCEAN

Choctaw Ft. Toulouse
Natchez Creek
Natchez Ft. Tombeche
Baton Rouge
Opelousas Mobile
Atakapas Pensacola
New Orleans

SOUTH CAROLINA

GEORGIA

Charles Town

Savannah

St. Augustine

SPANISH FLORIDA

Gulf of Mexico

Mississippi R.

St. Lawrence R.

Lake Michigan *Lake Huron*

	English claims
	French claims
	Spanish claims
——	French trade routes
■	French forts
●	Settlements
Chickasaw	Selected Native American groups

French North America, 1608–1763 The vast region west of the Appalachian Mountains claimed by France was thinly settled by colonists, so how did the French manage to hold it?

Louisiana economy. African slaves mingled with Native American women, producing mixed-race children known locally as *grifs,* while African women made interracial liaisons with French immigrants, often soldiers in search of partners. By 1765, blacks outnumbered whites. The chance of gaining freedom in fluid French Louisiana, especially for those of mixed-race descent, exceeded that of any other colony in North America. When the Spanish took over the colony in 1769, they guaranteed slaves the right to buy freedom with money earned in their free time. A free black class emerged, but when Americans acquired the colony in 1803, they suppressed freedom purchase and discouraged manumission.

A Generation of War

The growth of French strength and ambitions brought British America and New France into deadly conflict beginning in the late seventeenth century. Protestant New Englanders regarded Catholic New France as a threat to their divinely sanctioned mission. When the European wars began in 1689, conflict between England and France quickly extended into every overseas theater where the two powers had colonies, including New York, New England, and eastern Canada.

In two wars, from 1689 to 1697 and 1702 to 1713, the English and French, while fighting in Europe, also sought to oust each other from the Americas. The zone of greatest importance was the Caribbean, where slave labor generated huge sugar fortunes. Both home governments deemed the North American settlements as secondary in importance, worthwhile for the timber and fish that sustained the more valuable West Indian colonies.

The English struck three times at the centers of French power—at Port Royal, which commanded the access to the St. Lawrence River, and at Quebec, the capital of New France. In 1690, during **King William's War** (1689–1697), a small flotilla captured Port Royal, the hub of Acadia (which was returned to France at the end of the war). The English assault on Quebec, however, failed disastrously. In **Queen Anne's War** (1702–1713), New England attacked Port Royal three times before finally capturing it in 1710. A year later, when England sent a flotilla of 60 ships and 5,000 men to conquer Canada, the land and sea operations foundered before reaching their destination.

With European-style warfare miserably unsuccessful in America, both England and France attempted to subcontract military tasks to their Indian allies. This policy occasionally succeeded, especially for the French, who gladly sent their own troops into the fray alongside Indian partners. In both wars, French and Native American allies wiped out frontier posts in New York and Maine and battered other towns along New England's fringes. Retaliating, the English-supplied Iroquois left New France "bewildered and benumbed" after a massacre near Montreal in 1689. Assessing their own interests, and too powerful to be bullied by either France or England, the Iroquois sat out the second war in the early eighteenth century. Convinced that neutrality served their purposes better than acting as mercenaries for the English, they held to the principle that "we are a free people uniting ourselves to what sachem we wish."

Though Britain had rebuffed France after a generation of war, New England suffered grievous economic and human losses. Massachusetts bore the heaviest burden. Probably one-fifth of all able-bodied males in the colony participated in the Canadian campaigns, and of these, about one-quarter never lived to tell of the terrors of New England's first major experience with international warfare. The war debt was £50,000 sterling in Massachusetts alone. At the end of the second conflict, in 1713, war widows were so numerous that the Bay Colony faced its first serious poverty problem. War at sea disrupted trade, cutting off markets and destroying shipping.

The burdens and rewards fell unevenly on the participants, as usually happens in wartime. Some lowborn men rose spectacularly. William Phips, the twenty-sixth child in his family, had been a poor sheep farmer and ship's carpenter in Maine who seemed destined to go nowhere. He then won a fortune by recovering a sunken Spanish treasure ship in the West Indies in 1687 and was given command of the expedition against Port Royal in 1690. Victory there catapulted him in 1691 to the governorship of Massachusetts. Other men, already rich, got richer. Andrew Belcher of Boston, who had grown wealthy on provisioning contracts during King Philip's War, supplied warships and outfitted the New England expeditions to Canada. He became a local titan, riding in London-built coaches, erecting a handsome mansion, and purchasing slaves. Most men, especially those who did the fighting, gained little, and many lost all. The least securely placed New Englanders supplied most of the voluntary or involuntary recruits, dying in numbers that seem staggering today.

In 1713, the Peace of Utrecht, which ended Queen Anne's War, capped a century-long rise for England and the decline of Spain in the rivalry for the sources of wealth outside Europe. Great Britain (recently formed out of the union of Scotland and England) won big, receiving Newfoundland and Acadia (renamed Nova Scotia). France recognized British sovereignty over the fur-rich Hudson Bay territory. France retained Cape Breton Island, controlling the entrance to the St. Lawrence River. In the Caribbean, France returned St. Kitts and Nevis. Suffering various Old World losses, Spain awarded the British the lucrative privilege of supplying the Spanish empire in America with African slaves.

Spain's Frail North American Grip

Spain's grip on its colonies in North America had always been tenuous. On the east coast, the growth of South Carolina slave-based plantation society in the late seventeenth century stemmed partly from the English use of Native American allies to attack Spanish Indian missions and outposts and sell the captives into slavery. From this time forward, English and French traders, with more attractive trade goods to offer, held sway over Florida Indians.

After 1713, Spain maintained a fragile hold on the southern tier of the continent. However, Spain learned how easily its thinly peopled missions and frontier outposts could be crippled or destroyed by chafing Native

A Chart of Mixed-Race Families The mixing of races in Spain's New World colonies is vividly displayed in paintings of interracial families, widely produced in Mexico in the eighteenth century. In each painting shown here, the mother and father of different racial ancestries produces a child who is indentified by a different racial term. In panel 5, for example, the mulatto mother and Spanish father produce a "Morisco" child. What was the message conveyed by paintings such as these, and why do you think they were so popular?

Americans and invading British. In the first half of the eighteenth century, the Spanish settlements stagnated, suffering from Spain's colonial policy that regarded them as marginal, money-losing affairs, useful only as defensive outposts.

Hispanics, *mestizos,* and detribalized Indians began to increase modestly in Texas, New Mexico, and California in the first half of the eighteenth century. In Florida, however, by 1745 they represented only one-tenth the population of British South Carolina. New Mexico's Hispanic population of about 10,000 at midcentury could not defend the vast region, but no European challenger appeared.

As in New France, there was more racial intermixture and social fluidity in New Spain than in the English colonies. Precisely how much is uncertain because the Spanish never defined racial groups as distinctly as the English. Social mobility was considerable: The Crown would raise even a commoner to the status of *hidalgo* (minor nobleman) as an inducement to settle and ranch in New Mexico.

Native Americans had mixed success resisting Spanish domination. In New Mexico, an early nineteenth-century Spanish investigator saw the key to Pueblo cultural autonomy as the underground *kivas*, which were "like impenetrable temples, where they gather to discuss mysteriously their misfortunes or good fortunes, their happiness or grief." California tribes had a harder time maintaining cultural cohesion. In the 1770s, the Spanish completed their western land and sea routes from San Diego to Yerba Buena (San Francisco) to block Russian encroachment. California's Spanish pioneers were Franciscan missionaries, accompanied by royal soldiers. The priests would choose a good location and attract a few Indians to be baptized and resettle around the mission. Visiting relatives would then be induced to stay. Over time, the Indians were reduced to virtual slaves. The California mission, with its extensive and profitable herds and grain crops, theoretically belonged to the Indian converts, but they did not enjoy the profits. Ironically, the spiritual motives of the priests brought a similar degradation of tribal Americans as elsewhere.

Cultural and Ecological Changes Among Interior Tribes

During the first half of the eighteenth century, the inland tribes proved their capacity to adapt to the contending European colonizers in their region while maintaining political independence. Yet extensive contact with Europeans slowly brought ominous changes. Trade goods, especially iron implements, textiles, firearms and ammunition, and alcohol, altered lifeways. Subsistence hunting turned into commercial hunting, propelled by the rising quantity of trade goods desired. Native American males, gradually wiping out deer and beaver east of the Mississippi River, spent far more time away from the villages trapping and hunting. Women were also drawn into the new economy, skinning animals and fashioning pelts into robes. Among some tribes, all this became so time-consuming that they had to procure food from others.

The fur trade altered much in traditional Native American life. Competition for furs sharpened intertribal tensions, often to the point of war. The introduction of European weaponry, which Indians quickly mastered, intensified these conflicts. Tribal political organization changed too. Earlier, most tribes had been loose confederations of villages and clans, with primary loyalty directed to the village. But trade, diplomatic contact, and war with Europeans required coordinated policies, so villagers gradually adopted more centralized leadership.

While incorporating trade goods into their material culture and adapting their economies and political structures to new situations, the interior tribes held fast to many traditions. They saw little reason to replace what they valued in their own culture. What they saw of the colonists' law and justice, religion, education, family organization, and child rearing usually convinced Native Americans that their own ways were superior. Their refusal to accept the superiority of white culture frustrated English missionaries, who expected little opposition to efforts to win Native Americans from "savage" ways.

Overall, interior tribes suffered from contact with the British colonizers. Decade by decade, the fur trade spread epidemic diseases, intensified warfare, depleted game animals, and drew Native Americans into a market economy where their trading partners gradually became trading masters.

The Urban World of Commerce and Ideas

Only about 5 percent of eighteenth-century colonists lived in towns as large as 2,500, and no city boasted a population above 16,000 in 1750 or 30,000 in 1775. Yet urban societies were at the leading edge of the transition to "modern" life. There, a barter economy first gave way to a commercial economy, a social order based on assigned status turned into one based on achievement, rank-conscious and deferential politics faded into participatory and contentious politics, and small-scale craftsmanship was gradually replaced by factory production. Into the cities flowed European ideas, which radiated outward to the hinterland.

Sinews of Trade

In the half century after 1690, Boston, New York, Philadelphia, and Charleston blossomed into thriving commercial centers. Their growth accompanied the development of the agricultural interior. As the colonial population rose and spread out, minor seaports such as Salem, Newport, Providence, Annapolis, Norfolk, and Savannah boasted 5,000 or more inhabitants.

Cities served as trade centers through which flowed colonial exports (tobacco, rice, furs, wheat, timber products, and fish) and the imported goods that colonists needed: manufactured and luxury goods from England (glass, paper, iron implements, and cloth); wine, spices, coffee, tea, and sugar; and laborers. The seaport merchant was a pivotal figure, frequently engaging in both retail and wholesale trade as well as serving as moneylender, shipbuilder, insurance agent, land developer, and often coordinator of artisan production.

See the Map
Colonial Products
at **www.myhistorylab.com**

By the eighteenth century, the American economy was integrated into an Atlantic trading system that connected settlers to Great Britain, western Europe, Africa, the West Indies, and Newfoundland. Britain, like other major trading nations of western Europe, pursued mercantilist trade policies. **Mercantilism**'s core idea was that a country gained wealth by increasing exports, taxing imports, regulating production and trade, and exploiting colonies. These policies governed British treatment of North America.

Colonists could never produce enough exportable raw materials to pay for the imported goods they craved, so they had to earn credit in Britain by supplying the West Indies with foodstuffs and timber products. They also accumulated credit by providing shipping and distribution services, which Yankee merchant seamen and Yankee-built ships dominated.

((●—[Hear the **Audio**
The Connecticut Peddler
at **www.myhistorylab.com**

The Artisan's World

Although merchants stood first in wealth and prestige in the colonial towns, artisans were far more numerous. About two-thirds of urban adult males (slaves excluded) labored at handicrafts. By the mid-eighteenth century, the colonial cities contained scores of specialized "leather apron men" besides the proverbial butcher, baker, and candlestick maker. Handicraft specialization increased as the cities matured, but every artisan worked with hand tools, usually in small shops. Work patterns for artisans were irregular, dictated by weather, length of daylight, erratic delivery of raw materials, and shifting consumer demand.

Urban artisans took fierce pride in their crafts. While deferring to those above them, they saw themselves as the backbone of the community, contributing essential products and services. "Our professions rendered us useful and necessary members of our community," the Philadelphia shoemakers asserted. "Proud of that rank, we aspired to no higher." This self-esteem and desire for community recognition sometimes jostled with the upper-class view of artisans as "mere mechanicks," part of the "vulgar herd."

Striving for respectability, artisans placed a premium on achieving economic independence. Every craftsman began as an apprentice, spending five or more teenage years in a master shop and then, after fulfilling his contract, becoming a "journeyman," selling his labor to a master and frequently living in his house, where he ate at his table and sometimes married his daughter. He hoped to complete within a few years the three-step climb from servitude to self-employment. In trades requiring greater organization and capital, such as distilling and shipbuilding, the rise from journeyman to master could prove impossible.

In good times, urban artisans did well. Success, however, was far from automatic, even for those following Poor Richard's advice. An advantageous marriage, luck in avoiding illness, and an ample inheritance were often critical. In Philadelphia, about half the artisans in the first half of the eighteenth century died leaving enough personal property to have ensured a comfortable standard of living. Their economy weaker, New England artisans did not fare as well.

Urban Social Structure

Population growth, economic development, and war altered the urban social structure between 1690 and 1765. Stately townhouses displayed fortunes built through trade, shipbuilding, war contracting, and—probably most profitable of all—urban land development. "It is almost a proverb," a Philadelphian observed in the 1760s, "that every great fortune made here within these 50 years has been by land." A merchant estate of £2,000 sterling was impressive in the early eighteenth century. Two generations later, North America's first millionaires were accumulating estates of £10,000 to £20,000 sterling.

Alongside urban wealth grew urban poverty. Ordinary laborers dreaded winter, for it was a season when cities had "little occasion for the labor of the poor," and firewood could cost several months' wages. From the beginning, every city had its disabled, orphaned, and widowed who required aid. But after 1720, poverty marred the lives of many more city dwellers, including war widows without means of support, rural migrants, or recent immigrants. Boston was hit especially hard. Its economy stagnated in the 1740s, and taxpayers groaned under the burden of paying for heavy war expenditures. Though cities devised new ways of helping the needy, many of the indigent preferred "to starve in their homes" rather than endure the discipline and indignities of the poorhouse or leave their children alone to labor in America's first textile factory.

Urban eighteenth-century tax lists reveal the increasing gap between the wealthy and the poor. The top 5 percent of taxpayers increased their share of the cities' taxable assets from about 30 to 50 percent between 1690 and 1770. The bottom half of the taxable inhabitants saw their share of the wealth shrink from about 10 to 4 percent. Except in Boston, the urban middle classes continued to gain ground. Still, the growth of princely fortunes amid increasing poverty made some urban dwellers reflect that Old World ills were appearing in the New.

The Entrepreneurial Ethos

As the cities grew, new values took hold. In the traditional view of society, economic life was supposed to operate according to what was fair, not what was profitable. Regulated prices and wages, quality controls, supervised public markets, and other such measures seemed natural because a community was defined as a single body of interrelated parts, where individual rights and responsibilities formed a seamless web.

In their commercialized cities, most urban dwellers grew to regard the subordinating of private interests to the commonweal as unrealistic. Prosperity required the encouragement of acquisitive appetites rather than self-denial. The new view held that if people were allowed to pursue their material desires competitively, they would collectively form a natural, impersonal market of producers and consumers that would advantage everyone. This change had profound consequences.

RECOVERING *the* PAST

Household Inventories

Historians use probate records to examine social changes in American society. They include wills, the legal disposition of estates, and household inventories taken by court-appointed appraisers that detail the personal possessions left at death. Inventories have been especially valuable in tracing the transformation of colonial communities.

Like tax lists, inventories can be used to show changes in a community's distribution of wealth. But they are far more detailed than tax lists, providing a snapshot of how people lived at the end of their life. Inventories list and value almost everything a person owned—household possessions, equipment, books, clothes and jewelry, cash on hand, livestock and horses, crops and stored provisions. Hence, through inventories, we can measure the quality of life at different social levels. We can also witness how people made choices about investing their savings—in capital goods of their trade such as land, ships, and equipment; in personal goods such as household furnishings and luxury items; or in real property such as land and houses.

Studied systematically (and corrected for biases, which infect this source as well as others), inventories show that by the early 1700s, ordinary householders were improving their standard of living. Finished furniture such as cupboards, beds, tables, and chairs turn up more frequently in inventories. Pewter dinnerware replaces wooden bowls and spoons, bed linen makes an appearance, and books and pictures are sometimes noted.

The estates of the elite included fashionable articles of consumption. The partial inventory of Robert Oliver, a wealthy merchant and officeholder living in a Boston suburb, is reproduced here. You can get some idea of the dignified impression Oliver wished to make by looking at his furniture and dishes and by noticing that he owned a mahogany tea table, damask linen, and a bed with curtains. The inventory further suggests the spaciousness of Oliver's house and shows how he furnished each room.

It is helpful when studying inventories to categorize the goods in the following way: those that are needed to survive (basic cooking utensils, for example); those that make life easier or more comfortable (enough plates and beds for each member of the family, for instance); and those that make life luxurious (slaves, silver plates, paintings, mahogany furniture, damask curtains, spices, wine, and so forth). Oliver had many luxury goods as well as items that contributed to his use of leisure time and his personal enjoyment. Which items in his inventory do you think were needed only to survive comfortably? Which were luxuries? What other conclusions can you draw about the lifestyle of rich merchants like Oliver?

Beyond revealing a growing social differentiation in colonial society, the inventories help the historian understand the reaction to what many ordinary colonists regarded as sinful pride displayed by the elite. By the 1760s, this distrust of affluence among simple folk had led to outright hostility toward men who surrounded themselves with the trappings of aristocratic life.

Such resentments take on their full meaning only when contrasted with what inventories tell us about life at the bottom of society. The hundreds of inventories for Bostonians dying in the decade before the American Revolution show that fully half of them died with less than £40 personal wealth and one-quarter with £20 or less. The inventories and wills of Jonathan and Daniel Chandler of Andover, Massachusetts, show the material circumstances of less favored Americans who suffered from the economic distress afflicting New England since the 1730s. Daniel Chandler was a shoemaker.

REFLECTING ON THE PAST How do the possessions of these brothers compare with Oliver's partial inventory shown on pages 116–117? Do these contrasting inventories help explain the class tension that figured in the revolutionary experience?

Household Inventory of Robert Oliver, Wealthy Merchant

Dorchester Jan.ry 11.th 1763.

Inventory of what Estates Real & Personall, belonging to Coll.o Robert Oliver [Esquire] late of Dorchester Deceased, that has been Exhibited to us the Subscribers, for Apprizement. Viz.t

In the Setting Parlour Viz.tt

a looking Glass	£4.—.—
a Small Ditto	0.6.0
12 Metzitens pictures Glaz'd @6/	3.12.—
8 Cartoons D.o Ditto	4.—.—
11 small Pictures	—.4.—
4 Maps	—.10.—
1 Prospect Glass	—.10.—
2 Escutchons Glaz'd	—.4.—
1 pair small hand Irons	—.6.—
1 Shovel & Tongs	—.8.—
1 Tobacco Tongs	—.1.—
1 pair Bellowes	—.2.—
1 Tea Chest	—.2.—
2 Small Waters	—.1.—
1 Mehogony Tea Table	1.—.—
8 China Cups & Saucers	—.2.—
1 Earthen Cream Pott	—.—.1
1 Ditto. Sugar Dish	—.—.4
1 Black Walnut Table	1.—.—
1 Black Ditto Smaller	0.6.—
1 Round painted Table	0.1.—
7 Leather Bottom Chairs @ 6/	2.2.—
1 Arm.d Chair Common	1.3.—
1 Black Walnut Desk	1.12.—
1 pair Candlesticks snuffers & Stand Base Mettle	—.4.—
6 Wine Glasses 1 Water Glass	—.1.—
a parcell of Books	1.—.—
a Case with Small Bottles	0.4.—
	22.1.5
In the Entry & Stair Case Viz.t 17 pictures	£0.10.—
	0.10.0
In the Kitchen Chamber Viz.t	
a Bedstead & Curtains Compleat	£4.—.—
a Bed Bolster & 2 pillows	5.—.—
a Under Bed & 1 Chair	0.1.—
2 Rugs & 1 Blankett @ 6/	0.18.—
	09.19.0
In the Dining Room Viz.t	
1 pair of andirons	£0.3.—
7 Bass Bottoms Chairs	0.7.—
1 Large Wooden Table	0.3.—

1 Small Ditto Oak		0.1.—
1 Small looking Glass		0.6.—
1 Old Desk		0.6.—
1 Case with 2 Bottles		0.2.—
1 Warming pan		0.12.—
		2. 0. 0

In the Marble Chamber Viz.t

1 Bedstead & Curtains Compleat		£8.—.—
1 feather Bed, Bolster & 2 pillows		8.—.—
1 Chest of Drawers		2.8.—
1 Buroe Table		1.—.—
6 Chairs Leather'd Bottoms @ 6/		1.16.—
1 Small dressing Glass		—.6.—
1 Small Carpett		1.—.—
1 White Cotton Counterpin		—.18.—
1 pair Blanketts		1.12.—
1 pair holland Sheets		1.4.—
3 pair Dowlases D.o New	@ 12S/p.r	1.16.—
3 pair & 1 Ditto Coarser	@ 4/	0.14.—
3 pair Cotton & Linnen D.o	@ 3/	0.9.—
4 pair Servants Ditto	@ 2/	0.8.—
4 Coarse Table Cloths	@ 1/	0.4.—
10 Ditto Kitchen Towels	@ 1/	0.1.—
5 Diaper Table Cloths	@ 12/	3.—.—
6 Damask Table Cloths	@ 18/	5.8.—
4 N: England Diaper D.o	@ 3	0.12.—
4 pair Linnen pillow Cases	@ 2/	0.8.—
5 Coarser Ditto	@ 1/	0.5.—
6 Diaper Towels	@ 6d	0.3.—
7 Damask Ditto	@ 2/	0.14.—
2 doz.n & 9 Damask Napkins	@ 24/doz.n	3.6.—
1 Gauze Tea Table Cover		0.1.—
		£43.13.0

Household Inventory of Jonathan Chandler	(d. 1745)
Cash	£18p
Gun	1p
Psalmbook	8p
£19p	
Debts	£5p
Total	£14p
Household Inventory of Daniel Chandler (d. 1752), Shoemaker	
Bible	
Shoe knife	
Hammer Total	£12
Last (shoe shaper)	
Various notes	

As the colonial port towns took their places in the Atlantic world of commerce, merchants became accustomed to making decisions according to the emerging commercial ethic that rejected traditional restraints on entrepreneurial activity. If wheat fetched eight shillings a bushel in the West Indies but only five in Boston, a grain merchant felt justified in sending all he could purchase from local farmers to the more distant buyer. The new transatlantic market responded only to the invisible laws of supply and demand.

Tension between the new economic freedom and the older concern for the public good erupted only with food shortages or galloping inflation. The American colonies experienced none of the famines that ravaged Europe in this period, so such crises were usually limited to wartime, when demand for provisions rose sharply. Nonetheless, the two conceptions of community and economic life continued to rub against each other for decades, until by the mid-eighteenth century, the pursuit of a profit was winning out over the old community-oriented social compact.

The American Enlightenment

Ideas about the prospects for the improvement of the human condition also filtered across the Atlantic. In the eighteenth century, an American version of the European intellectual movement called the **Enlightenment** emerged.

In what is called the Age of Reason, European thinkers rejected the Calvinist concept of innate human depravity, replacing it with the more optimistic notion that a benevolent God wanted all to be redeemed. In this view, humankind had been blessed with the supreme gift of reason. Thinkers like **John Locke**, in his influential *Essay Concerning Human Understanding* (1689), argued that God had not predetermined the content of the human mind but had instead given it the capacity to acquire knowledge. All Enlightenment thinkers prized this acquisition of knowledge, for it allowed humankind to improve its condition. As the great mathematician Isaac Newton demonstrated, systematic investigation could unlock the secrets of the physical universe. Such scientific knowledge could be applied to improve society.

The scientific and intellectual advances of the seventeenth and eighteenth centuries encouraged a belief in "natural law" and fostered debate about the "natural" human rights. These ideas spread in Europe and the Americas, eventually finding expression in movements for reform, democracy, and liberation—all of deep interest to those beginning to oppose slavery and the slave trade as abominations. Even as the traffic in slaves peaked, religious and humanitarian opposition to slavery rose. The idea grew in the 1750s that slavery contradicted the Christian concept of brotherhood and the Enlightenment notion of the natural equality of all humans. Only a few

The Quaker Benjamin Lay Benjamin Lay was regarded as eccentric and a troublemaker, even by his fellow Quakers. Known as a fervent opponent of slavery and the slave trade as early as the 1730s, he was also in the vanguard of many reform movements such as temperance and vegetarianism. What does the basket at bottom left symbolize? *(National Portrait Gallery, Smithsonian Institution/Art Resource, NY)*

hundred masters freed their slaves in the mid-eighteenth century, but the seeds of abolitionism had been planted.

Eighteenth-century Americans, including naturalist John Bartram of Philadelphia and Harvard Professor John Winthrop III, began to make significant contributions to the advancement of science. Foremost among them was Benjamin Franklin, whose spectacular (and dangerous) experiments with electricity, the properties of which were just becoming known, earned him an international reputation. Franklin's true genius as a figure of the Enlightenment came in his practical application of scientific knowledge. Among his inventions were the lightning rod; bifocal spectacles; and a stove that heated rooms more cost-effectively than the open fireplace. Franklin made his adopted city of Philadelphia a center of the Enlightenment. He helped found America's first circulating library in 1731, an artisans' debating club for "mutual improvement," and an intercolonial scientific association that in 1769 became the American Philosophical Society.

Most colonists were not educated enough to participate actively in the Enlightenment, and only a handful read French authors like Voltaire. But the efforts of men such as Franklin exposed thousands, especially in the cities, to new currents of thought. This kindled hopes that Americans, blessed by an abundant environment and relatively free of the shackles of tradition, might achieve the Enlightenment ideal of a perfect society.

The Great Awakening

Many of the social, economic, and political changes occurring in eighteenth-century colonial society converged in the Great Awakening, the first of many religious revivals that would sweep North America during the next two centuries. Though the timing and character of the Awakening varied from region to region, this quest for spiritual renewal challenged old sources of authority and produced patterns of thought and behavior that helped fuel a revolutionary movement in the next generation.

Religious Mosaic

Early eighteenth-century British America remained an overwhelmingly Protestant culture. The puritan tradition—institutionalized in Congregational churches—dominated all of New England except Rhode Island. The Church of England held sway in much of New York and throughout the South except the backcountry. In the mid-Atlantic and in the western settlements, German Mennonites, Dunkers, Moravians, and Lutherans; Scots–Irish Presbyterians; as well as Baptists and Quakers all mingled. Even so, half of the colonists went to no church at all, partly because in many areas, ministers and churches were simply unavailable. In the most populous colony, Virginia, only 60 parsons in 1761 served a population of 350,000—one for every 5,800 people.

As early as the 1660s, New England's Congregational clergy had adopted the **Half-Way Covenant** in order to maintain the church's centrality in the community. It allowed children of church members, if they adhered to the "forms of godliness," to join the church even if they could not demonstrate that they had undergone a conversion experience. They could not vote in church affairs or take communion, but they could have their own children baptized. Such innovations responded to the creeping religious apathy that many ministers feared was overtaking their society.

Most colonial churches were voluntary ("congregated") groups, formed for reasons of conscience rather than government compulsion. Though Catholics, Jews, and nonbelievers could not vote or hold office, the persecution of Quakers and Catholics had largely passed, and by 1720 some dissenting groups had gained the right to use long-obligatory church taxes to support their own congregations.

Most efforts to tighten church organization and discipline failed. For example, Anglican ministers had to be ordained in England and regularly report to the bishop of London. But in his Chesapeake parish, an Anglican priest faced wealthy planters who controlled the vestry (the local church governing body), set his salary, and would drive him out if he challenged them too forcefully. In Connecticut, the Saybrook Platform of 1708 created a network of Congregational churches, but individual churches still preserved much of their autonomy.

The Awakeners' Message

The Great Awakening was not a unified movement; rather, it was a series of revivals that swept different regions between 1720 and 1760 with varying degrees of intensity. Clergymen, worried that their communities were being overtaken by spiritual indifference, fueled the flames of revival. The first stirrings came in the 1720s in New Jersey, where a Dutch Reformed minister, Theodore Frelinghuysen, excited his congregation, forcefully preaching about the need to be saved.

From New Jersey, the Awakening spread to Pennsylvania in the 1730s, especially among Presbyterians, and then broke out in the Connecticut River Valley. There its greatest leader was Jonathan Edwards in Northampton, Massachusetts, who was later recognized as a philosophical giant. During the Northampton revival Edwards preached a powerful message that brought his trembling congregants to their knees. Fearful of remaining among the unrepentant, his neighbors were soon preparing frantically for the conversion by which they would be "born again." His *Faithful Narrative of the Surprizing Work of God* (1736), which described his town's awakening, was the first published revival narrative, a literary form that would be used many times in the future to fan the flames of evangelical religion.

○ View the Image
Jonathan Edwards
at **www.myhistorylab.com**

In 1739, these regional brushfires of evangelicalism were drawn together by a 24-year-old Church of England clergyman, George Whitefield. Inspired by John Wesley, the founder of English Methodism, Whitefield used his magnificent speaking voice in dynamic open-air preaching before huge gatherings. The charismatic Englishman barnstormed seven times along the American seaboard, beginning in 1739. In Boston, he preached to 19,000 in three days and at a farewell sermon left 25,000 writhing in fear of damnation. In his wake came American preachers whom he had inspired, mostly young men.

The appeal of the Awakeners lay both in the medium and the message. They preached that the established, college-trained clergy was too intellectual and tradition-bound. Congregations were dead, Whitefield declared, "because dead men preach to them." The fires of Protestant belief could be reignited only if individuals assumed responsibility for their own conversion.

An important form of individual participation was "lay exhorting," which meant that anyone—young or old, female or male, black or white—could spontaneously recount a conversion experience and preach "the Lord's truth." This defiance of assigned roles horrified trained clergy and threatened to shatter their monopoly. The oral culture of common people gained new importance, their impromptu outpourings contrasting sharply with the controlled literary culture of elites. Revivalists believed that many clergy, their energies drained by doctrinal disputes, appealed too much to the mind and not enough to the heart. As one Connecticut leader remembered it, "the spirit of God appeared to be awfully withdrawn."

•••◦ Read the Document
Jonathan Edwards, Sinners in
the Hands of an Angry God
at **www.myhistorylab.com**

How religion, social change, and politics became interwoven in the Great Awakening can be seen by examining two regions swept by revivalism. Both Boston, the heartland of New England, and interior Virginia, a land of struggling small planters and slave-rich aristocrats, experienced the Great Awakening, but in different ways and at different times.

Revivalism in the Urban North

In Boston, Whitefield-inspired revivalism blazed up amid political controversy about paper money and land banks. This battle pitted large merchants against local traders, artisans, and the laboring poor, who preferred the land bank. At first, Boston's elite applauded Whitefield's ability to call the people to worship. It seemed that the master evangelist might restore social harmony by redirecting people from earthly matters such as the currency dispute toward concerns for their souls. But when he left Boston in 1740, others followed him. Men such as James Davenport were more critical of the "unconverted" clergy and the self-indulgent accumulation of wealth. Finding every meetinghouse closed to him, even those whose clergy had embraced the Awakening, the 25-year-old Davenport preached daily on the Boston Common, aroused religious fervor among thousands like Hannah Heaton, and stirred up feeling against the city's leading figures. Respectable people decided that revivalism had gotten out of hand when ordinary people began verbally attacking opponents of the land bank in the streets as "carnal wretches, hypocrites, fighters against God, children of the devil, cursed Pharisees." A revival that had begun as a return to religion among backsliding Christians had overlapped with political affairs, threatening polite culture, which stressed order and discipline from ordinary people.

Southern Revivalism

Although aftershocks continued for years, by 1744, the Great Awakening was ebbing in New England and the middle colonies. In Virginia, where the initial religious earthquake was barely felt, tremors of enthusiasm rippled through society from the mid-1740s onward.

Whitefield stirred some religious zeal during his early trips through Virginia. Traveling "New Light" preachers were soon gathering large crowds both in the backcountry and in the older settled areas traditionally dominated by Anglicanism. By 1747, worried clergymen convinced the governor to issue a proclamation restraining "strolling preachers." As in other colonies, Virginia's leaders despised traveling evangelists, who, like lay exhorters, conjured up a world without properly constituted authority. When the Hanover County court gave the fiery James Davenport a license to preach in 1750, the governor ordered the suppression of all circuit riders.

Awakeners challenged the spiritual monopoly of the gentry-dominated Anglican church. New Light Presbyterianism spread in the 1750s. Then, in the 1760s, came the Baptists. Renouncing finery and ostentatious display and addressing each other as "brother" and "sister," the Baptists reached out to thousands of unchurched people. Like northern revivalists, they focused on the conversion experience. Many of their preachers were uneducated farmers and artisans who called themselves "Christ's poor" and insisted that heaven was populated more by the humble poor than by the purse-proud rich. Among the poorest—Virginia's 140,000 slaves in 1760— the evangelical movement began to take hold. The insurgent Baptist movement offered a personal, emotionally satisfying religion among ordinary folk and a rejection of gentry values. Established Anglican pulpits denounced the Awakeners as furiously as had conservative New England divines. In both regions, social changes had weakened the cultural authority of elites and, in the context of religious revival, produced a vision of a society drawn along more equal lines.

Legacy of the Awakening

By the time George Whitefield returned to North America for his third tour in 1745, the revival had burned out in the North. Its effects, however, were long-lasting. Notably, it promoted religious pluralism and nourished the idea that all denominations were equally legitimate, giving the dissenting Protestant groups that had sprung up in seventeenth-century England a basis for living together in relative harmony. This framework paved the way for a second change—the separation of church and state. Once a variety of churches gained legitimacy, it was hard to justify one denomination claiming special privileges. In the seventeenth century, Roger Williams had tried to sever church and state because he believed that ties with civil bodies would corrupt the Church. During the Awakening, groups such as the Baptists and Presbyterians in Virginia constituted their own religious bodies and broke the Anglican monopoly as the Church in the colony. This undermining of the church–state tie would be completed during the Revolutionary era.

A third effect of the revival was to legitimate community diversity, which had been valued in Rhode Island, the Carolinas, and the middle colonies almost from their beginnings. But uniformity had been prized elsewhere, especially in Massachusetts and Connecticut. There, the Awakening split Congregational churches into New Lights and Old Lights. Mid-Atlantic Presbyterian churches faced similar schisms. In hundreds of rural communities by the 1750s, two or three churches existed where only one had stood before. People learned that the fabric of community could be woven from threads of many hues.

The death in 1747 of a Mahican Indian who had converted to the Moravian faith and taken the name of Johannes inspired the church's leader with a vision of converts from many nations. Count Zinzendorf asked church member and artist Johann Haidt to paint this picture. What do the different figures in the painting represent? *("The First Fruits," oil on canvas by Johann Valentin Haidt (1700–1781), Moravian Archives Bethlehem)*

New eighteenth-century colonial colleges reflected the religious pluralism. Before 1740, there existed only Congregational Harvard (1636) and Yale (1701) and Anglican William and Mary (1693). Between 1746 and 1769, six new colleges were added: Dartmouth, Brown, Princeton, and what are now Columbia, Rutgers, and the University of Pennsylvania. None was controlled by an established church, all had governing bodies composed of men of different faiths, and all admitted students regardless of religion. Eager for students and funds, they made nonsectarian appeals and combined the traditional Latin and Greek curricula with natural sciences and natural philosophy.

Last, the Awakening nurtured a subtle change in values that crossed over into politics and daily life. Ordinary people assumed new responsibilities in religious affairs and became skeptical of dogma and authority. Many, especially the Baptists, decried the growing materialism and deplored the new acceptance of self-interested behavior. By learning to oppose authority and create new churches, thousands of colonists unknowingly rehearsed for revolution.

Political Life

"Were it not for government, the world would soon run into all manner of disorders and confusions," wrote a Massachusetts clergyman early in the eighteenth century. Few colonists or Europeans would have disagreed. Government existed to protect life, liberty, and property.

How should political power be divided—in Britain, between the British government and the American colonies, and within each colony? Colonists naturally drew heavily on inherited political ideas and institutions—almost entirely English ones, for it was English charters that sanctioned settlement, English governors who ruled, and English common law that governed the courts. But meeting unexpected circumstances in a new environment, colonists modified familiar political forms.

Structuring Colonial Governments

All societies consider it essential to determine the final source of political authority. In England, the notion of the God-given, supreme monarchical authority was crumbling during the early colonial period. In its place arose the belief that stable government depended on blending and balancing the three pure forms of government: monarchy, aristocracy, and democracy. Unalloyed, each would degenerate into oppression. Most colonists believed that the Revolution of 1688 in England had vindicated and strengthened a carefully balanced political system.

In the colonies, political balance was similarly valued but was achieved somewhat differently. The governor, as the king's agent (or, in proprietary colonies, the agent of the proprietor to whom the king delegated authority), represented monarchy. Bicameral legislatures arose in most of the colonies in the seventeenth century. In most provinces they had upper houses of wealthy men appointed by the governor, a pale equivalent of Britain's House of Lords. The assembly, elected by white male freeholders, replicated the House of Commons and injected a democratic element. Every statute required the governor's assent (except in Rhode Island and Connecticut), and all colonial laws required final approval from the king's Privy Council. This royal check operated imperfectly, however. A law took months to reach England and months more before word of its final approval or rejection. In the meantime, the laws took force in the colony.

Behind the formal structure of politics stood rules governing who could participate as voters and officeholders. In England, male property owners with property producing at least an annual rental income of 40 shillings could vote or hold office. The colonists closely followed this principle, except in Massachusetts, where until 1691 church membership was an additional requirement. As in England, the poor and propertyless were excluded, for they lacked the stake in society that supposedly produced responsible voters. In England, the 40-shilling freehold requirement kept the electorate small; but in the colonies, where land was cheap, it conferred the vote on 50 to 75 percent of the adult free males. As the proportion of landless colonists increased in the eighteenth century, however, the franchise contracted. Though voting rights were broadly based, most men assumed that the wealthy and socially prominent should hold the main political positions. Balancing this elitism, however, was the notion that the entire electorate should periodically judge the performance of those entrusted with political power and reject those who were found wanting.

The Power of the People

One way the people expressed their views was through crowd action, a tradition with a long history in Europe. Popular protests seldom faced effective police power. In the countryside, where most colonists lived, only the county sheriff insulated civil leaders from angry farmers. In the towns, the sheriff had only the night watch to keep order. In 1757, New York's night watch was described as a "parcell of idle, drinking vigilant snorers, who never quelled any nocturnal tumult in their lives." In theory, the militia stood ready to suppress public disturbances, but crowds usually included many militiamen.

Boston's Impressment Riot of 1747 vividly illustrates both the people's readiness to defend their privileges and the weakness of law enforcement. Commodore Charles Knowles brought royal navy ships to Boston for provisioning and to replenish the ranks of mariners thinned by death and desertion. Knowles sent press gangs—teams of seamen authorized to force men into maritime service—out to fill vacancies from Boston's waterfront population. But before the press gangs could hustle away their victims, a crowd of angry Bostonians seized several British officers, surrounded the governor's house, and demanded the release of their townsmen. When the sheriff and his deputies attempted to intervene, the mob mauled them. The militia refused to respond. An enraged Knowles threatened to bombard the town, but negotiations amid further tumult averted a showdown. Finally, Knowles released the impressed Bostonians. After the riot, a young politician named Samuel Adams defended Boston's defiance of royal authority. The people, he argued, had a "natural right" to band together against press gangs that deprived them of their liberty. Local magnates who had supported the governor were "tools to arbitrary power."

Another way the people expressed their will was through the legislative assemblies, which extended their reach in the eighteenth century.

Initially, royal and proprietary governors sharply limited the power of the elected legislatures. Governors could dissolve the lower houses and delay their sitting, control the election of their speakers, and in most colonies initiate legislation with their appointed councils. They had authority to appoint and dismiss judges at all levels of the judiciary and to create chancery courts, which sat without juries. Governors also controlled the expenditure of public monies and had authority to grant land to individuals and groups, which they sometimes used to confer vast estates on their favorites.

In the eighteenth century, nearly half the colonies had royal governors. Many of these appointees were competent military officers or bureaucrats, but some were corrupt recipients of patronage posts. A few never even came over, preferring to pay part of their salary to another man who served as lieutenant governor. One committed suicide a week after arriving. Most, however, were merely mediocre.

Eighteenth-century legislatures challenged the swollen powers of the colonial governors. Bit by bit, they won new rights: to initiate legislation, to elect their own speakers, to settle contested elections, to discipline members, and to nominate provincial treasurers who disbursed public funds. Most important, they won the "**power of the purse**"—the authority to initiate money bills, specifying how much money should be raised by taxes and how it should be spent. Thus, the elected assemblies gradually transformed themselves into governing bodies reflecting the interests of the electorate.

Binding elected officeholders to their constituents became an important feature of the colonial political system. In England, the House of Commons claimed to represent the entire nation, but few men could vote in the election of Members of Parliament and many seats went in uncontested elections as political appointments. American assemblies, by contrast, contained mostly representatives sent by voters who instructed them on particular issues and held them accountable.

Royal governors and colonial grandees who sat as councillors often deplored this localist, popular orientation. Sniffed one aristocratic New Yorker, the assemblies were crowded with "plain, illiterate husbandmen [small farmers], whose views seldom extended farther than the regulation of highways, the destruction of wolves, wildcats, and foxes, and the advancement of the other little interests of the particular counties which they were chosen to represent." In actuality, most lower-house members were merchants, lawyers, and substantial planters and farmers, who by the mid-eighteenth century constituted the political elite in most colonies. They took pride in upholding their constituents' interests, for they saw themselves as bulwarks against oppression and arbitrary rule. In any event, local government was usually more important to the colonists than provincial government. In the North, local political authority generally rested in the towns (which included surrounding rural areas). The New England town meeting decided a wide range of matters, arguing until it could express itself as a single unit.

In the South, the county was the primary unit of government, and by the mid-eighteenth century, a landed squirearchy of third- and fourth-generation families had achieved political dominance. They ruled the county courts and the legislature. Substantial farmers served in minor offices such as road surveyor and deputy sheriff. At court sessions, usually four times a year, deeds were read aloud and then recorded, juries impaneled and justice dispensed, elections held, licenses issued, and proclamations read. On election days, gentlemen treated their neighbors (on whom they depended for votes) to alcoholic treats.

The Spread of Whig Ideology

Whether in local or provincial affairs, a political ideology called Whig, or "republican," had spread widely by the mid-eighteenth century. This body of thought, inherited from England, rested on the belief that concentrated power was historically the enemy of liberty and that too much power lodged in any person or group usually produced corruption and tyranny. The best defenses against concentrated power were balanced government, elected legislatures adept at checking executive authority, prohibition of standing armies (almost always controlled by tyrannical monarchs to oppress the people), and vigilance by the people in watching their leaders for telltale signs of corruption.

Much of this **Whig ideology** reached the people through the 23 newspapers circulating in the colonies by 1763. Many papers reprinted pieces from English Whig writers railing against corruption and creeping despotism. Though limited to a few pages and published only once or twice a week, the papers passed from hand to hand and were read aloud in taverns and coffeehouses, so that their contents probably reached most urban households and a substantial minority of rural farms.

The new power of the press and its importance in guarding the people's liberties against would-be tyrants (such as haughty royal governors) were dramatically illustrated in the Zenger case in New York. Young John Peter Zenger, a printer's apprentice, had been hired in 1733 by the anti-government faction of Lewis Morris to start a newspaper. The *New-York Weekly Journal* aimed to publicize the tyrannical actions of Governor William Cosby.

Arrested for seditious libel, Zenger was defended brilliantly by Andrew Hamilton, a Philadelphia lawyer hired by the Morris faction to convince the jury that Zenger had been simply trying to inform the people of attacks on their liberties. Although the jury acquitted Zenger, the libel laws remained very restrictive. The acquittal reinforced the notion that the government was the people's servant, and it brought home the point that public criticism could keep people with political authority responsible to those they ruled. Such ideas about liberty and corruption, raised in the context of local politics, would shortly achieve a much broader significance.

Conclusion

America in 1750

The English colonies in North America, robust and expanding, matured rapidly between 1690 and 1750. Transatlantic commerce linked them closely to Europe, Africa, and other parts of the Americas. Churches, schools, and towns—the visible marks of the receding frontier—appeared everywhere. And everywhere people like Hannah Heaton had been energized by the Great Awakening. A balanced gender ratio and stable family life had been achieved throughout the colonies. Many men were able to move up in society despite frequent obstacles. Seasoned political leaders and familiar political institutions functioned from Maine to Georgia.

Yet the sinew, bone, and muscle of American society had not yet fully knit together. The polyglot population, one-fifth of it bound in chattel slavery and its Native American component still unassimilated and uneasily situated on the frontier, was a kaleidoscopic mixture of ethnic and religious groups. While developing rapidly, its economy showed weaknesses, particularly in New England, where land resources had been strained. As the social structure solidified, the consolidation of wealth by a landed and mercantile elite was matched by pockets of poverty appearing in the cities and some rural areas. Full of strength yet marked by awkward incongruities, how would colonial America approach an era of strife and momentous

The "Paxton Boys" in Philadelphia When frontier farmers marched on Philadelphia in 1763 to demand better defense, a miniature civil war almost broke out. Philadelphians had little use for the Paxton Boys, who had murdered 20 harmless Christian Indians in retaliation for frontier raids. Why are soldiers and mounted men commanding the public space?
(The Library Company of Philadelphia)

decisions? Much of that strife involved the growing power of France's inland empire in North America and the way that wars in Europe were becoming globe-encircling conflicts. In 1750, colonists could not envision breaking with Britain, so why would such a breech come only a quarter century later?

TIME*line*

1682	La Salle canoes down Mississippi River and claims Louisiana for France
1689–1697	King William's War
1700	Spanish establish first mission in Arizona
1702–1713	Queen Anne's War
1704	*Boston News-Letter*, first regular colonial newspaper, published
1712	First northern slave revolt erupts in New York City
1713	Peace of Utrecht
1714	Beginning of Scots–Irish and German immigration
1715–1730	Volume of slave trade doubles
1718	French settle New Orleans
1720s	Natural increase of African population begins
1732	Benjamin Franklin publishes first *Poor Richard's Almanack*
1734–1736	Great Awakening begins in Northampton, Massachusetts
1735	Zenger acquitted of seditious libel in New York
1739	Slave revolt in Stono, South Carolina
1739–1740	Whitefield's first American tour spreads Great Awakening
1740s	Slaves compose 90 percent of population on Carolina rice coast
	Indigo becomes staple crop in Lower South
1747	Impressment riot in Boston
1750s	Quakers initiate campaign to halt slave trade and end slavery
1760	Africans compose 20 percent of colonial population
1760s–1770s	Spanish establish California mission system
1769	American Philosophical Society founded at Philadelphia

✓●─|Study and Review at **www.myhistorylab.com**

Questions for Review and Reflection

1. Regional variations within colonial society created different social and economic systems in areas of North America. What were the key divisions, and what differences characterized the societies and economies in each?

2. Why did slavery become a widespread institution in eighteenth-century colonial North America, and how did it shape society?

3. Was the Great Awakening compatible with other changes occurring in society, or did it contradict most other trends? How do you see religious change relating to social, political, and intellectual changes?

4. Was colonial America more affected by transatlantic trends or local influences in the areas of politics, ideas, and social life?

5. What were the most important aspects of colonial society that enabled it to mature? Why do you think these particular factors most significant?

Key Terms

Enlightenment 118

Freehold tenure 94

Half-Way Covenant 120

John Locke 118

King William's War 108

Mercantilism 113

Power of the purse 127

Queen Anne's War 108

Whig ideology 128

5

Bursting the Bonds of Empire

American Stories

A Shoemaker Leads a Boston Mob

In 1758, when he was 21 years old, Ebenezer MacIntosh of Boston laid down his shoemaker's awl and enlisted in the Massachusetts expedition against the French on Lake Champlain. The son of a poor shoemaker who had fought against the French in a previous war, MacIntosh had known poverty all his life. Military service offered the hope of plunder or at least an enlistment bounty worth half a year's wages. One among thousands of colonists who fought against the "Gallic menace" in the Seven Years' War, MacIntosh did his part in the climactic struggle that drove the French from North America.

But a greater role lay ahead for the Boston shoemaker. Two years after the Peace of Paris in 1763, England imposed a stamp tax on the American colonists. In the massive protests that followed, MacIntosh emerged as the street leader of Boston's ordinary people. In two nights violent attacks on private property, a Boston crowd nearly destroyed the houses of two of the colony's most important officials. On August 14, they tore through the house of Andrew Oliver, a wealthy merchant and the appointed distributor of stamps for Massachusetts. Twelve days later, MacIntosh led the crowd in attacking the mansion of Thomas Hutchinson, a wealthy merchant who served as lieutenant governor and chief justice of Massachusetts. "The mob was so general," wrote the governor, "and so supported that all civil power ceased in an instant."

For the next several months, the power of the shoemaker grew. Called "General" MacIntosh and "Captain-General of the Liberty Tree," he soon sported a militia uniform of gold and blue and a hat laced with gold. Two thousand townsmen marched behind him in orderly ranks through the crooked streets of Boston on November 5 to demonstrate their solidarity in resisting the hated stamps.

Five weeks later, a crowd publicly humiliated stamp distributor Oliver. Demanding that he announce his resignation before the assembled citizenry, they marched

Chapter Outline

The Climactic Seven Years' War

The Crisis with Britain

On the Brink of Rebellion

Severing the Colonial Bonds

Conclusion: Coming of Revolution

him across town in a driving December rain. With MacIntosh at his elbow, he finally reached the "Liberty Tree," which had become a symbol of resistance to Britain's new policies. There the aristocratic Oliver recanted. He concluded his resignation remarks with bitter words, hissing sardonically that he would "always think myself very happy when it shall be in my power to serve the people."

"To serve the people" was an ancient idea embedded in English political culture, but it assumed new meaning in the American colonies during the epic third quarter of the eighteenth century. Few colonists in 1750 held even a faint desire to break the connection with Britain, and fewer still might have predicted the form of government that 13 independent states in an independent nation might fashion. Yet 2 million colonists moved haltingly toward a showdown with mighty Britain. Little-known men like Ebenezer MacIntosh as well as his celebrated townsmen Samuel Adams, John Hancock, and John Adams were part of the struggle. Collectively, ordinary people such as MacIntosh influenced—and, in fact, sometimes even dictated—the revolutionary movement in the colonies. Though we read and speak mostly of a small group of "founding fathers," the wellsprings of the American Revolution can be fully discovered only among a variety of people from different social groups, occupations, regions, and religions.

The tensions in late colonial society, exacerbated by the imperial settlement that followed the **Seven Years' War** (in the colonies, often called the French and Indian War), would lead ultimately to a break with Great Britain. How did the colonists, who called themselves British and took pride in their membership in the triumphant British Empire, come to endorse independence? Ebenezer MacIntosh helps to answer that question. In leading the Boston mob against Crown officers and colonial collaborators who tried to implement a new colonial policy after 1763, he contributed to a revolutionary movement to restore ancient liberties thought by the Americans to be under deliberate attack in England. This movement eventually escalated into the war for American independence.

MacIntosh's Boston followers were also venting years of resentment at the accumulation of wealth and power by Boston's elite. Behind every swing of the ax, shattered crystal goblet, and splintered mahogany chair lay the fury of a Bostonian who had seen conservative leaders try to dismantle the town meeting, had suffered economic hardship, and had lost faith that opportunity and just relations still prevailed in his town. This sentiment, flowing from resentment of what many believed was a corrupt, self-indulgent, and inequitable society, produced a commitment to reshape American society even while severing the colonial bond. Distinct from the war for independence, the uprising in favor of a better future for themselves and their children against any who stood in the way was the American Revolution.

The work of creating a new nation began during the revolutionary ferment that burst the colonial bonds. While the Declaration of Independence officially severed the tie with Britain, former colonists still had to create new governments that would function as independent states. How would these infant states, confronting a war against the most powerful nation in Europe, coordinate that war effort? State constitution making and the process of organizing a central government—accomplished through Articles of Confederation—were urgent matters, as war with Great Britain loomed. Inspired by republican ideology, the patriots labored to set the former colonies on a viable course. The challenges they faced were immense, but the hopes of many were equally high.

The Climactic Seven Years' War

After a brief period of peace following King George's War (1744–1748), France and Britain fought the fourth, largest, and by far most significant of the wars for empire that had begun in the late seventeenth century. Known

👁️ See the **Map**
The Seven Years' War
at **www.myhistorylab.com**

variously as the Seven Years' War, the French and Indian War, and the Great War for Empire, this global conflict in part represented a contest for control of North America between the Atlantic Ocean and the Mississippi River.

In North America, the Anglo-American forces ultimately prevailed, and their victory dramatically affected the lives of all the diverse people living in the huge region east of the Mississippi.

War and the Management of Empire

England began constructing a more coherent imperial administration after the Glorious Revolution of 1688. In 1696, a professional **Board of Trade** replaced the old Lords of Trade; the Treasury strengthened the customs service; and Parliament created overseas vice-admiralty courts, which functioned without juries to prosecute smugglers who evaded the trade regulations set forth in the Navigation Acts. Parliament began playing a more active role after the reign of Queen Anne (1702–1714) and continued to do so when the weak, German-speaking King George I came to the throne. Royal governors received greater powers, got more detailed instructions, and came under more insistent demands from the Board of Trade to enforce British policies. The government gradually installed the machinery of imperial management.

The best test of an effectively organized state is its ability to wage war. Four times between 1689 and 1763, England matched its strength against France, its arch rival in Europe, North America, and the Caribbean. These wars of empire had tremendous consequences for the home governments, their colonial subjects, and the North American Indian tribes.

The Peace of Utrecht (see Chapter 4), which ended Queen Anne's War (1702–1713), brought victor's spoils of great importance to Britain. The generation of peace that followed was really only a time-out, during which both Britain and France strengthened their war-making capacity. Britain's productive and efficiently governed New World colonies made important contributions.

Concerned mainly with economic regulation, Parliament added new articles to the list of items produced in the colonies that had to be shipped to England before being exported to another country. Parliament also curtailed colonial production of articles important to England's economy: woollen cloth (1699), beaver hats (1732), and finished iron products (1750). Most important, Parliament passed the Molasses Act in 1733, an attempt to stop New England from trading with the French West Indies for molasses to convert into rum. Parliament imposed a prohibitive duty of six pence per gallon on French slave-produced molasses. Many of New England's largest merchants and distillers became smugglers. Motivated out of self-interest, these men and their ship captains, crews, and allied waterfront artisans learned to defy royal authority.

The generation of peace ended abruptly in 1739 when Britain declared war on Spain. The immediate cause was the ear of sea captain Robert Jenkins, which had been cut off eight years earlier when Spanish authorities caught him smuggling. Encouraged by his government, Jenkins publicly displayed his pickled ear in 1738 to whip up war fever against Spain. The real cause of the war, however, was Britain's determination to continue its drive toward commercial domination of the Atlantic basin.

From 1744 to 1748, the Anglo-Spanish war merged into a much larger Anglo-French conflict, called King George's War in North America and the War of Austrian Succession in Europe. Its scale far exceeded previous conflicts, highlighting the need for increased discipline within the empire. Unprecedented military expenditures led Britain to ask its West Indian and American colonies to share in the costs of defending—and extending—the empire. For the most part, war was costly for American colonists. Though proud of their part in capturing the French fortress of Louisbourg, the losses for the Massachusetts volunteers were staggering. Furthermore, they became bitter at war's end when Britain returned Louisbourg to France in exchange for other concessions.

Outbreak of Hostilities

The tension between British and French colonists in North America, which reached back to the early seventeenth century, was intensified by the spectacular population growth of the British colonies: from 250,000 in 1700 to 1.25 million in 1750, and to 1.75 million in the next decade. Three-quarters of the increase came in the colonies south of New York, propelling thousands of land-hungry settlers westward.

Fur traders and land speculators promoted this westward rush. In the 1740s and 1750s, speculators (including many future revolutionary leaders) formed land companies to capitalize on the seaboard population explosion. Penetration of the Ohio valley in the 1740s established the first British outposts in the continental heartland, challenging French interests.

The French resisted. They attempted to block further expansion west of the Alleghenies by constructing new forts in the Ohio valley and by prying some tribes loose from their new British alliances. By 1753, the French were driving British traders out of the Ohio River valley and establishing a line of forts between Lake Erie and the forks of the Ohio River, near present-day Pittsburgh. There, near Fort Duquesne on May 28, 1754, the French smartly rebuffed an ambitious 21-year-old Virginia militia colonel named George Washington, dispatched by his colony's government to expel them from the region.

Men in the capitals of Europe, not in the colonies, made the decision to force a showdown in the interior of North America. Britain's powerful merchants, supported by American clients, had been emboldened by the earlier success in overwhelming the mighty French fortress at Louisbourg. Now, they argued, the time was ripe to destroy the French overseas trade. Convinced, the government ministry ordered several thousand troops to North America in 1754; in France, 3,000 regulars embarked to meet this challenge.

With war looming, the colonial governments attempted to coordinate efforts. Representatives of seven colonies met at Albany, New York, in June 1754 to plan a union and regain the allegiance of the Iroquois. Both failed. The 150 Iroquois chiefs left with 30 wagonloads of gifts but made no firm commitment to fight the French. Benjamin Franklin designed a plan for an intercolonial government to manage Native American affairs, provide for defense, pass laws, and levy taxes. Even the clever woodcut displayed in the *Pennsylvania Gazette* that pictured a chopped-up snake with the insignia "Join or Die" failed to overcome long-standing jealousies, and the colonies rejected his plan.

With his newly arrived British regiments and hundreds of colonial recruits, General Edward Braddock slogged across Virginia in the summer of 1755, each day cutting a few miles of road through forests and across mountains. A headstrong professional soldier who regarded his European battlefield experience as sufficient for war in the American wilderness, Braddock had contempt for the woods-wise French regiments and their Native American allies.

As Braddock neared Fort Duquesne, the entire French force and the British suddenly surprised one another in the forest. The French had 218 soldiers and Canadian militiamen and 637 Native American allies; Braddock commanded 1,400 British regulars, supported by 450 Virginians and a few Indian scouts commanded by Washington. Pouring murderous fire into Braddock's tidy lines, the French and their allies won. Braddock perished, and two-thirds of the British were killed or wounded. Washington, his uniform pierced by four bullets, had two horses shot from beneath him. Although they had 1,000 men in reserve down the road, the Anglo-American force beat a hasty retreat. This ignominious defeat brought almost every tribe north of the Ohio River to the French side. For the next two years, French-supplied Native American raiders torched the backcountry.

Farther north, the Anglo-American forces had more success, overpowering Fort Beauséjour, the French fort on the neck of land that connected Nova Scotia and the French-controlled mainland. This victory quickly led to the expulsion of the French Acadians, Catholics who lived under British rule in Nova Scotia but refused to swear oaths of allegiance to the British king. The British rounded up about 6,000 Acadians, herded them aboard ships, and dispersed them among their other colonies, giving their confiscated land to New Englanders. They justified forcibly relocating this civilian population as a wartime security measure.

In 1756, Britain officially declared war on France, and the French and Indian War in North America turned into a world war with France, Austria, and Russia pitting themselves against Britain and Prussia. The turning point in the war came after the energetic William Pitt became the British secretary of state in 1757. "I believe that I can save this nation and that no one else can," he boasted, abandoning Europe as the main theater of action against the French and throwing his nation's military might into the American campaign. The forces he dispatched to North America in 1757 and 1758 dwarfed all preceding commitments: about 23,000 British troops and a huge fleet with 14,000 mariners. But even forces of this magnitude, when asked to engage the enemy in the forests of North America, were not necessarily sufficient to the task without Native American support, or at least neutrality.

Tribal Strategies

The Iroquois knew that their interest lay in playing off one European power against the other. Anglo-American leaders realized that the support of the Iroquois and their tributary tribes was crucial and could be secured in only two ways: through purchase or by a demonstration of power that would convince the tribes that the British would prevail with or without their assistance.

The first stratagem failed. In 1754, colonial negotiators heaped gifts on the Iroquois chiefs, but received only tantalizing half-promises of support against the French. The second alternative fizzled because, for the first three years of the war, the French campaign was superior to that of the British. In 1758, however, the huge military buildup began to produce British victories. Troops under Sir Jeffrey Amherst captured Louisbourg on Cape Breton Island, and Fort Duquesne fell to another army of 6,000. These successes, and the fact that the British navy had cut the Iroquois off from French trade goods, finally moved the Iroquois away from neutrality. Added incentive to join the Anglo-American side came. By early 1759, foreseeing a French defeat in North America, the Iroquois pledged 800 warriors for an attack on Fort Niagara, the strategic French trading depot on Lake Ontario.

Dramatic Anglo-American victories did not always guarantee Indian support. Backcountry skirmishes with the Cherokee from Virginia to South Carolina turned into a costly war from 1759 to 1761. In 1760, the Cherokee mauled a British army of 1,300 under Amherst. The following summer, a much larger Anglo-American force invaded Cherokee country, burning towns and food supplies. British control of the sea interrupted the Native Americans' supply of French arms. Beset by food shortages, lack of ammunition, and a smallpox epidemic, the Cherokee finally sued for peace.

Other Anglo-American victories in 1759, the "year of miracles," decided the outcome of the bloodiest war yet known in the Americas. The British captured Fort Niagara, the critical link in the system of forts that joined the French inland empire with the Atlantic, then conquered sugar-rich Martinique in the West Indies. The culminating stroke came at Québec. Led by 32-year-old General James Wolfe, 5,000 troops scaled a rocky cliff and overcame the French. The capture of Montréal late in 1760 completed the shattering of French power in North America. While fighting continued for three more years in the Caribbean and in Europe, in the American colonies, the old dream of destroying the Gallic menace had finally come true.

Consequences of the Seven Years' War

The Treaty of Paris, ending the Seven Years' War in 1763, brought astounding changes to European and native peoples in North America. Spain acquired New Orleans, the vast Louisiana territory west of the Mississippi, and Havana, and in turn surrendered Spanish Florida to the British. The interior tribes, which had adeptly forced Britain and France to compete for their support, suffered a severe setback when the French disappeared and the British became their sole source of trade goods. In response, the Ottawa chief Pontiac, concerned that the elimination of the French threatened the old treaty and gift-giving system, gathered together many of the northern tribes that had aided the French assaults during the Seven Years' War. Although Pontiac's pan-Indian movement to drive the British out of the Ohio valley collapsed in 1764, it served notice that the interior tribes would fight for their lands.

After making peace, the British government launched a new policy designed to separate Native Americans and colonizers by creating a boundary roughly following the crest of the Appalachian Mountains from Maine to Georgia. The Proclamation of 1763 reserved all land west of the line for Native American nations. White settlers who were already there were told to withdraw.

This well-meaning attempt to protect their Indian allies from further encroachment failed completely. London could not enforce the proclamation. Staggering under an immense wartime debt, Britain decided to maintain only small army garrisons to regulate the interior. Nor could royal governors stop land speculators and settlers from privately purchasing land from trans-Appalachian tribes or simply taking their land. The western frontier seethed after 1763.

War also had important social and economic effects on colonial society. It convinced the colonists of their growing strength, yet left them debt-ridden and weakened in manpower. The war spurred economic development and poured British capital into the colonies, yet rendered them more vulnerable to cyclic fluctuations in the British economy. When the war ended, so did the military contracts that had brought prosperity during the war years. Gone were the huge orders for ships, arms, uniforms, and provisions that had enriched northern merchants and provided good prices for farmers.

The war also required heavy taxes and took a huge human toll, especially in New England, which bore the brunt of the fighting. When peace

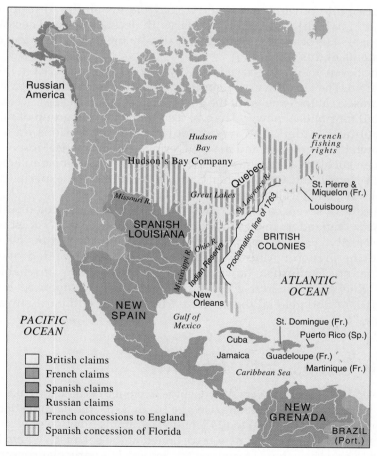

North America After 1763 At the Treaty of Paris in 1763, France surrendered huge claims west of the Mississippi River to Spain and east of the river to Great Britain. Britain also acquired Florida from Spain. How would these altered geopolitical circumstances affect Native Americans, British colonists, and the French-speaking settlers living in what is now called Canada?

came, Boston had a deficit of almost 700 men in a town of about 2,000 families. The high rate of war widowhood feminized poverty and required expanded poor relief to maintain husbandless women and fatherless children. Peace ended the casualties but also brought depression. When the bulk of the British forces left North America in 1760, the economy slumped badly, especially in the coastal towns.

Although some wealthy merchants went bankrupt, the greatest hardships after 1760 fell on laboring people. Established craftsmen and shopkeepers were caught between rising prices and reduced demand for their goods and services. A New York artisan expressed a common lament in 1762. Thankfully, he still had employment, he wrote in the *New-York Gazette*. But despite every effort at unceasing labor and frugal living, he had fallen into poverty and found it "beyond my ability to support my family . . . [which] can scarcely appear with decency or have necessaries to subsist." His situation, he added, "is really the case with many of the inhabitants of this city."

The Seven Years' War paved the way for a far larger conflict in the next generation. The legislative assemblies, for example, which had been flexing their muscles at the expense of the governors in earlier decades, accelerated their bid for political power. The war also trained a new group of military and political leaders. In carrying out military operations on a scale unknown in the colonies and in shouldering heavier political responsibilities, men such as George Washington, Samuel Adams, Benjamin Franklin, Patrick Henry, and Christopher Gadsden acquired the experience that would serve them well in the future.

In spite of severe costs, the Seven Years' War left many colonists buoyant. New Englanders rejoiced at the final victory over the "Papist enemy of the North." Frontiersmen, fur traders, and land speculators also celebrated the French withdrawal, for the West now appeared open for exploitation. The British, however, thought the colonists unreliable and poor fighters. He "could take a thousand grenadiers to America," boasted one officer, "and geld all the males, partly by force and partly by a little coaxing."

The Crisis with Britain

At the end of the Seven Years' War, George Grenville became the chief minister of Britain's 25-year-old king, George III. By 1763, the national debt had ballooned from £75 million to £145 million, straining a nation of weary taxpayers. Grenville proposed new taxes aimed at the colonists, whom he expected to bear their share of running the empire. His particular concern was financing the 10,000 British regulars left in North America after 1763 to police Canada and the Native Americans—and to remind unruly Americans that they were still subjects. In so doing, he opened a rift that in a dozen years would become a revolution.

Sugar, Currency, and Stamps

In 1764, Grenville pushed through Parliament several bills that in combination pressed hard on colonial economies. First came the Revenue Act (or Sugar Act) of 1764. While reducing the tax on imported French molasses from six to three pence per gallon, it added various colonial products to the list of commodities that could be sent only to England. It also required American shippers to post bonds guaranteeing observance of the trade regulations before loading their cargoes, and it strengthened the vice-admiralty courts to prosecute violators of the trade acts.

•‣•⊣Read the **Document**
James Otis, An American Colonist Opposes New Taxes and Asserts the Rights of the Colonists *(1764)*
at **www.myhistorylab.com**

Many colonial legislatures grumbled about the Sugar Act because a strictly enforced duty of three pence per gallon on molasses pinched more than the loosely enforced six-pence duty. But only New York objected that any tax by Parliament to raise revenue (rather than to control trade) violated the rights of overseas subjects who were unrepresented in Parliament.

Next came the Currency Act. In 1751, Parliament had forbidden the New England colonies to issue paper money as legal tender, and now it extended that prohibition to all the colonies. In a colonial economy chronically short of cash, this policy constricted trade.

The move to tighten up the machinery of empire confused the colonists because many of the new regulations came from Parliament. For generations, colonists had viewed Parliament as a bastion of English liberty. Now they began to see Parliament as a threat to their rights. Colonial leaders were uncertain about where Parliament's authority began and ended.

⊙‣⊣View the **Image**
Stamp Act Stamps
at **www.myhistorylab.com**

After Parliament passed the Sugar Act in 1764, Grenville announced his intention to extend to America the stamp duties—imposed in England decades earlier—on every newspaper, pamphlet, almanac, legal document, liquor license, college diploma, pack of playing cards, and pair of dice. He gave the colonies a year to suggest alternative ways of raising revenue. Colonial governments objected, but none provided another plan. Knowing that colonial property taxes were slight compared with those in England, Grenville drove the bill through Parliament. The Stamp Act became effective in November 1765.

Colonial reaction to the Stamp Act ranged from disgruntled submission to mass defiance. The breadth of the reaction shocked the British government—and many Americans as well. In many cases, resistance involved not only discontent over tightening the imperial screws but also internal resentments born out of local events. Especially in the cities, the defiance of authority and destruction of property by people from the middle and lower ranks redefined the dynamics of politics, setting the stage for a 10-year internal struggle for control among the various social elements alarmed by the new policies.

•‣•⊣Read the **Document**
Benjamin Franklin, Testimony against the Stamp Act *(1766)*
at **www.myhistorylab.com**

Stamp Act Riots

The first legislature to react to the news of the Stamp Act, in late 1764, Virginia's House of Burgesses strenuously objected. The burgesses argued that it was their "inherent" right to be taxed only by their own consent. Virginians were already worried by a severe decline in tobacco prices and heavy war-related taxes. Many planters were mired in debt. Led by newly elected 29-year-old Patrick Henry, in May 1765, the House debated seven strongly worded resolutions. Old-guard burgesses regarded some of them as treasonable, and they were revised. Many burgesses had left for home before Henry introduced his resolutions, so less than a quarter of Virginia's legislators voted for the four moderate resolves. Within a month, newspapers of other colonies published all seven resolutions. They included an assertion that Virginians did not have to pay externally imposed taxes and branded as an "enemy to this, his Majesty's colony" anyone who denied Virginia's exclusive right to tax itself.

Governor Francis Bernard of Massachusetts called the Virginia resolves an "alarm bell for the disaffected." August 1765 events in Boston confirmed his view. On August 14, Bostonians hung a rag-dressed effigy of stamp distributor Andrew Oliver. When the sheriff tried to remove it by order of Lieutenant Governor Thomas Hutchinson, Oliver's brother-in-law, a hostile crowd intervened. In the evening, workingmen cut down Oliver's effigy, carried it boisterously through the streets, leveled his new brick office, and reduced his luxurious mansion to a shambles. The stamp distributor promptly asked to be relieved of his commission. Twelve days later, MacIntosh led the crowd as they destroyed the handsomely appointed homes of two British officials as well as that of the unpopular Hutchinson, a descendent of Anne Hutchinson.

In attacking the property of men associated with the stamp tax, the Boston crowd demonstrated not only its opposition to parliamentary policy but also its resentment of local elites. For decades, ordinary Bostonians had aligned politically with the Boston "caucus," which led the colony's "popular party" against conservatives such as Hutchinson and Oliver. But the "rage-intoxicated rabble" had suddenly broken away from the leaders of the popular party and gone farther than they had intended. Hutchinson was one of their main targets. Characterized by young lawyer John Adams as "very ambitious and avaricious," Hutchinson was, in the popular view, chief among the "mean mercenary hirelings" of the British. The more cautious political leaders had to struggle to regain control of the protest movement.

View the Image
Bostonians Paying the Excise Man (Cartoon)
at **www.myhistorylab.com**

Protest took a more dignified form at the October 1765 **Stamp Act Congress** in New York. Imperial authorities branded this first self-initiated intercolonial convention a "dangerous tendency." The delegates formulated 12 restrained resolutions that accepted Parliament's right to legislate for the colonies but denied its right to tax them directly.

Groups calling themselves the **Sons of Liberty**, composed mostly of artisans, shopkeepers, and other ordinary citizens, led violent protests against the Stamp Act in New York and Newport, Rhode Island. By late 1765, effigy-burning crowds up and down the seaboard were convincing stamp distributors to resign. Colonists defied British authority even more directly by forcing most customs officers and court officials to open the ports and courts for business after November 1 without using the hated stamps required after that date. This effort could take months of pressure and sometimes mob action, but the Sons of Liberty, frequently led by new faces in local politics, got their way by going outside the law.

In March 1766, Parliament debated the American reaction to the Stamp Act. Lobbied by many merchants friendly to the colonies, Parliament voted to repeal it, bowing to expediency. At the same time, it passed the Declaratory Act, which asserted Parliament's power to enact laws for the colonies in "all cases whatsoever."

The crisis had passed, yet nothing was resolved. Colonists feared a grasping government trampling subjects' rights. The Stamp Act, one New England clergyman foresaw, "diffused a disgust through the colonies and laid the basis of an alienation which will never be healed." Stamp Act resisters had politicized their communities as never before. People lower down the social ladder often displaced generally cautious established leaders.

Gathering Storm Clouds

Ministerial instability in Westminster hampered the quest for a coherent, workable imperial policy. Attempting to be a strong king, George III chose

Patrick Henry, Forceful Patriot Orator From the time of his election to the Virginia House of Burgesses at the age of 29, Patrick Henry was an outspoken proponent of American rights. Do you notice any unusual features in this portrait, in which he pleads a case at a county courthouse crowded with local planters?

RECOVERING *the* PAST

Poetry

Poetry is one of the most ancient and universal of the arts. Making its effect by the rhythmic sound and imagery of its language, poetry often expresses romantic love, grief, and responses to nature. But other kinds of poetry interest historians: reflections of human experience, often expressed with deep emotion; and political verses, often written to serve propagandistic goals. For generations, American historians have drawn on poetry to recapture feelings, ideas, and group experiences.

The revolutionary generation created such poetry. Many newspapers published weekly "Poet's Corner" satires, drinking songs, and versed commentary on issues of the day. Verse was widely used to provoke public discussion; in 1767, poets prompted the boycott of British goods to obtain Parliament's reversal of the Townshend duties.

A year later, Philadelphia's John Dickinson composed a "Liberty Song," the first set of verses learned in all the colonies. Boston's Sons of Liberty used this "Liberty Song" in annual ceremonies celebrating their resistance to the Stamp Act. Set to music and easily learned, the verses cultivated anti-British feeling and a sense of the need for intercolonial cooperation.

Of all the revolutionary-era poets, none has fascinated historians more than Phillis Wheatley, a slave in Boston who wrote her first poem at age 14. In 1774, she became North America's first published black poet. Boston's "Ethiopian poetess" had been brought from Africa to Boston at age 7 and purchased by a prospering tailor named John Wheatley. Soon her master and his wife discovered that she was a prodigy. Learning English in 16 months so well that she could read the Bible, she showed an uncanny gift for writing. Much of her writing was inspired by deep religious feelings, but she was soon caught up in the dramatic events in Boston leading toward revolution. In "To the King's Most Excellent Majesty," she saluted King George III in poetry for repealing the Stamp Act; in "On the Death of Mr. Snider [Seider], Murder'd by Richardson," she lambasted the British customs officer who murdered a Boston teenager.

Wheatley was anything but radical. She had so thoroughly imbibed Christianity from her master and mistress that she wrote in one of her first poems that "Twas mercy brought me from my Pagan land." Many times she used poetry to implore slaves to "fly to Christ." But by 1772, she was inserting a muffled plea for an end of slavery in her odes to American rights and American resistance to British policies.

That Wheatley's poems were published in London in 1773 is remarkable. Women were not supposed to write publicly in the eighteenth century, especially not black women. Nonetheless, her master shipped a sheaf of poems to a bookseller in England, who obtained the support of the Countess of Huntingdon for publishing them. They appeared under the title Poems on Various Subjects, Religious and Moral. Even more remarkable was that Wheatley, only 20 years old, took ship to London to see her book come off the press. Her master and mistress financed the trip, hoping that sea air would clear her clogged lungs. There she was introduced to public dignitaries, received a copy of Milton's *Paradise Lost* from the lord mayor of London, and met with Benjamin Franklin.

Read the two poems that follow: "On the Death of Mr. Snider [Seider], Murder'd by Richardson" and her poem addressed to the King's minister for colonial affairs, penned in 1772.

On the Death of Mr. Snider, Murder'd by
*   Richardson (1770)*
In heaven's eternal court it was decreed
How the first martyr for the cause should
*   bleed*
To clear the country of the hated
*   brood*

We whet his courage for the common
*   good.*
Long hid before, a vile infernal here
Prevents Achilles in his mid career
Wherev'r this fury darts his Poisonous
*   breath*
All are endanger'd to the shafts of death

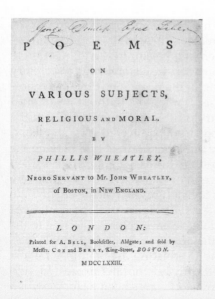

Wheatley worshiped at Old South Meeting House, where people frequently gathered for political rallies and deliberations. This partly explains her growing interest in the political battles raging in Boston. Wheatley's patroness in England requested a drawing of Phillis for the frontispiece of this volume.

To the Right Honourable William, Earl of Dartmouth, His Majesty's Principal Secretary of State for North America (1772)

HAIL, happy day, when, smiling like the morn,
Fair Freedom rose New-England to adorn:
The northern clime beneath her genial ray,
Dartmouth, congratulates thy blissful sway:
Elate with hope her race no longer mourns,
Each soul expands, each grateful bosom burns,
While in thine hand with pleasure we behold
The silken reigns, and Freedom's charms unfold.
No more, America, in mournful strain
Of wrongs, and grievance unredress'd complain,
No longer shalt thou dread the iron chain,

Which wanton Tyranny with lawless hand
Had made, and with it meant t' enslave the land.
Should you, my lord, while you peruse my song,
Wonder from whence my love of Freedom sprung,
Whence flow these wishes for the common good,
By feeling hearts alone best understood,
I, young in life, by seeming cruel fate
Was snatch'd from Afric's fancy'd happy seat:
What pangs excruciating must molest,
What sorrows labour in my parent's breast?
Steel'd was that soul and by no misery mov'd
That from a father seiz'd his babe belov'd:
Such, such my case. And can I then but pray
Others may never feel tyrannic sway?

REFLECTING ON THE PAST You may find the poetry stilted, but Wheatley's style was modeled on poetic conventions of the eighteenth century. What change can you discern in Wheatley's political consciousness between 1770 and 1772? Do you consider her poem on Seider's murder propagandistic? How does she relate the plight of enslaved Africans to the American colonists' struggle? More generally, how effective do you think poetry is in arousing sentiment and mobilizing political energy? Can you think of verse serving as lyrics in popular protest music today?

145

ministers who commanded little respect in Parliament. Strife between Parliament and the king's chief ministers created a generally chaotic political situation just as the king was trying to overhaul the empire's administration. His goals included reorganizing the customs service, establishing a secretary of state for American affairs, and installing in the port cities three new vice-admiralty courts, which would try accused smugglers without juries. Still hard-pressed for revenue, the new ministry pushed through Parliament the relatively small Townshend duties on paper, lead, painters' colors, and tea. A final law suspended New York's assembly until that body ceased defying the Quartering Act of 1765, which required public funds for support of British troops garrisoned in the colony since the end of the Seven Years' War. New York knuckled under in order to save its legislature. Massachusetts led the colonial protests against the Townshend Acts. Its House of Representatives sent a circular letter written by Samuel Adams to each colony objecting to the new Townshend duties. Adams attacked the duties as unconstitutional.

Showing more restraint than they had in resisting the Stamp Act, most colonists only grumbled and petitioned. But Bostonians protested stridently. In the summer of 1768, after customs officials seized a sloop owned by John Hancock for violating trade regulations, an angry crowd mobbed them; for months, the officials took refuge on a British warship in Boston harbor. Newspapers warned of new measures designed to "suck the life blood" from the people and predicted that Britain would send troops to "dragoon us into passive obedience." The belief grew that the British were plotting "designs for destroying our constitutional liberties."

Troops indeed came. The attack on the customs officials convinced the government that Bostonians were insubordinate and selfish. It decided to subdue their rebellion and make them an example. On October 1, 1768, redcoats marched into Boston without resistance.

Thereafter, the colonists' main tactic of protest against the Townshend Acts became economic boycott. First in Boston and then in New York and Philadelphia, merchants and consumers adopted nonimportation and non-consumption agreements, pledging neither to import nor to use British goods. These measures promised to bring politically influential English merchants to their aid, for half of British shipping was engaged in commerce with the colonies, and one-quarter of all English exports were consumed there. When the southern colonies also adopted nonimportation agreements in 1768, the move represented a new step toward intercolonial union.

Many colonial merchants, however, especially those with official connections, refused to be bound by nonimportation agreements. They had to be persuaded otherwise by street brigades, usually composed of artisans for whom nonimportation was a boon to home manufacturing. Crowd action welled up again in the seaports, as bands attacked the homes and warehouses of offending merchants and "rescued" incoming contraband goods seized by customs officials.

Britain's attempts to discipline its colonies and oblige them to share the costs of governing their empire lay in shambles by the end of the 1760s. Using troops to restore order undermined the very respect needed for acceptance of imperial authority. The Townshend duties had failed miserably, yielding less than £21,000 by 1770 while costing British business £700,000 through the colonial nonimportation movement. On March 5, 1770, Parliament repealed all the Townshend duties except the one on tea.

On that same evening in Boston, British troops fired on an unruly crowd of heckling citizens. When the smoke cleared, five bloody bodies, including that of Ebenezer MacIntosh's brother-in-law, stained the snow-covered street. Bowing to furious popular reaction, Thomas Hutchinson, recently appointed governor, ordered the British troops out of town and arrested the commanding officer and the soldiers involved. They were later acquitted, with two young lawyers, John Adams and Josiah Quincy, Jr., providing a brilliant defense.

Read the Document
Boston Gazette Description of the Boston Massacre (1770)
at **www.myhistorylab.com**

In spite of the potential of the "Boston Massacre" for galvanizing the colonies into further resistance, opposition, including boycotts, subsided in 1770. Popular leaders such as Samuel Adams in Boston and Alexander McDougall in New York, who had made names for themselves as the standard-bearers of American liberty, had few issues left, especially when the depression that had helped sow discontent ended. Yet the fires of revolution had not been extinguished but merely dampened.

View the Image
Paul Revere Etching of Boston Massacre
at **www.myhistorylab.com**

On the Brink of Rebellion

Even as the imperial crisis seemed to abate, fears and tensions continued to seethe through colonial society. Concerns that imperial officials intended to deprive colonists of their liberty circulated widely, and such fears helped to explain the vehement reaction of colonists to seemingly minor threats. At the same time, social tensions kept the dampened fires of revolt from going out entirely. When the imperial struggle resumed, these fears and tensions would shape the conflict that brought the British Empire to the brink of crisis.

Protesting Farmers

In most of the agricultural areas of the colonies, where the majority of settlers made their livelihoods, passions over imperial policies awakened only slowly. After about 1740, farmers had benefited from a sharp rise in the demand for foodstuffs in England, southern Europe, and the West Indies. Rising prices and brisk markets brought a higher standard of living to thousands of rural colonists, especially south of New England. Living far from harping British customs officers, impressment gangs, and occupying armies, the colonists of the interior had to be drawn gradually into the resistance movement by their urban cousins. Even in Concord, Massachusetts, only a dozen miles from the center of colonial agitation, townspeople found little to protest in British policies through the 1760s and early 1770s.

Still, other parts of rural America seethed with social tension in the prewar era. The dynamics of conflict, shaped by the social development of particular regions, would eventually become part of the momentum for revolution. In three western counties of North Carolina and in the Hudson River valley of New York, for example, widespread civil disorder marked the prerevolutionary decades.

For years, the small farmers of western North Carolina had suffered exploitation by corrupt county court officials appointed by the governor and a legislature dominated by eastern planter interests. Sheriffs and justices, allied with land speculators and lawyers, seized property when farmers could not pay their taxes and sold it, often at a fraction of its worth, to their cronies. The legislature rejected western petitions for lower taxes, paper currency, and lower court fees. In the mid-1760s, frustrated at getting no satisfaction from legal forms of protest, the farmers formed associations—the so-called **Regulators**—that forcibly closed the courts, attacked the property of their enemies, and whipped judges and lawyers. When their leaders were arrested, the Regulators stormed the jails and released them.

In 1768 and again in 1771, Governor William Tryon led troops against the Regulators. Bloodshed was averted on the first occasion. On the second, at the Battle of Alamance, two armies of more than 1,000 fired on each other. Nine men died on each side before the Regulators fled the field. Six leaders were executed in the ensuing trials. Though the Regulators lost the battle, their protests drew upon the language of the larger imperial struggle. They railed against the self-interested behavior of a wealthy elite and asserted the necessity for people of humble rank to throw off deference and assume political responsibility.

Rural insurgency over land holdings in New York flared up in the 1750s, subsided, and then erupted again in 1766. A few wealthy families with enormous landholdings, acquired as virtually free gifts from royal governors, controlled the Hudson River valley. The Van Rensselaer manor, for example, totaled a million acres. Hundreds of tenants with their families paid substantial annual rents for the right to farm on these lands. When tenants resisted rent increases or purchased land from Indians who swore that manor lords had extended the boundaries of their manors by fraud, the landlords began evicting them.

As the wealthiest men of the region, the landlords had the power of government, including control of the courts, on their side. Organizing themselves and going outside the law became the tenants' main strategy, as with the Carolina Regulators. By 1766, while New York City was absorbed in the Stamp Act furor, tenants led by William Prendergast began resisting sheriffs who tried to evict them from lands they claimed. The militant tenants threatened landlords with death and broke open jails to rescue friends. British troops from New York were used to break the tenant rebellion. Prendergast was tried and sentenced to be hanged, beheaded, and quartered. Although he was pardoned, the bitterness of the Hudson River tenants endured for decades. Most of them, unlike the Carolina Regulators, would ultimately fight for the British against their landlords.

The Growing Rift

In June 1772, the Crown created a new furor by announcing that it, rather than the provincial legislature, would henceforth pay the salaries of the royal governor and superior court judges in Massachusetts. Even though the measure saved the colony money, it looked like a scheme to impose despotic government. Judges paid from Westminster presumably would obey Westminster.

Boston's town meeting protested loudly and created a Committee of Correspondence to win other colonies' sympathy. By the end of 1772, another 80 towns in Massachusetts had created committees. In the next year, all but three colonies established **Committees of Correspondence** in their legislatures.

Samuel Adams was the leader of the Boston radicals, the influence of laboring men like Ebenezer MacIntosh having declined. Adams was an experienced caucus politicker and a skilled journalist. Despite his Harvard degree, Adams had deep roots among laboring people. He was equally adept at organizing workers and securing the financial support of wealthy merchants such as John Hancock.

In 1772, Rhode Island gave Adams a new issue. The commander of the royal ship *Gaspee* was roundly hated by the fishermen and small traders of Narragansett Bay. When his ship ran aground while pursuing a suspected smuggler, Rhode Islanders burned it. A local court convicted the captain of illegally seizing what he was convinced had been smuggled sugar and rum. Westminster reacted with outrage. Investigators found Rhode Islanders' lips sealed. The event was tailor-made for Samuel Adams, who used it to "awaken the American colonies, which have been too long dozing upon the brink of ruin."

The final plunge into revolution began when Parliament passed the Tea Act in early 1773, allowing the practically bankrupt East India Company to ship its tea directly to North America with the colonists paying only a small tax. Americans would get inexpensive tea, the Crown a modest revenue, and the East India Company a new lease on life. But colonists reacted furiously. American merchants who competed with the East India Company denounced the monopoly. Many colonists suspected that the government's true object was to gain acceptance of Parliament's taxing power. As Americans drank the taxed tea, they would be swallowing the right to tax them. Showing that their principles were not entirely in their pocketbooks, Americans staged mass meetings that soon forced the resignation of East India Company agents. Some colonists vowed to stop the obnoxious tea at the water's edge.

•••[Read the Document

A Retrospect on the Boston Tea Party' (1834)

at **www.myhistorylab.com**

The major contribution of colonial women to the resistance movement revolved around the boycott of tea and other goods. The success of the non-consumption pacts depended on substituting homespun cloth for English textiles on which colonists of all classes relied. From Georgia to Maine, women and children began spinning yarn and weaving cloth. Towns often vied patriotically in the manufacture of cotton, linen, and woollen cloth, the women staging spinning contests to publicize their commitment. With the Tea Act, the interjection of politics into the household economy increased as patriotic women boycotted their favorite drink. Newspapers carried recipes for tea substitutes and recommendations for herbal teas. In Wilmington, North Carolina, women paraded solemnly through the town and then made a ritual display of their patriotism by burning their imported tea.

In the face of widespread opposition, Governor Hutchinson brought the tea crisis to a climax, convinced that to yield again to popular pressure would forever cripple British sovereignty in North America. Samuel Adams's Patriot party had been urging Bostonians to demonstrate that they would not accept the "yoke of slavery" by sending the tea away. When Hutchinson refused, a band of Bostonians, dressed as Native Americans, boarded the tea ships and flung £10,000 worth of the East India Company's property into the harbor.

Now the die was cast. Lord North, the king's chief minister, argued that the dispute was no longer about taxes but about whether Britain had any authority over the colonies. Parliament passed the Coercive Acts, stern laws that Bostonians promptly labeled the "Intolerable Acts." The acts closed the port of Boston to all shipping until the colony paid for the destroyed tea.

American Liberty Abused Liberty always had to struggle against power, as American colonists saw it; in this cartoon, Britain (power) forces Liberty (America in the form of a woman) to drink the "Bitter Draught" of tea. Uncompliant, America spits the tea into Britain's face. What other signs of the political and moral corruption of the British does this image convey?

They also barred local courts from trying British soldiers and officials for acts committed while suppressing civil disturbances. Parliament amended the Massachusetts charter, transforming the council into a body appointed by the governor and without veto power over the governor's decisions.

The act also struck at local government by authorizing the governor to prohibit all town meetings except one annual meeting to elect local officers of government. Finally, General Thomas Gage, commander in chief of British forces in America, replaced Thomas Hutchinson as governor.

The colonists found their maneuvering room severely narrowed. When the Intolerable Acts arrived in May 1774, Boston's town meeting urged all the colonies to ban trade with Britain. While this met with faint support, a second call, for a meeting in Philadelphia of delegates from all colonies, received a better response. Called the **Continental Congress**, it began to transform a 10-year debate conducted by separate colonies into a unified American cause.

In September 1774, 55 delegates from all the colonies except Georgia converged on Carpenters' Hall in Philadelphia. The discussions centered not on how to prepare for a war that many sensed was inevitable but on how to resolve sectional differences that most delegates feared were irreconcilable.

The Continental Congress was by no means a unified body. Some delegates, led by cousins Samuel and John Adams from Massachusetts and Richard Henry Lee and Patrick Henry of Virginia, argued for outright resistance to Parliament's Coercive Acts. Moderate delegates from the middle colonies urged restraint and further attempts at reconciliation. After weeks of debate, the delegates agreed to a modest Declaration of Rights and Resolves, which attempted to define American grievances and justify the colonists' defiance. Congress had a more concrete agreement on a plan of resistance. If Britain did not rescind the Intolerable Acts by December 1, 1774, all imports and exports between the colonies and Great Britain, Ireland, and the British West Indies would be banned. To keep reluctant southern colonies in the fold, some exceptions were made for the export of southern staple commodities.

By the time the Congress adjourned in late October, leaders from different colonies had transformed Boston's cause into a national movement. Patrick Henry argued dramatically, "Government is dissolved [and] we are in a state of nature. . . . I am not a Virginian, but an American." Many other delegates were a long way from his conclusion; still, the Congress agreed to reconvene in May 1775.

When the Second Continental Congress met, the fabric of government was badly torn in most colonies. Illegal revolutionary committees, conventions, and congresses were replacing legal governing bodies. Assuming authority in defiance of royal governors, who suspended truculent legislatures in many colonies, they often operated on instructions from mass meetings where everyone, not just those entitled to vote, gave voice. These extralegal bodies created and armed militia units, bullied merchants and shopkeepers refusing to obey popularly authorized boycotts, levied taxes, operated the courts, and obstructed customs officials. By the end of 1774, all but three colonies defied their own charters by appointing provincial assemblies without royal authority. In the next year, this independently created power became evident when trade with Britain practically ceased.

The Role of Urban People

Although the cities contained only about 5 percent of the colonial population, they were the core of revolutionary agitation. As centers of communications, government, and commerce, they led the way in protesting policy, and they soon contained the most politicized people in America. Local politics could be rapidly transformed as the struggle against Britain meshed with calls for internal reform.

Philadelphia offers a good example of popular empowerment. Before the Seven Years' War, craftsmen had usually acquiesced to local leadership by merchant and lawyer politicos. But economic difficulties in the 1760s and 1770s led them to band together within their craft and community. Artisans played a central role in forging and enforcing a nonimportation agreement in 1768. Cautious merchants complained that mere artisans had "no right to give their sentiments respecting an importation" and called the craftsmen a "rabble." But artisans, casting off their customary deference, forged ahead. By 1772, they were filling elected municipal positions and insisting on their right to participate equally with their social superiors in nominating assemblymen and other officeholders. They also began lobbying for reform laws, calling for elected representatives to be more accountable to their constituents. Genteel Philadelphians muttered, "It is time the tradesmen were checked—they ought not to intermeddle in state affairs—they will become too powerful."

By 1774, the Philadelphia working people's meddling in state affairs reached a bold new stage—de facto assumption of governmental powers by committees created by the people at large. Artisans had first assumed such extralegal authority in policing the nonimportation agreement in 1768. Now, responding to the Intolerable Acts, they proposed a radical slate of candidates for a committee to enforce a new economic boycott. Their ticket drubbed one nominated by conservative merchants.

The political support of the new radical leaders centered in the 31 companies of the Philadelphia militia, composed mostly of laboring men, and in the extralegal committees now controlling the city's economic life. Their leadership helped overcome the conservatism of the regularly elected Pennsylvania legislature, which was resisting the movement of the Continental Congress toward independence. The new radical leaders demanded internal reforms: curbing the accumulation of wealth by "our great merchants . . . at the expense of the people"; abolishing the property requirement for voting; allowing militiamen to elect their officers; and imposing stiff fines, to be used for the support of the families of poor militiamen, on men who refused militia service.

Philadelphia's radicals never controlled the city. They always jostled for position with prosperous artisans and shopkeepers of more moderate views and with cautious lawyers and merchants. But mobilization among artisans, laborers, and mariners, in other cities as well as Philadelphia, became part of the chain of events that led toward independence. Whereas most of the Patriot elite fought only to change colonial policy, the ordinary people of the cities also struggled for internal reforms. They raised notions of how an independent American society might be reorganized.

The Final Rupture

The final spark to the revolutionary powder keg was struck in April 1775. Royal government ordered General Gage, commander of the British troops occupying Boston, to arrest "the principal actors and abettors" of insurrection. Under cover of night, he sent 700 redcoats out of Boston to seize colonial arms in nearby Concord. But Americans learned of the plan, and when the troops reached Lexington at dawn, 70 armed Minutemen—townsmen available on a minute's notice—were waiting. In the ensuing skirmish, 18 Massachusetts farmers fell, 8 of them mortally wounded.

Marching farther west, to Concord, the British encountered another firefight. Withdrawing, the redcoats made their way back to Boston, harassed by militiamen firing from farmhouses and from behind stone walls. Before the bloody day ended, 273 British and 95 Americans lay dead or wounded. News of the bloodshed swept through the colonies. Within weeks, thousands of men besieged the British troops in Boston. According to one colonist, everywhere "you see the inhabitants training, making firelocks, casting mortars, shells, and shot."

As fighting erupted around Boston, the Second Continental Congress assembled in May 1775 in Philadelphia. Many delegates knew one another from the earlier Congress. But fresh faces appeared, including Boston's wealthy merchant John Hancock; a young planter-lawyer from Virginia, Thomas Jefferson; and Benjamin Franklin, who had recently arrived from London.

Meeting in the statehouse where the king's arms hung over the entrance and the inscription on the tower bell read "Proclaim liberty throughout the land unto all the inhabitants thereof," the Second Congress set to work. Though its powers were unclear and its legitimacy uncertain, the desperate situation required action. After a spirited debate, Congress authorized a continental army of 20,000 and, partly to cement Virginia to the cause, chose George Washington as commander in chief. Over succeeding weeks, it issued a "Declaration of Causes of Taking-up Arms," sent the king an "Olive Branch Petition" begging him to remove the obstacles to reconciliation, made moves to secure the neutrality of the interior Indian tribes, issued paper money, and approved plans for a military hospital.

While debate continued over whether the colonies ought to declare independence from Britain, military action grew more intense. The fiery Ethan Allen and his Green Mountain Boys from eastern New York captured

Fort Ticonderoga, controlling the Champlain valley, in May 1775. On New Year's Day in 1776, the British shelled Norfolk, Virginia. Still, many members of Congress hoped for reconciliation. Such hopes finally crumbled at the end of 1775 when news arrived that the king, rejecting the Olive Branch Petition and proclaiming the colonies in "open and avowed rebellion," had dispatched 20,000 additional troops to quell the insurrection. Those fatal words made Congress's actions treasonable and turned all who obeyed the Congress into traitors.

Thomas Paine's *Common Sense*

As the crisis deepened, a pamphlet surfaced that would speed the move toward independence. Published in Philadelphia on January 9, 1776, Thomas Paine's *Common Sense* soon appeared in bookstalls all over the colonies. In scathing language, Paine denied the very legitimacy of monarchy. "Of more worth is one honest man to society," he scoffed, "than all the crowned ruffians that ever lived." It was Paine's unsparing rejection of monarchy that made his pamphlet seem so radical. From that it was a logical step to call openly for Americans to act in defense of their liberties. "O ye that love mankind," he declared. "Ye that dare oppose not only the tyranny, but also the tyrant, stand forth!"

The pamphlet's astounding popularity—it went through 25 editions in 1776 and sold more copies than any printed piece in colonial

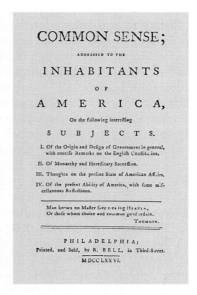

Thomas Paine and the Title Page of *Common Sense* In *Common Sense*, Thomas Paine took the radical step of attacking George III and the entire concept of monarchy in plain but muscular language that common folk could understand. Why do you suppose Paine did not put his name on the title page (though he was quickly identified as the author)?

history—stemmed not only from its argument but also from its style. Shunning the elaborate, legalistic language of most pamphlets written by lawyers and clergymen, Paine wrote for the common people who read little more than the Bible. Using biblical imagery and plain language, he appealed to their Protestant heritage and millennial yearnings: "We have it in our power to begin the world over again," he exulted. "The birthday of a new world" is at hand. It was language that could be understood on the docks, in the taverns, on the streets, and in the farmyards.

Many Whig leaders found his pungent rhetoric and egalitarian call for ending hereditary privilege and leadership by the colonial elite too strong. Some denounced the disheveled immigrant as a "crack-brained zealot for democracy" who appealed to "every silly clown and illiterate mechanic." But thousands who read or listened to *Common Sense* were radicalized by it and came to believe not only that independence could be wrestled from Great Britain, but also that a new social and political order could be created in North America.

Severing the Colonial Bonds

By 1776, tension between the colonies and Britain was at the breaking point. In each of the colonies, extralegal committees and assemblies organized resistance to the Intolerable Acts, while in England, Parliament and the king's ministers prepared to crush the colonial challenge to British authority. The outbreak of fighting at Lexington and Concord had transformed the imperial crisis. No longer was it limited to a struggle over competing theories of parliamentary authority and colonial rights, for now the firing had commenced and men on both sides were dying. Within a year of that fateful event, Britain's empire was severed. The subjects of George III were remade as citizens, and they faced the task of creating a new nation even as they entered a war to secure the independence their representatives had declared.

Declaring Independence

By the time Paine's hard-hitting pamphlet appeared, members of Congress were talking less gingerly about independence. When England embargoed all trade to the colonies and ordered the seizure of American ships, Congress declared American ports open to all countries. "Nothing is left now," Joseph Hewes of North Carolina admitted, "but to fight it out."

((•─[Hear the **Audio**
The Liberty Song
at **www.myhistorylab.com**

It was almost anticlimactic when Richard Henry Lee introduced a congressional resolution on June 7 calling for independence. After two days of debate, Congress ordered a committee chaired by Jefferson to begin drafting such a document.

Though it would become revered as the new nation's birth certificate, the Declaration of Independence was not a highly original statement. It drew heavily on Congress's earlier justifications of American resistance.

●─[View the **Image**
*Independence Hall: The Signing
of the Declaration of
Independence, Copy of John
Trumbull Painting (1817–1818)*
at **www.myhistorylab.com**

Tearing Down the Statue of George III In celebration of American independence, Patriots and their slaves toppled the statue of King George III that stood at Bowling Green in New York City. How might this symbolic act have been understood in Britain?

The ringing phrases that "all men are created equal, that they are endowed by their Creator with certain unalienable Rights, that among these are Life, Liberty, and the pursuit of Happiness" were familiar in the writing of many American pamphleteers. Much of the document rehearses a long list of the abuses perpetrated by George III against his colonial subjects.

Congress began to debate the proposed declaration on Monday, July 1. The following day 12 delegations voted "yes," with New York abstaining, thus allowing Congress to say that the vote for independence was unanimous. Two more days were spent polishing the document. The major change was the elimination of a long argument blaming the king for slavery in America. On July 4, Congress sent the document to the printer.

Four days later, Philadelphians thronged to the statehouse to hear the Declaration of Independence read aloud. They "huzzahed" the reading, tore the king's arms from above the statehouse door, and later that night, amid cheers, toasts, and clanging church bells, hurled this symbol of more than a century and a half of colonial dependency into a roaring fire. Independence had been declared; the war, however, was yet to be won.

Congress and the Articles of Confederation

As the Declaration made its way through committee, the Continental Congress turned to the task of creating a more permanent and effective national government. It was a daunting assignment, for prior to independence the colonies had quarreled over conflicting boundaries, control of the Indian trade, and commercial advantage within the empire. The crisis with Britain had forced them together, and Congress was the initial embodiment of that tenuous union.

As long as hope of reconciliation lingered, Congress's uncertain authority posed no serious problems. But as independence and the prospects of an extended war loomed, pressure to establish a more durable central government increased. On June 20, 1776, shortly before independence was declared, Congress appointed a committee, chaired by John Dickinson of Pennsylvania, to draw up a plan of perpetual union. So urgent was the crisis that the committee responded in a month's time and debate on the proposed Articles of Confederation soon began.

The delegates promptly clashed over whether to form a strong, consolidated government or a loose confederation of sovereign states. As discussions went on, those differences sharpened. Dickinson's draft, outlining a government of considerable power, generated strong opposition. American experience with a "tyrannous" king and an overreaching Parliament had revealed the dangers of central governments unmindful of the people's liberties.

As finally approved, the Articles of Confederation represented a compromise. Article 9 gave Congress sole authority to regulate foreign affairs, declare war, mediate interstate boundary disputes, manage a post office, and administer relations with Indians living outside state boundaries.

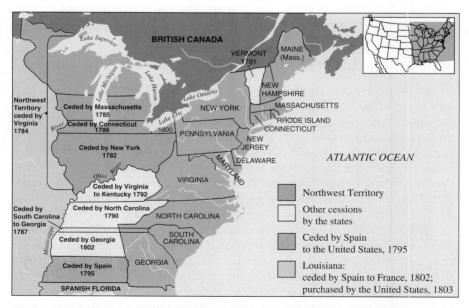

Western Land Claims Ceded by the States, 1782–1802 Seven of the original states laid claim, based on their colonial charters, to lands west of the Appalachian Mountains. Eventually those states ceded those lands to Congress, thus making ratification of the Articles of Confederation and the creation of new states possible. Why were the western claims such a problem?

The Articles also stipulated that the inhabitants of each state were to enjoy the "privileges and immunities" of the citizens of every other state. Embedded in that clause was the basis for national, as distinguished from state, citizenship.

But the Articles sharply limited what Congress could do and reserved broad governing powers to the states. For example, Congress could neither raise troops nor levy taxes, but only ask the states for support. Article 2 stipulated that each state was to retain "its sovereignty, freedom and independence," as well as "every power . . . which is not by this confederation expressly delegated to the United States in Congress assembled." And the Articles could be amended only by the unanimous agreement of the 13 states.

Though Congress sent the Articles to the states for approval in November 1777, they were not ratified until March 1781. Ratification required approval by all 13 states, and that was hard to obtain. The biggest impediment was a bitter dispute over control of lands west of the Appalachian Mountains. Some states had western claims tracing back to their colonial charters, but other states, such as Maryland and New Jersey, did not. In December 1778, the Maryland assembly announced that it would not ratify until all the western lands had been ceded to Congress. For several years, ratification hung in the balance while politicians and land speculators jockeyed. Finally, in 1780, New York and Virginia agreed to give up their western lands. Those decisions paved the way for Maryland's ratification in early 1781. Approval of the Articles was now assured.

Mobilizing the People

Under the pressure of revolutionary events, politics absorbed people's energies as never before. The politicization of American society was evident in the flood of printed material issuing from American presses. Newspapers multiplied and pamphlets by the thousands fanned political debate. The expansion of popular politics resulted from an explosive combination of circumstances: the momentous events of revolution and war; the efforts of Patriot leaders to mobilize popular support for the struggle; and the determination of artisans, workingmen, farmers, and other common folk to apply the principles of liberty to the conditions of their own lives.

Pulpits rocked with political exhortations as well. While religion and politics had never been sharply separated in colonial America, the Revolution drew them more tightly together. In countless sermons, Congregational, Presbyterian, and Baptist clergy exhorted the American people to repent the sins that had brought British tyranny upon them and urged them to rededicate themselves to God's purposes by fighting for American freedom. It was language that people nurtured in Protestant piety and the Great Awakening instinctively understood.

The belief that God sanctioned their revolution strengthened Americans' resolve. It also encouraged them to equate their own interests with divine intent, and thus offered justification for whatever they believed necessary. This was not the last time Americans would make that dangerous equation.

By contrast, clergy loyal to the Crown, such as Maryland's Jonathan Boucher, urged their parishioners to support the king as head of the Church of England. During the months preceding independence, as the local Committee of Safety interrupted worship to harass him, Boucher carried a loaded pistol into the pulpit while he preached submission to royal authority.

Belief in the momentous importance of what they were doing increased the intensity of revolutionary politics. As independence was declared, people throughout the land raised toasts to the great event: "Liberty to those who have the spirit to preserve it," and "May Liberty expand sacred wings, and, in glorious effort, diffuse her influence o'er and o'er the globe." Inspired by the searing experience of rebellion, war, and nation-building, Americans believed they held the future of human liberty in their hands. Small wonder they took their politics so seriously.

The expanding array of crowds and committees of safety and correspondence that formed during the 1770s and 1780s provided the most dramatic evidence of the people's political commitment. Prior to independence, crowds had taken to the streets to protest measures such as the Stamp Act. After 1776, direct political action increased as people gathered to administer rough-hewn justice to Loyalists, and, as one individual protested, even to direct "what we shall eat, drink, wear, speak, and think."

Patriots of more radical temperament defended these activities as legitimate expressions of the popular will. More cautious souls, however, worried that such behavior threatened political stability. Direct action by the people had been necessary in the struggle against Britain, but why such restlessness now, after the yoke of tyranny had been thrown off? Even Thomas Paine expressed concern. "It is time to have done with tarring and feathering," he wrote in 1777. "I never did and never would encourage what may properly be called a mob, when any legal mode of redress can be had."

A Republican Ideology

In addition to the rejection of monarchy that Paine had so eloquently expressed in *Common Sense*, the American people also rejected the system of hierarchical authority on which monarchy was based. Under a republican system, by contrast, the people, contracting together, created public authority for their mutual good. The ideology of **revolutionary republicanism**, pieced together from British political ideas, Enlightenment theories, and religious beliefs, constituted a revolution in thought.

Basic to republican belief was the notion that governmental power, when removed from the people's close oversight, threatened to expand at the expense of liberty. Recent experience with Britain had made that lesson unmistakably clear. Although excessive liberty could degenerate into political chaos, history seemed to demonstrate that trouble most often arose from too much, not too little government.

Given the need to limit governmental power, how could political order be maintained? The revolutionary generation offered an extraordinary answer to that question. Order was not to be imposed from above through traditional agencies of control such as monarchies and state churches. In a republic, explained one pamphleteer, "each individual gives up all private interest that is not consistent with the general good." This radical principle of "**public virtue**" was an essential ingredient of republican belief.

By contrast, political "**faction**," or organized self-interest, constituted the "mortal disease" to which popular governments throughout history had succumbed. Given the absence in republics of a strong central authority capable of imposing political order, factional conflict could easily spin out of control. This fear added to the intensity of political conflict in revolutionary America, for it encouraged people to attribute the worst motives to their political opponents.

The idea of placing responsibility for political order with the people and counting on them to act selflessly for the good of the whole alarmed countless Americans. What if the people proved unworthy? If the attempt was made, warned one individual darkly, "the bands of society would be dissolved, the harmony of the world confused, and the order of nature subverted." A strong incentive toward Loyalism lurked in such concerns.

Few Patriots were so naive as to believe that the American people were altogether virtuous. During the first years of independence, when revolutionary enthusiasm ran high, however, many believed that public virtue was sufficiently widespread to support republican government. Others argued that the American people would learn public virtue by its practice. The revolutionary struggle would serve as a "furnace of affliction," refining the American character as it strengthened people's capacity for virtuous behavior. It was an extraordinarily hopeful but risk-filled undertaking.

The principle of political equality was another controversial touchstone of republicanism. It was broadly assumed that republican governments must be grounded in popular consent, that elections must be frequent, and that citizens must be vigilant in defense of their liberties. But there agreement often ended.

Some Americans took the principle of political equality literally, arguing that every citizen should have an equal voice and that public office should be open to all. This position was most forcefully articulated by tenants and small farmers in the interior, as well as workers and artisans in the coastal cities who had long struggled to claim a political voice. More cautious citizens emphasized that individual liberty must be balanced by political order, arguing that stable republics required leadership by men of ability and experience, an "aristocracy of talent" that could give the people direction. Merchants, planters, and large commercial farmers who were used to providing such leadership saw no need for radical changes in the existing distribution of political power.

Forming New Governments

Differences of ideology and self-interest burst through the surface of American politics during debates over new state constitutions. Fashioning new governments would not be easy, for the American people had no experience with government-making on such a scale and had to undertake it in the midst of a disruptive war. In addition, there were sharp divisions over the kinds of governments they wanted to create. One person thought it the "most difficult and dangerous business."

Rather than create new written constitutions, Connecticut and Rhode Island continued under their colonial charters, simply deleting all reference to the British Crown. The other 11 states, however, set their charters aside and started anew. By 1778, all but Massachusetts had completed the task. Two years later, it had done so as well.

Constitution makers began with two overriding concerns: to limit the powers of government and to make public officials closely accountable. The only certain way of accomplishing these goals was by establishing a fundamental law, in the form of a written constitution that could serve as a standard for controlling governmental behavior.

In most states, the provincial congresses, extralegal successors to the defunct colonial assemblies, wrote the first constitutions. But this made people uneasy. If governmental bodies wrote the documents, they could change them as well, and what would then protect liberty against the abuse of governmental power? Some way had to be found of grounding the fundamental law not in the actions of government, but directly in the people's sovereign will. Massachusetts first perfected the new procedures. In 1779, its citizens elected a special convention for the sole purpose of preparing a new constitution, which was then returned to the people for ratification.

Through trial and argumentation, the revolutionary generation gradually worked out a clear understanding of what a constitution was and how it should be created. In the process it established some of the most basic doctrines of American constitutionalism: that sovereignty resides in the people rather than government; that written constitutions embody the people's sovereign will; and that governments must function within clear constitutional limits. No principles have been more important to the preservation of American liberty.

Different Paths to the Republican Goal

Constitution-making generated heated controversy, especially over how democratic the new governments should be. In Pennsylvania, a coalition of western farmers, Philadelphia artisans, and radical leaders pushed through the most democratic state constitution of all. Drafted less than three months after independence, during the most intense period of political reform, it rejected the familiar English model of two legislative houses and an independent executive. Republican governments, the radicals insisted, should be simple and easily understood. The constitution thus provided for a single, all-powerful legislative house, its members annually elected, its debates open to the public. A truly radical assumption underlay this unitary design: that "only the interest of society" and not "separate and jarring private interests" should be represented in public affairs.

There was to be no governor—legislative committees would handle executive duties. Property-holding requirements for public office were abolished, and the franchise was opened to every white, taxpaying male over 21. A bill of rights guaranteed every citizen religious freedom, trial by jury, and freedom of speech. The most radical proposal of all called for the partial redistribution of property. Alarmed conservatives just managed to fend off that dangerous proposal.

Debate over the proposed constitution polarized the state. Men of wealth condemned the document's supporters as "coffee-house demagogues" seeking to introduce a "tyranny of the people." The constitution's proponents—tradesmen, farmers, and other small producers—shot back that their critics were "the rich and great men" who had "no common interest with the body of the people."

In 1776, the radicals had their way, and the document was approved. For the moment, the lines of political power had been decisively redrawn. The Pennsylvania constitution, together with its counterparts in Vermont and Georgia, represented the most radical thrust of revolutionary republicanism.

In Massachusetts, constitution-making followed a more cautious course. There the disruptions of war were less severe and the continuity of political leadership was greater. The constitution's main architect, John Adams, readily admitted that the new government must be firmly grounded in the people, yet he warned against "reckless experimentation" and regarded the Pennsylvania constitution as far too democratic. Believing that society was inescapably divided between "democratic" and "aristocratic" forces, Adams sought to isolate each in separate legislative houses where they could guard against each other. The constitution also provided for a governor empowered to veto legislation, make appointments, command the militia, and oversee state expenditures.

When the convention sent the document to the town meetings for approval on March 2, 1780, farmers and Boston artisans attacked it as "aristocratic." But when the convention reconvened in June, it declared the constitution approved, and the document went into effect four months later.

Women and the Limits of Republican Citizenship

While men of the revolutionary generation battled over sharing political power, they were virtually unanimous in the belief that women should be excluded from public politics. Though women participated in revolutionary crowds and other political activities, they continued to be denied the

Mercy Otis Warren
Though women were discouraged from public writing, Mercy Otis Warren published pamphlets and plays dealing with revolutionary politics. Do you think her relationship by birth and marriage to leading Massachusetts Patriots affected her ability to publish despite the strictures against women doing so? *(John Singleton Copley (American, 1738–1815), "Mrs. James Warren (Mercy Otis)," ca.1763. Oil on canvas. 49 5/8 × 39 1/2 in. (126 × 100.3 cm). Bequest of Winslow Warren. Courtesy Museum of Fine Arts, Boston (31.212). Reproduced with permission. © 1999 The Museum of Fine Arts, Boston. All Rights Reserved.)*

franchise. Except on scattered occasions, colonial women had neither voted nor held public office. Nor, with rare exceptions, did they do so in revolutionary America. In New Jersey, the constitution of 1776 opened the franchise to "all free inhabitants" meeting property and residence requirements, and in the 1780s numerous women took advantage of that opening to vote, leading one disgruntled man to protest that "women, generally, are neither by nature, nor habit, nor education . . . fitted to perform this duty with credit to themselves, or advantage to the public." Reflecting that widely held belief, the New Jersey assembly in 1807 again disfranchised women. Not until the twentieth century would women secure the vote, the most fundamental attribute of citizenship.

Prior to independence, most women had accepted the principle that political involvement fell outside the female sphere. Women, however, felt the urgency of the revolutionary crisis as intensely as men, writing and speaking to each other about public events, especially as their own lives were affected. As the war progressed, growing numbers of women spoke out publicly. A few, such as Mercy Otis Warren and Esther DeBerdt Reed, published essays explaining women's urgent desire to contribute to the Patriot cause. In her 1780 broadside, "The Sentiments of an American Woman," Reed declared that women wanted to serve like "those heroins of antiquity, who have rendered their sex illustrious," and called on women to renounce "vain ornament" as they had earlier renounced imported tea. The money not spent on clothing and hairstyles would be the "offering of the Ladies" to Washington's army. In Philadelphia, women responded by collecting $300,000 in continental currency from more than 1,600 individuals. Refusing Washington's proposal that the money be mixed with general funds in the national treasury, they insisted on using it to purchase materials for shirts so that each soldier might know he had received a contribution directly from the women.

Even women's traditional roles took on new political meaning. With British imports cut off and the army badly in need of clothing, spinning and weaving assumed patriotic significance. Coming together as Daughters of Liberty, women made shirts and other items. Charity Clarke, a New York teenager, acknowledged that she "felt Nationaly" as she knitted "stockens" for the soldiers.

Most women did not press for full political equality, since the idea flew in the face of long-standing social convention and its advocacy exposed a person to public ridicule. Women did, however, speak out in defense of their rights. Choosing words that had resonated so powerfully during the protests against Britain, Abigail Adams urged her husband John not to put "unlimited power" in the hands of husbands. Remember, she warned, that "all men would be tyrants if they could." John consulted Abigail on many things but ignored this admonition.

In the years ahead, new challenges to male political hegemony would emerge. When they did rebel, women would find guidance in the universal principles enshrined in the Declaration of Independence that the women of the Revolution had helped to defend.

Conclusion

Coming of Revolution

The colonial Americans who lived in the third quarter of the eighteenth century participated in an era of political tension and conflict that changed the lives of nearly everyone. The Seven Years' War removed French and Spanish challengers and nurtured the colonists' sense of separate identity. Yet it left them with difficult economic adjustments, heavy debts, and growing social divisions. The colonists heralded the Treaty of Paris in 1763 as the dawning of a new era, but it led to a reorganization of Great Britain's triumphant yet debt-torn empire that had profound repercussions in America.

In the prerevolutionary decades, as England and the colonies moved from crisis to crisis, a dual disillusionment penetrated ever deeper into the colonial consciousness. Pervasive doubt arose concerning both the colonies' role in the economic life of the empire and the sensitivity of the government in Westminster to the colonists' needs. Meanwhile, the colonists began to perceive British policies—instituted by

Watch the **Video**

The American Revolution as Different Americans Saw It
at **www.myhistorylab.com**

Parliament, the king, and his advisors—as a systematic attack on the fundamental liberties of British subjects in North America. In the course of resisting British policy, many previously inactive colonists, such as the humble shoemaker Ebenezer MacIntosh, entered public life to challenge elite control of political affairs. Ahead lay not only war but protracted arguments about how the American people, if they prevailed in their war for independence, should refashion their society.

The break with Britain came as something of a surprise, as defiance of imperial policy led to bloodshed and then, finally, to a declaration of independence. With that declaration and the first halting steps to form a political alternative to the colonial past, American citizens would struggle over the meaning of their revolution and the future shape of their newly formed nation. In the meantime, however, they would fight a long and grueling war against the most powerful nation in Europe. The challenges they faced were immense.

TIME*line*

1696	Parliament establishes Board of Trade
1701	Iroquois set policy of neutrality
1702–1713	Queen Anne's War
1713	Peace of Utrecht
1733	Molasses Act
1739–1742	War of Jenkins's Ear
1744–1748	King George's War
1754	Albany Conference
1755	Braddock defeated by French and Indian allies
	Acadians expelled from Nova Scotia
1756–1763	Seven Years' War
1759	Wolfe defeats the French at Québec
1759–1761	Cherokee War against the English
1760s	Economic slump
1763	Treaty of Paris ends Seven Years' War
	Proclamation Line limits westward expansion
1764	Sugar and Currency acts
	Pontiac's Rebellion in Ohio valley
1765	Colonists resist Stamp Act
	Virginia House of Burgesses issues Stamp Act resolutions
1766	Declaratory Act
	Tenant rent war in New York
	Slave insurrections in South Carolina

1767	Townshend duties imposed
1768	British troops occupy Boston
1770	"Boston Massacre"
	Townshend duties repealed (except on tea)
1771	North Carolina Regulators defeated
1772	*Gaspee* incident in Rhode Island
1773	Tea Act provokes Boston Tea Party
1774	"Intolerable Acts"
	First Continental Congress meets in Philadelphia
1776	Publication of *Common Sense*
	Declaration of Independence
1780	Massachusetts constitution ratified
1781	Articles of Confederation ratified by states

✓•⌐Study and **Review** at **www.myhistorylab.com**

Questions for Review and Reflection

1. What roles did Native Americans play in the imperial conflicts of the eighteenth century?

2. How did the Seven Years' War help pave the way for the colonies' break with Britain?

3. The British government pursued policies toward its colonies that it thought reasonable and just in the aftermath of the Treaty of Paris. Why did many colonists see these policies in an entirely different light?

4. What events caused the final break with Britain?

5. What actions did the newly independent states immediately take, and what challenges did they face?

Key Terms

Board of Trade 134

Committees of Correspondence 149

First Continental Congress 166

Faction 160

Public virtue 160

Regulators 148

Revolutionary republicanism 159

Seven Years' War 133

Sons of Liberty 142

Stamp Act Congress 142

6

A People in Revolution

American Stories

Safeguarding the Revolution

Timothy Bloodworth of New Hanover County, North Carolina, experienced the American Revolution first-hand. A man of humble origins, Bloodworth had known poverty as a child. Lacking formal education, he worked as an innkeeper and ferry pilot, self-styled preacher and physician, blacksmith and farmer. Through hard work, he came to own nine slaves and 4,200 acres of land, considerably more than most of his neighbors.

His unpretentious manner and commitment to political equality earned Bloodworth the confidence of his community. In 1758, at the age of 22, he was elected to the North Carolina assembly. From that time forward, he remained deeply involved in politics. When the colonies' troubles with England drew toward a crisis, Bloodworth spoke ardently of American rights and mobilized support for independence. In 1775, he helped form the Wilmington Committee of Safety. Filled with revolutionary fervor, he endorsed republican political reform and, as commissioner of confiscated property for the district of Wilmington, harassed local Loyalists.

Shortly after the war ended, the North Carolina assembly named Bloodworth one of the state's delegates to the Confederation Congress. There he learned about the problems of governing a new nation. As Congress struggled through the middle years of the 1780s with foreign trade, war debt, and control of the trans-Appalachian interior, Bloodworth shared the growing conviction that the Articles of Confederation were too weak. He supported Congress's call for a special convention to meet in Philadelphia in May 1787 for the purpose of taking action necessary "to render the constitution of the federal government adequate to the exigencies of the Union."

Chapter Outline

The War for American Independence

The Experience of War

Peacetime Opportunities and Challenges

Toward a New National Government

Conclusion: Completing the Revolution

Like thousands of Americans, Bloodworth eagerly awaited the convention's work. He was stunned by the result, for the proposed constitution described a government that seemed designed not to preserve republican liberty but to threaten it.

Once again sniffing political tyranny in the wind, Bloodworth resigned his congressional seat and in August 1787 hurried back to North Carolina to help organize opposition to the proposed constitution. For several years, he worked tirelessly for its defeat, protesting that "we cannot consent to the adoption of a Constitution whose revenues lead to aristocratic tyranny, or monarchical despotism, and open a door wide as fancy can point, for the introduction of dissipation, bribery and corruption to the exclusion of public virtue." Had Americans so quickly forgotten the dangers of consolidated power? Were they already prepared to turn aside their brief experiment in republicanism?

At the very least, Bloodworth demanded the addition of a federal bill of rights to protect individual liberties. Echoing the language of revolutionary republicanism, he warned the North Carolina ratifying convention that "without the most express restrictions, Congress may trample on your rights. Every possible precaution should be taken when we grant powers," he continued, for "Rulers are always disposed to abuse them."

Bloodworth feared the sweeping authority granted to Congress, the power to make "all laws which shall be necessary and proper" for carrying into execution "all other powers vested . . . in the government of the United States." That language, he insisted, "would result in the abolition of the state governments." In North Carolina, the arguments of Bloodworth and his Anti-Federalist colleagues carried the day. By a vote of 184 to 84, the ratifying convention declared that a bill of rights "asserting and securing from encroachment the great Principles of civil and religious Liberty, and the unalienable rights of the People" must be approved before North Carolina would concur. The convention was true to its word. Not until November 1789, well after the new federal government had gotten under way and Congress had forwarded a national bill of rights to the states for approval, did North Carolina, with Timothy Bloodworth's cautious endorsement, finally enter the new union.

The Revolutionary War was only the first step toward the creation of a new nation. Beyond finally severing the bond with Britain, how did war itself shape the new United States? The war lasted longer than any other of America's wars until Vietnam nearly two centuries later. And unlike the nation's twentieth-century conflicts, it was fought on American soil. It called men by the thousands from shops and fields, disrupted families, destroyed communities, spread disease, and made a shambles of the economy. Soldiers lost their lives or suffered crippling injuries; slaves used the war as an opportunity to gain their freedom; and those who remained loyal to Britain clung to the colonial world they had known even as war tore that world asunder. Exploring the different consequences of the war for various groups reveals a great variety of experiences.

Against huge odds, the Americans finally succeeded in defeating the British rulers. They did so with the help of their allies the French, who were driven by their own imperial ambitions and the realities of European power politics to join in the conflict. The Treaty of Paris (1783) that ended the war not only secured American independence, but also redrew the contours of empire in North America and recast relations between Britain and the nations of western Europe.

Victory in war ensured independence, while at the same time it presented opportunities and posed challenges. Timothy Bloodworth and many other politically active Americans addressed these issues over the decade that followed the war. Americans could now flood the western lands that Britain had tried to keep free of settlers. Once again, expansion brought conflicts with Native Americans. It also forced the new nation to confront its need for a foreign policy. The citizens of the newly United States struggled to define a revolutionary people's relationship to slavery and to the older institution of a state church, and some embraced innovative solutions to those thorny issues. This euphoric sense of possibility was counterbalanced by the many struggles of veterans and other ordinary citizens who faced economic stagnation and the potential loss of their lands.

By 1786, countless Americans were caught up in an escalating debate between **Federalists**, who believed that the Articles of Confederation were failing and must be replaced by a stronger national government, and **Anti-Federalists**, who were alarmed by what they perceived to be the dangers to individual liberty posed by governmental power. An uprising of western Massachusetts farmers, many of them veterans, revealed the hardships faced by many at the same time that it proved to some that a stronger government was desperately needed. That debate over the future of America's republican experiment came to a head in the momentous Philadelphia convention of 1787, with its proposal for dramatic changes in the national government. With ratification of the new Constitution, the American people opened a portentous new era in their history and launched a dialogue over the very nature of American politics and government that continues to our own time.

The War for American Independence

•**•**•―[Read the **Document**

Joseph Warren, Account of the
Battle of Lexington *(1775)*
at **www.myhistorylab.com**

The war, although it had begun in Massachusetts in 1775, shifted south to the middle states within a year. After 1779, the South became the primary theater. Why did this geographic pattern develop, what was its significance, and why did the United States ultimately win?

The War in the North

For a brief time following Lexington and Concord, British officials thought of launching forays out from Boston into the surrounding countryside. They soon reconsidered, however, for the growing size of the continental army and the absence of significant Loyalist strength in the New England region urged caution. More important, Boston became untenable after the Americans placed artillery on the strategic Dorchester Heights.

On March 7, 1776, the British commander, General William Howe, decided to evacuate the city. Fearing retaliation against Loyalists and wishing not to destroy lingering hopes of reconciliation, Howe spared the city from the torch, but the departing British left it in shambles. "Almost everything here, appears gloomy and melancholy," lamented one returning resident. For half a dozen years after Boston's evacuation, British ships prowled the New England coast, confiscating supplies and attacking coastal towns. Yet away from the coast, there was little fighting. Most New Englanders had reason to be thankful.

The British established their new military headquarters in New York City, which offered important strategic advantages: a fine harbor, control of the Hudson River route to the interior, and access to the abundant grain and livestock of the mid-Atlantic states. Loyalist sentiment ran deep there, too. When, in the summer of 1776, Washington challenged the British for control of New York City, he was badly defeated. By late October, the city was firmly in British hands. It would remain so until the war's end.

In the fall of 1776, King George III instructed his two chief commanders in North America, the brothers General William Howe and Admiral Richard Howe, to make a final effort at reconciliation. In early September, the Howes met with three delegates from Congress on Staten Island in New York Harbor. The Howes demanded revocation of the Declaration of Independence before negotiations could begin, and all hope of reconciliation vanished.

For the next two years, the war swept back and forth across New Jersey and Pennsylvania. Reinforced by German mercenaries hired in Europe, the British moved virtually at will. Neither the state militias nor the continental army—weakened by losses, low morale, and inadequate supplies—offered serious opposition. At Trenton, New Jersey, in December 1776 and at Princeton the following month, Washington surprised the British and scored victories

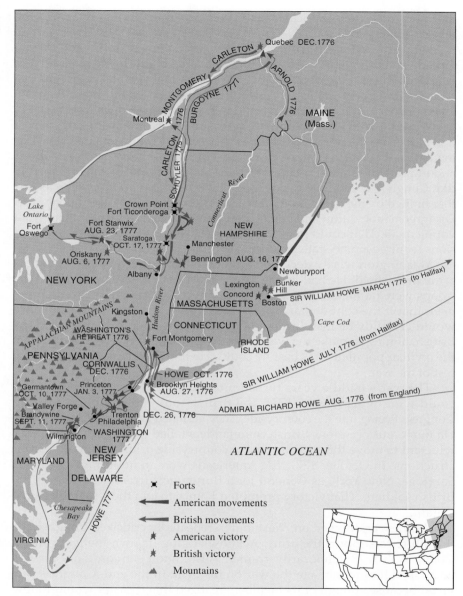

Military Operations in the North, 1776–1780 During the early years of the war, fighting was most intense in upper New York and the mid-Atlantic states. There, as in the South, the British and their Native American allies opened a second front far to the interior. Why did they do so, and how did this complicate American strategy?

that prevented the American cause's collapse. But survival remained the rebels' primary goal.

American efforts during the first year of the war to invade British Canada and bring it into the rebellion also fared badly. In November 1775, American forces took Montreal. But the subsequent assault against Québec ended with almost 100 Americans killed or wounded and more than 300 taken prisoner. American forces could not survive many such losses.

Working with Washington, Congress managed the war effort as best it could, using the unratified Articles as a guide. Events quickly proved its inadequacy, because Congress could do little more than pass resolutions and implore the states for support. If the states refused, as they frequently did, Congress could only urge cooperation. Its ability to function was further limited by the stipulation that each state's delegation cast but one vote. Disagreements within state delegations sometimes prevented them from voting at all. That could paralyze Congress, because most important decisions required a nine-state majority.

Washington wisely decided to avoid major battles while keeping his army in the field. He had learned the painful lesson at New York that his troops were no match for the British in direct combat. He realized, moreover, that if the continental army was defeated, American independence would certainly be lost. Instead of direct engagements, he harassed the British, aiming to make the war as costly for them as possible and protect the civilian population as best he could. He followed that strategy for the rest of the war.

The war's middle years turned into a deadly chase that neither side could win. In September 1777, the British took Philadelphia, sending Congress fleeing into the countryside. They hesitated to press their advantage. On numerous occasions British commanders failed to act decisively, either reluctant to move through the hostile countryside or uncertain of their instructions. In October 1777, the Americans won an important victory at Saratoga, New York, as General John Burgoyne surrendered with 5,700 British soldiers. That victory prompted France to join the struggle against Britain.

As the war dragged on, Washington repeatedly criticized Congress for its failure to support the army. Acknowledging its own ineffectiveness, Congress in 1778 temporarily granted Washington extraordinary powers and asked him to manage the war on his own. In the end, Congress survived because enough of its members realized that disaster would follow its collapse.

The War Moves South

Once the war in the North bogged down in a costly stalemate, Britain adopted an alternative strategy: invasion and pacification of the southern states. Royal officials in the South encouraged the move with predictions that thousands of Loyalists would rally to the British standard. Moreover, if the slaves could be lured to the British side, the balance might tip in Britain's favor. Even the threat of slave rebellion would weaken white southerners' will to resist. Persuaded by these arguments, the British shifted the war's focus southward for its last three years.

Georgia—small, isolated, and largely defenseless—was the initial target. In December 1778, Savannah, the state's major port, fell to a seaborne attack. For nearly two years, the Revolution in the state virtually ceased. Encouraged, the British turned to the Carolinas, with equally impressive results. On May 12, 1780, Charleston surrendered after a month's siege. At a cost of only 225 casualties, the British captured the entire 5,400-man American garrison. It was the costliest American defeat of the war.

After securing Charleston, the British quickly extended their control north and south along the coast. At Camden, South Carolina, the British killed nearly 1,000 Americans and captured 1,000 more, temporarily crippling the American forces in the South. Scarcely pausing, the British pushed on into North Carolina. There, however, British officers quickly learned the difficulty of extending their lines into the interior: distances were too great, problems of supply too challenging, the reliability of Loyalist troops too uncertain, and popular support for the Revolutionary cause too strong.

In October 1780, Washington sent Nathanael Greene south to lead the continental forces. It was a fortunate choice, for Greene knew the region and the kind of war that had to be fought. Determined, like Washington, to avoid large-scale encounters, Greene divided his army into small, mobile bands. Employing what today would be called guerrilla tactics, he harassed the British and their Loyalist allies at every opportunity, striking by surprise and then disappearing into the interior. Nowhere was the war more fiercely contested than in Georgia and Carolina. Neither British nor American authorities could restrain the violence. Bands of private marauders, roving the land and seizing advantage from the war's confusion, compounded the chaos.

In time, the tide began to turn. At Cowpens, South Carolina, in January 1781, American troops under General Daniel Morgan won a decisive victory, suffering fewer than 75 casualties to 329 British deaths, and taking 600 prisoners. In March, at Guilford Court House in North Carolina, the British commander Cornwallis won, but at a cost that forced him to retreat to Wilmington, near the sea.

In April 1781, convinced that British authority could not be restored in the Carolinas while the rebels used Virginia as a supply and staging area, Cornwallis moved north. With a force of 7,500, he raided deep into Virginia, chasing Governor Jefferson and the state legislature from Charlottesville. But again Cornwallis found the costs of victory high, and turned back toward the coast for protection. On August 1, he reached Yorktown.

Cornwallis's position was secure as long as the British fleet controlled Chesapeake Bay, but that advantage did not last long. In 1778, the French government, still smarting from its defeat in the Seven Years' War

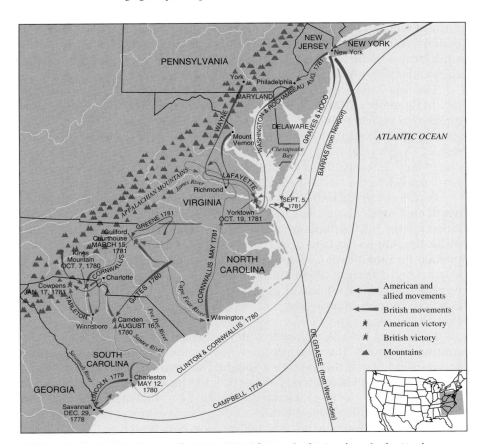

Military Operations in the South, 1778–1781 The war in the South, as in the North, was fought along the coast and in the interior while British and French forces battled as well in the West Indies. Important water routes shaped the course of the war from beginning to end. Why was this so?

and buoyed by the American victory at Saratoga, had signed an alliance with Congress, promising to send its naval forces into the war. Initially, the French concentrated their fleet in the West Indies, hoping to seize some of the British sugar islands. But on August 30, 1781, after repeated American urging, the French admiral Comte de Grasse arrived in the Chesapeake Bay and established naval supremacy. At the same time, Washington's continentals, supplemented by a French army, marched south from Pennsylvania.

As Washington had foreseen, French entry turned the tide of war. Cut off from the sea and pinned down on a peninsula between the York

●〔View the Image

Surrender at Yorktown

at **www.myhistorylab.com**

and James rivers by 17,000 French and American troops, Cornwallis's fate was sealed. On October 19, 1781, near the hamlet of Yorktown, he surrendered.

Learning the news in London a month later, Lord North, the king's chief minister, exclaimed: "Oh, God! It is all over." On February 27, 1782, the House of Commons cut off further support for the war. North resigned the following month. In Philadelphia, citizens poured into the streets to celebrate while Congress held a solemn ceremony of thanksgiving. Though the preliminary articles of peace were not signed until November 1782, everyone knew after Yorktown that the Americans had won independence.

Native Americans in the Revolution

The Revolutionary War drew in countless Native Americans as well as colonists and British troops. By 1776, the major coastal tribes had been decimated by warfare and disease, their villages displaced by white settlement. Powerful tribes, however, still dominated the interior. The Iroquois Six Nations, a confederation numbering 15,000 people, controlled the area from the Hudson River to the Ohio valley. Five tribes—the Choctaw, Chickasaw, Seminole, Creek, and Cherokee, 60,000 people in all—dominated the southern interior. As the imperial crisis between Britain and the colonies deepened, Native and European Americans eyed each other warily.

When the Revolutionary War began, British and American officials urged neutrality on the Indians. The Native Americans, however, were too important militarily for either side to ignore. By the spring of 1776, both were seeking Indian alliances. Recognizing their stake in the conflict, Native Americans up and down the interior debated their options.

Alarmed by encroaching settlements, Cherokee bands led by the warrior Dragging Canoe launched a series of raids in 1776 in what is now eastern Tennessee. In retaliation, Virginia and Carolina militias laid waste a group of Cherokee towns, effectively ending Cherokee opposition. "I hope that the Cherokees will now be driven beyond the Mississippi," declared Jefferson. "Our contest with Britain is too . . . great to permit any possibility of [threat] . . . from the Indians." Seeing what had befallen their neighbors, the Creek stayed aloof. Their time for resistance awaited the early nineteenth century, when settlers pushed onto their land.

In the Ohio country, the struggle lasted longer. For several decades before the Revolution, colonists—including Daniel Boone—had contested the Shawnee and others for control of the region bordering the Ohio River. The Revolutionary War intensified these conflicts. In February 1778, George Rogers Clark led a ragtag band of Kentuckians across 180 miles of forbidding terrain to attack a British outpost at Vincennes, in present-day Indiana. Clark fooled the British troops and their Indian allies into believing that his force was much larger than it was, and the British surrendered without a shot. Clark's victory tipped the balance in the war's western theater.

To the northeast, an even more deadly scenario unfolded. The initial Iroquois decision at a meeting of tribal leaders in Albany, New York, to ignore the Revolution as a "family affair" between Britain and its colonies did not last long. In 1776, after American troops raided deep into Mohawk territory west of Albany, the British urged the Iroquois to join them against the rebels. Most did so in the summer of 1777 at the urging of Joseph Brant, a Mohawk warrior who had visited England several years earlier and proclaimed Britain's value as an ally against American expansion.

It was a fateful decision for Indians and whites alike. Over the next several years, the Iroquois and their British allies devastated large areas in central New York and Pennsylvania. Revenge came in the summer of 1779, when American troops launched a series of punishing raids into the Iroquois country, burning villages, killing men, women, and children, and destroying fields of corn. By war's end, the Iroquois had lost as many as one-third of their people as well as countless towns. Their domination of the northeastern interior was permanently shattered.

Not all the Eastern Woodland tribes sided with Britain in the Revolutionary War. The Oneida and Tuscarora, once members of the Iroquois confederation, fought with the revolutionaries, their decision driven by intertribal politics and effective diplomacy by emissaries of the Continental Congress. Indians who fought for American independence, however, reaped little reward. Though the Americans spared the Oneida and Tuscarora villages, the British and their Iroquois allies destroyed them in turn. Tribes allied with the victors, moreover, gained no protection from the accelerating spread of Euro-American settlement.

Joseph Brant Mohawk chief Joseph Brant (Thayendanegea) played a major role in the Iroquois' decision to enter the war on the side of Britain. Can you identify the symbols of authority in his dress?

Most Indians had sound reason for opposing the independence movement. Britain provided them with trade goods, arms, and markets for their furs. The royal government, moreover, had promised protection against colonial expansion, as the Proclamation Line of 1763 had demonstrated. Yet at the peace talks that ended the Revolutionary War, the British ignored their Indian allies. They received neither compensation for their losses nor guarantees of their land. The boundary of the United States was set far to the west, at the Mississippi River.

Though the Indians' struggle against white expansion would continue, their war of liberation had failed. The American Revolution, declared a gathering of Indian chiefs to the Spanish governor at St. Louis in 1784, had been "the greatest blow that could have been dealt us."

Negotiating Peace

In September 1781, formal peace negotiations began in Paris between the British commissioner and the American emissaries, Benjamin Franklin, John Adams, and John Jay. Negotiations were complicated by involvement in the war of several European countries, seeking to weaken Great Britain. The Americans' main ally, France, had entered the war in February 1778. Eight months later, Spain joined the war against Britain, though it declined to recognize American independence. Between 1780 and 1782, Russia, the Netherlands, and six other European countries formed a League of Armed Neutrality aimed at protecting their maritime trade against British depredations. America's Revolutionary War had become internationalized. It could hardly have been otherwise, given Britain's role in the European balance of power and the long-standing competition among Europeans for dominance in North America.

Dependent on French support, Congress instructed the American commissioners to follow the advice of French foreign minister Vergennes. But as the American commissioners soon learned, he was prepared to let the exhausting war continue in order to weaken Britain further and tighten America's dependence on France. Even more alarming, Vergennes suggested that the new nation's boundary should be set no farther west than the crest of the Appalachian Mountains and hinted that the British might retain any areas they controlled at the war's end. That would have left New York City and other coastal enclaves in British hands.

In the end, the American commissioners ignored their instructions and, without a word to Vergennes, arranged a provisional peace agreement with the British emissaries. The British were prepared to be generous. In the Treaty of Paris, signed in September 1783, they recognized American independence and agreed to set the western boundary of the United States at the Mississippi River. Britain also promised U.S. fishermen the right to fish the waters off Newfoundland; and they committed to evacuate their forces from American territory "with all convenient speed." In return, Congress would recommend that the states restore the rights and property of the Loyalists. Both sides agreed that prewar debts owed the residents of one country by those of the other would remain valid. Each of these issues would trouble Anglo-American relations in the years ahead, but for the moment it seemed a splendid outcome to a long and difficult war.

The Ingredients of Victory

In spite of British fears and congressional hopes, only half of Britain's New World colonies (13 out of 26) joined the rebellion. Congressional efforts to enlist Canadian support foundered because Canada's location at the western end of the North Atlantic sea routes made it a center of British military force. The colony's French Catholic majority, moreover, harbored bitter memories of conflicts during the Seven Years' War with the Protestant colonists to the south.

Congress made overtures as well to planters on Jamaica and other British sugar islands in the Caribbean. But the islands' sugar economies were heavily dependent on British markets. Planters relied as well on British military force for protection against Spanish and Dutch raiders, to say nothing of the slave majorities in their midst. Also, reports that slavery was being questioned in some of the rebellious colonies struck fear into planters' hearts.

Even without the support of Canada and the Caribbean islands, the 13 weak and disunited North American states were able to defeat Great Britain, the most powerful nation in the Atlantic world. How was that so? Certainly Dutch loans and French military resources were crucially important. At the height of the war, France fielded a force of more than 10,000 men in North America.

More decisive, though, was the American people's determination not to submit. Often the Americans were disorganized and uncooperative. Repeatedly, the war effort seemed about to collapse as continental troops drifted away, state militias refused to march, and supplies failed to materialize. Yet as the war progressed, the people's estrangement from Britain deepened and their commitment to independence grew stronger. To subdue the colonies, Britain would have had to occupy the entire eastern third of the continent, and that it could not do.

The American victory owed much to Washington's organizational talents. Against massive odds, often by the sheer force of his will, he held the continental army together. It endured as a military force capable of winning selected encounters and surviving over time. Had he failed, the Americans could not possibly have won. Though state militias engaged in relatively few battles after the first months of the war, they provided a reservoir of manpower capable of intimidating Loyalists, gathering intelligence, and harassing British forces. Washington frequently disparaged the militias' fighting qualities, but he gradually learned to utilize them in the war effort.

In the end, however, it is as accurate to say that Britain lost the war as that the United States won it. With vast economic and military resources, Britain enjoyed clear military superiority. Its troops were more numerous, better armed and supplied, and more professionally trained. Until the closing months of the contest, Britain enjoyed naval superiority as well, enabling its forces to move up and down the coast virtually at will.

Britain, however, could not capitalize on its advantages. It had difficulty extending its command structures and supply routes across several thousand miles of ocean. As a result, decisions were often based on outdated intelligence. Given the difficulties of supply, British troops frequently lived off the land, thus reducing their mobility and increasing the resentment of Americans whose crops and animals were commandeered.

Faced with these circumstances, British leaders were often overly cautious. Burgoyne's attempt in 1777 to isolate New England by invading from Canada failed because Sir William Howe decided to attack Philadelphia rather than move northward up the Hudson River to join him. Similarly, neither Howe nor Cornwallis pressed his advantage in the central states during the middle years of the war, when more aggressive action might have crushed the continentals.

Just as important, British commanders generally failed to adapt European battlefield tactics to the realities of the American war. They were willing to fight only during specified times of the year and used formal battlefield maneuvers, even though the wooded American terrain was better suited to the use of smaller units and irregular tactics. Washington and Greene were more flexible, often employing a patient strategy of raids, harassment, and strategic retreat. They knew that popular support for the revolutionary cause would grow and that the costs of subduing the rebellion would become greater than the British government could bear. As a later war in Vietnam would also reveal, a guerrilla force can win if it does not lose, while a regular army loses if it does not consistently win.

The American strategy proved sound. As the war dragged on and its costs escalated, Britain wavered. After France and Spain entered the conflict, Britain had to worry about the European, Caribbean, and Mediterranean theatres, as well as North America. Unrest in Ireland and food riots in London tied down additional troops. As the cost in money and lives increased and the prospects of victory dimmed, political support for the war eroded. With the defeat at Yorktown, it finally collapsed.

The Experience of War

In terms of the loss of life and destruction of property, the Revolutionary War pales by comparison with America's more recent wars. Yet modern comparisons are misleading, for the War of American Independence proved terrifying and disruptive to the people caught up in it.

Recruiting an Army

Estimates vary, but on the American side as many as 250,000 men may at one time or another have borne arms. That amounted to one out of every two or three adult, white males. Though a majority of recruits were native born, many who fought for American freedom came from the thousands of British and European immigrants who streamed into North America during the middle decades of the eighteenth century. Of the 27 men enrolled in Captain John Wendell's New York company, for example, more than half had been born abroad, the majority in Ireland but others in Germany and the Netherlands. While the motives of these men varied, many had come seeking to better their lives and eagerly embraced the Revolution's democratic promise.

As the war began, most state militias were not effective fighting forces. This was especially noted in the South, where Nathanael Greene complained that the men came "from home with all the tender feelings of domestic life" and were not "sufficiently fortified . . . to stand the shocking scenes of war, to march over dead men, [or] to hear without concern the groans of the wounded." The militia served, however, as an efficient recruiting system, for men were already enrolled and could be called into the field on short notice. It held special importance early in the war, before the continental army took shape. Given its grounding in local community life, the militia also legitimated the war among the people and secured their commitment to the revolutionary cause. What better way to separate Patriots from Loyalists, moreover, than by mustering the local company and seeing who turned out?

During the early years of the war, when enthusiasm ran high, men of all ranks—from the rich and middling ranks as well as the poor—volunteered to fight. As the war went on, however, casualties increased, enlistment terms grew longer, military discipline became more harsh, and the army filled with conscripts. Eventually, the war was transformed, as wars so often are, into a poor man's fight as wealthier men hired substitutes and communities filled their quotas with strangers lured by enlistment bonuses. Convicts, out-of-work laborers, free and unfree blacks, even occasional British deserters filled the continental army with an array of "Tag, Rag, and Bobtail" soldiers.

●◦●⌐Read the Document

Letter from a Revolutionary
War Soldier (1776)
at **www.myhistorylab.com**

For the poor and the jobless, whose ranks the war rapidly swelled, military bonuses and the promise of board and keep proved attractive. But often the bonuses failed to materialize, pay was long overdue, and soldiers frequently learned of their families' distress. As the war dragged on and desertion rose as high as 25 percent, Washington imposed harsher discipline in an effort to hold his troops in line.

The Hardships of War

Throughout the war, soldiers suffered from shortages of supplies. At Valley Forge during the terrible winter of 1777–1778, men went without shoes or coats. Declared one despairing soul in the midst of that winter's gloom,

RECOVERING *the* PAST

Military Muster Rolls

In all of America's wars, patriotism and impassioned rhetoric have inspired citizens to arms. The American Revolutionary War was no exception, but people often fought for more than patriotic reasons. It is always difficult to assess human motivations in something as complex as war. If we knew which Americans bore arms, however, it would help us understand why people fought and what the war meant to them.

As we see in this chapter, the social composition of the revolutionary army changed as the war went along. At the beginning, men from all walks of life and every class fought in defense of American liberty. As the war lengthened and its costs increased, however, men who could afford to hired substitutes or arranged to go home, while men of less wealth and influence increasingly carried the burden of fighting. Many of them did so out of choice, for the army promised adventure, an escape from the tedium of daily life, and even, occasionally, a chance to rise in the world. Such a decision was attractive to them because other opportunities were limited.

Enlistment lists of the continental army and state militias offer an important source for studying the social history of the Revolutionary War. Although eighteenth-century records are imperfect by modern standards, recruiting officers did keep track of the men they signed on so that bounties and wages could be paid accurately. These lists usually give the recruit's name, age, occupation, place of birth, residence, and length of service.

Such lists exist for some of America's earlier wars. The muster rolls for New York City and Philadelphia during the Seven Years' War, for example, show that most of the enlistees from these two cities in that conflict were immigrants—about 90 percent of New York's recruits and about 75 percent of Philadelphia's. Their occupations—mariner, laborer, shoemaker, weaver, tailor—indicate that they came primarily from the lowest ranks of society. Many were former indentured servants, while others were servants who ran away from their masters to answer the recruiting sergeant's drum. In these mid-Atlantic port towns, successful, American-born artisans left the bloody work of bearing arms against the French to those beneath them on the social ladder. Enlistment lists for Boston, however, reveal that soldiers from that city were drawn from higher social classes.

A comparison of Revolutionary War muster rolls from different towns and regions provides a view of the social composition of the revolutionary army and how it changed over time. It also offers clues to how social conditions in different regions might have affected military recruitment.

The muster rolls shown here of Captain Wendell's and Captain White's companies from New York and Virginia give "social facts" on several dozen men. (Because of space limitations, only portions of each roster are included here.) What kind of group portrait can you draw from the data? Some occupations, such as tanner, cordwainer, and chandler, may be unfamiliar to modern readers, but they are defined in standard dictionaries. How many of the recruits came from middling occupations (bookkeeper, tobacconist, shopkeeper, and the like)? How many were skilled artisans? How many were unskilled laborers? What proportions were foreign and native born? Analyze the ages of the recruits. What does that tell you about the kind of fighting force that was assembled? How did the New York and Virginia companies differ in terms of these social categories and occupations? Can you explain these differences?

To extract the full meaning of the soldiers' profile, you would have to learn more about the economic and social conditions prevailing in the communities from which these men were drawn. But already you have glimpsed how social historians go beyond the history of military strategy, tactics, and battles to understand the "internal" social history of the Revolutionary War.

REFLECTING ON THE PAST **How would social historians describe and analyze more recent American wars? What would a social profile of soldiers who fought in Vietnam or Iraq—including their age, region, race, class, and extent of education—suggest to a social historian of these wars?**

New York Line—1st Regiment
Captain John H. Wendell's Company, 1776–1777

Men's Names	Age	Occupation	Place of Birth	Place of Abode
Abraham Defreest	22	Yeoman	N. York	Claverack
Benjamin Goodales	20	do [ditto]	Nobletown	do
Hendrick Carman	24	do	Rynbeck	East Camp
Nathaniel Reed	32	Carpenter	Norwalk	Westchester
Jacob Crolrin	29	do	Germany	Beaver Dam
James White	25	Weaver	Ireland	Rynbeck
Joseph Battina	39	Coppersmith	Ireland	Florida
John Wyatt	38	Carpenter	Maryland	
Jacob Reyning	25	Yeoman	Amsterdam	Albany
Patrick Kannely	36	Barber	Ireland	N. York
John Russell	29	Penman	Ireland	N. York
Patrick McCue	19	Tanner	Ireland	Scholary
James J. Atkson	21	Weaver	do	Stillwater
William Burke	23	Chandler	Ireland	N. York
Wm Miller	42	Yeoman	Scotland	Claverack
Ephraim H. Blancherd	18	Yeoman	Ireland	White Creek
Francis Acklin	40	Cordwainer	Ireland	Claverack
William Orr	29	Cordwainer	Ireland	Albany
Thomas Welch	31	Labourer	N. York	Norman's Kill
Peter Gasper	24	Labourer	N. Jersey	Greenbush
Martins Rees	19	Labourer	Fishkill	Flatts
Henck Able	24	do	Albany	Flatts

Virginia Line—6th Regiment

Captain Tarpley White's Company, December 13th, 1780

Name	Age	Trade	Where Born		Place of Residence	
			State or Country	Town or County	State or Country	Town or County
Win Bails, Serjt	25	Baker	England	Burningham	Virg.	Leesburg
Arthur Harrup	24	Carpenter	Virg.	Southampton	Virg.	Brunswick
Charles Caffatey	19	Planter	"	Caroline	"	Caroline
Elisha Osborn	24	Planter	New Jersey	Trenton	"	Loudon
Benj Allday	19	"	Virg.	Henrico	"	Pawhatan
Wm Edwards Senr	25	"	"	Northumberland	"	Northumberland
James Hutcherson	17	Hatter	Jersey	Middlesex	"	P. Williams
Robert Low	31	Planter	"	Powhatan	"	Powhatan
Cannon Row	18	Planter	Virg.	Hanover	Virg.	Louisa
Wardon Pulley	18	"	"	Southampton	"	Hallifax
Richd Bond	29	Stone Mason	England	Cornwell	"	Orange
Tho Homont	17	Planter	Virg.	Loudon	"	Loudon
Tho Pope	19	Planter	"	Southampton	"	Southampton
Tho Morris	22	Planter	"	Orange	"	Orange
Littlebury Overby	24	Hatter	"	Dinwiddie	"	Brunswick
James [Pierce]	27	Planter	"	Nansemond	"	Nansemond
Joel Counsil	19	Planter	"	Southampton	"	Southampton
Elisha Walden	18	Planter	"	P. William	"	P. William
Wm Bush	19	S Carpenter	Virg.	Gloucester	Virg.	Glocester
Daniel Horton	22	Carpenter	"	Nansemond	"	Nansemond
John Soons	25	Weaver	England	Norfolk	"	Loudon
Mara Lumkin	18	Planter	Virg.	Amelia	"	Amelia
Wm Wetherford	27	Planter	"	Goochland	"	Lunenburg
John Bird	16	Planter	"	Southampton	"	Southampton
Tho Parsmore	22	Planter	England	London	"	Fairfax
Josiah Banks	27	Planter	Virg.	Gloucester	"	Gloucester
Richd Roach	28	Planter	England	London	"	Culpeper

"I am sick, discontented, and out of humour. Poor food, hard lodging, cold weather, fatigue, nasty cloathes, nasty cookery, vomit half my time, smoaked out of my senses. The Devil's in't, I can't Endure it. Why are we sent here to starve and freeze?"

Neither state governments nor Congress could effectively administer a war effort of such magnitude. Though many individuals served honorably as supply officers, others exploited the army's distress. Washington commented bitterly on the "speculators, various tribes of money makers, and stock-jobbers" whose "avarice and thirst for gain" threatened the country's ruin.

Legions of camp followers further complicated army life. Wives and prostitutes, personal servants and slaves, con men and provisioners swarmed around the continental army camps. While often providing essential services, they slowed its movement and threatened its discipline.

Medical treatment, whether for wounds or the diseases that raged through military camps, frequently did more harm than good. Casualties poured into hospitals, overcrowding them beyond capacity. Surgeons, operating without anesthetics and with the crudest of instruments, threatened life as often as they preserved it. Few understood the causes or proper treatment of infection. Doctoring consisted mostly of bleeding, blistering, and vomiting. One doctor reported that "we lost no less than from 10 to 20 of camp diseases, for one by weapons of the enemy."

No one kept accurate records of how many soldiers died. But the most conservative estimate runs to 25,000, a higher percentage of the total population than for any other American conflict except the Civil War. For Revolutionary War soldiers, death was an imminent reality.

Civilians and the War

While the experience of war varied from place to place, it touched the lives of virtually every American. Noncombatants felt the burden of war most heavily in densely settled areas along the coast. The British concentrated their military efforts there, taking advantage of their naval power and striking at the political and economic centers of American life. At one time or another, British troops occupied every major port city.

While British men-of-war prowled the coast, American ships rocked idly at empty wharves, New England's once-booming shipyards grew quiet, and communities whose livelihood depended on the sea sank into depression. Virginia tobacco planters, their British markets gone and their plantations open to seaborne attack, struggled to survive. Farmers in the middle and New England states often prospered when hungry armies were nearby, but their profits plummeted when the armies moved on.

But even as some prospered, countless others saw their affairs fall into disarray. Intractable issues such as price and wage inflation, skyrocketing taxation, and mushrooming debt set people sharply against each other. The issue of taxation, seared into Americans' consciousness by their troubles with Britain, generated similarly heated controversy. As the costs of the war mounted, so did taxes. Between 1774 and 1778, Massachusetts levied more than £400,000 in taxes, a stunning increase over colonial days. As taxes skyrocketed, farmers, artisans, and others of modest means argued that the taxes should be payable in depreciated paper money or government securities. Lacking the hard money that states required in payment, they faced foreclosure of their property. Officials responded that allowing payment in depreciated paper would deprive governments of critically needed revenue.

Controversy swirled as well around efforts to control soaring prices. The upward spiral of prices was staggering. In Massachusetts, a bushel of corn that sold for less than $1 in 1777 went for nearly $80 two years later, and in Maryland the price of wheat increased several thousandfold. Every state experimented with price controls at one time or another. Seldom were such efforts effective; always they generated controversy. In Boston, a crowd of women angered by the escalating cost of food tossed a merchant suspected of monopolizing commodities into a cart and dragged him through the city's streets while "a large concourse of men stood amazed." Individuals not yet integrated into the market economy supported price controls. They believed that goods should carry a "just price" that was fair to buyer and seller alike.

Disputes over paper money also divided the American people. Faced with the uncontrollable escalation of wartime expenses, Congress and the states did what colonial governments had done before and American governments have done ever since: they printed money. In the first year of the war alone, they issued more than $400 million in various kinds of paper money, and that was just the beginning. Citizens' willingness to accept such money at face value disappeared as the flood of paper increased. Congressional bills of credit that in 1776 were pegged against gold at the ratio of 1.5 to 1 had slipped five years later to 147 to 1. State currencies depreciated just as drastically.

The social consequences of such depreciation were at times alarming. James Lovell reported nervously that "sailors with clubs" were parading the streets of Boston "instead of working for paper." With property values in disarray, it seemed at times as if the very foundations of society were coming unhinged. The poor suffered most severely, for they were most vulnerable to losses in the purchasing power of wages and military pay. But they were not alone. Farmers, merchants, planters, and artisans also faced growing debt and uncertainty.

Urban dwellers suffered profound dislocations. About half of New York City's inhabitants fled when the British occupation began. An American officer somberly reported the scene as his troops entered the city at the war's end: "Close on the eve of an approaching winter, with an heterogeneous set of inhabitants, composed of almost ruined exiles, disbanded soldiery, mixed foreigners, disaffected Tories, and the refuse of the British army, we took possession of a ruined city."

New York City Burning In 1776, as the British took control of New York, nearly a quarter of the city was destroyed by a fire apparently set by a defiant Patriot woman. Among the gutted buildings was the elegant Trinity Church, the tallest structure in the city. Not until the British evacuated in 1783 did reconstruction of the city begin. What did the artist intend to convey with the various figures in this scene?

In Philadelphia, the occupation was shorter and disruptions less severe, but the shock of invasion was no less real. Elizabeth Drinker, living alone after local Patriots had exiled her Quaker husband, found herself the unwilling landlady of a British officer and his friends. Though the officer's presence may have protected her from the plundering that went on all around, she was constantly anxious, confiding to her journal that "I often feel afraid to go to Bed." British soldiers frequently tore down fences for their campfires and confiscated food. Even Loyalists complained about the "dreadful consequences" of British occupation.

Along the coastal plain, British landing parties descended without warning, seizing supplies and terrorizing inhabitants. In 1780 and 1781, the British mounted punishing attacks in Connecticut. The southern coast, with its broad, navigable rivers, was even more vulnerable. In December 1780, Benedict Arnold, the American traitor who by then was fighting for the British, ravaged Virginia's James River valley, uprooting tobacco, confiscating slaves, and creating panic among whites. Such onslaughts sent civilians fleeing into the interior.

Not all the refugee traffic, however, was away from the coast. In western New York, Pennsylvania, Virginia, and the Carolinas, frontier settlements collapsed under British and Indian assaults, sending their residents fleeing to the east. Wherever the armies went, they generated a swirl of refugees who spread vivid tales of the war's devastation. Displaced populations, together with the constant movement of soldiers between army and civilian life, brought the war home to countless people who did not experience it firsthand.

Disease, spread by the movement of people, ravaged populations as well. During the 1770s and 1780s, a smallpox epidemic surged across North America, wreaking its devastating effects from the Atlantic coast to the Pacific, and from the Southwest to Hudson's Bay in Canada. The human toll cannot be measured exactly, but the virus may have killed more than 130,000 people. Because a crash program of inoculation launched by Washington in 1777 (the first large-scale immunization program in American history) protected much of the continental army and because many British troops carried immunity from earlier exposure to the disease, the plague did not significantly affect the war's outcome. Still, it took a terrible toll. In New England and the mid-Atlantic states, it was spread by returning soldiers and Britain's disease-infested prison ships. In the Chesapeake region, thousands of black Loyalists succumbed, while in the backcountry the virus raced through Native populations, reducing the ability to resist. Beyond the Mississippi, agricultural tribes such as the Mandan, Hidatsa, and Arikara were virtually wiped out. The pox, declared one observer gloomily, "spread its destructive and desolating power, as the fire consumes the dry grass of the field."

The Loyalists

Among the Americans suffering the most grievous losses were those who remained loyal to the Crown. Some 50,000 colonists fought against the rebels. Though many Loyalist émigrés established successful lives in England, the Maritime Provinces of Canada, and the British West Indies, others found the uprooting an ordeal from which they never recovered. Several thousand Loyalists, appearing after the war before a royal commission in London appointed to hear their claims, gained partial reimbursement for their losses. But it proved meager compensation for the confiscation of house and property, expulsion from a familiar community, and relocation to a distant land. The vast majority of Loyalists never appeared before the commission and thus secured nothing.

Although we do not know how many colonists remained loyal, tens of thousands evacuated with British troops at the end of the war. At least as many slipped away while fighting was still going on. Additional thousands who wished the Revolution had never occurred stayed on in the new nation, struggling to rebuild their lives. The incidence of Loyalism differed from region to region. Loyalists were fewest in New England and most numerous around New York City, where British authority was most stable.

In each state, revolutionary assemblies exacted revenge against those who had rejected the revolutionary cause by depriving Loyalists of the vote, confiscating their property, and banishing them from their homes. In 1778, the Georgia assembly expelled 117 persons on pain of death. Probably not more than a few dozen Loyalists died at the hands of the revolutionary regimes, but thousands found their livelihoods destroyed, their families ostracized, and themselves subject to physical attack.

Punishing Loyalists—or people accused of being loyal, a distinction that was often unclear in the confusion of the times—was politically popular. Most Patriots argued that such "traitors" had put themselves outside the protection of American law. No other wartime issue raised so starkly the nettlesome question of balancing individual liberty against the requirements of public security. That issue would return to trouble the nation in the years ahead.

Why did so many Americans remain loyal to the Crown, often at the cost of personal danger and loss? Royal appointees such as customs officers, members of the governors' councils, and Anglican clergy often remained with the king. Loyalism was common, as well, among groups dependent on the British presence—for example, settlers on the Carolina frontier holding long-standing grievances against the planter elite along the coast and ethnic minorities, such as Germans, who feared persecution by the Anglo-American majority. Others were Loyalist because they feared British military power, or doubted that independence could be won.

Still others based their Loyalism on principle. "Every person owes obedience to the laws of the government," insisted Samuel Seabury, "and is obliged in honour and duty to support them. Because if one has a right to disregard the laws of the society to which he belongs, all have the same right; and then government is at an end." Another Loyalist worried about the kind of society independence would bring when revolutionary crowds showed no respect for the rights of dissenters such as he. "If I differ in opinion from the multitude," he asked, "must I therefore be deprived of my character, and the confidence of my fellow-citizens; when in every station of life I discharge my duty with fidelity and honour?" Such individuals claimed to be upholding reason and the rule of law against disorder. Their defeat weakened conservatism in American society and promoted revolutionary change.

African Americans and the War

The Revolution caught up thousands of American blacks. In the northern states, free and enslaved blacks were enlisted in support of the revolutionary cause. The South's nearly 400,000 slaves were viewed by the British as a resource to be exploited and by southern whites as a source of vulnerability and danger. Sizing up the opportunities provided by the war's confusion, slaves struck out for their own freedom by seeking liberty behind British lines, journeying to the north, or fleeing to mixed-race settlements in the interior. Before the war was over, the conflict generated the largest slave rebellion in American history prior to the Civil War.

Hearing their masters' talk about liberty, growing numbers of black Americans questioned their own oppression. In the North, slaves petitioned state legislatures for their freedom, while in the South pockets of insurrection appeared. In 1765, more than 100 South

●●●─[Read the Document

Slave Petition to the Massachusetts House of Reps (1774)

at **www.myhistorylab.com**

Carolina slaves, most of them young men in their twenties and thirties, fled their plantations. The next year, slaves paraded through the streets of Charleston chanting, "Liberty, liberty!"

In November 1775, Lord Dunmore, Virginia's royal governor, issued a proclamation offering freedom to all slaves and servants "able and willing to bear arms," who would leave their masters and join the British at Norfolk. Within weeks, 500 to 600 slaves responded. Among them was Thomas Peters, an African who had been brought to Spanish Louisiana about 1760. He resisted enslavement so fiercely that his master sold him into the English colonies. By the 1770s, he was toiling on William Campbell's plantation on the Cape Fear River, near Wilmington, North Carolina.

Peters's plans for his own declaration of independence may have ripened as a result of the rhetoric of liberty he heard around his master's house, for William Campbell was a leading member of Wilmington's Sons of Liberty and talked enthusiastically about inalienable rights. By mid-1775, the Cape Fear region, like many areas of the coastal South, buzzed with rumors of slave uprisings. In July, the state's revolutionary government imposed martial law when the British commander of Fort Johnston, near Wilmington, encouraged blacks to "elope from their masters." When 20 British ships entered the Cape Fear River in March 1776 and disembarked royal troops, Peters seized the moment to redefine himself as a man, instead of William Campbell's property, and escaped. Before long, he was fighting with the British-officered Black Pioneers.

As many as 20 percent of African Americans may have sought liberty behind British lines. Unlike their masters, blacks saw in Britain the promise of freedom, not tyranny. As the war dragged on, British commanders pressed blacks into service. A regiment of black soldiers formed from Virginia slaves who responded to Dunmore's proclamation and marched into battle, their chests covered by sashes emblazoned "Liberty to Slaves."

Some of the blacks who joined the British achieved their freedom. At the war's end, several thousand were evacuated to Nova Scotia. But their reception by the inhabitants was generally hostile. By 1800, most had left Canada to help establish the free black colony of Sierra Leone in West Africa. Thomas Peters was a leader among them.

Many of the slaves who fled behind British lines never won their freedom. Under the terms of the peace treaty, hundreds were returned to their American owners. Several thousand others, their value as field hands too great to be ignored, were transported to work on harsh West Indian sugar plantations.

Other blacks took advantage of the war's confusion to flee. Some went north, following rumors that slavery had been abolished there. Others sought refuge among Indians in the southern interior. The Seminoles of Georgia and Florida generally welcomed black runaways and through intermarriage absorbed them into tribal society. Blacks met a more uncertain reception from the Cherokee and Creek. While some were taken in, others were returned to their owners for bounties, and still others were held in slave-like conditions by new Indian masters.

Fewer blacks fought on the American side than on Britain's, in part because neither Congress nor the states were eager to see them armed. Faced with the increasing need for troops, however, Congress and all the states except Georgia and South Carolina eventually relented, pressing blacks into service. Of those who served the Patriot cause, many received the freedom they were promised. The patriotism of others, however, went unrewarded.

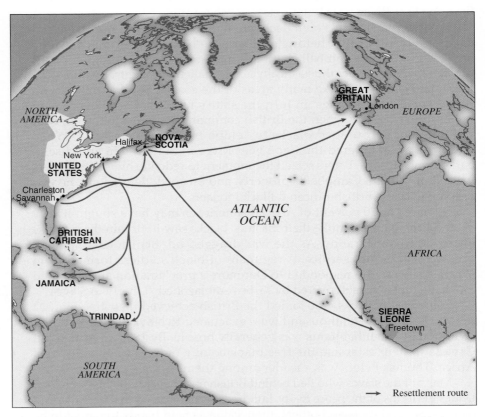

Resettlement of Black Loyalists After the Revolution Thousands of American blacks departed the new nation with British troops at the end of the Revolutionary War. As the map indicates, their destinations differed. How did resettlement outside the United States reshape the lives of black Loyalists?

The Challenge of Demobilizing the Army

The final challenge of the war involved bringing it to a close. When the fighting stopped, many of the troops refused to go home until Congress redressed their grievances. Trouble first arose in early 1783 when officers at the continental army camp in Newburgh, New York, sent a delegation to complain about arrears in pay and other benefits that Congress had promised them during the dark days of the war. When Congress called on the army to disband, an anonymous address circulated among the officers, attacking the "coldness and severity" of the Congress and hinting darkly at more direct action if grievances were not addressed.

Washington moved quickly to calm the situation. Promising that Congress would treat the officers justly, he counseled patience and urged his comrades not to tarnish the victory they had so recently won. His efforts succeeded, for the officers reaffirmed their confidence in Congress and agreed to disband.

Officers were not the only ones to take action. In June, several hundred disgruntled continental soldiers and Pennsylvania militiamen gathered in front of Philadelphia's Independence Hall, where Congress and Pennsylvania's Executive Council were meeting. When state authorities would not guarantee Congress's safety, it fled to Princeton, New Jersey. Once there, tension eased when it issued the soldiers three months' pay and furloughed them until they could be formally discharged. By early November, the crisis was over.

Peacetime Opportunities and Challenges

War's end meant that independence was won, a reality that brought with it both opportunities and challenges. Long-standing goals, like freedom to take up western lands, could be achieved, although expansion engendered further conflicts with Native Americans. Some of the inhabitants of the new United States worked to expand the realm of liberty, arguing for the elimination of slavery and for religious freedom. Creating a new nation, especially in a time of economic malaise and international conflict, proved difficult. These obstacles challenged the people of the new United States to look for solutions, and they often bitterly debated the best way to move forward.

Separating Church and State

The revolutionary settlement ultimately promoted the radical idea that the church and state ought to be separated. Prior to 1776, Rhode Island, New Jersey, Pennsylvania, and Delaware had allowed full religious liberty. They had done so because local diversity made any other policy impossible or because of an ideological commitment to religious freedom. Other colonies followed the more common practice in Europe, with established churches endorsed by the government and supported by public taxes. Although civil authorities grudgingly tolerated "dissenters" such as Methodists and Baptists in these colonies, their numbers were growing rapidly. On the eve of the Revolution, they noisily pressed their case for full religious liberty.

With independence, pressure built for severing all ties between church and state. Isaac Backus, the most outspoken of New England's Baptists, protested that "many, who are filling the nation with the cry of *liberty* and against *oppressors* are at the same time themselves violating that dearest of all rights, *liberty of conscience*." Such arguments were strengthened by the belief that throughout history, alliances between government and church authorities had brought religious oppression, and that voluntary choice was the only safe basis for religious association.

In New England, Congregationalists fought to preserve their long-established privileges. To separate church and state, they argued, was to risk infidelity and disorder. Massachusetts's 1780 constitution guaranteed everyone the right to worship God "in the manner and season most agreeable to the dictates of his own conscience." But it also empowered the legislature to require towns to tax their residents to support local ministers. Backus argued that official support should be ended completely; "religious toleration," he insisted, fell far short of true religious freedom. Not until 1833 were laws linking church and state finally repealed in Massachusetts.

In Virginia, Baptists pressed their cause against the Protestant Episcopal Church, successor to the Church of England. The adoption in 1786 of Thomas Jefferson's Bill for Establishing Religious Freedom, rejecting all connections between church and state and removing all religious tests for public office, decisively settled the issue. Three years later, that statute served as a model for the First Amendment to the new federal Constitution.

But even the most ardent supporters of religious freedom were not prepared to extend it universally. The wartime alliance with Catholic France together with Congressional efforts to entice Catholic settlers in Québec to join the resistance against Britain had weakened long-established prejudices. Still, anti-Catholic biases remained strong, especially in New England. The people of Northbridge, Massachusetts, wanted to exclude "Roman Catholics, pagons, or Mahomitents" from public office. The legal separation of church and state did not end religious discrimination, but it implanted the principle of religious freedom firmly in American law.

Slavery Under Attack

The place of slavery in a republican society also vexed the revolutionary generation. How, wondered many, could slavery be reconciled with the inalienable right to life, liberty, and the pursuit of happiness?

During the several decades preceding 1776, the trade in human chattels had flourished. The 1760s witnessed the largest importation of slaves in colonial history. The Revolutionary War, however, halted the slave trade almost completely. Though southern planters talked of replacing their lost chattels once the war ended, a combination of revolutionary principles, a reduced need for field hands in the depressed Chesapeake tobacco economy, natural increase among the slave population, and anxiety over black rebelliousness argued for the slave trade's permanent extinction. By 1790, every state except South Carolina and Georgia had outlawed slave importations.

Ending the trade had powerful implications, for it reduced the infusion of new Africans into the black population. As a result, an ever higher proportion of blacks was American born, thus speeding the cultural transformation by which Africans became African Americans.

Slavery itself came under attack during the Revolutionary era, with immense consequences for blacks and the nation's future. As the crisis with Britain heated up, catchwords such as *liberty* and *tyranny*, mobilized against imperial policies, reminded citizens that one-fifth of the colonial population was in chains. Samuel Hopkins, a New England clergyman, accosted his compatriots for "making a vain parade of being advocates for the liberties of mankind, while . . . continuing this lawless, cruel, inhuman, and abominable practice of enslaving your fellow creatures." Following independence, antislavery attacks intensified.

In Georgia and South Carolina, where blacks outnumbered whites more than two to one and where slave labor remained essential to the production of rice, slavery went largely unchallenged. Instead, planters tightened local slave codes, shuddering at the prospect of black freedom.

In Virginia and Maryland, by contrast, whites openly argued whether slavery was compatible with republicanism, and in these states significant change did occur. The weakened demand for slave labor in the depressed tobacco economy facilitated the debate. Though neither state abolished slavery, both passed laws making it easier for owners to free their slaves without continuing responsibility for them. Moreover, increasing numbers of blacks purchased their own or their families' freedom, or simply ran away. By 1800, more than one of every ten blacks in the Chesapeake region was free, a dramatic increase from 30 years before. Opportunities for free blacks were limited, however.

The majority of free blacks lived and worked in towns such as Richmond and Baltimore, where they formed communities that served as centers of African American society, as well as havens for slaves escaping from the countryside. In the Chesapeake region, the conditions of life for black Americans slowly changed for the better.

The most dramatic breakthrough occurred in northern states, where slavery was either abolished or put on the road to gradual extinction. Such actions were possible because blacks were a numerical minority—in most areas, they constituted less than 4 percent of the population—and slavery had neither the economic nor social importance that it did in the South. In 1780, the Pennsylvania assembly passed a law stipulating that all newborn slaves were to be free when they reached age 21. It was a cautious but decisive step. Other northern states adopted similar policies of gradual emancipation.

In scattered instances, free blacks participated actively in revolutionary politics. In a debate over the Massachusetts constitution's provisions for voting, William Gordon, a white minister, demanded: "Would it not be ridiculous . . . and unjust to exclude freemen from voting . . . though otherwise qualified, because their skins are black? . . . Why not . . . for being long-nosed, short-faced, or . . . lower than five feet nine?" In the end, the new state constitution made no mention of race, and black men occasionally cast their ballots.

If civic participation by blacks was scattered and temporary in the North, it was almost totally absent in the South. With the brief exception of North Carolina, free African Americans could neither vote nor enjoy protection of their persons and property under the law. In the South, blacks remained almost entirely without political voice, other than the petitions against slavery and mistreatment that they pressed on the state governments.

Still, remarkable progress had been made. Prior to the Revolution, slavery had been an accepted fact of life. After the Revolution, it no longer was. That change made a vast difference in the lives of countless black Americans. The abolition of slavery in the North, moreover, widened the sectional divergence between North and South, with enormous consequences for the years ahead. A coherent, publicly proclaimed antislavery argument now existed, and it was closely linked in Americans' minds with the nation's founding. Activists created the first antislavery organizations during this era as well. Although another half century would pass before antislavery became a powerful force in American politics, the groundwork for slavery's final abolition had been laid.

Opening the West

Another major undertaking of the 1780s was the opening of the western lands to settlement. Availability of that land had been one of the points of contention between Britain and the colonists in the years leading up to the Revolution. The Confederation Congress, as the central government of the new United States, passed two great land ordinances in 1785 and 1787. The first provided for the systematic survey and sale of the region west of Pennsylvania and north of the Ohio River. The area was to be laid out in townships six miles square, which were in turn to be subdivided into lots of 640 acres each. Thus began the rectangular grid pattern of land survey and settlement that to this day characterizes the Midwest, and distinguishes it so markedly from the irregular settlement patterns of the eastern sector.

Two years later, Congress passed the **Northwest Ordinance**. It provided for the political organization of the same interior region, first under congressionally appointed officials, then under popularly elected territorial assemblies, and ultimately as new states incorporated into the Union "on an equal footing with the original states in all respects whatsoever."

These laws represented a dramatic change from Britain's colonial administration. Rather than seeking to restrain white settlement as Parliament had attempted to do in the Proclamation Line of 1763, the new central government sought ways to promote settlement's expansion via land laws and Indian policies. Remarkably, settlements in the American West would not remain colonies subordinate to an imperial power, but would be fully incorporated into the expanding American nation.

Both ordinances enjoyed broad political support, for they opened land to settlers and profits to speculators. Income from land sales, moreover, promised to help reduce the national debt. While permitting slave

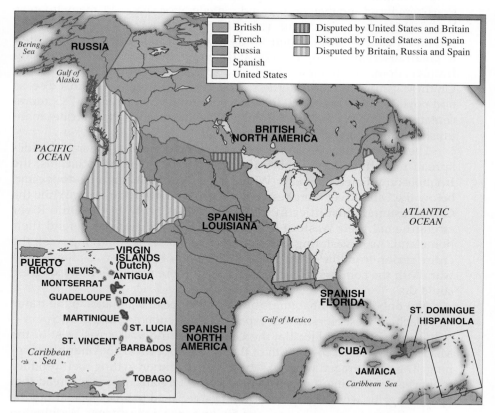

North America After the Treaty of Paris, 1783 Though victorious in its struggle for independence, the United States was surrounded by British and Spanish possessions, while Russia and France continued to harbor imperial ambitions in the Americas as well. What problems and opportunities did European claims on areas of North America pose for the United States?

owners already living north of the Ohio River to retain their chattels, the Ordinance of 1787 prohibited the importation of new slaves into the region. This policy made the area more attractive to white farmers who worried about competing with slave labor and living among blacks. Southern delegates in Congress accepted the restriction because they could look forward to slavery's expansion south of the Ohio River. During the 1780s, the country's interior seemed large enough to accommodate everyone's needs.

Support for expansion naturally put the new government and the migrants to the west on a collision course with the Native inhabitants of the region. During the postwar years, Congress operated as if the Native Americans of the interior were "conquered" peoples—allies of Britain who had lost the war and thus come under U.S. control. Initially, the conquest strategy seemed to work. During the mid-1780s, Congress imposed land treaties on the interior tribes, among them the Iroquois. Their numbers sharply reduced and their once-proud confederation shattered, many Iroquois had fled into Canada. At the Treaty of Fort Stanwix in 1784, those who remained ceded most of their lands to the United States and retreated to small reservations. By the 1790s, little remained of the once-imposing Iroquois domain but a few islands in a spreading sea of white settlement. On these "slums in the wilderness," the Iroquois struggled against disease and poverty, their traditional lifeways undermined. In January 1785, representatives of the Wyandotte, Chippewa, Delaware, and Ottawa tribes relinquished claim to most of present-day Ohio.

The treaties, often exacted under the threat of force, generated widespread resentment. Two years after the Fort Stanwix negotiations, the Iroquois repudiated the treaty. Within a few years, tribal groups above and below the Ohio River were resisting expansion into the interior. While the Creek resumed hostilities in Georgia, Indians north of the Ohio River strengthened their Western Confederacy and prepared to defend their homeland. As devastating Indian raids greeted settlers moving west, the entire region from the Great Lakes to the Gulf of Mexico was aflame with war. With the continental army disbanded, there was little that Congress could do.

Not only Indian inhabitants but also European claimants to the trans-Appalachian west blocked this expansionist agenda. In June 1784, Spain—still in possession of Florida, the Gulf Coast, and vast areas west of the Mississippi—closed the mouth of the Mississippi River to American shipping. The act outraged western settlers dependent on getting their produce to market by floating it downstream to New Orleans. Rumors spread that Spanish agents were urging American frontiersmen to break away from the new nation and seek affiliation with Spain. Sensing the danger, Washington commented uneasily that settlers throughout the West were "on a pivot." "The touch of a feather," he warned, "would turn them away."

Opening the West was essential to the plans of many Americans. Speculators facing the loss of their investment worried that the lands might not be available for sale. Those who hoped to move west were similarly anxious: farmers wanting to leave the crowded lands of the East and revolutionary soldiers eager to start afresh on the rich soil of Kentucky and Ohio that they had been promised as payment for military service. Thomas Jefferson, who believed that America's "empire of liberty" depended on an expanding nation of yeoman farmers, thought that continued expansion was essential to creating the kind of society the American Revolution made possible.

Surviving in a Hostile Atlantic World

Even after the United States had formally won independence, Britain, France, and Spain continued to harbor imperial ambitions in North America. Before the century was over, France would regain vast areas west of the Mississippi. Meanwhile, Great Britain's Union Jack still flew over Canada and British troops continued to occupy military outposts on American soil, while Spain held the southern half of the continent.

The reason for America's diplomatic troubles during the 1780s was clear: The country was new, weak, and republican in an Atlantic world dominated by strong, monarchical governments and divided into exclusive, warring empires. Nothing revealed the difficulties of national survival more starkly than Congress's futile efforts to rebuild America's overseas commerce. When the war ended, familiar British goods once again flooded American markets. Few American goods, however, flowed the other way. John Adams learned why. In 1785, he arrived in London as the first American minister to Britain, carrying instructions to negotiate a commercial treaty. After endless rebuffs, he reported in frustration that the British had no intention of reopening the empire's ports to American shipping. British officials testily reminded him that Americans had desired independence and must now live with its consequences.

While Britain remained intractable, wartime allies such as France and Spain returned to a policy of maritime restrictions against American commerce. Congressional efforts to secure authorization from the states to regulate foreign trade were unavailing, because each state wanted to channel its trade for its own advantage. As a result, overseas trade continued to languish and economic hardship deepened.

By the late 1780s, the per capita value of American exports had fallen a startling 30 percent from the 1760s. No wonder that merchants and artisans, carpenters and shopkeepers, sailors and dockworkers—all dependent on shipbuilding and overseas commerce—suffered. In an Atlantic world divided into exclusive, imperial trading spheres, the United States lacked the political unity and economic muscle to protect its basic interests.

In this context of hardship and division, the nation also faced a major war debt. Estimated at $35 million, much was held by French and Dutch bankers. Unable to make regular payments against the loan's principal, Congress had to borrow additional money just to pay the accumulating interest.

Things were no better at home. In response to the incessant demands of its creditors, the government could only delay and try to borrow more.

In 1781, Congress appointed Robert Morris, a wealthy Philadelphia merchant, as superintendent of finance and gave him broad authority to deal with the nation's troubled affairs. Morris urged the states to stop issuing paper money and persuaded Congress to demand that the states pay their requisitions in specie (gold and silver coin). In addition, he encouraged Congress to charter the Bank of North America and took steps to make federal bonds more attractive to investors.

Though Morris made considerable progress, the government's finances remained shaky. Lacking authority to tax, Congress depended on the states' willingness to meet their financial obligations. This arrangement, however, proved unworkable. In October 1781, a desperate Congress requested $8 million from the states. Two and a half years later, less than $1.5 million had come in. In January 1784, Morris resigned. By 1786, federal revenue totaled $370,000 a year, not enough, one official lamented, to provide "the bare maintenance of the federal government."

Not all Americans were alarmed. Some noted approvingly that several state governments, having brought their own financial affairs under control, were beginning to assume portions of the national debt. Others, however, saw this as additional evidence of Congress's weakening condition and wondered how long a government unable to maintain its credit could endure. Rarely has the American economy been in such disarray. Problems of debt, taxation, price control, and paper money seemed to exceed the capacity of politics for compromise and resolution.

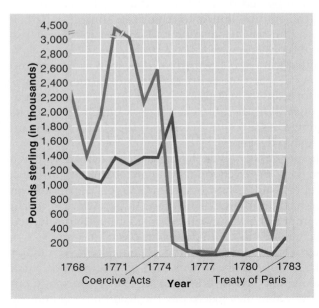

Exports and Imports, 1768–1783
Nonimportation affected colonial commerce during the late 1760s and early 1770s, but both exports and imports plummeted in 1774 and 1775. Why? Can you explain why imports recovered somewhat beginning in 1778, while American exports remained flat?
(Source: U.S. Bureau of the Census)

Conservative Resurgence and Shays's Rebellion

In a pattern that would frequently recur in American history, the postwar era witnessed growing social and political conservatism. Exhausted by the war, many Americans focused their energies on their personal lives. And with the patriotic crusade against Britain successfully concluded, the initial surge of republican reform subsided. As a consequence, political leadership fell increasingly to men convinced that republican experimentation had gone too far, that individual liberty threatened to overbalance political order, and that the "better sort" of men, not democratic newcomers, should occupy public office.

The most dramatic change occurred in Pennsylvania, where the democratic constitution of 1776 was replaced in 1790 by a far more conservative document. The new constitution provided for a strong governor who could veto legislation and control the militia, and a conservative senate designed to balance the more democratic assembly. Gaining control even of the assembly by the mid-1780s, the conservatives proceeded to dismantle much of the radicals' program, stopped issuing paper money, and rechartered the Bank of North America. Pennsylvania's experiment in radical republicanism was over.

The conservative resurgence generated little controversy in Pennsylvania. Elsewhere, however, popular opposition to hard money and high-tax policies spawned vigorous protest. Nowhere was the situation more volatile than in Massachusetts. The controversy that erupted there in 1786 echoed strongly of equal rights and popular consent, staples of the rhetoric of 1776.

By the mid-1780s, increasing numbers of Massachusetts citizens found that they had to borrow money simply to pay their taxes and support their families. Those who were better off borrowed to speculate in western land and government securities. Because there were no commercial banks in the state, people borrowed from each other in a complicated, highly unstable pyramid of credit that reached from wealthy merchants along the coast to shopkeepers and farmers in the interior.

Trouble began when British goods glutted the American market, forcing down prices. In 1785, a number of British banks, heavily overcommitted in the American trade, called in their American loans. When American merchants tried in turn to collect debts due them by local shopkeepers, a credit crisis surged through the state's economy.

Hardest hit were farmers and laboring people in the countryside and small towns. Caught in a tightening financial bind, they turned to the state government for "stay laws" suspending the collection of private debts, thus easing the threat of foreclosure against their farms and shops. They also demanded new issues of paper money with which to pay debts and taxes. The largest creditors, most of whom lived in commercial towns along the coast, fought such relief proposals because they wanted repayment in hard money. They also feared that new paper money would quickly depreciate, further confounding economic affairs.

By 1786, Massachusetts farmers, desperate in the face of mounting debt and a lingering agricultural depression, were petitioning the Massachusetts assembly for relief in words that echoed the colonial protests of the 1760s. Their appeals, however, fell on deaf ears, for commercial and creditor interests now controlled the government. Turning aside appeals for tax relief, the government passed a law calling for full repayment of the state debt and levied a new round of taxes that would make repayment possible. No matter that, as one angry citizen charged, "there was not . . . the money in possession or at command among the people" to pay what was due. Between 1784 and 1786, 29 towns defaulted on their tax obligations.

As frustrated Americans had done before and would do again when the law proved unresponsive to their needs, Massachusetts farmers took matters into their own hands. A Hampshire County convention of delegates from 50 towns condemned the state senate, court fees, and tax system. It advised against violence, but crowds began to form.

The county courts drew much of the farmers' wrath, because they issued the writs of foreclosure that private creditors and state officials demanded. In September 1786, armed men closed the court at Worcester. When farmers threatened similar actions elsewhere, the alarmed governor dispatched 600 militiamen to protect the state Supreme Court, then meeting in Springfield.

About 500 insurgents had gathered nearby under the leadership of Daniel Shays, a popular Revolutionary War captain recently fallen on hard times. A "brave and good soldier," Shays had returned home in 1780, tired and frustrated, to await payment for his military service. Like thousands of others, he had a long wait. Meanwhile, his farming went badly, debts accumulated, and, as he later recalled, "the spector of debtor's jail . . . hovered close by." Most of the men who gathered around Shays were also veterans and debtors.

The insurrection, known as **Shays's Rebellion**, collapsed in eastern Massachusetts in late November, but to the west it was far from over. When several insurgent groups refused Governor James Bowdoin's order to disperse, he called out a force of 4,400 men, financed by worried eastern merchants. On January 26, 1787, Shays led 1,200 men toward the federal arsenal at Springfield. When they arrived, its frightened defenders opened fire, killing four of the attackers and sending the Shaysites into retreat. By the end of February, the rebellion was over. In March, the legislature pardoned all but Shays and three other leaders; in another year, they too were forgiven.

Similar challenges to public authority, fired by personal troubles and frustration over unresponsive governments, erupted in other states. In Charles County, Maryland, a "tumultuary assemblage" rushed into the courthouse and closed it down. The governor condemned the "riotous" proceedings and warned against further "violence and outrages." In South Carolina, an incensed Hezekiah Mayham, being served by the sheriff with a writ of foreclosure, forced him to eat it on the spot.

Across the states, politics was in turmoil. While many felt betrayed by the Revolution's promise of equal rights and were angered by the "arrogant unresponsiveness" of government, others were alarmed by the "democratic excesses" that the Revolution appeared to have unleashed. What the immediate future held in store seemed exceedingly uncertain.

Toward a New National Government

By 1786, belief was spreading among members of Congress that the nation was in crisis and the republican experiment was in danger of foundering. Explanations for the crisis and prescriptions for its resolution varied, but attention focused on the inadequacies of the Articles of Confederation. Within two years, following a deeply divisive political struggle, a new constitution had replaced the Articles, altering forever the course of American history.

The Rise of Federalism

The supporters of a stronger national government called themselves Federalists (leading their opponents to adopt the name Anti-Federalists). Led by men such as Washington, Hamilton, Madison, and Jay, whose experiences in the continental army and Congress had strengthened their national vision, the Federalists believed that the nation's survival was at stake. Such men had never been comfortable with the more democratic impulses of the Revolution. While committed to moderate republicanism, they believed that democratic change had carried too far, property rights needed greater protection, and elite men such as themselves should lead the country.

Federalist leaders feared the loss of their own political power, but they were concerned as well about the collapse of the orderly world they believed essential to the preservation of republican liberty. In 1776, American liberty had required protection against overweening British power. Now, however, danger arose from excessive liberty that threatened to degenerate into license. "We have probably had too good an opinion of human nature," concluded Washington somberly. "Experience has taught us, that men will not adopt and carry into execution measures the best calculated for their own good, without the intervention of a coercive power." What America now needed was a "strong government, ably administered."

The Federalists regarded outbursts like Shays's uprising not as evidence of genuine social distress but as threats to social and political order. Although they were reassured by the speed with which the Shaysites had been dispatched, the episode persuaded them of the need for a stronger national government managed by the "better sort."

Congress's inability to handle the national debt, establish public credit, and restore overseas trade also troubled the Federalists. Sensitive to America's economic and military weakness, smarting from French and British arrogance, and aware of continuing Anglo-European designs on North America, Federalists called for a new national government capable of extending American trade, spurring economic recovery, and protecting the national interest. Beyond that, Federalists shared a vision of an expanding commercial republic, its people spreading across the rich lands of the interior, its merchant ships connecting America with the markets of Europe and beyond. That vision, so rich in promise, seemed clearly at risk.

The Grand Convention

The first step toward governmental reform came in September 1786, when delegates from five states who were gathered in Annapolis, Maryland, to discuss interstate commerce issued a call for a convention to revise the Articles of Confederation. In February, the Confederation Congress cautiously endorsed the idea. Before long, it became clear that far more than a revision of the Articles was afoot.

During May 1787, delegates representing every state except Rhode Island began assembling in Philadelphia. The city bustled with excitement as they gathered, for the roster read like an honor roll of the Revolution. Proponents of the convention had held their breath while Washington considered whether to attend. His presence vastly increased the prospects of success. Fellow Virginian James Madison was equally significant in his own way. No one, with perhaps the single exception of New York delegate Alexander Hamilton, was more committed to nationalist reform. No one had worked harder to prepare for the convention. Poring over treatises on republican government and natural law that his friend Thomas Jefferson sent from France, Madison brought to Philadelphia a clear design for a new national government. That design, presented to the convention as the **Virginia Plan**, would serve as the basis for the new constitution. Nor did anyone rival the diminutive Madison's contributions to the convention's work. He also kept extensive notes of the debates in his personal shorthand. Those notes constitute the essential record of the convention's proceedings. The venerable Benjamin Franklin was also present; too old to contribute significantly to the debates, he remained able to call quarreling members to account and to inspire them in their work.

Meeting in Independence Hall, where the Declaration of Independence had been proclaimed little more than a decade earlier, the convention elected Washington as its presiding officer, adopted rules of procedure, and, after spirited debate, voted to close the doors and conduct its business in secret.

Drafting the Constitution

Delegates presented two plans for a revised government to the convention in its first weeks. The Virginia Plan, introduced on May 29, 1787, by Edmund Randolph, outlined a potentially powerful national government and

James Madison, Father of the Constitution James Madison of Virginia, only 36 years old when the Philadelphia convention met, worked tirelessly between 1786 and 1788 to replace the Articles of Confederation with a new and more effective national constitution. Why was he painted in relatively simple clothing? What information does the viewer gain from the objects in this portrait?

effectively set the convention's agenda. The smaller states quickly objected to the Virginia Plan's call for proportional rather than equal representation of the states. In response, on June 15, William Paterson introduced a counterproposal, the **New Jersey Plan**. It urged retention of the Articles of Confederation as the basic structure of government while conferring on Congress the long-sought powers to tax and to regulate foreign and interstate commerce. After three days of heated debate, by a vote of seven states to three, the delegates adopted the Virginia Plan as the basis for further discussions. It was now clear that the convention would replace the Articles with a much stronger national government. The only question was how powerful the new government would be.

At times over the next four months, it seemed that the Grand Convention would collapse under the weight of its own disagreements and the oppressive summer heat. How were the conflicting interests of large and small states to be reconciled? How should the balance of power between national and state governments be struck? How could an executive be created that was strong enough to govern but not so strong as to endanger republican liberty? And what, if anything, would the convention say about slavery and the slave trade, issues on which northerners and southerners, antislavery and proslavery advocates so passionately disagreed?

The delegates divided over the answers to such questions. Hamilton strongly favored a conservative and powerful government, while at the other extreme stood the ardent Anti-Federalist Luther Martin of Maryland, who opposed anything that threatened state sovereignty or smacked of aristocracy.

By early July, with tempers frayed and frustration growing over an apparent deadlock, the delegates agreed to recess, ostensibly for Independence Day but actually to let Franklin, Roger Sherman of Connecticut, and several others make a final effort at compromise. All agreed that only a bold stroke could prevent a collapse.

That stroke came on July 12, as part of what has become known as the **Great Compromise**. The reassembled delegates settled one major point of controversy by agreeing that representation in the lower house should be based on the total of each state's white population plus three-fifths of its blacks. Though African Americans were not accorded citizenship and could not vote, the southern delegates argued that they should be fully counted for this purpose. Delegates from the northern states, where relatively few blacks lived, did not want them counted at all. Hence a bargain was struck. As part of this compromise, the convention agreed that direct taxes would also be apportioned on the basis of population and that blacks would be counted similarly in that calculation. On July 16, the convention accepted the principle that the states should have equal votes in the Senate. Thus the interests of both large states and small were effectively accommodated.

Watch the Video
Slavery and the Constitution
at **www.myhistorylab.com**

The convention then submitted its work to a committee for drafting in proper constitutional form. That group reported on August 6, and for the next month the delegates hammered out the language of the document's seven articles. Determined to give the new government the stability that state governments lacked, the delegates created an electoral process designed to bring persons of wide experience and solid reputation into national office. An **Electoral College** of wise and experienced leaders, selected at the direction of state legislatures, would meet to choose the president. The process functioned that way during the first several presidential elections. Selection of the Senate would be similarly indirect, for its members were to be named by the state legislatures. (Not until 1913, with ratification of the Seventeenth Amendment, would the American people elect their senators directly.) Only the House of Representatives would be popularly elected.

The delegates' final set of compromises touched the fate of black Americans. At the insistence of southerners, the convention agreed that the federal government would not discuss the slave trade for another 20 years. As drafted, the Constitution did not contain the words *slavery* or *slave trade*, but spoke more vaguely about not prohibiting the "migration or importation of such persons as any of the states now existing shall think proper to admit." The meaning, however, was entirely clear.

Despite Gouverneur Morris's impassioned charge that slavery was a "nefarious institution" that would bring "the curse of Heaven on the states where it prevails," the delegates firmly rejected a proposal to abolish slavery, thereby tacitly acknowledging its legitimacy. More than that, they guaranteed slavery's protection, by writing in Section 2 of Article 4 that

"No person held to service or labour in one state, . . . [and] escaping into another, shall, in consequence of any law . . . therein, be discharged from such service, but shall be delivered up on claim of the party to whom such service or labour may be due." Through such convoluted language, the delegates provided federal sanction for the capture and return of runaway slaves. This **fugitive slave clause** would return to haunt northern consciences in the years ahead. At the time, however, it seemed a small price to pay for sectional harmony and a new government.

Although the Constitution's unique federal system of government called for shared responsibilities between the nation and the states, it decisively strengthened the national government. Congress would now have the authority to levy and collect taxes, regulate commerce with foreign nations and between the states, devise uniform rules for naturalization, administer national patents and copyrights, and control the federal district in which it would eventually be located. Conspicuously missing was any statement reserving to the states all powers not explicitly conferred on the central government. Such language had proved crippling in the Articles of Confederation. On the contrary, the Constitution contained a number of clauses bestowing vaguely defined grants of power on the new government. Section 8 of Article 1, for example, granted Congress the authority to "provide for the . . . general welfare of the United States" as well as to "make all laws . . . necessary and proper for carrying into execution . . . all . . . powers vested by this Constitution in the government of the United States." Later generations would call these phrases "elastic clauses" and would use them to expand the federal government's activities.

In addition, Section 10 of Article 1 contained a litany of powers now denied the states, among them issuing paper money and entering into agreements with foreign powers without the consent of Congress. A final measure of the Federalists' determination to ensure the new government's supremacy over the states was the assertion in Article 6 that the Constitution and all laws and treaties passed under it were to be regarded as the "supreme Law of the Land."

When the convention had finished its business, 3 of the 42 remaining delegates refused to sign the document. The other 39, however, affixed their names and forwarded it to the Confederation Congress along with the request that it be sent on to the states for approval. On September 17, the Grand Convention adjourned.

Federalists Versus Anti-Federalists

Ratification presented the Federalists with an even more difficult problem than they had faced at Philadelphia. The debate now shifted to the states, where sentiment was sharply divided and the political situation was more difficult to control. Recognizing the unlikelihood of gaining quick agreement by all 13 states, the Federalists stipulated that the Constitution should go into effect when any nine agreed to it. Other states could then enter the

Union as they were ready. Ratification was to be decided by specially elected conventions rather than by the state assemblies. Approval by such conventions would give the new Constitution greater legitimacy by grounding it in the consent of the people.

Opposition to the proposed Constitution was widespread and vocal. Some critics warned of the threat to state interests. Others, like Timothy Bloodworth, charged the Federalists with betraying revolutionary republicanism. Like all "energetic" governments, the one being proposed would be corrupted by its own power. Far from the watchful eyes of the citizenry, its officials would behave as power wielders always had, and American liberty, so recently preserved at such high cost, would again come under attack.

Anti-Federalists were aghast at their opponents' vision of an expanding "republican empire." "The idea of . . . [a] republic, on an average of 1,000 miles in length, and 800 in breadth, and containing 6 millions of white inhabitants all reduced to the same standards of morals, . . . habits . . . [and] laws," exclaimed one incredulous critic, "is . . . contrary to the whole experience of mankind." Such an extended republic would quickly fall prey to factional conflict and internal disorder. Anti-Federalists continued to believe that republican liberty could be preserved only in small, homogeneous societies, where the seeds of faction were few and public virtue guided citizens' behavior. They saw the states as a better basis for government.

Nor did Anti-Federalists believe that the proposed separation of executive, legislative, and judicial branches or the intended balance between state and national governments would prevent power's abuse. Government, they insisted, must be kept simple, for complexity only confused the people and cloaked selfish ambition. Many Anti-Federalists believed that if government was to be safe, it must be tied closely to the people.

Federalist spokesmen moved quickly to counter the attacks, for many of the criticisms carried the sanction of the revolutionary past. Their most important effort was a series of essays penned by James Madison, Alexander Hamilton, and John Jay and published in New York under the pseudonym Publius. The **Federalist Papers**, as they came to be called, were written to promote ratification in New York but were quickly reprinted elsewhere.

Madison, Hamilton, and Jay moved systematically through the Constitution, explaining its virtues and responding to the Anti-Federalists' charges. In the process, they described a political vision fundamentally different from that of their Anti-Federalist opponents. No difference was more dramatic than the Federalists' treatment of governmental power. Power, the Federalists now argued, was not the enemy of liberty but its guarantor. Where government was not sufficiently "energetic" and "efficient," demagogues and disorganizers would find opportunity to do their nefarious work. It is far better, Hamilton wrote in *Federalist No. 26*, "to hazard the abuse of . . . confidence than to embarrass the government and endanger the public safety by impolitic restrictions of . . . authority."

The authors of the *Federalist Papers* also countered Anti-Federalists' warning that a single, extended republic would lead inevitably to factional conflict and the end of republican liberty. Turning the Anti-Federalists' republican argument on its head, they explained that political divisions were the inevitable accompaniment of human liberty. Earlier emphasis on public virtue as the guarantor of political order, Federalists affirmed, had been naive, for few people would consistently put the public good ahead of their own interests. Politics had to heed this harsh fact of human nature and provide for peaceful compromise among conflicting groups. That could best be accomplished by expanding the nation so that it included innumerable factions. Out of the clash and accommodation of multiple social and economic interests would emerge compromise and the best possible approximation of the public good.

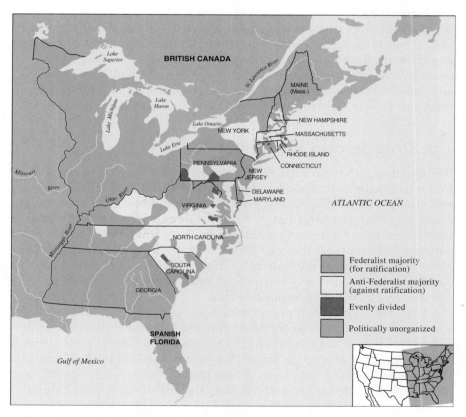

Federalist and Anti-Federalist Areas, 1787–1788 Distinct geographic patterns of Federalist and Anti-Federalist strength appeared during the ratification debate. This map shows areas whose delegates to the state ratifying conventions voted for and against the Constitution. What do the patterns suggest concerning the economic and social bases of Federalist and Anti-Federalist support?

In that argument is to be found the basic rationale for modern democratic politics, but it left Anti-Federalists sputtering in frustration. Where in the Federalists' scheme was there a place for that familiar abstraction, the public good? What would become of public virtue in a system built on the notion of competing, private interests? In such a system, Anti-Federalists warned, the wealthy and powerful would thrive, while ordinary folk would suffer.

As the ratification debate revealed, the two camps held sharply different visions of the new republic. Anti-Federalists remained much closer to the original republicanism of 1776, with its suspicion of power and wealth, its emphasis on the primacy of local government, and its fears of national development. They envisioned a decentralized republic filled with citizens who were self-reliant, guided by public virtue, and whose destiny was determined primarily by the states rather than the nation. Anxious about the future, they longed to preserve the political world of an idealized past.

Federalists, persuaded that America's situation had changed dramatically since 1776, embraced the idea of nationhood and looked forward eagerly to the development of a rising "republican empire," fueled by commercial development and led by men of wealth and talent. Both Federalists and Anti-Federalists claimed to be heirs of the Revolution, yet they differed fundamentally in what they understood that heritage to be.

The Struggle over Ratification

No one knows what most Americans thought of the proposed Constitution, for no national plebiscite on it was ever taken. Probably no more than several hundred thousand people participated in the elections for the state ratifying conventions, and many of the delegates carried no binding instructions from their constituents on how they should vote. It's likely that a majority of the people opposed the document, either out of indifference or alarm. Fortunately for the Federalists, they did not have to persuade most Americans but needed only to secure majorities in nine of the state ratifying conventions, a much less formidable task.

They set about it with determination. As soon as the Philadelphia Convention adjourned, its members hurried home to organize the ratification movement in their states. In Delaware and Georgia, New Jersey and Connecticut, where the Federalists were confident of their strength, they pressed quickly for a vote. Where the outcome was uncertain, as in New York, Massachusetts, and Virginia, they delayed, hoping that word of ratification elsewhere would work to their benefit.

It took less than a year to secure approval by the necessary nine states. Delaware, Pennsylvania, and New Jersey ratified first, in December 1787. Approval came a month later in Georgia and Connecticut. Massachusetts ratified in February 1788, but only after Federalist leaders agreed to forward a set of amendments outlining a federal bill of rights along with notice of ratification. The strategy worked, for it brought Samuel Adams and John Hancock into line, and with them the crucial convention votes that they controlled.

Maryland and South Carolina were the seventh and eighth states to approve. That left New Hampshire and Virginia vying for the honor of being ninth and putting the Constitution over the top. Sensing that they lacked the necessary votes, Federalists adjourned the New Hampshire convention and worked feverishly to build support. When the convention reconvened, it took but three days to secure a Federalist majority.

Two massive gaps in the new Union remained—Virginia and New York. Clearly, the nation could not endure without them. In Virginia, Madison gathered support by promising that the new Congress would immediately consider a bill of rights. Other Federalists spread the rumor that Patrick Henry, among the most influential Anti-Federalist leaders, had changed sides, a charge that Henry angrily denied. His oratory, however, proved no match for the careful politicking of Madison and others. On June 25, the Virginia convention voted to ratify by a mere 10 votes.

The New York convention gathered on June 17 at Poughkeepsie, with the Anti-Federalist followers of Governor Clinton firmly in command. Hamilton worked for delay, hoping that news of the results in New Hampshire and Virginia would turn the tide. For several weeks, approval hung in the balance. On July 27, approval squeaked through, 30 to 27. That left two states still uncommitted: North Carolina finally ratified in November 1789; Rhode Island did not enter the Union until May 1790, more than a year after the new government had gotten under way.

The Social Geography of Ratification

Federalist strength in the ratifying conventions was concentrated in areas along the coast and navigable rivers and was strongest in cities and towns. Merchants and businessmen supported the Constitution most ardently. Enthusiasm also ran high among urban laborers, artisans, and shopkeepers. In the troubled circumstances of the late 1780s, they worried primarily about their livelihoods and believed that a stronger government could better promote overseas trade and protect American artisans from foreign competition.

On July 4, 1788, a grand procession celebrating the Constitution's ratification wound through the streets of Philadelphia. Seventeen thousand strong, it graphically demonstrated the breadth of support for the Constitution. At the head of the line marched lawyers, merchants, and others of the city's elite. Close behind came representatives of virtually every trade in the city, from ship's carpenters to shoemakers. For the moment, declared the democratic-minded physician Benjamin Rush in amazement, "rank . . . forgot all its claims." Within a few years, political disputes would divide merchants and artisans once again. For the moment, however, people of all ranks joined in celebrating the new Constitution.

Outside coastal cities, political alignments were more sharply divided. The Constitution found support among commercial farmers and southern planters eager for profit and anxious about overseas markets. But in the interior, Federalist enthusiasm waned and Anti-Federalist sentiment increased. Among ordinary farmers living outside the market economy, local loyalties and the republicanism of 1776 still held sway. They found Federalist visions alarming.

Why did the Federalists prevail when their opponents had only to tap into people's deep-seated fears of central government and appeal to their local loyalties? The Federalists won, in part, because of the widespread perception that the Articles of Confederation were inadequate and that America's experiment in republican independence was doomed unless decisive action was taken. More than anything, however, the Federalists succeeded because of their determination and political skill. Most of the Revolution's major leaders were Federalists. Time and again they spoke out for the Constitution, and time and again their support proved decisive. Their experience in the continental army and as members of the Continental and Confederation Congresses fired their vision of what the nation might become. They brought that vision to the ratification process and asked others to share it. Their success turned the American Republic in a new and fateful direction.

Conclusion
Completing the Revolution

The period from the Declaration of Independence to the ratification of the Federal Constitution, although it covered only 13 years, encompassed the formative period of American nation building. When Congress launched its struggle for national liberation in July 1776, it steered the American people into uncharted seas. The break with Britain and accompanying war redrew the contours of American life and changed the destinies of countless Americans. Though the war ended in victory, liberty had its costs, as lives were lost, property destroyed, and local economies damaged. The conflict altered relationships between Indians and whites, for it left the Iroquois and Cherokee severely weakened and opened the floodgates of western expansion.

By 1783, a new nation had come into being, one based not on age-encrusted principles of monarchy and aristocratic privilege but on the doctrines of republican liberty. That was the greatest change of all. The political transformations that were set in motion generated angry disputes whose outcome could be only dimly foreseen. How might individual liberty be reconciled with the need for public order? Who should be accorded full republican citizenship, and to whom should it be denied? How should constitutions be written and republican governments be organized? Thomas Paine put the matter succinctly: "The answer to the question, can America be happy under a government of her own, is short and simple— as happy as she pleases; she hath a blank sheet to write upon." The years immediately ahead would determine whether America's republican experiment, launched with such hopefulness in 1776, would succeed.

The challenges and opportunities faced by the new nation were enormous. In keeping with the Revolution's roots in a struggle over liberty, some citizens of the new nation endorsed religious liberty and they questioned the institution of slavery. Given the colonial opposition expressed against the Proclamation Line of 1763, it was unsurprising that a major goal of the new nation was to facilitate settlement to the West. This goal created conflict with Native Americans and with European powers that had a presence in the trans-Appalachian west. The new nation's position in a hostile Atlantic world was insecure. Wartime alliances had revealed that North America remained an object of imperial ambition and European power politics, while the cutoff of Atlantic trade had made clear how dependent the nation still was on overseas commerce. The postwar era saw economic crisis, as the new nation struggled with debt and inflation. Amidst the resulting political turmoil, Americans continued to argue over how democratic their experiment in republicanism could safely be—even whether it could survive.

At the same time, the American people retained an immense reservoir of optimism about the future. Had they not defeated mighty Britain? Was not their Revolution destined to change the course of history and provide a model for all mankind? Did not America's wonderfully rich interior contain the promise of limitless economic and social opportunity? Though many Anti-Federalists continued to worry, other citizens, still filled with the enthusiasm of their new beginning, answered with a resounding "Yes." Much would depend on their new Constitution and the government soon to be created under it. As the ratification debate subsided and the Confederation Congress prepared to adjourn, the American people looked eagerly and anxiously ahead.

TIME*line*

1777	Washington's army winters at Valley Forge
1778	French treaty of alliance and commerce
1779	Sullivan destroys Iroquois villages in New York
1780	Massachusetts constitution ratified
	Pennsylvania begins gradual abolition of slavery
1781	Cornwallis surrenders at Yorktown
	Articles of Confederation ratified by states

1783	Peace treaty with Britain signed in Paris
1784	Spain closes the Mississippi River to American navigation
1786	Virginia adopts "Bill for Establishing Religious Freedom"
	Annapolis Convention calls for revision of the Articles of Confederation
1786–1787	Shays's Rebellion
1787	Northwest Ordinance
	Constitutional Convention
	Federalist Papers published by Hamilton, Jay, and Madison
1788	Constitution

✓•⸻Study and Review at **www.myhistorylab.com**

Questions for Review and Reflection

1. Wars often produce unintended consequences. How was that the case for the American people during and after the Revolutionary War?

2. Some African Americans supported the struggle for American independence, but countless others did not. Explain the difference.

3. The peace treaty ending the Revolutionary War set the western boundary of the United States at the Mississippi River. What problems did the new territory west of the Appalachian Mountains pose for the new nation, and how effectively did Congress handle those problems during the 1780s?

4. With independence, the United States had to develop its own ways of dealing with other nations. What foreign policy problems did Congress face during the 1780s, and how effectively did it deal with them?

5. The successful struggle for independence encouraged many Americans to apply the language of rights and equality, used against Britain, to the conditions of political, social, and religious life in the American states. Identify three examples of this during the 1780s and describe the outcomes.

6. The new American Constitution in 1787–1788 has been interpreted as a conservative reaction to the more democratic pressures of the Revolution. Is this an accurate judgment? Explain.

Key Terms

Anti-Federalists 169

Electoral College 204

Federalist Papers 206

Federalists 169

Fugitive Slave Clause 205

Great Compromise 204

New Jersey Plan 203

Northwest Ordinance 194

Shays's Rebellion 200

Virginia Plan 202

7

Creating a Nation

American Stories

Creating New Lives

In April 1795, Ben Thompson started north from Queen Anne's County, Maryland, for New York City. Ben knew little beyond farming, but he was ambitious, and when he arrived in New York he listened intently to the ships' captains as they talked about life at sea and recruited men for their crews. Ben was lucky, for he arrived just as American overseas commerce was entering a decade of unprecedented prosperity. Sailors were in demand, pay was good, and few questions were asked. For five years Ben sailed the seas. Having enough of travel, he returned to New York and hired out as an apprentice to a ship's carpenter.

About the same time, Phyllis Sherman left Norwalk, Connecticut. She also headed for New York, where she took a job as a maid in the household of one of the city's wealthy merchants. As fate would have it, Phyllis and Ben met, fell in love, and in the spring of 1802 were married.

There is little remarkable in their stories, except that Ben and Phyllis were former slaves and were married in the African Methodist Episcopal Zion Church. Ben had cast off his slave name, Cato, as a sign of liberation, while Phyllis kept the name her master had given her. Ben was doubly fortunate, for he had purchased his freedom just as cotton production began to expand through the southern interior, creating an accelerating demand for field hands shipped in from the Chesapeake region. In another decade, he would have faced greater difficulty securing his independence. Phyllis had been freed as a child when slavery ended in Connecticut. As she grew up, she tired of living as a servant with her former owner's family and longed for the companionship of other blacks. She had heard that there were people of color in New York, and she was correct. In 1800, it was home to 6,300 African Americans, more than half of them free.

Though life in New York was better than either Ben or Phyllis had known before, it was hardly easy. They shared marginally in the city's commercial prosperity.

Chapter Outline

Launching the National Republic

Society in the Early American Republic

A Nation Divided

Jeffersonian-Republican Triumph

Conclusion: A Period of Trial and Transition

In 1804, they watched helplessly as yellow fever carried off their daughter and many of their friends. And while they found support in newly established African American churches and the expanding black community, they had to be constantly on guard because slave ships still moved in and out of the port and slave catchers pursued southern runaways in the city's streets.

Free blacks, whether in the north or the south, faced special challenges. But they were among the Americans who took the opportunities presented in the new nation to build lives for themselves. Along with others like them, they focused on recreating their lives amidst the political debates that occupied many in the early Republic.

In the early republic, thousands of Americans seized opportunities to improve their lives. Some, like Ben Thompson and Phyllis Sherman, moved from the countryside to the nation's burgeoning cities; others would join the swelling tide of westward expansion. By their actions, such migrants contributed to a process that strengthened American values of individual initiative, social equality, and personal autonomy. That process was powered in part by an accelerating movement of people across the land that disrupted families, weakened long-established communities, and created countless new settlements. It was also encouraged by waves of religious revivalism known as the Second Great Awakening, which swept through American society, strengthening belief in the equality of all believers before God and the individual's responsibility for his or her own soul. African Americans found their lives constrained in the South by a revitalized system of slavery, while in the North free blacks such as Phyllis and Ben faced an increasingly racist society. West of the Appalachians, Native Americans confronted a swelling tide of white settlement.

These social changes occurred against a backdrop of political controversy that severely divided the nation over its direction and its position on the conflicts among European nations. The Washington administration moved to exercise the new powers of the federal government, developing policies to guide the new nation. Those policies revealed deep-seated conflicts between economic interests and raised urgent questions of how the new Constitution should be interpreted. What was the proper balance of power between state and national governments? How should governing authority be allocated between the executive branch and Congress?

Into this already heated discussion was interjected disagreement over the French Revolution and the relationship of the new American Republic to the revolution itself, to a related revolution in Haiti, and to the efforts of other European states to contain France. By the last years of the 1790s, the prospect of war with France and Federalist security measures such as the Alien and Sedition Acts brought the nation to the brink of political upheaval. That prospect was narrowly avoided by the Federalists' defeat and Thomas Jefferson's election as president in 1800. The election of Jefferson reversed some of the less popular Federalist policies, but over time much of the Federalist economic program was implemented.

Finally, the new Republic turned its attentions toward the West. The Louisiana Purchase vastly increased the territory claimed by the United States, while the War of 1812 removed the British presence in the interior. By 1815, the Federalist–Jeffersonian political system had collapsed. This quarter century from the passage of the Bill of Rights through the War of 1812 saw the Republic set upon the path it would henceforth follow. An expansive nation, with a commitment to a strong economic program but increasingly divergent approaches to the issue of slavery, emerged out of this period.

Launching the National Republic

Once the Constitution had been ratified, the nation embarked upon the new government that the framers had designed. In keeping with the concerns of the Anti-Federalists, a Bill of Rights was immediately passed. The Washington administration soon erected new federal policies, most notably having to do with the economy and Native Americans. Discontent with the impact of the new economic policies taxing whiskey galvanized western farmers to rebel, bringing a swift response from the newly empowered federal government. The political nation did not agree on the best way forward.

Beginning the New Government

On April 16, 1789, George Washington, unanimously elected president by the Electoral College, started north from Virginia to be inaugurated first president of the United States. His feelings were mixed as he set forth. "I bade adieu to Mount Vernon, to private life, and to domestic felicity," he confided to his diary, "and with a mind oppressed with more anxious and painful sensations than I have words to express, set out for New York . . . with the best disposition to render service to my country in obedience to its call, but with less hope of answering its expectations." For the moment, his sense of foreboding seemed unwarranted.

View the Image
Washington Taking the Oath of Office
at **www.myhistorylab.com**

The president-elect was the object of adulation as he journeyed north. In villages and towns, guns boomed their salutes, children danced in the streets, church bells pealed, and local dignitaries toasted his arrival. On April 23, he was rowed on a flower-festooned barge from the New Jersey shore to New York City, where throngs of citizens and newly elected members of Congress greeted him. That evening, bonfires illuminated the city.

President-Elect Washington Travels to New York This imaginative scene of Washington's reception in Trenton, New Jersey, during his trip from Virginia to New York City for his first inauguration depicts the popular adulation that surrounded him. What other messages can you find in the picture's details?

Inaugural day was April 30. Shortly after noon, on a small balcony overlooking Wall Street, Washington took the oath of office. "It is done," exulted New York's chancellor, Robert Livingston. "Long live George Washington, President of the United States!"With the crowd roaring its approval and 13 guns booming in the harbor, the president bowed his way off the balcony. Celebrations lasted late into the night.

Though hopefulness attended the new government's beginning, the first weeks were tense. Everyone knew how important it was that the government be set on a proper republican course. When Washington addressed the first Congress, republican purists complained that it smacked too much of a British monarch's speech from the throne at the opening of Parliament. Congress then had to decide whether it should accord Washington a title. Vice President Adams proposed "His Most Benign Highness," while others suggested the even gaudier "His Highness, the President of the United States, and Protector of the Rights of the Same." Howls of outrage arose from those who thought titles had no place in a republic. Good sense finally prevailing, Congress settled on the now familiar "Mr. President." The belief that such decisions might determine the new government's direction for years to come gave politics a special intensity.

The Bill of Rights

Among Congress's first tasks was consideration of the constitutional amendments that several states had made a condition of their ratification. Although Madison and other Federalists had argued that a national bill of rights was unnecessary, they were ready to keep their promise that such amendments would be considered. That would reassure the fearful, fend off calls for a second constitutional convention, and build support for the new regime.

From the variety of proposals offered by the states, Madison culled a set of specific propositions. After extensive debate, Congress reached agreement in September 1789 on 12 amendments and sent them to the states for approval. By December 1791, 10 had been ratified and became the national Bill of Rights. Among other things, they guaranteed freedom of speech, press, and religion; pledged the right of trial by jury and due process of law; forbade "unreasonable searches and seizures"; and protected individuals against self-incrimination in criminal cases. The Bill of Rights was the most important achievement of these early years, for it has protected citizens' rights ever since.

New Federal Economic Policies

During its first months, Washington's administration enjoyed almost universal support. It moved to implement new policies in keeping with the vision of the Federalist supporters of the Constitution. These policies were intended to strengthen the government, develop the economy, and support westward expansion.

Economic policy was largely the work of Washington's new Secretary of the Treasury, Alexander Hamilton. Seldom in the nation's history has a single official so dominated public affairs as did Hamilton in these years. An ardent proponent of economic development, Hamilton, perhaps more than any of the nation's founders, foresaw the country's future strength and was determined to promote its growth by encouraging domestic manufacturing and overseas trade. The United States, he was fond of saying, was a "Hercules in the cradle." At the same time, Hamilton's politics were profoundly conservative. Hamilton distrusted the people and feared their purposes. "The people," he asserted, "are turbulent and changing: they seldom judge or determine right." Recognizing the potential importance of his office, he determined to build the kind of nation he envisioned.

•••—Read the Document

Alexander Hamilton, Report on Manufactures (1791)

at **www.myhistorylab.com**

In his first "Report on the Public Credit," Hamilton recommended funding the remaining Revolutionary War debt by enabling the government's creditors to exchange their badly depreciated securities at face value for new interest-bearing government bonds. Second, he proposed that the federal government assume responsibility for the $21.5 million in remaining state war debts. These actions, he hoped, would stabilize the government's

Alexander Hamilton Hamilton used the office of secretary of the treasury during the administration of President Washington to shape national policy during the early 1790s. What personal qualities was the portraitist attempting to convey in this painting?

finances, establish its credit, build confidence in the new nation at home and abroad, and tie business and commercial interests firmly to the new government.

The proposal to fund the foreign debt aroused little controversy, but Hamilton's plans for handling the government's domestic obligations generated immediate opposition. In the House of Representatives, James Madison, Hamilton's recent ally in the ratification process, protested the unfairness of funding depreciated securities at their face value because speculators, some anticipating Hamilton's proposals, had acquired many of them at a fraction of their initial worth. Madison and his southern colleagues also knew that northern businessmen held most of the securities and that funding would bring little benefit to the South. Despite such criticisms, Congress ultimately endorsed the funding plan.

Hamilton then called for the federal government to assume responsibility for the remaining state debts. States with the largest unpaid obligations, such as Massachusetts, thought assumption a splendid idea. But others, such as Virginia and Pennsylvania, which had already retired much of their debt, were opposed. Critics also warned that assumption would further strengthen the central government at the expense of the states. Moreover, with its increased need for revenue to pay off the accumulated debt, the federal government would have additional reason to exercise its newly acquired power of taxation. Whereas critics saw this as a flaw in the plan, Hamilton intended to use this and other measures to precisely that end.

Once again, Congress endorsed Hamilton's bill, in good measure because Madison and Jefferson supported it as part of a deal to move the seat of government from New York to Philadelphia, and eventually to a new federal district on the Potomac River. Southerners hoped that moving the government away from northern commercial centers would enable them to align it with their own agrarian interests.

Hamilton then introduced the second phase of his financial program: a national bank capable of handling the government's financial affairs and pooling private investment capital for economic development. He had the Bank of England and its ties to the royal government in mind, though he did not say so publicly. Opposition to the bank came almost entirely from the South. It seemed obvious that the bank would serve the needs of northern merchants and manufacturers far better than those of southern planters. Still, in February 1792, Congress approved the bank bill.

When Washington asked his cabinet whether he should sign the bill, Hamilton urged him to do so. Following the constitutional doctrine of "implied powers"—the principle that the government had the authority to make any laws "necessary and proper" for exercising the powers specifically granted it by the Constitution—Hamilton argued that Congress could charter such a bank under its power to collect taxes and regulate trade. Secretary of State Jefferson, however, urged a veto. He saw in Hamilton's argument a blueprint for the indefinite expansion of federal authority and insisted that the government possessed only those powers specifically listed in the Constitution. Because the Constitution said nothing about chartering banks, the bill was unconstitutional and should be rejected. To Jefferson's distress, Washington took Hamilton's advice and signed the bank bill into law.

In December 1790, in his second "Report on the Public Credit," Hamilton proposed a series of **excise taxes**, including one on the manufacture of distilled liquor. This so-called Whiskey Tax signaled the government's intention to use its taxing authority to increase federal revenue. The power to tax and spend, Hamilton knew, was the power to govern. The Whiskey Tax became law in March 1791.

Those who had opposed the creation of a stronger central government in the Constitution watched with mounting alarm as Hamilton worked to expand the federal power. They joined with others to block some aspects of Hamilton's plan, such as a cluster of initiatives designed to promote American manufacturing. Although numerous elements of his vision were implemented, the political nation was divided over whether to follow the path being laid out by Hamilton.

Federal Indian Policies

The new government also turned its attention to the need for an Indian policy that would prevent continual warfare while also opening lands to the West to settlement. Intended in part to promote the assimilation of Native Americans, the policies speeded the transfer of Indian land to white settlers and set the stage for later, large-scale Indian removal. With the government's initial "conquest" theory rendered obsolete by the Indians' refusal to regard themselves as a conquered people (see Chapter 6), U.S. officials shifted course by recognizing Indian rights to the land they inhabited and declaring that all future land transfers would come through treaty agreements.

Henry Knox, Washington's first Secretary of War, laid out the government's new position in 1789. The Indians, he explained, "being the prior occupants of the soil, possess the right of the soil." It should not be taken from them "unless by their free consent, or by the right of conquest in case of just war." The Indian Intercourse Act of 1790 declared that public treaties, ratified by Congress, would henceforth be the only legal means of obtaining Indian land. Though it promised a more humane Indian policy, the acquisition of land remained the overarching goal.

The new, treaty-based strategy proved effective in the short term. Native American leaders frequently ceded land in return for trade goods, yearly annuity payments, and assurances that there would be no further demands. Reluctant tribal leaders could often be persuaded to cooperate by warnings about the inevitable spread of white settlement, or more tractable chieftains could be found. In these ways, vast areas of tribal land passed to settlers.

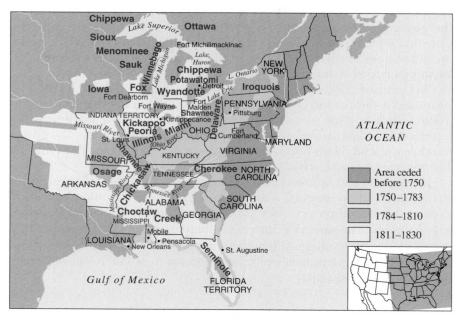

Indian Land Cessions, 1750–1830 As white settlers streamed across the nation's interior, state and federal governments wrung land cessions from the Indians. What region was the last in which native peoples held onto significant areas of their ancestral land east of the Mississippi River? (Labels in blue indicate the major Native American tribes.)

A second objective of federal Indian policy was to "civilize" and Christianize the Native Americans, then assimilate them into white society. With the government's blessing, Moravians, Baptists, and other religious groups sent scores of missionaries to live among the Indians, preach the Gospel, and teach white ways. Among the most selfless were Quakers who labored with the Iroquois in New York. In spite of the missionaries' best efforts, however, most Native Americans remained aloof. The chasm between Christianity and their own religions was too wide.

Education was the other weapon of assimilation. In 1793, Congress appropriated $20,000 to promote literacy, agriculture, and vocational instruction among Indians. Federal officials encouraged missionaries to establish schools in which Indian children could learn the three R's and vocational skills. But the vast majority of Indian children never attended, they and their parents distrusting the schools' alien environment.

Although white assimilationists cared deeply about the physical and spiritual fate of Native American people, they showed little sympathy for Indian culture. They demanded that Native Americans give up their language, religion, and extended family arrangements. Assimilation or removal were the stark alternatives posed by even the most benevolent whites.

Faced with the loss of land and tribal autonomy, Native Americans devised various strategies of resistance and survival. Among the Iroquois, a prophet named Handsome Lake led his people through a religious renewal and cultural revitalization. In 1799, following a series of visions, he preached a combination of Indian and white ways: temperance, peace, land retention, and a new religion combining elements of Christianity and traditional Iroquois belief. His vision offered renewed pride in the midst of the Iroquois' radically changed lives.

Other Native peoples, most notably the Cherokee, embraced the assimilationist option as the best means to stave off encroachments on their land. After a bitter internal struggle, accommodationists in the community won. They brought the tribe's scattered villages under a common government, the better to protect their freedom and prevent the further loss of land. In 1808, the Cherokee National Council adopted a written legal code combining elements of U.S. and Indian law. Working from that basis, the Cherokee nation proceeded to use the legal system to attempt to shelter the autonomy and property of their people.

At the same time, a process of social and cultural accommodation, encouraged by Cherokee leaders such as mixed-blood John Ross and promoted by missionaries and government agents, went forward. As the Cherokee turned from their traditional hunting, gathering, and farming economy to settled agriculture, many moved from village settlements onto individual farmsteads. Others established sawmills, stores, and blacksmith shops. In place of traditional practices of communal ownership, the concept of private property took hold. The majority of Cherokee kept their crude log cabins and continued to live a hand-to-mouth existence. But some mixed-bloods who learned English and understood how to deal with white authorities accumulated hundreds of acres of fertile land and scores of black slaves. Initially, the strategy of peaceful accommodation brought clear rewards. Tribal government was stronger and the sense of Cherokee identity was reasonably secure. But success would prove the Cherokee people's undoing. As their self-confidence grew, so did the hostility of neighboring whites impatient to acquire their land. That hostility would erupt in a campaign to drive the Cherokee from their land forever (see Chapter 10).

Not all tribes proved so accommodating to white expansion. In the late 1780s, chieftains such as Little Turtle of the Miami and Blue Jacket of the Shawnee had led devastating raids across Indiana, Ohio, and western Pennsylvania, panicking white settlers and challenging U.S. control of the Old Northwest. In 1794, President Washington, determined to smash the Indians' resistance once and for all, sent a federal army led by the old Revolutionary War general Anthony Wayne into the area. It won a decisive victory over 2,000 Indian warriors in the **Battle of Fallen Timbers** that summer. Shortly after, in the Treaty of Greenville, the assembled chiefs ceded the southern two-thirds of Ohio. That cession opened the heart of the Old Northwest to white control. Subsequent treaties further reduced the Indians' land base, driving the tribes more tightly in upon each other. Further South, the Shawnee and Creek, faced with growing threats to their political and cultural survival, rose in armed resistance. Conflict, smoldering as the nineteenth century began, burst into open flame during the War of 1812.

The Whiskey Rebellion

While western farmers applauded efforts to contain the threat of Native American resistance through treaties or warfare, they rejected policies that harmed their economic interests. They vigorously opposed the new Whiskey Tax, which directly affected their livelihoods. They transported their surplus grain over the Appalachian Mountains to eastern markets in distilled form, because shipping it in bulk was prohibitively expensive. The Whiskey Tax threatened to make this trade unprofitable. The farmers also protested that people charged with tax evasion had to stand trial in federal court hundreds of miles away in Philadelphia.

•◆•⌐Read the Document

George Washington, Proclamation Regarding the Whiskey Rebellion *(1794)*

at **www.myhistorylab.com**

Westerners also sensed control of their local affairs slipping away as the backcountry became caught up in a market economy and political system dominated by the more populous, commercialized areas to the east. In southern states such as South Carolina, the integration of coastal and interior regions went more smoothly because of similar agricultural interests and a shared antipathy to enslaved Africans. In the more economically diverse and racially homogenous states of the north, however, conflicts between coastal and backcountry regions sharpened.

Hamilton cared little what western farmers thought about the Whiskey Tax. The government needed revenue, and the farmers would have to bear the cost. Angered by Federalist arrogance as much as the tax, farmers quickly made their resentment known. In the summer of 1792, citizens began gathering in mass meetings across western Pennsylvania. In August, a convention at Pittsburgh declared its intention to prevent the tax's collection. Like opponents of the Stamp Act in 1765 and the Shays rebels in Massachusetts, they concluded that liberties would be lost if resistance did not soon begin. Alarmed, Washington issued a proclamation warning against such "unlawful" gatherings and insisting that the tax would be enforced. As collections began, the farmers took matters into their own hands.

In July 1794, when a federal marshal and a local excise inspector attempted to serve papers on several recalcitrant farmers near Pittsburgh, an angry crowd cornered a dozen federal soldiers in the marshal's house. After an exchange of gunfire, the troops surrendered, and the house was torched. Similar episodes involving the erection of liberty poles reminiscent of the Revolution erupted across the state, while a convention of 200 delegates debated armed resistance and talked about seceding from the United States.

Fearing that the protests might spread through the entire backcountry from Maine to Georgia and alarmed by talk of secession, Washington called out federal troops to restore order. For more than a year, Hamilton had been urging the use of force against the protesters. To him, the insurrection was not evidence of an unjust policy needing change, but a test of the administration's ability to govern. He eagerly volunteered to accompany the troops west.

In late August 1794, a federal force of nearly 13,000 men marched into western Pennsylvania. At its head rode both the president and secretary of the treasury. Persuaded of the danger to his safety, Washington returned to Philadelphia, but Hamilton pressed ahead. The battle for which he hoped never materialized, for as the army approached, the "Whiskey Rebels" dispersed. Of 20 prisoners taken, 2 were convicted of treason and sentenced to death. Later, in a calmer mood, Washington pardoned them both.

As people soon realized, the **Whiskey Rebellion** had never threatened the government. "An insurrection was . . . proclaimed," Jefferson scoffed, "but could never be found." Even such an ardent Federalist as Fisher Ames was uneasy at the sight of federal troops marching against American citizens. "Elective rulers," he warned, "can scarcely ever employ the physical force of a democracy without turning the moral force or the power of public opinion against the government." The federal government had the resources necessary to suppress armed insurrection, but the use of coercion against the American people was a troubling indication of serious divisions over political and economic policies in the new republic.

RECOVERING *the* PAST

Foreign Travel Journals

Historians utilize many different kinds of sources in their quest to recover the American past. Among the most revealing are travel accounts penned by foreign visitors eager to learn about the United States and record their impressions. From the days of earliest explorations to our own time, travelers have been fascinated by the people, customs, institutions, and physical setting of North America. Out of this continuing interaction between America and its foreign visitors has emerged a rich and fascinating travel literature that reveals much not only about America but about the travelers who have visited it as well.

The American Revolution fanned similar interest in the minds of Europeans in the decades after its completion. One of the most opinionated and engaging of these earlier commentators was the Frenchman Moreau de Saint Méry. His curiosity aroused by the Revolution, he was fascinated by the newly independent nation and anxious to discern its implications for European society.

Born on the French island of Martinique in January 1750, de Saint Méry established a successful legal practice before moving to France, where relatives introduced him to polite Parisian society. In the late 1780s, he became an ardent champion of political reform during the early days of the French Revolution. As the revolution entered its radical phase, however, he was forced to flee to the United States for safety. Arriving at Norfolk, Virginia, with his wife and two children, de Saint Méry settled in Philadelphia, where he remained from October 1794 to August 1798. While there, he mingled with civic and cultural leaders, opened a bookstore that served as a rendezvous for French émigrés who also had fled the revolution's turmoil, and published a French-language paper that reported the latest news from home. In the late summer of 1798, de Saint Méry returned safely to France.

As with all such travel accounts, de Saint Méry's commentary must be read with a critical eye, for travelers disagreed over what they thought important and worth reporting, and interpreted what they saw in very different ways. In nearly 400 pages of commentary, de Saint Méry touched on numerous aspects of American life, but none in more frank and compelling fashion than relations between the sexes. The selections that follow (somewhat rearranged for greater continuity) provide tantalizing insights into the behavior and sexual mores of American men and women in the early years of the republic.

What did de Saint Méry find most interesting about gender relations in Philadelphia? How did religion, class, and ethnicity shape men's and women's behavior? Of what forms of behavior did he approve and disapprove?

The explicit commentary of de Saint Méry is unique among the numerous accounts left by foreign travelers in the early republic, most of whom showed far more interest in America's racial makeup, political practices, and physical environment. Thus, de Saint Méry's observations may be idiosyncratic and should be approached with caution.

What other kinds of sources might enable us to evaluate the accuracy of such travel accounts? In what ways is a traveler's own nationality, gender, religion, or class likely to shape his or her impressions of the United States? Similarly, how important is it to know travelers' motives for coming, how long they stayed, which parts of the country they visited, and with whom they associated while here?

REFLECTING ON THE PAST Does the gendered world of late eighteenth-century Philadelphia, as described by de Saint Méry, seem strange or familiar, attractive or distasteful to your own sensibilities? If you were to live for a few years in another country today, how accurate do you think you could be in assessing the social behavior and cultural values of its people? To what extent would your values, perhaps like those of Moreau de Saint Méry, color your impressions? Might it be more difficult to understand some foreign cultures than others? Why?

Moreau de Saint Méry's American Journal

American men, generally speaking, are tall and thin . . . [and] seem to have no strength. . . . They are brave, but they lack drive. Indifferent toward almost everything, they sometimes behave in a manner that suggests real energy; then follow it with a "Oh-to-hell-with-it" attitude which shows that they seldom feel genuine enthusiasm. . . .

American women are pretty, and those of Philadelphia are prettiest of all. . . . Girls ordinarily mature in Philadelphia at the age of fourteen, and reach that period without unusual symptoms. . . . But they soon grow pale. . . . After eighteen years old they lose their charms. . . . Their hair is scanty, their teeth bad. . . . In short, while charming and adorable at fifteen, they are faded at twenty-three, old at thirty-five, decrepit at forty or forty-five. . . .

American women carefully wash their faces and hands, but not their mouths, seldom their feet and even more seldom their bodies. . . . They are greatly addicted to finery and have a strong desire to display themselves—a desire . . . inflamed by their love of adornment. They cannot, however, imitate that elegance of style possessed by Frenchwomen. . . .

One is struck by the tall and pretty young girls one sees in the streets, going and coming from school. They wear their hair long, and skirts with closed seams. But when nubility has arrived they put up their hair with a comb, and the back of the skirt has a placket. At this time, they . . . become their own mistresses, and can go walking alone and have suitors. . . .

They invariably make their own choice of a suitor, and the parents raise no objection because that's the custom of the country. The suitor comes into the house when he wishes; goes on walks with his loved one whenever he desires. On Sunday he often takes her out in a cabriolet, and brings her back in the evening without anyone wanting to know where they went. . . . Although in general one is conscious of widespread modesty in Philadelphia, . . . the disregard . . . of some parents for the manner in which their daughters form relationships to which they . . . have not given their approval is an encouragement to indiscretions. . . .

When one considers the unlimited liberty which young ladies enjoy, one is astonished by their universal eagerness to be married. . . . When a young woman marries, she enters a wholly different existence. She is no longer a . . . butterfly who denies herself nothing and whose only laws are her whims and her suitor's wish. She now lives only for her husband, and to devote herself without surcease to the care of her household and her home. . . . The more her husband is capable of multiplying . . . the pleasures of matrimony . . . the more her health may suffer, most of all when she has a child; for sometimes while nursing it, or as soon as it is weaned, she has already conceived another. . . .

Divorce is obtained with scandalous ease. From this alone one can judge the extent of loose habits. . . .

Bastards are extremely common in Philadelphia. There are two principal reasons for this. In the first place, the city is full of religious sects, but none of them give their clergymen any authority to enforce obedience. Consequently there is no way of inspiring shame in women who become mothers for no reason except the pleasure they get out of it. In the second place, once an illegitimate child is twelve months old, a mother can disembarrass herself of him by farming him out for twenty-one years. This makes it possible for her to commit the same sin for a second time. It never occurs to her that her child can never know her, and that the whole business is shameful. . . .

There are streetwalkers . . . in Philadelphia. These are very young and very pretty girls, elegantly dressed, who promenade two by two, arm in arm and walking very rapidly, at an hour which indicates that they aren't just out for a stroll. . . . Anyone who accosts them is taken to their home . . . [where] they fulfill every desire for two dollars, half of which is supposed to pay for the use of the room. Quaker youths are frequent visitors in the houses of ill fame, which have multiplied in Philadelphia and are frequented at all hours. There is even a well-known gentleman who leaves his horse tied to the post outside one of these houses, so that everyone knows when he is there and exactly how long he stays. . . .

Source: From *Moreau de St. Méry's American Journey*, by Moreau de St. Méry's, translated by Kenneth Roberts and Anna M. Roberts, copyright 1947 by Kenneth Roberts and Anna M. Roberts. Used by permission of Doubleday, a division of Random House, Inc.

Society in the Early American Republic

In the early Republic, the vast majority of Americans drew their living from the land. As the nineteenth century began, fully 83 percent of the labor force was engaged in agriculture, a figure that had hardly changed 25 years later. Cities grew more rapidly than the general population, greeting new residents from various sources, including free blacks such as Phyllis Sherman and Ben Thompson. In this expansive and diverse nation, improvements in long-distance communication and travel made minor gains. Still, the society shared some common experiences, participating in widespread revivals and in patriotic celebrations that expressed attachment to the new nation and, often, admiration for its first president.

Regional Differences in an Agricultural Society

Agriculture was the primary occupation, yet across the nation, people occupied the land in very different ways. In the Northeast, stretching from New Jersey and eastern Pennsylvania to New England, family farms dominated the landscape. On New England's rock-strewn land, farmers often abandoned field crops for the greater profits to be made from livestock. On the richer agricultural lands of New York and Pennsylvania, farmers cultivated the land intensively, planting crops year after year rather than following the time-honored practice of allowing worn-out fields to lie fallow and recover their productivity.

Most farms were not large. By 1800, the average farm in longer-settled areas was no more than 100 to 150 acres, down substantially from half a century before. Such shrinkage was primarily a result of the continuing division of farm property from fathers to sons. Even in southeastern Pennsylvania, the most productive agricultural region in the Northeast, opportunity was declining. Continuous cropping had robbed the soil of fertility, forcing farmers to bring more marginal land under cultivation, thus bringing a steady decline in productivity. Nearly 20 percent of male taxpayers in southeastern Pennsylvania were single, clear evidence that young men were delaying marriage until they could establish themselves financially.

Whereas the majority of northeasterners made their living from the land, growing numbers of rural folk also worked for wages as artisans or day laborers in nearby towns, or toiled in the small-scale manufactories—grain and saw mills, potash works, and iron forges—that dotted the rural landscape. Farm women contributed to the family economy by helping with the livestock, preserving food, and making clothes for sale or exchange with neighbors. As the practice of men working for wages outside the family setting grew, women's unwaged domestic labor began to be regarded as less valuable.

Life was different in the South, a region stretching from Maryland to Georgia along the coast and west to the newly forming states of Alabama and Mississippi. In 1800, much of southern agriculture was in disarray. Low prices, worn-out land, war, and the loss of slaves had left the Chesapeake tobacco economy in shambles. In response, southern planters experimented with wheat and other grains in hopes of boosting their sagging fortunes. Regional recovery began in earnest, however, when they turned to a new staple crop—cotton.

In 1790, the South had produced 3,135 bales of cotton; by 1820, output had mushroomed to 334,378 bales. In 1805, cotton accounted for 30 percent of the nation's agricultural exports; by 1820, it exceeded half. Across the coastal South and the newly developing states of Alabama, Mississippi, and Tennessee, cotton was becoming king. A fortuitous combination of circumstances fueled the transformation: the growing demand of textile mills in England and the American Northeast; wonderfully productive virgin soil; a long, steamy growing season; ample slave labor; and southern planters' long experience in producing and marketing staple crops.

Eli Whitney's cotton gin speeded the process as well. The silky fibers of long-staple cotton could be easily separated from the cotton's seeds. The delicate, long-staple plant, however, grew only in the hot, humid climate along the southern coast. The hardier short-staple variety could be successfully cultivated in the southern interior, but its fibers clung tenaciously to the plant's sticky, green seeds. A slave could clean no more than a pound of short-staple cotton a day. Whitney's cotton gin was little more than a box containing a roller equipped with wire teeth designed to pull the fibers through a comb-like barrier, thus stripping them from the seeds. A hand crank activated the mechanism. With this crude device, a laborer could clean as many as 50 pounds of short-staple cotton a day.

The swing to cotton marked a momentous turning point in the South's, and the nation's, history. It raised the value of southern land and opened economic opportunity for southern whites. It also increased the demand for black field hands and breathed new life into slavery. Some of the escalating demand for slave labor was met from overseas. In 1803, Georgia and South Carolina together imported 20,000 new slaves, as southern planters and northern suppliers rushed to fill the demand before 1808, the moment when the federal government was free to take action on the slave trade. Much of the demand for agricultural labor, however, was met by the internal slave trade that moved black labor from the worn-out lands of the Chesapeake to the lush cotton fields of the southern interior.

A third significant region of white settlement was forming west of the Appalachian Mountains as the nineteenth century began. Trans-Appalachia, extending from the mountains to the Mississippi River and from the Great Lakes to the Gulf of Mexico, housed scarcely 100,000 white settlers in 1790. By 1810, their number had swollen to nearly a million. They came by wagon through mountain passes such as the Cumberland Gap and by flatboat down the Ohio River.

The human tide seemed to grow with each year. The woods were full of new settlers, wrote an amazed observer near Batavia in western New York in 1805. "Axes are resounding, and the trees literally falling around us as we passed." America, he exclaimed, is "breaking up and going west!" Settlers were drawn by the promotions of speculators seeking their fortunes in the sale of western land. Between 1790 and 1820, land companies hawked vast areas of New York, Ohio, and Kentucky to prospective settlers. Many ventures failed, but countless others proved profitable. Settlers joined in the speculative fever, often going deeply into debt to buy extra land for resale when population increased and land values rose.

North of the Ohio River, settlement followed the grid pattern prescribed in the Land Ordinance of 1785. There, free-labor agriculture took hold and towns such as Cincinnati emerged as service and cultural centers for the surrounding population. South of the Ohio, white settlers and their black slaves distributed themselves more randomly across the land. In Kentucky and Tennessee, free-labor agriculture was soon challenged by the spread of slavery-based cotton.

As settlers arrived, they began the long process of transforming the region's heavily forested land. Farmers cut girdles of bark off groves of trees, and then set them on fire or left them to die while planting crops around the decaying hulks. By this method, a family could clear from three to five acres a year for cultivation. As expanding areas of Trans-Appalachia came under the farmer's plow, forests and wildlife gave way. The relentless demand for wood generated by the growing white population continued the assault on the region's forests that had begun in the colonial era.

The Nation's Cities

Though most Americans lived on the land or in small towns, increasing numbers dwelt in the nation's expanding cities. From 1790 to 1820, the nation's population increased by 84 percent, but urban places of more than 2,500 residents grew almost twice as fast.

Patterns of urban development differed from region to region. The most dramatic growth occurred in the port cities of the Northeast. By 1820, the region contained three cities of more than 50,000. New York alone held over 100,000 people, while inland towns such as Cincinnati, Ohio, and Albany, New York, proliferated as service centers for their surrounding areas.

Though increasing rapidly in population, America's urban places remained small in area. In these "walking cities," residents could easily stroll from one side of town to the other. Rapid growth, however, brought increasing congestion, together with serious problems of public health and safety. Philadelphia led the way in street paving, but dust and mud constantly plagued urban life. More than mud clogged urban streets in the early nineteenth century, for residents dumped their garbage there, privies leached into open drains, and livestock roamed the streets, leaving their droppings behind. Though one urban dweller thought the scavenging hogs she encountered "disgusting," she acknowledged that without them the streets would soon be choked with filth. Under such conditions, typhoid and dysentery, spread by contaminated water, took a continuous toll.

Economic life still centered on the wharves, where sailing ships from around the world docked, and on the warehouses, where their cargoes were unloaded. At the same time, by the 1820s manufacturing was beginning to transform urban life. Philadelphia was becoming a textile manufacturing center, while New York produced shoes and iron goods. As these enterprises expanded, artisan production slowly gave way to factory-based wage labor.

Such changes widened the gap between richer and poorer inhabitants. Prosperous merchants sat at the top of the social pyramid, their households graced by fine table linens and store-bought furniture, the artifacts of an expanding consumer economy. Below them came an aspiring middle class of artisans, shopkeepers, and professional men whose families shared modestly in the general prosperity. At the bottom spread a growing underclass of common laborers, dockworkers, and the unemployed, their lives a continuous struggle for survival. Whereas rich and poor had often lived close together in colonial cities, rising land values now forced the poor into crowded alleys and tenements, while more prosperous urban dwellers began clustering in fashionable neighborhoods.

In other regions, cities were smaller although still important nexuses. Southeast urban development centered in long-established ports such as Charleston and Savannah. As during the colonial period, they continued to serve as commercial *entrepots*, exporting agricultural products and importing manufactured goods. Half their population was black, the majority of them slaves. In Trans-Appalachia, fledgling cities such as Pittsburgh and Cincinnati dotted the region's rivers and lakes. The largest of these in 1820 was New Orleans, which reflected its multinational origins.

Established as a French colony in 1718, New Orleans came under Spanish rule in 1763. When it became part of the United States in 1803, urban life was dominated by French and Spanish Creole families. For several decades, U.S. citizens remained a minority among the white population. Of the city's 27,000 people, nearly 13,000 were black.

Forming Free Black Communities

During the half century following independence, vibrant black communities, fed by emancipation in the Northeast and the increasing numbers of freed men and women in the Upper South, appeared in eastern port cities. In 1776, 4,000 slaves and several hundred free blacks had called the major port cities home; 50 years later, more than 40,000 African Americans did so.

Black men worked as laborers and dock hands, and black women as domestics. Family formation was eased by the fact that many of the urban migrants were women, thus correcting a long-standing imbalance in the black urban population. Former slaves often created extended households that included relatives, friends, and boarders. As circumstances allowed, single-family units were formed. By 1820, most blacks in northern cities lived in autonomous households.

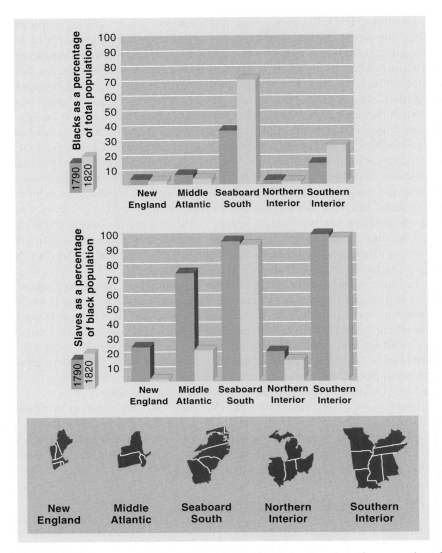

Blacks and Slavery, 1790–1820 In 1790, regions differed significantly in the proportion of blacks in their population and in the percentage of slaves among black residents. In the ensuing decades, those differences increased. Can you explain why? *(Source: U.S. Bureau of the Census)*

As their numbers grew, African Americans created organizations independent of white control and capable of serving the needs of black communities. Schools educated black children excluded from white academies, mutual aid societies offered help to the down-and-out, and fraternal associations provided fellowship and mutual support.

Black churches quickly emerged as the cornerstones of black community life. Following the Revolution, growing numbers of free blacks joined integrated Methodist and Baptist congregations, drawn by their strongly biblical theology, enthusiastic forms of worship, and antislavery stand. As the number of black communicants grew, however, they found themselves segregated in church galleries, excluded from leadership roles, and even denied communion. In 1794, a small group of black Methodists led by Richard Allen, a slave-born itinerant preacher, organized the Bethel African American Methodist Church in Philadelphia. Originally established within American Methodism, Allen's congregation moved toward separatism by requiring that only "Africans and descendents of the African race" be admitted to membership. In 1815, it rejected all oversight by the white Methodist leadership, and a year later joined a similar congregation in Baltimore to form the African Methodist Episcopal Church—the first independent black denomination in the United States. Black Baptists also formed separate churches during the early nineteenth century.

Located in the heart of black communities, these churches nurtured distinctive African American forms of worship and provided education for black children and burial sites for families excluded from white cemeteries. Equally important, they offered secure places where the basic rituals of family and community life—marriages and births, funerals and anniversaries—could be celebrated, and where community norms could be enforced. A rich cultural and institutional life took root in the black neighborhoods of northeastern cities.

Black life was far different in southern cities, where the vast majority remained enslaved. Of Charleston's 14,127 blacks (over half the city's population), 90 percent were slaves. That circumstance, together with the South's rigid Black Codes, frustrated black community building. In New Orleans, by contrast, policies established during Spanish colonial rule had produced the largest free black (*libre*) and mixed-race (mulatto) population in North America. While racial hierarchies existed, *libres*, their numbers augmented by slaves who had been manumitted (freed) by their masters and by refugees fleeing revolutionary Haiti, prospered. By 1820, *libres* made up 46 percent of the black population. They constituted a uniquely prosperous and independent black community.

Yet several developments threatened their privileges. Among them were the thousands of new slaves imported to provide labor for the burgeoning sugar economy—what one historian has called the "re-Africanization" of Louisiana—as well as alarm over the black rebellion in nearby Haiti, and the introduction of rigid racial ideologies by new white settlers.

Conquering Distance

It has been estimated that within half an hour of President Kennedy's assassination in Dallas, Texas, in 1963, 68 percent of the American people had learned the news. By contrast, when George Washington died in December 1799 in Alexandria, Virginia, it took five days for word to reach Philadelphia (scarcely 140 miles away), 11 days to get as far as Boston, and over three weeks to penetrate west to Lexington, Kentucky. In the absence of modern technologies such as telephones, television, and the Internet, human travel was the only way of communicating across space. Gradually over the course of the early nineteenth century, however, improvements in transportation and communication began to knit the nation more effectively together.

A flurry of turnpike construction in the northeastern states contributed to the improvements. Most consisted of little more than dirt roadways cut through the woods, with tree stumps sawed off low enough to clear wagon axles. Still, when a pike from Philadelphia to Lancaster, Pennsylvania, proved profitable, dozens of others quickly followed. By 1811, New York had chartered 137 turnpike companies and the New England states 200 more. Construction of such roads reduced travel time along these pathways by half.

In the first federal road building project, Congress in 1806 authorized construction of a National Road from Cumberland, Maryland, to the West. By 1818, it had reached Wheeling on the Ohio River and had reduced travel time between its terminals from eight days to three.

Given the difficulties of overland routes, Americans traveled by water whenever possible. During the early years of the century, the first steamboats appeared along the Atlantic coast and began to ply the waters of the Ohio and Mississippi rivers. In 1807, Robert Fulton launched his 160-ton sidewheeler *Clermont*, demonstrating the feasibility of steam travel. Four years later, the *New Orleans* made the first successful run over the falls of the Ohio River at Cincinnati, and then continued down the Mississippi to New Orleans. Within a few decades, steamboats would revolutionize transportation on the nation's interior river system.

Between 1790 and 1810, significant breakthroughs occurred in print communication as well. Fewer than three dozen newspapers were published in the colonies on the eve of the Revolution. When Washington assumed the presidency, 92 newspapers existed. Most were weeklies; virtually all were printed in cities along the Atlantic coast. The majority had no more than 600 subscribers. By 1810, the number of newspapers had increased to almost 400, with a significant minority of them dailies. Some were published in places as far inland as Pittsburgh and St. Louis. By 1820, the ratio of newspapers to population was higher in the United States than in Great Britain.

The swelling demand for newspapers was spurred by rising literacy rates, the desire for information generated by the nation's expanding market economy, the democratic belief in the importance of an informed citizenry, and the growing importance of newspapers as instruments of party politics. The circulation of papers brought information about distant people and events into formerly isolated communities, expanding citizens' horizons and strengthening their sense of shared experience. Only a newspaper, noted one observer, "can drop the same thought into a thousand minds at the same moment."

During these years, the American postal system expanded similarly. When Washington was inaugurated, there were only 75 post offices in the entire country. As late as 1792, there were none in the trans-Appalachian West. By 1820, nearly 8,500 post offices lay scattered throughout the nation, while the number of letters carried by the postal system had increased nine-fold. Though it cost 25 cents to send a letter 30 miles or more—a prohibitive sum for most folks when daily wages averaged only a dollar—the rate had declined by half.

Religious Revival and Patriotic Celebration

As travel and communication gradually knit the nation together, so, too, did shared cultural experiences. Once again, religious revival swept through broad areas, creating a sense of community and heightening inter-est in social reform. With reference to the colonial-era revivals, these later bouts of religious enthusiasm came to be known as the Second Great Awakening. The revivals began in the 1790s and continued sporadically for decades. In settings ranging from the Cane Ridge district of backwoods Kentucky to the cities of the Northeast, Americans by the tens of thousands sought personal salvation and social belonging in the shared experience of religious revivalism. Revivals tied Americans together in networks of shared religious identity, woven by the hundreds of itinerant ministers

A Camp Meeting During the Second Great Awakening, religious enthusiasts gathered at count-less camp meetings to seek salvation and serve other needs as well. What does this depiction suggest about who attended and what took place?

who carried the Gospel message into communities in every part of the country. The flood of printed tracts circulated by religious organizations reinforced the sense of religious unity.

Displayed most spectacularly at Methodist and Baptist camp meetings, the revivals crossed boundaries of class and race. Rough-hewn itinerant preachers, black as well as white, many of them theologically untrained but afire with religious conviction, spread the Gospel message. Offering a simple message that ordinary folks could readily grasp, the Awakening emphasized the equality of all believers before God, held out the promise of salvation, and declared each individual responsible for his or her soul. The Awakening also called on believers to demonstrate their faith by going into the world to perfect American society and uplift the downtrodden. That mandate would provide much of the energy for later reforms such as temperance and abolition

People also came together around rituals of patriotic celebration. Occasions such as Washington's birthday and the Fourth of July also helped unify the country. Citizens from varied political perspectives, northerners and southerners, black and white Americans filled these occasions with their own, often conflicting meanings, yet all were eager to claim a voice in shaping the nation's heritage. Reports of these local celebrations, carried across the land via newspapers and correspondence, knitted communities together in a national conversation of patriotism.

A Nation Divided

Even as the new nation took steps toward great integration and shared common experiences, older differences and new challenges combined to create an intense period of political conflict. The French Revolution, while welcomed by many as a sign that Europe was shrugging off its old ways, threatened to draw the young Republic into international war. Citizens of the United States disagreed vehemently about whether to support Britain or France in the ensuing struggle. Similarly divisive eventually was the Haitian Revolution, which created the first anti-slavery republic in the Americas. Opposition to both the foreign and domestic policies of the government crystallized in Democratic Republican Societies, the first organized opposition within American politics.

The Promise and Peril of the French Revolution

France's revolution began in 1789 as an effort to reform an arbitrary but weakened monarchy. Pent-up demands for social justice, however, quickly outran initial attempts at moderate reform, and in January 1793, when the recently proclaimed republican regime beheaded Louis XVI, France plunged into a genuinely radical revolution. Soon Europe was locked in a deadly struggle between revolutionary France and a coalition led by Prussia and

Britain. For more than a decade, the French Revolution dominated European affairs. It also cut like a plowshare through the surface of American politics, dividing Americans.

The outbreak of European war posed thorny diplomatic problems for Washington's administration. By the 1790s, American merchants were earning handsome profits from "neutral trade" with both Britain and France. In 1800, American ships carried an astonishing 92 percent of all commerce between America and Europe. The economic benefits were most evident in the coastal cities, but radiated as well into the surrounding countryside, where cargoes of agricultural and forest goods and the provisions required by the ships' crews were produced.

America's expanding commerce, however, generated problems as well. While Britain and France sought access to American goods, each was determined to prevent those goods from reaching the other, if necessary by stopping American ships and confiscating their cargoes. America's relations with Britain were additionally complicated by the Royal Navy's practice of forcibly impressing American sailors into service aboard its warships to meet the growing demand for seamen. Washington faced the difficult problem of protecting the country's citizens without getting drawn into the European conflict.

The French treaty of 1778 compounded the government's dilemma. It required that the United States come to the aid of France, much as France had assisted the American states a decade and a half earlier. Americans sympathetic to the French cause argued that the commitment still held. Others, fearing the consequences of involvement and the political infection that closer ties with revolutionary France might bring, insisted that the treaty had lapsed when the French king was overthrown.

The American people's intense reaction to the revolution in France further complicated the situation. At first, many saw it as an extension of America's own struggle for liberty. Even the swing toward social revolution did not immediately dampen American enthusiasm. By the mid-1790s, however, especially after the revolutionary regime launched its attack on organized Christianity, many Americans pulled back in alarm. What connection could there be between the principles of 1776 and the chaos so evident in France? The differences were indeed profound.

To Federalists—who since the ratification of the Constitution endorsed the centralizing policies of the Washington administration—revolutionary France represented social anarchy and threatened the European order on which they believed America's commercial and diplomatic well-being depended. With increasing vehemence, they castigated the revolution, championed Britain as the defender of European civilization, and sought ways of linking Britain and the United States more closely together.

Many Americans, however, continued to support France. While decrying the revolution's excesses, they believed that liberty would ultimately emerge from the turmoil. Though Jefferson regretted the shedding of innocent blood, he thought it necessary if true liberty was to be achieved.

Haiti and the Promise of African Liberty in the Americas

The revolution in France made possible an array of political insurgencies that challenged aristocratic power and promoted democratic values during the 1790s. Supported by invading armies of revolutionary France and inspired by the doctrine of natural rights voiced during the American and French revolutions, rebellions against long-entrenched privilege erupted from the Netherlands to the Italian peninsula. Democratic insurgencies broke out as well in Latin America and the Caribbean. The most important occurred on the island of Saint Domingue, soon to be known as Haiti.

On this French island in the Caribbean, a multiracial coalition rose in rebellion against French colonial rule beginning in 1791. Conflict quickly developed between white landowners seeking to preserve their privileges while throwing off the colonial yoke, poor whites demanding access to land, mixed-race people chafing under years of discrimination, and black slaves angered by brutal repression. For more than a decade, black and white Haitians conducted a furious struggle against a French force of nearly 30,000. (Britain, fearing rebellion among the 300,000 slaves on Jamaica, its nearby possession, offered France military support, even though France was its mortal enemy in Europe.) The conflict devastated Haiti's sugar economy and caused more than 100,000 casualties among whites and blacks alike.

In 1798, the island's black majority, led by the charismatic Toussaint L'Ouverture, seized control of the rebellion, making the abolition of slavery its primary goal. Six years later, the victorious rebels established Haiti as an independent state.

While Haitian rebels celebrated the Declaration of Independence as a manifesto of universal freedom, North American whites divided over how to respond to the events on that troubled island. On one hand, the Haitian revolt appeared to affirm the universal relevance of America's own struggle for liberty and struck another blow against European colonialism in the New World. During the height of the Haitian insurgency, American warships ferried black troops from one part of the island to another in preparation for battle. On the other hand, U.S. slaveholders contemplated with dread the effect on North American slaves of a successful black rebellion.

White southerners were especially anxious. The governor of North Carolina issued a proclamation warning Haitians fleeing the island to stay away. When Haitian officials appealed "in the name of humanity" for "fraternal aid," Congress demurred. If Haiti became an independent state, warned a senator, it might become "a dangerous neighbor" offering asylum to runaway slaves. When the Haitian republic was proclaimed in 1804, the U.S. government withheld recognition. Not until after the American Civil War were diplomatic relations established.

These fears appeared to have been confirmed in the summer of 1800, when a rebellion just outside Richmond, Virginia, was nipped in the bud. A 24-year-old slave named Gabriel devised a plan to arm 1,000 slaves for an assault on the city. Gabriel and his accomplices were American-born blacks who spoke English and worked at skilled jobs that provided considerable personal autonomy. They fashioned their own ideology of liberation by appropriating the revolutionary traditions of Virginia's whites and news of the Haitian revolt. A drenching downpour delayed the attack, giving time for several house servants (later granted their freedom by the Virginia Assembly) to sound the alarm. No whites died in the abortive rebellion, but scores of slaves and free blacks were arrested and 25 suspects, including Gabriel, were hanged at the order of Governor James Monroe.

Though each of the democratic insurgencies that erupted during the 1790s was inspired by local experiences of injustice, they shared a common dedication to human liberty. News of these far-flung revolutions circulated in the United States via newspapers, networks of personal correspondence, and an expanding human traffic of soldiers, émigrés, and political idealists who crisscrossed the Atlantic during these tumultuous years. In the mid-1790s, Joel Barlow and other Americans, motivated by curiosity and democratic principle, journeyed to France, eager to witness the further unfolding of universal liberty. At the same time, a stream of French émigrés, bringing vivid tales of political turmoil, sought sanctuary in North America.

The Democratic–Republican Societies

Political clubs—providing safe havens where dissidents could gather to read tracts and plot change—served as weapons of democratic reform throughout the Atlantic world during the 1790s. The Jacobin clubs in France were the best known, but similar groups sprouted up in the United States.

As early as 1792, ordinary citizens began to form "constitutional societies" dedicated to "watching over the rights of the people" and giving the alarm in case of governmental encroachment on American liberties. Several dozen societies, modeled after the Sons of Liberty and Committees of Correspondence that had mobilized Patriots 20 years earlier, formed in opposition to Hamilton's financial program.

The French Revolution stoked the fires of democratic enthusiasm and spurred the societies' growth, as did the arrival in 1793 of Citizen Edmond Genêt, the French republic's new minister to the United States. Genêt landed at Charleston, South Carolina, to a tumultuous reception. His instructions were to court popular support and negotiate a commercial treaty with the United States. Shortly after his arrival, however, he began commissioning American privateers to attack British shipping in the Caribbean and enlisting American seamen for expeditions against Spanish Florida, clear violations of American neutrality.

As he traveled north toward Philadelphia, Genêt met more enthusiastic receptions. His popularity, however, soon led him into trouble. In open defiance of diplomatic protocol, he urged Congress to reject Washington's recently issued Neutrality Proclamation and side with revolutionary France. On August 2, the president demanded Genêt's recall.

Though Genêt failed as a diplomat, he succeeded in fanning popular enthusiasm for revolutionary France. With his encouragement, the largest and most influential of the new societies, the Democratic Society of Pennsylvania, was founded in Philadelphia in June 1793. It called immediately for the formation of similar societies to join in supporting France and promoting "freedom and equality" at home. Washington and his colleagues might have wondered whether that challenge was aimed at them.

About 40 popular societies scattered from Maine to Georgia sprang up during the next several years. Working people—artisans and laborers in the cities, small farmers and tenants in the countryside—provided the bulk of membership. Federalist critics derided them as "the lowest orders of . . . draymen . . . broken hucksters, and trans-Atlantic traitors." That canard referred to the growing tide of Irish immigrants, fleeing hard times and political repression at home, who combined demands for Irish independence with a commitment to political equality and an appreciation for rough-and-tumble politics.

The societies' leaders were often doctors, lawyers, and tradesmen—men of acknowledged respectability. All were united by a determination to preserve the "principles of '76" against the "royalizing" tendencies of Washington's administration. Committed to an awakened citizenry, the societies organized public celebrations, issued ringing addresses, and fired off petitions sharply critical of administration policies. Washington's proclamation of neutrality they labeled a "pusillanimous truckling to Britain, despotically conceived and unconstitutionally promulgated." Several of the societies openly urged the United States to enter the war on France's behalf.

West of the Appalachians, local democratic societies agitated against Britain's continuing occupation of the frontier posts south of the Great Lakes and berated Spain for closing the Mississippi River at New Orleans to American shipping. Everywhere, they protested the Excise Tax, opposed the administration's overtures to England, and called for a press free from control by Federalist "aristocrats."

President Washington and his supporters were incensed by the societies' support of Genêt and criticism of the government. Such "nurseries of sedition," thundered one Federalist, threatened to revolutionize America as the Jacobins had revolutionized France. Such polemics indicated how inflamed public discourse had become.

Deepening Political Crisis

With an organized opposition challenging Washington's policies, his administration ended in political conflict, which carried over into the administration of his successor, John Adams. An effort to resolve differences with Great Britain, which resulted in a controversial treaty negotiated by Chief Justice John Jay, was one area of controversy. The treaty that Jay brought home in early 1795 contained British promises on a number of sensitive matters but ignored a host of other problems. When its terms were made public, they triggered an explosion of protest.

The administration's pleas that the agreement headed off an open breach and was the best that could be obtained failed to pacify its critics. In New York City, Hamilton was stoned while defending the treaty at a mass meeting. Southern planters were angry because the agreement brought no compensation for their lost slaves. Westerners complained that the British were not evacuating the military posts, while merchants and sailors railed against Jay's failure to stop **impressments** and open the British West Indies to American trade. After a long and acrimonious debate, the Senate ratified the treaty by a narrow margin.

By mid-decade, political harmony had disappeared as divisions deepened on virtually every important issue of foreign and domestic policy. Jefferson, increasingly estranged from the administration, resigned as secretary of state, joining Madison and others in open opposition to Washington's administration. In September 1796, in what came to be called his Farewell Address, Washington deplored the deepening political divisions, warned against entangling alliances with foreign nations, and announced that he would not accept a third term. He had long been contemplating retirement, for he was now 64 and wearied by political attacks. "As to you, sir," fumed Thomas Paine in a letter published in an opposition newspaper, "treacherous in private friendship . . . and a hypocrite in public life, the world will be puzzled to decide, whether you . . . have abandoned good principles, or whether you ever had any." The contrast between his triumphant progress to take up the presidency eight years earlier could not have been more stark.

John Adams John Adams, Washington's vice president, won a narrow victory over Jefferson for the presidency in 1796. His administration foundered on conflicts over foreign policy abroad and the suppression of political dissent at home. How would you interpret the various items included in this portrait?

Elected narrowly to the presidency in 1796, John Adams was a committed Federalist. He believed in a vigorous national government, was appalled by the French Revolution, and feared "excessive" democracy. The election of 1796 bound Adams to his onetime friend and ally Thomas Jefferson in a deeply strained and ill-fated alliance. The two men disagreed politically. Jefferson, while firmly supporting the Constitution, was alarmed by Hamilton's financial program, viewed France's revolution as a hopeful if chaotic extension of America's struggle for freedom, and aimed to expand democracy at home. Even though by 1796 Jefferson was the leader of an increasingly vocal opposition, the Jeffersonian Republican party, he served as Adams's vice president. While Adams received 71 electoral votes and became president, Jefferson, by virtue of coming in second with 68 votes, assumed the vice presidency.

Adams had no sooner taken office than he confronted a deepening crisis with France generated by French naval vessels interfering with American merchant ships in the Caribbean. That crisis would push the nation to the brink of civil conflict.

Hoping to ease relations between the two countries, Adams sent three commissioners to Paris to negotiate an accord. When they arrived in Paris, agents of the French foreign minister Talleyrand (identified only as "X, Y, and Z") made it clear that the success of the American mission depended on a loan to the French government and a $240,000 "gratuity" (more accurately, a bribe) for themselves. The two staunchly Federalist commissioners, John Marshall and Charles Pinckney, indignantly sailed home. Elbridge Gerry, the third commissioner, alarmed by Talleyrand's intimation that France would declare war if all three Americans departed, stayed on.

●◆●─**Read the Document**

*The Treaty of San Lorenzo
(or Pinckney's Treaty) (1796)*
at **www.myhistorylab.com**

When Adams reported the so-called **XYZ Affair** to Congress, Federalists quickly exploited the French blunder. Secretary of State Pickering urged an immediate declaration of war, while Federalist congressmen thundered, "Millions for defense, but not one cent for tribute!" Caught up in the anti-French furor and emboldened by petitions of support that flooded in, Adams lashed out at "enemies" at home and abroad. Emotions were further inflamed by the so-called Quasi War, a series of naval encounters between American and French ships on the high seas.

For the moment, the Republicans were in disarray. Publicly, they deplored the French government's behavior and pledged to uphold the nation's honor. But they were alarmed about Federalist intentions—with good reason, because the Federalists soon mounted a program to repel invaders from abroad and root out "traitors" at home.

The Alien and Sedition Acts

In May 1798, Congress called for a naval force capable of defending the American coast against French attack. In July, it moved closer to an open breach by repealing the treaty of 1778 and calling for the formation of a 10,000-man army. The army's stated mission was to deter a French invasion, but this seemed an unlikely danger given France's desperate struggle in Europe. The Jeffersonians, remembering the speed with which the Federalists had deployed troops against the Whiskey Rebels, feared the army would be used against them.

•🎧•Read the Document

The Alien and Sedition Acts (1798)

at **www.myhistorylab.com**

As criticism of the army bill mounted, Adams had second thoughts. He continued to fear the dangers of standing armies, just as he had done during the Revolution. "This damned army," he exclaimed, "will be the ruin of the country." He was further angered when members of his party sought to put Hamilton in command of the troops. To the dismay of hard-line Federalists, Adams issued only a few of the officers' commissions that Congress had authorized. Without officers, the army could not be mobilized.

Fearful of foreign subversion and aware that French and Irish immigrants were active in the Jeffersonian opposition, the Federalist-dominated Congress acted to curb the flow of aliens into the country. In June 1798, the Naturalization Act raised the residence requirement for citizenship from 5 to 14 years, while the Alien Act authorized the president to expel aliens whom he judged "dangerous to the peace and safety of the United States." Another bill, the Alien Enemies Act, empowered the president in time of war to arrest, imprison, or banish the subjects of any hostile nation without specifying charges against them or providing opportunity for appeal. A Federalist congressman explained that there was no need "to invite . . . the turbulent and disorderly of all parts of the world, to come here with a view to distract our tranquility."

The implications of these acts for political liberties were ominous enough, but the Federalists had not yet finished. In a move aimed directly at the Jeffersonians, Congress passed the Sedition Act, making it punishable by fine and imprisonment for anyone to conspire in opposition to "any measure or measures of the government," or to aid "any insurrection, riot, unlawful assembly, or combination." Fines and prison also awaited those who dared to "write, print, utter, or publish . . . any false, scandalous and malicious writing" bringing the government, Congress, or the president into disrepute. The Federalist moves stunned the Jeffersonians, for they threatened to smother all political opposition.

Under the terms of the Alien Act, Secretary of State Pickering launched investigations intended to force foreigners to register with the government. He noted approvingly that large numbers of aliens were leaving the country. As Sedition Act prosecutions went forward, 25 people were arrested. Fifteen were indicted, and 10 were ultimately convicted, the majority of them Jeffersonian printers and editors. In Congress, Representative Matthew Lyon, a cantankerous, Irish-born, acid-tongued Jeffersonian from Vermont, became embroiled in a heated debate over the Sedition Act and spat in the face of a Federalist opponent, Roger Griswold of Connecticut. Two weeks later, Griswold caned Lyon on the House floor. Later that year, Lyon was hauled into court, fined $1,000, and sentenced to four months in prison. His crime? Referring in a personal letter to President Adams's "unbounded thirst for ridiculous pomp, foolish adulation, and selfish avarice."

The Alien and Sedition Acts generated a firestorm of protest across the country. On November 16, 1798, the Kentucky assembly passed a resolution declaring that the government had violated the Bill of Rights. Faced with such an arbitrary exercise of federal power, each state had "an equal right" to judge of infractions and "the mode and measure of redress." Nullification (declaring a federal law invalid within a state's borders) was the "rightful remedy" for unconstitutional laws. Similar resolutions, written by Madison and passed the following month by the Virginia Assembly, asserted that when the central government threatened the people's liberties, the states were "duty bound to interpose for arresting the progress of the evil." It would not be the last time in American history that state leaders would claim authority to set aside a federal law. The Kentucky and Virginia resolutions received little support elsewhere, and as it turned out the Alien and Sedition Acts were not enforced in the South. Still, the resolutions indicated the depth of popular opposition to the Federalist program.

Although as 1799 began, the country seemed on the brink of upheaval, within a year, the crisis had been averted. From Europe, the president's son, John Quincy Adams, sent assurances that Talleyrand was prepared to negotiate an honorable accord. Fearful that war with France "would convulse the attachments of the country," Adams seized the opening and determined to appoint new peace commissioners. "The end of war is peace," he explained, "and peace was offered me." He chose to pursue peace, though it would be unpopular with his supporters. After Secretary of State Pickering ignored presidential orders to dispatch the new commissioners, Adams dismissed him and ordered them to depart. By year's end, the envoys had secured an agreement releasing the United States from the 1778 alliance and restoring peaceful relations.

Jeffersonian-Republican Triumph

The election of 1800, which brought an end to the Federalist hold on the executive branch, demonstrated the strength and resiliency of the new government. With Jefferson as President, the repressive legislation of the Federalists was overturned. Jefferson and his successor in the White House, fellow Virginian James Monroe, turned attention away from the Atlantic and the controversies raging in Europe, concentrating instead on westward expansion. Increased engagement in the West brought war, first with Native peoples and eventually with Britain. The War of 1812 ended British occupation and ensured continued American expansion.

Watch the **Video**

Mr. Jefferson's Wall: The Changing Meaning of Separation of Church and State in the Early Republic at **www.myhistorylab.com**

The "Revolution of 1800"

As the election of 1800 approached, the Federalists were in disarray, having squandered the political advantage handed them by the XYZ Affair. With peace a reality, they stood before the nation charged with exercising federal power unconstitutionally, suppressing dissent, and threatening to use a federal army against American citizens. Adams's opponents within the **Federalist party** were furious at his "betrayal." When he stood for reelection, they plotted his defeat.

Emotions ran high as the election approached. In Philadelphia, gangs of young Federalists and Jeffersonians clashed in the streets. "A fray ensued," one observer reported, "the light horse [troops] were called in, and the city was so filled with confusion . . . that it was dangerous going out." In Virginia, rumors of a slave insurrection briefly interrupted the political feuding, but the scare subsided. Federalists and Jeffersonians were soon at each others' throats once again. This election, Jefferson warned, would determine whether republicanism or aristocracy would prevail.

Election day was tense throughout the country but passed without serious incident. As the results were tallied, it became clear that the Jeffersonians had won a decisive victory. The party's two candidates for president, Jefferson and Aaron Burr, each had 73 electoral votes. Adams trailed with 65.

Because of the tie vote, the election was thrown into the House of Representatives, as provided in the Constitution, where a deadlock quickly developed. After a bitter struggle, the House finally elected Jefferson, 10 states to 4, on the thirty-sixth ballot. (Seeking to prevent a recurrence of such a crisis, the next Congress passed and the states then ratified the Twelfth Amendment, providing for separate Electoral College ballots for president and vice president.) The magnitude of the Federalists' defeat was even more evident in congressional elections, where they lost their majorities in both the House and Senate.

The election's outcome revealed strong sectional divisions. The Federalists dominated New England because of regional loyalty to Adams, the area's commercial ties with Britain, and fears that the Jeffersonians intended to import social revolution from France. From Maryland south, political control by the Jeffersonians was almost as complete. In the middle states, the election was more closely contested.

The Federalist–Jeffersonian conflict was rooted as well in socioeconomic divisions among the American people. Federalist strength was greatest among merchants, manufacturers, and commercial farmers situated within easy reach of the coast. In New York City and Philadelphia, Federalists were most numerous in the wards where assessments were highest, houses largest, and addresses most fashionable. All had supported the Constitution in 1787–1788.

The Jeffersonian coalition included most of the old Anti-Federalists, but was broader than that. It found support among urban workers and artisans, many of whom had once been staunch Federalists.

View the Image
Thomas Jefferson, First Inaugural Address (1801)
at **www.myhistorylab.com**

The coalition, moreover, was led by individuals such as Madison who had helped create the Constitution. Unlike the Anti-Federalists, the Jeffersonians were ardent supporters of the Constitution, but they insisted that it be implemented in ways consistent with political liberty and a strong dependence on the states.

Not all Jeffersonians were democratic in sympathy. Some argued for leadership by a "natural aristocracy of talent," most southern Jeffersonians found no inconsistency between black slavery and white liberty, and virtually all continued to believe that politics should remain an exclusively male domain. Still, the Jeffersonian coalition included countless individuals committed to the creation of a more democratic society. Motivated by electoral self-interest, political principle, and the determination of ordinary people to claim their rights as republican citizens, the Jeffersonian Republican party ushered in a growing tide of popular politics.

((•—[Hear the **Audio**
Jefferson and Liberty
at **www.myhistorylab.com**

In the election of 1800, control of the federal government passed for the first time from one political party to another, not easily but at least peacefully. The "revolution of 1800," Jefferson claimed, was "as real a revolution in the principles of our government as that of 1776 was in its form." Although the election did not permanently bring in a different approach to governance to the extent that Jefferson averred, the successful transfer of power was significant for the way that it demonstrated the staying power of the United States in the face of vigorous political debate.

[View the **Image**
*New Capitol—Congress'
First Meeting—1800*
at **www.myhistorylab.com**

Opening the Trans-Mississippi West

Jefferson's policy with regard to the West was perhaps his most successful, even though it helped lay the groundwork for war and seemed to violate his commitment to small government. Believing that political liberty could survive only under conditions of broad economic and social equality, Jefferson rested his hopes in the independent, yeoman farmer. His self-reliance, industriousness, and concern for the public good were deemed essential to democratic citizenship. In order to maintain the conditions for such a society, Jefferson and others looked to territorial expansion that would provide land for the nations' citizen farmers, draw restless people out of crowded eastern cities, and preserve the social equality that democratic liberty required.

The goal of securing agrarian democracy by territorial expansion explains Jefferson's most dramatic accomplishment, the Louisiana Purchase of 1803. It nearly doubled the nation's size. In 1800, Spain ceded the vast trans-Mississippi region called Louisiana to France. Jefferson was disturbed at this evidence that European nations still coveted North American territory. His fears were well grounded, for in October 1802, the Spanish commander at New Orleans, which Spain had retained, again closed the Mississippi to American commerce. Spain's action raised consternation both in Washington and the West.

[See the **Map**
The Louisiana Purchase
at **www.myhistorylab.com**

In response, Jefferson instructed Robert Livingston, the American minister to France, to purchase a tract of land on the lower Mississippi that might serve as an American port, thus guaranteeing free transit for American shipping. By the time James Monroe arrived in April 1803 to assist in the negotiations, the French ruler, Napoleon Bonaparte, had decided to sell all of Louisiana. Faced with the threat of renewed war with Britain, as well as the successful black rebellion against French rule in Haiti, Napoleon feared American designs on Louisiana and knew he could not long keep American settlers out. Soon the deal was struck. For $15 million, the United States obtained nearly 830,000 square miles of new territory.

Territorial expansion did not stop with Louisiana. In 1810, American adventurers fomented a revolt in Spanish West Florida and proclaimed an independent republic. Two years later, over vigorous Spanish objections, Congress annexed the region. In the Adams-Onís (or Transcontinental) Treaty of 1819, Spain ceded East Florida. As part of that agreement, the United States also extended its territorial claims to include the Pacific Northwest.

If America's expanding domain was to serve the needs of the agrarian nation, it would have to be explored and prepared for white settlement. In the summer of 1803, Jefferson dispatched an expedition led by Meriwether Lewis and William Clark to explore the far Northwest, make contact with the Native Americans there, open the fur trade, and bring back scientific information. For nearly two and a half years, the intrepid

View the **Image**
Meriwether Lewis, Portrait
at **www.myhistorylab.com**

View the **Image**
William Clark, Portrait
at **www.myhistorylab.com**

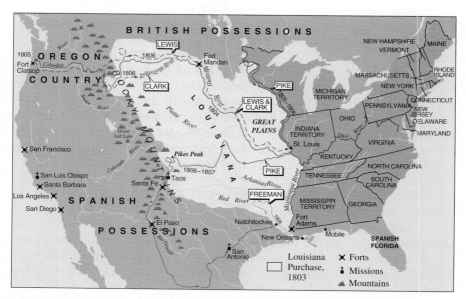

Exploring the Trans-Mississippi West, 1804–1807 During his two administrations, Jefferson sent several exploring expeditions into the vast Louisiana Territory and beyond. Why did he send them, and what did they accomplish?

explorers, assisted by the Shoshone woman Sacajawea, made their way across thousands of miles of hostile and unmapped terrain. Lewis and Clark's journey fanned American interest in the trans-Mississippi West, and demonstrated the feasibility of an overland route to the Pacific.

In 1805 and 1806, Lieutenant Zebulon Pike explored the sources of the Mississippi River in northern Minnesota, and then undertook an equally bold venture into the Rockies, where he traversed the peak that still bears his name. In the following decade, the government established a string of military posts from Minnesota to Arkansas, all intended to secure the frontier, promote the fur trade, and support white settlement.

⊙ Watch the Video

Lewis and Clark: What Were They Trying to Accomplish? at **www.myhistorylab.com**

Struggling for Neutral Rights

After a brief interlude of peace, European war resumed in 1803. Once again Britain and France seized American shipping. Britain's naval superiority made its attacks especially serious. Its continuing refusal to stop impressment, vacate its military posts south of the Great Lakes, and allow trade with its West Indian islands heightened the tension.

In response to British seizures of American shipping, Congress passed the Non-Importation Act in April 1806, banning British imports that could be produced domestically or acquired elsewhere. A month later, Britain blockaded the European coast, thus shutting off American trade there. In retaliation, Napoleon forbade all commerce with the British Isles.

Tension between Britain and the United States reached the breaking point in June 1807, when the British warship *Leopard* stopped the American frigate *Chesapeake* off the Virginia coast and demanded that four crew members be handed over as British deserters. When the American commander refused, protesting that the sailors were U.S. citizens, the Leopard opened fire, killing 3 men and wounding 18. After the *Chesapeake* limped back into port with the story, cries of outrage rang across the land.

Knowing that the United States was not prepared to confront Britain, Jefferson proposed withdrawing American ships from the Atlantic. In December 1807, Congress passed the Embargo Act, forbidding American vessels from sailing for foreign ports. The embargo was one of Jefferson's most ill-fated decisions.

Embargo had relatively little effect on Britain, since British shipping profited from the withdrawal of American competition, and British merchants found new sources of agricultural produce in Latin America. The embargo's impact on the U.S., however, was far-reaching. Exports plummeted 80 percent in a year, while imports dropped by more than half. New England was hardest hit. In ports such as Boston and Providence, ships lay idle and thousands of jobs were lost. Economic depression settled in.

Up and down the coast, communities openly violated the embargo. As attempts to police it failed, goods were smuggled in across the Canadian border. Throughout the Federalist Northeast, bitterness threatened to escalate into rebellion. When federal officials declared martial law and sent in troops in an effort to control the situation near Lake Champlain in upstate New York, local citizens fired on U.S. revenue boats and recaptured confiscated goods. In language reminiscent of the **Virginia and Kentucky Resolutions,** Connecticut's Federalist governor declared that states were duty-bound "to interpose their protecting shield" between the liberties of the people and oppressive acts of the central government. Faced with the embargo's ineffectiveness abroad and disastrous political consequences at home, Congress repealed the measure in 1809.

Jefferson's efforts to achieve neutrality strained the nation, but did not resolve the challenges the nation faced from Europe. How could American rights on the high seas be protected and the country's honor upheld without being drawn into a European war and without further inflaming American politics? An uneasy peace continued for some years after Jefferson left office, but the nation would eventually be drawn into war.

Native American Resistance to Westward Expansion

Expansion to the West sparked periodic confrontation with the regions' Native American inhabitants, as it had done since the colonial period. Native resistance to white encroachment, having been curbed in the Ohio River Valley in the Battle of Fallen Timbers in 1794, re-emerged after the turn of the century.

Tecumseh Though Tecumseh's vision of a pan-Indian alliance reaching from the Great Lakes to the Gulf of Mexico never materialized, he led Indian tribes of the Old Northwest in militant opposition to white territorial expansion. How does this portrait compare to the earliest depictions of Native Americans?

By 1809, two Shawnee leaders, the brothers Tecumseh and Elskwatawa, the latter known to whites as "the Prophet," were traveling among the region's tribes warning of their common dangers and forging an alliance against the invading whites. They established headquarters at an ancient Indian town named Kithtippecanoe in northern Indiana. Soon it became a gathering point for Native Americans from across the region responding to the messages of cultural pride, land retention, and pan-Indian resistance proclaimed by the Shawnee brothers.

Between 1809 and 1811, Tecumseh carried his message south to the Creek and the Cherokee. His speeches rang with bitterness. "The white race is a wicked race," he said. "Since the days when the white race first came in contact with the red men, there has been a continual series of aggressions. The hunting grounds are fast disappearing, and they are driving the red men farther and farther to the west." The only hope was a "war of extermination." Though the southern tribes refused to join, by 1811, more than 1,000 fighting men had gathered at Kithtippecanoe.

Alarmed, the governor of the Indiana Territory, William Henry Harrison, surrounded the Indian stronghold with a force of 1,000 soldiers. After an all-day battle, he burned Kithtippecanoe to the ground. The Indians, however, were not yet defeated. Tecumseh's followers, taking advantage of the recent outbreak of the War of 1812 between the United States and Britain and aided by British troops from Canada, mounted devastating raids across Indiana and southern Michigan. With the British, they crushed American forces at Detroit and followed up with an attack on Fort Wayne. The tide turned, however, at the Battle of the Thames near Detroit. There Harrison inflicted a grievous defeat on a combined British and Indian force. Among those slain was Tecumseh.

The American victory at the Thames signaled the collapse of Tecumseh's confederacy and an end to Indian resistance in the Old Northwest. Beginning in 1815, American settlers surged once more across Ohio and Indiana, then on into Illinois and Michigan. The balance of power in the Old Northwest had shifted decisively.

To the south, the Creek challenged white intruders with similar militancy. As the nineteenth century began, white settlers were pushing onto Creek lands in northwestern Georgia and central Alabama. Although some Creek leaders urged accommodation, others, called Red Sticks, prepared to fight. The embers of this conflict were fanned into flame by an aggressive Tennessee militia commander named Andrew Jackson. Citing Creek atrocities against "defenseless women and children," Jackson urged President Jefferson to endorse a campaign against the "ruthless foe." He got his chance in the summer of 1813, when the Red Sticks devastated the frontier and assaulted Fort Mims on the Alabama River, killing 500 men, women, and children. News of the tragedy elicited bitter cries for revenge. At the head of 5,000 Tennessee and Kentucky militia, augmented by warriors from other tribes eager to punish their traditional Creek enemies, Jackson attacked.

As he moved south, the fighting grew more ferocious. Davey Crockett, one of Jackson's soldiers, later reported that the militia volunteers shot down the Red Sticks "like dogs." The Indians gave like measure in return.

The climactic fight of the Creek War came in March 1814 at the **Battle of Horseshoe Bend** in central Alabama. Over 800 Native Americans died, more than in any other Indian-white battle in American history. Jackson followed up his victory with a scorched-earth sweep through the remaining Red Stick towns. He allowed the Creek survivors to return home, but exacted his final revenge by constructing Fort Jackson on the Creek nation's most sacred spot. During the following months, he seized 22 million acres, nearly two-thirds of the Creek domain. Before his Indian-fighting days were over, Jackson would acquire, through treaty or conquest, nearly three-fourths of Alabama and Florida, a third of Tennessee, and a fifth of Georgia and Mississippi.

Just as Tecumseh's death had signaled the end of Indian resistance in the North, so Jackson's defeat of the Creek at Horseshoe Bend broke the back of Indian defenses in the South. With all possibility of armed resistance gone, Native Americans gave way before the swelling tide of white settlement.

The War of 1812

These battles between the United States and various native peoples had become caught up in a war with Great Britain. The immediate origins of the war, however, were continued conflicts at sea. During Madison's presidency, American ships once more ventured into the Atlantic following the embargo's collapse. As the British Navy renewed its depredations, war fever continued to mount, especially in the West and South. The election of 1810 brought to Congress a new group of leaders, firmly Jeffersonian in party loyalty but impatient with the administration's bumbling foreign policy and demanding tougher measures. These War Hawks included such future political giants as Henry Clay of Kentucky and John C. Calhoun of South Carolina.

For too long, the War Hawks cried, the United States had tolerated Britain's presence on American soil, encouragement of Indian raids, and attacks on American commerce. They talked freely of expanding the nation's boundaries north into Canada and south into Spanish Florida. Most of all, these young nationalists resented British arrogance and America's continuing humiliation. No government or political party, they warned, could long endure unless it protected the people's interests and upheld the nation's honor.

Responding to the pressure, President Madison finally asked Congress for a declaration of war on June 1, 1812. Opposition came entirely from the New England and mid-Atlantic states—ironically, the regions British policies affected most adversely—whereas the South and West voted solidly for war. Rarely had sectional alignments been more sharply drawn.

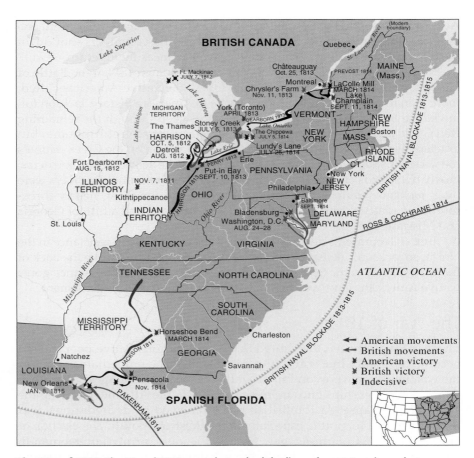

The War of 1812 The War of 1812 scarcely touched the lives of most Americans, but areas around the Great Lakes, Lake Champlain, Chesapeake Bay, and the Gulf Coast witnessed significant fighting. Why was the fighting concentrated in these areas?

The war proved a strange affair. Britain beat back several American forays into Canada and launched a series of attacks along the Gulf Coast. As it had done during the Revolutionary War, the British navy blockaded American coastal waters, while landing parties launched punishing attacks along the eastern seaboard. On August 14, a British force occupied Washington, torched the Capitol and president's mansion (soon to be called the White House after being repaired and whitewashed), and sent the president, Congress, and panic-stricken American troops fleeing into Virginia. Britain, however, did not press its advantage, for it was preoccupied with Napoleon's armies in Europe and wanted to end the American quarrel.

Emotions ran high among Federalist critics and Jeffersonian supporters of the war. In June 1812, during bloody riots in Baltimore, several people, including an old Federalist Revolutionary War general, were badly beaten in the streets. In Federalist New England, opposition to the war veered toward outright disloyalty. In December 1814, delegates from the five New England states met at Hartford, Connecticut, to debate proposals for secession. Cooler heads prevailed, but before adjourning, the **Hartford Convention**, echoing the Kentucky and Virginia Resolutions of 1798, asserted the right of a state "to interpose its authority" against "unconstitutional" acts of the government. As the war dragged on, Federalist support soared in the Northeast, while elsewhere bitterness grew over New England's disloyalty.

Before the war ended, American forces won several impressive victories, among them Commander Oliver Hazard Perry's defeat of the British fleet on Lake Erie in 1813. The most dramatic American triumph was Andrew Jackson's victory in 1815 over an attacking British force at New Orleans, though it occurred after preliminary terms of peace had already been signed. The war made Andrew Jackson a national hero and established him as a major political leader. With his success not only in New Orleans but also in the war against the Creeks, Jackson cemented his reputation.

Increasingly concerned about Europe, the British government offered to begin peace negotiations. Madison eagerly accepted, and on Christmas Eve in 1814, at Ghent, Belgium, the two sides reached agreement. While Britain promised to evacuate the western posts, the treaty ignored other long-standing issues, including impressment, neutral rights, and American access to Canadian fisheries. It simply declared the fighting over, called for the return of prisoners and captured territory, and provided for joint commissions to deal with lingering disputes.

The war left its mark on the American nation. Four thousand African American sailors, constituting nearly 20 percent of American seamen, fought in the war, demonstrating their patriotism and challenging white stereotypes. At least as many blacks served the British as spies, messengers, and guides, much as had occurred during the American Revolution. A hundred or so newly liberated slaves accompanied the British troops that burned the Capitol and president's house in 1814.

The American people regarded the contest as a "Second War of American Independence" that finally secured the nation from outside interference. In the years following 1815, the nation focused its energies on the task of internal development—occupying the continent, building the economy, and reforming American society. At the same time, Europe entered what would prove to be nearly a century free of general war. In the past, European wars had drawn America in; in the twentieth century, they would do so again. For the rest of the nineteenth century, however, that fateful link was broken. European colonialism was now shifting to Africa and Asia, and that diverted European attention from the Americas as well.

The Collapse of the Federalist–Jeffersonian Party System

For a while following the election of 1800, both Jeffersonian-Republican and Federalist division continued to influence politics, albeit to a lesser extent. Federalists continued to garner votes, and they maintained a drumfire of attack on the Jeffersonians, including the charge published by a Federalist editor in 1803 that Jefferson had sired several children by his slave Sally Hemings.

The Jeffersonians' overwhelming political success after the War of 1812 proved their undoing. No single party could contain the nation's swelling diversity of economic and social interests, deepening sectional differences, and personal ambitions of new political leaders. At the same time, Federalists—discredited by accusations of disloyalty during the War of 1812—proved unable to maintain an effective opposition. Their party gradually collapsed.

In response to growing pressures from the West and Northeast, as well as to nationalist sentiment stimulated by the War of 1812, Madison's admin- istration launched a Federalist-like program of national development. In March 1816, he signed a bill creating a second Bank of the United States (the first bank's charter had expired in 1811), intended to stimulate economic expansion and regulate the loose currency-issuing practices of countless state-chartered banks. At Madison's urging, Congress passed America's first **protective tariff**, a set of duties on imported goods intended to protect America's "infant industries." Madison also launched a federally subsi- dized network of roads and canals.

Several key decisions of the Supreme Court during the early decades of the century supported this move toward a stronger central government. In a series of trailblazing cases, the Court, led by Chief Justice John Marshall, laid down some of the most basic doctrines of American constitutional law. In *Marbury v. Madison* (1803), the Court established the principle of judicial review, the assertion that the Court had the authority to judge the constitu- tionality of congressional laws and executive actions. In the case of *Martin v. Hunter's Lessee* (1816), the Court claimed appellate jurisdiction over the de- cisions of state courts.

Three years later, in another landmark decision, *McCulloch v. Mary- land*, the Court set aside claims that Congress had exceeded its authority in chartering the Second Bank of the United States (1816). In a unani- mous decision, Marshall issued a ringing endorsement of the doctrine of loose, as opposed to strict, construction of the Constitution. "Let the end (of a Congressional law) be legitimate," he declared, "let it be within the scope of the constitution, and all means which are appropriate . . . to that end, which are not prohibited, but consist with the letter and spirit of the constitution, are constitutional." The Bank's charter would thus stand.

No state, he further argued, possessed the right to tax a branch of the nationally chartered bank, as Maryland had attempted to do, because "the power to tax involves the power to destroy." The principle of national supremacy lay at the very center of Marshall's findings. The doctrines elab- orated in these path-breaking decisions would continue to shape the nation's history in the years ahead.

Conclusion

A Period of Trial and Transition

The quarter century after the founding of the new national government was a time of trial and transition. Shortly after the new government had been formed, divisions appeared, initially among political leaders at the capital, but increasingly among the people at large. The domestic policies authored by Washington's secretary of the treasury, Hamilton, generated conflict first. The French Revolution, European war, Jay's Treaty, and Federalist war program galvanized political energies and set Federalists and **Jeffersonian Republicans** against each other. The Democratic insurgencies, particularly the Haitian rebellion, further inflamed the country's politics. The conflict of

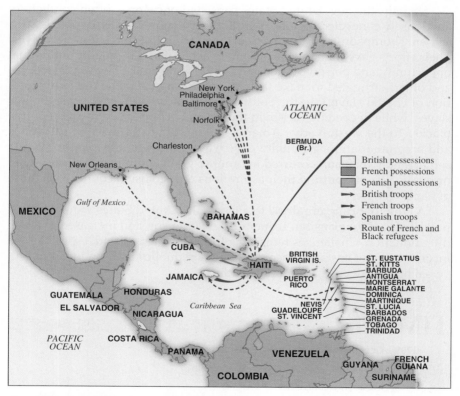

The Haitian Revolution Not only did the Haitian Revolution resonate with issues of racial ideology, it also proved a focal point of European imperial competition in the Americas and of French political battles at home. For white Americans, the Haitian Revolution conjured up frightening visions of black rebellion and cast doubt on the universal relevance of America's own revolution. In what ways was the United States sympathetic or unsympathetic to the Haitian Revolution?

the 1790s ended with the election of 1800, the first successful transfer of power from one major political party to another in the country's history.

In control of the federal government from 1800, the Jeffersonians labored to reverse some Federalist policies. At home, they fashioned domestic policies designed to redirect authority to the states and promote the country's agrarian expansion. Abroad they attempted, with more ambiguous results and at considerable political cost, to protect American rights in a hostile Atlantic world, all the while avoiding European entanglements. These foreign policy challenges and especially the continued presence of various European nations in the continental interior led finally to a second war with Britain. With the War of 1812, the United States achieved independence from British encroachments and greater control over the West. This set the stage for the full exploitation of the lands acquired in the Louisiana Purchase.

Socially, the new United States consisted of diverse, often conflicting, and loosely connected regions. Within those regions, ordinary people such as Ben Thompson, and Phyllis Sherman struggled to fashion new lives. Their efforts gave human expression to values of social equality, individual opportunity, and personal autonomy. At the same time, however, free blacks and others struggled to make their way in the new nation. The reinvigoration of chattel slavery in the South imperiled the lives of countless black slaves, while deepening racism in the North circumscribed the lives of free blacks. To the west, Native Americans, pursuing strategies of resistance and accommodation, gradually gave way in the face of expanding white settlement. Expansion occurred in order to grant continued opportunity to ordinary citizens, putting their aspirations on a collision course with those of native peoples.

As the founding era drew to a close, the United States would enter a period of rapid expansion, economic development, and increased regional differentiation. Challenges remaining from this early period, especially the inconsistency of enslaving people within a republic based on ideals of universal liberty, awaited a future resolution.

TIME*line*

1789	George Washington inaugurated as first president
1790	Hamilton's "Reports on the Public Credit"
	Indian Intercourse Act
1794	Whiskey Rebellion in Pennsylvania
1795	Controversy over Jay's Treaty with England
1796	John Adams elected president
1797	XYZ Affair
1798	Alien and Sedition Acts
	Virginia and Kentucky Resolutions

✓●─Study and Review at **www.myhistorylab.com**

Questions for Review and Reflection

1. How did the nation's regions differ in the early republic? To what extent were these differences grounded in the colonial period, and to what extent did they reflect developments since the end of the Revolutionary War?

2. How did Federalists and Jeffersonians differ in political principles? In the kind of economy they envisioned for the nation?

3. Tensions between the demands of national security and the protection of citizens' rights has also been a recurrent theme of our history. Why did that tension become so severe during the 1790s?

4. Name three foreign policy crises of the years 1790–1811, and explain why each was so controversial.

5. Why did some Indian tribes follow the path of accommodation to white expansion, while others rose in armed resistance? Which strategy was more successful?

Key Terms

Battle of Fallen Timbers 222

Battle of Horseshoe Bend 249

Excise taxes 219

Federalist party 243

Hartford Convention 251

Impressment 239

Jeffersonian Republicans 253

Protective tariff 252

Virginia and Kentucky Resolutions 247

Whiskey Rebellion 223

XYZ affair 240

8

Currents of Change in the Northeast and the Old Northwest

American Stories

Discovering Success in the Midst of Financial Ruin

For her first 18 years, Susan Warner was little touched by the economic and social changes transforming the country and her own city of New York. Some New Yorkers made a living by taking in piecework; others responded to unsettling new means of producing goods by joining trade unions to agitate for wages that would enable them to "live as comfortable as others." But Susan was surrounded by luxuries. Much of the year was spent in the family's townhouse in St. Mark's Place. There Susan acquired the social graces and skills appropriate for a girl of her position: dancing, singing, Italian and French lessons, and the etiquette of receiving visitors and making calls. When hot weather made life in New York unpleasant, the Warners escaped to their summer house. Like any girl of her social class, Susan realized that marriage, which she confidently expected some time in the future, would bring significant new responsibilities but not the end of her comfortable life.

It was not marriage and motherhood that disrupted the pattern of Susan's life but financial disaster. Sheltered as she had been from the far-reaching and unsettling economic and social changes of the early nineteenth century, Susan found that she, too, was at the mercy of forces beyond her control. Her hitherto successful father lost most of his fortune in the Panic of 1837. Like others experiencing a sharp economic reversal, the Warners had to make radical adjustments. The fashionable home in St. Mark's Place and the pleasures of New York gave way to a modest existence on an island in the Hudson River. Susan turned "housekeeper" and learned tasks once relegated to others: sewing and making butter, pudding sauces, and johnny cake.

The change of residence and Susan's attempt to master domestic skills did not halt the family's financial decline. Prized possessions went up for auction. "When at last the men and the confusion were gone," Susan's younger sister, Anna, recalled, "then we woke up to life."

Waking up to life meant facing the necessity of making money. But what could Susan do? True, some women labored as factory operatives, domestics, seamstresses, or schoolteachers, but it was doubtful Susan could even imagine herself in any of these occupations. Her Aunt Fanny, however, had a more congenial suggestion. Knowing that the steam-powered printing press had revolutionized the publishing world and created a mass readership, much of it female, Aunt Fanny told her niece, "Sue, I believe if you would try, you could write a story." "Whether she added 'that . . . would sell,' I am not sure," recalled Anna later, "but of course that was what she meant."

Taking Aunt Fanny's advice, Susan started to write a novel that would sell. She constructed her story around the trials of a young orphan girl, Ellen Montgomery. As Ellen suffered one reverse after another, she learned lessons that allowed her to survive and eventually triumph: piety, self-denial, discipline, and the power of a mother's love. Entitled *The Wide, Wide World*, the novel was accepted for publication only after the mother of the publisher, George Putnam, read it and told her son, "If you never publish another book, you must make *The Wide, Wide World* available for your fellow men." The cautious Putnam printed 750 copies. Much to his surprise, if not to his mother's, 13 editions appeared within two years. *The Wide, Wide World*, the first American novel to sell more than a million copies, became one of the best-sellers of the century.

Long before she realized the book's success, Susan, always aware of the need to make money, was working on a new story. Drawing on her own experience, Susan described the spiritual and intellectual life of a young girl thrust into poverty after an early life of luxury in New York. It was also a great success.

Though her fame as a writer made Susan Warner unusual, her books' popularity suggested how well they spoke to the concerns and interests of a broad readership. The background of social and financial uncertainty, with its sudden changes of fortune so prominent in several of the novels, captured the reality and fears of a fluid society in the process of transformation. While one French writer was amazed that "in America a three-volume novel is devoted to the history of the moral progress of a girl of thirteen," pious heroines like Ellen Montgomery, who struggled to master their passions and urges toward independence, were shining exemplars of the new norms for middle-class women. Their successful efforts to mold themselves heartened readers who believed that the future of the nation depended on virtuous mothers and those who strove to live up to new ideals. Susan's novels validated their efforts and the importance of the domestic sphere. "I feel strongly impelled to pour out to you my most heartful thanks," wrote one woman. None of the other leading writers of the day had been able to minister "to the highest and noblest feelings of my nature so much as yourself."

Susan Warner's life and her novels introduce the far-reaching changes that this chapter explores. Between 1820 and 1860, as Warner discovered, economic transformations in the Northeast and the Old Northwest reshaped economic, social, cultural, and political life. Between 1840 and 1860, industrialization and economic growth increasingly knit the two regions together.

After placing American economic change in an international context, one of the foci of this text, and discussing the factors that fueled antebellum growth, the chapter examines the industrial world, where so many new trends appeared. What new patterns of work emerged? How did class arrangements and values change and what evidence of rising social and racial tensions do you notice? As you read the chapter, also consider how economic growth and the new industrial mode of production affected the majority of Americans who still lived in rural settings. What goods, opportunities, and markets did they enjoy?

Economic Growth

Between 1820 and 1860, the American economy entered a new and more complex phase as it shifted from reliance on agriculture as the major source of growth toward an industrial and technological future. Amid general national expansion, real per capita output grew an average of 2 percent annually between 1820 and 1840 and slightly less between 1840 and 1860. This doubling of per capita income over a 40-year period suggests that many Americans were enjoying a rising standard of living.

⊙ See the **Map**

Expanding America and Internal Improvements

at **www.myhistorylab.com**

But the economy was also unstable, as the Warners discovered. Periods of boom (1822–1834, mid-1840s–1850s) alternated with periods of bust (1816–1821, 1837–1843). As never before, Americans faced dramatic and recurrent shifts in the availability of jobs and goods and in prices and wages. Particularly at risk were working-class Americans, a third of whom lost their jobs in depression years. And because regional economies were increasingly linked, problems in one area tended to affect conditions in others.

The Trans-Atlantic Context for Growth

American economic growth was linked to and influenced by events elsewhere in the world, particularly in Great Britain. Britain was the home of the Industrial Revolution, the event that some historians believe to be among the most important of human history in terms of its impact on material life. For the first time, production of goods proceeded at a faster pace than the growth of population.

The Industrial Revolution beginning in Britain in the eighteenth century involved many technological innovations that spurred new developments and efficiencies. Among the most important developments was the discovery in the 1780s of a way to eliminate carbon and other substances from pig iron. This opened the way for cheap, durable iron machines that led to the increased production of goods. Another milestone, the improvement of the steam engine, originally used to pump water out of coal mines, eventually led to railroads and steamboats, thus revolutionizing transportation. Steam-powered machinery also transformed cloth production, moving it from cottages to factories. The British textile industry was the giant of the early Industrial Revolution. The use of machinery allowed the production of more and cheaper textiles. The industry became a prime market for American cotton as well as cotton from India and Brazil. British demand for raw cotton helped to cement the South's attachment to slavery.

By 1850, Great Britain was the most powerful country in the world, and its citizens were the richest. In the following decades, its factories and mines churned out most of the world's coal and over half of its iron and textiles. Not surprisingly, Americans would look to England and English know-how as they embarked on their own course of industrialization. While American industrial development did not mimic the British, there were many similarities between the two countries' experiences.

Factors Fueling Economic Development

As the following table suggests, abundant natural resources and a growing population provided the basis for economic expansion. Because the size of American families was gradually shrinking, European immigrants played an essential role in supplying the workers, households, and consumers essential to economic development. They also contributed capital and technological ideas that helped shape American growth.

Improved transportation played a key role in promoting economic and geographical expansion. Early in the century, high freight rates discouraged production for distant markets and the exploitation of resources, while primitive transportation hindered western settlement. The construction of canals dramatically transformed this situation during the 1820s and 1830s. The most impressive was the 363-mile-long Erie Canal, the last link in a chain of waterways connecting New York City to the Northwest. The volume of goods and people it carried at low cost demonstrated the economic benefits of this mode of transportation and encouraged the construction of over 3,000 miles of canals by 1840.

•••⌐Read the **Document**
Erie Canal (1819)
at **www.myhistorylab.com**

((••⌐Hear the **Audio**
The Erie Canal
at **www.myhistorylab.com**

But even at the height of the canal boom, politicians and promoters, impressed by Britain's success with railways, supported the construction of railroads. Canals froze in the winter, but railroads could operate all year round and could be built almost anywhere. These advantages encouraged

Significant Factors Promoting Economic Growth, 1820–1860

Factor	Important Features	Contribution to Growth
Abundant natural resources	Acquisition of new territories (Louisiana Purchase, Florida, trans-Mississippi West); exploitation and discovery of eastern resources	Provided raw materials and energy vital to economic transformation
Substantial population growth	Increase from 9 million in 1820 to over 30 million in 1860—due to natural increase of population and, especially after 1840, to rising immigration; importance of immigration from Ireland, Germany	Provided workers and consumers necessary for economic growth; immigration increased diversity of workforce with complex results, among them supply of capital and technological know-how
Transportation revolution	Improvement of roads; extensive canal building, 1817–1837; increasing importance of railroad construction thereafter; by 1860, 30,000 miles of tracks; steamboats facilitate travel on water	Facilitated movement of people, goods, and information; drew people into national economic market; stimulated agricultural expansion, regional crop specialization; decreased costs of shipping goods; strengthened ties between Northeast and Midwest
Capital investment	Investments by European investors and U.S. interests; importance of mercantile capital and banks, insurance companies in funneling capital to economic enterprises	Provided capital to support variety of new economic enterprises, improvements in transportation
Government support	Local, state, and national legislation; loans favoring enterprise; judicial decisions	Provided capital, privileges, and supportive climate for economic enterprises

Baltimore merchants, envious of New York's water link to the Northwest, to begin the Baltimore & Ohio Railroad in 1828.

The first trains jumped their tracks and their sparks set fields ablaze, but such technical difficulties were quickly overcome. By 1840, there were 3,000 miles of track, mostly in the Northeast. Ten years later, total mileage soared to 30,000. Like canals, railroads strengthened links between the Old Northwest and the East and eventually fostered shared political outlooks.

Some historians use the term "Transportation Revolution" to suggest the importance of improved transportation for economic development.

Goods, people, and information flowed more predictably, rapidly, and cheaply. Canals and railroads gave farmers, merchants, and manufacturers inexpensive, reliable access to distant markets and goods and fostered technological innovations that, in turn, spurred production. Transportation links stimulated regional specialization and agricultural expansion as farmers began to plant larger, more specialized crops for the market—grain in the Old Northwest, dairy goods and produce in New England. By 1860, American farmers were producing four to five times as much wheat, corn, cattle, and hogs as in 1810. American workers had plentiful, cheap food, and farmers had more income to spend on new consumer goods.

Improved transportation encouraged Americans to settle the frontier. Railroads exerted enormous influence in shaping the pattern of western settlement. As the railroads followed—or led—settlers westward, their routes could determine whether a city, a town, or even a homestead survived and prospered. The railroad transformed Chicago from a small settlement into a bustling commercial and transportation center.

◄•►[Watch the Video

Coming of Age in 1833 (a Great Period of Change/ Reinvention of the World)

at **www.myhistorylab.com**

Capital and Government Support

Internal improvements, the exploitation of natural resources, and the cultivation of new lands demanded capital. American mercantile capital contributed to the development of enterprises ranging from canals to textile factories. Europeans also played an important role in stimulating expansion. Between 1790 and 1861, Europeans invested more than $500 million in the United States. These funds, along with savings brought by immigrant families, financed as much as a third of all canal construction and purchased almost a quarter of all railroad bonds.

Local and state government enthusiastically supported economic growth. States often helped new ventures raise capital by passing laws of incorporation, by awarding entrepreneurs tax breaks or monopolies, by underwriting bonds for improvement projects (which increased their investment appeal), and by providing loans for internal improvements. New York, Pennsylvania, Ohio, Indiana, Illinois, and Virginia publicly financed almost 75 percent of the canal systems in their states between 1815 and 1860.

The national government also encouraged economic expansion by cooperating with states on some internal improvements, such as the national road from Maryland to Illinois. Federal tariff policy shielded American products, and the second Bank of the United States provided the financial stability investors required. So widespread was the enthusiasm for growth that the line separating the public sector from the private often blurred.

The law also undergirded aggressive economic growth. Judicial decisions created a new understanding of property rights and increased predictability in the conduct of business. The case of *Palmer* v. *Mulligan*, decided by the New York State Supreme Court in 1805, determined that property ownership included the right to develop property for business purposes. Land was increasingly defined as a productive asset for exploitation, not merely subsistence. Contracts lay at the heart of commercial relationships, but contract law hardly existed in 1800. Between 1819 and 1824, major Supreme Court decisions established the basic principle that contracts were binding. In *Dartmouth College* v. *Woodward*, the Court held that a state charter could not be modified unless both parties agreed, and in *Sturges* v. *Crowninshield* it declared unconstitutional a New York law allowing debtors to repudiate debts.

A New Mentality

Economic expansion also depended on intangible factors. When a farmer decided to specialize in apples for the New York market rather than to concentrate on raising food for his family, he was thinking in a new way. So was a merchant who invested in banks that would, in turn, finance a variety of economic enterprises. The entrepreneurial outlook—the *"universal desire,"* as one newspaper editor put it, *"to get forward"*—was shared by millions of Americans. By encouraging investment, new business and agricultural ventures, and land speculation, it played a vital role in antebellum development.

Europeans often recognized other intangibles. As one Frenchman observed in 1834, Americans were energetic and open to change. "All here is circulation, motion, and boiling agitation. Experiment follows experiment; enterprise succeeds to enterprise." Some saw an American mechanical "genius." "In Massachusetts and Connecticut," one Frenchman insisted, "there is not a labourer who had not invented a machine or tool." He exaggerated (many American innovations drew on British precedents and were introduced by immigrants familiar with the British originals), but every invention did attract scores of imitators.

Mechanically minded Americans prided themselves on devising efficient tools and machines. The McCormick harvester, the Colt revolver, Goodyear vulcanized rubber products, and the sewing machine—all were developed, refined, and further improved. The process cut labor costs and increased efficiency. By 1840, the average American cotton textile mill was about 10 percent more efficient and 3 percent more profitable than its British counterpart.

Although the labor shortage in the United States stimulated technological innovations that replaced humans with machines, the rapid spread of education after 1800 also spurred innovation and productivity. By 1840, most whites were literate, and public schools were educating 38.4 percent of white children between the ages of 5 and 19. The belief that education meant economic growth fostered enthusiasm for public education, particularly in the Northeast.

The development of the Massachusetts common school illustrates the connections many saw between education and progress. Although several states had decided to use tax monies for education by 1800, Massachusetts was the first to move toward mass education. In 1827, it mandated that taxes pay the whole cost of the state's public schools, and in 1836 it forbade factory managers to hire children who had not spent 3 of the previous 12 months in school. Still, the Massachusetts school system limped along with run-down school buildings, nonexistent curricula, and students with nothing to do.

Under the leadership of **Horace Mann**, the reform of state education for white children began in earnest in 1837. He and others pressed for graded schools, uniform curricula, and teacher training and fought the local control that often blocked progress. Mann's success inspired reformers everywhere. For the first time in American history, primary education became the rule for most children outside the South between ages 5 and 19. The expansion of education created a whole new career of schoolteaching, mostly attracting young women.

Mann believed that education promoted inventiveness. Businessmen often agreed. Prominent industrialists in the 1840s were convinced that education produced reliable workers who could handle complex machinery without undue supervision. Manufacturers valued education not merely because of its intellectual content, but also because it encouraged habits necessary for a disciplined and productive workforce.

Ambivalence Toward Change

While supporting education as a means to economic growth, many Americans also firmly believed in its social value. They expected public schools to mold student character and promote "virtuous habits." Rote learning taught discipline and concentration. The content of schoolbooks reinforced classroom goals.

This concern with education and character suggests that while Americans welcomed economic progress, they also feared its unsettling results. The improvements in transportation that encouraged trade and emigration also raised concerns that civilization might disintegrate as people moved far from familiar institutions. Others worried that rapid change undermined the American family. Schools, which taught students to be deferential, obedient, and punctual, could help counter the worst by-products of change.

Other signs of cultural uneasiness appeared. Popularizers in the 1830s reinforced Benjamin Franklin's message of hard work. As a publishing revolution lowered costs and speeded up printing, out poured tracts, stories, and self-help manuals touting diligence, punctuality, temperance, and thrift. All these habits probably assisted economic growth. But the success of early nineteenth-century economic ventures frequently depended on the ability to take risks. The emphasis these publicists gave to the safe but stolid virtues suggests their fear of social disintegration. Their books and tracts aimed to counter unsettling effects of change and reinforce **middle-class values**.

The Advance of Industrialization

As had been true for Great Britain in the eighteenth century, the advance of industrialization in the United States fueled economic growth in the decades before the Civil War. As was also the case in Britain, economic changes spilled over to transform many other aspects of life. The types of work people did, the places where they labored, and the relationships they had with their bosses were all affected by new modes of production. The American class system was modified as a new working class dependent on wages emerged and as a new middle class took shape.

Factory production moved away from the decentralized system of artisan or family-based manufacturing using hand tools and reorganized work by breaking down the manufacture of an article into discrete steps. Manufacturers farmed out some steps to workers, both urban and rural, in shops and homes, paying them by the piece. This was the "putting-out" system. But other steps in the production process were consolidated in central shops, and eventually all the steps of production came under one roof, with hand labor gradually giving way to power-driven machinery such as "spinning jennies."

Sometimes, would-be American manufacturers sought the help of British immigrants with the experience and know-how that no American yet possessed. Thus in 1789 William Ashley and Moses Brown, Rhode Island merchants, hired 21-year-old Samuel Slater, a former apprentice in an English cotton textile mill, to devise a water-powered, yarn-spinning machine. Slater did that, but he also developed a machine capable of carding, or straightening, the cotton fibers. Within a year, Ashley and Brown's spinning mill had begun operations in Pawtucket, Rhode Island. Its initial workforce consisted of nine children, ranging in age from 7 to 12. Ten years later, their number had grown to more than 100. As factory workers replaced artisans and home manufacturers, the volume of goods rose, and prices dropped dramatically. The price of a yard of cotton cloth fell from 18 to 2 cents during the 45 years preceding the Civil War.

The transportation improvements that gave access to large markets after 1820 also encouraged the reorganization of production and the use of machinery. The simple tastes and rural character of the American people suggested the wisdom of manufacturing inexpensive everyday goods such as cloth and shoes rather than luxuries for the rich.

Between 1820 and 1860, textile manufacturing became the country's leading industry. Textile mills sprang up across the New England and middle Atlantic states. These regions had swift-flowing streams to power the mills, capitalists eager to finance ventures, children and women willing to tend machines, and numerous cities and towns with ready markets for cheap textiles. Early mills were small, containing only the machines for carding and spinning. The thread was then put out to home workers, who wove it into cloth. The early mechanization of cloth production supplemented, but did not replace, home manufacture.

Experiments were under way that would further transform the industry. In 1813, Boston merchant Francis Cabot Lowell and mechanic Paul Moody devised a power loom to weave cloth, based on Lowell's study of mechanical looms in England and Scotland. Eventually, they installed their loom in a mill at Waltham, Massachusetts, capitalized at $300,000 by Lowell and his Boston Associates.

The most important innovation of the Waltham operation was Lowell's decision to combine all the steps of cotton cloth production and all the workers under one roof. The Waltham mill thus differed from mills in Rhode Island and Great Britain, which separated spinning and weaving. Centralization allowed the profitable mass production of inexpensive cloth. In 1823, the Boston Associates expanded their operations to Lowell, a renamed village on the Merrimack River. The Lowell system became the prototype for most New England mills. Although most of the South's cotton went to England, an increasing share flowed to northeastern mills.

The cumulative impact of the rise of the textile industry was to supplant the home production of cloth, though some women would continue to spin and weave for their families and hand-loom weavers would survive for another generation. More and more, Americans abandoned earth-colored homespun garments for clothes made of colorful manufactured cloth.

Textile mills and other manufacturing such as shoemaking gave the Northeast an increasingly industrial character. By 1860, fully 71 percent of all manufacturing workers lived there. Elsewhere, in communities of 200 families or more, power-driven machinery processed wheat, timber, and hides. Although a third of them were clustered in Philadelphia, paper mills were widespread. Ironworking and metalworking stretched from Albany, New York, to Maryland and Cincinnati.

THE MANCHESTER PRINT WORKS, AT MANCHESTER, N. H.

A New Hampshire Printing Factory Gleason's Pictorial, one of the many modestly priced publications that the introduction of steam-powered printing presses put within reach of the reading public, pictures the Manchester Print Works in New Hampshire in 1854. How has the mill complex been depicted? What signs of pollution does the picture suggest? Men appear in the foreground, but over half the workers in this calico factory were female.

Environmental Consequences

Although canals, railroads, steamboats, and the growth of industry stimulated economic growth, their impact on the environment was far-reaching.
Dams and canals supporting industrial activities contributed to erosion.
Wood used as fuel for steamboats, early railroads, and household stoves
meant the destruction of eastern forests and their wildlife. Better transportation, which encouraged western migration, contributed to the disappearance of forest cover as settlers cleared land for crops and cut wood for
housing. Sawmills and milldams interfered with the spawning of fish and
changed the flow of rivers.

As late as 1840, wood provided for most of the country's energy
needs. But its high price and the discovery of anthracite coal in Pennsylvania signaled the beginning of a shift to coal as the
major power source. While the East gradually regained some of its forest cover, the heavy use of coal
polluted the air. Acrid smells and black soot were part
of urban life.

View the Image

*Anti-Railroad Poster in
Philadelphia (1839)*

at **www.myhistorylab.com**

Some Americans recognized the environmental consequences of rapid
growth and change. "Industrial operations," declared the Vermont fish commissioner in 1857, are "destructive to fish that live or spawn in fresh water."
Novelist James Fenimore Cooper had one of his characters in *The Pioneers*
condemn those who destroyed nature "without remorse and without shame."
Yet most Americans accepted a changing environment as the price of progress.

Early Manufacturing

Industrialization created a more efficient means of producing more goods at
a much lower cost. A Philadelphian's diary described the new profusion and
range of goods that he saw at an exhibition of American manufactures in
1833. "More than 700 articles have been sent," he noted. "Among this great
variety, I distinguished the Philadelphia porcelains, beautiful Canton cotton,
made at York in this state, soft and capacious blankets, silver plate, cabinet
ware, marble mantels, splendid pianos and centre tables, chymical drugs,
hardware, saddlery, and the most beautiful black broadcloth I ever saw."

Two examples illustrate how industrialization transformed American
life in both simple and complex ways. Before the nineteenth century, local
printing shops used manual labor to produce relatively expensive books
and newspapers. Many literate families had little to read other than a Bible
and an almanac. Between 1830 and 1850, however, the adoption and improvement of British inventions revolutionized the American printing
and publishing industries. Like other changes in production, the transformation of publishing involved not only technological innovations, but also
managerial and marketing changes. A $2.5 million market in 1830, the book
business quintupled by 1850.

As books and magazines dropped in cost and grew in number, far more people could afford them. This new mass market of readers provided the basis for Susan Warner's literary success. Inexpensive reading material inspired and nourished literacy, and it encouraged a new sort of independence. Freed of depending on the "better sort" for information, people could form their own views from what they read. At the same time, however, readers everywhere were exposed repeatedly to the mainstream norms expressed in magazines and books. Even pioneer women could study inexpensive ladies' magazines or draw inspiration from *The Wide, Wide World*. Their husbands could follow political news, prices, and theories about scientific farming; their children learned to read from the moralistic McGuffey readers.

Meanwhile, the making of inexpensive timepieces affected the pace and rhythms of American life. Before the 1830s, owning a clock was a luxury, making exact planning and scheduling almost impossible. But by midcentury, inexpensive mass-produced clocks could be found everywhere, encouraging a more disciplined use of time. Timepieces were essential for the successful operation of railroads and steamboats and imposed a new rhythm in many workplaces—for some Americans, representing a new form of oppression.

A New England Textile Town

The process of industrialization and its impact on work and the workforce are well illustrated by Lowell, the "model" Massachusetts textile town, and Cincinnati, a bustling midwestern industrial center. Though the communities shared certain traits, there were also significant differences. Lowell reveals the importance of women in the early stages of industrialization, while Cincinnati shows that industrialization was often an uneven and complex process.

•**⟨**Read the Document

"Visit to the Shakers,"
Lowell Offering (1841)

at **www.myhistorylab.com**

Lowell was planned and built for industrial purposes in the 1820s. Planners focused on its shops, mills, and worker housing, but the bustling town had a charm that prompted visitors to see it as a model factory community. In 1836, Lowell, with 17,000 inhabitants, was the country's most important textile center.

Lowell's planners, understanding the difficulty of luring men away from farming, realized that they might recruit unmarried women relatively cheaply for a stint in the mills. Unlike factory owners farther south, they decided not to depend on child labor. By hiring women who would work only until marriage, they hoped to avoid the "depraved" and depressed workforce so evident in Great Britain. They envisioned New England factory communities as models for the world. By 1830, women composed nearly 70 percent of the Lowell textile workforce. As the first women to labor outside their homes in large numbers, they were also among the first Americans to experience the full impact of the factory system.

Working and Living in a Mill Town

At the age of 15, Mary Paul wrote to her father asking him "to consent to let me go to Lowell if you can." This young woman from Vermont was typical of those drawn to work in Lowell. In 1830, more than 63 percent of Lowell's population was female, and most were between the ages of 15 and 29.

Women workers came from New England's middling rural families to the mills for a variety of reasons, but desperate poverty was not one of them. The decline of home manufacture deprived many women, especially daughters in farming families, of their traditional productive role. Some had already earned money at home by taking in piecework. Millwork offered them a chance for economic independence, better wages than domestic service, and an interesting environment. Few made a permanent commitment by coming to Lowell. They came to work for a few years, felt free to go home or to school for a few months, and then return to millwork. Once married—and the majority of women did marry—they left the mill workforce forever.

Millwork was regimented and exhausting. Six days a week, the workers began their 12-hour day at dawn or earlier with only a half hour for breakfast and lunch. Within the factory, the organization of space facilitated production. In the basement was the waterwheel, the source of power. Above, successive floors were completely open, each containing the machines necessary for the different steps of cloth making. Elevators moved

View the Image

Mill in West Virginia
at **www.myhistorylab.com**

materials from one floor to another. Under the watchful eyes of male overseers, the women tended their machines. Work spaces were noisy, poorly lit, and badly ventilated, the windows often nailed shut.

Millwork required the women to adapt to both new work and new living situations. Hoping to attract respectable and productive female workers, mill owners built company boardinghouses for them. Headed by female housekeepers, the boardinghouse maintained strict rules, including a 10 P.M. curfew, and afforded little personal privacy. The cramped quarters encouraged close ties and a sense of community. Group norms dictated acceptable behavior, clothing, and speech. Shared leisure activities included lectures, night classes, sewing and literary circles, and church.

Female Responses to Work

Millwork offered better wages than other occupations open to women, but female workers had limited job mobility and received lower wages than men. Even those with the best female positions never earned as much as senior male employees. Economic and job discrimination characterized the American industrial system from the beginning.

Job discrimination generally went unquestioned; but the sense of sisterhood, so central to the Lowell work experience, encouraged protest against a system that workers feared was turning them into dependent wage earners.

Lowell women's critique of the new industrial order drew on both the sense of female community and the revolutionary tradition.

Trouble began when hard times hit Lowell in February 1834. Falling prices, poor sales, and rising inventories prompted managers to announce a 15 percent wage cut. The millworkers sprang into action, threatening a strike. At one lunchtime gathering, the company agent, hoping to end the protests, fired an apparent ringleader. But, as the agent reported, "she declared that every girl in the room should leave with her," then "made a signal, and . . . they all marched out and few returned the ensuing morning." Strikers roamed the streets appealing to other workers and visited other mills. In all, about a sixth of the workforce turned out.

> •••—Read the Document
> *"A Second Peep at Factory Life,"*
> *Lowell Offering (1841–1845)*
> at **www.myhistorylab.com**

Though this work stoppage was brief and failed to prevent the wage reduction, it demonstrated women workers' concern about the impact of industrialization on the labor force. Viewing wage reductions as an attack on their economic independence, strikers linked their protest to their fathers' and grandfathers' struggles against British oppression during the Revolution.

During the 1830s, wage cuts, long hours, increased workloads, and production speedups mandated by owners' desire to protect profits constantly reminded Lowell women and other textile workers of the possibility of "wage slavery." In Dover, New Hampshire, 800 women formed a union in 1834 to protest wage cuts. In the 1840s, women in several New England states agitated for the 10-hour day, and petitions from Lowell prompted the Massachusetts legislature to hold the first official hearings on industrial working conditions.

> •••—Read the Document
> *"A Week in the Mill,"* Lowell
> *Offering, Vol. V (1845)*
> at **www.myhistorylab.com**

The Changing Character of the Workforce

Most protest efforts had limited success. The short tenure of most women millworkers prevented permanent labor organizations, and owners could easily replace strikers. Increasingly, owners found that they could do without the Yankee women altogether. The waves of immigration that deposited so many impoverished foreigners in northeastern cities in the 1840s and 1850s created a new pool of labor, desperate for jobs and willing to work for less than New England farm girls. By 1860, Irish men composed nearly half the workers. A permanent workforce, once the owners' nightmare, became a reality by 1860. Lowell's reputation as a model factory town faded away.

The transformation of the Lowell workforce suggests the far-reaching impact of massive immigration on antebellum life. Immigration, of course, had been a constant part of the country's experience from the early seventeenth century. But what had been a trickle in the 1820s—some 128,502 foreigners came to U.S. shores during that decade—became a torrent in the 1850s, with more than 2.8 million migrants to the United States. The majority of the newcomers were young European men of working age.

This vast movement of people, which continued throughout the nineteenth century, resulted from dramatic changes in European life. Between

1750 and 1845, Europe experienced a population explosion. New farming and industrial practices undermined or destroyed traditional means of livelihood. Agricultural disaster uprooted the Irish from their homeland. In 1845, a terrible blight attacked and destroyed the potato crop, the staple of the Irish peasant diet. Years of famine followed. One million Irish starved to death between 1841 and 1851; another million and a half emigrated. The Irish were the most numerous of all newcomers to America in the two decades preceding the Civil War, usually arriving penniless and with only their unskilled labor to sell.

German immigrants, the second-largest group of immigrants during this period (1,361,506 arrived between 1840 and 1859), were not driven to the United States by the same kind of desperate circumstances as the Irish. Some even arrived with sufficient resources to go west and buy land. Others had the training to join the urban working class as shoemakers, cabinetmakers, and tailors.

The arrival of so many non-British newcomers made American society more diverse. Because more than half of the Irish and German immigrants were Roman Catholics, religious differences exacerbated economic and ethnic tensions.

Factories on the Frontier

Cincinnati, a small Ohio River settlement of 2,540 in 1810, grew to be the country's third-largest industrial center by 1840. With a population of 40,382, it had a variety of industries at different stages of development. Manufacturers who turned out machines, machine parts, hardware, and furniture quickly mechanized. Other trades, like carriage making and cigar making, moved far more slowly toward mechanization. Artisans still labored in small shops, using traditional hand tools. The new and the old coexisted in Cincinnati, as in most manufacturing towns.

No uniform work experience prevailed in Cincinnati. Some craftsmen continued to employ a wide array of skills to produce goods in time-honored ways. Others used their skills in new factories, focusing on more specialized tasks. Though in the long run machines threatened to replace them, skilled factory workers often had reason in the short run to praise the factory's opportunities. Less fortunate was the new class of unskilled factory laborers who performed limited operations at their jobs, with or without machinery. Having no skills, they were easily replaced, and during business slowdowns were casually dismissed.

Cincinnati's working women had a different work experience. A majority of black women labored as washerwomen, cooks, or maids. Many white women earned money as "outworkers" for the city's growing ready-to-wear clothing industry. Manufacturers purchased the cloth, cut it into basic patterns, and then contracted out the finishing work to women in small workshops or at home. Like many other urban women, Cincinnati women sought such employment because their husbands or fathers did not bring

Cincinnati and the Ohio River In 1848, a photographer took this picture of Cincinnati. What indications are there of the causes of the city's growth? While the countryside is visible in the background, what are the signs of Cincinnati's status as a bustling urban center?

in enough to support the family and because outwork allowed them to earn money at home. Middle-class domestic ideology prescribed that home, not the workplace, was the proper sphere for women. Many working men supported these views because they feared female labor would undercut their wages and destroy order in the family.

Paid by the piece, female **outworkers** were among the most exploited of Cincinnati's workers. Long days of sewing in darkened rooms not only often failed to bring an adequate financial reward, but also led to ruined eyes and curved spines. The introduction of sewing machines in the 1850s made stitching easier, increasing both the pool of potential workers and the volume of work expected.

Cincinnati employers claimed that the new industrial order offered great opportunities to most of the city's male citizens. Manufacturing work encouraged the "manly virtues" necessary for the "republican citizen." Not all Cincinnati workers agreed. The workingman's plight, as Cincinnati labor leaders analyzed it, stemmed from his loss of independence. The reorganization of work meant that few could expect to rise from apprentice to independent craftsman. The new worker, with only his raw labor to sell, toiled for others rather than for himself. His "**wage slavery**," or dependence on wages, promised to be lifelong.

Workers also resented attempts to control their lives. In the new factories, owners insisted on a steady pace of work and uninterrupted production. Artisans accustomed to working in spurts, stopping for a few moments of conversation or a drink, disliked the new routines. Those who took a dram or two at work got fired. Even outside the workplace, manufacturers attacked Cincinnati's working-class culture. Middle-class crusades to abolish "nonproductive" volunteer fire companies and saloons suggested how little equality the Cincinnati worker enjoyed in an industrializing society.

The fact that workers' wages in Cincinnati, as in other cities, lagged behind food and housing costs compounded discontent. The working class sensed it was losing ground just as the city's rich were visibly growing richer. In 1817, the top tenth of the city's taxpayers owned over half the wealth, whereas the bottom half possessed 10 percent. In 1860, the share of the top tenth had increased to two-thirds, and the bottom half's share had shrunk to 2.4 percent.

In the decades before the Civil War, Cincinnati workers, like workers in other communities, formed unions, struck for fair wages, and rallied for the 10-hour day. Like the Lowell mill girls, they cloaked their protest with the mantle of the Revolution. Because the Republic depended on a free and independent citizenry, male workers warned that their bosses' policies undermined the Republic itself.

Only in the early 1850s did Cincinnati workers begin to suspect that their employers formed a distinct class of parasitic "nonproducers." Although most strikes still revolved around familiar issues of better hours and wages, signs appeared of the more hostile labor relations that would emerge after the Civil War.

As elsewhere, skilled workers were in the forefront of Cincinnati's labor protest and union activities. But they won only temporary victories. Depression and bad times always hurt labor organizations and canceled employers' concessions. Furthermore, Cincinnati workers did not readily unite, for the uneven pace of industrialization meant that they, unlike the Lowell mill women, had no common working experience. Growing cultural, religious, and ethnic diversity compounded workplace differences. By 1850, almost half the people in the city were foreign-born (mostly German), whereas only 22 percent had been in 1825. Ethnic and religious tensions simmered. Immigrants faced limited job choices and cultural suspicions, which exploded in Cincinnati in the spring of 1855. Americans attacked barricades in German neighborhoods, shouting death threats. Their wrath visited the Irish as well. Ethnic, cultural, and social differences often drove workers apart, enabling businesses to maximize productivity and profits.

Urban Life

Americans experienced the impact of economic growth most dramatically in the cities. In the four decades before the Civil War, the rate of **urbanization** in the United States rose faster than ever before or since. In 1820, about 9 percent of Americans lived in cities (defined as areas with a population of 2,500 or more). Forty years later, almost 20 percent of them did. Older cities such as Philadelphia and New York mushroomed, while new cities such as Cincinnati, Columbus, and Chicago sprang up "as if by enchantment." Urban growth was most dramatic in the East. By 1860, more than a third of the people living in the Northeast were urban residents, compared with only 14 percent of westerners and 7 percent of southerners.

Urbanization played an important role in sustaining economic expansion. The growing number of urban dwellers represented new markets for farmers and for manufacturers of shoes and clothing, furniture and carriages, and cast-iron stoves. City governments purchased cast-iron pipes for sewers and water supply, and city merchants erected cast iron buildings.

The Process of Urbanization

Three distinct types of cities—commercial centers, mill towns, and transportation hubs—emerged during these years of rapid economic growth. Although a lack of waterpower limited industrial development, commercial seaports such as Boston, Philadelphia, and Baltimore expanded steadily and developed diversified manufacturing to supplement the older functions of importing, exporting, and providing services and credit. New York replaced Philadelphia as the country's largest and most important city. The completion of the Erie Canal allowed New York merchants to gain control of much of the trade with the West. By 1840, they had also seized the largest share of the country's import and export trade.

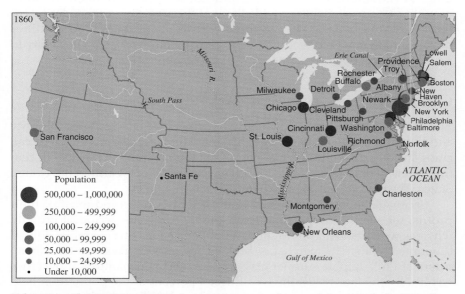

Urban Growth in 1820 and 1850 In 1820, there were few very large cities in the United States, and most of them were located along the Atlantic coast. This map shows urban growth by 1850. What are the important features of the map, and what forces lie behind them? *(Data Source: Statistical Abstract of the United States)*

Access to waterpower spurred the development of a second kind of city, exemplified by Lowell, Massachusetts; Trenton, New Jersey; and Wilmington, Delaware. Situated inland along the waterfalls and rapids that provided the power to run their mills, these cities burgeoned.

A third type of city arose between 1820 and 1840, west of the Appalachian Mountains, where one-quarter of the nation's urban growth occurred. Louisville, Cleveland, and St. Louis typified cities that served as transportation and distribution centers from the earliest days of frontier settlement. In the 1850s, Chicago's most significant business was selling lumber to prairie farmers.

Until 1840, the people eagerly crowding into cities came mostly from the American countryside. Then ships began to spill their human cargoes into eastern seaports. Immigrants who could afford it, many of them Germans or Scandinavians, left crowded port cities for the interior. Those without money sought work in eastern cities. By 1860, fully 20 percent of those living in the Northeast were immigrants; in some of the largest cities, they and their children comprised more than half the population. The Irish were the largest foreign group in the Northeast.

•••─Read the **Document**

Samuel F.B. Morse, Dangers of Foreign Immigration *(1835)* at **www.myhistorylab.com**

While a few cities, such as New York and Boston, provided parks where residents could escape from the sounds, noises, and smells of urban life, much about urban life was grimy and difficult, especially for those who belonged to the working class. Speculators, finding the grid pattern the cheapest and most efficient way to divide land for development, created miles of monotonous new streets and houses. Overwhelmed by rapid growth, city governments provided few of the services we consider essential today, and usually only to those who paid for them. Poor families devoted many hours to securing necessities, including water. The ability to pay for services determined not only comfort, but health.

Class Structure in the Cities

The drastic differences in the quality of urban life reflected social fluidity and the growing economic inequality that characterized many American cities. In contrast to the colonial period, the first half of the nineteenth century witnessed a dramatic rise in the **concentration of wealth** in the United States. The pattern was most extreme in cities.

Because Americans believed that capitalists deserved most of their profits, the well-to-do profited handsomely from this period of growth, whereas workers lost ground. Philadelphia provides one example of these economic trends. The merchants, brokers, lawyers, bankers, and manufacturers of Philadelphia's upper class gained increasing control of the city's wealth. By the late 1840s, the wealthiest 4 percent of the population held about two-thirds of the wealth. Because more wealth was being generated, the widening gap between the upper class and the working class did not cause mass suffering. But growing inequality hardened class lines and contributed to labor protests.

Between 1820 and 1860, a new working and middle class took shape in Philadelphia and elsewhere. As preindustrial ways of producing goods yielded to factory production and as the pace of economic activity quickened, some former artisans and skilled workers seized newly created opportunities. Perhaps 10 to 15 percent of Philadelphians in each decade before the Civil War improved their occupations and places of residence. Increasingly, membership in this middle class meant having a nonmanual occupation and a special place of work suited to activities depending on brainpower rather than brawn. But downward occupational mobility increased. Former artisans or journeymen became part of a new class of permanent manual workers, dependent on wages. Fed by waves of immigrants, the lower class grew at an accelerating rate. The percentage of unskilled wage earners living in poverty or on its brink increased from 17 to 24 percent between 1820 and 1860, while the proportion of craftsmen, once the heart of the laboring class, shrank from 56 to 47 percent.

The Urban Working Class

As with so much else in urban life, housing patterns reflected social and economic divisions. Behind substantial houses on the main streets lay slums in back unpaved alleys and streets, where garbage accumulated and privies overflowed. The poorest rented quarters in crowded, flimsy shacks and two-room houses. Because they moved often, it was difficult for them to create close-knit neighborhoods and support networks.

Slums were not just abodes of poverty; they represented the transformation of working-class family life. Men could no longer be sure of supporting their wives and children; even when they were employed, they felt that they had lost much of their authority and power in the family. The shortage of money contributed to family tensions and misunderstandings. Some men thought their wives too independent or careless with money. One woman angered her husband by failing to explain clearly what she had done with the grocery money. This squabble over grocery money ended in murder. Although this was an extreme case, family violence that spilled out onto the streets was not uncommon in working-class quarters.

Middle-Class Life and Ideals

Members of the new middle class profited from the dramatic increase in wealth in antebellum America. They lived in pleasantly furnished houses, enjoying more peace, more privacy, and more comfort. Franklin stoves gave warmth in winter, and iron cookstoves made cooking easier. New lamps made it possible to read after dark. Bathing stands and bowls ensured higher standards of cleanliness. Genteel behavior, proper dress, and an elegantly furnished parlor all identified one as middle class.

New expectations about male and female roles, prompted partly by economic change, also shaped middle-class life. In the seventeenth and

African Americans in Philadelphia This cartoon was one of a series entitled "Life in Philadelphia." Philadelphia had a large, free African American community that often became the target for racial animosity. In what ways has the cartoonist presented a negative picture of the man and woman in the cartoon? Notice the exaggerated racial features of the two figures and the overelaborate clothing of the dandified man passing his card to the woman coming up from the basement. The verbal message reinforced the visual one. The man asks, "Is Miss Dinah at home?" The woman replies, "Yes sir but she bery potickly engaged in washing de dishes." He replies, "Ah! I'm sorry I cant have the honour to pay my devours to her. Give her my card."

eighteenth centuries, the labor of men and women, adults and children, had all been necessary for the family's economic welfare. But in the nineteenth century, improved transportation, new products, and the rise of factory production and large businesses changed the family economy. Falling prices for processed and manufactured goods such as soap, candles, clothing, and even bread made it unnecessary for women (except those on the frontier) to continue making these items at home.

As men increasingly involved themselves in a money economy, whether through commerce or market farming, women's and children's economic contributions to the family welfare became relatively less significant. Even the rhythm of their lives, oriented to housework rather than the demands of the clock, separated them from their husbands' bustling commercial world. By 1820, these changing circumstances supported the conventional wisdom that the sexes had different innate characteristics and occupied separate spheres.

Men were seen as naturally aggressive, intellectual, and active, at home in the public world of politics, business, and commerce. They were responsible for supporting their families in middle-class comfort—not always an easy duty, as Susan Warner's family experience suggested. Women, by contrast, were perceived as innately pious, virtuous, unselfish, and modest. This conception, based upon ideas first advanced in revolutionary days, suggested that women should operate in the private or domestic sphere, where they would train children in the virtues and habits necessary for the welfare of the Republic and society. Just as important, they were expected to create peaceful retreats for husbands returning from the cares and harried rhythms of the public world.

No longer producers but housekeepers, women discovered both pleasures and frustrations in their new role. Susan Warner celebrated the coziness of domestic life in her novels. Yet it was sometimes impossible to create a harmonious home and meet the new standards of cleanliness, order, and beauty. Catharine Beecher's "Words of Comfort for a Discouraged Housekeeper" listed just some of the problems—inconvenient houses, sick children, poor domestics—that undermined efforts to meet the domestic ideal.

In actuality, the notion of separate spheres was far more flexible in real life than on paper. There was considerable overlap in the activities and roles of men and women. Many middle-class men were involved in child rearing and domestic life, for example, and some middle-class women, like Susan Warner, actually became breadwinners for their families. Furthermore, some aspects of reinterpretation of women's role and nature could encourage women to extend their interest in the public world.

Although the concept of domesticity emphasized women's domestic role, "Woman," as Sarah Hale, editor of the popular magazine *Godey's Lady's Book*, pointed out, was "God's appointed agent of *morality*." This insistence on women's moral nature encouraged women to join voluntary female associations that mushroomed in the early nineteenth century. Although initially most involved religious and charitable activities, women undertook activities in the public world as well, supporting orphanages, paying for and distributing religious tracts and Bibles, establishing Sunday schools, and ministering to the poor. By the 1830s, as we shall see in Chapter 10, women added specific moral concerns including the abolition of slavery to their missionary and benevolent efforts. As these women took on more active and controversial tasks, they often clashed with men and with social conventions about "woman's place."

While domesticity described norms rather than the actual conduct of white middle-class women, the ideas, expressed so movingly by novelists like Susan Warner, influenced how women thought of themselves. They also promoted "female" behavior by encouraging particular choices and helped many women make psychological sense of their lives. New standards for behavior also operated as a way of clarifying social boundaries between the middle class and those below them on the social scale.

Still, the new norms, effectively spread by the publishing industry, also influenced rural and urban working women. The insistence on marriage and service to family discouraged married women from entering the workforce.

RECOVERING *the* PAST

Family Paintings

Although paintings are often admired and studied for artistic reasons alone, their value as historical documents should not be overlooked. In an age before the camera, paintings, sketches, and even pictures done in needlework captured Americans at different moments of life and memorialized their significant rituals. Paintings of American families in their homes, for example, reveal both an idealized conception of family life and the details of its reality. In addition, the paintings provide us with a sense of what the houses of the middle and upper classes (who could afford to commission art) were like.

Artists trained in the European tradition of realism painted family scenes and portraits, but so did many painters who lacked formal academic training, the so-called primitive artists. Their art was abstract in the sense that the artists tended to emphasize what they knew or felt rather than what they actually saw.

Some primitive artists were women who had received some drawing instruction at school. They often worked primarily for their own pleasure. Other artists were craftsmen, perhaps house or sign painters, who painted pictures in their leisure time. Some traveling house decorators made a living by making paintings and wall decorations. Many primitive paintings are unsigned, and even when we know the painter's identity, we rarely know more than a name and perhaps a date. Primitive artists flourished in the first three-quarters of the nineteenth century, eventually supplanted by the camera and inexpensive prints.

We see here a painting of the Sargent family by an unknown artist around 1800. Though not an exact representation of reality, it does convey what the artist and the buyer considered important and how the family wished to be viewed. Like any piece of historical evidence, this painting must be approached critically and carefully. First, study the family itself. How many family members are there, and what is each one doing? What objects are associated with each person? What seems to be the relationship between husband and wife? Why do you think Mr. Sargent is painted with his hat on? Who seems to dominate the painting, and how is this dominance conveyed?

Why do you think the artist included a ball and a dog in this scene of family life? What do these choices suggest about attitudes toward children and their upbringing? What seems to be the role of the children in the family?

Finally, observe the objects and decoration of the room. Make an inventory of the objects and furnishings and compare it to present-day interiors. How comfortable was the family? What nonessential items did they own? Why do you think the chairs are placed near the window and door? What kind of scene does the window frame? What can we learn about daily life from the painting?

Reverend John Atwood and His Family, painted by Henry F. Darby in 1845, is a more detailed painting showing a larger family gathering several decades later. Similar questions can be asked about this painting, especially about new expectations for middle-class children. The family's living room can be contrasted with the Sargent family's room to reveal some of the changes brought about by industrialization. How many items does the family have that were manufactured? What does this family have that the Sargent family does not?

Note the depiction of husband and wife in the two paintings. How do they differ?

REFLECTING ON THE PAST As you compare these two paintings, can you find hints that the position of middle-class women was changing as the nineteenth century progressed? What do the paintings reveal about new consumption habits in the middle class?

The Sargent Family, 1800. *("The Sargent Family," gift of Edgar William and Bernice Chrysler Garbisch, Image © 2003 Board of Trustees, National Gallery of Art, Washington, D.C.)*

Henry Darby, "Reverend John Atwood and His Family," 1845. *(Henry F. Darby, "Reverend John Atwood and His Family". 1845. Oil on Canvas. 72: × 96 1/4". Gift of Maxim Karolik to the M. and M. Karolik Collection of American Paintings, 1815–1865, 1962. Courtesy, Museum of Fine Arts, Boston. Reproduced with permission. © 2003 Museum of Fine Arts, Boston. All Rights Reserved.)*

Those who had to work often harbored guilty feelings. Many accepted badly paid piecework in order to stay home. Though the new feminine ideal may have suited middle-class women in cities and towns, it created difficult tensions in the lives of working-class women.

As family roles were reformulated, a new view of childhood emerged. Middle-class children were no longer expected to contribute economically to the family. Middle-class parents now came to see childhood as a special stage of life, a period of preparation for adulthood. In a child's early years, mothers were to impart important values, including the necessity of behaving in accordance with gender prescriptions. Harsh punishments lost favor. Children's fiction, which poured off the printing presses, reinforced maternal training, picturing modest youngsters happily making the correct choices of playmates and activities, obeying their parents, and being dutiful, religious, loving, and industrious. Schooling also prepared a child for the future, and urban middle-class parents supported the public school movement.

New notions of family life that emphasized a child's need for affection and careful preparation for adulthood suggested smaller families and the use of contraception. The declining birthrate evident first in the Northeast, particularly in cities and among the middle class, shows that families were limiting births. Abortion, which was legal in many states until 1860, terminated perhaps as many as a third of all pregnancies. Other birth control methods included coitus interruptus and abstinence. The success of these methods that relied on self-control suggests that many men and women may have internalized the view of the female sex as naturally affectionate but passionless and sexually restrained.

Mounting Urban Tensions

The social and economic changes transforming American cities and festering ethnic and racial tensions in the half century before the Civil War produced unprecedented urban violence. Mob actions sometimes lasted for days because there was no force strong enough to quell group disorder. Traditional constables and night watches did not try to stop crimes, discover offenses, or "prevent a tumult," and cities were slow to establish modern police forces.

An unsavory riot in Philadelphia in August 1834 revealed not only racial and social antagonisms but also the inability of the city's police force to control the mob. Starting off with the destruction of a merry-go-round patronized by both blacks and whites, the riot turned into an orgy of destruction, looting, and intimidation of black residents. In the several days of violence, at least one black was killed and numerous others injured. As one shocked eyewitness reported, "The mob exhibited more than fiendish brutality, beating and mutilating some of the old, confiding and unoffending blacks with a savageness surpassing anything we could have believed men capable of."

This racial explanation overlooked the range of causes underlying the rampage of fury and destruction. The rioters were young and generally of low social standing. Many were Irish; some had criminal records. A number of those arrested, however, were from a "class of mechanics of whom better things are expected," and middle-class onlookers egged the mob on. The rioters revealed that in the event of an "attack by the city police, they confidently counted" on the assistance of these bystanders.

The mob's composition hints at some of the reasons for participation. Many of the rioters were newly arrived Irish immigrants at the bottom of the economic ladder who competed with blacks for jobs. Subsequent violence against blacks suggested that economic rivalry was an important component of the riot. But if blacks threatened the dream of advancement of some whites, this was not the complaint of the skilled workers. These men were more likely to have believed themselves injured by a changing economic system that undermined the small-scale mode of production. Dreams of a better life seemed increasingly illusory as declining wages pushed them closer to unskilled workers than to the middle class. Like other rioters, they were living in one of the poorest and most crowded parts of the city. Their immediate scapegoats were blacks, but the intangible villain was the economic system itself.

Urban expansion also figured as a factor in the racial violence. Most of the rioters lived either in the riot area or nearby. Racial tensions generated by squalid surroundings and social proximity go far to explain the outbreak of violence. The same area would later become the scene of race riots and election trouble and became infamous for harboring criminals and juvenile gangs. The absence of middle- or upper-class participants did not mean that these groups were untroubled during times of growth and change, but their material circumstances cushioned them from some of the more unsettling forces.

Philadelphia, like other eastern cities, was beginning to build a police force, but only continued disorder would convince residents and city officials there (and in other large cities) to support an expanded, quasi-military, preventive, and uniformed police force. By 1855, most sizable eastern cities had such forces.

Finally, the character of the free black community itself was a factor in producing those gruesome August events. Not only was the community large and visible, but it also had created its own institutions and its own elite. The mob vented its rage against black affluence by targeting the solid brick houses of middle-class blacks and robbing them of silver and watches. Black wealth threatened the notion of the proper social order held by many white Philadelphians and seemed unspeakable when whites could not afford life's basic necessities or lacked jobs.

The Black Underclass

Despite the emergence of small African American elites, most blacks failed to benefit from economic expansion and industrial progress. Black men, often with little or no education, held transient and frequently dangerous jobs. Black women, many of whom headed their households because men were away working or had died, held jobs before and after marriage. In Philadelphia in 1849, almost half of the black women washed clothes for a living. Others took boarders into their homes, adding to their domestic chores.

Northern whites, like southerners, believed in black inferiority and depravity and feared black competition for jobs and resources. Although northern states had passed gradual abolition acts between 1780 and 1803 and the national government had banned slaves from the Northwest Territory, nowhere did any government extend equal rights and citizenship or economic opportunities to free blacks. In the 1830s, black men in most northern states began losing the right to vote, and by 1840 fully 93 percent of the northern free black population lived in states where law or custom kept them from the polls. In five northern states, blacks could not testify against whites or serve on juries. In most states, the two races were thoroughly segregated in railway cars, steamboats, hospitals, prisons, and other asylums. In some states, they could enter public buildings only as personal servants of white men. They sat in "Negro pews" in churches and took communion only after whites had left the church.

As the Philadelphia riot revealed, whites were driving blacks from their jobs. In 1839, *The Colored American* blamed the Irish. "These impoverished and destitute beings . . . are crowding themselves into every place of business . . . and driving the poor colored American citizen out." Increasingly after 1837, these "white niggers" became coachmen, stevedores, barbers, cooks, house servants—all occupations blacks had once held.

Educational opportunities for blacks were also severely limited. Only a few school systems admitted blacks, in separate facilities. In 1833, when Prudence Crandall, a Quaker schoolmistress in Canterbury, Connecticut, tried to admit "young colored ladies and Misses" to her private school, townspeople used intimidation and violence to block her. Eventually she was arrested, and after two trials—in which free blacks were declared to have no citizenship rights—she finally gave up and moved to Illinois.

Crandall likely did not find the Old Northwest much more hospitable. The fast-growing western states were intensely committed to white supremacy and black exclusion. In 1829, in Cincinnati, where evidence of freedom papers and a $500 bond were demanded of blacks who wanted to live in the city, white rioters ran nearly 2,000 blacks out of town. An Indiana senator proclaimed in 1850 that a black could "never live together equally" with whites because "the same power that has given him a black skin, with less weight or volume of brain, has given us a white skin with greater volume of brain and intellect." Abraham Lincoln in neighboring Illinois, soon to be a nationally prominent politician, would not have disagreed.

Rural Communities

Although the percentage of families involved in farming fell from 72 to 60 percent between 1820 and 1860, agriculture represented the country's most significant economic activity and the source of most of its exports. The small family farm still characterized eastern and western agriculture.

Agriculture changed in the antebellum period, however. Vast new tracts of land came under cultivation in the West. Railroads, canals, and better roads drew rural Americans into a wider world. Some crops were shipped to regional markets; others, such as grain, hides, and pork, stimulated industrial processing. Manufactured goods, ranging from cloth to better tools, flowed in return to farm families. Like city dwellers, farmers and their families read books, magazines, and papers that exposed them to new ideas. Commercial farming encouraged different ways of thinking and acting and lessened the isolation that was so typical before 1820.

Farming in the East

Antebellum economic changes created new rural patterns in the Northeast. Marginal lands in New England, New York, and Pennsylvania, cultivated as more fertile lands ran out, yielded discouraging returns. Gradually, after 1830, farmers abandoned these farms, forest reclaimed farmland, and the New England hill country began a slow decline.

Those farmers who did not migrate west had to transform production. Unable to compete with western grain, they embraced new agricultural opportunities created by better transportation and growing urban markets. The extension of railroad lines into rural areas, for example, allowed farmers as far away as Vermont to ship cooled milk to the city. Other farmers used the new railroads to ship fruit and vegetables to the cities. By 1837, a Boston housewife could buy a wide variety of fresh vegetables and fruits, ranging

Preparing for Market This 1856 print shows the farm as a center of human and animal activity. What signs of the shifts in eastern agriculture can you find as farmers responded to competition from the Midwest? The rise of commercial farming also encouraged technological innovations like the McCormick reaper, patented in 1834.

from cauliflower to raspberries, at the central market. Cookbooks began to include recipes calling for fresh ingredients.

As northern farmers adopted new crops, they began to regard farming as a scientific endeavor. After 1800, northern farmers started using manure as fertilizer; by the 1820s, some farmers were rotating their crops and planting new grasses and clover to restore fertility to the soil. These techniques recovered worn-out wheat and tobacco lands in Maryland and Delaware for livestock farming. While farmers in the Delaware River valley were leaders in adopting new methods, interest in scientific farming was widespread. New journals informed readers of modern farming practices, and many states established agricultural agencies. Although wasteful farming practices did not disappear, they became less characteristic of the Northeast. Improved farming methods contributed to increased agricultural output and helped reverse a 200-year decline in farm productivity in some of the oldest areas of settlement. A "scientific" farmer in 1850 could often produce two to four times as much per acre as in 1820. Experimentation and the exchange of information also led to the development of thousands of special varieties of plants for local conditions by 1860.

Rural attitudes also changed. Cash transactions replaced the exchange of goods. Country stores became more reluctant to accept wood, rye, corn, oats, and butter as payment for goods instead of cash. As some farmers adopted the "get-ahead" ethic and entered the market economy, those who were content with just getting along fell behind. Wealth inequality increased throughout the rural Northeast.

Frontier Families

In 1820, less than one-fifth of the American population lived west of the Appalachians. By 1860, almost half did, and Ohio and Illinois had become two of the nation's most populous states.

After the War of 1812, Americans flooded into the Old Northwest, settling first along the Ohio River and sending corn and pork down the Ohio and

●●●—[Read the Document

The Western Country, Letters in Nile's Weekly Register, 19th Century at **www.myhistorylab.com**

Mississippi to southern buyers. By 1830, Ohio, Indiana, and southern Illinois were heavily settled, but Michigan, northern Illinois, Wisconsin, and parts of Iowa and Missouri were still frontier.

The 1830s were boom times in the Old Northwest. Changes in federal land policy, which reduced both prices and the minimum acreage a settler had to buy, helped stimulate migration. Eastern capital contributed to the boom with loans, mortgages, and speculative buying. Inter-

●—[View the Image

American Stage Wagon at **www.myhistorylab.com**

nal improvement schemes after 1830 facilitated settlement and tied the Old Northwest firmly to the East. These links increasingly encouraged farmers to ship wheat east rather than concentrating on corn and hogs for the southern market. Between 1840 and 1860, Illinois, southern Wisconsin, and eastern Iowa became the country's fastest-growing grain regions.

Although the Old Northwest passed rapidly through the frontier stage between 1830 and 1860, its farming families faced severe challenges. Western farms were small, for there were limits to what a family with hand tools could manage. A family with two healthy men could care for about 50 acres. In wooded areas, it took several years to get even that much land under cultivation, for only a few acres could be cleared in a year.

It took capital to begin farming—a minimum initial investment of perhaps $100 for 80 acres of government land, $300 for basic farming equipment, and another $100 or $150 for livestock. To buy an already "improved" farm cost more, and free bidding at government auctions could drive the price of unimproved federal land far above the minimum price. Once farmers moved onto the prairies of Indiana and Illinois, they needed an initial investment of about $1,000, because they had to buy materials for fencing, housing, and expensive steel plows. If farmers invested in the new horse-drawn reapers, they could cultivate more land, but all their costs also increased.

Opportunities in the Old Northwest

It was possible to begin farming with less, however. Some farmers borrowed; others rented land from farmers with more acres than they could manage. Tenants furnishing their own seeds and animals could expect to keep about a third of the yield, and within a few years some could buy their own farms. Those without capital could earn good wages as farmhands. Five to ten years of frugal living and steady work would bring the sum needed to get started. Probably about a quarter of the western farm population consisted of young men laboring as tenants or hired hands.

Widespread ownership of land characterized western rural communities. Unlike in the cities, there was no growing class of propertyless wage earners. But there were inequalities. In Butler County, Ohio, for example, 16 percent of people leaving wills in the 1830s held half the wealth; by 1860, the wealthiest 8 percent held half the wealth. Nevertheless, the Northwest offered many American families the chance to become independent producers and to enjoy a "pleasing competence." The rigors of frontier life faded with time.

Commercial farming brought new patterns of family life. As one Illinois farmer told his wife and daughter, "Store away . . . all of your utensils for weaving cloth up in the loft. The boys and I can make enough by increasing our herds." Many farm families had money to spend on new goods. As early as 1836, the *Dubuque Visitor* was advertising the availability of ready-made clothing and "Calicoes, Ginghams, Muslins, Cambricks, Laces and Ribbands."

Agriculture and the Environment

Shifting agricultural patterns in the East and expanding settlement into the Old Northwest contributed to the changing character of the American landscape. John Audubon, the naturalist, mused in 1826 that "a century hence," the rivers, swamps, and mountains "will not be here as I see them." A French visitor remarked that Americans would never be satisfied until they had subdued nature.

More than the subjugation of nature was involved, however. When eastern farmers abandoned marginal lands, the process of reforestation was under way. When they changed their agricultural practices as they became involved in the market economy, their decisions left an imprint on the land. Selling wood and potash stimulated clearing of forests. So did the desire for new tools, plow castings, threshing machines, or wagon boxes, which were produced in furnaces fueled by charcoal. As forests disappeared, so did their wildlife. Even using mineral manures such as gypsum or lime or organic fertilizers such as guano to revitalize worn-out soil and increase crop yields depleted land elsewhere.

When farmers moved into the Old Northwest, they used new steel plows, like the one developed in 1837 by Illinois blacksmith John Deere. Unlike older eastern plows, the new ones could cut through the dense, tough prairie cover. Deep plowing and the intensive cultivation of large cash crops had immediate benefits. But these practices could rob the soil of necessary minerals. When farmers built new timber houses as frontier conditions receded, they speeded the destruction of the country's forests.

Conclusion

The Character of Progress

Between 1820 and 1860, the United States experienced tremendous growth and economic development. Transportation improvements facilitated the movement of people, goods, and ideas. Larger markets stimulated both agricultural and industrial production. There were more goods and ample food for the American people. Cities and towns were established and thrived. Visitors constantly remarked on the amazing bustle and rapid pace of American life. The United States was, in the words of one Frenchman, "one gigantic workshop, over the entrance of which there is the blazing inscription 'no admission here, except on business.'"

Although the wonders of American development dazzled foreigners and Americans alike, economic growth had its costs, as the example of Susan Warner suggested at the chapter's beginning. Expansion was cyclic, and financial panics and depression punctuated the era. Even middle-class families like the Warners might face financial ruin. Workers discovered that industrial profits derived partly from low wages paid to them. Time-honored routes to economic independence disappeared, and a large class of unskilled, impoverished workers appeared in U.S. cities. Growing inequality characterized urban and rural life, prompting some labor activists to criticize new economic and social arrangements. But workers, still largely unorganized, did not speak with one voice. Ethnic, racial, and religious diversity divided Americans in new and troubling ways.

Yet a basic optimism and sense of pride also characterized the age. To observers, however, it frequently seemed as if the East and the Old Northwest were responsible for the country's achievements. During these decades, many noted that the paths between the East, Northwest, and South seemed to diverge. The rise of King Cotton in the South, where slave rather than free labor formed the foundation of the economy, created a new kind of tension in American life that would prove increasingly disruptive as time passed.

TIME*line*

1820	Lowell founded by Boston Associates
	Land Act of 1820
	The expression "woman's sphere" becomes current
1824–1850	Construction of canals in the Northeast
1825–1856	Construction of canals linking the Ohio, the Mississippi, and the Great Lakes
1828	Baltimore & Ohio Railroad begins operation
1830s	Boom in the Old Northwest
	Increasing discrimination against free blacks
	Public education movement spreads
1837–1844	Financial panic and depression
1840s–1850s	Rising tide of immigration

✓•⌐Study and Review at **www.myhistorylab.com**

Questions for Review and Reflection

1. List what you consider the most significant factors underlying American economic growth, and explain why you think those factors were so important.

2. Explain the ways in which Great Britain contributed to American economic development. How was American industry both similar to and different from British industry?

3. Compare and contrast industrialism in Lowell and Cincinnati.

4. How did economic changes transform the American class system and the relationship between classes?

Key Terms

Concentration of wealth 274

Horace Mann 263

Internal improvements 261

Middle-class values 263

Outworkers 271

Urbanization 272

Wage slavery 271

9

Slavery and the Old South

American Stories

A Young Slave Discovers the Path to Freedom

As a young slave, Frederick Douglass was sent by his master to live in Baltimore. When he first met his mistress, Sophia Auld, he was "astonished at her goodness" as she began to teach him to read. Her husband, however, ordered her to stop. Maryland law forbade teaching slaves to read. Master Auld's opposition, however, inspired Douglass "with a desire" to learn.

In the seven years he lived with the Aulds, young Frederick used "various stratagems" to teach himself to read and write. In the narrative of his early life, written after his escape to the North, Douglass acknowledged that his master's "bitter opposition" had helped him achieve his freedom as much as did Mrs. Auld's "kindly aid."

Most slaves did not, like Douglass, escape. But all were as tied to their masters as Douglass was to the Aulds. Nor could whites in antebellum America escape the influence of slavery. Otherwise decent people were often compelled by the "peculiar institution" to act inhumanely. After her husband's interference, Sophia Auld, Douglass observed, was transformed into a demon by the "fatal poison of irresponsible power." Her formerly tender heart turned to "stone" when she ceased teaching him. "Slavery proved as injurious to her," Douglass wrote, "as it did to me."

A slavebreaker, Mr. Covey, to whom Douglass was sent in 1833 to have his will broken, also paid the cost of slavery. Covey succeeded for a time, Douglass reported, in breaking his "body, soul, and spirit" by brutal work and discipline. But one hot August day in 1833, the two men fought a long, grueling battle. Douglass won. Victory, he said, "rekindled the few expiring embers of freedom, and revived within me a sense of my own manhood." Although it would be four more years before his

Chapter Outline

Building a Diverse Cotton Kingdom

Missouri Compromise

Morning: Master and Mistress in the Big House

Noon: Slaves in House and Fields

Night: Slaves in Their Quarters

Resistance and Freedom

Conclusion: Douglass's Dream of Freedom

escape north, the young man never again felt like a slave. The key to Douglass's resistance to Covey's power was not just his strong will, or even the magical root he carried in his pocket, but rather his knowledge of how to jeopardize Covey's livelihood as a slavebreaker. The oppressed survive by knowing their oppressors.

As Mrs. Auld and Covey discovered, as long as some people were not free, no one was free. Douglass observed, "You cannot outlaw one part of the people without endangering the rights and liberties of all people. You cannot put a chain on the ankle of the bondsman without finding the other end of it about your own necks." After quarreling with a house servant, one plantation mistress complained that she "exercises dominion over me—or tries to do it. One would have thought . . . that I was the Servant, she the mistress." Many whites lived in constant fear of a slave revolt. A Louisiana planter recalled that he had "known times here when there was not a single planter who had a calm night's rest; they then never lay down to sleep without a brace of loaded pistols at their sides." In slave folktales, the clever Brer Rabbit usually outwitted the more powerful Brer Fox or Brer Wolf, thus reversing the roles of oppressed and oppressor.

Slavery in America was both an intricate web of human relationships and a labor system. After tracing the economic development of the Old South in a global context, in which slavery and cotton played vital roles, this chapter considers the institution's impact on diverse social groups and the patterns that contributed to the tremendous economic growth of the South from 1820 to 1860. How did slavery affect those who were not members of the planter class? How did it encourage migration to the West? Then we turn to the daily lives and relationships of masters and slaves who, like Douglass and the Aulds, lived, loved, learned, worked, and struggled with one another in the years before the Civil War.

Perhaps no issue in American history has generated as many interpretations or as much emotional controversy as slavery. Three interpretive schools developed over the years, each adding to our knowledge of the peculiar institution. The first saw slavery as a relatively humane and reasonable institution in which plantation owners took care of helpless, childlike slaves. The second depicted slavery as a harsh and cruel system of exploitation. The third, and most recent, interpretation has described slavery from the perspective of the slaves, who did indeed suffer brutal treatment yet nevertheless survived with integrity, self-esteem, and a sense of community and culture.

The first two interpretive schools emphasized sunup to sundown interactions among masters and mostly passive, victimized slaves; the third, however, focuses on the creative energies, agency, and vibrant life in the slave quarters from sundown to sunup. In a unique structure, this chapter follows these masters and slaves through their day, from morning in the Big House through hot afternoon in the fields to the slave cabins at night. In what ways do you see the three interpretive views of slavery reflected here?

Building a Diverse Cotton Kingdom

Many myths obscure our understanding of the **antebellum South**. It was not a monolithic society composed of large cotton plantations worked by hundreds of slaves. While large-plantation agriculture was dominant, most southern whites were not even slaveholders. Most southern farmers lived in two-room cabins. Cotton was the key cash crop in the South, but it was not the only crop grown. Some masters were kindly, but many were not; some slaves were contented, but most were not.

Watch the Video

Moonlight and Magnolias: Creating the Old South

at **www.myhistorylab.com**

There were many Souths. The older Upper South of Virginia, Maryland, North Carolina, and Kentucky grew different staple crops from the newer, Lower or "Black Belt" South, stretching from South Carolina to eastern Texas. Within each state, the economies of flat coastal areas and inland up-country pine forests differed. Further diversity existed between these areas and the Appalachian highlands. Cities such as New Orleans, Charleston, and Richmond differed dramatically from rural areas.

Although the South was diverse, agriculture dominated its economy. Southerners thus placed a high value on agricultural labor and the system of slavery that furnished that labor. Although slavery was also a paternalistic institution, with masters and slaves owing mutual obligations, it increasingly became a capitalistic enterprise intended to maximize profits for its owners.

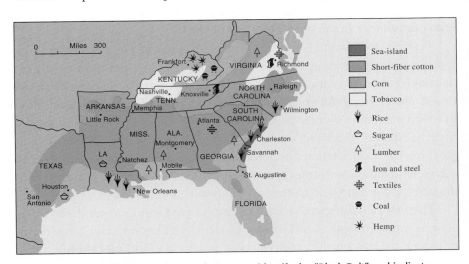

The Varied Economic Life in the South Can you identify the "Black Belt" and indicate which two states had more African slaves than whites? If short-fiber cotton was "king," what crop was "queen"—second most important? Why do you think so?

The Expansion of Slavery in a Global Economy

In the 20 years preceding the Civil War, the South's economy grew slightly faster than the North's. If the South had won independence in 1860, it would have ranked as one of the wealthiest countries in the world per capita, a wealth based mainly on cotton.

◉ See the **Map**
Slavery in the South
at **www.myhistorylab.com**

The world was deeply involved in the tremendous economic growth of the South in the early nineteenth century. The expansion of cotton depended on five factors: technological developments, demand, a global system of trade, land, and labor. The technological breakthrough was the cotton gin, which separated cotton fibers from the sticky seeds in the hardier "short staple" cotton plant. The gin wedded the southern economy to cotton production, increased the need for more land and labor, stimulated slavery's southwestward expansion into vast new territories, and brought the South deeper into a global economy of trade.

Cotton's importance in the worldwide system of trade dated to the late eighteenth century. The inventions of the spinning jenny, flying shuttle, and steam engine led to a flourishing textile industry especially in England. At the same time, European working classes were demanding inexpensive, lightweight cotton clothing to replace heavy linen and woolen clothes. As British textile manufacturers sought to supply this need, they eagerly bought all the cotton they could from the American South. Compared to the importation of 22 million pounds of cotton in the pre–cotton gin year of 1787, by 1840, England imported 366 million pounds!

To meet this demand, southern farmers rushed to the fresh, fertile lands of the Gulf states to plant cotton. Large-plantation owners, who alone could afford to purchase the gins, slaves, and vast lands needed for cotton cultivation, spread the plantation system southwestward. Despite the abolition of slavery in the North and occasional talk of emancipation in the South, slavery became more entrenched in southern life. Thoughts of ending slavery were dispelled by one word: cotton.

Although more acreage was planted in corn, cotton was the largest cash crop and for that reason was called "king." In 1820, the South became the world's largest cotton producer, and from 1815 to 1860, cotton represented more than half of all American exports. Cotton spurred economic growth throughout the country. New England textile mills bought it; northern merchants profitably shipped, insured, and marketed it; and northern bankers acquired capital from cotton sales. The supply of American cotton to Old and New England grew at an astonishing rate. Cotton production soared from 461,000 bales in 1817 to 4.8 million bales in 1860, a more than tenfold jump.

Slavery in Latin America

Slavery in the Americas was not confined to the United States. Africans were enslaved not only in Virginia and the Carolinas but also in Jamaica, Barbados, Cuba, and other European-owned islands in the West Indies, in

Spanish Mexico and Central America, and throughout South America, including Portuguese Brazil, which at 1 million in 1800 had the largest slave population in all the Americas.

Slavery emerged in Latin America from the need for labor where the indigenous population of Indians, decimated by both disease and intermarriage, could not be replaced. Sugar was to Latin America as cotton was to the southern United States, doubling in output at the beginning of the nineteenth century. In the Caribbean and Brazil, slaves were indispensable to the sugarcane industry, providing refined sugar for a growing global market that included rum and other liquor distilleries. By 1840, Cuba was the world's largest producer of cane sugar.

Enslaved Africans also toiled in Peruvian and Chilean vineyards and in cacao, coca, cotton, and tobacco fields throughout Central and South America. They labored in Mexican and South American gold, silver, and copper mines; as construction menials, cowboys, tradesmen, dockworkers, and muleteers for overland and maritime transportation; and as servants to royal and religious officials. Women were generally expected to perform the same physical labor as men.

◉ View the Image

Slave Dockworkers (1860),
Brady Photo
at **www.myhistorylab.com**

Working conditions in Bolivian mines or Brazilian sugar fields were as harsh as in American cotton fields. Slaves labored in gangs yet were held accountable as individuals. With increasing demands for sugar, growers pressured slaves to increase their productivity, which rose from 1,500 to 2,500 pounds per year. Slaves were literally worked to debilitation and death, the average working life in the fields falling from 15 to 7 years. Whippings were used to enforce obedience, and strict supervision and control were maintained to prevent Africans from mixing with Indians or Europeans and from fleeing to communities of escaped slaves in nearby jungles, called maroons.

Perhaps the most distinctive aspect of Latin American slavery compared to the United States was the preponderance of enslaved African men and the absence of women and families. By the nineteenth century, the gender ratio was three men to every two women, with a 2:1 ratio on the sugar estates of Brazil and Cuba; as late as 1875, only one in six Brazilian slaves was recorded as married. The death rate in Latin America was appalling, the result of overwork, tropical diseases, malnutrition, and an extremely high infant mortality rate. With low birthrates and lower life expectancy (age 23 in Brazil, 35 in the United States), the slave population in Latin America actually dropped in the nineteenth century. In 1860, Brazil's slave population reached 1,510,000 compared to over 4 million in the United States.

In the United States, natural births increased the slave population, but Latin Americans used the African slave trade to replenish lost labor. Between 1810 and 1870, after Great Britain and the United States abolished their slave trade in 1807, nearly 2 million Africans were taken to the Americas, 60 percent to Brazil and 32 percent to Cuba and Puerto Rico (2.7 percent were smuggled illegally to the American South). The last American countries to abolish slavery were Cuba (1880) and Brazil (1888). Although Latin America was slow to end slavery officially, intermarriages among Europeans, Indians, and Africans increased the population of free people of color, who by midcentury vastly outnumbered slaves (80 percent in Brazil). It was strikingly different in the United States, where free blacks constituted only 12 percent of all African Americans.

Latin American slaves obtained their freedom in various ways: racial intermarriage, as payment for special favors, in wills upon a master's death, and by purchasing their own freedom by extra work and hiring out. Many Latin American slaves enjoyed relative autonomy and incentives such as presents, privileges, extra rations, holidays, and their own gardens. As one slaveholder manual explained: "the slave who owns neither flees nor causes disorder." Thus, although slave conditions in Latin America were often harsher than in the American South, rights were more fluid, shifting with changing economic and demographic conditions.

White and Black Migrations

Conditions changed in the United States, too. Seeking profits from the British and worldwide demand for cotton, southerners migrated southwestward between 1830 and 1860, pushing the southeastern Indians and Mexicans in Texas out of the way. Like northern grain farmers, southern farmers followed parallel migration paths westward. From the coastal states they trekked westward into the lower Midwest and into the Lower South. By the 1830s, the center of cotton production had shifted from the Southeast to Alabama and Mississippi. This process continued in the 1850s as southerners forged into Arkansas, Louisiana, and eastern Texas.

Not only were these migrating southern families pulled by the prospect of fresh land and cheap slave labor, but they also were pushed westward by deteriorating economic conditions. A long depression in the Upper South beginning in the 1820s affected tobacco and cotton prices, as years of constant use exhausted formerly fertile lands. In a society that valued land ownership, farmers could move west or stay and diversify. Farmers of the Upper South shifted to grains—mainly corn and wheat, which required less slave labor—and to the sale of slaves.

The internal slave trade from Virginia "down the river" to the Old Southwest became a multimillion-dollar "industry" in the 1830s. Between 1830 and 1860, an estimated 300,000 Virginia slaves were transported south for sale. One of the busiest routes was from Alexandria, Virginia, almost within view of the nation's capital, to a huge depot near Natchez, Mississippi. Although most southern states occasionally attempted to control the traffic in slaves, these efforts were poorly enforced. Besides, the

◉ View the Image
Nat Turner Rebellion (1831)
at **www.myhistorylab.com**

reason for outlawing the slave trade was generally not humanitarian, but rather reflected fear of a rapid increase in the slave population. Alabama, Mississippi, and Louisiana all banned the importation of slaves after the

Nat Turner revolt in Virginia in 1831 (described later in this chapter), resuming only in the profitable 1850s.

Congress formally ended external slave imports on January 1, 1808, the earliest date permitted by the Constitution. Enforcement by the United States was weak, and Africans continued to be smuggled to North America until the end of the Civil War. The tremendous increase in the slave population was the result not of this illegal trade, however, but of natural reproduction, often encouraged by slave owners.

The Missouri Compromise

Since 1789, politicians had labored to keep the explosive issue of slavery tucked safely beneath the surface of political life, for they understood how quickly it could jeopardize the nation. But the growing cotton kingdom forced politicians to confront the issue. In 1819, Missouri applied for admission to the Union, raising anew the question of slavery's extension. The Northwest Ordinance of 1787 had prohibited slavery north of the Ohio River while allowing its expansion to the south. But Congress had said nothing about slavery's place in the vast Louisiana territory west of the Mississippi.

Though there were already several thousand slaves in the Missouri Territory, Senator Rufus King of New York demanded that Missouri prohibit slavery before entering the Union. The proposal triggered a fierce debate over Congress's authority to regulate slavery in the trans-Mississippi West. Southerners were adamant that the area must remain open to their slave property and were determined to preserve the equal balance of slave and free states in the Senate. Already by 1819, the more rapidly growing population of the free states had given them a 105-to-81 advantage in the House of Representatives. Equality in the Senate offered the only sure protection for southern interests. Northerners, however, vowed to keep the territories west of the Mississippi open to free labor, which meant closing them to slavery.

For nearly three months, Congress debated the issue. "This momentous question," worried the aged Jefferson, "like a fire-bell in the night, [has] awakened and filled me with terror." In the end, compromise prevailed. Missouri gained admission as a slave state, while Maine (formerly part of Massachusetts) came in as a counterbalancing free state. A line was drawn west from Missouri at latitude 36°30′ to the Rocky Mountains. Land south of that line would be open to slavery; areas to the north would not. For the moment, the issue of slavery's expansion had been put to rest.

Southern Dependence on Slavery

Slavery became ever more important to the South. The rapidly increasing slave population, from 1.5 million in 1820 to 4 million in 1860, fostered southern economic growth and its dependence on slavery. A Tennessee senator declared that slavery was "sacred," the basis of civilization, and an English traveler noted that it would be easier to attack popery in Rome or Islam in Constantinople than slavery in the American South.

View the Image
Slave Dealers
at www.myhistorylab.com

Although most slaves worked on plantations and medium-size farms, they were found in all segments of the southern economy. In 1850, some 75 percent of all slaves performed agricultural labor: 55 percent growing cotton, 10 percent tobacco, and 10 percent rice, sugar, and hemp. Of the remaining one-fourth, about 15 percent were domestic servants, while others were involved in mining, lumbering, construction, dock and steamship labor, and iron and tobacco factories. A visitor to Natchez in 1835, noting that slaves were "trained to every kind of manual labour," saw them working as "mechanics, draymen, hostelers, labourers, hucksters, and washwomen."

The Tredegar Iron Company of Richmond decided in 1847 to shift from white labor "almost exclusively" to slave laborers, who were cheaper and unlikely to organize. This strategy foreshadowed the many future companies that exploited black labor while putting an economic squeeze on organized white workers who, along with white artisans, were threatened by black slave competition. Some white workers even opposed slavery.

Whether in factories, mines, or cotton fields, slavery was profitable as labor and as an investment. In 1859, the average plantation slave produced $78 in cotton earnings for his master annually while costing only about $32 for food, clothing, and housing. Enslaved women were likely to bear from two to six children, increasing their value. A slave owner could prosper by buying slaves, working them for several years, and then selling them for a profit. In 1844, a "prime field hand" sold for $600. A cotton boom beginning in 1849 raised this price to $1800 by 1860.

The economic growth of the South was impressive, but dependence on a cotton and slave economy was limiting. Generally, agricultural growth spurs the rise of cities and industry, but not in the Old South. In 1860, the South had 35 percent of the U.S. population but only 15 percent of its manufacturing. Just before the Civil War, 1 southerner in 14 was a city dweller, compared with 1 of every 3 northerners.

Some southerners worried about the single focus on cotton. *De Bow's Review*, an important journal published in New Orleans, called for more economic independence in the South through agricultural diversification, industrialization, and an improved transportation system. De Bow urged using slave labor in factories. But the planter class disagreed. As long as money could be made through an agricultural slave system that also valued honor and regulated race and gender relationships, plantation owners saw no reason to risk capital in new ventures.

Paternalism and Honor in the Planter Class

The aversion to industrialism in the South stemmed from the fact that most southerners, inheriting traditions of medieval chivalry from their Celtic

Scots–Irish cultural heritage, espoused a code of refined paternalism based on a rigid sense of social-class hierarchy and obligations. Wealthy planters, emulating the aristocratic English landowning class, claimed a privileged status as social "betters" and insisted on deferential treatment from those below them. This was especially important for those living in elegant mansions in isolated areas surrounded by black slaves and envious poor whites, circumstances that led to a violent undercurrent throughout the South.

The head of the plantation was to care for his "inferiors," much like a kindly father. He should provide the necessities of life to slaves (and white overseers), treat them as humanely as he could, and expect faithful obedience, loyalty, and hard work in return. The plantation wife was an essential part of this culture. Expected to uphold genteel values of sexual purity, spiritual piety, and submissive patience, she managed the household and extended gracious hospitality to social equals. She also had to endure a double sexual standard and the hypermasculinity of plantation life, which made it all the more important that she reflect ladylike virtues and be fiercely protected.

This masculine code valued activities such as politics, war, hunting, horse racing, cockfighting, and gambling, and embraced a rigid sense of honor. Southern men were sensitive to lapses of appropriate, chivalrous behavior and to insults and challenges to their honor. Such slights led to duels, regulated by strict rules. One southern visitor said that the "smallest breach of courtesy" was "sufficient grounds for a challenge." Although duels were eventually outlawed in most states, the laws were routinely ignored.

Slavery, Class, and Yeoman Farmers

Slavery clearly served both social and economic purposes. Although the proportion of southern white families that owned slaves slowly declined from 40 to 25 percent, the ideal of slave ownership permeated all classes and determined southern society's patriarchal and hierarchical character. At the top stood the planter aristocracy, much of it new wealth, elbowing its way among old established families. Some 10,000 rich families owned 50 or more slaves in 1860; of these about 3,000 owned over 100. A slightly larger group of small planters held from 10 to 50 slaves. But the biggest group, 70 percent of all slaveholders in 1860, comprised 270,000 middle-level farm families with fewer than 10 slaves. The typical slaveholder worked a small family farm of about 100 acres with less than 10 slaves. The typical slave, however, was more likely to be one of 20 or more on a large farm or small plantation.

In 1841, a young white North Carolinian, John Flintoff, went to Mississippi dreaming of wealth and prestige. Beginning as an overseer managing an uncle's farm, he bought a "negro boy 7 years old" even before he owned any land. After several years of unrewarding struggle, Flintoff married and returned to North Carolina. There he finally bought 124 acres and a few cheap, young blacks, and by 1860 he had a modest farm with several slaves growing corn, wheat, and tobacco. Although he never realized his grandest dreams, his son went to college, and his wife, he reported proudly, "has lived a Lady." Economic, social, and political standing for middle-level farmers like Flintoff depended on owning slaves. Aspiring southern whites hoped to purchase one slave, preferably a female who would bear children, and then climb the socioeconomic ladder.

Middling white southerners defended slavery not only for economic reasons but also because it gave them feelings of superiority over blacks and of kinship, if not quite equality, with other whites. Although a few southern whites believed in emancipation, most did not. An Alabama farmer told a northern visitor in the 1850s that if the slaves got their freedom, "they'd all think themselves just as good as we. . . . How would you like to hev a nigger feelin' just as good as a white man?"

Yeoman farmers also stoutly defended their independence (from both the national government and local elites), their property and lands as "self-working farmers," and their "households of faith." They believed in an evangelical Christianity that endorsed the divine sanctity of both the male-headed family and slavery.

The Nonslaveholding South

Below Flintoff and other yeoman farmers lived the majority of white southerners, with no slaves at all. Some 30 to 50 percent were landless. This nonslaveholding class, 75 percent of all southerners, was scattered throughout the South. Newton Knight, for example, worked a harsh piece of land cut out of the pines of southern Mississippi. He and his wife lived in a log cabin, scratching out their livelihood by growing corn and sweet potatoes and raising chickens and hogs. A staunch Baptist given to fits of violence, Knight had once killed a black.

Living throughout the South but especially in the Appalachian highlands, whites like Knight worked poorer lands than yeomen and planters. Far from commercial centers, they were largely self-sufficient, raising almost all their food and trading hogs, eggs, small game, and homemade items for cash and necessary manufactured items like kettles and rifles. With the indispensable help of their wives and children, they maintained a subsistence household economy, making soap, shoes, candles, whiskey, coarse textiles, and ax handles. They lived in two-room log houses separated by a "dog run." Their drab, isolated life was brightened when neighbors and families gathered at corn huskings and quilting parties, logrolling and wrestling matches, and political stump and revivalist Baptist or Methodist camp meetings.

These nonslaveholding farmers were in the majority. In 1860, in North Carolina and even in the large plantation states of Mississippi and Louisiana, 60 to 70 percent of farms were less than 100 acres. Despite numerical majorities, these farmers were politically marginalized. Resenting the tradition of political deference to "betters," they were unable to challenge planters for political power. Most fought with the Confederacy during the Civil War; a few silently harbored Unionist views.

Another group was herdsmen raising hogs and other livestock, fed on corn or allowed to roam in the woods. These whites supplied bacon and pork to local slaveholders (who often thought hog growing beneath their dignity) and drove herds to stockyards in Nashville, Louisville, and Savannah. The South raised two-thirds of the nation's hogs. In 1860, the value of southern livestock was $500 million, twice that of cotton. Although the hog business was large and valued, hog herdsmen were low on the southern social ladder.

Below them were the poorest whites of the South, about 10 percent of the population. Often sneeringly called "crackers," they eked out a living in isolated, inhospitable areas. Some made corn whiskey, and many hired out

The Life of Yeoman Farm Families Study these two images and describe what you see. What do the pictures tell you about the daily lives of women and men in southern non-plantation rural cultures? How self-sufficient do they seem to be? How isolated are they? What many social purposes did the quilting party fulfill (other than revealing a uniquely female American work of useful art)? Note that men were also at the party, talking (politics, perhaps) by the stove, bouncing a baby, carrying food, and courting a young woman by the quilt.
(Left: North Wind Picture Archives)

as farmhands for an average wage of $14 per month. Because of poor diet and bad living conditions, these poor whites often suffered from hookworm and malaria. This, along with the natural debilitation of heat and poverty, gave them a reputation as lazy, shiftless, and illiterate.

Poor whites stayed poor partly because the slave system allowed the planter class to accumulate a disproportionate amount of land and political power. High slave prices made entry into the planter class increasingly difficult, raising class tensions. Because large planters dominated southern life and owned the most slaves, slavery and the relations between slaves and masters are best understood by looking closely at this group.

Morning: Master and Mistress in the Big House

It is early morning in the South. Imagine four scenes. In the first, William Waller of Virginia is preparing to leave with 20 choice slaves on a long trip to the slave market in Natchez, Mississippi. Waller is making this "intolerable" journey to sell some of his slaves in order to ease his heavy debts. Although he "loaths the vocation of slave trading," he must recover some money to see his family "freed" from the "bondage" of indebtedness. To ease his conscience, he intends to supervise the sale personally, thus securing the best possible deal not only for himself but also for his departing slaves.

On another plantation, owned by the wealthy James Hammond of South Carolina, the horn blows an hour before daylight to awaken slaves for fieldwork. Hammond rises soon after, aware that to run an efficient plantation he must hold his slaves "in complete check." "In general 15 to 20 lashes will be sufficient flogging" for most offenses, but "in extreme cases" the punishment "must not exceed 100 lashes in one day."

On an Alabama plantation, Hugh Lawson is up early, writing a sorrowful letter about the death of a "devotedly attached and faithful" slave, Jim. A female slave, already awake, "walked across a frosty field in the early morning . . . to the big house to build a fire" for her mistress. As the mistress wakes up, she says to the slave, a grown woman taking care of two families, "Well, how's my little nigger today?"

In a fourth household, a middling farm in upcountry Georgia, Charles Brock awakens at dawn to join two sons and four slaves digging up stumps and plowing fields of grains and sweet potatoes, while Brock's wife and a female slave tend cows.

As these diverse scenes suggest, slavery thoroughly permeated the lives of southern slaveholders. For slaves, morning was a time for getting up early for a long day of tedious, hard work. But for white slaveholders, morning involved contact with slaves in many ways: as burdens of figuring profit and loss, as objects to be kept obedient and orderly, as intimates and fellow workers, but also as ever-present reminders of fear, hate, and uncertainty.

The Burdens of Slaveholding and the Plantation Mistress

Robert Francis Withers Allston (1801–1864) was a major rice planter in the Georgetown district of South Carolina, a low, swampy, mosquito-infested tidal area. It was a perfect spot for growing rice, but so unhealthy that few whites wanted to live there. The death rate among slaves was appallingly high. Robert was the fifth generation of Allstons to live in this inhospitable land. By 1860, he owned seven plantations along the Peedee River, totaling some 4,000 acres, and another 9,500 acres of pasture and timberland. He held nearly 600 slaves. The total value of his land and slaves in the 1850s was approximately $300,000. Rich in land and labor, he had large mortgages and debts.

Allston was an enlightened, talented, public-spirited man. Educated at West Point but trained in the law, he both practiced agriculture and served South Carolina many years as state senator and governor. His political creed, he wrote in 1838, was based on "the principles of Thomas Jefferson." The core of his conviction was a "plain, honest, commonsense reading of the Constitution," which for Allston meant the constitutionality of slavery and the illegitimacy of abolitionism and the United States Bank. Allston also reflected Jefferson's humane side. Active in the Episcopal Church, he advocated the liberalization of South Carolina's poor laws; an improved system of public education open to rich and poor; humanitarian care of the disabled; and the improvement of conditions for the Catawba Indians.

In 1832, Allston married the equally enlightened Adele Petigru. She participated fully in the management of the plantation and ran it while Robert was away doing politics. In a letter to her husband in 1850, Adele demonstrated her diverse interests by reporting on family affairs and the children's learning, sickness among the slaves, the status of spring plowing, the building of a canal, the bottling of wine, and current politics. After Robert's death during the Civil War, she would assume control of the Allston plantations, abandoned when Union troops arrived (see Chapter 14). Except

Watch the Video
The Lives of Southern Women
at **www.myhistorylab.com**

during the worst periods of mosquitoes and heat, both Allstons were fully engaged in plantation operations. Managing thousands of acres of rice required not only an enormous investment in labor and equipment, but also careful supervision of slaves. Although working rice rather than cotton, Allston's concerns were typical of large planters.

His letters frequently expressed the burdens of owning slaves. Although Allston carefully distributed enough cloth, blankets, and shoes to his slaves and gave them rest, the sickness and death of slaves, especially young field-workers, headed his list of concerns. "I lost in one year 28 negroes," he complained. He tried to keep slave families together, but sold slaves when necessary. In a letter to his son Benjamin, he expressed concern over the bad example set by a slave driver who was "abandon'd by his hands" because he had not worked with them the previous Sunday. In the same letter, Allston urged Benjamin to keep up the "patrol duty," less to guard against runaway slaves, he said, than to restrain "vagabond whites." Clearly, the planter class felt a duty to control lower-class whites as well as black slaves.

Other planters likewise saw slavery as both a duty and a burden. Many insisted that they worked harder than their slaves to feed and clothe them. R. L. Dabney of Virginia exclaimed, "there could be no greater curse inflicted on us than to be compelled to manage a parcel of Negroes." Curse or not, Dabney and other planters profited from their burdens, a point they seldom admitted.

Their wives experienced other kinds of burdens. "The mistress of a plantation," wrote one, "was the most complete slave on it." Another complained, "It is the slaves who own me. Morning, noon, and night, I'm obliged to look after them," burdens Adele Allston would have understood. In accord with the southern code of honor, plantation mistresses were expected to improve their husbands' morals and beautify their parlors. They also suffered under a double standard of morality. Expected themselves to act as chaste ladies, their husbands had nearly unrestricted sexual access to slave women. "God forgive us, but ours is a monstrous system," Mary Boykin Chesnut wrote in her diary. "Any lady is ready to tell you who is the father of all the mulatto children in everybody's household but her own. Those, she seems to think, drop from the clouds." But plantation wives had their own double standard: a former slave woman said of her mistress that, "though a warm-hearted woman, [she] was a violent advocate of slavery. I have . . . puzzled how to reconcile this with her otherwise Christian character."

Chesnut called the sexual dynamics of slavery "the sorest spot." There were others. Together with female slaves, plantation mistresses had to tend to the food, clothing, health, and welfare of not just their husbands and children, but the slaves, too. The plantation mistress, then, served many roles: as a potential humanizing influence on men; as a resourceful, responsible manager of numerous plantation affairs; as a perpetuator of the system; and sometimes as a victim herself.

Justifying Slavery

The behavior of Douglass's mistress discussed at the beginning of this chapter suggests that slavery led otherwise good people to act inhumanely. Increasingly attacked as immoral, slaveholders felt compelled to justify slavery, not only to opponents of the "peculiar institution" but perhaps also to themselves. Until the 1830s, they explained away slavery as a "necessary evil." After abolitionist attacks in that decade, however, they shifted to justifying slavery in five arguments as a "positive good."

A biblical justification was based in part on the curse that had fallen upon the son of Ham, one of Noah's children, and in part on Old and New Testament admonitions to servants to obey their masters. In a historical justification, southerners claimed slavery had always existed and formed the basis for all the great ancient civilizations.

A Slave Coffle This engraving of a group of slaves in chains depicts the stark inhumanity of the institution of slavery. Note the white man (in the right corner) raising the whip to hurry the slaves along. In front of him are a woman and child, and another woman stares at him in moral disbelief. What is your response to this engraving?

The legal justification rested on the U.S. Constitution's refusal to forbid slavery and on three passages clearly implying its legality: the "three-fifths" clause, the protection of the overseas slave trade for 20 years, and the mandate for returning fugitive slaves.

A fourth justification for slavery was pseudoscientific. Until the 1830s, most white southerners believed that blacks were degraded not by nature but by African climate and their slave condition. With the rise of the "positive good" defense in the 1830s, southerners began to argue that blacks had been created separately as an inherently inferior race, and therefore the destiny of the inferior Africans was to work for the superior Caucasians. At best, the patriarchal slave system would domesticate uncivilized blacks. As Allston put it, "The educated master is the negro's best friend upon earth."

A sociological defense of slavery was implicit in Allston's paternalistic statement. **George Fitzhugh**, a leading advocate of this view, argued, "the Negro is but a grown child and must be governed as a child," and so needed the paternal guidance and protection of a white master. Many southerners believed that chaos and miscegenation would ensue if slaves were freed. Fitzhugh compared the treatment of southern slaves favorably with that of free laborers working in northern factories. These "wage slaves," he argued, worked as hard as slaves, yet with their

Read the Document

George Fitzhugh, Slavery Justified *(1854)*

at **www.myhistorylab.com**

paltry wages they had to feed, clothe, and shelter themselves. Since southern masters took care of these necessities, to free their slaves would be a heartless burden on both blacks and whites.

Southern apologists for slavery faced the difficult intellectual task of justifying a system that ran against the main ideological directions of nineteenth-century American society: the expansion of individual liberty, economic opportunity, and democratic political participation. The southern defense of slavery had also to take into account the 75 percent of white families who owned no slaves but envied those who did. To deflect potential for class antagonisms among whites, wealthy planters developed a justification of slavery that emphasized white superiority regardless of class.

The underlying but rarely admitted motive behind all these justifications was that slavery was profitable. As the southern defense of slavery intensified in the 1840s and 1850s, it aroused greater opposition from northerners and from slaves themselves. Perhaps slavery's worst cruelty was not physical but psychological: to be enslaved and barred from participation in a nation that espoused freedom and equality of opportunity.

Noon: Slaves in House and Fields

It is two o'clock on a hot July afternoon on the plantation. The midday lunch break is over, and the slaves are returning to work in the fields. Lunch was the usual cornmeal and pork. The slaves now work listlessly, their low stamina resulting from a deficient diet and suffocating heat and humidity. Douglass remembered that "we worked all weathers. . . . It was never too hot, or too cold." Mary Reynolds, a Louisiana slave, recalled that she hated most having to pick cotton "when the frost was on the bolls," which made her hands "git sore and crack open and bleed."

Daily Toil

The daily work schedule for most slaves, whether in the fields or the Big House, was long and demanding. Awakened before daybreak, they worked on an average day 14 hours in the summer and 10 hours in the winter; during harvest, an 18-hour workday was not uncommon. Depending on the size of the workforce and the crop, the slaves were organized either in gangs or according to tasks. Gangs, usually of 20 to 25, worked the cotton rows under the watchful eye and quick whip of a driver. Ben Simpson, a Georgia slave, remembered vividly his master's "great, long whip platted out of rawhide" that struck any slave who would "fall behind or give out."

Under the **task system**, which slaves preferred and negotiated for cleverly, each slave had a specific task to complete daily. It gave slaves incentive to work hard enough to finish early, but their work was scrutinized constantly. An overseer's weekly report to Robert Allston in 1860 noted that he had "flogged for hoeing corn bad Fanny 12 lashes, Sylvia 12, Monday 12,

Phoebee 12, Susanna 12, Salina 12, Celia 12, Iris 12." Black slave drivers were no less demanding.

An average slave was expected to pick 130 to 150 pounds of cotton per day; work on sugar and rice plantations was even harder. Sugar demanded constant cultivation, digging ditches in snake-infested fields. At harvest time, cutting, stripping, and carrying the cane to the sugar house for boiling was exhausting, as was cutting and hauling huge quantities of firewood. Working in the low-country rice fields was worse: slaves spent long hours standing in water up to their knees.

House slaves, mostly women, had relatively easier assignments, though they were regularly called on to help with the harvest. Their usual work was in or near the Big House as maids, "mammies," cooks, seamstresses, laundresses, coachmen, drivers, and gardeners. Slaves did most of the skilled artisan work on the plantation. More intimacy between whites and blacks occurred near the house. House slaves ate and dressed better than those in the fields. But there were disadvantages: close supervision, duty day and night, and conflicts with whites that could range from being given unpleasant jobs to insults, spontaneous angry whippings, and sexual assault. The most feared punishment, however, other than sale to the Deep South, was to be sent to the fields.

Slave Health and Punishments

Although slave owners had an interest in keeping their workforce healthy, slaves led sickly lives. Home was a crude, one-room log cabin with a dirt floor and a fireplace. Mosquitoes found easy entry through cracks and holes. Typical furnishings included a table, some stools or boxes to sit on, an iron pot and wooden dishes, and perhaps a bed. Cabins were crowded, usually housing more than one family. Clothing was shabby and uncomfortable.

Studies on the adequacy of slave diet disagree. But compared with Latin American slaves, American slaves were fed well. Once a week, each slave got an average ration of a peck of cornmeal, three to four pounds of salt pork or bacon, some molasses, and perhaps some sweet potatoes. The mainstay was corn. While some slaves were able to grow vegetables and to fish or hunt, they rarely enjoyed fresh meat, dairy products, fruits, or vegetables. The limitations of their diet led to theft of food and the practice of eating dirt, which caused worms. The slave diet also resulted in skin disorders, cracked lips, sore eyes, vitamin deficiency diseases, and even mental illness.

Enslaved women especially suffered weaknesses caused by vitamin deficiency, hard work, and disease, as well as those associated with menstruation and childbirth. Women were expected to do the same tasks in the fields as the men, in addition to cooking, sewing, child care, and traditional female jobs in the quarters when the fieldwork was finished. "Pregnant women," the usual rule stated, "should not plough or lift" and had a three-week recovery period following birth. But these guidelines were often violated. Mortality of slave children under five years of age was twice as high as for white children.

Life expectancy for American slaves in 1850 was 21.4 years as compared to 25.5 years for whites. In part because of poor diet and the climate, slaves were highly susceptible to epidemics. Despite some resistance as a result of the sickle-cell trait, many slaves died from malaria, yellow fever, cholera, and other diseases spread by mosquitoes or bad water. Slaves everywhere suffered and died from intestinal ailments in the summer and respiratory diseases in the winter. An average of 20 percent (and sometimes more than 50 percent) of the slaves on a given plantation would be sick at one time, and no overseer's report was complete without recording sicknesses and days of lost labor.

The relatively frequent incidence of whippings and other physical punishments aggravated the poor physical condition of the slaves. Many slaveholders offered rewards—a garden plot, an extra holiday, hiring out, and passes—as inducements for faithful labor and withheld these privileges as punishment. But southern court records, newspapers, plantation diaries, and slave memoirs reveal that sadistic punishments were frequent. Slaveholders had many theories on the appropriate kind of lash to inflict sufficient pain and punishment without damaging a valuable laborer. Other punishments included confinement in stocks and jails during leisure hours, chains, muzzling, salting lash wounds, branding, burning, and castration.

Nothing testifies better to the physical brutality of slavery than the advertisements for runaways that slaveholders printed in antebellum newspapers. In searching for the best way to describe the physical characteristics or brands of a missing slave, slave owners unwittingly condemned their own behavior. A Mississippi runaway was described as having "large raised scars . . . in the small of his back and on his abdomen nearly as large as a person's finger." A female fugitive, Betty, was described as recently "burnt . . . with a hot iron on the left side of her face. I tried to make the letter M," her master admitted in his diary.

> •**•**—[Read the **Document**
> *Runaway Slave Advertisements*
> *(1838–1839)*
> at **www.myhistorylab.com**

Slave Law and the Family

Complicating master–slave relationships was the status of slaves as both human and property, a legal and psychological ambiguity the South never resolved. On the one hand, the slaves had names, personalities, families, and wills of their own, making them fellow humans. On the other hand, they were items of property, purchased to perform specific profit-making tasks.

> •**•**—[Read the **Document**
> *Poem, "The Slave Auction," by*
> *Frances E.W. Harper (1854)*
> at **www.myhistorylab.com**

This ambiguity led to confusion in the laws governing treatment of slaves. Until the early 1830s, some southern abolitionist activity persisted, primarily in the Upper South, and slaves had slight hopes of being

> •**•**—[Read the **Document**
> *The Confessions of*
> *Nat Turner (1831)*
> at **www.myhistorylab.com**

A Slave Market The breakup of families and friendships was an ever-present fear for slaves, who could be sold for economic reasons or for uncooperative behavior. Study this painting of a slave market by an unidentified artist, and describe what you see. Note the varied colors and conditions of the African Americans in the painting, and note the varied classes of whites—and blacks. What differences between the two women do you see? How many different men are gazing at them, and in what ways? What conclusions do you draw about slavery from this one complex image?

freed. But they also suffered careless, often brutal treatment. This confusion changed with the threatening convergence in 1831 of Nat Turner's revolt and William Lloyd Garrison's publication of the abolitionist newspaper the *Liberator*. After 1831, the South tightened up the slave system. Laws prohibited manumission, and slaves' hopes of freedom other than by revolt or escape vanished. At the same time, laws protecting them from overly severe treatment were strengthened.

Treatment varied with individual slaveholders and depended on their mood and other circumstances. Most planters, like Robert Allston, encouraged their slaves to marry and sought to keep families intact; they believed that families made enslaved males more docile and less inclined to run away. But some masters failed to respect slave marriages or broke them up because of financial problems, which southern law permitted them to do.

Adding to the pain of forced breakup of the slave family was the sexual abuse of black women. Although the frequency of such abuse is unknown, the presence of thousands of mulattoes in the antebellum era points to the practice. White men in the South took advantage of black enslaved women by offering gifts for sexual "favors," by threatening those who refused sex with physical punishment or the sale of a child or loved one, by purchasing concubines, and by outright rape.

To obtain cheap additional slaves for the workforce, slaveholders encouraged young enslaved women to bear children, whether married or not. If verbal prodding and inducements such as less work and more rations did not work, masters would force mates on slave women. Massa Hawkins, for example, selected Rufus to bed with an unwilling 16-year-old Rose Williams. At first, Rose repulsed him by shoving him on the floor with her feet, but when Rufus persisted, she took a poker and "lets him have it over de head." Hawkins then threatened Rose with a "whippin' at de stake" or sale away "from my folks." This was too much for her. "What am I's to do?"

Slaves, however, usually chose their own mates on the basis of mutual attraction during a courtship complicated by the threat of white interference. As among poor whites, premarital intercourse was frequent, but promiscuous behavior was rare. Most couples maintained affectionate, lasting relationships. This, too, led to numerous sorrows. Members of slave families, powerless to intervene, had to witness the flogging or physical abuse of loved ones. William Wells Brown remembered that "cold chills ran over me and I wept aloud" when he saw his mother whipped. For this reason, some slaves preferred to marry a spouse from another plantation.

Although motherhood was the key event in an enslaved woman's life, bearing children and the double burden of work and family responsibilities challenged her resourcefulness. Some masters provided time off for nursing mothers, but the more common practice was for them to work in the fields with their newborn infants lying nearby. Women developed support networks, looking after one another's children; meeting to sew, quilt, cook, or do laundry; and attending births, caring for the sick and dying, and praying together.

The worst trauma for slaves was the separation of families, a haunting fear rarely absent from slave consciousness. Although many slaveholders had both moral and economic reasons to maintain families, inevitably they found themselves destroying them. One study of 30 years of data from the Deep South shows that masters dissolved one-third of all slave marriages. Even then, the slaves tried to maintain contact with loved ones sold elsewhere. "My Dear Wife for you and my Children my pen cannot Express the Griffe I feel to be parted from you all," wrote Abream Scriven.

There was a sound basis, in fact, for the **abolitionists'** contention that slavery was a harsh, brutal system. However, two points need to be emphasized. First, although slavery led otherwise decent human beings to commit inhumane acts, many slaveholders throughout the South were not cruel; they did what they could for their slaves, out of both economic self-interest and Christian morality. Second, whether under kind or cruel masters, the slaves endured with dignity, communal strength, and occasional joy. If daytime in the fields describes slavery at its worst, nighttime in the quarters, as examined from the black perspective, reveals noble survival powers and the capacity to mold an African American community culture even under slavery.

Night: Slaves in Their Quarters

It is near sundown, and the workday is almost over. Some slaves begin singing the gentle spiritual "Steal Away to Jesus," and others join in. To the unwary overseer or master, the song suggests happy slaves, looking forward to heaven. To the slaves, however, the song is a signal that, as ex-slave Wash Wilson put it, they are to "steal away to Jesus" because "dere gwine be a 'ligious meetin' dat night."

In the slave quarters, away from whites and daily work, a black community helped the slaves make sense out of and cope with their lives. In family life, religion, song, dance, the playing of musical instruments, and the telling of stories, the slaves both sought release from suffering and created a vibrant community and culture.

Black Christianity

As suggested by the scene Wash Wilson described, Christian worship was indispensable to life in the slave quarters. The revivals of the early nineteenth century led to an enormous growth of Christianity among black Americans. Independent black Baptist and Methodist churches, especially in border states and cities, served slaves, free blacks, and occasionally even whites. These black churches steered a careful path to maintain their autonomy and avoid white interference. The vast majority of southern blacks, however, were slaves, attending plantation churches set up by their masters.

Robert Allston built a prayer house for his slaves, reporting with pride that they were "attentive . . . and greatly improved in intelligence and morals." For the slaveholders, religion represented a form of social control. Black religious gatherings were usually forbidden unless white observers were present or white preachers led them. Whether in slave or white churches (where blacks sat in the back), sermons emphasized the importance of work, obedience, honesty, and respect for the master's property. "All that preacher talked about," one slave remembered, "was for us slaves to obey our master and not to lie and steal."

There were limits, however, to white control. Although some slaves accommodated to the master's brand of Christianity and patiently waited for heavenly deliverance, others rebelled and sought earthly liberty. Not far from Allston's plantation, several slaves were discovered—and imprisoned—for singing "We'll soon be free / We'll fight for liberty / When de Lord will call us home." Douglass had an illegal Sabbath school on one plantation, "the sweetest engagement with which I was ever blessed," where he and others risked whippings while learning about Christianity and how to read. In religious meetings like these, the slaves created an "invisible" church. On Sunday morning, they dutifully sat through the master's service and waited for "real preachin'" later that night.

Long into the night, they would sing, dance, shout, and pray. "Ya' see," one enslaved woman explained, "niggers lack ta shout a whole lot an' wid de white fo'ks al'round 'em, dey couldn't shout jes' lack dey want to." But at night they could, taking care to deaden the sound to keep the whites away. Dance, forbidden by Methodists, was transformed into the "ecstatic shout," praising the Lord. The religious ceremony itself, with its camp meeting features, relieved the day's burdens and expressed communal religious values when blacks "really did have they freedom of spirit," one recalled.

Although many of the expressive forms were African, the message stressed the Judeo-Christian themes of suffering and deliverance from bondage. "We prayed a lot to be free," Anderson Edwards recalled, but the freedom the slaves sought was a complex blend of a peaceful soul and an earthly escape from slavery, as reflected in spirituals.

The Power of Song

A group of slaves gathers at night in the woods behind their quarters to sing and shout together. Two moods are expressed. First, they mourn being stolen from Africa, with families "sold apart." But second, they sing: "There's a better day a-coming. / Will you go along with me? / There's a better day a-coming. / Go sound the jubilee."

Music was a crucial form of expression in the slave quarters on both secular and religious occasions. The slaves were adept at creating a song, as one woman recalled, "on de spurn of de moment." Jeanette Robinson Murphy described a process of spontaneous creation that, whether in rural church music or urban jazz, describes black music to this day. "We'd all be at the 'prayer house' de Lord's day," she said, when all of a sudden in the midst of a white preacher's sermon, "de Lord would come a-shinin' thoo dem pages and revive dis ole nigger's heart." She continued, "I'd jump up dar and den and holler and shout and sing and pat, and dey would all cotch de words and I'd sing it to some ole shout song I'd heard 'em sing from Africa, and dey'd all take it up and keep at it, and keep a-addin' to it, and den it would be a spiritual."

Spirituals reiterated a basic Judeo-Christian theme: a chosen people, the children of God, were held in bondage but would be delivered. What they meant by deliverance often had a double meaning: freedom in heaven and freedom in the North. Where, exactly, was the desired destination of "Oh Canaan, sweet Canaan / I am bound for the land of Canaan"? Was it heaven? Was it the North? Was it a literal reference to the terminus of the Underground Railroad in Canada? Or was it freedom "anyplace else but here"? For different slaves, and at different times for the same person, it meant all of these.

Slave songs did not always contain hidden meanings. Sometimes slaves gathered simply for music, to play fiddles, drums, and other instruments fashioned in imitation of West African models. Some musicians were invited to perform at white ceremonies and parties, but most played for the slave community. Weddings, funerals, holiday celebrations, family reunions, and a successful harvest were all occasions for a communal gathering, usually with music.

So, too, was news of external events that affected their lives—a crisis in the master's situation, a change in the slave code, a Civil War battle, or emancipation. "The songs of the slave," Douglass wrote, "represent the sorrows of his heart." But they also expressed joy, triumph, and deliverance. Each expression of sorrow usually ended in an outburst of eventual liberation and justice: from "sometimes I feel like a motherless chile" to "a eagle in de air. . . . / Gonna spread my wings an' Fly, fly, fly."

The Enduring Family

The role of music in all milestones of family life suggests the centrality of the family to life in the slave quarters. Although sexual abuse and family separation were real, so was the hope for family continuity. Naming practices, for example, show that children were connected to large extended families.

The benefits of family cohesion were those of any group: love, protection, education, moral guidance, cultural transmission, role models, and basic support. All existed in the slave quarters. In this way, blacks preserved cultural traditions, which enhanced the identity and self-esteem of parents and children alike. Parents taught their children how to cope with slavery and survive in the world. As young ones neared the age for full-time field-work, parents instructed them in the best ways to pick cotton, how to avoid the overseer's whip, whom to trust and learn from, and ways of fooling their master.

Opportunities existed on many plantations for parents to perform extra work for money to buy sugar or clothing; to hunt and fish, thereby adding protein to their family's diet; or to tend a small garden to grow vegetables. In such small ways, they improved the welfare of their families.

Slaves were not always totally at the mercy of abusive masters and overseers. Harriet Jacobs fended off her master's sexual advances partly by her cleverness and sass, and partly by a threat to use her free black grandmother's considerable influence in the community against him. When family intervention, appeals for mercy, or conjurers' magic failed, some slaves resorted to force. In 1800, a slave called Ben shot dead a white man for living with Ben's wife, and another slave killed an overseer in 1859 for raping his wife. Enslaved women risked serious consequences to protect themselves or family members. When Cherry Loguen was attacked by a knife-wielding would-be rapist, she knocked him out with a large branch.

Slave Families in Their Quarters In these two photographs of the slave quarters at "night," men, women, and children, despite separation, sale, and sexual abuse by white masters, created a vibrant black community and provided love, support, and pride to family members. How many generations do you see in the 1862 photograph of a Hilton Head, South Carolina, family at the top, and what activities are going on in the bottom picture? What do you observe about gender roles from these two photographs? *(Bottom: Collection of the New York Historical Society)*

Despite numerous incidents of mutual support, the love and affection that slaves had for each other was sometimes a liability. Many slaves, women especially, were reluctant to run away because they did not want to leave their families. Those who fled were easily caught because, as an overseer near Natchez, Mississippi, told a northern visitor, they "almost always kept in the neighborhood, because they did not like to go where they could not sometimes get back and see their families."

As these episodes suggest, violence, sexual abuse, and separation constantly threatened slave families. Yet slave parents continued to serve as protectors, providers, comforters, transmitters of culture, and role models for their children.

Resistance and Freedom

Songs, folktales, and other forms of cultural expression enabled slaves to articulate their resistance to slavery. For example, in the song "Ole Jim," on Jim's "journey" to the "kingdom," he invited others to "go 'long" with him, taunting his owner: "O blow, blow, Ole Massa, blow de cotton horn / Ole Jim'll neber wuck no mo' in de cotton an' de corn." From refusal to work, it was a short step to outright revolt. In another song, "Samson," the slaves stated their determination to abolish the house of bondage: "An' if I had-'n my way / I'd tear the buildin' down! / . . . And now I got my way / And I'll tear this buildin' down." Every defiant song, story, or event, like Douglass's victory over Covey, was an act of resistance.

Forms of Black Protest

Slaves protested the burdensome demands of continuous forced labor in various "day-to-day" actions. These ranged from breaking tools to burning houses, from stealing food to defending fellow slaves from punishment, from self-mutilation to work slowdowns, and from poisoning masters to feigning illness.

Slave women, aware of their childbearing value, were adept at missing work on account of "disorders and irregularities." They established networks of support while winnowing and pounding rice or shucking corn, sharing miseries but also encouraging each other in private but subtle defiance like ruining the master's meals and faking sickness or painful menstrual cramps.

Overseers also suffered from such disobedience, for their job depended on productivity, which in turn depended on the goodwill of the slave workers. Slaves adeptly played on the frequent struggle between overseer and master.

Many slaveholders resorted to using black drivers rather than overseers, but this created other problems. Slave drivers, "men between," had the tricky job of getting the master's work done without alienating fellow slaves or compromising their own loyalties. Although some drivers were as brutal as white overseers, many became leaders and role models for other slaves. A common practice of the drivers was to appear to punish without really doing so. Solomon Northrup reported that he "learned to handle the whip with marvelous dexterity and precision, throwing the lash within a hair's breadth of the back, the ear, the nose, without, however, touching either of them."

Another form of resistance was flight. The typical runaway was a young male who ran off alone and hid out in a nearby wood or swamp. He left to avoid a whipping or because he had just been whipped, to protest excessive work demands, or, as one master put it, for "no cause" at all. But there was a cause—the need to experience a period of freedom away from the restraints and discipline of the plantation. Many runaways snuck back to the quarters for food, and after a few days, if not tracked down by hounds, returned, perhaps to be whipped, but also perhaps with some concessions for better treatment.

Some slaves fled repeatedly. Remus and his wife Patty ran away from their master in Alabama. Caught and jailed three times, each time they escaped again. Runaways hid out for months and years in communities of escaped slaves, especially in Florida, where Seminole Indians befriended them. In these maroons, black Seminoles intermarried and shared a common hostility to whites, though sometimes other southeastern natives were hired to track down runaway slaves.

The means of escape were manifold: forging passes, posing as master and servant, disguising one's sex, sneaking aboard ships, and pretending loyalty until taken by the master on a trip to the North. One slave even had himself mailed to the North in a large box. The Underground Railroad, organized by abolitionists, was a series of safe houses and stations where runaway slaves could rest, eat, and spend the night before continuing. Harriet Tubman, who led around 70 slaves out of the South on 11 or 12 separate trips, was the railroad's most famous "conductor." It is difficult to know exactly how many slaves actually escaped to the North and Canada, but the numbers were not large. One estimate suggests that in 1850, about 1,000 slaves (out of over 3 million) attempted to run away, and most were returned. Nightly patrols by white militiamen reduced the chances for any slave to escape and probably deterred many from even trying.

Other ways in which slaves sought their freedom included petitioning Congress and state legislatures, bringing suit against their masters that they were being held in bondage illegally, and persuading masters to provide for emancipation in their wills. Many toiled to purchase their own freedom by hiring out to do extra work at night and on holidays.

Slave Revolts

The ultimate act of resistance was rebellion. Countless slaves committed individual acts of revolt. In addition, there were hundreds of conspiracies whereby slaves met to plan a group escape and often the massacre of whites. Most of these conspiracies never led to action, either because circumstances changed, or the slaves lost the will to follow through, or, more often, because some fellow slave—perhaps planted by the master—betrayed the plot. Such spies thwarted the elaborate conspiracies of Gabriel in Virginia in 1800 and Denmark Vesey in South Carolina in 1822. Both men were skilled, knowledgeable leaders who planned their revolts in hopes that larger events would support them—a possible war with France in 1800 and the Missouri debates in 1820. Both conspiracies were thwarted before revolts could begin, and both resulted in severe reprisals by whites, including mass executions of leaders and the random killing of innocent blacks. The severity of these responses indicated southern whites' enormous fear of slave revolt.

Only a few organized revolts actually occurred. Nat Turner led the most famous slave revolt in Southampton County, Virginia, in 1831. Turner, an intelligent, skilled, unmarried, and religious slave who had experienced many visions of "white spirits and black spirits engaged in battle," believed himself "ordained for some great purpose in the hands of the Almighty." He and his followers intended, Turner said, "to carry terror and devastation" throughout the country. They crept into the home of Turner's "kind master" with "the greatest confidence in me" and killed the entire family. Before the insurrection was finally put down, 55 white men, women, and children had been murdered and twice as many blacks killed in the aftermath. Turner hid for two weeks before he was apprehended and executed, but not before dictating a chilling confession to a white lawyer. The Nat Turner revolt was a crucial moment for southern whites. A Virginia legislator said that he suspected there was "a Nat Turner . . . in every family."

The fact that Turner was an intelligent and trusted slave and yet led such a shocking revolt suggests again how difficult it is to generalize about slavery and slave behavior. Slaves, like masters, had diverse personalities and changeable moods, and their behavior could not be predicted easily. Sometimes humble and deferential, at other times obstinate and rebellious, the slaves made the best of a bad situation and did what they needed to do to survive with a measure of self-worth.

Free Blacks: Becoming One's Own Master

Frederick Douglass said of the slave, "Give him a bad master, and he aspires to a good master; give him a good master, and he wishes to become his own master." In 1838, Douglass forged a free black's papers as a seaman and sailed from Baltimore to become his own master in the North, where he found "great insecurity and loneliness." Apart from the immediate difficulties of finding food, shelter, and work, he realized that he was a fugitive in a land "whose inhabitants are legalized kidnappers" who could at any moment seize and return him to the South. Douglass thus joined the 11 to 12 percent of the African American population who were not slaves.

	British colonies
	Former Portuguese colonies
	Former Spanish colonies
✗	Slave revolts
■	Maroon communities

Virginia, 1831 (Nat Turner)

UNITED STATES

Virginia, 1800 (Gabriel Prosser)

New Orleans, 1811

South Carolina, 1822 (Denmark Vesey)

Gulf of Mexico

ATLANTIC OCEAN

MEXICO Cuba, 1820 (Spanish)

Cuba, 1805, 1812, 1842–1844 (Spanish)

Jamaica, 1795, 1831 (British West Indies)

Santo Domingo, 1791; Haitian independence, 1804

BELIZE

St. Croix, 1848 (Denmark)

St. Kitts, 1835 (British)

GUATEMALA HONDURAS

Caribbean Sea

Martinique, 1831 (French)

EL SALVADOR

Barbados, 1816 (British West Indies)

NICARAGUA

COSTA RICA

Grenada, 1795 (British West Indies)

PANAMA VENEZUELA Demerara, 1823

PACIFIC OCEAN

Choco, 1820

BRITISH GUIANA FRENCH GUIANA

COLOMBIA

DUTCH GUIANA

ECUADOR

Abolition of Slavery

1777–1802	U.S. Northern states (effective gradually)
1794	French West Indies (revoked in Haiti in 1802, finally in 1848)
1804	Haitian independence
1808–1825	Revolutionary movements throughout South and Central America for independence from Spain and Portugal (Brazil)
1823	Chile
1824	Central American republics
1829	Mexico (gradually)
1820s–1850s	Venezuela, Colombia, Ecuador (gradually)
1833	British West Indies (effective in 1834)
1848	Virgin Islands
1853	Argentina
1854	Peru
1861	Russian serfs
1865	United States
1873	Puerto Rico
1886	Cuba
1888	Brazil

PERU

Peru, 1848–1851

Bahia, 1800–1835

BRAZIL

BOLIVIA

CHILE

PARAGUAY

Brazil 1854, 1865, 1880s

ARGENTINA

URUGUAY

Slave Revolts, Maroons, and the Abolition of Slavery in the Americas, 1790–1888
Throughout the Americas, enslaved Africans found many ways to protest their enslavement, including revolt, escape, and petitioning the abolition of slavery altogether. Maroons were communities of successful runaway slaves who fled to dense forested and largely inaccessible areas where they often intermarried with Native Americans. Some carried on a kind of guerilla warfare with Europeans who tried to track them down. Do you see any patterns in the outbreaks of this partial mapping of slave revolts, either by place or time? What relationships do you see, if any, between slave revolts and abolition, or between national independence movements and abolition? What other observations would you make about the data on this map?

Between 1820 and 1860, the number of free blacks in the United States doubled, from 233,500 to 488,000. This rise resulted from natural increase, successful escapes, "passing" as whites, purchasing of freedom, and manumission.

Frederick Douglass The young Douglass, shown here in a photograph from about 1855, understood as well as any American the profound human, social, and political complexities and consequences of slavery. What qualities do you see in his face? Do they match the Douglass whose words and actions are described in this chapter?

More than half the free blacks lived in the South, most (85 percent in 1860) in the Upper South. They were found scattered on impoverished rural farmlands and in small towns, feared by whites as an inducement to slave unrest. One-third of the southern free African American population lived in cities or towns. In part because it took a long time to buy freedom, free blacks tended to be older, more literate, and lighter-skinned than other African Americans. In 1860, more than 40 percent of free blacks were mulattoes (compared with 10 percent of the slaves). With strong leadership, Baltimore, Richmond, Charleston, New Orleans, and other southern cities developed black communities—their churches, schools, and benevolent societies vibrant in the midst of white hostility.

Most free African Americans in the antebellum South were poor farmhands, day laborers, or woodcutters. In the cities, they worked in factories and lived in poverty. A few skilled jobs, such as barbering, shoemaking, and plastering, were reserved for black men, but they were barred from more than 50 other trades. Women worked as cooks, laundresses, and domestics. The 15 percent of free African Americans who lived in the Lower South were divided into two distinct castes. Most were poor. But in New Orleans, Charleston, and other southern cities, a small, mixed-blood free black elite emerged, closely connected to white society and distant from poor blacks. A handful even owned land and slaves.

Most free blacks had no such privileges. In most states, they could not vote, bear arms, buy liquor, assemble, speak in public, form societies, or testify against whites in court. Nevertheless, the African American persistence in supporting each other in prayer meetings, burial societies, and back alleys was stronger than white efforts to impede it.

RECOVERING *the* PAST

Folktales

A frequent activity of family life in the slave quarters was telling stories. The folktale was an especially useful and subtle way in which older slaves could express defiance toward their masters, impart wisdom and ways of survival to the young, and have a little entertainment. Folktales, cleverly indirect, reveal to historians a great deal about the enslaved Africans' view of their experience and aspirations.

Although the tales took many forms, perhaps the best known are the "Brer [brother] Rabbit" animal stories. The trickster rabbit, who existed originally in West African folklore (and in Brazilian African fables as an Amazonian tortoise), appeared weak and careless, often looked down on by the other animals. Like the slaves, he seemed a victim. But he was also boastful, outwardly happy, and full of mischief. He knew how to use cleverness and cunning to outwit stronger foes, usually by knowing them better than they knew him, a psychological necessity for all who are oppressed.

In one story, the powerful Brer Tiger took all the water and food for himself during a time of famine, leaving the weaker animals miserable. Brer Rabbit, however, turned things around. He played on Brer Tiger's fears that he would be blown away by a "big wind," which was secretly manufactured by the rabbit with the help of other creatures. The tiger was so afraid of the wind (perhaps the winds of revolt?) that he begged Brer Rabbit to tie him "tightly" to a tree to keep from being blown away. Brer Rabbit, although initially resistant in order to make Brer Tiger beg harder, was finally happy to oblige, after which all the creatures of the forest were able to share the cool water and juicy pears that the tiger had denied them.

In another folktale, Brer Rabbit fell into a well but then got out by tricking Brer Wolf into thinking it was better to be in the cool bottom of the well than outside where it was hot. As the wolf lowered himself down in one bucket, Brer Rabbit rose up in the other, laughingly saying as he passed Brer Wolf, "Dis am life; some go up and some go down." In these stories, the weaker animal usually switched roles with the more powerful adversary.

The accompanying story excerpt is from perhaps the most famous animal tale, "The Wonderful Tar Baby Story," written in 1881 by a southern white writer, Joel Chandler Harris, as told by a fictional old black plantation storyteller, Uncle Remus. In this way Harris sought to "preserve the legends themselves in their original simplicity" and capture the "genuine flavor of the old plantation." Therefore, he used dialect, which is best understood if you read the tale out loud as if you were an Uncle Remus reading to a group of children.

We enter the story as a wily but thwarted Brer Fox has decided on a plan to catch the lazy but happy-go-lucky Brer Rabbit, who has been stealing cabbages from a local garden, skillfully avoiding Brer Fox.

REFLECTING ON THE PAST When you have finished the story on pages 318–319, ask yourself what you learned about slavery from it. Why a "tar baby"? Did violence work for Brer Rabbit, or did it only make things worse? What finally worked? How do you interpret the ending? Brer Rabbit returned to the briar patch, a place where he was "bred en bawn." Is the briar patch, with all its thorns, scratches, and roots, a symbol of Africa or slavery? Or something else?

Think about the stories you heard as a child or now find yourself telling others. How do they express the values and dreams, strengths and flaws of the American people? The same question applies to the songs we sing, the art we make, the rhythms we move to, and the jokes we tell: What do they tell us about ourselves and our values? Answering these questions deepens our knowledge of history.

The Wonderful Tar Baby Story

"Didn't the fox never catch the rabbit, Uncle Remus?" asked the little boy the next evening.

"He come mighty nigh it, honey, sho's you born—Brer Fox did. One day atter Brer Rabbit fool 'im wid dat calamus root, Brer Fox went ter wuk en got 'im some tar, en mix it wid some turkentime, en fix up a contrapshun w'at he call a Tar-Baby, en he tuck dish yer Tar-Baby . . . in de big road, en den he lay off in de bushes fer to see what de news wuz gwine ter be. En he didn't hatter wait long, nudder, kaze bimeby here come Brer Rabbit pacin' down de road—lippity-clippity, clippity-lippity—dez ez sassy ez a jay-bird. Brer Fox, he lay low. Brer Rabbit come prancin' 'long twel he spy de Tar-Baby, en den he fotch up on his behime legs like he wuz 'stonished. De Tar Baby, she sot dar, she did, en Brer Fox, he lay low.

"'Mawnin'!' sez Brer Rabbit, sezee—'nice wedder dis mawnin',' sezee.

"Tar-Baby ain't sayin' nuthin', en Brer Fox he lay low.

. . . "'Is you deaf?' sez Brer Rabbit, sezee. 'Kaze if you is, I kin holler louder,' sezee. "Tar-Baby stay still, en Brer Fox, he lay low.

"'You er stuck up, dat's w'at you is,' says Brer Rabbit, sezee, 'en I'm gwine ter kyore you, dat's w'at I'm a gwine ter do,' sezee.

"Brer Fox, he sorter chuckle in his stummick, he did, but Tar-Baby ain't sayin' nothin'.

"'I'm gwine ter larn you how ter talk ter 'spectubble folks ef hit's de las' ack,' sez Brer Rabbit, sezee. 'Ef you don't take off dat hat en tell me howdy, I'm gwine ter bus' you wide open,' sezee.

"Tar-Baby stay still, en Brer Fox, he lay low.

"Brer Rabbit keep on axin' 'im, en de Tar-Baby, she keep on sayin' nothin', twel present'y Brer Rabbit draw back wid his fis', he did, en blip he tuck 'er side er de head. Right dar's whar he broke his merlasses jug. His fis' stuck, en he can't pull loose. De tar hilt 'im. But Tar-Baby, she stay still, en Brer Fox, he lay low.

"'Ef you don't lemme loose, I'll knock you agin,' sez Brer Rabbit, sezee, en wid dat he fotch 'er a wipe wid de udder han', en dat stuck. Tar-Baby, she ain'y sayin' nuthin', en Brer Fox, he lay low.

"'Tu'n me loose, fo' I kick de natal stuffin' outen you,' sez Brer Rabbit, sezee, but de Tar-Baby, she ain't sayin' nuthin'. She des hilt on, en de Brer Rabbit lose de use er his feet in de same way. Brer Fox, he lay low. Den Brer Rabbit squall out dat ef de Tar-Baby don't tu'n 'im loose he butt 'er cranksided. En den he butted, en his head got stuck. Den Brer Fox, he sa'ntered fort', lookin' dez ez innercent ez wunner yo' mammy's mockin'-birds.

"'Howdy, Brer Rabbit,' sez Brer Fox, sezee. 'You look sorter stuck up dis mawnin',' sezee, en den he rolled on de groun', en laft en laft twel he couldn't laff no mo'. 'I speck you'll take dinner wid me dis time, Brer Rabbit. . . .' sez Brer Fox, sezee."

Here Uncle Remus paused, and drew a two-pound yam out of the ashes.

"Did the fox eat the rabbit?" asked the little boy to whom the story had been told.

"Dat's all de fur de tale goes," replied the old man . . . "I hear Miss Sally callin'. You better run 'long."

Urban whites sought to restrain free blacks from mixing with whites in working-class grogshops, gambling halls, and brothels, as well as to confine them to certain sections of the city or (increasingly by the 1850s) to compel them to leave altogether. Those who stayed had trouble finding work, were required to carry papers, and had to have their actions supervised by a white guardian. Southern whites especially feared contact between free blacks and slaves.

The key institution in these developments was the African American church, "the Alpha and Omega of all things," Martin Delaney wrote to Douglass. Welcoming the freedom from white control, the independent African Methodist Episcopal (AME) church grew enormously in the two decades before the Civil War. By 1860, Baltimore had 15 African

"Uncle Remus," said the little boy one evening, when he had found the old man with little or nothing to do, "did the fox kill and eat the rabbit when he caught him with the Tar-Baby?"

"Law, honey, ain't I tell you 'bout dat?" replied the old darkey, chuckling slyly. "I 'clar ter grashus I ought er tole you dat, but old man Nod wuz ridin' on my eyeleds. . . .

"W'at I tell you w'en I fus' begin? I tole you Brer Rabbit wuz a monstus soon creetur; leas'ways dat's w'at I laid out fer ter tell you. . . . 'Fo' you begins fer ter wipe yo' eyes 'bout Brer Rabbit, you wait en see whar'bouts Brer Rabbit gwineter fetch up at. But dat's needer yer ner dar.

"W'en Brer Fox fine Brer Rabbit mixt up wid de Tar-Baby, he feel mighty good, en he roll on de groun' en laff. Bimeby he up'n say, sezee:

"'Well, I speck I got you dis time, Brer Rabbit,' sezee; 'maybe I ain't, but I speck I is. You been runnin' 'roun' here sassin' atter me a mighty long time, but I speck you done come ter de een' er de row. You bin cuttin' up yo' capers en bouncin' 'roun' in dis neighborhood ontwel you come ter b'leeve yo'se'f de boss er de whole gang,' . . . sez Brer Fox, sezee. 'Who ax you fer ter come en strike up a 'quaintance wid dish yer Tar-Baby? En who stuck you up dar whar you iz? Nobody in de roun' worril. You des tuck en jam yo'se'f on dat Tar-Baby widout waitin' fer enny invite,' sez Brer Fox, sezee, 'en dar you is, en dar youll stay twel I fixes up a bresh-pile and fires her up, kaze rm gwineter bobby-cue you dis day, sho,' sez Brer Fox, sezee.

"Den Brer Rabbit talk mighty 'umble.

"'I don't keer w'at you do wid me, Brer Fox,' sezee, 'so you don't fling me in dat brier-patch. Roas' me, Brer Fox' sezee, 'but don't fling me in dat brierpatch,' sezee.

"'Hit's so much trouble fer ter kindle a fier,' sez Brer Fox, sezee, 'dat I speck I'll hatter hang you,' sezee.

"'Hang me des ez high as you please, Brer Fox,' sez Brer Rabbit, sezee, 'but do fer de Lord's sake don't fling me in dat brier-patch,' sezee.

"'I ain't got no string,' sez Brer Fox, sezee, 'en now I speck I'll hatter drown you,' sezee.

"'Drown me des ez deep ez you please, Brer Fox,' sez Brer Rabbit, sezee, 'but do don't fling me in dat brier-patch,' sezee.

"'Dey ain't no water nigh,' sez Brer Fox, sezee, 'en now I speck I'll hatter skin you,' sezee.

"'Skin me, Brer Fox,' sez Brer Rabbit, sezee, 'snatch out my eyeballs, t'ar out my years by de roots, en cut off my legs,' sezee, 'but do please, Brer Fox, don't ffing me in dat brier-patch,' sezee.

"Co'se Brer Fox wanter hurt Brer Rabbit bad ez he kin, so he cotch 'im by de behime legs en slung 'im right in de middle er de brier-patch. Dar wuz a considerbul flutter whar Brer Rabbit struck de bushes, en Brer Fox sorter hang 'roun' fer ter see w'at wuz gwineter happen. Bimeby he hear somebody call 'im, en way up de hill he see Brer Rabbit settin' crosslegged on a chinkapin log koamin' de pitch outen his har wid a chip. Den Brer Fox know dat he bin swop off mighty bad. Brer Rabbit wuz bleedzed fer ter fling back some er his sass, en he holler out:

"'BRED EN BAWN IN A BRIER-PATCH, BRER FOX—BRED EN BAWN IN A BRIER-PATCH!' EN WID DAT HE SKIP OUT DES EZ LIVELY EZ A CRICKET IN DE EMBERS."

American churches representing five different denominations, and in Virginia 14 new black Baptist churches were founded between 1841 and 1860. These institutions gave spiritual solace, set community standards, and offered a host of educational, insurance, self-help, and recreational opportunities.

Nor were African American Catholics left out. Baltimore and New Orleans had strong black Catholic communities made up of Creoles, converts, former slaves, and refugees from Haiti. The Sisters of the Holy Family and other Catholic black women started schools and ministered to the infirm and aged in community religious work reaching Louisville and St. Louis.

African American churches were centers of vital urban black community activities and springboards for activist black preachers seeking larger changes in American society. The Reverend J. C. Pennington, an escaped slave, attended lectures at Yale Divinity School (though he was denied the right to enroll or borrow books). Licensed to preach in 1838, he headed prominent black churches in New Haven, Hartford, and New York City. Pennington started several schools, was an abolitionist leader of the National Negro Convention movement (described in Chapter 10), and founded a black missionary society focused on Africa. Such black religious leaders prepared the way not only for Civil War, but also for an unprecedented postwar growth of African American churches.

A young AME minister, Henry Turner, proclaimed in the 1850s, "We, as a race, have a chance to be Somebody, and if we are ever going to be a people, now is the time." As free blacks became more of a "people," they faced a crisis in the 1850s. The worsening conflict between the North and South over slavery in the territories caused many white southerners to be even more concerned than usual with the presence of free blacks. Pressures increased in the late 1850s either to deport or enslave them. Some black leaders, not surprisingly, began to look more favorably on migration to Africa. That quest was interrupted, however, by the outbreak of the Civil War, rekindling in Douglass the "expiring embers of freedom."

Conclusion

Douglass's Dream of Freedom

When Frederick Douglass forged a free black sailor's pass and escaped to the North, in a real sense he wrote himself into freedom. *The Narrative of the Life of Frederick Douglass*, "written by himself" in 1845, was a way for Douglass both to expose the many evils of slavery and to create his own identity, even choosing his own name. Ironically, Douglass had learned to value reading and writing from his Baltimore masters, the Aulds. This reminds us again of the intricate ways in which the lives of slaves and masters were tied together in the antebellum South. Our understanding of the complexities of this relationship is enhanced as we consider the variations of life in the Big House in the morning, in the fields during the afternoon, in the slave quarters at night, and in the degrees of freedom blacks achieved through resistance and revolt.

•••[Read the Document

Passages from The Autobiography of Frederick Douglass *(1883)* at **www.myhistorylab.com**

In a poignant moment in his *Narrative*, Douglass described his boyhood dreams of freedom as he looked out at the boats on the waters of Chesapeake Bay. Contrasting his own enslavement with the boats he saw as "freedom's swift-winged angels," Douglass vowed to escape: "This very bay shall yet bear me into freedom. . . . There is a better day coming." Many other Americans also were concerned with various evil aspects in their society, slavery among them, and sought ways of shaping a better America. We now turn to these other dreams.

TIME*line*

1787 Constitution adopted with proslavery provisions

1793 Eli Whitney invents cotton gin

1820 South becomes world's largest cotton producer

1830s Southern justification of slavery changes from a necessary evil to a positive good

1831 Nat Turner's slave revolt in Virginia

1845 *Narrative of the Life of Frederick Douglass* published

1852 Harriet Beecher Stowe publishes best-selling *Uncle Tom's Cabin*

1860 Cotton production and prices peak

✓● Study and Review at www.myhistorylab.com

Questions for Review and Reflection

1. How much variety—social and economic—existed in the Old South? In what ways—social and economic—was the South dependent on slavery and cotton, and what were the consequences of this dependency?

2. Compare and contrast North American with Latin American slavery. In which country was slavery most brutal?

3. Show your understanding of the morning, noon, and night structure of this chapter by explaining it to a friend not in the course. How does this structure reflect three different interpretations of slavery?

4. List five or six different ways in which slaves resisted their enslavement and achieved a measure of autonomy, agency, and self-esteem. Can you identify in any way with these methods of resistance?

5. What does the author of this chapter—and Frederick Douglass—think was the worst thing about slavery? What do you think? What does the institution of slavery suggest about American values and how they have changed over time?

Key Terms

Abolitionists 307

Antebellum South 290

Cotton kingdom 290

George Fitzhugh 302

Missouri Compromise 294

Nat Turner revolt 294

Task system 303

10

Shaping America in the Antebellum Age

American Stories

Experiencing the Costs of a Commitment

In November 1836, as the second term of Andrew Jackson neared its end, 30-year-old Marius Robinson and Emily Rakestraw were married near Cincinnati, Ohio. Two months later, Marius went on the road to speak against slavery and organize abolitionist societies in Ohio. Emily stayed in Cincinnati to teach in a school for free blacks. During their 10-month separation, their affectionate letters told of their love and work.

Writing to Emily after midnight from Concord, Ohio, Marius complained of the "desolation of loneliness" he felt without her. Emily responded that she felt "about our separation just as you do" and confessed that her "womanish nature" did not enjoy self-denial. In their letters, each imagined the "form and features" of the other and chided the other for not writing more often. Each thought of the burdens of the other's work. Each expressed comfort, doubted his or her own abilities ("a miserable comforter I am"), and agreed that in their separation "we must look alone to God."

With such love for each other, what prompted this painful early separation? Emily wrote of their duty "to labor long in this cause so near and dear to us both," together if possible, but apart if so decreed by God. Marius, who had been converted by revivalist Charles G. Finney and his abolitionist disciple Theodore Weld, described the reason for their separation: "God and humanity bleeding and suffering demand our services apart." Driven by a strong religious commitment to serve others, these two young reformers dedicated themselves to several social causes: the abolition of slavery, equal rights and education for free blacks, temperance, and women's rights.

Their commitments cost more than separation. When Emily went to Cincinnati to work with other young reformers, her parents disapproved. When she married

Chapter Outline

Religious Revival and Reform Philosophy

The Political Response to Change

Perfectionist Reform and Utopianism

Reforming Society

Abolitionism and Women's Rights

Conclusion: Perfecting America

Marius, who already had a reputation as a "rebel," her parents disowned her. Emily wrote with sadness that her sisters and friends also "love me less . . . than they did in by-gone days." Marius responded that he wished he could "dry your tears" and sought to heal the rift. Although Emily's family eventually accepted their marriage, there were other griefs. Teaching at the school in Cincinnati was demanding, and Emily could not get rid of a persistent cough. Furthermore, the white citizens of the city treated the school and the young abolitionists in their midst with contempt. Earlier in the year, Marius had escaped an angry mob by disguising himself and mingling with the crowd that came to sack the offices of a reformist journal edited by James G. Birney. Emily, meanwhile, tirelessly persisted in the work of "our school" while worrying about the health and safety of her husband.

She had good reason for concern, for Marius's letters were full of reports of mob attacks, disrupted meetings, stonings, and narrow escapes. At two lectures, he was "mobbed thrice, once most rousingly," by crowds of "the veriest savages I ever saw," armed with clubs and intense hatred for those speaking against slavery. In June, he was dragged from his Quaker host's home, beaten, and tarred and feathered. Never quite recovering his health, Marius spent six months in bed, weak and dispirited. For nearly 10 years after that, the Robinsons lived on an Ohio farm, only slightly involved in abolitionist activity. Despite the joyous birth of two daughters, they felt lonely, restless, and guilt-ridden, "tired of days blank of benevolent effort and almost of benevolent desires."

The work of Emily and Marius Robinson represents one response by the American people to the rapid social and economic changes of the antebellum era described in the last two chapters. In September 1835, a year before the Robinsons' marriage, the Niles Register commented on some 500 recent incidents of mob violence and social upheaval. "Society seems everywhere unhinged, and the demon of 'blood and slaughter' has been let loose upon us. . . . [The] character of our countrymen seems suddenly changed." How did Americans adapt to these changes? In a world that seemed everywhere "unhinged," in which old rules and patterns no longer provided guidance, how did people maintain some sense of control over their lives? How did they seek to shape their altered world? How could they both adopt the benefits of change and reduce the accompanying disruptions?

One way was to embrace the changes fully. Thus, some Americans became entrepreneurs in new industries; invested in banks, canals, and railroads; bought more land and slaves; and invented new machines. Others went west or to the new textile mills, enrolled in common schools, joined trade unions, specialized their labor in the workplace and the home, and celebrated modernization's practical benefits. Marius Robinson eventually went into life insurance, though he and Emily never fully gave up their reformist efforts and idealism.

But many Americans were uncomfortable with the character of the new era. Some worried about the unrestrained power and materialism symbolized by the slavemaster's control over his slaves. Others feared that institutions like the U.S. Bank represented an "aristocracy capable of undermining the country's honest producers." Seeking positions of leadership and authority, these critics of the new order tried to shape a nation that retained the benefits of economic change without sacrificing humane principles of liberty, equality of opportunity, and community virtue. What do the explorations of religious revivalism, party politics, utopian communitarianism, and social reform reveal about the varied ways in which the American people attempt to influence their country's development?

Religious Revival and Reform Philosophy

When the Frenchman Alexis de Tocqueville visited the United States in 1831 and 1832, he remarked that there was "no country in the whole world in which the Christian religion retains a greater influence over the souls of men than in America." Tocqueville was describing a new and powerful religious enthusiasm among American Protestants. Religious rebirth gave some Americans a mooring in a fast-changing world; others determined to refashion their society, working through new political parties to shape an agenda for the nation or through reform associations targeting a particular social evil. Although not all evangelicals agreed about politics or even about what needed reform, religion was the lens through which they viewed events and sought change.

Finney and the Second Great Awakening

From the late 1790s until the late 1830s, a wave of religious revivals matching the intensity of the Great Awakening in the 1730s and 1740s swept through the United States. While there were many links between Protestant denominations in the United States and in Great Britain, the popular character of American revivalism made it distinctive. British religion was becoming more conservative, while American Protestantism was becoming more democratic.

The turn-of-the-century frontier camp meeting revivals and the New England revivals sparked by Lyman Beecher took on a new emphasis and location after 1830. Led by the spellbinding **Charles G. Finney**, revivalism shifted to upstate New York and the Old Northwest. Both areas had been gripped by profound economic and social changes.

Rochester, New York, was typical. Located on the Erie Canal, it was changed by the canal from a sleepy village of 300 in 1815 to a bustling city of nearly 20,000 by 1830. As in other cities, booming economic growth created a gulf between masters and workers. As that gulf widened, masters' control over laborers weakened. Saloons and unions sprang up, and workers became more transient, following opportunities westward.

In 1830, prompted partly by their concerns about poverty and absenteeism, both caused presumably by alcohol, prominent Rochester citizens invited Charles Finney to the city. He led what became one of the most successful revivals of the Second Great Awakening. Finney preached nearly every night and three times on Sundays, first converting the city's business elite, often through their wives, and then many workers. For six months, Rochester experienced a citywide prayer meeting in which one conversion led to another.

Jonathan Edwards had believed that revivals were God's miracles. Revivalist preachers like Finney emphasized the role of human effort and faith in bringing about individual salvation and highlighted emotion over doctrine. Understanding that the human "agency" of the minister was crucial in causing a revival, Finney even published a do-it-yourself manual for revivalists. But few could match his powerful preaching style that relied upon both logic and emotion to trigger conversions. When he threw an imaginary brick at the Devil, people ducked.

The Rochester revival was part of a wave of religious enthusiasm in America that contributed to the tremendous growth of Methodists, Baptists, and other evangelical denominations in the first half of the nineteenth century. By 1844, Methodism became the country's largest denomination with over a million members.

American Catholics also caught the revival fervor in the 1830s. Scattered in small but growing numbers, urban Catholic leaders recognized that survival as a small, often despised religion depended on constant reinvigoration and evangelism. Focusing on the parish mission, energetic retreats and revivals gathered Catholics from miles around to preserve a religious heritage seriously threatened by life in Protestant America.

Finney believed that humans were not passive objects of God's predestined plan, but moral free agents who could choose good over evil and thereby eradicate sin. Unlike Catholic and southern revivalism, which sought personal conversion and personal salvation, Finney revivals insisted that conversion and salvation were not the end of religious experience but the beginning. Finney encouraged not only individual reformation but also the commitment on the part of converted Christians to embrace the sacred duty of reforming society.

The Transcendentalists

No one knew this better than Ralph Waldo Emerson, a Concord, Massachusetts, essayist and the era's foremost intellectual figure. Emerson's essays of the 1830s influenced the midcentury generation of reformist American intellectuals, artists, and writers. The small but influential group of New England intellectuals living near Emerson were called Transcendentalists because they believed that truth was found beyond (transcended) experience. Shedding European intellectual traditions, Emerson urged Americans to look inward and to nature for self-knowledge, self-reliance, and the spark of divinity within them. Such examinations would lead to social reform. "What is man born for," Emerson asked, "but to be a Reformer?"

Inspired by self-reflection, Transcendentalists asked troublesome questions. They challenged not only slavery, an obvious evil, but also the obsessive, competitive pace of economic life, the overriding materialism, and the restrictive conformity of social life.

When Emerson wrote, "Whoso would be a man, must be a nonconformist," he described his friend Henry David Thoreau. No one thought more deeply about the virtuous natural life than Thoreau. On July 4, 1845, he went to live in a small hut by Walden Pond, near Concord, to confront the "essential facts of life"—to discover who he was and how to live well. When Thoreau left Walden two years later, he protested against slavery and the Mexican War by refusing to pay his taxes. He went to jail briefly and wrote an essay, "On Civil Disobedience" (1849), and a book, *Walden* (1854), both classic statements of what one person can do to protest unjust laws and wars and live a life of principle.

The Political Response to Change

Although transcendentalism touched only a few elite New Englanders, evangelical Protestantism affected perhaps 40 percent of Americans. Evangelical values and religious loyalties colored many people's understanding of the appropriate role of government and influenced their politics. As politics became more a popular than an elite vocation, it was not surprising that religious commitments spilled over into it.

At the heart of American politics was the concern for the continued health of the republican experiment. As American society changed, so did the understanding of what was needed to maintain that health. In the late 1850s, a Maine newspaper warned that the preservation of the nation's freedom depended on the willingness of its citizens to go to the polls. This insistence on voting as crucial to the well-being of the country was a new emphasis in the United States and unique in the world at that time.

Before the 1820s, politics in both the United States and Europe primarily engaged the social and economic elite. In the United States, however, the power of the Revolution's ideas and the relative weakness of the country's upper classes led to a gradual extension of the franchise to all white men. During the early nineteenth century, many states were voluntarily removing voting restrictions even though the majority of white men did not trouble themselves with political matters. But the Panic of 1819 and the spirited presidential campaigns for Andrew Jackson helped create widespread interest in politics and a distinctive American political style. For many Americans, political participation became an important way of asserting and supporting important values and promoting their vision of the republic.

Changing Political Culture

Jackson's presidency was crucial in bringing politics to the center of many Americans' lives. Styling himself the people's candidate in 1828, Jackson derided the Adams administration as corrupt and aristocratic and promised a more democratic political system. He told voters he would "purify" and "reform the Government," purging all "who have been appointed from political considerations or against the will of the people." Most Americans believed campaign rhetoric. Four times more men turned out to vote in the election of 1828 than four years earlier. They gave Jackson a resounding 56 percent of their ballots. No other president in the century would equal that percentage of popular support.

⊙┤**View** the **Image**
Andrew Jackson's
Inauguration (Lithograph)
at **www.myhistorylab.com**

Despite campaign rhetoric and his image as a democratic hero, Jackson was not personally very democratic, nor did the era he symbolized involve any significant redistribution of wealth. Jackson owned slaves, defended slavery, and condoned mob attacks on abolitionists like Marius Robinson. He disliked Indians and ordered the forcible removal of southeastern Native Americans to west of the Mississippi River in blatant disregard of treaty rights and a Supreme Court decision. Belying promises of widening opportunity, the rich got richer during the Jacksonian era, and most farming and urban laboring families did not prosper.

But the nation's political life changed in important ways. The old system of politics, based on elite coalitions and dependent on voters deferring to their "betters," largely disappeared. In its place emerged a competitive party system, begun early in the republic but now oriented toward heavy voter participation. The major parties grew adept at raising money, selecting and promoting candidates, and bringing voters to the polls. A new "democratic" style of political life emerged as parties sponsored conventions, rallies (much like evangelical revivals), and parades to encourage political identification and participation. Party politics became a central preoccupation for many adult white males. In both the North and South, even women who were formally excluded from voting might become caught up in party politics and turn up at rallies and speeches.

Political parties appealed to popular emotions, religious views, and ethnic prejudices. Party-subsidized newspapers regularly indulged in scurrilous attacks on political candidates. The language of politics became contentious and militaristic. Jackson defined an opponent as the "enemy," while politicians described elections as battles. Strong party identification and loyalty became part of the new political culture.

Jackson's Path to the White House

The early career of Andrew Jackson gave few hints of his future political importance. Orphaned at age 14, young Jackson was often in trouble. As a law student, he was "a most roaring . . . horse-racing, card-playing, mischievous fellow." Still, he passed the bar and set out to seek his fortune in frontier Nashville. There he built a successful law practice and became state attorney general, a substantial landowner, and a prominent citizen of Nashville.

Jackson's national reputation stemmed mainly from his military exploits, primarily against Indians. As major general of the Tennessee militia, he proved able and popular, winning the nickname of "Old Hickory." His savage victory over the Creek in 1813 and 1814 brought notoriety and an appointment as major general in the U.S. Army. Victory at New Orleans in 1815 made him a national hero. Within two years, he was talked of as a presidential candidate. While aggressive military forays into Spanish Florida in 1818 bothered rival politicians and added to Jackson's reputation for scandal, they increased both his popularity and interest in the presidency. Jackson recognized that his greatest appeal lay with ordinary people, whom he cultivated. But he also secured effective political backing. Careful political maneuvering in Tennessee in the early 1820s brought him election as U.S. senator and nomination for the presidency in 1824.

Jackson won both the popular and the electoral votes in 1824, but lost in the House of Representatives to John Quincy Adams. This failure highlighted

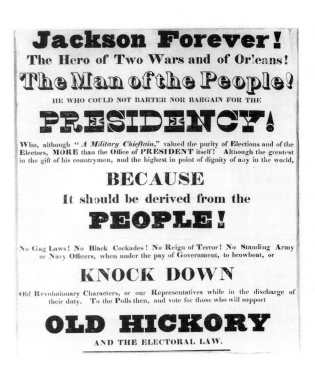

The Man of the People
Unlike rivals J. Q. Adams and Henry Clay, who deprived Jackson of the presidency in 1824, Jackson (nicknamed "Old Hickory" after America's toughest hardwood) claimed to honor the constitutional electoral system and the will of the people. To what historical events does this poster refer? Was Jackson a man of the people?

the importance of political organization. Confident of his strength in the West and helped by Adams's vice president, John C. Calhoun, in the South, Jackson organized his campaign by setting up committees and newspapers in many states and by encouraging efforts to undermine Adams and Clay.

A loose coalition promoting Jackson's candidacy began to call itself the Democratic party. Politicians of diverse views from all sections of the country were drawn to it, including Martin Van Buren of New York. Jackson masterfully waffled on controversial issues. He concealed his dislike of banks and paper money and vaguely advocated a "middle and just course" on the tariff. He also promised to cleanse government of corruption and privilege.

The Jackson–Adams campaign in 1828 degenerated into a nasty but entertaining contest. The Democrats whipped up enthusiasm with barbecues, mass rallies, and parades and distributed buttons and hats with hickory leaves attached. Few people discussed issues. Both sides indulged in slanderous personal attacks. Supporters of Adams and Clay, who called themselves National Republicans, branded Jackson "an adulterer, a gambler . . . a drunkard, and a murderer" and maligned his wife Rachel as immoral.

The Jacksonians charged Adams with buying Clay's support in 1824 and described him as a "stingy, undemocratic" aristocrat determined to destroy the people's liberties. Worse yet, they said, Adams was an intellectual. Campaign slogans contrasted the hero of New Orleans, "a man who can fight," with a wimpy Adams, "a man who can write."

Jackson's supporters in Washington worked to ensure his election by devising a tariff bill to win necessary support in key states. Under the leadership of Van Buren, who hoped to replace Calhoun as Jackson's heir apparent, the Democrats in Congress managed to pass what opponents called the **"Tariff of Abominations."** It arbitrarily raised rates to protect New England textiles, Pennsylvania iron, and some agricultural goods, securing voters in those states where the Democrats needed more support.

The efforts of Jackson and his party paid off as he won an astonishing 647,286 votes, about 56 percent of the total. Organization, money, effective publicity, and a popular style of campaigning had brought the 60-year-old Jackson to the presidency. His inauguration, however, horrified many. Washington was packed for the ceremonies. When Jackson appeared to take the oath of office, wild cheering broke out. Few heard him, but many hoped to shake the new president's hand, and Jackson was all but mobbed. At the White House reception, the crowd got completely out of hand. As Justice Joseph Story observed, a throng of people, "from the highest and most polished, down to the most vulgar and gross," poured into the White House, overturning furniture in a rush for food and punch. Jackson had to leave by a side door. When wine and ice cream were carried out to the lawn, many guests followed by diving through the windows. The inauguration, to Story, represented the "reign of King Mob." But another observer called it a "proud day for the people." Their contrasting views on the inauguration captured the essence of the Jackson era.

Old Hickory's Vigorous Presidency

Although Jackson adopted vague positions on important issues during the campaign, as president he needed to confront many of them. His decisions, often controversial, helped sharpen what it meant to be a Democrat.

A few key convictions, drawn from Jeffersonian principles—the principle of majority rule, the limited power of the national government, the obligation of the national government to defend the interests of the nation's average people against the "monied aristocracy"—guided Jackson's actions as president. As he drew upon Jeffersonian ideals, Jackson helped to transform them and to create a new political environment. Seeing himself as the people's most authentic representative (only the president was elected by all the people), Jackson intended to be a vigorous executive. More than any predecessor, Jackson used presidential power in the name of the people and justified his actions by appeals to the voters. Jackson asserted his power most dramatically through the veto. His six predecessors had cast only nine vetoes, mostly against measures that they had believed unconstitutional. Jackson vetoed 12 bills during his two terms, often because they conflicted with his political agenda.

Jackson had promised to correct what he called an undemocratic and corrupt system of government officeholding. Too often, "unfaithful or incompetent" men clung to government jobs for years. Jackson proposed to throw these "scoundrels" out and establish rotation of office. The duties of public office were so "plain and simple," he said, that ordinary men could fulfill them.

Jackson's rhetoric was more extreme than his actions. He did not replace officeholders wholesale. In the first year and a half of his presidency, he removed 919 officeholders of a total of 10,093, mostly for corruption or incompetence. Nor were the new Democratic appointees especially plain, untutored, or honest; they were much like their predecessors. Still, Jackson's rhetoric helped create a new democratic political culture for most of the nineteenth century.

His policy on internal improvements—roads, canals, and other forms of transportation—was less far-seeing. Like most Americans, Jackson recognized their economic importance. But he opposed infringement on states' rights. When proposals for federal support for internal improvements seemed to rob local and state authorities of their proper function, he opposed them. In 1830, he vetoed the Maysville Road bill, which recommended federal funding for a road in Henry Clay's Kentucky. But projects of national significance, like river improvements or lighthouses, were different. During his presidency, Jackson supported an annual average of $1.3 million in internal improvements.

In a period of rapid economic change, tariffs stirred heated debate. New England and the mid-Atlantic states, the center of manufacturing, favored tariffs. The South had long opposed them because they made it more expensive to buy northern and European manufactured goods and threatened to provoke retaliation against southern cotton and tobacco exports. Feelings ran particularly high in South Carolina. Some of that state's leaders mistakenly believed the tariff was the prime reason for the depression hanging over their state. In addition, some worried that the federal government might eventually interfere with slavery, a frightening prospect in a state where slaves outnumbered whites.

Vice President Calhoun, a brilliant political thinker opposed to the tariff, provided the appropriate theory to check federal power and protect minority rights. "We are not a nation," he once remarked, "but a Union, a confederacy of equal and sovereign states." In 1828, the same year as the hateful tariff, Calhoun anonymously published "Exposition and Protest," presenting nullification as a way for southern states to protect themselves from harmful national action by declaring legislation null and void.

Two years later, Calhoun's doctrine was aired in a Senate debate over public land policy. South Carolina's Robert Hayne defined nullification and urged western states to adopt it. New England's Daniel Webster responded. The federal government, he said, was no mere agent of the state legislatures. It was "made for the people, made by the people, and answerable to the people." Aware that nullification could mean a "once glorious Union . . . drenched . . . in fraternal blood," Webster cried in his powerful closing words that the appropriate motto for the nation was not "Liberty first and Union afterwards, but Liberty and Union, now and forever, one and inseparable!"

•••⌐**Read** the **Document**

South Carolina's Ordinance of Nullification (1832)

at **www.myhistorylab.com**

The drama was repeated a month later in a dinner toast, when President Jackson declared his position. Despite his support of states' rights, Jackson did not believe that any state had the right to reject the will of the majority or to destroy the Union. Jackson rose for a toast, held high his glass, and said, "Our Union—it must be preserved." Challenged, Calhoun followed: "The Union—next to our liberty most dear." The split between them widened over personal as well as ideological issues, and in 1832, Calhoun resigned as vice president. The final rupture came in a collision over the tariff and nullification.

In 1832, hewing to Jackson's "middle course," Congress modified the tariff of 1828 by retaining high duties on some goods but lowering other rates to an earlier level. A South Carolina convention later that year adopted an **Ordinance of Nullification**, voiding the tariffs of 1828 and 1832 in the state. The legislature funded a volunteer army and threatened secession if the federal government tried to force the state to comply.

South Carolina had attacked the principles of union and majority rule, and Jackson responded forcefully. To the "malcontents" in South Carolina, he proclaimed emphatically that "the laws of the United States must be executed. . . . Disunion by armed force is treason. . . . The Union will be preserved and treason and rebellion promptly put down."

Jackson's proclamation stimulated an outburst of patriotism all over the country. South Carolina stood alone, abandoned even by other southern states.

Jackson asked Congress for legislation to enforce tariff duties (the Force Bill of 1833), and new tariff revisions, engineered by Clay and supported by Calhoun, called for reductions over a 10-year period. Having secured its objective, South Carolina quickly repealed its nullification of the tariff laws. But the state saved face by nullifying the Force Bill, which Jackson ignored. The crisis was over, but left unresolved were the constitutional issues it raised. Was the Union permanent? Was secession a valid way to protect minority rights? Such questions would trouble Americans for three decades.

Jackson's Native American Policy

Jackson threatened force on South Carolina; he used it on southeastern Indians. His policy of forcible relocation defined governmental and private practice toward Native Americans for the rest of the century.

In the early nineteenth century, the vast lands of the five "civilized nations" of the Southeast (the Cherokee, Choctaw, Chickasaw, Seminole, and Creek) had been seriously eroded by land-hungry whites supported by military campaigns led by professional Indian fighters like Jackson. The Creek lost 22 million acres in Georgia and Alabama after Jackson defeated them in 1814. Cessions to the government and private sales accounted for even bigger losses: Cherokee holdings of more than 50 million acres in 1802 dwindled to only 9 million 20 years later.

A Supreme Court decision in 1823 declaring that Indians could occupy but not hold title to land in the United States bolstered the trend. Seeing that their survival was threatened, Indian nations acted to protect tribal lands. By 1825, the Creek, Cherokee, and Chickasaw restricted land sales to government agents. The Cherokee, having already assimilated such elements of white culture as agricultural practices, slaveholding, Christianity, and constitutionalism, established a police force to prevent local leaders from selling tribal lands.

Jackson's election in 1828 boosted white efforts to relocate the Indians west of the Mississippi, however. In 1829, Jackson recommended to Congress removal of the southeastern tribes. Appealing at first to sympathy, Jackson argued that because the Indians were "surrounded by the whites," they were inevitably doomed to "weakness and decay." "Humanity and national honor" justified removal. He also insisted that state laws should prevail over the claims of either Indians or the federal government (thus contradicting his tariff policy).

The crisis came to a head that same year, when the Georgia legislature declared the Cherokee tribal council illegal and claimed jurisdiction over both the tribe and its lands. In 1830, the Cherokee were forbidden to bring suits or testify against whites in the Georgia courts. The Cherokee protested to the Supreme Court. In 1832, Chief Justice Marshall supported them in *Worcester* v. *Georgia*, saying that state laws could "have no force" over the Cherokee.

●●●─Read the Document

Memorial of the Cherokee Nation (1830)

at **www.myhistorylab.com**

Legal victory did not suppress white land hunger. With Jackson's blessing, Georgia defied the Court ruling. By 1835, harassment, intimidation,

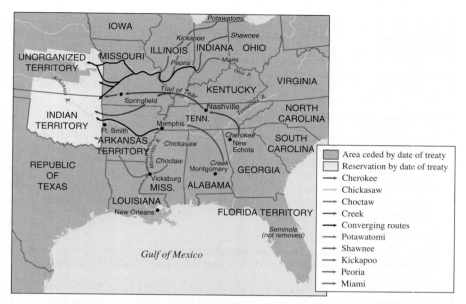

Native American Removals: Southeast and Midwest This map shows the westward routes of Indians removed from the Southeast to the new Indian territory in Oklahoma and from the Midwest (Old Northwest Territory) to present-day Kansas. Why Kansas and Oklahoma? Who already lived there?

and bribery had persuaded a minority of chiefs to sign a removal treaty. That year, Jackson informed the Cherokee, "You cannot remain where you are. Circumstances . . . render it impossible that you can flourish in the midst of a civilized community." But most Cherokee refused to leave. Chief John Ross protested to Congress that the treaty was illegitimate. "We are stripped of every attribute of freedom. . . . Our property may be plundered . . . our lives may be taken away." His words did no good. So in 1837 and 1838, the U.S. Army gathered the terrified Indians in stockades before herding them west to the "Indian Territory" in present-day Oklahoma.

The removal, whose $6 million cost was deducted from the $9 million awarded the Cherokee for its eastern lands, killed perhaps a quarter of the 15,000 who set out. The Cherokee, following the earlier experiences of the Creek, Choctaw, and Chickasaw, remember this as the **"Trail of Tears."**

Between 1821 and 1840, tribes in the Old Northwest, as well as the southeast, were also forced westward to Kansas and Oklahoma. Despite resistance from some tribes, most nations were removed. Although both Jackson and the Removal Act of 1830 had promised to protect and forever guarantee the Indian lands in the West, within a generation those promises, like others before and since, would be broken. Indian removal left the eastern United States open for the enormous economic expansion already described.

View the **Image**

Cherokee Trail of Tears (Painting)
at **www.myhistorylab.com**

Key Court Cases on Indian Rights

These Supreme Court cases decided in the nineteenth century have provided the legal basis for Native American activism in the twentieth century. Although Indian victories in court during the Jacksonian period did not halt the determination of whites to take over tribal lands, in the twentieth century, these court decisions allowed Indian tribes to win numerous court victories.

1823: *Johnson & Graham's Lessee* v. *William Mcintosh*

This case focused on the status of a land grant from an Indian tribe to an individual person. The decision recognized tribal sovereignty and the tribe's rights to land. The court stated that only the federal government was competent to negotiate with tribes for their lands.

"It has been contested that the Indian claims amounted to nothing. Their right of possession has never been questioned . . . the Court is decidedly of the opinion, that the plaintiffs do not exhibit a title which can be sustained in the Courts of the United States."

1831: *Cherokee Nation v. Georgia*

This case involved the status of state law within the Cherokee nation. The court classified the Indian tribes as domestic dependent nations whose relationship was like that of a ward to a guardian.

"Though the Indians are acknowledged to have an unquestionable, and, heretofore, unquestioned right to the lands they occupy until that right shall be extinguished by a voluntary cession to our government, yet it may well be doubted whether those tribes . . . can, with strict accuracy, be denominated as foreign nations. They may more correctly, perhaps, be denominated as domestic dependent nations."

1832: *Worcester v. Georgia*

This case was prompted by the state of Georgia's attempt to extend state law over the Cherokee nation. The decision reaffirmed Indian political rights, stating that Georgia laws had no force in Native American territories and that only the federal government had jurisdiction in Indian territories.

"The Indian nations had always been considered as distinct, independent, political communities . . . the settled doctrine of the law of nations is, that a weaker power does not surrender its independence—its rights to self-government—by associating with a stronger."

1835: *Mitchell v. The United States*

This decision affirmed the rights Native Americans have as occupants (not owners) of the land. "It is enough to consider as a settled principle, that the right of occupancy is considered as sacred as the fee simple of the white."

Jackson's Bank War and "Van Ruin's" Depression

As the (white) people's advocate, Jackson could not ignore the Second Bank of the United States, which in 1816 had received a charter for 20 years. The bank generated intense feelings. Jackson called it a "monster" threatening the people's liberties. But it was not so irresponsible as Jacksonians imagined.

Guided since 1823 by the aristocratic Nicholas Biddle, the Philadelphia bank and its 29 branches generally played a responsible economic role in an expansionary period. As the nation's largest commercial bank, "the B.U.S." could shift funds around the country as needed and could influence state banking activity. It restrained state banks from making unwise loans by insisting that they back their notes with specie (gold or silver coin) and by calling in its loans to them. The bank accepted federal deposits, made commercial loans, and bought and sold government bonds. Businessmen, state bankers needing credit, and nationalist politicians such as Webster and Clay, who were on the bank's payroll, all favored it.

Other Americans, led by the president, distrusted the bank. Businessmen and speculators in western lands disliked its careful control over state banking and wanted cheap, inflated money to finance new projects and expansion. Some state bankers resented its power over their actions. Southern and western farmers regarded it as immoral because it dealt with paper rather than landed property. Others simply thought it was unconstitutional.

Jackson had long opposed the B.U.S. He hated banks in general because of a near financial disaster in his own past, and also because he and his advisers considered the B.U.S. the chief example of a special privilege monopoly that hurt the common man—farmers, craftsmen, and debtors. Jackson called the bank a threat to the Republic. Its power and financial resources, he thought, made it a "vast electioneering engine."

Aware of Jackson's hostility, Clay and Webster persuaded Biddle to ask Congress for a new charter in 1832, four years ahead of schedule. They reasoned that in an election year, Jackson would not risk a veto. The bill to recharter the bank swept through Congress. Jackson took up the challenge. "The bank . . . is trying to kill me," he told Van Buren, "but I will kill it."

•••▶Read the **Document**

Jacksonian Democracy: Andrew Jackson, Veto of the Bank Bill (1832)
at **www.myhistorylab.com**

Jackson determined not only to veto the bill, but also to carry his case to the public. His veto message, condemning the bank as undemocratic, un-American, and unconstitutional, was meant to stir up voters. He presented the bank as a dangerous monopoly that gave the rich special privileges and harmed "the humble members of society." He also pointed to the high percentage of foreign investors in the bank. Jackson's veto message turned the rechartering issue into a struggle between the people and the aristocracy. His oversimplified analysis made the bank into a symbol of everything that worried many Americans in a time of change.

The bank furor helped to clarify party differences. In 1832, the National Republicans, now calling themselves **Whigs**, nominated Henry Clay, and they and Biddle spent thousands of dollars trying to defeat "King Andrew." Democratic campaign rhetoric pitted Jackson, the people, and democracy against Clay, the bank, and aristocracy. The Anti-Masons, the first third party in American political life and the first to hold a nominating convention, expressed popular resentments against the elitist Masonic order (Jackson was a member) and other secret societies.

Jackson won handsomely, with 124,000 more popular votes than the combined total for Clay and the Anti-Mason candidate, William Wirt. "He may be President for life if he chooses," said Wirt of Jackson.

Jackson, seeing the election as a victory for his bank policy, closed in on Biddle, even though the bank's charter had four years to run. He decided to weaken the bank by transferring $10 million in government funds to state banks. Although two secretaries of the treasury balked at the request as financially unsound, Jackson persisted until he found one, Roger Taney, willing to do it.

Jackson's war with Biddle and the bank had serious economic consequences. A wave of speculation in western lands and ambitious new state internal-improvement schemes in the mid-1830s produced inflated land prices and a flood of paper money. Even Jackson was concerned, and he tried to curtail irresponsible economic activity. In July 1836, he issued the Specie Circular, announcing that the government would accept only gold and silver in payment for public lands. Panicky investors rushed to change paper notes into specie, and banks started calling in loans. The result was the Panic of 1837. Jackson was blamed for this rapid monetary expansion followed by sudden deflation, but international trade problems probably contributed more to the panic and to the ensuing seven years of depression.

Whatever the primary cause, Jackson left his successor, Martin Van Buren, elected in 1836 over a trio of Whig opponents, with an economic crisis. Van Buren had barely taken the oath of office in 1837 when banks and businesses began to collapse. "Van Ruin's" presidency was dominated by a severe depression. As New York banks suspended credit and began calling in loans, some $6 million was lost on defaulted debts. By the fall of 1837, one-third of America's workers were unemployed, and thousands of others had only part-time work. Those who kept their jobs saw wages fall by 30 to 50 percent within two years. The price of necessities nearly doubled. As winter neared in 1837, a journalist estimated that 200,000 New Yorkers were "in utter hopeless distress with no means of surviving the winter but those provided by charity." They took to the streets, but as one worker said, most laborers called "not for the bread and fuel of charity, but for Work!"

((•—[Hear the **Audio**

Van Buren

at **www.myhistorylab.com**

The pride of workers was dampened as soup kitchens and breadlines grew faster than jobs. Laboring families found themselves defenseless, for the depression destroyed the trade union movement begun a decade earlier—a demise hastened by employers who imposed longer hours, cut wages and piece rates, and divided workers. Job competition, poverty, and ethnic animosities led to violent clashes in other eastern cities, as we have seen.

The Second American Party System

By the mid-1830s, a new two-party system and a lively national political culture had emerged in the United States. The parties had taken shape amid the conflicts of Jackson's presidency and the religious fervor and commitments stimulated by the Second Great Awakening. Although both parties included wealthy and influential leaders and mirrored the nation's growing diversity, Democrats had the better claim to be "the party of the common man," with support in all sections of the country.

Whigs represented greater wealth than Democrats and were strongest in New England and in areas settled by New Englanders across the Upper Midwest. Appealing to businessmen and manufacturers, Whigs generally endorsed Clay's American System: a national bank, federally supported internal improvements, and tariff protection for industry. Many large southern cotton planters joined the Whig party because of its position on bank credit and internal improvements. Whigs ran almost evenly with Democrats in the South for a decade, and artisans and laborers belonged equally to each party. The difficulty in drawing clear regional or class distinctions between Whigs and Democrats suggests that ethnic, religious, and cultural background also influenced party choice.

In the Jeffersonian tradition, the Democrats espoused liberty and local rule. They wanted freedom from those who legislated morality, from religious tyranny, from special privilege, and from too much government. For them, the best society was one in which all Americans were free to follow individual interests. The Democrats appealed to members of denominations that had suffered discrimination in colonies and states where there had been an established church. Scots–Irish, German, French, and Irish Catholic immigrants, as well as freethinkers and labor organizers, tended to be Jacksonians. Democrats were less moralistic than Whigs on matters like drinking and slavery. Their religious background generally taught the inevitability of sin and evil, and they sought to separate politics from moral issues.

By contrast, for many Whigs, religious and moral commitments shaped political goals and the ways they understood issues. Calling themselves the party of law and order, most Whigs did not think Americans needed more freedom; rather, they had to learn to use the freedom they already had. If all men were to vote, they should learn how to use their political privileges. Old-stock Yankee Congregationalists and Presbyterians were usually Whigs. So were Quakers and evangelical Protestants, who believed in government action to change moral behavior and eradicate sin. Whigs supported a wide variety of reforms, such as temperance, public education, and strict observance of the Sabbath, as well as government action to promote economic development.

Party identification played an increasingly large part in the lives of American men. Gaudy new electioneering styles were designed to recruit new voters into the political process and ensure loyalty. Politics offered excitement, entertainment, camaraderie, and a way to shape the changing world.

The election of 1840 illustrated the new political culture. Passing over Henry Clay, the Whigs nominated William Henry Harrison, the aging hero of the Battle of Tippecanoe of 1811. Virginian John Tyler was nominated as vice president to underline the regional diversity of the party. The Democrats had no choice but to renominate Van Buren, who conducted a quiet campaign. The Whig campaign, however, used every form of popularized appeal: songs, cartoons, barbecues, and torchlight parades.

The Whigs reversed conventional images by labeling Van Buren an aristocratic dandy and their man as a simple candidate. Harrison reminded voters of General Jackson, and they swept him into office, with 234 electoral votes to Van Buren's 60. In one of the largest turnouts in American history, over 80 percent of eligible voters marched to the polls. A Democratic party

The Second American Party System

	Democrats	**Whigs**
Leaders	Andrew Jackson John C. Calhoun Martin Van Buren Thomas Hart Benton	Henry Clay Daniel Webster John Quincy Adams William Henry Harrison
Political tradition	Republican party (Jefferson, Madison)	Federalist party (Hamilton, John Adams)
Major Political Beliefs	State and local autonomy Opposition to monopoly and privilege Low land prices and tariffs Freedom from government interference	National power Support for U.S. Bank, high tariff Internal improvements Broad government role in reforming America
Primary Sources of Support		
Region	South and West	New England, Middle Atlantic, Upper Midwest
Class	Middle-class and small farmers, northeastern urban laborers and artisans	Big southern planters and wealthy businessmen, pockets of middling farmers in Midwest and South, artisans
Ethnicity	Scots–Irish, Irish, French, German, and Canadian immigrants	English, New England old stock
Religion	Catholics, frontier Baptists and Methodists, free thinkers	Presbyterians, Congregationalists, Quakers, moralists, reformers

journal acknowledged that the Whigs had out-Jacksoned the Jacksonians: "We taught them how to conquer us."

During the campaign, one man had complained that he was tired of all the hoopla over "the Old Hero. Nothing but politics . . . mass-meetings are held in every groggery." The implied criticism of the role that alcohol played in party politics highlights the moral and religious perspective many Americans, especially Whigs, brought to politics. Others, however, rejected the political route and sought other means to impose order and morality on American society.

Perfectionist Reform and Utopianism

"Be ye therefore perfect even as your Father in heaven is perfect," commanded the Bible. Mid-nineteenth-century reformers, inspired by the Finney revivals, took the challenge seriously. Eventually, a perfected millennial era—1,000 years of peace, harmony, and Christian brotherhood—would bring the Second Coming of Christ.

This perfectionist thrust in religion fit America's sense of itself as chosen by God to reform the world.

Watch the Video

Evangelical Religion and Politics, Then and Now

at **www.myhistorylab.com**

Motivations and Causes of Reform in America, 1830–1850

- Changing relationships between men and women, masters and workers as a result of the market economy, growth of cities, and increasing immigration
- Finney and other religious revivalists in the Second Great Awakening
- Social activist and ethical impulses of the Whig party
- Psychological anxieties over shifting class and ethnic relationships
- Family traditions and youthful idealism
- Puritan and Revolutionary traditions of the American mission to remake the world
- Republican ideology and Enlightenment emphasis on virtue and good citizenship
- Romantic literary influences such as Transcendentalism

The impulse to reform in the 1830s had deep-rooted causes: the Puritan idea of American mission; the secular examples of founding fathers like Benjamin Franklin to do good, reinforced by Republican ideology and romantic beliefs in the natural goodness of human nature; the social activist tendencies in Whig political ideology; anxiety over shifting class relationships and socio-economic change; family influence and the desire of young people to choose careers of principled service; and the direct influence of the revivals.

The International Character of Reform

Yet not all the forces leading to reformism came from within. During the early decades of the nineteenth century, the Atlantic Ocean was a highway for reform ideas and reformers. Many of the conditions that troubled Americans, often spawned by industrialization, also concerned Europeans. Women organized in Britain and the United States to reform prostitutes. Societies to encourage temperance flourished in Germany, Ireland, and England as well as the United States. French and British liberals agitated to end the slave trade as did their American counterparts.

A steady stream of men and women traveled from one side of the Atlantic to the other, raising money, publicizing their ideas, studying what had been done outside of their own country, and setting up social experiments. Abolitionists Frederick Douglass and William Lloyd Garrison visited England to gain support for their struggle against slavery, while English abolitionist George Thompson toured in the northern states to assist abolitionists there. Scottish cotton mill owner Robert Owen came to the United States in the 1820s to set up a socialist community after having created a model factory town in Scotland.

There was cross-fertilization across national boundaries of ideas and reform strategies. Owen's *The Book of the Moral World* (1820) inspired cooperative efforts of many kinds, while the work of female antislavery societies in Britain and Scotland served as models for American women. Letters between reformers in different countries also helped to firm the reform commitment and inspire action. Hearing of a success elsewhere gave faith that change might come at home, while hearing about failures prompted discussions of appropriate strategies.

The Dilemmas of Reform

Throughout the Atlantic world, reformers faced timeless dilemmas about how best to effect change. Is it more effective to appeal to people's minds in order to change bad institutions, or to change institutions first, assuming that altered behavior will then change attitudes? Taking the first path, the reformer relies on education, sermons, tracts, literature, argument, and personal testimony. Following the second, the reformer acts politically and institutionally, seeking to pass laws, win elections, encourage unions, boycott goods, and create or abolish institutions. Reformers must also decide whether to attempt to bring about limited, piecemeal, practical change on a single issue or whether to go for perfection. Should they use or recommend force or enter into coalitions with less principled potential allies?

As Marius and Emily Robinson understood, promoting change has its costs. Reformers invariably disagree on appropriate ideology and tactics, and so they end up quarreling with one another. Although reformers suffer pressure to conform and cease questioning things, their duty to themselves, their society, and their God sustains their commitment.

Utopian Communities: Oneida and the Shakers

Thoreau tried to lead an ideal solitary life. Others tried to redeem a flawed society that was losing the cohesion and traditional values of small community life by creating miniature utopian societies—alternatives to a world of factories, foreigners, immorality, and entrepreneurs. Many also rejected the new middle-class ideals of marriage and family.

Watch the Video
Religious Troublemakers of the 19th Century
at **www.myhistorylab.com**

In 1831, as Jackson and the nullifiers squared off, as Nat Turner planned his revolt, and as the citizens of Rochester sought ways of controlling their workers' drinking habits, a young man in Putney, Vermont, heard Charles Finney preach. John Humphrey Noyes was an instant, if unorthodox, convert.

Noyes believed that spiritual conversion led to perfection and complete release from sin. But his earthly happiness was soon sorely tested when a woman he loved rejected both his doctrine and his marriage offer. Among those who were perfect, he argued, all men and women belonged equally to each other. Others called his doctrines "free love" and socialism. Noyes recovered from his unhappy love affair and married a loyal follower. When she bore four stillborn babies within six years, Noyes again revised his unconventional ideas about sex.

Read the Document
John H. Noyes on Free Love at Oneida Community (1865)
at **www.myhistorylab.com**

In 1848, Noyes and 51 followers founded a "perfectionist" community at Oneida, New York. Under his strong leadership, it prospered, although many Americans found the community's rejection of middle-class marriage norms immoral. Sexual life at the commune was subject to many regulations, including male abstinence except under carefully prescribed conditions. Only certain spiritually advanced males (usually Noyes) could father children. Other controversial practices included communal child rearing, sexual equality in work, the removal of the competitive spirit from both work and play, and an elaborate program of "mutual criticism" at community meetings presided over by "Father" Noyes. Wise economic decisions bound community members in mutual prosperity. Noyes opted for modern manufacturing, first producing steel animal traps and later silverware.

Noyes greatly admired the Shakers, who also believed in perfectionism, communal property, and bringing on the millennial kingdom of heaven. Unlike the Oneidans, Shakers condemned sexuality and demanded absolute chastity, so that only conversions could bring in new members. Founded by an Englishwoman, Mother Ann Lee, Shaker conversions grew in the Second Great Awakening and peaked around 6,000 souls by the 1850s, with communities from Maine to Kentucky. Shakers believed that God had a dual personality, male and female, and that Mother Ann was the female counterpart to the masculine Christ. Shaker communities, some of which survived long into the twentieth century, were known for their communal ownership of property, equality of women and men, simplicity, and beautifully crafted furniture.

Other Utopias

Over 100 utopian communities were founded. Some were religiously motivated; others were secular. Most were small, lasting only a few months or years. All eventually collapsed, but not before giving birth to significant social ideas.

While pietist German-speaking immigrants founded the earliest utopian communities in America to preserve their language, spirituality, and ascetic lifestyle, other antebellum utopian communities focused on the regeneration of this world or responded more directly to the social misery and wretched working conditions accompanying industrialization. Evil, these communities assumed, came from bad environments, not from individual sin.

Robert Owen was the best-known of the secular communalists. A Scottish industrialist who saw the miserable lives of cotton mill workers, he envisioned a society of small towns with good schools and healthy work. In 1824, he established his first town in America at New Harmony, Indiana. But little harmony prevailed, and it failed within three years.

Brook Farm, founded by two Concord friends of Emerson, tried to integrate "intellectual and manual labor." Residents would hoe for a few hours each day and then recite poetry. Although the colony lasted less than three years, it produced some notable literature in a journal, *The Dial*, edited by Margaret Fuller. Nathaniel Hawthorne briefly lived at Brook Farm and wrote a novel, *The Blithedale Romance* (1852), criticizing the utopians' naive optimism.

◉─See the **Map**

Utopian Communities
Before the Civil War
at **www.myhistorylab.com**

The utopian communities fell apart for similar reasons. Americans seemed unwilling to share either their property or their spouses. Nor did celibacy arouse much enthusiasm. Other recurring problems included unstable leadership, financial bickering, local hostility toward sexual experimentation and other unorthodox practices, the indiscriminate admission of members, and waning enthusiasm. As Emerson said of Brook Farm, "It met every test but life itself."

Millerites and Mormons

If utopian communities failed to bring about the peaceful millennium, an alternative hope was to leap directly to the Second Coming of Christ. William Miller, a shy farmer from upstate New York, figured out its exact time: 1843, probably in March. A sect gathered around him to prepare for Christ's return and the Day of Judgment. Excitement and fear grew as the day came closer. Some people gave away all their belongings, put on robes, and flocked to high hills and rooftops. When 1843 passed without the end of the world, Miller recalculated. Each new disappointment diminished his followers, and he died discredited in 1848. But a small Millerite sect, the Seventh-Day Adventists, abandoned predicting the date of the Second Coming, living rather with the expectation that it will be "right soon." That sect continues and has millions of believers today.

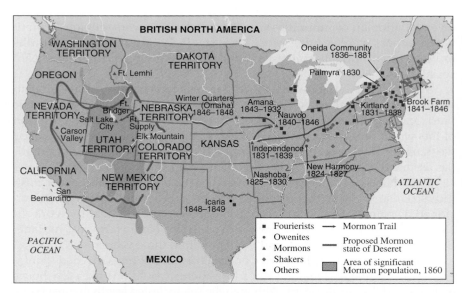

Utopian Communities Before 1860 The Mormons migrated to the trans-Mississippi West to realize their vision of a better society, but most communitarians did not go so far away from "civilization" to establish their experiments. Where were the communities located? Why did members not flee more settled and ordinary communities? Why did they avoid the South?

RECOVERING *the* PAST

Slave Narratives

In the 1840s and 1850s, abolitionists eagerly sought out and published book-length accounts of slavery written by runaway slaves themselves. These chilling stories of captivity and successful escapes, in the voices of former slaves, were instrumental in influencing public opinion to end slavery. Over 100 book-length "slave narratives" were published, selections from two of which are included here.

These narratives were derived from three American autobiographical traditions: spiritual confessionals by Puritans; the rags-to-riches individualistic success story of Benjamin Franklin; and Native American captivity narratives. The last tradition, popular reading in the early nineteenth century, described the three-part process of white captives (usually women) being taken from their villages by Indians, then suffering the trials and coping adaptations of living in a Native American village, and finally returning home. Some women refused to be "redeemed," preferring to stay, often with an Indian husband.

The African American slave narratives followed a similar three-stage pattern, beginning with either a childhood in a West African village or the relative innocence of childhood on a southern plantation. Aimed at northern white readers, these stories, in vivid detail, described the brutal oppressions of slave captivity, dwelling on the horrors of the slave ships, slave auctions and the breakup of families, and the daily beatings, punishments, and harsh rigors of life on the plantation. But the narratives also described a creative and self-empowering will to survive: cunning strategies for avoiding work, sassing one's owner, connecting with loved ones, and learning how to read and write.

The narratives usually concluded with the story of escape and adopting a new identity in freedom. As William L. Andrews put it in *To Tell a Free Story*, for blacks to write their story was "in some ways uniquely self-liberating, the final, climactic act in the drama of their lifelong quests for freedom." Other themes included poignant appeals to white readers to agitate for the abolition of slavery; contrasts between the slaveholder's use of religion to justify slavery and the spiritually based Christianity of the slaves themselves; and the supportive strength of the slave community and the white and black underground network in facilitating a successful runaway.

Although not the first, the prototypical slave narrative was that of Frederick Douglass, whose story is told in Chapter 9. Douglass grew up witnessing the horrors of slavery on a Maryland plantation and in Baltimore, learned to read and write, successfully defied the cruel Mr. Covey's efforts to break his will, and finally escaped to fight for abolitionism. Similar stories were told by William Wells Brown, Olaudah Equiano, Mary Prince, Solomon Northup, Sojourner Truth, and many others; all provided gory details of whippings, the wrenching loss of loved ones, and eventual escape to freedom.

The two short selections on pages 344–345—from James W. C. Pennington's *Fugitive Blacksmith* (1849) and Harriet Jacobs's *Incidents in the Life of a Slave Girl* (1861)—focus on the initial process of planning an escape. Jacobs wrote under the pseudonym Linda Brent. As background to this passage, she discovers that her two children are to be taken to her master's plantation to be "broke in." As you read, look for restraints on running away, anticipated difficulties, sources of support, and the cleverness of the runaways.

REFLECTING ON THE PAST **What role does religion play in their efforts? What about issues of family, trust, safety, and self-reliance? What do you learn about slavery in these brief descriptions of the first moments of self-emancipation? Can you imagine the impact they had on northern readers, and why abolitionists avidly used the narratives as part of their attack on slavery?**

Pennington's "The Flight"—from Fugitive Blacksmith

It was the Sabbath: the holy day which God in his infinite wisdom gave for the rest of both man and beast. In the state of Maryland, the slaves generally have the Sabbath, except in those districts where the evil weed, tobacco, is cultivated; and then, when it is the season for setting the plant, they are liable to be robbed of this only rest.

. . . It was a bright day, and all was quiet. Most of the slaves were resting about their quarters; others had leave to visit their friends on other plantations, and were absent. The evening previous I had arranged my little bundle of clothing, and had secreted it at some distance from the house. I had spent most of the forenoon in my workshop, engaged in deep and solemn thought.

It is impossible for me now to recollect all the perplexing thoughts that passed through my mind during that forenoon; it was a day of heartaching to me. But I distinctly remember the two great difficulties that stood in the way of my flight: I had a father and mother whom I dearly loved,—I had also six sisters and four brothers on the plantation. The question was, shall I hide my purpose from them? moreover, how will my flight affect them when I am gone? Will they not be suspected? Will not the whole family be sold off as a disaffected family, as is generally the case when one of its members flies? But a still more trying question was, how can I expect to succeed, I have no knowledge of distance or direction. I know that Pennsylvania is a free state, but I know not where its soil begins, or where that of Maryland ends? Indeed, at this time there was no safety in Pennsylvania, New Jersey, or New York, for a fugitive, except in lurking-places, or under the care of judicious friends, who could be entrusted not only with liberty, but also with life itself.

With such difficulties before my mind . . . I had resolved to let no one into my secret; but the other difficulty was now to be met. . . . The consequences of a failure would be most serious. Within my recollection no one had attempted to escape from my master; but I had many cases in my mind's eye, of slaves of other planters who had failed, and who had been made examples of the most cruel treatment, by flogging and selling to the far South, where they were never to see their friends more. I was not without serious apprehension that such would be my fate. The bare possibility was impressively solemn; but the hour was now come, and the man must act and be free, or remain a slave for ever. . . . The emotions of that moment I cannot fully depict. Hope, fear, dread, terror, love, sorrow, and deep melancholy were mingled in my mind together; my mental state was one of most painful distraction. When I looked at my numerous family—a beloved father and mother, eleven brothers and sisters, &c.; but when I looked at slavery as such; when I looked at it in its mildest form, with all its annoyances; and above all, when I remembered that one of the chief annoyances of slavery, in the most mild form, is the liability of being at any moment sold into the worst form; it seemed that no consideration, not even that of life itself, could tempt me to give up the thought of flight. And then when I considered the difficulties of the way—the reward that would be offered—the human blood-hounds that would be set upon my track—the weariness—the hunger—the gloomy thought, of not only losing all one's friends in one day, but of having to seek and to make new friends in a strange world. But, as I have said, the hour was come, and the man must act, or for ever be a slave.

Harriet Jacobs—from Incidents in the Life of a Slave Girl

I was meditating upon some means of escape for myself and my children. My friends had made every effort that ingenuity could devise to effect our purchase, but all their plans had proved abortive. Dr. Flint was suspicious, and determined not to loosen his grasp upon us. I could have made my escape alone; but it was more for my helpless children than for myself that I longed for freedom. Though the boon would have been precious to me, above all price, I would not have taken it at the expense of leaving them in slavery. Every trial I endured, every sacrifice I made for their sakes, drew them closer to my heart, and gave me fresh courage to beat back the dark waves that rolled and rolled over me in a seemingly endless night of storms. . . .

My plan was to conceal myself at the house of a friend, and remain there a few weeks till the search was over. My hope was that the doctor would get discouraged, and, for fear of losing my value, and also of subsequently finding my children among the missing, he would consent to sell us; and I knew somebody would buy us. I had done all in my power to make my children comfortable during the time I expected to be separated from them. . . .

Mr. Flint was hard pushed for house servants, and rather than lose me he had restrained his malice. I did my work faithfully, though not, of course, with a willing mind. They were evidently afraid I should leave them. Mr. Flint wished that I should sleep in the great house instead of the servants' quarters. . . . I did as I was ordered. But now that I was certain my children were to be put in their power, in order to give them a stronger hold on me, I resolved to leave them that night. I remembered the grief this step would bring upon my dear old grandmother; and nothing less than the freedom of my children would have induced me to disregard her advice. I went about my evening work with trembling steps. Mr. Flint twice called from his chamber door to inquire why the house was not locked up. I replied that I had not done my work. "You have had time enough to do it," said he. "Take care how you answer me!"

I shut all the windows, locked all the doors, and went up to the third story, to wait till midnight. How long those hours seemed, and how fervently I prayed that God would not forsake me in this hour of utmost need! I was about to risk every thing on the throw of a die; and if I failed, O what would become of me and my poor children? They would be made to suffer for my fault.

At half past twelve I stole softly down stairs. I stopped on the second floor, thinking I heard a noise. I felt my way down into the parlor, and looked out of the window. The night was so intensely dark that I could see nothing. I raised the window very softly and jumped out. Large drops of rain were falling, and the darkness bewildered me. I dropped on my knees, and breathed a short prayer to God for guidance and protection. I groped my way to the road, and rushed towards the town with almost lightning speed. I arrived at my grandmother's house, but dared not see her. She would say, "Linda, you are killing me;" and I knew that would unnerve me. [She therefore stayed with another woman.]

. . . My grandmother's house was searched from top to bottom. As my trunk was empty, they concluded I had taken my clothes with me. Before ten o'clock every vessel northward bound was thoroughly examined, and the law against harboring fugitives was read to all on board. At night a watch was set over the town. Knowing how distressed my grandmother would be, I wanted to send her a message; but it could not be done. Every one who went in or out of her house was closely watched. The doctor said he would take my children, unless she became responsible for them; which of course she willingly did. The next day was spent in searching. Before night, the following advertisement was posted at every corner, and in every public place for miles round:—

$300 Reward! Ran away from the subscriber, an intelligent, bright, mulatto girl, named Linda, 21 years of age. Five feet four inches high. Dark eyes, and black hair inclined to curl; but it can be made straight. Has a decayed spot on a front tooth. She can read and write, and in all probability will try to get to the Free States. All persons are forbidden, under penalty of law, to harbor or employ said slave. $150 will be given to whoever takes her in the state, and $300 if taken out of the state and delivered to me, or lodged in jail.

Dr. Flint

Note: James Pennington successfully escaped to New York, where he became a Presbyterian minister and later performed Frederick Douglass's marriage rites. Harriet Jacobs hid for seven years in a cramped, tiny attic in her grandmother's house before finally escaping in disguise by ship; she eventually was reunited with her children.

Other groups that emerged from the same religiously active area of up-state New York were more successful. As Palmyra, New York, was being swept by Finney revivalism, young Joseph Smith, a recent convert, claimed to be visited by the angel Moroni, who led him to golden tablets buried near his home. On these were inscribed The Book of Mormon, which described the one true church and a "lost tribe of Israel" missing for centuries. The book also predicted the appearance of an American prophet who would establish a new and pure kingdom of Christ in America. Smith published his book in 1830 and soon founded the Church of Jesus Christ of Latter-Day Saints (the Mormons). His visionary leadership attracted thousands of ordinary people trying to escape what they viewed as social disorder, religious impurity, and commercial degradation in the 1830s.

Smith and a steadily growing band of converts migrated first to Ohio, next to Missouri, and then back to Illinois. The frequent migrations were partly a consequence of the ridicule, persecution, and violence that they encountered. Hostility stemmed in part from their active missionary work, in part from their beliefs and support for local Indian tribes, and in part from rumors of unorthodox sexual practices.

Despite persecution and dissension over Smith's strong leadership style, the Mormons prospered. Converts from England and northern Europe added substantially to their numbers. By the mid-1840s, Nauvoo, Illinois, with a thriving population of nearly 15,000, was the showplace of Mormonism. Smith petitioned Congress for territorial status and ran for president of the United States in 1844. His behavior proved too much for local citizens. Violence culminated in Smith's trial for treason and his lynching. Under the brilliant leadership of his successor, Brigham Young, the Mormons headed west in 1846.

View the **Image**

Mormon Emigrants (1879)
at **www.myhistorylab.com**

Reforming Society

The Mormons and the utopian communitarians had as their common goal, in Young's words, "the spread of righteousness upon the earth." Most people, however, preferred to focus on a specific social evil.

"We are all a little wild here," Emerson wrote in 1840, "with numberless projects of social reform." Mobilized in part by their increased participation in the political parties of Jacksonian America, the reformers created and joined all kinds of social-uplift societies. The reform ranks were swelled by thousands of women, stirred to action by the religious revivals and freed from domestic burdens by delayed marriage and smaller families. In hundreds of voluntary societies, people like Emily Rakestraw and Marius Robinson tackled such issues as alcohol, diet and health, sexuality, the institutional treatment of social outcasts, education, the rights of labor, slavery, and women's rights.

Temperance

On New Year's Eve in 1831, a Finney disciple, Theodore Dwight Weld, delivered a four-hour temperance lecture in Rochester. Graphically he described the awful fate of those who refused to stop drinking and urged his audience not only to cease their tippling, but also to stop others. Several were converted on the spot. The next day, the largest whiskey providers in Rochester smashed their barrels as cheering Christians applauded.

Nineteenth-century Americans drank heavily. It was said that "a house could not be raised, a field of wheat cut down, nor could there be a log rolling, a husking, a quilting, a wedding, or a funeral without the aid of alcohol." With drinking came poverty, crime, illness, insanity, battered and broken families, and corrupt politics.

Early efforts at curbing alcohol emphasized moderation. Local societies agreed to limit what they drank. Some met in taverns to toast moderation. But, influenced by the revivals, the movement achieved better organization and clearer goals. The **American Temperance Society**, founded in 1826, aimed at the "teetotal" pledge. Within a few years, thousands of local and state societies had formed.

Temperance advocates copied revival techniques. Fiery lecturers expounded on the evil consequences of drink and urged group pressure on the weak-willed. A deluge of graphic and sometimes gory temperance tracts poured out. One "intemperate man," it was claimed, died when his "breath caught fire by coming in contact with a lighted candle."

By 1840, disagreements split the temperance movement into many separate organizations. In depression

Watch the Video
Drinking and the Temperance Movement in Nineteenth-Century America
at **www.myhistorylab.com**

times, when jobs and stable families were harder to find than whiskey and beer, laboring men and women moved more by practical concerns than religious fervor joined the crusade. The Washington Temperance Society, founded in a Baltimore tavern in 1840, was enormously popular with unemployed young workers and grew to an estimated 600,000 members in three years. The Washingtonians, arguing that alcoholism was a disease rather than moral failure, changed the shape of the temperance movement. They replaced revivalist techniques with those of the new party politics by organizing parades, picnics, melodramas, and festivals to encourage people to take the pledge.

Tactics in the 1840s also shifted away from moral suasion to political action. Temperance societies lobbied for local option laws, which allowed communities to prohibit the sale, manufacture, and consumption of alcohol. The first such law in the nation was passed in Maine in 1851. Fifteen other states followed with similar laws before the Civil War. Despite weak enforcement, per capita drinking fell dramatically in the 1850s. Interrupted by the Civil War, the movement reached its ultimate objective with passage of the Eighteenth Amendment in 1919.

Temperance Propaganda This piece of temperance propaganda comes from a journal entitled *Cold Water Magazine.* Why that title? What does the picture suggest are the effects of drinking?

The temperance crusade reveals the many practical motivations for Americans to join reform societies. For some, as in Rochester, temperance provided an opportunity for the Protestant middle class to exert some control over laborers, immigrants, and Catholics. Perfectionists saw abstinence as a way of practicing self-control. For many women, the temperance effort represented a way to control drunken abusers. For many young men, especially after the onset of the depression of 1837, a temperance society provided entertainment, fellowship, and contacts to help their careers. In temperance societies as in political parties, Americans found jobs, purpose, support, spouses, and relief from loneliness and uncertainty.

Health and Sexuality

It was a short step from the physical and psychological ravages of alcohol to other potentially harmful practices. Reformers were quick to attack too much eating, too many stimulants, and, above all, too much sex. Many endorsed a variety of special diets and exercise programs for maintaining good health. Some promoted panaceas, including hydropathy (bathing and water purges), hypnotism, phrenology (the study of bumps on the head), and "spiritualist" seances.

Sylvester Graham, inventor of the graham cracker, combined all these enthusiasms. In 1834, he delivered a series of lectures on chastity, later published as an advice book. To those "troubled" by sexual desire, he recommended cold baths and open-air exercise. Women were advised to "have intercourse only for procreation." Although females learned to control sexuality for their own purposes, male "sexual purity" advocates urged restraint to protect various male interests. One doctor argued that women ought not to be educated because blood needed for the womb would be diverted to the head, thus breeding "puny men."

The authors of antebellum "health" manuals advocated abstinence from sex as vehemently as from alcohol. Semen must be saved for reproductive purposes and should not be wasted, either in masturbation or intercourse. Such waste would cause enervation, disease, insanity, and death. Some argued that the "expenditure" of sperm meant a loss of energy from the economy.

Humanizing the Asylum

Struggling to restore order to American society, some reformers preferred to work not to influence individuals but to change institutions like asylums, almshouses, prisons, schools, and even factories. Dealing with social outcasts presented special challenges. Colonial families or communities had looked after orphans, paupers, the insane, and even criminals. Beginning early in the nineteenth century, states built various institutions to uplift and house social victims. In some, like prisons and almshouses, the sane and the insane, children and hardened adult criminals, were thrown together. In 1843, Dorothea Dix reported to a horrified Massachusetts legislature that the state's imprisoned insane people lived in the "extremest state of degradation and misery," confined in "cages, closets, stalls, pens! Chained, naked, beaten with rods, and lashed into obedience!" Dix recommended special asylums where the insane could be "humanly and properly controlled" by trained attendants.

Many perfectionist reformers like Dix believed that asylums could reform outcasts. Convinced that bad institutions corrupted basically good human beings, they reasoned that reformed institutions could rehabilitate them. In 1853, Charles Loring Brace started a Children's Aid Society in New York City that was a model of change through effective education and self-help. Reformers like Dix and Brace, as well as Samuel Gridley Howe and Thomas Gallaudet, who founded institutions for the care and education of the blind and deaf, achieved remarkable results.

But all too often, results were disappointing. Reformers believed that a proper penitentiary could bring a criminal "back to virtue." Some preferred the prison at Auburn, New York, with its tiny cells and common workrooms; others praised Pennsylvania's penitentiaries, each inmate in solitary confinement. All prison reformers assumed that "penitents" in isolated cells, studying the Bible and reflecting on their wrongdoing, would eventually decide to become good citizens. In fact, many inmates went mad or committed suicide. Institutions built by well-intentioned reformers became dumping places for society's outcasts. By midcentury, American prisons and mental asylums had become what they remain today: sadly impersonal, understaffed, and overcrowded.

Working-Class Reform

Efforts to improve the institutional conditions of American life were not all top-down movements initiated and led by middle-class reformers. For working-class Americans, as in England, the institution most in need of transformation was the factory. Workers, many of them involved in other issues such as temperance, peace, and abolitionism, tried to improve their own lives.

Between 1828 and 1832, dozens of workingmen's parties arose. They advocated free, tax-supported schools, free public lands in the West, equal rights for the poor, and elimination of monopolistic privilege. Trade union activity began in Philadelphia in 1827 as skilled workers organized journeymen carpenters, plasterers, printers, weavers, tailors, and other tradesmen. That same year, 15 unions combined into a citywide federation, a process followed in other cities. The **National Trades Union**, founded in 1834, was the first attempt at a national labor organization.

Trade unions fared better than labor parties as Jacksonian Democrats siphoned off workers' votes. Union programs set more practical goals, including shorter hours, wages that would keep pace with rising prices, and ways (such as the closed shop) of warding off the competitive threat of cheap labor. In addition, both workers and their middle-class supporters sought free public education, improved living conditions for workers, and the right to organize as well as the elimination of imprisonment for debt and compulsory militia duty (both often cost workers their jobs). Discouraged by anti-union decisions of New York State courts, workers compared themselves to the rebels of the Boston Tea Party.

Fired by revolutionary tradition, rising political influence, and a union membership of near 300,000, workers struck some 168 times between 1834 and 1836. Over two-thirds of the strikes were over wages (see Chapter 8); the others were for shorter hours. The Panic of 1837 ushered in a depression that dashed the hopes and efforts of American workers. But the organizational work of the 1830s promised that the labor movement would reemerge, strengthened, later in the century.

Abolitionism and Women's Rights

As American workers struggled for better wages and hours in 1834, Emily and Marius Robinson arrived in Cincinnati to fight for their causes. Along with many other young idealists, they had been attracted by the newly founded Lane Seminary, a center of reformist activity. When nervous citizens persuaded the school's president, Lyman Beecher, to crack down, 75 "Lane rebels" fled to Oberlin in northern Ohio.

◉ Watch the Video

The Women's Rights Movement in 19th Century America at **www.myhistorylab.com**

The rebels turned Oberlin College into the first institution in the United States open to women and men, blacks and whites. The movements to abolish slavery and for equal rights for women and free blacks coalesced.

The goals of the struggle against slavery and subtle forms of racism and sexism often seemed as distant as the millennium itself. Yet antislavery and feminist advocates persisted in their efforts to abolish what they believed were visible, ingrained social wrongs. Whether seeking to eliminate coercion in the cotton fields or in the kitchen, they faced the dual challenge of pursuing elusive goals while achieving practical changes.

Tensions Within the Antislavery Movement

Although the antislavery movement was smaller than the temperance movement, it revealed more clearly the difficulties of pursuing significant social change. William Lloyd Garrison passionately desired to improve, if not to perfect, a flawed world. On January 1, 1831, eight months before Nat Turner's revolt, Garrison published the first issue of the Liberator, soon to become the leading antislavery journal in the United States. "I am in earnest," he wrote. "I will not equivocate—and I will be heard." After organizing the New England Anti-Slavery Society with a group of blacks and whites, in 1833 Garrison and 62 others established the American Anti-Slavery Society, which called for an immediate end to slavery.

Until then, most antislavery whites had advocated gradual emancipation by individual slave owners. Many joined the American Colonization Society, founded in 1816, which sent a few ex-slaves to Liberia. But these efforts proved inadequate and racist, the main goal being to rid the country of free blacks. Rejected by African Americans and violently attacked by Garrisonians, colonization lost much of its support.

Garrison and others in the American Anti-Slavery Society viewed slavery as a sin that had to be eliminated and called for immediate emancipation in uncompromising language. As Garrison declared, "I do not wish to think, or speak, or write, with moderation." There could be "no Union with slaveholders," he argued, condemning the Constitution that perpetuated slavery as "an agreement with Hell." Inspired by the Liberator and antislavery lecturers like Garrison and Marius Robinson, dozens of local male and female abolitionist societies dedicated to the immediate emancipation of the slaves arose, mostly in the Northeast and Northwest. Yet others who opposed slavery found the Garrisonian abolitionists far too radical for their tastes.

Abolitionists also differed over tactics. Their primary method was to convince slaveholders and their supporters that slavery was a sin. Slaveholding whites, black abolitionist David Walker declared, were morally inferior. But as Marius wrote to Emily Robinson, "The spirit of slavery is not confined to the South." His Ohio trip suggests that northerners were equally guilty in providing the ships and support necessary to maintain the slave system.

By 1837, the abolitionists had flooded the nation with over a million pieces of antislavery literature. Their writing described slave owners as

An Abolitionist Gathering This woodcut illustration of an abolitionist convention from *Harper's Weekly* magazine in 1859 shows the mixture of both black and women delegates in the hall. The black man on the stage could be Frederick Douglass. How many other black (and female) abolitionists do you see, and where are they sitting? *(Courtesy of the Trustees of the Boston Public Library/Rare Books)*

"manstealers" who gave up all claim to humanity. In 1839, Weld published *American Slavery as It Is*, which described in the goriest possible detail the inhumane treatment of slaves.

Other abolitionists preferred more direct methods. Some brought antislavery petitions before Congress and formed third parties. Boycotting goods made by slave labor was another tactic. Still another approach, although rare, was to call for slave rebellion, as did two northern blacks, David Walker in an 1829 pamphlet and Henry Highland Garnet in a speech at a convention of black Americans in 1843. As Garnet recognized, Walker's work represented "among the first, and . . . the boldest and most direct appeals in behalf of freedom" of the early abolitionist movement.

Abolitionists' tactical disagreements helped splinter the movement. Garrison's unyielding style and commitment to even less popular causes such as women's rights offended many abolitionists. In 1840, at its annual meeting in New York, the American Anti-Slavery Society split. Several delegates walked out when a woman, Abby Kelley, was elected to a previously all-male committee. One group, which supported multiple issues and moral suasion, stayed with Garrison; the other left to pursue political action and the Liberty party.

Class differences and race further divided abolitionists. Northern workers, though fearful of the potential job competition with blacks implicit in emancipation, nevertheless saw their "wage slavery" as similar to chattel

may expect a felon's death." One widely circulated book in 1836 described opponents of slavery as "crack-brained enthusiasts" and "female fanatics." Jackson denounced abolitionists in his annual message in 1835 as "incendiaries" who deserved to have their "unconstitutional and wicked" activities broken up by mobs, and he urged Congress to ban antislavery literature from the U.S. mails. A year later, southern Democratic congressmen, with crucial support from Van Buren, passed a "gag rule" to stop the flood of abolitionist petitions in Congress.

By the 1840s the antislavery movement had gained significant strength. Many northerners, including workers otherwise unsympathetic to ending slavery, decried mob violence, supported free speech, and denounced the South and its northern defenders as undemocratic. The gag rule, interference with the mails, and Lovejoy's killing seemed proof of the growing influence of an evil slave power. Former president John Quincy Adams, now a Massachusetts congressman, devoted himself for

◉|View the Image

Illustrations from the American Anti-Slavery Almanac for 1840 at **www.myhistorylab.com**

several years to the repeal of the gag rule, which he finally achieved in 1844, keeping the matter alive until the question of slavery in the territories became the dominant political issue of the 1850s (see Chapter 12). Meanwhile, black and white abolitionists struggled on with many different tactics.

Women Reformers and Women's Rights

As a young Quaker teacher in Massachusetts in 1836, Abby Kelley circulated petitions for the local antislavery society. She came to reform through religious conviction. In 1838, she braved a crowd in Philadelphia by delivering an abolitionist speech to a convention of antislavery women so eloquently that Weld told her that if she did not join the movement full time, "God will smite you." Before the convention was over, a mob, incensed by both abolitionists and women speaking in public, burned the hall to the ground.

After a soul-searching year, Kelley left teaching to focus on antislavery and women's rights. When she married, she retained her own name and went on lecture tours of the West while her husband stayed home to care for their daughter. Other young women were also defining unconventional new relationships while illustrating the profound difficulty of both fulfilling traditional roles and speaking out for change. Angelina and Sarah Grimké, outspoken Quaker sisters from Philadelphia who had grown up in South Carolina, went to New England in 1837 to lecture on abolitionism. Criticized for speaking to audiences containing both men and women, Angelina defended women's rights to speak in public. After the tour, Angelina married Theodore Weld and stopped her public lectures to show that she could also be a good wife and mother. But she and Sarah, who moved in with her, undertook most of the research and writing for Weld's book attacking American slavery.

Young couples like these, while pursuing reform, also experimented with equal relationships in an age that assigned distinctly unequal roles to husbands and wives. On the one hand, women were told that their sphere was the home, upholding piety and virtue. On the other hand, they were

Marriage Expectations Examine the respective marital requirements of husband and wife detailed in this certificate (you may need a magnifying glass). What are male responsibilities and what are female duties? How might the views expressed here relate to the meeting the same year at Seneca Falls, New York?

assured that their ethical influence would be "felt around the globe." Not surprisingly, many women joined the perfectionist movement to cleanse America of its sins. Active in every reform movement, women discovered the need to improve their own condition.

To achieve greater personal autonomy, antebellum American women, like their English counterparts, pursued several paths depending on their class, cultural background, and situation. In 1834, Lowell textile workers went on strike against wage reductions while looking to marriage as an escape from millwork. Catharine Beecher argued that it was by accepting marriage and the home as a woman's sphere and by mastering domestic duties there that women could best achieve power and autonomy. In another form of feminism, American wives exerted considerable control over their bodies by convincing their husbands to practice abstinence, coitus interruptus, and other forms of birth control.

Other women found an outlet for their role as moral guardians by attacking the sexual double standard. In 1834, a group of Presbyterian women formed the New York Female Moral Reform Society. Inspired by revivalism, they visited brothels, opened a refuge to convert prostitutes, and even publicly identified brothel patrons. Within five years, there were 445 auxiliaries of the society.

Lowell millworkers and New York moral reformers generally accepted the duties—and attractions—of female domesticity. Other women, usually from upper-middle-class families, did not. They sought to devote their lives to working directly for more legally protected rights. Campaigns to secure married women's control of their property and custody of their children involved many of them. Others gained from abolitionism a growing awareness of similarities between the oppression of women and of slaves. Collecting antislavery signatures and speaking out publicly, they continually faced denials of their right to speak or act politically. American women "have good cause to be grateful to the slave," Kelley wrote, for in "striving to strike his iron off, we found most surely, that we were manacled ourselves."

The more active women became in antislavery activities, the more hostility they encountered, especially from conservative clergymen. Sarah Grimké was criticized once too often. She struck back in 1837 with *Letters on the Condition of Women and the Equality of the Sexes*, concluding that she sought "no favors for my sex. I surrender not our claim to equality. All I ask of our brethren is, that they will take their feet from off our necks and permit us to stand upright on that ground which God designed us to occupy."

Grimké's strong message was soon translated into an active movement for women's rights, and, illustrative of its international character, the American movement was born in London. At the World Anti-Slavery Convention in London in 1840, attended by many American abolitionists, male delegates refused to let women participate. Two of the women, Elizabeth Cady Stanton and Lucretia Mott, had to sit behind curtains and were forbidden to speak. When they returned home, they resolved to "form a society to advocate the rights of women." In 1848, in Seneca Falls, New York, their intentions, though delayed, were fulfilled in one of the most significant antebellum protest gatherings.

In preparing for the meeting, Mott and Stanton drew up a list of women's grievances. For example, even though some states had awarded married women control over their property, they still had no control over their earnings. Modeling their "Declaration of Sentiments" on the Declaration of Independence, the women at Seneca Falls proclaimed it a self-evident truth that "all men and women are created equal" and that men had usurped women's freedom and dignity. The remedy was expressed in 11 resolutions calling for equal opportunities in education and work, equality before the law, and the right to appear on public platforms. The most controversial resolution called for women's "sacred right to the elective franchise." The convention approved Mott and Stanton's list of resolutions.

Throughout the 1850s, led by Stanton and Susan B. Anthony, women held annual conventions, working by resolution, persuasion, and petition campaign to achieve equal political, legal, and property rights with men. The right to vote, however, was considered the cornerstone of the movement. It remained so for 72 years of struggle until 1920. The **Seneca Falls convention** was crucial in beginning the campaign for equal public rights. The seeds of psychological autonomy and self-respect, still continuing, were sown in the struggles of countless women like Abby Kelley, Sarah Grimké, and Emily Robinson.

Conclusion

Perfecting America

Inspired by religious revivalism, advocates for women's rights and temperance, abolitionists like Marius and Emily Robinson, and other reformers carried on very different crusades from those waged by Andrew Jackson against Indians, nullificationists, and the U.S. Bank. In fact, Jacksonian politics and antebellum reform were often at odds. Most abolitionists and temperance reformers were anti-Jackson Whigs. Jackson and most Democrats repudiated the passionate moralism of reformers.

Yet both sides shared more than either side would admit. Reformers and political parties were both organized rationally. Both mirrored new tensions in a changing, growing society. Both had an abiding faith in change and the idea of progress yet feared that sinister forces jeopardized that progress. Whether ridding the nation of alcohol or the national bank, slavery or nullification, mob violence or political opponents, both forces saw these responsibilities in terms of patriotic duty. Whether inspired by religious revivalism or political party loyalty, both believed that by stamping out evil forces, they could shape a better America. In this effort, they turned to politics, religion, reform, and new lifestyles. Whether politicians like Jackson and Clay, religious community leaders like Noyes and Ann Lee, or reformers like Garrison and the Grimkés, these antebellum Americans sought to remake their country politically and morally as it underwent social and economic change.

As the United States neared midcentury, slavery emerged as the most divisive issue. Against much opposition, the reformers had made slavery a matter of national political debate by the 1840s. Although both major political parties tried to evade the question, westward expansion and the addition of new territories to the nation increasingly made avoidance impossible. Would new states be slave or free? The question aroused the deepest passions of the American people. Yet for the pioneer family, who formed the driving force behind the westward movement, questions involving their fears and dreams seemed more important.

TIME*line*

1828	Jackson defeats Adams for the presidency
	Tariff of Abominations
1830–1831	Charles Finney's religious revivals
1832	Jackson vetoes U.S. Bank charter
	Jackson reelected
	Worcester v. Georgia

✓•⎯Study and Review at www.myhistorylab.com

Questions for Review and Reflection

1. How does the story of Marius Robinson and Emily Rakestraw introduce the major themes and structure of the chapter?

2. What social, economic, and political forces motivated Americans to seek ways of controlling their lives? How did they try to shape both their own lives and also America?

3. What were the major issues of Jackson's administration? Was he primarily a unifier or divider? Did he advance or set back the development of American democracy? Explain your responses.

4. Explain the key differences between Democrats and Whigs and their basis of support. Which party would you have supported and why?

5. Describe the role of religion in antebellum American life and the ways in which revivalism sought to effect social change. Do you agree that this was a proper function for religion?

6. Characterize three or four major antebellum reform movements, pointing out what motivations, values, challenges, and resources were common to each of them. Would you have been a reformer? Why or why not?

Key Terms

American Temperance Society 347

Bank War 334

Charles G. Finney 324

Jacksonian Democrats 336

National Trades Union 350

Ordinance of Nullification 331

Seneca Falls Convention 357

Tariff of Abominations 329

Trail of Tears 333

Whigs 335

11

Moving West

((•—Hear the Audio *Chapter 11 Audio File*
at **www.myhistorylab.com**

American Stories

The Surprises of a Missionary Life

It was July 4, 1836, but nothing in her 28 years had prepared Narcissa Whitman for the sights and sounds marking this particular holiday. Earlier in the day, Narcissa and the party with which she was traveling had crossed over the South Pass of the Rocky Mountains, a memorable milestone for the nation's birthday. Now, evening had come, and the caravan set up camp for the night. Suddenly, wild cries and the sound of gunshots and galloping horses broke the silence. Fourteen or fifteen men, most dressed as Indians, advanced toward the camp. Frightened by the threatening appearance of the horsemen, the noise, and the bullets whizzing over her head, Narcissa may well have wondered if her journey and even her life were to end. But as the horsemen approached, the anxious travelers could make out a white flag tied to one of the rider's rifles. These were not foes but friends who had ridden out from the annual fur traders' rendezvous to greet the caravan.

Two days later, Narcissa reached the rendezvous site where hundreds of Indians as well as 200 whites, mostly traders and trappers, were gathered to exchange furs, tell stories, drink, and enjoy themselves. Some of the mounted Indians, "carrying their war weapons, wearing their war emblems and implements of music," put on a special display. The exhibition was a novelty for Narcissa, as was her presence for the Indians. Narcissa found herself the center of attention "in the midst of [a] gazing throng" of curious Indians. The experience was not unpleasant, and Narcissa's impression of the Indians was favorable. "They all like us and that we have come to live with them."

Narcissa Whitman was one of the first white women to cross the Rocky Mountains and live in Oregon territory in the 1830s. While many more Americans would follow her, only a few would share her reasons for coming west. They would come to farm, dig for gold, speculate in land, open a store, or practice law. However, Narcissa

Chapter Outline

Probing the Trans-Mississippi West

Winning the Trans-Mississippi West

Going West and East

Living in the West

Cultures in Conflict

Conclusion: Fruits of Manifest Destiny

and her husband, Dr. Marcus Whitman, did not go west to better their lives but to carry God's word to the Native Americans. Inspired by the revivals of the Second Great Awakening and convinced that all non-Christians were headed toward eternal damnation, Narcissa and her husband came to settle among the Indians in Oregon territory and to convert them to Christianity and the American way of life.

This dream of becoming a missionary was one Narcissa had nourished since her early teens. But once the Whitmans reached their mission station in the Walla Walla valley, Narcissa slowly discovered that missionary work was nothing like her youthful fantasies. Although the Cayuse Indians listened to the missionaries and adopted some Christian practices, they never lived up to the Whitmans' high standards. None experienced conversion. They continued to consult their medicine men and refused to settle permanently next to the mission station. Cayuse women seemed little interested in the middle-class domestic skills Narcissa wished to teach them. Narcissa's positive impression of Native Americans disappeared. The Cayuse, she wrote, were "insolent, proud, domineering, arrogant, and ferocious."

There were other disappointments and personal tragedies. Marcus was often away from the mission on medical business, leaving Narcissa lonely and sometimes frightened. Her only daughter fell into the river and drowned.

As time passed, however, Narcissa's dismay and depression faded as hopeful signs of new possibilities other than Indian missionary work appeared. As she wrote to her mother in 1840, "a tide of immigration appears to be moving this way rapidly." In the following years, many American families passed the mission station. One wagon train included a family of children orphaned during their journey. The Whitmans adopted all seven children. Narcissa threw herself into caring for them and found herself too busy to work actively with the Cayuse.

The Indians were troubled by the numbers of whites coming into the territory, but the Whitmans, convinced that the future of the West lay with the emigrants, welcomed them. The day of the Indians had passed. As a "hunted, despised and unprotected" people, the Whitmans believed that the Native Americans were headed toward "entire extinction." But in an unexpected turn of events, some of the Cayuse rejected this vision, turned against the Whitmans, and killed them both. Such violent actions did nothing to slow the swarm of Americans heading west.

Narcissa Whitman and her husband, Marcus, were among thousands of Americans participating in the nation's expansion into the trans-Mississippi West. While the religious faith that drove them west differentiated them from many emigrants, the Whitmans' cultural beliefs about the inferiority of the Native Americans and the necessity of American settlement were widely shared. Shared too was the conviction that the American values and way of life were superior to those of the Native Americans and Mexicans who occupied the land.

This chapter explores the trans-Mississippi West between 1830 and 1865. First we will consider how and when Americans moved west, by what means the United States acquired the vast territories that in 1840 belonged to other nations, and the meaning of "Manifest Destiny," the slogan used to defend the conquest of the continent west of the Mississippi River. How important were the various factors that stimulated expansion? As we explore the nature of life on the western farms, in western mining communities where Latin American, Chinese, and European adventurers mingled with American fortune seekers, and in western cities, consider the ways in which communities and settlers in the West were similar and diverse. The chapter concludes by examining the responses of Native Americans and Mexican Americans to expansion, and exploring how different cultural traditions intersected. What were the values and beliefs that energized each group as they confronted one another in the West?

Probing the Trans-Mississippi West

Until the 1840s, most Americans lived east of the Mississippi. By 1860, however, some 4.3 million Americans had moved beyond the great river into the trans-Mississippi West.

The International Context for American Expansionism

When the Whitmans arrived in Oregon territory, they stayed at a bustling British fur trading post with hundreds of workers: French Canadians, English, Scots, and many from mixed European-Indian backgrounds. The establishment symbolized the international setting within which American expansionism occurred. The shifting interests and fortunes of several European nations helped to shape the character and timing of westward emigration even though individual settlers might not recognize the large forces affecting their experiences.

In 1815, except for Louisiana territory, Spain held title to most of the trans-Mississippi West. For hundreds of years, Spaniards had marched north from Mexico to explore, settle, and spread Spanish culture to native peoples. Eventually, Spanish holdings included present-day Texas, Arizona, New Mexico, Nevada, Utah, western Colorado, California, and parts of Wyoming, Kansas, and Oklahoma. Spanish rulers tried to exclude foreigners from these frontier areas but increasingly found this policy difficult to enforce. The area was vast, and Spain itself was experiencing internal difficulties that weakened its hold on its New World colonies. In 1820, the conservative Spanish monarch faced liberal revolt at home. Its ideas sparked liberation movements in the New World.

In 1821, Mexico declared its independence and acquired Spain's territories in the trans-Mississippi West with a population that included 75,000 Spanish-speaking inhabitants and numerous Native American tribes. While maintaining control of this distant region and its peoples would have been difficult under any circumstances, Mexico was not successful in forming a strong or a stable government until the 1860s. It was in a weak position to resist the avid American appetite for expansion.

North of California lay Oregon country, a vaguely defined area extending to Alaska. Russia, Spain, and Great Britain all had claims to Oregon, but negotiations with Russia and Spain in 1819 and 1824 left just the United States and Britain contending for the territory. Joint British-American occupation, agreed upon in 1818 and 1827, delayed settling the boundary question. With only a handful of Americans in the territory, Oregon's future would depend partly on how Britain, the world's richest and most powerful country, defined its interests there as Americans began to stream into Oregon in the 1840s.

Early Interest in the West

Some Americans penetrated the trans-Mississippi West long before the great migrations of the 1840s and 1850s. The fur business attracted American trappers and traders to Oregon by 1811 and a decade later to the Rockies. Many married Indian women and established valuable connections with Indian tribes involved in trapping. Along with their wives, they occupied a cultural middle ground characterized by elements from both American and native ways of life. Some ultimately became guides for Americans who emigrated later to the West.

Like the Whitmans, Methodist missionaries established early outposts in Oregon territory to teach native tribes Christian and American practices. Roman Catholic priests, sent from Europe, also worked among the native peoples. More tolerant of Indian culture than their Protestant counterparts, the Catholics had greater initial success in converting native peoples to Christianity.

The collapse of the Spanish Empire in 1821 provided Americans with a variety of opportunities. Each year American caravans followed the Santa Fe Trail, loaded with goods for New Mexico's 40,000 inhabitants. Eventually, some "Anglos" settled there. In Texas, cheap land for cotton attracted settlers and squatters just as the small local Tejano (the Spanish word for "Texan") population was adjusting to Mexico's independence. By 1835, almost 30,000 had migrated to Texas, the largest group of Americans living outside the nation's boundaries.

On the Pacific, a handful of New England traders carrying sea-otter skins to China anchored in the harbors of Spanish California in the early nineteenth century. By the 1830s, as the near extermination of the animals ruined this trade, a commerce exchanging California cowhides and tallow for clothes, boots, hardware, and furniture manufactured in the East developed.

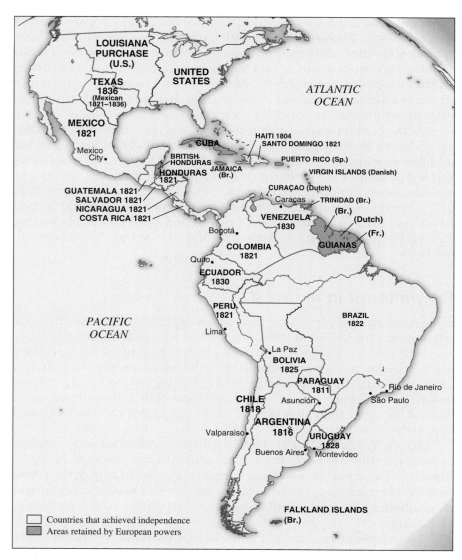

North and South America, 1800–1836 Events in Europe had a dramatic impact on the Americas. Napoleon's defeat of the Spanish king in 1808 and the popularization of the ideas of the French Revolution contributed to ending Spanish rule in the New World. Note how rapidly countries claimed their independence in the southern hemisphere and Latin America. How did the changing political landscape of the Americas affect the power and influence of the United States in the region?

Tribes driven from the South and the Old Northwest by the American government into present-day Oklahoma and Kansas were among the earliest easterners in the trans-Mississippi West. Ironically, some of these tribes acted as agents of white civilization by introducing cotton, the plantation system, black slavery, and schools. Other tribes triggered conflicts that weakened the western tribes with whom they came into contact. These disruptions foreshadowed white incursions later in the century.

The fact that much of the trans-Mississippi West lay outside U.S. boundaries and that the government had guaranteed Indian tribes permanent possession of some western territories did not deter American economic or missionary activities. By the 1840s, a growing volume of detailed published information about the interior made emigration feasible. Lansford Hastings's *Emigrants' Guide to Oregon and California* (1845) provided practical information and a rationale for emigration, arguing that Americans would bring "genuine Republicanism and unsophisticated Democracy" to the West, replacing "ignorance, superstition, and despotism."

Hastings's vision rapidly materialized. During the 1840s the United States used war and diplomacy to acquire Mexico's possessions in the West as well as the title to the Oregon country up to the 49th parallel. The 1853 Gadsden Purchase secured yet another chunk of Mexican territory for the nation.

Manifest Destiny

Florid rhetoric accompanied territorial growth, and Americans used the slogan "Manifest Destiny" to justify it. The phrase, coined in 1845, suggested that the country's superior institutions and culture constituted a God-given right, even an obligation, to spread American civilization across the continent. Rooted in Puritan utopianism and revolutionary republicanism, this sense of uniqueness and mission also stemmed from the rapid growth and progress of the early nineteenth century. The idea that the nation could and should expand enjoyed wide popular support.

Winning the Trans-Mississippi West

Manifest Destiny justified expansion, but events in Texas triggered the national government's determination to move west of the Mississippi. The Texas question dated back to the years of Spanish control. Primarily a buffer zone for Mexico, the sparsely populated Southwest had scattered centers of Spanish settlement, distant from one another and thousands of miles from Mexico City. Vulnerable as this defensive perimeter of the Spanish Empire was, the United States had recognized its legal status with the Adams-Onis Treaty of 1819, which, in return for Florida, specifically conceded Texas to Spain.

Annexing Texas, 1845

By the time that treaty was ratified in 1821, Mexico was independent but unable to defend its borderlands or to develop powerful bonds of national identity. Mexicans soon had reason to wonder whether Americans would honor the 1819 treaty as American politicians like Henry Clay called for "reannexation" of Texas.

◉ Watch the Video
The Annexation of Texas
at **www.myhistorylab.com**

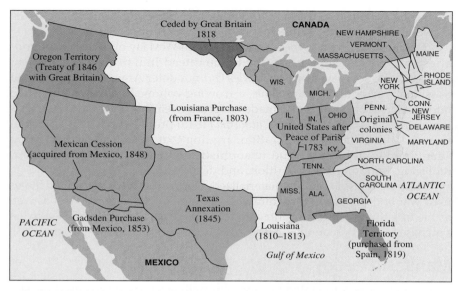

United States Territorial Expansion by 1860 What does this map suggest about the time involved in acquiring the Far West?

In 1823, the Mexican government resolved to strengthen Texas by increasing its population. In return for token payments and pledges to adopt Catholicism and Mexican citizenship, settlers were promised land. **Stephen F. Austin** was among the first Americans to take up the offer. Most settlers were southerners, and some brought slaves. By the end of the decade, some 15,000 white Americans, 1,000 slaves, but just 5,000 Tejanos lived in Texas.

Mexican officials began to question the wisdom of their policies. Although Austin converted to Roman Catholicism, few settlers honored their bargain. Some were malcontents who disliked Mexican laws and limitations on their opportunities. In late 1826, a small group declared the Republic of Fredonia. Although Stephen Austin helped crush the brief uprising, American newspapers praised the rebels as "apostles of democracy."

Mexican anxiety rose. Secretary of Foreign Relations Lucas Aláman branded American settlers advance agents of the United States. In 1829, the Mexican government determined to curb American influence by abolishing slavery in Texas. In 1830, it forbade further American emigration. But little changed. American residents evaded the mandate to abolish slavery while emigrants still crossed the border into Texas.

Tensions escalated, and in October 1835, a skirmish between the colonial militia and Mexican forces opened hostilities. Sam Houston, onetime governor of Tennessee and army officer, headed the Texas forces. Although Texans called the war a revolution, it was in fact, as one Vermont soldier observed, "a rebellion."

Mexican dictator and general Antonio López de Santa Anna hurried north with an army of 6,000 conscripts, many of them Mayan Indians who spoke no Spanish. All were exhausted by the long march. Supply lines were spread thin. Nevertheless, Santa Anna and his men won initial engagements. They took the Alamo in San Antonio, defended by 187 Americans—all of whom were killed—and then the fortress of Goliad, to the southeast, where more than 300 Americans lost their lives.

•**Read** the **Document**
William Barret Travis, Letter from the Alamo *(1836)*
at **www.myhistorylab.com**

As he pursued Houston and the Texans toward the San Jacinto River, carelessness proved Santa Anna's undoing. Although anticipating an American attack, the Mexican general and his men settled down to their usual siesta on April 21, 1836, without posting an adequate guard. As the Mexicans dozed, the Americans attacked. With cries of "Remember the Alamo! Remember Goliad!" the Texans overcame the army, captured its commander in his slippers, and won the war within 20 minutes. American casualties were minimal, but 630 Mexicans lay dead.

Watch the **Video**
The Alamo
at **www.myhistorylab.com**

Vanquished and threatened with lynching, Santa Anna signed treaties recognizing Texan independence. When news of the disaster reached Mexico City, however, the Mexican Congress repudiated an agreement carried out under "threat of death," insisting that Texas was still part of Mexico.

The new republic, financially unstable with a questionable diplomatic status, sought admission to the United States. Jackson was reluctant to act quickly. With 13 free and 13 slave states, many northerners violently opposed taking in another slave state. Petitions poured into Congress in 1837 opposing annexation. Soon the explosive idea was dropped.

For the next few years, the Lone Star Republic limped along. Mexico refused to recognize it, but sent only an occasional raiding party across the border. Texans failed ignominiously in their attempt to capture Santa Fe in 1841. While diplomatic maneuvering in European capitals for financial aid and recognition was only moderately successful, financial ties with the United States increased.

Texas made headline news again in 1844. One Alabama expansionist rightly predicted that it would "agitate the country more than all the other public questions ever have." Hoping to ensure his reelection, President John Tyler reopened the annexation issue. Powerful sectional, national, and political tensions exploded, demonstrating the divisiveness of the slavery-expansion question. Southern Democrats insisted that their region's future hinged on annexing Texas.

Other wings of the Democratic party capitalized more successfully on the issue, however. Stephen Douglas of Illinois, among others, vigorously supported annexation not because it would expand slavery (a topic he avoided), but because it would spread American civilization. Such arguments, classic examples of Manifest Destiny, put the question into a national context of expanding American freedom. So powerfully did these Democrats link Texas to Manifest Destiny that their candidate, James Polk of Tennessee, secured the

1844 Democratic nomination. Polk called for both "the reannexation of Texas at the earliest practicable period" and the occupation of the Oregon Territory.

Fearing the addition of another slave state, most Whigs opposed annexation. They accused the Democrats of exploiting Manifest Destiny to gain office rather than to bring freedom to Texas. As the Whigs feared, Polk rode the issue to win a close election in 1844.

But by the time Polk assumed office in March 1845, Tyler had resolved the question of annexation by pushing through Congress a joint resolution admitting Texas to the Union. Unlike a treaty, requiring the approval of two-thirds of the Senate, a joint resolution needed only majority support. Nine years after its revolution, Texas finally joined the Union, with the right to split into five states if it chose.

●◖▪┤Read the Document

John O'Sullivan, Annexation *(1845)* at **www.myhistorylab.com**

War with Mexico, 1846–1848

When Mexico learned of Texas's annexation, it severed diplomatic ties with the United States. Mexicans could easily interpret events from the 1820s on as part of a gigantic American plot to steal Texas. During the war for Texas independence, American papers, especially those in the South, had hailed the rebels, while southern money and volunteers assisted the Texans. Now, in his inaugural address in 1845, Polk was arguing "that our system may easily be extended to the utmost bounds of our territorial limits, and that as it shall be extended the bonds of our Union, so far from being weakened

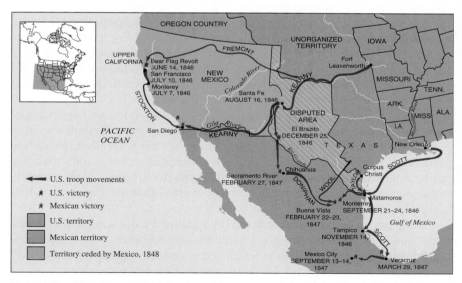

The Mexican-American War What does this map reveal about the movements of American troops during the Mexican-American war? Would you consider American actions equivalent to an invasion? How large an area was in dispute between the Americans and the Mexicans?

will become stronger." Did his remarks suggest further territorial designs, this time on Mexico?

Like many Americans, Polk failed to appreciate how the annexation of Texas humiliated Mexico and encouraged its government to respond belligerently. The president anticipated that a weak Mexico would grant his grandiose demands: Texas bounded by the Rio Grande rather than the Nueces River 150 miles to its north, as well as California and New Mexico.

As a precaution, Polk ordered General Zachary Taylor to move "on or near the Rio Grande." By October 1845, Taylor and 3,500 American troops had reached the Nueces River. The positioning of an American army in Texas did not mean that Polk expected war. Rather, he hoped that a show of military force, coupled with secret diplomacy, would bring the desired concessions. In November, the president sent his secret agent, John L. Slidell, to Mexico City with instructions to secure the Rio Grande border and to buy Upper California and New Mexico. When the Mexican government refused to receive Slidell, Polk decided to make Mexico accept American terms. He ordered Taylor south to the Rio Grande, a move Mexicans saw as an act of war. Democratic newspapers and expansionists enthusiastically hailed Polk's provocative decision; Whigs opposed it.

In late April, the Mexican government declared a state of defensive war. Two days later, a skirmish between Mexican and American troops resulted in 16 American casualties. When Polk heard the news, he quickly drafted a war message for Congress. Despite the fact that the skirmish had occurred on both contested and Mexican territory, Polk claimed that Mexico had "invaded our territory and shed American blood upon American soil." "Notwithstanding all our efforts to avoid it," Polk asserted, war "exists by act of Mexico."

Although Congress declared war, the conflict was bitterly divisive. Many Whigs, including Abraham Lincoln, questioned Polk's truthfulness, and, with time, their opposition grew more vocal. Lincoln declared the war one "of conquest brought into existence to catch votes." The American Peace Society revealed sordid examples of army misbehavior in Mexico, and Frederick Douglass accused the country of "cupidity and love of dominion." Many workers also censured the war.

Debate continued as American troops swept toward Mexico City. The Mexican government refused to admit defeat or to negotiate an end to the conflict. Yet even as some Americans criticized the inconclusive war, expansionists enthusiastically supported the president. Some even urged permanent occupation of Mexico.

In the end, chance helped end hostilities. Mexican moderates approached Polk's diplomatic representative, Nicholas Trist, who accompanied the American army in Mexico. In Trist's baggage were detailed, though out-of-date, instructions outlining Polk's requirements: the Rio Grande boundary, Upper California, and New Mexico. Although the president lost confidence in Trist and ordered him home in chains, Trist stayed in Mexico to negotiate an end to the war.

California and New Mexico

While Texas and Mexico dominated the headlines, Polk considered California and New Mexico part of any resolution of the Mexico crisis. Serious American interest in California dated from the late 1830s. Before then, few Americans were living in Californio. Many had married into California families and taken Mexican citizenship. But gradual recognition of California's fine harbors, its favorable position for the China trade, and suspicion that Great Britain had designs on it fed the conviction that California must become part of the United States. The arrival of 1,500 overland emigrants in the 1840s increased the likelihood that California would not long remain a Mexican outpost.

In 1845, Polk appointed Thomas Larkin, a successful American merchant in Monterey, as his confidential agent. "If the people [of California] should desire to unite their destiny with ours," wrote Polk's secretary of state, James Buchanan, to Larkin, "they would be received as brethren." Polk's efforts to buy California suggested that he was sensitive to the fragility of American claims to the region. But Santa Anna, carrying the burden of having lost Texas, was in no position to sell.

New Mexico was also on Polk's list. Profitable economic ties with the United States dating back to the 1820s stimulated American territorial ambitions. As part of the oldest and largest Mexican community in North America, however, most New Mexicans had little desire for annexation. The unsuccessful Texan assault on Santa Fe in 1841 and border clashes in the two following years did not enhance the attractiveness of Anglo neighbors. But standing awkwardly in the path of westward expansion and further isolated from Mexico by the annexation of Texas in 1846, New Mexico's future was uncertain.

In June 1846, shortly after the declaration of war with Mexico, American troops led by Colonel Stephen W. Kearney left Fort Leavenworth, Kansas, for New Mexico. Kearney had orders to occupy Mexico's northern provinces and to protect the lucrative Santa Fe trade. Two months later, the army took Santa Fe without a shot. Having already made strategic alliances with Americans, New Mexico's upper class readily accepted the new rulers. However, ordinary Mexicans and Pueblo Indians did not take conquest so lightly. After Kearney departed for California, resistance erupted first in New Mexico and then in California. Kearney was wounded, and the first appointed American governor of New Mexico was killed. In the end, superior American military strength won the day. By January 1847, both California and New Mexico were firmly in American hands.

The Treaty of Guadalupe Hidalgo, 1848

Negotiated by Trist and signed on February 2, 1848, the **Treaty of Guadalupe Hidalgo** resolved the original issues by setting the Rio Grande as the boundary between Mexico and the United States and by transferring the Southwest and California into American hands. At a cost of 13,000 American lives, mostly from disease, the United States gained 75,000 Spanish-speaking inhabitants, 150,000 Native Americans, and 529,017 square miles, almost a third of prewar Mexico. It paid Mexico $15 million (and another $10 million in 1853 for the Gadsden Purchase), agreed to honor American claims against Mexico, and guaranteed the civil, political, and property rights of former Mexican citizens. Although sporadic violence would continue for years in the Southwest as Mexicans protested the outcome, the war was over, and the Americans had won.

The Oregon Question, 1844–1846

In the Pacific Northwest, the presence of mighty Great Britain suggested the wisdom of diplomacy rather than war. Glossing over the disputed nature of American claims to the Oregon Territory, Polk assured the inauguration day crowd that "our title to the country of Oregon is 'clear and unquestionable.'" The British did not agree.

Though the British considered the president's speech belligerent, Polk correctly noted that Americans had begun to settle in the disputed territories. Between 1842 and 1845, the number of Americans in Oregon grew from 400 to more than 5,000, mostly south of the Columbia River in the Willamette valley. By 1843, these settlers had written a constitution and soon after elected a legislature. At the same time, declining British interest in the area set the stage for an eventual compromise. The near destruction of the beaver undermined the fur trade, while the riches created by Britain's Industrial Revolution reduced the appeal of colonies. Britain had already granted Canada self-rule. Attractive commercial opportunities were opening up in other parts of the world like India and China, while New Zealand, annexed in 1840, and Australia became magnets for British emigration.

Polk's flamboyant posture and the expansive American claims made mediation difficult, however. His campaign slogan claimed a boundary of 54°40'. But Polk was not willing to go to war with Great Britain for Oregon. Privately, he considered reasonable a boundary at the 49th parallel, which would extend the existing Canadian-American border to the Pacific.

Soon after his inauguration, Polk offered his compromise to Great Britain, but his tone antagonized the British. In his year-end address to Congress in 1845, the president increased diplomatic tensions by again claiming Oregon and giving the required one-year's notice of American intention to cancel the joint occupation.

Despite slogans, most Americans did not want to fight for Oregon. As war with Mexico loomed, the task of resolving the disagreement became urgent. The British, too, were eager to settle, and in June 1846, they agreed to the 49th parallel boundary if Vancouver Island remained British. Polk ended the crisis just weeks before the declaration of war with Mexico; he escaped some of the responsibility for retreating from slogans by sharing it with the Senate, who approved the compromise.

As these events show, Manifest Destiny was an idea that supported and justified expansionist policies. It corresponded to Americans' basic belief that expansion was necessary and right. As early as 1816, American geography books pictured the nation's western boundary at the Pacific and included Texas. Popular literature typically described Indians as a dying race and Mexicans as "injurious neighbor[s]." Only whites could make the wilderness flower. Thus, as lands east of the Mississippi filled up, Americans automatically called on familiar ideas to justify expansion.

Going West and East

Americans lost little time in moving into the new territories. Between 1841 and 1867, thousands of Americans left their homes for the West. By 1860, California alone had 380,000 settlers. At the same time, thousands of Chinese headed south and east to destinations like Australia, Hawaii, and North and South America to escape the unrest caused by opium wars with Great Britain, internal unrest, and poor economic conditions. Sixty-three thousand had come to the United States by 1870, most settling in California.

View the **Image**

A Forty-Niner's Covered Wagon
at **www.myhistorylab.com**

One Chinese folk song depicted the "perilous journey" to the United States "sailing [in] a boat with bamboo poles across the sea." The Chinese, of course, had little choice on their travel route to the American West, but American migrants did. Some chose the expensive sea route from Atlantic or Gulf Coast ports around South America to the West Coast or across Panama and then by sea to the coast. Most American emigrants, however, chose land routes. In 1843, the first large party succeeded in crossing the plains and mountains to Oregon. More followed. Between 1841 and 1867, some 350,000 traveled the overland trails to California or Oregon, while others trekked part of the way to intermediate points like Colorado and Utah.

Unlike earlier migrations west, the trip to the Far West involved considerable expense: $600 paid for one person on the relatively comfortable Cape Horn voyage or for four people overland. (If emigrants sold their wagons and oxen at the journey's end, the final expenses might be only $220.) Such outlays ruled out the very poor. Migration to the Far West (with the exception of group migration to Utah) was a movement of middle-class Americans.

See the **Map**

U.S. Territorial Expansion in the 1850s
at **www.myhistorylab.com**

The Emigrants

Most of the emigrants to the Far West, where slavery was prohibited, were white and American-born. They came from the Midwest and the Upper South. A few free blacks made the trip as well. Emigrants from the Deep South usually headed for Arkansas or Texas, many with their slaves. By 1840, over 11,000 slaves toiled in Texas and 20,000 in Arkansas.

Except for the Gold Rush, white migration was a family experience, usually involving men and women from their late twenties to early forties. A sizable number had recently married. For most, migration to the Far West was the latest in a series of moves, often as children or as newlyweds. But this time, vast distances seemed to mean a final separation from home.

Migrants' Motives

While emigrant expectations varied, many believed that the West would offer rich opportunities. Thousands sought gold. Others anticipated making their fortune as merchants, shopkeepers, and peddlers. Some intended to speculate in land, acquiring large blocks of public lands and reselling to later settlers at a handsome profit. Practicing law or medicine on the frontier attracted still others.

Most migrants dreamed of bettering their life by farming, and government policies made it easier to get land. During the 1830s and 1840s, **preemption acts** allowed "squatters" to settle public lands before the government offered them for sale and then to purchase them at the minimum price once they came on the market. The amount of land a family had to buy shrank to only 40 acres. (In 1862, the Homestead Act would offer 160 acres of government land free to citizens or future citizens over 21 who lived on the property, improved it, and paid a small registration fee.) Oregon's land policy was even more generous. It awarded a single man 320 acres of free land and a married man 640 acres, provided he occupied his claim for four years and made improvements.

Some emigrants went west for their health. Others pursued religious or cultural missions in the West. Missionary couples like David and Catherine Blaine, who settled in frontier Seattle, were determined to bring Protestantism and education to white settlers. Stirred by stories of the "deplorable morals" on the frontier, they left the comforts of home to evangelize and educate westerners. Still others, like the **Mormons**, made the long trek to Utah to establish a society conforming to their religious beliefs.

Like Americans, Chinese migrants also dreamed of bettering their condition. Most were married men facing limited opportunities in their villages. Labor circulars insisted that Americans "want the Chinaman to come and make him very welcome. . . . Money is in great plenty and to spare in America." Emigrants to Hawaii and the United States reinforced the message when they returned with money in their pockets. In the 1860s, Chinese laborers could earn $30 a month working for the railroad, far more than the $3 to $5 they might earn at home.

The Overland Trails

The trip for American emigrants began at starting points in Iowa and Missouri. When the grass was up for the stock in the late spring, the emigrant trains set out. Making only 15 miles a day, emigrants first followed the valley of the

RECOVERING *the* PAST

Personal Diaries

Nineteenth-century journals kept by hundreds of ordinary men and women traveling west on the overland trails constitute a rich source for exploring the nature of the westward experience. They are also an example of how private sources can be used to deepen our understanding of the past. Diaries, journals, and letters all provide us with a personal perspective on major happenings. These sources tend to focus on the concrete, so they convey the texture of daily life in the nineteenth century, daily routines and amusements, clothing, habits, and interactions with family and friends. They also offer evidence of the varied concerns, attitudes, and prejudices of the writers, thus providing a test of commonly accepted generalizations about individual and group behavior.

Like any historical source, personal documents must be used carefully. It is important to note the writer's age, gender, class, and regional identification. Although this information may not be available, some of the writer's background can be deduced from what he or she has written. It is also important to consider for what purpose and for whom the document was composed. This information will help explain the tone or character of the source and what has been included or left out. It is, of course, important to avoid generalizing too much from one or even several similar sources. Only after reading many diaries, letters, and journals is it possible to make valid generalizations about life in the past.

Here we present excerpts from two travel journals of the 1850s. Few of the writers considered their journals to be strictly private. Often, they were intended as a family record or as information for friends back home. Therefore, material of a personal nature has often been excluded. Nineteenth-century Americans referred to certain topics, such as pregnancy, only indirectly or not at all.

One excerpt comes from Mary Bailey's 1852 journal. Mary was 22 years old when she crossed the plains to California with her 32-year-old doctor husband. Originally a New Englander, Mary had lived in Ohio for six years before moving west. The Baileys were reasonably prosperous and were able to restock necessary supplies on the road west. The other writer, Robert Robe, was 30 years old when he crossed along the same route a year earlier than the Baileys, headed for Oregon. Robert was a native of Ohio and a Presbyterian minister.

REFLECTING ON THE PAST As you read these brief excerpts, notice what each journal reveals about the trip west. What kinds of challenges did the emigrants face on their journey? Can you see indications of the divisions of work based on gender? How is the focus of their interests different? What sorts of interactions seem to have occurred between men and women?

Even these short excerpts suggest that men and women, as they traveled west, had different concerns and different perspectives on the journey. How are the two accounts similar and different?

Journal of Robert Robe

[May] [1851]

29. Have arrived in the region abounding in Buffalo. At noon a considerable herd came in sight. The first any of us had ever seen. Thus now for the chase—the horsemen proved too swift in pursuit and frightened them into the Bluffs without capturing any. Footmen pursued however and killed three pretty good success for the first.

30. Nothing remarkable today.

31. Game being abundant we resolved to rest our stock and hunt today—Started in the morning on foot. Saw probably 1,000 Buffalo. Shot at several and killed one. Where ever we found them wolves were prowling around as if to guard them. Their real object is however no

doubt to seize the calves as their prey. Saw a town of Prairie dogs, they are nearly as large as a gray squirrel. They bark fiercely when at a little distance but on near approach flee to their holes. Wherever they are we see numerous owls. After a very extensive ramble and having seen a variety of game we returned at sunset with most voracious appetites.

[June]

1. The Bluffs became beautifully undulating losing their precipitous aspect and the country further back is beautifully rolling prairie.
2. In the evening camped beside our old friends Miller and Dovey. They had met with a great loss this morning their 3 horses having taken fright at a drove of buffalo and ran entirely away. Some of our company killed more buffalo this evening & a company went in the night with teams to bring them in.
3. Spent the forenoon in an unsuccessful search for the above mentioned horses. In the afternoon pursued & caught our company after.
4. Crossed the south fork of the Platte at 2 p.m.

Source: "Robert Robe's Diary While Crossing the Plains in 1851," WHQ Volume 19, Number 1, January 1928.

Journal of Mary Stuart Bailey

Wednesday, April 13, 1852

Left our hitherto happy home in Sylvania amid the tears of parting kisses of dear friends, many of whom were endeared to me by their kindness shown to me when I was a stranger in a strange land, when sickness and death visited our small family & removed our darling, our only child in a moment, as it were. Such kindness I can never forget. . . .

Friday, 21st [May]

Rained last night. Slept in the tent for the first time. I was Yankee enough to protect myself by pinning up blankets over my head. I am quite at home in my tent.

12:00 Have traveled in the rain all day & we are stuck in the mud. I sit in the wagon writing while the men are at work doubling the teams to draw us out. . . .

Sunday, 23rd.

Walked to the top of the hill where I could be quiet & commune with nature and nature's God. This afternoon I was annoyed by something very unpleasant & shed many tears and felt very unhappy. . . .

Sunday, 4th [July]

Started at 3 o'clock to find feed or know where it was. Had to go 4 or 5 miles off the road. Found water & good grass. Camped on the sand with sage roots for fuel. It is wintery, cold & somewhat inclined to rain, not pleasant. Rather a dreary Independence Day. We speak of our friends at home. We think they are thinking of us. . . .

Monday, 12th.

Stayed in camp another day to get our horse better. He is much improved. It is cold enough. Washed in the morning & had the sick headache in the afternoon. . . .

Saturday, 18th [September]

Very pleasant, delightful weather. Feel much better today. We are not stirring this afternoon. We have heard to a great deal of suffering, people being thrown out on the desert to die & being picked up & brought to the hospital. . . .

Tuesday, November 8th

Sacramento city has been nearly consumed. The Dr. has had all his instruments & a good deal of clothing burned, loss not exceeding $300. It really seems as though it was not right for us to come to California & lose so much. I do not think that we shall be as well off as at home.

Source: From Ho for California! Women's Overland Diaries, Sandra L. Meyers, ed. Reprinted with the permission of the Henry E. Huntington Library.

A Mormon Wagon Train What does this view of a Mormon wagon train in the 1850s suggest about the terrain that emigrant families encountered as they went west? The Mormon migrations were the most organized of the migrations into the trans-Mississippi West, although not all Mormons were lucky enough to travel by wagon. Some emigrants to Utah pushed handcarts across the plains to their destination.

Platte River up to South Pass in the Rockies. This part of the trip seemed novel, even enjoyable. Until the 1850s, conflict with Indians was rare. The traditional division of labor persisted: Men did "outdoor" work like driving and repairing wagons, and women handled domestic chores. Young children stayed out of the way in wagons, while older brothers and sisters walked alongside and lent a hand. Wagon trains might stop to observe the Sabbath, allowing for rest and laundry.

Later, difficulties multiplied. Cholera often took a heavy toll. Deserts and mountains replaced rolling prairies. Emigrants had to cross the final mountain ranges—the Sierras and the Cascades—before the first snowfall, so they pushed on relentlessly. Animals weakened by travel, poor feed, and bad water sickened and often died. Families had to lighten wagons by throwing out treasured possessions. Food supplies dwindled, and the familiar division of responsibilities often collapsed. Women found themselves loading and driving wagons, even helping to drag them over rocky mountain trails. Their husbands worked frantically with the animals and the wagons as the time of the first snowfall approached. Tempers frayed. Family harmony often collapsed. Mary Power, who with her husband and three children crossed in 1853, revealed exasperation and depression in her journal: "I felt my courage

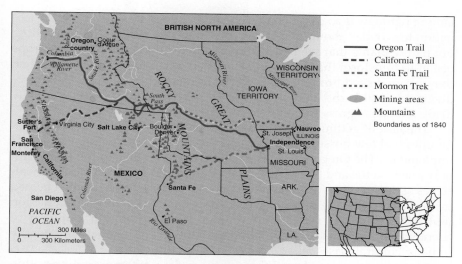

Overland Trails to the West The various trails over which thousands of Americans traveled during the 1840s, 1850s, and 1860s are depicted on this map. What natural obstacles do the map's geographic features suggest the travelers faced, and at what point during their trip did travelers encounter them?

must fail me, for there we were in a strange land, almost without anything to eat, [with] a team that was not able to pull an empty wagon."

Finally, five or six months after setting out, emigrants arrived, exhausted and often penniless, in Oregon or California. As one wrote at the end of her journey in 1854, its "care, fatigue, tediousness, perplexities and dangers of various kinds, can not be excelled."

Living in the West

Whether elated or depressed after months of travel, emigrants had no choice but to start anew. As they did so, they naturally drew on their experiences back East. "Pioneers though we are, and proud of it, we are not content with the wilds . . . with the idleness of the land, the rudely construct[ed] log cabin," one Oregon settler explained.

Watch the Video
The Real West Is an Urban West
at **www.myhistorylab.com**

Farming in the West

Pioneer farmers faced the urgent task of establishing homesteads and beginning farming. First, they had to locate a suitable claim, then clear land, and construct a shelter. Only then could they plant crops.

As farmers labored "to get the land subdued and the wilde nature out of it," they repeated a process occurring on earlier frontiers. The goal of taming nature was so central and difficult that there was little time or inclination to wonder about long-range consequences. Felling timber, pulling out native plants that seemed without value, and planting familiar crops began to transform the landscape, often with unanticipated results. When they planted seed brought from home, farmers unknowingly also introduced weeds that did all too well, like the Canadian thistle that gradually displaced native grass and rendered land useless for grazing.

The task of getting started presented many challenges. Since emigrant families had few possessions, they had to work without familiar tools and implements. The Oregon bride who set up housekeeping in the 1840s with only a stew kettle and three knives was not unusual. Men often found themselves assisting wives in unfamiliar domestic chores, while women helped men with their heavy outdoor work. After months of intense interaction with other travelers, families often felt lonely and thought longingly of friends and family back home. Although they might interact with nearby Indians, cultural biases made close friendships difficult.

One pioneer remembered that "in those days anyone residing within twenty miles was considered a neighbor." But the isolation usually ended within a few years as new emigrants arrived and old settlers sought better claims. As rural communities grew, settlers established schools, churches, and clubs. These organizations redefined acceptable forms of behavior and enforced conventional standards.

Determination to reestablish familiar institutions was most apparent in law and politics. In Oregon, pioneers set up a political system based on eastern models before territorial status was resolved. Before permanent schools or churches existed, men resumed familiar political rituals of electioneering, voting, and talking politics. They went to court to ensure law and order.

Establishing a common school system and churches was more difficult and less urgent than beginning political life. Schools operated sporadically and only for students paying at least part of the fees. While confirmed believers attended early church services, they often discovered that there were too few members of individual denominations to support separate churches. Nor were converts plentiful, for many settlers had lost the habit of regular churchgoing. David Blaine learned the "unwelcome lesson" that "separation from gospel influences" had left many "quite indifferent to gospel truth."

The chronic shortage of cash on the frontier hampered the growth of both schools and churches. Until farmers could send their goods to market, they had little cash to spare. Geographic mobility also contributed to institutional instability. Up to three-quarters of the population of a frontier county might vanish within a 10-year period. Some farmed in as many as four locations before finding a satisfactory claim. Institutions relying on continuing personal and financial support suffered accordingly.

Yet newspapers, journals, and books, which circulated early on the frontier, reinforced familiar norms and determination. As more settlers arrived, support for educational, religious, and cultural institutions grew. In the end, as one pioneer pointed out, "We have a telegraph line from the East, a daily rail road train, daily mail and I am beginning to feel quite civilized. And here ended my pioneer experience." Only 16 years had passed since she had crossed the Plains.

Although the belief in frontier economic and social opportunities encouraged emigration, the dream was often illusory. Western society rapidly acquired a social and economic structure resembling that of the East. Frontier newspapers referred to leading settlers as the "better" sort, while workers for hire and tenant farmers appeared. Widespread geographic mobility also suggests that many failed to capitalize on the benefits of homesteading. Those who left communities were generally less successful than the core of stable residents, who became economic and social leaders. Those on the move believed that fortune would finally smile at their next stop. Said one wife when her husband announced another move: "I seemed to have heard all this before."

Mining Western Resources

In 1848, news of the discovery of gold in California swept the country and prompted thousands to abandon their ordinary lives in hopes of a fortune. Within a year, California's population ballooned from 14,000 to almost 100,000. By 1852, that figure more than doubled.

Unlike farming pioneers, the "forty-niners" were mostly unmarried young men. (In 1850, over half the people in California were in their twenties.) Of those pouring into California in 1849, about 80 percent came from the United States and 13 percent from Mexico and South America; the rest were Europeans and Asians. California was thus one of the most diverse places in the country. Few, however, thought of settling in the West; instead, they dreamed of going home rich.

California was only the first and most dramatic of the western mining discoveries. In 1858, 25,000 to 30,000 emigrants, many from California, hurried to British Columbia; the next year gold strikes in Colorado precipitated another frantic rush. Precious metals lured prospectors to the Pacific Northwest, Montana, and Idaho in the 1860s and, in the next decade, to the Black Hills of South Dakota.

Unlike isolated farming settlements, the mining communities sprang up almost overnight after a strike. Often hastily constructed, the camps soon housed hundreds or even thousands of miners and the merchants, saloonkeepers, cooks, druggists, gamblers, and prostitutes serving them. Usually about half of the residents were there to prospect the miners.

Given the motivation, character, and ethnic diversity of those flocking to boomtowns and the feeble attempts to set up local government in what were perceived as temporary communities, it was hardly surprising that mining life was disorderly. Racial antagonisms led to ugly riots and lynchings. Miners had few qualms about eliminating Indians and others who got in the way. Fistfights, drunkenness, and murder occurred often enough to become part of the lore of the gold rush. In less than a month, one woman wrote, "we have had murders, fearful accidents, bloody deaths, a mob, whippings, a hanging, an attempt at suicide, and a fatal duel."

Mining life was not usually this violent, but it did tolerate behavior unacceptable farther east. Miners were trying to get rich, not to recreate eastern communities. Married men, knowing the raucous and immoral character of mining communities, hesitated to bring wives and families west.

Although the lucky few struck it rich or at least made enough money to return home with pride intact, miners' journals and letters reveal that many made only enough to keep going. Easily mined silver and gold deposits soon ran out. Although Chinese miners proved adept at finding what early miners overlooked, the remaining rich deposits lay deeply embedded in rock or gravel. Extraction required capital, technological experience, and expensive machinery. Eventually, mining became a corporate industrial concern and miners industrial wage workers.

Probably 5 percent of early gold rush emigrants to California were women and children. Many of the women also anticipated getting "rich in a hurry." Because there were so few of them, the cooking, nursing, laundry, and hotel services women provided had a high value. When Luzena Wilson arrived in Sacramento, a miner offered her $10 for a biscuit. Yet the work was tiring, and some wondered if the money compensated for the exhaustion. Mary Ballou thought it over and decided, "I would not advise any Lady to come out here and suffer the toil and fatigue I have suffered for the sake of a little gold." As men's profits shrank, so, too, did those of the women who served them.

Some of the first women on the mining frontier were prostitutes, hoping to capitalize on the shortage of women. Prostitutes may have constituted as much as 20 percent of California's female population in 1850, probably vastly outnumbering other women in early mining camps. During boom days, they made good money and sometimes won a recognized place in society. But prostitution was a risky business in such a disorderly environment.

The Mexicans, South Americans, Chinese, and small numbers of blacks seeking their fortunes in California soon discovered that although they contributed substantially to California's growth, racial discrimination flourished vigorously. At first, American miners tried to force foreigners out of the gold fields altogether. An attempt to declare mining illegal for all foreigners failed, but a high tax on them was more successful. Thousands of Mexicans left the mines, and the Chinese found other jobs in San Francisco and Sacramento. As business stagnated in mining towns, however, white miners reduced the levy. By 1870, when the tax was declared unconstitutional, the Chinese, paying 85 percent of it, had "contributed" $5 million to California for the right to prospect. The hostility that led to this legislation also fed widespread violence against Chinese and Mexicans.

Black Americans found that their skin color placed them in a situation akin to that of foreigners. Deprived of the vote, forbidden to testify in civil or criminal cases involving whites, excluded from the bounties of the state's homestead law, blacks led a precarious existence in Golden California.

For the Native American tribes of the interior, the mining rushes were disasters. Accustomed to foraging for food, they found fish and game increasingly scarce as miners diverted streams, hunted game, or drove it from mining areas altogether. When Indians responded by raiding mining camps, miners erupted with fury. They stalked and killed native men and women, sometimes collecting bounties offered by some mining communities for their scalps. Indian women were raped; children were kidnapped and offered as apprentices. As one miner pointed out, "Indians seven or eight years old are worth $100 . . . [and] it is a damn poor Indian that's not worth $50." Without legal recourse because of their skin color, Native Americans could not withstand the onslaught of white society. Subjected not only to violence but to white disease, Indians died by the thousands. In 1849, there had been about 150,000 Indians in California. In just over 20 years, numbers had tumbled to fewer than 30,000.

In fact, fantasies of riches rarely came true. Western ghost towns testified to the typical pattern: boom, bust, decay, death. The landscape bore the scars of careless exploitation. Forests were devastated to provide timber for the flumes miners constructed to divert rivers from their channels in the hopes of exposing gold in dry riverbeds. During heavy rains, mounds of debris oozed over fields and choked waterways.

Yet for all the negative consequences, gold had many positive effects on the country and the West. Between 1848 and 1883, California mines supplied two-thirds of the country's gold. Gold transformed sleepy San Francisco into a bustling metropolis. It fueled the agricultural and commercial development of California and Oregon, as miners provided a market for goods and services. Gold built harbors, railroads, and irrigation systems all over the West. Though few people made large fortunes, both the region and the nation profited from gold.

Establishing God's Kingdom

In the decades before 1860, many emigrants heading for the Far West stopped to rest and buy supplies in Salt Lake City, the heart of the Mormon state of Deseret. There they encountered a society both familiar and also shockingly foreign. Visitors admired the attractively laid-out town, but they also gossiped about **polygamy** and searched the faces of Mormon women for signs of rebellion—and were amazed that so few Mormon women seemed interested in escaping the bonds of plural marriage, which outsiders equated with slavery.

Violence drove the Mormons to the Great Basin area. Two years after Joseph Smith's murder in 1844, angry mobs had chased the last of the "Saints" out of Nauvoo, Illinois. Smith's successor, Brigham Young, believed the Saints' best hope for survival lay in situating the Kingdom of God somewhere in the West, far removed from the United States. The Mexican-American War unexpectedly furthered his plans. By raising 500 Mormon young men for Kearney's Army of the West, Young acquired sorely needed capital. The battalion's advance pay bought wagonloads of supplies for starving and sick Mormons strung out along the trail between Missouri and Iowa and helped finance the impending great migration.

Young selected the Great Basin area, technically part of Mexico, for the future settlement. One thousand miles from its nearest "civilized" neighbors, it was remote and arid. But if irrigated, Mormon leaders concluded it might prove as fertile as ancient Israel. In April 1847, Young led an exploratory expedition west. After reaching Salt Lake in late July, he exclaimed, "This is the place," and announced his land policy. Settlers would receive virtually free land on the basis of a family's size and ability to cultivate it. While he returned to lead the main body, the expeditionary group dug irrigation ditches and began planting.

Young's organizational talents and his followers' cooperative abilities were fully tested. By September 1847, fully 566 wagons and 1,500 Saints made the arduous trek to Salt Lake City; more came the next year. Church leaders directed everything. By 1850, the Mormon frontier had over 11,000 settlers. Missionary efforts in the United States, Great Britain, and Scandinavia drew thousands of converts to the Great Basin, with a Church-administered loan fund facilitating the journey for many. By the end of the decade, over 30,000 Saints lived in Utah, not only in Salt Lake City but also in more than 90 village colonies. Despite hardship, the Mormons thrived.

Most Mormons were farmers; many came from New England and the Midwest and shared many customs, attitudes, and political structures with other Americans. But "Gentile" outsiders perceived profound differences, for the heart of Mormon society was not the individual farmer on his own homestead, but the cooperative village. Years of persecution had promoted a strong group identity and acceptance of Church guidance. With Church leaders making essential decisions, farming became a collective enterprise. All farmers received land and access to community water. During Sunday services, the local bishop might provide farming instructions along with his sermon.

Nothing separated Church and state in Utah. Church leaders occupied all of the important political posts. Young's Governing Quorum included the Church's high priests, who made both religious and political decisions. When it became clear that Utah would become a territory, however, Mormon leaders drew up a constitution separating religious and political power. But little changed. As one Gentile pointed out, "This intimate connection of church and state seems to pervade everything that is done. The supreme power in both being lodged in the hands of the same individuals, it is difficult to separate their two official characters, and to determine whether in any one instance they act as spiritual or merely temporal officers." The Treaty of Guadalupe Hidalgo officially incorporating Utah into the United States hardly affected political and religious arrangements. Young became territorial governor. Bishops continued as spiritual and civil leaders.

Although most Gentiles accepted some of the peculiarities of the Mormon settlement, few could tolerate polygamy. Smith and other Church leaders had secretly practiced it in the early 1840s, but Young only publicly revealed the doctrine in 1852, when the Saints were safely in Utah. Smith believed that the highest or "celestial" form of marriage brought special rewards in the afterlife. Because wives and children contributed to these rewards, plural marriage was a means of sanctification. From a practical standpoint, polygamy incorporated into Mormon society single female converts who had left their families to come to Utah.

Although most Mormons accepted the doctrine and its religious justification, perhaps only 10 to 20 percent of Mormon families were polygamous. Few men had more than two wives. Personal strains and the expense of maintaining several families ensured that usually only the most successful and visible Mormon leaders practiced plural marriage during the 40 years in which polygamy was practiced openly.

Polygamous family life hardly resembled outsiders' fantasies of sexual excess. Since jealousy among wives could destroy families, Mormon leaders minimized romantic love and sexual attraction in courtship and marriage. Instead, they encouraged marriages founded on mutual attachment, with sex primarily for procreation.

To the shock of outsiders, Mormon women considered themselves not slaves but highly regarded members of the community. Whether plural wives or not, they saw polygamy as the cutting edge of their society and defended it to outsiders. Polygamy was preferable to monogamy, which left the single woman outside family life and forced some into prostitution.

Although they faced obvious difficulties, many plural wives found rewards in polygamy. Without the constant presence of husbands, they had an unusual opportunity for independence. Many treated visiting husbands as revered friends, deriving day-to-day emotional satisfaction from their children. Occasionally, plural wives lived together and became close friends.

The Mormon frontier succeeded in terms of its numbers, its growing prosperity, and its unity. Long-term threats loomed, however, once the area became part of the United States. Attacks on Young's power as well as heated verbal denunciations of polygamy proliferated. Efforts began in Congress to outlaw polygamy. In the years before the Civil War, Mormons withstood these assaults. But as Utah became more connected to the rest of the country, the pressures on the institution of plural marriage would increase.

Cities in the West

Many emigrants went west not to farm or pan for gold but to live in cities like San Francisco, Denver, and Portland. There they pursued business and professional opportunities or perhaps speculated in real estate.

Cities were integral to frontier life. Some, like St. Joseph, Missouri, which catered to the emigrant trade, preceded agricultural settlement. Others, like Portland, were destinations for overland travelers or were market and supply centers for emigrant farmers. San Francisco and Denver were "instant cities," transformed as the discovery of precious metals sent thousands of miners to and through them. Once the strike ran out, many miners returned to these cities to make a new start. In San Francisco, a Chinese community took shape as Chinese laborers abandoned mining and railroad work. In 1860, almost 3,000 Chinese lived in Chinatown; 10 years later, that number grew to 12,022.

Bustling commercial life offered residents a wide range of occupations and services. As a Portland emigrant remarked in 1852, "In many ways life here . . . was more primitive than it was in the early times in Illinois and Missouri. But in others it was far more advanced. . . . We could get the world's commodities here which could not be had then, or scarcely at all, in the interior of Illinois or Missouri."

Young, single men seeking their fortunes made up a disproportionate share of urban populations. Frontier Portland had more than three men for every woman. Predictably, urban life was often noisy, rowdy, and occasionally violent. Some women tried to reform the atmosphere by attempting to close stores on Sunday or to prohibit drinking. Others, of course, enjoyed all the attention that came with so many young men. Eventually, the gender ratio became balanced, but as late as 1880, fully 18 of the 24 largest western cities had more men than women.

Western cities soon lost their distinctiveness. The history of Portland suggests the common pattern of development. In 1845, it was only a clearing in the forest, with lively speculation in town lots. By the early 1850s, Portland had become a small trading center with a few rough log structures and muddy tracks for streets. As farmers poured into Oregon, the city became a regional commercial center. More permanent structures were built, giving it an "eastern" appearance.

The belief that western cities offered special opportunities initially drew many young men to Portland and other urban areas. Success was greatest, however, for those arriving with assets. By the 1860s, when the city's population had reached 2,874, Portland's Social Club symbolized the emergence of an elite. Portland's businessmen, lawyers, and editors controlled an increasing share of the community's wealth and set its social standards, showing how rapidly and far Portland had traveled from its raw frontier beginnings.

Cultures in Conflict

Looking at westward expansion through the eyes of white emigrants provides only one view of the frontier experience. In such a diverse region, many other views existed.

Some of those heading to the American West came from south China. Mostly men, they planned to work for a few years and then return home. Initially, California welcomed them. One San Francisco merchant reported in

A View of Chinese Miners This magazine illustration shows Chinese miners searching for gold deposits in areas probably abandoned by other miners. How does the illustration highlight the foreign character of these miners? What point of view towards the miners does this illustration seem to convey?

1855 that the Chinese were "received like guests" and treated "with politeness." However, tolerance disappeared as more Chinese arrived on the West Coast and took jobs in mining camps, on the railroads, and elsewhere. A telegram from Chinese miners in the California mountains betrayed anxieties many must have felt: "Am afraid there will be big fight." Increasingly whites perceived the Chinese as racial threats, calling them "nagurs" only slightly removed "from the African race." Chinese workers faced many forms of harassment. In 1880, California legislators expressed white hostility by passing a law that made any marriage between a white person and a "negro, mulatto, or Mongolian" illegal.

Confronting the Plains Tribes

Some likened the Chinese to the Native Americans, another group that viewed the western experience differently from white emigrants. An entry from an Oregon Trail journal hints at what one such perspective might be. On May 7, 1864, Mary Warner, a bride of only a few months, described a frightening event. That day, a "fine-looking" Indian had visited the wagon train and tried to buy her. Mary's husband, probably uncertain how to handle the situation, played along, agreeing to trade his wife for

View the Image
Oregon Trail Marker
at **www.myhistorylab.com**

two ponies. The Indian generously offered three. "Then," wrote Mary, "he took hold of my shawl to make me understand to get out [of the wagon]. About this time I got frightened and really was so hysterical [that] I began to cry." Everyone laughed at her, she reported, though surely the Indian found the whole incident no more amusing than she had.

This ordinary encounter on the overland trail suggests the social and cultural differences separating white Americans moving west and the peoples they met. Confident of their values and rights, emigrants had little regard for those who had lived in the West for centuries and no compunction in seizing their lands. Many predicted that the Indians would soon disappear from the continent.

During the 1840s, white Americans for the first time came into extensive contact with the powerful Plains tribes, whose culture differed from that of the more familiar eastern Woodland peoples. Probably a quarter-million Native Americans occupied the Plains. "Border" tribes along the Plains' eastern edge lived in villages and raised crops, supplemented with buffalo meat during summer months. On the Central Plains lived Brulé and Oglala Sioux, Cheyenne, Shoshone, and Arapaho, all aggressive tribes who followed the buffalo and often raided the border tribes. In the Southwest were Comanche, Ute, Navajo, and some Apache bands; northern and western Texas were hunting grounds for the Kiowa, Wichita, Apache, and southern Comanche. Many southwestern tribes had adopted aspects of Spanish culture and European domestic animals such as cattle, sheep, and horses.

The Plains tribes shared certain characteristics. Most became nomads after the introduction of Spanish horses in the sixteenth century increased their seasonal mobility from 50 to 500 miles. Horses allowed Indian men to hunt the buffalo so successfully that tribes (with the exclusion of the border groups) came to depend on the beasts for food, clothing, fuel, teepee dwellings, and trading purposes. Women were responsible for processing buffalo products, and some men had more than one wife to tan skins for trading.

Mobility also increased tribal contact and conflict. War was central to the lives of the Plains tribes. Unlike whites, Indians sought not to exterminate their enemies or to claim territory but to steal horses and prove individual prowess. They considered it braver to touch an enemy than to kill or scalp him. Under such conditions, political unity was difficult. No male became a fully accepted member of his tribe until proven in battle, and chiefs, who enjoyed only limited authority, often could not restrain young men intent on proving their courage.

With guns, fast ponies, and skills in warfare and raiding, the Plains tribes posed a fearsome obstacle to white expansion. They had signed no treaties with the United States and had few friendly feelings toward whites. While their contact with white society had brought gains through trade in skins, it had also brought alcohol and epidemics.

When the first emigrants drove their wagons across the plains and prairies in the early 1840s, Indian-white relations were peaceable. But the intrusion of whites set in motion an environmental cycle that eventually made for

An Indian Contrast
This drawing, done by an unknown Indian artist sometime in the 1840s, contrasts the traditionally clad Indians and the wild animals they hunted with the formally dressed white men and their stock animals. Has the artist depicted whites in a sympathetic manner? *(Archives de Jesuites, St. Jerome, Québec)*

conflict. Indians depended on the buffalo but respected this source of life. The grasses that nourished the buffalo also sustained the Indians' ponies and the animals that supported horse traders like the Cheyenne.

●●●—Read the Document

Elizabeth Dixon Smith Greer,
Journal (1847, 1848)
at **www.myhistorylab.com**

Whites, however, fed their oxen and horses on the grass that the Indians' ponies and the buffalo needed. And they adopted that "most exciting sport," the buffalo hunt. As the great herds began to shrink, Native American tribes began to battle one another for hunting grounds and food. The powerful Sioux swooped down into the hunting grounds of their enemies and mounted destructive raids against the Pawnee and other smaller tribes.

In 1846, the Sioux petitioned President Polk for compensation for damages to their hunting grounds caused by emigrating whites. When the president denied their request, they tried to tax emigrants, who were outraged at what they considered Indian effrontery. However, little was done to relieve the suffering of the tribes bearing the brunt of Sioux aggression, the dismay of the Sioux at the white invasion, or the fears of the emigrants themselves.

The discovery of gold in California, luring over 20,000 across the Plains in 1849 alone, prompted federal action. The horde of gold seekers and their animals wrought such devastation in the Platte valley that it rapidly became a wasteland for the Indians. Cholera spread from whites to Indians, killing thousands.

Government officials devised a two-pronged plan. The government would construct a chain of forts to protect emigrants and, simultaneously, call the tribes to a general conference. Officials expected that in return for generous presents, Indians would end tribal warfare and limit their movements. They instructed tribes to select chiefs to speak for them at the conference.

The Fort Laramie Council, 1851

In 1851, the council convened at Fort Laramie. As many as 10,000 Indians gathered, hopeful of ending the destruction of their way of life and eager for the presents. Tribal animosities simmered, however. Skirmishes occurred on the way to the fort. Border tribes, fearful of the Sioux, refused to come; so did the Comanche, Kiowa, and Apache because their Sioux and Crow enemies would be there.

Whites informed the tribes that times had changed. In the past, "you had plenty of buffalo and game . . . and your Great Father well knows that war has always been your favorite amusement and pursuit. He then left the question of peace and war to yourselves. Now, since the settling of the districts West . . . by the white men, your condition has changed." In return for compensation for the destruction of grass, timber, and buffalo and annual payments of goods and services, tribes must give up their rights of free movement. The government drew tribal boundaries, and chiefs promised to stay within them. Some tribal lands were sold.

The Fort Laramie Treaty was the first agreement between the Plains tribes and the United States government. It expressed whites' conviction that Indians must stay apart in clearly defined areas. But even during the conference, ominous signs of trouble appeared. The Sioux refused to remain north of the Platte, for south of the river lay their recently conquered lands. "These lands once belonged to the Kiowas and the Crows," one Sioux explained, "but we whipped those nations out of them and in this we did what the white men do when they want the lands of the Indians." Elsewhere in the trans-Mississippi West, other tribes, like the fierce Navajo of New Mexico, also resisted white Americans' attempts to restrict them.

Overwhelming the Mexican Settlers

In the Southwest, in Texas, and in California, Americans encountered a Spanish-speaking population and Hispanic culture. Americans regarded Mexicans, whom they often outnumbered and usually disparaged, as the "dregs of society." Although Anglo-Mexican interaction differed from place to place, few Anglos heeded the Treaty of Guadalupe Hidalgo's assurances that Mexicans would have citizens' rights.

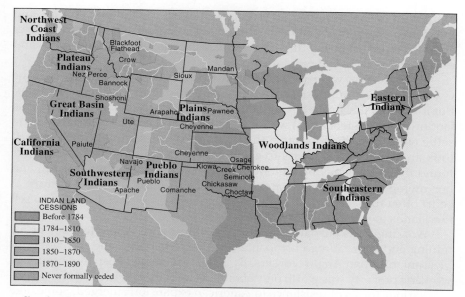

Indian land Cessions in 1840 This map of Indian tribes and groupings reveals locations in 1840, but it presents too static a picture of tribal territories. Some of the Indian groups in the West had been forced across the Mississippi by events in the Midwest. What does the map show about the pace of Indian land cessions in the nineteenth century, especially in the trans-Mississippi West?

Most Spanish-speaking people lived in New Mexico, and, of all former Mexican citizens, they probably fared the best. Most were of mixed blood, living marginally as ranch hands for rich landowners or as farmers and herdsmen in small villages dominated by a *patron*, or headman. As the century wore on, Americans produced legal titles and took over lands long occupied by peasant farmers and stock raisers. But despite economic reversals, New Mexicans survived, carrying their rural culture well into the twentieth century.

Disinterested in the situation of their poor rural countrymen, upper-class landowners looked out for themselves. Even before the conquest, rich New Mexicans had protected their future by establishing contacts with American businessmen and sending their sons east to American schools. When the United States annexed New Mexico, they made strategic marriage and business alliances with the Anglo men who slowly trickled in and thus retained much of their influence and prestige.

In Texas, the Spanish-speaking residents, only 10 percent of the population in 1840, shrank to a mere 6 percent by 1860. Although the upper class also intermarried with Americans, they lost most of their power. Poor, dark-skinned Hispanics clustered in low-paying and largely unskilled jobs.

In California, the discovery of gold transformed California life. In 1848, there were 7,000 Californios (Californians from an Hispanic background) and about twice as many Anglos; by 1860, the Anglo population reached 360,000. Californios were hard pressed to cope with these numbers. At first, along with several thousand Mexican citizens, they joined Anglos and others in the gold fields. But competition fed antagonism and conflict. Taxes and terrorism ultimately drove most Spanish speakers from the mines and established new racial boundaries.

Other changes were even more disastrous. In 1851, Congress passed the Gwin Land Law, supposedly validating Spanish and Mexican land titles. But it violated the Treaty of Guadalupe Hidalgo because it forced California landowners to defend what was already theirs and encouraged squatters to settle on land in the hopes that the Californios' titles would prove false. It took an average of 17 years to establish clear title to land. Landowners found themselves paying American lawyers large fees, often in land, and borrowing at high interest rates to cover court proceedings. A victory at court often turned into a defeat when legal expenses forced owners to sell their lands to pay debts.

Working-class Hispanic Americans, laboring for Anglo farmers or for mining and later railroad companies, earned less money and did more unpleasant jobs than Anglo workers. By 1870, the average Hispanic American worker's property was worth only about a third of its value of 20 years earlier.

Various forms of resistance to American expansion emerged. Some, like Tiburcio Vásquez in southern California, became *bandidos*. As he explained, the American presence provoked a "spirit of hatred and revenge . . . I believed we were unjustly and wrongfully deprived of the social rights that belonged to us." Others, like the members of Las Gorras Blancas in New Mexico, ripped up railroad ties and cut the barbed wire fences of Anglo ranchers and farmers, while the religiously oriented Penitentes tried to work through the ballot box. Ordinary men, women, and children resisted efforts to convert them to Protestantism and held on to familiar customs and beliefs while learning some of the skills they hoped would enable them to flourish in a changing culture.

Conclusion

Fruits of Manifest Destiny

Like Narcissa Whitman and her husband, many nineteenth-century Americans decided that they had a unique right to settle the West and make it flower. They were not much concerned with the fate of those who had lived for centuries on the land. The process of acquiring the western half of the continent was so swift that there seemed little point in worrying about the losers. The tale of western expansion loomed large in the imagination of the American people for many years. Some western settlers became folk heroes. The Whitmans were remembered by the founding of Whitman College in Walla Walla, Washington. All white Americans could be thankful for the special opportunities and the new chance that the West seemed to hold out. Certainly, the nation did gain vast natural wealth in the trans-Mississippi

West. But only a small fraction of the hopeful emigrants heading for the frontier realized their dreams of success. And the move west and east had a dark side, as the acquisition of new territories fueled the controversy over the future of slavery.

TIME*line*

1818	Treaty on joint U.S.–British occupation of Oregon
1821	Mexican independence
	Opening of Santa Fe Trail
	Stephen Austin leads American settlement of Texas
1836	Texas declares independence
1840s	Emigrant crossings of overland trail
1846	Mexico declares defensive war
	United States declares war and takes Santa Fe
	Resolution of Oregon question
1848	Treaty of Guadalupe Hidalgo
1849	California Gold Rush begins
1851	Fort Laramie Treaty

✓•─Study and **Review** at **www.myhistorylab.com**

Questions for Review and Reflection

1. Explain how and why the westward movement entangled the United States in the affairs of foreign powers.

2. Compare and contrast the acquisition of Texas and the Southwest with the annexation of Oregon.

3. What racial and ethnic tensions emerged in the West because of American expansionism?

4. What factors caused problems and tensions between Native Americans and whites?

5. What were the important American beliefs and values that were involved in the westward movement? How did they shape the westward experience?

Key Terms

54-40 or Fight 371

Fort Laramie Council 388

Mexican American War 368

Mormons 373

Overland Trails 373

Polygamy 381

Preemption acts 373

Stephen F. Austin 366

Treaty of Guadalupe Hidalgo 370

12

The Union in Peril

American Stories

Four Men Respond to the Union in Peril

The autumn of 1860 was a time of ominous rumors. The election was held on November 6 in an atmosphere of crisis. In Springfield, Illinois, Abraham Lincoln, taking coffee and sandwiches prepared by the "ladies of Springfield," waited as the telegraph brought in the returns. By 1 A.M., victory was certain. "I went home, but not to get much sleep, for I then felt, as I never had before, the responsibility that was upon me." He and the American people faced the most serious crisis since the founding of the Republic.

Lincoln won a four-party election with only 39 percent of the popular vote. He appealed almost exclusively to northern voters in a blatantly sectional campaign, defeating his three opponents by carrying every free state except New Jersey. Only Illinois Senator Stephen Douglas campaigned actively in every section of the country. For his efforts, he received the second-highest number of votes. Douglas's appeal, especially in the closing days of the campaign, was "on behalf of the Union," which he feared—correctly—was in imminent danger of splitting apart.

That fall, other Americans sensed the crisis and faced their own fears and responsibilities. A month before the election, South Carolina plantation owner Robert Allston wrote his oldest son, Benjamin, that "disastrous consequences" would follow from a Lincoln victory. Although his letter mentioned the possibility of secession, he dealt mostly with plantation concerns: a new horse, the mood of the slaves, ordering supplies from the city, instructions for making trousers on a sewing machine. After Lincoln's election, Allston corresponded with a southern colleague about the need for an "effective military organization" to resist "Northern and Federal aggression." In his shift from sewing machines to military ones, Allston prepared for what he called "the crisis."

Chapter Outline

Frederick Douglass greeted the election of 1860 with characteristic optimism. Not only was this an opportunity to "educate . . . the people in their moral and political duties," he said, but "slaveholders know that the day of their power is over when a Republican President is elected." But no sooner had Lincoln's victory been determined than Douglass's hopes turned sour. He noted that Republican leaders, who were trying to keep border states from seceding, sounded more antiabolitionist than antislavery. They vowed not to touch slavery in areas where it already existed (including the District of Columbia), not to enforce the hated Fugitive Slave Act, and to put down slave rebellions. In fact, Douglass bitterly concluded, slavery would "be as safe, and safer" with Lincoln than with a Democrat.

Iowa farmer Michael Luark was not so sure. Born in Virginia, he was a typically mobile nineteenth-century American. Growing up in Indiana, he followed the mining booms of the 1850s to Colorado and California, and then returned to the Midwest to farm. Luark sought a good living and resented the furor over slavery. He could not, however, avoid the issue. Writing in his diary on the last day of 1860, Luark looked ahead to 1861 with a deep sense of fear. "Startling" political changes would occur, he predicted, perhaps even the "Dissolution of the Union and Civil War with all its train of horrors." He blamed abolitionist agitators, perhaps reflecting his Virginia origins. On New Year's Day, he expressed his fears that Lincoln would let the "most ultra sectional and Abolition" men disturb the "vexed Slavery question" even further, as Frederick Douglass wanted. But if this happened, Luark warned, "then farewell to our beloved Union of States." Within four months, the guns of the Confederate States of America fired on a U.S. fort in South Carolina. The Civil War had begun.

The firing on Fort Sumter made real Luark's fears, Douglass's hopes, and Lincoln's and Allston's preparations for responsibility. America's shaky democratic political system faced its worst crisis. The explanation of the peril and dissolution of the Union forms the theme of this chapter.

Such a calamitous event as the Civil War had numerous causes, large and small. The reactions of Allston, Douglass, and Luark to Lincoln's election suggest some of them: moral duties, sectional politics, growing apprehensions over emotional agitators, and a concern for freedom and independence on the part of blacks, white southerners, and western farmers. But as Douglass understood, by 1860 it was clear that "slavery is the real issue . . . between all parties and sections. It is the one disturbing force, and explains the confused and irregular motion of our political machine."

This chapter analyzes how the momentous issue of slavery disrupted the political system and eventually the Union itself. Four major developments between 1848 and 1861 contributed to the Civil War: first, a sectional dispute over the extension of slavery into the western territories; second, the breakdown of the political party system; third, growing cultural differences in the views and lifestyles of southerners and northerners; and fourth, intensifying emotional and ideological polarization between the two regions over losing their way of life and sacred republican rights at the hands of the other. How did each development contribute to growing tensions? A preview of civil war occurred in Kansas in 1855 to 1856. In what ways did that conflict express the intersection of the various causes tearing the Union apart? Eventually, emotional events, mistrust, and irreconcilable differences made conflict inevitable. Lincoln's election was the spark that touched off the conflagration of civil war, with all its "train of horrors."

Slavery in the Territories

As Narcissa Whitman sadly discovered with the Cayuse Indians in eastern Washington (see Chapter 11), white migration westward was discouraging and downright dangerous. It was especially damaging to the lives, lands, and cultural integrity of Native Americans and Mexicans. Moreover, the westward movement imperiled freedom and eventually the Union by causing a collision between Yankees and southern slaveholders.

The North and the South had mostly contained and compromised their differences over slavery for 60 years after the Constitutional Convention. Compromise in 1787 had resolved questions of the slave trade and how to count slaves for congressional representation. Although slavery threatened the uneasy sectional harmony in 1820, the Missouri Compromise had established a workable balance of free and slave states and defined a geographic line (36°30′) across the Louisiana Purchase to determine future decisions. In 1833, compromise had defused South Carolina's attempt at nullification, and the gag rule in 1836 had kept the abolitionists' antislavery petitions off the floor of Congress.

Each apparent resolution, however, raised the level of emotional tension between North and South and postponed ultimate settlement of the slavery question. One reason these compromises temporarily worked was the two-party system, with Whigs and Democrats in both North and South. The parties differed over cultural and economic issues, but they kept slavery largely out of political campaigns and congressional debates. This changed in the late 1840s.

Free Soil or Constitutional Protection?

When war with Mexico broke out in 1846, Pennsylvania congressman David Wilmot added an amendment to an appropriations bill, declaring that "neither slavery nor involuntary servitude shall ever exist" in any territories acquired from Mexico. Legislators debated the **Wilmot Proviso** not as Whigs and Democrats, but as northerners and southerners.

A Boston newspaper prophetically observed that Wilmot's resolution "brought to a head the great question which is about to divide the American people." When the war ended, several solutions were presented to deal with slavery in the territories. First was the "**free-soil**" idea of preventing any extensions of slavery. Two precedents suggested that Congress could do this. One was the Northwest Ordinance, which had barred slaves from the Upper Midwest; the other was the Missouri Compromise.

Free-Soilers had mixed motives. For some, slavery was an evil to be destroyed. But for many northern white farmers looking westward, the threat of economic competition with an expanding system of large-scale slave labor was even more serious. Nor did they wish to compete with free blacks. As Wilmot put it, his proviso was intended to preserve the area for the "sons of toil, of my own race and own color." Other northerners supported it as a means of restraining the growing political power and "insufferable arrogance" of the "spirit and demands of the Slave Power."

South Carolina Senator John C. Calhoun offered an opposing position to the Free-Soilers. Congress not only lacked the constitutional right to exclude slavery from the territories, he argued, but also had a duty to protect it. Therefore, the Wilmot Proviso was unconstitutional. So were the Missouri Compromise and other federal acts that prevented slaveholders from taking their slave property into the territories.

Economic, political, and moral considerations stood behind Calhoun's position. Many southerners hungered for new cotton lands in the West and

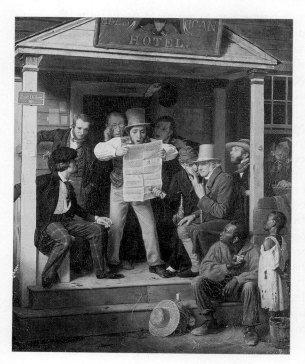

War News Describe what you see in this 1848 painting by Richard Caton Woodville, titled *War News from Mexico*. What do you suppose the men are hearing about the war in Mexico, and how are they reacting? Do you think this "American Hotel" is in the North or South? How would the war news be heard in each place? What are the black man and little girl doing there, and how do you think they are responding to the news? Why would the Mexican War and its outcomes interest them? *(© 2004 Board of Trustees, National Gallery of Art, Washington, D.C.)*

Southwest, even in Central America and the Caribbean. Southerners feared that northerners wanted to trample their right to protect their institutions. Southern leaders saw the Wilmot Proviso as a moral issue touching basic Republican principles. One congressman called it "treason to the Constitution," and Senator Robert Toombs of Georgia warned that if Congress passed the proviso, he would favor disunion rather than "degradation."

Popular Sovereignty and the Election of 1848

With such divisive potential, naturally many Americans sought a compromise solution to exclude slavery from politics. Polk's secretary of state, James Buchanan, proposed extending the Missouri Compromise line to the Pacific Ocean, thereby avoiding thorny questions about the morality of slavery and the constitutionality of congressional authority. So would **"popular sovereignty,"** the proposal of Michigan Senator Lewis Cass to leave decisions about permitting slavery to territorial legislatures. The idea appealed to the American democratic belief in local self-government, but it left many details unanswered. At what point in the progress toward statehood could a territorial legislature decide about slavery?

Democrats, liking popular sovereignty because it could mean all things to all people, nominated Cass for president in 1848. Cass denounced abolitionists and the Wilmot Proviso, but otherwise avoided the slavery issue. The Democrats printed two campaign biographies of Cass, one for the South and one for the North.

The Whigs found an even better way to maintain party unity. Rejecting Henry Clay, they nominated the Mexican-American War hero General Zachary Taylor, a Louisiana slaveholder. Taylor compared himself to Washington as a "no party" man above politics. This was about all he stood for. Southern Whigs supported Taylor because they thought he might understand the burdens of slaveholding, and northern Whigs were pleased that he took no stand on the Wilmot Proviso.

The evasions of the two major parties disappointed Calhoun, who tried to create a new, unified southern party. His "Address to the People of the Southern States" threatened secession and called for a united stand against further attempts to interfere with the southern right to extend slavery. Although only 48 of 121 southern representatives signed the address, Calhoun's argument raised the specter of secession and disunion.

Warnings also came from the North. A New York Democratic faction bolted to support Van Buren for president. At first, the split had more to do with state politics than moral principles, but it soon involved the question of slavery in the territories. Disaffected "conscience" Whigs from Massachusetts also explored a third-party alternative. These groups met in Buffalo, New York, to form the Free-Soil party and nominated Van Buren. The platform of the new party, an uneasy mixture of ardent abolitionists and opponents of free blacks moving into western lands, pledged to fight for "free soil, free speech, free labor and free men."

Taylor won easily, largely because defections from Cass to the Free-Soilers cost the Democrats New York and Pennsylvania. Although weakened, the two-party system survived. Purely sectional parties had failed. The Free-Soilers took only about 10 percent of the popular vote.

The Compromise of 1850

Taylor won the election by avoiding slavery questions. But as president, he had to face them. When he was inaugurated in 1849, four issues confronted the nation. First, the rush of some 80,000 gold miners to California qualified it for statehood. But California's entry as a free state would upset the slave–free state balance in the Senate. The unresolved status of the Mexican cession in the Southwest posed a second problem. The longer the area remained unorganized, the more local inhabitants called for an application of either the Wilmot Proviso or the Calhoun doctrine. The Texas–New Mexico boundary was also disputed, with Texas claiming everything east of Santa Fe. Northerners feared that Texas might split into five or six slave states. A third problem, especially for abolitionists, was the existence of slavery and a huge slave market in the nation's capital. Fourth, southerners resented the lax federal enforcement of the Fugitive Slave Act of 1793. They called for a stronger act to end protection for runaways fleeing to Canada.

Taylor was a political novice (he had never voted in a presidential election before 1848) and tackled these problems somewhat evasively. Sidestepping the issue of slavery in the territories, he invited California and New Mexico to seek statehood immediately, presumably as free states. But soon he alienated both southern supporters such as Calhoun and mainstream Whig leaders such as Clay and Webster.

Early in 1850, the old compromiser Henry Clay sought to regain control of the Whig party by proposing solutions to the divisive national issues. With Webster's support, Clay introduced a series of resolutions in an omnibus package intended to settle these issues once and for all. The stormy debates, great speeches, and political maneuvering that followed made up a crucial and dramatic moment in American history. Yet after 70 speeches on behalf of the compromise, the Senate defeated Clay's Omnibus Bill. Tired and disheartened, the 73-year-old Clay left Washington and died two years later. Into the gap stepped Senator Stephen Douglas of Illinois, who saw that Clay's resolutions had a better chance of passing if voted on individually. Under Douglas's leadership, in variously strange political alignments and with the support of Millard Fillmore, who succeeded to the presidency upon Taylor's sudden death, a series of bills finally passed.

The "Compromise of 1850" put Clay's resolutions, slightly altered, into law. First, California entered the Union as a free state, ending the balance of free and slave states. Second, territorial governments were organized in New Mexico and Utah, letting local people decide whether to permit slavery. The Texas–New Mexico border was settled, denying Texas the disputed area.

In return, the federal government gave Texas $10 million to pay debts owed to Mexico. Third, the slave trade, but not slavery, was abolished in the District of Columbia.

The fourth and most controversial part of the compromise was a new **Fugitive Slave Act**, containing many provisions that offended northerners. One denied alleged fugitives a jury trial, leaving special cases for decision by commissioners (who were paid $5 for setting a fugitive free, but $10 for returning a fugitive). An especially repugnant provision compelled northern citizens to help catch runaways.

Consequences of Compromise

The Compromise of 1850 was the last attempt to keep slavery out of politics. Voting on the different bills followed sectional lines on some issues and party lines on others. Douglas felt pleased with his "final settlement" of the slavery question.

But the Compromise only delayed more serious sectional conflict, and it added two new ingredients to American politics. First, political realignment along sectional lines moved closer. Second, although repudiated by most ordinary citizens, ideas like secessionism, disunion, and a "higher law" than the Constitution entered political discussions. People wondered whether the question of slavery in the territories could be "compromised away" next time.

Others were immediately upset. The new fugitive slave law angered many northerners. Owners of runaway slaves hired agents (labeled "kidnappers" in the North) to hunt down fugitives. In a few dramatic episodes, notably in

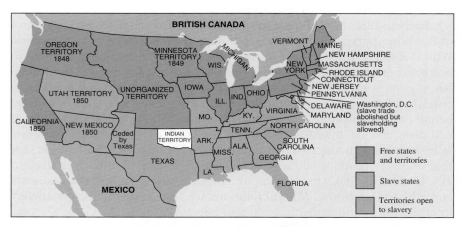

The Compromise of 1850 "I have seen many periods of great anxiety, of peril, and of danger in this country," Henry Clay told the Congress in February of 1850, "and I have never before risen to address any assemblage so oppressed, so appalled, and so anxious." What followed were the debates that led eventually to the passage of his great compromise. Can you find three of the four major parts of the bill on the map? What was the fourth, and how might you represent it on the map?

Boston, literary and religious intellectuals led mass protests to resist slave hunters. When Webster supported
the law, New England abolitionists denounced him.
Emerson said that he would not obey the "filthy law."

View the Image
Hypocrisy of Fugitive Slavery Act (cartoon, 1851)
at **www.myhistorylab.com**

Frederick Douglass would not obey it either. As a
runaway slave, he faced arrest and return to the South until friends overcame
his objections and purchased his freedom. Douglass still risked harm by his
strong defiance of the Fugitive Slave Act. Arguing the "rightfulness of forcible resistance," he urged free blacks to arm themselves. "The only way to
make the Fugitive Slave Law a dead letter," he said in Pittsburgh in 1853, "is
to make a half dozen or more dead kidnappers." Douglass raised money for
black fugitives, hid runaways in his home, helped hundreds escape to Canada, and supported black organizations such as the League of Freedom in
Boston.

Other northerners, both white and black, stepped up work for the Underground Railroad and helped runaway slaves evade capture. Several
states passed "**personal liberty laws**" that prohibited using state officials
and institutions in the recovery of fugitive slaves. But
most northerners complied. Of some 200 blacks arrested in the first six years of the law, only 15 were rescued, and only 3 of these by force. Failed rescues, in
fact, had more emotional impact than did successful

Read the Document
Frederick Douglass, Independence Day Speech (1852)
at **www.myhistorylab.com**

ones. In two cases in the early 1850s, angry mobs of abolitionists in Boston
failed to prevent the forcible return of blacks to the South. These celebrated
cases aroused antislavery emotions in more northerners than abolitionists
had been able to do by their tracts and speeches.

But the spoken and written word also fueled emotions over slavery in
the aftermath of 1850. In an Independence Day speech in 1852, Douglass
wondered aloud: "What, to the American slave, is your 4th of July?" It was,
he said, the day that revealed to the slave the "gross injustice and cruelty to
which he is the constant victim. To him, your celebration is a sham; your
boasted liberty, an unholy license; your national greatness, swelling vanity;
your sounds of rejoicing are empty and heartless; your denunciation of
tyrants, brass-fronted impudence; your shouts of liberty and equality,
hollow mockery." Douglass's speeches, like those of another ex-slave,
Sojourner Truth, became increasingly strident.

At a women's rights convention in 1851 in Akron, Ohio, Truth made one
of the decade's boldest statements for minority rights. The convention was
attended by clergymen who heckled female speakers. Sojourner Truth stood
up to speak words still debated by historians. She pointed to her many years
of childbearing and hard, backbreaking work as a slave, crying out a refrain,
"And ar'n't I a woman? Where had Jesus came from? From God and a
woman: Man had nothing to do with Him." Referring to Eve, she concluded,
"If the first woman God ever made was strong enough to turn the world
upside down all alone, these women together ought to be able to turn it
back, and get it right side up again! And now they is asking to do it, the men
better let them." She silenced the hecklers.

As Truth spoke, another American woman, Harriet Beecher Stowe, was finishing a novel, *Uncle Tom's Cabin*, that would go far toward turning the world upside down. As politicians were hoping the American people would forget slavery, Stowe's novel brought it to the attention of thousands. In gripping emotional style with heartbreaking cruelty, daring escapes, and reunited family members, she gave readers an absorbing indictment of the horrors of slavery and its impact on both northerners and southerners. Published initially as a newspaper serial, each chapter ended at a nail-biting moment.

••◆—⌐Read the Document

Harriet Beecher Stowe,
Uncle Tom's Cabin *(1852)*
at **www.myhistorylab.com**

Although outraging the white South when published in full in 1852, *Uncle Tom's Cabin* became one of the all-time best-sellers in American history. In the first year, more than 300,000 copies were printed, and Stowe's novel was eventually published in 20 languages. When President Lincoln met Stowe in 1863, he is reported to have said to her, with a twinkle in his eye, "So you're the little woman who wrote the book that made this great war!"

⌐Watch the Video

Harriet Beecher Stowe and the
Making of Uncle Tom's Cabin
at **www.myhistorylab.com**

Political Disintegration

The response to *Uncle Tom's Cabin* and the Fugitive Slave Act indicated that politicians had congratulated themselves too soon for saving the Republic in 1850. Political developments, not all dealing with slavery, were already weakening the ability of political parties—and ultimately the nation—to withstand the passions slavery aroused.

Weakened Party Politics in the Early 1850s

As we see in modern elections, political parties attempt to convince voters that they stand for moral values and economic policies crucially different from those of the opposition. Between 1850 and 1854, these differences blurred, undermining party loyalty.

Both parties scrambled to convince voters that they had favored the Compromise of 1850. In addition, several states rewrote their constitutions and remodeled their laws. These changes reduced the number of patronage jobs that politicians could dispense and regularized the process for securing banking, railroad, and other corporate charters, ending the role formerly played by the legislature and undermining the importance of parties in citizens' lives. The return of prosperity in the early 1850s also weakened parties. For almost a quarter of a century, Whigs and Democrats had disagreed over the tariff, money and banking, and government-supported internal improvements. Now, in better times, party distinctions over economic policies seemed less important.

The election of 1852 illustrated the decreasing significance of political parties. Hoping to repeat Taylor's success four years earlier, the Whigs nominated General Winfield Scott, another Mexican-American War hero. With the passing prominence of Clay and Webster (who died in 1852),

Celebrating a Political Victory In George Caleb Bingham's *Verdict of the People* (after 1855), the American flag flies proudly over a happy throng celebrating the outcome of democratic politics. How well did the political process work in the 1850s? In an earlier version of this same painting, the women on the hotel balcony in the upper right display a banner announcing (ironically?) "Freedom for Virtue." What do you think that means?

Senator William Seward of New York aspired to party leadership and desired a president he could influence more successfully than the moderate Fillmore. Still, it took 52 ballots to nominate Scott over Fillmore, alienating southern Whigs. Democrats had their own problems. After 49 ballots, the party turned to a lackluster compromise candidate, Franklin Pierce of New Hampshire.

The two parties offered little choice and downplayed issues so as not to widen intraparty divisions. Voter interest diminished. "Genl. Apathy is the strongest candidate out here," was a typical report from Ohio. Democratic leaders resorted to bribes and drinks to buy the support of thousands of new Catholic immigrants from Ireland and Germany, who could be naturalized and were eligible to vote after only three years. Pierce won easily, 254 to 42 electoral votes.

The Kansas–Nebraska Act

The Whig party's final disintegration came in February 1854 when southern Whigs, choosing to be more southern than Whig, supported Stephen Douglas's Nebraska bill. The Illinois senator had many reasons for introducing a bill organizing the Nebraska Territory (which included Kansas). An ardent nationalist, he was interested in the continuing development of the West.

He wanted the eastern terminus for a transcontinental railroad in Chicago rather than in rival St. Louis. This meant organizing the lands west of Iowa and Missouri.

Politics also played a role. Douglas hoped to recapture the party leadership he had held in passing the Compromise of 1850 and win the presidency. Although he had replaced Cass as the great advocate of popular sovereignty, thus winning favor among northern Democrats, he needed southern Democratic support. Many southerners, especially neighboring Missouri slaveholders, opposed organizing the Nebraska Territory unless open to slavery. But the Nebraska Territory lay north of the Missouri Compromise line prohibiting slavery.

Douglas's bill, introduced early in 1854, in effect repealed the Missouri Compromise restriction by declaring that the states created out of the Nebraska Territory would enter the Union "with or without slavery, as their constitution may prescribe at the time of their admission." It proposed using popular sovereignty to organize two territories, Kansas and Nebraska. Inhabitants thus could vote slavery in. Douglas reasoned, however, that Kansas and Nebraska would never support slavery-based agriculture and that the people would choose to be a free state. Therefore, he could win the votes he needed for the railroad without also getting slavery.

Douglas miscalculated. Northerners from his own party immediately attacked him and his bill as a "criminal betrayal of precious rights" and as part of a plot promoting his own presidential ambitions by turning free Nebraska over to "slavery despotism." Whigs and abolitionists were even more outraged. Frederick Douglass branded the act the result of the "audacious villainy of the slave power."

But the more Stephen Douglas was attacked, the harder he fought. Eventually his bill passed, but it seriously damaged the party system. What began as a railroad measure ended in reopening the question of slavery in the territories, which Douglas had thought finally settled in 1850. What began as a way of avoiding conflict ended in violence over whether Kansas would enter the Union slave or free. What began as a way of strengthening party lines ended up destroying one party (Whigs), planting irreconcilable divisions in another (Democrats), and creating two new parties (Know-Nothings and Republicans).

Expansionist "Young America" in the Larger World

The Democratic party was weakened in the early 1850s not only by the Kansas–Nebraska Act, but also by an expansive energy that led Americans to adventures far beyond Kansas. Americans had hailed the European revolutions of 1848 as evidence that republicanism was the wave of the future. "Young America" was the label assumed by patriots eager to spread Americanism abroad; however, these ardent republican nationalists ironically abetted the spread of the idea of slavery.

Pierce's platform in 1852 reflected this nationalism, declaring that the war with Mexico had been "just and necessary." Many Democrats took

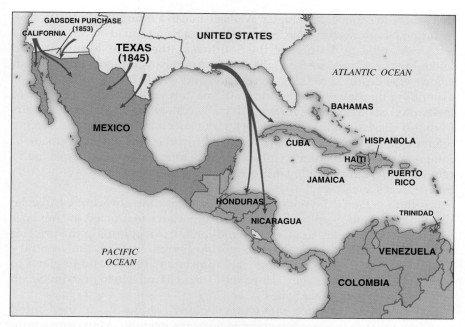

Expansionist "Young America" in the 1850s: Attempted Raids into Latin America
Note the flurry of expansionist American raids and forays southward into Mexico and the
Caribbean between the mid-1840s and the mid-1850s. What major events and motives
caused the expansionist interest? Why was Cuba a key target?

their overwhelming victory as a mandate to continue adding territory. A
Philadelphia newspaper in 1853 described the United States as bound on
the "East by sunrise, West by sunset, North by the Arctic Expedition, and
South as far as we darn please."

Many of Pierce's diplomatic appointees were southerners interested in
adding new cotton-growing lands to the Union. Pierce's ambassador to
Mexico, for example, South Carolinian James Gadsden, had instructions
to negotiate with Mexican president Santa Anna to acquire large parts
of northern Mexico. While Gadsden did not get all he wanted, he managed
to buy a strip of southwestern desert for a transcontinental railroad linking
the Deep South with the Pacific Coast.

Failure to acquire more territory from Mexico legally did not discourage expansionist Americans. During the 1850s, Texans and Californians
staged dozens of illegal raids ("filibusters") into Mexico. The most daring
such adventurer was William Walker, a tiny Tennessean with a zest for danger and power. In 1853, he invaded Mexican Baja California with fewer than
300 men and declared himself president of the Republic of Sonora. Arrested
and tried in the United States, he was acquitted in eight minutes. Two years
later, he invaded Nicaragua, where he proclaimed himself dictator and
legalized slavery. When the Nicaraguans, with British help, regained control,
the U.S. Navy rescued Walker. After a triumphant tour in the South, he tried

twice more to conquer Nicaragua. Walker came to a fitting end in 1860 when, invading Honduras this time, he was shot by a firing squad.

Undaunted by failures in the Southwest, the Pierce administration looked to the acquisition of Cuba. Many Americans thought this Spanish colony was destined for U.S. annexation and would be an ideal place for expanding the slave-based economy. Some argued that Cuba belonged to the United States because it was physically connected by alluvial deposits from the Mississippi River. In the 1840s, the Polk administration had vainly offered Spain $10 million for Cuba. Unsuccessful efforts were then made to foment a revolution among Cuban sugar planters, who were expected to request annexation by the United States, which might then divide Cuba into several slave states.

Although Pierce did not support these illegal efforts to acquire Cuba, he wanted the island. Secretary of State William Marcy instructed the minister to Spain, Pierre Soulé, to offer $130 million for Cuba, upping the price. If that failed, Marcy suggested stronger measures. In 1854, the secretary arranged for Soulé and the American ministers to France and England to meet in Belgium, where they issued the Ostend Manifesto to pressure Spain to sell Cuba to the United States.

The manifesto argued that Cuba "belongs naturally" to the United States and that they were "one people with one destiny." Moreover, southern slaveholders feared that a slave rebellion would "Africanize" Cuba, like Haiti, and suggested all kinds of "horrors to the white race" in the nearby southern United States. American acquisition of Cuba was necessary, therefore, to "preserve our rectitude and self-respect." If Spain refused to sell, the ministers at Ostend threatened a Cuban revolution with American support. If that failed, "we should be justified in wresting it from Spain."

Even Marcy was shocked, and he quickly repudiated the manifesto. As with the Kansas–Nebraska Act, Democrats supported the Ostend Manifesto in order to further the expansion of slavery. The outraged reaction of northerners in both cases divided and further weakened the Democratic party.

Nativism, Know-Nothings, and Republicans

Increasing immigration also damaged an already enfeebled Whig party and alarmed many native-born Americans. To the average hardworking Protestant American, the foreigners pouring into the nation and following the railroads westward spoke unfamiliar languages rather than English, wore funny clothes, drank alcohol freely, and bred crime and pauperism. Moreover, they seemed content with a lower standard of living and thus threatened to take jobs away from native-born American workers, themselves descended from former immigrants.

Worst of all from the Protestant perspective, Irish and German immigrants spearheaded an unprecedented growth of American Catholicism. By the 1850s, there were nearly 3 million Catholics in the United States, not

Immigration and Politics Describe what you see in this cartoon from the mid-1850s (top). What stereotypes of Irish and Germans are shown? What does it mean that they are stealing the ballot box, and what is going on in the background by the "election polls"? The Know-Nothing flag (bottom) makes starkly clear that party's view on the origins of the danger. Who are the "Native Americans" referred to on the flag, and what do you think the original "Native" Americans would think of this flag and its warning?

only in eastern cities but expanding westward and—to the shocked surprise of many old-stock Americans—converting Protestants. A wave of Catholic revivals to gain converts and the opening of Catholic schools compounded their offensiveness to Protestants.

Many Protestants charged that Catholic immigrants corrupted American politics. Indeed, most Catholics did prefer the Democratic party, which was less inclined than the Whigs to interfere with religion, schooling, drinking, and other aspects of personal behavior and rights. It was mostly former Whigs, therefore, who in 1854 founded the American party to oppose the new immigrants. Members wanted a longer period of naturalization to guarantee the "vital principles of Republican Government" and pledged never to vote for Irish Catholics, whose highest loyalty was supposedly to the pope. They also agreed to keep information about their order secret. If asked, they would say, "I know nothing." Hence, they were dubbed the Know-Nothing party.

The Know-Nothings appealed to the middle and lower classes—to workers worried about their jobs and to farmers and small-town Americans nervous about change. A New Yorker said in 1854, "Roman Catholicism is feared more than American slavery." It was widely believed that Catholics slavishly obeyed their priests, who represented a Church associated with European despotism. In the 1854 and 1855 elections, the Know-Nothings gave anti-Catholicism as well as anti-immigration a national political focus for the first time.

To other northerners, however, the "slave power" seemed a more serious threat than alleged schemes of the pope. No sooner had debates over Nebraska ended than the nucleus of another new party appeared: the Republican party. Drawn almost entirely from "conscience" Whigs and disaffected Democrats (including ex–Free-Soilers), the **Republicans** combined four main elements.

Moral fervor led the first group, headed by senators William Seward, Charles Sumner (Massachusetts), and Salmon P. Chase (Ohio), to demand prohibiting slavery in the territories, freeing slaves in the District of Columbia, repealing the Fugitive Slave Act, and banning the internal slave trade. There were, however, limits to most Republicans' idealism. A more moderate and larger group, typified by Abraham Lincoln, opposed slavery in the western territories, but would not interfere with it where it already existed. This group also opposed equal rights for northern free blacks.

Many Republicans were anti-Catholic as well as antislavery. A third element of the party, true to traditional Whig reformist impulses, wanted to cleanse America of intemperance, impiety, parochial schooling, and other forms of immorality—including voting for Democrats, who catered to the "grog shops, foreign vote, and Catholic brethren" and combined the "forces of Jesuitism and Slavery."

The fourth element of the Republican party, a Whig legacy from Clay's American System, included those who wanted the federal government to promote economic development and the dignity of labor. This group, like the antislavery and anti-Catholic elements, idealized free labor. At the heart of both the new party and the future of America were hardworking, middle-class, mobile, free white laborers—farmers, small businessmen, and independent craftsmen, people who, in the words of the Springfield, Illinois, *Republican*, valued "work with their hands" and "home and family."

The strengths of the Republican and Know-Nothing (American) parties were tested in 1856. The American party nominated Fillmore, who had strong support in the Upper South. The Republicans chose John C. Frémont, an ardent Free-Soiler from Missouri with virtually no political experience but with fame as an explorer of the West and a military record against the Mexicans in California. The Democrats nominated Pennsylvanian James Buchanan, a "northern man with southern principles." Frémont carried several free states, while Fillmore took only Maryland. Buchanan, benefiting from a divided opposition, won with only 45 percent of the popular vote.

After 1856, the Know-Nothings died out, largely because Republican leaders cleverly redirected nativist fears—and voters—to their broader program. Moreover, Know-Nothing secrecy, hatreds, and occasional violent attacks on Catholic voters damaged their image. Still, the Know-Nothings represented a powerful current in American politics that would return each time social and economic changes seemed to threaten. It became convenient to label certain people "un-American" or "illegal" immigrants, and try to root them out. The Know-Nothing party disappeared, but nativist hostility to new immigrants did not, as we clearly see in the current opposition to Mexican and Central American migrants.

Kansas and the Two Cultures

The slavery issue also would not die. As Democrats sought to expand slavery and other American institutions westward across the Plains and south into Cuba, Republicans wanted to halt the advance of slavery. In 1854, Lincoln worried that slavery "deprives our republican example of its just influence in the world." The specific cause of his concern was the likelihood that slavery might be extended into Kansas as a result of the passage that year of Stephen Douglas's Kansas–Nebraska Act.

Competing for Kansas

During the congressional debates over the Kansas–Nebraska bill, Seward accepted the challenge of slave-state senators to "engage in competition for the virgin soil of Kansas." No sooner had the Kansas–Nebraska Act passed Congress in 1854 than the Massachusetts Emigrant Aid Society was founded to recruit free-soil settlers for Kansas. By the summer of 1855, about 1,200 New England colonists had migrated to Kansas.

One migrant was Julia Louisa Lovejoy, a Vermont minister's wife. As a riverboat carried her into a slave state for the first time in her life, she wrote of the dilapidated plantation homes on the monotonous Missouri shore as the "blighting mildew of slavery." By the time she and her husband arrived in the Kansas Territory, Julia had concluded that the "morals" of the slaveholding Missourians moving into Kansas were of an *"indescribably repulsive and undesirable character."* To her, northerners came to bring the "energetic Yankee" virtues of morality and economic enterprise to drunken, unclean slaveholders.

Perhaps she had in mind David Atchison, Democratic senator from Missouri. Atchison believed that Congress must protect slavery in the territories, allowing Missouri slaveholders into Kansas. In 1853, he pledged "to extend the institutions of Missouri over the Territory at whatever sacrifice of blood or treasure." He recommended to fellow Missourians if need be "to kill every God-damned abolitionist in the district."

Under Atchison's inflammatory leadership, secret societies sprang up in the Missouri counties adjacent to Kansas dedicated to combating the Free-Soilers. One editor exclaimed that northerners came to Kansas "for the express purpose of stealing, running off and hiding runaway negroes from Missouri [and] taking to their own bed . . . a stinking negro wench." Not slaveholders, he said, but New Englanders were immoral, uncivilized, and hypocritical. Rumors of 20,000 such Massachusetts migrants spurred Missourians to action. Thousands poured across the border late in 1854 to vote on permitting slavery in the territory. Twice as many ballots were cast as the number of registered voters.

The proslavery forces overreacted. The permanent population of Kansas consisted primarily of migrants from Missouri and other border states, people more concerned with land titles than slavery. They opposed any blacks—slave or free—moving into their state.

In March 1855, a second election was held to select a territorial legislature. The pattern of border crossings, intimidation, and illegal voting was repeated. Atchison himself, drinking "considerable whiskey," led an armed band across the state line to vote and frighten away would-be Free-Soil voters. Not surprisingly, swollen numbers of illegal voters elected a proslavery territorial legislature. Free-Soilers, meanwhile, held their own convention in Lawrence and created a Free-Soil government at Topeka. It banned blacks from the state. The proslavery legislature settled eventually in Lecompton, giving Kansas two governments.

The struggle shifted to Washington. Although Pierce could have nullified the illegal election, he did nothing. Congress debated and sent an investigating committee to Kansas, which further inflamed passions. Throughout 1855, the call to arms grew more strident. In South Carolina, Robert Allston wrote his son Benjamin that he was "raising men and money . . . to counteract the effect of the Northern hordes. . . . We are disposed to fight the battle of our rights . . . on the field of Kansas."

Both sides saw Kansas as a holy battleground. An Alabaman sold his slaves to raise money to hire an army of 300 men to fight for slavery in Kansas, promising free land to his recruits. A Baptist minister blessed their departure from Montgomery, promised them God's favor, and gave each man a Bible. Northern Christians responded in kind. At Yale University, the noted minister Henry Ward Beecher presented 25 Bibles and 25 Sharps rifles to young men who would go fight for the Lord in Kansas. "There are times," he said, "when self-defense is a religious duty." Beecher suggested that rifles would be of greater use than Bibles. Missourians dubbed them "Beecher's Bibles" and vowed, as one newspaper put it, "Blood for Blood!"

"Bleeding Kansas"

As civil war threatened in Kansas, a Brooklyn poet, Walt Whitman, heralded American democracy in his epic poem *Leaves of Grass* (1855). Whitman celebrated average Americans "of every hue and caste . . . of every rank and religion" but his faith in the democratic American masses faltered in the mid-1850s. He worried that a knife plunged into the "breast" of the Union would bring on the "red blood of civil war."

Blood indeed flowed in Kansas. In May 1856, supported by a pro-southern federal marshal, a mob entered Lawrence, smashed the offices and presses of a Free-Soil newspaper, fired several cannonballs into the Free State Hotel, and destroyed homes and shops. Three nights later, believing he was doing God's will, John Brown led a small New England band, including four of his sons, to a proslavery settlement near Pottawatomie Creek and hacked five men to death with swords.

That same week, abolitionist senator Charles Sumner delivered a tirade known as "The Crime Against Kansas." He lashed out at the "incredible atrocities of the Assassins and . . . Thugs" from the South. He accused proslavery Senate leaders, especially Andrew Butler of South Carolina and Stephen Douglas, of cavorting with the "harlot, Slavery." Two days later, Butler's cousin, Congressman Preston Brooks, avenged his honor by viciously beating Sumner senseless with his cane as he sat at his Senate desk.

The sack of Lawrence, the Pottawatomie massacre, and the caning of Sumner set off a minor civil war in "Bleeding Kansas" that lasted throughout the summer. Crops were burned, homes destroyed, fights broke out in saloons and streets, and night raiders murdered enemies. Charles Lines, who just wanted to farm in peace, hoped his neighbors near Lawrence would avoid "involving themselves in trouble." But it was impossible to remain neutral. When proslavery forces tortured a neighbor to death, Lines joined the battle. "Blood," he wrote, "must end in the triumph of the right."

Even before the bleeding of Kansas began, the New York *Tribune* warned, "We are two peoples. We are a people for Freedom and a people for Slavery. Between the two, conflict is inevitable." As the rhetoric and violence in Kansas demonstrated, competing visions of two separate cultures for the future destiny of the United States were at stake. Despite many similarities between the North and the South, the gap between the two sides widened with the hostilities of the 1850s.

Northern Views and Visions

As Julia Lovejoy suggested, the North saw itself as a prosperous land of bustling commerce and expanding, independent agriculture. Northern farmers and workers were self-made free men who believed in individualism and democracy. The "free labor system" of the North, as both Seward and Lincoln often said, offered equality of opportunity and upward mobility. Both generated more wealth. Although the North contained many growing cities, northerners revered the values of the small towns that spread from New England across the Upper Midwest. These values included a respect for the rights of the people, tempered by the rule of law; individual enterprise, balanced by a concern for one's neighbors; and a fierce morality, rooted in Protestantism. Northerners would regulate morality—by persuasion if

Scenes from North and South Describe the socioeconomic contrasts in these two pictures. How many differences can you identify? Any similarities? Chicago (top) was a rapidly growing, bustling northern city in the 1850s; situated on the Great Lakes and a developing railroad hub, Chicago became the distribution center for industrial and agricultural goods throughout the Midwest. The vital unit of southern commerce was, by contrast, the individual plantation (bottom), with steamboats and flatboats carrying cotton and sugar to port cities for trade with Europe. Are there examples today of cultural contrasts similar to this?

possible, by legislation if necessary—to purge irreligion, illiteracy, and intemperance from American society.

Northerners valued the kind of republican government that guaranteed the rights of free men, enabling them to achieve economic progress. This belief supported government action to promote free labor, industrial growth, some immigration, foreign trade (protected by tariffs), and the extension of railroads and free farm homesteads westward across the continent. Energetic mobility, both westward and upward, would dissolve state, regional, and class loyalties and increase the sense of nationhood. A strong Union could achieve national and even international greatness. These were the conditions, befitting a chosen people, who would, as Seward put it, spread American institutions around the world and "renovate the condition of mankind." These were also the principles of the Republican party.

Only free men could achieve economic progress and moral society. In northerners' eyes, therefore, the worst sin was the loss of one's freedom. Slavery was the root of evil. It was, Seward said, "incompatible with all . . . the elements of the security, welfare, and greatness of nations." The South was the antithesis of everything that such northerners saw as good. Southerners were unfree, backward, economically stagnant, uneducated, lawless, immoral, and in conflict with the values and ideals of the nineteenth century. Julia Lovejoy's denunciation of slaveholding Missourians was mild. Other Yankee migrants saw southerners as "wild beasts" who guzzled whiskey, ate dirt, swore, raped slave women, and fought or dueled at the slightest excuse. In the slang of the day, they were "Pukes."

The Southern Perspective

Southerners were a diverse people who, like northerners, shared certain broad values, generally those of the planter class. If in the North the values of economic enterprise were most important, southerners revered social values most. They admired the English gentry and saw themselves as courteous, refined, hospitable, and chivalrous—and saw "Yankees" as rude, aggressive, and materialistic. In a society where one person in three was a black slave, racial distinctions and paternalistic relationships were crucial in maintaining order and white supremacy. Fear of slave revolt was ever-present. The South had five times as many military schools as the North. Northerners educated the many for economic utility; southerners educated the few for character. In short, the white South saw itself as an ordered society guided by the planters' genteel code.

Southerners agreed with northerners that republican sovereignty rested in the people, who created a government of laws to protect life, liberty, and property. But unlike northerners, southerners believed that the democratic principle of self-government was best preserved in local political units such as the states. They were ready to fight to resist any tyrannical encroachment on their liberty, as they had in 1776. They saw themselves as true revolutionary patriots. Like northerners, southerners cherished the Union. But they preferred the loose confederacy of the Jeffersonian past, not Seward's centralized nationalism.

To southerners, Yankees were in too much of a hurry—to make money, to reform others' behavior, to put dreamy theories (like racial equality) into practice. Two images dominated the white South's view of northerners: either they were stingy, hypocritical, moralizing Puritans, or they were grubby, slum-dwelling, Catholic immigrants. These northerners, one paper said, "are devoid of society fitted for well-bred gentlemen."

Each side saw the other threatening its freedom and degrading proper republican society. Each saw the other imposing barriers to its vision for America's future, which included the economic systems described in the last two chapters. As hostilities rose, the views each section had of the other grew steadily more rigid and conspiratorial. Northerners saw the South as a "slave power," determined to foist the slave system on free labor throughout the land. Southerners saw the North as full of "black Republicanism," resolved to destroy their way of life.

Polarization and the Road to War

The struggle over Kansas solidified the image of the Republicans as a northern party and seriously weakened the Democrats. Further events, mostly over the question of slavery in the territories, soon split the Democrats irrevocably into sectional halves: the *Dred Scott* decision of the Supreme Court (1857), the constitutional crisis in Kansas (1857), the Lincoln–Douglas debates in Illinois (1858), John Brown's raid in Virginia (1859), and Lincoln's election (1860). These incidents further polarized the negative images each culture held of the other and accelerated the nation down the road to civil war.

The Dred Scott Case

The events of 1857 reinforced the arguments of those who believed in a slave power conspiracy. Two days after James Buchanan's inauguration, the Supreme Court ruled in *Dred Scott* v. *Sanford*, a case that had been before the Court for nearly three years. Back in 1846, Dred and Harriet Scott had filed suit in Missouri for their freedom. They argued that their master had taken them into territories where the Missouri Compromise prohibited slavery, and therefore they should be freed. By the time the case reached the Supreme Court, slavery in the territories was a hot political issue.

●●●—Read **the Document**

Opinion of the Supreme Court for Dred Scott v. Sanford (1857) at **www.myhistorylab.com**

When the Court, with its southern majority, issued a 7–2 decision, it made three rulings. First, because blacks were, as Chief Justice Roger Taney put it, "beings of an inferior order [with] . . . no rights which white men were bound to respect," Dred Scott was not a citizen and had no right to sue in federal court. The second ruling stated that the Missouri Compromise was unconstitutional because Congress had no power to ban slavery in a territory.

●—View **the Image**

Dred Scott at **www.myhistorylab.com**

Third, the Court decided that the Scotts being taken in and out of free states did not affect their status.

The implications of these decisions went far beyond the Scotts' personal freedom. The arguments about black citizenship infuriated many northerners. Frederick Douglass called the ruling "a most scandalous and devilish perversion of the Constitution." Many citizens worried about the few rights free blacks still held. Even more troubling, the decision hinted that slavery might be legal in the free states of the North. People who suspected a conspiracy were not calmed when Buchanan endorsed the *Dred Scott* decision as a final settlement of the right of citizens to take their "property of any kind, including slaves, into the common Territories . . . and to have it protected there under the Federal Constitution." Far from settling the issue of slavery in the territories, as Buchanan had hoped, *Dred Scott* threw it back into American politics. It opened new questions and increased sectional hostilities.

Constitutional Crisis in Kansas

The *Dred Scott* decision and Buchanan's endorsement fed northern suspicions of a slave power conspiracy to impose slavery everywhere. Events in Kansas, which still had two governments, heightened these fears. In the summer of 1857, Kansas had yet another election, with so many irregularities that only 2,000 out of a possible 24,000 voters participated. A proslavery slate of delegates was elected to a constitutional convention meeting at Lecompton to prepare for statehood. The convention barred free blacks from the state, guaranteed the property rights of the few slaveholders in Kansas, and asked voters to decide in a referendum whether to permit more slaves.

Watch the Video
Dred Scott and the Crisis that Led to the Civil War
at **www.myhistorylab.com**

The proslavery Lecompton constitution, clearly unrepresentative of the wishes of the majority of the people of Kansas, was sent to Congress for approval. Eager to retain southern Democratic support, Buchanan endorsed it. Stephen Douglas challenged the president's power and jeopardized his standing with southern Democrats by opposing it. Facing reelection to the Senate in 1858, Douglas needed to hold the support of the northern wing of his party. Congress sent the Lecompton constitution back to the people of Kansas for another referendum. This time they defeated it, which meant that Kansas remained a territory rather than becoming a slave state. While Kansas lingered in an uncertain status, the larger political effect of the struggle was to split the Democratic party almost beyond repair.

No sooner had Douglas settled the Lecompton question than he faced reelection in Illinois. Douglas's opposition to the Lecompton constitution had restored his prestige in the North as an opponent of the slave power. This weakened the Republican party's claim that only it could stop the spread of southern power. Party leaders from the West, however, had a candidate who understood the importance of distinguishing Republican moral and political views from those of the Democrats.

Lincoln and the Illinois Debates

Although relatively unknown nationally and out of elective office for several years, by 1858, Abraham Lincoln emerged in Illinois to challenge Seward for leadership of the Republican party. Lincoln's character was shaped on the midwestern frontier, where he had educated himself, developed mild abolitionist views, and dreamed of America's greatness.

Douglas was clearly the leading Democrat, so the 1858 Senate election in Illinois gave a preview of the presidential election of 1860. The other

Douglass, Frederick, observed, "the slave power idea was the ideological glue of the Republican party." Lincoln's handling of this idea would be crucial in distinguishing him from Stephen Douglas. The Illinois campaign featured seven debates between Lincoln and Douglas, which took place in different cities. Addressing a national as well as a local audience, the debaters confronted the heated racial issues before the nation.

Lincoln set a solemn tone when he accepted the Republican senatorial nomination. The American nation, he said, was in a "crisis" and building toward a worse one. "A House divided against itself cannot stand. I believe this government cannot endure, permanently half *slave* and half *free*." Lincoln said he did not expect the Union "to be dissolved" or "the house to fall," but rather that "it will become *all* one thing, or *all* the other." Then he rehearsed the history of the South's growing influence over national policy since the Kansas–Nebraska Act, which he blamed on Douglas. Lincoln stated his firm opposition to the *Dred Scott* decision, which he believed part of a conspiracy involving Pierce, Buchanan, Taney, and Douglas. He and others like him opposing this conspiracy wished to place slavery on a "course of ultimate extinction."

•◦•⎡Read the Document

The Lincoln-Douglas Debates of 1858

at **www.myhistorylab.com**

Debating Douglas, Lincoln reiterated these controversial themes. Although far from a radical abolitionist, in these debates Lincoln also skillfully staked out a moral position on race and slavery not just in advance of Douglas but well ahead of his time.

Lincoln was also a part of his time. He believed in white superiority, opposed granting specific equal civil rights to free blacks, and said that differences between whites and blacks would "forever forbid the two races from living together on terms of social and political equality." "Separation" and colonization in Liberia or Central America was the best solution. But Lincoln differed from most contemporaries in his deep commitment to the equality and dignity of all human beings. Countering Douglas's racial slurs, Lincoln said that he believed not only that blacks were "entitled to all the natural rights . . . in the Declaration of Independence," but also that they had many specific economic rights, like "the right to put into his mouth the bread that his own hands have earned." In these rights, blacks were "my equal and the equal of Judge Douglas, and the equal of every living man."

Unlike Douglas, Lincoln hated slavery. "I contemplate slavery as a moral, social, and political evil." The difference between a Republican and a Democrat was simply whether one thought slavery wrong or right. Douglas was more equivocal and dodged the issue in Freeport, pointing out that slavery would not exist if local legislation did not support it. But Douglas's moral indifference was clear: he did not care if a territorial legislature voted it "up or down." Republicans did care, Lincoln answered, and said that by stopping the expansion of slavery, the course toward "ultimate extinction" had begun. Although barred by the Constitution from interfering with slavery where it already existed, Lincoln said that Republicans believed slavery wrong, and "we propose a course of policy that shall deal with it as a wrong."

What Lincoln meant by "policy" was not yet clear, not even to himself. However, he did succeed in affirming that Republicans were the only moral and political force capable of stopping the slave power. It seems ironic now (though not then) that Douglas won the election. Elsewhere in 1858, however, Democrats did poorly, losing 18 congressional seats to the Republicans.

John Brown's Raid

Unlike Lincoln, John Brown was prepared to act decisively against slavery. On October 16, 1859, he and a band of 22 men attacked the federal arsenal at Harpers Ferry, Virginia (now West Virginia). He hoped to provoke a general uprising of slaves through-out the Upper South or at least provide arms for slaves to make their way to freedom. Federal troops soon overcame him. Nearly half his men died, including two sons. Brown was captured, tried, and hanged. So ended a lifetime of failures.

View the Image
John Brown (ca.1850)
at **www.myhistorylab.com**

In death, however, Brown was not a failure. His daring if foolhardy raid and his dignified behavior during his trial and speedy execution unleashed powerful passions. The North–South gap widened. Although Brown's death was widely condemned, many northerners responded with an outpouring of sympathy. Thoreau compared him to Christ. Abolitionist William Lloyd Garrison, a pacifist, wished "success to every slave insurrection" in the South. Ministers called slave revolt a "divine weapon" and glorified Brown's treason as "holy." Brown's raid, Frederick Douglass said, showed that slavery was a "system of brute force" that would only be ended when "met with its own weapons."

Read the Document
John Brown's Address Before Sentencing (1859)
at **www.myhistorylab.com**

John Brown as an Avenging Hero Describe the many images in this modern mural of John Brown. What do you see? What are the opposing forces? How violent is this depiction? Is the angry, stormy sky God's wrath? What do you think about John Brown? *(Kansas State Historical Society)*

Southerners felt "dread and terror" over the possibility of a wave of slave revolts led by hundreds of imaginary John Browns and Nat Turners, and concluded that northerners would stop at nothing to free the slaves. This suspicion further eroded freedom of thought and expression. A North Carolinian described a "spirit of terror, mobs, arrests, and violence" in his state. Twelve families in Berea, Kentucky, were evicted from the state for their mild abolitionist sentiments. A Texas minister who criticized the treatment of slaves in a sermon got 70 lashes.

With Brown's raid, southerners also became more convinced, as the governor of South Carolina put it, of a "black Republican" plot in the North "arrayed against the slaveholders," now a permanent minority. Southern Unionists lost their influence, and power passed to those favoring secession.

The Election of 1860

When the Democratic convention met in Charleston, South Carolina, a secessionist hotbed, it sat for a record 10 days and went through 59 ballots without being able to name a candidate. Reconvening in Baltimore, the Democrats acknowledged their irreparable division by choosing two candidates at two separate conventions: Douglas for northern Democrats, and John C. Breckinridge, Buchanan's vice president, for the proslavery South. The Constitutional Union party, made up of former southern Whigs and border-state nativists, claimed the middle ground and nominated John Bell, a slaveholder from Tennessee who favored compromise.

With Democrats split and a new party in contention, the Republican strategy aimed at keeping the states carried by Frémont in 1856 and adding

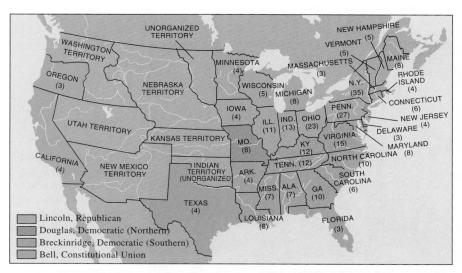

The Presidential Election of 1860 Lincoln's election, the first of a Republican, was on the basis of a totally northern sectional victory; he received only 40 percent of the popular vote. How do you explain each candidate's success in each section of the country? Why didn't Douglas do better? Why did Lincoln win the election? Who would you have voted for in 1860?

Pennsylvania, Illinois, and Indiana. Seward, the leading candidate, had been tempering his antislavery views to appear more electable. So had Lincoln, who seemed more likely than Seward to carry those key states. After shrewd maneuvers emphasizing his "availability" as a moderate, Lincoln was nominated.

The Republican platform exuded moderation, opposing only slavery's extension. Mostly it spoke of tariff protection, subsidized internal improvements, free labor, and a homestead bill. Republicans, like southern Democrats, defended their view of what republican values meant for America's future, which did not include the equal rights envisioned by Frederick Douglass. An English traveler in 1860 observed that in America "we see, in effect, two nations—one white and another black—growing up together within the same political circle, but never mingling on a principle of equality."

The Republican moderate strategy worked as planned. Lincoln was elected by sweeping the entire Northeast and Midwest. Although he got less than 40 percent of the popular vote nationwide, his triumph in the North was decisive. Even a united Democratic party could not have defeated him. With victory assured, Lincoln finished his sandwich and coffee on election night in Springfield and prepared for his awesome responsibilities. They came even before his inauguration.

The Divided House Falls

The Republicans overestimated Unionist sentiment in the South. A year earlier, some southern congressmen had walked out in protest when the House chose an antislavery speaker. A Republican leader, Carl Schurz, recalling this, said that the southerners had taken a drink and then come back. Now, Schurz predicted, they would walk out, take two drinks, and come back again. He was wrong.

Secession and Uncertainty

On December 20, 1860, South Carolina seceded, declaring the "experiment" of putting people with "different pursuits and institutions" under one government a failure. By February 1, the other six Deep South states (Mississippi, Florida, Alabama, Georgia, Louisiana, and Texas) also left. A week later, delegates meeting in Montgomery, Alabama, created the Confederate States of America and elected Jefferson Davis, a Mississippi senator and cotton planter, its provisional president. The divided house had fallen, as Lincoln had predicted. But it was not yet certain whether the house could be put back together, or whether there would be civil war.

The government in Washington had three options. First was compromise, but the emotions of the time ruled that out, as the compromises were mostly pro-southern. Second, as suggested by New York *Tribune* editor Horace Greeley, Washington might let the seven states "go in peace," taking

⟨⟩⟨Watch the Video
What Caused the Civil War?
at **www.myhistorylab.com**

care not to lose the border states. This was opposed by northern businessmen, who would lose profitable economic ties with the South, and by those
who believed in an indissoluble Union. The third option was to compel
secessionist states to return, which probably meant war.

Republican hopes that southern Unionism would assert itself and
avoid all these options seemed possible in February 1861. No more states
seceded. The nation waited, wondering what Virginia and the border states
would do, what outgoing President Buchanan would do, and what Congress would do. Determined not to start a civil war in the last weeks of his
already dismal administration, Buchanan did nothing. Congress made some
feeble efforts to pass compromise legislation, waiting in vain for the support
of the president-elect. And as Union supporters struggled with secessionists,
Virginia and the border states, like the entire nation, waited for Lincoln.

Frederick Douglass waited, too, without much hope. He wanted the "complete and universal *abolition* of the whole slave system," as well as equal suffrage and other rights for free blacks. His momentary expectation during the
presidential campaign, that Lincoln and the Republicans had the will to do this,
had been thoroughly dashed. Douglass foresaw northern politicians and businessmen "granting the most demoralizing concessions to the Slave Power."

In his despair, Douglass began to explore possibilities for emigration
and colonization in Haiti, an idea he had long opposed. To achieve full freedom and citizenship in the United States for all blacks, he said in January
1861, he would "welcome the hardships consequent upon a dissolution of
the Union." In February, Douglass said, "Let the conflict come." He opposed
all compromises, hoping that with Lincoln's inauguration in March, it would
"be decided, and decided forever, which of the two, Freedom or Slavery, shall
give law to this Republic."

Lincoln and Fort Sumter

As Douglass penned these thoughts, Lincoln began a long, slow train
ride from Springfield to Washington, writing and rewriting his inaugural
address. Lincoln's quietness in the period between his election and his
inauguration led many to judge him weak and indecisive. He was not.
Lincoln firmly opposed secession and any compromise with the principle
of stopping the extension of slavery. He would neither conciliate secessionist southern states nor force their return.

Lincoln believed in his constitutional responsibility to uphold the laws
of the land. The focus of his attention was a federal fort in the harbor of
Charleston. Major Robert Anderson, the commander of Fort Sumter, was
running out of provisions and had requested new supplies from Washington.
Lincoln would enforce the laws and protect federal property at Fort Sumter.

As the new president delivered his inaugural address on March 4, he
faced a tense and divided nation. Lincoln asserted his unequivocal intention to enforce the laws of the land, arguing that the Union was "perpetual"
and indissoluble. He reminded the nation that the "only substantial dispute" was that "one section of our country believes slavery is *right*, and
ought to be extended, while the other believes it is *wrong*, and ought not to

The Causes of the Civil War

Starting with the seven items at the top of this chart, how would you explain the primary cause of the Civil War? Which four or five of the following "specific issues and events" would you use to support your argument? Can you make a distinction between underlying causes and immediate sparks?

Date	Issues and Events	Deeper, Underlying Causes of Civil War
1600s–1860s	Slavery in the South	Slavery as major, underlying, pervasive cause
1700s–1860s	Development of two distinct socioeconomic systems and cultures	Further reinforced slavery as fundamental socioeconomic, cultural moral issue
1787–1860s	States' rights, nullification doctrine	Ongoing political issue, less fundamental as cause
1820	Missouri Compromise (36°30′)	Background for conflict over slavery in territories
1828–1833	South Carolina tariff nullification crisis	Background for secession leadership in South Carolina
1831–1860s	Antislavery movements, southern justification	Thirty years of emotional preparation for conflict
1846–1848	War with Mexico (Wilmot Proviso, Calhoun, popular sovereignty)	Options for issue of slavery in territories

Date	Specific Issues and Events	Specific Impact on the Road to War
1850	Compromise of 1850	Temporary and unsatisfactory "settlement" of divisive issue
1851–1854	Fugitive slaves returned and rescued in North; personal liberty laws passed in North; Harriet Beecher Stowe's *Uncle Tom's Cabin*	Heightened northern emotional reactions against the South and slavery
1852–1856	Breakdown of Whig party and national Democratic party; creation of a new party system with sectional basis	Made national politics an arena where sectional and cultural differences over slavery were fought
1854	Ostend Manifesto and other expansionist efforts in Central America; formation of Republican party; Kansas–Nebraska Act	Reinforced image of Democratic party as favoring slavery; major party identified as opposing the extension of slavery; reopened "settled" issue of slavery in the territories
1856	"Bleeding Kansas"; Senator Sumner physically attacked in Senate	Foretaste of Civil War (200 killed, $2 million in property lost) inflamed emotions and polarized North and South
1857	*Dred Scott* decision; proslavery Lecompton constitution in Kansas	Made North fear a "slave power conspiracy," supported by President Buchanan and the Supreme Court
1858	Lincoln–Douglas debates in Illinois; Democrats lose 18 seats in Congress	Set stage for election of 1860
1859	John Brown's raid and reactions in North and South	Made South fear a "black Republican" plot against slavery; further polarization and irrationality
1860	Democratic party splits in half; Lincoln elected president; South Carolina secedes from Union	Final breakdown of national parties and election of "northern" president; no more compromises
1861	Six more southern states secede by February 1; Confederate Constitution adopted February 4; Lincoln inaugurated March 4; Fort Sumter attacked April 12	Civil War begins

RECOVERING *the* PAST

Senate Speeches

The history of ordinary Americans is recovered in letters, diaries, and folktales. But in times of political conflict, as in the years before the Civil War, historians turn to more conventional sources such as congressional speeches. Recorded in the *Congressional Globe,* these speeches are a revealing means of recovering the substance, tone, and drama of political debate.

The mid-nineteenth century was an era of giants in the U.S. Senate: Daniel Webster, Henry Clay, John C. Calhoun, William Seward, and Stephen Douglas. When Congress debated a major issue, such as nullification or the extension of slavery, large crowds packed the Senate galleries. These spectacular oratorical events provided mass entertainment and political instruction. Such was the case with the Senate speeches over the Compromise of 1850. The three principal figures early in the debates were Clay (Kentucky), Calhoun (South Carolina), and Webster (Massachusetts), each of whom delivered memorable speeches to crown brilliant careers.

Born within five years of each other, each man began his political career in the House of Representatives in the War of 1812 era. Each served a term as secretary of state, and each served in the Senate for an average of 16 years. Clay and Webster were leaders of the Whig party, and Calhoun was a leader of the Democrats. All three were failing candidates for president between 1824 and 1844. All three clashed with and spent most of their careers in the political shadow of Andrew Jackson.

Forty years of political and ideological conflict with each other not only sharpened their oratorical skills but also led to mutual respect. Webster said of Calhoun that he was "the ablest man in the Senate. He could have demolished Newton, Calvin, or even John Locke as a logician." Calhoun said of Clay, "He is a bad man, but by god, I love him." And "Old Man Eloquent" himself, John Quincy Adams, said of Webster that he was "the most consummate orator of modern times."

Therefore, it was a momentous event when they each prepared speeches and met for one last encounter in 1850. Clay was over 70 years old and in failing health, but he sought to keep the Union together by defending his compromise proposals in a four-hour speech spread over two days in February. The Senate galleries were so packed that listeners were pushed into hallways and even into the rotunda of the Capitol. Copies of his speech were in such demand that over 100,000 were printed.

A month later, on March 7, Webster rose to join Clay in defending the compromise, three days after a seriously ill Calhoun had "tottered into the Senate" on the arm of a friend to hear James Mason of Virginia read his rejection of the compromise. Within a month, Calhoun was dead. Clay and Webster followed him to the grave two years later.

REFLECTING ON THE PAST As you read these brief excerpts from each speech, try to imagine yourself sitting in the gallery overlooking the Senate floor absorbing the drama. What oratorical devices does each speaker use? How do they differ? To what extent does each man reflect his region, especially on the fugitive slave issue? To what extent do they appeal to an indivisible Union? On whom do they put the burden of resolving the conflicts? Which speaker is most persuasive to you? Why?

Henry Clay
February 5–6, 1850
I have seen many periods of great anxiety, of peril, and of danger in this country, and I have never before risen to address any assemblage so oppressed, so appalled, and so anxious. . . .
Mr. President, it is passion, passion-party, party, and intemperance—that is all I dread in the adjustment of the great questions which unhappily at this time divide our distracted country. Sir, at this moment we have in the legislative bodies of this Capitol and in the States, twenty old furnaces in full blast, emitting heat, and passion, and intemperance, and

diffusing them throughout the whole extent of this broad land. Two months ago all was calm in comparison to the present moment. All now is uproar, confusion, and menace to the existence of the Union, and to the happiness and safety of this people. . . .

Sir, when I came to consider this subject, there were two or three general purposes which it seemed to me to be most desirable, if possible, to accomplish. The one was, to settle all the controverted questions arising out of the subject of slavery. . . . I therefore turned my attention to every subject connected with this institution of slavery, and out of which controverted questions had sprung, to see if it were possible or practicable to accommodate and adjust the whole of them. . . .

We are told now, and it is rung throughout this entire country, that the Union is threatened with subversion and destruction. Well, the first question which naturally rises is, supposing the Union to be dissolved,—having all the causes of grievance which are complained of,—How far will a dissolution furnish a remedy for those grievances? If the Union is to be dissolved for any existing causes, it will be dissolved because slavery is interdicted or not allowed to be introduced into the ceded territories; because slavery is threatened to be abolished in the District of Columbia, and because fugitive slaves are not returned, as in my opinion they ought to be, and restored to their masters. These, I believe, will be the causes; if there be any causes, which can lead to the direful event to which I have referred. . . .

Mr. President, I am directly opposed to any purpose of secession, of separation. I am for staying within the Union, and defying any portion of this Union to expel or drive me out of the Union.

John C. Calhoun
March 4, 1850
Having now, Senators, explained what it is that endangers the Union, and traced it to its cause, and explained its nature and character, the question again recurs—How can the Union be saved? To this I answer, there is but one way by which it can be—and that is—by adopting such measures as will satisfy the States belonging to the Southern section, that they can remain in the Union consistently with their honor and their safety. . . .

But will the North agree to this? It is for her to answer the question. But, I will say, she cannot refuse, if she has half the love of the Union which she professes to have, or without justly exposing herself to the charge that her love of power and aggrandizement is far greater than her love of the Union. At all events, the responsibility of saving the Union rests on the North, and not on the South. . . .

Daniel Webster
March 7, 1850
Mr. President: I wish to speak to-day, not as a Massachusetts man, nor as a Northern man, but as an American, and a member of the Senate of the United States. . . .

I speak to-day for the preservation of the Union. "Hear me for my cause." I speak to-day, out of a solicitous and anxious heart, for the restoration to the country of that quiet and that harmony which make the blessing of this Union so rich, and so dear to us all. . . . I shall bestow a little attention, Sir, upon these various grievances existing on the one side and on the other. I begin with complaints of the South . . . and especially to one which has in my opinion just foundation; and that is, that there has been found at the North, among individuals and among legislators, a disinclination to perform fully their constitutional duties in regard to the return of persons bound to service who have escaped into the free States. In that respect, the South, in my judgment, is right, and the North is wrong. Every member of every Northern legislature is bound by oath, like every other officer in the country, to support the Constitution of the United States; and the article of the Constitution which says to these States they shall deliver up fugitives from service is as binding in honor and conscience as any other article. . . .

WHERE IS THE LINE TO BE DRAWN? WHAT STATES ARE TO SECEDE? WHAT IS TO REMAIN AMERICAN? WHAT AM I TO BE? AN AMERICAN NO LONGER? AM I TO BECOME A SECTIONAL MAN, A LOCAL MAN, A SEPARATIST, WITH NO COUNTRY IN COMMON WITH THE GENTLEMEN WHO SIT AROUND ME HERE, OR WHO FILL THE OTHER HOUSE OF CONGRESS? HEAVEN FORBID! WHERE IS THE FLAG OF THE REPUBLIC TO REMAIN? WHERE IS THE EAGLE STILL TO TOWER? OR IS HE TO COWER, AND SHRINK, AND FALL TO THE GROUND?

be extended." Still appealing to Unionist strength among southern moderates, Lincoln said that he would make no attempts to interfere with existing slavery and would respect the law to return fugitive slaves. Nearing the end, Lincoln put the burden of initiating civil war on the "dissatisfied fellow-countrymen" who had seceded. As if foreseeing the horrible events that would follow, he closed his speech eloquently:

> I am loath to close. We are not enemies, but friends. We must not be enemies. Though passion may have strained, it must not break our bonds of affection. The mystic chords of memory, stretching from every battlefield, and patriot grave, to every living heart and hearthstone, all over this broad land, will yet swell the chorus of the Union, when again touched, as surely they will be, by the better angels of our nature.

Frederick Douglass was not impressed with Lincoln's "honied phrases" and accused him of "weakness, timidity and conciliation." Also unmoved, Robert Allston wrote his son from Charleston, where he was watching the crisis over Fort Sumter, that the Confederacy's "advantage" was in having a "much better president than they have."

On April 6, Lincoln notified the governor of South Carolina that he was sending "provisions only" to Fort Sumter. No effort would be made "to throw in men, arms, or ammunition" unless the fort were attacked. On April 10, Jefferson Davis directed General P. G. T. Beauregard to demand the surrender of Fort Sumter. Davis told Beauregard to reduce the fort if Major Anderson refused.

On April 12, as Lincoln's relief expedition neared Charleston, Beauregard's batteries began shelling Fort Sumter, and the Civil War began. Frederick Douglass was about to leave for Haiti when he heard the news. He immediately changed his plans: "This is no time . . . to leave the country." He announced his readiness to help end the war by aiding the Union to organize freed slaves "into a liberating army" to "make war upon . . . the savage barbarism of slavery." The Allstons had changed places, and it was Benjamin who described the events in Charleston harbor to his father. On April 14, Benjamin reported the "glorious, and astonishing news that Sumter has fallen." With it fell America's divided house.

Conclusion
The "Irrepressible Conflict"

Lincoln had been right. The nation could no longer endure half-slave and half-free. The collision between North and South, William Seward said, was not an "accidental, unnecessary" event, but an "irrepressible conflict between opposing and enduring forces." Those forces had been at work for many decades, but developed with increasing intensity after 1848 over the question of the extension of slavery into the territories. Although economic, cultural, political, constitutional, and emotional forces all contributed to the developing opposition between North and South, slavery was the fundamental, enduring force that underlay all others, causing what Walt Whitman called the "red blood of civil war." Abraham Lincoln, Frederick Douglass, the Allston family, Michael Luark, and the American people all faced a radically altered national scene. All wondered whether the American democratic system would be able to withstand this challenge.

TIME*line* ▬▬▬▬▬

1848	Arguments over slavery in the territories gained from Mexico
1850	Compromise of 1850, including Fugitive Slave Act
1854	Kansas–Nebraska Act
	Republican and Know-Nothing parties formed
1855–1856	Bleeding Kansas
1857	*Dred Scott* case
1859	John Brown's raid at Harpers Ferry
1860	Abraham Lincoln elected president
1861	Confederate States of America founded
	Attack on Fort Sumter begins Civil War

✓●─Study and Review at **www.myhistorylab.com**

Questions for Review and Reflection

1. What options existed for dealing with slavery in the territories, and what compromises did Congress propose? How well did they work?

2. How did political party alignments change in the 1850s, and how did that affect the path to civil war?

3. Examine how southerners and northerners viewed each other, especially in and after Kansas. How did cultural stereotypes and emotional attitudes contribute to the outbreak of civil war?

4. Can you explain four basic, underlying causes of the American Civil War? Which one cause do you think was most significant, and what specific events would you use to support your choice?

5. To what extent was the American democratic political system flexible enough to handle the issues of the 1850s? Could the Civil War have been avoided, or was it inevitable?

Key Terms

Bleeding Kansas 408

Dred Scott case 412

Free soil 395

Fugitive Slave Act 398

John Brown's raid 415

Kansas-Nebraska Act 401

Personal liberty laws 399

Popular sovereignty 396

Republican party 406

Wilmot Proviso 394

13

The Union Severed

American Stories

A War That Touched Lives

In his remarks to Congress in 1862, Abraham Lincoln reminded congressmen that "We cannot escape history. We of this Congress and this administration will be remembered in spite of ourselves. No personal significance, or insignificance, can spare . . . us. The fiery trial through which we pass, will light us down, in honor or dishonor, to the latest generation." Lincoln's conviction that Americans would long remember him and other major actors of the Civil War was correct. Jefferson Davis, Robert E. Lee, Ulysses S. Grant—these are the men whose characters, actions, and decisions have been the subject of continuing discussion and analysis, whose statues and memorials dot the American countryside and grace urban squares. Whether seen as heroes or villains, great men have dominated the story of the Civil War.

 ☀️-View the Image
Robert E. Lee on Horseback
at **www.myhistorylab.com**

Yet from the earliest days, the war touched the lives of even the most uncelebrated Americans. From Indianapolis, 20-year-old Arthur Carpenter wrote to his parents in Massachusetts, begging for permission to volunteer: "I have always longed for the time to come when I could enter the army and be a military man, and when this war broke out, I thought the time had come, but you would not permit me to enter the service . . . now I make one more appeal to you." The pleas worked, and Carpenter enlisted, spending most of the war fighting in Kentucky and Tennessee.

In that same year, in Tennessee, George and Ethie Eagleton faced anguishing decisions. Though not an abolitionist, George, a 30-year-old Presbyterian preacher, was unsympathetic to slavery and opposed to secession. But when his native state left the Union, George felt compelled to follow and enlisted in the 44th Tennessee Infantry. Ethie, his 26-year-old wife, despaired over the war, George's decision, and her own forlorn situation:

Chapter Outline

Organizing for War

Clashing on the
Battlefield, 1861–1862

The Tide Turns, 1863–1865

Changes Wrought by War

Conclusion: An
Uncertain Future

Mr. Eagleton's school dismissed—and what for? O my God, must I write it? He has enlisted in the service of his country—to war—the most unrighteous war that ever was brought on any nation that ever lived. Pres. Lincoln has done what no other Pres. ever dared to do—he has divided these once peaceful and happy United States. And Oh! the dreadful dark cloud that is now hanging over our country—'tis enough to sicken the heart of any one. . . . Mr. E. is gone. . . . What will become of me, left here without a home and relatives, a babe just nine months old and no George.

Both Carpenter and the Eagletons survived the war, but it transformed their lives. Carpenter had difficulty settling down. Filled with bitter memories of the war years in Tennessee, the Eagletons moved to Arkansas. Ordinary people like Carpenter and the Eagletons are historically anonymous. Yet their actions on and off the battlefield helped to shape the course of events, as their leaders realized, even if today we tend to remember only the famous and influential.

For thousands of Americans, from Lincoln and Davis to Carpenter and the Eagletons, war was both a profoundly personal and a major national event. Its impact reached far beyond the four years of hostilities. As you read about the war that was fought to conserve two political, social, and economic visions, ask yourself how it ultimately changed familiar ways of political, social, and economic life in both North and South. In what ways was war a transforming force, both destructive and creative in its effect on the structure and social dynamics of society and on the lives of ordinary people? This question underlies this chapter's analysis of the war's three stages: the initial months of preparation; the years of military stalemate between 1861 and 1865; and, finally, resolution.

Organizing for War

The Confederate bombardment of **Fort Sumter** on April 12, 1861, and the surrender of Union troops the next day ended uncertainties. The North's response to Fort Sumter was a virtual declaration of war as President Lincoln called for state militia volunteers to crush the "insurrection." His action pushed Virginia, North Carolina, Tennessee, and Arkansas into the secessionist camp. Three other slave states (Maryland, Kentucky, and Missouri) agonizingly debated which way to go. The "War Between the States" was a reality.

Many Americans were dismayed. Southerners like George Eagleton reluctantly followed their states out of the Union. When he enlisted, Eagleton complained of the "disgraceful cowardice" of those who were "now refusing self and means for the prosecution of war." Robert E. Lee of Virginia hesitated to resign his federal commission but finally decided that he could not "raise [a] hand against . . . relatives . . . children . . . home." Whites in the southern uplands (where blacks were few and slaveholders were heartily disliked), yeomen farmers in the Deep South (who owned no slaves), and many border state residents opposed secession and war. Many would eventually join the Union forces.

In the North, large numbers supported neither the Republicans nor Lincoln. Irish immigrants fearing the competition of free black labor and southerners living in Illinois, Indiana, and Ohio opposed war. Northern Democrats at first blamed Lincoln and the Republicans almost as much as the secessionists for the crisis.

Nevertheless, the days following Fort Sumter and Lincoln's call for troops saw an outpouring of support on both sides, fueled in part by relief at decisive action, in part by patriotism and love of adventure, and in part by unemployment. The conviction that the conflict would rapidly come to a glorious conclusion also fueled the eagerness to enlist. Lincoln's call for 75,000 state militiamen for only 90 days of service, and a similar enlistment term for Confederate soldiers, supported the notion that the war would be short.

The war fever produced so many volunteers that officials could not handle the throng. Both sides sent thousands of white would-be soldiers home.

The Balance of Resources

The Civil War was one of several military conflicts during the nineteenth century that sought national independence. In Europe, Italian and German patriots struggled to create new nations out of individual states. Unlike their European counterparts, however, southern nationalists proclaimed their independence by withdrawing from an already unified state. Likening their struggle to that of the Revolutionary generation that had broken away from Great Britain's tyranny, southerners argued that they were "now enlisted in The Holy Cause of Liberty and Independence." While they legitimized secession by appealing to freedom, however, southerners were also preserving freedom's antithesis, slavery.

The outcome of the southern bid for autonomy was uncertain. Although statistics of population and industrial development suggested a northern victory, Great Britain with similar advantages in 1775 had lost that war. Many northern assets would become effective only with time.

The North's white population greatly exceeded the South's, giving the appearance of a military advantage. Yet early in the war, the armies were more evenly matched. Almost 187,000 Union troops bore arms in July 1861, while just over 112,000 men marched under Confederate colors. Southerners believed that their army would prove to be superior fighters. Many northerners feared so, too. And slaves could carry on vital work behind the lines, freeing most adult white males to serve the Confederacy.

The Union also enjoyed impressive economic advantages. In the North, 1 million workers in 110,000 manufacturing concerns produced goods valued at $1.5 billion annually, while 110,000 southern workers in 18,000 manufacturing concerns produced goods valued at only $155 million a year. But northern industrial resources had to be mobilized. That would take time, especially because the government did not intend to direct production. A depleted northern treasury made the government's first task the raising of funds to pay for military necessities.

The South depended on imported northern and European manufactured goods. If Lincoln cut off that trade, the South would have to create its industry almost from scratch. Its railroad system was organized to move cotton, not armies and supplies. Yet the agricultural South did have important resources of food, draft animals, and, of course, cotton, which southerners believed would secure British and French support. By waging a defensive war, the South could tap regional loyalty and enjoy protected lines. Because much of the South raised cotton and tobacco rather than food crops, Union armies could not live off the land, and extended supply lines were always vulnerable. The Union had to conquer and occupy; the South merely had to survive until its enemy gave up.

The Border States

Uncertainty and divided loyalties produced indecision in the **border states**. When the seven Deep South states seceded in 1860 and 1861, all the border states except Unionist Delaware adopted a wait-and-see attitude. Their decisions were critically important to both North and South.

The states of the Upper South could provide natural borders for the Confederacy along the Ohio River, access to its river traffic, and vital resources,

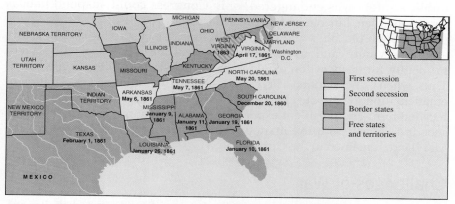

Secession of the Southern States The map provides a chronology of secession and shows the geographical importance of the border states. In what ways does the map highlight the vulnerable position of Washington and explain many of Lincoln's actions in the early days of the war?

wealth, and population. The major railroad link to the West ran through Maryland and western Virginia. Virginia boasted the South's largest ironworks, and Tennessee provided its principal source of grain. Missouri opened the road to the West and controlled Mississippi River traffic.

For the North, every border state remaining loyal was a psychological triumph. Nor was the North unaware of the economic and strategic advantages of keeping the border states with the Union. However, Lincoln's call for troops precipitated the secession of Virginia, Arkansas, Tennessee, and North Carolina between April 17 and May 20, 1861. Maryland, precariously balanced between the pro-Confederate southern and Eastern Shore counties and Unionist western and northern areas, and with pro-southern enthusiasts abounding in Baltimore, vividly demonstrated the significance of border state loyalty.

On April 19, a mob of some 10,000 southern sympathizers, some carrying Confederate flags, attacked the 6th Massachusetts Regiment, headed for Washington, as it marched through Baltimore. The bloody confrontation and confusion allowed would-be secessionists to burn the railroad bridges to the north and south, isolating Washington temporarily from the rest of the Union.

Lincoln took stern measures to secure Maryland. The president agreed temporarily to route troops around Baltimore. In return, the governor called the state legislature into session at Frederick in Unionist western Maryland. This action and Lincoln's swift violation of civil liberties dampened secessionist enthusiasm. Hundreds of southern sympathizers, including 19 state legislators and Baltimore's mayor, were imprisoned without trial. Although Chief Justice Roger B. Taney challenged the president's action and issued a writ of habeas corpus for the release of a southern supporter, Lincoln ignored him. A month later, Taney ruled in *Ex Parte Merryman* that if the public's safety was endangered, only Congress could suspend habeas corpus. By then, Lincoln had secured Maryland.

Although Lincoln's quick and harsh response ensured Maryland's loyalty, he was more cautious elsewhere. Above all, he had to deal with slavery prudently, for hasty action would push border states into the Confederacy. Thus, when General John C. Frémont issued an unauthorized declaration of emancipation in Missouri in August 1861, Lincoln revoked the order and recalled him. The president expected a chain reaction if certain key states seceded. After complex maneuvering, Kentucky and Missouri, like Maryland, remained in the Union.

Challenges of War

The tense weeks after Fort Sumter spilled over with unexpected challenges. Both North and South faced enormous organizational problems.

Southerners had to create a nation–state and devise everything from a constitution to a flag. An important question hovered behind the frantic organizational efforts: could the new political entity succeed in creating bonds of nationhood and inspire the feelings of patriotism that would be necessary if the conflict proved long and difficult?

In February 1861, the original seceding states began the work of creating a nation. The first task was to establish a provisional framework and choose a provisional president and vice president. The delegates swiftly wrote a constitution, much like the federal constitution but emphasizing the "sovereign and independent character" of the states and explicitly recognizing slavery. Provisional President Jefferson Davis tried to assemble a balanced and moderate cabinet. His appointees took on the daunting challenge of creating government departments from scratch. When an army captain came to the treasury with a warrant from Davis for blankets, he found only one clerk. After reading the warrant, the clerk offered the captain a few dollars of his own, explaining, "This, Captain, is all the money that I will certify as being in the Confederate Treasury at this moment."

Despite the challenges, the new Confederate government enjoyed enthusiastic civilian support and a growing sense of nationalism. Ordinary people spoke proudly of the South as "our nation" and referred to themselves as the "southern people." Georgia's governor insisted that "poor and rich, have a common interest, a common destiny." Southern Protestant ministers encouraged a sense of collective identity and reminded southerners that they were God's chosen people. The conflict was a sacred one.

While Lincoln inherited the federal government, he lacked administrative experience and, like his Confederate counterpart, faced organizational problems. Military officers and government clerks defected daily to the South. The treasury was empty. Floods of Republican office seekers thronged into the White House. Unacquainted with many of the "prominent men of the day," Lincoln appointed important Republicans to cabinet posts whether they agreed with him or not. Several scorned him as a backwoods bumbler. Treasury Secretary Salmon P. Chase hoped to replace Lincoln as president in four years' time. Secretary of State William Seward sent Lincoln a memo condescendingly offering to oversee the formulation of presidential policy.

Lincoln and Davis

A number of Lincoln's early actions, however, illustrated that he was no fool. As his Illinois law partner, William Herndon, pointed out, Lincoln's "mind was tough—solid—knotty—gnarly, more or less like his body." The president firmly told Seward that he would run his own administration. After Sumter, he mobilized state militias, expanded the navy, suspended habeas corpus, blockaded the South, and approved spending funds for military purposes—all without congressional sanction, because Congress was not in session. As Lincoln told legislators later, "The dogmas of the quiet past are inadequate to the stormy present. . . . As our case is new, so must we think anew, and act anew." This willingness to "think anew" was a valuable personal asset, even though some criticized his expansion of presidential power as despotic.

By coincidence, Lincoln and his rival, Jefferson Davis, were born only 100 miles apart in Kentucky. However, the course of their lives diverged radically. Lincoln's father migrated north and eked out a simple existence as a farmer. Lincoln himself had only a rudimentary education. Davis's family moved to Mississippi to become cotton planters. Davis grew up in comfortable circumstances, went to West Point, fought in the Mexican-American War, was elected to the U.S. Senate, and served as secretary of war under Franklin Pierce.

Although Davis had not been eager to accept the presidency, he had loyally responded to the call of the provisional congress in 1861 and worked tirelessly as chief executive. As his wife observed, "the President hardly takes time to eat his meals and works late at night." Some, however, criticized this endless busyness as the result of Davis's inability to delegate details. Others found him sickly, reserved, humorless, and sensitive to criticism. He was hardly the kind of magnetic leader who might serve as a national symbol for the new nation. But Davis, like Lincoln, found it necessary to "think anew." He reassured southerners in his inaugural address that his aims were conservative, "to preserve the Government of our fathers in spirit." Yet under the pressure of events, he moved toward creating a new kind of South.

Clashing on the Battlefield, 1861–1862

The Civil War was the most brutal and destructive conflict in American history. Much of the bloodshed resulted from inadequate communications combined with changing military technology. The range of rifles had increased from 100 to 500 yards, in part owing to the new French minié bullet, which had tremendous velocity and accuracy. Because it was no longer possible to move artillery close enough to enemy lines to support an infantry charge, attacking infantry soldiers faced a 500-yard dash into deadly fire.

((•—[Hear the **Audio**

When This Cruel War Is Over

at **www.myhistorylab.com**

As it became clear that infantry charges produced horrible carnage, military leaders increasingly valued strong defensive positions. Although Confederate soldiers at first criticized General Lee as "King of Spades," the epithet evolved into one of affection as it became obvious that earthworks saved lives. Union commanders followed suit.

War in the East

The war's brutal character only gradually revealed itself. The Union's commanding general, 70-year-old Winfield Scott, initially pressed for a cautious, long-term strategy, the Anaconda Plan. Scott proposed weakening the South slowly through blockades on land and sea until the northern army was strong enough for the kill. The public, however, hungered for quick victory. So did Lincoln: He knew that the longer the war lasted, the more embittered

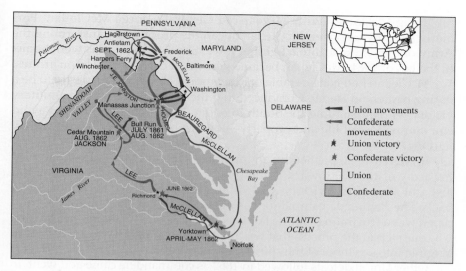

Eastern Theater of the Civil War, 1861–1862 The map reveals the military actions in the East during the early years of the war. Initially, military planners hoped to end the war quickly by capturing Richmond. They soon discovered that the Confederate army was too powerful to allow them an easy victory. Eventually, Lincoln decided to combine military pressure on Virginia with efforts in the West.

the South and the North would both become, making reunion ever more difficult. So 35,000 partially trained men led by General Irwin McDowell left Washington in sweltering July weather, heading for Richmond.

On July 21, 1861, only 25 miles from the capital at Manassas Creek (also called **Bull Run**), inexperienced northern troops confronted 25,000 raw Confederate soldiers commanded by Brigadier General P. G. T. Beauregard, a West Point classmate of McDowell's. Although sightseers, journalists, and politicians gaily accompanied the Union troops, Bull Run was no picnic. The battle was inconclusive until the arrival of 2,300 fresh Confederate troops, brought by trains, decided the day. Terrified and bewildered Union soldiers and sightseers fled toward Washington. Defeated though the Union forces were, inexperienced Confederate troops failed to turn the rout into a quick, decisive victory. As General Joseph E. Johnston pointed out, his men were disorganized, confused by victory, and insufficiently supplied with food to pursue the Union army to Washington.

In many ways, the Battle of Bull Run was prophetic. Victory would be neither quick nor easy. Both armies were unprofessional. Both sides faced problems with short-term enlistments and with the logistical problems involved in moving and supplying the largest American armies ever put in the field.

South Carolinian Robert Allston viewed the battlefield at Bull Run and decided it had been a "glorious tho bloody" day. For the Union, the loss was sobering. Lincoln began his search for a winning commander by replacing McDowell with 34-year-old General George McClellan. Formerly an army engineer, McClellan began the process of transforming the Army of the Potomac into a fighting force. Short-term militias went home. In the fall of 1861, McClellan became general in chief of the Union armies.

McClellan had considerable organizational ability but no desire to be a daring battlefield leader. Convinced that the North must combine military victory with persuading the South to rejoin the Union, he sought to avoid embittering loss of life and property—to win "by maneuvering rather than fighting."

In March 1862, pushed by an impatient Lincoln, McClellan finally led his army of 130,000 toward Richmond, now the Confederate capital. But just as it seemed that victory was within grasp, Lee drove the Union forces back. The Peninsula campaign was abandoned. For the Union, the campaign was a frustrating failure. For Lee, the success in repelling the invasion was one step in the process that was making him and the Army of Northern Virginia into a symbol of the spirit of the new nation.

Other Union defeats followed in 1862 as commanders came and went. In September, the South took the offensive with a bold invasion of Maryland. But after a costly defeat at **Antietam**, in which more than 5,000 soldiers were slaughtered and another 17,000 wounded on the grisliest day of the war, Lee withdrew to Virginia. The war in the East was stalemated.

War in the West

The early struggle in the East focused on Richmond, the Confederacy's capital and one of the South's most important railroad, industrial, and munitions centers. But the East was only one of three theaters. Between the Appalachians and the Mississippi lay the western theater. The Mississippi River, with its vital river trade and its great port, New Orleans, was a major strategic objective. Here both George Eagleton and Arthur Carpenter served. Beyond lay the trans-Mississippi West—Louisiana, Arkansas, Missouri, Texas, and the Great Plains—where Native American tribes joined the conflict on both sides.

Union objectives in the West were twofold. The army sought to dominate Kentucky and eastern Tennessee, the avenues to the South and West, and to win control of the Mississippi in order to split the South in two.

In the western theater, Ulysses S. Grant rose to prominence. His modest military credentials included education at West Point, service in the Mexican-American War, and an undistinguished stint in the peacetime army. After his resignation, he went bankrupt. Shortly after Fort Sumter, Grant enlisted as a colonel in an Illinois militia regiment. Within two months, he was a brigadier general. He proved to be a military genius, able to see beyond individual battles to larger goals. In 1862, he realized that the Tennessee and Cumberland rivers offered pathways for the successful invasion of Tennessee. A premature Confederate invasion of Kentucky allowed Grant to bring his forces into that state without arousing sharp local

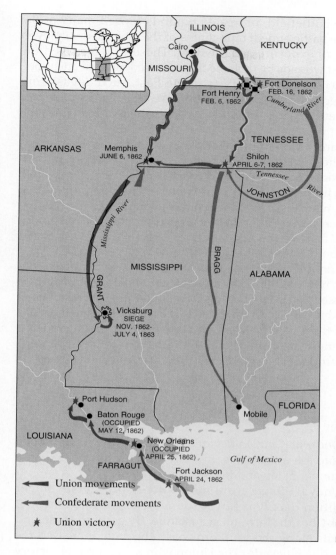

Trans-Mississippi Campaign of the Civil War What does this map suggest about the objectives of the Union campaigns in the Mississippi valley and the ultimate goal of Union military strategy there?

opposition. Assisted by gunboats, Grant was largely responsible for the capture of Fort Henry and Fort Donelson, key points on the rivers, in February 1862. His successes there raised fears among Confederate leaders that southern mountaineers, loyal to the Union, would rush to Grant's support.

Despite Grant's grasp of strategy, his army was nearly destroyed by a surprise Confederate attack at Shiloh Church in Tennessee. The North won, but at enormous cost. In that two-day engagement, the Union suffered over 13,000 casualties, while 10,000 Confederates lay dead or wounded. More American men fell in this single battle than in the American Revolution, the War of 1812, and the Mexican-American War combined. Because neither army offered sufficient care on the battlefield, untreated wounds caused many of the deaths. A day after the battle ended, nine-tenths of the wounded still lay in the rain, many dying of exposure or drowning. Those who survived the downpour had infected wounds by the time they received medical attention.

Though more successful than efforts in the East, such devastating Union campaigns failed to bring decisive results. Western plans were never coordinated with eastern military activities. Victories there did not force the South to its knees.

The war in the trans-Mississippi West was a sporadic, far-flung struggle. California was the prize that lured both armies into the Southwest. Confederate Texan troops held Albuquerque and Santa Fe briefly in 1862, but a mixed force, including volunteer soldiers from the Colorado mining fields and Mexican Americans, drove them out. A Union force recruited in California arrived after the Confederates were gone. It spent the remainder of the Civil War years fighting the Apache and the Navajo, and with brutal competence crushed both Native American nations.

Farther east was another prize, the Missouri River, which flowed into the Mississippi River, bordered Illinois, and affected military campaigns in Kentucky and Tennessee. Initially, Confederate troops were successful here, as they had been in New Mexico. But in March 1862, at Pea Ridge in northern Arkansas, Union forces whipped a Confederate army that included a brigade of Native Americans from the Five Civilized Nations. Missouri entered the Union camp for the first time in the war, but fierce guerrilla warfare continued.

Naval Warfare

At the beginning of the war, Lincoln decided to strangle the South with a naval blockade. But success was elusive. In 1861, the navy intercepted only about one blockade runner in ten and in 1862, one in eight.

Other northern naval efforts were more successful. In November 1861, a Union expedition took Port Royal Sound, where it freed the first slaves, and the nearby South Carolina sea islands. By gaining these and other important points along the southern coast, the navy increased the possibility of an effective blockade. The Union won a major naval victory with the capture of the South's biggest port, New Orleans, in 1862. The success of this amphibious effort stimulated other joint attempts to cut the South in two.

The Confederates, recognizing that they could not match the Union fleet, concentrated on developing new weapons like torpedoes and ironclad vessels. The *Merrimac* was one key to southern naval strategy. Originally a U.S. warship that had sunk as the federal navy hurriedly abandoned the Norfolk Navy Yard early in the war, the Confederates raised the vessel and covered it with heavy iron armor. Rechristened the *Virginia*, the ship steamed out of Norfolk in March 1862, heading directly for the Union ships blocking the harbor. Using its 1,500-pound ram and guns, the *Virginia* drove one-third of the vessels aground and destroyed the squadron's largest ships. But the victory was short-lived. The next day, the *Virginia* confronted the *Monitor*, a newly completed Union iron vessel. They dueled inconclusively, and the *Virginia* withdrew. It was burned during the evacuation of Norfolk that May. Southern attempts to buy ironclad ships abroad faded and, with them, southern hopes of escaping the northern noose.

Confederate attacks on northern commerce enjoyed some success. Southern raiders, many of them built in Britain, wreaked havoc on northern shipping. In its two-year career, the *Alabama* destroyed 69 Union merchant vessels valued at more than $6 million. But such blows did not seriously damage the North's war effort.

Thus the first two years brought victories to both sides, but the war remained deadlocked. The South was far from defeated; the North was equally far from giving up. Costs in manpower and supplies drastically exceeded what either side had expected.

Cotton Diplomacy

Both sides realized that attitudes in Europe could be decisive. Diplomatic recognition would give the Confederacy international credibility, and European loans and assistance might bring the South victory—just as French and Dutch aid had helped the American colonies win independence. If the European powers refused to recognize the South, however, the fiction of the Union was kept alive. Such a refusal undermined both long-term Confederate survival and the critical process of knitting the Confederacy together as one nation. European powers, of course, consulted their own interests. Neither Britain nor France wished to back a loser. Nor did they wish to upset Europe's delicate balance of power by hasty intervention in American affairs. One by one, therefore, the European states declared neutrality.

Southerners were sure that cotton would be their trump card. British and French textile mills needed cotton, and southerners believed that their owners would eventually force their governments to recognize the Confederacy and to end the northern blockade. But a glut of cotton in 1860 and 1861 left foreign mill owners oversupplied. As stockpiles dwindled, European industrialists found cotton in India and Egypt. The faith that cotton was "king" was unfounded.

Union Secretary of State Seward's goal was to prevent diplomatic recognition of the Confederacy. The North had its own economic ties with Europe, so the Union was not as disadvantaged as southerners thought. Seward threatened Great Britain with war if it interfered. Some called his boldness reckless, but it succeeded. Although Britain allowed the construction of Confederate raiders in its ports, it did not intervene in American affairs in 1861 or 1862. Nor did the other powers. Unless the military situation changed dramatically, Europeans would sit on the sidelines.

Common Problems, Novel Solutions

As the conflict dragged on into 1863, unanticipated problems arose. In response, Union and Confederate leaders devised novel approaches to solve them.

One challenge of the long conflict was monetary. Both treasuries had been empty initially, and the war proved extraordinarily expensive. Neither side considered imposing direct taxes, which would have alienated support, but both introduced taxation on a small scale. Ultimately, taxes financed 21 percent of the North's war expenses but only 1 percent of southern expenses. Both treasuries also tried borrowing. Northerners purchased over $2 billion worth of bonds, but southerners proved reluctant to buy their government's securities. As in the American Revolution, printing paper money provided the unwelcome solution. In August 1861, the Confederacy put into circulation $100 million in crudely engraved bills. Millions more followed the next year. Five months later, the Union issued $150 million in paper money, soon nicknamed "**greenbacks**." The result of this paper money policy was inflation. Inflation was particularly bad in the Confederacy, but even a "modest" 80 percent increase in food prices brought Union city families near starvation and contributed to wartime urban misery.

Both sides faced manpower problems as initial enthusiasm for the war evaporated. Soldiering, with its carnage and deadly diseases along with the

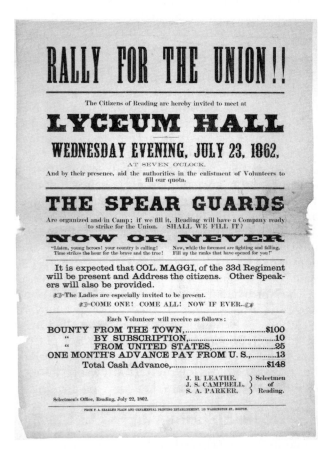

Recruiting the Troops This 1862 poster invites "one" and "all" to come to the rally in Reading, Massachusetts. While there would be speeches and perhaps even patriotic music, the point of the meeting was to fill the town's military quota with "volunteers." How does the poster encourage young men to enlist? Can you discover how much $148 would be worth today?

boredom of life in camp, was nothing like militia parades familiar to most American males. Those in the service longed to go home. The swarm of volunteers disappeared. Rather than filling their military quotas from within, rich northern communities began offering bounties of $800 to $1,000 to outsiders who would join up.

Arthur Carpenter's letters give a good picture of life in the ranks and his growing disillusionment with the war. As Carpenter's regiment moved into Kentucky and Tennessee in 1862, his spirits sank. "Soldiering in Kentucky and Tennessee is not so pretty as it was in Indianapolis. . . . We have been half starved, half frozen, and half drowned. The mud in Kentucky is awful." Soldiering often meant marching with 50 or 60 pounds of equipment and insufficient food, water, or supplies. One blanket was insufficient in the winter. In the summer, stifling woolen uniforms attracted lice. Poor food, bugs, inadequate sanitation, and exposure invited disease. Carpenter marched through Tennessee suffering from diarrhea and fever. His regiment left him behind in a convalescent barracks in Louisville, which he fled as soon as he could. "[Ninety-nine] Surgeons out of a hundred," he wrote his parents, "would not know whether his patient had the horse distemper, lame toe, or any other disease."

Confederate soldiers, even less well supplied than their northern foes, complained similarly. In 1862, a Virginia captain described what General Lee called the best army "the world ever saw":

> During our forced marches and hard fights, the soldiers have been compelled to throw away their knapsacks and there is scarcely a private in the army who has a change of clothing of any kind. Hundreds of men are perfectly barefooted and there is no telling when they can be supplied with shoes.

Such circumstances often led to desertion. An estimated one of every nine Confederate soldiers and one of every seven Union troopers deserted.

As manpower problems became critical, both governments resorted to the draft. Despite sacrosanct states' rights, the Confederate Congress passed the first conscription act in American history in March 1862. Four months later, the Union Congress also approved a draft measure. Both laws encouraged men already in the army to reenlist and sought volunteers rather than men forced to serve. Ultimately, over 30 percent of the Confederate army and 6 percent of the Union forces were draftees. The South relied more heavily on the draft because the North's manpower pool was larger and growing. During the war, 180,000 foreigners of military age poured into the northern states. Some came specifically to claim bounties and fight. Immigrants made up at least 20 percent of the Union army.

Although necessary, draft laws were very unpopular. The first Confederate conscription declared all able-bodied men between the ages of 18 and 35 eligible for military service but allowed numerous exemptions and the purchase of substitutes. The exemption from military service granted to every planter with more than 20 slaves fed class tension and encouraged disloyalty and desertion, particularly among mountaineers. The advice one woman shouted after her husband as he was dragged off to the army was hardly unique: "You desert again, quick as you kin. . . . Desert, Jake!"

Northern legislation was neither more popular nor more fair. The 1863 draft allowed the hiring of substitutes, and $300 bought an exemption from military service. Workers, already suffering from inflation, resented the ease with which moneyed citizens could avoid army duty. In July 1863, the resentment boiled over in New York City in the largest civil disturbance of the nineteenth century, a three-day riot that erupted a month after a work stoppage on the New York waterfront. Events spun out of control as a mob (mainly Irish workmen) burned draft records and the armory, plundered the houses of the rich, and looted jewelry stores. Blacks, hated as economic competitors and the cause of the war, became special targets. Mobs beat and lynched blacks and burned the Colored Orphan Asylum. More than 100 people died. There was much truth in the accusation that the war on both sides was a rich man's war but a poor man's fight.

Political Dissension, 1862

As the war continued, rumbles of dissension grew louder. On February 24, 1862, the *Richmond Examiner* summarized many southerners' frustration. "The Confederacy has had everything that was required for success but one, and that one thing it was and is supposed to possess more than anything else, namely Talent." Criticism of Confederate leaders mounted. Vice President Alexander Stephens became one of the administration's most bitter accusers.

Because the South had no party system, dissatisfaction with Davis's handling of the war tended to be factional, petty, and personal. Detractors rarely offered alternative policies. Without a party leader's traditional weapons and rewards, Davis had no mechanism to generate political support.

Although Lincoln has since become a folk hero, at the time of the Civil War, many northerners derided his performance. Peace Democrats, called **Copperheads**, claimed that Lincoln betrayed the Constitution and that working-class Americans bore the brunt of his conscription policy. Immigrant workers in eastern cities and citizens in the southern Midwest had little sympathy for abolitionism or blacks, and they supported the antiwar Copperheads. Even pro-war Democrats found Lincoln arbitrary and tyrannical, and worried that extremist Republicans would push Lincoln into making the war an antislavery crusade. Some Republicans judged Lincoln indecisive and inept.

Republicans were themselves divided. Moderates favored a cautious approach toward winning the war, fearing the possible consequences of emancipating slaves, confiscating Confederate property, or arming blacks. The radicals, however, urged Lincoln to make emancipation a wartime objective. They sought a victory that would revolutionize southern social and racial arrangements. The reduction of the congressional Republican majority in the fall elections of 1862 made it imperative that Lincoln heed both factions as well as the Democratic opposition.

The Tide Turns, 1863–1865

Harsh political realities and Lincoln's sense of the public's mood help explain why he delayed action on emancipation until 1863. Many northerners supported a war for the Union, not for emancipation. Most whites saw blacks as inferior and feared that emancipation would lure former slaves north to steal white jobs and political rights. Northern urban race riots dramatized white attitudes.

The Emancipation Proclamation, 1863

If the president moved too fast on emancipation, he risked losing the allegiance of northern racists, offending the border states, and increasing the Democrats' chances for political victory. Moreover, he at first hoped that pro-Union sentiment would emerge in the South and compel its leaders to abandon their rebellion. But if Lincoln did not move at all, he would alienate abolitionists and lose the support of radical Republicans, which he could ill afford.

So Lincoln proceeded cautiously. At first, he thought the border states might take the initiative. In the early spring of 1862, he urged Congress to pass a joint resolution offering federal compensation to states beginning a

A French View of Emancipation This depiction of African Americans celebrating the Emancipation Proclamation appeared in the French publication *Le Monde Illustre*. How has the artist provided a triumphant and sympathetic picture of rejoicing freed people? What does this picture, published in France, suggest about the diplomatic importance to the Union cause of the Emancipation Proclamation?

"gradual abolishment of slavery." Border state opposition killed the idea. Abolitionists and northern blacks, however, greeted Lincoln's proposal with a "thrill of joy."

That summer, Lincoln told his cabinet he intended to emancipate the slaves. Secretary of State Seward urged the president to delay any general proclamation until the North won a decisive military victory. Otherwise, Lincoln would appear to be urging racial insurrection behind the Confederate lines to compensate for northern military bungling. Lincoln took Seward's advice, using the summer and fall to prepare the North for the shift in the war's purpose. To counteract white fears of free blacks, he promoted schemes for establishing black colonies in Haiti and Panama. In August, Horace Greeley, the influential abolitionist editor of the New York *Tribune,* printed an open letter to Lincoln attacking him for failing to act on slavery. Replying, Lincoln linked emancipation to military necessity:

> If I could save the Union without freeing any slave, I would do it; and if I could save it by freeing all the slaves, I would do it; and if I could do it by freeing some and leaving others alone, I would also do that. What I do about Slavery and the colored race, I do because I believe it helps to save this Union.

If Lincoln attacked slavery, then, it would be only because emancipation would save white lives, preserve the democratic process, and restore the Union.

In September 1862, the Union victory at Antietam gave Lincoln the opportunity to issue a preliminary emancipation proclamation. It stated that unless rebellious states (or parts of states in rebellion) returned to the Union by January 1, 1863, the president would declare their slaves "forever free." Although supposedly aimed at bringing the southern states back into the Union, Lincoln never expected the South to lay down arms after two years of bloodshed. Rather, he was preparing northerners to accept the eventuality of emancipation on the grounds of necessity. Frederick Douglass greeted the president's action with jubilation. But not all northerners shared Douglass's joy. The September proclamation probably harmed Republicans in the fall elections.

Although the elections of 1862 weakened the Republicans' grasp on the national government, they did not destroy it. Still, cautious cabinet members begged Lincoln to forget about emancipation. His refusal demonstrated his vision and humanity. So did his efforts to reduce racial fears. "Is it dreaded that the freed people will swarm forth and cover the whole land?" he asked. "Are they not already in the land? Will liberation make them any more numerous? Equally distributed among the whites of the whole country, and there would be but one colored to seven whites. Could the one, in any way, greatly disturb the other?"

Finally, on New Year's Day, 1863, Lincoln issued the final **Emancipation Proclamation** as he had promised. It was an "act of justice, warranted by the Constitution upon military necessity." Thus, what began as a war to save the Union became a struggle that, if victorious, would free the slaves. Yet the proclamation had no immediate impact on slavery. It affected only slaves living in the unconquered portions of the Confederacy and said nothing about slaves in the border states and in parts of the South already in northern hands. These limitations led Elizabeth Cady Stanton and Susan B. Anthony to establish the Woman's Loyal National League to lobby Congress to emancipate all southern slaves.

Yet the Emancipation Proclamation had a tremendous symbolic importance. On New Year's Day, blacks gathered outside the White House to cheer the president and tell him that if he would "come out of that palace, they would hug him to death." They realized that the proclamation had transformed the nature of the war. For the first time, the government had committed itself to freeing slaves. Jubilant blacks could only believe that the president's action heralded a new era for their race. More immediately, the proclamation sanctioned the policy of accepting blacks as soldiers. Blacks also hoped that the news would reach southern slaves, encouraging them either to flee to Union lines or subvert the southern war effort.

Diplomatic concerns also lay behind the Emancipation Proclamation. Lincoln and his advisers anticipated that the commitment to abolish slavery would favorably impress foreign powers. European statesmen did not abandon their cautious stance toward the Union. However, important segments of the British public who opposed slavery now came to regard any attempt to help the South as immoral. Foreigners could better understand and sympathize with a war to free the slaves than they could with a war to save the Union. In diplomacy, where image is so important, Lincoln had created a more attractive picture of the North. The Emancipation Proclamation became the North's symbolic call for human freedom.

Unanticipated Consequences of War

The Emancipation Proclamation was but one example of the war's surprising consequences. In the final two years of the war, both North and South experimented on the battlefields and behind the lines in desperate efforts to win.

One of the Union's experiments involved using black troops in combat. Blacks had offered themselves as soldiers in 1861 but had been rejected. They were serving as cooks, laborers, teamsters, and carpenters in the army, however, and composed as much as a quarter of the navy. As white casualties mounted, so did pressure for black service on the battlefield. The Union government allowed states to escape draft quotas if they enlisted enough volunteers, and they allowed them to count southern black enlistees on their state rosters. Northern governors grew increasingly interested in black military service.

Anticipating blacks' postwar interests, Frederick Douglass pressed for military service. "Once let the black man get upon his person the brass letter, U.S., let him get an eagle on his button, and a musket on his shoulder and bullets in his pocket," Douglass believed, "there is no power on earth that can deny that he has earned the right to citizenship." By the war's end, 186,000 blacks (10 percent of the army) had served the Union cause, 134,111 of them fugitives from slave states.

But the black experience in the army highlighted some of the obstacles to racial acceptance. Black soldiers, usually led by white officers, were second-class soldiers for most of the war, receiving lower pay, poorer food, often more menial work, and fewer benefits than whites. Even whites working to equalize black and white pay often considered blacks inferior.

The army's racial experiment had mixed results. But the faithful and courageous service of black troops helped modify some of the most demeaning white racial stereotypes of blacks. The black soldiers who conquered the South, many of them former slaves, felt pride and dignity. Wrote one, "We march through these fine thoroughfares where once the slave was forbid being out after nine P.M. . . . Negro soldiers!—with banners floating."

As the conflict continued, basic assumptions about how it should be waged weakened. One wartime casualty was the courtly idea that war involved only armies. Early in the war, many officers tried to protect civilians and their property. Such concern for rebel property soon vanished. Southern troops, on the few occasions when they came North, also lived off the land.

Changing Military Strategies, 1863–1865

In the early war years, southern strategy combined defense with selected maneuvers. Until the summer of 1863, the strategy seemed to be succeeding, at least in the East. But an occasional victory over the invading northern army, such as at Fredericksburg in December 1862, did not change the course of the war. Realizing this, Lee concluded, "There is nothing to be gained by this army remaining quietly on the defensive." Without victories in the North, he believed, it could not prevail.

In the summer of 1863, Lee led the Confederate army of northern Virginia into Maryland and southern Pennsylvania. His goal was a victory that would threaten Philadelphia and Washington; he even dreamed of capturing a northern city. Such feats would surely win diplomatic recognition and might force the North to sue for peace.

At **Gettysburg** on a hot and humid July 1, Lee confronted a Union army led by General George Meade. During three days of fighting, the fatal obsession with the infantry charge returned as Lee ordered costly assaults that probably lost him the battle. On July 3, Lee sent about 15,000 men against the Union center. The assault, known as Pickett's Charge, was gallant but futile. At 700 yards, the Union artillery opened fire. One southern officer described the scene: "Pickett's division just seemed to melt away in the blue musketry smoke which now covered the hill. Nothing but stragglers came back."

●◦●─Read the Document

Abraham Lincoln, The Gettysburg Address *(1863)*

at **www.myhistorylab.com**

Despite his losses, Lee did procure the food and fodder he needed and captured thousands of prisoners. Gettysburg was a defeat, but neither Lee, nor his men, nor southern civilians regarded it as conclusive. Fighting would continue for another year and a half. In 1864, one high army officer revealed his continuing belief in the struggle's outcome. "Our hearts are full of hope," he wrote. "Oh! I do pray that we may be established as an independent people, . . . [and] recognized as God's Peculiar People!" While many remained hopeful, Lee's Gettysburg losses were so heavy that he could never mount another southern offensive.

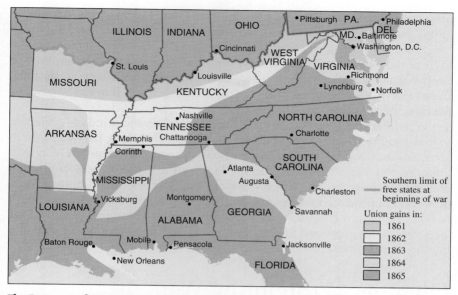

The Progress of War, 1861–1865 In this map you can see the very slow progression of the North's effort to defeat the South. For much of the war, the South controlled large areas of contiguous territory. This control of the southern homeland helped southerners to feel that it was possible for them to win the war. At what point in time might the realities depicted in this map have made southerners decide their cause was lost?

Despite the Gettysburg victory, Lincoln was dissatisfied with General Meade, who had failed to finish off Lee's retreating army. His disappointment faded with news of a great victory on July 4 at Vicksburg in the western theater. The capture of the city completed the Union campaign to gain control of the Mississippi River and to divide the South. Ulysses S. Grant, who was responsible for the victory, demonstrated the boldness and flexibility that Lincoln had been looking for in a commander.

By the summer of 1863, the military situation finally looked promising for the North. The Union controlled much of Arkansas, Louisiana, Mississippi, Missouri, Kentucky, and Tennessee. In March 1864, Lincoln appointed Grant general in chief of all Union armies. Grant planned for victory within a year. "The art of war is simple enough," he reasoned. "Find out where your enemy is. Get at him as soon as you can. Strike at him as hard as you can, and keep moving on."

As an outsider to the prewar military establishment, Grant had no difficulty rejecting conventional military wisdom: "If men make war in slavish observance of rules, they will fail." He sought not one decisive engagement but rather a grim campaign of annihilation, using the North's superior resources to grind down the South. Although Grant's plan entailed large casualties on both sides, he justified it by arguing that "now the carnage was to be limited to a single year."

A campaign of annihilation involved the destruction not only of enemy armies but also of enemy resources. Although the idea of cutting the enemy off from needed supplies was implicit in the naval blockade, economic or "total" warfare was a relatively new and shocking idea. Grant, however, "regarded it as humane to both sides to protect the persons of those found at their homes, but to consume everything that could be used to support or supply armies." Following this policy, he set out after Lee's army in Virginia. General William Tecumseh Sherman, striking from Tennessee toward Atlanta, refined this plan.

War, Sherman believed, must also be waged on the minds of civilians, to make southerners "fear and dread" their foes. Therefore, his campaign to seize Atlanta and his march to Savannah spread destruction and terror. Ordered to forage "liberally" on the land, his army left desolation in its wake. This destruction, with its goal of total victory, showed once more how conflict produced the unexpected. The war that both North and South had hoped would be quick and relatively painless was ending after four long years with great cost to both sides. But the grimness of warfare during that final year threatened Lincoln's hopes for reconciliation.

Changes Wrought by War

As bold new tactics emerged both on and off the battlefield, both governments took steps that changed their societies in surprising ways. Of the two, the South, which had left the Union to preserve a traditional way of life, experienced the more radical transformation.

A New South

The expansion of the central government's power in the South, starting with the passage of the 1862 Conscription Act, continued in the last years of the war. States' rights had inspired secession, but winning demanded centralization. Many southerners denounced Davis as a despot because he recognized the need for the central government to take the lead. Despite the accusations, the Confederate Congress cooperated with him and established important precedents, including serious interference with property rights. For example, government impressment of slaves for war work in 1863 affected the very form of private property that had originally driven the South from the Union.

The Conscription Act of 1862 did not solve the Confederate army's manpower problems. By 1864, the southern armies were only one-third the size of the Union forces. Hence, in February 1864, an expanded conscription measure made all white males between the ages of 17 and 50 subject to the draft. By 1865, the necessities of war had led to the unthinkable: arming slaves as soldiers. Black companies were recruited, but the war was over before any blacks could fight for the Confederacy.

In a message sent to Congress in November 1864, Davis speculated on some of the issues involved in arming slaves. "Should a slave who had served his country" be kept in servitude, he wondered, "or should his emancipation be held out to him as a reward for faithful service, or should it be granted at once on the promise of such service . . . ?" The South had begun the war to preserve slavery but ended it contemplating emancipation.

Southern agriculture also changed under the pressure of war. Earlier, the South had imported food from the North, concentrating on producing cotton and tobacco for market. Now, more and more land was turned over to food crops. Some farmers voluntarily shifted crops, but others responded only to state laws reducing the acreage permitted for cotton and tobacco cultivation. These measures raised enough food to feed southerners adequately, but they helped dramatically cut the production of cotton.

The South had always depended on imported manufactured goods. Although some blockade runners evaded Union ships, the noose tightened after 1862. The Confederacy could not, in any case, rely on blockade runners to equip the army. Thus, war triggered the expansion of military-related industries in the South. Here, too, the government played a crucial role. The war and navy offices directed industrial development, awarding contracts to private manufacturing firms like Richmond's Tredegar Iron Works and operating other factories themselves. The number of southerners working in industry rose dramatically. At the end of the war, rebel soldiers were better supplied with arms and munitions than with food.

Although the war did not transform the southern class structure, relations between the classes began to change. The pressures of the struggle undermined white solidarity, based on racism, and the supposed political unanimity that masked class differences. Draft resistance and desertion reflected growing alienation from a war perceived as serving only the interests of plantation owners. More and more yeoman families suffered grinding poverty as the men went to war and officials requisitioned resources.

The Victorious North

Although changes in the South were more noticeable, the Union's government and economy also responded to the demands of war. Like Davis, Lincoln was accused of being a dictator. Although he rarely tried to control Congress, veto its legislation, or direct government departments, Lincoln freely exercised executive power. He violated the writ of habeas corpus by locking up more than 13,000 northerners without trials; he curbed press freedom by suppressing supposedly disloyal and inflammatory articles; he established conscription; he issued the Emancipation Proclamation; and he fired generals. Lincoln argued that this vast extension of presidential power was temporarily justified because, as president, he was responsible for defending and preserving the Constitution.

Many changes in government proved more permanent than Lincoln had imagined. Wartime financial necessities helped revolutionize the country's banking system. Ever since Jackson's destruction of the Bank of the United States, state banks had served American financial needs. Treasury Secretary Chase found this system inadequate and chaotic and proposed to

RECOVERING *the* PAST

Photography

The invention of photography in 1839 expanded the visual and imaginative world of nineteenth-century Americans. For the first time, Americans could visually record events in their own lives and see the images of unfamiliar people and places. Photographs also expand the boundaries of the historian's world. As photographic techniques became simpler, more and more visual information about the nineteenth century was captured. Historians can use photographs to discover many aspects of daily life: what people wore; how they celebrated events like marriages and funerals; what their families, houses, and cities looked like. Pictures of election campaigns, parades, strikes, and wars show the texture of public life. But historians also study photographs, as they do paintings, to glean information about attitudes and values. The choice of subjects, the way in which people and objects are arranged, and the relationships between people in the photographs all provide clues to the social and cultural values of the past.

Some knowledge of the early history of photography helps place the visual evidence in the proper perspective. The earliest type of photograph, the daguerreotype, was not a print but the negative itself on a sheet of silver-plated copper. The first daguerreotypes required between 15 and 30 minutes for the proper exposure. The long exposure time explains why nineteenth-century images often seem stiff and formal. Glass ambrotypes (negatives on glass) and tintypes (negatives on gray iron bases), developed after the daguerreotypes, were easier and cheaper to produce. But both techniques produced only one picture and required what to us would seem an interminable time for exposure.

A major breakthrough came in the 1850s with the development of the wet-plate process. In this process, the photographer coated a glass negative with a sensitive solution, exposed the negative (that is, took the picture), and then quickly developed it. The new procedure required a relatively short exposure time of about five seconds outside and one minute indoors. The resulting photographs looked more natural, but action shots were not yet possible. The entire process tied the photographer to the darkroom. Traveling photographers carried their darkrooms with them. The advantage of the wet-plate process was that it was possible to make many paper prints from one negative, opening new commercial vistas for professional photographers.

Mathew Brady, a fashionable Washington photographer, realizing that the camera was the "eye of history," asked Lincoln for permission to record the war with his camera. He and his team of photographers left about 8,000 glass negatives, currently stored in the Library of Congress and the National Archives, as their record of the Civil War. Shown are two photographs. In the photograph entitled "Confederate Captives," study and describe the soldiers. How are they posed? What kinds of clothes are they wearing? What do you notice about their equipment? Their health? This one photograph just begins to suggest what can be discovered through the study of images. In family attics and cellars, there may well be photograph albums that, when examined carefully, will reveal many aspects of your own family's history.

The second picture was taken in April 1865, about a year after the battle at Cold Harbor. In the background, you can see two Union soldiers digging graves. In the foreground are the grisly remains of the battle. What do you think is the intent of the photograph? The choice of subject matter shows clearly that photography reveals attitudes as well as facts. Why is the burial taking place a full year after the battle? What does this tell us about the nature of civil warfare? Notice that the soldiers ordered to undertake this ghastly chore are black, as was customary. What might this scene suggest about the experience of black soldiers in the Union army?

Top: Mathew Brady, "Confederate Captives," Gettysburg. **Bottom:** Mathew Brady, "Burial Party at Cold Harbor."

REFLECTING ON THE PAST Using these photographs as evidence, what might you conclude about the southern soldiers' physical condition? What attitudes are conveyed through the men's facial expressions and poses? What kind of mood was the northern photographer trying to create? What attitude toward war and death is conveyed?

replace it. In 1863 and 1864, Congress reestablished a federal banking system by passing legislation that set up a national currency issued by federally chartered banks and backed by government bonds.

Northern agriculture expanded to feed soldiers and civilians, and so did investment in farm machinery. With so many men off soldiering, farmers were short of labor. Mechanical reapers performed the work of four to six men, and farmers began to buy them; McCormick sold 165,000 during the war. Northern farming, especially in the Midwest, was well on the way to becoming mechanized. Farmers even accumulated a surplus for export.

The war selectively stimulated manufacturing, although overall it retarded economic growth by consuming rather than generating wealth. Between 1860 and 1870, the annual rate of increase in real manufacturing value added was only 2.3 percent, in contrast with 7.8 percent for the years between 1840 and 1860 and 6 percent for the period from 1870 to 1900. However, war industries, especially those with advantages of scale, expanded and made large profits. Each year, the Union army required 1.5 million uniforms and 3 million pairs of shoes; the woolen and leather industries grew accordingly. Meatpackers and producers of iron, steel, and pocket watches all profited from wartime opportunities.

On the Home Front, 1861–1865

Events on the battlefield were intimately connected to life behind the lines. As both northern and southern leaders realized, civilian morale was crucial to the war's outcome. If civilians lost faith, they would lack the will to continue the conflict.

The war stimulated religious efforts to generate enthusiasm and loyalty on the home front. On both sides, Protestant clergymen threw themselves behind the war effort. As northern preacher Henry Ward Beecher proclaimed, "God hates lukewarm patriotism as much as lukewarm religion, and we hate it too." Southern ministers gave similar messages and urged southerners to reform their lives, for victory could not come without moral change. In North and South, every defeat was a cause for soul searching. Fast days and revivals provided a spiritual dimension to the conflict and helped people deal with discouragement and death.

In numerous, less tangible ways, the war transformed northern and southern society. The very fact of conflict established a new perspective for most civilians. They read newspapers and national weekly magazines with a new eagerness, and used the mail often. As one North Carolina woman explained, "I never liked to write letters before, but it is a pleasure as well as a relief now." Distant events became almost as real and vivid as those at home. The war helped make Americans part of a larger world.

For some northerners like John D. Rockefeller and Andrew Carnegie, war brought unanticipated riches from army contracts. The New York *Herald* reported that New York City had never been "so gay, . . . so crowded, so prosperous," as in March 1864. Southern blockade runners made fortunes slipping in luxury goods.

The Impact of the War in the South The dislocations caused by the war were many. These southerners, forced to leave their home by invading troops, have packed what few belongings they could transport and stand ready to evacuate their homestead. How many children can you find in the picture? What does the fact that the woman in the foreground is smoking a pipe suggest about the social class of this group? *(Library of Congress)*

For the majority of Americans, however, war meant deprivation. The war effort gobbled up a large part of each side's resources and, ultimately, ordinary people suffered. To be sure, the demand for workers ended unemployment and changed employment patterns. Many women and blacks entered the workforce, as they would in all future American wars. But whereas work was easy to get, real income declined. Inflation, especially destructive in the South, was largely to blame. By 1864, eggs sold in Richmond for $6 a dozen; butter brought $25 a pound. Strikes and union organizing pointed to working-class discontent.

Low wages compounded the problem of declining income and particularly harmed women workers. Often forced into the labor market because husbands could save little or nothing from small army stipends, army wives and other women took what pay they could get. As more women entered the workforce, employers cut costs by slashing wages.

In the South, which bore the brunt of the fighting, conflict and wartime dislocation drastically affected civilian life. Most white southerners suffered shortages in food, manufactured goods, and medicine. Farming families without slaves fared poorly, but food riots in Richmond and other cities suggest that urban conditions were the most dismal. Thousands of southerners fleeing from the advancing Union armies lost their homes at least temporarily. "The country for miles around is filled with refugees," noted an officer in 1862. "Every house is crowded and hundreds are living in churches, in barns and tents." Caught up in the effort of mere survival, worried about what had happened to homes and possessions left behind, these southerners must have wondered if the cause was worth the sacrifices. Life was probably just as agonizing for those who chose to stay put when Union troops arrived.

White flight also disrupted slave life. Even the arrival of Union forces could prove a mixed blessing. White soldiers were unknown quantities and might be hostile to blacks whom they were supposed to be liberating. One slave described the upsetting arrival of the Yankees at his plantation in Arkansas: "Them folks stood round there all day. Killed hogs . . . killed cows . . . Took all kinds of sugar and preserves . . . Tore all the feathers out of the mattresses looking for money. Then they put Old Miss and her daughter in the kitchen to cooking." The next day found the Yanks gone and the Confederates back.

Throughout the South, insubordination, refusal to work, and refusal to accept punishment testified to the discontent of slaves, especially the field hands. Probably 20 percent of all slaves, many of them women, fled toward Union lines after the early months of the war. Their flight pointed to the changing nature of race relations and the harm slaves could do to the southern cause. Reflected one slave owner, "The 'faithful slave' is about played out."

Women and the War

The war made it impossible for many women to live according to conventional norms, which exalted their domestic role and minimized their economic importance. With so many men in the armies, women had to find jobs and sustain farms. During the war years, southern women who had no slaves to help with the farmwork and northern farm wives who labored without the assistance of husbands or sons carried new physical and emotional burdens.

•••—Read the Document

Chesnut Diary CW (1861)
at **www.myhistorylab.com**

Women also participated in numerous war-related activities. North and South, they entered government service in large numbers. In the North, hundreds of women became military nurses. Under the supervision of Drs. Emily and Elizabeth Blackwell; Dorothea Dix, superintendent of army nurses; and Clara Barton, northern women nursed the wounded and dying for low or even no pay. They also fought the red tape that worsened hospital conditions. In the South, men largely staffed southern military hospitals, but Confederate women played an important part in caring for the sick and wounded in their homes and in makeshift hospitals behind battle lines. Grim though the work was, many women felt that they were participating in the real world for the first time in their lives.

Women moved outside the domestic sphere in other forms of volunteer war work. Some women gained administrative experience in soldiers' aid societies and in the United States Sanitary Commission. Many others made bandages and clothes, put together packages for soldiers at the front, and helped army wives and disabled soldiers find jobs. Fund-raising activities realized substantial sums. By the end of the war, the Sanitary Commission had raised $50 million for medical supplies, nurses' salaries, and other wartime necessities.

Many of the changes women experienced during the war years ended when peace returned. Jobs disappeared when men reclaimed them. Women turned over the operation of farms to returning husbands. But for women whose men came home maimed or did not come home at all, the work had not ended. Nor had the discrimination. Trying to pick up the threads of their former lives, they found it impossible to forget what they had done in the war effort. Some of them were sure they had equaled their men in courage and commitment.

The Election of 1864

In the North, the election of 1864 brought some of the transformations of wartime into the political arena. The Democrats, capitalizing on war weariness, nominated General McClellan, branded the war a failure, and demanded an armistice. Democrats accused Lincoln of arbitrarily expanding executive power and denounced sweeping economic measures like the banking bills. Arguing that the president had transformed the war from one for Union into one for emancipation, they insinuated that a Republican victory would mean race mixing.

Although Lincoln controlled the party machinery and easily gained the Republican renomination, his party did not unite behind him. The outcome of the presidential election was much in doubt. Lincoln seemed to please no one. His veto of the radical reconstruction plan for the South, the Wade–Davis Bill, led to cries of "usurpation." The Emancipation Proclamation did not sit well with conservatives. In August 1864, a gloomy Lincoln, recognizing the many internal conflicts that divided northerners, told his cabinet that he expected to lose. As late as September, some Republicans hoped to reconvene the convention and select another candidate.

Sherman's capture of Atlanta in September 1864 and his march to Savannah helped swing voters to Lincoln. In the end, Republicans had no desire to see the Democrats oust their party. Lincoln won 55 percent of the popular vote and swept the Electoral College.

Why the North Won

In the months after Lincoln's reelection, the war drew to an agonizing conclusion. Sherman moved north from Georgia to North Carolina, while Grant pummeled Lee in Virginia. Grant's losses were staggering, but new recruits replaced the dead. On April 9, 1865, Grant accepted Lee's surrender at Appomattox. Southern soldiers and officers were allowed to go home with their personal equipment after promising to remain there peaceably. The war was over.

Grant's military strategy succeeded because the Union's manpower and economic resources could survive staggering losses of men and equipment while the Confederacy's could not. Naval strategy eventually paid off because the North could build enough ships to make its blockade work.

The South had taken tremendous steps toward satisfying war needs. But despite the impressive growth of manufacturing and food production, southern troops and southern people were poorly fed and clothed. New industries could not meet the extraordinary demands of wartime, and advancing Union forces destroyed many of them. Women working alone or with disgruntled slaves could not produce enough food. Worn-out farm equipment was not replaced. Impressments of slaves and animals and the flight to Union lines of half a million blacks cut production. A Confederate officer in northern Virginia described the consequences. "Many of our soldiers are thinly clothed and without shoes and in addition to this, very few of the infantry have tents. With this freezing weather, their sufferings are indescribable." Skimpy rations—only one-third of a pound of meat for each soldier a day by 1864—weakened the Confederate force, whose trail was "traceable by the deposit of dysenteric stool." By that time, the Union armies were so well supplied that soldiers often threw away extra blankets and coats.

The South's woefully inadequate transportation system also contributed to defeat. Primitive roads deteriorated and became all but impassable without repairs. The railroad system was inefficient. When tracks wore out or were destroyed, they were not replaced. Food intended for the army rotted awaiting shipment, while soldiers went hungry and cities rioted.

Ironically, measures that the Confederacy took to strengthen its ability to win the war, as one Texan later observed, "weakened and paralyzed it." Conscription, impressment, and taxes bred resentment and even open resistance. The proposal to use slaves as soldiers called into question the war's purpose. The many southern governors who refused to contribute men, money, and supplies on the scale Davis requested implicitly condoned disloyalty and undermined any sense of southern nationalism. The belief in states' rights and the sanctity of private property that gave birth to the Confederacy also helped kill it.

By the final months of the war, Davis had recognized how dangerous defeatism was to the Confederacy's cause. But such realization did not prompt any vigorous attempts to influence public opinion or to control internal dissent.

It is tempting to compare Lincoln and Davis as war leaders. There is no doubt that Lincoln's humanity, his awareness of the terrible costs of war, his determination to save the Union, and his eloquence set him apart as one of this country's most extraordinary presidents. Yet the men's personal characteristics were probably less important than the differences between the political and social systems of the two regions. Without the support of a party behind him, Davis failed to engender enthusiasm or loyalty. Even though the Republicans rarely united behind Lincoln, they uniformly wanted to keep the Democrats from office. Despite squabbles, Republicans tended to support Lincoln's policies in Congress and back in their home districts. Commanding considerable resources of patronage, Lincoln was able to line up federal, state, and local officials behind his party and administration.

Just as the northern political system provided Lincoln with more flexibility and support, its social system also proved more able to meet the war's extraordinary demands. Although both societies innovated to secure victory, northerners were more cooperative and disciplined. In the southern states, old attitudes impeded the war effort. Wedded to states' rights, southern governors undermined the Confederate government. When Sherman approached Atlanta, Georgia's governor would not turn over the 10,000 men in the state army to Confederate commanders. Slaveholders resisted the impressment of their slaves for war work.

Read the Document
William T. Sherman, The March Through Georgia (1875)
at **www.myhistorylab.com**

In the end, the Confederacy collapsed, exhausted and bleeding. The belief that the southern cause might triumph disappeared. Hungry soldiers got letters revealing desperate situations at home. Some were perhaps horrified by the possibility that black troops might join the struggle. Soldiers in the Army of Virginia feared that Lee, who, rather than Davis, had symbolized their new nation, might take another post. Hungry, worried, and uncertain, the men slipped away. By December 1864, the Confederate desertion rate exceeded 50 percent. Replacements could not be found. Farmers hid livestock and produce from tax collectors. Many southerners resigned themselves to defeat, but some fought to the end. One Yankee described them as they surrendered at Appomattox:

View the Image
Ruins of Atlanta (1864)
at **www.myhistorylab.com**

> Before us in proud humiliation stood the embodiment of manhood: men whom neither toils and sufferings, nor the fact of death, nor disaster, nor hopelessness could bend from their resolve; standing before us now, thin, worn, and famished, but erect, and with eyes looking level into ours, waking memories that bound us together as no other bond.

The Costs of War

The war was over, but its memories would fester for years. About 3 million American men, one-third of all free males between the ages of 15 and 59, had served in the army. Each would remember his personal history of the war. For George Eagleton, who had worked in army field hospitals, the history was one of "Death and destruction! Blood! Blood! Agony! Death! Gaping flesh wounds, broken bones, amputations, bullet and bomb fragment extractions." Of all American wars, none has been more deadly. The death rate was more than five times that of World War II. About 360,000 Union soldiers and another 258,000 Confederate soldiers died, about one-third of these because their wounds were either improperly treated or not treated at all. Disease claimed more lives than combat.

Thousands upon thousands of men would be reminded of the human costs of war by the injuries they carried with them to the grave and by the missing limbs that marked them as Civil War veterans. About 275,000 on each side were maimed. Another 410,000 (195,000 northerners and 215,000 southerners) would recall their time in wretchedly overcrowded and unsanitary prison camps. The lucky ones would remember only the boredom. The worst memory was of those who rotted in prison camps, such as Andersonville in Georgia, where 31,000 Union soldiers were confined. At the war's end, over 12,000 graves were counted there.

Some Americans found it hard to readjust to peace. As Arthur Carpenter's letters suggest, he gradually grew accustomed to army life. War provided him with a sense of purpose, and afterward he felt aimless. A year after the war's end, he wrote, "Camp life agrees with me better than any other." Many others had difficulty returning to civilian routines. Even those who adjusted successfully discovered that they looked at life from a different perspective. The experience of fighting, of mixing with all sorts of people from many places, and of traveling far from home had lifted former soldiers out of their familiar local world and widened their vision. Fighting the war made the concept of national union real.

●●●—Read the Document

Susie King Taylor, Reminiscences of an Army Laundress *(1902)* at **www.myhistorylab.com**

Unanswered Questions

What had the war accomplished? Certainly death and destruction. Physically, the war devastated the South. Historians have estimated a 43 percent decline in southern wealth during the war years, exclusive of the value of slaves. Great cities like Atlanta, Columbia, and Richmond lay in ruins. Fields were weed-choked and uncultivated. Tools were worn out. One-third or more of the South's mules, horses, and swine were gone. Two-thirds of the railroads had been destroyed. Thousands were hungry, homeless, and bitter about their four years of what now appeared useless sacrifice. More than 3 million slaves, a vast financial investment, were free.

Watch the Video

The Meaning of the Civil War for Americans at **www.myhistorylab.com**

On the other hand, the war had resolved the question of union and ended the debate over the relationship of the states to the federal government. Republicans had seized the opportunity to pass legislation that would foster national union and economic growth: the Pacific Railroad Act of 1862, which set aside huge tracts of public land to finance the transcontinental railroad; the Homestead Act of 1862, which was to provide yeoman farmers cheaper and easier access to the public domain; the Morrill Act of 1862, which established support for agricultural (land-grant) colleges; and the banking acts of 1863 and 1864.

The war had also resolved the issue of slavery that for so long had plagued American life. Yet uncertainties outnumbered certainties. What would happen to ex-slaves? When blacks had fled to Union lines, commanders had not known what to do with them. Now the problem became more pressing. Should blacks have the same civil and political rights as whites? In the Union army, they had been second-class soldiers. The behavior of Union forces toward liberated blacks in the South showed how deep the stain of racism went. Would blacks now get land and economic independence? What would be their relations with their former owners?

What, indeed, would be the status of the conquered South in the nation? Should it be punished for the rebellion? Some people thought so. Should southerners keep their property? Some people thought not. There were clues to Lincoln's intentions. As early as December 1863, the president had announced a generous plan of reconciliation. He was willing to recognize the government of former Confederate states established by a group of citizens equal to 10 percent of those voting in 1860, as long as the group swore to support the Constitution and to accept the abolition of slavery. He began to restore state governments in three former Confederate states on that basis. But some northerners disagreed with this leniency, and the debate continued.

In his 1865 inaugural address, Lincoln urged Americans to harbor "malice towards none . . . and charity for all." "Let us strive," he urged, "to finish the work we are in; to bind up the nation's wounds . . . to do all which may achieve a just and lasting peace." Privately, the president said the same thing. Generosity and goodwill would pave the way for reconciliation. On April 14, he pressed the point home to his cabinet. His wish was to avoid persecution and bloodshed. That same evening, only five days after the surrender at Appomattox, the president attended a play at Ford's Theatre. And there, said an eyewitness,

> ○○○─Read the Document
> *Abraham Lincoln,* Second
> Inaugrual Address *(1865)*
> at **www.myhistorylab.com**

> a pistol was heard and a man . . . dressed in a black suit of clothes leaped onto the stage apparently from the President's box. He held in his right hand a dagger whose blade appeared about 10 inches long. . . . Every one leaped to his feet, and the cry of "the President is assassinated" was heard—Getting where I could see into the President's box, I saw Mrs. Lincoln . . . in apparent anguish.

John Wilkes Booth had killed the president.

Conclusion
An Uncertain Future

As the war ended, many Americans grieved for the man whose decisions had so marked their lives for five years. "Strong men have wept tonight & the nation will mourn tomorrow," wrote one eyewitness to the assassination. Many more wept for friends and relations who had not survived the war, but whose actions had in one way or another contributed to its outcome. The lucky ones, like Arthur Carpenter and George and Ethie Eagleton, now faced the necessity of putting their lives back together and moving forward into an uncertain future. Perhaps not all Americans realized how drastically the war had altered their lives, their prospects, their nation. It was only as time passed that the war's impact became clear to them. And it was only with time that they recognized how many problems the war had left unsolved. It is to these years of Reconstruction that we now turn.

TIME*line*

1861	Lincoln calls up state militia and suspends habeas corpus
	First Battle of Bull Run
	Union blockades the South
1862	Battles at Shiloh, Bull Run, and Antietam
	First black regiment authorized by Union
	South institutes military draft
1863	Lincoln issues Emancipation Proclamation
	Congress adopts military draft
	Battles of Gettysburg and Vicksburg
1864	Sherman's march through Georgia
	Lincoln reelected
1865	Lee surrenders at Appomattox
	Lincoln assassinated

✓●─Study and Review at **www.myhistorylab.com**

Questions for Review and Reflection

1. Assess the strengths and weaknesses of the North and South at the beginning of the war. What northern strengths actually led to northern victory, and what Confederate weaknesses explain southern defeat?

2. What were the most important transformations in the Union and Confederacy during the war, and why, in your opinion, were these changes so significant?

3. Compare and contrast Lincoln and Davis as war leaders and the two governments over which they presided.

4. What role did race play during the war?

5. Consider the Civil War as a struggle between differing beliefs and values, and assess the importance of northern victory for this struggle. In what ways did the war's outcome realize or fail to realize the founding principles of this nation?

Key Terms

Antietam 432

Border states 427

Bull Run 431

Copperheads 438

Cotton diplomacy 435

Emancipation Proclamation 439

Fort Sumter 425

Gettysburg 442

Greenbacks 436

Radical Republicans 439

14

The Union Reconstructed

American Stories

Blacks and Whites Redefine Their Dreams and Relationships

In April 1864, a year before Lincoln's assassination, Robert Allston died, leaving his wife Adele and his daughter Elizabeth to manage their many rice plantations. With Union troops moving through coastal South Carolina in the winter of 1864–1865, Elizabeth's sorrow turned to "terror" as Union soldiers arrived and searched for liquor, firearms, and valuables. The women fled. Later, Yankee troops encouraged the Allston slaves to take furniture, food, and other goods from the Big House. Before they left, the Union soldiers gave the keys to the crop barns to the semifree blacks.

After the war, Adele Allston swore allegiance to the United States and secured a written order for the newly freed African Americans to relinquish those keys. She and Elizabeth returned in the summer of 1865 to reclaim the plantations and reassert white authority. She was assured that although the blacks had guns, "no outrage has been committed against the Whites except in the matter of property." But property was the issue. Possession of the keys to the barns, Elizabeth wrote, would be the "test case" of whether former masters or former slaves would control land, labor, and its fruits, as well as the subtle aspects of interpersonal relations.

Nervously, Adele and Elizabeth Allston confronted their ex-slaves at their old home. To their surprise, a pleasant reunion took place as the Allston women greeted the blacks by name and caught up on their lives. A trusted black foreman handed over the keys to the barns. This harmonious scene was repeated elsewhere.

But at one plantation, the Allston women met defiant and armed African Americans, who ominously lined both sides of the road as the carriage arrived. An old black driver, Uncle Jacob, was unsure whether to yield the keys to the barns full

Chapter Outline

The Bittersweet Aftermath of War

National Reconstruction Politics

The Lives of Freedpeople

Reconstruction in the Southern States

Conclusion: A Mixed Legacy

of rice and corn, put there by slave labor. Mrs. Allston insisted. As Uncle Jacob hesitated, an angry young man shouted: "If you give up the key, blood'll flow." Uncle Jacob slowly slipped the keys back into his pocket.

The African Americans sang freedom songs and brandished hoes, pitchforks, and guns to discourage anyone from going to town for help. Two blacks, however, slipped away to find some Union officers. The Allstons spent the night safely, if restlessly, in their house. Early the next morning, they were awakened by a knock at the unlocked front door. There stood Uncle Jacob. Silently, he gave back the keys.

The story of the keys reveals most of the essential human ingredients of the Reconstruction era. Defeated southern whites were determined to resume control of both land and labor. The law and federal enforcement generally supported property owners. The Allston women were friendly to the blacks in a maternal way and insisted on restoring prewar deference in black–white relations. Adele and Elizabeth, in short, both feared and cared about their former slaves.

The African American freedpeople likewise revealed mixed feelings toward their former owners: anger, loyalty, love, resentment, and pride. They paid respect to the Allstons but not to their property and crops. They wanted not revenge, but economic independence and freedom.

Northerners played a most revealing role. Union soldiers, literally and symbolically, gave the keys of freedom to the freed men and women but did not stay around long enough to guarantee that freedom. Despite initially encouraging blacks to plunder the master's house and seize the crops, in the crucial encounter after the war, northern officials had disappeared. Understanding the limits of northern help, Uncle Jacob ended up handing the keys to land and liberty back to his former owner. Before long, however, blacks realized that if they wanted to ensure their freedom, they had to do it themselves.

This chapter describes what happened to the conflicting goals and dreams of three groups as they sought to redefine new social, economic, and political relationships during the postwar Reconstruction era. Amid vast devastation and bitter race and class divisions, Civil War survivors sought to put their lives back together. But how could victorious but variously motivated northern officials, defeated but defiant southern planters, and impoverished but hopeful African Americans each fulfill their conflicting goals? The Reconstruction era would be divisive, leaving a mixed legacy of human gains and losses.

The Bittersweet Aftermath of War

"There are sad changes in store for both races," the daughter of a Georgia planter wrote in the summer of 1865. To understand the bittersweet nature of Reconstruction, we must look at the state of the nation after the assassination of President Lincoln.

The United States in April 1865

Constitutionally, the "Union" faced a crisis in April 1865. What was the status of the 11 former Confederate states? The North had denied the South's constitutional right to secede but needed four years of war and more than 600,000 deaths to win the point. Lincoln's official position had been that the southern states had never left the Union and were only "out of their proper relation" with the United States. The president, therefore, as commander in chief, had the authority to decide how to set relations right again. Lincoln's

The United States in 1865: Crises at the End of the Civil War

Given the enormous casualties, costs, and crises of the immediate aftermath of the Civil War, what attitudes, goals, dreams, and behaviors would you predict for white southerners, white northerners, and black freedpeople?

Military Casualties

360,000 Union soldiers dead
260,000 Confederate soldiers dead
620,000 Total dead
375,000 Seriously wounded and maimed
995,000 Casualties nationwide in a total male population of 15 million (nearly 1 in 15)

Physical and Economic Crises

The South devastated; its railroads, industry, and some major cities in ruins; its fields and livestock wasted

Constitutional Crisis

Eleven former Confederate states not a part of the Union, their status unclear and future states uncertain

Political Crisis

Republican party (entirely of the North) dominant in Congress; a former Democratic slaveholder from Tennessee, Andrew Johnson, in the presidency

Social Crisis

Nearly 4 million freedpeople throughout the South facing challenges of survival and freedom, along with thousands of hungry demobilized white southern soldiers and displaced white families

Psychological Crisis

Incalculable stores of resentment, bitterness, anger, and despair throughout North and South congressional opponents retorted that the ex-Confederate states were now "conquered provinces" and that Congress should resolve the constitutional issues and direct Reconstruction.

Politically, differences between Congress and the White House over Reconstruction mirrored a wider struggle between the two branches of the national government. During war, as has usually been the case, the executive branch assumed broad powers. Many believed, however, that Lincoln had far exceeded his constitutional authority, and his successor, Andrew Johnson, was worse. Would Congress reassert its authority?

In April 1865, the Republican party ruled nearly unchecked. Republicans had made immense achievements in the eyes of the northern public: winning the war, preserving the Union, and freeing the slaves. They had enacted sweeping economic programs on behalf of free labor and free enterprise. But the party remained an uneasy grouping of former Whigs, Know-Nothings, Unionist Democrats, and antislavery idealists.

The Democrats were in shambles. Republicans depicted southern Democrats as rebels, murderers, and traitors, and they blasted northern Democrats as weak-willed, disloyal, and opposed to economic growth and progress. Nevertheless, in the election of 1864, needing to show that the war was a bipartisan effort, the Republicans nominated a Tennessee Unionist Democrat, Andrew Johnson, as Lincoln's vice president. Now the tactless Johnson headed the government.

Economically, the United States in the spring of 1865 presented stark contrasts. Northern cities and railroads hummed with productive activity; southern cities and railroads lay in ruins. Southern financial institutions were bankrupt; northern banks flourished. Mechanizing northern farms were more productive than ever; southern farms and plantations, especially those along Sherman's march, resembled a "howling waste." The widespread devastation in the South affected southern attitudes. As a later southern writer explained, "If this war had smashed the Southern world, it had left the essential Southern mind and will . . . entirely unshaken." Many white southerners braced to resist Reconstruction and restore their former life and institutions; others, the minority who had remained quietly loyal to the Union, sought reconciliation.

Socially, nearly 4 million newly freedpeople faced the challenges of freedom. After initial joy and celebration in jubilee songs, freedmen and freedwomen quickly realized their continuing dependence on former owners. A Mississippi woman said:

> I used to think if I could be free I should be the happiest of anybody in the world. But when my master come to me, and says, Lizzie, you is free! it seems like I was in a kind of daze. And when I would wake up in the morning I would think to myself, Is I free? Hasn't I got to get up before day light and go into the field of work?

For Lizzie, and 4 million other blacks, everything—and nothing—had changed.

Hopes Among the Freedpeople

Throughout the South in the summer of 1865, optimism surged through the old slave quarters. The slavery chain, however, broke slowly, link by link. After Union troops swept through an area, "we'd begin celebratin'," one man said, but Confederate soldiers would follow, or master and overseer would return and "tell us to go back to work." The freedmen and women learned, therefore, not to rejoice too quickly or openly.

Gradually, though, African Americans began to test the reality of freedom. Typically, their first step was to leave the plantation, if only for a few hours or days. "If I stay here I'll never know I am free," said a South Carolina woman who went to work as a cook in a nearby town. Some freedpeople cut their ties entirely—returning to an earlier master, or, more often, going into towns and cities to find jobs, schools, churches, and association with other blacks, safe from whippings and retaliation.

((•—[Hear the **Audio**

Free at Last

at **www.myhistorylab.com**

Many blacks left the plantation in search of a spouse, parent, or child sold away years before. Advertisements detailing these sorrowful searches filled African American newspapers. For those who found a spouse or who had been living together in slave marriages, freedom meant getting married legally, sometimes in mass ceremonies common in the first months of emancipation. Legal marriage was important morally, but it also established the legitimacy of children and meant access to land titles and other economic opportunities. Marriage brought special burdens for black women,

Consequences of War
This 1867 engraving shows two southern women and their children soon after the Civil War. In what ways are they similar and in what ways different? Is there a basis for sisterhood bonds? What separates them, if anything? From *Frank Leslie's Illustrated Newspaper*, February 23, 1867.

who assumed the double role of housekeeper and breadwinner. Their determination to create a traditional family life and care for their children resulted in the withdrawal of women from plantation field labor.

Freedpeople also demonstrated their new status by choosing surnames. Names connoting independence, such as Washington, were common. Revealing their mixed feelings toward their former masters, some would adopt their master's name while others would pick "any big name 'ceptin' their master's." Emancipation changed black manners around whites as well. Masks fell, and expressions of deference—tipping a hat, stepping aside, calling whites "master" or "ma'am"—diminished. For African Americans, these changes were necessary expressions of selfhood, proving that race relations had changed; whites, however, saw such behaviors as "insolence" and "insubordination."

The freedpeople made education a priority. A Mississippi farmer vowed to "give my children a chance to go to school, for I consider education next best ting to liberty." One traveler through the South counted "at least five hundred" schools "taught by colored people." Other than a persisting desire for education, the primary goal for most freedpeople was getting land. "All I want is to git to own fo' or five acres ob land, dat I can build me a little house on and call my home," a Mississippi black said. Through a combination of educational and economic independence, basic American means of controlling one's own life, labor, and land, freedpeople like Lizzie would make sure that emancipation was real.

During the war, some Union generals had put liberated slaves in charge of confiscated and abandoned lands. In the Sea Islands of South Carolina and Georgia, blacks had been working 40-acre plots of land and harvesting their own crops for several years. Farther inland, freedmen who received land were the former slaves of the Cherokee and the Creek. Some blacks held title to these lands. Northern philanthropists had organized others to grow cotton for the Treasury Department to prove the superiority of free labor. In Mississippi, thousands of ex-slaves worked 40-acre tracts on leased lands that ironically had formerly been owned by Jefferson Davis. In this highly successful experiment, they made profits sufficient to repay the government for initial costs, then lost the land to Davis's brother.

Many freedmen and women expected a new economic order as fair payment for their years of involuntary work. "Give us our own land," said one, "and we take care ourselves; but widout land, de ole massas can hire us or starve us, as dey please." Freedmen had every expectation that "forty acres and a mule" had been promised. Once they obtained land, family unity, and education, some looked forward to civil rights and the vote—along with protection from vengeful defeated Confederates.

▶ View the Image
Freedmen at Rest on a Levee
at **www.myhistorylab.com**

The White South's Fearful Response

White southerners had equally strong dreams and expectations. Middle-class (yeoman) farmers and poor whites stood beside rich planters in bread lines, all hoping to regain land and livelihood. White southerners responded with feelings of outrage, loss, and injustice. Said one man, "My pa paid his own money for our niggers; and that's not all they've robbed us of. They have taken our horses and cattle and sheep and everything."

A dominant emotion was fear. The entire structure of southern society was shaken, and the semblance of racial peace and order that slavery had provided was shattered. Having lost control of all that was familiar, whites feared everything—from losing their cheap labor to having blacks sit next to them on trains. Ironically, given the rape of black women during slavery, southern whites' worst fears were of rape and revenge. African American "impudence," some thought, would lead to legal intermarriage and "Africanization," the destruction of the purity of the white race. African American Union soldiers seemed especially ominous. These fears were greatly exaggerated, as demobilization of black soldiers came quickly, and rape and violence by blacks against whites was extremely rare.

Believing their world turned upside down, the former planter aristocracy tried to set it right again. To reestablish white dominance, southern legislatures passed "Black Codes" in the first year after the war. Many of the codes granted freedmen the right to marry, sue and be sued, testify in court, and hold property. But these rights were qualified. Complicated passages explained under exactly what circumstances blacks could testify against whites, own property (mostly they could not), or exercise other

●●●─ Read the Document

The Mississippi Black Code (1865)

at **www.myhistorylab.com**

The End of Slavery? The Black Codes, widespread violence against freedpeople, and President Johnson's veto of the civil rights bill gave rise to the sardonic title "Slavery Is Dead?" in this Thomas Nast cartoon. What do you see in the two scenes? Describe the two images of justice. What is Nast saying?

rights of free people. Forbidden rights were racial intermarriage, bearing arms, possessing alcoholic beverages, sitting on trains (except in baggage compartments), being on city streets at night, or congregating in large groups. Many of the qualified rights guaranteed by the Black Codes were only passed to induce the federal government to withdraw its remaining troops from the South. This was a crucial issue, for in many places marauding whites were terrorizing virtually defenseless African Americans.

Key provisions of the Black Codes regulated freedpeople's economic status. "Vagrancy" laws provided that any blacks not "lawfully employed" (by a white employer) could be arrested, jailed, fined, or hired out to a man who would assume responsibility for their debts and behavior. The codes regulated black laborers' work contracts with white landowners, including severe penalties for leaving before the yearly contract was fulfilled. A Kentucky newspaper was mean and blunt: "The tune . . . will not be 'forty acres and a mule,' but . . . 'work nigger or starve.'"

National Reconstruction Politics

The Black Codes directly challenged the national government in 1865. Would it use its power in the South to uphold the codes, white property rights, and racial intimidation, or to defend the liberties of freedpeople? Although the primary drama of Reconstruction pitted white landowners against African American freedmen over land and labor in the South, in the background of these local struggles lurked the debate over Reconstruction policy among politicians in Washington. This dual drama would extend to the civil rights struggles of the 1960s and beyond.

Presidential Reconstruction by Proclamation

After initially demanding that the defeated Confederates be punished for treason, President Johnson adopted a more lenient policy. On May 29, 1865, he issued two proclamations setting forth his Reconstruction program. Like Lincoln's, it rested on the claim that the southern states had never left the Union.

Johnson's first proclamation continued Lincoln's policies by offering "**amnesty** and pardon, with restoration of all rights of property" to most former Confederates who would swear allegiance to the Constitution and the Union. Johnson revealed his Jacksonian hostility to "aristocratic" planters by exempting ex–Confederate government leaders and rebels with taxable property valued over $20,000. They could, however, apply for individual pardons, which Johnson granted to nearly all applicants.

In his second proclamation, Johnson accepted the reconstructed government of North Carolina and prescribed the steps by which other southern states could reestablish state governments. First, the president would appoint a provisional governor, who would call a state convention representing those "who are loyal to the United States," including persons who took the oath of allegiance or were otherwise pardoned. The convention must ratify the Thirteenth Amendment, which abolished slavery; void secession; repudiate Confederate debts; and elect new state officials and members of Congress.

Under Johnson's plan, all southern states completed Reconstruction and sent representatives to Congress, which convened in December 1865. Defiant southern voters elected dozens of former officers and legislators of the Confederacy, including a few not yet pardoned. Some state conventions hedged on ratifying the Thirteenth Amendment, and some asserted former owners' right to compensation for lost slave property. No state convention provided for black suffrage, and most did nothing to guarantee civil rights, schooling, or economic protection for the freedmen. Eight months after Appomattox, the southern states were back in the Union, freedpeople were working for former masters, and the new president was firmly in charge. Reconstruction seemed to be over.

Congressional Reconstruction by Amendment

Late in 1865, northern leaders painfully saw that almost none of their moral or political postwar goals were being fulfilled and that the Republicans were likely to lose their political power. Would Democrats and the South gain by postwar elections what they had lost by civil war?

●●●—Read the **Document**

Reconstruction Era: Thirteenth, Fourteenth, and Fifteenth Amendments (1864)

at **www.myhistorylab.com**

Some Congressional Republicans, led by Thaddeus Stevens of Pennsylvania and Senator Charles Sumner of Massachusetts, advocated policies aimed at providing full civil, political and economic rights for blacks. Labeled "radicals," their efforts were frustrated by the more moderate majority of Republicans, who were less committed to freedmen's rights.

At first, rejecting Johnson's position that the South had already been reconstructed, Congress exercised its constitutional authority to decide on its own membership. It refused to seat the new senators and representatives from the old Confederate states. It also established the Joint Committee on Reconstruction to investigate conditions in the South. Its report documented white resistance, disorder, and the appalling treatment and conditions of freedpeople.

Congress passed a civil rights bill in 1866 designed to protect the fragile new economic freedoms of African Americans and extended for two more years the **Freedmen's Bureau**, an agency providing emergency assistance at the end of the war. Johnson vetoed both bills and called his congressional opponents "traitors." His actions drove moderates into the radical camp, and Congress passed both bills over his veto—both, however, watered down by weakening the power of enforcement. Southern courts regularly disallowed black testimony against whites, acquitted whites of violence, and sentenced blacks to compulsory labor.

Reconstruction Amendments

What three basic rights were guaranteed in these three amendments? What patterns do you see? How well were the dreams of the freedpeople fulfilled? Was that fulfillment immediate or deferred? For how long?

Substance	Outcome of Ratification Process	Final Implementation and Enforcement
Thirteenth Amendment—Passed by Congress January 1865		
Prohibited slavery in the United States	Ratified by 27 states, including 8 southern states, by December 1865	Immediate, although economic freedom came by degrees
Fourteenth Amendment—Passed by Congress June 1866		
(1) Defined equal national citizenship; (2) reduced state representation in Congress proportional to number of disfranchised voters; (3) denied former Confederates the right to hold office	Rejected by 12 southern and border states by February 1867; Congress made readmission depend on ratification; ratified in July 1868	Civil Rights Act of 1964
Fifteenth Amendment—Passed by Congress February 1869		
Prohibited denial of vote because of race, color, or previous servitude	Ratification by Virginia, Texas, Mississippi, and Georgia required for readmission; ratified in March 1870	Voting Rights Act of 1965

In such a climate, southern racial violence erupted. In a typical outbreak, in May 1866, white mobs in Memphis, encouraged by local police, rampaged for over 40 hours of terror, killing, beating, robbing, and raping virtually helpless African American residents and burning houses, schools, and churches. Forty-eight people, all but two of them black, died. The local Union army commander took his time restoring order, arguing that his troops had "hated Negroes too." A congressional inquiry concluded that Memphis blacks had "no protection from the law whatever."

A month later, Congress sent to the states for ratification the Fourteenth Amendment, the single most significant act of the Reconstruction era. The first section of the amendment promised permanent constitutional protection of the civil rights of blacks by defining them as citizens. States were prohibited from depriving "any person of life, liberty, or property, without due process of law," and citizens were guaranteed the "equal protection of the laws." Section 2 granted black male suffrage in the South, inserting the word "male" into the Constitution for the first time. Other sections of the amendment barred leaders of the Confederacy from national or state offices (except by act of Congress), repudiated the Confederate debt, and denied claims of compensation to former slave owners. Johnson urged the southern states to reject the Fourteenth Amendment, and 10 immediately did so.

The Fourteenth Amendment was the central issue of the 1866 midterm election. Johnson barnstormed the country asking voters to throw out the radical Republicans and trading insults with hecklers. Democrats north and south appealed openly to racial prejudice in attacking the Fourteenth Amendment. Republicans responded by attacking Johnson personally and freely "waved the bloody shirt," reminding voters of the Democrats' treason. Self-interest and local issues moved voters more than fiery speeches, and the Republicans won an overwhelming victory. The mandate was clear: presidential Reconstruction had not worked, and Congress could present its own.

Early in 1867, Congress passed three Reconstruction acts. The southern states were divided into five military districts, whose commanders had broad powers to maintain order and protect civil and property rights. Congress also defined a new process for readmitting a state. Qualified voters—including blacks but excluding unreconstructed rebels—would elect delegates to state constitutional conventions that would write new constitutions guaranteeing black suffrage. After the new voters of the states had ratified these constitutions, elections would be held to choose governors and state legislatures. When a state ratified the Fourteenth Amendment, its representatives to Congress would be accepted, completing its readmission to the Union.

The President Impeached

Congress also restricted presidential powers and established legislative dominance over the executive branch. The Tenure of Office Act, designed to prevent Johnson from firing the outspoken Secretary of War Edwin Stanton, limited the president's appointment powers. Other measures trimmed his power as commander in chief.

Johnson responded exactly as congressional Republicans had anticipated. He vetoed the Reconstruction acts, hindered the work of Freedmen's Bureau agents, limited the activities of military commanders in the South, and removed cabinet officers and other officials sympathetic to Congress. The House Judiciary Committee charged the president with "usurpations of power" and of acting in the "interests of the great criminals" who had led the rebellion. But moderate House Republicans defeated the impeachment resolutions.

In August 1867, Johnson dismissed Stanton and asked for Senate consent. When the Senate refused, the president ordered Stanton to surrender his office, which he refused, barricading himself inside. The House quickly approved impeachment resolutions, charging the president with "high crimes and misdemeanors." The three-month trial in the Senate in 1868 featured impassioned oratory, similar to the trial of President Bill Clinton 130 years later. And, as with Clinton, evidence was skimpy that Johnson had committed any constitutional crime justifying his removal. With seven moderate Republicans joining Democrats against conviction, the effort to find the president guilty fell one vote short of the required two-thirds majority.

RECOVERING *the* PAST

Novels

We usually read novels, short stories, and other forms of imaginative literature for pleasure, for the enjoyment of plot, style, symbolism, and character development. "Classic" novels such as *Moby Dick, Huckleberry Finn, The Great Gatsby, The Invisible Man,* and *Beloved,* for example, are not only written well, but also explore timeless questions of good and evil, of innocence and knowledge, of noble dreams fulfilled and shattered. We enjoy novels because we often find ourselves identifying with one of the major characters. Through that person's problems, joys, relationships, and search for identity, we gain insights about our own.

Even though they may be historically untrue, we can also read novels as historical sources, for they reveal much about the attitudes, dreams, fears, and everyday experiences of human beings in a particular period. In addition, they show how people responded to the major events of that era. The novelist, like the historian, is a product of time and place and has an interpretive point of view. Consider the two novels about Reconstruction quoted here. Neither is reputed for great literary merit, yet both reveal much about the various interpretations and impassioned attitudes of the post–Civil War era. *A Fool's Errand* was written by Albion Tourgée, a northerner; *The Clansman,* by Thomas Dixon, Jr., a southerner.

Tourgée was a young northern teacher and lawyer who fought with the Union army and moved to North Carolina after the war to begin a legal career. He became a judge and was an active Republican, supporting black suffrage and helping to shape the new state constitution. Because he boldly criticized the Ku Klux Klan, his life was threatened many times. When he left North Carolina in 1879, he published an autobiographical novel about his experiences as a judge challenging the Klan's campaign of violence and intimidation against the freedpeople.

The "fool's errand" in the novel is that of the northern veteran, Comfort Servosse, who, like Tourgée, seeks to fulfill humane goals on behalf of both blacks and whites in post–Civil War North Carolina. His efforts are thwarted, however, by threats, intimidation, a campaign of violent "outrages" against Republican leaders in the county, and a lack of support from Congress. Historians have verified the accuracy of many of the events in Tourgée's novel. While exposing the brutality of the Klan, Tourgée features loyal southern Unionists, respectable planters ashamed of Klan violence, and even guilt-ridden poor white Klansmen who try to protect or warn intended victims.

In the year of Tourgée's death, 1905, another North Carolinian published a novel with a very different analysis of Reconstruction and its fate. Thomas Dixon, Jr., was a lawyer, state legislator, Baptist minister, pro-Klan lecturer, and novelist. *The Clansman,* subtitled *A Historical Romance of the Ku Klux Klan,* reflects turn-of-the-century attitudes most white southerners still had about Republican rule during Reconstruction. According to Dixon, a power-crazed, vindictive, radical Congress, led by scheming Austin Stoneman (Thaddeus Stevens), sought to impose corrupt carpetbagger and brutal black rule on a helpless South. Only through the inspired leadership of the Ku Klux Klan was the South saved from the horrors of rape and revenge.

Dixon dedicated *The Clansman* to his uncle, a Grand Titan of the Klan in North Carolina during the time when two crucial counties were being transformed from Republican to Democratic through intimidation and terror. No such violence shows up in Dixon's novel. When the novel was made the basis of D. W. Griffith's film classic *Birth of a Nation* in 1915, its attitudes were firmly implanted in the twentieth-century American mind.

Both novels convey Reconstruction attitudes toward the freedpeople. Both create clearly defined heroes and villains. Both include exciting chase scenes, narrow escapes, daring rescues, and tragic deaths. Both include romantic subplots. Yet the two novels are strikingly different.

A Fool's Errand
Albion Tourgée (1879)

When the second Christmas came, Metta wrote again to her sister:

"The feeling is terribly bitter against Comfort on account of his course towards the colored people. There is quite a village of them on the lower end of the plantation. They have a church, a sabbath school, and are to have next year a school. You can not imagine how kind they have been to us, and how much they are attached to Comfort. . . . I got Comfort to go with me to one of their prayer-meetings a few nights ago. I had heard a great deal about them, but had never attended one before. It was strangely weird. There were, perhaps, fifty present, mostly middle-aged men and women. They were singing in soft, low monotone, interspersed with prolonged exclamatory notes, a sort of rude hymn, which I was surprised to know was one of their old songs in slave times. How the chorus came to be endured in those days I can not imagine. It was—

'Free! free! free, my Lord, free!
An' we walks de hebben-ly way!

"A few looked around as we came in and seated ourselves; and Uncle Jerry, the saint of the settlement, came forward on his staves, and said, in his soft voice,

"'Ev'nin', Kunnel! Sarvant, Missuss! Will you walk up, an' hev seats in front?'

"We told him we had just looked in, and might go in a short time; so we would stay in the back part of the audience.

"Uncle Jerry can not read nor write; but he is a man of strange intelligence and power. Unable to do work of any account, he is the faithful friend, monitor, and director of others. He has a house and piece of land, all paid for, a good horse and cow, and, with the aid of his wife and two boys, made a fine crop this season. He is one of the most promising colored men in the settlement: so Comfort says, at least. Everybody seems to have great respect for his character. I don't know how many people I have heard speak of his religion. Mr. Savage used to say he had rather hear him pray than any other man on earth. He was much prized by his master, even after he was disabled, on account of his faithfulness and character."

The Clansman
Thomas Dixon, Jr. (1905)

At noon Ben and Phil strolled to the polling-place to watch the progress of the first election under Negro rule. The Square was jammed with shouting, jostling, perspiring negroes, men, women, and children. The day was warm, and the African odour was supreme even in the open air. . . .

The negroes, under the drill of the League and the Freedman's Bureau, protected by the bayonet, were voting to enfranchise themselves, disfranchise their former masters, ratify a new constitution, and elect a legislature to do their will. Old Aleck was a candidate for the House, chief poll-holder, and seemed to be in charge of the movements of the voters outside the booth as well as inside. He appeared to be omnipresent, and his self-importance was a sight Phil had never dreamed. He could not keep his eyes off him. . . .

[Aleck] was a born African orator, undoubtedly descended from a long line of savage spell-binders, whose eloquence in the palaver houses of the jungle had made them native leaders. His thin spindle-shanks supported an oblong, protruding stomach, resembling an elderly monkey's, which seemed so heavy it swayed his back to carry it.

The animal vivacity of his small eyes and the flexibility of his eyebrows, which he worked up and down rapidly with every change of countenance, expressed his eager desires.

He was already mellow with liquor, and was dressed in an old army uniform and cap, with two horse-pistols buckled around his waist. On a strap hanging from his shoulder were strung a half-dozen tin canteens filled with whiskey.

Source: Clansman: An Historical Romance of the Ku Klux Klan by Thomas Dixon. Copyright 1905 by University Press of Kentucky. Reproduced with permission of University Press of Kentucky via Copyright Clearance Center.

REFLECTING ON THE PAST **Even in these brief excerpts, what differences of style and attitude do you see in the depictions of Uncle Jerry and Old Aleck? What emotional responses do you have to these passages? How do you think late nineteenth-century and early twentieth-century Americans might have responded?**

Not until the late twentieth century (Nixon and Clinton) would an American president again face the threat of removal from office through impeachment.

Moderate Republicans were fearful that by removing Johnson, they might get Ohio Senator Benjamin Wade, a leading radical Republican, as president. Wade had endorsed woman suffrage, rights for labor unions, and civil rights for African Americans in both southern and northern states. As moderate Republicans gained strength in 1868 through their support of the eventual presidential election winner, Ulysses S. Grant, radicalism lost much of its power within Republican ranks.

What Congressional Moderation Meant for Rebels, Blacks, and Women

Congress's political battle against President Johnson was not matched by an idealistic resolve on behalf of the freedpeople. State and local elections of 1867 showed that voters preferred moderate Reconstruction policies. It is important to look not only at what Congress did during Reconstruction, but also at what it did not do.

With the exception of Jefferson Davis, Congress did not imprison Confederate leaders, and only one person, the commander of the infamous Andersonville prison camp, was executed. Congress did not insist on a long probation before southern states could be readmitted. It did not reorganize southern local governments. It did not mandate a national program of education for the freedpeople. It did not confiscate and redistribute land to the freedmen. It did not prevent Johnson from taking land away from those who had gained titles during the war. It did not, except indirectly and with great reluctance, provide economic help to the new black citizens.

Congress did, however, halfheartedly grant citizenship and suffrage to freedmen, but not to freedwomen. White northerners were no more prepared than white southerners to make African Americans equal citizens. Proposals to give black men the vote gained support in the North only after the presidential election of 1868, when General Grant, the supposedly invincible military hero, barely won the popular vote in several states. To ensure grateful black votes, Congressional Republicans, who had twice rejected a suffrage amendment, took another look at the idea. After a bitter fight, the Fifteenth Amendment, forbidding all states to deny the vote to anyone "on account of race, color, or previous condition of servitude," became part of the Constitution in 1870.

One casualty of the Fourteenth and Fifteenth Amendments was the goodwill of women who had worked for suffrage for two decades. They had hoped that male legislators would recognize their wartime service in support of the Union and were shocked that black males got the vote but not loyal white (or black) women. Elizabeth Cady Stanton and Susan B. Anthony, veteran suffragists and opponents of slavery, campaigned against the Fourteenth Amendment, breaking with abolitionist allies such as Frederick Douglass, who had long supported woman suffrage yet declared that this was "the Negro's hour."

When the Fifteenth Amendment was proposed, many suffragists wondered why gender was still a barrier to the right to vote. Disappointment over the suffrage issue helped split the women's movement in 1869. Anthony and Stanton continued their fight for a national amendment for woman suffrage and a long list of other rights, while other women concentrated on securing the vote state-by-state. Abandoned by radical and moderate men alike, women had few champions in Congress, and their efforts did not bear fruit for half a century.

Congress compromised the rights of African Americans as well as women. It gave blacks the vote but not land, the opposite of what they wanted first. Thaddeus Stevens argued that "forty acres . . . and a hut would be more valuable . . . than the . . . right to vote." But Congress never seriously considered his plan to confiscate the land of the "chief rebels" and give a small portion of it, divided into 40-acre plots, to freedpeople, which would have violated deeply held beliefs of the Republican party and the American people on the sacredness of private property. Moreover, northern business interests looking to develop southern industry and invest in southern land liked the prospect of a large pool of propertyless African American workers.

Congress did pass the Southern Homestead Act of 1866, making public lands available to blacks and loyal whites in five southern states. But the land was poor and inaccessible, and most black laborers were bound by contracts that prevented them from making claims before the deadline. Only about 4,000 African American families even applied for the Homestead Act lands, and fewer than 20 percent of them saw their claims completed. White claimants did little better.

The Lives of Freedpeople

Union army major George Reynolds boasted late in 1865 that in the area of Mississippi under his command, he had "kept the negroes at work, and in a good state of discipline." Clinton Fisk, a well-meaning white who helped found a black college in Tennessee, told freedmen in 1866 that they could be "as free and as happy" working again for their "old master . . . as any where else in the world." Such pronouncements reminded blacks of white preachers' exhortations during slavery to work hard and obey masters. Ironically, Fisk and Reynolds were agents of the Freedmen's Bureau, the agency intended to aid the black transition from slaves to freedpeople.

The Freedmen's Bureau

Never in American history has one small agency—underfinanced, understaffed, and undersupported—been given a harder task than was the Bureau of Freedmen, Refugees, and Abandoned Lands. Controlling less than 1 percent of southern lands, the Bureau's name is telling; its fate epitomizes Reconstruction.

The Freedmen's Bureau performed many essential services. It issued emergency food rations, clothed and sheltered homeless victims of the war, and established medical and hospital facilities. It provided funds to relocate thousands of freedpeople. It helped blacks search for relatives and get legally married. It represented African Americans in local civil courts to ensure that they got fair trials and learned to respect the law. Working with northern missionary aid societies and southern black churches, the Bureau became responsible for an extensive program of education, and by 1870 there were almost 250,000 pupils in 4,329 agency schools.

Watch the Video

The Schools that the Civil War and Reconstruction Created

at **www.myhistorylab.com**

The Bureau's largest task was to promote African Americans' economic well-being. This included settling them on abandoned lands and getting them started with tools, seed, and draft animals, as well as arranging work contracts with white landowners. But in this area the Freedmen's Bureau, determined not to instill a new dependency, more often than not supported the needs of white landowners to find cheap labor rather than of blacks to become independent farmers.

Although a few agents were idealistic New Englanders eager to help freedpeople adjust to freedom, most were Union army officers more concerned with social order than social transformation. Working in a postwar climate of resentment and violence, Freedmen's Bureau agents were overworked, underpaid, spread too thin (at its peak only 900 agents were scattered across the South), and constantly harassed by local whites. Even the best-intentioned agents would have agreed with Bureau commissioner General O. O. Howard's belief in the nineteenth-century American values of self-help, minimal government interference in the marketplace, the sanctity of private property, contractual obligations, and white superiority.

On a typical day, overburdened agents would visit local courts and schools, file reports, supervise the signing of work contracts, and handle numerous complaints, most involving contract violations between whites and blacks or property and domestic disputes among blacks. A Georgia agent wrote that he was *"tired out* and *broke down. . . .* Every day for 6 months, day after day, I have had from 5 to 20 complaints, *generally trivial* and of no moment, yet requiring consideration & attention coming from both Black & White." To find work for freedmen, agents implored freedwomen to hold their husbands accountable as providers and often sided with white landowners by telling blacks to obey orders, trust employers, and accept disadvantageous contracts. One agent sent a man who had complained of a severe beating back to work: "Don't be sassy [and] don't be lazy when you've got work to do."

Read the **Document**

Southern Skepticism of the Freedmen's Bureau (1866)

at **www.myhistorylab.com**

Despite numerous constraints, the agents accomplished much. In little more than two years, the Freedmen's Bureau issued 20 million rations (nearly one-third to poor whites), reunited families and resettled some 30,000 displaced war refugees, treated some 450,000 people for illness and injury, built 40 hospitals and 4,000 schools, provided books, tools, and furnishings—and even some land—to the freedmen, and occasionally protected their economic and civil rights. The great African American historian and leading black intellectual of the twentieth century, W. E. B. Du Bois, wrote that, "In a time of perfect calm, amid willing neighbors and streaming wealth," it "would have been a herculean task" for the bureau to fulfill its many purposes. But in the midst of hunger, sorrow, spite, suspicion, hate, and cruelty, "the work of any instrument of social regeneration was . . . foredoomed to failure." But Du Bois, reflecting the varied views of freedpeople themselves, recognized that in laying the foundation for black labor, future land ownership, a public school system, and recognition before courts of law, the Freedmen's Bureau was "on the whole successful beyond the dreams of thoughtful men."

Economic Freedom by Degrees

Despite the best efforts of the Freedmen's Bureau, the failure of Congress to provide the promised 40 acres and a mule forced freedmen and women into a new dependency on former masters. Blacks made some progress, however, in degrees of economic autonomy and were partly responsible, along with international economic developments, for forcing the white planter class into making major changes in southern agriculture.

First, a land-intensive system replaced the labor intensity of slavery. Land ownership was concentrated into fewer and even larger holdings than before the war. From South Carolina to Louisiana, the wealthiest tenth of the population owned about 60 percent of the real estate in the 1870s. Second, these large planters increasingly specialized in one crop, usually cotton, and were tied into the international market. This resulted in a steady drop in postwar food production (both grain and livestock). Third, one-crop farming created a new credit system whereby most farmers, black and white, were forced into dependence on local merchants for renting land, housing, seed, and farm implements and animals. These changes affected race relations and class tensions.

This new system took a few years to develop after emancipation. At first, most African Americans signed **contracts** with white landowners and worked in gangs as during slavery. All members of the family had to work to receive their rations. The freedpeople resented this new semiservitude, refused to sign the contracts, and sought a measure of independence working the land themselves. Freedwomen especially wanted to send their children to school rather than to apprenticeships, and insisted on "no more outdoor work," preferring small plots of land to grow vegetables rather than plantation labor.

Many blacks therefore broke contracts, ran away, engaged in work slowdowns or strikes, burned barns, and sought other means of negotiation. In the Sea Islands and rice-growing regions of coastal South Carolina and Georgia, where slaves had long held a degree of autonomy, resistance was especially

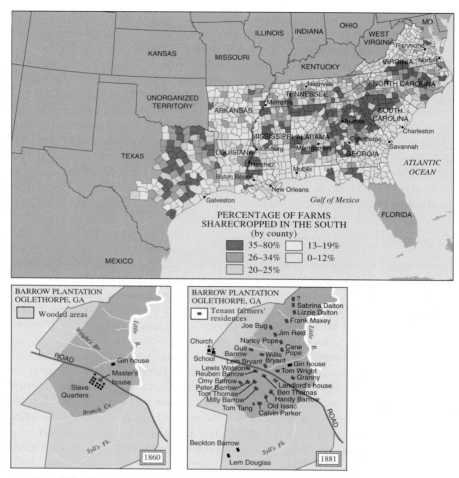

The Rise of Tenancy in the South, 1880 Although no longer slaves and after resisting labor contracts and the gang system of field labor, the freedmen (as well as many poor whites) became tenant farmers, working on shares, in the New South. The former slaves on the Barrow plantation in Georgia, for example, moved their households to individual 25- to 30-acre tenant farms, which they rented from the Barrow family in annual contracts requiring payment in cotton and other cash crops. Where was the highest percentage of tenant farms, and how do you explain it? How would you explain the low-percentage areas? What do you notice about how circumstances have changed—and not changed—on the Barrow plantation?

strong. On the Heyward plantations, near those of the Allstons, the freedmen "refuse work at any price," a Freedman's Bureau agent reported, and the women "wish to stay in the house or the garden all the time."

Blacks' insistence on autonomy and land of their own was the major impetus for the change from the contract system to tenancy and **sharecropping**. Families would hitch mules to their old slave cabin and drag it to their plot, as far from the Big House as possible. Sharecroppers received seed, fertilizer, implements, food, and clothing. In return, the landlord (or a local merchant) told them what and how much to grow, and he took a share—usually half—of the harvest. The cropper's half usually went to pay for goods bought on credit (at high interest rates) from the landlord. Thus sharecroppers remained tied to the landlord.

●●●⊢Read the Document

Post-Civil War, United States:

A Sharecropper's Contract (1882)

at **www.myhistorylab.com**

Tenant farmers had only slightly more independence. Before a harvest, they promised to sell their crop to a local merchant in return for renting land, tools, and other necessities. From the merchant's store they also had to buy goods on credit (at higher prices than whites paid) against the harvest. At "settling up" time, income from sale of the crop was compared to accumulated debts. It was possible, especially after an unusually bountiful season, to come out ahead and eventually to own one's own land. But tenants rarely did; in debt at the end of each year, they had to pledge the next year's crop. World cotton prices remained low, and whereas big landowners still generated profits through their large scale of operation, sharecroppers rarely made much money. When they were able to pay their debts, landowners frequently altered loan agreements. Thus **peonage** replaced slavery, ensuring a continuing cheap labor supply to grow cotton and other staples in the South.

Despite this bleak picture, painstaking, industrious work by African Americans helped many gradually accumulate a measure of income, personal property, and autonomy, especially in the household economy of producing eggs, butter, meat, food crops, and other staples. Debt did not necessarily mean a lack of subsistence. In Virginia, the declining tobacco crop forced white planters to sell off small parcels of land to blacks. Throughout the South, a few African Americans became independent landowners—about 3 to 4 percent by 1880, but closer to 25 percent by 1900.

White Farmers During Reconstruction

Changes in southern agriculture affected middle-class and poor white farmers as well, and planters worried about a coalition between poor black and pro-Unionist white farmers. As a Georgia farmer said in 1865, "We should tuk the land, as we did the niggers, and split it, and giv part to the niggers and part to me and t'other Union fellers." But confiscation and redistribution of land was no more likely for white farmers than for the freedmen. Poor whites, too, had to concentrate on growing staples, pledging their crops against high-interest credit, and facing perpetual indebtedness. In the upcountry piedmont area of Georgia, for example, the number of whites working their own land dropped from nine in ten before the Civil War to seven in ten by 1880, while cotton production doubled.

Reliance on cotton meant fewer food crops and greater dependence on merchants for provisions. In 1884, Jephta Dickson of Jackson County, Georgia, purchased over $50 worth of flour, meal, meat, syrup, peas, and corn from a local store; 25 years earlier, he had been almost completely self-sufficient. Fencing laws seriously curtailed the livelihood of poor whites raising pigs and hogs, and restrictions on hunting and fishing reduced the ability of poor whites and blacks alike to supplement incomes and diets. In the worn-out flatlands and barren mountainous regions of the South, the poverty, health, and isolation of poor whites worsened after the war. They lived a marginal existence, hunting, fishing, and growing crops that, as a North Carolinian put it, were "puny." Some became farmhands at $6 a month (with board). Others fled to low-paying jobs in cotton mills.

The cultural life of poor southern whites reflected their lowly position and their pride. Their religion centered on camp meeting revivals in backwoods clearings. Their ballads and folklore told of debt, chain gangs, and herbal remedies for poor health. Their quilt making and house construction reflected a culture of scarcity in which everything was saved and reused.

In part because their lives were so hard, poor whites clung to their belief in white superiority. Many joined the Ku Klux Klan and other southern white terror groups that emerged between 1866 and 1868. A federal officer reported, "The poorer classes of white people . . . have a most intense hatred of the Negro," which expressed itself in midnight raids on teachers in black schools, Republican voters, and any black whose "impudence" caused him not to "bow and scrape to a white man, as was done formerly."

Black Self-Help Institutions

But however hard life was for poor whites, things were even worse for blacks, whose hopes slowly soured. Recalled an African American Texan, "We soon found out that freedom could make folks proud but it didn't make 'em rich." Many African American leaders realized that because white institutions could not fulfill the promises of emancipation, freedpeople would have to do it themselves.

Black community self-help survived in the churches and schools of the antebellum free Negro communities and in the "invisible" cultural institutions of the slave quarters. Emancipation brought a rapid increase in the growth of membership in African American churches. The Negro Baptist Church grew from 150,000 members in 1850 to 500,000 in 1870, while the membership of the African Methodist Episcopal Church increased fourfold in the postwar decade, from 100,000 to over 400,000 members. African American ministers continued to exert community leadership. Many led efforts to oppose discrimination, some by entering politics; over one-fifth of the black officeholders in South Carolina were ministers. Most preachers, however, focused on sin, salvation, and revivalist enthusiasm. An English visitor to the South in 1867 and 1868 noted the intensity of black "devoutness." As one woman explained: "We make noise 'bout ebery ting else . . . I want to go to Heaben in de good ole way."

The freedpeople's desire for education was as strong as for religion. A school official in Virginia said that the freedmen were "down right crazy to learn." In addition to black teachers from the churches, "Yankee school-marms taught black children and adults." Sent by aid societies such as the American Missionary Association, these high-minded young women sought to convert blacks to Congregationalism and their version of moral behavior. In October 1865, Esther Douglass found "120 dirty, half naked perfectly wild black children" in her schoolroom near Savannah, Georgia. Eight months later, she reported that they could read, sing hymns, and repeat Bible verses and had learned "about right conduct which they tried to practice."

Such glowing reports waned as white teachers grew frustrated with crowded facilities, limited resources, local opposition, and absenteeism caused by fieldwork. In Georgia, for example, only 5 percent of black children went to school for part of any one year between 1865 and 1870, as opposed to 20 percent of white children. As white teachers left, they were increasingly replaced by blacks, who boarded with families and were more persistent and positive. Charlotte Forten, for example, noted that even after a half day's "hard toil" in the fields, her older pupils were "as bright and as anxious to learn as ever," showing "a desire for knowledge, and a capability for attaining it." Under

Black Schoolchildren with Their Books and Teacher Along with equal civil rights and land of their own, what the freedpeople wanted most was education. Despite white opposition, one of the most positive outcomes of the Reconstruction era was education in Freedmen's Bureau schools. What do you see in this photograph? Is it sad or uplifting? Why?

teachers like Forten, by 1870 there was a 20 percent gain in adult literacy, a figure that, against difficult odds, continued to grow for all ages to the end of the century, when more than 1.5 million black children attended school. To train African American teachers and preachers, northern philanthropists founded Howard, Atlanta, Fisk, Morehouse, and other black universities in the South after 1865.

African American schools, like churches, became community centers. They published newspapers, provided training in trades and farming, and promoted political participation and land ownership. These efforts made black schools objects of local white hostility. As a Virginia freedman told a congressional committee, in his county, anyone starting a school would be killed and blacks were "afraid to be caught with a book." In 1869, in Tennessee alone, 37 black schools were burned to the ground.

White opposition to black education and land ownership stimulated African American nationalism and separatism. In the late 1860s, Benjamin "Pap" Singleton, a former Tennessee slave, urged freedpeople to abandon politics and migrate westward. He organized a land company in 1869, purchased public property in Kansas, and in the early 1870s took several groups from Tennessee and Kentucky to establish separate black towns in the prairie state. In following years, thousands of "exodusters" from the Lower South bought some 10,000 infertile acres in Kansas. But natural and human obstacles to self-sufficiency often proved insurmountable. By the 1880s, despairing of ever finding economic independence in the United States, Singleton and other nationalists advocated emigration to Canada and Liberia. Other black leaders like Frederick Douglass continued to press for full citizenship rights within the United States.

Reconstruction in the Southern States

Douglass's confidence in the power of the ballot seemed warranted in the enthusiastic early months under the Reconstruction Acts of 1867. With President Johnson neutralized, Republican congressional leaders finally could prevail. Local Republicans, taking advantage of the inability or refusal of many southern whites to vote, overwhelmingly elected their delegates to state constitutional conventions in the fall of 1867. Guardedly optimistic and sensing the "sacred importance" of their work, black and white Republicans began creating new state governments.

Republican Rule

Contrary to early pro-southern historians, southern state governments under Republican rule were not dominated by illiterate black majorities intent on "Africanizing" the South. Nor were these governments unusually corrupt or extravagant, nor did they use massive numbers of federal troops to enforce their will. By 1869, only 1,100 federal soldiers remained in Virginia,

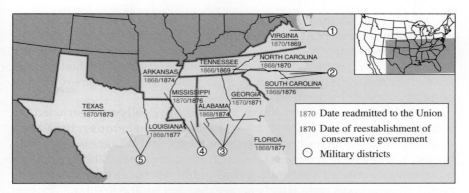

The Return of Conservative Democratic Control in Southern States During Reconstruction Note that the duration of Republican governments in power to implement even moderate Reconstruction programs varied from state to state. In North Carolina and Georgia, for example, Republican rule was very brief, while in Virginia it never took place at all. "Redemption," the return of conservative control, took longest in three Deep South states. How would you explain these variations among the southern states?

and most federal troops in Texas were guarding the frontier against Mexico and hostile Indians. Lacking strong military backing, the new state governments faced economic distress and increasingly violent harassment.

Diverse coalitions made up the new governments elected under congressional Reconstruction. The "black and tan" legislatures (as opponents called them) were actually predominantly white, except for South Carolina's lower house. Many of the new leaders were local bankers, industrialists, and others interested more in economic growth and sectional reconciliation than in radical social reforms. A second group consisted of northern Republican capitalists who headed south to invest in land, railroads, and new industries. Others included Union veterans, and missionaries and teachers inspired to work in Freedmen's Bureau schools. Such people were unfairly labeled "carpetbaggers."

Moderate African Americans made up a third group in the Republican state governments. Many were well-educated, biracial mulattos representing a new class of preachers and teachers from the North. Others were self-educated tradesmen and small landowners. In South Carolina, for example, of some 255 African American state and federal officials elected between 1868 and 1876, two-thirds were literate and one-third owned real estate; only 15 percent owned no property at all. This class composition meant that black leaders often supported policies that largely ignored the economic needs of the African American masses. Their goals fit squarely into the American republican tradition. Black leaders reminded whites that they were also southerners, seeking only, as an 1865 petition put it, "that the same laws which govern white men shall govern black men [and that] we be dealt with as others are—in equity and justice."

The primary accomplishment of Republican rule in the South was to eliminate undemocratic features from prewar state constitutions. All states provided universal male suffrage and loosened requirements for holding office. Underrepresented counties got more legislative seats. Automatic imprisonment for debt was ended, and laws were enacted to relieve poverty and care for the disabled. Many southern states passed their first divorce laws and provisions granting property rights to married women. Lists of crimes punishable by death were shortened.

Republican governments financially and physically reconstructed the South by overhauling tax systems and approving generous railroad and other capital investment bonds. Harbors, roads, and bridges were rebuilt; hospitals and asylums were established. Most important, the Republican governments created the South's first public school systems. As in the North, these schools were largely segregated, but for the first time rich and poor, black and white alike had access to education. By the 1880s, African American school attendance increased from 5 to over 40 percent, and white from 20 to over 60 percent. All this cost money, so the Republicans also increased tax rates and state debts.

These considerable accomplishments came in the face of opposition like that expressed at a convention of Louisiana planters, which labeled the Republican leaders the "lowest and most corrupt body of men ever assembled in the South." There was some corruption, mostly in land sales, railway bonds, and construction contracts. Such graft had become a way of life in postwar American politics, South and North. Given their lack of experience with politics, the black role was remarkable. As Du Bois put it, "There was one thing that the White South feared more than negro dishonesty, ignorance, and incompetence, and that was negro honesty, knowledge, and efficiency."

The Republican coalition did not survive. It lasted for different periods in different states, surviving longest in the Deep South, where the black population was equal to or greater than the white. In Virginia, Republicans ruled hardly at all, joining with Democrats to encourage northern investors to rebuild shattered cities and develop industry. In South Carolina, African American leaders' unwillingness to use their power to help black laborers contributed to their loss of political control to the Democrats, and class divisions among blacks in Louisiana helped weaken the Republican regime there. But the primary reason for the return of Democrats to power was the use of violence.

Violence and "Redemption"

A southern editor said, "We must render this either a white man's government, or convert the land into a Negro man's cemetery." The Ku Klux Klan was only one of several secret organizations that forcibly drove black and white Republicans from office. Although violence was pervasive throughout the South, North Carolina and Mississippi typified an intentional pattern of terrorism.

After losing a close election in North Carolina in 1868, conservatives concentrated on several piedmont counties, areas of strong Unionist support. If the Democrats could win these counties in 1870, they would most likely win statewide. In the year before the election, several prominent Republicans were killed, including a white state senator and a leading black Union League organizer, who was hanged in the courthouse square with a sign pinned to him: "Bewar, ye guilty, both white and black." Scores of citizens were flogged, fired from their jobs, or driven at night from burning homes and barns. The courts consistently refused to prosecute anyone for these crimes, which local papers blamed on "disgusting negroes and white Radicals." The campaign of terror worked. In the election of 1870, some 12,000 fewer Republicans voted in the two crucial counties than had voted two years earlier, and the Democrats swept back into power.

In Mississippi's state election in 1875, Democrats used similar tactics in what became known as the "Mississippi Plan." Local Democratic clubs formed armed militias, marching defiantly through black areas, breaking up Republican meetings, and provoking riots to justify killing hundreds. Armed men posted during voter registration intimidated Republicans. At the election itself, voters were either "helped" by gun-toting whites to cast a Democratic ballot or chased away. Counties that had given Republicans majorities in the thousands managed a total of less than a dozen votes in 1875!

Ensuring Votes for the Democratic Ticket Despite the Fourteenth and Fifteenth Amendments, white southerners opposed to black suffrage found many illegal ways of influencing and eventually depriving them of that vote, thus returning white Democrats to office. In this cartoon, titled "Of course he wants to vote the Democratic Ticket," one of the two pistol-wielding men is saying: "You're as free as air, ain't you? Say you are, or I'll blow your black head off!" Note that another freedman is being led down the street to the polling place. How do you think he will vote? Was Reconstruction a success or failure?

Democrats called their victory "redemption." Their resumption of control of states throughout the South succeeded from a combination of persistent white southern resistance, including violence and coercion, and a failure of northern will.

Congress and President Grant did not totally ignore southern violence. Three **Force Acts**, passed in 1870 and 1871, gave the president strong powers to use federal supervisors to ensure that citizens were not prevented from voting by force or fraud. The third act, also known as the Ku Klux Klan Act, declared illegal secret organizations that used disguise and coercion to deprive others of equal protection of the laws. Congress created a joint committee to investigate Klan violence, and in 1872 its report filled 13 huge volumes with horrifying testimony. Grant sent messages to Congress proclaiming the importance of the right to vote and condemning lawlessness, and dispatched additional troops to South Carolina, where violence against blacks was the worst. However, Republicans lost interest in defending African Americans, deciding that they could keep political power without black votes. In 1875, Grant's advisers told him that Republicans might lose important Ohio elections if he continued protecting African Americans, so he rejected appeals by Mississippi blacks for troops to guarantee free elections. He and the nation, Grant said, "had tired of these annual autumnal outbreaks."

The success of the Democrats' Mississippi Plan in 1875, repeated a year later in South Carolina and Louisiana, indicated that congressional reports, presidential proclamations, and the Force Acts did little to stop the reign of terror against black and white Republicans throughout the South. Despite hundreds of arrests, all-white juries refused to find whites guilty of crimes against blacks. The U.S. Supreme Court backed them in two 1874 decisions throwing out cases against whites convicted of preventing blacks from voting and declaring key parts of the Force Acts unconstitutional. Officially, the Klan's power ended, but the attitudes (and tactics) of Klansmen would continue long into the next century.

Shifting National Priorities

White Americans, like their leaders, were tired of battles over the freedpeople. The easiest course was to give citizenship and the vote to African Americans, and leave them to fend for themselves. Americans of increasing ethnic diversity were primarily interested in starting families, finding work, and making money. Slovak immigrants fired furnaces in Pittsburgh; Chinese men pounded in railroad ties for the Central Pacific over the Sierra Nevada mountains and across the Nevada desert; Yankee women taught in one-room schoolhouses in Vermont for $23 a month; Mexican *vaqueros* drove Texan cattle herds to Kansas; and Scandinavian families battled heat, locusts, and high railroad rates on farmsteads in the Dakotas.

American priorities had shifted, at both the individual and national levels. Failing to effect a smooth transition from slavery to freedom for freedpeople, northern leaders focused their efforts on accelerating and solidifying programs of economic growth and industrial and territorial expansion.

As North Carolina Klansmen convened in dark forests in 1869, the Central Pacific and Union Pacific railroads met in Utah, linking the Atlantic and the Pacific. As southern cotton production revived, northern iron and steel manufacturing and western settlement of the mining, cattle, and agricultural frontiers also surged. As black farmers haggled over work contracts with landowners in Georgia, white workers were organizing the National Labor Union in Baltimore. As Elizabeth and Adele Allston demanded the keys to their barns in the summer of 1865, the Boston Labor Reform Association was demanding that "our . . . education, morals, dwellings, and the whole Social System" needed to be "reconstructed." If the South would not be reconstructed, labor relations might be.

The years between 1865 and 1875 featured not only the rise (and fall) of Republican governments in the South, but also a spectacular surge of working-class organization. Stimulated by the Civil War to improve working conditions in northern factories, trade unions, labor reform associations, and labor parties flourished, culminating in the founding of the National Labor Union in 1866. Before the depression of 1873, an estimated 300,000 to 500,000 American workers enrolled in some 1,500 trade unions, the largest such increase in the nineteenth century. This growth inevitably stirred class tensions. In 1876, hundreds of freedmen in the rice region along the Combahee River in South Carolina went on strike to protest a 40-cent-per-day wage cut, clashing with local sheriffs and white Democratic rifle clubs. A year later, also fighting wage cuts, thousands of northern railroad workers went out in a nationwide wave of strikes, clashing with police and the National Guard.

As economic relations changed, so did the Republican party, changing from a party of moral reform to one of material interest. In the continuing struggle in American politics between "virtue and commerce," self-interest was again winning. Abandoning the Freedmen's Bureau as an inappropriate federal intervention, Republican politicians had no difficulty handing out huge grants of money and land to the railroads. As freedpeople were told to fend for themselves, the Union Pacific was getting subsidies of between $16,000 and $48,000 for each mile of track it laid. As Susan B. Anthony and other women tramped through the snows of upstate New York with petitions for women's rights, Boss Tweed and other politicians defrauded New York taxpayers of millions of dollars. As Native Americans in the Great Plains struggled to preserve the sacred Black Hills from gold prospectors protected by U.S. soldiers, corrupt government officials in the East "mined" public treasuries.

Read the Document

Trial of Susan B. Anthony, on the Charge of Illegal Voting, at the Presidential Election in November 1872 at **www.myhistorylab.com**

By 1869, the year financier Jay Gould almost cornered the gold market, the nation was increasingly defined by its sordid, materialistic "go-getters." President Grant's cabinet was filled with his old army cronies and rich friends to whom he owed favors. Henry Adams, descended from two former presidents, charged that Grant's administration "outraged every rule of decency." Honest himself, Grant showed poor judgment of others. The scandals of his administration touched his relatives, his cabinet, and two vice presidents. Outright graft, loose prosecution, and generally negligent administration flourished in a half dozen departments. The Whiskey Ring affair, for example, cost the public millions of dollars in tax revenues siphoned off to government officials. Gould's gold scam was aided by Grant's Treasury Department and by the president's brother-in-law.

Nor was Congress pure. Crédit Mobilier, a dummy corporation supposedly building the transcontinental railroads, received generous bonds and contracts in exchange for giving congressmen money, stock, and railroad lands. An Ohio congressman described the House of Representatives in 1873 as an "auction room where more valuable considerations were disposed of under the speaker's hammer than any place on earth."

The election of 1872 showed the public uninterested in moral issues. "Liberal" Republicans, disgusted with Grant, formed a third party calling for lower tariffs and fewer grants to railroads, civil service reform, and the removal of federal troops from the South. Their candidate, Horace Greeley, editor of the New York *Tribune*, was also nominated by the Democrats, whom he had spent much of his career condemning. Despite his wretched record, Grant easily won a second term.

The End of Reconstruction

Soon after Grant's second inauguration, a financial panic, caused by railroad mismanagement and the collapse of some eastern banks, started a terrible depression that lasted throughout the mid-1870s. In these hard times, economic issues dominated politics, further diverting attention from freedpeople. As Democrats took control of the House of Representatives in 1874 and looked toward winning the White House in 1876, politicians talked about new Grant scandals, unemployment and public works, the currency, and tariffs. No one said much about freedpeople. In 1875, a guilt-ridden Congress did pass Senator Charles Sumner's civil rights bill to put teeth into the Fourteenth Amendment. But the act was not enforced, and eight years later the Supreme Court declared it unconstitutional. Congressional Reconstruction, long dormant, was over. The election of 1876, the closest in American history until 2000, sealed the end.

As their presidential candidate in 1876, the Republicans chose a former governor of Ohio, Rutherford B. Hayes, partly because of his reputation for honesty; partly because he had been a Union officer (a necessity for post–Civil War candidates); and partly because, as Henry Adams put it, he was "obnoxious to no one." The Democrats nominated Governor Samuel J. Tilden of New York, a well-known civil service reformer who had broken the corrupt Tweed ring.

Watch the Video

The Promise and Failure of Reconstruction

at **www.myhistorylab.com**

The End of Reconstruction This 1868 Thomas Nast cartoon ran under a caption quoting a Democratic party newspaper, "This is a white man's government." Describe each of the four (stereotyped) figures in this cartoon. Note the details in what each person carries in his raised (or outstretched) arm. You will see symbols of Irish workers in the "5 Points" neighborhood of New York City, the "lost cause" of the CSA, Confederate general Nathan Bedford Forrest, capitalist wealth, a Union soldier's uniform, and the ballot box. Note also the images in the background. In short, what do you see, and what does it mean? No single image better captures the story of the end of Reconstruction. Why?

Tilden won a popular-vote majority and appeared to have enough electoral votes for victory—except for 20 disputed electoral votes, all but one in Louisiana, South Carolina, and Florida, where some federal troops remained and where Republicans still controlled the voting apparatus despite Democratic intimidation. To settle the dispute, Congress created a commission of eight Republicans and seven Democrats who voted along party lines to give Hayes all 20 votes and a narrow electoral college victory, 185 to 184.

Outraged Democrats protested the outcome and threatened to stop the Senate from officially counting the electoral votes, preventing Hayes's inauguration. There was talk of a new civil war. But unlike in the 1850s, a North–South compromise emerged. Northern investors wanted the government to subsidize a New Orleans-to-California railroad. Southerners wanted northern dollars but not northern political influence—no social agencies, no federal enforcement of the Fourteenth and Fifteenth amendments, and no military occupation, not even the symbolic presence left in 1876.

As the March 4 inauguration date approached, the forces of mutual self-interest concluded the "compromise of 1877." On March 2, Hayes was declared president-elect. After his inauguration, he ordered the last federal troops out of the South, sending them west to fight Plains Indians; appointed a former Confederate general to his cabinet; supported federal aid for economic and railroad development in the South; and promised to let southerners handle race relations themselves. On a goodwill trip to the South, he told blacks that "your rights and interests would be safer if this great mass of intelligent white men were let alone by the general government." The message was clear: Hayes would not enforce the Fourteenth and Fifteenth Amendments, initiating a pattern of executive inaction that lasted to the 1960s. But the immediate crisis was averted, officially ending Reconstruction.

Conclusion
A Mixed Legacy

In the 12 years between Appomattox and Hayes's inauguration, victorious northern Republicans, defeated white southerners, and hopeful black freedpeople each wanted more than the others would give. Each got something. The compromise of 1877 cemented the reunion of North and South, providing new opportunities for economic development in both regions. The Republican party achieved its economic goals and generally held the White House, though not always Congress, until 1932. The ex-Confederate states came back into the Union, and southerners retained their grip on southern lands and black labor, though not without struggle and some changes. The Allstons' freedpeople refused to sign work contracts, even when offered livestock and other favors, and in 1869, Adele Allston had to sell much of her lands, albeit to whites.

In 1880, Frederick Douglass wrote: "Our Reconstruction measures were radically defective. . . . To the freedmen was given the machinery of liberty, but there was denied to them the steam to put it in motion. . . . The old master class . . . retained the power to starve them to death, and wherever this power is held there is the power of slavery." The wonder, Douglass said, was "not that freedmen have made so little progress, but, rather, that they have made so much; not that they have been standing still, but that they have been able to stand at all."

Freedpeople had made strong gains in education and in economic and family survival. Despite sharecropping and tenancy, black laborers organized themselves to achieve a measure of autonomy and opportunity in their lives. The three great Reconstruction amendments, despite flagrant violation over the next 100 years, held out the promise that equal citizenship and political participation would yet be realized.

TIME*line*

1865	Civil War ends
	Thirteenth Amendment ratified
	Freedmen's Bureau established
1865–1866	Black Codes
	Repossession of land by whites
	Ku Klux Klan formed
1867	Reconstruction acts passed over Johnson's veto
1868	Fourteenth Amendment ratified
1868–1870	Ten former Confederate states readmitted to the Union
1870	Fifteenth Amendment ratified
1876–1877	Three remaining former Confederate States of America readmitted to the Union
1880s	Tenancy and sharecropping prevail in the South
	Disfranchisement and segregation of southern blacks begins

✓●─┤Study and Review at **www.myhistorylab.com**

Questions for Review and Reflection

1. At the end of the Civil War, what were the goals and dreams of defeated southern whites, victorious northerners, and emancipated freedpeople? Can you name three for each group?

2. How did each group pursue its goals and dreams, what resources did each have, and how did they conflict with each other between 1865 and 1877?

3. What differences existed *within* each of the three major groups?

4. What were the major differences between northern presidential and congressional plans for reconstruction? In your judgment, which was more important—reconstruction politics in the North, or daily life, race relations, and politics in the South?

5. What is your assessment of how well American democratic politics and values served the dreams of diverse American peoples in the postwar era?

Key Terms

Amnesty 464

Contract labor 473

Debt peonage 475

Force Acts 482

Freedmen's Bureau 465

Presidential Reconstruction 464

Reconstruction Acts 459

Redemption 480

Sharecropping 474

15

The Realities of Rural America

American Stories

Realizing Dreams: Life on the Great Plains

In 1873, Milton Leeper, his wife Hattie, and their baby Anna climbed into a wagon piled high with their possessions and set out to homestead in Boone County, Nebraska. Like others, the Leepers believed the opportunities offered by the western plains were vital to continued national health as well as individual well-being. Once on the claim, the Leepers dreamed confidently of their future. Wrote Hattie to her sister in Iowa, "I like our place the best of any around here." "When we get a fine house and 100 acres under cultivation," she added, "I wouldn't trade with any one." But Milton had broken in only 13 acres when disaster struck. Hordes of grasshoppers appeared, and the Leepers fled their claim and took refuge in the nearby town of Fremont.

There they stayed for two years. Milton worked first at a store, and then hired out to other farmers. Hattie sewed, kept a boarder, and cared for chickens and a milk cow. The family lived on the brink of poverty but never gave up hope. "Times are hard and we have had bad luck," Hattie acknowledged, but "I am going to hold that claim . . . there will [be] one gal that won't be out of a home." In 1876, the Leepers triumphantly returned to their claim with $27 to help them start over.

The grasshoppers were gone, there was enough rain, and preaching was only half a mile away. The Leepers, like others, began to prosper. Two more daughters were born. The sod house was "homely" on the outside, but plastered and cozy within. Hattie thought that the homesteaders lived "just as civilized as they would in Chicago."

Their luck did not last. Hattie died in childbirth along with her infant son. Heartbroken, Milton buried his wife and child and left the claim. The last frontier had momentarily defeated him, although he would try farming in at least four other locations before his death in 1905.

Chapter Outline

Modernizing Agriculture

The West

Resolving the Native American Question

The New South

Farm Protest

Conclusion: Farming in the Industrial Age

The same year that the Leepers established their Boone County homestead, another family tried their luck in a Danish settlement about 200 miles west of Omaha. Rasmus and Ane Ebbesen and their 8-year-old son, Peter, had arrived in the United States from Denmark in 1868, lured by the promise of an "abundance" of free land "for all willing to cultivate it." By 1870, they had made it as far west as Council Bluffs, Iowa. There they stopped to earn the capital they needed to begin farming. Rasmus dug ditches for the railroad, Ane worked as a cleaning woman in a local boarding-house, and young Peter brought water to thirsty laborers digging other ditches.

Like the Leepers, the Ebbesens eagerly took up their homestead and began to cultivate the soil. Peter later recalled that the problems the family had anticipated never materialized. Even the rumors that the Sioux, "flying demons" in the settlers' eyes, were on the rampage proved false. The real obstacles facing the family were unexpected: rattlesnakes, prairie fires, grasshoppers—the latter just as devastating as they had been to the Leeper homestead. But unlike the Leepers, the Ebbesens stayed on the claim. Although the family "barely had enough" to eat, they survived the three years of grasshopper infestation.

In the following years, the Ebbesens thrived. Rasmus had almost all the original 80 acres under cultivation and purchased an additional 80 acres from the railroad. A succession of sod houses rose on the land and finally even a two-story frame house, paid for with money Peter earned teaching school. By their fifties, Rasmus and Ane could look with pride at their "luxurient and promising crop." But once more natural disaster struck, a "violent hailstorm . . . which completely devastated the whole lot."

The Ebbesens were lucky, however. A banker offered to buy them out, for $1,000 under what the family calculated was the farm's "real worth." But it was enough for the purchase of a "modest" house in town. Later, there was even a "dwelling of two stories and nine rooms . . . with adjacent park."

The stories of the Leepers and the Ebbesens, though different in their details and endings, hint at some of the problems confronting rural Americans in the last quarter of the nineteenth century. As a mature industrial economy transformed agriculture and shifted the balance of economic power permanently away from America's farmlands to the country's cities and factories, many farmers found it impossible to realize the traditional dream of rural independence and prosperity. Even bountiful harvests no longer guaranteed success. "We were told two years ago to go to work and raise a big crop; that was all we needed," said one farmer. "We went to work and plowed and planted; the rains fell, the sun shone, nature smiled, and we raised the big crop they told us to; and what came of it? Eight cent corn, ten cent oats, two cent beef and no price at all for

◉ View the Image

Red Cloud (Maqpeya-luta),
Chief of the Oglala Sioux
at **www.myhistorylab.com**

butter and eggs—that's what came of it." Native Americans also discovered that changes threatened their values and dreams. As the Sioux leader Red Cloud told railroad surveyors in Wyoming, "We do not want you here. You are scaring away the buffalo."

This chapter explores several of this book's basic themes as it analyzes the agricultural transformation of the late nineteenth century in the West and the South. In discovering the ways in which rural Americans—red, white, and black—joined the industrial world, ask yourself how diverse groups responded to new economic and social conditions. In what ways did the rise of large-scale agriculture in the West, the exploitation of its natural resources, and the development of the Great Plains shape the relationship between white settlers and the western tribes? How well were native peoples able to preserve their culture and traditions? In the South, what measures of success did the proponents of a **"New South"** enjoy in light of the underlying realities of race and cotton? Although the chapter shows that discrimination and economic peonage scarred the lives of most black southerners during this period, it also describes the rise of new black protest tactics and ideologies. Finally, the chapter highlights the ways in which agricultural problems of the late nineteenth century, which would continue to characterize much of agricultural life in the twentieth century, led American farmers to become reformers.

Modernizing Agriculture

Between 1865 and 1900, the nation's farms more than doubled in number as Americans flocked west of the Mississippi. Farmers raised specialized crops with modern machinery and relied on railroads to speed them to market. As one farmer explained, agriculture now was "a business."

While small family farms still typified American agriculture, vast mechanized operations devoted to one crop appeared, especially west of the Mississippi River. Bonanza wheat farms, established in the late 1870s on the northern plains, symbolized the trend to large-scale agriculture. Thousands of acres in size, these farms required large capital investments; corporations owned many of them. Like factories, they depended on machinery, hired hundreds of workers, and relied on efficient managers. Although **bonanza farms** were not typical, they dramatized the agricultural changes that were occurring everywhere on a smaller scale.

Despite their success in adapting farming to modern conditions, farmers were slipping from their dominant position in the workforce. In 1860, they represented almost 60 percent of the labor force; by 1900, less than 37 percent of employed Americans farmed. At the same time, farmers' contribution to the nation's wealth declined from one-third to one-quarter.

American Agriculture and the World

The expansion of American agriculture was tied to changing global patterns and demands. During the nineteenth century, as the population of Europe exploded, increasing numbers abandoned farming for urban industrial work. In Britain, farmers, only 10 percent of the total workforce, could not produce enough to feed the nation. Like other European countries, Great Britain imported substantial food supplies for its citizens. The growing demand prompted American farmers, along with their counterparts in eastern Europe, Australia, and New Zealand, to expand their operations for the European market.

In their attempts to improve crop yields and livestock, American farmers both benefited from and contributed to global trends in agriculture. German scientists facilitated agricultural expansion after 1850 by developing better seeds, livestock, and chemical fertilizers. The land-grant university system in the United States, established during the Civil War, ensured research into and development of better strains of crops and animals and more effective farming methods. For their part, American farmers led the way in using farm machinery such as the horse-drawn harvester, showing farmers elsewhere the way to raise bigger harvests.

A Vision of the Lackawanna Valley George Inness's *Lackawanna Valley*—with the reclining figure in the foreground, the train, and puffing smokestacks in the background—suggests that there need be no conflict between technology and agriculture. What other signs of technology besides the train can you see in this 1855 painting? *(George Inness, "The Lackawanna Valley." 1858. Oil on canvas, 33 7/8" × 50 3/16". Image © 2010 Board of Trustees, National Gallery of Art, Washington)*

This integration into the wider world depended on improved transportation at home and abroad. Reliable, cheap transportation in the United States allowed farmers to specialize: wheat on the Great Plains, corn in the Midwest. Eastern farmers turned to vegetable, fruit, and dairy farming—or sold out. Cotton, tobacco, wheat, and rice dominated in the South, while grain, fruits, and vegetables prevailed in the Far West. The development of steamships and an ever-expanding European network of railroad systems ensured that Americans goods and products could move swiftly, efficiently, and cheaply across land and sea to distant markets.

As farmers specialized for national and international markets, their success depended increasingly on outside forces and demands. Bankers and investors, many of them European, provided the capital to improve transportation and expand operations; middlemen stored and sometimes sold produce; and railroads and steamships carried it to market. A prosperous economy at home and abroad put money into laborers' pockets for food purchases. But when several European countries banned American pork imports between 1879 and 1883, fearing trichinosis, American stock raisers suffered. As Russian, Argentinean, and Canadian farmers turned to wheat cultivation, increased competition in the world market affected the United States' chief **cash crop**. Moreover, the worldwide **deflation** of prices for crops such as wheat and corn affected all who raised these crops for the international market, including American farmers.

The Character of American Agriculture

Technological innovation played a major role in facilitating American agricultural expansion. Harvesters, binders, and other new machines, pulled by work animals, diminished much of the drudgery of farming life, making the production of crops easier, more efficient, and cheaper. Moreover, they allowed a farmer to cultivate far more land than was possible with hand tools. But machinery was expensive, and many American farmers borrowed to buy it. In the decade of the 1880s, mortgage indebtedness grew two and a half times faster than agricultural wealth.

Only gradually did farmers realize the perils of their new situation. Productivity rose 40 percent between 1869 and 1899. But so large were the harvests for crops such as wheat that the domestic market could not absorb them. Foreign competition and deflation further affected steadily declining prices. In 1867, corn sold for 78 cents a bushel; by 1889, it had tumbled to 23 cents. Wheat similarly plummeted from about $2 a bushel in 1867 to only 70 cents a bushel in 1889. Cotton profits also spiraled downward, the value of a bale depreciating from $43 in 1866 to $30 in the 1890s.

Falling prices did not automatically hurt all farmers. Because the supply of money rose more slowly than productivity, all prices declined—by more than half between the end of the Civil War and 1900. Farmers received less for their crops but also paid less for their purchases. But deflation may have encouraged overproduction. To make the same amount of money, many farmers believed they had to raise larger and larger crops. As they did, prices fell even lower. Furthermore, deflation increased the real value of debts. In 1888, it took 174 bushels of wheat to pay the interest on a $2,000 mortgage at 8 percent. By 1895, it took 320 bushels. Declining prices thus affected most negatively farmers in newly settled areas who borrowed heavily to finance their new operations.

The West

In 1893, the young American historian Frederick Jackson Turner addressed historians gathered at Chicago's World's Fair. His message was startling. The age of the American frontier had ended, Turner declared, pointing to recent census data that suggested the disappearance of vacant land in the West. Although Turner overstated his case (for even in the twentieth century much of the West remained uninhabited), his analysis reflected rapid expansion into the trans-Mississippi West after the Civil War. Between 1870 and 1900, acreage devoted to farming tripled west of the Mississippi, while from 1880 to 1900, the western population grew at a faster rate than the nation as a whole.

The Frontier Thesis in National and Global Context

Turner considered the end of the frontier a milestone in the nation's history. The frontier had played a central role, he argued, in shaping American character and American institutions. Over the course of American history, the struggle to tame the wilderness had changed settlers from Europeans into Americans and created a rugged individualism that "promoted democracy." Turner's thesis, emphasizing the unique nature of the American experience and linking it to the frontier, won many supporters. His interpretation complemented long-held ideas about the exceptional nature of American society and character. It accorded with what many saw as a long struggle to conquer what Turner called the "wilderness."

But the American westward movement was less unusual than Turner suggested. The settlement of the trans-Mississippi West was part of a global pattern that redistributed European populations into new areas of the world. Paralleling their American counterparts, farmers, miners, and ranchers were claiming land in Argentina, Brazil, New Zealand, Australia, Canada, and South Africa. Like Americans, they argued that native occupants had failed to make the land productive, and they used their technological superiority to wrest the land from them. Around the world, many native peoples were facing domination by settler societies or retreating as far away from "civilization" as they could.

Turner's frontier scheme honored the frontier farmer who transformed and civilized the wilderness. Before the Civil War, however, real farmers avoided many parts of the West, especially the Great Plains, an area from

200 to 700 miles wide, extending from Canada to Texas. Much of this region, especially beyond the 98th meridian, had little rain. The absence of trees seemed to symbolize the plains' unsuitability for agriculture.

The Cattleman's West, 1860–1890

While the Great Plains initially discouraged farmers, its grasses provided the foundation for the cattle kingdom. Cattle raising dated back to Spanish mission days, but the commercial cattle frontier resulted from the Union's success in separating Texas from Confederate cattle markets. By war's end, millions of longhorns roamed the Texas range. The postwar burst of railroad construction allowed cattle to be turned into dollars. By the 1870s, cowboys were herding thousands of longhorns north to towns such as Abilene, Kansas, where they were loaded on trains for Chicago and Kansas City packinghouses.

((•─Hear the **Audio**
Cowboys and Cattle
at **www.myhistorylab.com**

Ranchers on the Great Plains bought some of the cattle and bred them with Hereford and Angus cows to create animals acclimatized to severe winters. In the late 1870s and early 1880s, huge ranches, many owned by eastern or European investors, arose from eastern Colorado to the Dakotas. These ventures paid handsomely since cattle grazed cheaply on public lands and then commanded good prices. Cowboys (a third of them Mexican and black) who herded the steers came cheap, earning paltry wages of $25 to $40 a month.

By the mid-1880s, the first phase of the cattle frontier was ending as farmers moved onto the Plains, buying and fencing public lands once used for grazing. But the arrival of farmers was only one factor in transforming the cattle frontier. Ranchers overstocked herds in the mid-1880s, and malnourished cattle weakened. Fierce blizzards followed the very hot summer of 1886. By spring, 90 percent of the cattle were dead. Frantic owners dumped their remaining animals on the market, getting $8 or even less per head.

Ranchers who survived the disaster adopted new techniques. Experimenting with new breeds, they began to fence in their herds and feed them grain during the winter. Consumers wanted tender beef rather than tough cuts from free-range animals, and these new methods satisfied the market. Ranching, like farming, was becoming a modern business.

Farmers on the Great Plains, 1865–1890s

Views of the agricultural possibilities of the Great Plains brightened after the Civil War, with railroads playing a key role in publicizing the region's potential. Now that rail lines crossed the continent, they needed customers, settlers, and freight to make a profit. Along with town boosters and land speculators, also hoping to capitalize on their investments, railroads joined in promotional campaigns. "This is the sole remaining section of paradise in the western world," promised one newspaper. Such propaganda reached beyond the United States to Scandinavians, Germans, and others.

Domestic Work in the West This photograph shows some of the hard physical labor involved in homesteading. How many steps were involved in doing the family laundry? The clothing of these women, probably settlers in North Dakota, identifies them as immigrants. Their presence reminds us that the West was the home of diverse peoples including Asians, European newcomers, Native Americans, black migrants, and Hispanics whose families had lived in the West for generations.

Dismissing the fear that the plains lacked adequate rainfall, promotional material assured readers that "All that is needed is to plow, plant, and attend to the crops properly; the rains are abundant." Above-average rainfall in the 1880s strengthened the case.

In the first boom period of settlement from 1879 to the early 1890s, tens of thousands of eager families began farming the Great Plains. The majority came from Illinois, Iowa, and Missouri. Like the Ebbesens, many others were immigrants. The largest numbers came from Germany, the British Isles, and Canada, but Scandinavians, Czechs, and Poles also arrived. Unlike many immigrating to American cities, they came in family groups and intended to stay.

Some claimed land under the Homestead Act, which granted 160 acres to any family head or adult who lived on the claim for five years or paid $1.25 an acre after six months of residence. Because homestead land was frequently less desirable, however, most settlers bought land from railroads or land companies. Start-up costs were thus higher than the Homestead Act would suggest. Although western land was cheap compared with eastern

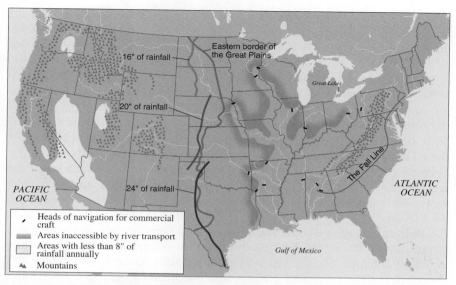

The Natural Environment of the West Study the patterns of rainfall and the natural features of the West, including rivers and mountain ranges. What do these patterns suggest about native vegetation and the prospects for farming? What is revealed about the role of water and irrigation in the West? What difficulties facing the settlers are revealed?

farmland, a farmer was lucky to buy a good quarter section for under $500. Machinery added another $700. Although some thought leasing rather than buying land made economic sense, many rented only because they lacked capital. In 1880, some 20 percent of the Plains farmers were tenants, and this percentage rose over time.

Late-nineteenth-century industrial innovations helped settlers overcome some natural obstacles. The shortage of timber for fencing and housing had encouraged early emigrants to go elsewhere. But in the 1870s, Joseph Glidden developed barbed wire as a cheap alternative to timber fencing. Twine binders, which speeded up grain harvesting, reduced the threat of losing crops to the unpredictable weather. And mail-order steel windmills for pumping water from deep underground wells relieved some of the water shortages by the 1890s.

Industrial innovations, however, could not resolve all of the problems confronting settlers. Wrote one Kansas homesteader:

> I tell you Auntie no one can depend on farming for a living in this country. Henry is very industrious and this year had in over thirty acres of small grain, 8 acres of corn and about an acre of potatoes. We have sold our small grain . . . and it come to $100; now deduct $27.00 for cutting, $16.00 for threshing, $19.00 for hired help . . . and where is your profit. I sometimes think this a God forsaken country, the [grass]hopper hurt our corn and we have ½ a crop and utterly destroyed our garden. If one wants trials, let them come to Kansas.

This letter highlights the uncertainties of frontier life: high costs, market fluctuations, pests, and natural disasters. Since many Plains pioneers took up homesteads with only a few dollars in their pockets, survival often depended on how well families managed during the crucial first years.

The first boom on the Great Plains fizzled in the late 1880s and early 1890s. Falling prices cut profits; one wheat farmer reported in 1890 earnings of $41.48 and expenses of $56.00. Then a devastating drought replaced the unusual rainfall that had lured farmers west. The destitute survived on boiled weeds, a few potatoes, and a little bread and butter. Many lost their farms to creditors. Some stayed as tenants. Homesteaders like the Leepers gave up. By 1900, two-thirds of homestead farms had failed. In western Kansas, the population fell by half between 1888 and 1892, and eastward-bound wagons bore a sad epitaph: "In God We Trusted: In Kansas We Busted."

Both ranching and agriculture had a long-term impact on the region's environment. Ranchers disrupted a complex natural balance when they killed off antelope, elk, wolves, and other wildlife. As cattle on overstocked ranges devoured perennial grasses, less nutritious annual grasses sprang up and, in turn, sometimes disappeared altogether. Lands once a lush home for large herds of cattle turned into parched deserts of sagebrush, weeds, and dust. Farmers who bought steel windmills to pump water from deep underground depleted the water table level. When they removed sod to build their houses and plowed, they removed the earth's protective covering. Heavy winds, common on the prairies, could lift topsoil and carry it miles away. Deep plowing, essential for dry farming techniques introduced after the drought of the 1880s, worsened the situation. The 1930s dust bowl was the eventual outcome of such human interventions.

Cornucopia on the Pacific

Although Americans rushed West when gold was discovered in California, one father advised his son, "Plant your lands; these be your best gold fields." He was right; completion of a national railroad system made farming California's greatest asset. But California farming resembled neither the traditional picture of rural life nor the dreams of homesteaders.

Little of California's land was homesteaded or developed as family farms. When California entered the Union, speculators acquired much of the land held by Mexican ranchers and sold it at prices beyond the reach of many small farmers. Those small farmers and ranchers who existed found it hard to compete with large, mechanized operators using cheap migrant laborers, usually Mexican or Chinese. One San Joaquin Valley wheat farm was so vast that workers started plowing in the morning at one end of the 17-mile field, ate lunch at its halfway point, and camped at its end that night. By 1900, farms of 1,000 acres or more made up two-thirds of the state's farmland.

The value of much of California's agricultural land, especially the southern half of the Central Valley, depended on water. By the 1870s, water, land, and railroad companies, using the labor and expertise of Chinese workers, were building dams, headgates, and canals—at high costs that they passed on to buyers eager to acquire hitherto barren land and water rights. By 1890, over a quarter of California's farms were irrigated. The irrigation ditches symbolized the importance of both technology and the managerial attitude toward the land characterizing late-nineteenth-century agriculture.

Although grain was initially California's most valuable crop, it faced stiff competition from farmers on the Plains and abroad. Some argued that land capable of raising luscious fruits "in a climate surpassing that of Italy, is too valuable for the cultivation of simple cereals." But high railroad rates and lack of refrigeration limited the volume of fresh produce sent to market. As railroad managers in the 1880s realized the potential profit that California's produce represented, they cut rates and introduced refrigerated cars. Fruit and vegetable production rose, benefiting from the agricultural expertise of Chinese laborers, tenant farmers, and Chinese entrepreneurs. So important were their contributions that some have argued that Chinese know-how was mainly responsible for the shift to produce farming. Before long, California fruit was sold as far away as London.

The Mining West

Mining hastened rapid western growth and development. The first and best-known mining rush occurred in 1848 when gold was discovered in California, but others followed as precious metals—silver, iron, copper, coal, lead, zinc, and tin—lured thousands west to Colorado, Montana, Idaho, and Nevada as well as to states such as Minnesota. Mining discoveries were transformative events, for they attracted people and businesses west, often to places far away from agricultural settlements. Hastily built mining communities might be eyesores, but they had bustling urban characters. If and when the strike was over, however, residents abandoned the mining camps and towns as fast as they had rushed into them. The pattern of boom and bust characterized much of mining life.

The reality of late-nineteenth-century mining was nothing like the popular stereotype of the independent miner panning for gold. Retrieving minerals from rock was difficult, expensive, and dangerous, requiring a large labor force, industrial tools, and railroad links. Miners worked way below the earth's surface in poorly ventilated tunnels, with no means for removing human or animal waste. Temperatures could reach as high as 120 degrees. Accidents were part of the job that involved blasting equipment and industrial machinery. In 1884, a Montana miner drilled into an unexploded dynamite charge and lost his eyes and ear. He received no compensation, for the court decided that the accident "was the result of an unforeseen and unavoidable accident incident to the risk of mining." In time, western miners became one of the most radical groups of industrial workers.

Exploiting Natural Resources

Mining was a big business with high costs and a basic dynamic that encouraged rapid and thorough exploitation of the earth's resources. The destruction of forests accompanied large-scale mining and the railroads that provided the links to markets. Both railroads and mining depended on wood—railroads for wooden ties, mines for shaft timber and ore reduction. In California, the California State Board of Agriculture estimated in the late 1860s that one-third of the state's forests had already disappeared.

👁 See the **Map**

Resources and Conflict in the West

at **www.myhistorylab.com**

When lumber companies cut down timber, they affected the flow of streams and destroyed the habitat supporting birds and animals. Like the activities of farmers and cattle owners, the companies stripping the earth of its forest cover were also contributing to soil erosion. The idea that the federal public lands ought to be rapidly developed supported such exploitation of natural resources. Often, in return for royalties, the government leased parts of the public domain to companies that hoped to extract valuable minerals, not to own the land permanently. In other cases, companies bought land, but not always legally. In 1878, Congress passed the Timber and Stone Act, which initially applied to Nevada, Oregon, Washington, and California. This legislation allowed the sale of 160-acre parcels of the public domain that were "unfit for cultivation" and "valuable chiefly for timber." Timber companies quickly took advantage of the new law. They hired men willing to register for claims and then to turn them over to timber interests. By the end of the century, more than 3.5 million acres of the public domain had been acquired under the legislation; most of it was in corporate hands.

The rapacious and rapid exploitation of resources combined with the increasing pace of industrialization made some Americans uneasy. Many believed that forests played a part in causing rainfall and that their destruction would have an adverse impact on the climate. Others, like John Muir, lamented the destruction of the country's great natural beauty. In 1868, Muir came upon the Great Valley of California, "all one sheet of plant gold, hazy and vanishing in the distance . . . one smooth, continuous bed of honey-bloom." He soon realized, however, that a "wild, restless agriculture" would destroy this vision of loveliness. Muir became a preservation champion. He played a part in the creation of Yosemite National Park in 1890, participated in a successful effort to allow President Benjamin Harrison to classify certain parts of the public domain as forest reserves (the Forest Reserve Act of 1891), and in 1892, established the Sierra Club. At the same time, conservation ideas were also emerging. Gifford Pinchot, a leading advocate of these ideas, was less interested in the preservation of the nation's wilderness areas than in careful management of its natural resources. "Conservation," he explained, "means the wise use of the earth and its resources for the lasting good of man." Both perspectives, however, were more popular in the East than in the West, where the seeming abundance of natural resources and the profit motive diminished support.

Resolving the Native American Question

Black Elk, an Oglala Sioux, listened to a story his father had heard from his father.

> A long time ago . . . there was once a Lakota [Sioux] holy man, called Drinks Water, who dreamed what was to be; and this was long before the coming of the Wasichus [white men]. He dreamed . . . that a strange race had woven a spider's web all around the Lakotas. And he said: "When this happens, you shall live in square gray houses, in a barren land, and beside those square gray houses you shall starve."

So great was the wise man's sorrow that he died soon after his strange dream. But Black Elk lived to see it come true.

As farmers settled the west and became entangled in a national economy, they clashed with the Indians who lived on the land. In California, disease and violence killed 90 percent of the Native Americans in the 30 years following the gold rush. Elsewhere, the struggle among Native Americans, white settlers, the U.S. Army, government officials, and reformers was prolonged and bitter. Some tribes moved onto government reservations with little protest. But most—including the Nez Percé in the Northwest, the Apache in the Southwest, and the Plains Indians—resisted stubbornly.

Background to Hostilities

The lives of most Plains Indians revolved around the buffalo. As migration to California and Oregon increased in the 1840s and 1850s, tribal life and animal migration patterns were disrupted. Initially, the federal government tried to persuade the tribes to stay away from white wagon trains and settlements. They did not have much success.

During the Civil War, some of the eastern tribes that had relocated across the Mississippi sided with the Confederacy; others with the Union. But after the war all were "treated as traitors." The federal government callously nullified pledges and treaties, leaving Indians defenseless against incursions. As settlers pushed into Kansas, tribes there were shunted into Oklahoma.

The White Perspective

When the Civil War ended, red and white men on the Plains were already at war. In 1864, the Colorado militia massacred a band of friendly Cheyenne at Sand Creek. Cheyenne, Sioux, and Arapaho soon responded in kind. The Plains wars had begun.

Although not all whites condoned this butchery, the congressional commission authorized to make peace viewed Native Americans' future narrowly. The commissioners accepted as fact that the West belonged to an "industrious, thrifty, and enlightened population" of whites. Native Americans, the commission believed, must relocate to western South Dakota or Oklahoma to learn white ways. Annuities, food, and clothes would ease their transition to "civilized" life.

At two major conferences in 1867 and 1868, chiefs listened to these drastic proposals spelling the end of traditional native life. Some agreed; others, like a Kiowa chief, insisted, "I don't want to settle. I love to roam over the prairies." In any case, the agreements were not binding because no chief had authority to speak for his tribe. For its part, the U.S. Senate dragged its feet in approving the treaties. Supplies promised to Indians who settled in the arid reserved areas failed to materialize, and wildlife proved too sparse to support them. These Indians soon drifted back to their former hunting grounds.

The commander of the army in the West, William T. Sherman, warned, "All who cling to their old hunting ground are hostile and will remain so till killed off." When persuasion failed, the army went to war. "The more we can kill this year," Sherman remarked, "the less will have to be killed the next war." In 1867, he ordered General Philip Sheridan to deal with the tribes. Sheridan introduced winter campaigning, aimed at seeking out Indians who divided into small groups during the winter and exterminating them.

Completion of the transcontinental railroad in 1869 intensified pressure for "solving" the Indian question. Transcontinental railroads wanted rights-of-way through tribal lands and needed white settlers to make their operations profitable. Few whites considered Native Americans had any right to lands they wanted.

In his 1872 annual report, the commissioner for Indian affairs, Francis Amasa Walker, addressed two fundamental questions: how to prevent Indians from blocking white migration to the Great Plains, and what to do with them over the long run. Walker suggested buying off the "savages" with promises of food and gifts, luring them onto reservations, and there imposing a "rigid reformatory discipline" on Indians who were "unused to manual labor." Though Walker wanted to save the Indians from destruction, he offered only one grim choice: "yield or perish."

The Tribal View

Native Americans defied such attacks on their ancient traditions. Black Elk remembered that in 1863, when he was only three, his father had his leg broken in a fierce battle with white men. "When I was older," he recalled,

> I learned what the fighting was about. . . . Up on the Madison Fork the Wasichus had found much of the yellow metal that they worship and that makes them crazy, and they wanted to have a road up through our country . . . but my people did not want the road. It would scare the bison and make them go away, and also it would let the other Wasichus come in like a river. They told us that they wanted only to use a little land, as much as a wagon would take between the wheels; but our people knew better.

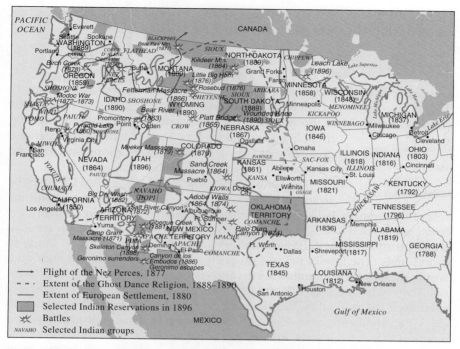

Native Americans, 1850–1896 What does this map reveal about the widespread appeal of the Ghost Dance movement and the result of efforts to force Native Americans onto reservations?

Black Elk's father and many others soon realized fighting was their only recourse. "There was no other way to keep our country."

Broken promises fueled Indian resistance. In 1875, the government allowed gold prospectors into the Black Hills, one of the Indians' sacred places and part of the Sioux reservation. Chiefs such as Sitting Bull led the angry Sioux on the warpath. At the Battle of Little Big Horn in 1876, they vanquished the army's most famous Indian fighter, George Custer. But bravery and skill could not permanently withstand the well-supplied, well-armed, and determined U.S. Army.

The wholesale destruction of the buffalo so central to Indian life contributed significantly to white victory. Plains Indians could be wasteful of buffalo when the animals were abundant, but white miners and hunters wiped out the herds. Sportsmen shot the beasts from trains. Railroad crews ate the meat. Ranchers' cattle competed for grass. And demand for buffalo bones for fertilizer and hides for robes and shoes encouraged decimation. The slaughter of 13 million animals by 1883 appears disgraceful today. Certainly, the Indians considered white men demented. "They just killed and killed because they like to do that," said one, whereas when "we hunted the bison . . . [we] killed only what we needed." But the destruction pleased whites because it helped control the Indians.

The Dawes Act, 1887

Changing federal policy was aimed at ending Indian power and culture. In 1871, Congress stopped the practice, in effect since the 1790s, of treating the tribes as sovereign nations. Other measures contributed to undermining tribal integrity and leaders. Federal authorities extended government jurisdiction to reservations and warned tribes not to gather for religious ceremonies.

●●●─Read the Document

The General Allotment Act (Dawes Act) (1887)
at **www.myhistorylab.com**

The **Dawes Severalty Act** of 1887 pulled together the strands of federal Indian policy and set its course for the rest of the century. Believing that tribal bonds kept Indians in savagery, reformers intended to destroy them. Rather than allotting reservation lands to tribal groups, the act allowed the president to distribute these lands to individuals. The lure of private property, the framers of the bill reasoned, would undermine communal norms and encourage Indians to settle as farmers. Those who accepted allotments would become citizens and presumably shed their tribal identity. But the support of speculators for the legislation suggested another force was at work. Even if each Indian family head claimed a typical share of 160 acres, millions of "surplus" acres would remain for sale to whites. Within 20 years of the Dawes Act, Native Americans lost 60 percent of their lands. The federal government held the profits from land sales "in trust" for the "civilizing" mission.

The Ghost Dance: An Indian Renewal Ritual

By the 1890s, their grim plight prepared many Native Americans for the message of Paiute prophet Wovoka. Predicting the destruction of the white race through natural disasters, Wovoka promised that Indians who performed the **Ghost Dance** would survive and gain new strength as their ancestors and wild game returned to life. Wovoka's ideas spread rapidly. Believers expressed their hope for change through new rituals of ghost dancing, hypnosis, and meditation.

●●─Watch the Video

Sioux Ghost Dance
at **www.myhistorylab.com**

American settlers were uneasy even though the prophet did not encourage Native Americans to harm whites. Indian agents tried to prevent ghost dances and filed hysterical reports. One agent determined that the Sioux medicine man Sitting Bull, a strenuous opponent of American expansion, was a leading troublemaker and decided to arrest him. In the confusion, Indian police killed Sitting Bull. Bands of Sioux fled the reservation with the army in swift pursuit. In late December 1890, the army caught up with them at Wounded Knee Creek. Although the Sioux had raised a flag of truce and started turning over weapons, a scuffle led to a

●●─View the Image

Sioux Encampment (early 1890s)
at **www.myhistorylab.com**

bloody massacre. Using the most up-to-date machine guns and Hotchkiss cannons, the army killed more than 200 men, women, and children.

With such measures, white Americans defeated the western tribes. Once proud, independent, and strong, Native Americans suffered dependency, poverty, and cultural disorganization on reservations, in Indian schools, or in urban slums.

The New South

The trans-Mississippi West was transformed as native peoples were subdued, the Great Plains settled, and commercial agriculture helped knit the region into the larger world. Mining camps became industrial centers. Western cities grew at a fast pace; by 1900, nearly 40 percent of westerners lived in cities. The large number of itinerant workers who toiled in mines, forests, and fields provided a flexible workforce that supported economic growth.

In contrast to this pattern, the southern economy sputtered. Of all the nation's agricultural regions, the South was the poorest. The agricultural labor force lacked efficiency, mobility, and capital for needed improvements. And while some southerners dreamed of making the agricultural South rival the industrial North, the region remained dependent on the North. Southern industrial workers were poorly paid, caught in dead-end jobs with little hope of advancement.

Postwar Southerners Face the Future

After the painful war and Reconstruction, compelling arguments for regional self-sufficiency emerged. Those dreaming of a "New South" argued that southern backwardness did not stem from the war, as many southerners wished to believe, but from southern conditions, especially the cotton-based economy. Defeat only highlighted the reality that power and wealth came from factories, machines, and cities, not cotton.

In hundreds of speeches, editorials, pamphlets, articles, and books, New South spokesmen tried to persuade fellow southerners to replace genteel prewar ideals with the ethic of hard work. In response, middle-class southerners increasingly accepted new entrepreneurial values. Because the South was short of capital, New South advocates held out attractive investment possibilities to northern bankers and manufacturers. Several southern state governments offered tax exemptions and the cheap labor of leased convicts. Texas and Florida awarded the railroads land grants, and cities including Atlanta and Louisville mounted huge industrial exhibitions. These enticements helped to lure northern capital to the South. In the 1880s, northerners increased investments in the cotton industry sevenfold and financed an expansion of southern railroads. Northern money fueled southern urban expansion. The percentage of southerners living in cities

RECOVERING *the* PAST

Magazines

Weekly and monthly magazines constitute a rich primary source for the historian, offering a vivid picture of the issues of the day and useful insights into popular tastes and values. With advances in the publishing industry and an increasingly literate population, the number of these journals soared after the Civil War. In 1865, only 700 periodicals were published. Twenty years later, there were 3,300. As the *National Magazine* grumbled, "Magazines, magazines, magazines! The newsstands are already groaning under the heavy load, and there are still more coming."

Some of these magazines were aimed at the mass market. *Frank Leslie's Illustrated Newspaper,* established in 1855, was one of the most successful. At its height, circulation reached 100,000. Making skillful use of pictures (sometimes as large as two by three feet and folded into the magazine), the weekly covered important news of the day as well as music, drama, sports, and books. Although Leslie relied more heavily on graphics and sensationalism than do modern newsweeklies, his publication was a forerunner of *Newsweek* and *Time.*

Other Journals sought middle- and upper-class readers. Editors such as Edwin Lawrence Godkin of *The Nation,* with a circulation of about 30,000, hoped to influence those in positions of authority and power by providing a forum for the discussion of reform issues. In contrast, the more popular *Scribner's* expressed a more conservative, middle-of-the-road point of view. Each month the magazine offered readers a wide variety of articles, ranging from essays to short stories, serialized novels, biographies, book reviews, and poetry. The magazine also had an elaborate art program, using images as another way to enlarge its readership. The formula was successful; by 1880, circulation surpassed 100,000. The following year, the name of the magazine was changed to *Century.* The number of subscribers continued to rise, topping out at over 200,000 by the end of the decade. Unlike some journals, like *Atlantic Monthly*, *Century* appealed to both northern and southern audiences.

One reason for the journal's success in the South was its policy of publishing articles about the South and the work of southern writers who often set their stories in the prewar period. Here you see the first page of a short story entitled "Two Runaways," by the popular southern author Henry Stillwell Edwards. It appeared in 1886.

REFLECTING ON THE PAST **What messages does the picture suggest about plantation masters and their slaves? In what ways has the illustrator hinted at the inferiority of the child? Do you think the depiction is stereotyped? In what ways does the text reinforce the messages conveyed by the graphics? How does this story, appearing in a very popular middle-class journal, help explain the racial situation in the late nineteenth century, both north and south? In what ways does "Two Runaways" reveal the challenges facing those who desired to create a New South? By considering the choice of graphics and text, you can begin to discover how magazines provide insight, not only into the events of the day but also into the ways magazines shaped the values and perspectives of nineteenth-century men and women. If you are intrigued by the possibilities offered by exploring popular middle-class monthlies, you can pursue this interest by consulting the site "Making of America," which contains digital reproductions of all the important magazines of the late nineteenth century.**

Harper's Weekly delivered powerful messages about the Native Americans in its choice of illustrations.

Two Runaways *(Century Magazine,* v. 32 (July 1886), p. 378)

rose from 7 percent in 1860 to 15 percent in 1900 (as compared to national averages of 20 and 40 percent).

Birmingham, Alabama, symbolized the New South. In 1870 it was a cornfield. The next year, two northern real estate speculators arrived, attracted by rich iron deposits. Despite cholera and the depression of the 1870s, Birmingham rapidly became the center of the southern iron and steel industry. By 1890, a total of 38,414 people lived there. Coke ovens, blast furnaces, rolling mills, iron foundries, and machine shops belched smoke. Mills and factories poured out millions of dollars of finished goods, and eight railroad lines carried them away.

Other southern cities flourished, too. Memphis prospered from its lumber industry and the manufacturing of cottonseed products, while Richmond became the country's tobacco capital even as its flour mills and iron and steel foundries continued to produce wealth. Augusta, Georgia, led the emerging textile industry of Georgia, the Carolinas, and Alabama.

The Other Side of Progress

New South enthusiasts, a small group of merchants, industrialists, and planters, bragged about their iron and textile industries and paraded statistics to prove the success of modernization. But progress was slow, and older values lingered. Even New South spokesmen romanticized the recent past, impeding full acceptance of a new economic order. Despite modernization, southern schools lagged far behind the North's.

Although new industries and signs of progress abounded, two of the new industries depended on tobacco and cotton, crops long at the center of rural life. As they had before the war, commerce and government work drove urban growth. The South's economic achievements, though not insignificant, did not improve its position in relation to the North. While southern industry grew in absolute terms, it declined in relative terms.

Moreover, the South failed to reap many of industrialization's possible benefits. The South remained an economic vassal of the North. Southern businessmen grew in number, but except for the American Tobacco Company, no great southern corporations arose. Instead, southerners worked for northern corporations, which absorbed southern businesses or dominated them financially. Profits and critical decision-making power flowed north. In many cases, southern mills and factories were allowed to handle only the early stages of processing. Northern factories finished the goods.

Individual workers in the new industries may have preferred factory life to sharecropping, but the rewards were meager. The presence of thousands of women and children in factories highlighted their husbands' and fathers' inability to earn a "family wage." As usual, women and children earned less than men. Justifying these policies, one Augusta factory president explained that child labor was "a matter of charity with us; some of them would starve if they were not given employment. . . . The work we give children is very light." Actually, many children at his factory performed adults' work for children's pay.

In general, workers earned less and toiled longer in the South than elsewhere. Per capita income was the same in 1900 as in 1860—and half the national average. In North Carolina in the 1890s, workers averaged 50 cents a day, with a 70-hour week. Black workers, who made up 6 percent of the southern manufacturing force in 1890 (but were excluded from textile mills), usually had the worst jobs and the lowest wages.

Cotton Still King

Although New South advocates envisioned the South's transformation from a rural to an industrial society, they always recognized the need for agricultural change. "It's time for an agricultural revolution," proclaimed Henry Grady, the New South's most vocal spokesman. Overdependence on "King Cotton" hobbled southern agriculture by making farmers the victims of faraway market forces and an oppressive credit system. Subdivide old cotton plantations into small diversified farms, Grady urged. Raising choice produce for urban markets could result in "simply wonderful profits."

A new agricultural South with new class and economic arrangements did emerge, but not the one Grady envisioned. Despite the breakup of some plantations, large landowners were resourceful in keeping their property and dealing with postwar conditions, as we have seen. As they adopted new agricultural arrangements, former slaves sank into peonage.

White farmers on small and medium-size holdings fared only slightly better than black tenants and sharecroppers. Immediately after the war, high cotton prices tempted them to raise as much cotton as they could. Then prices began a disastrous decline, from 11 cents a pound in 1875 to less than 5 cents in 1894. Yeoman farmers became entangled in debt. Each year, farmers bought supplies on credit from merchants so they could plant the next year's crop and support their families until harvest. In return, merchants demanded their exclusive business and acquired a lien (claim) on their crops. But when farmers sold their crops at declining prices, they usually discovered that they had not earned enough to settle with the merchant, who had charged dearly for store goods and whose annual interest rates might exceed 100 percent. Each year, thousands of farmers fell farther behind. By 1900, over half the South's white farmers and three-quarters of its black farmers were tenants. Tenancy increased all over rural America, but nowhere faster than in the Deep South.

These patterns had baneful results for individual southerners and for the South as a whole. Caught in a cycle of debt and poverty, few farmers could think of improving techniques or diversifying crops. Desperate to pay debts, they concentrated on cotton despite falling prices. Landowners pressured tenants to raise a market crop. Far from diversifying, farmers increasingly limited their crops. By 1880, the South was not growing enough food to feed its people adequately. Poor nutrition contributed to chronic bad health.

The Nadir of Black Life

Grady and other New South advocates expected that their region could deal with the race issue without the interference of any "outside power." He had few regrets over the end of slavery, which he thought had contributed to southern economic backwardness. Realizing that black labor would be crucial to the transformation he sought, he advocated racial cooperation. But racial cooperation did not mean equality. Grady assumed that blacks were inferior and supported informal segregation.

By the time of Grady's death in 1889, a much harsher perspective on southern race relations was appearing. Congressional leaders' decision in 1890 to shelve a proposed act protecting black civil rights and the defeat of a bill giving federal assistance for educational institutions rendered black Americans vulnerable. The traditional sponsor of freed people's rights, the Republican party, left blacks to fend for themselves. The courts also abandoned them: in 1878, the Supreme Court ruled unconstitutional a Louisiana statute banning discrimination in transportation. In 1882, the Court voided the Ku Klux Klan Act of 1871, finding that the civil rights protections of the Fourteenth Amendment applied to states, not to individuals. In 1883, provisions of the Civil Rights Act of 1875 that ensured for blacks equal rights in public places were similarly voided.

Rather than opposing these actions, northerners increasingly promoted negative stereotypes of blacks as lazy, ignorant, and childlike. Clearly, blacks could hardly enjoy the same rights and freedoms as whites; they needed the paternal protection of the superior white race. Such stereotypes filled magazines and newspapers and were popularized in advertisements, cartoons, and theater. Encouraged by northern public opinion, and with the blessing of Congress and the Supreme Court, southern whites sought to make blacks permanently second-class citizens.

In the political sphere, white southerners amended state constitutions to disfranchise black voters. By various legal devices—the poll tax, literacy tests, "good character" and "understanding" clauses administered by white voter registrars, and all-white primary elections—blacks lost the right to vote. The most ingenious method was the "grandfather clause," which specified that only citizens whose grandfathers were registered to vote on January 1, 1867, could cast ballots. This virtually excluded blacks. Although the Supreme Court outlawed such blatantly discriminatory laws, other constitutional changes, beginning in Mississippi in 1890 and spreading to all 11 former Confederate states by 1910, effectively eliminated the black vote.

In a second tactic in the 1890s, southern state and local laws legalized segregation in public facilities. Beginning with railroads and schools, **"Jim Crow" laws** soon covered libraries, hotels, hospitals, prisons, theaters, parks,

Lynching In 1896, an African American named William Biggerstaff was hanged for what was labeled the murder of a white man. The picture cannot reveal the innocence or guilt of the accused. Lynching and violence aimed at blacks became common in the late nineteenth century. What does the presence of the people in the background suggest about lynchings?

cemeteries, toilets, sidewalks, drinking fountains— nearly every place where blacks and whites might mingle. The Supreme Court upheld these laws in 1896 in *Plessy* v. *Ferguson*, ruling that "separate but equal" facilities did not violate the Fourteenth Amendment's equal protection clause. The decision opened the way for as many forms of legal segregation as southern lawmakers could devise.

●◆●—Read the Document

Legalizing Racial Segregation: From Plessy v. Ferguson *(1896)*

at **www.myhistorylab.com**

Political and social discrimination made it easier to keep blacks permanently confined to agricultural and unskilled labor and dependent on whites. In 1900, nearly 84 percent of black workers nationwide either did some form of agricultural labor or had service jobs, mostly as domestic servants and in laundries. These had been the primary slave occupations. The remaining 16 percent worked in forests, sawmills, mines, and, with northward migration, in northern cities. As whites systematically excluded blacks from trades, the percentage of blacks laboring in these jobs dropped to under 10 percent, although at the end of the Civil War, at least half of all skilled craftsmen in the South had been black. Such factory work

◉—View the Image

Plessy v. Ferguson *(1896)*

at **www.myhistorylab.com**

as blacks had been doing was also reduced, largely to separate poor blacks from whites and to undercut unionization. Exclusion of blacks from industry prevented them from acquiring the skills and habits that facilitated the entry of European immigrants and their children into the middle class by the mid-twentieth century.

Blacks did not accept their decline passively. In the mid-1880s, they enthusiastically joined the Knights of Labor (discussed in the next chapter), making up at least a third of the membership in the South. But southern whites feared that the Knights' policies of racial and economic cooperation might lead to social equality. The Charleston *News and Courier* warned darkly about "mongrels and hybrids." As blacks continued to join, whites fled the organization. White violence finished it off.

Lynching and other violence against blacks increased. On February 21, 1891, the *New York Times* reported that in Texarkana, Arkansas, a mob caught a 32-year-old black man, Ed Coy, charged with raping a white woman, tied him to a stake, and burned him. As Coy pleaded his innocence to a large crowd, his alleged victim somewhat hesitatingly put the torch to his oil-soaked body. The *Times* report concluded that only by the "terrible death such as fire . . . can inflict" could other blacks "be deterred from the commission of like crimes." Ed Coy was one of more than 1,400 black men lynched or burned alive during the 1890s. About a third were charged with sex crimes. The rest were accused of a variety of "crimes" related to not knowing their place: marrying or insulting a white woman, testifying in court against whites, or having a "bad reputation." Such violence operated not only to keep blacks but also white women in their "places."

Diverging Black Responses

White discrimination and exploitation nourished new protest tactics and ideologies among blacks. For years, Frederick Douglass had urged blacks to remain loyal Americans and count on the Republican party. In 1895, his dying words were allegedly "Agitate! Agitate! Agitate!"

Calls for black separatism rang out. Insisting that blacks must join together to fight the rising tide of discrimination, T. Thomas Fortune in 1891 organized the Afro-American League. The League (the precursor of the NAACP) encouraged independent voting, opposed segregation and lynching, and urged the establishment of black institutions such as banks to support black businesses. In the 1890s, black leaders lobbied to make the Oklahoma Territory, recently opened to white settlement, an all-black state. Blacks founded 25 towns there, as well as in other states and even Mexico. But these attempts, like earlier ones, were short-lived.

There were more radical black voices, too. Bishop Henry McNeal Turner, a former Union soldier and prominent black leader, despaired of ever securing equal rights for American blacks. The Constitution, he said, was "a dirty rag, a cheat, a libel" that "every Negro in the land" should "spit upon." In 1894, he organized the International Migration Society to return blacks to Africa, arguing that "this country owes us forty billions of dollars" to help. He sent two boatloads of emigrants to Liberia, but this effort worked no more successfully than those earlier in the century.

Douglass had long argued that no matter how important African roots might be, blacks had been in the Americas for generations and would have to win justice and equal rights here. W. E. B. Du Bois, the first black to receive a Ph.D. from Harvard, agreed. Yet in 1900, at the first Pan-African Conference in London, he argued that blacks must lead the struggle for liberation both in Africa and in the United States. It was at this conference that Du Bois first made his prophetic comment that "the problem of the Twentieth Century" would be "the problem of the color line."

Despite such militancy, many blacks worked patiently but persistently within white society for equality and social justice. In 1887, J. C. Price formed the Citizens Equal Rights Association, which supported various petitions and direct-action campaigns to protest segregation. Other blacks boycotted segregated streetcars in southern cities. Most black Americans continued to follow the slow, moderate self-help program of Booker T. Washington, the best-known black leader in America. Born a slave, Washington had risen through hard work to become the founder in 1881 and principal of Tuskegee Institute in Alabama, which he made the nation's largest and best-known industrial training school. At Tuskegee, young blacks received a highly disciplined education in scientific agriculture and skilled trades. Washington believed that economic self-help and the familiar Puritan virtues of hard work, frugality, cleanliness, and moderation would help African Americans succeed despite racism. He spent much time traveling through the North to secure philanthropic gifts for Tuskegee, becoming a favorite of the American entrepreneurial elite, whose capitalist assumptions he shared.

In 1895, Washington delivered a speech at the Cotton States and International Exposition in Atlanta—his invitation had been a rare honor for a former slave—in which he proclaimed black loyalty to southern economic development while accepting the lowly status of southern blacks. "It is at the bottom of life we must begin, and not at the top," he declared. Although Washington worked behind the scenes for black civil rights, in Atlanta he publicly renounced black interest in the vote, civil rights, or social equality. Whites throughout the country enthusiastically acclaimed Washington's address, but many blacks considered his "**Atlanta Compromise**" a serious setback.

Washington has often been charged with conceding too quickly that political rights should follow rather than precede economic well-being. In 1903, Du Bois confronted Washington directly in *The Souls of Black Folk*, arguing for the "manly assertion" of a program of equal civil rights, suffrage, and higher education in the ideals of liberal learning. A trip through Dougherty County, Georgia, showed Du Bois the "forlorn and forsaken" condition of southern blacks. Although "here and there a man has raised his head above these murky waters . . . a pall of debt hangs over the beautiful land." The lives of most blacks were still tied to the land of the South. To improve their lives, rural blacks would have to organize.

Watch the Video

The Conflict Between Booker T. Washington and W.E.B. Du Bois at **www.myhistorylab.com**

Farm Protest

During the post–Civil War period, many farmers, black and white, began to realize that only collective action could improve rural life. Not all were dissatisfied; midwestern farmers and those near city markets adjusted to changing economic conditions. Southern and western farmers, however, faced new problems that led to the first mass organization of farmers in American history.

The Grange in the 1860s and 1870s

The earliest effort to organize white farmers came in 1867 when Oliver Kelley founded the Order of the Patrons of Husbandry. Originally a social and cultural organization, it soon was protesting the powerlessness of the "immense helpless mob" of farmers, victims of "human vampires." The depression of the 1870s (discussed in the next chapter) sharpened discontent. By 1875, an estimated 800,000 had joined Kelley's organization, now known as the National Grange.

View the Image

The Purposes of the Grange at **www.myhistorylab.com**

The Grangers recognized some, but not all, of the complex changes that had created rural problems. Some of their "reforms" attempted to bypass middlemen by establishing buying and selling cooperatives. Although many cooperatives failed, they indicated that farmers realized the need for unified action. Midwestern farmers also accused grain elevator operators of cheating them, and they pointed to the railroads, America's first big business, as the worst offenders. Although cutthroat competition among railroad companies generally brought lower rates nationwide, railroads often raised rates in rural areas. Their rebates to large shippers also discriminated against small operators.

Read the Document

Advice on Keeping Children on the Farm (1881) at **www.myhistorylab.com**

Farmers realized that a confrontation with the mighty railroads demanded both cooperation with others, like western businessmen whose interests railroads also hurt, and political action. Between 1869 and 1874, businessmen and farmers successfully pressed Illinois, Iowa, Wisconsin, and Minnesota to pass so-called Granger laws (an inaccurate name, for the Grangers did not deserve complete credit for them) establishing maximum rates that railroads and grain elevators could charge. Other states set up railroad commissions to regulate railroad rates, or outlawed railroad pools, rebates, passes, and other practices that seemed to represent "unjust discrimination and distortion."

Railroad companies and grain elevators quickly challenged the new laws. In 1877, the Supreme Court upheld them in *Munn* v. *Illinois*. Even so, it soon became apparent that state commissions might control local rates but not long-haul rates. While Granger laws did not control the railroads and raised questions difficult to resolve on the local level, they established an important principle. The Supreme Court had made it clear that state legislatures could regulate businesses of a public nature such as the railroads. When the Court reversed its ruling in *Wabash* v. *Illinois* in 1886, pressure increased on Congress to continue the struggle.

The Interstate Commerce Act, 1887

In 1887, Congress passed the Interstate Commerce Act, requiring that railroads establish "reasonable and just" rates, publicize their rate schedules, and discontinue rebates and similar practices. The act also created the first federal regulatory agency, the **Interstate Commerce Commission** (ICC), empowered to investigate and prosecute lawbreakers. But the legislation limited its authority to commerce crossing state lines.

Like state railroad commissions, the ICC found it hard to define a reasonable rate, and thousands of cases overwhelmed its tiny staff. The ICC could only bring offenders into the federal courts for lengthy legal proceedings. Few railroads worried about defying it. When they appeared in court four or five years later, they often won their cases from judges suspicious of new federal authority. Between 1887 and 1906, the Supreme Court decided 15 of 16 such cases in the railroads' favor.

The Southern Farmers' Alliance in the 1880s and 1890s

The Grange declined in the late 1870s as the nation recovered from depression. But farm protest did not die. Depression struck farmers once again in the late 1880s and worsened in the early 1890s. Official statistics told the familiar, dismal story of falling grain prices on the plains and prairies. The national currency shortage, which usually reached critical proportions at harvest time, helped drive agricultural prices ever lower. Debt and shipping costs, however, climbed. It sometimes cost a farmer as much as one bushel of corn to send another bushel to market. Distraught farmers again tried organization, education, and cooperation.

The Southern Farmers' Alliance became one of the most important reform organizations of the 1880s. Its ambitious organizational drive sent lecturers across the South and onto the Plains. Alliance lecturers proposed programs that would help realize their slogan: "Equal rights to all, special privileges to none." Among the Alliance's efforts were experiments with cooperatives to free farmers from the clutches of supply merchants, banks, and other credit agencies. While cooperatives often failed, the Alliance also supported legislative efforts to regulate powerful monopolies and corporations that, they believed, gouged farmers. Many Alliance members believed that increasing the money supply was critical to improving the position of farmers and supported a national banking system empowered to issue paper money. Finally, the Alliance called for a variety of measures to improve the quality of rural life. Better rural public schools, state agricultural colleges, and improvements in the status of women were all on its agenda.

By 1890, rural discontent swept more than a million farmers into the Alliance. Included in this burst of organization growth were black as well as white farmers. Organized in 1888, the Colored Farmers' Alliance recognized that farmers of both races shared common economic problems and therefore must cooperate. But many southern cotton farmers, depending on black labor, disagreed. In 1891, black cotton pickers on plantations near Memphis went on strike. Revealing the racial tensions simmering just below the surface, white posses chased the strikers and lynched 15 of them.

The Ocala Platform, 1890

In December 1890, the National Alliance gathered in Ocala, Florida, to develop a platform. Believing that the federal government had failed to address the farmers' problems, delegates attacked both parties as subservient to the "will of corporation and money power."

Much of the Alliance's program was radical in the context of late-nineteenth-century political life. Calling for the direct election of U.S. senators, it supported lowering the tariff (a topic much debated in Congress) with the dangerous-sounding justification that prices must be reduced for the sake of the "poor of our land." The money plank surpassed what any national legislator would consider, boldly envisioning a new banking system controlled by the federal government. The platform called for the government to take an active economic role by increasing the amount of money in circulation through treasury notes and silver. More money would cause inflation and help debtors pay off loans.

The platform also called for subtreasuries (federal warehouses) in agricultural regions where farmers could store their produce at low interest rates until market prices favored selling. To tide farmers over, the federal government would lend them up to 80 percent of the current local price for their produce. Other demands included a graduated income tax and the regulation of transportation and communication networks—or, if regulation failed, their nationalization.

•ᵇ•─Read the Document

Ocala Platform, 1890
at **www.myhistorylab.com**

Although the Alliance was not formally in politics, it supported sympathetic candidates in the fall elections of 1890. A surprising number of them won. But before long, many Alliance members were pressing for an independent political party. Legislators elected with Alliance support did not necessarily bring action on issues of interest to farmers, or even respect. On the national level, no one had much interest in the Ocala platform.

Formation of the People's Party, 1892

Two years later, in February 1892, the People's, or Populist, party was established with Leonidas Polk, president of the National Farmers Alliance, as its presidential candidate. "The time has arrived," he thundered, "for the great

West, the great South, and the great Northwest, to link their hands and hearts together and march to the ballot box and take possession of the government . . . and run it in the interest of the people." But by July, at the party convention in Omaha, Polk had died and the party nominated James B. Weaver, Union army veteran from Iowa, for president and a former Confederate soldier for vice president.

The platform preamble for the new political party blazed with the urgent spirit of the agrarian protest movement, proclaiming that in the midst of political and corporate corruption "the people are demoralized. . . . The fruits of the toil of millions are boldly stolen to build up colossal fortunes . . . we breed two great classes—paupers and millionaires." To heal that divide, it was necessary to eliminate "the controlling influences dominating the old political parties."

The Omaha demands expanded the Ocala platform of 1890. They included more direct democracy (popular election of senators, direct primaries, the initiative and referendum, and the secret ballot) and several pro-labor planks (the eight-hour day, immigration restriction, and condemnation of the use of Pinkerton agents). The Populists also endorsed a graduated income tax, the free and unlimited coinage of silver at a ratio of 16 to 1, and government ownership of railroads, telephone, and telegraph. "The time has come," the platform said, "when the railroad corporations will either own the people or the people must own the railroads."

Although attempting to widen political debate by promoting a new vision of government activism to resolve farmers' problems, the Populists faced monumental obstacles: weaning the South from Democrats, encouraging southern whites to work with blacks, and persuading voters of both parties to abandon familiar political ties. But the new party pressed ahead. Weaver campaigned actively in the South, where he faced egg- and rock-throwing Democrats, who fanned racial fears in opposing his efforts to include blacks in the People's party. Despite hostile opposition, Weaver won over 1 million popular votes (the first third-party candidate to do so), and he carried four states (Kansas, Colorado, Idaho, and Nevada) and parts of Oregon and North Dakota, for a total of 22 electoral votes.

The Populists' support was substantial but regional, coming from western miners and mine owners who favored the demand for silver coinage and from rural Americans from the Great Plains. But the People's party failed to break the Democratic stranglehold on the South, and it did not appeal to city workers of the Northeast, who were suspicious of the party's anti-urban tone and its desire for higher agricultural prices (which meant higher food prices). Perhaps most damaging, the Populists made few inroads among Midwestern farmers, who were relatively better off than farmers elsewhere and saw little value in the Omaha platform. Although the Populists were not yet finished, most discontented farmers in 1892 voted for Cleveland and the Democrats, not for the Populists.

Conclusion

Farming in the Industrial Age

The late nineteenth century brought turbulence to rural America. The "Indian problem," which had plagued Americans for 200 years, was tragically solved for a while, but not without resistance and bloodshed. Few whites found these events troubling. Most were caught up in the challenge of responding to a fast-changing world. Believing themselves to be the backbone of the nation, white farmers brought Indian lands into cultivation, modernized their farms, and raised bumper crops. But success and a comfortable competency eluded many, like Milton Leeper, who were caught up in a cycle of poverty and debt. Some turned to collective action and politics in an attempt not merely to react to events but to shape them. Still others fled to cities, where they joined the industrial workforce in an attempt to find a better life for themselves and their families.

TIME*line*

1865–1867	Sioux wars on the Great Plains
1869–1874	Granger laws
1873	Financial panic triggers economic depression
1875	Black Hills gold rush incites Sioux war
1880s	"New South"
1884	Southern Farmers' Alliance founded
1887	Dawes Severalty Act
	Interstate Commerce Act
1890	Sioux Ghost Dance movement
	Massacre at Wounded Knee
	Ocala platform
	Yosemite National Park established
1890s	Black disfranchisement in the South

✓•⸤Study and Review at **www.myhistorylab.com**

Questions for Review and Reflection

1. Compare and contrast farming on the Great Plains with farming in California.
2. How did technology affect agriculture and mining in the West?
3. Describe the differing viewpoints of Native Americans and whites and the differing cultural values underlying these viewpoints.

4. What were the reasons that the New South did not achieve its goals?
5. Compare and contrast the treatment of Native Americans and African Americans in this period. Are there any similarities?
6. In what ways did agricultural life in the West and South create conditions that did not mesh with the ideals of American life?

Key Terms

Atlanta Compromise 513
Bonanza farms 491
Cash crops 493
Dawes Severalty Act 504
Deflation 493
Ghost Dance 504

Interstate Commerce Commission 515
Jim Crow laws 510
New South 491
Plessy v. Ferguson 511

16

The Rise of Smokestack America

American Stories

Telling His Story: O'Donnell and the Senators

By 1883, Thomas O'Donnell, an Irish immigrant, had lived in the United States for over a decade. He was 30 years old, married with two young children, and in debt for the funeral of his third child, who had died the year before. Money was scarce, for O'Donnell was a textile worker in Fall River, Massachusetts, and not well educated. "I went to work when I was young," he explained, "and have been working ever since." However, O'Donnell worked only sporadically at the mill, whose owners preferred to hire man-and-boy teams. Because O'Donnell's children were only one and three, he often saw others preferred for day work. Once, when he was passed over, he recalled, "I said to the boss . . . 'what am I to do; I have got two little boys at home . . . how am I to get something for them to eat; I can't get a turn when I come here. . . .'" I says, "Have I got to starve; ain't I to have any work?"

O'Donnell and his family were barely getting by. He said that he had earned only $133 the previous year. Rent came to $72. The family spent $2 for a little coal, but depended on driftwood for heat. Clams were a major part of the family diet, but on some days, there was nothing to eat at all.

The children "got along very nicely all summer," but it was now November, and they were beginning to "feel quite sickly." It was hardly surprising. "One has one shoe on, a very poor one, and a slipper, that was picked up somewhere. The other has two odd shoes on, with the heel out." His wife was healthy, but not ready for winter. She had two dresses, one saved for church, and an "undershirt that she got given to her, and . . . an old wrapper, which is about a mile too big for her; somebody gave it to her."

O'Donnell was testifying to a Senate committee, which was gathering testimony in Boston in 1883 on the relations between labor and capital. The senators asked

Chapter Outline

The Texture of Industrial Progress

Industrial Work and the Laboring Class

Capital Versus Labor

Strive and Succeed

The Politics of the Gilded Age

Conclusion: The Complexity of Industrial Capitalism

Gap Between Rich and Poor The threat of social upheaval is dramatically illustrated in this turn-of-the-century work, called "From the Depths." What do you think will happen next in this scene?

him why he did not go west. "It would not cost you over $1,500," said one. The gap between the worlds of the senator and the worker could not have been more dramatic. O'Donnell replied, "Well, I never saw over a $20 bill . . . if some one would give me $1,500 I will go." Asked by the senator if he had friends who could provide him with the funds, O'Donnell sadly replied no.

The senators, of course, were far better acquainted with the world of comfort and leisure than with the poverty of families like the O'Donnells. For them, the fruits of industrial progress were clear, and political leaders supported its continued expansion. As the United States became a world industrial leader in the years after the Civil War, its factories poured forth an abundance of ever-cheaper goods ranging from steel rails and farm reapers to mass-produced parlor sets. Manufacturing replaced agriculture as the leading source of economic growth between 1860 and 1900. By 1890, a majority of the American workforce held nonagricultural jobs; over a third lived in cities. A rural nation of farmers was becoming a nation of industrial workers and city dwellers.

As O'Donnell's appearance before the senatorial committee illustrates, industrial and technological advances profoundly changed American life. For O'Donnell and others like him, the benefits of this transformation were hard to see. Although no nationwide studies of poverty existed, estimates suggest that half the American population was too poor to take advantage of the new goods of the age. Eventually, the disparity between the reality of life for families like the O'Donnells and American ideals would give rise to attempts to improve conditions for working-class Americans, but it is unlikely that O'Donnell ever profited from such efforts.

This chapter examines the new order that resulted from the maturing of the American industrial economy. Focusing on the years between 1865 and 1900, it describes the rise of big business and heavy industry, the organization and character of the new industrial workplace, as well as the politics of this era known as the **Gilded Age**. As the United States built up its railroads, cities, and factories, how did its production and profit orientation affect the distribution of wealth and power? How did industrial capitalists build their wealth, and what actions did workers take to protest inequalities? How did national political leaders respond to this era of great transformation? Across the spectrum of American life, these were years of tremendous growth and broad economic and social change.

The Texture of Industrial Progress

When the Civil War began in 1861, agriculture was its leading source of economic growth. Forty years later, manufacturing had taken its place. During these years, the production of manufactured goods outpaced population growth. Per capita income increased by over 2 percent a year. But these aggregates disguise the fact that many people won no gains at all.

Big businesses became the characteristic form of economic organization. They could raise the capital to build huge factories, acquire the most efficient machinery, hire hundreds of workers, and use the most up-to-date methods. The result was more goods at lower prices.

New regions grew in industrial importance. From New England to the Midwest lay the country's industrial heartland. New England remained a center of light industry, and the Midwest still processed natural resources. Now, however, the production of iron, steel, and transportation equipment joined older manufacturing operations there. In the Far West, manufacturers concentrated on processing the region's natural resources, but heavy industry made strides as well. In the less industrialized South, the textile industry put down roots by the 1890s.

Although many factors contributed to the dramatic rise in industrial productivity, the changing nature of the industrial sector itself explains many of the gains. Pre–Civil War manufacturers had concentrated either on producing textiles, clothing, and leather goods or on processing agricultural and natural resources. Although these enterprises remained important, heavy industry grew rapidly after the war. The manufacturing of steel, iron, and machinery, meant for other producers rather than consumers, fueled economic growth.

Technological Innovations

An accelerating pace of technological change contributed to and was shaped by the industrial transformation of the late nineteenth century. Technological breakthroughs allowed more efficient production that, in turn, helped to generate new needs and further innovation. Developments in the steel industry exemplify this process and highlight the important role of entrepreneurs.

View the **Image**
Edison with Phonograph (1878), Matthew Brady
at **www.myhistorylab.com**

Before the Civil War, skilled workers used a slow and expensive process to produce an iron that was so soft that iron train rails wore out within a few years. The need for a harder metal supported the development and introduction of new technology. The Bessemer converter transformed iron into steel by forcing air through the molten iron, thus reducing the carbon. The converter had the added advantage of reducing the need for highly paid skilled workers.

Steel magnate Andrew Carnegie was neither an inventor nor an engineer, but he recognized the possibilities of the new process and new ways to organize industry effectively. Steel companies like Carnegie's acquired access to both raw materials and markets and brought all stages of steel manufacturing into one mill. Output soared and prices fell. When Carnegie introduced the Bessemer process in his plant in the mid-1870s, the price of steel dropped from $100 to $50 a ton. By 1890, it cost only $12 a ton.

In turn, the production of a cheaper, stronger, more durable material than iron created new goods, new demands, and new markets, and it stimulated further technological changes. Bessemer furnaces, geared toward making steel rails, did not produce steel appropriate for building. Experimentation with the open-hearth process using high temperatures yielded steel usable by bridge builders, engineers, architects, and even designers of subways. Steel use increased dramatically, from naval vessels to screws.

New power sources facilitated American industry's shift to mass production and also suggest the importance of new ways of organizing research and innovation. In 1869, about half the industrial power came from water. The opening of new anthracite deposits, however, cut the cost of coal, and American industry rapidly converted to steam. By 1900, steam engines generated 80 percent of the nation's industrial energy

Read the **Document**
Thomas Edison, The Success of the Electric Light (1879)
at **www.myhistorylab.com**

supply. Then electricity began to replace steam as a power source. Its development owed much to Thomas Edison, who had decided in 1878 to solve

The Homestead Steel Works The Homestead Steel Works, pictured here in about 1890, were located near Pittsburgh, Pennsylvania. The vast scale of the enterprise suggests the ways in which technological innovation stimulated the expansion of the steel industry in the late nineteenth century. Although the two small figures in the foreground humanize the picture, what does this picture suggest about the character of work in the steel mills?

the problem of electric lighting. Rather than relying on individual creativity, Edison believed that professional collaboration fostered successful innovation. His research lab had a range of specialists and facilities that included an advanced library, a chemical lab, and eventually a glassblowing lab. From these beginnings eventually came the electric generator.

Railroads: Pioneers of Big Business

Railroads were the pioneers of big business and a great modernizing force in the economy. Efficient national transportation and communications networks encouraged mass production and mass marketing and promoted new management techniques.

The creation of a national railway system was facilitated by the largesse of both federal and state governments that granted railroads lands from the public domain. Eventually, railroads received lands one and a half times the size of Texas. Benefiting from such incentives, the first transcontinental railroad was finished in 1869. Four additional transcontinental lines and miles of feeder and branch roads were laid down in the 1870s and 1880s, with telegraph lines running alongside them.

Railroad companies were large, complicated organizations presenting both new opportunities and new problems. The costs of construction required unprecedented amounts of capital, while the numbers of workers and the operation of the business demanded new management techniques.

In 1854, the Erie Railroad hired engineer and inventor Daniel McCallum to discover how to make managers and employees more accountable. McCallum realized that large organizations needed to be handled differently than small ones. The system he devised separated responsibilities and ensured a regular flow of information. Other large-scale businesses copied both the new procedures that effectively distributed work and separated management from operations and many of the ruthless techniques railroads adopted.

Unlike small businesses, railroads' high costs and heavy indebtedness encouraged aggressive business practices that could contribute to instability. Slashing workers' wages was one tactic that often led to powerful worker unrest. To meet competition, railroads might offer customers lower rates or secret rebates (cheaper fares in exchange for all of a company's business). While rivalry between railroads lowered freight rates steadily, they might result in bankruptcy. Hoping to impose some order on the railroad business in the 1870s, railroad leaders set up "pools"—informal arrangements that established uniform rates—or agreed to divide up the traffic. Yet these deals never completely succeeded. Too often, companies broke them, especially during business downturns.

Growth in Other Industries

By the last quarter of the century, the textile, metal, and machinery industries equaled the railroads in size. By 1900, more than 1,000 American factories had giant labor forces ranging between 500 and 1,000, and another 450 employed more than 1,000 workers. Big business had come of age.

Business expansion was accomplished in one of two ways (or a combination of both). Some owners such as steel magnate Andrew Carnegie engage in **vertical integration** adding operations either before or after the production process. Even though he had introduced the most up-to-date innovations in his steel mills, Carnegie realized he needed his own sources of pig iron, coal, and coke—"backward" integration—to avoid dependence on suppliers. When Carnegie acquired steamships and railroads to transport his finished products, he was integrating "forward." Companies that integrated vertically frequently achieved economies of scale.

Other companies copied the railroads and integrated horizontally by combining similar businesses. They did not intend to control all stages of production, but rather, by monopolizing the market, hoped to eliminate competition and stabilize prices. John D. Rockefeller used **horizontal integration** to control the oil market. Rockefeller bought or drove out competitors of his Standard Oil of New Jersey. Although his company never achieved a complete monopoly, by 1898 it refined 84 percent of the nation's oil. While horizontal integration occasionally stimulated economies and greater profits, it was the monopolistic control over prices that boosted earnings.

In the oil business, Rockefeller observed, "the day of individual competition . . . is past and gone." As giant businesses competed intensely, often cutting wages and prices, they absorbed smaller, weaker producers. Business ownership became increasingly concentrated. In 1870, 808 American iron and steel firms were operating, but by 1900, fewer than 70 were left.

As businesses grew, like the railroads, they recognized the many advantages of legal incorporation. A corporation could raise money for large-scale operations by selling stocks. Its legal identity allowed it to survive the death of original and subsequent shareholders, while the principle of limited liability protected the personal assets of both shareholders and officials. Such characteristics made investments in corporations more attractive.

These economic transformations demanded huge amounts of capital and the willingness to accept financial risks. Building the railroad system cost over $1 billion by 1859 (the prewar canal system's price tag was under $2 million); after the war, another $10 billion went to complete the national railroad network. Foreign investors contributed a third of that. Americans, too, began to invest an increasing percentage of the national income.

Although savings and commercial banks continued to invest depositors' capital, investment banking houses like Morgan & Co. played a new and significant role in transferring resources to economic enterprises. Stocks, which paid dividends only if a company made a profit, were riskier investments than bonds. When J. Pierpont Morgan, a respected investment banker, began to market stocks, they caught on. The market for industrial securities expanded rapidly in the 1880s and 1890s. Although some Americans feared the powerful investment bankers and distrusted the financial market, both were integral to late-nineteenth-century economic expansion.

American Industry and the World

The industrialization of the late nineteenth century represented the second stage of the great transformation that began in eighteenth-century Great Britain. By reorganizing production, often through the use of machinery, early manufacturers turned out more and cheaper goods than at any time in human history. Innovation created the textile, mining, and metal industries and stimulated changes in transportation and communications. From Britain, industrialization spread to other European countries and the United States.

The second stage of the Industrial Revolution was marked by the application of science and technology to manufacturing and by the creation of new ways to mass-produce goods. The United States was the leader in developing techniques of mass production, while Germany excelled in using science and technology to reshape production. Technological innovations transformed German industry. As in the United States, giant firms turned out goods (especially heavy machinery and chemicals) for ever lower prices. Along with Great Britain, Germany and the United States produced two-thirds of the world's manufactured products between 1870 and 1930.

Great Britain, the world's most powerful nation during the nineteenth century, had long been its economic leader. But the balance of power began to shift as German and American businesses developed large new enterprises, introduced new ways of organizing and efficiently managing them, invested heavily in equipment, and promoted research. Great Britain lost ground, preferring traditional ways of organizing businesses rather than the new corporate structure. British manufacturing continued to be centered in older industries such as textiles, while British investors channeled their capital away from domestic industries toward investment opportunities abroad. American railroads and subways were constructed partly with the assistance of British investors.

The full impact of the changed position of the United States in the world, triggered by its industrial might, only became fully apparent in the twentieth century. But the importance of connections with other nations was obvious. Standard Oil sent two-thirds of the kerosene it refined to overseas markets. Firms manufacturing sewing machines, a range of office machines such as typewriters, and farm machinery came to dominate the world market. Singer Sewing Machine had a factory in Scotland in the 1880s and two decades later manufactured over 400,000 machines in Moscow, employing 2,500 workers and 300 managers. American locomotives were exported to South America, parts of Africa and Europe, the Middle East, and Asia. The Baldwin Locomotive Works of Philadelphia produced as many engines as any other locomotive company in the world.

These connections between American business and other nations meant that events overseas could affect the American economy. Furthermore, they suggested the intricate ties binding American business to other parts of the world. American industrial production contributed to the economic development of countries around the globe, while American business also competed with foreign producers.

An Erratic Global Economy

Affected by national and worldwide economic trends, the transformation of the economy was neither smooth nor steady. Two depressions, from 1873 to 1879 and from 1893 to 1897, surpassed the severity of pre–Civil War downturns. Collapsing land values, unsound banking practices, and changes in the money supply had caused antebellum depressions. In the larger and more interdependent late-nineteenth-century economy, depressions were industrial, intense, and accompanied by widespread unemployment, a phenomenon new to American life. They were also related to economic declines in European industrial nations.

The business cycle had a recurring rhythm. The global pattern of falling prices and fierce competition encouraged overproduction and the flooding of markets with goods. When the market was saturated, sales and profits declined and the economy spiraled downward. Owners laid off workers (who lived solely on their wages); and when workers economized on food, farm prices plummeted. Farmers, like wage workers, cut purchases. Business stagnated. Finally, the railroads were hurt. Eventually the cycle bottomed out, but millions of workers had lost jobs, thousands of businesses had gone bankrupt, and many Americans had suffered hardship.

One of the worst depressions ever to grip the American economy, from 1893 to 1897, was heightened by the growth of the national economy and economic interdependence. The depression started in Europe and spread to the United States as overseas buyers cut back on purchases of American products. Shrinking markets abroad soon crippled American manufacturing. Foreign investors, worried about the stability of American currency, dumped some $300 million of their securities in the United States. As gold left the country to pay for these securities, the nation's money supply declined. At the same time, falling prices hurt farmers, who discovered that it cost more to raise their crops and livestock than they could make in the market. Workers fared no better: wages fell faster than the price of food and rent.

The collapse in 1893 was also caused by an overextension of the domestic economy, especially in railroad construction. Farmers, troubled by falling prices, planted more, hoping that the market would pick up. As the realization of overextension spread, confidence faltered, and then gave way to financial panic. When Wall Street crashed early in 1893, investors frantically sold their shares, companies plunged into bankruptcy, and disaster spread. People rushed to exchange paper notes for gold, reducing gold reserves and confidence in the economy even further. Banks called in loans, which by the end of the year led to 16,000 business bankruptcies and 500 bank failures.

The capital crunch and the diminished buying power of rural and small-town Americans (still half the population) forced massive factory closings. Within a year, an estimated 3 million Americans—20 percent of the workforce—lost jobs. People fearfully watched tramps going from city to city, looking for work.

Despite the magnitude of despair, national politicians and leaders were reluctant to respond. When an army of unemployed led by Jacob Coxey marched on Washington in the spring of 1894 to press for public work relief, its leaders were arrested for walking on the Capitol grass. In American cities, only mass demonstrations forced authorities to provide soup kitchens and places for the homeless to sleep.

Industrial Work and the Laboring Class

The huge fortunes accumulated by Andrew Carnegie and John D. Rockefeller during the late nineteenth century dramatized the pattern of wealth concentration that began in the early period of industrialization. In 1890, the top 1 percent of American families possessed over a quarter of the wealth, and the top 10 percent owned about 73 percent. But what of the workers who tended machines that created industrial wealth?

Industry still needed skilled workers and paid them well. Average real wages rose more than 50 percent between 1860 and 1900. But wages for the unskilled increased by only 31 percent—a substantial differential that widened as the century drew to a close. But for workers without steady employment, rising real wages meant little. Work also could be sporadic, subject to layoffs when times were slow or economic conditions depressed. Working-class Americans made up the largest segment of the labor force (more than 50 percent), so their experience reveals important facets of the American social and economic system and American values.

The New Immigration, 1880–1900

In the 40 years before the Civil War, 5 million immigrants poured into the United States; from 1860 to 1900, that volume almost tripled. Three-quarters of them stayed in the Northeast, while many of the rest settled in cities across the nation, where they soon outnumbered native-born whites.

Until 1880, three-quarters of the immigrants, so-called "old immigrants," hailed from the British Isles, Germany, and Scandinavia. Then the pattern slowly changed. By 1890, "old immigrants" composed only 60 percent of the total number of newcomers, with **"new immigrants"** from southern and eastern Europe making up most of the rest. Italian Catholics and eastern European Jews were most numerous, followed by Slavs (mostly Russians and Poles).

A variety of forces prompted the tide of migration. Better and cheaper transportation made the trip possible. Trains reached deep into eastern and southern Europe. Even steerage passengers on transatlantic vessels could expect a bed and communal washroom. The modernization of European economies also stimulated immigration. New agricultural techniques led landlords to consolidate their land, evicting longtime tenants. Some moved to European cities, others to Canada or South America, but the largest group headed to the United States. Artisans, their skills made obsolete by machinery, also pulled up stakes. But dissatisfaction with life at home also played a part. Especially in Russia, government persecution and the expansion of military drafts drove millions of Jews and other minorities to emigrate.

Opportunity in "golden" America was the lure. State commissioners of immigration and American railroad and steamship companies wooed potential immigrants. Friends and relatives wrote optimistic letters promising help in finding work, often including passage money or pictures of friends in fashionable clothes.

Like rural and small-town Americans, Europeans came primarily to work. Most were young, single men with few skills. Jews, however, came most often in family groups, and women predominated among the Irish. When times were good and American industry needed unskilled laborers, migration was heavy. In bad times, the numbers fell off. Immigrants hoped to earn enough money in America to realize ambitions at home, and as many as a third eventually went back.

Although the greatest influx of Mexicans would come in the twentieth century, Mexican laborers also migrated to the United States. Like Europe, Mexico was modernizing. Overpopulation and new land policies uprooted many inhabitants, while the construction of a 900-mile railroad from central Mexico to the Texas border facilitated migration. Many Mexicans ended up in the Southwest and West, often working on railroads and in mines.

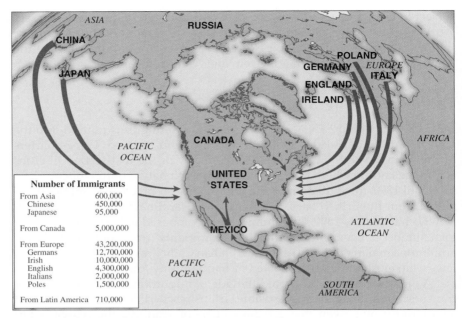

Number of Immigrants	
From Asia	600,000
Chinese	450,000
Japanese	95,000
From Canada	5,000,000
From Europe	43,200,000
Germans	12,700,000
Irish	10,000,000
English	4,300,000
Italians	2,000,000
Poles	1,500,000
From Latin America	710,000

Migration to the United States, 1860–1910 This map makes clear the many parts of the world that sent population to the United States. Many of those who came were dislodged by economic changes in their home countries. What were the most important short-term consequences of these migratory streams? What have been the long-term consequences?

Overpopulation, turmoil, unemployment, and crop failures brought Asians, mostly from south China, to the "Land of the Golden Mountains." Although only 264,000 Chinese came to the United States between 1860 and 1900, they constituted a significant minority on the West Coast. Most were unskilled male contract laborers, away from wives and families for years. They held some of the worst jobs in the West. They worked in mining and agriculture, on railroad and levee construction, and labored in factory and laundry work. To serve them, contractors brought in Chinese women to serve as prostitutes. Virtually enslaved, few of these women could pay off the costs of their passage or escape brothel life.

By the 1870s and 1880s, white workers in the West began to blame the Chinese for economic hardships. A meeting of San Francisco workers in 1877 in favor of the eight-hour day exploded into a rampage against the Chinese. In following years, angry mobs killed Chinese workers in Tacoma, Seattle, Denver, and Rock Springs, Wyoming. Local hostility was expressed at the national level when, in 1882, Congress passed the Chinese Exclusion Act, prohibiting the immigration of Chinese workers for a 10-year period. It was extended in 1892 and made permanent in 1902.

•••—Read the Document
William B. Farwell, The Chinese at Home and Abroad *(1885)*
at **www.myhistorylab.com**

•••—View the Image
Chinese-Americans in California
at **www.myhistorylab.com**

•••—Read the Document
Chinese Exclusion Act (1882)
at **www.myhistorylab.com**

The importance of migration from Europe, Mexico, and Asia can hardly be overestimated. Immigrants contributed to the country's rapid urbanization and provided much of the labor needed to accomplish the economic transformation of the late nineteenth century. Their presence also helped transform American society. The American population became far more heterogeneous in terms of ethnicity and religion than any other industrial nation.

The Impact of Ethnic Diversity

Late-nineteenth-century immigrants formed 20 percent of the labor force and over 40 percent of laborers in the manufacturing and extractive industries. They tended to settle in cities and made up more than half the working-class population. The fact that more than half the urban industrial class was foreign, unskilled, and often unable to speak English influenced industrial work, urban life, labor protest, and local politics. Immigrants often had little in common with native-born workers or even with one another.

There were many gradations within the working class. Atop the working-class hierarchy, native-born Protestant whites held most of the well-paying skilled jobs. Their occupations bore the mark of late-nineteenth-century industrialism: machinists, iron puddlers and rollers, engineers, foremen, conductors, carpenters, plumbers, mechanics, and printers. Skilled northern European immigrants filled most middle-rank positions. Often they had held similar jobs in their homelands. Jews, who had tailoring experience, became the backbone of the garment industry (where they faced little competition because American male workers considered it unmanly to work on women's clothes). But most "new immigrants" from southern and central Europe lacked urban industrial

•꞉•⎯Read the **Document**

Charles Loring Brace, The Dangerous Classes of New York *(1872)*
at **www.myhistorylab.com**

experience. They got the unskilled, dirty jobs near the bottom of the occupational ladder: relining blast furnaces, carrying raw materials or finished products, or cleaning up. Often, they were day laborers on the docks, ditch-diggers, or construction workers. Hiring was often done on a daily basis, usually arranged through middlemen such as the Italian *padrone*. Unskilled work seldom gave much job stability or paid much money.

At the bottom, blacks occupied the most marginal positions as janitors, servants, porters, and laborers. Racial discrimination generally kept them from industrial jobs, even though their occupational background differed little from that of rural white immigrants. There were always plenty of whites eager to work, so it was not necessary to hire blacks except occasionally as scabs during a strike.

Work Settings and Experiences

A majority of American manufacturing workers now labored not in shops but in factories dominated by the unceasing rhythms of machinery. Industrial jobs became increasingly specialized and monotonous. Even skilled workers did not produce a complete product, and the range of their skills narrowed. Those still toiling in small shops and basement, loft, or tenement sweatshops shared the monotony and the relentless pressure to produce—volume, not hours, determined pay.

The organization of work kept workers apart. In large factories, workers were divided into small work groups often defined by ethnicity, and the entire workforce rarely mingled. Those paid by the piece competed in speed, agility, and output.

What workers shared in common was a very long working day—usually 10 hours a day, six days a week—and unhealthy, dangerous, and uncomfortable workplaces. A few states passed laws to regulate work conditions, but enforcement was spotty, and owners were unconcerned with workers' health or safety. Women bent over sewing machines developed digestive illnesses and curved spines. In some mines, workers labored in temperatures above 120 degrees, handled dynamite, and died in cave-ins caused by inadequate timber supports. When new drilling machinery was introduced, the air was filled with tiny particles that caused lung disease.

Accident rates in the United States far exceeded those of Europe's industrial nations. Nationwide, nearly 25 percent of the men reaching the age of 20 in 1880 would not live to see 44, compared with 7 percent today. The law placed the burden of avoiding accidents on workers, who were expected to quit if they thought conditions unsafe.

The Family Economy

Although nineteenth-century ideology pictured men as breadwinners, many working-class married men could not earn enough to support their families alone. In the nineteenth century, married women did not usually take outside employment, although they contributed to family income by taking in sewing, laundry, and boarders. In 1890, only 3.3 percent of married women were in the paid labor force. A working-class family's standard of living thus often depended on the work of children. The laborer whose annual earnings amounted to only $384 depended on his 13-year-old son, not his wife, to earn an extra $196, critical to the family's welfare. In 1880, one-fifth of the nation's children between the ages of 10 and 14 held jobs.

Child labor was closely linked to a father's income, which in turn depended on skill, ethnic background, and occupation. Immigrant families more frequently sent their young children out to work (and also had more children) than native-born families. Middle-class reformers who sentimentalized childhood disapproved of parents who put their children to work. "Father never attended school, and thinks his children will have sufficient schooling before they reach their tenth year, thinks no advantage will be gained from longer attendance at school, so children will be put to work as soon as able," said one. Such a father condemned his children to future poverty, reformers believed. Actually, sending children to

[View the Image
Children Working in Coal Mine
(Lewis Hine, Photo)
at **www.myhistorylab.com**

work was a means of handling the immediate threat of poverty, of financing the education of one of the children, or even of ensuring that children stayed near their family.

Many more young people over the age of 14 were working for wages than was the case for children. Half of all Philadelphia's students had quit school by that age. Daughters as well as sons were expected to take jobs, although young women from immigrant families were more likely to work than young American women.

Women at Work

By 1900, nearly 20 percent of American women were in the labor force. Discrimination, present from women's earliest days in the workforce, persisted. An experienced female factory worker might be paid $5 or $6 a week, whereas an unskilled male laborer could make about $8. Still, factory jobs were desirable because they often paid better than other kinds of work open to women.

Employment opportunities for women were limited, and ethnic taboos and cultural traditions helped shape choices. About a quarter of working women secured factory jobs. Italian and Jewish women (whose cultural backgrounds virtually forbade their going into domestic service) clustered in the garment industry, and Poles and Slavs went into textiles, food processing, and meatpacking. In some industries, such as textiles, women composed an important segment of the workforce. With the introduction of the typewriter, other sorts of employment opportunities opened up. By 1900, nearly all typists were female. Specialized skills such as stenography also meant more office work for working-class young women, while big department stores needed scores of clerks to wait on middle-class shoppers. But about 40 percent of working-class women, especially those from Irish, Scandinavian, or black families, were maids, cooks, laundresses, and nurses.

●●●─Read the **Document**

Massachusetts Bureau of Statistics of Labor, from The Working Girls of Boston *(1884)*

at **www.myhistorylab.com**

Domestic service was arduous, and domestics could not count on much sympathy from their employers. "Do not think it necessary to give a hired girl as good a room as that used by members of the family," said one lady of the house. "She should sleep near the kitchen and not go up the front stairs or through the front hall to reach her room." A servant received room and board plus $2 to $5 a week. The fact that so many women took such work speaks clearly of their limited opportunities.

The difficult situation facing working women drove some, like Rose Haggerty, into prostitution. Burdened with a widowed and sickly mother and four young brothers and sisters, at 14 Rose started work at a New York paper bag factory. She earned $10 a month, of which $6 went for rent. Her fortunes improved when a friend helped her buy a sewing machine. Rose then sewed shirts at home, often working as many as 14 hours a day to support her family. Suddenly, the piecework rate for shirts was slashed in half.

Domestic Servants Wearing their best clothes, these domestics pose for the camera. What do the women appear to be holding and why? In what room does the picture appear to have been taken? Although there is no way to ascertain the background of these young women, a majority of domestic servants were Irish or Irish American. Domestic work was often exhausting and provided little privacy or free time, but many women were attracted by the opportunity to live in a middle-class home and have regular meals. In addition, domestic work often paid better than factory work. Still, some young women avoided service, explaining that "it's freedom that we want when the day's work is done."

Rose contemplated suicide. But when a sailor offered her money for spending the night with him, she realized that she had an alternative. Prostitution meant food, rent, and heat for her family. "Let God Almighty judge who's to blame most," the 20-year-old Rose reflected, "I that was driven, or them that drove me to the pass I'm in."

Prostitution appears to have increased in the late nineteenth century, although there is no way of knowing the actual numbers of women involved. Probably most single women accepted the respectable jobs open to them. They tolerated discrimination and low wages because their families depended on their contributions. They also knew that when they married, they would probably leave the paid workforce forever.

Marriage hardly ended women's work, however. Like colonial families, late-nineteenth-century working-class families operated as economic units. The unpaid domestic labor and management skills of working-class wives were critical to family survival. With husbands away for 10 to 11 hours a day, women bore the burden of caring for children and doing all domestic chores, made more difficult by the lack of conveniences and urban services.

Black women's working lives reflected the obstacles African Americans faced in late-nineteenth-century cities. Although few married white women (about 7 percent) worked outside the home, many black women did. In southern cities in 1880, about three-quarters of single black women and one-third of married black women worked outside the home. Because industrial employers would not hire black women, most served as domestics or laundresses. The high percentage of married black women in the labor force reflected the marginal wages their husbands earned. But it may also be explained partly by the lesson learned during slavery that children could thrive without the constant attention of their mothers.

Capital Versus Labor

Class conflict colored late-nineteenth-century industrial life. Although workers welcomed the progress the factory made possible, many rejected their employers' values, which emphasized individual gain at the expense of collective good. While owners reaped most of the profits, workers were becoming wage slaves. Fashioning their arguments from their republican legacy, workers claimed that the degradation of the country's citizen laborers threatened to undermine the Republic itself.

On-the-Job Protests

Workers and employers struggled over control of the workplace. Many workers staunchly resisted unsatisfactory working conditions. They resented being "like any other piece of machinery, to be made to do the maximum amount of work with the minimum expenditure of fuel." Because skilled workers had indispensable practical knowledge, they were well positioned to direct on-the-job actions. Sometimes they tried to control critical work decisions or to humanize work. Cigar makers clung to their custom of having one worker read to others as they performed their tedious chores.

Workers also sought to control the pace of production. Too many goods meant an inhuman work pace and might result in overproduction, massive layoffs, and a reduction in piecework prices. So an experienced worker might whisper to a new hand, "See here, young fellow, you're working too fast. You'll spoil our job for us if you don't go slower."

Absenteeism, drunkenness at work, and general inefficiency—all widespread—contained elements of protest. In three industrial firms in the late nineteenth century, one-quarter of the workers stayed home at least one day a week. Some lost days were due to layoffs, but not all. The efforts of employers to impose stiff fines on absent workers suggested their frustration with uncooperative employees.

To a surprising extent, workers made the final protest by quitting their jobs altogether. Most employers responded by penalizing workers who left without sufficient notice—to little avail. A Massachusetts labor study in

1878 found that although two-thirds of them had the same occupation for more than 10 years, only 15 percent of the workers surveyed held the same job. A similar rate of turnover occurred in the industrial workforce in the early twentieth century. Workers unmistakably and clearly voted with their feet.

Strike Activity After 1876

The most direct and strenuous attempts to change conditions in the workplace came in the form of thousands of strikes punctuating the late nineteenth century. In 1877, railroad workers staged the first and bloodiest nationwide industrial strike of the nineteenth century. The immediate cause was the railroad owners' decision to reduce wages. But the rapid spread of the strike all over the country, as well as the violence of the strikers, who destroyed railroad property and kept trains idle, indicated more fundamental discontent.

An erratic economy, high unemployment, and the lack of job security all fed the conflagration. More than 100 people died before federal troops ended the strike. The frenzied response of the propertied class, which saw the strike as the beginning of revolution and applauded military intervention, forecast the pattern of later conflicts. Time and time again, middle- and upper-class Americans would turn to state power to crush labor activism.

A wave of confrontations followed the strike of 1877. Between 1881 and 1905, there were 36,757 strikes involving over 6 million workers. Such numbers show widespread working-class discontent, involving more than just those at the very bottom. Strikes, as well as sabotage and violence, were most often linked to demands for higher wages and shorter hours. Nineteenth-century strike activity underwent important changes as the consciousness of American workers expanded. In the post–Civil War period, local and national unions played a more important role in organizing protest, conducting 60 percent of the strikes between 1881 and 1905. Coordination between strikers in different companies improved. Finally, wages among the most highly unionized workers became less of an issue. Workers sought more humane conditions. By the early 1890s, over one-fifth of strikes involved workplace rules.

In 1892, silver miners in Coeur d'Alene, Idaho, struck when their employers installed machine drills in the mines, reduced skilled workers to shovelmen, and cut wages. The owners, supported by state militiamen and the federal government, successfully broke the strike by using scabs, but not without fighting. Several hundred union men were eventually tried and found guilty of a wide variety of charges. Out of the defeat emerged the Western Federation of Miners (WFM), whose chief goal was an eight-hour law for miners.

The Coeur d'Alene struggle set the pattern for many subsequent strikes. Mine owners fought strikes by shutting off credit to union men, hiring strikebreakers and armed guards, and infiltrating unions with spies. Violence was frequent, usually ending with the arrival of state militia, arrests or intimidation, legal action, and blacklisting. Despite this, the WFM won as many strikes as it lost.

Labor's worst setback came in 1892 at the Homestead steel mills near Pittsburgh. Carnegie had purchased the Homestead plant and put Henry Clay Frick in charge. Together, they wanted to break the union that threatened to extend its organization of the steel industry. After three months of stalemated negotiations over a new wage contract, Frick issued an ultimatum. Workers must accept wage cuts or be replaced. Frick barricaded the entire plant and hired 300 armed Pinkerton guards. As they arrived on July 6, they and armed steelworkers fought a daylong gun battle. Several men on both sides were killed, and the Pinkertons retreated. Then, at Frick's request, the governor of Pennsylvania sent 8,000 troops to crush the strike and the union. Two and a half weeks later, a New York anarchist tried to assassinate Frick.

Labor Organizing, 1865–1900

Civil War experience colored postwar labor organizing. As one working-class song pointed out, workers had borne the brunt of that struggle. "You gave your son to the war/ The rich man loaned his gold/ And the rich man's son is happy to-day,/ And yours is under the mold." Workers who had fought to save the Union argued that wartime sac-rifices justified efforts for justice and equality in the workplace.

⊙ See the **Map**
Organizing American Labor
in the Late 19th Century
at **www.myhistorylab.com**

Labor leaders quickly realized the need for national as well as local organizations to protect the laboring class against "despotic employers." In 1866, several craft unions and reform groups formed the National Labor Union (NLU). Claiming 300,000 members by the early 1870s, the organization supported a range of causes including temperance, women's rights, and the establishment of cooperatives to bring the "wealth of the land" into "the hands of those who produce it."

The call for an eight-hour day reveals some of the basic assumptions of the organized labor movement. Few workers saw employers as a hostile class or wanted to destroy the economic system. But they did believe bosses were often tyrants whose demands for their time threatened to turn citizens into slaves. The eight-hour day would curb the power of owners and al-low workers the time to cultivate the qualities necessary for republican citizenship.

•●•Read the **Document**
Address to 1894 Convention
of American Railway Union
by Jennie Curtis
at **www.myhistorylab.com**

Many of the NLU's specific goals survived, although the organization did not. An unsuccessful attempt to create a political party and the depression of 1873 decimated the NLU. Survival and job searches took precedence over union causes.

The Knights of Labor and the AFL

As the depression wound down, a new mass organization, the Noble and Holy Order of the Knights of Labor, rose to prominence. Founded as a secret society in 1869, the order became public and national when Terence V. Powderly was elected Grand Master Workman in 1879. The Knights of Labor sought "to secure to the workers the full enjoyment of the wealth they create." Because the industrial system denied workers their fair share as producers, the Knights of Labor proposed a cooperative system of production paralleling the existing system. Cooperative efforts would provide workers with the economic independence necessary for citizenship, and an eight-hour day would allow them time for moral, intellectual, and political pursuits.

The Knights of Labor was open to all American "producers," defined as all contributing members of society—skilled and unskilled, black and white, men and women, even merchants and manufacturers. Only the idle and the corrupt (gamblers, saloonkeepers, speculators, bankers, lawyers) were excluded. Many shopkeepers joined, advertising themselves as a "friend of the workingman." This inclusive membership policy provided the organization with the potential power of great numbers. The organization grew in spurts, attracting miners between 1874 and 1879, skilled urban tradesmen between 1879 and 1885, and unskilled workers thereafter.

Although Powderly frowned on strikes, the organization reaped the benefit of grassroots strike activity. Local struggles proliferated after 1883. In 1884, unorganized workers of the Union Pacific Railroad walked off the job when management announced a wage cut. Within two days, the company caved in, and the men joined the Knights. The next year, a successful strike against the Missouri Pacific Railroad brought in another wave of members. Then, in 1886, the **Haymarket Riot** in Chicago caused such a growth in labor militancy that in that single year the membership of the Knights of Labor ballooned from 100,000 to 700,000.

The "riot" at Haymarket was, in fact, a peaceful protest meeting connected with a lockout at the McCormick Reaper Works. When the Chicago police arrived to disperse the crowd, a bomb exploded. Seven policemen died. Although no one knows who planted the bomb, eight anarchists were tried and convicted. Three were executed, one committed suicide, and the others served prison terms.

The Knights could not sustain momentum. Alerted by the Haymarket Riot, employers were determined to break the organization. A strike against Jay Gould's southwestern railroad system in 1886 collapsed. Consumer and producer cooperatives fizzled; the policy of accepting both black and white workers led to strife and discord in the South. The two major parties co-opted labor politicians. Furthermore, national leaders also failed. Powderly could neither unify his diverse following nor control militants opposing him. By 1890, membership plummeted to 100,000, although the Knights continued to play a role well into the 1890s.

The **American Federation of Labor** (AFL), founded in 1886, became the nation's dominant union in the 1890s. The history of the Knights pointed up the problems of a national union that admitted all who worked for wages, but officially rejected strikes in favor of the ballot box and arbitration. The leader of the AFL, Samuel Gompers, had a different notion of effective worker organization. He was convinced that skilled workers should put their specific occupational interests first, so that they could control the supply of skilled labor and keep wages up.

Gompers organized the AFL as a federation of skilled trades—cigar makers, iron molders, ironworkers, carpenters, and others—each one autonomous, yet linked through an executive council to work together for pro-labor national legislation and mutual support during boycott and strike actions. He repudiated dreams of a cooperative commonwealth or of ending the wage system, instead focusing on immediate "bread and butter" issues—higher wages, shorter hours, industrial safety, and the right to organize. Although Gompers rejected direct political action as a means of obtaining labor's goals, he believed in the value of the strike. A shrewd organizer, he knew from bitter experience the importance of dues high enough to sustain a strike fund through a long, tough fight.

Under Gompers's leadership, the AFL grew from 140,000 in 1886 to nearly 1 million by 1900. Although his notion of a labor organization was elitist, he steered his union through a series of crises, fending off challenges from socialists on his left and corporate opposition to strikes on his right. But there was no room in his organization for the unskilled or for blacks. The AFL did make a brief, halfhearted attempt to unionize women in 1892, but men resented women as coworkers and preferred them to stay in the home. The AFL agreed. In 1900, the International Ladies' Garment Workers Union (ILGWU) was established. Although women were its backbone, men dominated the leadership.

Strive and Succeed

The social ethic of the age stressed that economic rewards were available to anyone who fervently sought them. Many Americans, particularly those who began well, did rise rapidly. Between 1865 and 1890, average middle-class income rose about 30 percent. Middle-class Americans enjoyed more leisure time and greater access to consumer goods. They were able to purchase dozens of products, manufactured, packaged, and promoted in an explosion of technological inventions and shrewd marketing techniques. Among still-familiar products and brands invented or mass-produced for the first time in the 1890s were Jell-O, Wesson oil, the Hershey bar, Aunt Jemima pancake mix, and Coca-Cola.

Popular novels by Horatio Alger, Jr., such as *Strive and Succeed*, taught a generation of American youth that upward mobility from "rags to riches" was entirely possible. But unlimited and equal opportunity for upward advancement has never been as easy as the stories maintained. For the most part, native-born, middle-class whites tended to have the skills, resources, and connections that opened up the most desirable jobs and the greatest chance for success.

New Freedoms for Middle-Class Women

As many middle-class women acquired leisure time and enhanced purchasing power, they also won new freedoms. Several states granted women more property rights in marriage, adding to their growing sense of independence.

Casting off confining crinolines, they now wore shirtwaist blouses and ankle-length skirts that were more comfortable for working, school, and sports. The "new woman" was celebrated as *Life* magazine's attractively active, slightly rebellious "Gibson girl."

Using their new freedom, women joined organizations of all kinds— literary societies, charity groups, reform clubs. There they gained organizational experience, awareness of their talents, and contact with people and problems outside their traditional family roles.

After the Civil War, educational opportunities for women expanded. New women's colleges offered programs similar to those at competitive men's colleges, while midwestern and western state schools dropped prohibitions against women. In 1890, some 13 percent of all college graduates were women; by 1900, nearly 20 percent were. Higher education prepared middle-class women both for conventional female roles and work and public service.

Job opportunities for these educated middle-class women were generally limited to the social services and teaching. Still regarded as a suitable female occupation, teaching was a highly demanding but poorly paying field that grew as urban schools expanded under the pressure of a burgeoning population. By the 1890s, the willingness of middle-class women to work for low pay opened up new forms of employment in office work, nursing, and department stores. But moving up to high-status jobs proved difficult, even for middle-class women.

One reason for the greater independence of American women was that they were having fewer babies. This was especially true of educated women. In 1900, nearly one married woman in five was childless. Advances in birth control technology (the modern diaphragm was developed in 1880) helped make new patterns possible. But decreasing family size and an increase in the divorce rate (1 out of 12 marriages in 1905) also fueled male responses. Arguments against the new woman intensified as many men reaffirmed Victorian stereotypes of "woman's sphere." Male campaigns against prostitution and for sex hygiene also suggested they feared female passions might weaken male vigor.

Male Mobility and the Success Ethic

The postwar economy opened up many new opportunities for middle-class men. As the lower ranks of the white-collar world became more specialized, the number of middle-class jobs increased.

Because these new careers required more education, the educational system expanded. Public high schools increased from 160 in 1870 to 6,000 in 1900. By that year, most states and territories had compulsory school attendance laws. Enrollments in colleges and universities nearly doubled, from 53,000 in 1870 to 101,000 in 1900. Universities gained a new stature in American life. Land-grant state colleges expanded, and philanthropists established research universities such as Johns Hopkins, Stanford, and the University of Chicago.

These developments led to greater specialization and professionalism. By the 1890s, government licensing and the rise of professional schools helped to give the word *career* its modern meaning. No longer were tradesmen likely to read up on medicine in their spare time and become doctors. Organizations such as the American Medical Association and the American Bar Association were regulating and professionalizing membership.

The need for lawyers, bankers, architects, and insurance agents to serve business and industry expanded opportunities. Large companies required many more managers, while the growing public sector provided new positions in social services and government. Young professionals with graduate training in the social sciences filled many of them.

The Gospel of Wealth

For most Americans in the late nineteenth century, Christianity supported the competitive individualistic ethic. Philadelphia Baptist preacher Russell Conwell's famous sermon "Acres of Diamonds," delivered 6,000 times to an estimated 13 million listeners, praised riches as a sure sign of "godliness" and stressed the power of money to "do good."

Andrew Carnegie expressed the ethic most clearly. In an article, "The **Gospel of Wealth**" (1889), Carnegie celebrated competition for producing better goods at lower prices. The concentration of wealth in a few hands, he concluded, was "not only beneficial but essential to the future of the race." The fittest would bring order and efficiency out of the chaos of rapid industrialization. Carnegie insisted that the rich must spend some of their wealth to benefit their "poorer brethren." Carnegie built hundreds of libraries and promoted world peace.

Carnegie's ideas reflected an ideology known as **Social Darwinism**, based on the work of naturalist Charles Darwin. In his *Origin of Species*, published in 1859, Darwin concluded that plant and animal species evolved through natural selection. Some managed to adapt to their environment and survived; others failed to adapt and perished. Herbert Spencer, an English social philosopher, applied this "survival of the fittest" notion to human society.

The scientific vocabulary of Social Darwinism injected scientific rationality into what often seemed a baffling economic order. Spencer argued that underlying social laws, like those of the natural world, dictated economic affairs. Social Darwinists also believed in the superiority of the Anglo-Saxon race, which they maintained had reached the highest stage of evolution. Their theories were used to justify race supremacy and imperialism, as well as the monopolistic efforts of American businessmen. "The growth of a large business," John D. Rockefeller, Jr., told a YMCA class, "is merely the survival of the fittest."

The Politics of the Gilded Age

Co-authoring a satirical book in 1873, Mark Twain coined the expression "Gilded Age" to describe corruption during the presidency of Ulysses S. Grant. The phrase has come to characterize social and political life in the last quarter of the nineteenth century. Although politics was marred by corruption, and politicians avoided fundamental issues in favor of a politics of mass entertainment, voter participation in national elections between 1876 and 1896 hovered at an all-time high of 73 to 82 percent of all registered voters.

Behind the glitter, two gradual changes occurred that would greatly affect twentieth-century politics. First was the development of a professional bureaucracy. In congressional committees and executive branch offices, elite specialists and experts emerged as a counterfoil to the perceived dangers of majority rule represented by high voter participation, especially by the millions of immigrant "newcomers alien to our traditions," as a New England poet put it. Second, after a period of close elections and party stalemate, new issues and concerns fostered a party realignment in the 1890s.

Politics, Parties, Patronage, and Presidents

Political leaders of the 1870s and 1880s favored governmental passivity that would allow industrial expansion and wealth creation. The Republican and Democratic parties diverged mostly over patronage (control over government jobs) rather than principles. As one disgusted student of legislative politics, Woodrow Wilson, wrote in 1879: "No leaders, no principles; no principles, no parties." A British observer, Lord Bryce, concluded that the two parties, like two bottles, bore different labels, yet "each was empty."

Yet these characterizations were not entirely accurate. There were differences, as party professionals solidified their popular base to achieve political ends. Republican votes came from northeastern Yankee industrial interests, New England migrants, and Scandinavian Lutherans across the Upper Midwest. Democrats depended on southern whites, northern workers, and urban immigrants. Affiliation reflected interest in important cultural, religious, and ethnic questions. Because the Republican party was willing to mobilize the power of the state to reshape society, people who wanted to regulate moral and economic life were attracted to it. Catholics and various immigrant groups preferred the Democratic party because it opposed government efforts to regulate morals. Said one Chicago Democrat, "A Republican is a man who wants you t' go t' church every Sunday. A Democrat says if a man wants t' have a glass of beer on Sunday he can have it."

For a few years, Civil War and Reconstruction issues generated party differences. But after 1876, the two parties were evenly matched, and they avoided controversial stands on national issues. In three of the five presidential elections between 1876 and 1892, a mere 1 percent of the vote separated the two major candidates. In 1880, James Garfield won by only 7,018 votes; in 1884, Grover Cleveland squeaked by Blaine by a popular vote margin of 48.5 to 48.2 percent. In two elections (1876 and 1888), the electoral vote winner had fewer popular votes. Only twice, each time for only two years, did one party control the White House and both houses of Congress. Although all the presidents in the era except Cleveland were Republicans, Democrats controlled the House of Representatives in 8 of 10 sessions of Congress between 1875 and 1895.

Gilded Age presidents were undistinguished and played a minor role in national life. None of them—Rutherford B. Hayes (1877–1881), Garfield (1881), Chester A. Arthur (1881–1885), Cleveland (1885–1889 and 1893–1897), and Benjamin Harrison (1889–1893)—served two consecutive terms. The only Democrat in the group, Cleveland, differed little from the Republicans. When Cleveland violated the expectation that presidents should not initiate ideas by devoting his entire annual message in 1887 to a call for a lower tariff, Congress did nothing. Voters turned him out of office a year later.

One of the issues that did rouse attention on the national level was civil service reform. The worst feature of the spoils system was that parties financed themselves by assessing holders of patronage jobs, often as much as 1 percent of their annual salaries. Reformers, mostly genteel native white Protestants, demanded competitive examinations to create an honest and professional civil service—but also one that would bar immigrants and their urban political machine bosses from the spoils of office.

Most Americans expected their presidents to reward the faithful with government jobs, but Garfield's assassination by a crazed office seeker in 1881 created a public backlash. "My God! Chet Arthur in the White House!" someone exclaimed, knowing that the new president was closely identified with New York Senator Roscoe Conkling's corrupt political machine. Arthur surprised doubters by being a capable and dignified president, responsive to growing demands for civil service reform. Congress found itself forced into passing the Pendleton Act of 1883, mandating merit examinations for about one-tenth of federal offices. Gradually, more bureaucrats fell under its coverage, but parties became no more honest. As campaign contributions from government employees dried up, parties turned to huge corporate contributions, which in 1888 helped elect Benjamin Harrison.

National Issues

Four issues, all related to the distribution of wealth and power, were important at the national level in the Gilded Age: currency, the tariff, civil service, and government's role in regulating business. In confronting these issues, legislators tried to serve both their own self-interest and the national interest of an efficient, productive, growing economy.

Major Legislative Activity of the Gilded Age

In the table, note the kinds of issues dealt with at the different levels: mostly money, tariff, immigration, and civil service legislation at the national level and "hot button" emotional, social, and value issues in the states and localities. Which three or four issues would you have been most concerned with? Which still exist today?

National

1871	National Civil Service Commission created
1873	Coinage Act demonetizes silver
	"Salary Grab" Act (increased salaries of Congress and top federal officials) partly repealed
1875	Specie Resumption Act retires greenback dollars
1878	Bland-Allison Act permits partial coining of silver
1882	Chinese Exclusion Act
	Federal Immigration Law restricts certain categories of immigrants and requires head tax of all immigrants
1883	Standard time (four time zones) established for the entire country
	Pendleton Civil Service Act
1887	Interstate Commerce Act sets up Interstate Commerce Commission
	Dawes Act divides Indian tribal lands into individual allotments
1890	Dependent Pension Act grants pensions to Union army veterans
	Sherman Anti-Trust Act
	Sherman Silver Purchase Act has government buy more silver
	McKinley Tariff sets high protective tariff
	Federal elections bill to protect black voting rights in South fails in Senate
	Blair bill to provide support for education defeated
1891	Immigration law gives federal government control of overseas immigration
1893	Sherman Silver Purchase Act repealed
1894	Wilson-Gorman Tariff lowers duties slightly
1900	Currency Act puts United States on gold standard

State and Local

1850s–1880s	State and local laws intended to restrict or prohibit consumption of alcoholic beverages
1871	Illinois Railroad Act sets up railroad commission to fix rates and prohibit discrimination
1874	Railroad regulatory laws in Wisconsin and Iowa
1881	Kansas adopts statewide prohibition
1882	Iowa passes state prohibition amendment
1880s	Massachusetts, Connecticut, Rhode Island, Montana, Michigan, Ohio, and Missouri all pass local laws prohibiting consumption of alcohol
	Santa Fe ring dominates New Mexico politics and land grabbing
1889	New Jersey repeals a county-option prohibition law of 1888
	Laws in Wisconsin and Illinois mandate compulsory attendance of children at schools in which instruction is in English
	Kansas, Maine, Michigan, and Tennessee pass antitrust laws
1889–1890	Massachusetts debates bill on compulsory schooling in English
1899–1902	Eleven former Confederate states amend state constitutions and pass statutes restricting the voting rights of blacks
1890–1910	Eleven former Confederate states pass segregation laws
1891	Nebraska passes eight-hour workday law
1893	Colorado adopts woman suffrage
1894–1896	Woman suffrage referenda defeated in Kansas and California

The "money question" became a fixture of American politics for nearly three decades. During the Civil War, the federal government had circulated paper money (greenbacks) that could not be exchanged for gold or silver (specie). In the late 1860s and 1870s, politicians debated whether the United States should return to a metallic standard, which would allow paper money to be exchanged for specie. "Hard-money" advocates supported either withdrawing all paper money from circulation or making it convertible to specie. They opposed increasing the volume of money, fearing inflation. "Soft-money" Greenbackers argued that there was not enough currency in circulation for an expanding economy and urged increasing the supply of paper money in order to raise farm prices and cut interest rates.

Hard-money interests had more clout. In 1873, Congress demonetized silver. In 1875, it passed the Specie Resumption Act, gradually retiring greenbacks from circulation and putting the nation firmly on the gold standard. But as large supplies of silver were mined in the West, pressure resumed for increasing the money supply by coining silver. Soft-money advocates pushed for the unlimited coinage of silver in addition to gold. In an 1878 compromise, the Treasury was required to buy between $2 million and $4 million of silver each month and coin it as silver dollars. Despite this increase in the money supply, the period was not inflationary. Prices fell, disappointing supporters of soft money. They pushed for more silver, continuing the controversy into the 1890s.

Political Advertisements of the 1880s Although the tariff protectionist Harrison defeated Cleveland in 1888 (the results were reversed in 1892), all Gilded Age presidents were essentially "preservers" rather than innovators. None had approached the greatness of Washington, Lincoln, and the other presidents hovering over Harrison and Morton in this illustration. In a second image from 1888, titled "The Presidential B. B. Club," politics and business are merged in a tobacco advertisement, which shows Cleveland the fielder tagging out Harrison the batter—true enough for the election of 1892 but not for 1888, which Harrison won. Why baseball? What other images do you see in these two campaign visuals?

Recognizing the appeal of **free silver** to agrarian debtors, Republican leaders feared their party might be destroyed by the issue. In 1890, Congress approved a compromise that momentarily satisfied almost everyone. The Sherman Silver Purchase Act ordered the Treasury to buy 4.5 million ounces of silver monthly and to issue treasury notes for it. Silverites were pleased by the proposed increase in the money supply. Opponents felt they had averted the worst—free coinage of silver. The gold standard still stood.

The currency compromise was part of a swift wave of legislation during the first six months of 1890, when Republicans gained control of both houses of Congress. The Sherman Anti-Trust Act passed with only one nay vote. It declared illegal "every contract, combination . . . or conspiracy in restraint of trade or commerce." Although the Sherman Act was vague and not really intended to break up big corporations, it was an initial attempt to restrain large business combinations. But in *United States* v. *E. C. Knight* (1895), the Supreme Court ruled that the American Sugar Refining Company, which controlled more than 90 percent of the nation's sugar-refining capacity, was not in violation of the Sherman Act.

A tariff bill introduced in 1890 by Ohio Republican William McKinley raised taxes on imports higher than ever before. Republicans favored high tariffs as a means of protecting American business from foreign competition. Despite heat from agrarian interests, whose products were generally not protected, the bill passed the House and, after nearly 500 amendments, also the Senate.

To pass the McKinley Tariff, Republican leaders bargained away an elections bill, proposed by Massachusetts Senator Henry Cabot Lodge, that sought to ensure African American voter registration and fair elections. Since 1877, the South had become a Democratic stronghold, where party victories could be traced to fraud and intimidation of black Republican voters. Lodge's legislation, then, was intended to honor old commitments to the freedpeople and improve party fortunes in the South. Without it, major-party efforts to protect African American voting rights in the South ended until the 1960s.

In a second setback for black southerners, the Senate, fearful of giving the federal government a role in education, defeated a bill to provide federal aid to black schools in the South that received a disproportionately small share of local and state funds. "The plain truth is," said the New York *Herald*, "the North has got tired of the negro," foreshadowing a similar abandonment of civil rights legislation 100 years later.

The Crucial Election of 1896

The campaign of 1896, waged during the depression and featuring a climactic battle over the currency, was one of the most critical in American history. In the 1894 midterm elections, voters had abandoned the Democrats in droves, giving both Populists (introduced in Chapter 15) and Republicans high hopes for the next presidential election. Although Cleveland was in disgrace for ignoring depression woes, few leaders in either major party thought the federal government was responsible for alleviating the suffering of the people. But the disadvantaged, unskilled, and unemployed everywhere wondered where relief might be found. Would either major party respond to the pressing human needs of the depression? Would the People's party set a new national agenda for politics? These questions were raised and largely resolved in the election of 1896.

As the election approached, Populist leaders emphasized the silver issue and debated whether to fuse with one of the major parties by agreeing on a joint ticket, which meant abandoning much of the Populist platform. Influenced by silver mine owners, many Populists became convinced that they must make a single-issue commitment to the free and unlimited coinage of silver at the ratio of 16 to 1.

In the throes of the depression in the mid-1890s, silver took on enormous importance as the symbol of the many grievances of downtrodden Americans. Popular literature captured the rural, moral dimensions of the silver movement. L. Frank Baum's *The Wonderful Wizard of Oz* (1900) was a free-silver allegory of rural values (Kansas, Auntie Em, the uneducated but wise scarecrow, and the good-hearted tin woodsman) and Populist attitudes and policies (the wicked witch of the East and the magical silver shoes in harmony with the yellow brick road in "Oz"—ounces).

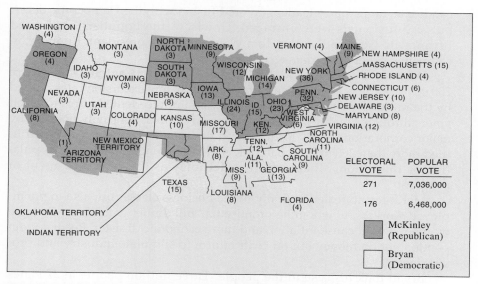

	ELECTORAL VOTE	POPULAR VOTE
McKinley (Republican)	271	7,036,000
Bryan (Democratic)	176	6,468,000

The Presidential Election of 1896 In his sweep of the densely populated urban Northeast and Midwest, McKinley beat Bryan by the largest popular vote margin since 1872. In his cabled congratulations, Bryan wrote, "We have submitted the issues to the American people and their will is law." How does the country divide politically today? Was there a "red states" and "blue states" similarity in 1896?

The Republicans nominated William McKinley. As a congressman and governor of Ohio, McKinley was identified with the high protective tariff that bore his name. Citing the familiar argument that prosperity depended on the gold standard and protection, Republicans blamed the depression on Cleveland's attempt to lower the tariff.

The excitement of the Democratic convention in July contrasted with the staid, smoothly organized Republican gathering. With Cleveland already repudiated by his party, state after state elected convention delegates pledged to silver. Gold Democrats, however, had enough power to wage a close battle for the platform plank on money. The Democrats' surprise nominee was an ardent young silverite, William Jennings Bryan, a 36-year-old congressman from Nebraska. Few saw him as presidential material, but Bryan arranged to give the closing argument for a silver plank himself. His dramatic speech swept the convention for silver and ensured his nomination. Concluding one of the most famous political speeches in American history, Bryan attacked the "goldbugs":

> Having behind us the producing masses of this nation . . . and toilers everywhere, we will answer their demand for a gold standard by saying to them: "You shall not press down upon the brow of labor this crown of thorns, you shall not crucify mankind upon a cross of gold."

Bryan stretched out his arms as if on a cross, and the convention exploded in applause.

Populist strategy lay in shambles when the Democrats named a silver candidate. Some party leaders favored fusion with the Democratic ticket, but anti-fusionists were outraged. Unwisely, the Populists nominated Bryan, with Georgia Populist Tom Watson for vice president. Running on competing silver slates damaged Bryan's chances.

During the campaign, McKinley stayed home in Canton, Ohio, where 750,000 admirers came to visit him, brought by low excursion rates offered by the railroads. The Republicans made an unprecedented effort to reach voters through a highly sophisticated media campaign, heavily financed by major corporations. Party leaders hired thousands of speakers and distributed more than 200 million pamphlets in 14 languages to a voting population of 15 million, all advertising McKinley as the "advance agent of prosperity."

McKinley appealed not only to the business classes but also to unemployed workers, to whom he promised a "full dinner pail." Free silver, he warned, would cause inflation and more economic disaster. Recovery depended not on money but on tariff reform to stimulate industry and provide jobs.

Bryan took his case to the people. Three million people in 27 states heard him speak as he traveled over 18,000 miles, giving as many as 30 speeches a day. Bryan's message was simple: prosperity required free coinage of silver, and government should attend to the needs of the producing classes rather than the vested interests.

Voters turned out in record numbers. In key states such as Illinois, Indiana, and Ohio, 95 percent of those eligible to went to the polls. McKinley won 271 electoral votes to Bryan's 176, the largest margin of victory since Grant trounced Greeley in 1872. Millionaire Mark Hanna jubilantly wired McKinley: "God's in his heaven, all's right with the world."

Although Bryan won over 6 million votes (47 percent of the total), more than any previous Democratic winner, he failed to carry the Midwest or the urban industrial masses, who had little confidence that the Democrats could stimulate economic growth or cope with industrialism. McKinley's promise of a "full dinner pail" was more convincing. Northern laborers feared that inflation would leave them even poorer—that prices and rents would rise faster than their wages. Catholic immigrants distrusted Populist Protestantism. Chance also played a part in Bryan's defeat. Bad wheat harvests in India, Australia, and Argentina drove up world grain prices, and many of the complaints of American farmers evaporated.

The New Shape of American Politics

The landslide Republican victory broke the stalemate in post–Civil War American politics. Republicans dropped their identification with the politics of piety and strengthened their image as the party of prosperity and national greatness, which gave them a party dominance that lasted until the 1930s. The Democrats, under Bryan's leadership until 1912, put on the mantle of Populist moralism, but were largely reduced to a sectional party, reflecting narrow southern views on money, race, and national power. The 1896 election demonstrated that the Northeast and Great Lakes states had acquired so many immigrants that they now controlled the nation's political destiny. The demoralized Populists disappeared, yet within the next 20 years many Populist issues were adopted by the two major parties.

Another result of the election of 1896 was a change in political participation. Because the Republicans were so dominant outside of the South and Democrats so powerful in the South, most states did not have vigorous two-party political battles and therefore could not mobilize large numbers of voters. With results so predictable, voters had little motivation to cast a ballot. The tremendous rate of political participation that had characterized the nineteenth century since the Jackson era gradually declined.

McKinley had promised that Republican rule meant prosperity, and as soon as he took office, the economy recovered. Discoveries of gold in the Yukon and the Alaskan Klondike increased the money supply, ending the silver mania. Industrial production returned to full capacity. Touring the Midwest in 1898, McKinley spoke to cheering crowds about the shift from "industrial depression to industrial activity."

RECOVERING *the* PAST

Congressional Hearings

Students of history can discover fascinating materials on nineteenth-century life by exploring the published records of the American political system. Privately published from 1833 to 1873, the *Congressional Globe* details the proceedings of the Senate and the House, revealing the nature of congressional deliberations in an era when debate, such as that over the Compromise of 1850 in the Senate, was the focus of the national political process. After 1873, the government published these proceedings in the *Congressional Record*. The *Record* is not a literal transcription of debate, for members can edit their remarks, insert speeches, and add supporting materials. Still, it gives a good sense of the proceedings of both the Senate and the House.

Much of the serious work of government, past and present, takes place in congressional committees. One foreign observer called Congress "not so much a legislative assembly as a huge panel from which committees are selected." The committee system is almost as old as the constitutional system itself and is rooted in the Constitution's granting of lawmaking power to Congress. From the start, Congress divided into assorted committees to gather information, enabling members to evaluate legislative proposals intelligently.

Two kinds of committees existed in the House and Senate. Standing committees had permanent responsibility for reviewing legislative proposals on a host of financial, judicial, foreign, and other affairs. By 1892, the Senate had 44 standing committees and the House had 50. Select committees were temporary, often charged with investigating specific problems. In the late nineteenth century, congressional committees investigated such problems as Ku Klux Klan terrorism, the sweatshop system, tenement house conditions, and relations between labor and capital. In each case, extensive hearings were held.

Congressional hearings have become increasingly important sources of historical evidence in recent years. They show the Senate and the House of Representatives in action as they seek to translate popular sentiment into law. But they also reveal public attitudes as they record the voices of Americans testifying in committee halls. Because one function of legislative hearings is to enable diverse groups to express their frustrations and desires, they often contain the testimony of witnesses drawn from many different social and economic backgrounds. Included here is the partial testimony of a Massachusetts laborer who appeared before the Senate Committee on Education and Labor in 1883. Because working-class witnesses like this man usually left no other record of their experiences or thoughts, committee reports and hearings provide valuable insight into the lives and attitudes of ordinary people.

Hearings also reveal the attitudes and social values of committee members. Hence, caution is needed in the use of hearings. Witnesses often have vested interests and are frequently coached and cautious in what they communicate on the stand. Rather than seeking to illuminate issues, committee members often speak and explore questions for other—usually political—reasons.

Despite these limitations, committee hearings are rich sources of information. In this excerpt on pages 551–552, what can you learn about the life of the witness testifying before the committee? In what way do the values of the committee members conflict with those of the witness? Why is the chairman so harsh toward the witness? Is he entirely unsympathetic? Why do you think the questioner overemphasizes the relationship between moral beliefs and economic realities? What kind of social tensions does the passage reveal?

Hearings on the Relations Between Labor and Capital

Q. You get a dollar a day, wages?—A. That is the average pay that men receive. The rents, especially in Somerville, are so high that it is almost impossible for the working men to live in a house.

Q. What rent do you pay?—A. For the last year I have been paying $10 a month, and most of the men out there have to pay about that amount for a house—$10 a month for rooms.

Q. For a full house, or for rooms only?—A. For rooms in a house.

Q. How many rooms?—A. Four or five.

Q. How much of your time have you been out of work, or idle, for the last full year, say?—A. I have not been out of work more than three weeks altogether, because I have been making a dollar or two peddling or doing something, when I was out of work, in the currying line.

Q. Making about the same that you made at your trade?—A. Well, I have made at my trade a little more than that, but that is the average.

Q. Are you a common drunkard?—A. No, sir.

Q. Do you smoke a great deal?—A. Well, yes, sir; I smoke as much as any man.

The CHAIRMAN. I want to know how much you have got together in the course of a year, and what you have spent your money for, so that folks can see whether you have had pay enough to get rich on.

The WITNESS. A good idea.

The CHAIRMAN. That is precisely the sort of idea that people ought to know. How much money do you think you have earned during this last year; has it averaged a dollar a day for three hundred days?

The WITNESS. I have averaged more than that; I have averaged $350 or $400. I will say, for the year.

Q. You pay $10 a month rent; that makes $120 a year?—A. Yes, sir.

The CHAIRMAN. I have asked you these questions in this abrupt way because I want to find out whether you have spent much for practices that might have been dispensed with. You say you smoke?

The WITNESS. Yes, sir.

Q. How much a week do you spend for that?—A. I get 20 cents worth of tobacco a week.

Q. That is $10.40 a year?—A. Yes, sir.

Q. And you say you are not a common drunkard?—A. No, sir.

Q. Do you imagine that you have spent as much more for any form of beer, or ale, or anything of that kind, that you could have got along without?—A. No, sir.

Q. How much do you think has gone in that way?—A. About $1 or $2.

Q. During the whole year?—A. Yes, sir.

Q. That would make $11.40 or $12.40—we will call it $12—gone for wickedness. Now, what else, besides your living, besides the support of your wife and children?—A. Well, I don't know as there is anything else.

Q. Can you not think of anything else that was wrong?—A. No, sir.

Q. Twelve dollars have gone for sin and iniquity; and $120 for rent; that makes $132?—A. Yes.

Q. How many children have you?—A. Two.

Q. Your family consists of yourself, your wife, and two children?—A. Yes.

Q. One hundred and thirty-two dollars from $400 leaves you $268, does it not?—A. Yes, sir.

Q. And with that amount you have furnished your family?—A. Yes, sir.

Q. You have been as economical as you could, I suppose?—A. Yes.

Q. How much money have you left?—A. Sixty dollars in debt.

Q. How did you do that?—A. I don't know, sir.

Q. Can you not think of something more that you have wasted?—A. No, sir.

Q. Have you been as careful as you could?—A. Yes, sir.

Q. And you have come out at the end of the year $60 in debt?—A. Yes, sir.

Q. Have you been extravagant in your family expenses?—A. No, sir; a man can't be very extravagant on that much money. . . .

Q. And there are four of you in the family?—A. Yes, sir.

Q. How many pounds of beefsteak have you had in your family, that you bought for your own home consumption within this year that we have been speaking of?—A. I don't think there has been five pounds of beefsteak.

Q. You have had a little pork steak?—A. We had a half a pound of pork steak yesterday; I don't know when we had any before.

Q. What other kinds of meat have you had within a year?—A. Well, we have had corn beef twice I think that I can remember this year—on Sunday, for dinner.

Q. Twice is all that you can remember within a year?—A. Yes—and some cabbage.

Q. What have you eaten?—A. Well, bread mostly, when we could get it; we sometimes couldn't make out to get that, and have had to go without a meal.

Q. Has there been any day in the year that you have had to go without anything to eat?—A. Yes, sir, several days.

Q. More than one day at a time?—A. No.

Q. How about the children and your wife—did they go without anything to eat too?—A. My wife went out this morning and went to a neighbor's and got a loaf of bread and fetched it home, and when she got home the children were crying for something to eat.

Q. Have the children had anything to eat to-day except that, do you think?—A. They had that loaf of bread—I don't know what they have had since then, if they have had anything.

Q. Did you leave any money at home?—A. No, sir.

Q. If that loaf is gone, is there anything in the house?—A. No, sir; unless my wife goes out and gets something; and I don't know who would mind the children while she goes out.

REFLECTING ON THE PAST **Have you observed any recent hearings of congressional investigating committees on television? Are moral behavior and hunger still topics of concern for Americans? How is the interaction between modern "haves" and "have-nots" similar to and different from the interaction between this laborer and the committee members in 1883? Do ethical beliefs and economic realities still separate social classes?**

Conclusion
The Complexity of Industrial Capitalism

The rapid growth of the late nineteenth century made the United States one of the world's industrial giants. Many factors contributed to the "wonderful accomplishments" of the age. They ranged from sympathetic government policies to the rise of big business and the emergence of a cheap industrial workforce. Many Americans benefited only marginally from the new wealth. Some of them protested by joining unions, by walking out on strike, or by initiating on-the-job actions. Some launched a new political party. Most lived their lives more quietly without Thomas O'Donnell's opportunity to tell their story. But middle-class Americans began to wonder about the O'Donnells of the country. This period of growth was also a time of tension and turbulence, especially in the nation's rapidly growing cities.

TIME*line*

1843–1884	"Old immigration"
1869	Knights of Labor founded
1870s–1880s	Consolidation of continental railroad network
1873	Bethlehem Steel begins using Bessemer process
1873–1879	Depression
1885–1914	"New immigration"
1886	American Federation of Labor founded
	Haymarket Riot in Chicago
1890	Sherman Anti-Trust Act
1892	Formation of People's (Populist) party
1893–1897	Depression
1896	People's party fuses with Democrats
	William McKinley elected president

✓•⎯Study and Review at **www.myhistorylab.com**

Questions for Review and Reflection

1. What explains the United States' rise to industrial and economic prominence in the late nineteenth century?

2. Explain which groups were able to realize the American dream of success and which were not and why.

3. Which factors undermined the working-class efforts at collective action and which promoted them? In your opinion, which were the most important factors underlying the failures of the working class? Why?

4. How would you characterize the politics of the Gilded Age? How does it compare with present-day politics?

5. Why was the election of 1896 crucial in the development of American political parties?

Key Terms

American Federation of Labor 538

Free silver 546

Gilded Age 522

Gospel of Wealth 541

Haymarket Riot 538

Horizontal integration 525

New immigrants 529

Social Darwinism 541

Vertical integration 525

17

The New Metropolis

American Stories

A Journalist Marvels at the Growth of Cities

Julian Ralph was a New Yorker accustomed to the pace of urban life, but he was nevertheless amazed by what he saw in Chicago in 1891. At precisely 5:30 each afternoon, the central business district erupted in a convulsion of activity. Office workers poured from tall office buildings into the streets. The sidewalks filled with a torrent of pedestrians. Cable cars and electric streetcars scraped, screeched, and sparked into action to convey the city's business population to outlying residences. Even for a New Yorker like Ralph, "the energy, roar, and bustle of the place were yet sufficient to first astonish and then fatigue me."

Ralph was on a journey across the United States and Canada as a correspondent for *Harper's Magazine.* Traveling by rail between 1891 and 1893, he documented the spectacular transformations taking place not only in Chicago but across the continent in Minneapolis and St. Paul, Denver, San Francisco, and other cities in the West. As an experienced reporter for one of the leading newspapers of the day, the New York *Sun,* he had an eye for revealing details as well as the broad trends of urbanization. His flair as a writer attracted magazine commissions, such as this tour on behalf of *Harper's,* launching him on a new career as a traveling correspondent. Born in New York City in 1853, Ralph tended to measure each place he encountered against his home city—and in the 1890s, he found many American cities beginning to measure up.

In his travels, Ralph recorded the experiences of city-dwellers as new technologies reshaped their lives and work. Consider, for example, the wonders of the elevator. Ralph described being "loaded into one of those frail-looking baskets of steel netting, and the next instant the elevator-boy touches the trigger, and up goes the whole load as a feather is caught up by a gale." And then, to descend, "Something lets go, and you fall from ten to twenty stories as it happens. There is sometimes a

Chapter Outline

The Industrial City

The New Urban Geography

Reforming the City

Conclusion: Cities Transformed

jolt, which makes the passenger seem to feel his stomach pass into his shoes, but, as a rule, the mechanism and management both work marvelously towards ease and gentleness." In Chicago, the pace of business demanded express elevators so that time would not be wasted stopping at every floor.

The newly electrified streetcars were marvels as well, carrying commuters farther and faster than anyone would have dreamed even a few years before. In Denver, Ralph noted that the streetcars "whiz along so fast that men do not hesitate to build their homes five or six miles from their stores and offices, where they can get garden and elbow room." He predicted, correctly, that "we are going to see all our cities shoot out in this way. It promotes beauty in residence districts, and pride in the hearts of those who own the pretty homes. It carries the good health that comes with fresh air." But this would also come with a cost for increasing city services to build and maintain streets, water mains, sewer lines, and police.

Across the West from one city to the next, so much seemed to be brand new. Ralph found that the leading businessmen were young, streets were freshly paved, and new, substantial structures were rising downtown. Much of the population was new as well, as cities swelled with arrivals from abroad or from the American countryside. Each city eagerly promoted its advantages over the others, and everything seemed to be moving quickly, from the new transit lines to the waiters in restaurants who hustled diners to their tables.

Ralph's essays were published in three books, *On Canada's Frontier* (1892), *Our Great West* (1893), and *Chicago and the World's Fair* (1893). He went on to become a foreign correspondent in Europe and covered the Boer War in South Africa. His newspaper stories about coronations and battles produced more exciting headlines, but his travels across the American continent in the 1890s documented the significant growth and transformation of cities at the end of the nineteenth century.

As Julian Ralph discovered, American cities in the late nineteenth century were booming. As immigrants and rural migrants added to urban populations, cities grew upward and outward, aided by new technologies of construction and transportation. Downtowns reached toward the sky as structural steel provided the strong skeletons necessary for the first skyscrapers, and elevators carried businesspeople and shoppers to new heights in offices and department stores. Meanwhile, streetcars radiating out from the downtown opened new neighborhoods for the middle class, especially after horsepower gave way to electrification in the 1890s. Commuter railways allowed the most prosperous Americans to move to fashionable suburbs even farther away from the center of business and industry, the source of their wealth. Left behind were the industrial neighborhoods, where immigrants and rural newcomers invigorated the city but also struggled to make a living in deteriorating and increasingly crowded conditions.

This chapter explores the new shape and circumstances of urban life in the decades following the Civil War. How and why did cities grow so much during this period? What opportunities and challenges did they present? What were the consequences for city people and their environment? As the middle and upper classes separated themselves from the heart of industrial, immigrant neighborhoods, how did reformers tackle the issues of urban poverty and governance? By exploring these questions, we uncover the history of cities in the late nineteenth century, but we also find the foundations of issues that continue to challenge urban and suburban communities today.

The Industrial City

American cities grew rapidly in the last part of the nineteenth and the first part of the twentieth centuries. In 1870, some 25 percent of Americans lived in cities; by 1900, fully 40 percent of them did. As manufacturing shifted from water to steam power, most factory owners also favored urban locations, which offered workers, specialized services, local markets, and railroad links to raw materials and distant markets.

Newcomers streamed into the cities from abroad and from the nation's small towns and farms. New York, which had a population of 1.2 million in 1880, grew to 3.4 million by 1900 and 5.6 million in 1920. Los Angeles, a town of 11,000 in 1880, multiplied 10 times by 1900 and then increased another 5 times, to more than a half million, by 1920. Smaller cities, especially in the industrial Midwest and the South, shared in the growth; far western cities increased explosively.

Growing Populations, Expanding Boundaries

Much of the population growth in northern industrial cities consisted of the "new immigrants" from southern and eastern Europe (see Chapter 16) who arrived in East Coast ports, especially New York. The Statue of Liberty, placed on its pedestal in 1886, became a symbol of welcome to new arrivals. The Ellis Island immigration station, opened in 1892, became their first experience of America. Many Europeans stayed in eastern cities, but railroads also carried immigrants west to Pittsburgh, St. Louis, Chicago, and to cities and towns across the country. In the West, meanwhile, immigrants from Asia and Mexico added to the urban populations. When the Chinese met with a backlash of violence in California, many moved east and created Chinatowns in New York, Philadelphia, Chicago, and other cities.

View the Image
Immigrants at Ellis Island
at **www.myhistorylab.com**

Lower East Side, New York Here is a picture of life on Hester Street on New York's Lower East Side. Study the photograph to see what it reveals about living conditions in the city. What indications are there of commercial activity? Why are there so many women on the street and so few men? What is suggested about children? What impression does the picture give of city services to this poor neighborhood?

Immigrants in cities were joined by rural Americans, who were pushed from the farm as agricultural machinery replaced human hands. They were lured by the promise of employment. Urban jobs were often dirty, dangerous, and exhausting, but so was farmwork.

Watch the Video
Immigrants to America
at **www.myhistorylab.com**

Furthermore, by 1890, manufacturing workers were earning hundreds of dollars more a year than farm laborers. Higher urban living costs gobbled up some of the differential between rural and urban wages but not all of it. The "gilded metropolis" also offered marvels absent from rural life. Shops, theaters, restaurants, department stores, baseball games, and the crowds amazed and amused young people coming from towns and farms.

One of the most astounding examples of city growth was Chicago, the city founded on the southwest shore of Lake Michigan in 1833. Its location in the nation's midsection helped to make Chicago a crossroads for trade and for the railroads. Lumber, livestock, and grain from the nation's heartland came to Chicago to be processed and sold, a process that turned natural resources into commodities and marked Chicago as a commercial center. Although devastated by a great fire in 1871, Chicago in the last decades of the nineteenth century became a phoenix reborn from its ashes. From a population of about 300,000 at the time of the fire, Chicago by 1900 was a city of more than 1.6 million people, and its territory had expanded by annexation from 36 to 169 square miles. The city put its success on display in 1893 when it became the improbable mid-American site for the **World's Columbian Exposition**, a grand world's fair commemorating the arrival of Christopher Columbus in the New World.

⊙⊣**See the Map**
Foreign-Born Population, 1890
at **www.myhistorylab.com**

Like Julian Ralph, visitors to Chicago in the late nineteenth century found it both dazzling and dizzying. A writer for *Harper's* magazine in 1880 called the city rebounding after the fire "one of the wonders of the world." For the architect Frank Lloyd Wright, his arrival to look for a job in 1887 was his first encounter with a city. "Chicago!" he later wrote in his autobiography, recalling his first impressions. "Immense gridiron of noisy streets. Dirty . . . Heavy traffic crossing both ways at once, managing somehow: Torrential noise. . . . Were all American cities like this one, so casual, so monotonous in their savage, outrageous attempts at variety? All competing for the same thing in the same way? Another senseless competition never to be won?"

Chicago's counterpart in the West was San Francisco, where commercial growth and industrialization had followed the boom of the Gold Rush of 1849. The wealth produced by mining was reinvested in real estate development, in the manufacture of products from iron pipes to blankets, in refineries for sugar grown in Hawaii, and in the Central Pacific Railroad. The city's population more than doubled between 1870 and 1900. And San Francisco was just the most prominent of the growing cities in the West, where railroad promoters played a major role in the urbanization of small towns (like El Paso, Texas) and in the creation of entirely new cities (like Cheyenne, Wyoming, and Billings, Montana).

●⊷⊣**Read the Document**
Adna Weber, Growth of Cities in the Nineteenth Century *(1899)*
at **www.myhistorylab.com**

In the South, Atlanta was known as the "Chicago of the South" because of its position as a railroad hub. But in general, southern cities grew at a slower pace. Less industrial than cities in the North, they drew fewer

The Progress of Chicago In this advertisement, a Chicago manufacturer displays contrasting images to show the growth of the city from 1833 to 1883. Look closely at the details in the images. Why would a company sponsor this type of advertisement? What do the images reveal about the reasons for Chicago's phenomenal growth?

immigrants but nevertheless gained population from the migration of rural southerners, especially African Americans seeking new lives and opportunities after the end of slavery. Urbanization quickened after 1880, when railroad expansion triggered new industry. Birmingham, Alabama, became an industrial center of iron mines and steel mills once the railroads provided connections between its rich iron deposits and Atlanta and other major cities. With little more than 3,000 residents in 1880, Birmingham added more than 100,000 to its population by 1910. Memphis, Tennessee, gained seven new rail lines in the 1880s and saw its population increase 92 percent in just 10 years. Norfolk, Virginia, grew after the Norfolk and Western Railroad connected the port with coal fields in Virginia and West Virginia.

As populations grew and spread, many of the nation's older cities expanded their boundaries by annexing adjacent towns and countryside. Philadelphia began the trend in 1854 by expanding its boundaries to all of Philadelphia County, increasing its territory from 2 to 130 square miles and instantly quadrupling its population. Boston created new territory by filling in part of the Back Bay to create fashionable Commonwealth Avenue and by annexing adjacent towns such as Dorchester, Charleston, and Brighton. St. Louis, Baltimore, and New Orleans were among the many other expanding cities. Portland, Oregon, became the second-largest city in the West—behind only San Francisco—when the "Great Consolidation of 1891" incorporated adjacent East Portland and Albina into a single municipality.

At the end of the nineteenth century, the most phenomenal example of territorial expansion was New York, which in 1898 consolidated Manhattan, part of Westchester County (the Bronx), Brooklyn, Queens, and Staten Island into a single giant metropolis. The move reinforced New Yorkers' sense of their city's importance. "This consolidation makes of New York, topographically considered, a city unique in the history of cities," wrote E. Idell Zeisloft in *The New Metropolis,* published in 1899. "The metropolis of the Western World, stronger and more progressive than ever, is launched on a new cycle of its history."

Urban Bosses and Local Politics

Governing the often chaotic, rapidly growing cities presented new challenges and opportunities for a rising class of professional politicians. Urban politics during the late nineteenth century functioned at the hands of tightly controlled single-party "machines," operated by charismatic and often corrupt bosses who had come up through the ranks from their neighborhoods. They operated at the center of a web of favors and payback, a system that provided benefits for their constituents while also adding to their own power and wealth.

Political organizations operated block by block in urban neighborhoods. They built allegiance not only through political appeals but also by providing badly needed assistance, such as a connection for a job, a Christmastime turkey, or the arrangements for proper burial for a deceased family member. They could turn out the vote for their favored candidates—sometimes electing the political bosses themselves—and thereby gain access to lucrative municipal contracts at a time when the expanding cities were building sewer lines, streetcar lines, parks, roads, and bridges. One of New York's political bosses, George Washington Plunkitt, defended the profits of politics, saying there was nothing wrong with earning a little "honest graft" from inside knowledge of the system.

Favors from a Party Boss Political machine bosses exerted enormous influence over urban life and politics, as this cartoon from Puck magazine indicates. What good did bosses do? Did the good outweigh the bad? What would reformers criticize and want to change?

"I seen my opportunities and I took 'em," he declared. By the time he died, he was a millionaire.

New York's Tammany Hall, the Democratic Party operation in New York City, was one of the most famous of the political machines. As a political society, Tammany (named for the Lenni Lenape Indian chief Tamanend) had existed since the 1780s, but it became a disciplined machine in the decades after the Civil War. Tammany controlled votes and provided services through a system of precinct captains and ward leaders who maintained close ties with their neighborhoods. Led by Irish Americans, the Tammany Democrats wielded power in New York and national politics into the 1920s and 1930s.

Read the Document

Tammany Hall, Excerpt from Niles Weekly Register (1835)

at **www.myhistorylab.com**

At a time when national politics avoided controversial issues, local politics generated the interest and excitement necessary to move voters to the polls. Far more eligible voters turned out in the late nineteenth century than at any time since. The 78.5 percent average turnout to vote for president in the 1880s contrasts sharply with the 56.8 percent of eligible Americans who voted in 2008.

"Big Tim" Sullivan, one of the Tammany bosses in New York, showed how politics could be combined with the theatrics of urban culture to build voter loyalty. A former saloon owner, he invested in new entertainments such as vaudeville houses and movie theaters, and he befriended their owners. His showmanship went on display each summer in an extravaganza for thousands, including a parade, a steamboat ride up the East River to picnic grounds, contests, music and dancing, plentiful food, and fireworks.

American men were drawn to the polls in part by the hoopla but also by local issues. This was true in rural areas as well as cities. Iowa farmers turned out to vote for state representatives who favored curbing the power of the railroads. But emotional issues of race, religion, nationality, and alcohol often overrode economic self-interest. Voters expressed strong interest in temperance, anti-Catholicism, compulsory school attendance and Sunday laws, aid to parochial schools, racial issues, immigration restriction, and "bloody shirt" reminders of the Civil War.

Prohibition provoked spirited local contests. Many Americans considered drinking a serious social problem. Annual consumption of brewery beer had risen from 2.7 gallons per capita in 1850 to 17.9 in 1880. In one city, saloons outnumbered churches 31 to 1. Such statistics shocked those who believed that drinking would destroy character, corrupt politics, and cause poverty, crime, and unrestrained sexuality. Because they were often the targets of violent drunken men, women especially supported temperance. Rather than try to persuade individuals to give up drink, as the pre–Civil War temperance movement had done, many now sought to ban drinking by putting the question of prohibition on the ballot.

The battle in San Jose, California, illustrates the strong passions such efforts aroused. In the 1870s, temperance reformers put on the ballot a local option referendum to ban the sale of liquor in San Jose. Women erected a temperance tent where they held daily meetings. Despite denunciations from clergymen and heckling from some local drinkers, the women refused to retreat to their homes. On election eve, a large crowd appeared at the temperance tent, but a larger one turned up at a pro-liquor rally. In the morning, women roamed the streets, urging men to adopt the referendum. Children marched to the polls and saloons, singing, "Father, dear father, come home with me now." By afternoon, the mood grew ugly; the women were harassed and threatened by drunken men, and the proposal lost by a vote of 1,430 to 918.

Party leaders used local and ethnic issues to solidify party affiliation and mobilize voters for their national agendas. In New Mexico, for example, the Santa Fe ring, a small group of Anglo-Protestant Republican bankers, lawyers, and politicians, had long exploited local anti-Mexican feelings to grab lands. The ring controlled judges, legislators, and the business interests of the state, including many Spanish-speaking voters. When desperate Mexican-American tenant farmers turned to violence in the 1880s, the ring used the situation to dispossess Mexican Americans, Native Americans, and poor white squatters from enormous tracts of land.

In American cities, political machines survived into the twentieth century. Their influence over such cities as St. Louis, Minneapolis, Pittsburgh, and Chicago became the subject of an exposé by journalist Lincoln Steffens, who published his essays from *McLure's* magazine in the book *The Shame of the Cities* in 1904. After visiting Philadelphia, Steffens declared the city to be "corrupt and contented." In his view, the situation could not be blamed entirely on the bosses or on the immigrant neighborhoods they controlled. All of the citizens must share in the blame, he said, because they had ceded control to the political machines, had given up on democracy, and had ceased to care.

••••–Read the Document

Lincoln Steffens, from The Shame of the Cities *(1904)*

at **www.myhistorylab.com**

Pollution and Public Health

Living in cities also meant living with widespread pollution, a byproduct of the industrial age. Promotional maps and lithographs of cities in the nineteenth century displayed smokestacks as a sign of economic prosperity, but smoky skies adversely affected the environment. In the iron and steel city of Birmingham, Alabama, for example, the production of these metals befouled the air with smoke, soot, and ashes. Coal tar, a byproduct of the process, was dumped, making the soil so acid that nothing would grow in it.

The effects of urban pollution did not stop at the city limits. Factories often were constructed near waterways so that water would be available for production processes and for use in steam boilers. When industrial, human, and animal wastes were channeled into rivers, they killed fish and other forms of marine life and plants that were part of that ecosystem. By the late nineteenth century, pollution was evident in eastern and Midwestern rivers and lakes.

The intellectual rationale of the times stressed growth, development, and the rapid exploitation of resources—not conservation. Presidents Grover Cleveland and Benjamin Harrison both set aside forest reserves, and there was growing interest in creating national parks. But such activities were limited in scope and did not begin to touch the problems created by the rise of heavy industry and the rapid urban expansion that it stimulated.

In the densely packed neighborhoods of industrial cities, piles of garbage, foul odors, and disease were common. Outdoor privies, shared by several families, were the rule. Water came from outdoor hydrants, and had to be carried inside for cooking, washing, and cleaning. When there were indoor fixtures, they frequently emptied waste directly into unpaved alleys and courts served by inadequate sewage systems or none at all. Accumulated garbage and waste stank in the summer and froze in the winter.

These conditions placed an additional burden on women, for whom housekeeping was a constant battle against dust and grime. In factory neighborhoods, no amount of scrubbing could maintain clean windows or floors, let alone clean children. Even when people could keep their own living quarters clean, their outside environment was unsanitary and unhealthy. Outbreaks of diseases such as yellow fever and typhoid occurred, and urban death rates were high. Only at the turn of the century did the public health movement, particularly the efforts to treat water supplies with germ-killing chemicals, begin to ameliorate these living conditions.

The New Urban Geography

The late-nineteenth-century industrial city had new physical and social arrangements that attracted widespread comment. Slums, not new, seemed disturbing because so many people lived in them. Yet cities also contained grand mansions, handsome business and industrial buildings, grandiose civic monuments, parks, and acres of substantial middle-class homes.

By the last quarter of the nineteenth century, the antebellum "**walking city**," whose size and configuration had been limited by the necessity of walking to work, disappeared. Where once substantial houses, businesses, and small artisan dwellings had stood side by side, central business districts emerged. Here were banks, shops, theaters, professional firms, and businesses. Few people lived downtown, although many worked or shopped there. Surrounding the business center were areas of light manufacturing and wholesale activity with housing for workers. Beyond these working-class neighborhoods stretched middle-class residential areas. Then came the suburbs, with "pure air, peacefulness," and "natural scenery." Scattered throughout the city were pockets of industrial activity surrounded by crowded working-class housing.

This new pattern, with the poorest city residents clustered near the center, reversed the early nineteenth-century urban form in which much of the most desirable housing was in the heart of the city. New living arrangements were also more segregated by race and class than those in the preindustrial walking city. Homogeneous social and economic neighborhoods emerged, and it became more unusual than before for a poor, working-class family to live near a middle- or upper-class family.

Neighborhoods and Neighborhood Life

Working-class neighborhoods clustered near the center of most industrial cities. Here lived newcomers from the American countryside and, because most immigrants settled in cities, crowds of foreigners as well.

Ethnic groups frequently gathered in particular neighborhoods, often located near industries requiring their labor. In Detroit in 1880, for example, 37 percent of the city's native-born families lived in one area, whereas 40 percent of the Irish inhabited the "Irish West Side." More than half of the Germans and almost three-quarters of the Poles settled on the city's east side. Although such neighborhoods often had an ethnic flavor, with small specialty shops and foreign-language signs, they were not ethnic ghettos. Immigrants and native-born Americans often lived in the same neighborhoods, on the same streets, and even in the same houses. The Chinatowns that sprang up in western cities and in places like New York were exceptions to this pattern. Hostility from whites kept most Chinese secluded in Chinatowns where they felt safe among their own people.

Working-class neighborhoods were often what would be called slums today. They were crowded and unsanitary, with inadequate public services. Many workers lived in houses once occupied by middle- and upper-class residents, now divided and subdivided to accommodate more people than the original builders had intended. Others squeezed into tenements, which were specially constructed to house as many families as possible. Small apartments were dark and stuffy and often had window-less rooms.

●┤View the Image
Hester Street, New York City
at **www.myhistorylab.com**

Not every working-class family lived in abject circumstances. Skilled workers might rent comfortable quarters, and a few even owned their own homes. A study of working-class families in Massachusetts found the family of one skilled worker living "in a tenement of five rooms in a pleasant and healthy locality, with good surroundings. The apartments are well furnished and [the] parlor carpeted." The family even had a sewing machine. But unskilled and semiskilled workers were not so fortunate. The Massachusetts survey describes the family of an unskilled ironworker crammed into a tenement of four rooms,

> in an overcrowded block, to which belong only two privies for about fifty people. When this place was visited the vault had overflowed in the yard and the sink-water was also running in the same place, and created a stench that was really frightful. . . . The house inside, was badly furnished and dirty, and a disgrace to Worcester.

Drab as their neighborhoods usually were, working families created a community life that helped alleviate some of their dreary physical surroundings. The expense of moving around the city helped encourage a neighborhood and family focus. Long working hours meant that precious free time was apt to be spent close to home.

The wide range of institutions and associations that came to life in urban neighborhoods demonstrates that working-class men and women were not just victims of their environment. Frequently rooted in religious and ethnic identities, these organizations helped residents feel at home in the city. But they also could separate ethnic groups from one another and from native-born Americans. A Lithuanian worker in Chicago found companionship in a Lithuanian Concertina Club and a Lithuanian society that gave two picnics and two balls each year. Irish collective life focused around the Roman Catholic parish church, Irish nationalist organizations, ward politics, and Irish saloons. Jews gathered in their synagogues, Hebrew schools, and Hebrew- and Yiddish-speaking literary groups. Germans had their family saloons and educational and singing societies. Various Chinese organizations provided benefits, including education, health, and religious services. Although such activities may have slowed assimilation into American society and discouraged inter-group contact, they provided companionship, a social network, spiritual consolation, and a bridge between life in the "old country" and life in America.

Beyond working-class neighborhoods lay streets of middle-class houses. Here lived the urban lower middle class: clerks, shopkeepers, bookkeepers, salespeople, and small tradespeople. Their salaries allowed them to buy or rent houses with some privacy and comfort. Separate spaces for cooking and laundry work kept hot and often odorous housekeeping tasks away from other living areas. Many houses boasted up-to-date gas lighting and bathrooms. Outside, the neighborhoods were cleaner and more attractive than in the inner city. Residents could pay for garbage collection, gaslights, and other improvements.

African Americans faced the most wretched living conditions of any group in the city. In the North, they often lived in segregated black neighborhoods. In southern cities, they gathered in back alleys and small streets. Many could afford only rented rooms. In cases where predominantly black neighborhoods formed in southern cities, they received few if any benefits from expanding municipal services such as water and sewer lines or streetcar transportation.

A rich religious and associational life tempered the suffering. African American churches enjoyed phenomenal growth. Black members of mainline Protestant denominations separated from their white counterparts to establish autonomy and self-respect. The African Methodist Episcopal Church, with a membership of 20,000 in 1856, founded churches in every city and sizable town, and by 1900 claimed more than 400,000 members. African American worship continued to express the emotional exuberance that had characterized slave religion. Energetic preaching and expressive music helped make churchgoing a fulfilling spiritual experience. Often associated with churches were mutual-aid and benevolent societies that helped needy members of the community. Outreach activities also included support for missionaries in Africa.

Some urban African Americans in the late nineteenth century rose into the middle class. In spite of the heavy odds against them, they created the nucleus of professional life. Ministers, businessmen, doctors, and lawyers became leaders of their communities. However, their housing options often were limited to the same dense and impoverished neighborhoods occupied by other, less prosperous African Americans.

Conditions in Philadelphia's Seventh Ward, documented by **W. E. B. Du Bois** in *The Philadelphia Negro* (1899), demonstrated the trends and limitations of African American life in a northern city. Du Bois found that racial discrimination in hiring and housing had disastrous effects, but that white Philadelphians did not understand or even recognize the problem. Blocks near the nation's first African American churches, which since the 1790s had served as the vibrant center of black life, had descended into "the worst Negro slums of the city," he found. Prosperous African Americans tended to move westward within the ward, but the swelling population followed and defeated their attempts at residential respectability.

Railroad and Streetcar Suburbs

Cities still held some enclaves for the wealthy in neighborhoods such as San Francisco's Nob Hill and Boston's Beacon Hill, and beginning in the 1870s, elegant apartment houses also provided homes for the elite. But it became increasingly common for people of means to move to countryside suburbs and commute into the city by rail. By the end of the nineteenth century, suburban possibilities also opened up along trolley lines and allowed the middle class to separate from the city's industrial core. These changes in transportation led to increasing separation of classes and land uses, with lasting impact on cities and suburbs.

Railroad companies promoted the development of new suburbs for the elite in previously remote areas such as the North Shore of Chicago and Westchester County north of Manhattan. West of Philadelphia, the Pennsylvania Railroad developed the "Main Line" suburbs after acquiring properties in the 1870s to straighten its tracks. The railroad bestowed new, picturesque names on existing towns (Humphreysville became Bryn Mawr) and enticed the wealthy to venture into the countryside for summer retreats at fashionable hotels. Railroad executives built estates for themselves along the line, and others followed. The pattern was similar in Westchester County, New York, where three rail lines transformed a region known as a summer retreat into a suburban haven for more than 100,000 commuters who rode the rails into Manhattan's Grand Central Station.

In the railroad suburbs, new and more diverse communities also formed near the commuter rail stations. This was because the elite did not come alone; with them came the servants, gardeners, and small businesses necessary to sustain a comfortable life. Unlike their wealthy employers and customers, who could afford the train fares and had the time for commuting, these domestic and service workers needed to live close to their workplaces.

People of somewhat lesser means also moved out from the shadows of the factories as mass transportation expanded. At midcentury, public transportation consisted of streetcars, also known as horsecars because they were pulled by horses along rails through city streets. The cost of a fare limited ridership to the prosperous classes, but enabled some to move to newly constructed, more distant neighborhoods.

For example, Robert Work, a modestly successful cap and hat merchant, moved his family to a $5,500 house in West Philadelphia in 1865 and commuted more than four miles to work. Fifteen years later, the 1880 census revealed the Work family's comfortable life. The household contained two servants, two boarders, Robert's wife, and their son, who was still in school. The Works' house had running hot and cold water, indoor bathrooms, central heating, and other modern conveniences of the age. Elaborately carved furniture, rugs, draperies, and lace curtains probably graced the downstairs, where the family entertained and gathered for meals. Upstairs, comfortable bedrooms provided a maximum of privacy for family members. The live-in servants, who did most of the housework, shared little of this space or privacy, however. They were restricted to the kitchen, the pantry, and bedrooms in the attic.

Additional suburban horizons opened with the introduction of cable cars in the 1870s and especially the electrified streetcar in the 1890s. Cable cars operated by gripping a moving cable underground, while the new streetcars, or trolleys, gained power from overhead electric lines. As trolleys connected cities with nearby towns, the populations of the towns grew with middle-class commuters. New "**streetcar suburbs**" developed along the line, creating communities such as Houston Heights, Denver's Curtis Park, Cincinnati's Norwood, and Atlanta's Kirkwood.

The trolleys carried people to and from work during the week, but they did not remain idle on the weekends. To promote weekend travel, streetcar companies created attractions such as racetracks, beer gardens, and amusement parks at the farthest reaches of the transit lines. City-dwellers flocked to these new destinations to socialize, compete in carnival games, and listen to band concerts. For young working people, the amusement parks offered inexpensive opportunities for mingling with the opposite sex away from the controls of family and neighborhood. By the end of the century, parks such as Coney Island presented a spectacle of electrified, mechanical amusements such as carousels and the Ferris wheel, first introduced at the World's Columbian Exposition in Chicago in 1893.

Central Business Districts

As outlying residential suburbs developed, the central city became increasingly devoted to business and industry. During the last three decades of the nineteenth century, many American cities developed specialized business districts for the first time. In these new downtowns, tall office buildings provided workplaces for the white-collar bureaucracy, and retail stores offered goods from around the world to eager consumers. Banks, hotels, theaters, and grand railroad stations rose in place of older, rundown residential buildings. In the city's desirable commercial center, land values soared.

The first skyscraper was built in 1885 in Chicago's central business district, which later became known as "the Loop" when it was encircled by an elevated railway. The 10-story Home Insurance Building, designed by William LeBaron Jenney, was the first to employ a structural steel skeleton.

By the end of the century, buildings from 10 to 20 stories in height changed the look and experience of cities. The overall effect required a new term, "skyline," which appeared for the first time in 1896 in *Harper's* magazine to describe lower Manhattan.

Among the major attractions of the business district were the department stores, a new form of retailing based on European precedents such as Le Bon Marché in Paris. At the Emporium in San Francisco, Marshall Field's in Chicago, Wanamaker's in Philadelphia, Macy's in New York, and Filene's in Boston, shoppers found an array of specialized shops all under one roof. The department stores offered such marvels as air conditioning, elevators, and escalators, and they staged holiday pageants and fashion shows. They imported goods from around the world, especially Europe. Elaborate window displays beckoned shoppers in from the street, and even those who could not afford to buy could browse, desire, and dream. The department stores also offered employment that was considered respectable for young middle-class women, who worked as clerks.

The numerous young clerks and office workers needed to support the business districts also needed convenient housing, which many found in new apartment buildings or residential hotels on the fringe of the downtown. These single young adults, living apart from family or community, were considered by some to be leading unacceptably isolated and potentially immoral lives. They found companionship in the workplace and in

Sharing the Streets
This photograph taken in 1896 shows electrified streetcars in the business district of Atlanta, Georgia. How did the introduction of this new form of mass transportation impact American cities? Who traveled on streetcars, where, and why? What does this photograph suggest about changes in transportation and the interactions of vehicles and pedestrians?

the saloons, dance halls, and restaurants of cities rather than in the more supervised setting of home.

Industrial Suburbs: Pullman's Model Town

Most industries were located in cities near their workforces, and the railroads needed to carry their goods to market. But the labor conflicts of the late nineteenth century, combined with the deteriorating conditions of cities, led some factory owners to seek new locations outside the urban core. High land costs in cities also led industrialists to seek nearby but less expensive factory sites. In California, for example, the oil industry expanded near Los Angeles in El Segundo and Long Beach. Outside Pittsburgh, the steel industry spread to McKeesport, Homestead, and Allegheny.

Industrial suburbs consisted of newly built factories, homes for employees, and community services and institutions such as libraries and hotels. This arrangement might provide more pleasant surroundings, but it also gave employers a high degree of control over local government and their workers' lives.

The model town of Pullman, Illinois, was widely admired as an alternative to the typically dense and grimy factory neighborhood. The town south of Chicago was created as the setting for the Pullman Palace Car Company, which manufactured railroad cars with sleeping compartments. Workers lived in tidy row houses, all owned by the company, with larger residences provided for managers. The residents all paid rent to the company. Pullman had a fine hotel, churches, and schools. It was such a novelty that visitors to Chicago arranged for side trips to see Pullman's industrial utopia.

But Pullman's geographic distance from the city could not separate it from the realities of the economy and struggles between labor and capital. Late in 1893, in the midst of the worsening depression, the Pullman Company cut wages by one-third and laid off many workers without reducing rents or prices in its stores. Forced to pay in rent what they could not earn in wages, working families struggled through the winter. Those working experienced speedups, threats, and further wage cuts.

Desperate Pullman workers joined the American Railway Union (ARU) in the spring of 1894 and went on strike. Recounting the workers' outlook later to a government commission, one of the strikers declared that "Pullman, both the man and the town, is an ulcer on the body politic. He owns the houses, the schoolhouses, the churches of God. . . . The wages he pays out with one hand . . . he takes back with the other."

In late June, after Pullman refused to submit the dispute to arbitration, labor organizer **Eugene V. Debs** led the ARU into a sympathy strike in support of the striking Pullman workers. Remembering the ill-fated railroad strike of 1877, Debs advised his lieutenants to "use no violence" and "stop no trains." Rather, he sought to boycott trains handling Pullman cars throughout the West. As the boycott spread, the General Managers

Industrial Experiment At a shift change, workers spill out of the Pullman Palace Car Company. Notice the date over the factory entrance, which indicates this is a new industrial setting. The model town of Pullman was intended to create a superior environment for workers, but conflict erupted in a strike in 1893. What does this photograph suggest about the working conditions in Pullman? Why did the experiment fail?

Association (GMA), which ran the 24 railroads centered in Chicago, came to Pullman's support. Hiring 2,500 strikebreakers, the GMA appealed to the state and federal governments for military and judicial support in stopping the strike.

Governor Richard Altgeld of Illinois, sympathizing with the workers and believing that local law enforcement was sufficient, opposed using federal troops. But U.S. Attorney General Richard Olney, a former railroad lawyer, obtained a court injunction on July 2 to end the strike as a "conspiracy in restraint of trade." Two days later, President Grover Cleveland ordered federal troops to crush the strikers. Violence escalated rapidly. Local and federal officials hired armed guards, and the railroads paid them to help the troops. Within two days, strikers and guards were fighting bitterly. As troops poured into Chicago, the violence worsened, leaving scores of workers dead.

Debs's resources would run out unless he could enlist wider labor support. "We must all stand together or go down in hopeless defeat," he warned other unions. When American Federation of Labor leader Samuel Gompers refused support, the strike collapsed. Debs and several other leaders were found guilty of contempt of court. Hitherto a lifelong Democrat, Debs became a staunch socialist. His arrest and the defeat of the **Pullman strike** killed the American Railway Union. In 1895, in *In Re Debs*, the Supreme Court upheld the legality of using an injunction to stop a strike, giving management a powerful weapon against unions.

Reforming the City

Although most middle-class Americans avoided reformist politics, urban corruption and labor violence of the late nineteenth century frightened many out of their aversion to politics. Middle-class activists worried about the degradation of life and labor in America's cities, factories, and farms.

These urban reformers were influenced by middle-class English socialists; by European social prophets such as Karl Marx, Leo Tolstoy, and Victor Hugo; and by the ethical teachings of Jesus. Their message was highly idealistic, ethical, and Christian. They preferred a society marked by cooperation rather than competition—where, as they liked to say, people were guided by the "golden rule rather than the rule of gold." Some preferred to put their goals in more secular terms, speaking of radically transforming American society. Most, however, worked within existing institutions. As middle-class intellectuals and professionals, they tended to stress an educational approach to problems. But they were also practical, seeking tangible improvements by running for public office, crusading for legislation, mediating labor disputes, and living among the poor.

Settlements and Social Gospel

In 1889, Jane Addams, then 29 years old, and her college friend Ellen Starr rented a rundown mansion on the West Side of Chicago. They intended to live there—but that was not all. The pair had recently visited London, where they had encountered the idea of the "**settlement house**," a place where reformers lived in a working-class neighborhood,

•••⌐Read the **Document**

Jane Addams, "Ballots Necessary for Women" (1906)

at **www.myhistorylab.com**

provided services to the poor, and studied urban conditions. In Chicago, Addams and Starr followed this model by establishing Hull House, not the first settlement house in the United States but one of most famous and influential. Its purpose, Addams said, was "to aid in the solution of the social and industrial problems which are engendered by the modern conditions of life in a great city."

Settlement houses in the United States differed from the English model in two important respects: Women were more involved in operating them, and the neighborhoods they served were far more diverse with large populations of recent immigrants. The reformers' efforts at

•●⌐View the **Image**

Jane Addams, Portrait

at **www.myhistorylab.com**

instilling middle-class values among the immigrant working class could be paternalistic, but among their many activities they helped to organize programs that celebrated and preserved the immigrants' heritage. They also documented their neighborhoods and pushed for local ordinances and state laws to improve urban conditions.

The settlement house movement typified 1890s middle-class reformers' blend of idealism and practicality. The primary purpose of settlement houses was to help immigrant families, especially women, adapt Old World rural styles of child rearing and housekeeping to American urban life. Settlement houses launched day nurseries, kindergartens, and boarding rooms for working women; they offered classes in sewing, cooking, nutrition, health care, and English; and they tried to keep young people out of saloons by organizing sports clubs and coffeehouses.

A second purpose of the settlement house movement was to give college-educated women meaningful work at a time when they faced professional barriers and to allow them to preserve the strong feelings of sisterhood they had experienced at college. A third goal was to gather data exposing social misery in order to spur legislative action—developing city building codes for tenements, abolishing child labor, and improving factory safety. The settlement house movement, with its dual emphasis on the scientific gathering of facts and spiritual commitment, blended academic study and Christian beliefs and nourished the new discipline of sociology.

The Lower East Side of Manhattan saw the opening of the first settlement houses in the United States, the Neighborhood Guild (1886) and the College Settlement (1889), followed soon thereafter by Hull House in Chicago. By the end of the century, more than one hundred settlement houses existed in the United States, most of them in the largest cities. With so many Catholics among the immigrant population, Catholic women countered the Protestant influence of institutions like Hull House by founding Catholic settlements such as the Madonna Center on Chicago's West Side and the St. Elizabeth Settlement in St. Louis.

Read the Document
Jane Addams, "From Twenty Years at Hull House" (1910)
at **www.myhistorylab.com**

Religious leaders also addressed urban problems. Dwight Moody preached a traditional evangelical Christianity in cities, leading hundreds

Settlement House Service (left) What is being taught to immigrant women in this typical settlement house poster? The health clinic (right) is in Vida Scudder's Denison House in Boston. Settlement house work, Scudder wrote, fulfilled "a biting curiosity about the way the Other Half lived, and a strange hunger for fellowship with them." What evidence do you see of cross-cultural, cross-class bonding? Do you have opportunities to engage in this kind of service learning today? *(Right: Schlesinger Library, Radcliffe Institute, Harvard University)*

of urban revivals in the 1870s. Discovering his mission while in England for the YMCA, Moody mastered the art of the folksy sermon filled with Bible and family stories, the easy path from sin to salvation by filling out a decision card, and the importance of music in making converts. The revivals appealed to lower-class, rural folk who were both drawn to the city by their hopes and pushed there by economic ruin. Supported by businesspeople who believed that religion would make workers and immigrants more docile, revivalists battled sin through individual conversion. The revivals helped to nearly double Protestant church membership in the last two decades of the century. Although some urban workers drifted into socialism, most remained conventionally religious.

Unlike Moody, many Protestant ministers embraced the **Social Gospel movement** of the 1890s, which tied salvation to social betterment. Like the settlement house workers, they sought to make Christianity relevant to urban conditions. Congregational minister Washington Gladden advocated collective bargaining and corporate profit sharing. A young Baptist minister in the notorious Hell's Kitchen area of New York City, Walter Rauschenbusch, raised an even louder voice. Often called on to conduct funeral services for children killed by the airless, disease-ridden tenements and sweatshops, Rauschenbusch scathingly attacked capitalism and church ignorance of socioeconomic issues. His progressive ideas for social justice and a welfare state were later published in two landmark books, *Christianity and the Social Crisis* (1907) and *Christianizing the Social Order* (1912).

View the Image
Tenement Families
(Jacob Riis, Photo)
at **www.myhistorylab.com**

Perhaps the most influential book promoting social Christianity was a best-selling novel *In His Steps*, published in 1897 by Charles Sheldon. The novel portrayed the dramatic changes made possible by a few community leaders who resolved to base all their actions on a single question: "What would Jesus do?" For a minister, this meant seeking to "bridge the chasm between the church and labor." For the idle rich, it meant settlement house work and reforming prostitutes. For landlords and factory owners, it meant improving the living and working conditions of tenants and laborers. Although filled with naive sentimentality characteristic of much of the Social Gospel, Sheldon's novel prepared thousands of influential middle-class Americans for progressive civic leadership after 1900.

In Pursuit of Good Government

No late-nineteenth-century institution needed reforming more than urban government, called by the president of Cornell University "the worst in Christendom—the most expensive, the most inefficient, and the most corrupt." A Philadelphia committee pointed to years of "inefficiency, waste, badly paved and filthy streets, unwholesome and offensive water, and slovenly and costly management." New York and Chicago were even worse.

Rapid urban growth swamped city leaders with new demands for service. As city governments struggled, they raised taxes and incurred vast debts, which bred graft and the rise of the political boss. Bossism deeply offended these ethnocentric, well-intentioned middle-class urban reformers. "Goo-goos" (as bosses called advocates of "good government") opposed not only graft and vice, but also the perversion of democracy by the exploitation of ignorant immigrants. The immigrants, said one, "follow blindly leaders of their own race, are not moved by discussion, and exercise no judgment of their own"—and so were "not fit for the suffrage."

Urban reformers' programs were similar in most cities. They not only worked for the "Americanization" of immigrants in public schools (and opposed parochial schooling), but also formed voters' leagues to discuss the failings of municipal government. They delighted in exposing electoral irregularities and large-scale graft. These discoveries led to strident calls for replacing the mayor, especially an Irish Catholic, with an Anglo-Saxon Protestant reformer.

Politics colored every reform issue. Anglo-Saxon men favored prohibition partly to remove ethnic saloon owner influence from politics and supported woman suffrage partly to gain a middle-class political advantage against male immigrant voters. Most urban reformers disdained the "city proletariat mob." They proposed to replace bosses with expert city managers, who would bring honest professionalism to city government. They hoped to make government cheaper and thereby lower taxes. One effect of their emphasis on cost efficiency was to cut services to the poor. Another was to disfranchise working-class and ethnic groups, whose political participation depended on the boss system.

Not all urban reformers were elitist. Samuel Jones, for example, both opposed bossism and passionately advocated political participation by urban immigrants. He himself had begun as a poor Welsh immigrant in the Pennsylvania oil fields but worked his way up to the ownership of several oil fields and a factory in Toledo, Ohio. Influenced by a combination of firsthand contact with the "piteous appeals" of unemployed workers and by his reading of social reformers and the New Testament, in 1894, Jones decided to "apply the Golden Rule as a rule of conduct" in his factory, with an eight-hour day, a $2 minimum daily wage (50 to 75 cents higher than the local average for 10 hours), cooperative insurance, and a Christmas dividend. He hired social outcasts, offered employees cheap lunches and recreational facilities, and established Golden Rule Hall, where social visionaries could speak.

In 1897, Jones was elected to the first of an unprecedented four terms as mayor of Toledo. A maverick Republican who antagonized prominent citizens, Jones advocated municipal ownership of utilities, public works jobs and housing for the unemployed, more civic parks and playgrounds, and free vocational education and kindergartens. A pacifist, he took away policemen's side arms and heavy clubs. In police court, Jones regularly dismissed most cases of petty theft and drunkenness on grounds that the accused were victims of social injustice, and he often released prostitutes after fining every man in the room 10 cents—and himself a dollar—for condoning prostitution. Crime in notoriously sinful Toledo fell. When "Golden Rule" Jones died in 1904, nearly 55,000 tearful people filed past his coffin.

RECOVERING *the* PAST

World's Fairs

International expositions during the nineteenth and twentieth centuries were amazing spectacles of arts and manufacturing from around the world. It is tempting to focus on their novelties, like the midway sideshows, the introduction of the ice cream cone, or the first demonstration of the telephone. But for historians, these periodic grand events also provide a rich resource for understanding such topics as imperialism, nationalism, race and gender relations, and city planning. They were also important booster projects for their host cities.

World's fairs originated in 1851 in London, where the Crystal Palace Exhibition displayed the treasures and products of Queen Victoria's British Empire. A similar Crystal Palace was created in New York City in 1853–54, but the first full-scale world's fair in the United States was the Centennial Exhibition in Philadelphia in 1876. Although staged to commemorate the 100th anniversary of the Declaration of Independence, the Philadelphia fair emphasized technological progress, especially the achievements of the United States.

The World's Columbian Exposition held in Chicago in 1893 is one of the most studied of the world's fairs. It is especially notable as an example of architecture and city planning ideas that were emerging during the 1890s as part of the "City Beautiful" movement. Its exhibition buildings communicate their designers' hopes for cities in the future. What if a city could be designed from scratch? What would it look like? What benefits would it offer to its citizens? Could these ideas be applied to existing cities? The answers, as expressed by the buildings at the fair, show a great contrast with the realities of American cities in the 1890s.

Chicago's fair also offers insights into prevailing ideas about race. On the midway, various peoples of the world were presented as "anthropology" exhibits, arranged in order from those that were considered the most to the least "civilized." European people were displayed as highest on the civilization scale, followed by darker-skinned peoples of Asia and Africa. At the end of the sequence came Native Americans. The fairs in Chicago and Philadelphia provided little if any representation (or employment) for African Americans.

World's fairs were immensely popular attractions well into the twentieth century. Held predominantly in Europe and the United States, they celebrated technology and progress and became increasingly commercialized. Chicago's second world's fair, in 1933, was called the Century of Progress Exposition, in honor of the city's achievements since its founding. The fairs celebrated the conquest of new territory and peoples, as in the 1904 St. Louis World's Fair, which commemorated the Louisiana Purchase, and the 1915 Panama-Pacific Exposition in San Francisco, which celebrated the opening of the Panama Canal. Expositions continually looked toward the future. In 1939, the New York World's Fair offered the theme "World of Tomorrow" and transformed a former ash dump in Queens into Flushing Meadow Park.

World's fairs continue to be held, but draw far less popular attention today. Perhaps the world has become too familiar, or travel too easy, for a world's fair to seem exciting. By the late twentieth century, world's fairs focused more on environmental issues—important, but less entertaining and less spectacular. The closest equivalent to the early world's fairs today may be Epcot Center at Disney World in Orlando, Florida, where pavilions around a lagoon represent the nations of the world.

Historical documents of world's fairs, many of which have been digitized by libraries and archives, include photographs, guidebooks, diaries, and souvenirs. Artifacts from the fairs may be found in museums and private collections. Most of the buildings and exhibits of world's fairs were temporary. But the documents and artifacts they left behind present many opportunities for exploring cities, nations, and the world in the nineteenth and twentieth centuries.

REFLECTING ON THE PAST What do these photographs reveal about the conditions and desires for cities during the 1890s? Do you see continuities between the two world's fair photographs from Chicago in 1893 and Atlanta in 1895? What impact would these ideas for improving city life have on city-dwellers, such as the children pictured playing in the street near Hull House? If you explore digital collections of photographs and documents about world's fairs, do you notice similarities or differences over time? What else can you discover about the cities that hosted world's fairs and about the nations that participated?

Spectators overlook the "White City" of the World's Columbian Exposition in 1893.

Children play on the street near Hull House, less than a mile from the 1893 fair in Chicago.
(Courtesy of the Library of Congress)

A panoramic view shows the buildings and monuments of the Cotton States Exposition in Atlanta, 1895.

Housing and Civic Improvement

The physical environment of the city also seemed in need of reform, especially to middle- and upper-class Americans who recoiled from the unruliness, ugliness, and unsanitary conditions festering in populous industrial cities. The streets, buildings, and neighborhoods of the rapidly expanding cities had grown as a matter of private enterprise, without coordinated plans. Over the last decades of the nineteenth century, a variety of projects aimed at improving urban health and aesthetics set the stage for a new profession of city planning in the twentieth century.

Among the first targets for reform were the crowded tenements of New York City, where the poor and other newcomers lived in deep, narrow buildings four to six stories high with four apartments per floor. Interior rooms had no windows to let in light or air, and sanitation consisted of outdoor privies in back lots. The Tenement Reform Law of 1879 required light and air for every room, but the resulting "dumbbell" tenements with narrow air shafts were otherwise not much of an improvement.

The continuing squalid conditions in tenement neighborhoods were easily ignored by most of the middle and upper classes, who lived in distant parts of the city or suburbs. However, in 1890, a new impetus toward reform appeared with the publication of Jacob Riis's exposé *How the Other Half Lives.* Subsequent investigations documented tenement conditions and led to New York state legislation in 1901 that required open courtyards instead of air shafts, fire escapes, and sanitation for each apartment.

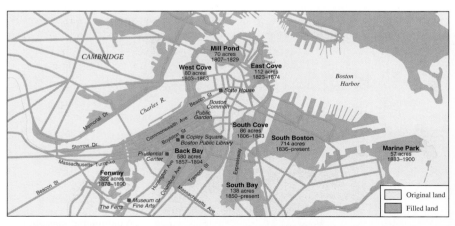

The City Beautiful: Enlarging Boston As part of the "city beautiful" movement, Boston filled in coastal, swampy lowlands with gravel, thus adding the fashionable Back Bay along Commonwealth Avenue. What is the effect of beautifying cities on different classes and ethnicities? Who benefits?

Sanitation and civic improvement became popular causes in many cities. At the urging of engineers, architects, and reformers, cities put in water mains and sewers, built parks, and planted trees along broadened boulevards lined by elegant homes and public buildings. These transformations of urban space rarely reached the squalid sections of the city inhabited by recent immigrants and rural transplants, but reformers believed that they would be morally uplifting as well as pleasing to the eye.

Settlement house workers took the lead in establishing neighborhood parks and public playgrounds. In Chicago, Hull House established the city's first public playground in 1893. In New York, the Henry Street Settlement campaigned in New York for small parks and the opening of schoolyards on weekends. By the end of the century, reformers persuaded municipal authorities in 13 cities to operate supervised public playgrounds.

Numerous projects to encourage public art and civic beautification emerged during the 1890s, especially in older industrial cities. Some were large-scale projects such as the design of Copley Square in Boston and a movement to encourage decorative art, sculpture, and murals for public buildings in New York. Others, initiated in smaller cities and towns, were more limited civic improvement projects as simple as planting flowers or removing eyesore buildings or signs.

By the end of the decade, initiatives such as these coalesced into the "City Beautiful" movement, which promoted monumental city planning and large-scale, neoclassical architecture. A prime example was the "White City" of exhibition buildings created for the World's Columbian Exposition in 1893. Most of the world's fair buildings were temporary, but early in the twentieth century, the City Beautiful movement had longer-lasting impact with such projects as the new civic centers created for Denver and San Francisco and the Benjamin Franklin Parkway in Philadelphia. American artists and art critics took the term "city beautiful" from the arts and crafts movement in England—which was fitting, because this ideal was distinctly European in seeking to emulate such cities as London, Paris, and Rome.

Conclusion

Cities Transformed

If Julian Ralph, the journalist who introduced us to cities at the start of this chapter, revisited the same cities today, he would find much that would be familiar. He would recognize public buildings and plazas that were inspired by the **City Beautiful movement**. Amid the skyscrapers of the twenty-first century, he would be able to pick out the ten-story buildings that were the tallest structures of his day. He might be able to walk through a department store, although it would likely have a different name along with vastly different merchandise. He would surely notice the lasting effects of the separation of social classes that resulted when new forms of mass transportation made suburban living possible for those who could afford it.

Cities grew in spectacular ways, but many Americans also found urban conditions troubling. Calls for change did not necessarily lead to change. But in the areas of personal action and the philosophical bases for social change, intellectual middle-class reformers such as Jane Addams, "Golden Rule" Jones, and many others foreshadowed the progressive reforms in the new century.

Because of their lasting presence and influence, the cities of the late nineteenth century are relevant to the present as well as to the past. They also reflect a history that is both local and global, involving immigrant populations, European cultural influences, and international commerce. The United States entered the twentieth century as a more urban nation, poised to take an even greater role in the world.

TIME*line*

1870s–1900	City populations grow
	Tammany Hall political machine dominates New York
	Development of railroad suburbs
	Creation of central business districts
1870s	Evangelical revivals
	Cable cars introduced
1871	Great Fire in Chicago
1879	Tenement Reform Law, New York
1886–1889	First U.S. settlement houses founded
1890s	Electrification of streetcars
	Creation of streetcar suburbs
	Social Gospel movement
	City Beautiful movement
1890	Jacob Riis, *How the Other Half Lives*
1892	Ellis Island Immigration Station opens
1893	World's Columbian Exposition, Chicago
	Pullman strike
1897	Charles Sheldon, *In His Steps*
1898	Consolidation of New York City boroughs
1899	W. E. B. DuBois, *The Philadelphia Negro*
1904	Lincoln Steffens, *The Shame of the Cities*

✓●─Study and Review at www.myhistorylab.com

Questions for Review and Reflection

1. Who were the newcomers to American cities in the late nineteenth century, and why did they relocate?

2. What role did political machines play? Did they help or hurt cities and city-dwellers?

3. How did new forms of public transportation change cities? How did these changes in technology affect where people lived and worked?

4. What role did middle-class reformers, especially women, play in dealing with social and political problems?

5. In what ways did urban populations, reform movements, and trends in architecture and city planning create connections between the United States and the world?

Key Terms

City Beautiful movement 579

Eugene V. Debs 570

Pullman strike 571

Settlement house 572

Social Gospel movement 574

Streetcar suburbs 568

W. E. B. Du Bois 566

Walking city 564

World's Columbian Exposition 558

18

Becoming a World Power

American Stories

Private Grayson Kills a Soldier in the Philippines

On the night of February 4, 1899, Privates William Grayson and David Miller of Company B, 1st Nebraska Volunteers, were on patrol near the capital of the Philippines, an ocean and a world away from the United States. In a neutral area of Santa Mesa, a Manila suburb surrounded on three sides by insurgent trenches, American soldiers had orders to shoot any Filipino soldiers they encountered. Cautiously, the two Americans worked their way to a bridge over the San Juan River. They heard a Filipino signal whistle, answered by another. Then a red lantern flashed from a nearby blockhouse.

The Americans froze as four Filipinos emerged from the darkness on the road ahead. "Halt!" Grayson shouted. The Filipino lieutenant in charge answered, "Halto!," either mockingly or because he had similar orders. Standing less than 15 feet apart, the two men repeated their commands. After a moment's hesitation, Grayson fired, killing his opponent with one bullet. The other Filipinos jumped out at them and Grayson and Miller shot two more. Then they turned and ran back to their own lines shouting warnings of attack. A full-scale battle followed.

It was a pivotal moment at a pivotal time for the United States as an emerging world power. Until recent weeks, the Americans and Filipinos had been allies in the Spanish-American War, together defeating the Spanish to liberate the Philippines. The American fleet under Admiral George Dewey had destroyed the Spanish naval squadron in Manila Bay on May 1, 1898. Three weeks later, an American ship brought from exile the native Filipino insurrectionary leader, Emilio Aguinaldo, to lead rebel forces on land while U.S. gunboats patrolled the seas.

At first, the Filipinos looked on the Americans as liberators. Although the intentions of the United States were never clear, Aguinaldo believed that, as in Cuba, the

Americans had no territorial ambitions. They would simply drive the Spanish out and then leave. In June, therefore, Aguinaldo declared the independence of the Philippines and began setting up a constitutional government. American officials pointedly ignored the independence ceremonies. When an armistice ended the war in August, American troops denied Aguinaldo's Filipino soldiers an opportunity to liberate their own capital city and shunted them off to the suburbs. The armistice agreement recognized American rights to the "harbor, city, and bay of Manila," while the proposed Treaty of Paris gave the United States the entire Philippine Islands archipelago.

As a result, tension mounted in the streets of Manila and along 14 miles of trenches separating American and Filipino soldiers. Taunts, obscenities, and racial epithets were shouted across the neutral zone. Barroom skirmishes and knifings filled the nights; American soldiers searched houses without warrants and looted stores. Their behavior was not unlike that of the English soldiers in Boston in the 1770s.

The battle ignited by Private Grayson's shots occurred as the United States Senate was locked in a dramatic debate over whether to ratify the Treaty of Paris concluding the recent war with Spain over Cuban independence. The outbreak of hostilities ended the Senate debates. Commodore Dewey cabled Washington that the "insurgents have inaugurated general engagement" and promised a hasty suppression of the insurrection. On February 6, 1899, the Senate ratified the Treaty of Paris, thus formally annexing the Philippines and sparking a war between the United States and Filipino nationalists.

In a guerrilla war similar to those fought later in Vietnam, Afghanistan, and Iraq, Aguinaldo's Filipino nationalists tried to undermine the American will by hit-and-run attacks. American soldiers remained in heavily garrisoned cities and undertook search-and-destroy missions to root out rebels and pacify the countryside. The **Filipino-American War** lasted until July 1902, three years longer than the Spanish-American War that caused it, and involved far more troops, casualties, and monetary and moral costs.

How did all this happen? What brought Private Grayson to "shoot my first nigger," as he put it, halfway around the world? For the first time in history, regular American soldiers found themselves fighting outside North America. The "champion of oppressed nations," as Aguinaldo said, had turned into an oppressor nation itself, imposing the American way of life and American institutions on faraway peoples against their will. It would not be the last time.

The war in the Philippines marked a critical transformation of America's role in the world. As the United States sought to exert its influence on the world, so also did global events influence America. Within a few years at the turn of the century, the United States acquired an empire, however small by

European standards, and established itself as a world power. In this chapter, we will review the historical dilemmas of America's role in the world, especially those of the expansionist nineteenth century. What motivated the intensified expansionism of the 1890s, and what happened in Cuba, the Philippines, and elsewhere as a result? How did events of the early twentieth century establish the fundamental patterns of modern American foreign policy toward Latin America, Asia, and Europe? In pursuing these questions, we will see that the tension between idealism and self-interest that has permeated America's domestic history has also guided its foreign policy.

Steps Toward Empire

The circumstances that brought Privates Grayson and Miller from Nebraska to the Philippines originated deep in American history. As early as the seventeenth-century Puritan migration, Americans worried about how to do good in a world that does wrong. John Winthrop sought to set up a "city on a hill" in the New World, a model community of righteous living for the rest of the world to imitate. "Let the eyes of the world be upon us," Winthrop had said. That wish, reaffirmed during the American Revolution, became a permanent goal of American policy toward the outside world.

America as a Model Society

Nineteenth-century Americans continued to believe in the nation's special mission. The Monroe Doctrine in 1823 warned Europe's monarchies to keep out of the republican New World. In succeeding decades, distinguished European visitors came to observe the "great social revolution." They found widespread democracy, representative and responsive political and legal institutions, a Protestant religious commitment to human perfectibility, unlimited energy, and an ability to apply unregulated economic activity and inventive genius to produce more things for more people.

View the Image
"Uncle Sam Teaching the World" (Puck Cartoon)
at **www.myhistorylab.com**

In an evil world, Americans then, as now, believed that they stood as a transforming force for good. But how could a nation in the western hemisphere do the transforming? One way was to encourage other nations to observe and imitate the good example set by the United States. Often, however, other nations and peoples were attracted to competing models of modernization, like socialism, or preferred their own religious traditions, like Islam.

Americans have rarely just focused on perfecting the good example at home and waiting for others to copy it, which requires patience and passivity, two traits not characteristic of Americans. Rather, the American people have actively and sometimes forcefully imposed their ideas and institutions on others. The international crusades of the United States, usually well intentioned if not always well received, have been motivated by a mixture of noble idealism and crass self-interest. Hence, the effort to spread the American model to an imperfect world has been both a blessing and a burden—for others as well as for the American people.

Early Expansionism

Persistent expansionism marked the first century of American independence. Jefferson's purchase of Louisiana in 1803, the removal of Native Americans westward, and the midcentury pursuit of "Manifest Destiny" into Mexico spread the United States across North America. In the 1850s, Americans began to look beyond their own continent as Commodore Perry in 1853 "opened" Japan and southerners sought more cotton lands in the Caribbean. After the Civil War, Secretary of State William Seward spoke of an America that would hold a "commanding sway in the world," destined to exert commercial domination "on the Pacific ocean, and its islands and continents." He purchased Alaska from Russia in 1867 for $7.2 million and acquired a coaling station in the Midway Islands near Hawaii, where missionaries and merchants were already active. He advocated annexing Cuba and other West Indian islands, tried to negotiate a treaty for an American-built canal through Panama, and dreamed of "possession" of the entire North and Central American continent and ultimately "control of the world."

Uncle Sam's Imperial Stretch Citing the Monroe Doctrine as justification, U.S. imperial interests at the turn of the century spread American economic, political, and military influence from Alaska across the Caribbean to South America. Uncle Sam is looking westward. Why? Compare this cartoon to others in this chapter.

In 1870, foreshadowing the Philippine debates 30 years later, supporters of President Grant tried to persuade the Senate to annex Santo Domingo (the Dominican Republic) on the island of Hispaniola. They cited the strategic importance of the Caribbean and argued forcefully for the economic value that Santo Domingo would bring. Opponents responded that expansionism violated American principles of **self-determination** and government by the consent of the governed. They claimed that the Caribbean peoples could not be assimilated. Expansionism might also involve foreign entanglements, a large and expensive navy, bigger government, and higher taxes; the Senate rejected the annexation treaty.

Although reluctant to add territory outright, Americans eagerly sought commercial dominance in Latin America and Asia. But American talk of building a canal across Nicaragua produced only Nicaraguan suspicions. In 1881, Secretary of State James G. Blaine sought to convene a conference of American nations to promote hemispheric peace and trade. Latin Americans may have wondered what Blaine intended, for in 1881 he intervened in three separate border disputes in Central and South America, in each case at the cost of goodwill. After an incident and threat of war with Chile in 1889, Blaine's efforts resulted in the first Pan-American Conference to improve economic ties among the nations of the Americas.

American economic influence spread to the Pacific. In the mid-1870s, American sugar-growing interests in the Hawaiian Islands were strong enough to put whites in positions of influence over the monarchy. In 1875, they obtained a treaty admitting Hawaiian sugar duty-free to the United States, and in 1887, the United States also won exclusive rights to build a naval base at Pearl Harbor. Native Hawaiians resented the influence of American sugar interests, especially as they brought in Japanese to replace native people—many of whom died from white diseases—in the sugarcane fields. In 1891, the nationalistic queen Liliuokalani assumed the throne and pursued a policy of "Hawaii for the Hawaiians." In 1893, white planters staged a coup with the help of U.S. gunboats and marines and imprisoned the queen. An annexation treaty was presented to the Senate by the Harrison administration. But when Grover Cleveland, who opposed imperial expansion, returned to the presidency for his second term, he stopped the move. The white sugar growers waited patiently for a more desirable time for annexation, which came during the war in 1898.

American Expansionism in Global Context

American forays into the Pacific and Latin America brought the United States increasingly into contact and conflict with European nations. The nineteenth century was marked by European imperial expansionism throughout much of the world. In southern and southeastern Asia, the British were in India, Burma, and Malaya; the French in Cambodia, Vietnam, and Laos; the Dutch in Singapore and the East Indies; and the Spanish in the

See the **Map**

World Colonial Empires, 1900

at **www.myhistorylab.com**

Philippines. These and other colonial powers divided China, its Manchu dynasty weakened by the opium trade, internal conflicts, and European pressure, into spheres of economic influence. A China newspaper editorial complained that other nations "all want to satisfy their ambitions to nibble at China and swallow it." The Russians wrested away Manchuria, and Japan took Korea after intervention in a Korean peasant rebellion in 1894. In addition, China was forced to cede Taiwan and southern Manchuria to Japanese influence and control.

In Africa, Europeans scrambled to gain control of both coastal and interior areas, with England, France, Germany, Portugal, and Belgium grabbing the most land and exploiting African peoples. Only two independent African nations existed in the late nineteenth century: Liberia, founded in 1822 by Americans to resettle free blacks, and the fragmented kingdom of Ethiopia, which thrashed the Italians when they invaded in 1896. With nearly all of Africa divided, the only way imperial powers could acquire more land was to fight each other. Thus, in 1899, war broke out in southern Africa between the British and the Boers, descendants of Dutch settlers—a war waged with a savagery Europeans usually reserved for indigenous peoples. The English destroyed Boer farms and property and drove civilians into camps where an estimated 20,000 women and children perished from starvation and malnutrition. The British won, but at a horrific cost.

Africa was not then of interest to the United States, but in the Pacific and Caribbean, it was inevitable that the United States, a late arrival to **imperialism**, would bump into European rivals. Moving outward from Hawaii closer to the markets of eastern Asia, the United States acquired a naval and coaling station in the Samoan Islands in 1878. American and German naval forces almost fought each other there in 1889—before a typhoon ended the crisis by wiping out both navies. Troubles in the Pacific also occurred in the late 1880s over the American seizure of several Canadian ships in fur seal and fishing disputes in the Bering Sea, settled only by the threat of British naval action and an international arbitration commission ruling, which ordered the United States to pay damages.

Closer to home, the United States sought to replace Great Britain as the most influential nation in Central America and northern South America. In 1895, a boundary dispute between Venezuela and British Guiana threatened to bring British intervention against the Venezuelans. President Cleveland, needing a popular political issue during the depression, asked Secretary of State Richard Olney to send a message to Great Britain. Invoking the Monroe Doctrine, Olney's note (stronger than Cleveland intended) called the United States "practically sovereign on this continent" and demanded international arbitration to settle the dispute. The British ignored the note, and war loomed. Both sides realized that war would be an "absurdity," and the boundary dispute was settled.

Despite these expansionist efforts, the United States in 1895 had neither the means nor a consistent policy for enlarging its role in the world. The diplomatic service was small and unprofessional. No U.S. embassy official in Beijing spoke Chinese. The U.S. Army, with about 28,000 men, was smaller than Bulgaria's. The navy, dismantled after the Civil War and partly rebuilt under President Arthur, ranked no higher than tenth in the world and included dangerously obsolete ships. By 1898, things would change.

Expansionism in the 1890s

In 1893, historian Frederick Jackson Turner wrote that for three centuries "the dominant fact in American life has been expansion." The "extension of American influence to outlying islands and adjoining countries," he thought, indicated still more expansionism. Turner struck a responsive chord in a country that had always been restless and optimistic. With the western frontier closed, Americans would surely look for new frontiers, for mobility and markets as well as for morality and missionary activity. The motivations for the expansionist impulse of the late 1890s resembled those that had prompted Europeans to settle the New World in the first place: greed, glory, and God. We will examine expansionism as a reflection of profits, patriotism, piety, and politics.

Profits: Searching for Overseas Markets

Senator Albert Beveridge of Indiana bragged in 1898 that "American factories are making more than the American people can use; American soil is producing more than they can consume. Fate has written our policy for us; the trade of the world must and shall be ours." Americans like Beveridge revived older dreams of an American commercial empire in the Caribbean Sea and the Pacific Ocean. American businessmen saw huge profits beckoning in heavily populated Latin America and Asia and wanted to get their share of these markets, as well as access to the sugar, coffee, fruits, oil, rubber, and minerals that were abundant in these lands.

Understanding that commercial expansion required a stronger navy and coaling stations and colonies, business interests began to shape diplomatic and military strategy. But not all businessmen in the 1890s liked commercial expansion or a vigorous foreign policy. Some preferred traditional trade with Canada and Europe rather than risky new ventures in Asia and Latin America. Some thought it more important to recover from the depression than to annex islands.

Despite the 1890s depression and a drop in domestic consumption, products spewed from American factories at a staggering rate. The United States moved from fourth place in the world in manufacturing in 1870 to first place in 1900, doubling the number of factories and tripling the value of farm output. Manufactured goods grew nearly fivefold between 1895 and 1914. The total value of American exports tripled, from $434 million in 1866 to nearly $1.5 billion in 1900. By 1914, exports had risen to $2.5 billion, a 67 percent increase over 1900. The increased trade continued to go mainly to Europe

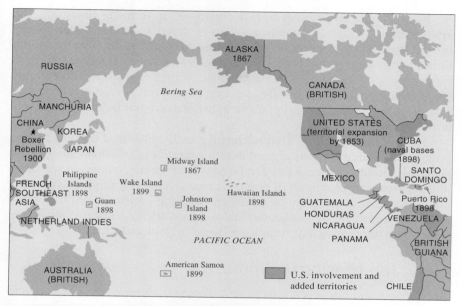

United States Territorial Expansion to 1900 By 1900, U.S. involvement expanded beyond North America to include (in green) islands in the Pacific and the Caribbean as well as parts of South America. How did this happen? What patterns and problems do you see?

rather than Asia. In 1900, for example, only 3 to 4 percent of U.S. exports went to China and Japan. Nevertheless, interest in Asian markets grew, especially as agricultural output continued to increase and prices stayed low.

Investments followed a similar pattern. American direct investments abroad increased from about $634 million to $2.6 billion between 1897 and 1914. Although investments were largest in Britain, Canada, and Mexico, most attention focused on actual and potential investment in Latin America and eastern Asia. Central American investment increased from $21 million in 1897 to $93 million by 1914, mainly in mines, railroads, and banana and coffee plantations. At the turn of the century came the formation and growth of America's biggest multinational corporations, including du Pont, Alcoa, and the United Fruit Company. Although slow to respond to investment and market opportunities abroad, these companies soon supported an aggressive foreign policy.

Patriotism: Asserting National Power

In 1898, a State Department memorandum stated that "we can no longer afford to disregard international rivalries now that we ourselves have become a competitor in the world-wide struggle for trade." The national state, it was argued, should support commercial interests.

More Americans, however, saw expansion in terms of national glory and greatness. In the late 1890s, a group centered around Assistant Secretary of the Navy Theodore Roosevelt and Massachusetts Senator Henry Cabot Lodge emerged as highly influential leaders of a changing American foreign policy. These intensely nationalistic young men shifted official policy to what Lodge called the "large policy." Roosevelt agreed that economic interests should take second place to questions of what he called "national honor."

Naval strategist Alfred Thayer Mahan greatly influenced the new foreign policy elite. Mahan's books argued that in a world of Darwinian struggle for survival, national power depended on naval supremacy, control of sea lanes, and vigorous development of domestic resources and foreign markets. He advocated colonies in both the Caribbean and the Pacific, linked by a canal built and controlled by the United States. In a world of constant "strife," he said, it was imperative that Americans begin "to look outward."

Piety: The Missionary Impulse

As Mahan's and Roosevelt's statements suggest, a strong sense of duty and the missionary ideal of doing good for others also motivated expansionism—and sometimes rationalized the exploitation and oppression of weaker peoples. As a missionary put it in 1885, "The Christian nations are subduing the world in order to make mankind free." A former Secretary of State, Richard Olney, agreed, saying in 1898, "the mission of this country is . . . to forego no fitting opportunity to further the progress of civilization" as defined by American values and political interests.

Josiah Strong, a Congregationalist minister, was another ardent advocate of American missionary expansionism. He argued that in the struggle for survival among nations, the United States had emerged as the center of Anglo-Saxonism and was "divinely commissioned" to spread political liberty, Protestant Christianity, and civilized values over the earth. "This powerful race," he wrote, "will move down upon Mexico, down upon Central and South America, out upon the islands of the sea, over upon Africa and beyond." In a cruder statement of the same idea, Senator Beveridge said in 1899 that God had prepared English-speaking Anglo-Saxons to become "the master organizers of the world to establish and administer governments among savages and senile peoples."

●●●—Read the Document

Theodore Roosevelt, "Our Poorer Brother" (1897)
at **www.myhistorylab.com**

Missionaries carried Western values to non-Christian lands around the world, especially China. The number of American Protestant missionaries in China increased from 436 in 1874 to 5,462 in 1914, and the estimated number of Christian converts in China jumped from 5,000 in 1870 to nearly 100,000 by 1900. Although this was much less than missionaries hoped, this tiny fraction of the Chinese population included young reformist intellectuals who, absorbing Western ideas, in 1912 helped overthrow the Manchu dynasty. Economic relations between China and the United States increased at approximately the same rate as missionary activity.

Politics: Manipulating Public Opinion

Although less significant than the other factors, politics also played a role. As in the past, public opinion on international issues helped shape presidential politics. The psychological tensions and economic hardships of the 1890s depression jarred national self-confidence. Foreign adventures provided an emotional release from domestic turmoil and promised to restore patriotic pride—and maybe even win votes.

This process was helped by the growth of a highly competitive popular press, which brought international issues before a mass readership. When New York City newspapers, notably William Randolph Hearst's *Journal* and Joseph Pulitzer's *World*, competed in stirring up public support for the Cuban rebels against Spain, politicians dared not ignore the outcry. Daily reports of Spanish atrocities in 1896 and 1897 kept public moral outrage constantly a part of political discourse.

Politics, then, joined profits, patriotism, and piety in motivating the expansionism of the 1890s. These four impulses interacted to produce the Spanish-American War, the annexation of the Philippine Islands and subsequent war, and the energetic foreign policy of President Theodore Roosevelt.

War in Cuba and the Philippines

Lying 90 miles off Florida, Cuba had been the object of intense American interest for a half century. Spain could not halt the continuing struggle of the Cuban people for a measure of autonomy and relief from exploitive labor in the sugar plantations, even after slavery itself ended. The most recent uprising, which lasted from 1868 to 1878, raised tensions between Spain and the United States, just as it whetted the Cuban appetite for complete independence.

The Road to War

When the Cuban revolt flared up anew in 1895, the Madrid government again failed to implement reforms. Instead, it sent General Weyler, dubbed the "butcher" by the American press, with 50,000 troops to quell the disturbance. When Weyler began herding rural Cubans into "reconcentration" camps, Americans were outraged. An outpouring of sympathy swept the nation, especially as sensationalist reports of horrible suffering and the deaths of thousands in the camps filled American newspapers.

The Cuban struggle appealed to a country convinced of its role as protector of the weak and defender of the right of self-determination. Motivated in part by genuine humanitarian concern and a sense of admiration for the heroic Cuban freedom fighters, many Americans held rallies to raise money and food for famine relief and called for land reform and even armed intervention. But neither Cleveland nor McKinley wanted war.

Self-interest also played a role. For many years, Americans had noted the profitable resources and strategic location of the island. American companies had invested extensively in Cuban sugar plantations. Appeals for reform had much to do with ensuring a stable environment for further investments and trade ($27 million in 1897), as well as for protecting the sugar fields.

The election of 1896 only temporarily diverted attention from Cuba. A new government in Madrid made halfhearted concessions. Conditions worsened in the reconcentration camps, and the American press kept harping on the plight of the Cuban people. McKinley, eager not to upset recovery from the depression, skillfully resisted war pressures. But he could not control Spanish misrule or Cuban aspirations for freedom.

Events early in 1898 sparked the outbreak of hostilities. Rioting in Havana intensified both Spanish repression and American outrage. A letter from the Spanish minister to the United States, Depuy de Lôme, calling McKinley a "weak," hypocritical politician, was intercepted and made public. Americans fumed.

A second event was more serious. When the rioting broke out, the battleship the *U.S.S. Maine* was sent to Havana harbor to protect American citizens. On February 15, a tremendous explosion blew up the *Maine*, killing 262 men. Newspapers trumpeted slogans such as "Remember the *Maine*! To hell with Spain!"

Assistant Secretary of the Navy Theodore Roosevelt had been preparing for war for many years. He said that he believed the *Maine* had been sunk "by an act of dirty treachery on the part of the Spaniards" and would "give anything if President McKinley would order the fleet to Havana tomorrow." When the president did not, Roosevelt privately declared that McKinley had "no more backbone than a chocolate éclair" and continued readying the navy for action. Although a board of inquiry at the time concluded that an external submarine mine caused the disaster, it is probable that a faulty boiler or some other internal problem set off the explosion. Even Roosevelt later conceded this possibility.

After the sinking of the *Maine*, Roosevelt took advantage of Secretary of the Navy John Long's absence from the office one day to cable Commodore George Dewey, commander of the United States' Pacific fleet at Hong Kong. Roosevelt ordered Dewey to fill his ships with coal and, "in the event" of a declaration of war with Spain, to sail to the Philippines and make sure "the Spanish squadron does not leave the Asiatic coast." "The Secretary is away and I am having immense fun running the Navy," Roosevelt wrote in his diary that night.

Roosevelt's act was consistent with policies he had been urging on his more cautious superior for more than a year. As early as 1895, the navy had contingency plans for attacking the Philippines. Influenced by Mahan and Lodge, Roosevelt wanted to enlarge the navy. He also believed that the United States should construct an interoceanic canal, acquire the Danish West Indies (the Virgin Islands), annex Hawaii, and oust Spain from Cuba. As Roosevelt told McKinley late in 1897, he was putting the navy in "the best possible shape" for the day "when war began."

Waging War in the Philippines Describe what is happening in these two visuals. How did it happen that the United States went to war against Spain to free Cuba from colonial domination yet ended up committing many similar atrocities in the Philippines?

The public outcry over the Maine drowned out McKinley's efforts to avoid war. With the issues politicized, McKinley pressured the Madrid government to make concessions. Spain did, though refusing to grant full independence to the Cubans, and the president finally acted. On April 11, 1898, he sent an ambiguous message to Congress that seemed to call for war.

Two weeks later, Congress authorized using troops against Spain and recognized Cuban independence, actions amounting to a declaration of war. In a significant additional resolution, the Teller Amendment, Congress stated that the United States had no intention of annexing Cuba. A Cuban revolutionary general was more cautious, saying, "I expect nothing from the Americans. We should trust everything to our efforts. It is better to rise or fall without help than to contract debts of gratitude with such a powerful neighbor."

"A Splendid Little War": Various Views

The outbreak of war between Spain and the United States did not go unnoticed in Europe. German Kaiser Wilhelm II sarcastically offered to join with other European monarchs to help Spain resist the efforts of "the American-British Society for International Theft and Warmongering . . . to snatch Cuba from Spain." But Spain was left to face the United States alone, fully expecting a defeat. When war broke out, a Spanish rear admiral said that the ruptured relations with the United States "would surely be fatal."

Indeed, the war was short and relatively easy for the Americans and "fatal" for the Spanish, who at the war's conclusion were left with "only two major combat vessels." The Americans won naval battles almost without return fire. At both major engagements, Manila Bay and Santiago Bay in Cuba, only two Americans died, one of them from heat prostration while stoking coal. Guam and Puerto Rico were taken virtually without a shot. Only 385 men died from Spanish bullets, but more than 5,000 succumbed to tropical diseases. As the four-month war neared its end in August, Secretary of State John Hay wrote Roosevelt that "it has been a splendid little war; begun with the highest motives, carried on with magnificent intelligence and spirit."

The Spanish-American War seemed splendid in other ways, as letters from American soldiers suggest. One young man wrote that his comrades were all "in good spirits" because oranges and coconuts were plentiful and "every trooper has his canteen full of lemonade all the time." Another wrote his brother that he was having "a lot of fun chasing Spaniards."

But the war was not much fun for other soldiers. One said, "Words are inadequate to express the feeling of pain and sickness when one has the fever. For about a week every bone in my body ached and I did not care much whether I lived or not." Another described a fellow soldier shot in the head as "a mass of blood." Nor was the war splendid for African American soldiers, who fought in segregated units and noted stark differences between receiving rude treatment in the American South yet warm greetings in Cuba and Puerto Rico.

For Colonel Roosevelt, who resigned from the Navy Department to lead a cavalry unit as soon as war was declared, the war was excitement and political opportunity. After a close brush with death in Cuba, Roosevelt declared with delight that he felt "the wolf rise in the heart" during "the power of joy in battle." But ironically, he needed help from African

Watch the Video

Roosevelt's Rough Riders
at **www.myhistorylab.com**

American soldiers to achieve his goals. His celebrated charge up Kettle Hill near Santiago was made possible by black troops first clearing the hill and then protecting his flank. The "charge" made three-inch headlines and propelled him toward the New York governor's mansion. "I would rather have led that charge," he said later, "than served three terms in the U.S. Senate." More than anyone, Roosevelt used the war to advance not only his political career but also the glory of national expansionism.

The Philippines Debates and War

Roosevelt's ordering Admiral Dewey to Manila initiated a chain of events that led to the annexation of the Philippines. The most crucial battle of the Spanish-American War occurred on May 1, 1898, when Dewey destroyed the Spanish fleet in Manila Bay and cabled McKinley for additional troops. He sent twice as many troops as Dewey had asked for and began shaping American public opinion to accept the "political, commercial [and] humanitarian" reasons for annexing the Philippines. The Treaty of Paris gave the United States the islands in exchange for a $20 million payment to Spain.

The treaty went to the Senate for ratification during the winter of 1898–1899. Senators hurled arguments across the floor of the Senate as American soldiers hurled oaths and taunts across the neutral zone at Aguinaldo's insurgents near Manila. Private Grayson's encounter, as we have seen, led to the passage of the treaty in a close Senate vote—and began the Filipino-American War and the debates over what to do with the Philippines.

The entire nation joined the argument. At stake were two very different views of foreign policy and of America's vision of itself. After several months of quietly seeking advice and listening to public opinion, McKinley finally recommended annexation. Many Democrats supported the president out of fear of being labeled disloyal. At a time when openly racist thought flourished in the United States, fellow Republicans confirmed McKinley's arguments for annexation, adding even more insulting ones. Filipinos were described as childlike, dirty, and backward. "The country won't be pacified," a Kansas veteran of the Sioux wars told a reporter, until the Filipinos are "killed off like the Indians."

A small but prominent and vocal **Anti-Imperialist League** vigorously opposed war and annexation. These dignitaries included ex-presidents Harrison and Cleveland, Andrew Carnegie, Jane Addams, and Mark Twain. In arguments heard again recently about Iraq, anti-imperialists contended that taking over other countries contradicted American ideals. First, the annexation of territory without postwar planning or steps toward statehood was unprecedented and unconstitutional.

Read the Document

Mark Twain, "Incident in the Phillippines" (1924)
at **www.myhistorylab.com**

Second, to occupy and govern a foreign people without their consent violated American ideals. Third, social reforms needed at home demanded American energies and money: "Before we attempt to teach house-keeping to the world," one writer said, we needed "to set our own house in order."

Not all anti-imperialist arguments were so noble. A racist position alleged that Filipinos were nonwhite, Catholic, inferior in size and intelligence, and therefore unassimilable. A practical argument suggested that once in possession of the Philippines, the United States would have to occupy and defend them, necessitating the acquisition of more territories—in turn leading to higher taxes and bigger government, and perhaps requiring that American troops fight distant Asian wars.

The last argument became fact when Private Grayson's encounter started the Filipino-American War. Before it ended in 1902, some 126,500 American troops served in the Philippines, 4,234 died there, and 2,800 more were wounded. The cost was $400 million. Filipino casualties were much worse. In addition to 18,000 killed in combat, perhaps 200,000 Filipinos died of famine and disease as American soldiers burned villages and destroyed crops and livestock. General Jacob H. Smith told his troops that "the more you kill and burn, the better you will please me." Insurgent ineptness, Aguinaldo's inability to extend the fight across ethnic boundaries, and atrocities on both sides increased the frustrations of a lengthening war. The American "water cure" and other tortures were especially brutal.

As U.S. treatment of the Filipinos became more like Spanish treatment of the Cubans, the hypocrisy of American behavior became even more evident. This was especially true for black American soldiers who fought in the Philippines. They identified with the dark-skinned insurgents, whom they saw as tied to the land, burdened by debt, and pressed by poverty like themselves. "I feel sorry for these people," a sergeant in the 24th Infantry wrote. "You have no idea the way these people are treated by the Americans here."

The war starkly exposed the hypocrisies of shouldering the **white man's burden**. On reading a report that 8,000 Filipinos had been killed in the first year of the war, Carnegie wrote a letter, dripping with sarcasm, congratulating McKinley for "civilizing the Filipinos. . . . About 8,000 of them have been completely civilized and sent to Heaven. I hope you like it." Another writer penned a devastating one-liner: "Dewey took Manila with the loss of one man—and all our institutions."

●●●─┤Read the Document

Ernest Howard Crosby, "The Real 'White Man's Burden'" (1899) at **www.myhistorylab.com**

The anti-imperialists failed both to prevent annexation and to interfere with the war effort. However prestigious and principled, they had little political power and were out of tune with the period of exuberant expansionist national pride, prosperity, and promise.

Expansionism Triumphant

By 1900, Americans had ample reason to be patriotic. Within a year, the United States had acquired several island territories in the Pacific and Caribbean. But several questions arose over what to do with the new territories. Were they colonies? Would they be granted statehood, or would they develop gradually from colonies to constitutional parts of the United States? Did Hawaiians,

Puerto Ricans, and Filipinos have the same rights as American citizens on the mainland? Were they protected by the Constitution?

Although slightly different governing systems were worked out for each new territory, the solution in each case was to define its status somewhere between a colony and a candidate for statehood. The indigenous people were usually allowed to elect their own legislature, but had governors and other judicial and administrative officials appointed by the president. The first full governor of the Philippines, McKinley appointee William Howard Taft, effectively moved the Filipinos toward self-government, although the island nation did not achieve independence until 1946.

The question of constitutional rights was resolved by deciding that Hawaiians and Puerto Ricans, for example, would be treated differently from Texans and Oregonians. In the "insular cases" of 1901, the Supreme Court ruled that the people in these new territories would achieve citizenship and constitutional rights only when Congress said they were ready.

In the election of 1900, William Jennings Bryan was again the Democratic nominee and tried to make imperialism the "paramount issue" of the campaign. He failed, in part because the country strongly favored annexing

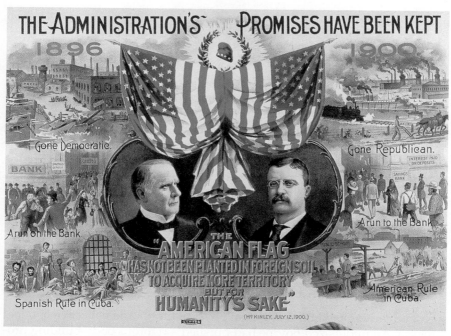

Republican Campaign Poster Analyze this 1900 campaign poster for McKinley showing Republican claims for what had changed in four years. Why would voters want to vote again for McKinley and why not for the Democrats? What several arguments are made in this poster, including the rationale for expansion? Note McKinley's vice presidential nominee to his right. What role does the flag play in this poster? *(From the David J. and Janice L. Frent Collection/Corbis)*

the Philippines. In the closing weeks of the campaign, Bryan shied away from imperialism and focused on domestic issues.

That did Bryan no good either. Prosperity returned with the discovery of gold in Alaska, and cries for reform fell on deaf ears. The McKinley forces rightly claimed that four years of Republican rule had brought more money, jobs, thriving factories, and manufactured goods, as well as the tremendous growth in American prestige abroad. As Tom Watson put it, noting the end of the Populist revolt with the war fervor over Cuba, "The blare of the bugle drowned out the voice of the reformer."

He was more right than he knew. Within one year, expansionist Theodore Roosevelt went from assistant secretary of the navy to colonel of the Rough Riders to governor of New York. For some Republican politicos, who thought he was too vigorous and independent, this quick rise as McKinley's potential rival came too fast. One way to eliminate Roosevelt politically, or at least slow him down, was to make him vice president, which they did in 1900. But six months into McKinley's second term, an anarchist killed him, the third presidential assassination in less than 40 years. "Now look," exclaimed party boss Mark Hanna, who had opposed putting Roosevelt on the ticket, "that damned cowboy is President of the United States!"

Theodore Roosevelt's Energetic Diplomacy

At a White House dinner party in 1905, a guest told a story about visiting the Roosevelt home when "Teedie" was a baby. "You were in your bassinet, making a good deal of fuss and noise," the guest reported, "and your father lifted you out and asked me to hold you." Secretary of State Elihu Root looked up and asked, "Was he hard to hold?" Whether true or not, the story reveals much about President Roosevelt's principles and policies on foreign affairs. As president from 1901 to 1909, and as the most dominating American personality for the 15 years between 1897 and 1912, Roosevelt made a lot of noise about the activist role the United States should play in the world, and he often seemed "hard to hold." Roosevelt's energetic foreign policy in Latin America, Eastern Asia, and Europe paved the way for a century and more of the United States as a world power.

Foreign Policy as Darwinian Struggle

Roosevelt advocated both individual physical fitness and collective national strength. An undersized boy, he had pursued a rigorous body-building program, and as a young man on his North Dakota ranch he learned to value the "strenuous life." Reading Darwin taught him that life was a constant struggle for survival. As president, his ideal was a "nation of men, not weaklings." Although he believed in Anglo-Saxon superiority, he admired—and feared— Japanese military prowess. Powerful nations, like individuals, Roosevelt

TR as Caribbean Policeman Compare this cartoon with others in the chapter. What images are conveyed in the cartoon? What symbols and stereotypes are portrayed?

believed, had a duty to cultivate vigor, strength, courage, and moral commitment to civilized values. In practical terms, this meant developing natural resources, building large navies, and being ever prepared to fight.

Although famous for saying "Speak softly and carry a big stick," Roosevelt often not only wielded a large stick but spoke loudly as well. In a speech in 1897, he used the word *war* 62 times, saying, "no triumph of peace is quite so great as the supreme triumphs of war." But despite his bluster, Roosevelt was usually restrained in exercising force. He won the Nobel Peace Prize in 1906 for helping end the Russo-Japanese War. The big stick and the loud talk were meant to preserve order and peace.

Roosevelt divided the world into "civilized" and "uncivilized" nations. The civilized ones had a responsibility to "police" the uncivilized, not only maintaining order but also spreading "superior" values and institutions. Taking on the "white man's burden," civilized nations sometimes had to wage war on the uncivilized—justly so, he argued, because the victors bestowed the blessings of culture and racial superiority on the vanquished. A war between two civilized nations (for example, Germany and Great Britain) would be foolish. Above all, Roosevelt believed in the balance of power. Strong, advanced nations had a duty to use their power to preserve order and peace. With a booming economy and population, Americans could no longer "avoid responsibilities" to exercise a greater role in world affairs.

RECOVERING *the* PAST

Political Cartoons

One of the most enjoyable ways of recovering the values and attitudes of the past is through political cartoons. Ralph Waldo Emerson once said, "Caricatures are often the truest history of the times." A deft drawing of a popular or unpopular politician can freeze ideas and events in time, conveying more effectively than columns of print the central issues—and especially the hypocrisies and misbehaviors—of an era. Cartoonists are often at their best when they are critical, exaggerating a physical feature of a political figure or capturing public sentiment against the government.

The history of political cartoons in the United States goes back to Benjamin Franklin's "Join or Die" cartoon calling for colonial cooperation against the French in 1754. But political cartoons were rare until Andrew Jackson's presidency. Even after such cartoons as "King Andrew the First" in the 1830s, they did not gain notoriety until the advent of Thomas Nast's cartoons in *Harper's Weekly* in the 1870s. Nast drew scathing cartoons exposing the corruption of William "Boss" Tweed's Tammany Hall, depicting Tweed and his men as vultures and smiling deceivers. "Stop them damn pictures," Tweed ordered. "I don't care so much what the papers write about me. My constituents can't read. But, damn it, they can see pictures." Tweed sent some of his men to Nast with an offer of $100,000 to "study art" in Europe. The $5,000-a-year artist negotiated up to a half million dollars before refusing Tweed's offer. "I made up my mind not long ago to put some of those fellows behind bars," Nast said, "and I'm going to put them there." His cartoons helped to drive Tweed out of office.

The emergence of the United States as a world power and the rise of Theodore Roosevelt gave cartoonists plenty to draw about. At the same time, the rise of cheap newspapers such as William Randolph Hearst's *Journal* and Joseph Pulitzer's *World* provided a rich opportunity for cartoonists, whose clever images attracted more readers. When the Spanish-American War broke out, newspapers whipped up public sentiment by having artists draw fake pictures of fierce Spaniards stripping

"The Spanish Brute Adds Mutilation to Murder," by Grant Hamilton, in *Judge*, July 9, 1898.

"Liberty Halts American Butchery in the Philippines," from *Life*, 1899.

American women at sea and killing helpless Cubans. Hearst used these tactics to increase his paper's daily circulation to 1 million copies.

By the time of the debates over Philippine annexation, many cartoonists took an anti-imperialist stance, pointing out American hypocrisy. Within a year, cartoonists shifted from depicting "The Spanish Brute Adds Mutilation to Murder" (1898) to "Liberty Halts American Butchery in the Philippines" (1899), both included here. Note the similarities in that both cartoons condemn the "butchery" of native peoples. But the villain has changed. Although Uncle Sam as a killer is not nearly as menacing as the figure of Spain as an ugly gorilla, both cartoons share similarities of an aggressive stance, blood-covered swords, and a trail of bodies behind.

REFLECTING ON THE PAST **Describe each cartoon. What is the apparent message of each cartoonist? What symbols and images do you see in these two cartoons? Who is the woman figure, and what does she represent? How would you explain the change of bloodied sword bearer within one year? In addition to these two cartoons, look at cartoons in this and other chapters. How do the images and symbols used in these reflect the cartoonist's point of view? How are various nationalities depicted in the Theodore Roosevelt cartoon? Check some recent newspapers: Who is criticized today and how do cartoonists reveal their attitudes and political positions? Is American imperialism still an issue?**

When threats failed to accomplish his goals, Roosevelt used direct personal intervention. When he wanted Panama, Roosevelt bragged later, "I took the Canal Zone" rather than submitting a long "dignified State Paper" for congressional debate. And while Congress debated, he pointed out, the building of the canal began. Roosevelt's executive activism in foreign affairs influenced later presidents from Woodrow Wilson to George W. Bush.

Taking the Panama Canal

To justify the intervention of 2,600 American troops in Honduras and Nicaragua in 1906, Philander Knox, later a secretary of state, said, "because of the Monroe Doctrine" the United States is "held responsible for the order of Central America." The closeness of the canal, he said, "makes the preservation of peace in that neighborhood particularly necessary." The Panama Canal was not yet finished when Knox spoke, but it had already become a cornerstone of U.S. policy.

Three problems had to be surmounted in order to dig an interoceanic connection. First, an 1850 treaty bound the United States to build a canal jointly with Great Britain, a problem resolved in 1901 when the British canceled the treaty in exchange for an American guarantee that the canal would be open to all nations. A second problem was where to dig it. American engineers rejected a long route through Nicaragua in favor of a shorter, more rugged path across Panama, where a French firm had already begun work. This raised the third problem: Panama was a province of Colombia, which rejected the terms the United States offered. Roosevelt called the Colombians "Dagoes" who tried to "hold us up" like highway robbers.

Aware of Roosevelt's fury, encouraged by hints of American support, and eager for the economic benefits that a canal would bring, Panamanian nationalists in 1903 staged a revolution led by several rich families and Philippe Bunau-Varilla of the French canal company. An American warship deterred Colombian intervention, and local troops were separated from their officers, who were bought off. A bloodless revolution occurred on November 3; on November 4, Panama declared its independence; and on November 6 the United States recognized it. Two weeks later, a treaty established the American right to build and operate a canal through Panama and to exercise "titular sovereignty" over the 10-mile-wide Canal Zone. The Panamanian government protested, calling it a "treaty that no Panamanian signed." Roosevelt later claimed that the diplomatic and engineering achievement, completed in 1914, would "rank . . . with the Louisiana Purchase and the acquisition of Texas."

View the Image

Teddy Roosevelt at Panama Canal, 1906

at **www.myhistorylab.com**

Policing the Caribbean

As late as 1901, the Monroe Doctrine was still regarded, according to Roosevelt, as the "equivalent to an open door in South America." To the United States, this meant that although no nation had a right "to get territorial possessions," all nations had equal commercial rights in the Western Hemisphere south of the Rio Grande. But as American investments poured into Central America and the Caribbean, the policy changed to one of asserting U.S. dominance in the Caribbean basin.

This change was demonstrated in 1902 when Germany and Great Britain blockaded Venezuela's ports to force the government to pay defaulted debts. Roosevelt was especially worried that German influence would replace the British. He insisted that the European powers accept arbitration and threatened to "move Dewey's ships" to the Venezuelan coast. The crisis passed, largely for other reasons, but Roosevelt's threat of force made very clear the paramount presence and self-interest of the United States in the Caribbean.

The United States kept liberated Cuba under a military governor until 1902, when the Cubans elected a congress and president. The United States honored Cuban independence, as it had promised to do, but through the Platt Amendment, which Cubans reluctantly added to their constitution in 1901, the United States obtained many economic rights in Cuba, a naval base at Guantanamo Bay (recently a government prison), and the right to intervene if Cuban sovereignty were ever threatened.

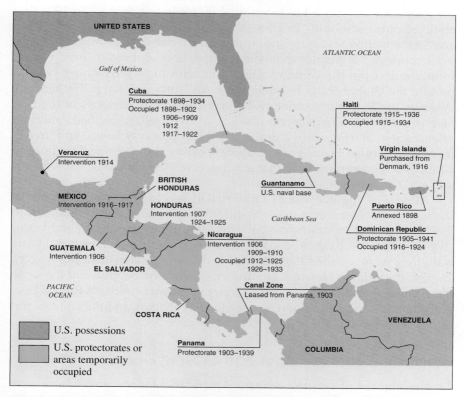

United States Involvement in Central America and the Caribbean, 1898–1939 Can you update the location of further interventions in Central America and the Caribbean since the 1950s? What do Latin Americans think of Norte Americanos today?

American policy intended to make Cuba a model of how a newly independent nation could achieve orderly self-government with only minimal guidance. Cuban self-government, however, was shaky. When, in 1906, a political crisis threatened to spiral into civil war, Roosevelt expressed his fury with "that infernal little Cuban republic." He sent warships to patrol the coastline and special commissioners and troops "to restore order and peace and public confidence." Along with economic development, which mostly benefited American companies, American political and even military involvement in Cuban affairs would continue for over a century.

The pattern was repeated throughout the Caribbean. The Dominican Republic, for example, suffered from unstable governments and great poverty. In 1904, as a revolt erupted, European creditors pressured the Dominican government for payment of $40 million in defaulted bonds. Sending its warships to discourage European intervention, the United States took over the collection of customs in the republic. Two years later, the United States intervened in Guatemala and Nicaragua, where American bankers controlled nearly 50 percent of all trade, the first of several twentieth-century interventions in those countries.

In a policy known as the **Roosevelt Corollary** to the Monroe Doctrine, the president announced in his annual message to Congress in 1904 that civilized nations should "insist on the proper policing of the world." The goal of the United States, he said, was to have "stable, orderly and prosperous neighbors." A country that paid its debts and kept order "need fear no interference from the United States." But "chronic wrong-doing" would require the United States to intervene as an "international police power." Whereas the Monroe Doctrine had warned European nations not to intervene in the Western Hemisphere, the Roosevelt Corollary justified American intervention. Starting with a desire to protect property, loans, and investments, the United States wound up supporting the tyrannical regimes of elites who owned most of the land, suppressed the poor, blocked reforms, and acted as American surrogates.

After 1904, the Roosevelt Corollary was invoked in several Caribbean countries. Intervention usually required the landing of U.S. Marines to counter a threat to American property. Occupying the capital and major seaports, Marines, bankers, and customs officials remained for several years until they were satisfied that stability had been reestablished. Roosevelt's successors, William Howard Taft and Woodrow Wilson, pursued the same interventionist policy, as did late-twentieth-century presidents Ronald Reagan (Grenada and Nicaragua), George Bush (Panama), and Bill Clinton and George W. Bush (Haiti).

Opening Doors to China and Closing Doors to America

Throughout the nineteenth century, American relations with China were restricted to a small but profitable trade. The British, in competition with France, Germany, and Russia, took advantage of the crumbling Manchu dynasty to force treaties on China creating "treaty ports" and granting exclusive trading privileges in various parts of the country. After 1898, Americans with dreams of exploiting the seemingly unlimited markets of China wanted to join the competition and enlarge their share. Those with moral interests, however, including many missionaries, reminded Americans of their revolutionary tradition against European imperialism. They made clear their opposition to U.S. commercial exploitation of a weak nation and supported China's political integrity as the other imperial powers moved toward partitioning the country.

Although a few Americans admired China's ancient culture, the dominant American attitude viewed the Chinese as heathen, exotic, backward, and immoral. The Exclusion Act of 1882 barring further immigration and riots against Chinese workers in the 1870s and 1880s reflected this negative stereotype. The Chinese, in turn, regarded the United States with a mixture of admiration, curiosity, resentment, suspicion, and disdain.

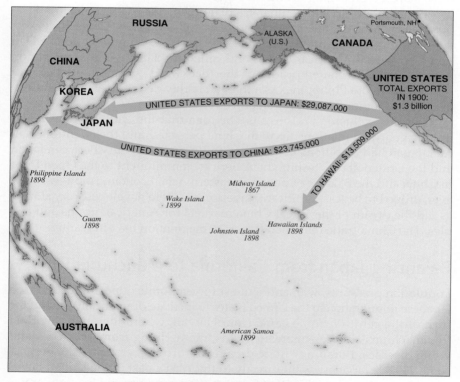

United States Involvement in the Pacific and Eastern Asia, 1898–1909 By 1898, the United States expanded far into eastern Asia and the Pacific. Which motivation do you think was most important in this expansion: profits, patriotism, piety, or politics? What major events in the past 100 years have followed American expansion into the Pacific and East Asia? Where else has the United States been involved? Hint: Get a world map.

The annexation of Hawaii and the Philippines in 1898 and 1899 convinced Secretary of State Hay that the United States should announce a China policy. He did so in the Open Door notes of 1899–1900, which became the cornerstone of U.S. policy in eastern Asia for half a century. The first note demanded an **open door policy** for American trade by declaring the principle of equal access to commercial rights in China by all nations. The second note, addressing Russian movement into Manchuria, called on all countries to respect the "territorial and administrative integrity" of China. This second principle announced a larger American role in Asia, offering China protection and preserving the East Asian balance of power.

An early test of this new role came during the Boxer Rebellion in 1900. The Boxers were a society of young traditionalist Chinese in revolt against both the Manchu dynasty and the growing Western presence in China. During the summer of 1900, Boxers killed some 242 missionaries and other foreigners and besieged the western quarter of Peking (Beijing). Eventually an international military force of 19,000 troops, including some 3,000 Americans, marched on Beijing to end the siege.

The relationship with China was plagued by the exclusionist immigration policy of the United States. Despite barriers and riots, Chinese workers kept coming to the United States illegally. In 1905, Chinese nationalists at home boycotted American goods and called for a change in immigration policy. Roosevelt, contemptuous of the "backward" Chinese, bristled and sent troops to the Philippines as a threat. Halfheartedly, he also asked Congress for a modified immigration bill, but nothing came of it.

Despite exclusion and insults, the idea that the United States had a unique guardian relationship with China persisted into the twentieth century. Japan had ambitions in China, so this created a rivalry between Japan and the United States, testing the American commitment to the Open Door in China and the balance of power in eastern Asia. Economic motives, however, proved to be less significant. Investments there developed very slowly, as did the dream of the "great China market" for American grains and textiles. The China trade remained larger in imagination than in reality.

Balancing Japan from California to Manchuria

Population pressures, war, and a quest for economic opportunities caused Japanese immigration to the United States to increase dramatically around the turn of the century. Some came from Hawaii, where they had "worked like machines" in the sugarcane fields, many dying from overwork and white diseases. Pursuing "huge dreams of fortune . . . across the ocean," some 200,000 Japanese went directly to the West Coast of the United States to work on railroads and in West Coast canneries, mines, and logging camps.

Others worked on farms in the valleys of Oregon and California, many successfully rising to own their own lands and turning marginal farmlands into productive agricultural businesses. Japanese-owned farms increased from 4,698 acres in 1900 to 194,742 by 1910, when they produced 70 percent of the California strawberry crop. Kinji Ushijima, for example, developed 10,000 acres of potato lands worth $500,000 in the fertile deltas between Stockton and Sacramento. By 1912, known then as Shima the "Potato King," he was praised by the *San Francisco Chronicle*. But when Shima moved to a well-to-do neighborhood in Berkeley, local newspapers and protesting professors complained of the "Yellow Peril in College Town." Shima refused to move.

Threatened by this competitive success, native white Californians sought ways to exclude Japanese immigrants, discriminate against them, and limit their ability to own or lease land. Japanese workers were barred from factory jobs. In 1906, the San Francisco school board, claiming that Japanese children were "crowding the whites out of the schools," segregated them into separate schools. Californians passed an anti-Japanese resolution and asked Roosevelt to persuade Japan to stop the emigration. Denouncing anti-Japanese rioting in San Francisco, Roosevelt favored restriction rather than exclusion. In the "Gentlemen's Agreement" notes of 1907–1908, the Japanese agreed to limit the migration of unskilled workers to the United States. In return, Californians repealed some of their anti-Japanese laws. Tensions continued.

It was one thing to check Japanese power in California but quite another to stop it in eastern Asia, where Roosevelt was determined to maintain the balance of power. The Boxer Rebellion of 1900 left Russia with 50,000 troops in Manchuria, making it the strongest regional power. Roosevelt's admiration for the Japanese as a "fighting" people and valuable factor in the "civilization of the future" contrasted with his low respect for the Russians. As Japan moved into Korea and Russia into Manchuria, Roosevelt hoped that each would check the other.

Roosevelt welcomed news in 1904 that Japan had successfully mounted a surprise attack, beginning the Russo-Japanese War. But as Japanese victories continued, Americans worried that Japan might play the game too well, shutting the United States out of Asian markets. Roosevelt tilted toward Russia. When the Japanese expressed an interest in ending the war, the American president was pleased to exert his influence.

Roosevelt's goal was to achieve peace and leave a balanced situation. Nothing better symbolized the new American presence in the world than the 1905 negotiation and signing of a peace treaty in Portsmouth, New Hampshire, ending a war between Russia and Japan halfway around the globe in Manchuria. The Treaty of Portsmouth left Japan dominant in Manchuria (as well as in Korea) and established the United States as the major balance to Japan's power. In the Root-Takahira Agreement of 1908, in return for recognizing these developments, Roosevelt got Japan's promise to honor U.S. control in the Philippines and to make no further encroachments into China.

Preventing War in Europe

The United States had stretched the Monroe Doctrine to justify sending Marines and engineers to Latin America and the navy and dollars to eastern Asia. Treaties, agreements, and the protection of territories and interests entangled the United States with foreign nations from Panama and

Nicaragua to the Philippines and China. Toward European nations, however, traditional neutrality continued.

Roosevelt believed that the most serious threats to world peace and civilized order lay in the relationships among Germany, Great Britain, and France. He established two fundamental policies toward Europe that defined the U.S. role throughout the century. The first was to make friendship with Great Britain the cornerstone of U.S. policy. The second was to prevent a general war in Europe among strong nations. Toward this end, Roosevelt depended on his personal negotiating skills with the leaders of major European nations.

Roosevelt supported British imperialism because he favored the dominance of the "English-speaking race" and believed that Britain was "fighting the battle of civilization." Furthermore, both nations worried about growing German power around the world. Roosevelt knew, as he wrote to Lodge in 1901, that the United States had "not the least particle of danger to fear" from Britain and that German ambitions and militarism represented the major threat to peace in Europe. As Roosevelt left the presidency in 1909, one of his final acts was to proclaim the special American friendship with Great Britain.

The relationship between Great Britain and Germany continued to deteriorate, and by 1914, a new American president, Woodrow Wilson, faced the terrible reality that Roosevelt had skillfully sought to prevent. When World War I finally broke out, no American was more eager to fight on the British side against the Germans than Colonel Roosevelt of the Rough Riders.

Conclusion
The Responsibilities of Power

The realities of power in the 1890s brought increasing international responsibilities. Roosevelt said in 1910 that because of "strength and geographical situation," the United States had itself become "more and more, the balance of power of the whole world." This ominous responsibility was also an opportunity to extend American economic, political, and moral influence around the globe.

As president in the first decade of the twentieth century, Roosevelt established aggressive American policies toward the rest of the world that President Bush would emulate in the first decade of the twenty-first century. The United States dominated and policed Central America and the Caribbean Sea to maintain order and protect its investments and other economic interests. In eastern Asia, Americans marched through Hay's Open Door with treaties, troops, navies, and dollars to protect the newly annexed Philippine Islands, to develop markets and investments, and to preserve the balance of power in Asia. In Europe, the United States sought to remain neutral and uninvolved in European affairs and at the same time to cement Anglo-American friendship and prevent "civilized" nations from going to war.

Making both friends and enemies, the fundamental ambivalence of America's sense of itself as an example to others remained. As questionable actions around the world—Private Grayson's in the Filipino-American War, for example—painfully demonstrated, it was increasingly difficult for the United States to be both responsible and good, both powerful and loved. The American people experienced, therefore, the satisfactions and burdens, the profits and costs, of their growing international responsibilities. How well these policies worked would unfold in the next century.

TIME*line*

1875–1877	United States acquires Hawaiian Islands
1898	Spanish-American War
	Annexation of Hawaiian Islands
	Treaty of Paris; annexation of the Philippines
1899–1902	Filipino-American War
1899–1900	Open Door notes and Boxer Rebellion in China
1902	U.S. military occupation of Cuba ends
	Platt Amendment
1903	Panamanian revolt and independence
1904	Roosevelt Corollary to the Monroe Doctrine
1904–1906	United States intervenes in Nicaragua, Guatemala, and Cuba
1907	"Gentleman's Agreement" with Japan
1914	Opening of the Panama Canal
	World War I begins

✓•⌐Study and Review at **www.myhistorylab.com**

Questions for Review and Reflection

1. What fundamental dilemma of American foreign policy was inherited from the Puritans, and to what extent do you think it applies today in America's relations with the rest of the world?

2. What motivated American expansionism in the 1890s—and perhaps still today?

3. What were the major differences and similarities in the causes and consequences of the Spanish-American and Filipino-American wars?

4. Give three or four justifications for annexing the Philippine Islands and three or four reasons opposing annexation. Which set of arguments do you think is most compelling? Can the United States be both powerful and good?

5. Outline the major principles, with examples, of President Roosevelt's foreign policy in the Caribbean, eastern Asia, and Europe. How well have these policies worked in the 100 years since Roosevelt's time?

6. Do you think American foreign policy has made America primarily an interventionist savior of other nations or an interfering expansionist into the affairs of other nations? Or some of both? Give examples.

Key Terms

Anti-Imperialist League 595

Filipino-American War 583

Imperialism 587

Josiah Strong 590

Open Door policy 606

Roosevelt Corollary 604

Self-determination 586

U.S.S. Maine 592

White man's burden 596

19

The Progressives Confront Industrial Capitalism

American Stories

A Professional Woman Joins the Progressive Crusade

Frances Kellor, a young woman who grew up in Ohio and Michigan, received her law degree in 1897 from Cornell University and became one of the small but growing group of professionally trained women. Deciding that she was more interested in solving the nation's social problems than in practicing law, she moved to Chicago, studied sociology, and trained herself as a social reformer. Kellor believed passionately that poverty and inequality could be eliminated in America. She also had the progressive faith that if Americans could only hear the truth about the millions of people living in urban slums, they would rise up and make changes. She was one of the experts who provided the evidence to document what was wrong in industrial America.

Like many progressives, Kellor believed that environment was more important than heredity in determining ability, prosperity, and happiness. Better schools and better housing, she thought, would produce better citizens. Even criminals, she argued, were simply victims of environment. Kellor demonstrated that poor health and deprived childhoods explained the only differences between criminals and college students. If it were impossible to define a criminal type, then it must be possible to reduce crime by improving the environment.

Kellor was an efficient professional. Like the majority of the professional women of her generation, she never married but devoted her life to social research and social reform. She lived for a time at Hull House in Chicago and at the College Settlement in New York, centers not only of social research and reform but also of lively community. For many young people the settlement, with its sense of commitment and its exciting conversation around the dinner table, provided an alternative to the nuclear family or the single apartment.

Chapter Outline

The Social Justice Movement

The Worker in the Progressive Era

Reform in the Cities and States

Theodore Roosevelt and the Square Deal

Woodrow Wilson and the New Freedom

Conclusion: The Limits of Progressivism

While staying at the College Settlement, Kellor researched and wrote a muck-raking study of employment agencies, published in 1904 as *Out of Work*. She revealed how employment agencies exploited immigrants, blacks, and other recent arrivals in the city. Kellor's book, like the writing of most progressives, sizzled with moral outrage. But Kellor went beyond moralism to suggest corrective legislation at the state and national levels. She became one of the leaders of the movement to Americanize the immigrants pouring into the country in unprecedented numbers. Between 1899 and 1920, over 8 million people came to the United States, most from southern and eastern Europe. Many feared that this flood of immigrants threatened the very basis of American democracy. Kellor and her coworkers repre-sented the side of progressivism that sought state and federal laws to protect the new arrivals from exploitation and to establish agencies and facilities to educate and Americanize them. Another group of progressives, often allied with organized labor, tried to pass laws to restrict immigration. Kellor was not entirely free of her generation's ethnic prejudice, but she did maintain that all immigrants could be made into useful citizens.

Convinced of the need for a national movement to push for reform legislation, Kellor helped to found the National Committee for Immigrants in America, which tried to promote a national policy "to make all these people Americans," and a fed-eral bureau to organize the campaign. Eventually, she helped establish the Division of Immigrant Education within the Department of Education. A political movement led by Theodore Roosevelt excited her most. More than almost any other single person, Kellor had been responsible for alerting Roosevelt to the problems the immigrants faced in American cities. When Roosevelt formed the new Progressive party in 1912, she was one of the many social workers and social researchers who joined him. She campaigned for Roosevelt and directed the Progressive Service Organization, educating voters in all areas of social justice and welfare after the election. After Roosevelt's defeat and the collapse of the Progressive party, Kellor continued to work for Americanization. She spent the rest of her life promoting justice, order, and efficiency and looking for ways of resolving industrial and international disputes.

Frances Kellor's life illustrates two important aspects of progres-sivism, the first nationwide reform movement of the modern era: first, a commitment to promote social justice, to ensure equal opportunity, and to preserve democracy; and second, a search for order and efficiency in a world complicated by rapid industrialization, immigration, and spectacu-lar urban growth. Like many progressives, she was part of a global move-ment to confront these problems, and she was influenced by writers and reformers in England and Germany as well as by those in the United States.

But no one person can represent all facets of so complex a movement. Borrowing from populism and influenced by a number of reformers from the 1890s as well as by social welfare legislation passed in several European countries, progressivism reached a climax in the years from 1900 to 1914. The **progressive movement** did not plot to overthrow the government; rather, it sought to reform the system in order to ensure the survival of the American way of life.

This chapter traces the important aspects of progressivism. Who were these reformers, whom did they seek to help, and what were their motives? How did reform movements strive to reduce chaos and promote order and democracy? How did voluntary action to solve social problems lead to passage of state and federal laws to promote social reform? In the early twentieth century, progressivism characterized the highest levels of government during the administrations of Theodore Roosevelt and Woodrow Wilson, the first thoroughly modern presidents.

The Social Justice Movement

Historians write of a "progressive movement." Actually there were a number of movements, some of them contradictory, but all focusing on the problems created by a rapidly expanding urban and industrial world. Some reformers, often from the middle class, sought to humanize the modern city—improving housing and schools and providing a better life for immigrants. Others focused on working conditions and the rights of labor. Still others sought to make politics responsive to popular interests, including those of women. Progressivism had roots in the 1890s, when many reformers were shocked by the devastation caused by the depression of 1893, and the progressives were influenced by Henry George's *Progress and Poverty* (1879); Edward Bellamy's *Looking Backward* (1888); a British pamphlet, *The Bitter Cry of Outcast London*; and the Social Gospel movement (see Chapter 17).

Watch the Video
Progressive Era
at **www.myhistorylab.com**

The Progressive Movement in a Global Context

Most progressives shared an international outlook. Many had studied in European universities. They attended international conferences on urban problems, belonged to organizations like the International Association for Labor Legislation, and read the latest sociological literature from Great Britain, France, Sweden, and Germany. Many were inspired by visiting Toynbee Hall, the pioneer social settlement in the slums of

London, and they observed municipal housing experiments in Glasgow and Dresden.

The United States lagged behind much of the industrialized world in passing social legislation, perhaps because it lacked Europe's strong labor and socialist movements. Germany had sickness, accident, and disability insurance by the 1880s. Great Britain passed workmen's compensation laws in the 1890s. But American cities were filled with immigrants with cultural adjustments and language barriers to overcome. Reform battles had to be fought first on the local and state levels, slowing the reform process in the United States.

Intellectually, the progressives were influenced by Darwinism. Believing that the world was in flux, they rebelled against the fixed and the formal. Progressive philosopher John Dewey wrote that ideas could become instruments for change. William James, in his philosophy of pragmatism, explained ideas in terms of their consequences. Most progressives were convinced that social environment was much more important than heredity in forming character. Building better schools and houses would make better people and a more perfect society. Yet even the more advanced reformers thought in racial and ethnic categories, convinced that some groups could be molded more easily than others. Progressivism did not usually mean progress for blacks.

In many ways, progressivism was the first modern reform movement. It sought to bring order and efficiency to a world that had been transformed by rapid growth and new technology. Yet elements of nostalgia infected the movement as reformers tried to preserve preindustrial handicrafts and to promote small-town and rural values in urban settings. Progressive leaders were almost always middle class, and they quite consciously tried to teach middle-class values to immigrants and working people. Often progressives seemed more interested in control than in reform; frequently, they displayed paternalism toward those they tried to help.

The progressives were part of a statistics-minded, realistic generation. They conducted surveys, gathered facts, wrote reports, and usually had faith that all this would lead to change. Their urge to document and to record came out in haunting photographs of young workers taken by Lewis Hine, in the stark and beautiful city paintings by John Sloan, and in the realist novels of Theodore Dreiser and William Dean Howells.

Optimistic about human nature, progressives believed that change was possible. They may seem naive or bigoted today, but they wrestled with many social questions, some of them old but fraught with new urgency in an industrialized society. What is the proper relation of government to society? In a world of large corporations and huge cities, how much should the government regulate and control? How much responsibility does society have for its poor and needy? Progressives could not agree on the answers, but for the first time in American history, they struggled with the questions.

The Muckrakers

Writers who exposed corruption and other social evils were labeled "**muckrakers**" by Theodore Roosevelt. Not all muckrakers were reformers—some just wrote for the money—but reformers learned from their techniques of exposé.

In part, the muckrakers were a product of the journalistic revolution of the 1890s. Nineteenth-century magazines had elite audiences. The new magazines had slick formats, more advertising, and wider sales. Competing for readers, editors eagerly published articles telling the public what was wrong in American society.

Lincoln Steffens, a young California journalist, wrote articles exposing the connections between respectable businessmen and corrupt politicians. When published as a book in 1904, *The Shame of the Cities* became a battle cry for people determined to clean up city government. Ida Tarbell, a teacher turned journalist, revealed the ruthlessness of John D. Rockefeller's Standard Oil Company. David Graham Phillips uncovered the alliance of politics and business in *The Treason of the Senate* (1906). Robert Hunter, a young settlement worker, shocked Americans in 1904 with his book *Poverty*. Upton Sinclair's novel *The Jungle* (1906) described the horrors of the Chicago meatpacking industry, and Frank Norris dramatized the railroads' stranglehold on farmers in *The Octopus* (1901).

Women and Children

Nothing disturbed the social justice progressives more than the sight of children as young as 8 or 10 working long hours in dangerous and depressing factories. Florence Kelley was one of the most important leaders in the crusade against child labor. Kelley had grown up in an upper-class Philadelphia family and was a member of the first generation of college women. Refused admission to an American graduate school because of her gender, she went to the University of Zurich in Switzerland and became a socialist. After her marriage failed, Kelley moved into Hull House and poured her energies into the campaign against child labor. When no Chicago attorney would argue child labor cases against prominent corporations, she went to law school, passed the bar exam, and argued the cases herself.

●**●─**Read the Document

Mother Jones, "The March of the Mill Children" (1903)

at **www.myhistorylab.com**

Kelley and other child labor reformers quickly recognized the need for state laws. Marshaling their evidence about the tragic effects on growing children of long working hours in dark and damp factories, they pressured the Illinois legislature into passing a child labor law. A few years later, however, the state supreme court ruled it unconstitutional, convincing reformers that action at the national level was essential. Kelley led the charge.

Newsboys Nothing disturbed the reformers more than the sight of little children, sullen and stunted, working long hours in factory, farm, and mine. But of all child laborers perhaps the newsboys caused the most concern. They often had to pick up their papers late at night or very early in the morning. They sometimes were home-less and slept wherever they could find a place. But even more troubling, they associated with unsavory characters and fell prey to bad habits. In this photo Lewis Hine captures three young newsboys in St. Louis in 1910. Why were reformers upset by photos like this? If you had to work, would you prefer the mine or the factory or would you become a newsboy? *(The Metropolitan Museum of Art, New York, NY, USA. Image copyright © The Metropolitan Museum of Art/Art Resource, N.Y.)*

The National Child Labor Committee was the brainchild of Edgar Gardner Murphy, a Social Gospel clergyman from Alabama. Headquartered in New York, it drew up a model state child labor law, encouraged state and city campaigns, and coordinated the movement around the country. Although two-thirds of the states passed some form of child labor law between 1905 and 1907, many had loopholes, and a national bill was de-feated in 1906. But reformers convinced Congress in 1912 to establish a Children's Bureau in the Department of Labor. Compulsory school atten-dance laws, however, did more to reduce the number of children who worked than federal and state laws, which proved difficult to pass and even more difficult to enforce.

The crusade against child labor was a typical social justice reform effort. Its origins lay in the moral indignation of middle-class reformers. But reformers went beyond moral outrage; they gathered statistics, took photographs, and used their evidence to push for legislation, first on the local level, then in the states, and eventually in Washington.

Like other progressive reform efforts, the battle against child labor was only partly successful. Too many businessmen profitably employed children. Too many politicians and judges were reluctant to regulate the work of children or adults. And some parents, desperately needing their child's wages, opposed the reformers and broke the law.

Reformers worried over the young people who got into trouble with the law, often for pranks that in rural areas would have seemed harmless. By setting up juvenile courts, the progressives hoped to separate young people from the criminal justice system while preventing them from being turned into hardened criminals by adult prisons. Yet juvenile courts frequently deprived young offenders of all rights of due process, as the Supreme Court finally recognized in 1967.

Closely connected with the anti–child labor movement was the effort to limit the hours of women's work. Florence Kelley and the National Consumers League led the campaign. It was foolish and unpatriotic, they argued, to allow the "mothers of future generations" to work long hours in dangerous industries. The most important court case on women's work came before the U.S. Supreme Court in 1908. Josephine Goldmark, Kelley's friend, wrote the brief for *Muller* v. *Oregon* that her brother-in-law, Louis Brandeis, used when he argued the case. The Court upheld the Oregon 10-hour law largely because Goldmark's sociological argument detailed the danger and disease that factory women faced. Brandeis opposed laissez-faire legal concepts, arguing that the government had a special interest in protecting citizens' health. Most states fell into line with the Supreme Court decision and passed protective legislation for women, though many companies managed to circumvent the laws. But even the 10 hours of work permitted by the law seemed too long for women who had to come home to child care and housekeeping.

Contending that "women are fundamentally weaker than men in all that makes for endurance," reformers won some protection for women workers. But their arguments would later be used to reinforce gender segregation at work.

Much more controversial than protective legislation was the birth control movement. Even many advanced progressives could not imagine themselves teaching immigrant women how to prevent conception (which was also illegal under federal law).

Margaret Sanger, a nurse who had watched poor women suffer from too many births and even die from dangerous, illegal abortions, was one of the founders of the modern American birth control movement. Middle-class Americans had limited family size in the nineteenth century through abstinence, withdrawal, abortion, and primitive birth control devices, but much ignorance remained, even among middle-class women. Sanger obtained the latest medical and scientific European studies and in 1914 explained in her magazine, *The Woman Rebel*, and in a

RECOVERING *the* PAST

Documentary Photographs

Photographs are a revealing way of recovering the past visually. But when looking at a photograph, especially an old one, it is easy to assume that it is an accurate representation of the past. Photographers, however, like novelists and historians, have a point of view. They take their pictures for a reason and often to prove a point. As one photographer remarked, "Photographs don't lie, but liars take photographs."

To document the need for reform in the cities, progressives collected statistics, made surveys, described urban problems, and even wrote novels. But they discovered that the photograph was often more effective than words. Jacob Riis, the Danish-born author of *How the Other Half Lives* (1890), a devastating exposure of conditions in New York City tenement house slums, was also a pioneer in urban photography. Others had taken pictures of dank alleys and street urchins before, but Riis was the first to photograph slum conditions with the express purpose of promoting reform. At first he hired photographers, but then he bought a camera and taught himself how to use it. He even tried a new German flash powder to illuminate dark alleys and tenement rooms in order to record the horror of slum life.

Riis made many of his photographs into lantern slides and used them to illustrate his lectures on the need for housing reform. Although he was a creative and innovative photographer, his pictures were often far from objective. His equipment was awkward, his film slow. He had to set up and prepare carefully before snapping the shutter. His views of tenement ghetto streets and poor children now seem like clichés, but they were designed to make Americans angry, to arouse them to reform.

Another important progressive photographer was Lewis Hine; like Riis, he taught himself photography. Trained as a sociologist, Hine used his camera to illustrate his lectures at the Ethical Culture School in New York. In 1908, he was hired as a full-time investigator by the National Child Labor Committee. His haunting photographs of children in factories helped convince many Americans of the need to abolish child labor. Hine's children were appealing human beings. He showed them eating, running, working, and staring wistfully out factory windows. His photographs avoided the pathos that Riis was so fond of recording, but just as surely they documented the need for reform.

Another technique that the reform photographer used was the before-and-after shot. The two photographs shown here of a one-room apartment in Philadelphia early in the century illustrate how progressive reformers tried to teach immigrants to imitate middle-class manners. The "before" photograph shows a room cluttered with washtubs, laundry, cooking utensils, clothes, tools, even an old Christmas decoration. In the "after" picture, much of the clutter has been cleaned up. A window has been installed to let in light and fresh air. The wallpaper, presumably a haven for hidden bugs and germs, has been torn off. The cooking utensils and laundry have been put away. The woodwork has been stained, and some ceremonial objects have been gathered on a shelf.

What else can you find that has been changed? How well do you think the message of the photographic combinations like this one worked? Would the immigrant family be happy with the new look and condition of their room? Could anyone live in one room and keep it so neat?

REFLECTING ON THE PAST As you look at these, or any photographs, ask yourself: What is the photographer's purpose and point of view? Why was this particular angle chosen for the picture? And why center on these particular people or objects? What does the photographer reveal about his or her purpose? What does the photographer reveal unintentionally? How have digital cameras changed photography? On what subjects do reform-minded photographers train their cameras today?

The reality of one-room tenement apartments (top) contrasted with the tidiness that reformers saw as the ideal (bottom).

pamphlet, *Family Limitation*, that women could separate sex from procreation. She was indicted for violation of the postal code and fled to Europe to avoid arrest.

Birth control long remained controversial—and in most states, illegal. Yet Sanger helped to bring sexuality and contraception out into the open. When she returned to the United States in 1921, she founded the American Birth Control League, which became the Planned Parenthood Federation in 1942.

The Struggle for Woman Suffrage

The social justice progressives also campaigned for woman suffrage. Like so much of progressivism, it was part of a global crusade. The women leading the American movement met their foreign counterparts at conventions of the International Suffrage Alliance. The United States lagged behind several other countries in granting female suffrage. Women in New Zealand

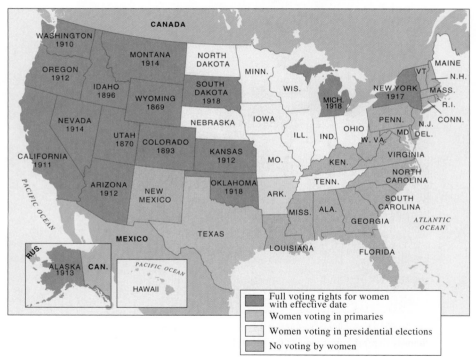

Woman Suffrage Before the Nineteenth Amendment Western states led the battle for women's right to vote, but key victories in New York (1917) and Michigan (1918) and a carefully organized campaign in all parts of the country finally led to the ratification of the Nineteenth Amendment. What patterns do you notice in the map, and how might they be explained?

won the vote in 1893, Australia in 1902, Finland in 1906, Norway in 1913, Denmark and Iceland in 1915, and Canada and Great Britain (for some local elections) in 1918.

In the United States, women's civil and political rights advanced very slowly after the Seneca Falls Convention in 1848. The political process that eventually led to woman suffrage in the United States was slowed by the difficulty of amending the Constitution and the need to fight the battle one state at a time. The earliest success came in the West where Wyoming (1869), Utah (1870), Colorado (1893), Idaho (1896), Washington (1910), California (1911), Arizona and Oregon (1912), and Montana and Nevada (1914) gave women the vote at least in some elections.

Many men in the East and Midwest feared that women, if given the vote, would support prohibition, while some women argued that the votes of middle-class women would cancel the vote of immigrant men. But progressives like Jane Addams supported votes for all women because, she argued, in an urban and industrial age women needed to be municipal housekeepers to protect their families. The progressive insistence that all women needed the vote helped to push woman suffrage toward victory during World War I.

In the 1890s, leading suffragists reexamined their situation. The two wings of the women's rights movement, split since 1869, combined in 1890 as the National American Woman Suffrage Association (NAWSA). Although Elizabeth Cady Stanton and Susan B. Anthony continued to head the association, both were in their seventies, and leadership passed to younger, more moderate women who concentrated on the single issue of the vote.

Changing leadership meant a shift in the arguments for the suffrage. Since 1848, suffragists had argued primarily from the principle of "our republican idea, individual citizenship." But the younger generation shifted to three expedient arguments. The first was that women needed the vote to pass self-protection laws to guard against rapists and unsafe industrial work. The second argument, Addams's notion of urban house-keeping, pointed out that political enfranchisement would further women's role in cleaning up immoral cities and corrupt politics. The third expedient argument reflected urban middle-class reformers' prejudice against non-Protestant immigrants who voted. Suffragists argued that educated, native-born American women should get the vote to counteract the undesirable influence of male immigrants. In a speech in Iowa in 1894, Carrie Chapman Catt, who succeeded Anthony as president of NAWSA in 1900, argued that the "Government is menaced with great danger . . . in the votes possessed by the males in the slums of the cities," a danger that could be averted only by cutting off that vote and giving it instead to women. In the new century, under the leadership of women like Catt, suffrage would finally be secured, and anti-immigrant attitudes continued.

Home and School

Reformers believed that better housing and education could transform the lives of the poor and create a better world. Books such as Jacob Riis's *How the Other Half Lives* (1890) horrified them. With vivid language and haunting photographs, Riis had documented the misery of New York's slums.

In the first decade of the twentieth century, the progressives took a new approach to the housing problems. They collected statistics, conducted surveys, organized committees, and constructed exhibits to demonstrate the effect of urban overcrowding. Tenement house laws, passed in several cities, were often ineffectual. In 1910, reformers organized the National Housing Association, and some hoped for federal laws and even government-subsidized housing. But the reformers' ideas often clashed with the values of those they tried to help.

Many middle-class women reformers who tried to teach working-class families how to live in their tenements had never organized their own homes. Those who lived in settlement houses never worried about cooking or chores.

Read the Document

Charlotte Perkins Gilman, "If I Were a Man" (1914)
at **www.myhistorylab.com**

Some, however, began to realize that domestic tasks kept women of all classes from taking their full place in society. Charlotte Perkins Gilman sketched an alternative to traditional notions of "the woman's sphere," suggesting that entrepreneurs build apartment houses with common dining facilities where women could combine motherhood with careers. However, most Americans of all political persuasions continued to view the home as sacred space where the mother ruled supreme.

Next to better housing, the progressives stressed better schools as a way to produce better citizens. Public school systems were often rigid and corrupt and seemed to reinforce old habits. A Chicago teacher told her students: "Don't stop to think; tell me what you know."

Progressive education, like many other aspects of progressivism, opposed the rigid in favor of flexibility. John Dewey was the key philosopher of progressive education. He tried to create in the city a sense of the small rural community of his native Vermont. He experimented with new educational methods, including seats that could be arranged in small groups rather than bolted down in rows.

Watch the Video

What Was the Progressive Education Movement?
at **www.myhistorylab.com**

Dewey insisted that the schools be child-centered, not subject-oriented. Teachers should teach children rather than teach history or mathematics. He did not mean that history and math should not be taught, but that those subjects should be related to the students' experience. Students should not just learn about democracy; the school itself should operate like a democracy.

Dewey also maintained, somewhat controversially, that the schools should become instruments for social reform. But like most progressives, Dewey was never clear whether he wanted the schools to help the students adjust to the existing world or to turn out graduates who would change the world. Although he wavered, the spirit of progressive education, like the spirit of progressivism in general, was optimistic. The reformers believed that the schools could create more flexible, better-educated adults who would eventually improve society.

Crusades Against Saloons, Brothels, and Movie Houses

Given their faith in the reforming potential of healthy and educated citizens, it was logical that most social justice progressives opposed the sale of alcohol. Some came from Protestant homes where drinking was considered a sin, but most favored prohibition for pragmatic reasons: to reform the city and conserve human resources.

Americans did drink a lot, and the amount they consumed rose rapidly after 1900, peaking between 1911 and 1915. Only three states still had prohibition laws dating from the 1850s. The modern anti-liquor movement was spearheaded in the 1880s and 1890s by the Women's Christian Temperance Union and after 1900 by the Anti-Saloon League and a coalition of religious leaders and social reformers. Seven states passed temperance laws between 1906 and 1912.

Progressives also saw the urban dance hall and movie theater as threats to youthful morals. The motion picture, invented in 1889, developed as an important form of entertainment only during the first decade of the twentieth century, at first appealing mainly to a lower-class and largely ethnic audience.

Not until World War I, when D. W. Griffith produced long feature films, did the movies begin to attract a middle-class audience. The most popular of these early films was Griffith's *The Birth of a Nation* (1915), a blatantly racist and distorted epic of black debauchery during Reconstruction. Many early films were imported from France, Italy, and Germany; because they were silent, they could be subtitled in any language. But viewers did not need to know the language, or even be able to read, to enjoy the action. That was part of early films' attraction. Many depicted premarital sex, adultery, and violence, and, unlike later films, many attacked authority and had tragic endings. *The Candidate* (1907) showed an upper-class reform candidate who gets dirt thrown at him when he tries to clean up the town. In *Down with Women* (1907), well-dressed men denounced woman suffrage and the incompetence of "the weaker sex," but throughout the film, only strong women were depicted.

Some of the films stressed slapstick humor or romance and adventure; others bordered on pornography. The reformers objected not only to the plots and content of the films, but also to the location of the theaters—near saloons and burlesque houses—and to their dark interiors, which could stimulate immoral activity. This disturbed reformers. But for young immigrant women, who made up the bulk of the audience at most urban movie theaters, the films provided rare exciting moments in their lives.

Saloons, dance halls, and movie theaters all seemed to progressives somehow connected with the worst evil of all: prostitution. Nineteenth-century anti-prostitution campaigns were nothing compared with the progressives' crusade to wipe out the "social evil." All major cities and many smaller ones appointed vice commissions, whose reports, often running to several thick volumes, were typical progressive documents, filled with elaborate statistical studies and moral outrage.

The progressive anti-vice crusade attracted many kinds of people, for often contradictory reasons. Racists and those who wanted to restrict immigration claimed that "inferior people"—blacks and recent immigrants—became prostitutes and pimps. Social hygiene progressives published vivid accounts of prostitution as part of their campaign to fight sexual ignorance. Some women reformers promoted a single moral standard for men and women. Others worried that prostitutes would spread venereal disease to unfaithful husbands, who would pass it on to wives and babies. Most progressives, however, stressed the environmental causes of vice. They believed that prostitution, like child labor and poor housing, could be eliminated through education and reform.

Watch the **Video**

Ellis Island Immigrants (1903)

at **www.myhistorylab.com**

Despite all their efforts, the progressives failed to end prostitution and did virtually nothing to address its roots in poverty. "Do you suppose I am going back to earn five or six dollars a week in a factory," one prostitute asked an investigator, "when I can earn that amount any night and often much more?" Reformers wiped out a few red-light districts, closed some brothels, and managed to push a bill through Congress (the Mann Act of 1910) that prohibited the interstate transport of women for immoral purposes. Perhaps more important, in several states, they got the age of consent for women raised, and in 20 states they made the Wassermann test for syphilis mandatory for both men and women before a marriage license could be issued.

The Worker in the Progressive Era

Progressive reformers sympathized with industrial workers, who struggled to earn a living for themselves and their families, and they sought legislation to protect working women and children. But often they had little understanding of what it was really like to sell one's strength by the hour. For example, they supported labor's right to organize at a time when labor had few friends, yet they often opposed the strike as a weapon against management. And neither organized labor nor the reformers, individually or in shaky partnership, had much power over industry in the years before World War I.

Adjusting to Industrial Labor

The nature of work continued to change in the early twentieth century as industrialists extended late-nineteenth-century efforts to make their factories and workers more efficient, productive, and profitable. In some industries, new machines revolutionized work and eliminated highly paid, skilled jobs. The moving assembly line, perfected by Henry Ford, transformed the nature of work and turned many laborers into unskilled machine-tenders.

The influence of the machine was uneven, having a greater impact in some industries than in others. Although some skilled weavers and glass-blowers were transformed into unskilled operators, the machines themselves created the need for new skilled workers. In the auto industry, for example, the new elite workers were the mechanics and the tool and die men who kept the assembly line running. But the trend toward mechanization was unstoppable, and even the most skilled workers were eventually removed from making decisions about production.

The principles of **scientific management** were also important in altering industrial work. Here the key figure was Frederick Taylor, the son of a prominent Philadelphia family. Taylor had a nervous breakdown as a youth, and his physicians prescribed manual labor as a cure. Working in a Philadelphia steel plant and studying engineering at night, he became chief engineer in the 1880s. Later he used this experience to rethink the organization of industry.

Taylor was obsessed with efficiency. He emphasized centralized planning, systematic analysis, and detailed instructions. He timed workers with a stopwatch to determine the most efficient way to perform a task. Although he overstated his data, many owners enthusiastically adopted his concepts of scientific management, seeing an opportunity to increase their profits and their control of the workplace. Not surprisingly, many workers resented "Taylorism."

Union Organizing

Samuel Gompers, head of the American Federation of Labor, quickly saw that Taylorism would reduce workers to "mere machines." Under his guidance, the AFL prospered during the progressive era. By 1914, the AFL alone had over 2 million members. Gompers's "pure and simple unionism" was most successful among coal miners, railroad workers, and the building trades. As we saw in Chapter 16, Gompers ignored unskilled and immigrant workers and concentrated on raising the wages and improving the working conditions of the skilled craftsmen who were members of unions affiliated with the AFL.

For a time, Gompers's strategy seemed to work. Several industries negotiated with the AFL to avoid disruptive strikes. But cooperation was short-lived. Labor unions were defeated in a number of disastrous strikes, and the National Association of Manufacturers (NAM) launched an aggressive counterattack. The NAM and other employer associations provided strikebreakers, used industrial spies, and blacklisted union members to bar them from other jobs.

The Supreme Court came down squarely on management's side, ruling in the *Danbury Hatters* case in 1908 that trade unions were subject to the

Sherman Anti-Trust Act. Thus union members could be held personally liable for money lost by a business during a strike. Courts at all levels often declared strikes illegal and were quick to issue restraining orders.

Working women and their problems aroused more sympathy among progressive reformers than the plight of working men. The number of women working outside the home increased steadily during the progressive era, from over 5 million in 1900 to nearly 8.5 million in 1920. But few belonged to unions, and the percentage had declined by 1910 before increasing a little after that date with aggressive organizing in the textile and clothing trades.

Of necessity, women continued to work to support themselves and their families. Many upper-class women reformers tried to help these working women. Tension and misunderstanding often developed between the reformers and the working women, but one organization in which there was genuine cooperation was the Women's Trade Union League. Founded in 1903, the league was organized by several progressive reformers but drew leaders from the working class such as Mary Kenney and Rose Schneiderman, a Jewish immigrant cap maker. The league established branches in most large eastern and midwestern cities and served for more than a decade as an important force in helping to organize women into unions. It forced the AFL to pay more attention to women, helped out in time of strikes, put up bail money for those arrested, and publicized the plight of working women.

Garment Workers and the Triangle Fire

Thousands of young women, most of them Jewish and Italian, were employed in the garment industry in New York City. Most were between the ages of 16 and 25. They worked a 56-hour, 6-day week that paid about $6. New York had over 600 shirtwaist (blouse) and dress factories employing more than 30,000 workers.

Like other industries, garment manufacturing had changed. Once conducted in thousands of dark and dingy tenement rooms, all operations were now centralized in large loft buildings in lower Manhattan. Though an improvement over the tenements, many were still overcrowded and had few safety features. Scientific management made life miserable for the workers. Most of the women rented their sewing machines and even paid for their electricity. They were penalized for mistakes or for talking loudly, and were usually supervised by a male contractor who badgered and sometimes sexually harassed them.

In 1909, some of the women went out on strike to protest the working conditions. The International Ladies' Garment Workers Union (ILGWU) and the Women's Trade Union League supported them. But strikers were beaten and sometimes arrested. On November 22, after an impassioned speech in Yiddish by a young shirtwaist worker who had been injured on the picket line, a mass meeting voted for a general strike.

Triangle Fire Victims The Triangle fire shocked the nation, and dramatic photographs, such as this candid shot showing bodies and bystanders waiting for more young women to jump, helped stimulate the investigation that followed. What event in your lifetime was as shocking as this photo?

This "uprising of the twenty thousand" startled the nation. Jews and Italians learned a little of each other's language so they could communicate on the picket line. A young state legislator, Fiorello La Guardia, later a congressman and mayor, was one of many public officials who joined clergy and social reformers in aiding the strikers.

The shirtwaist workers won, and in part, the success of the strike made the garment union one of the most powerful in the AFL. But some companies refused to go along, and work conditions remained oppressive and unsafe. That became dramatically obvious on Saturday, March 25, 1911, when a fire broke out on the eighth floor of the 10-story loft building housing the Triangle Shirtwaist Company. Within minutes, the top three floors of the factory were ablaze. The managers had locked many exit doors. The elevators broke down. With no fire escapes, 46 women jumped to their deaths and over 100 died in the flames of the **Triangle Shirtwaist fire**.

A shocked state legislature appointed a commission to investigate working conditions in the state. One investigator for the commission was a young social worker, Frances Perkins, who in the 1930s would become secretary of labor. She took politicians on a tour through the garment district to show them the miserable conditions under which young women worked. The result was state legislation limiting the work of women to 54 hours a week, prohibiting labor by children under the age of 14, and improving safety regulations in factories. One supporter of the bills was a young state senator named Franklin Delano Roosevelt.

The investigative commission was a favorite progressive tactic, and the Industrial Relations Commission, created in 1912, was one of the most important. The commission studied the causes of industrial unrest and violence and investigated a dramatic labor-management conflict in Colorado called the Ludlow Massacre. When the mine workers struck for an eight-hour day, better safety, and the removal of armed guards, the Rockefeller-dominated company refused to negotiate. The strike turned violent, and in the spring of 1914, strikebreakers and national guardsmen fired on the workers, killing 11 children and 2 women.

The Industrial Relations Commission forced John D. Rockefeller, Jr., to testify and implied that he was personally guilty of murder. Its report concluded that violent class conflict could be avoided only by limiting the use of armed guards and detectives, by restricting monopoly, by protecting workers' right to organize, and, most dramatically, by redistributing wealth through taxation. Not surprisingly, the report fell on deaf ears. Most progressives, like most Americans, denied its conclusion that class conflict was inevitable.

Radical Labor

Not everyone accepted the progressives' faith in investigations and protective labor legislation. Nor did everyone approve of Samuel Gompers's conservative tactics or his emphasis on getting better pay for skilled workers. About 200 radicals met in Chicago in 1905 to form a new union as an alternative to the AFL. They called it the Industrial Workers of the World (IWW). Like the Knights of Labor in the 1880s, the IWW welcomed all workers, regardless of skill, gender, or race.

Eugene Debs attended the organizational meeting. He had become a socialist after the Pullman strike of 1894 and emerged by 1905 as one of the outstanding radical leaders in the country. Also there was "Big Bill" Haywood of the Western Federation of Miners, and the legendary "Mother" Jones, who dressed like a society matron but attacked labor leaders "who sit on velvet chairs in conferences with labor's oppressors." Now in her sixties, she had been a dressmaker, a Populist, and a member of the Knights of Labor.

•••─Read the Document

Eugene Debs, "The Outlook for Socialism in America" (1900)

at **www.myhistorylab.com**

The IWW remained small and troubled by internal squabbling. Haywood dominated the movement, which played an important role in organizing the militant strikes of textile workers in Lawrence, Massachusetts, in 1912 and the following year in Paterson, New Jersey, and Akron, Ohio. The IWW had its greatest success organizing lumbermen and migrant workers in the Northwest. Elsewhere, especially in times of high unemployment, the "Wobblies" helped the unskilled workers vent their anger against their employers.

But most American workers did not feel, as European workers often did, that they were involved in a class struggle. Some immigrant workers, intent on earning enough money to go home, had no time to join the conflict. Most of those who stayed dreamed the American dream—a better job or moving up into the middle class—and avoided labor militancy. They believed that even if they failed, their sons and daughters would profit from the American way. The AFL, not the IWW, became the dominant American labor organization.

Reform in the Cities and States

The reform movements of the progressive era usually started at the local level, moved to the state, and finally reached the nation's capital. Progressivism in the cities and states had roots in the depression and discontent of the 1890s. The reform banners called for more democracy, more power for the people, and legislation regulating railroads and other businesses. Yet often the professional and business classes were the movement's leaders. They intended to bring order out of chaos and to modernize the city and the state during a time of rapid growth.

Municipal Reformers

The spectacular and continuing growth of the cities created a need for housing, transportation, and municipal services. But the kind of people who were filling the cities gave cause for worry. Fully 40 percent of New York's population and 36 percent of Chicago's were foreign-born in 1910; including immigrant children, the percentage approached 80 percent in some cities. "Beaten men from beaten races, representing the worst failures in the struggle for existence," was how the president of MIT described them.

Fear of the city and its new inhabitants motivated progressive municipal reform. Early twentieth-century reformers, mostly middle-class citizens, wanted to regulate the sprawling metropolis, restore democracy, cut corruption, and limit the power of bosses and their immigrant allies. When these reformers talked of restoring power to the people, they usually meant people like themselves.

Municipal reform movements varied from city to city. In Boston, reformers tried to strengthen the power of the mayor, break the hold of the city council, and eliminate council corruption. But in 1910 John Fitzgerald, grandfather of John F. Kennedy and a foe of reform, was elected mayor, defeating the reform candidate. Elsewhere reformers used different tactics, but they almost always conducted elaborate studies and campaigned to reduce corruption.

The most dramatic innovation was the replacement of both mayor and council with a nonpartisan commission of administrators. This innovation began quite accidentally when a hurricane devastated Galveston, Texas, in September 1900—one of the worst natural disasters in the nation's history, killing more than 6,000 people. The existing government was helpless to deal with the crisis, so the state legislature appointed five commissioners to run the city during the emergency.

The idea of government by commission spread rapidly, especially to the small and mid-sized cities in the Midwest and the Pacific Northwest. Dayton, Ohio, went one step further. After a disastrous flood in 1913, the city hired a city manager to run the city and to report to the elected council. Government by experts was the perfect symbol of what most municipal reformers had in mind.

In most large cities, however, the commission and the expert manager did not replace the mayor. One of the most flamboyant and successful of the progressive mayors was Tom Johnson of Cleveland, a wealthy man converted to reform by Henry George's *Progress and Poverty*. Elected mayor of Cleveland in 1901, he cut transit fares and built parks and municipal bathhouses throughout the city. He also broke the connection between the police and prostitution by promising "madams" and brothel owners that he would not bother them if they would not steal from customers or pay off the police. His most controversial move was to advocate city ownership of the street railroads and utilities. He was defeated in 1909, in part because he alienated many powerful business interests, but one of his lieutenants, Newton D. Baker, was elected mayor in 1911 and carried on many of his programs.

Reform in the States

The progressive movements in the states had many roots and took many forms. In some states, especially in the West, progressive attempts to regulate railroads and utilities were simply an extension of populism. In other states, progressivism bubbled up from urban reform efforts. Most states passed laws designed to extend democracy and give more authority to the people. Initiative and referendum laws allowed citizens to originate legislation and to overturn laws passed by the legislature, and recall laws gave the people a way to remove elected officials. Most of these "democratic" laws worked better in theory than in practice, but they did represent a genuine effort to remove special privilege from government.

Much progressive state legislation concerned order and efficiency, but many states passed social justice measures as well. Maryland enacted the first workers' compensation law in 1902, paying employees for days missed because of job-related injuries. Illinois approved a law aiding mothers with dependent children. Several states passed anti–child labor bills, and Oregon's law restricting women's labor to 10 hours per day became a model for other states.

States with the most successful reform movements elected strong governors: Charles Evans Hughes in New York, Hoke Smith in Georgia, Woodrow Wilson in New Jersey, and Robert La Follette in Wisconsin. After Wilson, La Follette was the most famous, and in many ways, the model progressive governor. Of small-town origin and an 1879 graduate of the University of Wisconsin, he began his career as a railroad lawyer and became a reformer only after the depression of 1893. Taking advantage of the general mood of discontent, he won the governorship in 1901. Ironically, La Follette owed his victory to his attack on the railroads. But he was a shrewd politician. He used professors from the University of Wisconsin to prepare reports and do statistical studies. Then he worked with the legislature to pass a state primary law and an act regulating the railroads. "Go back to the first principles of democracy; go back to the people" was his battle cry. Journalists touted Wisconsin as the "laboratory of democracy." La Follette became a national figure and was elected to the Senate in 1906.

The progressive movement did improve government and make it more responsible to the people in states like Wisconsin. For example, the railroads were brought under the control of a railroad commission. But by 1910, the railroads no longer complained about the new taxes and restrictions. They had discovered that it was to their advantage to make their operations more efficient, and they often convinced the commission that they should raise rates or abandon unprofitable lines. Progressivism in the states, like progressivism everywhere, had mixed results. But the spirit of reform that swept the country was real, and progressive movements on the local level did eventually have an impact on Washington.

Theodore Roosevelt and the Square Deal

Although early progressive reformers had attacked problems that they saw in their own communities, they gradually understood that some problems could not be solved at the state or local level. The emergence of a national industrial economy had spawned conditions that demanded national solutions. Progressives at the national level turned their attention to the economic system—the railroads and other large corporations, the state of the natural environment, and the quality of American industrial products. And as they fashioned legislation to remedy economic flaws, they vastly expanded the national government's power. Although reformers were not sure what to expect from Theodore Roosevelt when he became president in 1901, during his presidency progressivism reshaped the national political agenda.

A Strong and Controversial President

Roosevelt came to the presidency with considerable experience. He had run unsuccessfully for mayor of New York and served a term in the New York state assembly. He had spent four years as a U.S. civil service commissioner and two years as New York City police commissioner. His exploits in the Spanish-American War brought him to the public's attention, but he had also been an effective assistant secretary of the navy and a reform governor of New York. While police commissioner and governor, he had been influenced by progressives like his friend Jacob Riis and a group of New York City settlement workers.

⦿ **View** the **Image**

Collage Spanning the Career of Teddy Roosevelt

at **www.myhistorylab.com**

Roosevelt loved being president. He called the office a "bully pulpit," and he enjoyed talking to the people and reporters. His appealing personality and sense of humor made him a good subject for the new mass-market press. The public quickly adopted him as their favorite. They called him "Teddy" and named a stuffed bear after him. Sometimes his exuberance got a little out of hand. On one occasion, he took a foreign diplomat on a nude swim in the Potomac River. You have to understand, someone remarked, that "the president is really only six years old."

Roosevelt, however, was more than an exuberant child; he was the strongest president since Lincoln. By revitalizing the executive branch, reorganizing the army command structure, and modernizing the consular service, he made many aspects of the federal government more efficient.

TR's Bully Pulpit Theodore Roosevelt was a dynamic public speaker who used his position to influence public opinion. Despite his high-pitched voice, he could be heard at the back of the crowd in the days before microphones. Note the row of reporters decked out in their summer straw hats writing their stories as the president speaks. How have presidential speeches and the role of reporters changed since Roosevelt's time?

He established the Bureau of Corporations, appointed commissions staffed with experts, and enlisted talented men to work for the government. "TR" called a White House conference on the care of dependent children, and in 1905 he even summoned college presidents and coaches to discuss ways to limit violence in football. He angered many social justice progressives by not going far enough. But he was the first president to listen to the pleas of the progressives and to invite them to the White House.

Dealing with the Trusts

One of Roosevelt's first actions as president was to attempt to control the large industrial corporations. He took office amid an unprecedented wave of business consolidation. Between 1897 and 1904, some 4,227 companies combined to form 257 large corporations. U.S. Steel, the first billion-dollar corporation, was formed in 1901 by joining Carnegie Steel with its eight main competitors. The new company controlled two-thirds of the market, and J. P. Morgan made $7 million on the deal.

The Sherman Anti-Trust Act of 1890 had been virtually useless in controlling the trusts, but a new outcry from muckrakers and progressives called for regulation. Some even demanded the return to the age of small business. Roosevelt opposed neither bigness nor the right of businessmen to make money. "We draw the line against misconduct, not against wealth," he said.

To the shock of much of the business community, he directed his attorney general to file suit to dissolve the Northern Securities Company, a giant railroad monopoly put together by Morgan and railroad man James J. Hill. "If we have done anything wrong," Morgan suggested, "send your man to my man and they can fix it up." A furious Roosevelt let Morgan and other businessmen know that the president of the United States was not just another tycoon. The government won its case and proceeded to prosecute some of the largest corporations, including Standard Oil of New Jersey and the American Tobacco Company.

Roosevelt's antitrust policy did not end the power of the giant corporations or even alter their methods of doing business. Nor did it force down the price of kerosene, cigars, or railroad tickets. But it breathed some life into the Sherman Anti-Trust Act and increased the role of the federal government as regulator. It also caused large firms such as U.S. Steel to diversify to avoid antitrust suits.

Roosevelt tried to strengthen the regulatory powers of the federal government in other ways. He steered the Elkins Act through Congress in 1903 and the Hepburn Act in 1906, which together increased the power of the Interstate Commerce Commission (ICC). The first act eliminated the use of rebates by railroads; the second broadened the power of the ICC and gave it the right to investigate and enforce rates, though opponents in Congress weakened both bills.

Roosevelt firmly believed in corporate capitalism, detested socialism, and was not comfortable around labor leaders. Yet he saw his role as mediator and regulator. His view of the power of the presidency was illustrated in 1902 during the anthracite coal strike. Led by the United Mine Workers, coal miners went on strike to protest low wages, long hours, and dangerous conditions. In 1901, a total of 513 coal miners had died in industrial accidents. The mine owners refused to talk to the miners, hiring strikebreakers and using private security forces to intimidate workers. In the fall of 1902, schools began closing for lack of coal, and it looked like many citizens would suffer through the winter. Over the managers' protests about talking to "outlaws," Roosevelt called owners and union leaders to the White House and appointed a commission that included both union and community representatives. Within weeks, the miners were back at work with a 10 percent raise.

Meat Inspection and Pure Food and Drugs

Roosevelt's first major legislative reform began almost accidentally in 1904 when Upton Sinclair, a 26-year-old muckraking journalist, started to research Chicago's stockyards. His novel *The Jungle*, published in 1906, documented labor exploitation and tried to convert readers to socialism, but its description of contaminated meat turned stomachs and set off an outcry for better regulation of the meatpacking industry. Roosevelt, who read the book, reportedly could no longer enjoy his breakfast sausage. He ordered a study of the industry and used the report to pressure Congress and the meatpackers to accept a reform bill.

In the end, the Meat Inspection Act of 1906 was a compromise. It enforced some federal inspection and mandated sanitary conditions in all companies selling meat in interstate commerce. The meatpackers defeated a provision that would have required the dating of all meat. Some large companies supported the compromise bill because it gave them an advantage against smaller firms. But the bill was a beginning. It illustrates how muckrakers, social justice progressives, and public outcry eventually led to reform legislation. It also shows how Roosevelt used the public mood and manipulated the political process to get a bill through Congress. He was always willing to settle for half a loaf rather than none at all. Ironically, the Meat Inspection Act restored public confidence in the meat industry and helped it increase profits.

Publicity surrounding *The Jungle* generated legislation to regulate food and drug sales. Many packaged and canned foods contained dangerous chemicals and impurities. Americans consumed an enormous quantity of patent medicines; one popular remedy was revealed to be 44 percent alcohol, and often medicines were laced with opium. Many people unwittingly became alcoholics or drug addicts. The Pure Food and Drug Act (1906) was not perfect, but it corrected some of the worst abuses, including eliminating cocaine from Coca-Cola.

Conservation Versus Preservation

Roosevelt, an outdoorsman and amateur naturalist, considered his conservation program his most important domestic achievement. Using his executive authority, he more than tripled the land set aside for national forests, bringing the total to more than 150 million acres.

Roosevelt understood, as few easterners did, the problems created by limited water in the western states. In 1902, with his enthusiastic support, Congress passed the Newlands Act, setting aside the proceeds from the sale of public land in 16 western states to pay for the construction of irrigation projects in those states. Although it tended to help big farmers the most, the Newlands Act federalized irrigation for the first time.

More important, Roosevelt raised public consciousness about saving natural resources. He appointed a National Conservation Commission charged with making an inventory of the natural resources in the entire country, chaired by Gifford Pinchot, probably the most important conservationist in the country. An advocate of selective logging, fire control, and limited grazing on public lands, Pinchot became a friend and adviser to Roosevelt.

Pinchot's conservation policies pleased many in the timber and cattle industries and angered those who simply wanted to exploit the land. But the followers of John Muir, a passionate advocate of preserving wilderness, denounced Pinchot's philosophy and policies. Muir had founded the Sierra Club in 1862 and had led a successful campaign to create Yosemite National Park in California. He looked eccentric, but thousands agreed when he argued that to preserve the wilderness was a spiritual and psychological necessity for overcivilized city residents. Muir was one of the leaders in the turn-of-the-century "back-to-nature" movement, which also included the founding of the Boy Scouts (1910) and the Camp Fire Girls (1912).

The conflicting conservation philosophies of Pinchot and Muir were most dramatically demonstrated by the controversy over Hetch-Hetchy, a remote valley deep within Yosemite National Park. It was a pristine wilderness area, and Muir and his followers wanted to keep it that way. But in 1901, the mayor of San Francisco decided the valley would make a perfect place for a dam and reservoir to supply his growing city with water. Muir argued that wilderness soon would be scarcer than water, though more important for the nation's moral strength. Pinchot and other conservationists argued that it was immoral to sacrifice the welfare of the great majority to the aesthetic enjoyment of a tiny group. In the end, Roosevelt and Congress sided with the conservationists, and the valley became (and remains) a lake. The debate between conservationists and preservationists still goes on today.

Progressivism for Whites Only

Like most whites of his generation, Roosevelt believed that blacks, Indians, and Asians were inferior, and he feared that massive migrations from southern and eastern Europe threatened Anglo-Saxon dominance. But Roosevelt was a politician, so he made gestures of goodwill to most groups. He even invited Booker T. Washington to the White House in 1901, despite vicious southern protests, and appointed several qualified blacks to minor federal posts. But he could also be insensitive to African Americans, as he surely was in his handling of the Brownsville, Texas, riot of 1906. Members of a black army unit who were stationed there rioted, angered by discrimination against them. No one is sure exactly what happened, but one white man was killed and several were wounded. After the midterm elections of 1906, Roosevelt ordered all 167 members of three companies dishonorably discharged—an unjust punishment for an unproven crime. Sixty-six years later, the secretary of the army granted honorable discharges to the men, most of whom were dead by then.

The progressive era coincided with the years of greatest segregation in the South, but even the most advanced progressives seldom included blacks in their reform schemes. Like most settlements, Hull House was segregated, although Addams, more than most progressives, struggled to overcome the racist attitudes of her day. She helped found a settlement that served a black neighborhood in Chicago, and she spoke out repeatedly against lynching. In 1909, Addams supported the founding of the National Association for the Advancement of Colored People (**NAACP**), the most important organization of the progressive era aimed at promoting equality and justice for blacks.

The founding of the NAACP is the story of cooperation between a group of white social justice progressives and courageous black leaders. Even in the age of segregation and lynching, blacks in all parts of the country—through churches, clubs, and schools—worked to promote a better life for themselves.

The most important black leader who argued for equality and opportunity for his people was W. E. B. Du Bois. Du Bois differed dramatically with Booker T. Washington on the proper position of blacks in American life. Whereas Washington advocated vocational education, Du Bois argued that the "talented tenth" of the black population should get the best education possible. Against Washington's talk of compromise and accommodation to the dominant white society, Du Bois increasingly urged aggressive action for equality.

Denouncing Washington in 1905, Du Bois called a meeting of young and militant blacks across from Niagara Falls in Canada. "We believe in taking what we can get but we don't believe in being satisfied with it and in permitting anybody for a moment to imagine we're satisfied," said the Niagara movement's angry manifesto. Du Bois's small band was soon augmented by white liberals concerned with violence against blacks, including Jane Addams and Oswald Garrison Villard, grandson of abolitionist William Lloyd Garrison. In 1910, the Niagara movement merged with the NAACP, and Du Bois became editor of its journal, *The Crisis*. He toned down his rhetoric but tried to promote equality for all blacks. The NAACP

An American History Class Tuskegee Institute followed Booker T. Washington's philosophy of black advancement through accommodation to the white status quo. Here students study white American history, but most of their time was spent on more practical subjects. This photo was taken in 1902 by Frances Benjamin Johnston, a pioneer woman photographer. How have classrooms changed in the last hundred years? How have they stayed the same?

was a typical progressive organization, seeking to work within the American system to promote reform. But Roosevelt and many other progressives thought it dangerously radical.

William Howard Taft

After two terms as president, Roosevelt decided to step down and go big-game hunting in Africa. But he soon regretted leaving the White House. He was only 50 years old and at the peak of his popularity and power.

William Howard Taft, Roosevelt's choice for the Republican nomination in 1908 and winner over William Jennings Bryan for the election, was a distinguished lawyer and federal judge—the first civil governor of the Philippines and Roosevelt's secretary of war. In some ways, he was more progressive than Roosevelt. His administration instituted more suits against monopolies in one term than Roosevelt had in two. He supported the eight-hour workday and legislation to make mining safer. He supported the Mann-Elkins Act in 1910, which strengthened the ICC. Taft and Congress also authorized the first tax on corporate profits, and he encouraged the process that eventually led to the passage of the federal income tax, which was authorized under the Sixteenth Amendment and was ratified in 1913.

But Taft's presidency quickly ran into difficulties. His biggest problem was his style. He weighed over 300 pounds, wrote ponderously, and spoke with little inspiration. He also lacked Roosevelt's political skills and angered many of the progressives in the Republican party, especially the midwestern insurgents led by La Follette, when he signed the Payne-Aldrich Tariff of 1909. Many progressives thought it favored the eastern industrial interests and left the rates too high.

Even Roosevelt was infuriated when his successor reversed many of his conservation policies and fired Chief Forester Gifford Pinchot, who had attacked Secretary of the Interior Richard A. Ballinger for giving away rich coal lands in Alaska to mining interests. Roosevelt broke with Taft, letting it be known that he was willing to run again for president. This set up one of the most exciting and significant elections in American history.

The Election of 1912

Woodrow Wilson won the Democratic presidential nomination in 1912. The son and grandson of Presbyterian ministers, he grew up in a comfortable and intellectual southern household. He graduated from Princeton in 1879, got a Ph.D., and published *Congressional Government* (1885), which established his reputation as a shrewd political analyst. He taught history and became a Princeton professor. Less flamboyant than Roosevelt, he was a persuasive speaker. In 1902, he was elected president of Princeton University; during the next few years, he established a national reputation as an educational leader. He eagerly accepted the Democratic machine's offer to run for governor of New Jersey in 1910, but then showed courage by quickly alienating some of the conservatives who had helped elect him. Building a reform coalition, he put through a direct primary law and other progressive reforms. By 1912, Wilson had acquired the reputation of a progressive.

Roosevelt, who had been speaking out on a variety of issues since 1910, competed with Taft for the Republican nomination. As the incumbent president and party leader, Taft won it—but Roosevelt startled the nation by walking out of the convention and forming a new political party, the Progressive party. It appealed to progressives who had become frustrated with the conservative leadership in both major parties. Its platform contained provisions that reformers had been advocating for years: an eight-hour workday; a six-day workweek; abolition of child labor under age 16; federal accident, old age, and unemployment insurance; and—unlike the Democrats—woman suffrage.

Most supporters of the Progressives in 1912 hoped to organize a new political movement that would replace the Republican party, just as the Republicans had replaced the Whigs after 1856. Progressive leaders, led by Frances Kellor, had plans to apply the principles of social research by educating voters between elections.

The Progressive party convention in Chicago seemed like a religious revival or a social work conference. Delegates sang "Onward Christian Soldiers" and "The Battle Hymn of the Republic," and when Jane Addams seconded Roosevelt's nomination, a large group of women marched around the auditorium with a "Votes for Women" banner. The Progressive cause "is based on the eternal principles of righteousness," Roosevelt cried.

But behind the unified facade lurked many disagreements. Roosevelt had become more progressive on many issues since leaving the presidency. He even attacked the financiers "to whom the acquisition of untold millions is the supreme goal of life, and who are too often utterly indifferent as to how these millions are obtained." But he was less committed to social reform than some delegates. A number of social justice progressives fought hard to include a plank in the platform supporting equality for blacks and for seating a black delegation, but Roosevelt hoped to carry several southern states. In the end, no blacks were seated and the platform made no mention of black equality.

The 1912 campaign became a contest primarily between Roosevelt and Wilson, who vigorously debated the proper relationship of government to society in a modern industrial age. Advancing what he called the **New Nationalism**, Roosevelt argued that in a modern industrial society, large corporations were "inevitable and necessary." What was needed was a strong president and increased power in the hands of the federal government to regulate business and industry for the benefit of the people. He argued for using Hamiltonian means to ensure Jeffersonian ends, for using strong central government to guarantee the rights of the people.

Wilson responded with a program and a slogan of his own: the **New Freedom**. Drawing on the writings of Louis Brandeis, he emphasized the Jeffersonian tradition of limited government with open competition. He spoke of the "curse of bigness" and argued against too much federal power. "What I fear is a government of experts," Wilson declared, implying that Roosevelt's New Nationalism would mean regulated monopolies and even collectivism.

This was one of the few elections in American history in which important ideas were actually discussed. It also marked a watershed for political thought for liberals who rejected Jefferson's distrust of a strong central government. It is easy to exaggerate the differences between Roosevelt and Wilson. Both urged reform within the American system, defended corporate capitalism, and opposed socialism and radical labor organizations. Both wanted more democracy and stronger but conservative labor unions. Both were very different in style and substance from the fourth candidate, Eugene Debs, who ran on the Socialist party ticket in 1912.

Debs, at the time, was the most important socialist leader in the country. Socialism has always been a minority movement in the United States, but it stood at its pinnacle in the first decade of the twentieth century. Thirty-three cities had socialist mayors, and two socialists sat in Congress.

⦿—View the Image

Socialist Cartoon (1919)

at **www.myhistorylab.com**

The most important socialist periodical increased its circulation from about 30,000 in 1900 to nearly 300,000 in 1906. Its following was quite diverse. In the cities, some who called themselves socialists merely favored municipal ownership of street railways. Some reformers, such as Florence Kelley, joined out of frustration with the slow pace of reform. Many recent immigrants brought to the party a European sense of class and loyalty to socialism.

A tremendously appealing figure and a great orator, Debs had run for president in 1900, 1904, and 1908, but in 1912, he reached much wider audiences in more parts of the country. His message differed radically from that of Wilson or Roosevelt. Unlike the progressives, socialists argued for fundamental change in the American system. Debs polled almost 900,000 votes in 1912 (6 percent of the popular vote), the best showing ever for a socialist in the United States. Wilson received 6.3 million votes, Roosevelt a little more than 4 million, and Taft 3.5 million. Wilson garnered 435 electoral votes, Roosevelt 88, and Taft only 8.

Woodrow Wilson and the New Freedom

Wilson was elected largely because Roosevelt and the Progressive party split the Republican vote. But once elected, Wilson became a vigorous and aggressive chief executive who set out to translate his ideas about progres-

•⦿•—Read the Document

Woodrow Wilson, from The New Freedom *(1913)*

at **www.myhistorylab.com**

sive government into legislation. He was the first southerner elected president since Zachary Taylor in 1848 and only the second Democrat since the Civil War. Wilson, like Roosevelt, had to work with his party, and that restricted how progressive he could be. He was also constrained by his background and inclinations. Still, like Roosevelt, Wilson became more progressive during his presidency.

Tariff and Banking Reform

Wilson had a more difficult time than Roosevelt relating to small groups, but he was an excellent public speaker who dominated through the force of his intellect. He probably had an exaggerated belief in his ability to persuade and tended to trust his own intuition too much. His accomplishment in pushing a legislative program through Congress during his first two years in office was matched only by Franklin Roosevelt during the first months of the New Deal and by Lyndon Johnson in 1965. But his early success bred overconfidence, portending trouble.

Within a month of his inauguration, Wilson went before a joint session of Congress to outline his legislative program. He recommended reducing the tariff, freeing the banking system from Wall Street control, and restoring industrial competition. By appearing in person before Congress, he broke a precedent of written presidential messages established by Thomas Jefferson.

First on Wilson's agenda was tariff reform. The Underwood Tariff, passed in 1913, was not a free-trade bill, but it did reduce the schedule for the first time in many years. Attached to the Underwood bill was a provision for a small and slightly graduated income tax, recently allowed by passage of the Sixteenth Amendment. It imposed a modest rate of 1 percent on income over $4,000 (thus exempting a large portion of the population), with a surtax rising to 6 percent on high incomes. The income tax was enacted to replace the money lost from lowering the tariff. Wilson seemed to have no interest in using it to redistribute wealth.

A financial panic in 1907 had revealed the need for a central bank, and much of the private banking system was dominated by a few firms such as J. P. Morgan & Company, but few people could agree on what should be done. Progressive Democrats argued for a banking system and currency controlled by the federal government. But talk of banking reform raised the specter among conservative Democrats and the business community of socialism, populism, and the monetary ideas of William Jennings Bryan.

The **Federal Reserve System**, created by compromise legislation in 1913, was the first reorganization of the banking system since the Civil War. The law gave the federal government some control over the banking system. It also created a flexible currency, based on Federal Reserve notes, that could be expanded or contracted as need required. The Federal Reserve System was not without its flaws, as later developments would show, and it did not end the power of the large eastern banks; but it was an improvement, and it appealed to the part of the progressive movement that sought order and efficiency.

Wilson was not very progressive in some of his early actions. He failed to support a plan for long-term rural credit financed by the federal government. He opposed a woman suffrage amendment and refused to back an anti–child labor bill. And he ordered the segregation of blacks in several federal departments. "I sincerely believe it to be in their [the blacks'] best interest," he said in rejecting the NAACP's protests.

Moving Closer to a New Nationalism

Wilson and Roosevelt had vigorously debated how to control the great corporations. Wilson's solution was the Clayton Act, which prohibited various unfair trading practices, outlawed the interlocking directorate, and forbade corporations to purchase stock in other corporations if this tended to reduce competition. But the law was vague and hard to enforce, and the courts interpreted it to mean that labor unions remained subject to court injunctions during strikes.

More important was the creation of the **Federal Trade Commission** (FTC). Powerful enough to move directly against corporations accused of restricting competition, the FTC was the idea of Louis Brandeis. Wilson accepted it even though it seemed to move him more toward the philosophy of New Nationalism.

The FTC and the Clayton Act did not end monopoly. The success of Wilson's reform agenda appeared minimal in 1914, but the outbreak of war in Europe and the need to win the election of 1916 would force him into becoming more progressive.

Neither Wilson nor Roosevelt satisfied advanced progressives. Most of the efforts of the two progressive presidents were spent trying to regulate economic power rather than promoting social justice. Yet their most important legacy was their attempts to strengthen the office of president and the executive branch of the federal government. The nineteenth-century American presidents after Lincoln had been relatively weak, and much of the federal power had resided with Congress. The progressive presidents reasserted presidential authority, modernized the executive branch, and began the creation of the federal bureaucracy, which has had a major impact on the lives of Americans in the twentieth century.

Both Wilson and Roosevelt used the presidency to advertise and promote their reform agenda. TR called the office a "bully pulpit." He strengthened the Interstate Commerce Commission, and Wilson created the Federal Trade Commission, forerunners of many other federal regulatory bodies. By personally delivering his annual message before Congress, Wilson symbolized the new power of the presidency.

More than the increased power of the executive branch changed the nature of politics. The new bureaus, committees, and commissions brought to Washington a new kind of expert, trained in the universities, at the state and local level, and in the voluntary organizations. Julia Lathrop, a coworker of Jane Addams at Hull House, was typical. Appointed by President Taft in 1912 to become chief of the newly created Children's Bureau, she was the first woman ever named to such a position. She used her post not only to work for better child labor laws, but also to train a new generation of women experts who would take their positions in state, federal, and private agencies in the 1920s and 1930s. Other experts emerged in Washington during the progressive era to influence policy in subtle and important ways. The expert, the commission, the statistical survey, and the increased power of the executive branch were all legacies of the progressive era.

Conclusion
The Limits of Progressivism

The progressive era was a time when many Americans set out to promote reform because they saw poverty, despair, and disorder in the country transformed by immigration, urbanism, and industrialism. However, unlike the socialists, the progressives saw nothing fundamentally wrong with the American system. Progressivism, part of a global movement to regulate and control the worst aspects of industrialism, was largely a middle-class movement that sought to help the poor, the immigrants, and the working class. Yet the poor were rarely consulted about policy, and many groups, especially African Americans, were almost entirely left out of reform plans. Progressives had an optimistic view of human nature and an exaggerated faith in statistics, commissions, and committees. They talked of the need for more democracy, but they often succeeded in promoting bureaucracy and a government run by experts. Frances Kellor was one of those experts; she represented a growing group of well-educated women who found a role during the progressive era in the new government agencies and private foundations.

The progressives believed there was a need to regulate business, promote efficiency, and spread social justice, but these were often contradictory goals. In the end, their regulatory laws tended to aid business and to strengthen corporate capitalism, while social justice and equal opportunity remained difficult to achieve. By contrast, most of the industrialized nations of western Europe, especially Germany, Austria, France, and Great Britain, passed legislation during this period providing for old-age pensions and health and unemployment insurance.

Progressivism was a broad, diverse, and sometimes contradictory movement that had its roots in the 1890s and reached a climax in the early twentieth century. It began with many local movements and voluntary efforts to deal with the problems created by urban industrialism and moved to the state and finally the national level. Women played important roles in organizing reform, and many became experts at gathering statistics and writing reports. Eventually they began to fill positions in the new agencies in the state capitals and in Washington. Neither Theodore Roosevelt nor Woodrow Wilson was an advanced progressive, but during both their administrations, progressivism achieved some success. Both presidents strengthened the power of the presidency, and both promoted the idea that the federal government had the responsibility to regulate and control and to promote social justice. These positions would be evident as the United States became involved in the conflict later known as the First World War.

TIME*line*

1901 McKinley assassinated

Theodore Roosevelt becomes president

Robert La Follette elected governor of Wisconsin

Tom Johnson elected mayor of Cleveland

1903 Women's Trade Union League founded

Elkins Act

1904 Roosevelt reelected

Lincoln Steffens, *The Shame of the Cities*

1906 Upton Sinclair, *The Jungle*

Hepburn Act

Meat Inspection Act

Pure Food and Drug Act

1908 *Muller* v. *Oregon*

Danbury Hatters case

William Howard Taft elected president

1909 NAACP founded

1911 Frederick Taylor, *The Principles of Scientific Management*

Triangle Shirtwaist Company fire

1912 Progressive party founded by Theodore Roosevelt

Woodrow Wilson elected president

Children's Bureau established

Industrial Relations Commission founded

1913 Sixteenth Amendment (income tax) ratified

Underwood Tariff

Federal Reserve System established

Seventeenth Amendment (direct election of senators) passed

1914 Clayton Act

Federal Trade Commission Act

AFL has over 2 million members

Ludlow Massacre in Colorado

✓●─⌐**Study** and **Review** at **www.myhistorylab.com**

Questions for Review and Reflection

1. What social problems concerned the progressives and why?
2. What contributions did women make to the progressive movement?
3. Why did the United States lag behind several European countries in passing social legislation?
4. How did progressivism influence the policies of Theodore Roosevelt and Woodrow Wilson?

Key Terms

Federal Reserve System 641

Federal Trade Commission 642

Muckrakers 615

NAACP 636

New Freedom 639

New Nationalism 639

Progressive movement 613

Scientific management 625

Triangle Shirtwaist fire 627

20

The Great War

American Stories

A Young Man Enlists in the Great Adventure

On April 7, 1917, the day after the United States declared war on Germany, 22-year-old Edmund P. Arpin, Jr., from Grand Rapids, Wisconsin, enlisted in the army. The war seemed to provide a solution for his aimless drifting. It was not patriotism but his craving for adventure that led him to join the army. A month later, he was at Fort Sheridan, Illinois, along with hundreds of other eager young men, preparing to become an army officer. He felt pride, purpose, and especially comradeship, but the war was far away.

Arpin finally arrived with his unit in Liverpool, England, on December 23, 1917, aboard the *Leviathan*, a German luxury liner that the United States had seized and turned into a troop transport. American troops were not greeted as saviors. English hostility simmered partly because of the previous unit's drunken brawls. Despite the efforts of the U.S. government to protect soldiers from the sins of Europe, drinking seems to have been a preoccupation of Arpin's outfit. He also learned something about French wine and women, but he spent most of the endless waiting time learning to play contract bridge.

Arpin saw some of the horror of war when he went to the front with a French regiment, but his own unit did not go into combat until October 1918, when the war was almost over. He took part in the bloody Meuse-Argonne offensive, which helped end the war. But he discovered that war was not the heroic struggle of carefully planned campaigns that newspapers and books described. War was filled with misfired weapons, mix-ups, and erroneous attacks. Wounded in the leg in an assault on an unnamed hill and awarded a Distinguished Service Cross for his bravery, Arpin later learned that the order to attack had been recalled, but word had not reached him in time.

When the armistice came, Arpin was in a field hospital. He was disappointed that the war had ended so soon, but he was well enough to go to Paris to take part

Chapter Outline

The Early War Years

The United States
Enters the War

The Military Experience

Domestic Impact of the War

Planning for Peace

Conclusion: The Divided
Legacy of the Great War

in the victory celebration and to explore famous restaurants and nightclubs. In many ways, the highlight of his war experiences was not a battle or his medal, but his postwar adventure. With a friend, he went AWOL and explored Germany, making it back without being arrested.

Edmund Arpin was one of 4,791,172 Americans who served in the army, navy, or marines, one of the 2 million who went overseas, and one of the 230,074 who were wounded. Some of his friends were among the 48,909 who were killed. Mustered out in March 1919, he felt confused. Being a civilian was not nearly as exciting as being in the army and visiting exotic places.

In time, Arpin settled down. He became a successful businessman, married, and reared a family. A member of the American Legion, he periodically went to conventions and reminisced with men from his division about their escapades in France. Although the war changed their lives in many ways, most would never again feel the same sense of common purpose and adventure. "I don't suppose any of us felt, before or since, so necessary to God and man," one veteran recalled.

For Edmund P. Arpin, Jr., the Great War was the most important event of a lifetime. Just as war changed his life, so, too, did it alter the lives of most Americans. The power and influence of the federal government increased. Not only did the war promote woman suffrage, prohibition, and public housing, but it also helped create an administrative bureaucracy that blurred the lines between public and private, between government and business—a trend that continued through the twentieth century.

In this chapter, we examine the complicated circumstances that led the United States into war and share the wartime experiences of American men and women at home and abroad. How and why did the United States become involved with a war in Europe? How did war affect domestic policies and the lives of ordinary Americans? Why did a war "to make the world safe for democracy" also leave a legacy of prejudice and hate? The chapter concludes with a look at the idealistic efforts to promote peace at the end of the war, and the disillusion that followed. The Great War was a global war in every sense. It thrust the United States into world leadership, but was this a role that Americans desired?

The Early War Years

Few Americans expected the war that erupted in Europe in the summer of 1914 to affect their lives or to alter their comfortable world. But when a Serbian terrorist shot Archduke Franz Ferdinand of Austria-Hungary in Sarajevo, a place almost no Americans had even heard of, this precipitated a series of events that led to the most destructive war the world had ever known.

The Causes of War

The Great War, as everyone called it, was ultimately caused by intense rivalry over trade, empire, and military strength, yet it did not seem inevitable in 1914. There had been many wars throughout the nineteenth century, including the American Civil War, but most had been local conflicts. And there were many signs of international cooperation with agreements on telegraphs in 1865, postage in 1875, copyright in 1880, and even time zones by 1890. In addition, a World Court at The Hague in the Netherlands, set up in 1899, promised to solve international disputes, while politicians and diplomats predicted that improved technology and communications would lead to permanent peace.

Watch the Video
The Outbreak of World War I at **www.myhistorylab.com**

Paradoxically, this time of increased cooperation also witnessed a growing rivalry among nations, especially in Europe. A growing sense of nationalism, a pride in being French or English, intensified the competition to sustain and defend empires around the world. Germany, which was created in 1871

The Great War in Europe and the Middle East The Great War had an impact not only on Europe but also on North Africa and the Middle East. Even the countries that remained neutral felt the influence of global war. For most Americans, the war was in France on the western front. How did European empire expand the war into a global conflict?

from a number of small states, began to increase its navy, causing Great Britain to build more battleships. Rivalry and jealousy led to a series of treaties: Austria-Hungry and Germany (the **Central Powers**) became military allies and Britain, France, and Russia (the **Allied Powers**) agreed to assist one another in case of attack. Despite peace conferences and international agreements, many promoted by the United States, the European balance of power rested precariously on these treaties.

The assassination in Sarajevo destroyed that balance. The leaders of Austria-Hungary wanted to punish Serbia for killing Franz Ferdinand, the heir to the throne. Russia mobilized to aid Serbia. Germany, supporting Austria-Hungary, declared war on Russia and France. When Germany invaded Belgium to attack France, Britain declared war. The slaughter began. Within a few months, the Ottoman Empire (Turkey) and Bulgaria joined the Central Powers. Italy joined the Allies after being secretly promised additional territory after the war. Japan declared war on Germany in order to acquire German rights in China and the Pacific islands. Spain, Switzerland, the Netherlands, Denmark, Norway, Sweden, and initially the United States, remained neutral.

The American sense that the nation would never succumb to the barbarism of war, combined with the knowledge that they were insulated by the Atlantic, brought relief after the first shock wore off. President Woodrow Wilson's official proclamation of neutrality on August 4, 1914, reinforced the belief that the United States had no major stake in the outcome and would stay uninvolved. The president urged Americans to "be neutral in fact as well as in name . . . impartial in thought as well as in action." But it was difficult to stay uninvolved, at least emotionally.

American Reaction

Although many Americans worked to promote world peace and a few sought to end the war through mediation, others could hardly wait to leap into the adventure. Hundreds of young American men, mostly college students or recent graduates, joined ambulance units. Among the most famous were Ernest Hemingway, John Dos Passos, and e. e. cummings (as he spelled his name), who later turned their wartime adventures into literary masterpieces. Others volunteered for the French Foreign Legion or the Lafayette Escadrille—volunteer American pilots attached to the French army.

Many Americans saw war as a test of idealism and manhood because the only conflict they remembered was the "splendid little war" of 1898. Older Americans recalled the Civil War, whose horrors had faded, leaving only the memory of heroic triumphs. But Oliver Wendell Holmes, the Supreme Court justice who had been wounded in the Civil War, remarked, "War, when you are at it, is horrible and dull. It is only when time has passed that you see that its message was divine."

Early reports from the battlefields should have indicated that the message was anything but divine. This would be a modern war in which men died by the thousands, cut down by an improved and efficient technology of killing.

The New Military Technology

The Germans' plan called for a rapid strike through Belgium to attack Paris and the French army from the rear. However, the French stopped the Germans in September 1914, and the fighting bogged down. Soldiers on both sides dug miles of trenches and strung out barbed wire. Hundreds of thousands died in battles that gained only a few yards or nothing at all. Rapid-firing rifles, improved explosives, incendiary shells, and tracer bullets all added to the destruction. Most devastating of all was the improved artillery that could hit targets miles behind the lines. Machine guns neutralized frontal assaults, but generals on both sides continued to order their men to charge to almost certain death.

•●•─Read the Document

Adolf K.G.E. von Spiegel,
U-Boat 202 *(1919)*
at **www.myhistorylab.com**

The war was the last major conflict in which cavalry was used and the first to employ a new generation of military technologies. By 1918, airplanes were creating terror with their bombs. Tanks made a tentative appearance in 1916, but it was not until the last days of the war that this new offensive weapon began to neutralize the machine gun. Poison gas, first used in 1914, added special fear and horror to **trench warfare**.

The Great War was truly a global struggle. For most Americans, the war consisted of the western front in France and Belgium, but there was also bitter fighting in Russia and Italy, while submarines and battleships carried the fight around the world. European nations drew upon their empires for troops and supplies. On the western front, soldiers from New Zealand and Australia fought side by side with French-speaking black Africans. The British and the French fought in Africa, trying to capture the German colonies. The British occupied Mesopotamia (Iraq) and fought a bloody war against the Turks along the Black Sea. The Turks used the war to massacre an estimated 800,000 Armenians in one of the worst acts of genocide in history, but few protested at the time.

Neutrality in a Global Conflict

Despite Wilson's efforts to promote neutrality, most Americans favored the Allied cause. About 8 million people of German and Austro-Hungarian descent lived in the United States, and some supported the Central Powers. The anti-British feelings of some Irish Americans led them to side not so much with Germany as against England. A number of American scholars, physicians, and intellectuals fondly remembered studying in Germany, and they admired its culture and progressive social planning. For most Americans, however, the ties of language and culture tipped the balance toward the Allies. After all, did not the English-speaking people of the world have special bonds and responsibilities? Memories of Lafayette's role in the American Revolution and France's gift of the Statue of Liberty made many Americans pro-French.

Other reasons made real neutrality nearly impossible. The fact that U.S. trade with the Allies was much more important than with the Central Powers caused many American businesses to support the Allies. Wilson's advisers openly supported the French and British. Most newspaper owners and editors had close ethnic, cultural, and sometimes economic ties to the Allies. The newspapers were quick to picture the Germans as barbaric Huns and to accept atrocity stories, some of them planted by British propaganda experts. Gradually for Wilson, and probably for most Americans, the perception that England and France were fighting to preserve civilization from evil Prussians replaced the idea that all Europeans were decadent. But as for going to war to save civilization, let France and England do that.

Wilson sympathized with the Allies for practical and idealistic reasons. He wanted to keep the United States out of the war, but he did not object to using force to promote diplomatic ends. The war, he hoped, would show the futility of imperialism and would usher in a world of free trade in both products and ideas, a world in which the United States had a special role to play. Remaining neutral while maintaining trade with the belligerents became increasingly difficult. The need to trade and the desire to control the peace finally led the United States into the Great War.

World Trade and Neutrality Rights

The United States was part of an international economic community in 1914 in a way that it had not been during the nineteenth century. The outbreak of war in the summer of 1914 caused immediate economic panic in the United States. On July 31, 1914, the Wilson administration closed the stock exchange. It also discouraged loans by American banks to belligerent nations. Most difficult was the matter of neutral trade. Wilson insisted on Americans' right to trade with both sides and with other neutrals, but Great Britain instituted an illegal naval blockade, mined the North Sea, and began seizing American ships.

Although the illicit blockade interfered with free trade, Wilson eventually accepted British control of the sea. His conviction that the destinies of the United States and Great Britain were intertwined outweighed his idealistic belief in free trade and caused him to react more harshly to German than to British violations of international law. American trade with the Central Powers declined between 1914 and 1916 from $169 million to just over $1 million, whereas American trade with the Allies increased during the same period from $825 million to over $3 billion. At the same time, the U.S. government eased restrictions on private loans to belligerents. With dollars as well as sentiments, the United States gradually ceased to be neutral.

Germany retaliated against British control of the seas with submarine warfare. International law obligated a belligerent warship to warn a passenger or merchant ship before attacking, but a submarine rising to the surface to issue a warning would have been blown out of the water by an armed merchant ship. On February 4, 1915, Germany announced a submarine blockade of the British Isles. Until Britain gave up its campaign to starve the

German population, the Germans would sink even neutral ships. Wilson warned Germany that it would be held to "strict accountability" for illegal destruction of American ships or lives.

The escalating conflict placed American travelers at risk. In March 1915, a German submarine sank a British liner, killing 103 people, including one American. While Wilson's advisers debated how to respond, on May 7, 1915, a submarine torpedoed the British luxury liner *Lusitania* off the Irish coast. The unarmed liner, which was carrying war supplies, sank in 18 minutes with a loss of nearly 1,200 lives, including 128 Americans. Suddenly Americans realized that modern war killed civilians as easily as it killed soldiers.

Some Americans called for war. Wilson and most Americans had no intention of fighting, but the president rejected Secretary of State William Jennings Bryan's advice that Americans be prohibited from traveling on ships from the countries at war. Instead, he demanded reparation for the loss of American lives and a German pledge to cease attacking ocean liners without warning. Bryan resigned as secretary of state, charging that the United States was not being truly neutral. The president replaced him with Robert Lansing, a legal counsel at the State Department, who was more eager to oppose Germany, even at the risk of war.

The tense situation eased late in 1915. After a German submarine sank the British steamer *Arabic*, which claimed two American lives, the German ambassador promised that Germany would not attack ocean liners without warning. But the *Lusitania* crisis had riveted Americans' attention on the possibility of war. An outpouring of books and articles urged the nation to prepare for war, although a group of progressive reformers also formed the American Union Against Militarism.

Wilson sympathized with the preparedness groups to the extent of asking Congress on November 4, 1915, for an enlarged and reorganized army. The bill met great opposition, especially from southern and western congressmen, but the Army Reorganization Bill that Wilson signed in June 1916 increased the regular army to just over 200,000 and integrated the National Guard into the defense structure. Few Americans expected those young men to go to war. But soon Wilson used the army and the marines in Mexico and Central America.

Intervening in Mexico and Central America

Wilson envisioned a world purged of imperialism, a world of free trade, and a world where American ideas and American products would spread. Combining the zeal of a Christian missionary with the conviction of a college professor, he spoke of "releasing the intelligence of America for the service of mankind." Yet Wilson's administration used force more systematically than his predecessors.

At first, Wilson's foreign policy seemed to reverse the most callous aspects of dollar diplomacy in Central America. Secretary of State Bryan signed a treaty with Colombia in 1913 paying $5 million for the loss of Panama and virtually apologizing for Theodore Roosevelt's treatment of Colombia. But the Senate refused to ratify the treaty.

The change in spirit proved illusory. After a disastrous civil war in the Dominican Republic, the United States offered in 1915 to take over the country's finances and police force. When Dominican leaders rejected a treaty making their country virtually an American protectorate, Wilson ordered in the marines. They took control of the government in May 1916. Although Americans built roads, schools, and hospitals, the Dominican people resented their presence. Americans also intervened in Haiti, with similar results. In Nicaragua, Wilson kept the marines (sent by Taft in 1912) to prop up a pro-American regime and acquired the right through a treaty to intervene at any time to preserve order and protect American property. Except briefly in the mid-1920s, the marines remained until 1933.

Wilson's policy of intervention ran into its greatest difficulty in Mexico, a country that had been ruled by dictator Porfirio Díaz, who had long welcomed American investors. By 1910, more than 40,000 American citizens lived in Mexico, and more than $1 billion of American money was invested there. In 1911, however, Francisco Madero, a reformer who wanted to destroy the privileges of the upper classes, overthrew Díaz. Two years later, Madero was deposed and murdered by Victoriano Huerta, the head of the army.

To the shock of many diplomats and businessmen, Wilson refused to recognize the Huerta government and set out to remove what he called a "government of butchers." At first, he applied diplomatic pressure. Then, using a minor incident as an excuse, he asked Congress for power to involve American troops if necessary. Few Mexicans liked Huerta, but they liked North American interference even less, and they rallied around the dictator. The United States landed troops at Veracruz, Mexico. Mobs destroyed American property wherever they could find it. Wilson's action outraged many in Europe, Latin America, and the United States.

Wilson's intervention drove Huerta from power, but a civil war between the forces of Venustiano Carranza and those under General Francisco "Pancho" Villa ensued. The United States sent arms to Carranza, who was considered less radical than Villa, and Carranza's soldiers defeated Villa's. When Villa led what was left of his army in a raid on Columbus, New Mexico, in March 1916, Wilson sent an expedition under Brigadier General John Pershing to track down Villa and his men. An American army charged 300 miles into Mexico, but it was unable to catch the elusive villain. Mexicans feared that Pershing's army was planning to occupy northern Mexico. Carranza shot off a bitter note to Wilson, but Wilson refused to withdraw. Tensions rose. An American patrol attacked a Mexican garrison. Wilson finally agreed to recall the troops and to recognize the Carranza government. But this was in January 1917, and had it not been for the growing crisis in Europe, war would likely have resulted.

The United States Enters the War

A significant minority of Americans opposed going to war in 1917, and that decision would remain controversial when it was reexamined in the 1930s. But once involved, the government and the American people made the war into a patriotic crusade that influenced all aspects of American life.

Watch the **Video**

American Entry into World War I
at **www.myhistorylab.com**

The Election of 1916

In 1915 and 1916, Wilson had to think of reelection as well as preparedness, submarines, and Mexico. His chances seemed poor. If supporters of the Progressives in 1912 returned to the Republican fold, Wilson would probably lose. Because the Progressive party had done very badly in the 1914 congressional elections, Roosevelt seemed ready to seek the Republican nomination.

Wilson knew that he had to win over voters who had favored Roosevelt in 1912. In January 1916, he nominated Louis D. Brandeis to the Supreme Court. The first Jewish justice, Brandeis was confirmed over strong opposition. His appointment pleased the social justice progressives because he had always championed reform causes. They made it clear to Wilson that the real test for them was whether he supported the anti–child labor and workers' compensation bills pending in Congress.

Within a few months, Wilson reversed his earlier New Freedom doctrines, which called for limited government, and aligned the federal government on the side of reform. In August 1916, he pushed through Congress the Workmen's Compensation Bill, which gave some protection to federal employees, and the Keatings-Owen Child Labor Bill, which barred from interstate commerce goods produced by children under the age of 14 and in some cases under the age of 16. This bill, later declared unconstitutional, was a far-reaching proposal that for the first time used federal control over interstate commerce to dictate the conditions under which products could be manufactured. To attract farm support, Wilson backed the Federal Farm Loan Act to extend long-term credit to farmers. Urged on by organized labor as well as by many progressives, he supported the Adamson Act, establishing an eight-hour day for all interstate railway workers.

The flurry of legislation early in 1916 provided a climax to the progressive movement. The strategy seemed to work, for progressives of all kinds enthusiastically endorsed the president.

The election of 1916, however, turned as much on foreign affairs as on domestic policy. Ignoring Roosevelt, Republicans nominated staid Charles Evans Hughes, a former governor of New York and future Supreme Court chief justice. Their platform called for "straight and honest neutrality" and "adequate preparedness." Hughes attacked Wilson for not promoting American rights in Mexico more vigorously and for giving in to what he called labor's unreasonable demands. Wilson implied that electing Hughes would guarantee war with both Mexico and Germany and that his opponents were somehow not "100 percent Americans." As the campaign progressed, the peace issue became more important, and the cry "He kept us out of war" echoed through every Democratic rally. It was a slogan that would soon seem strangely ironic.

The election was extremely close. Wilson went to bed on election night thinking he had lost, and the result was not clear until he won California by less than 4,000 votes. Wilson triumphed by carrying the West as well as the South.

Deciding for War

Wilson's victory in 1916 seemed to be a mandate for staying out of the European war. But the campaign rhetoric made the president nervous. He had tried to emphasize Americanism, not neutrality.

•••⌐Read the **Document**
President Wilson's War Message to Congress (1917)
at **www.myhistorylab.com**

Those who supported Wilson as a peace candidate applauded in January 1917 when he went before the Senate to clarify the American position on a negotiated settlement of the war. The German government had indicated earlier that it might be willing to go to the conference table. Wilson outlined a plan for a negotiated settlement, without indemnities or annexations. The agreement Wilson outlined could have worked only if Germany and the Allies were willing to settle for a draw.

Early in 1917, however, German leaders thought they could win. On January 31, 1917, Berlin announced that any ship, belligerent or neutral, sailing toward Britain or France would be sunk on sight. A few days later, the United States broke diplomatic relations with Germany. An intercepted telegram from the German foreign secretary, Arthur Zimmermann, to the German minister in Mexico increased anti-German feeling. If war broke out, the German minister was to offer Mexico the territory it had lost in Texas, New Mexico, and Arizona. In return, Mexico would join Germany in a war against the United States. When this telegram was released to the press on March 1, 1917, many Americans demanded war against Germany. Wilson still hesitated.

As the country waited on the brink of war, news of revolution in Russia reached Washington. In an event as important as the war itself, Russian workers, housewives, and soldiers rose up in March 1917 against the tsarist government's inept conduct of the war. The army had suffered staggering losses. Civilian conditions were desperate. Food was scarce, and the railroads and industry had nearly collapsed. At first, Wilson and other Americans were enthusiastic about the new republic led by Alexander Kerensky, who promised to continue the struggle against Germany. But within months, the revolution took a more extreme turn. Vladimir Ilyich Ulyanov, known as Lenin, returned from exile in Switzerland and led the radical Bolsheviks to victory over the Kerensky regime in November 1917. The Bolsheviks replaced the Russian empire with four socialist republics, which later established the Union of Soviet Socialist Republics (the Soviet Union) in 1922.

Lenin, a brilliant revolutionary tactician, was a follower of Karl Marx (1818–1883). Marx was a German radical philosopher who had described the alienation of the working class under capitalism and predicted a growing split between the proletariat (unpropertied workers) and the capitalists. Lenin extended Marx's ideas and argued that capitalist nations eventually would be forced to go to war over raw materials and markets. Believing that capitalism and imperialism went hand in hand, Lenin argued that the only way to end imperialism was to end capitalism. Communism, Lenin predicted, would eventually dominate the globe. The Russian Revolution threatened Wilson's vision of the world and his plan to bring the United States into the war "to make the world safe for democracy."

Then in the North Atlantic, German submarines sank five American ships between March 12 and March 21, 1917. On April 2, Wilson urged Congress to declare war. "It is a fearful thing," he concluded, "to lead this great, peaceful people into war, into the most terrible and disastrous of all wars." The war resolution swept the Senate 82 to 6 and the House of Representatives 373 to 50.

A Patriotic Crusade

Once war was declared, most Americans forgot their doubts. Young men rushed to enlist, and women volunteered to become nurses or to serve in other ways. But not all Americans applauded. Some pacifists and socialists and a few others opposed the U.S. entry into the war. "To whom does war bring prosperity?" Senator George Norris of Nebraska asked on the Senate floor. "Not to the soldier, . . . not to the broken hearted widow, . . . not to the mother who weeps at the death of her brave boy. . . . I feel that we are about to put the dollar sign on the American flag."

To convince senators and citizens alike that the war was real and that American participation was just, Wilson appointed a Committee on Public Information, headed by journalist George Creel. His committee launched a gigantic campaign to persuade the American public that the United States had gone to war to promote democracy and prevent the "Huns" from overrunning the world.

View the Image
Gee! I Wish I Were a Man!
at **www.myhistorylab.com**

The patriotic crusade soon became stridently anti-German and anti-immigrant. Most school districts forbade teaching German. Sauerkraut was renamed "liberty cabbage." Many families Americanized German surnames. Several cities banned music by German composers. South Dakota prohibited speaking German on the telephone. The most notorious incident occurred in East St. Louis, Illinois, which had a large German population.

Read the Document
Joseph Buffington, "Friendly Words to the Foreign Born" (1917)
at **www.myhistorylab.com**

In April 1918, a mob seized Robert Prager, a young German American, stripped off his clothes, dressed him in an American flag, marched him through the streets, and lynched him. Brought to trial, the ringleaders were acquitted on the grounds that the lynching was a "patriotic murder."

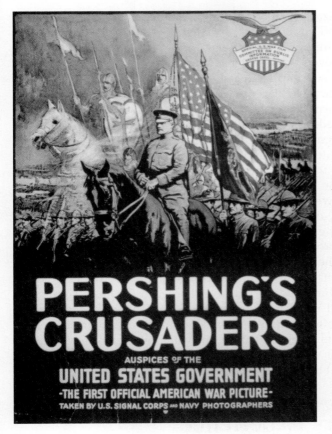

Pershing's Crusaders
This official 1917 U.S. government publication compares American soldiers to medieval knights. It makes explicit the American belief that by entering World War I, they were joining not only a war but also a crusade to make the world safe for democracy. How is this message conveyed by symbols and text? How do you suppose Europeans reacted to this American sense of mission and superiority?

The heated patriotism fanned by the war led to irrational hatreds and fears. Radicals, pacifists, and anyone with doubts about the American war efforts or the government's policies came under suspicion. The Los Angeles police ignored complaints that Mexicans were being harassed because they believed that all Mexicans were pro-German. Senator Robert La Follette, who had voted against declaring war, was burned in effigy and censured by the University of Wisconsin. At a number of universities, professors were dismissed, sometimes for questioning the morality or necessity of America's participation in the war.

On June 15, 1917, Congress, at Wilson's behest, passed the Espionage Act, providing imprisonment of up to 20 years or a fine of up to $10,000, or both, for people who aided the enemy or who "willfully cause . . . insubordination, disloyalty, mutiny or refusal of duty in the military . . . forces of the United States." The act also authorized the postmaster general to bar from the mails any matter he thought advocated treason or forcible resistance to U.S. laws.

Congress later added the Trading with the Enemy Act and a Sedition Act. The latter prohibited disloyal, profane, scurrilous, or abusive remarks about the form of government, flag, or uniform of the United States.

It even prohibited citizens from opposing the purchase of war bonds. In the most famous case tried under the act, Socialist Eugene Debs was sentenced to 10 years in prison for opposing the war. In 1919, the Supreme Court upheld the conviction, even though Debs had not explicitly urged violating the draft laws. While still in prison, Debs polled close to 1 million votes in the presidential election of 1920. Ultimately, the government prosecuted 2,168 people under the Espionage and Sedition Acts and convicted about half of them. These figures do not include the thousands who were persecuted informally. One woman was sentenced to prison for writing, "I am for the people and the government is for the profiteers." Ricardo Flores Magon, a leading Mexican American labor organizer and radical in the Southwest, got 20 years in prison for criticizing Wilson's Mexican policy and violating the **Neutrality Acts**.

●❖●[Read **the Document**

Eugene Debs, Critique
of World War I *(1916)*
at **www.myhistorylab.com**

The Civil Liberties Bureau, an outgrowth of the American Union Against Militarism, protested the blatant abridgment of freedom of speech during the war, but the protests fell on deaf ears at the Justice Department and in the White House. Rights and freedoms have been reduced or suspended during all wars, but the massive disregard for basic rights was greater during World War I than during the Civil War—especially ironic because Wilson had often written and spoken of the need to preserve freedom of speech and civil liberties. During the war, however, he tolerated the vigilante tactics of his own Justice Department. Wilson was so convinced his cause was just that he ignored the rights of those who opposed him.

The Military Experience

For years afterward, men and women who lived through the war (like Edmund Arpin and his friends) remembered nostalgically what it had meant to them. They sang the songs popular during the war, and they carefully preserved their wartime photos. For some, the war was a tragedy in which they saw the horrors of the battlefield firsthand. For others, it was liberating—the most exciting adventure in their lives.

The American Doughboy

The typical soldier stood 5 feet 7½ inches tall, weighed 141½ pounds, and was about 22 years old. He took a physical exam, an intelligence test, and a psychological test, and he probably watched a movie called *Fit to Fight*, warning about venereal disease. The majority of American soldiers had not attended high school. The median amount of education for native whites was 6.9 years, and for immigrants 4.7 years, but only 2.6 years for southern blacks. As many as 31 percent of the recruits were declared illiterate, but the tests were so primitive that they probably tested social class more than anything else. Fully 29 percent of the recruits were rejected as physically unfit for service, shocking health experts.

Trench Warfare World War I, especially on the western front, was a war of position and defense. Troops on both sides lived in elaborate trenches that turned into a sea of mud when it rained. The men tried to protect themselves with barbed wire and gas masks against new and terrifying technology. But there was little defense against the machine gun, which mowed down the troops as they charged from their trenches. Here American soldiers from the New York National Guard, part of the 42nd Division, dig in behind their sandbag-lined trenches in the woods near the Marne River in June 1918. What attitudes toward war might be formed among these soldiers?

Most World War I soldiers were ill-educated, unsophisticated young men from farms, small towns, and urban neighborhoods. Coming from all classes and ethnic groups, most were transformed into soldiers. The military experience changed the lives and often the attitudes of many young men. Women also contributed to the war effort as telephone operators and clerk-typists in the navy and the marines, as nurses, or with organizations such as the Red Cross. Yet the military experience was predominantly male. Even going to training camp was new and often frightening. A leave in Paris or London, or even in New York or New Orleans, was an adventure to remember for a lifetime. Many soldiers saw their first movie or their first truck in the army. Men learned to shave with the new safety razor and to wear the new wristwatch. The war also popularized the cigarette, which, unlike a pipe or cigar, could be smoked during a short break.

More than 75 percent of soldiers who served in the war were drafted. Wilson and his secretary of war, Newton Baker, both initially opposed the

View the Image
Soldiers Taking an IQ Test During World War I
at **www.myhistorylab.com**

RECOVERING *the* PAST

Government Propaganda

All governments produce propaganda. Especially in time of war, governments try to convince their citizens that the cause is important and worthwhile even if it means sacrifice. Before the United States entered the war, both Great Britain and Germany presented their side of the conflict through stories planted in newspapers, photographs, and other devices. Some historians argue that the British propaganda depicting the Germans as barbaric Huns who killed little boys and Catholic nuns played a large role in convincing Americans of the righteousness of the Allied cause.

When the United States entered the war, a special committee under the direction of George Creel did its best to persuade Americans that the war was a crusade against evil. The **Creel Committee** organized a national network of "four-minute men," local citizens with the proper political views, who could be used to whip up a crowd into a patriotic frenzy. These local rallies, enlivened by bands and parades, urged people of all ages to support the war effort and buy war bonds. The committee also produced literature for the schools, much of it prepared by college professors who volunteered their services. One pamphlet, titled *Why America Fights Germany*, described in lurid detail a possible German invasion of the United States. The committee also used the new technology of motion pictures, which proved to be the most effective propaganda device of all.

There is a narrow line between education and propaganda. As early as 1910, Thomas Edison made films instructing the public about the dangers of tuberculosis, and others produced movies that demonstrated how to avoid everything from typhoid to tooth decay. However, during the war, the government quickly realized the power of the new medium and adopted it to train soldiers, instill patriotism, and help the troops avoid the temptations of alcohol and sex.

After the United States entered World War I, the Commission on Training Camp Activities made a film called Fit to Fight that was shown to almost all male servicemen. It was an hour-long drama following the careers of five young recruits. Four of them, by associating with the wrong people and through lack of willpower, catch venereal disease. The film interspersed a simplistic plot with grotesque shots of men with various kinds of VD. The film also glorified athletics, especially football and boxing, as a substitute for sex. It emphasized the importance of patriotism and purity for America's fighting force. In one scene, Bill Hale, the only soldier in the film to remain pure, breaks up a peace rally and beats up the speaker. "It serves you right," the pacifist's sister remarks. "I'm glad Billy punched you."

Fit to Fight was so successful that the government commissioned another film, *The End of the Road*, to be shown to women who lived near military bases. The film is the story of Vera and Mary. Although still reflecting progressive attitudes, the film's message is somewhat different from that of *Fit to Fight*. Vera's strict mother tells her daughter that sex is dirty, leaving Vera to pick up "distorted and obscene" information about sex on the street. She falls victim to the first man who comes along

draft, but in the end concluded that it was the most efficient way to organize military manpower. Ironically, Theodore Roosevelt tipped Wilson in favor of the draft. With failing health and blind in one eye, the old Rough Rider wanted to recruit a volunteer division and lead it personally against the Germans. The thought of Roosevelt, whom Wilson considered his enemy, blustering about Europe so frightened Wilson that he supported the Selective Service Act in part, at least, to forestall such volunteer outfits as Roosevelt planned.

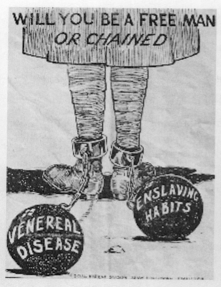

Anti-VD poster issued by the U.S. Commission on Training Camp Activities.

Scene from *Fit to Fight*.

and contracts a venereal disease. Mary, in contrast, has an enlightened mother who explains where babies come from. When Mary grows up, she rejects marriage and becomes a professional woman, a nurse. In the end, she falls in love with a doctor and gets married. *The End of the Road* has a number of subplots and many frightening shots of syphilitic sores. Several illustrations show the dangers of indiscriminate sex. Among other things, the film preached the importance of science and sex education and the need for self-control.

REFLECTING ON THE PAST What do the anti-VD films tell us about the attitudes, ideas, and prejudices of the World War I period? What images do they project about men, women, and gender roles? Would you find the same kind of moralism, patriotism, and fear of VD today? How have attitudes toward sex changed? Were you shown sex education films in school? Were they like these? Who sponsored them? What can historians learn from such films? Does the government produce propaganda today?

More than 24 million men registered for the draft, and more than 2.8 million of them were inducted. Draft protests erupted in a few places, the largest in Oklahoma, where a group of tenant farmers planned a march on Washington to take over the government and end the "rich man's war." A local posse arrested about 900 protesters and took them off to jail.

Some men escaped the draft. Thousands were deferred because of war-related jobs, and others resisted by claiming exemption for reasons of conscience. The Selective Service Act exempted men who belonged to pacifist religious groups, but religious motivation was often difficult to define, and nonreligious conscientious objection was even more complicated. Thousands of conscientious objectors were inducted. Some served in non-combat positions; others went to prison.

The African American Soldier

African Americans had served in all American wars, and many fought valiantly in the Civil War and the Spanish-American War. Yet black soldiers had most often performed menial work in segregated units. Black leaders hoped it would be different this time. W. E. B. Du Bois urged blacks to support the war, predicting that the war experience would cause the "walls of prejudice" to crumble gradually before the "onslaught of common sense." But the walls did not crumble.

View the Image

African American Soldiers Under French Command, World War I

at **www.myhistorylab.com**

The Selective Service Act made no mention of race, and African Americans in most cases registered without protest. Many whites, especially in the South, at first feared having too many blacks trained in the use of arms. In some areas, draft boards exempted single white men but drafted black fathers. Still, most southern whites found it difficult to imagine a black man in the uniform of the U.S. Army.

White attitudes toward African Americans sometimes led to conflict. In August 1917, violence erupted in Houston, Texas, involving soldiers from the regular army's all-black 24th Infantry Division. Harassed by the Jim Crow laws, which had been tightened for their benefit, a group of soldiers went on a rampage, killing 17 white civilians. More than 100 soldiers were court-martialed; 13 were condemned to death and hanged three days later before appeals could be filed.

Some African Americans were trained as junior officers and were assigned to the all-black 92nd Division, where the high-ranking officers were white. But blacks were officially considered unfit to fight. Most of the black soldiers, including about 80 percent of those sent to France, worked as stevedores and common laborers under white noncommissioned officers. Other black soldiers acted as servants, drivers, and porters for the white officers. It was a demeaning and ironic policy for a government that advertised itself as standing for justice, honor, and democracy.

Over There

The conflict that Wilson called the war "to make the world safe for democracy" became a contest of stalemate and slaughter. When the United States went to war in the spring of 1917, the fighting had dragged on for nearly three years. In one battle in 1916, a total of 60,000 British soldiers were killed or wounded in a single day, yet the battle lines did not move an inch. To this ghastly war, Americans made important contributions; without their

Hear the Audio

Over There

at **www.myhistorylab.com**

help, the Allies might have lost. But the American contribution was most significant only in the war's final months.

By the spring of 1917, the British and French armies were down to their last reserves. Italy's army had nearly collapsed. In the East, Russia plunged into a bitter internal struggle, and soon Lenin made a separate peace, which freed German divisions in the East to join in one final assault in the West. The Allies desperately needed fresh American troops, but those troops had to be trained, equipped, and transported to the front.

Token American regiments arrived in France in the summer of 1917 under the command of "Black Jack" Pershing, who had led the Mexican expedition in 1916. When they paraded in Paris on July 4, 1917, the crowd showered them with flowers. But the American commanders worried that many of their soldiers were so inexperienced they did not know how to march, let alone fight. The first American units saw action near Verdun in October 1917. By March 1918, more than 300,000 American soldiers reached France, and by November 1918, that number rose to more than 2 million.

One reason that the U.S. forces were slow to see combat was Pershing's insistence that they be kept separate from French and British divisions. An exception was made for four regiments of black soldiers who were assigned to the French army. Despite the American warning to the French not to "spoil the Negroes" by allowing them to mix with the French civilian population, these soldiers fought so well that the French later awarded three of the regiments the Croix de Guerre, their highest unit citation.

In the spring of 1918, with Russia out of the war and the British blockade becoming more and more effective, the Germans launched an all-out offensive to win the war before full American military and industrial power became a factor. By late May, the Germans pushed within 50 miles of Paris. American troops helped stem the German advance at Château-Thierry, Belleau Wood, and Cantigny, names that proud survivors later endowed with almost sacred significance. Americans also took part in the Allied offensive in the summer of 1918.

In September, more than a half million American troops fought near St. Mihiel, the first battle where large numbers of Americans went into action. One enlisted man "saw a sight which I shall never forget. It was zero hour and in one instant the entire front as far as the eye could reach in either direction was a sheet of flame, while the heavy artillery made the earth quake." The Americans suffered more than 7,000 casualties, but they captured more than 16,000 German soldiers.

In the fall of 1918, the combined British, French, and American armies drove the Germans back in the Meuse-Argonne offensive, the final battle of the war. Faced with low morale among the German soldiers and finally the mutiny of the German fleet and Austria-Hungary's surrender, Kaiser Wilhelm II abdicated, and the armistice was signed on November 11. More than a million American soldiers took part in the final offensive. Many were inexperienced, and some "90-day wonders" had never handled a rifle before arriving in France. Edmund Arpin was wounded in an unnecessary battle. There were many other mistakes, some disastrous. The most famous blunder was the "lost battalion," which advanced beyond its support and was cut off and surrounded. It suffered 70 percent casualties.

The performance of the all-black 92nd Division was also controversial. The 92nd had been deliberately dispersed around the United States and had never trained as a unit. Its higher officers were white, and they repeatedly asked to be transferred. Many of its men were partly trained and poorly equipped, and they were continually being called away to work as common laborers. At the last minute during the Meuse-Argonne offensive, the 92nd was assigned to a particularly difficult position on the line, without maps or wire cutters. Battalion commanders lost contact with their men, and several times the troops ran in the face of enemy fire. The division was withdrawn in disgrace. For years, politicians and military leaders used this incident to claim that black soldiers would never make good fighting men, ignoring the difficulties under which the 92nd fought and the valor shown by black troops assigned to the French army.

The war produced a few American heroes. Joseph Oklahombie, a Choctaw, overran several German machine gun nests and captured more than 100 German soldiers. Sergeant Alvin York, a former conscientious objector from Tennessee, single-handedly killed or captured 160 Germans using only his rifle and pistol. But his heroics were not typical. Artillery, machine guns, and, near the end, tanks, trucks, and airplanes won the war.

With few exceptions, the Americans fought hard and well. Although the French and British criticized the Americans' inexperience and disarray, they admired their exuberance, "pep," and ability to move large numbers of men and equipment efficiently. Sometimes the Americans simply overwhelmed the enemy with their numbers. They suffered over 120,000 casualties in the Meuse-Argonne campaign alone. One officer estimated that he lost 10 soldiers for every German his men killed in the final offensive.

The United States entered the war late but still lost 53,402 service personnel killed in battle and 63,114 who died from other causes, such as accidents, disease, and suicide. More than 200,000 Americans were wounded. But the British lost 900,000 men, the French 1.4 million, and the Russians 1.7 million. The United States contributed huge amounts of men and supplies in the last months of the war, and that finally tipped the balance. But it had entered late and sacrificed little compared with France and England. That would influence the peace settlement.

Thousands of American servicemen died from influenza, part of a pandemic that swept the world in the fall of 1918 and killed an estimated 50 million people. Unlike most epidemics, which were most deadly for children and the elderly, this one hit hardest among young adults. There were no antibiotics to treat the disease, and surgical masks, required in some cities, did not work. In a little more than a year, 675,000 people in the United States died from the flu. The speed with which the disease spread around the world was another reminder that in the modern age all countries were interconnected and isolation impossible.

Domestic Impact of the War

For at least 30 years before the United States entered the Great War, a debate raged over the proper role of the federal government in regulating industry and protecting people who could not protect themselves. Even within the Wilson administration, advisers disagreed on the proper role of the federal government. But the war and the problems it raised increased the power of the federal government. The wartime experience did not end the debate, but the United States emerged from the war a more modern nation, with more power residing in Washington.

Financing the War

The war, by one calculation, cost the United States more than $33 billion, and interest and veterans' benefits brought the total to nearly $112 billion. Early on, when an economist suggested that the war might cost the United States $10 billion, everyone had laughed. Yet many in the Wilson administration knew the war was going to be expensive, and they set out to raise the money by borrowing and by increasing taxes.

Secretary of the Treasury William McAdoo shouldered the task of financing the war. Studying the policies that Treasury Secretary Salmon Chase had followed during the Civil War, he decided that Chase should have appealed to popular emotions. His campaign to sell liberty bonds to ordinary American citizens at a very low interest rate stirred patriotism. "Lick a Stamp and Lick the Kaiser," one poster urged. Celebrities promoted the bonds, Boy Scouts sold them, and McAdoo implied that people who did not buy them were traitors.

The public responded enthusiastically, but they discovered after the war that their bonds had dropped to about 80 percent of face value. Because the interest on the bonds was tax-exempt, well-to-do citizens profited more from buying the bonds than did ordinary people. But the wealthy were not as pleased with McAdoo's other plan to finance the war by raising taxes. The War Revenue Act of 1917 boosted the tax rate sharply, taxed excess profits, and increased estate taxes. The next year, the tax rate on the largest incomes soared to 77 percent. The wealthy protested, but a number of progressives were just as unhappy, for they wanted the government to confiscate all income over $100,000 a year. Despite taxes and liberty bonds, however, World War I, like the Civil War, was financed in large part by inflation. Food prices, for example, nearly doubled between 1917 and 1919.

At first, Wilson tried to work through state agencies to mobilize resources. The need for more central control soon led Wilson to create a series of emergency federal agencies. To deal with food shortages caused by poor grain crops for two years and an increasing demand for American food in Europe, Wilson appointed Herbert Hoover, a young engineer who had won great prestige organizing relief for Belgium, to direct the Food Administration. He instituted "wheatless" and "meatless" days and urged housewives to cooperate. Women emerged during the war as the most important group of consumers.

The Wilson administration used the authority of the federal government to organize resources for the war effort. The War Industries Board, led by Bernard Baruch, a Wall Street broker, used government power to control scarce materials and, on occasion, to set prices and priorities. The government also went into the shipbuilding business and ran the railroads. When a severe winter and a lack of coordination brought the rail system near collapse in December 1917, Wilson put all the nation's railroads under the control of the United Railway Administration. The increasing power of the federal government led some businessmen to complain of "war socialism" and regulation.

War Workers

The Wilson administration sought to protect and extend the rights of organized labor during the war, while mobilizing workers to keep the factories running. The National War Labor Board insisted on adequate wages and reduced hours, and it tried to prevent exploitation of working women and children. If a munitions plant refused to accept the board's decision, the government seized it. When workers threatened to strike, the board often ruled that they either had to work or be drafted.

The Wilson administration favored the conservative labor movement of Samuel Gompers and his AFL. The Justice Department conducted massive raids on the offices of the more radical Industrial Workers of the World and arrested most of the leaders.

Gompers took advantage of the crisis to strengthen the AFL's position. He lent his approval to administration policies by making it clear that he opposed the IWW, socialists, and communists. As the AFL won a voice in home-front policy, its membership increased from 2.7 million in 1916 to over 4 million in 1917. Organized labor's wartime gains, however, would prove only temporary.

The war also created new employment opportunities for women. Posters and patriotic speeches urged women to do their duty for the war effort. One poster showed a woman at her typewriter, the shadow of a soldier in the background, with the message: "STENOGRAPHERS, WASHINGTON NEEDS YOU."

Women responded to these appeals out of both patriotism and a need to increase their earnings and to make up for inflation, which cut real wages. Women went into every kind of industry. They labored in brickyards and factories, as railroad conductors, and in munitions plants. The Woman's Land Army mobilized female labor for the farms. But even though women demonstrated that they could do "male" jobs, their wartime progress proved temporary. Only about 5 percent of the women employed during the war, mostly unmarried, were new to the workforce. For most, it meant a shift of

Icewomen Women proved during the war that they could do "men's work." These two young women deliver ice, a backbreaking task, but one that was necessary in the days before electric refrigerators. Despite women like these, the war did not change the American ideal that women's proper place was in the home. Has that ideal changed since 1918?

occupations or a move up to a better-paying position. Moreover, the war accelerated trends already under way. It increased the need for telephone operators, sales personnel, secretaries, and other white-collar workers, and in these occupations women soon became a majority. Telephone operator became an almost exclusively female job by 1917.

In the end, the war did provide limited opportunities for some women, but it did not change the dominant perception that a woman's place was in the home. After the war was over, the men returned, and women's gains almost disappeared. There were 8 million women in the workforce in 1910 and only 8.5 million in 1920.

The Great Migration

With 4 million men in the armed forces and the flow of immigrants ended by the war, factories for the first time hired African Americans in large numbers. By 1920, new industrial opportunities in the North encouraged more than 300,000 African Americans to seek an alternative to the discrimination, violence, and limitations on education in the South. The "Great Migration" transformed northern industrial cities including Chicago, Detroit, Cleveland, Pittsburgh, Philadelphia, and New York.

Northern labor agents actively recruited southern blacks, but the news from the North also spread by word of mouth and by reports in black newspapers such as the *Chicago Defender* and *Pittsburgh Courier*. Moving north required careful planning, not only because of the expense of travel but also because authorities in the South tried to prevent the outgoing tide of labor. Some migrants moved in stages, from the countryside to southern cities and then to the North. Some sent one family member ahead to find work before others followed. Organizations such as churches and the National Urban League, founded in 1911, helped migrants adjust to urban life.

The Great Migration set the stage for the cultural energy of the Harlem Renaissance in the 1920s and the rise of black political power in northern cities. But despite the hopes of migrants for a better life in the North, most found themselves limited to low-level jobs, in part because blacks were excluded from many unions representing skilled laborers. They also found that racial tension and violence existed in the North as well as the South. The worst of the violence occurred in 1917 in East St. Louis, Missouri, where whites retaliated against the employment of African Americans in a factory with government contracts. Forty blacks and eight whites died in the ensuing riot, which drove 6,000 African Americans from their homes.

•••—Read the Document

Letters from the Great Migration to Northern Cities (1917)

at **www.myhistorylab.com**

As African Americans trekked north, thousands of Mexicans crossed into the United States. Immigration officials relaxed regulations because of the need for labor in the farms and factories of the Southwest. Mexicans also found employment in the steel, cement, automotive, and meat-packing industries of the Midwest.

◉—See the Map

African American Population, 1910 and 1950

at **www.myhistorylab.com**

The Climax of Progressivism

Many progressives, especially the social justice progressives, opposed the entry of the United States into the war until a few months before Congress declared war. But after April 1917, many began to see the "social possibilities of war." They deplored the war's death and destruction, the abridgment of freedom of speech, and the extreme patriotism, but praised the social planning that war stimulated. They approved the Wilson administration's support of collective bargaining, the eight-hour day, and protection for women and children in industry. They welcomed government-owned housing projects, woman suffrage, and prohibition. Many endorsed the government takeover of the railroads and control of business. For many social justice progressives who had fought hard, long, and frustrating battles to humanize the industrial city, it was refreshing that suddenly people in high places were listening and approving.

One of the best examples of the progressives' influence on wartime activities was the Commission on Training Camp Activities, set up early in the war to mobilize, entertain, and protect American servicemen at home and abroad. It organized community singing and baseball, established post exchanges and theaters, and even provided university extension lectures. The overriding assumption was that the military experience would produce citizens ready to vote for social reform.

The Commission on Training Camp Activities also incorporated the progressive crusades against alcohol and prostitution. Laws banned liquor sales to men in uniform and prostitution and alcohol around military bases. "Fit to fight" was the motto. It was a typical progressive effort, combining moral indignation with scientific prophylaxis.

Suffrage for Women

In the fall of 1918, while American soldiers were mobilizing for the final offensive in France and hundreds of thousands of women were working in factories and serving as Red Cross and Salvation Army volunteers, Wilson asked the Senate to support woman suffrage as "vital to the winning of the war." Wilson had earlier opposed the vote for women. His positive statement at this late date was not necessary, but his voice was a welcome addition to a rising chorus of support for an amendment to the Constitution to permit the female half of the population to vote. Many still argued that voting would make women less feminine and less fit as wives and mothers. The National Association Opposed to Woman Suffrage declared that woman suffrage, socialism, and feminism were "three branches of the same Social Revolution."

Carrie Chapman Catt, an efficient administrator and tireless organizer, devised the strategy that finally secured the vote for women. In 1915, she became president of the National American Woman Suffrage Association (NAWSA), coordinating the state campaigns and directing a growing army of dedicated workers. The careful planning began to produce results, but a group of more militant reformers, impatient with the slow progress, broke off from NAWSA to form the National Woman's Party (NWP) in 1916. This group was led by Alice Paul, who had participated in suffrage battles in England. Paul and her group picketed the White House, chained themselves to the fence, and blocked the streets. They carried banners that asked, "MR. PRESIDENT, HOW LONG MUST WOMEN WAIT FOR LIBERTY?" In the summer of 1917, the government arrested more than 200 women and charged them with "obstructing the sidewalk." It was just the kind of publicity the militant group sought, and it made the most of it. Wilson, fearing more embarrassment, began to cooperate with moderate reformers.

The war did not cause the passage of the Nineteenth Amendment, but it did accelerate it. In 1917, 14 state legislatures petitioned Congress, urging enactment; an additional 26 states did the same in 1919. Early in 1919, the House of Representatives passed the amendment 304 to 90, and the Senate approved 56 to 25. Fourteen months later, the required 36 states had ratified, and women at last had the vote.

Planning for Peace

Wilson turned U.S. participation in the war into a crusade to make the world safe for democracy—and more. On January 8, 1918, partly to counter Bolshevik charges that the war was merely an imperialist struggle, he announced his plan. Called the **Fourteen Points**, it argued for "open covenants of peace openly arrived at," freedom of the seas, equality of trade, and the self-determination of all peoples. But his most important point, the fourteenth, called for a "league of nations" to preserve peace.

The Versailles Peace Conference

Late in 1918, Wilson announced that he would head the American delegation to Paris to attend the peace conference. Wilson and his entourage of college professors, technical experts, and advisers sailed for France on December 4, 1918. Secretary of State Lansing, Wilson's confidant Edward House, and a number of other advisers were there. Conspicuously missing was Henry Cabot Lodge, the most powerful man in the Senate, or any other Republican senator—a serious blunder, for the Republican-controlled Senate would have to approve the treaty. It is difficult to explain Wilson's lack of political insight, except to say that he hated Lodge and compromise with equal intensity and had supreme confidence in his ability to persuade.

Wilson's self-confidence grew during a triumphant tour through Europe before the conference. He was cheered enthusiastically by ordinary people, but he had greater difficulty convincing the political leaders at the peace conference.

Though Wilson was more naive and idealistic than his European counterparts, he won many concessions at the peace table, sometimes by threatening to go home. The Allied leaders were determined to punish Germany and enlarge their empires. Wilson believed that he could create a new kind of international relations based on his Fourteen Points. He did achieve limited endorsement of self-determination, his dream that each national group could have its own country and that people should decide in what country they wanted to live.

The peacemakers carved Austria, Hungary, and Yugoslavia out of what had been the Austro-Hungarian empire. They hoped that the new countries of Poland, Czechoslovakia, Finland, Estonia, Latvia, and Lithuania would help contain bolshevism in eastern Europe. France was to occupy Germany's industrial Saar region for 15 years, until a plebiscite determined whether its people wanted to be part of Germany or France. Italy gained the port of Trieste. Dividing up the map of Europe was difficult at best, but perhaps the biggest mistake that Wilson and other major leaders made was to give the small nations little power at the negotiating table and to exclude Soviet Russia entirely.

Europe and the Near East After World War I Led in part by President Wilson's goal to promote the self-determination of people and in part by a desire to block the expansion of Germany and the Soviet Union, the diplomats meeting at Versailles reconfigured the map of Europe and the Near East. How might these boundaries create future problems related to nationalism and ethnic conflict?

Wilson had to make major concessions at the peace conference. He was forced to agree that Germany should pay reparations (later set at $56 billion), lose much of its oil- and coal-rich territory, and admit war guilt. He accepted a mandate system that allowed France and Britain to take over portions of the Middle East and gave Germany's Pacific colonies as well as China's Shantung province to Japan. He acquiesced when the Allies turned Germany's African colonies into "mandate possessions" because they did not want to allow self-determination for blacks in Africa. Wilson did not envision a reordering of global race relations. He opposed a measure, introduced by Japan, that would have supported racial equality around the world. W. E. B. Du Bois, who was in Paris to attend the first Pan-African

Congress, supported the Japanese resolution and denounced colonialism. But Wilson and the others at Versailles ignored Du Bois.

This was not a "peace without victory," as Wilson had promised; and German feelings of betrayal would later have grave repercussions. Wilson did not achieve freedom of the seas or the abolition of trade barriers, but he did get the **League of Nations**, which he hoped would prevent future wars. The key to collective security was Article 10 of the league covenant, which pledged all members "to respect and preserve against external aggression the territorial integrity" of all other members.

Wilson's Failed Dream

While the statesmen met at Versailles to make peace and divide up Europe, a group of prominent and successful women (some from the Central Powers) convened in Zurich, Switzerland. The American delegation was led by Jane Addams and included Montana Congresswoman Jeannette Rankin, who had voted against war in 1917. They formed the **Women's International League** for Peace and Freedom with Addams as president and denounced the one-sided peace terms of the Versailles treaty that called for disarmament of only one side and exacted gigantic economic penalties from the Central Powers.

Hate and intolerance were legacies of the war. French Prime Minister Clemenceau especially wanted to humiliate Germany. The peace conference was also haunted by the Bolshevik success in Russia. This threat seemed so great that the Allies sent American and Japanese troops to Russia in 1919 to defeat bolshevism and create a moderate republic. By 1920, the mission had failed. The troops withdrew, but the Russians never forgot, and the threat of bolshevism remained.

Probably most Americans supported the concept of the League of Nations in the summer of 1919, yet the Senate refused to accept American membership. The League of Nations treaty, one commentator has suggested, was killed by its friends and not by its enemies.

First there was Lodge, who had earlier endorsed some kind of international peacekeeping organization. He objected to Article 10, claiming that it would force Americans to fight the wars of foreigners. Chairman of the Senate Foreign Relations Committee, Lodge (like Wilson) was a lawyer and a scholar as well as a politician. He disliked all Democrats, especially Wilson, whose missionary zeal infuriated him.

Then there was Wilson, whose only hope of passage of the treaty in the Senate was a compromise to bring moderate senators to his side. But Wilson refused to compromise or to modify Article 10. Angry at his opponents, who were exploiting the disagreement for political advantage, he stumped the country to convince the American people of the rightness of his plan. They did not need to be convinced. They greeted Wilson much the way the people of France had. Traveling by train, he gave 37 speeches in 29 cities in the space of three weeks. When he described the graves of American soldiers in France and announced that American boys would never again die in a foreign war, the people responded with applause.

After one dramatic speech in Pueblo, Colorado, Wilson collapsed. His health had been failing for some months, and the strain of the trip was too much. He was rushed back to Washington, where a few days later he suffered a massive stroke. For the final year and a half of his term, the president was incapable of running the government and could not lead a fight for the league.

The Senate finally killed the league treaty in March of 1920. Had the United States joined the League of Nations, it probably would have made little difference in the international events of the 1920s and 1930s, nor would American participation have prevented World War II. The United States did not resign from the world of diplomacy or trade, nor by that single act become isolated. But the rejection of the league treaty was symbolic of the refusal of many Americans to admit that the world and America's place in it had changed dramatically since 1914.

Conclusion
The Divided Legacy of the Great War

For Edmund Arpin and many of his friends who left small towns and urban neighborhoods to join the military forces, the war was a great adventure. For the next two decades, at American Legion conventions and Armistice Day parades, they continued to celebrate their days of glory. For others who served, the war's results were more tragic. Many died. Some came home injured, disabled by poison gas, or unable to cope with the complex world that had opened up to them.

In a larger sense, the war was both a triumph and a tragedy for the American people. The war created opportunities for blacks who migrated to the North, for women who found more rewarding jobs, and for farmers who suddenly discovered a demand for their products. But much of the promise and the hope proved temporary.

The war provided a certain climax to the progressive movement. The passage of the woman suffrage and prohibition amendments, and the use of federal power in a variety of ways to promote justice and order pleased reformers, who had been working toward these ends for many decades. But the results were often disappointing. Once the war ended, much federal legislation was dismantled or reduced in effectiveness, and votes for women had little initial impact on social legislation.

The Great War marked the coming of age of the United States as a world power, but the country seemed reluctant to accept the new responsibility. The war stimulated patriotism and pride in the country, but it also increased intolerance. With this mixed legacy from the war, the country entered the new era of the 1920s.

TIME*line*

1914	Archduke Franz Ferdinand assassinated
	World War I begins
	United States declares neutrality
	American troops invade Mexico and occupy Veracruz
1915	Germany announces submarine blockade of Great Britain
	Lusitania sunk
1916	Expedition into Mexico
	Wilson reelected
	Workmen's Compensation Bill
	Keatings-Owen Child Labor Bill
	Federal Farm Loan Act
	National Woman's Party founded
1917	Germany resumes unrestricted submarine warfare
	United States breaks relations with Germany
	Zimmermann telegram
	Russian Revolution
	United States declares war on Germany
	War Revenue Act
	Espionage Act
	Trading with the Enemy Act
	Selective Service Act
1918	Sedition Act
	Flu epidemic sweeps nation
	Wilson's Fourteen Points
	American troops intervene in Russian Revolution
1919	Paris peace conference
	Eighteenth Amendment prohibits alcoholic beverages
	Senate rejects Treaty of Versailles
1920	Nineteenth Amendment grants woman suffrage

✓•⌐Study and Review at **www.myhistorylab.com**

Questions for Review and Reflection

1. Why did the United States, so determined to stay out of the Great War in 1914, join the Allied cause enthusiastically in 1917?
2. Why did the war lead to hate, prejudice, and the abridgment of civil liberties?
3. How did the war affect women and minorities in America?

4. Why did Wilson's idealistic peace plan fail?
5. What were the long-range consequences of World War I? For the United States? For the world?

Key Terms

Allied Powers 649

Central Powers 649

Creel Committee 660

Fourteen Points 670

League of Nations 672

Lusitania 652

Neutrality Acts 658

Trench warfare 650

Women's International
League 672

21

Affluence and Anxiety

American Stories

Dreams and Setbacks in the Motor City

John and Lizzie Parker, who were among the many southern African Americans who sought a better life in the North during World War I, found their way to Detroit by the 1920s. They left behind lives as sharecroppers in central Alabama, where they lived in a "stubborn, ageless hut squatted on a little hill." Their first stop had been in West Virginia, where John Parker signed up with a mining company that offered free transportation out of the deep South. But the work was dirty and dangerous, and the houses were little better than the sharecroppers' cabins of Alabama.

John drifted to Detroit, where he got a job with the American Car and Foundry Company. It was 1918, and the pay was good, more than he had ever made before. After a few weeks, he rented an apartment and sent for his family. For the first time, Lizzie had a gas stove and an indoor toilet, and their seven-year-old daughter, Sally, started school. It seemed as if their dream had come true.

Detroit was not quite the dream, however. It was crowded with all kinds of migrants, attracted by the wartime jobs at the Ford Motor Company and other factories. The new arrivals increased racial tensions already present in the city. Sally was beaten up by a gang of white youths at school. Even in their neighborhood, which had been solidly Jewish before their arrival, the shopkeeper and the old residents made it clear that they did not like blacks moving in. The Ku Klux Klan, which gained many new members in Detroit, also made life uncomfortable for the blacks who had moved north to seek jobs and opportunity.

Almost immediately after the war ended, John lost his job. Then the landlord raised the rent, and the Parkers had to leave their apartment for housing in a section just outside the city near Eight Mile Road. The surrounding suburbs had paved streets, wide lawns, and elegant houses, but this black ghetto's dirt streets and shacks reminded the Parkers of the company town in West Virginia. Lizzie had to get along without her bathroom. There was no indoor plumbing and no electricity, only a pump in the yard and an outhouse.

The recession winter of 1921 to 1922 was particularly difficult. The auto industry and the other companies laid off most of their workers. John found only part-time employment, while Lizzie worked as a servant for white families. Because no bus route connected the black community to surrounding suburbs, she often had to trek miles through the snow. Their shack was freezing cold, and it was cramped because their older married daughter and her husband had joined them in Detroit.

Lizzie, however, did not give up her dream. With strength, determination, and a sense of humor, she kept the family together. In 1924, Sally entered high school. By the end of the decade, she had graduated from high school, and the Parkers finally had electricity and indoor plumbing, though the streets were still unpaved. Those unpaved streets symbolized their unfulfilled dream. The Parkers, like many African Americans in northern cities during the 1920s, had improved their lot, but they still lived outside Detroit—and, in many ways, outside America.

Like most Americans in the 1920s, the Parkers pursued the American dream of success. For them, a comfortable house, a steady job, a new bathroom, and an education for their younger daughter constituted that dream. For others during the decade, the symbol of success was a new automobile, a new suburban house, or perhaps making a killing in the stock market. The 1920s, the decade between the end of World War I and the stock market crash, has often been referred to as the "jazz age," a time when the American people had one long party complete with **flappers**, speakeasies, illegal bathtub gin, and young people doing the Charleston long into the night. This frivolous interpretation has some basis in fact, but most Americans did not share in the party, for they were too busy struggling to make a living.

In this chapter, we will explore some of the conflicting trends of an exciting decade. First, we will examine the intolerance that influenced almost all the events and social movements of the time. Why did such prejudices follow the intensely patriotic wartime years? We will also look at the booming economy and technological developments, especially the automobile, which changed life for almost everyone during the 1920s. How did the dramatic changes of the early twentieth century also create divisions in the culture? Who shared in the prosperity of the 1920s, and whose hopes were raised but not always fulfilled? We will close by considering the era's politics. What did President Calvin Coolidge mean when he said, "The chief business of the American people is business"?

Postwar Problems

Enthusiasm for social progress evaporated in 1919. The year after the war ended was marked by strikes and violence and by fear that Bolsheviks, blacks, foreigners, and others were destroying the American way of life. Some of the anxiety grew out of wartime patriotism, and some reflected the postwar economic and political turmoil that forced Americans to deal with new and immensely troubling situations.

Red Scare

Radicals and dissidents have often been feared as threats to the American way of life. In the early twentieth century, anarchists seemed the worst danger, but the Russian Revolution of 1917 suddenly made the Bolshevik the most dangerous radical, somehow mixed with that other villain, the German. In the spring of 1919, with the Bolsheviks advocating worldwide revolution, many Americans feared that the Communists planned to take over the United States.

Immediately after the war, there were perhaps 25,000 to 40,000 American Communists, but they never threatened the United States. Some were idealists such as John Reed, the son of a wealthy businessman, who had been converted to socialism in New York's Greenwich Village. Appalled by the carnage of the capitalistic war, Reed went to Russia as a journalist in 1917. His eyewitness account of the Bolshevik takeover, *Ten Days That Shook the World*, optimistically predicted a worldwide revolution. Seeing little hope for that revolution in postwar America, he returned to Moscow, where he died in 1920, disillusioned by the new regime's authoritarianism.

Though small in number, the Communists seemed to be a threat in 1919, especially as a series of devastating strikes erupted across the country. American workers had suffered from wartime inflation, which had almost doubled prices between 1914 and 1919, while most wages remained the same. In 1919, more than 4 million workers staged 4,000 strikes. Few wanted to overthrow the government; they demanded higher wages, shorter hours, and sometimes more control over the workplace.

From the beginning, corporate owners blamed the strikes on Bolsheviks, and the "bomb-throwing radical" became almost a cliché. On April 28, 1919, a bomb was discovered in a small package delivered to the home of the mayor of Seattle. The next day, the maid of a former senator opened a package and had her hands blown off. Other bombings occurred in June; one shattered the front of Attorney General A. Mitchell Palmer's home. The bombings seem to have been the work of a few misguided radicals who thought they might spark a revolution. But their effect was to convince many that revolution was a real and immediate threat.

No one was more convinced than Palmer. In the summer of 1919, he decided to destroy the Red network. He organized a special antiradical division within the Justice Department and put young J. Edgar Hoover in charge of coordinating information on domestic radical activities. Obsessed by the "Red Menace," Palmer instituted a series of raids to round up radical foreign workers. In December, 249 aliens, including the famous anarchist Emma Goldman, were deported, although few had any desire to overthrow the government of the United States.

The **Palmer raids**, probably the most massive violation of civil liberties in America up to that time, found few dangerous radicals but did increase fear and intolerance. Palmer briefly became a national hero, though in the end only about 600 aliens were deported out of more than 5,000 arrested. The worst of the "Red Scare" was over by the end of 1920, but fear of radicalism influenced almost every aspect of life during the 1920s.

The Red Scare promoted many patriotic organizations and societies determined to purge Communists. These organizations made little distinction between Communists, Socialists, progressives, and liberals, and they saw Bolsheviks everywhere. The best-known of the superpatriot organizations was the American Legion, but all provided a sense of purpose and belonging by attacking radicals and preaching patriotism.

A Rising Tide of Intolerance

The nation that had seemed to be so united during the Great War splintered into animosity along ethnic, religious, and racial lines. One result of the Red Scare and fear of foreign radicals was the conviction and sentencing of two Italian anarchists, Nicola Sacco and Bartolomeo Vanzetti. Arrested in 1920 for allegedly murdering a guard during a robbery in Massachusetts, Sacco and Vanzetti were sentenced to die in 1921 on what many liberals considered flimsy evidence. Indeed, it seemed to many that the two Italians, who spoke in broken English and were admitted anarchists, were punished because of their radicalism and foreign appearance.

The case took on symbolic significance as many intellectuals in Europe and America rallied to their defense. Appeal after appeal failed, and the two were electrocuted on August 23, 1927, despite massive protests and midnight vigils around the country. Recent evidence, including ballistic tests, suggests that they may have been guilty, but the trial and its aftermath pointed to the ethnic prejudice and divisions in American society.

Cases like **Sacco–Vanzetti** touched relatively few people, but intolerance affected millions of lives. Henry Ford published anti-Semitic diatribes. Barred from fashionable resorts, Jews built their own hotels in the Catskills in New York State and elsewhere. Many colleges, private academies, and medical schools had Jewish quotas, and many suburbs explicitly limited residents to "Christians." Catholics, too, were prohibited from many organizations, and few even tried to enroll in the elite colleges. Although prejudice and intolerance had always existed, during the 1920s much of that intolerance was made more formal; in some cases, it was translated into law.

Women of the Ku Klux Klan The Ku Klux Klan, with its elaborate rituals and uniforms, exploited the fear of blacks, Jews, liberals, and Catholics while preaching "traditional" values. The appeal of the Klan was not limited to the South, and many women joined. This is a photo of women Klan members marching in an America First Parade in Binghamton, New York. Why did so many women join the Klan? Is there anything like it today?

In race relations, intolerance accelerated into violence. Following the Great Migration of African Americans into northern cities during the war, racial friction sparked a "Red Summer" of riots in Chicago, Omaha, and more than twenty other cities during 1919. In Chicago the riot began on a hot July day when a black youth drowned in a white swimming area—hit by stones, blacks said, but the police refused to arrest any white men. When African Americans attacked the police, a four-day riot was on. Several dozen were killed, and hundreds were wounded.

A similarly explosive conflict occurred in 1921 in Tulsa, Oklahoma, after an African American man was accused of assaulting a white woman. The ensuing confrontations between blacks and whites around the city jail spread, leading to deaths, injuries, and the destruction of more than $1 million in property.

The wave of violence and racism angered and disillusioned W. E. B. Du Bois, who had urged African Americans to support the American cause during the war. In an angry editorial for *The Crisis*, he called on blacks to "fight a sterner, longer, more unbending battle against the forces of hell in our own land. We return. We return from fighting. We return fighting. Make way for Democracy; we saved it in France, and by the Great Jehovah, we will save it in the United States of America, or know the reason why."

Ku Klux Klan

Among the superpatriotic organizations claiming to protect the American way of life, the Ku Klux Klan was the most extreme. Postwar fear and confusion, along with aggressive recruiting, explained its explosive growth.

The Klan was revived in Georgia by William J. Simmons, a lay preacher, salesman, and member of many fraternal organizations. He adopted the name and white-sheet garb of the old anti-black Reconstruction organization that was glorified in 1915 in the immensely popular but racist film *Birth of a Nation*. Simmons appointed himself head ("Imperial Wizard") of the new Klan, which was thoroughly Protestant and antiforeign, anti-Semitic, and anti-Catholic. It opposed the teaching of evolution; glorified old-time religion; supported immigration restriction; denounced short skirts, petting, and "demon rum"; and upheld patriotism and the purity of women. The Klan was also militantly antiblack; its members took as their special mission the task of keeping blacks in their "proper place." They often used peaceful measures to accomplish their aim, but if those failed, they resorted to violence, kidnapping, and lynching. The Klan grew slowly until after the war, but added over 100,000 new members in 1920 alone.

View the **Image**
Ku Klux Klan on Parade (1928)
at **www.myhistorylab.com**

The Klan flourished in the small-town and rural South, but soon it spread throughout the country. It was especially strong in the working-class neighborhoods of Chicago, Detroit, Indianapolis, and Atlanta, where African Americans and other ethnic minorities were settling. At the peak of its power, it had several million members, many of them women who campaigned for more rights for white, Protestant women. The Klan also influenced politics, especially in Indiana, Oregon, Oklahoma, Louisiana, and Texas. The Klan declined after 1924, but widespread fear of everything "un-American" remained.

Read the **Document**
"Creed of Klanswomen,"
The Kluxer, *March 8, 1924*
at **www.myhistorylab.com**

A Prospering Economy

The decade after World War I was also a time of industrial expansion. After recovering from a postwar depression in 1921 and 1922, the economy took off. Fueled by new technology and more efficient management, industrial production almost doubled during the decade, but the benefits of prosperity were not equally distributed. A construction boom created new suburbs around American cities, and new skyscrapers transformed the cities themselves. While the American economy boomed, much of the rest of the world suffered in the aftermath of the war. As part of a global economy, the United States would eventually be affected by the economic stagnation in other parts of the world.

Watch the **Video**
Prosperity of the 1920s and the Great Depression
at **www.myhistorylab.com**

The Rising Standard of Living

Signs of the new prosperity abounded. Millions of homes and apartments were built and equipped with the latest conveniences. Perhaps the most tangible sign of the new prosperity was the modern American bathroom. In the early 1920s, the enameled tub, toilet, and washbasin became standard. The bathroom, with unlimited hot water, privacy, and clean white fixtures, symbolized American affluence, but a great many in rural America still used outdoor privies.

Many Americans now had more leisure time. Persistent efforts by labor unions had gradually reduced the 60-hour workweek of the late nineteenth century to a 45-hour week. Paid vacations, unknown in the nineteenth century, became prevalent. The American diet also improved. The consumption of cornmeal and potatoes declined, but the sale of fresh vegetables increased by 45 percent. Health improved and life expectancy lengthened. But not all Americans enjoyed better health and more leisure. A white male born in 1900 had a life expectancy of 48 years and a white female of 51 years. By 1930, these figures had increased to 59 and 63 years. For a black male born in 1900, however, the life expectancy was only 33 years, and for the black female, 35 years. These figures increased to 48 and 47 by 1930, but the discrepancy remained.

Yet almost all Americans benefited to some extent from the new prosperity. Some took advantage of expanding educational opportunities. In 1900, only 1 in 10 young people of high school age was in school. By 1930, that number had increased to 6 in 10, and much of the improvement came in the 1920s. College enrollment also grew, but only a small percentage went beyond high school during the decade.

The Rise of the Modern Corporation

The structure and practice of American business were transformed in the 1920s. After the economic downturn of 1920 to 1922, business boomed until the crash of 1929. Mergers increased during the decade at a rate greater than at any time since the end of the 1890s. What emerged were not monopolies but oligopolies (industry domination spread among a few large firms). By 1930, the 200 largest corporations—which were becoming more diversified—controlled almost half the corporate wealth.

Perhaps the most important business trend of the decade was the emergence of a new kind of manager. The prototype was Alfred P. Sloan, Jr., an engineer who reorganized General Motors and made marketing and advertising as important as production. Continuing the trends started earlier by efficiency expert Frederick Taylor, the new managers tried to keep employees working efficiently, but they also introduced pensions, recreation facilities, cafeterias, and even paid vacations and profit-sharing plans. This "**welfare capitalism**" was designed to reduce worker discontent and discourage labor unions.

Planning was the key to the new corporate structure, and planning often meant a continuation of the business-government cooperation that had developed during World War I. Even though all the planning failed to prevent the economic collapse in 1929, the modern corporation survived the depression to exert a growing influence on American life in the 1930s and after.

The Workers' Share

Even though hundreds of thousands of workers improved their standard of living in the 1920s, inequality grew. Between 1923 and 1929, real wages increased 21 percent, but corporate dividends went up by nearly two-thirds. The richest 5 percent of the population increased their share of the wealth from a quarter to a third, and the wealthiest 1 percent controlled a whopping 19 percent of all income. Workers did not profit from the increased production they helped generate.

Even among workers, there was great disparity. For example, those employed on auto assembly lines saw their wages go up and their hours go down. Yet the majority of American working-class families could not move much beyond subsistence. One study suggested that a family needed between $2,000 and $2,400 in 1924 to maintain an "American standard of living." That year, 16 million families earned under $2,000.

Although some workers prospered in the 1920s, organized labor did not. Union membership dropped from about 5 million in 1921 to under 3.5 million in 1929. The National Manufacturing Association carried on a vigorous campaign to restore the open shop, while many businesses added pensions and company unions to lure employees away from unions.

The conservative American Federation of Labor suffered during the 1920s, but so did the more aggressive unions like the United Mine Workers, led by the bombastic John L. Lewis. Internal strife weakened the union, and Lewis had to accept wage reductions in 1927. Organized labor, like so many other groups, struggled desperately to share in the prosperity of the 1920s. But affluence and a share of the American dream were beyond the reach of most workers.

A Global Automobile Culture

Automobile manufacturing grew spectacularly in the 1920s. The automobile was a major factor in the postwar boom. It stimulated and transformed the petroleum, steel, and rubber industries; it forced the construction and upgrading of streets and highways at the cost of millions of dollars for labor and concrete. From the beginning, the United States loved autos. There were nearly 1 million autos in 1912, and in the 1920s, autos came within the reach of the middle class. In 1929, Americans purchased 4.5 million cars, and by the end of that year, nearly 27 million were registered. The roads, mostly maintained by state and local governments, were often

View the Image
Downtown Scene with Cars (1911)
at **www.myhistorylab.com**

poor and sometimes impassable. European roads, maintained by national governments, were better, but there were not as many cars in Europe in the 1920s.

The auto created new suburbs and allowed families to live miles from work. Gasoline stations, diners, and tourist courts (forerunners of motels) became familiar landmarks on the American scene. But there was an environmental downside as oil and gasoline contaminated streams, piles of old tires and rusting hulks of discarded cars began to line the highways, and emissions from thousands and then millions of internal combustion engines fouled the air.

The auto transformed American life in other ways. Small crossroads stores and many small churches disappeared as rural families drove into town. Trucks and tractors changed farming. Buses began to eliminate the one-room school, and the tiny rural church began to disappear. Autos also changed courting habits by allowing young people to escape the watchful eyes of their parents.

Over the decade, the automobile became a sign of status. Advertising made it the symbol of the good life, sex, freedom, and speed. The auto transformed advertising and altered the way products were purchased. By 1926, three-fourths of the cars sold were bought on some kind of deferred-payment plan, and "buy now, pay later" was soon used to sell other consumer products. The auto industry, like most American businesses, consolidated. In 1908, more than 250 companies were making automobiles in the United States. By 1929, only 44 remained. But one name became synonymous with the automobile itself—Henry Ford.

Ford had a reputation as a progressive industrial leader and champion of ordinary people. As with all men and women who become symbols, the truth is less dramatic. For example, his famous assembly line was invented by a team of engineers. Introduced in 1913, it cut production time for a car from 14 hours to an hour and a half. The product of this carefully planned system was the Model T, the prototype of the inexpensive family car. By contrast, most European cars were custom made.

In 1914, Ford startled the country by increasing the minimum pay of the Ford assembly-line worker to $5 a day (almost twice the national average pay for factory workers). Ford was not a humanitarian. He wanted a dependable workforce and knew that skilled workers were less likely to quit if they were well paid. Ford was one of the first to appreciate that workers were also consumers who might buy Model Ts. But despite the high wages, work on the assembly line was numbing, and when the line closed down, workers were released without compensation.

The Model T, which cost $600 in 1912, was reduced gradually in price until it sold for only $290 in 1924. Except for adding a self-starter, offering a closed model, and making a few minor face-lifts, Ford kept the Model T in 1927 as he had introduced it in 1909. By that time, its popularity had declined as many people traded up to sleeker, more colorful, and, they

Watch the Video

The Rise and Fall of the Automobile Economy

at **www.myhistorylab.com**

thought, more prestigious autos put out by Ford's competitors; as a result, wages at Ford dipped below the industry average.

The Connected, Electrified Nation

The 1920s marked the climax of the "second Industrial Revolution," powered by electricity and producing a growing array of consumer goods. By 1929, electrical generators provided 80 percent of the power used in industry. Fewer than 1 of every 10 American homes had electricity in 1907; by 1929, more than two-thirds did, and workers were turning out twice as many goods as a similarly sized workforce had 10 years earlier.

Changing communications altered the way Americans lived as well as the way they conducted business. The telephone was first demonstrated in 1876, and by 1899, more than a million phones were in operation. During the 1920s, the number of homes with phones increased from 9 million to 13 million. Still, by the end of the decade, more than half of American homes lacked telephones.

> **Watch** the Video
>
> *1920s Media*
>
> at **www.myhistorylab.com**

Even more than the telephone, the radio symbolized the changes of the 1920s. The first station began commercial broadcasting in the summer of 1920, and that fall, election returns were broadcast for the first time. The next year a Newark station transmitted the World Series, beginning a process that would transform American sports. In 1922, a radio station in New York broadcast the first commercial.

Much early broadcasting consisted of classical music, but soon the programming also included news analysis and coverage of important events. Serials and situation comedies made radio a national medium, with millions tuning in to the same program. The record industry grew just as rapidly. By the end of the decade, people everywhere were humming the same popular songs, while actors and announcers became celebrities.

Even more dramatic was the phenomenon of the movies. Forty million viewers a week went to the movies in 1922, and by 1929 that total exceeded 100 million. To countless Americans, the stars were more famous and important than most government officials. Motion pictures before the war had attracted mostly the working class, but now they seemed to appeal to everyone. Many parents feared that they would dictate ideas about sex and life. One young college woman admitted that movies taught her how to smoke, and in some movies "there were some lovely scenes which just got me all hot 'n' bothered."

Sports heroes like Babe Ruth and Jack Dempsey were as famous as the movie stars. The great spectator sports of the decade owed much to the increase of leisure time and to the automobile, the radio, and the mass-circulation newspaper. Thousands drove to college towns to watch football; millions listened for scores or read about the results the next day. The popularity of sports, like the movies and radio, was a product of technology.

Electricity brought dozens of gadgets and labor-saving devices into the home. But the new machines did not reduce the time the average housewife spent doing housework. In many ways, the success of the electric revolution increased the contrast in American life. Urban "Great White Ways" symbolized progress, but they also made slums and rural hamlets seem even darker. For poor women, especially in rural America, the traditional female tasks of carrying water, pushing, pulling, and lifting continued.

The year 1927 seemed to mark the beginning of the new age of mechanization and progress. Henry Ford produced his 15 millionth car and introduced the Model A. Radio-telephone service linked San Francisco and Manila. The first radio network was organized (CBS), and the first sound movie was released (*The Jazz Singer*). The Holland Tunnel, the first underwater vehicular roadway, connected New York and New Jersey, and Charles Lindbergh flew his single-engine plane from New York to Paris and captured the world's imagination. When Americans cheered Lindbergh, they were reaffirming their belief in the American dream and their faith in individual initiative as well as in technology.

View the Image

Charles Lindbergh and Spirit of St. Louis at **www.myhistorylab.com**

Urban Growth and Rural Challenges

The automobile both pushed urban areas out into the countryside and brought industry to the suburbs. The great expansion of suburban population came in the 1920s. Shaker Heights, outside Cleveland, was typical. Two businessmen planned and built the new suburb on the site of a former Shaker community. No blacks were allowed. Curving roads and landscape design created a park-like atmosphere. Between 1919 and 1929, the population grew from 1,700 to over 15,000, and the price of lots multiplied by 10. Other suburbs grew just as rapidly—none more than Beverly Hills, California, whose population soared by 2,485 percent. The biggest land boom of all occurred in Florida, where Miami mushroomed from 30,000 people in 1920 to 75,000 in 1925. A plot in West Palm Beach sold for $800,000 in 1923, and two years later it was worth $4 million.

The automobile transformed every city, but the growth was most spectacular in two cities that the car virtually created. Detroit grew from 300,000 in 1900 to 1,837,000 in 1930. Los Angeles, held together by a network of roads, expanded from 114,000 in 1900 to 1,778,000 in 1930. In 1900, there were 52 metropolitan areas of over 100,000 people; by 1930, there were 115.

Cities expanded horizontally in the 1920s, sprawling into the countryside, but city centers grew vertically. A building boom that peaked near the end of the decade created new skylines for most urban centers. The most famous skyscraper of all, the 102-story Empire State Building in New York, was finished in 1931 but not completely occupied until after World War II.

In rural America, meanwhile, most farmers did not share in the decade's prosperity. During the war, farmers had responded to worldwide demand and rising commodity prices by investing in land and equipment. Then prices and farm income tumbled. Many farmers could not make payments on their mortgages, and they lost their farms.

The changing nature of farming was part of the problem. Chemical fertilizers and new hybrid seeds increased yields. Farming became more mechanized and efficient. Production swelled just as worldwide demand for American farm products tumbled.

Few farmers could afford the products of the new technology. Although many middle-class urban families were more prosperous than ever before, only 1 farm family in 10 had electricity in the 1920s. The lot of the farm wife had not changed for centuries.

Farmers tried to act collectively to solve their problems. Most of their effort went into passing the McNary–Haugen Farm Relief Bill, which provided for government support for key agricultural products. The government would buy crops at a "fair exchange value" and then sell the excess on the world market at a lower price. The bill passed Congress twice, in 1927 and 1928, and twice was vetoed by President Coolidge. But farm organizations across the country learned how to cooperate and influence Congress, with important future ramifications.

John Steuart Curry, *Baptism in Kansas* John Steuart Curry was one of the regionalist painters in the 1920s who found inspiration in the American heartland. In *Baptism in Kansas*, he depicts a religious ritual that reflects the strong hold of faith in rural America. Is there a religious split today between urban and rural America? Or is the cultural divide defined differently today? *(John Steuart Curry (1897–1946), "Baptism in Kansas." 1928. Oil on Canvas. 40" × 50". Collection of the Whitney Museum of American Art, New York)*

Farmers were particularly vulnerable to the power of nature, and that became apparent in the spring of 1927, when the worst flood in the nation's history devastated the Mississippi River valley. Despite efforts to improve the levies, over 27,000 square miles of land were flooded. Nearly a million people were made homeless. There was over a billion dollars in property damage, and 246 people died. The black sharecroppers, who often lived near the river, bore the brunt of the disaster. President Coolidge appointed Secretary of Commerce Herbert Hoover to coordinate flood relief. Hoover, who believed in voluntary efforts, enlisted the help of the Red Cross, the American Legion, and other groups, but the total relief efforts remained inadequate. The next year, Coolidge signed a flood control bill that for the first time committed the federal government to build levies to control the Mississippi River. But the debate continued about the best way to control nature and how to solve the farmers' problems.

Clashing Values

During the 1920s, radio, movies, advertising, and mass-circulation magazines promoted a national, secular culture. But this new culture of consumption, pleasure, upward mobility, and sex clashed with traditional values: hard work, thrift, church, family, home. This was not simply an urban-rural conflict, for many people clinging to old ways had moved into the cities. Still, many Americans feared that familiar ways of life were threatened by new values, scientific breakthroughs, bolshevism, relativism, Freudianism, and biblical criticism. Others found traditional values stifling and searched for alternatives.

((•─Hear the Audio
Hungarian Rag
at **www.myhistorylab.com**

Tradition and Modernity on Trial

In 1925, a trial over the teaching of evolution in a high school in the little town of Dayton, Tennessee, symbolized (even as it exaggerated) the clash of traditional versus modern, city versus country.

The scientific community and most educated people had long accepted Darwinian evolution. But the theory of evolution epitomized the challenge to traditional faith, and in some states its teaching was outlawed. John Scopes, a young biology teacher, broke the law, and Tennessee put him on trial. In the seminal **Scopes trial**, the famous lawyer Clarence Darrow defended Scopes, while the World Christian Fundamentalist Association hired former presidential candidate and Secretary of State William Jennings Bryan to assist the prosecution. Bryan was old and tired (he died only a few days after the trial), but he was deeply religious and still eloquent. In cross-examination, Darrow reduced Bryan's statements to intellectual rubble. Nevertheless, the jury declared Scopes guilty.

The national press covered the trial and upheld science and academic freedom. The journalist H. L. Mencken had a field day poking fun at Bryan and the fundamentalists. "Heave an egg out a Pullman window," Mencken wrote, "and you will hit a Fundamentalist almost anywhere in the United States today. . . . They are everywhere where learning is too heavy a burden for mortal minds to carry."

Many evangelical Protestants, who saw the Bible as literal truth, viewed the dramatic changes of the 1920s as a major spiritual crisis. Increasing numbers of Americans embraced religious fundamentalism. Enrollments in Christian colleges and the circulation of fundamentalist publications increased dramatically during the 1920s and 1930s, and popular preachers such as Billy Sunday and Aimee Semple McPherson attracted huge audiences on the radio.

Temperance, Triumphant but Temporary

The 1920s was the decade of Prohibition, when the "manufacture, sale, or transportation of intoxicating liquors" was prohibited by the Eighteenth Amendment to the Constitution. Temperance had been a social movement and political issue in the United States since the 1840s because of the many problems attributed to excessive drinking, including domestic violence, crime, and poverty. As a moral issue, temperance appealed to middle-class reformers, who pressed for state laws to control or ban the sale of alcohol. By 1917, more than three-fourths of Americans lived in dry states or counties. The First World War allowed anti-saloon advocates to link Prohibition and patriotism. At first, beer manufacturers supported limited Prohibition, but in the end, patriotic fervor prohibited the sale of all alcoholic beverages. "We have German enemies across the water," one prohibitionist announced. "We have German enemies in this country too. And the worst of all our German enemies, the most treacherous, the most menacing are Pabst, Schlitz, Blatz and Miller."

The Eighteenth Amendment was ratified in June 1919 and followed by the Volstead Act, an enforcement measure that banned the brewing and selling of beverages containing more than 0.5 percent alcohol. A social worker predicted that the Eighteenth Amendment would reduce poverty, nearly wipe out prostitution and crime, improve labor, and "substantially increase our national resources by setting free vast suppressed human potentialities."

The Prohibition experiment probably did reduce the total consumption of alcohol in the country, especially in rural areas and urban working-class neighborhoods. Fewer arrests for drunkenness were made, and deaths from alcoholism declined. But Prohibition showed the difficulty of using law to promote moral reform. Most people who wanted to drink during the "noble experiment" found a way. Speakeasies replaced saloons, and people consumed many strange and dangerous homemade concoctions. Bartenders invented the cocktail to disguise the poor quality of liquor, and middle- and upper-class women began to drink in public for the first time.

Prohibition also created great bootlegging rings, tied in many cities to organized crime. Chicago's Al Capone was the most famous underworld figure whose power and wealth were based on the sale of illegal alcohol. His organization grossed an estimated $60 million in 1927. Many Prohibition supporters slowly came to favor repeal, because Prohibition stimulated too much illegal activity and it did not seem worth the costs. An anti-Prohibition movement slowly gained strength through the 1920s and pointed toward the repeal of Prohibition with the Twenty-First Amendment in 1933.

((•—[Hear the **Audio**

Prohibition Is a Failure

at **www.myhistorylab.com**

Voices of Discontent

Many intellectuals, writers, and artists felt estranged from what they saw as the narrow materialism of American life during the 1920s. Some, like F. Scott Fitzgerald, Ernest Hemingway, e. e. cummings, and T. S. Eliot, moved to Europe—where they wrote novels, plays, and poems about America. Like so many American intellectuals in all periods, they had a love-hate relationship with their country. Because of their alienation, they became known as the **"Lost Generation."**

For many writers, disillusionment began with the war. Hemingway eagerly volunteered to go to Europe as an ambulance driver. But when he was wounded on the Italian front, he reevaluated the meaning of all the slaughter. His novel *The Sun Also Rises* (1926) is the story of the purposeless European wanderings of a group of Americans, as well as the story of Jake Barnes, who was made impotent by a war injury. His "unreasonable wound" symbolized the futility of postwar life. Fitzgerald, who loved the cafés and parties in Paris, became a celebrity during the 1920s. He epitomized some of the despair of his generation, which had "grown up to find all Gods dead, all wars fought, all faiths in man shaken." His best novel, *The Great Gatsby* (1925), was a critique of the American success myth.

It was not necessary to live in France to criticize American society. Sherwood Anderson created a fictional midwestern town in *Winesburg, Ohio* (1919), describing the dull, narrow, warped lives that seemed to provide a metaphor for American culture. Sinclair Lewis, another midwesterner, wrote scathing parodies of middle-class, small-town life in *Main Street* (1920) and *Babbitt* (1922). But no one had more fun laughing at the American middle class than Baltimore's H. L. Mencken, whose magazine the *American Mercury* overflowed with his assaults on "the booboisie." Harding's speeches reminded him of "a string of wet sponges, . . . of stale bean soup, of college yells, of dogs barking idiotically through endless nights."

•••—[Read the **Document**

John F. Carter, "'These Wild Young People' by One of Them" (1920)

at **www.myhistorylab.com**

Ironically, while intellectuals despaired over American society and complained that art could not survive in a business-dominated civilization, literature flourished. The 1920s was one of the most creative decades in American literature.

Hopes Raised, Promises Deferred

The 1920s was a time when all kinds of hopes seemed realizable. "Don't envy successful salesmen—be one!" one ad screamed. Buy a car. Build a house. Start a career. Invest in land or in stocks. Make a fortune. Not all Americans, of course, dreamed of making a killing on Wall Street; some merely wished to retain traditional values in a society that seemed to question them. Others wanted a steady job and a little respect. Many discovered, however, that even the most modest hopes lay tantalizingly out of reach.

Immigration Restriction

Immigrants and anyone else "un-American" seemed to threaten old ways. The fear and intolerance of the war years and the period right after the war resulted in major restrictive legislation.

The United States had acted previously to ban immigrants from China (with the Chinese Exclusion Act of 1882) and to limit immigration from Japan (with the Gentlemen's Agreement of 1907), but now attention turned toward the most recent waves of newcomers from southern and eastern Europe. More than 1 million immigrants poured into the country in 1920 and 1921, despite a 1917 law that banned radicals and required a literacy test. In Congressional hearings these newcomers, especially those who were Jewish or Italian, were labeled as inferior "degenerates" who threatened the racial purity of the country.

In 1921 and again in 1924, Congress imposed quotas on European immigration. The tighter 1924 quota allowed only 2 percent of those from each country who were in the United States in 1890—before the great flood of newcomers had begun arriving from southern and eastern Europe. All immigrants from Asia were banned. In 1927, a ceiling of 150,000 European immigrants a year was set; more than 60 percent could come from Great Britain and Germany, but fewer than 4 percent were allowed from Italy.

The immigration acts of 1921, 1924, and 1927 also cut off the streams of cheap labor that had provided muscle for industrialization since the early nineteenth century. At the same time, by exempting Western Hemisphere immigrants, the new laws opened the country to Mexicans eager to work in the fields and farms of California and the Southwest. Mexicans soon became the country's largest first-generation immigrant group. Mexican farmworkers often lived in primitive camps, where conditions were unsanitary and health care nonexistent. "When they have finished harvesting my crops I will kick them out on the country road," one employer announced.

Mexicans also migrated to industrial cities, recruited by northern companies that paid for their transportation. During the 1920s, El Paso became more than half Mexican. The Mexican population in California reached 368,000 in 1929, and Los Angeles was about 20 percent Mexican. Like African Americans, the Mexicans found opportunity by migrating, but they did not escape prejudice or hardship.

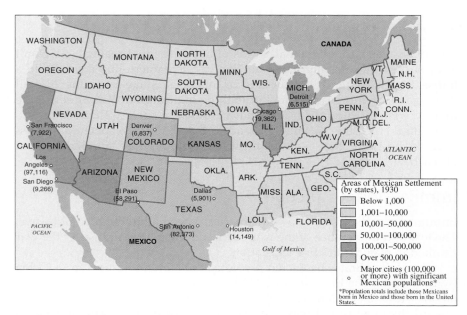

Mexican Population, 1930 Mexicans migrated across the border in great numbers in the 1920s; by 1930, they constituted a significant Spanish-speaking minority, especially in Texas, California, and Arizona. In an era of immigration restriction, why did Mexican immigration increase?

Marcus Garvey: Black Messiah

Marcus Garvey, a flamboyant Jamaican who arrived in New York at the age of 29, fed black pride. Although he never abandoned Booker T. Washington's self-help philosophy, Garvey thoroughly transformed it. Washington focused on economic betterment; Garvey saw self-help as political empowerment by which African peoples would reclaim their homelands.

In Jamaica, Garvey had founded the Universal Negro Improvement Association. By 1919, he had established 30 branches in the United States and the Caribbean. He also set up a newspaper, the Black Cross Nurses, and chains of stores and restaurants. His biggest project was the Black Star Line, a steamship company that was to be owned and operated by African Americans. Advocating blacks' return to Africa, he declared himself the "provisional president of Africa."

He won converts through the force of his oratory and powerful personality, but especially through his message of black pride. "Up you mighty race, you can accomplish what you will," Garvey thundered. Thousands of blacks cheered his Universal African Legions, marching in blue and red uniforms and waving a red-black-green flag. Thousands invested in the Black Star Line—which soon collapsed, in part because white entrepreneurs sold Garvey inferior ships. Garvey was arrested for using the mails to defraud shareholders and sentenced to five years in prison. Coolidge commuted the sentence. Ordered deported as an undesirable alien, Garvey left America in

Black Messiah Marcus Garvey (second from the right), shown dressed in his favorite uniform, became a hero for many black Americans. How did his appeal differ from that of other African American leaders?

1927. Despite his failures, he convinced thousands of black Americans, especially the poor and discouraged, and those who had recently migrated from the South, that they could unite and feel pride in their heritage.

The Harlem Renaissance

After the war, a group of black writers, artists, and intellectuals who settled in Harlem, an uptown neighborhood in New York City, led a movement related in some ways to Garvey's black nationalism crusade, and in the end, more important. They studied anthropology, art, history, and music, and in their novels, poetry, dance, and music explored the ambivalent role of blacks in America. Like Garvey, they expressed black pride and sought African and folk roots. Unlike Garvey, they wanted to be both black and American and had no desire to go back to Africa.

Watch the Video
The Harlem Renaissance
at **www.myhistorylab.com**

Alain Locke, the first black Rhodes scholar, was the father of the **Harlem Renaissance**. His *The New Negro* (1925) announced the movement to the outside world and outlined black contributions to American culture and civilization. Langston Hughes, a poet and novelist, wrote bitter but humorous poems, using black vernacular to describe the pathos and pride of African Americans. In *Weary Blues*, he adapted the rhythms of jazz and the blues.

Jazz was an important force in Harlem in the 1920s, and prosperous whites came to listen to Louis Armstrong, Duke Ellington, and other black musicians. Many brought up in Victorian white America were intrigued by what they saw as Harlem's primitive emotions and erotic atmosphere. American jazz was also exported to Europe. In Paris, jazz singer Josephine Baker, star of *Revue Négre*, was the toast of the town. Many Europeans criticized the United States for its materialism. They were not impressed with American literature or art, but they loved American jazz. It was the beginning of the export of American popular culture that would impress most of the rest of the world in the decades after World War II.

Jamaican Claude McKay wrote about the underside of life in Harlem in *Home to Harlem* (1925), one of the most popular "new Negro" novels. McKay portrayed two black men—one, Jake, who finds a life of simple and erotic pleasure in Harlem's cabarets, the other an intellectual unable to make such an easy choice and conscious that "My damned white education has robbed me of . . . primitive vitality." Many Harlem writers agonized about how to be both black and intellectual. They worried about white patrons who pressured them to conform to the white elite's idea of black authenticity, but they knew that patronage was their only hope to be recognized.

Like the white writers of the "Lost Generation," many African American writers felt alienated from American society. They tried living in Paris or Greenwich Village, but most felt drawn to Harlem, which in the 1920s was rapidly becoming the center of New York's black population. Over 117,000 whites left during the decade, while over 87,000 blacks moved in. Countee Cullen remarked, "In spite of myself I find that I am activated by a strong sense of race consciousness." So was Zora Neale Hurston, who came to New York to study at Barnard College, earned an advanced degree in anthropology from Columbia University, and used her interest in folklore to write stories of robust and passionate rural blacks. The Harlem writers were read by only a few people, but another generation of young black intellectuals in the 1960s would rediscover them.

Women Struggle for Equality

An indelible image of the 1920s is the flapper—a young woman with a short skirt, bobbed hair, and a boyish figure doing the Charleston, smoking, drinking, and being very casual about sex. Fitzgerald's heroines in novels like *This Side of Paradise* (1920) and *The Great Gatsby* (1925) provided role models for young people, and movie stars such as Clara Bow and Gloria Swanson, aggressively seductive on the screen, supplied even more vivid examples of provocative behavior.

Without question, women acquired more sexual freedom in the 1920s. "None of the Victorian mothers had any idea how casually their daughters were accustomed to being kissed," Fitzgerald wrote.

••• Read the Document

Changing Sexual Mores: Eleanor Rowland Wembridge, "Petting and the Campus" (Survey, July 1, 1925) at www.myhistorylab.com

However, it is difficult, if not impossible, to know how accustomed those daughters (and their mothers) were to kissing and enjoying other sexual activity. Contraceptives became more readily available, and Margaret Sanger (who had been indicted for sending birth control

Working Women of the 1920s Although the flapper look of short skirts and bobbed hair appeared in the workplace in the 1920s, for most working women of the era, employed in low-paying jobs as file clerks, typists, and telephone operators, the flapper lifestyle of freedom and equality was more illusion than reality. Does this workplace seem to empower or inhibit individual freedom?

information through the mail in 1914) organized the first American birth control conference in 1921. Birth control devices and literature, however, were still often illegal.

Family size declined during the decade (from 3.6 children in 1900 to 2.5 in 1930), and young people were apparently more inclined to marry for love than for security. More women expected sexual satisfaction in marriage (nearly 60 percent in one poll) and felt that divorce was the best solution for an unhappy marriage. Nearly 85 percent in another poll approved of sexual intercourse as an expression of love

●●─[Read the Document
Margaret Sanger, "Happiness in Marriage" (1926)
at **www.myhistorylab.com**

and affection, rather than simply for procreation. But these polls tended to be biased toward urban middle-class attitudes. Despite more freedom for women, the double standard persisted.

Middle-class women's lives were shaped by innovations like electricity, running water, and labor-saving devices. But as standards of cleanliness rose, they spent more time on housework while being bombarded with advertising urging them to make themselves better housekeepers yet still be beautiful. The young adopted new styles quickly, and they also learned to swim, play tennis, and ride bicycles.

More women worked outside the home—22 percent in 1933, compared to 17 percent in 1890. But their share of manufacturing jobs fell from 19 to 16 percent between 1900 and 1930. The greatest expansion of jobs was in white-collar occupations that were being feminized—secretary, bookkeeper, clerk, telephone operator. Although more married women had jobs (an increase of 25 percent during the decade), most held low-paying jobs, and most single women assumed that marriage would end their employment.

For some working women—secretaries and teachers, for example—marriage indeed often led to dismissal. Yet an office was a good place to meet eligible men, and a secretary learned endurance, self-effacement, and obedience—traits that many thought would make her a good wife.

Considering these attitudes, it is not surprising that the male-female pay disparity widened. By 1930, women earned only 57 percent of what men were paid.

The image of the flapper in the 1920s promised more freedom and equality for women than they actually achieved. The flapper was young, white, slender, and upper class, and most women did not fit those categories. Although the proportion of women lawyers and bankers increased slightly, the rate of growth declined. The number of women doctors and scientists dropped.

The promise of prewar feminists and suffrage advocates remained unfulfilled. In some states, women needed their husband's consent in order to hold office, own a business, or sign a contract. Women were usually held responsible for an illegitimate birth, and divorce laws almost always favored men.

Alice Paul, who had led the militant National Woman's Party in 1916, chained herself to the White House fence once again to promote an equal rights amendment to the Constitution. The amendment got support in several states, but many women opposed it, fearing that it would cancel the special legislation to protect women in industry. Feminists disagreed in the 1920s on the proper way to promote equality and rights for women, but the political and social climate was not conducive to feminism.

The Business of Politics

"Among the nations of the earth today America stands for one idea: *Business*," a popular writer announced in 1921. Bruce Barton, the head of the largest advertising firm in the country, published one of the best-selling nonfiction books of the decade. In *The Man Nobody Knows* (1925), he depicted Christ as "the founder of modern business." He took 12 men from the bottom of society and forged them into a successful organization.

Business, especially big business, prospered in the 1920s. The government reduced regulation, lowered taxes, and helped aid business expansion at home and abroad. Business and politics, always intertwined, became especially close during the decade. Wealthy financiers played important roles in formulating government policy. Even more significant, a new kind of businessman was elected president in 1928. Herbert Hoover, international engineer and efficiency expert, was the very symbol of modern business techniques and practices.

Harding and Coolidge

The Republicans, almost assured of victory in 1920 because of bitter reaction against Woodrow Wilson, might have preferred nominating their old standard-bearer, Theodore Roosevelt, but he had died the year before. Warren G. Harding, a former Ohio newspaper editor, captured the nomination after meeting late at night with some of the party's most powerful men in a Chicago hotel room. To balance the ticket, the Republicans chose as their vice presidential candidate Calvin Coolidge. Meanwhile, after 44 roll calls, the Democrats nominated Governor James Cox of Ohio and picked Franklin D. Roosevelt, the assistant secretary of the navy, for vice president.

Harding won in a landslide. His 60.4 percent of the vote was the widest margin yet recorded in a presidential election. More significant, fewer than 50 percent of the eligible voters went to the polls. Newly enfranchised women, especially in working-class neighborhoods, avoided the voting booths. So did large numbers of men. Many people did not care who was president.

In contrast to the reform-minded presidents Roosevelt and Wilson, Harding reflected the conservatism of the 1920s. A visitor to the White House found Harding and his cohorts discussing the problems of the day, with "the air heavy with tobacco smoke, trays with bottles containing every imaginable brand of whiskey." A few blocks away, Harry Daugherty, Harding's attorney general and longtime associate, did a brisk business in selling favors, taking bribes, and organizing illegal schemes.

Harding was not personally corrupt, and the nation's leading businessmen approved of his high-tariff, low-tax policies. Nor did Harding spend all his time drinking with his pals. He called a conference on disarmament and another on unemployment. Harding once remarked that he could never be considered a great president, but he thought perhaps he might be "one of the best loved." When he died suddenly in August 1923, the American people genuinely mourned.

Only after Coolidge became president did the full extent of the Harding scandals come out. A Senate committee discovered that Secretary of the Interior Albert Fall had illegally leased government-owned oil reserves in the Teapot Dome section of Wyoming to businessmen for over $300,000 in bribes. Illegal activities were turned up in the Veterans Administration and elsewhere. Harding's attorney general resigned in disgrace, the secretary of the navy barely avoided prison, two of Harding's advisers committed suicide, and Fall went to jail.

Coolidge was dour, taciturn—and honest. Born in a little town in Vermont, he was sworn in as president by his father, a justice of the peace, whom he was visiting when news of Harding's death came. To many, Coolidge represented old-fashioned values, simple religious faith, and personal integrity. But Coolidge felt ill at ease posing for photographers holding a pitchfork, and he was much more comfortable around corporate executives.

Coolidge ran for reelection in 1924 with the financier Charles Dawes as his running mate. There was little question that he would win. The Democrats were so equally divided between northern urban Catholics and southern rural Protestants that it took 103 ballots to nominate John W. Davis, an affable corporate lawyer.

Dissidents, mostly representing the farmers and laborers dissatisfied with both nominees, formed a new Progressive party. They adopted the name, but little else, from Theodore Roosevelt's party of 1912. Nominating Robert La Follette for president, their platform called for government ownership of railroads and ratification of an anti–child labor amendment. La Follette attacked the "control of government and industry by private monopoly." He received nearly 5 million votes, only 3.5 million short of Davis's total. But Coolidge and prosperity won easily.

Like Harding, Coolidge was immensely popular. Symbolizing his administration was his wealthy secretary of the treasury, Andrew Mellon. In 1922, Congress, with Mellon's endorsement, repealed the wartime excess profits tax. The federal income tax exempted most families by giving everyone a $2,500 exemption, plus $400 for each dependent. In 1928, Congress slashed taxes further, removed most excise taxes, and lowered the corporate tax rate. The 200 largest corporations increased their assets during the decade from $43 billion to $81 billion. "The chief business of the American people is business," Coolidge said. His idea of the proper role of the federal government was to have as little as possible to do with the functioning of business and the lives of the people. "No other president in my time slept so much," a White House usher remembered. But most Americans approved of their president.

Herbert Hoover

One bright light in the lackluster Harding and Coolidge administrations was Secretary of Commerce Herbert Hoover. He had made a fortune as a mining engineer before 1914 and earned the reputation of a great humanitarian during the war. Many progressives supported him as a presidential candidate in 1920.

Hoover was a dynamo. He expanded his department to regulate the airlines, radio, and other new industries. Through the Bureau of Standards, Hoover standardized the size of almost everything manufactured in the United States, from light bulbs to mattresses. He supported zoning codes, the eight-hour day in major industries, better nutrition for children, and conservation. He pushed through the Pollution Act of 1924, the first attempt to control coastal oil pollution.

While secretary of commerce, Hoover used the authority of the federal government to regulate, stimulate, and promote, but he believed first of all in American free enterprise and local volunteer action. In 1921, he convinced Harding of the need to do something about unemployment during the postwar recession. The president's conference on unemployment, convened in September 1921, marked the first time the national government had admitted any responsibility for the unemployed. The conference (the first of many that Hoover was to organize) unleashed a flood of publicity and expert advice. The conference report urged state and local governments and businesses to cooperate voluntarily to solve the problem. The primary responsibility of the federal government, Hoover believed, was to educate and promote, but not to initiate reform.

The Survival of Progressivism

The decade of the 1920s saw a reaction against reform, but progressivism did not simply die. Progressives interested in efficiency and order were perhaps happier during the 1920s than those who tried to promote social justice, but the fights against poverty and for better housing persisted, as did campaigns to protect children.

The greatest success of the social justice movement was the 1921 Sheppard–Towner Maternity Act, one of the first pieces of federal social welfare legislation and the product of long progressive agitation. The bill, controversial from the beginning, called for a million dollars a year to assist states in providing medical aid, and visiting nurses to teach expectant mothers how to care for themselves and their babies. The American Medical Association attacked it as socialism, and the opponents of woman suffrage argued that it was supported by extreme feminists and Communists. But the bill passed Congress and was signed by President Harding in 1921. The appropriation for the bill was only for six years, and the opposition, still trembling at a feminist-Socialist-Communist plot, got it repealed in 1929. Yet the Sheppard–Towner Act, promoted and fought for by a group of progressive women, indicated that concern for social justice was not dead in the age of Harding and Coolidge.

Global Expansion

The 1920s are often called a time of isolation. But the United States remained involved—indeed, increased its involvement—in international affairs. Although the United States never joined the League of Nations, and a few staunch isolationists blocked membership in the World Court, the United States cooperated with many league agencies. And it took the lead in trying to reduce naval armaments and to solve the problems of international finance caused in part by the war.

There were ominous clouds on the horizon. Germany was mired in economic and political chaos. Japan and Italy were unhappy with the peace settlement. Colonial powers still dominated Africa. Fascism was establishing a foothold in Italy and Spain, while Soviet communism was becoming more firmly entrenched in Russia. The Middle East was fragmented both economically and politically and presented problems that would persist for the rest of the twentieth century and beyond.

The sevenfold expansion of American corporate investments overseas turned the United States from a debtor to a creditor nation. Business, trade, and finance marked the decade as one of international expansion, and the United States increased its leadership in cable communications, wireless telegraphy, and film. Ninety-five percent of the movies shown in Great Britain and Canada and 70 percent of those shown in France in 1926 were American made. Yet the United States took up its role of international power reluctantly and with a number of contradictory and disastrous results.

"We seek no part in directing the destiny of the world," Harding announced in his inaugural address, but he discovered that international problems would not go away. One that required immediate attention was the naval arms race, for which purpose the United States convened the Washington Conference on Naval Disarmament, the first international disarmament conference, in November 1921.

Secretary of State Charles Evans Hughes startled the conference by proposing a 10-year "holiday" on warship construction and offering to sink or scrap 845,000 tons of American ships, including 30 battleships. He urged Britain and Japan to do the same. The delegates cheered Hughes's speech, and they sank more ships than all their admirals had managed to do in a century. The conference ultimately fixed the tonnage of capital ships at a ratio of the United States and Great Britain, 5; Japan, 3; and France and Italy, 1.67. Japan agreed only reluctantly, after the United States promised not to fortify its Pacific islands.

The Washington Conference has often been criticized in light of Pearl Harbor, but in 1921 it was appropriately hailed as the first time in history that the major nations of the world had agreed to disarm. The conference neither caused nor averted World War II. But it was a creative beginning to reducing tensions and to meeting the challenges of the modern arms race.

American foreign policy in the 1920s tried to reduce the risk of international conflict, resist revolution, and make the world safe for trade and investment. Nobody in the Republican administrations even suggested that the United States remain isolated from Latin America. American diplomats supported an open door to trade in China, but in Latin America, the United States had always assumed a special and distinct role. Throughout the decade, American investment increased in the Western Hemisphere. The United States bought nearly 60 percent of Latin America's exports and sold the region nearly 50 percent of its imports. By the end of the decade, the United States controlled the financial affairs of 10 Latin American nations.

Mexico frightened American businessmen in the mid-1920s by beginning to nationalize foreign holdings in oil and mineral rights. Fearing that further military activity would "injure American interests," businessmen and bankers urged Coolidge to negotiate. Coolidge did, and his ambassador's conciliatory attitude led to agreements protecting American investments.

The U.S. policy of promoting peace and trade was not always consistent, especially in Europe. The United States was owed more than $10 billion in war loans, three-fourths of it by Britain and France. Both countries, mired in economic problems, suggested that the United States forgive the debts, arguing that they had paid for the war in lives and property destroyed. But the United States, although adjusting the interest and the payment schedule, refused. "They hired the money, didn't they?" Coolidge supposedly asked.

The only way European nations could repay the United States was by exports, but Congress supported high tariffs. In 1930, the Hawley-Smoot Tariff raised rates even further, despite the protests of many economists.

The American policy of high tariffs (a counterproductive policy for a creditor nation) caused retaliation and restrictions on American trade, which American corporations were trying to increase.

Europeans' inability to export to the United States and repay their loans was intertwined with the reparation agreement made with Germany. The postwar German economy was beset by inflation and its industrial plant throttled by the peace treaty. By 1921, Germany was defaulting on reparations payments. Hoping to maintain international stability, the United States introduced the Dawes Plan, under which the German debt would be spread over a longer period while American bankers and the American government lent Germany hundreds of millions of dollars. This enabled Germany to pay reparations to Britain and France so that they could continue debt repayments to the United States.

Although the United States had displaced Great Britain as the dominant force in international finance, it was a reluctant and inconsistent world leader. The United States stayed out of the League of Nations and hesitated to join multinational agreements. But the Kellogg–Briand pact seemed irresistible. French foreign minister Aristide Briand suggested a Franco-American pact, to commemorate long years of friendship between the two countries, but Secretary of State Frank B. Kellogg in 1928 expanded the idea to a multinational treaty outlawing war. Fourteen nations initially signed the treaty and 62 eventually did, but the only power behind it was moral force, and moral force would not prevent World War II.

The Election of 1928

On August 2, 1927, President Coolidge announced, "I do not choose to run for President in 1928." Hoover immediately became the logical Republican candidate, and he easily got the nomination. Few doubted that the prospering country would elect him. The Democrats nominated Alfred Smith, the colorful, "wet," and Catholic governor of New York who seemed to contrast sharply with Hoover. Anti-Catholicism became a major component of the campaign. But the two candidates differed little. Both were self-made men, and both were progressives. Both sought women voters, favored organized labor, defended capitalism, and were advised by millionaires and corporate executives.

Hoover won in a landslide, receiving 444 electoral votes to Smith's 76. But the campaign revitalized the Democratic party. Smith polled nearly twice as many votes as Davis had in 1924, and for the first time Democrats carried the 12 largest cities.

Stock Market Crash

Hoover had only six months to apply his progressive, efficient methods to running the country. In the fall of 1929, the seemingly endless prosperity suddenly fizzled. In 1928 and 1929, rampant speculation made the stock market boom. Money could be made everywhere: in real estate, business

RECOVERING *the* PAST

Advertising

Have you ever noticed that television commercials can often be more interesting and creative than the programs? One authority has suggested that the best way for a foreign visitor to understand the American character and popular culture is to study television commercials. Television advertising, the thesis goes, appeals to basic cultural assumptions. The nature of advertising not only reveals for historians the prejudices, fears, values, and aspirations of a people but also makes an impact on historical development itself, influencing patterns of taste and purchasing habits. One modern critic calls advertising a "peculiarly American force that now compares with such long-standing institutions as the school and church in the magnitude of its social impact."

As long as manufacturing was local and limited, there was no need to advertise. Before the Civil War, for example, the local area could usually absorb all that was produced; therefore, a simple announcement in a local paper was sufficient to let people know that a particular product was available. But when factories began producing more than the local market could ordinarily consume, advertising came into play to create a larger demand.

Although national advertising began with the emergence of "name brands" in the late nineteenth century, it did not achieve the importance it now holds until the 1920s. In 1918, the total

Toothpaste advertisement.

Automobile advertisement (1929).

For Clean-up King
I Nominate . . .
by LOU GEHRIG

**New York Yankees' Clean-up Ace Makes
Novel Choice for All-Time Honor**

I DON'T need to tell baseball fans how important the "clean-up" (number four) man is in the batting line-up. With three reliable hitters batting ahead of him, it is his wallops that bring in the runs.

In my thirteen years of big league baseball I have watched some of the most famous "clean-up" men in the history of the game. But the other day in Boston I had the pleasure of seeing the "clean-up" king that gets my vote for the "all-time" honors. Strangely enough, this "clean-up" king isn't a slugger at all. Instead of cleaning up the bases, this one's specialty is cleaning up faces.

Here's how it happened. While in Boston playing the Red Sox, I made an inspection trip through the Gillette Safety Razor factory. There I discovered that what is true of baseball is also true of Gillette Blades. In baseball, the pick of the raw material is tried out, tested, and trained for the big league teams. At the Gillette factory I found that they buy only the finest steel, and put it through gruelling tests before it is made into Gillette Blades.

For instance, like a rookie baseball player, Gillette Blade steel has to be hardened and tempered.

To do this, Gillette uses electric furnaces, each one controlled by a device which can tell in an instant if the steel passing through the furnaces requires more heat or less heat. Faster than a speedball, the signal is flashed from the box to a great battery of switches, and the heat is raised or lowered accordingly. Then to make doubly sure that there is no possibility of error, they X-ray the steel with an electro-magnetic tester to detect hidden flaws.

A good ball player has to have precision and accuracy, too . . . and that's where Gillette chalks up a winning score. Grinding machines, adjustable to 1/10,000 of an inch give Gillette Blades shaving edges so keen you can't see them, even with the most powerful microscope.

These are some of the reasons why I nominate the Gillette Blade for all-time Clean-up King. For when it comes to cleaning up on stubborn bristles—with the greatest of ease and comfort—Gillette hits a home run with the bases loaded. Yes, Sir!—if baseball could only train players as accurately and efficiently as Gillette makes razor blades, we'd all find it easy to bat 1000.

With these important facts before you, why let anyone deprive you of shaving comfort by selling you a substitute! Ask for Gillette Blades and be sure to get them.

GILLETTE SAFETY RAZOR COMPANY, BOSTON, MASS.

Razor blade advertisement.

---

gross advertising revenue in magazines was $58.5 million. By 1920, it had more than doubled to $129.5 million, and by 1929, it was nearly $200 million. These figures should not be surprising in a decade that often equated advertising with religion. The biblical Moses was called the "ad-writer for the Deity," and in a best-selling book, Bruce Barton, a Madison Avenue advertiser, reinterpreted Jesus, the "man nobody knows," as a master salesman. Wrote Barton: "He would be a national advertiser today."

The designers of ads began to study psychology to determine what motives, conscious or unconscious, influenced consumers. One psychologist concluded that the appeal to the human instinct for "gaining social prestige" would sell the most goods. Another way to sell products, many learned, was to create anxiety in the mind of the consumer over body odor, bad breath, oily hair, dandruff, pimples, and other embarrassing ailments. In 1921, the Lambert Company used the term *halitosis* for bad breath in an ad for Listerine. Within six years, sales of Listerine had increased from a little more than 100,000 bottles a year to more than 4 million.

The appeal to sex also sold products, advertisers soon found, as did the desire for the latest style or invention. But perhaps the most important thing advertisers marketed was youth. "We are going to sell every artificial thing there is," a cosmetics salesman wrote in 1926, "and above all it is going to be young-young-young! We make women feel young." A great portion of the ads were aimed at women. As one trade journal announced: "The proper study of mankind is man . . . , but the proper study of markets is woman."

REFLECTING ON THE PAST Look at the accompanying advertisements carefully. What do they tell you about American culture in the 1920s? What do they suggest about attitudes toward women? Do they reveal any special anxieties? How are they similar to and different from advertising today?

ventures, and especially the stock market. "Everybody ought to be Rich," Al Smith's campaign manager proclaimed in an article in the *Ladies' Home Journal* early in 1929. A large number got into the game in the late 1920s because it seemed a safe and sure way to make money. The *New York Times* index of 25 industrial stocks reached 100 in 1924, moved up to 181 in 1925, dropped a bit in 1926, and rose again to 245 by the end of 1927.

Then the orgy started. During 1928, the market zoomed to 331. Many investors and speculators began to buy on margin (borrowing to invest). Money went into the market that would ordinarily have gone into houses, cars, and other goods. Yet even at the peak, probably only about 1.5 million Americans owned stock.

In early September 1929, the *New York Times* index peaked at 452 and then began to drift downward. On October 23, the market lost 31 points. The next day ("Black Thursday"), it first seemed that everyone was trying to sell, but at the end of the day, the panic appeared over. It was not. By mid-November, the market had plummeted to 224, about half what it had been two months before—a loss on paper of over $26 billion. Still, a month later, some businessmen got back into the market, thinking that it had reached its low point. But it continued to go down. Tens of thousands of investors lost everything. There was panic and despair, but the legendary stories of executives jumping out of windows were grossly exaggerated.

Conclusion

A New Era of Prosperity and Problems

Looking back, the 1920s may seem to be a golden era—an age of flappers, bootleg gin, constant parties, literary masterpieces, sports heroes, and easy wealth. The truth is much more complicated. More than most decades, the 1920s was a time of paradox and contradictions. It was a time of prosperity, yet a great many people, including farmers, blacks, and other ordinary Americans, did not prosper. It was a time of progress, when almost every year saw a new technological breakthrough, but it was also a decade of hate and intolerance.

The stock market crash ended the decade of prosperity. The crash did not cause the Great Depression, but the stock market debacle revealed the weakness of the economy. The Depression was related to the global economy and to problems created by the war and the peace settlement. The fruits of economic expansion had been unevenly distributed. African American families like the Parkers (the family we met at the beginning of this chapter) did not share much of the affluence created during the decade. Many other Americans, including many workers and farmers, could not afford to buy the autos, refrigerators, and other products pouring from American factories. Prosperity had been built on a shaky foundation. When that foundation crumbled in 1929, the nation slid into a major depression.

TIME*line*

1919 Treaty of Versailles

Strikes in Seattle, Boston, and elsewhere

Red Scare and Palmer raids

"Red Summer" race riots in Chicago and other cities

Marcus Garvey's Universal Negro Improvement Association spreads

1920 Warren Harding elected president

Women vote in national elections

First commercial radio broadcast

Sacco and Vanzetti arrested

Sinclair Lewis, *Main Street*

1921 Immigration Quota Law

Disarmament Conference

First birth control conference

Sheppard–Towner Maternity Act

1922 Fordney–McCumber Tariff

Sinclair Lewis, *Babbitt*

1923 Harding dies; Calvin Coolidge becomes president

Teapot Dome scandal

1925 Scopes trial in Dayton, Tennessee

F. Scott Fitzgerald, *The Great Gatsby*

Bruce Barton, *The Man Nobody Knows*

Alain Locke, *The New Negro*

Claude McKay, *Home to Harlem*

Five million enameled bathroom fixtures produced

1927 McNary–Haugen Farm Relief Bill

Sacco and Vanzetti executed

Lindbergh flies solo, New York to Paris

First talking movie, *The Jazz Singer*

Henry Ford produces 15 millionth car

1928 Herbert Hoover elected president

Kellogg–Briand Treaty

Stock market soars

1929 27 million registered cars in country

10 million households own radios

Stock market crash

✓●─⌐Study and **Review** at **www.myhistorylab.com**

Questions for Review and Reflection

1. What was the Harlem Renaissance?
2. Did the Prohibition experiment succeed or fail? Why?
3. In foreign policy during the 1920s, why did the United States try to isolate itself from the rest of the world?
4. What groups did not share in the prosperity of the decade?
5. Why are Harding and Coolidge often considered among our worst presidents?

Key Terms

Flapper 677
Harlem Renaissance 693
Lost Generation 690
Marcus Garvey 692

Palmer raids 679
Sacco–Vanzetti case 679
Scopes trial 688
Welfare capitalism 682

22

The Great Depression and the New Deal

American Stories

Coming of Age and Riding the Rails During the Depression

Flickering in a Seattle movie theater in the depths of the Great Depression, the Hollywood production *Wild Boys of the Road* captivated 13-year-old Robert Symmonds. The film, released in 1933, told the story of boys hitching rides on trains and tramping around the country. It was supposed to warn teenagers of the dangers of rail-riding, but for some it had the opposite effect. Robert, a boy from a middle-class home, already had a fascination with hobos. He had watched his mother give sandwiches to the transient men who sometimes knocked on the back door. He had taken to hanging around the "Hooverville" shantytown south of the King Street railroad station, where he would sit next to the fires and listen to the rail-riders' stories. Stoked for adventure, when school let out in 1934, Robert and a school friend hopped onto a moving boxcar on a train headed out of town. Hands reached out to pull them aboard the car, which already held 20 men. The two boys journeyed as far as Vancouver, Washington, and home to Seattle again. It was frightening, and exhilarating.

In 1938, under the weight of the Depression, the Symmonds family's security business failed. Years later, Robert recalled the effects on his father: "It hurt him bad when he went broke and all his friends deserted him. He did the best he could but never recovered his self-esteem and his pride." The loss of income forced Robert's family to accept a relative's offer of shelter in a three-room mountain cabin without electricity. Because of the move, Robert could no longer attend high school in Seattle. Once again, this time out of necessity, he turned to the rails, leaving his parents and three sisters behind.

Chapter Outline

The Great Depression

Economic Decline

Roosevelt and the First New Deal

One Hundred Days

The Second New Deal

The Last Years of the New Deal

The Other Side of the 1930s

Conclusion: The Mixed Legacy of the Great Depression and the New Deal

Robert faced a personal challenge of surviving difficult times, but he also was part of a looming problem that troubled the administration of President Franklin D. Roosevelt. Thousands of young people were graduating from high school, or leaving school earlier, with very few jobs open to them. An estimated 250,000 young people were among the drifters who resorted to the often dangerous practice of hitching rides on trains around the country. Robert rode the rails during summers to find work harvesting fruit up and down the West Coast. In 1939, his travels took him to Montana, where he encountered the **Civilian Conservation Corps** (CCC), the Roosevelt administration's solution to the problems of the young. When he enlisted in the CCC, Robert became one of nearly 3 million young men aged 17 and older who found work in government-sponsored conservation projects between 1933 and 1942. In exchange for their work, CCC workers earned $25 a month for their families back home, plus $5 a month spending money for themselves.

The CCC planted trees covering more than 2 million acres, improved more than 4 million acres of existing forest, and fought forest fires. In addition, the agency worked on a wide variety of conservation-related projects in a nation suffering from deforestation, erosion, drought, dust storms, and other environmental problems. CCC workers improved parks and recreation areas and even historic sites from the Civil War, including the notorious Andersonville prison camp in Georgia. In many ways, the CCC operated like a military organization, with workers wearing surplus World War I uniforms and following a fixed regimen of work and recreation that began with a bugler's call at 6 A.M. Many of its veterans credited the Corps with transforming them from boys into men, although others chafed under the discipline of the camps.

The greatest peacetime mobilization in U.S. history, the CCC set the stage for the wartime mobilization that followed. By the time Robert Symmonds joined the organization in 1939, war loomed in Europe. Like many CCC veterans, Robert's next stop in life was military service. He joined the navy and after the war became a merchant seaman. In later years, like many Americans of his generation, Robert remembered his experiences of the Great Depression grimly, but with some nostalgia. He even returned to hopping rides on railroad cars during his retirement years, out of a sense of adventure rather than necessity. "It's something that got into my blood years ago," he explained. "I guess it's a freedom thing."

The Great Depression changed the lives of all Americans and separated that generation from the one that followed. An exaggerated need for security, a fear of failure, a nagging feeling of guilt, and a real sense that economic catastrophe might happen again divided the Depression generation from people born after 1940. Like Robert Symmonds, most Americans never forgot those bleak years.

This chapter explores the causes and consequences of the Great Depression, and addresses such questions as: How effective were President Herbert Hoover's efforts to combat the crisis? How did Franklin Roosevelt revive a sense of confidence? How effective was the New Deal, Roosevelt's program of relief, recovery, and reform? And, in a time of great strides in technology, how did innovations in radio, movies, and the automobile affect the lives of most Americans?

The Great Depression

The United States had suffered other recessions and depression, notably in the 1830s, 1870s, and 1890s, but nothing compared to the devastating economic collapse of the 1930s. The Great Depression was all the more shocking because it came after a decade of unprecedented prosperity, when most experts assumed that the nation was immune to a business-cycle downturn. The Great Depression affected all areas of American life; perhaps most important, it destroyed American confidence in the future.

The Depression Begins

Few people anticipated the stock market crash in the fall of 1929. But even after that collapse, no one expected the entire economy to go into a tailspin. General Electric stock, selling for $396 in 1929, fell to $34 in 1932. By 1932, the median income had plunged to half what it had been in 1929. Construction spending fell to one-sixth of the 1929 level. By 1932, at least one of every four American breadwinners was out of work, and industrial production ground almost to a halt.

Why did the country sink deeper and deeper into depression? The prosperity of the 1920s was superficial. Farmers and coal and textile workers had suffered all through the 1920s from low prices, and the farmers were the first group in the 1930s to plunge into depression. But other economic sectors also lurched out of balance. Two percent of the population received about 28 percent of the national income, but the lower 60 percent got only 24 percent. Businesses increased profits while holding down wages and the prices of raw materials. This pattern depressed consumer purchasing power. Workers, like farmers, did not have the money to buy the goods they helped to produce. There was a relative decline in purchasing power in the late 1920s, unemployment was high in some industries, and the housing and automobile industries were already slackening before the crash.

Well-to-do Americans were investing a significant portion of their money in stock market speculation. Their illusion of permanent prosperity helped fire the boom of the 1920s, just as their pessimism and lack of confidence helped worsen the Depression in 1931 and 1932.

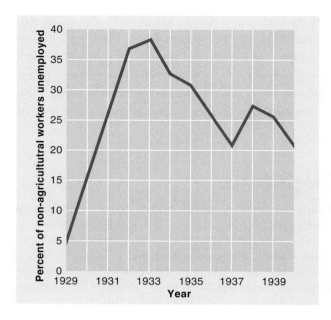

Unemployment Rate, 1929–1940 Although the unemployment rate declined during the New Deal years, the number still unemployed remained tragically high until World War II brought full employment. *(Source: U.S. Bureau of the Census)*

But there were other factors. The stock market crash revealed serious structural weaknesses in the financial and banking systems. The Federal Reserve Board, fearing inflation, tightened credit—the opposite of what it should have done. But the Depression was also caused by global economic problems. High American tariffs during the 1920s had reduced trade, and when American investment in Europe slackened in 1928 and 1929, European economies declined. As the European financial situation worsened, the American economy spiraled downward.

The federal government might have prevented the Wall Street crash and the Depression by more careful regulation of business and the stock market. Central planning might have ensured a more equitable distribution of income. But that kind of policy would have taken more foresight than most people had in the 1920s. It certainly would have required different people in power, and it is unlikely that the Democrats, had they been in control, would have altered the government's policies in fundamental ways.

Hoover and the Great Depression

Initial business and government reactions to the stock market crash were optimistic. "All the evidence indicates that the worst effects of the crash upon unemployment will have been passed during the next sixty days," Herbert Hoover predicted, but he did not sit idly by and watch the country drift toward disorder.

He acted aggressively. More than any president before him, he used the power of the federal government and the office of the president to deal with a crisis that seemed much like earlier cyclic recessions. Hoover called conferences of businessmen and labor leaders. He encouraged mayors and governors to speed up public works projects. He created agencies and boards, such as the National Credit Corporation and the Emergency Committee for Employment, to obtain voluntary action to solve the problem. Hoover even supported a tax cut, which Congress enacted in December 1929, but it did little to stimulate spending.

Economic Decline

Voluntary action and psychological campaigns could not stop the Depression. The stock market, after appearing to bottom out in the winter of 1930 and 1931, continued its decline, responding in part to the European economic collapse that threatened international finance and trade. Of course, not everyone lost money. Joseph Kennedy, film magnate, entrepreneur, and father of a future president, and a few others made millions as the market went down.

A Downward Spiral

More than a collapsing market afflicted the economy. Over 1,300 banks failed in 1930. Despite Hoover's pleas, many factories cut production, and some simply closed. The number of Americans out of work increased from 4 million in 1930 to 12 million in 1932. Foreclosures and evictions created thousands of personal tragedies. While the middle class watched in horror as life savings and dreams disappeared, the rich worried increasingly as the price of government bonds (the symbol of safety and security) dropped. They began to hoard gold and fear revolution.

There was never any real danger of violent upheaval. Some farmers organized to dump their milk to protest low prices, and when a neighbor's farm was sold, they gathered to hold a penny auction, bidding only a few cents for equipment and returning it to the dispossessed neighbor. But everywhere people despaired as the Depression deepened in 1931 and 1932. For most unemployed blacks and many tenant farmers, the Depression had little immediate effect because their lives were already so depressed. The 98 percent of Americans who did not own stock hardly noticed the crash; for them, the Depression meant a lost job or a foreclosure. Not everyone went hungry, stood in breadlines, or lost jobs, but almost everyone suffered, and many tended to blame themselves.

View the **Image**
Depression Era Breadlines
at **www.myhistorylab.com**

The Depression probably disrupted women's lives less than men's. When men lost their jobs, their identity and sense of purpose as the family breadwinner generally vanished. Some men helped out with family chores, usually with bitterness. For women, however, even when money was short,

Out of Work The worst result of the Great Depression was hopelessness and despair. Those emotions are captured in this painting of an unemployment office by artist Isaac Soyer. How does he convey a sense of anguish and dejection? How might these people have described what they were feeling? When did the unemployment crisis finally end? *(Isaac Soyer (1907–1981), "Employment Agency," 1937, Oil on canvas, 34 1/4 × 45 in. (87 × 114.3 cm.). Collection of the Whitney Museum of American Art, New York)*

there were still chores, and they were still in command of their households. Yet many women had to do extra work: taking in laundry, renting a room to a boarder, and making clothes they formerly would have bought. They also bore the psychological burden of unemployed husbands, hungry children, and unpaid bills. Many families moved in with relatives. The marriage rate, the divorce rate, and the birthrate all dropped during the decade, creating tensions that statistics cannot capture.

A Global Depression

Hoover kept urging more voluntary action. He insisted on maintaining the gold standard and a balanced budget, but so did almost everyone else. Hoover increasingly blamed the Depression on international economic problems, and he was partly right. The legacy of the war and the global economic policies of the 1920s were among the causes of the economic downturn in the United States. As the United States sank into Depression, the world followed. In May 1931, the

View the **Image**

"Migrant Mother"
(Dorothea Lange, Photo)
at **www.myhistorylab.com**

leading Austrian bank collapsed; by June, the German financial system was in chaos; and in September, England abandoned the gold standard. Soon most of the industrialized world, including Argentina, Brazil, and Japan, was caught in the Depression. Despite the global nature of the crisis, Americans began to blame Hoover. The president became isolated and bitter. The shanties that grew near all the large cities were called "Hoovervilles." Unable to admit mistakes and take a new tack, the President could not communicate personal empathy for the poor and the unemployed.

Hoover did try innovative schemes. More public works projects were built during his administration than in the previous 30 years. In the summer of 1931, he organized a pool of private money to rescue banks and businesses that were near failure. When that private effort failed, he turned reluctantly to Congress, which in 1932 authorized the Reconstruction Finance Corporation (RFC). It lent money to banks, insurance companies, farm mortgage companies, and railroads. Some critics charged that it was simply a trickle-down measure while the unemployed were ignored. Hoover, however, understood the immense costs to individuals and communities when a bank or mortgage company failed. The RFC helped shore up shaky financial institutions and remained the major government finance agency until World War II.

Hoover also asked Congress for a Home Financing Corporation to make mortgages more readily available. The Federal Home Loan Bank Act of 1932 became the basis for the Federal Housing Administration of the New Deal years. He also pushed the passage of the Glass–Steagall Banking Act of 1932, which expanded credit in order to make more loans available to businesses and individuals.

But Hoover rejected calls for the federal government to restrict production in hopes of raising farm prices—that, he believed, was too much federal intervention. He firmly believed in loans, not direct subsidies, and he thought it was the responsibility of state and local governments, as well as private charity, to provide direct relief to the unemployed and the needy.

Watch the Video

Dorothea Lange and Migrant Mother

at **www.myhistorylab.com**

The Bonus Army

Many World War I veterans lost their jobs during the Great Depression, and so, beginning in 1930, they lobbied for immediate payment of their veterans' bonuses that were due in 1945. In May 1932, about 17,000 veterans marched on Washington. Some took up residence in a shantytown, called Bonus City, outside town.

In mid-June, the Senate defeated the bonus bill, and most of the disappointed veterans accepted a free railroad ticket home. Several thousand remained, however, along with some wives and children, in the unsanitary shacks during the steaming summer heat. Among them were a few Communists and other radicals. Hoover, who exaggerated the subversive elements among those still camped out in Bonus City, refused to talk to the leaders, and finally called out the U.S. Army.

General Douglas MacArthur, the army chief of staff, ordered troops to disperse the veterans, whom he characterized as "a mob . . . animated by the essence of revolution." With tanks, guns, and tear gas, troops routed men who 15 years before had worn the same uniform. Two Bonus marchers died. Far from attacking revolutionaries in the streets of Washington, the army was routing bewildered, confused, unemployed men whose American dream had collapsed.

The Bonus army fiasco, breadlines, and shantytowns called Hoover-villes became the symbols of Hoover's presidency. He deserved better because he tried to use the power of the federal government to solve growing and increasingly complex economic problems. But his personality and background limited him. He could not understand why veterans marched on Washington to ask for a handout when they should have been back home working hard, practicing self-reliance, and cooperating. He believed that the greatest problem besetting Americans was a lack of confidence. He could not communicate with these people or inspire their confidence. Willing to give federal support to business, he could not accept giving federal aid to the unemployed. He feared an unbalanced budget and a large federal bureaucracy that would interfere with the "American way." Ironically, his actions and inactions soon led to a massive increase in federal power and in federal bureaucracy.

Roosevelt and the First New Deal

The first New Deal, from 1933 to early 1935, focused mainly on recovery and relief for the poor and unemployed. Some of its programs stemmed from the Hoover administration or from the progressive period. Others emerged from the nation's experiences in mobilizing for World War I. No single ideological position united all the programs, for Roosevelt, Hoover's successor, was a pragmatist who was willing to try different programs. More than Hoover, however, he believed in economic planning and in government spending to help the poor.

Roosevelt's caution and conservatism shaped the first New Deal. He did not promote socialism. The basic assumption of the New Deal was that a just society could be created by superimposing a welfare state on the capitalist system, leaving the profit motive in place. Roosevelt believed he could achieve this through cooperation with the business community. Later he moved toward reform, but at first his concern was primarily relief and recovery.

The Election of 1932

In the summer of 1932, the Republicans nominated Hoover for a second term, but the Depression and Hoover's unpopularity opened the way for the Democrats. Franklin D. Roosevelt won the nomination. Distantly related to

The Disabled President This is a rare photograph of Franklin Roosevelt in his wheelchair taken in a private moment with his dog, Fala, and a young friend. Usually FDR's advisers carefully arranged to have the president photographed only when he was seated or propped up behind a podium. Despite being paralyzed from the waist down, the president gave the impression of health and vitality until near the end of his life. Did his physical disability restrict his ability to be president?

Theodore Roosevelt, he had served as assistant secretary of the navy during World War I and was the Democratic vice presidential candidate in 1920. Crippled by polio not long after, he had recovered enough to serve as governor of New York for two terms. Despite his considerable experience, he was not especially well-known by the general public in 1932.

As governor, Roosevelt had promoted cheaper electric power, conservation, and old-age pensions, and he became the first governor to provide state aid for the unemployed. But it was difficult to tell during the campaign exactly what he stood for. Ambiguity was probably the best strategy in 1932, but Roosevelt had no master plan to save the country. Yet he won overwhelmingly, carrying more than 57 percent of the popular vote.

During the campaign, Roosevelt had promised a "new deal for the American people." But the New Deal had to wait for four months, because the Constitution provided for presidents to be inaugurated on March 4. (This was changed to January 20 by the Twentieth Amendment, ratified in 1933.) During the long interregnum, the state of the nation deteriorated badly. The banking system was near collapse, and hardship increased. Despite his bitter defeat, Hoover tried to cooperate with the president-elect and a hostile Congress. But he could accomplish little. Everyone waited for the new president to take office.

•‖ Read the Document

Franklin D. Roosevelt, First
Inaugural Address (1933)
at **www.myhistorylab.com**

⊙‖ Watch the Video

Franklin D. Roosevelt's
Inauguration
at **www.myhistorylab.com**

In his inaugural address, Roosevelt announced confidently, "The only thing we have to fear is fear itself." This, of course, was not true: The country faced the worst crisis since the Civil War. But Roosevelt's confidence and ability to communicate with ordinary Americans were obvious early in his presidency. He had clever speechwriters, a sense of pace and rhythm in his speeches, and an ability, in his "fireside chats" on the radio, to convince listeners that he was speaking directly to them. When he said "my friends," millions believed that he meant it.

Roosevelt's Advisers

During the interregnum, Roosevelt surrounded himself with intelligent and innovative advisers. His cabinet consisted of a mixture of people from different backgrounds who often did not agree with one another. Harold Ickes, the secretary of the interior, was a Republican lawyer from Chicago and onetime supporter of Theodore Roosevelt. Another Republican, Henry Wallace of Iowa, a plant geneticist and agricultural statistician, became the secretary of agriculture. Frances Perkins, the first woman ever appointed to a cabinet post, became the secretary of labor. A disciple of Jane Addams and Florence Kelley, she had been a settlement resident, the secretary of the New York Consumers League, and an adviser to Al Smith.

•‖ Read the Document

Frances Perkins and the Social
Security Act (1935, 1960)
at **www.myhistorylab.com**

In addition to the formal cabinet, Roosevelt had an informal "**Brain Trust**," including Adolph Berle, Jr., a young expert on corporation law, and Rexford Tugwell, a Columbia University authority on agricultural economics and a committed national planner. Roosevelt also listened to Raymond Moley, another Columbia professor who later became one of the president's severest critics, and to Harry Hopkins, an energetic man who loved to bet on horse races and was passionately concerned for the poor and unemployed.

Eleanor Roosevelt was a controversial first lady. She wrote a newspaper column, made radio broadcasts, traveled widely, and was constantly giving speeches and listening to the concerns of women, minorities, and ordinary Americans. Attacked by critics who thought she had too much power, she took courageous stands for social justice and civil rights, pushing the president toward social reform.

Roosevelt was an adept politician. He was not well read, especially on economic matters, but he demonstrated that he could learn from his advisers and yet not be dominated by them. He took ideas, plans, and suggestions from conflicting sources and combined them. An improviser who once likened himself to a quarterback who called one play and, if it did not work, called a different one, Roosevelt was an optimist by nature. And he believed in action.

One Hundred Days

In the midst of the crisis, Congress was ready to pass almost any legislation that Roosevelt put before it. In three months, it considered a bewildering number of bills, many hardly well-thought out or consistent with each other. But virtually all of the laws passed had far-reaching implications for the relationship of government to society. Unlike Hoover, Roosevelt was an opportunist willing to use direct government action against depression and unemployment. None of the bills passed during the first hundred days cured the Depression, but taken together, the **"First Hundred Days"** constituted one of the most innovative periods in American political history.

The Banking Crisis

The most immediate problem Roosevelt faced was the banking crisis. Many banks had closed, and citizens were hoarding money and gold. Roosevelt immediately declared a four-day bank holiday. Three days later, an emergency session of Congress approved his action and within hours gave the president broad powers over financial transactions, prohibited the hoarding of gold, and allowed for the reopening of sound banks, sometimes with RFC loans.

Over the next few years, Congress gave the federal government more regulatory power over the stock market and over the process by which corporations issued stock. The Banking Act of 1933 strengthened the Federal Reserve System, established the Federal Deposit Insurance Corporation (FDIC), and insured individual deposits up to $5,000. Although the American Bankers Association opposed the plan, banks were soon attracting depositors by advertising that they were protected by government insurance.

The Democratic platform in 1932 called for reduced government spending and an end to Prohibition. Roosevelt moved quickly on both issues. The Economy Act, which passed easily, called for a 15 percent reduction in government salaries and a reorganization of federal agencies to save money. The bill also cut veterans' pensions, despite the protests of veterans' organizations, though other bills called for additional spending. The Beer-Wine Revenue Act legalized 3.2-percent-alcohol beer and light wines and levied a tax on both. The Twenty-First Amendment, ratified on December 5, 1933, repealed the Eighteenth Amendment and officially ended Prohibition.

Congress gave the president broad power to devalue the dollar and induce inflation. Bankers and businessmen feared inflation, but farmers and debtors favored an inflationary policy to put more dollars in their pockets. Roosevelt rejected the more extreme plans of many congressmen from agricultural states, but he did take the country off the gold standard. No longer would paper currency be redeemable in gold. The action terrified some conservative businessmen, and even Roosevelt's director of the budget announced solemnly that it "meant the end of Western Civilization."

Devaluation neither ended Western civilization nor produced instant recovery. Roosevelt and his advisers fixed the price of gold at $35 an ounce in January 1934 (against the old price of $20.63), inflating the dollar by about 40 percent. Soon the country settled down to a slightly inflated currency and a dollar based on both gold and silver.

Relief Measures

Roosevelt believed in economy in government and in a balanced budget, but he also wanted to help the unemployed and the homeless. One survey estimated that in 1933 1.5 million Americans were homeless. A man with a wife and six children who was being evicted wrote, "I have 10 days to get another house, no job, no means of paying rent, can you advise me as to which would be the most humane way to dispose of myself and family, as this is about the only thing that I see left to do."

Roosevelt's answer was the Federal Emergency Relief Administration (FERA), which Congress authorized with an appropriation of $500 million in direct grants to cities and states. A few months later, Roosevelt created a Civil Works Administration (CWA) to put more than 4 million people to work on various state, municipal, and federal projects. Hopkins, who ran both agencies, believed it was much better to pay people to work than to give them charity. So did most people in need. An accountant working on a road project said, "I'd rather stay out here in that ditch the rest of my life than take one cent of direct relief."

The CWA was not always effective, but in just over a year, it built or restored a half-million miles of roads and constructed 40,000 schools and 1,000 airports. It hired 50,000 teachers to keep rural schools open and others to teach adult education courses in the cities. The CWA helped millions of people get through the bitterly cold winter of 1933 to 1934. It also put over a billion dollars of purchasing power into the economy. Roosevelt, who later would be accused of deficit spending, feared that the program was costing too much and might create a permanent class of relief recipients. In the spring of 1934, he ordered the CWA closed down.

The Public Works Administration (PWA), directed by Harold Ickes, lasted longer. Between 1933 and 1939, the PWA built hospitals, courthouses, and school buildings. Its projects included the port of Brownsville, Texas, two aircraft carriers, and low-cost slum housing. One purpose of the PWA was economic pump priming—to stimulate the economy through government spending. Afraid of scandals, Ickes spent money far too slowly and carefully. The PWA projects, worthwhile as most of them were, provided little economic stimulus.

Agricultural Adjustment Act

By 1933, most farmers were desperate, caught between mounting surpluses and falling prices. Some in the Midwest even talked of revolution. But most observers saw only despair in farmers who had worked hard but were still losing their farms.

Congress passed a number of bills in 1933 and 1934 to deal with the agricultural crisis, including foreclosures and evictions. But the New Deal's principal solution was the **Agricultural Adjustment Act (AAA)**, which sought to control the overproduction of basic commodities so that farmers might regain their pre-World War I purchasing power. To guarantee these "parity prices" (the average prices in the years 1909 to 1914), the production of major agricultural staples—wheat, cotton, corn, hogs, rice, tobacco, and milk—would be controlled by paying the farmers to reduce their acreage under cultivation. The AAA levied a tax at the processing stage to pay for the program.

The act caused great disagreement among farm leaders and economists, but the controversy was nothing compared with the public outcry in the summer of 1933, when, to boost prices, the AAA ordered 10 million acres of cotton plowed up and 6 million young pigs slaughtered. It seemed immoral to kill pigs and plow up cotton when millions of people were hungry and ill-clothed.

The Agricultural Adjustment Act did raise the prices of some agricultural products. But it helped the larger farmers more than the small operators, and it was often disastrous for the tenant farmers and sharecroppers. When they reduced their acreage, landowners often discharged tenant families. Many were simply cast out on the road with nowhere to go. Large farmers cultivated their fewer acres more intensely, so that the total crop was little reduced. In the end, the prolonged drought that hit the Southwest in 1934 did more than the AAA to limit production and raise agricultural prices. But the long-range significance of the AAA, which was later declared unconstitutional, was to establish the idea that the government should subsidize farmers for limiting production.

Industrial Recovery

The legislation during the first days of the Roosevelt administration contained something for almost every group. The National Industrial Recovery Act (NIRA) was designed to help business, raise prices, control production, and put people back to work. Its goal was to restrict competition, restrain profits, and produce labor-management harmony. The act established the **National Recovery Administration** (NRA), with the power to set fair competition codes in all industries. For a time, everyone forgot about antitrust laws and talked of cooperation. There were parades and rallies, a postage stamp, and "We Do Our Part" posters, featuring a blue eagle, for cooperating industries. But the results did not live up to the promise.

Section 7a of the NIRA, included at labor unions' insistence, guaranteed labor's right to organize and to bargain collectively. Even so, businessmen often interpreted the labor provisions of contracts loosely. In addition, small businessmen complained that the NIRA was unfair to their interests. Any attempt to set prices led to controversy.

Many consumers suspected that the codes and contracts were raising prices, while others feared the return of monopoly. When the Supreme

Court declared the NIRA unconstitutional in 1935, few complained. Still, the NIRA was an ambitious attempt to bring some order into a confused business situation, and its labor provisions provided a starting point for later legislation.

Civilian Conservation Corps

One of the most popular and successful New Deal programs, the Civilian Conservation Corps (CCC), combined work relief with the preservation of natural resources. It put young, unemployed men between the ages of 17 and 25—2.5 million of them—to work on reforestation, road and park construction, flood control, and other projects. The men lived in work camps and earned $30 a month, $25 of which had to be sent home to their families.

The CCC ran separate camps for young black men, and eventually a few camps were organized for unemployed young women, but the program was designed to help unemployed young men. Some complained that the camps were too military in their organization. Despite complaints, the CCC was one of the most successful and least controversial of all the New Deal programs.

Tennessee Valley Authority

Franklin Roosevelt, like his cousin Theodore Roosevelt, believed in conservation. He promoted flood-control projects and added millions of acres to the country's national forests, wildlife refuges, and fish and game sanctuaries.

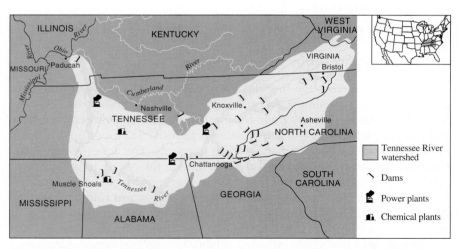

The Tennessee Valley Authority The TVA transformed the way the Tennessee valley looked; it replaced a wild river with a series of flood-control and hydroelectric dams and created a series of lakes behind the dams. It stopped short of the coordinated regional planning that some people wanted, but it was one of the most important New Deal projects, as it had an impact on portions of seven states.

But the most important New Deal conservation project, the **Tennessee Valley Authority** (TVA), owed more to Republican George Norris, a progressive senator from Nebraska, than to Roosevelt.

During World War I, the federal government had built a hydroelectric plant and two munitions factories at Muscle Shoals, on the Tennessee River in Alabama. The government tried unsuccessfully to sell these facilities to private industry, but all through the 1920s, Norris campaigned to have the federal government operate them for the benefit of the valley's residents. Twice Republican presidents vetoed bills providing for federal operation, but Roosevelt endorsed Norris's idea and expanded it into a regional development plan.

Congress authorized the TVA as an independent public corporation to sell electricity and fertilizer and to promote flood control and land reclamation. The TVA built nine major dams and many minor ones between 1933 and 1944, affecting parts of Virginia, North Carolina, Georgia, Alabama, Mississippi, Tennessee, and Kentucky. Some private utility companies claimed that the TVA unfairly competed with private industry, but it was an imaginative experiment in regional planning. For residents of the valley, it meant cheaper electricity and changed lifestyles. The largest federal construction project ever launched, it also created jobs for many thousands who helped build the dams. But government officials and businessmen who feared that the experiment would lead to socialism curbed the regional planning possibilities of the TVA.

•:•⊣**Read** the **Document**
Tennessee Valley Authority Act
at **www.myhistorylab.com**

Critics of the New Deal

The furious legislative activity during the first 100 days of the New Deal helped alleviate the country's pessimism and despair. The stock market rose slightly, and industrial production was up 11 percent at the end of 1933. Still, the country remained locked in depression, and nearly 12 million Americans lacked jobs.

Roosevelt captured the imagination of ordinary Americans everywhere, but conservatives became increasingly angry. Many businessmen who approved of Roosevelt's early economy measures and endorsed programs such as the NIRA began to fear that the president was leading the country toward socialism.

The conservative revolt against Roosevelt surfaced in the summer of 1934 as the congressional elections approached. A group of disgruntled politicians and businessmen formed the Liberty League. Led by Alfred E. Smith and John W. Davis, the league supported conservative or at least anti–New Deal candidates for Congress, but it had little influence. In the election of 1934, the Democrats increased their majority from 310 to 319 in the House and from 60 to 69 in the Senate (only the second time in the twentieth century that the party in power had increased its control of Congress in the midterm election). A few people were learning to hate "that man in the White House," but most Americans approved of what he was doing.

More disturbing than conservative critics were those on the left who maintained that the government had not done enough to help the poor. The Communist party increased its membership from 7,500 in 1930 to 75,000 in 1938. Communists organized protest marches and tried to reach out to the oppressed and unemployed. While a majority who joined the party came from the working class, communism had a special appeal to writers, intellectuals, and some college students during a decade when the American dream had turned into a nightmare.

More Americans, however, were influenced by other movements promising easy solutions. In Minnesota, Governor Floyd Olson accused capitalism of causing the Depression and thundered, "I hope the present system of government goes right to hell." In California, Upton Sinclair, the muckraking socialist and author of *The Jungle*, ran for governor on the EPIC platform ("End Poverty in California"). He promised to pay everyone over 60 years of age a pension of $50 a month, financed by higher income and inheritance taxes. He won the primary but lost the election, and his movement collapsed.

California also produced Dr. Francis E. Townsend, who claimed a national following of over 5 million. His supporters backed a scheme that promised $200 a month to all unemployed citizens over age 60 on the condition that they spend it in the same month they received it. Economists laughed, but followers organized thousands of Townsend Pension Clubs.

•⦿•⎯Read the **Document**

Father Charles E. Coughlin, "A Third Party" (1936) at **www.myhistorylab.com**

•⦿•⎯Read the **Document**

Huey Long, "Share Our Wealth" (1935) at **www.myhistorylab.com**

More threatening to Roosevelt and the New Deal were the protest movements led by Father Charles E. Coughlin and Senator Huey P. Long. Father Coughlin, a Roman Catholic priest from a Detroit suburb, attracted an audience of 30 million to 45 million to his national radio show. At first he supported Roosevelt's policies, but later he savagely attacked the New Deal as excessively pro-business. Mixing religious commentary with visions of a society without bankers and big businessmen, he roused his audience with blatantly anti-Semitic tirades.

Like Coughlin, Huey Long had a charisma that won support from the millions still trying to survive in a country where the continuing Depression made day-to-day existence a struggle. Elected governor of Louisiana in 1928, Long called his program "Share Our Wealth." He taxed the oil refineries and built hospitals, schools, and thousands of miles of new highways. By 1934, he was the virtual dictator of his state, personally controlling the police and the courts. Long talked about a guaranteed $2,000 to $3,000 income for all American families (18.3 million families earned less than $1,000 per year in 1936) and promised pensions for the elderly and college educations for the young, all to be paid for by soaking the rich. Had an assassin not killed Long in September 1935, he might have mounted a third-party challenge to Roosevelt.

The Second New Deal

Responding in part to lower-middle-class discontent and seeking as well to head off utopian schemes, Roosevelt moved in 1935 toward the goals of social reform and social justice. At the same time, he ceased trying to cooperate with the business community. "In spite of our efforts and in spite of our talk, we have not weeded out the overprivileged and we have not effectively lifted up the underprivileged," Roosevelt announced in his annual message to Congress in January 1935.

Work Relief and Social Security

The **Works Progress Administration** (WPA), authorized by Congress in April 1935, was the first massive attempt to deal with unemployment and its demoralizing effect on millions of Americans. The WPA employed about 3 million people a year (at wages below what private industry paid) on projects ranging from building bridges to putting on plays. It built nearly 6,000 schools, more than 2,500 hospitals, and 13,000 playgrounds, in addition to funding actors, artists, and writers.

View the Image
WPA's Federal Art Project
at **www.myhistorylab.com**

Only one member of a family could get a WPA job—always a man unless a woman headed the household. But eventually more than 13 percent of the people who worked for the WPA were women, usually making over old clothes. "For unskilled men we have the shovel. For unskilled women we have only the needle," one official explained.

The WPA was controversial from the beginning. Its initials, critics said, stood for "We Putter Around." Yet the WPA not only did useful work but also gave millions of unemployed Americans a sense of pride that they were working and supporting their families.

The National Youth Administration (NYA) supplemented the work of the WPA and assisted young men and women between the ages of 16 and 25 (including Richard Nixon, a young law student at Duke University). Lyndon Johnson began his political career as director of the Texas NYA.

By far the most enduring reform was the passage of the **Social Security Act** of 1935. Since the progressive period, reformers had argued for national health and unemployment insurance and old-age pensions. By the 1930s, the United States was the only major industrial country without such programs. Secretary of Labor Perkins argued most strongly for social insurance, but Roosevelt also wanted to head off popular schemes like the Townsend Plan.

The Social Security Act of 1935 was a compromise. To appease the medical profession, Congress quickly dropped a plan for federal health insurance. The act's central provision was old-age and survivor insurance, paid for by a tax of 1 percent on both employers and employees. The act also established a cooperative federal-state system of unemployment compensation, gave federal grants to the states for the disabled and the blind, and provided aid to dependent children—the provision that years later expanded to become the largest federal welfare program.

Conservatives denounced Social Security for regimenting people and destroying self-reliance. But in no other country was social insurance paid for in part by a regressive tax on the workers' wages. "With those taxes in there, no damn politician can ever scrap my Social Security program," Roosevelt later explained, insisting that by paying the taxes wage earners won a moral claim on their benefits. But farm laborers and domestic servants were not covered. The system discriminated against married women wage earners and failed to protect against sickness. Still, it was one of the most important New Deal measures, and it marked the beginning of the welfare state that expanded greatly after World War II.

Aiding the Farmers

The Social Security Act and the Works Progress Administration were only two signs of Roosevelt's greater concern for social reform. The flurry of legislation in 1935 and early 1936, often called the "second New Deal," also included an effort to help American farmers. The Resettlement Administration (RA), motivated in part by a Jeffersonian ideal of yeoman farmers working their own land, tried to relocate tenant farmers to land purchased by the government. But it failed to accomplish much, a victim of underfunding and of scare talk about Soviet-style collective farms.

Much more successful in improving the lives of farm families was the Rural Electrification Administration (REA), which was authorized in 1935 to lend money to cooperatives to generate and distribute electricity in isolated rural areas not served by private utilities. Only 10 percent of the nation's farms had electricity in 1936. When the REA's lines were finally attached, they dramatically changed the lives of millions of farm families who had only been able to dream about the radios, washing machines, and farm equipment advertised in magazines.

The Dust Bowl: An Ecological Disaster

Those who tried to farm on the Great Plains fell victim to years of drought and dust storms. Record heat waves and below-average rainfall in the 1930s turned the Oklahoma panhandle and western Kansas into a giant **dust bowl**. Thousands died of "dust pneumonia." By the end of the decade, 10,000 farm homes were abandoned, 9 million acres of farmland were reduced to wasteland, and 3.5 million people had joined a massive migration to find a better life. Many tenant farmers and hired hands were evicted, their plight immortalized by John Steinbeck in his novel *The Grapes of Wrath* (1939).

The dust bowl was a natural disaster, aided and exaggerated by human actions. The semiarid plains west of the 98th meridian were not suitable for intensive agriculture, and 60 years of improper land use had exposed the

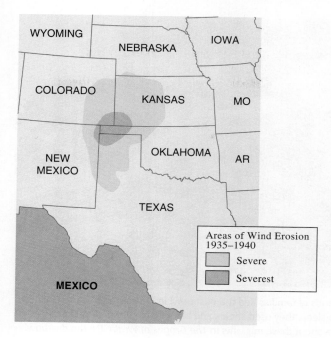

The Dust Bowl This map depicts the wide extent of damage caused by high winds and drought, the worst in the history of the country, according to the U.S. Weather Bureau. What options are open to residents of areas hit by such natural disasters?

thin soil to the elements. When the winds came, much of the land simply blew away. In the end, it was a matter of too little government planning and regulation and too many farmers using new technology to exploit nature. The Roosevelt administration did try to deal with the problem. The Taylor Grazing Act of 1934 restricted the use of the public range and established the principle that the remaining public domain was not for sale. The CCC planted trees and promoted soil conservation, but in the end it was too little too late.

Even worse, according to some authorities, government measures applied after the disaster of the 1930s encouraged farmers to return to raising wheat and other inappropriate crops, leading to more dust bowl crises in the 1950s and 1970s.

The New Deal and the West

The New Deal probably aided the West more than any other region. The CCC, the AAA, drought relief measures, and various federal agencies helped the region out of proportion to the number of people who lived there. Most important were the large-scale water projects, such as Boulder Dam (later renamed Hoover Dam) on the Colorado River and the massive Grand Coulee Dam on the Columbia River. These dams produced huge amounts of hydroelectric power, poured millions of dollars into the economy, and provided enormous amounts of water for urban and rural needs.

Dust Bowl Family Thousands of families fled the dust bowl in old cars and headed for California. With no place to sleep, they used sheets and blankets to turn their cars into tents. John Steinbeck wrote about these migrants in *The Grapes of Wrath.* Do the dustbowl migrants represent a failure of the American dream?

Despite all the federal aid to the region, many westerners bitterly criticized the regulation and the bureaucracy that came with the grants. The cattlemen in Wyoming, Colorado, and Montana desperately needed the help of the federal government, but even as they accepted the aid, they denounced the New Deal.

Controlling Corporate Power and Taxing the Wealthy

In the summer of 1935, Roosevelt set out to control the large corporations, and he even toyed with radical plans to heavily tax the well-to-do and redistribute wealth in the United States. The Public Utility Holding Company Act, passed in 1935, attempted to restrict the power of the giant utility companies, the 12 largest of which controlled more than half the country's power. It gave each company five years to demonstrate that its services were efficient or face being dissolved. This was one of the most radical attempts to control corporate power in American history.

In the same year, Roosevelt urged higher taxes on the rich and a heavy inheritance tax. When Congress dropped the inheritance tax provision, however, Roosevelt did not fight for it. Even the weakened bill angered many in the business community who thought that FDR was implementing Huey Long's "Share the Wealth" scheme.

The New Deal for Labor

Like many progressive reformers, Roosevelt was more interested in help-ing working people by passing social legislation than by strengthening unions. Yet he saw labor as an important balance to the power of industry, and he listened to his advisers, especially Frances Perkins and Senator Robert Wagner of New York, who persistently brought up the needs of organized labor.

Roosevelt supported the 1935 Wagner Act (officially the National Labor Relations Act), which outlawed blacklisting and a number of other practices and reasserted labor's right to organize and to bargain collectively. The act also established a National Labor Relations Board with the power to certify a properly elected bargaining unit. The act did not require workers to join unions, but it made the federal government a regulator in management-labor relations. That alone made the National Labor Relations Act one of the most important New Deal reform measures.

The Roosevelt administration's friendly attitude helped increase union membership from under 3 million in 1933 to 4.5 million by 1935. Many groups, however, were left out, including farm laborers, unskilled workers, and women. Only about 3 percent of working women belonged to unions, and they earned only about 60 percent of wages paid to men for equivalent work. Still, many resented women being employed at all. The AFL had never organized unskilled workers, but a new group of commit-ted and militant labor leaders emerged in the 1930s to take up that task: John L. Lewis of the United Mine Workers, David Dubinsky of the Interna-tional Ladies' Garment Workers, and Sidney Hillman of the Amalgamated Clothing Workers. The latter two were socialists who believed in economic planning and had worked closely with social justice progressives. These new progressive labor leaders formed the Committee of Industrial Organi-zation (CIO) within the AFL and set out to organize workers in the steel, auto, and rubber industries. Rather than separating workers by skill or craft as the AFL preferred, they organized industrywide unions.

In 1936, the workers at three rubber plants in Akron, Ohio, went on un-authorized strikes. Instead of picketing, they took over the buildings. The "sit-down strike" became a new protest technique, disorderly but largely nonviolent (as would be civil rights demonstrations in the 1960s). After sev-eral such strikes, General Motors finally accepted the United Auto Workers (UAW) as their employees' bargaining agent. The GM strike was the most important event in a critical period of labor upheaval. Labor's voice now began to be heard in the decision-making process in major industries where labor had long been denied any role, raising the status of organized labor in the eyes of many Americans.

Violence spread along with the sit-down strikes. Chrysler capitulated, but Ford fought back with armed guards, and it took a bloody struggle before the UAW became the bargaining agent. Militantly anti-union U.S. Steel agreed to a 40-hour week and an eight-hour day, but other steel companies refused to go along. In the "Memorial Day Massacre" in 1937, police fired into a crowd of workers and their families peacefully picketing the Republic Steel plant in Chicago. All 10 who died were shot in the back.

The CIO's aggressive tactics gained many members, to the horror of AFL leaders. They expelled the CIO leaders, only to see them form a separate **Congress of Industrial Organizations** (the initials stayed the same). Accepting unskilled workers, African Americans, and others who had never belonged to a union before, the CIO created a new spirit of optimism in the labor movement.

America's Minorities in the 1930s

A half-million African Americans joined unions through the CIO, and New Deal agencies aided many blacks. Yet familiar patterns of poverty, discrimination, and violence persisted. Lynchings in the South also increased in the New Deal years.

Throughout the decade, the nation was gripped by the "Scottsboro Boys" case in Alabama, which began in 1931 when two young white women accused nine black youths of rape. Convicted and condemned to death by an all-white jury, the blacks were given a new trial in 1933 by order of the Supreme Court on the grounds that they had not received proper legal counsel. Liberals and radicals (including the Communist party) mobilized in defense of the youths' civil rights, while many from the South saw the honor of white women at stake. Evidence supporting the alleged rapes was never presented, and eventually one of the women recanted. Yet in new trials, five of the young men were convicted and given long prison terms. Charges against the other four were dropped in 1937. Four of the remaining five were paroled in 1944, and the fifth escaped to Michigan.

The migration of blacks to northern cities, which had accelerated during World War I, continued during the 1930s. The collapse of cotton prices forced black farmers and farm laborers to flee north for survival. But since most were poorly educated, they soon became trapped in northern ghettos, where they got only the most menial jobs. The black unemployment rate was triple that of whites, and blacks often received less per person in welfare payments.

Black leaders attacked the Roosevelt administration for supporting or allowing segregation in government-sponsored facilities. Roosevelt, dependent on the vote of the South and afraid to antagonize powerful southern congressmen, refused to support the two major civil rights bills of the era: an anti-lynching bill and a bill to abolish the poll tax. Yet Ickes and Hopkins worked to ensure that blacks were given opportunities in New Deal agencies. By 1941, black federal employees totaled 150,000, more than three times the number during the Hoover administration. Most worked in the lower ranks, but some were lawyers, architects, office managers, and engineers.

Partly responsible for the presence of more black employees was the "black cabinet." It was a group of more than 50 young blacks working in various New Deal agencies, led by Mary McLeod Bethune, the daughter of a sharecropper and organizer of the National Council of Negro Women. She had a large impact on New Deal policy—speaking out forcefully, picketing and protesting, and intervening shrewdly to obtain civil rights and more jobs for African Americans.

Although FDR appointed some blacks to government positions, he was never particularly committed to civil rights. That was not true of Eleanor Roosevelt, who was educated in part by Bethune. In 1939, when the Daughters of the American Revolution denied black concert singer Marian Anderson their stage, the First Lady protested by resigning her DAR membership and arranged for Anderson to sing from the steps of the Lincoln Memorial before an audience of 75,000.

Hundreds of thousands of Mexicans, brought to the United States to work in the 1920s, lost their jobs in the Depression. Drifting to the Southwest or settling in urban *barrios*, they met signs like "No Niggers, Mexicans, or Dogs Allowed." Some New Deal agencies helped destitute Mexicans, but as aliens and migrants, most could not qualify for relief. The preferred solution was to ship them back to Mexico, often after illegal roundups. One estimate placed the number sent back in 1932 at 200,000, which included American citizens. But some who remained adopted militant tactics to obtain fair treatment.

Asians (Chinese, Japanese, and a smaller number of Koreans and Asian Indians) also suffered during the Depression. Most lived in ethnic enclaves and were treated like foreigners—not quite black, but not white either. Those who were part of the second generation were troubled by their "twoness." They were American citizens because they had been born in the United States, but their parents wanted them to retain their ties to the old country. One young Japanese woman wrote: "I became equally adept with knife and fork and with chopsticks. I said grace at mealtime in Japanese, and recited the Lord's Prayer in English." But to most Americans, who had difficulty distinguishing Japanese from Chinese from Korean, they were all foreigners.

Native Americans experienced hunger, disease, and despair, their plight compounded by years of exploitation. They had lost over 60 percent of the 138 million acres allocated to them under the Dawes Act in 1887 (see Chapter 17), and many who remained on the reservations were not even citizens. In 1924, Congress granted citizenship to all Indians born in the United States, but that did not end their suffering.

FDR brought a new spirit to Indian policy by appointing John Collier as commissioner of Indian affairs. Collier was primarily responsible for passage of the Indian Reorganization Act of 1934, which sought to restore tribes' political independence, to end the Dawes Act's allotment policy, and to promote the "study of Indian civilization." Not all Indians agreed with the new policies. Some Americans charged that the act was inspired by communism or would increase government bureaucracy, while missionaries claimed that the government was promoting paganism.

The paradox of U.S. policy toward the Indians can be illustrated by Collier's attempt to solve the Navajo problem. The Navajo lands, like most of the West, were overgrazed, and soil erosion threatened to fill the new lake behind Hoover Dam with silt. By supporting a policy of reducing the herds of sheep and goats on Indian land and by promoting soil conservation, Collier contributed to the change in the Navajo lifestyle and to the end of their self-sufficiency, something he wanted to support.

Women and the New Deal

Women made some gains during the 1930s, and more women occupied high government positions than in any previous administration. Some of these women had served as social workers and now joined government bureaus to continue the fight for social justice. But they were usually in offices where they did not threaten male prerogatives. Despite some gains, the early New Deal programs did nothing for an estimated 140,000 homeless women. Married women were often fired from their jobs on the grounds that they should be home caring for their families rather than depriving men of employment.

Despite the number of women working for the government, feminism declined in the 1930s. The older feminists died or retired, and younger women did not replace them. With some dramatic exceptions, the image of a woman's proper role in the 1930s continued to be that of a housewife and mother.

The Last Years of the New Deal

The New Deal was neither a consistent nor a well-organized effort to end the Depression and restructure society. A pragmatic politician, Roosevelt was concerned above all with addressing pressing problems as effectively as possible, and to that end, he frequently shifted course. The first New Deal in 1933 and 1934 had concentrated on relief and recovery; the legislation of 1935 and 1936 stressed social reform. In many ways, the election of 1936 marked the high point of Roosevelt's power and influence. After 1937, in part because of the growing threat of war but also because of increasing opposition in Congress, the pace of passing social legislation slowed. Yet several measures passed in 1937 and 1938 had such far-reaching significance that some historians refer to a third New Deal.

The Election of 1936

The Republicans in 1936 nominated a moderate, Governor Alfred Landon of Kansas. Although he attacked the New Deal, charging it with waste and too much bureaucracy, Landon promised to take the same approach, only more efficiently. The *Literary Digest* magazine predicted his victory on the basis of its "scientific" telephone poll.

Roosevelt, helped by signs of economic recovery and supported by a coalition of the Democratic South, organized labor, farmers, and urban voters, won easily. For the first time, a majority of African Americans deserted the GOP—"the party of Lincoln"—out of appreciation for New Deal relief programs. No viable candidate to the left of the New Deal materialized. Winning by over 10 million votes and carrying every state except Maine and Vermont, Roosevelt now had a mandate to continue his New Deal reforms.

The Battle of the Supreme Court

"I see one-third of a nation ill-housed, ill-clad, ill-nourished," Roosevelt declared in his second inaugural address, and he vowed to alter it. But the president's first action in 1937 was a plan to reform the federal judiciary and the Supreme Court, whose "nine old men" had struck down various important New Deal measures.

To create a more sympathetic Court, FDR asked for power to appoint an extra justice for each of the six justices over 70 years of age. He also called for modernizing the court system at all levels, but that plan got lost in the public outcry over the Court-packing scheme.

Roosevelt's plan foundered. Republicans accused him of subverting the Constitution. Many congressmen from his own party deserted him. Led by Vice President John Nance Garner of Texas, a number of southern Democrats broke with the president and formed a coalition with conservative Republicans that lasted for more than 30 years. Finally Roosevelt admitted defeat. He had perhaps misunderstood his mandate, and he certainly underestimated the respect, even reverence, that most Americans felt for the Supreme Court. Ironically, though he lost the battle of the Supreme Court, Roosevelt won the war. By the spring of 1937, the Court began to reverse its position and in a 5–4 decision upheld the National Labor Relations Act. When a conservative justice retired, Roosevelt made his first Supreme Court appointment, thus ensuring at least a shaky liberal majority on the Court. But Roosevelt triumphed at great cost. His attempt to reorganize the Court slowed the momentum of his legislative program. The most unpopular action he took as president, it made him vulnerable to criticism from New Deal opponents, and even some of his supporters were dismayed by what they regarded as an attack on the separation of powers.

The economy improved in late 1936 and early 1937, but then in August, the fragile prosperity collapsed. Unemployment shot back up, industrial production fell, and the stock market plummeted. Facing an embarrassing economic slump that evoked charges that the New Deal had failed, Roosevelt resorted to deficit spending as recommended by British economist John Maynard Keynes. Keynes argued that to get out of a depression, the government must spend massively on goods and services. This would spur demand and revive production. The economy responded slowly but never fully recovered until wartime expenditures, beginning in 1940, eliminated unemployment and ended the Depression.

Completing the New Deal

Despite increasing hostility, Congress passed a number of important bills in 1937 and 1938 that completed the New Deal reform legislation. The Bankhead-Jones Farm Tenancy Act of 1937 created the Farm Security Administration (FSA) to aid tenant farmers, sharecroppers, and owners who had lost their farms. The FSA, which provided loans to grain collectives, also set up camps for migratory workers. But the FSA never had enough money to make a real difference.

Congress passed a new Agricultural Adjustment Act in 1938 that tried to solve the problem of farm surpluses by controlling production. Under the new act, the federal treasury made direct payments to farmers. It introduced a soil conservation program and tried to market surplus crops. But only the outbreak of World War II ended the problem of farm surplus, and then only temporarily.

A shortage of urban housing continued to be a problem. Reformers who had worked in the first experiment with federal housing during World War I convinced FDR that federal low-cost housing should be part of New Deal reform. The National Housing Act of 1937 provided federal funds for slum clearance projects and the construction of low-cost housing. By 1939, however, only 117,000 units had been built—mostly bleak, boxlike structures.

New Deal housing legislation had a greater impact on middle-class housing policies and patterns. During the first 100 days of the New Deal, Congress created the Home Owners Loan Corporation (HOLC) at Roosevelt's urging, which over the next two years made more than $3 billion in low-interest loans and helped over a million people save their homes from foreclosure. The HOLC also introduced the first long-term fixed-rate mortgages (different from past loans, which usually ran no longer than five years and were subject to frequent renegotiation). The HOLC also introduced a uniform system of real estate appraisal that tended to undervalue urban property, especially in old, crowded, and ethnically mixed neighborhoods. The system gave the highest ratings to suburban developments in which the HOLC determined there had been no "infiltration of Jews" or other undesirable groups—the beginning of the practice later called "redlining" that made it nearly impossible for certain prospective homeowners to obtain a mortgage.

The Federal Housing Administration (FHA), created in 1934 by the National Housing Act, expanded and extended many HOLC policies. The FHA-insured mortgages, many of them for 25 or 30 years, reduced the minimum down payment from 30 percent to under 10 percent and allowed over 11 million families to buy homes between 1934 and 1972. It also tended to favor purchasing new suburban homes rather than repairing older urban residences.

An equally important reform measure was the Fair Labor Standards Act, passed in June 1938. Roosevelt's bill proposed for all industries engaged in interstate commerce a minimum wage of 25 cents an hour and a maximum workweek of 44 hours. Despite congressional watering down, when the act went into effect, 750,000 workers immediately got raises, and by 1940, some 12 million had them. The law also barred child labor in interstate commerce, making it the first permanent federal law to prohibit youngsters under 16 from working. And the law made no distinction between men and women, thus diminishing the need for special legislation for women.

The New Deal had many weaknesses, but it did dramatically increase government support for the needy. In 1913, local, state, and federal government spent $21 million on public assistance. By 1932, that had risen to $218 million; by 1939, it was $4.9 billion.

The Other Side of the 1930s

The Great Depression and the New Deal so dominate the history of the 1930s that it is easy to conclude that there were only breadlines and relief agencies. But there is another side of the decade. A communications revolution changed the lives of middle-class Americans. The sale of radios and attendance at movies increased during the 1930s, and literature flourished. Americans were fascinated by technology, especially automobiles. Many people traveled and looked ahead to a brighter future of streamlined appliances and gadgets that meant a better life.

Taking to the Road

"People give up everything in the world but their car," a banker in Muncie, Indiana, remarked during the Depression, and that seems to have been true all over the country. Although automobile production dropped off after 1929 and did not recover until the end of the 1930s, the number of motor vehicles registered, which declined from 26.7 million in 1930 to just over 24 million in 1933, increased to over 32 million by 1940. Even the "Okies" fled the dust bowl of the Southwest in cars—secondhand, run-down ones, to be sure, but automobiles nonetheless.

The American middle class traveled at an increasing rate after the low point of 1932 and 1933. In 1938, the tourist industry was the third largest in the United States, behind only steel and automobile production.

The Electric Home

If the 1920s was the age of the bathroom, the 1930s was the era of the modern kitchen. In 1930, the number of electric refrigerators produced exceeded the number of iceboxes for the first time, and refrigerator production peaked at 2.3 million in 1937. At first, the refrigerator looked like an icebox with a motor on top. In 1935, however, like most other appliances, it became streamlined. The Sears Coldspot, which quickly influenced the look of all other models, emphasized sweeping horizontal lines and rounded corners.

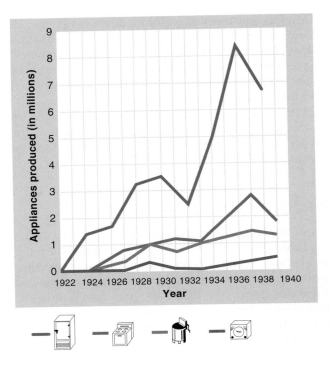

Household Appliance Production, 1922–1939
Electric appliances altered the lives of many American middle-class families during the 1930s. The replacement of the icebox with the electric refrigerator was especially dramatic. How did these appliances change the lifestyle of those who purchased them?
(U.S. Bureau of the Census)

Streamlining became the symbol of modern civilization in the 1930s. At the end of the decade, in 1939, the World's Fair in New York glorified the streamlined technology of the future.

Ironically, despite new conveniences, a great many middle-class families maintained their standard of living during the 1930s only because the women in the family learned to stretch and save and make do, and most wives spent as much time on housework as before. Some also took jobs outside the home to maintain their level of consumption. The number of married women who worked increased substantially during the decade.

The Age of Leisure

During the Depression, many middle-class people found themselves with time on their hands. The 1920s had been a time of spectator sports watched by huge crowds. Those sports continued during the Depression decade, although attendance suffered. Cheap forms of entertainment like softball and miniature golf also became popular. But leisure in the 1930s fascinated professionals, who published 450 new books on the subject.

Many popular games of the period had elaborate rules. Contract bridge swept the country. Monopoly was the most popular game of all, as Americans became fascinated by a game of building real estate and utility monopolies and bankrupting their opponents.

Literary Reflections of the 1930s

Though much of the literature of the 1930s reflected the decade's troubled currents, reading continued to be a popular and cheap entertainment. Novelist John Steinbeck described the plight of Mexican migrant workers in *Tortilla Flat* (1935), and in *The Grapes of Wrath* (1939) followed the deteriorating fortunes of an Okie family. His novels expressed his belief that there was in American life a "crime . . . that goes beyond denunciation"—the crime being the toleration of suffering and injustice.

Other writers also questioned the American dream. John Dos Passos's trilogy *U.S.A.* (1930–1936) conveyed a deep pessimism about American capitalism that many intellectuals shared. Less political were the novels of Thomas Wolfe and William Faulkner, who more sympathetically portrayed Americans caught up in the web of local life and in the face of modern complexities. Faulkner's fictional Yoknapatawpha County, brought to life in *The Sound and the Fury, As I Lay Dying, Sanctuary,* and *Light in August* (1929–1932), documented the South's racial problems, poverty, and stubborn pride. But a far more optimistic and far less complex book about the South became one of the decade's best-sellers—Margaret Mitchell's Civil War novel *Gone with the Wind* (1936). Its success showed that most Americans read to escape, not to explore their problems.

Radio's Finest Hour

The number of radios purchased increased steadily during the 1930s. In 1929, slightly more than 10 million households owned a radio; by 1939, the number had increased to 27.5 million. In Chicago's working-class neighborhoods in 1930, there was one radio for every two or three households, but often families and friends gathered together to listen. The radio became a focal point of the living room. Families listened to soap operas during the day and laughed at comedian Jack Benny at night. Radio allowed many people to feel connected to distant places and to believe they knew the performers personally. Radio was also responsible for one of the most widespread episodes of mass hysteria of all time. Orson Welles's Halloween 1938 broadcast of "The War of the Worlds" was so realistic that thousands actually believed that Martians had just landed in New Jersey. If anyone needed proof, that single program demonstrated the power of radio.

The Silver Screen

The era of the 1930s was the golden decade of the movies. Between 60 million and 90 million Americans went to the movies every week. Even in the depth of the Depression, film money was almost as important as food money for many families. City residents could go to an elaborate movie palace and live in a fantasy world far removed from the reality of Depression America.

RECOVERING *the* PAST

The Movies

Just as some historians have used fiction to help define the cultural history of a decade, others in the twentieth century have turned to film to describe the "spirit of an age." On an elementary level, the movies help us appreciate changing styles in dress, furniture, and automobiles. We can even get some sense of how a particular time defined a beautiful woman or a handsome man, and we can learn about ethnic and racial stereotypes and assumptions about gender and class.

The decade of the 1930s is sometimes called the "golden age of the movies." Careful selection among the 500 or so feature films Hollywood produced each year during the decade—ranging from gangster and cowboy movies to Marx Brothers comedies, from historical romances to Busby Berkeley musical extravaganzas—helps reveal important myths and assumptions of the Depression era. Films provided necessary amusement and entertainment in the midst of hard times. But they also helped create a new and different culture for many Americans as they struggled to get through the 1930s.

The year 1934 was a dividing line. The motion picture industry, like all other industries, had suffered during the Depression; 1933 marked the low point in attendance, with more than a third of the theaters in the country shut down. The next year, however, attendance picked up, heralding a revival that lasted until 1946. Also in 1934, the movie industry adopted a code for which the Catholic Legion of Decency and other religious groups had lobbied. The new code prohibited the depiction of "sex perversion, interracial sex, abortion, incest, drugs and profanity." Even married couples could not be shown together in a double bed. Although a movie could depict immoral behavior, sin always had to be punished. "Evil and good should never be confused," the code announced.

Before the code, Hollywood had indeed produced graphic films, such as *The Public Enemy* (1931) and *Scarface* (1932), with a considerable amount of violence; musicals, such as *Gold Diggers of 1933* (1933), filled with scantily clad young women; films featuring prostitutes, such as Jean Harlow in *Red Dust* (1932) and Marlene Dietrich in *Blond Venus* (1930); and other films that confronted the problems of real life. But after 1934, Hollywood concentrated on movies that created a mythical world where evil was always punished, family moral values won out in the end, and patriotism and American democracy were never questioned. Although the code was modified from time to time, it was not abandoned until 1966, when it was replaced by a rating system.

It Happened One Night (1934) and *Drums Along the Mohawk* (1939), two films out of thousands, illustrate some of the myths the movies created and sustained. Frank Capra, one of Hollywood's masters at entertaining without disturbing, directed *It Happened One Night*, a comedy-romance. A rich girl, played by Claudette Colbert, dives from her father's yacht off the coast of Florida and takes a bus for New York. She meets a newspaper reporter, played by Clark Gable, and they have a series of madcap adventures and fall in love. But mix-ups and misunderstandings make it appear that she will marry her old boyfriend. In the end, however, they are reunited and marry in an elaborate outdoor ceremony. Afterward, they presumably live happily ever after. The movie is funny and entertaining and presents a variation on the poor-boy-marries-rich-girl theme. Like so many movies of the time, this one suggests that life is fulfilled for a woman only if she can find the right man to marry.

Claudette Colbert also stars in *Drums Along the Mohawk*, this time with Henry Fonda. Based on a 1936 novel by Walter Edmonds, *Drums* is a sentimental story about a man who builds a house in the wilderness, marries a pretty girl, fights off the Indians, and works with the simple country folk to create a satisfying life in the very year the American colonies rebel against Great Britain. *Drums* was one of a number of films based on historical themes that Hollywood released just before World War II. *The Howards of Virginia* (1940), *Northwest Passage* (1939), and, most popular of all, *Gone with*

Top: A scene from *It Happened One Night*, 1934. **Bottom:** A scene from *Drums Along the Mohawk*, 1939.

the Wind (1939) were others in the same genre. Historical themes had been popular before, but with the world on the brink of war, the story of men and women in the wilderness struggling for family and country against the Indians (stereotyped as savages) proved comforting as well as entertaining.

REFLECTING ON THE PAST Can a historian use movies to describe the values and myths of a particular time, or are the complexities and exaggerations too great? Are the most popular or most critically acclaimed films more useful than others in getting at the "spirit of an age"? What films popular today tell us most about our time and culture? Is there too much sex and violence in movies today? Should the government control the language, themes, and values depicted in movies? Are movies as important today as they were in the 1930s in defining and influencing the country's myths and values?

In small towns across the country, for a quarter (a dime for those under age 12), people could see at least four movies during the week. Sometimes a double feature played, and there were always short subjects, a cartoon, and a newsreel. On Saturday there was usually a serial that left the heroine or hero in such a dire predicament that viewers just had to come back the next week. The animated cartoons of Walt Disney, one of the true geniuses of the movie industry, were so popular that Mickey Mouse was more famous and familiar than most politicians.

Conclusion
The Mixed Legacy of the Great Depression and the New Deal

The New Deal, despite its great variety of legislation, did not end the Depression, nor did it solve the problem of unemployment. For many Americans, like Robert Symmonds's father, the most vivid memory was the shame and guilt of being unemployed, or the despair and fear that came from losing a business or being evicted from a home or an apartment. Parents who lived through the decade urged their children to find a secure job, get married, and settle down. "Every time I've encountered the Depression it has been used as a barrier and a club," one daughter of Depression parents remembered; "older people use it to explain to me that I can't understand anything: I didn't live through the Depression."

Watch the Video

Responding to the Great Depression: Whose New Deal? at **www.myhistorylab.com**

New Deal legislation did not solve the country's problems, but it did strengthen the federal government, especially the executive branch. Federal agencies like the Federal Deposit Insurance Corporation and programs like Social Security influenced the daily lives of most Americans, and rural electrification, the WPA, and the CCC changed the lives of millions. The New Deal also established the principle of federal responsibility for the health of the economy, initiated the concept of the welfare state, and dramatically increased government spending to help the poor. Federally subsidized housing, minimum-wage laws, and a policy for paying farmers to limit production, all aspects of these principles, had far-reaching implications.

The New Deal was as important for what it did not do as for what it did. It did not promote socialism, and it did not redistribute income. It promoted social justice and social reform, but it provided little for people at the bottom of American society. In the long run, it probably strengthened corporate capitalism.

With his colorful personality and dramatic response to the nation's crisis, Roosevelt dominated his times in a way few presidents have done. Loved by many, hated by some, he left a powerful legacy. For the rest of the twentieth century, and even into the twenty-first, much of American political life has centered on preserving and extending or trying to abolish or revise legislation passed during the Depression decade. But the Depression was not America's problem alone. It was global in its impact and its consequences. The world-wide economic disaster in the 1930s contributed to the erosion of international harmony in the 1930s and was one of the causes of World War II.

TIME*line*

1929	Stock market crashes
	Agricultural Marketing Act
1932	Reconstruction Finance Corporation established
	Federal Home Loan Bank Act
	Glass-Steagall Banking Act
	Federal Emergency Relief Act
	Bonus march on Washington
	Franklin D. Roosevelt elected president
1933	Emergency Banking Relief Act
	Twenty-First Amendment repeals Eighteenth Amendment, ending Prohibition
	Agricultural Adjustment Act
	National Industrial Recovery Act
	Civilian Conservation Corps
	Tennessee Valley Authority established
	Public Works Administration established
1934	Federal Housing Administration established
	Indian Reorganization Act
1935	Works Progress Administration established
	Social Security Act
	Rural Electrification Act
	National Labor Relations Act
	Public Utility Holding Company Act
	Committee for Industrial Organization (CIO) formed
1936	United Auto Workers hold sit-down strikes against General Motors
	Roosevelt reelected president
	Economy begins to rebound
1937	Attempt to expand the Supreme Court
	Economic collapse
	Farm Security Administration established
	National Housing Act
1938	Fair Labor Standards Act
1939	John Steinbeck, *The Grapes of Wrath*

✓•—Study and **Review** at **www.myhistorylab.com**

Questions for Review and Reflection

1. Explain the origins of the Great Depression. How was the Depression in the United States related to global economic factors?
2. Explain the major phases of the New Deal. What programs were enacted in each phase, and what did they seek to accomplish?
3. Who criticized the New Deal and why?
4. How did communication technologies and popular culture change during the 1930s?
5. Why are the Depression and the New Deal considered to have a mixed legacy?

Key Terms

Agricultural Adjustment Act 719

Brain Trust 716

Civilian Conservation Corps 708

Congress of Industrial Organizations 728

Dust Bowl 724

First Hundred Days 717

National Recovery Administration 719

Social Security Act 723

Tennessee Valley Authority 721

Works Progress Administration 723

23

World War II

American Stories

A Native American Boy Plays at War

N. Scott Momaday, a Kiowa Indian born in Lawton, Oklahoma, in 1934, grew up on reservations. He was only 11 years old when World War II ended, yet the war changed his life. Shortly after the United States entered the war, Momaday's parents moved to New Mexico, where his father got a job with an oil company and his mother worked in the civilian personnel office at an army air force base. Like many couples, they had struggled through the hard times of the Depression. The war meant jobs.

Momaday's best friend was Billy Don Johnson. Together they played war, digging trenches and dragging themselves through imaginary minefields. They hurled grenades and fired endless rounds from their imaginary machine guns, pausing only to drink Kool-Aid from their canteens. At school, they were taught how to hate the enemy and be proud of America. They recited the Pledge of Allegiance to the flag and sang "God Bless America," "The Star-Spangled Banner," and "Remember Pearl Harbor." Like most Americans, they believed that World War II was a good war fought against evil empires. The United States was always right, the enemy always wrong. It was an attitude that would influence Momaday and his generation for the rest of their lives.

Momaday's only difficulty was that his Native American face was often mistaken for that of an Asian. Almost every day on the playground, someone yelled, "Hi ya, Jap," and a fight was on. Billy Don always came to his friend's defense, but it was disconcerting to be taken for the enemy. His father read old Kiowa tales to Momaday, who was proud to be an Indian but prouder still to be an American. On Saturday, he and his friends cheered at the movies as they watched a Japanese Zero or a German ME-109 go down in flames.

Chapter Outline

The Twisting Road to War

Battles and Bullets

The Impact of War

Insiders and Outsiders

Conclusion: Peace, Prosperity, and International Responsibility

Near the end of the war, Momaday's family, like many families, moved again, so that his father might get a better job. This time they lived right next door to an air force base, and Momaday fell in love with the B-17 "Flying Fortress," the bomber that military strategists thought would win the war in the Pacific and in Europe.

Looking back, Momaday reflected on the importance of the war in his growing up. "I see now that one experiences easily the ordinary things of life," he decided, "the things which cast familiar shadows upon the sheer, transparent panels of time, and he perceives his experience in the only way he can, according to his age." Though Momaday's life during the war differed from the lives of boys old enough to join the armed forces, the war for him was still vivid and real.

The Momadays fared better than most Native Americans. Although they had been made U.S. citizens by an act of Congress in 1924, like all Native Americans living in Arizona and New Mexico, they were denied the right to vote by state law. Jobs, even in wartime, were hard to find. Native American servicemen returning from the war discovered that as "Indians" they still faced blatant discrimination in many states. Still, Momaday thought of himself not so much as an Indian but as an American, and that too was a product of his generation. But as he grew to maturity, he became a successful writer and spokesman for his people. In 1969, he won the Pulitzer Prize for his novel *House Made of Dawn*. In his writing, he stresses the Indian's close identification with the land. Writing about his grandmother, he says: "The immense landscape of the continental interior lay like memory in her blood." For him, his sense of himself derived in part from the experience of war.

No American cities were bombed and the United States was never invaded, but World War II still influenced almost every aspect of American life. The war ended the Depression. Jobs were available, and even though prejudice was still prevalent in the workplace, blacks, Hispanics, women, and other minorities, such as Indians, now had new opportunities. Like World War I, this second global war expanded cooperation between government and industry and increased the influence of government in all areas of American life. The war also ended the last remnants of American isolationism. The United States emerged from the war in 1945 as the most powerful, most prosperous nation in the world.

This chapter traces the gradual involvement of the United States in the international events during the 1930s that finally led to participation in the most devastating war the world had ever seen. It examines such questions as: How did the United States react to the crises that led to war? How did the diplomatic and military struggles of the war affect the search for a secure peace? What was the war's impact on ordinary people and on American attitudes about patriotism, the American way of life, and the nation's connection to the world outside? What was the lasting impact on people like Momaday as they emerged from the war and embraced the new world that lay ahead?

The Twisting Road to War

As the United States faced the ravages of the Great Depression, it encountered equally serious problems in foreign affairs. The worldwide economic collapse caused near financial disaster in Europe. Germany had defaulted on its reparation payments, and most European countries were unable to pay their debts to the United States. Instability contributed to the rise of dictatorship in Italy and Germany. Meanwhile, in the Pacific, Japan was equally aggressive in invading other countries to help provide the raw materials the island nation lacked.

Watch the **Video**
Hitler and Roosevelt
at **www.myhistorylab.com**

Foreign Policy in a Global Age

Roosevelt had no master plan in foreign policy, just as he had none in the domestic sphere. In the first days of his administration, he gave conflicting signals about the international situation. First it seemed that FDR would cooperate in some kind of international economic agreement on tariffs and currency, which was to be negotiated in London. But then he refused to go along with any such agreement, wanting to keep control of economic issues in his own hands. He believed it was more important to solve the domestic economic crisis than to achieve international economic cooperation. Roosevelt did, however, alter some of the foreign policy decisions of previous administrations. He recognized the Soviet government. In reversing the 1920s nonrecognition policy (which rested largely on anti-Communist sentiments), Roosevelt hoped to gain a market for surplus American grain—a trade bonanza that never materialized. But diplomatic recognition opened communications between two emerging world powers.

The United States continued to support dictators, especially in Central America, because they promised to promote stability and preserve U.S. economic interests. But Roosevelt, extending the Good Neighbor policy Hoover had initiated, completed the removal of American military forces from Haiti and Nicaragua in 1934. In a series of pan-American conferences, he joined in pledging that no country in the hemisphere would intervene in the "internal or external affairs" of any other.

The new policy's first test came in Cuba, where a revolution threatened American investments of more than a billion dollars. But the United States did not send troops. Instead, Roosevelt dispatched envoys to work out a conciliatory agreement. A short time later, when a coup led by Fulgencio Batista overthrew the revolutionary government, the United States not only recognized the Batista government but also offered a large loan. The United States agreed to abrogate the Platt Amendment (which made Cuba a virtual protectorate of the United States) in return for continued rights to the Guantanamo naval base.

The Trade Agreements Act of 1934 empowered the president to lower tariff rates by as much as 50 percent. Secretary of State Cordell Hull negotiated a series of pacts that improved trade. By 1935, half of American cotton exports and a large proportion of other products were going to Latin America. So the Good Neighbor policy was also good business for the United States. But increased trade did not solve the economic problems for either the United States or Latin America.

Another test for Latin American policy came in 1938 when Mexico nationalized the property of American oil companies. Instead of intervening, as many businessmen urged, the State Department patiently worked out an agreement that included some compensation for the companies. Washington might have acted differently had not the threat of war in Europe in 1938 created a sense that all the Western Hemisphere nations should cooperate. At a pan-American conference held that year, the United States and most Latin American countries agreed to resist all foreign intervention in the hemisphere.

Europe on the Brink of War

Europe was an even greater foreign policy problem than Latin America. On January 30, 1933, about two months before Roosevelt's inauguration, Nazi leader Adolf Hitler became German chancellor. Born in Austria in 1889, he served in the army during World War I. Like so many other Germans, he was angered by the harsh terms of the Treaty of Versailles. But Hitler blamed the German defeat in the war on Jews and Communists. He had a charismatic style and a plan that attracted many followers. Shortly after he became chancellor, he suspended the constitution and made himself Fuehrer (leader) and dictator and set out to conquer Europe. As the first step, in 1934 he announced German rearmament, violating the Versailles Treaty. That same year, Italy's Fascist dictator Benito Mussolini (who had come to power a decade earlier) threatened to invade the East African country of Ethiopia. These ominous rumblings frightened Americans at the very time they were reexamining the history of American entry into the Great War and vowing that it would never happen again.

Senator Gerald P. Nye of North Dakota launched an investigation into the connection between corporate profits and American participation in World War I. His committee's public hearings revealed that many American businessmen had close relationships with the War Department. Although no conspiracy was proved, it was easy to conclude that the United States had been tricked into going to war by the people who profited heavily from it.

On many campuses, students demonstrated against war. They joined organizations like the Veterans of Future Wars and protested Reserve Officer

Training Corps programs on their campuses. They were determined never again to support a foreign war. But in Europe, Asia, and Africa, there were already rumblings of another great international conflict.

Ethiopia and Spain

In May 1935, Italy invaded Ethiopia after rejecting the League of Nations' offer to mediate disputes between the two countries. The remote Ethiopian war frightened Congress into passing a Neutrality Act, which authorized the president to prohibit all arms shipments to nations at war and to advise all U.S. citizens not to travel on belligerents' ships except at their own risk. Congress was determined to prevent America from entering another world war.

As the League of Nations condemned Italy as the aggressor, Roosevelt used the authority of the act to impose an arms embargo. But in the midst of depression, he was not willing to stop oil shipments to Italy or to join the fight. The embargo had little impact on Italy but was disastrous for the poor African nation. After defeating Ethiopia, Mussolini made an alliance with Germany, creating the Rome–Berlin Axis, in 1936.

"We shun political commitments which might entangle us in foreign war," Roosevelt announced in 1936. But isolation became more difficult when General Francisco Franco, supported by the Catholic church, large landowners, and reactionary politicians, revolted against the republican government of Spain. Germany and Italy aided Franco, sending planes and other weapons, while the Soviet Union supplied the Spanish republican Loyalists.

The war in Spain polarized the United States. Most Catholics and many anti-Communists sided with Franco. But many American liberals and radicals—even those who said they opposed all war—found the republican cause worth fighting for. Over 3,000 Americans joined the Abraham Lincoln Brigade, and hundreds died fighting fascism. "If this were a Spanish matter, I'd let it alone," wrote Sam Levenger, an Ohio State student. "But the rebellion would not last a week if it weren't for the Germans and the Italians." Levenger went to war and was killed in Spain in 1937 at the age of 20.

The U.S. government took neutrality seriously. Another Neutrality Act in 1936 extended the provisions of the first and included a ban on loans to belligerents. While the acts did not apply to civil war, Roosevelt asked Congress to extend the arms embargo to Spain. With the United States, Britain, and France neutral, Franco drew on German and Italian help to consolidate his own dictatorship. Then in 1937, Congress passed a third Neutrality Act, once more extending the provisions of the first two measures and now mandating that belligerents could buy nonmilitary items only on a cash-and-carry basis.

In a variety of ways, the United States tried to avoid repeating the mistakes that had led it into World War I. Unfortunately, World War II, which moved closer each day, was to be a different kind of war, and the lessons of the first war were of little use.

War in Europe

Roosevelt was no isolationist, but he wanted to keep the United States out of any European conflict. When he publicly announced, "I hate war," he meant it. Unlike his distant cousin Theodore Roosevelt, he did not view war as a test of manhood. In foreign policy, as in domestic affairs, he responded to events, but he moved reluctantly toward greater American involvement.

In March 1938, Hitler annexed Austria, and in September he occupied the Sudetenland, a part of Czechoslovakia. Within six months, Hitler seized the rest of that country. Little protest came from the United States. Most Americans sympathized with the victims of Hitler's aggression, and eventually some were horrified by rumors of the murder of hundreds of thousands of Jews. But because newspapers avoided intensive coverage of these well-documented but unpleasant stories, many Americans did not learn of the Holocaust until near the end of the war.

At first, almost everyone hoped that Europeans could find an alternative to war. But that notion evaporated on August 23, 1939, with the news of a **Nazi–Soviet pact**. Many Americans had hoped that Nazi Germany and Soviet Russia would destroy each other. Now these ideological enemies had signed a nonaggression pact. A week later, Hitler's army attacked Poland, marking the onset of World War II. Britain and France came to Poland's defense. "This nation will remain a neutral nation," Roosevelt said, "but I cannot ask that every American remain neutral in thought as well."

Roosevelt asked for repeal of the embargo section of the Neutrality Act and for approval of cash-and-carry arms sales to France and Britain. And he took some risks. In August 1939, physicist Albert Einstein, a Jewish refugee from Nazi Germany, warned him that German scientists were working on an atomic bomb. Fearing the consequences, FDR authorized an American atomic initiative. This top-secret effort, which came to be called the **Manhattan Project**, changed the course of human history.

There was a lull in the war after Germany and the Soviet Union crushed Poland in September 1939. Great Britain sent several divisions to aid the French against the expected German attack, but for months nothing happened. The "phony war" dramatically ended on April 9, 1940, when Germany attacked Norway and Denmark. At the beginning of May, the German *Blitzkrieg* ("lightning war") swept into the Low Countries. A week later, mechanized German forces stormed into France, sweeping around fortifications known as the Maginot line. France surrendered in June as the British army fled across the English Channel.

How should the United States respond to this desperate situation? Some concerned citizens organized the Committee to Defend America by Aiding the Allies, but others, including aviator Charles Lindbergh, supported a group called America First. They argued that the United States should forget England and concentrate on defending America. Roosevelt steered a cautious course. He sent Britain 50 old American destroyers in return for the right to establish naval and air bases from Newfoundland to Bermuda and British Guiana. Though British Prime Minister Winston Churchill wanted and needed more, Roosevelt hesitated. In July 1940, he authorized $4 billion for more American warships. In September, Congress passed the Selective Service Act, providing for America's first peacetime draft. Over 1 million men were to serve for one year, but only in the Western Hemisphere.

●●─Read the Document

Charles Lindbergh, Radio Address (1941)

at **www.myhistorylab.com**

The Election of 1940

Part of Roosevelt's reluctance to aid Great Britain more aggressively came from his genuine desire to keep the United States out of the war, but it also reflected the presidential campaign of 1940. Roosevelt broke tradition by seeking a third term. The increasing support he was drawing from the liberal wing of the Democratic party led him to select liberal farm economist Henry Wallace from Iowa as his running mate.

The Republicans nominated energetic Wendell Willkie of Indiana. Despite his big-business ties, Willkie approved of most New Deal legislation and supported aid to Great Britain. Willkie was the most exciting Republican candidate since Theodore Roosevelt. Yet amid the international crisis, the voters stayed with FDR—27 million to 22 million. Roosevelt carried 38 of the 48 states.

Lend-Lease

After the election, Roosevelt devised a **"lend-lease"** scheme for sending aid to Britain without demanding payment. He compared the situation to lending a garden hose to a neighbor whose house was on fire. Republican Senator Robert Taft thought it was more like lending chewing gum: "Once it had been used you did not want it back."

The Lend-Lease Act, which Congress passed in March 1941, destroyed the fiction of neutrality. By then, U-boats were sinking a half-million tons of Atlantic shipping each month. In June, Roosevelt proclaimed a national emergency. Then, on June 22, Germany attacked Russia.

When Roosevelt extended lend-lease aid to Russia, the former Communist enemy, in November 1941, many Americans were shocked. But most quickly shifted from viewing the Soviet Union as an enemy to treating it like a friend.

By the autumn of 1941, the United States was virtually at war with Germany in the Atlantic. On September 11, Roosevelt issued a "shoot on sight" order for all American ships operating in the Atlantic, and on October 30, a German submarine sank an American destroyer. Still, the war in the Atlantic was undeclared, and many Americans opposed it.

The Path to Pearl Harbor

Japan, not Germany, dragged the United States into World War II. Intent on becoming a major world power and desperate for natural resources, especially oil, Japan was willing to risk war to get them. It invaded Manchuria in 1931 and launched an all-out assault on China in 1937. But Japanese leaders wanted to put off attacking the Philippines, an American possession. For its part, the United States feared a two-front war and was willing to delay a confrontation with Japan until it had dealt with the German threat. Thus between 1938 and 1941, the United States and Japan engaged in diplomatic shadow boxing.

America exerted economic pressure on Japan in July 1939, giving the required six months' notice for cancellation of the 1911 commercial agreement between the two countries. In September 1940, the administration forbade shipping aircraft fuel and scrap metal to Japan. It added other items to the embargo list until by the spring of 1941 only oil could be shipped to Japan. The administration hoped that the threat of cutting off that important resource would force a diplomatic solution and avert a crisis. Japan opened negotiations with the United States, but there was little to discuss. Japan would not withdraw from China and occupied French Indochina. In July 1941, Roosevelt froze all Japanese assets in the United States, effectively embargoing trade with Japan.

Roosevelt had an advantage in negotiating with Japan, for Americans had broken the Japanese secret diplomatic code. But Japanese intentions were hard to decipher from the intercepted messages. American leaders knew that Japan planned to attack, but they didn't know where. In September 1941, the Japanese decided to strike sometime after November unless the United States offered real concessions.

On the morning of December 7, 1941, Japanese airplanes launched from aircraft carriers attacked the U.S. fleet at **Pearl Harbor**, in Hawaii. The surprise attack destroyed or disabled 19 ships (including five battleships) and 150 planes and killed 2,335 soldiers and sailors and 68 civilians. On the same day, Japan invaded the Philippines, Guam, Midway, and British Hong Kong and Malaya. The next day, Congress declared war on Japan.

December 7, 1941, was a date that would "live in infamy," Franklin Roosevelt told Congress and the nation as he asked for the declaration of war. It was also a day with far-reaching implications for American foreign policy and for American attitudes toward the world. The surprise attack united the country—even isolationists and "America Firsters"—as nothing else could have.

After the shock and anger subsided, Americans searched for a villain. Some targeted Roosevelt, who supposedly knew of the Japanese attack but failed to warn the military so that the American people might unite behind the war against Germany. But Roosevelt did not know. There was no warning that the attack was coming against Pearl Harbor, and the American ability to read Japanese coded messages was no help because the fleet kept radio silence.

The Americans underestimated the Japanese partly because of racial prejudice. They ignored many warning signals because they simply did not believe the Japanese capable of attacking a target as far away as Hawaii. Roosevelt and most experts expected the Japanese to attack the Philippines or Thailand. Many people blundered, but there was no conspiracy.

Even more important in the long run was the Japanese attack's effect on military and political leaders. Pearl Harbor became the symbol of unpreparedness. For a generation stunned by an unscrupulous enemy attack, the lesson was to be ready to stop an aggressor, anywhere in the world, before it struck.

Battles and Bullets

Pearl Harbor catapulted the country into war with Japan. On December 11, 1941, Hitler declared war on the United States. The reason why has never been fully explained. He was not required by his treaty with Japan to go to war with the United States, and without his action, the United States might have concentrated on fighting Japan. Hitler forced the United States into war against the **Axis powers** in both Europe and Asia.

War Aims and Priorities

Why was the United States fighting the war? In a speech before Congress in January 1941, Roosevelt had mentioned the **four freedoms**: freedom of speech and expression, freedom of worship, freedom from want, and freedom from fear. Roosevelt also spoke vaguely of extending democracy and establishing a peacekeeping organization, but unlike Woodrow Wilson, he never spelled out in any detail the political purposes for fighting. Others were more explicit. Henry Luce, the editor of *Life* magazine, published an essay before Pearl Harbor called "The American Century," where he argued that the United States had the responsibility to spread the American way of life around the world.

•◉•⌐Read the **Document**

*Franklin D. Roosevelt,
"The Four Freedoms" (1941)*
at **www.myhistorylab.com**

Roosevelt and his advisers decided on a holding action in the Pacific while concentrating efforts against Hitler in Europe. But the United States was not fighting alone. It joined the Soviet Union and Great Britain in a difficult, but ultimately effective, anti-Nazi alliance. Churchill and Roosevelt got along well, although they often disagreed on strategy. Roosevelt's relationship with Stalin was much more strained, but he frequently agreed with the Soviet leader about the way to fight the war. Stalin, who had murdered hundreds of thousands of potential or actual opponents, distrusted both the British and the Americans, but he needed them, just as they depended on him. Without the tremendous Russian sacrifices in 1941 and 1942, Germany would have won the war before the vast American military and industrial might could be mobilized. A major priority was keeping the alliance intact.

Year of Disaster, 1942

The first half of 1942 was disastrous for the Allies. The Japanese captured the resource-rich Dutch East Indies, swept into Burma, took Wake and Guam, and invaded Alaska's Aleutian Islands. They pushed American forces in the Philippines onto the Bataan peninsula and finally onto the tiny island of Corregidor, where General Jonathan Wainwright surrendered more than 11,000 men to the Japanese. American reporters tried to play down the disasters, concentrating on tales of American heroism against overwhelming odds.

In Europe, the Germans pushed deep into Russia, threatening to take all the industrial centers, the valuable oil fields, and even Moscow. In North Africa, General Erwin Rommel's mechanized Afrika Korps neared the Suez Canal. U-boats sank British and American ships faster than they could be replaced. For a few dark months in 1942, it seemed that the Axis would win before the United States got prepared for war.

The Allies could not agree on a military strategy in Europe. Churchill advocated tightening the ring around Germany, using bombing raids to weaken the enemy and encouraging resistance among the occupied countries. He wanted to avoid any direct assault on the continent until success was ensured. Stalin, on the other hand, demanded a second front, an invasion of Europe in 1942 to relieve the pressure on the Red Army, which faced 200 German divisions along a 2,000-mile front. Roosevelt agreed to an offensive in 1942. But the invasion in that year was not in France but in North Africa. The decision was probably right from a military point of view, but it led Russia to distrust Britain and the United States.

See the **Map**

World War II in Europe
at **www.myhistorylab.com**

Landing in North Africa in November 1942, American and British troops tried to link up with a beleaguered British army fighting westward from Egypt. The American army, enthusiastic but inexperienced, met little resistance until, at Kasserine Pass in Tunisia, the Germans counterattacked and destroyed a large American force, inflicting 5,000 casualties. Roosevelt, who launched the invasion in part to give the American people a victory to relieve dreary news from the Far East, learned that victories often came with long casualty lists.

Conquering French North Africa drew Roosevelt into unpleasant political compromises. To gain a cease-fire, the United States recognized a provisional government under Admiral Jean Darlan, a former Nazi collaborator. Did this mean that the United States would negotiate with Mussolini? Or with Hitler? The Darlan deal reinforced Soviet distrust of the Americans and angered many Americans.

Roosevelt tried to walk a tightrope. He never made a deal with Hitler, but he did aid Fascist Spain in return for safe passage of American shipping into the Mediterranean. At the same time, the United States supplied arms to the left-wing resistance in France, to the Communist guerrilla Tito in Yugoslavia, and to Ho Chi Minh, the anti-French resistance leader in Indochina.

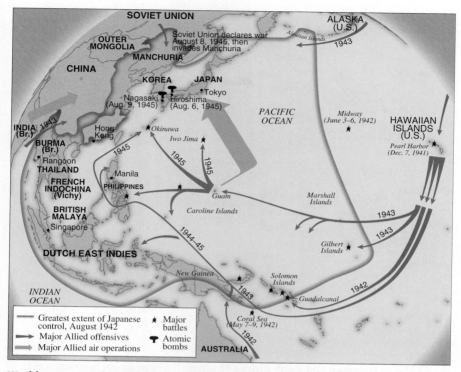

World War II: Pacific Theater After the surprise attack on Pearl Harbor, the Japanese extended their control in the Pacific from Burma to the Aleutian Islands and almost to Australia. But after American naval and air victories at Coral Sea and Midway in 1942, the Japanese were increasingly on the defensive. How did the great distances in the Pacific influence military plans for both sides? Why was the aircraft carrier more important than the battleship in the Pacific War? Was there any alternative to the American strategy of moving slowly from one Japanese-occupied island to another? Why did China play such a crucial role in the war against Japan?

Roosevelt also authorized large-scale, lend-lease aid to the Soviet Union. Although liberals criticized his support of dictators, Roosevelt was willing to do almost anything to win the war. Military expediency often dictated his political decisions.

Even on the issue of the plight of the Jews in Nazi-occupied Europe, Roosevelt's solution was to win the war as quickly as possible. By November 1942, confirmed information reached the United States that the Nazis were systematically exterminating Jews. Yet the administration did nothing for more than a year, and even then it did scandalously little. Only 21,000 refugees were allowed to enter the United States over a period of three and a half years, just 10 percent of those who could have been admitted under immigration quotas. The War Department refused to

Watch the Video
Nazi Murder Mills
at **www.myhistorylab.com**

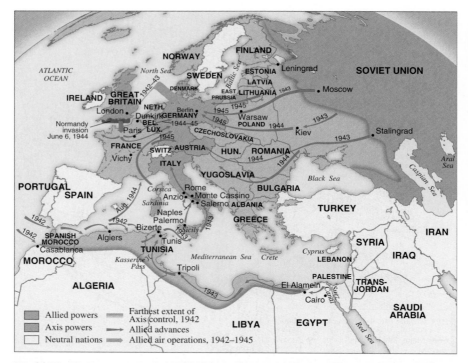

World War II: European and North African Theaters The German war machine swept across Europe and North Africa and almost captured Cairo and Moscow, but after major defeats at Stalingrad and El Alamein in 1943, the Axis powers were in retreat. Many lives were lost on both sides before the Allied victory in 1945. How was the African campaign important to the Allies' strategy to defeat Germany and Italy? Why was the invasion of France necessary even after the capture of North Africa and a portion of Italy? Why was the Soviet Union crucial to the war in Europe? Why was the war in Europe very different from the war in the Pacific?

bomb the Auschwitz gas chambers, and officials turned down many rescue schemes. Widespread anti-Semitism in the United States in the 1940s and fears of massive Jewish immigration partly explain the administration's policy. The failure of the media, Christian leaders, and even American Jews to bring effective pressure on the government does not excuse the president for his shameful indifference to the systematic murder of millions of people. Roosevelt could not have prevented the Holocaust, but vigorous action by him could have saved many thousands of lives.

A Strategy for Ending the War

Dwight D. Eisenhower, the commanding general of the Allied armies in the North African campaign, emerged as a genuine leader. Born in Texas, Eisenhower, often known as Ike, spent his boyhood in Abilene, Kansas.

Buchenwald Only at the end of the war did most Americans learn about the horrors of Nazi concentration camps and gas chambers. Senator Alben Barkley of Kentucky looks in disbelief at dead Jews stacked like wood at Buchenwald, April 24, 1945. Why didn't Americans learn about the Holocaust sooner?

His small-town background made it easy for the media to make him an American hero. Eisenhower, however, had not come to hero status easily. In World War I, he trained soldiers in Texas. He was only a lieutenant colonel when World War II erupted. But George Marshall, who became the army's top general in September 1939, had discovered Eisenhower's talents even before the war began. He quickly gained the rank of general and achieved a reputation as an expert planner and organizer. Gregarious and outgoing, Ike had a broad smile that made most people like him instantly. He was not a brilliant field commander and made mistakes in the African campaign, but he could get diverse people working together, which was crucial because British and American units had to cooperate.

The American army moved slowly across North Africa, linked up with the British, invaded Sicily in July 1943, and finally stormed ashore in Italy in September. The Italian campaign proved long and bitter. After the overthrow of Mussolini and Italy's surrender in September 1943, the Germans occupied the country and the American army bogged down. The Allies did not reach Rome until June 1944, and they never controlled all of Italy.

Despite the decision to make the war in Europe the first priority, American ships and planes halted the Japanese advance in the spring of 1942. In the Battle of Coral Sea in May 1942, American carrier-based planes inflicted heavy damage on the Japanese fleet and probably prevented the invasion of Australia. It was the first naval battle in history in which surface ships did not fire on each other; airplanes did all the damage. In World War II, aircraft carriers proved more important than battleships. A month later, at the Battle of Midway, American planes sank four Japanese carriers and destroyed nearly 300 planes. This first major Japanese defeat restored some balance of power in the Pacific and ended the threat to Hawaii.

In 1943, the American sea and land forces leapfrogged from island to island, retaking territory and building bases to attack the Philippines and eventually Japan. Progress often had terrible costs. In November 1943, about 5,000 marines landed on the coral beaches of the tiny island of Tarawa. Despite heavy naval bombardment and the support of hundreds of planes, they met massive resistance. The four-day battle killed more than 1,000 Americans and wounded over 3,000.

The Pacific war was often brutal and dehumanizing. American soldiers collected Japanese skulls and ears, something never done in the European war. Correspondent Ernie Pyle decided that soldiers saw the Japanese as something subhuman, like "cockroaches and mice."

The Invasion of France

Operation Overlord, the invasion Stalin had wanted in 1942, finally began on June 6, 1944. It was, according to Churchill, "the most difficult and complicated operation that has ever taken place." The initial assault along a 60-mile stretch of the Normandy coast unfolded with 175,000 men supported by 600 warships and 11,000 planes. Within a month, over 1 million troops and more than 170,000 vehicles had landed. It cost 2,245 killed and 1,670 wounded to secure the beachhead. "It was much lighter than anybody expected," one observer remarked. "But if you saw faces instead of numbers on the casualty list, it wasn't light at all."

The Allies dropped more than 1.5 million tons of bombs on Europe. Evidence gathered after the war suggests that this bombardment disrupted German war production less than Allied strategists expected. Often a plant or a rail center was back in operation days or hours after an attack, and the bombing of the cities may have strengthened the German people's resolve to fight to the bitter end. Nor did the destruction of German cities come cheaply. German fighter planes and antiaircraft guns shot down thousands of American and British planes.

The most destructive bombing raid of the war, against Dresden on the night of February 13–14, 1945, had no strategic purpose. The British and Americans launched the raid to help demonstrate to Stalin that they were aiding the Russian offensive. Dresden, a city of 630,000, was a communications center. Three waves of planes dropped 650,000 incendiary bombs, causing a firestorm that swept over eight square miles, destroying everything in its path and killing an estimated 100,000 civilians.

With eccentric General George Patton leading the charge and staid General Omar Bradley in command, the American army broke out of the Normandy beachhead in July 1944 and swept across France. American productive capacity and the ability to supply a mobile and motorized army eventually brought victory. But not all American equipment was superior. The American fighter plane, the P-40, could not compete early in the war with the German ME-109. The United States was far behind Germany in the development of rockets, but that was not as important as the American inability, until the end of the war, to develop a tank that could compete in armament or firepower with the German tanks. The American army partly made up for the deficiency of its tanks by having superior artillery. Perhaps even more important, most American soldiers had grown up tinkering with cars and radios. Children of the machine age, they managed to keep tanks, trucks, and guns functioning under difficult circumstances, which gave the American army superior mobility.

By late 1944, the American and British armies had driven across France, while the Russian military had pushed far into eastern Europe. The war seemed nearly over. Then, just before Christmas in 1944, the Germans launched a massive counterattack on the western front against thinly dispersed and inexperienced American troops. The Germans drove 50 miles inside the American lines before they were checked. During this Battle of the Bulge, Eisenhower was so desperate for additional troops that he offered to pardon any military prisoners in Europe who would go into battle. Most declined. Eisenhower also promised any black soldiers in the service and supply outfits an opportunity to become infantrymen in the white units, though usually with a lower rank. His chief of staff pointed out that this was the "most dangerous thing I have seen in regard to race relations." Eisenhower recanted, not wishing to start a social revolution.

The Politics of Victory

As American and British armies assaulted Germany in the winter and spring of 1945, the political and diplomatic aspects of the war began to overshadow military concerns. Relations between the Soviet Union and the other Allies had been badly strained at times during the war; with victory in sight, the tension grew worse. Although the American press idealized Stalin and the Russian people, a number of high-level American diplomats and presidential advisers distrusted the Russians and anticipated a postwar confrontation. They urged Roosevelt to make military decisions with the postwar political situation in mind.

The main issue in the spring of 1945 was who would capture Berlin. The British wanted to beat the Russians to the capital city. Eisenhower, however, fearing that the Germans might hold out indefinitely in the Alps, ordered the armies south rather than toward Berlin. He also wanted to avoid unnecessary American casualties, and he planned to meet the Russian army at an easily marked spot to avoid any unfortunate incidents. British and American forces could probably not have arrived in Berlin before the Russians, but Eisenhower's decision generated controversy after the war. Russian and American troops met on April 25, 1945, at the Elbe River. On May 2, the Russians took Berlin. Hitler committed suicide. The long war in Europe finally ended on May 8, 1945.

Meanwhile, throughout 1944, the United States had tightened the noose on Japan. Long-range B-29 bombers began sustained strikes on the Japanese mainland in June, and by November, they were firebombing Tokyo. In a series of naval and air engagements, especially at the Battle of Leyte Gulf, American planes destroyed most of the remaining Japanese navy. By the end of 1944, an American victory in the Pacific was all but ensured. American forces recaptured the Philippines early the next year. Yet it might take years to conquer the Japanese home islands.

While the military campaigns reached a critical stage, Roosevelt ran for a fourth term. He dropped Vice President Henry Wallace from the ticket because some thought him too radical and impetuous. To replace him, the Democratic convention selected a relatively unknown senator from Missouri. Harry S Truman's only fame had come from leading a Senate investigation of war contracts.

The Republicans nominated Thomas Dewey, the colorless and moderate governor of New York, who had a difficult time criticizing Roosevelt without appearing unpatriotic. Roosevelt seemed haggard and ill during much of the campaign, but he won easily. He would need all his strength to deal with the difficult problems of ending the war and constructing a peace settlement.

The Big Three at Yalta

Roosevelt, Churchill, and Stalin met at Yalta in the Crimea in February 1945 to discuss the problems of the peace settlements. Most of the Yalta agreements were secret, and during the subsequent Cold War they became controversial. Roosevelt wanted Soviet help in ending the Pacific war, to avoid the slaughter of American men in an invasion of Japan. In return for a promise to enter the war within three months after the war in Europe was over, the Soviet Union was granted the Kurile Islands, the southern half of Sakhalin Island, and railroads and port facilities in Korea, Manchuria, and Mongolia. That later seemed like a heavy price to pay, but realistically the Soviet Union controlled most of this territory and could not have been dislodged without going to war.

When the provisions of the secret treaties were revealed much later, many people accused Roosevelt of trusting Stalin too much. But Roosevelt wanted to retain a working relationship with Moscow to preserve the peace, and he hoped to get Soviet agreement to cooperate with the new peace-preserving United Nations organization after the war.

The European section of the Yalta agreement proved even more controversial. The diplomats decided to partition Germany and to divide Berlin. The Polish agreements were even more difficult to swallow. Stalin demanded that eastern Poland be given to the Soviet Union. Churchill and Roosevelt finally agreed to the Russian demands with the proviso that Poland be compensated with German territory on its western border. A Polish government-in-exile in London was militantly anti-Communist and looked forward to returning home after the war. Stalin finally agreed to include some London Poles in a new pro-Soviet Polish government and to "free and unfettered elections as soon as possible."

The Polish settlement proved divisive after the war, for it quickly became clear that what the British and Americans wanted in eastern Europe contrasted with what the Soviet Union intended. Yet at the time it seemed imperative that Russia enter the war in the Pacific, and the reality was that in 1945 the Soviet army occupied most of eastern Europe.

The most potentially valuable accomplishment at Yalta was Stalin's agreement to join Roosevelt and Churchill in calling a conference in San Francisco in April 1945 to draft a United Nations charter. The charter gave primary responsibility for keeping global peace to the Security Council, composed of five permanent members (the United States, the Soviet Union, Great Britain, France, and China) and six other nations elected for two-year terms.

Just as important was the Bretton Woods Conference held in the summer of 1944 in New Hampshire. It established the World Bank and the International Monetary Fund and fixed the rate for international exchange using dollars as the standard, in the process recognizing that the United States, not Great Britain, would be the dominant economic power in the postwar world.

The Atomic Age Begins

Two months after Yalta, on April 12, 1945, Roosevelt died suddenly. Hated and loved to the end, he was replaced by Harry Truman, who was both more difficult to hate and harder to love. In the beginning, Truman seemed tentative and unsure. Yet it fell to him to make some of the most difficult decisions of all time.

The Manhattan Project to create an atomic bomb was one of the best-kept secrets of the war. Scientists worked in 37 facilities in the United States and Canada to build an atomic weapon before Germany did. But by the time the bomb was successfully tested in the New Mexico desert on July 16, 1945, the war in Europe had ended.

The scientists working on the bomb assumed they were perfecting a military weapon. Yet when they first saw its ghastly power, remembered J. Robert Oppenheimer, a leading scientist on the project, "some wept, a few cheered. Most stood silently." They realized its revolutionary power and worried about the future reputation of the United States if it unleashed this new force. But a presidential committee made up of scientists, military leaders, and politicians recommended that it be dropped on a military target in Japan as soon as possible.

"The final decision of where and when to use the atomic bomb was up to me," Truman later remembered. "Let there be no doubt about it. I regarded the bomb as a military weapon and never had any doubt that it should be used." But the decision had military and political ramifications. Even though Japan had lost most of its empire by the summer of 1945, it still had several million troops and thousands of kamikaze planes, whose pilots gave their lives by crashing planes, heavily laden with bombs, into American ships. There was little defense against them.

Even with the Russian promise to enter the war, it appeared that an amphibious landing on the Japanese mainland would be necessary. The monthlong battle for Iwo Jima, nearly 700 miles from Tokyo, had killed nearly 7,000 Americans and wounded nearly 20,000, and the battle for Okinawa was even more costly. Invading the Japanese mainland would presumably be far worse. The bomb, many thought, could end the war without an invasion. Some people involved in the decision wanted to avenge Pearl Harbor, and still others felt they needed to justify spending over $2 billion, then a huge sum of money, on the project in the first place. Some policymakers also hoped to impress the Russians and ensure that they had little to do with the peace settlement in the Far East. In the end, Truman chose to go ahead and use the new weapon because the United States had always assumed it would be dropped once it was ready.

Though some questioned whether the use of the atomic bomb on Japanese cities was necessary to end the war, the hundreds of thousands of American troops waiting to invade Japan did not doubt the rightness of the decision. They believed that it saved their lives. On August 6, 1945, two days before the Soviet Union had promised to enter the war against Japan, a B-29 bomber, the *Enola Gay,* dropped a single atomic bomb over Hiroshima. It killed or severely wounded 140,000 civilians and destroyed four square miles of the city. The Soviet Union entered the war on August 8. When Japan refused to surrender, a second bomb destroyed Nagasaki on August 9. The Japanese surrendered five days later. The war was over, but the problems of the atomic age and the postwar world had just begun.

The Impact of War

Wars embrace more than just leaders, grand strategy, and elaborate campaigns. They affect all people—the soldiers who fight and the women and children and men who stay home. World War II especially had an impact on all aspects of society: economy, entertainment, even attitudes toward women and blacks. For many people, the war represented opportunity and the end of the Depression. For others, it left lasting scars.

Mobilizing for War

Converting American industry to war production was a complex task. Shortly after Pearl Harbor, Roosevelt created the War Production Board (WPB) and appointed Donald Nelson, executive vice president of Sears, Roebuck, to mobilize resources for an all-out war effort. The Roosevelt administration tried hard to gain the cooperation of businessmen, many of them alienated by New Deal policies. The president appointed many business executives to key positions and abandoned antitrust actions in any industry that was remotely war related.

The policy worked. Industrial production and net corporate profits nearly doubled during the war. Large commercial farmers also profited. The war years accelerated the mechanization of the farm and dramatically increased the use of fertilizer, but between 1940 and 1945, the farm population declined by 17 percent.

Many government agencies besides the War Production Board helped run the war effort efficiently. The Office of Price Administration (OPA) set prices to control inflation and rationed products—and because it affected so many lives so disagreeably, many Americans regarded it as oppressive. The National War Labor Board (NWLB) had the authority to set wages and hours and to monitor working conditions, and it could seize plants whose owners refused to cooperate.

Union membership grew rapidly, aided by government policy. In return for a "no-strike pledge," the NWLB allowed agreements that required workers to retain their union membership through the life of a contract. When labor leaders complained about wage controls, the NWLB finally allowed a 15 percent cost-of-living increase on some contracts, but not on overtime pay.

Besides wage and price controls and rationing, the government fought inflation by selling war bonds and increasing taxes. The Revenue Act of 1942 raised tax rates, broadened the tax base, boosted corporate taxes to 40 percent, and set the excess-profits tax at 90 percent. In addition, the government initiated payroll deductions, making the income tax a reality for most Americans for the first time.

Despite some unfairness and much confusion, the American economy turned out the equipment and supplies that eventually won the war. American industries built 300,000 airplanes, 88,140 tanks, and 3,000 merchant ships. In 1944 alone, American factories produced 800,000 tons of synthetic rubber to replace natural rubber, cut off by the Japanese. By the war's end, the American economy was turning out an astonishing 50 percent of all the world's goods.

Although the national debt grew from about $143 billion in 1943 to $260 billion in 1945, taxes paid for about 40 percent of the war's cost. At the same time, full employment and the increase in two-income families, together with forced savings, helped amass capital for postwar expansion. In a limited way, the tax policy also tended to redistribute wealth, which the

New Deal had failed to do. The top 5 percent income bracket, which controlled 23 percent of the disposable income in 1939, accounted for only 17 percent in 1945.

The war stimulated the growth of the federal bureaucracy and accelerated the trend, begun during World War I and extended in the 1920s and 1930s, toward a major federal government role in the economy. The war also increased the cooperation between industry and government, creating what came to be called a military-industrial complex. But for most Americans, despite their anger at the OPA and the income tax, the war meant the end of the Depression.

Wartime Opportunities

More than 15 million American civilians moved during the war. Like the Momadays, many left home seeking better jobs. For Native Americans, and for others, wartime opportunities caused a migration into the cities. California alone gained more than 2 million people during the war. But Americans also moved from the rural South into northern cities, and a smaller number moved from the North to the South. Two hundred thousand came to the Detroit area, nearly a half-million to Los Angeles, and about 100,000 to Mobile, Alabama.

Watch the Video
The Great Migration
at **www.myhistorylab.com**

Nowhere was the change more striking than in the West, which the wartime boom transformed more dramatically than any development since the nineteenth-century economic revolution created by the railroads and mining. The federal government spent over $70 billion in California (one-tenth of the total for the entire country) on army bases, shipyards, supply depots, and testing sites. Private industry built so many facilities that the region became the center of a growing military-industrial complex. San Diego, for example, changed from a sleepy port into a sprawling metropolis. This spectacular growth created housing shortages and overwhelmed schools, hospitals, and municipal services. Crime, prostitution, and racial tension all increased.

For the first time in years, many families had money to spend, but they had nothing to spend it on. The last new car rolled off the assembly line in February 1942. There were no washing machines, refrigerators, or radios in the stores, little gasoline, and few tires. Even when people had time off, they tended to stay home, go to the movies, or listen to the radio.

The war required major adjustments in American family life. With several million men in the service or working at faraway defense jobs, the number of households headed by women increased dramatically. The number of marriages also rose sharply. Early in the war, a young man could be deferred if he had a dependent, such as a wife. Later, many servicemen got married, often to women they barely knew, because they wanted a little excitement and perhaps someone waiting at home. Reversing a decline that extended back to the colonial period, the birthrate also began to rise in 1940, as young couples started families as fast as they could. Since birthrates had been especially low during the Depression, the shift marked a significant change. The number of births outside marriage rose, and the divorce rate also went up sharply. Yet most wartime marriages survived, and many of the women left behind looked ahead to a normal life after the war.

Patriotic Fervor

The war, so devastating elsewhere, was remote in the United States— except for the thousands of families that received the official telegram telling of a loved one killed. The government tried to keep the conflict alive in Americans' minds and to keep the country united behind the war effort. The **Office of War Information** promoted patriotism and controlled the news that the public received about the war. The government also sold war bonds, not only to help pay for the war and reduce inflation but also to sell the war to the American people. Schoolchildren purchased war stamps

Fighting for Freedom Norman Rockwell, a popular illustrator, created four paintings to illustrate the Four Freedoms that President Roosevelt mentioned in his 1941 address to spell out what the United States was fighting for: freedom of worship, freedom of speech, freedom from fear, and freedom from want. Commissioned by the *Saturday Evening Post*, these paintings were turned into posters and used to support the sale of war bonds. What does this poster reveal about American freedom?

and pasted them in an album until they had accumulated stamps worth $18.75, enough to buy a $25 bond (redeemable 10 years later). Their bonds, they were told, would purchase bullets or airplane parts to kill "Japs" and Germans. Working men and women purchased bonds through payroll deduction plans and looked forward to spending the money on consumer goods after the war. In the end, the government sold over $135 billion in war bonds. While the bond drives did help control inflation, they were most important in making millions of Americans feel that they were contributing to the war effort.

Those too old or too young to join the armed forces served as air raid wardens or civilian defense and Red Cross volunteers. They raised victory gardens, contributed to scrap drives, and did without. Anyone resisting heard the popular refrain: "Don't you know there's a war on?"

Wartime Entertainment

According to one survey, Americans listened to the radio an average of four and a half hours a day during the war. The major networks increased their news programs from less than 4 percent to nearly 30 percent of broadcasting time. Americans heard Edward R. Murrow broadcasting from London during the German air blitz with air-raid sirens in the background. Often static made listening difficult, but the live broadcasts had an authenticity never before possible.

The war intruded on almost all programming. Serials, the standard fare of daytime radio, adopted wartime themes. Popular music, which occupied a large share of radio programming, reflected the war. There was "Goodbye, Mama (I'm Off to Yokohama)," but more numerous were songs of romance, love, separation, and hope for a better time after the war. The danceable tunes of Glenn Miller and Tommy Dorsey became just as much a part of wartime memories as ration books and far-off battlefields.

For many Americans, the motion picture became the most important leisure activity. Movie attendance averaged about 100 million viewers a week. There might not be gasoline for Sunday drives, but the whole family could go to the movies. Even those in the military could watch American movies on-board ship or at a remote outpost. "Pinups" of Hollywood stars decorated barracks, tanks, and planes wherever American troops went.

The war engulfed Hollywood. Newsreels offering a visual synopsis of war news, always with an upbeat message and a touch of human interest, preceded most movies. Their theme was that the Americans were winning, even if early on there was little evidence to that effect. Many feature films also had a wartime theme, picturing the Pacific war complete with grinning Japanese villains (usually played by Chinese or Korean actors). Movies set in Europe differed somewhat from those depicting the Pacific war. British and American heroes behind enemy lines outwitted Nazis at every turn, sabotaged installations, and made daring escapes from prison camps. Many wartime movies featured a multicultural platoon led by a veteran sergeant with a Protestant, a Catholic, a Jew, an African American, a farmer, and a city resident. The message was that we could all get along and cooperate to defeat the enemy. But in the real army, blacks served in segregated platoons.

Religion in Time of War

"Freedom of worship," according to President Roosevelt, was one of the freedoms threatened by the war. According to one poll, 30 percent of Americans said the war had strengthened their religious faith. Most thought of the United States as a "Christian nation," and by that they usually meant Protestant. The war increased religious tolerance, but anti-Semitism and anti-Catholicism remained. Those who joined the armed forces had to identify themselves as Protestant, Catholic, or Jew. There was no room for Hindu, Buddhist, Muslim, or atheist. Over 70,000 men claimed exemption from service on religious grounds. The government honored about half those claims with assignments to noncombat military service.

Many clergymen of all faiths volunteered to serve as chaplains. A few remained pacifist, but far fewer than in World War I. One influential minister and theologian who argued for force to combat evil was Reinhold Niebuhr. In books like *The Children of Light and the Children of Darkness* (1944), he opposed what he saw as a naïve faith in the goodness of man, a faith that permeated the Social Gospel movement, progressivism, and the New Deal. In a world gone mad, he saw all men as sinful and argued for the use of force against evil. His Christian realism influenced the continuing debate in the 1930s, 1940s, and 1950s over the proper American response to evil around the world.

Insiders and Outsiders

Millions of Americans fought in the war, and some paid the ultimate price. But millions more at home had their own issues to confront, and outsiders in America, often treated as second-class citizens, tried to move ahead in the midst of the cataclysmic struggle.

The GIs' War

GI, short for *government issue*, became the affectionate designation for the ordinary soldier in World War II. The GIs came from every background and ethnic group. Some served reluctantly, some eagerly. A few became genuine heroes, and all were turned into heroes by the press and the public, who seemed to believe that one American could easily defeat at least 20 Japanese or Germans. Ernie Pyle, a war correspondent who chronicled the authentic story of the ordinary GI, wrote of soldiers "just toiling from day to day in a world full of insecurity, discomfort, homesickness, and a dulled sense of danger."

In the midst of battle, the war was no fun, but only one soldier in eight ever saw combat, and even for many of them the war was a great adventure (as World War I had been). "When World War II broke out I was delighted," Mario Puzo, author of *The Godfather*, remembered. "My country called." It was a glorious crusade.

Because the war lasted longer than World War I, its impact was greater. In all, over 16 million men and women served in the military. About 322,000 were killed, and more than 800,000 were wounded. The 12,000 listed as missing just disappeared. The war claimed many more lives than World War I and was the nation's costliest after the Civil War. But penicillin, blood plasma, sulfa drugs, and rapid battlefield evacuation made it twice as likely for the wounded in World War II to survive as in World War I. Penicillin also minimized the threat of venereal disease, but all men who served still saw an anti-VD film.

Women at War

Women served in support roles, just as in past wars. Some were nurses and cooks. In April 1943, women physicians won the right to join the Army and Navy Medical Corps. Despite some objections, Congress authorized full military participation (except combat duty) for women because they would free men for combat. World War II thus became the first U.S. war in which women received regular military status. About 350,000 women joined up, most in the Women's Army Corps (WACS) and the women's branch of the Navy (WAVES), but there were others in the coast guard, marines, and the air force.

Still, men and women were not treated equally. Women were explicitly kept out of combat situations and were often underused by male officers who found it difficult to view women in nontraditional roles. Army nurses with officer rank were forbidden to date enlisted men. Despite difficulties, women played important roles during the war, and when they left the service, they had the same rights as male veterans. The women in the service did not permanently alter the military or the public's perception of women's proper role, but they did change a few minds, and many of these women had their lives altered and their horizons broadened.

Meanwhile, thousands of women took jobs in heavy industry once considered unladylike. They built tanks, airplanes, and ships, but they still earned less than men. At first, women had difficulty finding positions because, as the war in Europe pulled American industry out of its long slump, unemployed men snapped up the newly available positions. But by 1943, with many men drafted and male unemployment virtually nonexistent, the government suggested that it was women's patriotic duty to join the assembly line. A popular song was "**Rosie the Riveter**," who helped her marine boyfriend by overtime on the riveting machine."

◉ Watch the Video

Rosie the Riveter
at **www.myhistorylab.com**

"Rosie the Riveter" Many African Americans moved north, lured by jobs in war industries. Prejudice remained even in the North, and some blacks were denied employment or were given the most menial tasks. Others, like these welders, found good jobs, improved their lives, and helped change the dynamics of race relations in the United States. What other developments resulted from the wartime employment of women and minorities?

At the end of the war, the labor force included 19.5 million women. New women war workers tended to be older than those already in the labor force, and they were more often married than single. Some worked for patriotic reasons. "Every time I test a batch of rubber, I know it's going to help bring my three sons home quicker," said a female worker in a rubber plant. But others worked for the money or to have something useful to do. Yet in 1944, women's weekly wages averaged $31.21, compared with $54.65 for men, reflecting women's menial tasks and low seniority as well as outright discrimination. Still, many women enjoyed factory work.

Black women faced the most difficult situation. Often, when they applied for work, they were told something like "We have not yet installed separate toilet facilities." Not until 1944 did the telephone company in New York City hire a black operator. Still, some black women moved during the war from domestic jobs to higher-paying factory work.

Many women war workers quickly left their jobs after the war ended. Some left by choice, but dismissals ran twice as high for women as for men. Some women who learned what an extra paycheck meant for the family's standard of living would have preferred to keep working. But most women, and even more men, agreed at the war's end that women should not compete with men for jobs.

View the Image

Women in an Airplane Factory

at **www.myhistorylab.com**

The African American Struggle

The United States remained a segregated society during World War II. Black Americans profited little from the wartime revival of prosperity and the expansion of jobs early in the war. Those who joined the military were usually assigned to menial jobs, always in segregated units with whites as the high-ranking officers. The myth persisted that black soldiers had failed to perform well in World War I. At the same time, African Americans, who served throughout the war in segregated units and faced prejudice everywhere, gained from the military experience. Fewer blacks were sent overseas (about 79,000 out of 504,000 blacks in the service in 1943), and fewer were in combat outfits, so the percentage of black soldiers killed and wounded was low. Many illiterate blacks, especially from the South, learned to read and write. Blacks who went overseas began to realize that not everyone viewed them as inferior. Most realized the paradox of fighting for freedom when they themselves had little freedom and hoped things would improve after the war.

●●●─┤Read the Document

A. Philip Randolph, "Why Should We March" (1942) at **www.myhistorylab.com**

Some black leaders demanded an end to racism. A labor union head, A. Philip Randolph, decided to act. Randolph had worked with the first wave of African Americans migrating from the South to the northern cities during and just after World War I. Afterwards he organized and led the Brotherhood of Sleeping Car Porters and in 1937 finally won grudging recognition of the union from the Pullman Company.

Admired by black leaders of all political persuasions, Randolph convinced many of them in 1941 to join him in a march on Washington to demand equal rights. Alarmed, Roosevelt talked to Randolph and finally struck a bargain. The president refused to desegregate the armed forces, but in return for Randolph's calling off the march, he issued Executive Order 8802, which stated that it was government policy that "there shall be no discrimination in the employment of workers in defense industries or government because of race, creed, color or national origin." To enforce the order, he established the **Fair Employment Practices Committee** (FEPC).

By threatening militant action, the black leaders wrested a major concession from the president. But the executive order did not end prejudice, and the FEPC (which its chairman described as the "most hated agency in Washington") had limited success in erasing the color line. Many black soldiers were angered and humiliated throughout the war by being made to sit in the back of buses and being barred from hotels and restaurants. Years later, one former black soldier recalled being refused service in a restaurant in Salina, Kansas, while the same restaurant served German prisoners from a camp nearby. "We continued to stare," he recalled. "This was really happening. . . . The people of Salina would serve these enemy soldiers and turn away black American GI's."

●●●─┤Read the Document

Sterling A. Brown, "Out of Their Mouths" (1942) at **www.myhistorylab.com**

Jobs in war industries helped many African Americans improve their economic circumstances. Continuing the migration that had begun during World War I, about 1 million southern blacks moved to northern and western cities. Some became skilled workers, and a few became professionals. The new arrivals increased pressure on overcrowded housing and other facilities, accentuating tension among all hard-pressed groups. In Detroit, a major race riot broke out in the summer of 1943 after Polish Americans protested a public housing development that promised to bring blacks into their neighborhood. A series of incidents led to fights between black and white young people and then to looting in the black community. Before federal and state troops restored order, 25 blacks and 9 whites had been killed and more than $2 million worth of property destroyed. Groups of whites roamed through the city attacking blacks, overturning cars, setting fires, and sometimes killing wantonly. Other riots broke out in Mobile, Alabama, Los Angeles, New York, and Beaumont, Texas. In all these cities, and in many others where the tension did not lead to open violence, the legacy of hate lasted long after the war.

View the Image

African American Family on the Road

at **www.myhistorylab.com**

Other Outsiders

Mexican Americans, like most minority groups, benefited from wartime job opportunities, both in military service and back home. They were drafted and volunteered in great numbers. A third of a million served in all branches of the military, a larger percentage than for many other ethnic groups. Although they encountered prejudice, they probably found less in the armed forces than at home, and many returned to civilian life with new ambitions and self-esteem. On the home front, however, even as they embraced new job opportunities, they faced continuing prejudice. In California and in many parts of the Southwest, Mexicans could not use public swimming pools and certain restaurants. Usually they held menial jobs and faced constant harassment from the police.

In Los Angeles, anti-Mexican prejudice flared into violence. Most of the anger focused on Mexican gang members wearing zoot suits—long, loose coats with padded shoulders, ballooned pants, and wide-brimmed hats. Zoot-suiters especially angered soldiers and sailors in Los Angeles. After many provocative incidents, violence peaked on June 7, 1943, when gangs of servicemen attacked all the young zoot-suiters they could find or anyone who looked Mexican. The police looked the other way or arrested the victims.

Many Native Americans also served, often recruited for special service in the Marine Signal Corps. One group of Navajo completely befuddled the Japanese with a code based on their native language. But the Navajo code talkers and all other Indians who chose to return to reservations after the war were ineligible for benefits like veterans' loans and hospitalization. They lived on federal land, and that, by law, canceled the advantages that other veterans enjoyed.

Asian Americans likewise played a role in the war. The Pacific conflict made China an ally of the United States, but Congress did not repeal the Chinese Exclusion Act until 1943, and then only 105 Chinese a year were allowed to enter the United States. Despite this, over 13,000 Chinese Americans joined the U.S. Army, while others took jobs in war industries. The Korean, Filipino, and Asian Indian population also contributed to the war effort, though they constantly faced prejudice and were often denied service in restaurants.

Japanese Americans Interned

Japanese Americans had a far worse time. They were easier than the Germans to hate.

The attack on Pearl Harbor created a special animosity toward them, but depicting them as warlike and subhuman owed something to a long-standing American distrust of all Asians. Still, Japanese were different, since other Asians were allies. Two weeks after Pearl Harbor, *Time* magazine told Americans how to distinguish the friendly Chinese from "the Japs": "The Chinese expression is likely to be more kindly, placid, open; the Japanese more positive, dogmatic, arrogant."

Racial stereotypes played a role in the treatment of Japanese Americans during the war. They were the only group confined in concentration camps, in the greatest mass abridgment of civil liberties in American history.

At the time of Pearl Harbor, about 127,000 Japanese Americans lived in the United States, most on the West Coast. About 80,000 were *Nisei* (Japanese born in the United States and holding American citizenship) and *Sansei* (the sons and daughters of *Nisei*); the rest were *Issei* (aliens born in Japan who were ineligible for U.S. citizenship). They had long suffered from prejudice—barred, for example, from intermarriage with other groups and excluded from various clubs, restaurants, and recreation facilities. Many worked as tenant farmers, fishermen, or small businessmen, or were landowning farmers, but some belonged to a small professional class of lawyers, teachers, and doctors.

Although many retained cultural ties to Japan and spoke Japanese, these people posed no more threat to the country than did the much larger groups of Italian Americans and German Americans. But their appearance made them stand out. After Pearl Harbor, an anti-Japanese panic seized the West Coast. West Coast politicians and citizens urged the War Department to remove the Japanese. The president capitulated and issued Executive Order 9066, authorizing the evacuation in February 1942. "The continued pressure of a largely unassimilated, tightly knit racial group, bound to an enemy nation by strong ties of race, culture, custom and religion, constituted a menace which had to be dealt with," General John De Witt argued, justifying the removal on military grounds. But racial fear and hatred, not military necessity, explained the order.

The Enemy During the war, American magazines and newspapers often depicted the Japanese as monkeys, insects, or rodents. Germans were rarely pictured this way. This December 12, 1942, issue of *Collier's* magazine pictures Japanese prime minister Hideki Tojo as a vampire bat carrying a bomb to drop on the United States. The Japanese, on the other hand, often pictured Americans and British as bloated capitalists and imperialists. What effect, do you suppose, did these caricatures have on attitudes and actions during the war?

"The Japs live like rats, breed like rats, and act like rats. We don't want them," the governor of Idaho announced. Because of that perception, the government built primitive "relocation centers" in remote, often arid sections of the West. "When I first entered our room, I became sick to my stomach," a Japanese American woman remembered.

The government evacuated about 110,000 Japanese, including about 60,000 American citizens. Farmers left their crops to be harvested by their American neighbors. Store owners sold out for a small percentage of what their goods were worth. Japanese Americans lost virtually all of their personal possessions, and something more—their pride and respect.

The evacuation was unjustified. In Hawaii, with its much larger Japanese American population, there was no evacuation, and no sabotage and little disloyalty occurred. Late in the war, the government allowed Japanese American men to volunteer for military service, and many served bravely in the European theater. The 442nd Infantry Combat Team, made up entirely of *Nisei*, became the most decorated unit in all the military service—another indication of the loyalty and patriotism of the Japanese Americans. In 1988, Congress belatedly apologized and voted limited compensation for Japanese Americans relocated during World War II.

RECOVERING *the* PAST

History, Memory, and Monuments

In recent years, historians have been studying collective memory—the stories people tell about the past. Collective memory is closely related to national regional identity and is often associated with patriotism and war. But memory is usually selective and often contested. The generation that lived through World War II is getting older, and often these people fear that few remember or care about their war. One veteran of the Italian campaign recently remarked: "Today they don't even know what Anzio was. Most people aren't interested." The collective memory of World War II may include letters, photos, old uniforms, and stories told to grandchildren (oral history), but the collective memory of war often includes monuments as well.

Almost every small town and city in the Northeast, the Midwest, and the South has a monument to the soldiers who fought and died in the Civil War; often it is a statue of a common soldier with rifle at rest. In the South, a statue of Robert E. Lee on horseback came to symbolize the "Lost Cause." Usually monuments to war symbolize triumph or fighting for a just cause, even in defeat.

A large monument to World War II veterans finally opened on the mall in Washington in 2004 after years of controversy. There have been many other attempts to honor the World War II generation. The Air and Space Museum of the Smithsonian Institution in Washington, D.C., planned a major exhibit for 1995 to commemorate the fiftieth anniversary of the dropping of the first atomic bomb on Hiroshima and the end of World War II. The *Enola Gay*, the B-29 that dropped the bomb, was to be the centerpiece of the exhibit, but the historians and curators who organized the exhibit also planned to raise a number of questions that historians had been debating for years. Would the war have ended in days or weeks without the bomb? How was the decision to drop the bomb made? Was there a racial component to the decision? Would the United States have dropped the bomb on Germany? Was the bomb dropped more to impress the Soviet Union than to force the Japanese to surrender? What was the impact of the bomb on the ground? What implications did dropping the bomb have on the world after 1945?

The exhibit (except in greatly modified form) never took place. Many veterans of World War II and other Americans denounced it as traitorous and un-American. For these critics, the decision to drop the bomb was not something to debate. For them, World War II was a contest between good and evil, and the bomb was simply a way to defeat the evil empire and save American lives. The controversy over the *Enola Gay* exhibit demonstrated that 50 years later, memory and history were at odds and that the memory of the war was still contested. The main reason the exhibit did not satisfy those who remembered the war was that it did not commemorate triumph but instead seemed to question the motives of those who fought and died.

The Vietnam Veterans Memorial erected in Washington in 1982 was initially controversial for similar reasons. Designed by Maya Lin, a young artist and sculptor, it consists of a wall of polished granite inscribed with the names of 58,000 dead. There are no soldiers on horseback; in fact, there are no figures at all, not even a flag. Critics called it a "black gash of shame." Even the addition of a sculpture of three "fighting men" did not satisfy many. But to almost everyone's surprise, hundreds of thousands of veterans and friends of veterans found the monument deeply moving, and they left photos, flowers, poems, and other objects. For them, the memorial successfully represented collective memory. Still the critics were dissatisfied; they wanted something more like the Iwo Jima monument.

Iwo Jima was a tiny, desolate island nearly 700 miles from Tokyo, important only because it was a base for Japanese fighters to attack American bombers on their way to the Japanese mainland. The Fourth and Fifth Marine Divisions invaded the island on February 17, 1945. After bitter fighting, the marines captured Mt. Suribachi, the highest point on the island, on February 23 and completed the conquest of the island on March 17. But it was a costly victory, with nearly 7,000 Americans dead and almost 20,000 wounded.

Dedication of the Iwo Jima Memorial Monument in Washington, D.C., November 10, 1954.

Associated Press photographer Joe Rosenthal was one of several journalists who went ashore with the marines and one of three photographers assigned to record the raising of the American flag on top of Mt. Suribachi. A group of marines raised the flag twice so the photographers could get their pictures. It was Rosenthal's photograph of the second flag raising that became famous. On February 25, 1945, his photograph of the five marines and a navy corpsman raising the flag was on the front page of Sunday newspapers across the country. "Stars and Stripes on Iwo," "Old Glory over Volcano," the captions read. Within months, the image of the flag raising appeared on a war bond poster with the caption "Now All Together" and also on a postage stamp. Three of the six flag raisers were killed in the battle for Iwo Jima, but those who survived became heroes, and their images were used to sell war bonds. Clearly, the flag-raising image had touched American emotions and quickly became part of the collective memory of the war, a symbol of the country pulling together to defeat the enemy.

In November 1954, a giant statue of the flag raising, designed by Felix De Weldon, was dedicated as a memorial to the U.S. Marine Corps on the edge of Arlington National Cemetery. Vice President Richard Nixon, speaking at the dedication, said that the statue symbolized "the hopes and dreams of the American people and the real purpose of our foreign policy." The flag-raising image played an important role in two movies: *The Sands of Iwo Jima* (1949), starring John Wayne, and *The Outsider* (1960), starring Tony Curtis. During the 1988 presidential campaign, George H. W. Bush chose to make a speech in front of the marine monument urging a constitutional amendment to ban the desecration of the flag. The image of the flag raising in photograph, drawing, film, and cartoon remains part of the collective memory of World War II.

REFLECTING ON THE PAST **Why did the Iwo Jima monument mean so much to the World War II generation? Was the monument more important than the photograph? What makes a monument meaningful? Is it the size? The accuracy? The ability to arouse emotion? Why do some monuments and symbols become part of collective memory, while others become controversial or forgotten? There are more than 15,000 outdoor sculptures and monuments in the country, most created since the Civil War. What monuments can you locate in your community? What collective memory do they symbolize?**

Conclusion

Peace, Prosperity, and International Responsibility

The United States emerged from World War II with an enhanced reputation as the world's most powerful industrial and military nation. The demands of the war had finally ended the Great Depression and brought prosperity to most Americans. Even N. Scott Momaday's family found better jobs because of the war, but like many Americans, they had to relocate in order to take those jobs. The war had also increased the power of the federal government. The payroll deduction of federal income taxes, begun during the war, symbolized the growth of a federal bureaucracy that affected the lives of all Americans. Ironically, the war to preserve freedom was fought with a segregated army, and some American citizens, notably Japanese Americans, suffered the loss of their freedom. Yet the war had also ended American isolationism and made the United States into the dominant international power. Of all the nations that fought in the war, the United States had suffered the least. No bombs were dropped on American factories, and no cities were destroyed. Although more than 300,000 Americans lost their lives, even this carnage seemed minimal when compared with the more than 20 million Russian soldiers and civilians who died or the 6 million Jews and millions of others systematically exterminated by Hitler.

Americans greeted the end of the war with joy and relief. They looked forward to the peace and prosperity for which they had fought. Yet within two years, the Cold War eroded the peace and led the United States to rearm its former enemies, Japan and Germany, to oppose its former friend, the Soviet Union. The irony of that situation reduced the joy of the hard-won peace and made the American people more suspicious of their government and its foreign policy. Yet the memory of World War II and the perception that the country was united against evil enemies—indeed, that World War II was a "good war"—had an impact on American foreign policy, and even on Americans' perception of themselves, for decades to come.

TIME*line*

1931–1932 Japan seizes Manchuria

1933 Hitler becomes German chancellor

United States recognizes the Soviet Union

Roosevelt extends Good Neighbor policy

1934 Germany begins rearmament

1935 Italy invades Ethiopia

First Neutrality Act

1936	Spanish Civil War begins
	Second Neutrality Act
	Roosevelt reelected
1938	Hitler annexes Austria, occupies Sudetenland
	German persecution of Jews intensifies
1939	Nazi–Soviet Pact
	German invasion of Poland; World War II begins
1940	Roosevelt elected for a third term
	Selective Service Act
1941	FDR's "Four Freedoms" speech
	Proposed black march on Washington
	Executive Order 8802 outlaws discrimination in defense industries
	Lend-Lease Act
	Germany attacks Russia
	Japanese assets in United States frozen
	Japanese attack Pearl Harbor; United States declares war on Japan
	Germany declares war on United States
1942	Internment of Japanese Americans
	Second Allied front in Africa launched
1943	Invasion of Sicily
	Italian campaign; Italy surrenders
	Race riots in Detroit and other cities
1944	Normandy invasion (Operation Overlord)
	Roosevelt elected for a fourth term
1945	Yalta Conference
	Roosevelt dies; Harry Truman becomes president
	Germany surrenders
	Successful test of atomic bomb
	Hiroshima and Nagasaki bombed; Japan surrenders

✓•—Study and Review at **www.myhistorylab.com**

Questions for Review and Reflection

1. Considering the series of international events that led to the U.S. entry into World War II, could the nation have stayed neutral?

2. Why did the United States intern Japanese Americans in the aftermath of the attack on Pearl Harbor? Was the internment justified?

3. How did the war change the lives of women, African Americans, and Hispanic Americans?

4. What were the war aims of the United States, and how were they achieved?

5. What led the United States to develop the atomic bomb? What were the consequences of this new weapon for the Japanese, for Americans, and for the outcome of World War II?

Key Terms

Axis powers 749

Fair Employment Practices Committee 766

Four freedoms 749

Lend-lease 747

Manhattan Project 746

Nazi–Soviet Pact 746

Office of War Information 761

Pearl Harbor 748

Rosie the Riveter 764

24

Chills and Fever During the Cold War, 1945–1960

American Stories

A Government Employee Confronts the Anti-Communist Crusade

Val Lorwin was in France in November 1950 when he learned of the charges against him. A State Department employee on leave of absence after 16 years of government service, he was in Paris working on a book. Now he had to return to the United States to defend himself against the accusation that he was a member of the Communist party and thus a loyalty and security risk. Suspicions of the Soviet Union had escalated after 1945, and a wave of paranoia swept through the United States.

Lorwin was an unlikely candidate to be caught up in the fallout of the Cold War. He had begun to work for the government in 1935, serving in a number of New Deal agencies, then in the Labor Department and on the War Production Board before he was drafted during World War II. While in the army, he was assigned to the Office of Strategic Services, an early intelligence agency, and he was frequently granted security clearances.

Lorwin, however, did have a left-wing past as an active socialist in the 1930s. He had supported Socialist party causes, particularly the unionization of southern tenant farmers and the provision of aid to the unemployed. He and his wife, Madge, drafted statements and stuffed envelopes to support their goals. But that activity was wholly open and legal, and Lorwin had from the start been aggressively anti-Communist in political affairs.

Suddenly, Lorwin, like others in the period, faced a nightmare. Despite his spotless record, Lorwin was told that an unnamed accuser had identified him as a Communist. The burden of proving his innocence was entirely on him. He was entitled to a hearing if he chose, or he could resign.

Chapter Outline

Origins of the Cold War

Containing the Soviet Union

Containment in Asia, the Middle East, and Latin America

Atomic Weapons and the Cold War

The Cold War at Home

Conclusion: The Cold War in Perspective

Lorwin requested a hearing that was held late in 1950. Still struck by the absurdity of the situation, he refuted all accusations but neglected to cite his own positive achievements. At the conclusion, he was informed that the government no longer doubted his loyalty but considered him a security risk, likewise grounds for dismissal from his job.

When he appealed the judgment, Lorwin was again denied access to the identity of his accuser. This time, however, he thoroughly prepared his defense. At the hearing, a total of 97 witnesses either spoke under oath on Lorwin's behalf or left sworn written depositions testifying to his good character and meritorious service.

The issues in the hearings might have been considered comic in view of Lorwin's record, had not a man's reputation been at stake. The accuser had once lived with the Lorwins in Washington, D.C. Fifteen years later, he claimed that in 1935 Lorwin had revealed that he was holding a Communist party meeting in his home and had even shown him a party card.

Lorwin proved all the charges groundless. He also showed that in 1935 the Socialist party card was red, the color the accuser reported seeing, while the Communist party card was black. In March 1952, Lorwin was finally cleared for both loyalty and security.

Lorwin's troubles were not yet over, however. His name appeared on one of the lists produced by Senator Joseph McCarthy of Wisconsin, and he was indicted for making false statements to the State Department Loyalty-Security Board. The charges this time proved as specious as before. Finally, in May 1954, admitting that its special prosecutor had deliberately lied to the grand jury and had no legitimate case, the Justice Department asked for dismissal of the indictment. Cleared at last, Lorwin went on to become a distinguished labor historian.

Val Lorwin was more fortunate than some victims of the anti-Communist crusade. Caught up in a global conflict that engulfed most of the world, he managed to weather a catastrophe that threatened to shatter his life. People rallied around him and gave him valuable support. Despite considerable emotional cost, he survived the witch hunt of the early 1950s, but his case still reflected vividly the ugly domestic consequences of the breakdown in relations between the Soviet Union and the United States.

The Cold War, which unfolded soon after the end of World War II and lasted for nearly 50 years, powerfully affected all aspects of American life. Rejecting for good the isolationist impulse that had governed foreign policy in the 1920s and 1930s, the United States began to play a major role in the world in the postwar years. Doubts about intervention in other lands faded as the nation acknowledged its dominant international position and resolved to do whatever was necessary to maintain it. The same sense of mission that had infused the United States in the Spanish-American War,

World War I, and World War II now appeared in a revived evangelical faith and committed most Americans to the struggle against communism at home and abroad.

This chapter explores that continuing sense of mission and its consequences. It examines such questions as: What were the roots of the Cold War? How did the idealistic aim to keep the world safe for democracy relate to the pursuit of economic self-interest that had long fueled American capitalism? How did American policymakers come to consider vast parts of the world as pivotal to American security and determine to act accordingly, particularly in Korea and Vietnam? How did the Cold War foster American economic development? And what were the tragic consequences of the effort to promote ideological unity in a rigid and doctrinaire version of the American dream that led to excesses threatening the principles of democracy itself?

Origins of the Cold War

The **Cold War** developed by degrees. It stemmed from divergent views about the shape of the post–World War II world as the colonial empires in Asia, Africa, and the Middle East began to crumble. The United States, strong and secure, was intent on spreading its vision of freedom and free trade around the world to maintain its economic hegemony. The Soviet Union, concerned about security after a devastating war, demanded politically sympathetic neighbors on its borders to preserve its own autonomy. Suppressed during World War II, these differences now surfaced in a virulent Soviet–American confrontation.

The American Stance

The United States emerged from World War II more powerful than any nation ever before, and it sought to use that might to achieve a world order that could sustain American aims. American policymakers hoped to spread the values—liberty, equality, and democracy—underpinning the American dream. They did not always recognize that what they considered universal truths were rooted in specific historical circumstances in their own country and might not flourish elsewhere.

At the same time, American leaders sought a world where economic enterprise could thrive. With the American economy operating at full speed as a result of the war, world markets were needed once the fighting stopped. Government officials wanted to eliminate trade barriers—imposed by the Soviet Union and other nations—to provide outlets for industrial products and for surplus farm commodities such as wheat, cotton, and tobacco. As the largest source of goods for world markets, with exports totaling $14 billion in 1947, the United States required open channels for growth to continue. Americans assumed that their prosperity would benefit the rest of the world, even when other nations disagreed.

Soviet Aims

The Soviet Union formulated its own goals after World War II. Russia had usually been governed in the past by a strongly centralized government, and that tradition, as well as Communist ideology, guided Soviet policy.

During the war, the Russians had played down talk of world revolution, which they knew their allies found threatening, and had mobilized domestic support with nationalistic appeals. As the struggle drew to a close, the Soviets still said little about world conquest, emphasizing socialism within the nation itself.

Rebuilding was the first priority. Devastated by the war, Soviet agriculture and industry lay in shambles. But revival required internal security. At the same time, the Russians felt vulnerable along their western flank. Twice in the twentieth century, invasions had come from the west, most recently when Hitler had attacked in 1941. Haunted by fears of a quick German recovery, the Soviets demanded defensible borders and neighboring regimes sympathetic to Russian aims. They insisted on military and political stability in the regions nearby.

Early Cold War Leadership

Both the United States and the Soviet Union had strong leadership in the early years of the Cold War. On the American side, presidents Harry Truman and Dwight Eisenhower accepted the centralization of authority Franklin Roosevelt had begun, as the executive branch became increasingly powerful in guiding foreign policy. In the Soviet Union, first Joseph Stalin, then Nikita Khrushchev provided equally forceful direction.

Truman was an unpretentious man who took a straightforward approach to public affairs. Ill prepared for the office he assumed in the final months of World War II, he matured rapidly. A sign on his White House desk read "The Buck Stops Here," and he was willing to make quick decisions on issues, even if associates sometimes wondered if he understood all the implications. As World War II drew to an end, Truman grew increasingly hostile to Soviet actions. Viewing collaboration as a wartime necessity, he was uncomfortable with what he believed were Soviet designs in Eastern Europe and Asia as the struggle wound down.

Eisenhower stood in stark contrast to Truman. His easy manner and warm smile made him widely popular. Though he lacked formal political background, his military experience gave him a real ability to get people to compromise and work together. Like Truman, Eisenhower saw communism as a monolithic force struggling for world supremacy and agreed that the Kremlin in Moscow was orchestrating subversive activity around the globe. Yet Eisenhower was more willing than Truman to practice accommodation when it served his ends.

Both Truman and Eisenhower subscribed to traditional American attitudes about self-determination and the superiority of American political institutions and values. Both were determined to stand firm in the face of the Soviet threat.

Joseph Stalin, the Soviet leader at the war's end, possessed almost absolute powers. He had presided over ruthless purges against his opponents in the 1930s. He had weathered a ferocious war that left 20 million Russians dead. Now he was determined to rebuild Soviet society and to keep Eastern Europe within the Russian sphere of influence.

Stalin's death in March 1953 left a power vacuum in Soviet political affairs that was eventually filled by Nikita Khrushchev, who by 1958 held the offices of both prime minister and party secretary. A crude man with a peasant background, Khrushchev once famously used his shoe to pound a table at the United Nations. Like Stalin, he was determined to keep Soviet interests front and center, even when compromise sometimes became necessary. During his regime, the Cold War continued, but for brief periods of time Soviet–American relations became less hostile.

Disillusionment with the USSR

American support for the Soviet Union faded quickly after the war. As Americans soured on Russia, they began to equate the Nazi and Soviet systems. Just as they had in the 1930s, authors, journalists, and public officials pointed to similarities, some of them legitimate, between the regimes. Both states, they contended, maintained total control over communications and could eliminate political opposition. Both states used terror to silence dissidents, and Stalin's labor camps in Siberia could be compared with Hitler's concentration camps. After the U.S. publication in 1949 of George Orwell's frightening novel *1984*, *Life* magazine noted in an editorial that the ominous figure Big Brother was but a "mating" of Hitler and Stalin. Truman spoke for many Americans when he said in 1950 that "there isn't any difference between the totalitarian Russian government and the Hitler government. . . . They are all alike."

The lingering sense that the nation had not been quick enough to resist totalitarian aggression in the 1930s heightened American fears. Many people believed that the free world had not responded promptly when the Germans, Italians, and Japanese first caused international trouble, and the United States was determined never to repeat the same mistake.

The Troublesome Polish Question

The first clash between East and West came, even before the war ended, over Poland. Soviet demands for a government willing to accept Russian influence clashed with American hopes for a more representative structure patterned after the Western model. The Yalta Conference of February 1945 provided a loosely worded and correspondingly imprecise agreement (see Chapter 23), and when Truman assumed office, the Polish situation remained unresolved.

Truman's unbending stance on Poland was clear in an April 1945 meeting with Soviet foreign minister Vyacheslav Molotov. Concerned that the Russians were breaking the Yalta agreements, vague as they were, the American leader demanded a new democratic government there. Truman later recalled that when Molotov protested, "I have never been talked to like that in my life," he himself retorted bluntly, "Carry out your agreements and you won't get talked to like that." Such bluntness contributed to the deterioration of Soviet–American relations.

Truman and Stalin met face-to-face for the first (and last) time at the Potsdam Conference in July 1945, the final wartime Big Three meeting of the United States, the Soviet Union, and Great Britain. There, outside devastated Berlin, the two leaders sized each other up as they considered the Russian–Polish boundary, the fate of Germany, and the American desire to obtain an unconditional surrender from Japan. It was Truman's first exposure to international diplomacy at the highest level, and it left him confident of his abilities. When he learned during the meeting of the first successful atomic bomb test in New Mexico, he became even more determined to insist that the Soviets behave in the ways he wanted.

Economic Pressure on the USSR

One major source of controversy in the last stages of World War II was the question of U.S. aid to its allies. Responding to congressional pressure to limit foreign assistance as hostilities ended, Truman acted impulsively. Six days after the end of the European war in May 1945, he issued an executive order cutting off lend-lease supplies to the Allies. Though the policy affected all nations receiving aid, it hurt the Soviet Union most of all.

The United States used economic pressure in other ways as well. The USSR desperately needed financial assistance to rebuild after the war and, in January 1945, had requested a $6 billion loan. Roosevelt hedged, hoping to win concessions in return. In August, the Russians renewed their application, but this time for only $1 billion. Truman dragged his heels, seeking to use the loan as a lever to gain access to markets in areas traditionally dominated by the Soviet Union. Stalin refused a loan under such conditions and launched his own five-year plan instead.

Declaring the Cold War

As Soviet–American relations deteriorated, both sides stepped up their rhetorical attacks. In 1946, Stalin spoke out first, arguing that capitalism and communism were on a collision course, that a series of cataclysmic disturbances would tear the capitalist world apart, and that the Soviet system would inevitably triumph. Supreme Court Justice William O. Douglas called Stalin's speech the "declaration of World War III."

•**Read** the **Document**
Churchill's "Iron Curtain"
Speech (March 5, 1946)
at **www.myhistorylab.com**

The West's response to Stalin's speech came from England's former prime minister, Winston Churchill. Speaking in Fulton, Missouri, in 1946, with Truman on the platform during the address, Churchill declared that "from Stettin in the Baltic to Trieste in the Adriatic, an iron curtain has descended across the Continent." A vigilant association of English-speaking peoples was necessary to contain Soviet designs.

Containing the Soviet Union

Containment formed the basis of postwar American policy. While the fledgling United Nations, established in 1945, might have provided a forum to ease tensions, both the United States and the Soviet Union acted unilaterally, and with the aid of allies, in pursuit of their own ends.

Containment Defined

George F. Kennan, chargé d'affaires at the American embassy in the Soviet Union, was primarily responsible for defining the new policy of containment. After Stalin's speech in February 1946, Kennan sent an 8,000-word telegram to the State Department. In it he argued that Soviet hostility stemmed from the "Kremlin's neurotic view of world affairs," which in turn came from the "traditional and instinctive Russian sense of insecurity." The stiff Soviet stance was not so much a response to American actions as a reflection of the Russian leaders' own efforts to maintain their autocratic rule.

The Contagion of Communism Americans in the early postwar years were afraid that communism was a contagious disease spreading around the globe. In this picture from the spring of 1946, *Time* magazine pictured the relentless spread of an infection that would need to be contained. Why would such a map seem frightening to people who looked at it?

Russian fanaticism would not soften, regardless of how accommodating American policy became. Therefore, it had to be opposed at every turn.

Kennan's "long telegram" struck a resonant chord in Washington. Soon he published an extended analysis, under the pseudonym "Mr. X," in the prominent journal *Foreign Affairs*. Soviet pressure, he suggested, had to "be contained by the adroit and vigilant application of counter-force at a series of constantly shifting geographical and political points." The concept of containment provided the philosophical justification for the hard-line stance that the United States adopted.

The First Step: The Truman Doctrine

The **Truman Doctrine** represented the first major application of containment policy. The Soviet Union was pressuring Turkey for joint control of the Dardanelles, the passage between the Black Sea and the Mediterranean. Meanwhile, a civil war in Greece pitted Communist elements against the ruling English-aided right-wing monarchy. Revolutionary pressures threatened to topple the government.

●◆●[Read the Document
Truman Doctrine (1947)
at **www.myhistorylab.com**

In February 1947, Britain—still reeling from the war—informed the State Department that it could no longer give Greece and Turkey economic and military aid. Administration officials willing to move into the void knew they needed bipartisan support to accomplish such a major policy shift. Senator Arthur Vandenberg of Michigan, a key Republican, aware of the need for bipartisanship, told top policymakers that they had to begin "scaring hell out of the country" if they wanted support for a bold new containment policy.

Truman complied. On March 12, 1947, he told Congress, in a statement that came to be known as the Truman Doctrine, "I believe that it must be the policy of the United States to support free peoples who are resisting subjugation by armed minorities or by outside pressures." Unless the United States acted, the free world might not survive. To avert that calamity, he urged Congress to appropriate $400 million for military and economic aid to Turkey and Greece.

Not everyone approved of Truman's request. Autocratic regimes controlled Greece and Turkey, some observers pointed out. And where was the proof that Stalin had a hand in the Greek conflict? Others warned that the United States could not by itself stop encroachment in all parts of the world. Nonetheless, Congress passed Truman's foreign aid bill. In assuming that Americans could police the globe, the Truman Doctrine was a major step in the advent of the Cold War.

The Next Steps: The Marshall Plan, NATO, and NSC-68

The next step for American policymakers involved sending extensive economic aid for postwar recovery in Western Europe. At the war's end, most of Europe was economically and politically unstable, and administration

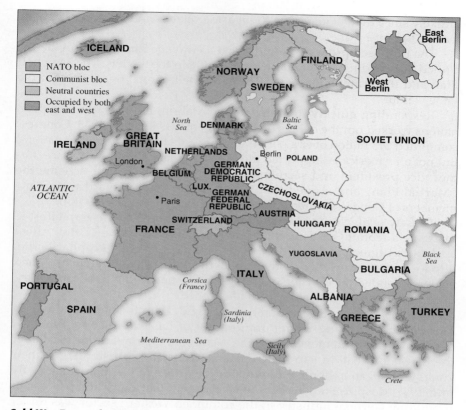

Cold War Europe in 1950 This map shows the rigid demarcation between East and West during the Cold War. Although there were a number of neutral countries in Europe, the other nations found themselves in a standoff, as each side tried to contain the possible advances of the other. The small inset map in the upper-right-hand corner shows the division of Berlin that paralleled the division of Germany itself after World War II. How widespread was the policy of neutrality in Cold War Europe? How powerful was the NATO bloc? How easily could one side move against the other in divided Europe?

officials believed that the Soviet Union might easily intervene. Another motive for decisive action was to bolster the European economy to provide markets for American goods. Excellent customers earlier, Western Europeans in the aftermath of the war were able to purchase less at a time when the United States was producing more.

George Marshall, the new secretary of state, revealed the administration's willingness to assist European recovery in a Harvard University commencement address in June 1947. He asked all troubled European nations to draw up an aid program that the United States could support, a program "directed not against any country or doctrine but against hunger, poverty, desperation, and chaos." Soviet-bloc countries were welcome to participate, Marshall announced, aware that their involvement was unlikely since they would have to set aside secrecy and disclose economic records to join.

The proposed program would assist the ravaged nations, provide the United States with needed markets, and contain the Soviets. The **Marshall Plan** and the Truman Doctrine, Truman noted, were "two halves of the same walnut."

Responding quickly to Marshall's invitation, the Western European nations worked out the details of massive requests. In early 1948, Congress committed $13 billion over a period of four years to 16 cooperating nations. But not all Americans supported the Marshall Plan. Henry A. Wallace, former vice president and secretary of agriculture, called the scheme the "Martial Plan" and argued that it was another step toward war. Some members of Congress feared spreading American resources too thin.

Closely related to the Marshall Plan was a concerted Western effort to integrate a rebuilt Germany into a reviving Europe. At war's end, Allied leaders had agreed to divide the defeated Nazi nation and its capital, Berlin, into four occupation zones (Soviet, American, British, and French). Allied leaders intended the division of both Germany and Berlin to be temporary, until a permanent peace treaty could be signed.

But the lines of demarcation became rigid. With the onset of the Cold War and the growing Soviet domination of Eastern Europe, the West became worried and moved to fill the vacuum in Central Europe to counter the Russian threat. In late 1946, the Americans and British merged their zones and began assigning administrative duties to German citizens. By mid-1947, despite French fears of a resurgent Germany, the process of rebuilding German industry in the combined Western sector was under way. Meanwhile, the same increasingly rigid separation into two separate cities occurred in Berlin.

The Soviet Union was furious. In mid-1948, a crisis erupted when the Soviets attempted to force the Western powers out of Berlin by refusing to allow them land access to their part of the city and banning all shipments through eastern Germany. In what became known as the Berlin airlift, the United States and the British Royal Air Force flew supplies to the beleaguered Berliners. Over the next year, more than 200,000 flights provided 13,000 tons daily of food, fuel, and other necessary materials. The airlift proved to be a public relations disaster for the Soviet Union and a triumph for the West. The Soviets finally ended the blockade, but Berlin remained a focal point of conflict, and there were now two separate German states: the Federal Republic of Germany, or West Germany, and the German Democratic Republic, or East Germany.

The next major link in the containment strategy was the creation of a military alliance in Europe in 1949 to complement the economic program. After the Soviets tightened their control over Hungary and Czechoslovakia, the United States took the lead in establishing the North Atlantic Treaty Organization (**NATO**). Twelve nations formed the alliance, vowing that an attack against any one member would be considered an attack against all, to be met by appropriate armed force. Despite George Washington's warning in 1796 against "entangling alliances," the United States established its first military treaty ties with Europe since the American Revolution. Congress also voted military aid for its NATO allies.

Two dramatic events in 1949—the Communist victory in the Chinese civil war and the Russian detonation of an atomic device—shocked the United States. While the fall of China (described in the next section) was frightening, the erosion of the American atomic monopoly was horrifying. Although American scientists had understood that the Soviets could create a bomb of their own, many people believed it would take the Russians at least a decade and a half. President Truman thought they might never be able to accomplish such a feat at all. In September 1949, an air force reconnaissance plane detected atmospheric radioactivity, indicating that the Soviets had tested their own bomb, just four years after the United States had ushered in the atomic age. Now a nuclear arms race beckoned.

Truman asked for a full-fledged review of U.S. foreign and defense policy. Responding to his request, the National Security Council, organized in 1947 to provide policy coordination, produced a document called **NSC-68**, which shaped U.S. policy for the next 20 years.

NSC-68 built on the Cold War rhetoric of the Truman Doctrine, describing challenges facing the United States in cataclysmic terms. "The issues that face us are momentous," the paper said, "involving the fulfillment or destruction not only of this Republic but of civilization itself." Conflict between East and West, the document assumed, was unavoidable. Negotiation was useless, for the Soviets could never be trusted to bargain in good faith. NSC-68 then argued that, to meet the Russian challenge, the United States must increase defense spending dramatically from the $13 billion set for 1950 to as much as $50 billion per year.

Containment in the 1950s

Because containment required detailed information about Communist moves, the government relied increasingly on the Central Intelligence Agency (CIA). Established by the National Security Act of 1947, which had also created the National Security Council, the CIA conducted espionage in foreign lands, some of it visible, more of it secret. With President Eisenhower's approval, by 1957, 80 percent of the CIA's budget went toward covert activities. More and more, Eisenhower relied on clandestine CIA actions to undermine foreign governments and assist those who supported the American stance in the Cold War.

The civil rights movement that was gaining momentum in the 1950s had an effect on Cold War policy. American policymakers were aware of the impact of stories about racial discrimination in other nations, particularly nations moving toward independence in sub-Saharan Africa. Leaders sought to portray the struggle in the best possible light in propaganda aimed abroad.

At the same time, the administration reassessed the impact of the containment policy itself. For most of Eisenhower's two terms, John Foster Dulles was secretary of state. A devout Presbyterian, he sought to move beyond containment and counter the "Godless terrorism" of communism with a holy crusade to promote democracy and to free the countries under Soviet domination. Dulles also advocated immediate retaliation in the face of hostile Soviet ventures: "There is one solution and only one: that is for the free world to develop the will and organize the means to retaliate instantly against open aggression by Red armies, so that, if it occurred anywhere, we could and would strike back where it hurts, by means of our own choosing."

Eisenhower's own rhetoric was equally strong, yet he was more conciliatory than Dulles and recognized the impossibility of changing the governments of the USSR's satellites. In mid-1953, when East Germans mounted anti-Soviet demonstrations in a challenge that foreshadowed the revolt against communism three and a half decades later, the United States maintained its distance. In 1956, when Hungarian "freedom fighters" rose up against Russian domination, the United States again stood back as Soviet forces smashed the rebels. Because Western action could have precipitated a more general conflict, Eisenhower refused to translate rhetoric into action. The policy of containment remained in effect.

Containment in Asia, the Middle East, and Latin America

In a dramatic departure from its history of noninvolvement, the United States extended the policy of containment to meet challenges around the globe. Colonial empires were disintegrating, and countries seeking and attaining their independence now found themselves caught in the middle of the superpower struggle. In Asia, the Middle East, and Latin America, the United States discovered the tremendous appeal of communism and found that ever greater efforts were required to advance American aims.

The Shock of the Chinese Revolution

The U.S. commitment to global containment became stronger with the Communist victory in the Chinese civil war in 1949. An ally during World War II, China had struggled against the Japanese, while simultaneously fighting a bitter civil war. **Mao Zedong** (Mao Tse-tung),* founder of a branch of the Communist party, gathered followers who wanted to reshape China in a distinctive Marxist mold. Opposing the Communists were the Nationalists, led by Jiang Jieshi (Chiang Kai-shek), who wanted to preserve their power and governmental leadership. By the early 1940s, Jiang's inefficient

---

*Chinese names are rendered in their modern pinyin spelling. At first occurrence, the older but perhaps more familiar spelling (usually Wade-Giles) is given in parentheses.

A New Chinese Leader Mao Zedong, chairman of the Chinese Communist party, was a powerful and popular leader who drove Jiang Jieshi from power in 1949 and established a stronghold over the People's Republic of China. How was Mao able to defeat his opponents and win the revolutionary war?

and corrupt regime was exhausted. Mao's movement, meanwhile, grew stronger as he opposed the Japanese invaders and won the loyalty of the peasantry. Mao finally prevailed, as Jiang fled in 1949 to the island of Taiwan (Formosa). Mao's proclamation of the People's Republic of China on October 1, 1949, fanned fears of Russian domination, for he had already announced his regime's support for the Soviet Union against the "imperialist" United States.

Events in China caused near hysteria in America. Staunch anti-Communists argued that Truman and the United States were to blame for Jiang's defeat because they failed to provide him with sufficient support. Secretary of State Dean Acheson briefly considered granting diplomatic recognition to the new government but backed off after the Communists seized American property, harassed American citizens, and openly allied China with the USSR.

Stalemate in the Korean War

The Korean War highlighted growing U.S. concern about Asia. The conflict in Korea stemmed from tensions lingering after World War II. Korea, long under Japanese control, hoped for independence after Japan's defeat.

But the Allies temporarily divided Korea along the 38th parallel to expedite the transition to peace after the rapid end to the Pacific struggle when the atomic bombs were dropped on Japan. The Soviet–American line, initially intended as a matter of military convenience, hardened after 1945, just as a similar division became rigid in Germany. In time, the Soviets set up one Korean government in the north and the Americans another government in the south. Each Korean government hoped to reunify the country on its own terms.

North Korea moved first. On June 25, 1950, North Korean forces crossed the 38th parallel and invaded South Korea. While the North Koreans used Soviet-built tanks, they operated on their own initiative. Kim Il Sung, the North Korean leader, had visited Moscow earlier and gained Soviet acquiescence in the idea of an attack, but both the planning and the implementation occurred in Korea.

Taken by surprise and certain that Russia had masterminded the North Korean offensive and was testing the American policy of containment, Truman responded by telling the public that "if this was allowed to go unchallenged it would mean a third world war, just as similar incidents had brought on the second world war."

Truman directed General Douglas MacArthur, head of the American occupation in Japan, to supply South Korea. The United States also went to the United Nations Security Council and secured a unanimous resolution branding North Korea an aggressor, then another resolution calling on members of the organization to assist South Korea in repelling aggression and restoring peace. This was the largest UN operation to date, and MacArthur became leader of all UN forces. While the United States and South Korea provided over 90 percent of the manpower, 15 other nations were involved in the UN effort.

Air and naval forces, then ground forces, went into battle south of the 38th parallel. Following a daring amphibious invasion that pushed the North Koreans back to the former boundary line, UN troops crossed the 38th parallel, hoping to reunify Korea under an American-backed government. Despite Chinese signals that this movement toward their border threatened their security, the UN troops pressed on. In October, Chinese troops appeared briefly in battle, then disappeared. The next month, the Chinese mounted a full-fledged counterattack, which pushed the UN forces back below the dividing line.

The resulting stalemate provoked a bitter struggle between the brilliant but arrogant General MacArthur, who called for retaliatory air strikes against China, and President Truman, who remained committed to conducting a limited war. MacArthur's statements, issued from the field, finally went too far. In April 1951, he argued that the American approach in Korea was wrong and asserted publicly that "there is no substitute for victory." Truman had no choice but to relieve the general for insubordination. The decision outraged many Americans. After the stunning victories of World War II, limited war was frustrating and difficult to understand.

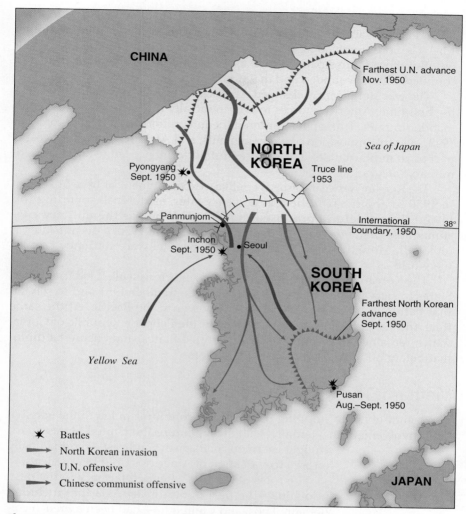

The Korean War This map shows the ebb and flow of the Korean War. North Korea crossed the 38th parallel first, then the UN offensive drove the North Koreans close to the Chinese border, and finally the Chinese Communists entered the war and drove the UN forces back below the 38th parallel. The armistice signed at Panmunjom in 1953 provided a dividing line very close to the prewar line. How far did both North Korea and South Korea penetrate into the territory of the other nation? What role did China play in the Korean War?

The Korean War dragged on into Eisenhower's presidency. Campaigning in 1952, Ike promised to go to Korea, and three weeks after his election, he did so. When UN truce talks bogged down in May 1953, the new administration privately threatened the Chinese with the use of atomic weapons. This brought about renewed UN negotiations, and on July 27, 1953, an armistice was signed. After three long years, the unpopular war had ended.

American involvement carried a heavy price: over 33,000 Americans killed in action and more than 142,000 American casualties in all. The other 15 UN nations involved in the struggle accounted for another 17,000 casualties. But those figures paled beside as many as 2 million Koreans dead and countless others wounded and maimed.

The war significantly changed American attitudes and institutions. For the first time, American forces fought in racially integrated units. As commander in chief, Truman had ordered the integration of the armed forces in 1948, over the opposition of many generals, and African Americans became part of all military units. Their successful performance led to acceptance of military integration.

The Korean War years also saw military expenditures soar from $13 billion in 1950 to about $47 billion three years later, as defense spending followed the guidelines proposed in NSC-68. Whereas the military consumed less than one-third of the federal budget in 1950, a decade later, it took half. More than a million military personnel were stationed around the world.

The Korean War had important political effects as well. It led the United States to sign a peace treaty with Japan in September 1951 and to rely on that nation to maintain the balance of power in the Pacific. At the same time, the struggle poisoned relations with the People's Republic of China, which remained unrecognized by the United States, and ensured a diplomatic standoff that lasted more than 20 years.

Vietnam: The Roots of Conflict

The commitment to stopping the spread of communism led to the massive U.S. involvement in Vietnam. That struggle tore the United States apart, wrought enormous damage in Southeast Asia, and finally forced a reevaluation of America's Cold War policies.

•••–Read the Document

Policy Statement about U.S. Objectives in Southeast Asia (1954) at **www.myhistorylab.com**

The roots of the war extended far back in the past. Indochina—the part of Southeast Asia that included Vietnam, Laos, and Cambodia—had been a French colony since the mid-nineteenth century. During World War II, Japan occupied the region, but an independence movement, led by the Communist organizer and revolutionary **Ho Chi Minh**, sought to expel the Japanese conquerors from Vietnam. In 1945, the Allied powers had to decide how to deal with Ho and his nationalist movement.

France was determined to regain its colony as a way of preserving its status as a great power. Meanwhile, Ho established the Democratic Republic of Vietnam in 1945. The new government's Declaration of Independence harkened back to its American counterpart. It declared: "All men are created equal. They are endowed by their Creator with certain inalienable rights, among these are Life, Liberty and the pursuit of Happiness." Despite widespread popular support, the United States refused to recognize the new government.

A long, bitter struggle broke out between French and Vietnamese forces, which became entangled with the larger Cold War. Truman needed France to check the Soviets in Europe, and that meant cooperating with France in Vietnam.

Although Ho did not have close ties to the Soviet Union and was committed to his independent nationalist crusade, Truman and his advisers assumed wrongly that Ho took orders from Moscow. Hence, in 1950, the United States formally recognized the French puppet government in Vietnam, and by 1954, was paying over three-quarters of the cost of France's Indochina war.

After Eisenhower took office, France's position in Southeast Asia deteriorated, but the president refused to intervene directly. He understood the lack of American support for intervention in that far-off land. As a French fortress at Dien Bien Phu in the north of Vietnam finally fell to Ho's forces, an international conference in Geneva sought to prevent Ho Chi Minh from gaining control of the entire country. The final declaration of the conference divided Vietnam along the 17th parallel, with elections promised in 1956 to unify the country and determine its political fate.

Two separate Vietnamese states emerged. Ho Chi Minh held power in the north, while in the south, Ngo Dinh Diem, a fierce anti-Communist

Father Ho Ho Chi Minh waged a long struggle first against France, then Japan, and finally the United States for the independence of Vietnam. The Vietnamese people viewed him as the father of the country. How does this picture of him with children contribute to that impression?

who had been in exile in the United States, returned to form a government. Diem enjoyed the full support of the United States, which saw him as a way of securing stability in Southeast Asia and avoiding further Communist incursions. When he decided not to hold the elections mandated in the Geneva accord, the United States backed him in that decision. In the next few years, American aid increased and military advisers—675 by the time Eisenhower left office—began to assist the South Vietnamese. The United States had taken its first steps toward direct involvement in a ruinous war halfway around the world that escalated out of control.

The Creation of Israel and Its Impact on the Middle East

The creation of the state of Israel also became intertwined with larger Cold War issues. Jews had longed for a homeland for years, and the Zionist movement had sought a place in Palestine, in the Middle East, since the latter part of the nineteenth century. Jewish settlers who began to gravitate to Palestine were not welcomed by the Turks, who dominated the region, or by the British, who exercised control after World War I.

•••–[Read the Document

*Press Release Announcing
U.S. Recognition of Israel*
at **www.myhistorylab.com**

Then the Holocaust—and the slaughter of 6 million Jews—during World War II created new pressure for a Jewish state. The unwillingness—and inability—of the Western powers to intervene in time to stop the Nazi genocide created a groundswell of support, particularly among American Jews, for a Jewish homeland in the Arab-dominated Middle East.

In 1948, the fledgling United Nations attempted to partition Palestine into an Arab state and a Jewish state. Truman officially recognized the new state of Israel 15 minutes after it was proclaimed. But American recognition could not end bitter animosities between Arabs, who believed they had been robbed of their territory, and Jews, who felt they had finally regained a homeland after the horrors of the Holocaust. As Americans looked on, Arab forces invaded Israel in the first of a continuing series of conflicts that dominated the Middle East in the second half of the twentieth century. The Israelis, fighting for the survival of the new nation, won the war and added territory to what the UN had given them, but the struggle continued.

While sympathetic to Israel, the United States tried at the same time to maintain stability in the rest of the region, which had tremendous strategic importance as the supplier of oil for industrialized nations. In 1953, the CIA helped the Iranian army overthrow the government of Mohammed Mossadegh, which had nationalized oil wells formerly under British control, and placed the shah of Iran securely on the throne. After the coup, British and American companies regained command of the wells.

As it cultivated close ties with Israel, the United States also tried to maintain the friendship of oil-rich Arab states or, at the very least, to prevent them from falling into the Soviet orbit. In Egypt, the policy ran into trouble when Arab nationalist General Gamal Abdel Nasser planned a huge dam on the Nile River to produce electric power and proclaimed his country's neutrality in the Cold War. Although Dulles offered U.S. financial support for the Aswan Dam project, Nasser also began discussions with the Soviet Union. Furious, the secretary of state withdrew the American offer. Left without funds for the dam, in July 1956, Nasser seized and nationalized the British-controlled Suez Canal and closed it to Israeli ships. Now Great Britain was enraged, and Europe worried about a continuing supply of oil.

In the fall, Israeli, British, and French military forces invaded Egypt. Eisenhower, who had not been consulted, was irate. Realizing that the strike might push Nasser into Moscow's arms, the United States sponsored a UN resolution condemning the attack and persuaded other nations not to send petroleum to England and France. These actions convinced the invaders to withdraw.

Before long, the United States again intervened in the Middle East. Concerned about the region's stability, the president declared in 1957, in what came to be called the Eisenhower Doctrine, that "the existing vacuum in the Middle East must be filled by the United States before it is filled by Russia." A year later he authorized the landing of 14,000 soldiers in Lebanon to prop up a right-wing government being challenged from within.

Restricting Revolt in Latin America

The Cold War also led to intervention in Latin America, the United States' traditional sphere of influence. In 1954, Eisenhower ordered CIA support for a right-wing coup aimed at ousting the elected government of reform-minded Colonel Jacobo Arbenz Guzmán in Guatemala. The takeover succeeded and established a military dictatorship that responded to U.S. wishes. These actions demonstrated again the shortsighted American commitment to stability and private investment, whatever the internal effect or ultimate cost. The interference in Guatemala fed anti-American feeling throughout Latin America.

View the **Image**

A Case History of Communist Penetration in Guatemala (1957)

at **www.myhistorylab.com**

In 1959, when Fidel Castro overthrew the dictatorship of Fulgencio Batista in Cuba, the shortsightedness of American policy became even clearer. Nationalism and the thrust for social reform were powerful forces in Latin America, as in the rest of the developing world formerly dominated by European powers. But when Castro confiscated American property in Cuba, the Eisenhower administration cut off exports and severed diplomatic ties. In response, Cuba turned to the Soviet Union for support.

Atomic Weapons and the Cold War

Throughout the Cold War, the atomic bomb was a crucial factor that hung over all diplomatic discussions and military initiatives. Atomic weapons were destructive enough, but when the United States and the Soviet Union both developed hydrogen bombs, an age of overkill began.

Sharing the Secret of the Bomb

The United States, with British aid, had built the first atomic bomb and attempted to conceal the project from its wartime ally, the Soviet Union. Soviet spies, however, learned about the effort and, even before the war was over, the Soviets had initiated a program to create their own bomb.

The United States briefly considered sharing the atomic secret. Just before he retired, Secretary of War Henry L. Stimson pushed for cooperating with the Soviet Union. Recognizing the futility of trying to cajole the Russians while "having this weapon ostentatiously on our hip," he warned that "their suspicions and their distrust of our purposes and motives will increase." Only mutual accommodation could bring international cooperation.

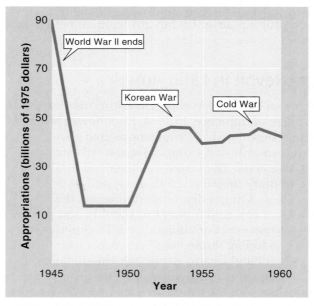

Defense Expenditures, 1945–1960 Defense spending plummeted after World War II, only to quadruple with the onset of the Korean War. After that increase, spending levels never dropped dramatically, even after the end of the war. Why was the United States willing to spend so much more for defense after 1950? Why did levels of spending remain relatively constant after that? *(Source: U.S. Bureau of the Census.)*

Yet as negotiations to develop a system of international arms control broke down, the United States gave up on the idea of sharing atomic secrets. Intent on retaining the technological advantage until the creation of a "foolproof method of control," Truman endorsed the Atomic Energy Act, passed by Congress in 1946. It established the Atomic Energy Commission (AEC) to supervise all atomic energy development in the United States and, under the tightest security, to authorize all nuclear activity in the nation at large. It also opened the way to a nuclear arms race once Russia developed its own bomb.

Nuclear Proliferation

As the atomic bomb found its way into popular culture, Americans at first showed more excitement than fear. In Los Angeles, the "Atombomb Dancers" wiggled at the Burbank Burlesque Theater. In 1946, the Buchanan Brothers released a record called "Atomic Power," noting the brimstone fire from heaven that was "given by the mighty hand of God."

Nevertheless, anxiety lurked beneath the exuberance, though it did not surface dramatically as long as the United States held a nuclear monopoly. Then, in September 1949, when the Soviet Union tested its own bomb, the security of being the world's only atomic power vanished. People wondered whether the Soviet test foreshadowed a nuclear attack and speculated when it might come. The editors of the *Bulletin of the Atomic Scientists*, the nation's foremost publication dealing with nuclear affairs, moved the minute hand of the "doomsday clock" on the cover of the journal from seven minutes before midnight to three minutes before midnight to reflect their fear of proliferation.

In early 1950, Truman authorized the development of a new hydrogen superbomb, potentially far more devastating than the atomic bomb, and by 1953 both the United States and the Soviet Union had unlocked the secret of fusion—joining atoms together in a reaction like that on the surface of the sun. A far more powerful reaction could do far more damage. As kilotons gave way to megatons, the stakes rose higher and higher. After the 1954 BRAVO test of a hydrogen device, Lewis Strauss, Atomic Energy Commission chairman, admitted that "an H-bomb can be made . . . large enough to take out a city," even New York. Then, in 1957, shortly after the news that the Soviets had successfully tested their first intercontinental ballistic missile (ICBM), Americans learned that the Soviets had lifted the first satellite, *Sputnik*, into outer space—with a rocket that could also deliver a hydrogen bomb.

⬤ View the Image

U.S. Hydrogen Bomb Test over Uninhabited Pacific Island (1952) at **www.myhistorylab.com**

The discovery of radioactive fallout made matters worse. Fallout became publicly known after the BRAVO blast showered Japanese fishermen on a ship called the *Lucky Dragon* 85 miles away with radioactive dust. They became ill with radiation sickness, and several months later, one of the seamen died. Everywhere people began to realize the terrible consequences of the new weapons. Fallout had become a serious international problem—in the words of physicist Ralph Lapp, "a peril to humanity."

Authors in both the scientific and the popular press focused attention on radioactive fallout. Radiation, Lapp observed, "cannot be felt and possesses all the terror of the unknown. It is something which evokes revulsion and helplessness—like a bubonic plague." Nevil Shute's best-selling 1957 novel *On the Beach*, and the film that followed, also sparked public awareness and fear. The story described a war that released so much radioactive waste that all life in the Northern Hemisphere disappeared, while the Southern Hemisphere awaited the same deadly fate. In 1959, when *Consumer Reports*, the popular magazine that tested and compared various products, warned of the contamination of milk with the radioactive isotope strontium-90, the public grew even more alarmed.

Watch the Video
Duck and Cover
at **www.myhistorylab.com**

The discovery of fallout provoked a shelter craze. *Good Housekeeping* magazine carried a full-page editorial in November 1958 urging the construction of family shelters. More and more companies advertised

An Awesome Atomic Blast The spectacular mushroom cloud resulting from an atomic blast became a familiar sight as it accompanied hundreds of nuclear tests in the postwar years. This picture shows the hydrogen blast at Eniwetok in the Pacific in 1952. While the cloud was beautiful, it also filled the atmosphere with fallout that contaminated people, plants, and animals below. What makes this image so imposing? Why might it appear terrifying at the same time?

ready-made shelters. *Life* magazine in 1955 featured an "H-Bomb Hide-away" for $3,000. By late 1960, the Office of Civil and Defense Mobilization estimated that a million family shelters had been built.

The Nuclear West

The bomb stimulated more than shelter building. It sparked an enormous increase in defense spending and created a huge nuclear industry, particularly in the West. Contractors liked the region because of its antiunion attitudes; labor stability, they argued, would make it easier to meet government deadlines.

During World War II, a number of the Manhattan Project's major centers were located in the West. The plant at Hanford, Washington, was one of the most important producers of fissionable material, and the first atomic weapon had been produced at Los Alamos, New Mexico. Development in this area expanded after the war: Hanford continued to produce plutonium, a facility outside Denver made plutonium triggers for thermonuclear bombs, the new Sandia National Laboratory in Albuquerque provided the production engineering of nuclear bombs, and the Los Alamos laboratory remained a major atomic research center. In 1951, the United States opened the Nevada Test Site, 65 miles north of Las Vegas, and the facility had a major impact on the city. The Chamber of Commerce offered schedules of test shots, and the mushroom cloud became the logo for the Southern Nevada telephone directory.

Defense spending promoted other development as well. Naval commands had headquarters in Seattle, San Francisco, San Diego, and Honolulu. Radar sites, aimed at tracking incoming missiles, stretched all the way up to Alaska. The Boeing Company, located in Seattle, stimulated tremendous development in that city as it produced B-47 and B-52 airplanes that were the U.S. Air Force's main delivery vehicles for nuclear bombs.

"Massive Retaliation"

As Americans grappled with the implications of nuclear weapons, government policy came to depend increasingly on an atomic shield. Truman authorized the development of a nuclear arsenal but also stressed conventional forms of defense. Eisenhower, concerned with controlling the budget and cutting taxes, decided to rely on atomic weapons rather than combat forces as the key to American defense.

Secretary of State Dulles developed the policy of threatening "massive retaliation." The United States, he declared, was willing and ready to use nuclear weapons against Communist aggression on whatever targets it chose. The policy allowed troop cutbacks and promised to be cost effective by giving "more bang for the buck."

Massive retaliation provided for an all-or-nothing response, leaving no middle course, no alternatives between nuclear war and retreat. Critics called the policy "brinkmanship" and wondered what would happen if the line was crossed in the new atomic age. Eisenhower himself was horrified when he saw reports indicating that a coordinated atomic attack could leave a nation "a smoking, radiating ruin at the end of two hours." With characteristic caution, he did his best to ensure that the rhetoric of massive retaliation did not lead to war.

Atomic Protest

As the arms race spiraled, critics demanded that it end. In 1956, Democratic presidential candidate Adlai Stevenson pointed to "the danger of poisoning the atmosphere" and called for a halt to nuclear tests. Eisenhower did not respond, but Vice President Richard Nixon called Stevenson's suggestion "catastrophic nonsense," while Dulles minimized the hazards of radiation by arguing, "From a health standpoint, there is greater danger from wearing a wrist watch with a luminous dial."

In 1957, activists organized SANE, the National Committee for a Sane Nuclear Policy. Several years later, women who had worked with SANE took the protest movement a step further. To challenge continued testing, which dropped lethal radiation on all inhabitants of the globe, the protesters called on women throughout the country to suspend normal activities for a day and strike for peace. An estimated 50,000 women marched in 60 communities around the nation. Their slogans included "Let the Children Grow" and "End the Arms Race—Not the Human Race."

Pressure from many groups produced a political breakthrough and sustained it for a time. The superpowers began a voluntary moratorium on testing in the fall of 1958. It lasted until the Soviet Union resumed testing in September 1961 and the United States began again the following March.

The Cold War at Home

The Cold War also affected domestic affairs and led to the creation of an internal loyalty program that seriously violated civil liberties. Americans had feared radical subversion before and after the Russian Revolution. Now the Soviet Union appeared ever more ominous in confrontations around the globe. As Americans began to suspect Communist infiltration at home, some determined to root out all traces of communism inside the United States.

Truman's Loyalty Program

In mobilizing support for its containment program, the Truman administration used increasingly shrill rhetoric. For Truman, the issue confronting the world was one of "tyranny or freedom." Attorney General J. Howard McGrath spoke of "many Communists in America," each bearing the "germ of death for society." Meanwhile, Truman appointed a Temporary Commission on Employee Loyalty to head off Republican charges that Democrats were "soft on communism."

On the basis of its report, Truman established a new Federal Employee Loyalty Program in 1947. In the same week that he announced his containment policy, he ordered the FBI to check its files for evidence of subversive activity and to bring suspects before a new Civil Service Commission Loyalty Review Board. Initially, the program included safeguards and assumed that a challenged employee was innocent until proven guilty. But as the Loyalty Review Board assumed more power, it ignored individual rights, and suspects had little chance to fight back. Val Lorwin, whose story was told at the start of the chapter, was just one of many victims.

The Truman loyalty program examined several million employees and found grounds for dismissing only several hundred. Nonetheless, it bred the unwarranted fear of subversion, led to the assumption that absolute loyalty could be achieved, and legitimated investigatory tactics that were used irresponsibly to harm innocent individuals.

The Congressional Loyalty Program

At the same time, Congress launched its own program. In the early years of the Cold War, the law became increasingly explicit about what was illegal in the United States. The requirement that members of Communist organizations had to register with the attorney general led to the decline of the American Communist party. Membership, numbering about 80,000 in 1947, fell to 55,000 in 1950 and to 25,000 in 1954.

The investigations of the House Un-American Activities Committee (HUAC) contributed to that decline. Intent on rooting out subversion, HUAC probed the motion picture industry in 1947, claiming that left-wing sympathizers were corrupting the American public. A frequent refrain in congressional hearings was "Are you now or have you ever been a member of the Communist party?" Altogether, HUAC called 19 Hollywood figures to testify. When 10 of them refused to answer accusatory questions by invoking their constitutional right to remain silent, Congress issued contempt citations, and they went to prison and served sentences ranging from six months to one year. At that point, Hollywood knuckled under and blacklisted anyone with even a marginally questionable past. No one on the blacklist could find a job at the studios, although some managed to work secretly under other names.

•••—[Read the **Document**

Ronald Reagan, Testimony before HUAC (1947)

at **www.myhistorylab.com**

Congress made a greater splash with the Hiss–Chambers case. Whittaker Chambers, a former Communist who had broken with the party in 1938, charged that **Alger Hiss** had been a Communist in the 1930s. Hiss was a distinguished New Dealer who had served in the Agriculture Department before becoming assistant secretary of state. Now out of the government, he denied Chambers's charge, and the matter might have died there had not freshman congressman Richard Nixon taken up the case. Nixon finally extracted from Hiss an admission that he had once known Chambers. Hiss sued Chambers for libel, whereupon Chambers changed his story and charged that Hiss was a Soviet spy.

Hiss was indicted for perjury for lying under oath about his former relationship with Chambers, for the statute of limitations prevented prosecution for espionage. The sensational case made front-page news around the nation. Chambers appeared unstable and changed his story several times. Yet Hiss, too, seemed contradictory in his testimony and never adequately explained how he had such close ties with members of the Communist party or how some copies of stolen State Department documents had been typed on his typewriter. The first trial ended in a hung jury; the second trial, in January 1950, sent Hiss to prison for almost four years. He continued to assert his innocence for the remainder of his life, although later evidence makes his involvement clear. For many Americans, the Hiss case proved that a Communist threat indeed existed in the United States and helped justify the even worse witch hunts that followed.

Congress also charged that homosexuals posed a security risk. The issue surfaced in February 1950, when Undersecretary of State John Peurifoy mentioned in testimony before the Senate Appropriations Committee that most of the 91 employees the State Department had dismissed for reasons of "moral turpitude" were homosexuals. Then, in December, the Senate released a report that painted a threatening picture of the problems of homosexuals in the civil service. They lacked moral and emotional stability, the report suggested, and were therefore likely candidates for blackmail, which threatened national security.

Senator Joe McCarthy

The key anti-Communist warrior in the 1950s was Joseph R. McCarthy, Republican senator from Wisconsin. He capitalized on the fear sparked by congressional and executive investigations and made the entire country cognizant of the Communist threat.

McCarthy came to the Communist issue almost accidentally. Elected to the Senate in 1946, he had an undistinguished career for much of his first term. He first gained national attention with a speech before a Republican women's club in Wheeling, West Virginia, in February 1950, not long after the conviction of Alger Hiss. In that address, McCarthy brandished in his hand what he said was a list of 205 known Communists in the State Department. Pressed for details, McCarthy first said that he would release his list only to the president, and then reduced the number of names to 57.

((•—[Hear the Audio
Joseph R. McCarthy Speech
at **www.myhistorylab.com**

Early reactions to McCarthy were mixed. A subcommittee of the Senate Foreign Relations Committee, after investigating, called his charge a "fraud and a hoax." As his support grew, however, Republicans realized his partisan

McCarthy's Anti-Communist Campaign Senator Joseph McCarthy's spurious charges inflamed anti-Communist sentiment in the 1950s. Here he uses a chart of Communist party organization in the United States to suggest that the nation would be at risk unless subversives were rooted out. How does the chart contribute to the impression McCarthy wanted to convey?

value and egged him on. Senator John Bricker of Ohio allegedly told him, "Joe, you're a dirty s.o.b., but there are times when you've got to have an s.o.b. around, and this is one of them."

McCarthy selected assorted targets in his crusade to wipe out communism. He called Dean Acheson the "Red Dean of the State Department" and slandered George C. Marshall, the architect of victory in World War II and a powerful figure in formulating both Far Eastern policy and the Marshall Plan for European recovery, as a "man steeped in falsehood . . . who has recourse to the lie whenever it suits his convenience."

A demagogue throughout his career, McCarthy gained visibility through extensive press and television coverage. He knew how to issue press releases just before newspaper deadlines and to provide reporters with leaks that became the basis for stories. Playing on his tough reputation, he did not mind appearing disheveled, and he used obscenity freely as part of his effort to appear as an ordinary man of the people.

McCarthy's tactics worked because of public alarm about the Communist threat. The arrest in 1950 of Julius and Ethel Rosenberg fed fears of internal subversion. The Rosenbergs, a seemingly ordinary American couple with two small children, were charged with stealing and transmitting atomic secrets to the Russians. To many Americans, it was inconceivable

RECOVERING *the* PAST

Public Opinion Polls

In recent years, historians have used a new source of evidence: the public opinion poll. People have always been concerned with what others think, and leaders have often sought to frame their behavior according to the preferences of the populace. As techniques of assessing the mind of the public have become more sophisticated, the poll has emerged as an integral part of the analysis of social and political life. Polls now measure opinion on many questions—social, cultural, intellectual, political, and diplomatic. Because of polls' increasing importance, it is useful to know how to use them in an effort to understand and recover the past.

The principle of polling is not new. In 1824, the *Harrisburg Pennsylvanian* sought to predict the winner of that year's presidential race, and in the 1880s, the *Boston Globe* sent reporters to selected precincts on election night to forecast final returns. In 1916, *Literary Digest* began conducting postcard polls to predict political results. By the 1930s, Elmo Roper and George Gallup had further developed the field of market research and public opinion polling. Notwithstanding an embarrassing mistake by *Literary Digest* in predicting a Landon victory over FDR in 1936, polling had become a scientific enterprise by World War II.

According to Gallup, a poll is not magic but "merely an instrument for gauging public opinion," especially the views of those often unheard. As Elmo Roper said, the poll is "one of the few ways through which the so-called common man can be articulate." Polling, therefore, is a valuable way to recover the attitudes, beliefs, and voices of ordinary people.

Yet certain cautions should be observed. Like all instruments of human activity, polls are imperfect and may even be dangerous. Historians using information from polls need to be aware of how large the samples were, when the interviewing was done, and how opinions might have been molded by the form of the poll itself. Questions can be poorly phrased. Some hint at the desirable answer or plant ideas in the minds of those interviewed. Polls sometimes provide ambiguous responses that can be interpreted many ways. More seriously, some critics worry that human freedom itself is threatened by the pollsters' manipulative and increasingly accurate predictive techniques.

Despite these limitations, polls have become an ever-present part of American life. In the late 1940s and early 1950s, Americans were polled frequently about topics ranging from foreign aid, the United Nations, and the occupation of Germany and Japan to labor legislation, child punishment, and whether women should wear slacks in public (39 percent of men said no, as did 49 percent of women). Such topics as the first use of nuclear arms, presidential popularity, national defense, and U.S. troop intervention in a troubled area of the world remain as pertinent today as they were then.

REFLECTING ON THE PAST A number of the polls included here deal with foreign policy during the Cold War in the early 1950s. How did people respond to Soviet nuclear capability? How did they regard Russian intentions, and what did they feel was the appropriate American response? How do you analyze the results of these polls? What do you think is the significance of rating responses by levels of education? In what ways are the questions "loaded"? How might the results of these polls influence American foreign policy? These polls show the challenge-and-response nature of the Cold War. How do you think Americans would respond today to these questions? Polls also shed light on domestic issues. Consider the poll on professions for young men and women taken in 1950. What does it tell us about the attitudes of the pollster on appropriate careers for men and women? Why do you think both men and women had nearly identical views on this subject? How do you think people today would answer these questions? Would they be presented in the same way? Also observe the poll on women in politics. To what extent have attitudes on this issue changed in the intervening years?

Foreign Policy Polls

December 2, 1949—Atom Bomb

Now that Russia has the atom bomb, do you think another war is more likely or less likely?

More likely	45%
Less likely	28%
Will make no difference	17%
No opinion	10%

By Education
College

More likely	36%
Will make no difference	23%
Less likely	35%
No opinion	6%

High School

More likely	44%
Will make no difference	19%
Less likely	28%
No opinion	9%

Grade School

More likely	50%
Will make no difference	12%
Less likely	26%
No opinion	12%

May 1, 1950—National Defense

Do you think United States government spending on defense should be increased, decreased, or remain about the same?

Increased	63%
Same	24%
Decreased	7%
No Opinion	6%

September 18, 1953—Indochina

The United States is now sending war materials to help the French fight the Communists in Indochina. Would you approve or disapprove of sending United States soldiers to take part in the fighting there?

Approve	8%
Disapprove	85%
No opinion	7%

January 11, 1950—Russia

As you hear and read about Russia these days, do you believe Russia is trying to build herself up to be the ruling power of the world—or is Russia just building up protection against being attacked in another war?

Rule the world	70%
Protect herself	18%
No opinion	12%

By Education
College

Rule the world	73%
Protect herself	21%
No opinion	6%

High School

Rule the world	72%
Protect herself	18%
No opinion	10%

Grade School

Rule the world	67%
Protect herself	17%
No opinion	16%

February 12, 1951—Atomic Warfare

If the United States gets into an all-out war with Russia, do you think we should drop atom bombs on Russia first—or do you think we should use the atom bomb only if it is used on us?

Drop A-bomb first	66%
Only if used on us	19%
No opinion	15%

The greatest difference was between men and women—72% of the men questioned favored our dropping the bomb first, compared to 61% of the women.

Source: George H. Gallup, "Foreign Policy Polls," in *The Gallup International Public Opinion Polls Great Britain, 1937–1975,* Vol. 2. Originally published by Random House, 1972. Reproduced by permission of ABC-CLIO, LLC, Santa Barbara, CA. All rights reserved.

Domestic Policy Polls

October 29, 1949—Women in Politics

If the party whose candidate you most often support nominated a woman for President of the United States, would you vote for her if she seemed qualified for the job?

Yes	48%
No	48%
No opinion	4%

By Sex
Men

Yes	45%
No	50%
No opinion	5%

Women

Yes	51%
No	46%
No opinion	3%

By Political Affiliation
Democrats

Yes	50%
No	48%
No opinion	2%

Republicans

Yes	46%
No	50%
No opinion	4%

Would you vote for a woman for Vice President of the United States if she seemed qualified for the job?

Yes	53%
No	43%
No opinion	4%

May 5, 1950—Most Important Problem

What do you think is the most important problem facing the entire country today?

War, threat of war	40%
Atomic bomb control	6%
Economic problems, living costs, inflation, taxes	15%
Strikes and labor troubles	4%
Corruption in government	3%
Unemployment	10%
Housing	3%
Communism	8%
Others	11%

July 12, 1950—Professions

Suppose a young man came to you and asked your advice about taking up a profession. Assuming that he was qualified to enter any of these professions, which one of them would you first recommend to him?

Doctor of medicine	29%
Government worker	6%
Engineer, builder	16%
Professor, teacher	5%
Business executive	8%
Banker	4%
Clergyman	8%
Dentist	4%
Lawyer	8%
Veterinarian	3%
None, don't know	9%

July 15, 1950—Professions

Suppose a young girl came to you and asked your advice about taking up a profession. Assuming that she was qualified to enter any of these professions, which one of them would you first recommend?

Choice of Women

Nurse	33%
Teacher	15%
Secretary	8%
Social service worker	8%
Dietitian	7%
Dressmaker	4%
Beautician	4%
Airline stewardess	3%
Actress	3%
Journalist	2%
Musician	2%
Model	2%
Librarian	2%
Medical, dental technician	1%
Others	2%
Don't know	4%

The views of men on this subject were nearly identical with those of women.

Source: George H. Gallup, "Atomic Warfare Polls," in *The Gallup International Public Opinion Polls Great Britain, 1937–1975,* Vol. 2. Originally published by Random House, 1972. Reproduced by permission of ABC-CLIO, LLC, Santa Barbara, CA. All rights reserved.

that the Soviets could have developed the bomb on their own. Treachery helped explain the Soviet detonation of an atomic device.

The next year, the Rosenbergs were found guilty of espionage. Their execution in the electric chair after numerous appeals reflected a national commitment to respond to the Communist threat. For years, supporters of the Rosenbergs claimed that they were innocent victims of the anti-Communist crusade. More recent evidence indicates that Julius was guilty. Ethel, cognizant of his activities but not involved herself, was arrested, convicted, and executed in a futile government attempt to make Julius talk.

When the Republicans won control of the Senate in 1952, McCarthy's power grew. He became chairman of the Government Operations Committee and head of its Permanent Investigations Subcommittee. He now had a stronger base and two dedicated assistants, Roy Cohn and G. David Schine, to help him.

McCarthy finally went too far. In 1953, after the army drafted Schine and then refused to allow him preferential treatment, McCarthy began to investigate army security and even top-level army leaders. When the army complained, the Senate investigated the complaint.

The **Army–McCarthy hearings** began in April 1954 and lasted 36 days. Beamed to a fascinated nationwide audience, they demonstrated the power of television to shape people's opinions. Americans saw McCarthy's savage tactics on screen. He came across as irresponsible and destructive, particularly in contrast to Boston lawyer Joseph Welch, who argued the army's case and showed McCarthy as the demagogue he was. At a climactic point in the hearings, Welch asked McCarthy dramatically: "Have you no sense of decency, sir, at long last? Have you left no sense of decency?"

The hearings shattered McCarthy's mystical appeal. In broad daylight, his ruthless tactics offended millions. The Senate, which had earlier backed off confronting McCarthy, finally summoned the courage to condemn him for his conduct. Although McCarthy remained in office, his influence disappeared. Three years later, at the age of 48, he died a broken man.

Yet for a time he had exerted a powerful hold in the United States. "To many Americans," radio commentator Fulton Lewis, Jr., said, "McCarthyism is Americanism." As his appeal grew, he put together a following that included both lower-class ethnic groups, whose members responded to the charges against established elites, and conservative midwestern Republicans. But his real power base was the Senate, where conservative Republicans saw McCarthy as a means of reasserting their own authority.

The Casualties of Fear

The anti-Communist campaign kindled pervasive suspicion in American society. In the late 1940s and early 1950s, dissent no longer seemed safe.

Civil servants, government workers, academics, and actors all came under attack and found that the right of due process often evaporated amid the Cold War Red Scare.

This paranoia affected American life in countless ways. In New York, subway workers were fired when they refused to answer questions about their own political actions and beliefs. Navajos in Arizona and New Mexico, facing starvation in the bitter winter of 1947–1948, were denied government relief because of charges that their communal way of life was communistic and therefore un-American. Racism became intertwined with the anti-Communist crusade when African American actor Paul Robeson was accused of Communist leanings for criticizing American foreign policy. Black author W. E. B. Du Bois, who joined the Communist party, encountered even more virulent attacks. Latino laborers faced deportation for membership in unions with left-wing sympathies. In 1949, the Congress of Industrial Organizations (CIO) expelled 11 unions with a total membership of more than 1 million for alleged domination by Communists. Val Lorwin weathered the storm of malicious accusations and was finally vindicated, but others were less lucky. They were the unfortunate victims as the United States became consumed by the passions of the Cold War.

Conclusion
The Cold War in Perspective

The Cold War dominated international relations in the post–World War II years. Tensions grew after 1945 as the United States and the Soviet Union found themselves engaged in a bitter standoff that affected all diplomatic discourse, encouraged an expensive arms race, and limited the resources available for reform at home. For the United States, it was a first experience with the fiercely competitive international relations that had long plagued the nations of Europe. And while there was seldom actual shooting, the struggle required warlike measures and imposed costs on all countries involved.

What caused the Cold War? Historians have long argued over the question of where responsibility should be placed. In the early years after the Second World War, policymakers and commentators who supported their actions justified the American stance as a bold and courageous effort to meet the Communist threat. Later, particularly in the 1960s, as the war in Vietnam eroded confidence in American foreign policy, revisionist historians began to argue that American actions were misguided, insensitive to Soviet needs, and at least partially responsible for escalating friction. As with most historical questions, there are no easy answers, but both sides must be weighed.

The Cold War stemmed from a competition for international influence between the two great world powers. After World War II, the U.S. goal was to exercise economic and political leadership in the world and thus to establish capitalist economies and democratic political institutions throughout Europe and in nations emerging from colonial rule. But these goals put the United States on a collision course with the Soviet Union, which had a different vision of what the postwar world should be like, and with anticolonial movements in emerging countries around the globe. Perceiving threats from the Soviet Union, China, and other Communist countries, the United States clung to its deep-rooted sense of mission and embarked on an increasingly aggressive effort at containment, based on its reading of the lessons of the past. American efforts culminated in the ill-fated war in Vietnam as the Communist nations of the world defended their own interests with equal force. The Cold War, which had a profound impact not simply on foreign policy questions but on economic and social initiatives at home, was the unfortunate result.

TIME*line*

1946	Churchill's "Iron Curtain" speech
1947	Truman Doctrine
	Federal Employee Loyalty Program
1948	Marshall Plan launched
1949	North Atlantic Treaty Organization (NATO) established
	Mao Zedong's forces win Chinese civil war
1950	Joseph McCarthy's Wheeling (West Virginia) speech on subversion
	NSC-68
1950–1953	Korean War
1954	Fall of Dien Bien Phu ends French control of Indochina
1959	Castro deposes Batista in Cuba

✓•⎼|Study and Review at **www.myhistorylab.com**

Questions for Review and Reflection

1. What were the roots of the conflict that turned into the Cold War?
2. Why did the United States and the Soviet Union find it so difficult to get along in the years after World War II?
3. How did Cold War policy change in the 1950s from what it had been in the late 1940s?
4. What impact did the Cold War have on American society at home?
5. Could the Cold War have been avoided?

Key Terms

25

Postwar America at Home, 1945–1960

American Stories

An Entrepreneur Franchises the American Dream

Ray Kroc, an ambitious salesman, headed toward San Bernardino, California, on a business trip in 1954. For more than a decade he had been selling "multimixers"—stainless steel machines that could make six milkshakes at once—to restaurants and soda shops around the United States. On this trip, he was particularly interested in checking out a hamburger stand run by Richard and Maurice McDonald, who had bought eight of his "contraptions" and could therefore make 48 shakes at the same time.

Always eager to increase sales, Kroc wanted to see the McDonalds' operation for himself. The 52-year-old son of Bohemian parents had sold everything from real estate to radio time to paper cups before peddling the multimixers but had enjoyed no stunning success. Yet he was still on the alert for the key to the fortune that was part of the American dream. As he watched the lines of people at the San Bernardino McDonald's, the answer seemed at hand.

The McDonald brothers sold only standard hamburgers, french fries, and milkshakes, but they had developed a system that was fast, efficient, and clean. It drew on the automobile traffic that moved along Route 66. And it was profitable indeed. Sensing the possibilities, Kroc proposed that the two owners open other establishments as well. When they balked, he negotiated a 99-year contract that allowed him to sell the fast-food idea and the name—and their golden arches design—wherever he could.

On April 15, 1955, Kroc opened his first McDonald's in Des Plaines, a suburb of Chicago. Three months later, he sold his first franchise in Fresno, California. Others soon followed. Kroc scouted out new locations, almost always on highway "strips," persuaded people to put up the capital, and provided them with specifications guaranteed to ensure future success. For his efforts, he received a percentage of the gross take.

McDonald's Golden Arches McDonald's provided a model for other franchisers in the 1950s and the years that followed. The golden arches, shown here in an early version, were virtually the same wherever they appeared. Initially found along highways around the country, they were later built within cities and towns as well. How did the golden arches contribute to McDonald's popularity?

From the start, Kroc insisted on standardization. Every McDonald's was the same—from the two functional arches supporting the glass enclosure that housed the kitchen and take-out window to the single arch near the road bearing a sign indicating how many 15-cent hamburgers had already been sold. All menus and prices were exactly the same, and Kroc demanded that everything from hamburger size to cooking time be constant. He insisted, too, that the establishments be clean. No pinball games or cigarette machines were permitted; the premium was on a good, inexpensive hamburger, quickly served, at a nice place.

McDonald's, of course, was an enormous success. In 1962, total sales exceeded $76 million. In 1964, before the company had been in operation for 10 years, it had sold over 400 million hamburgers and 120 million pounds of french fries. By the end of the next year, there were 710 McDonald's stands in 44 states. In 1974, only 20 years after Kroc's vision of the hamburger's future, McDonald's did $2 billion worth of business. When Kroc died in 1984, a total of 45 billion burgers had been sold at 7,500 outlets in 32 countries. Ronald McDonald, the clown who came to represent the company, became known to children around the globe after his Washington, D.C., debut in November 1963. When McDonald's began to advertise, it became the country's first restaurant to buy television time. Musical slogans like "You deserve a break today" and "We do it all for you" became better known than some popular songs.

The success of McDonald's provides an example of the development of new economic and technological trends in the United States in the post–World War II years. Ray Kroc capitalized on the changes of the automobile age. He understood that a restaurant had a better chance of success not in the city but along the highways, where it could draw on heavier traffic. Kroc understood, too, that the franchise notion provided the key to rapid economic growth. Finally, he sensed the importance of standardization and uniformity. He understood the mood of the time—the quiet conformity of people searching for the key to the American dream of prosperity and stability. The McDonald's image may have been monotonous, but that was part of its appeal. Customers always knew what they would get wherever they found the golden arches. If the atmosphere was "bland," that too was deliberate. As Kroc said, "Our theme is kind of synonymous with Sunday school, the Girl Scouts and the YMCA. McDonald's is clean and wholesome." It was a symbol of the age.

This chapter describes the structural and political changes in American society in the 25 years following World War II. Even as the nation became involved in the global confrontations of the Cold War with the Soviet Union, Americans were preoccupied with the shifts in social and economic patterns that were taking place. This chapter examines such questions as: How did economic growth, spurred by technological advances, transform the patterns of work and daily life in the United States? How did self-interest intersect with idealism, as most people gained a level of material comfort previously unknown? How did the political world reflect the prosperity and affluence that followed years of depression and war? How did political commitments in the decade and a half after the war create the groundwork for the welfare state that emerged in the 1960s? At the same time, what was the connection between prosperity and the serious social and economic divisions among the nation's diverse peoples that surfaced in these years? How can we explain the enormous gaps between rich and poor, and understand the considerable income disparity and persistent prejudice that African Americans (like members of other minority groups) encountered in their efforts to share in the postwar prosperity? And, finally, to what degree did their frustrations highlight the limits of the postwar American dream and propel the reform movements that changed American society?

Economic Boom

Most Americans were optimistic after 1945. As servicemen returned home from fighting in World War II, their very presence caused a change in family patterns. A **baby boom** brought unprecedented population growth.

The simultaneous and unexpected economic boom had an even greater impact. Large corporations increasingly dominated the business world, but unions grew as well, and most workers improved their lives. Technology appeared triumphant, with new products flooding the market and finding their way into most American homes. Prosperity convinced the growing middle class that all was well in the United States.

The Thriving Peacetime Economy

The wartime return of prosperity after the Great Depression continued in the postwar years, and the United States solidified its position as the richest nation in the world with a sustained economic expansion. Other nations struggled with the aftereffects of World War II. Yet in the United States, which produced half the world's goods, prosperity was the norm.

The statistical evidence of economic success was impressive. The gross national product (GNP) jumped dramatically between 1945 and 1960, while per capita personal income likewise rose—from $1,087 in 1945 to $2,026 in 1960. Almost 60 percent of all families in the country were now part of the middle class, a dramatic change from the class structure in the nineteenth and early twentieth centuries.

Personal resources fueled economic growth. During World War II, American consumers had been unable to spend all they earned because factories were producing for war. With accumulated savings of $140 billion at the end of the struggle, consumers were ready to buy whatever they could. Equally important was the 22 percent rise in real purchasing power between 1946 and 1960. Families now had far more discretionary income—money to satisfy wants as well as needs—than before. At the end of the Great Depression, fewer than one-quarter of all households had any discretionary income; in 1960, three of every five did.

This new consumer power, in contrast to the underconsumption of the 1920s and 1930s, spurred the economy. Most homes now had an automobile, a television set, a washing machine, and a vacuum cleaner. But consumers could also indulge themselves with electric can openers and automatic transmissions for their cars.

The automobile industry played a key part in the boom. Just as cars and roads transformed America in the 1920s when mass production came of age, so they contributed to the equally great transformation three decades later. Limited to the production of military vehicles during World War II, the auto industry expanded dramatically in the postwar period. Seventy thousand cars were made in 1945; 8 million were manufactured in 1955; and not quite 7 million were produced in 1960. Customers now chose from a wide variety of engines, colors, fancy styles, and optional accessories.

The development of a massive interstate highway system also stimulated auto production and so contributed to prosperity. Through the Interstate Highway Act of 1956, the Eisenhower administration poured $26 billion, the largest public works expenditure in American history, into building over 40,000 miles of federal highways, linking all parts of the United States. Federal officials claimed the system would make evacuation quicker in the event of nuclear attack. President Dwight D. Eisenhower boasted that "the amount of concrete poured to form these roadways would build . . . six sidewalks to the moon. . . . More than any single action by the government since the end of the war, this one would change the face of America." Significantly, this massive effort helped create a nation dependent on oil.

A housing boom also fed economic growth as home-ownership rates rose from 53 percent in 1945 to 62 percent in 1960. Much of the stimulus came from the GI Bill of 1944. In addition to giving returning servicemen priority for many jobs and providing educational benefits, it offered low-interest home mortgages. Millions of former servicemen from all social classes eagerly purchased their share of the American dream.

The government's increasingly active economic role both stimulated and sustained the expansion. Businesses were allowed to buy almost 80 percent of the factories built by the government during the war for much

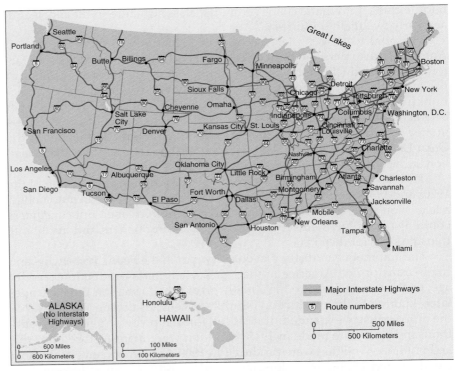

U.S. Interstate Highway System The interstate highway system, established by legislative action in 1956, created an extensive network of roads that changed the landscape and living patterns of people throughout the United States. How fully did the interstate highway network cover the entire country? Which areas were most extensively built? Why were there more roads in some parts of the country than in others?

less than they cost. Even more important was the dramatic rise in defense spending as the Cold War escalated. In 1947, Congress passed the National Security Act creating the Department of Defense and authorized an initial budget of $13 billion. With the onset of the Korean War, the defense budget rose to $22 billion in 1951 and to about $47 billion in 1953. Approximately half of the total federal budget went to the armed forces. This spending, in turn, helped stimulate the aircraft and electronic industries. The government underwrote 90 percent of aviation and space research, 65 percent of electricity and electronics work, and 42 percent of scientific instrument development. Meanwhile, the close business–government ties of World War II grew stronger.

Most citizens welcomed the huge expenditures, not only because they supported the American stance in the struggle against communism but also because they understood the economic impact of military spending. Columnist David Lawrence noted in 1950, "Government planners figure they have found the magic formula for almost endless good times. Cold war is an automatic pump primer. Turn a spigot, and the public clamors for more arms spending."

Postwar American growth avoided some of the major problems that often bedevil periods of economic expansion—inflation and the enrichment of a few at the expense of the many. Inflation, a problem in the immediate postwar period, slowed from an average of 7 percent per year in the 1940s to a gentle 2 to 3 percent per year in the 1950s. And though the concentration of income remained the same—the bottom half of the population still earned less than the top tenth—the ranks of middle-class Americans grew.

American products were sold around the world. People in other countries had developed a taste for Coca-Cola during the war. Now numerous other goods became available overseas. American books, magazines, movies, and records promoted the spread of American culture and provided still more profits for American entrepreneurs.

A major economic transformation had occurred in the United States. Peaceful, prosperous, and productive, the nation had became what economist John Kenneth Galbraith called the "affluent society."

Postwar Growth Around the World

Elsewhere in the world, postwar reconstruction began but affluence took longer to arrive. Both European and Asian countries had suffered greater casualties than the United States, and some nations, even those on the winning side, had to deal with enormous devastation.

Great Britain was ravaged by the war, and rationing—necessary to provide the equitable distribution of scarce resources—lasted until the early 1950s. British factories, which had been the first to industrialize, were now inefficient and outdated. Meanwhile, Britain lagged behind other European nations in developing a modern superhighway system that could spur industrial development.

In the general election of 1945, British voters ousted Winston Churchill and the Conservative party in favor of the Labour party, which was committed to social change. It took over the coal and railroad industries and began to nationalize the steel industry. While owners were compensated, some critics argued that the government's actions stifled industrial progress. Nevertheless, Great Britain began an economic and social recovery. It even provided a system of socialized medicine far in advance of anything in the United States.

While France was on the winning side of the war, it had suffered the indignity of occupation. It, too, experienced recovery, thanks in part to a rising birthrate, which was also occurring in the United States. At the same time, France, like Britain, was struggling with the demands of its colonial empire to be free. Brutal struggles in Indochina and Algeria caused financial instability and helped undermine economic development until France pulled out of both areas in the 1950s.

Defeated nations showed the most dramatic development of all. As the United States decided that a strong West Germany was necessary as a buffer against the Soviet Union, it helped cause what came to be known as "the German miracle." Because much of German industrial capacity had been destroyed by the war, new factories could be built with modern technological equipment. In the early 1950s, the West German rate of growth reached 10 percent a year, while the gross national product rose from $23 billion in 1950 to $103 billion in 1964.

Japan likewise revived quickly. Like Germany, it suffered tremendous wartime destruction, due both to conventional bombing and to the new atomic bombs that devastated Hiroshima and Nagasaki in 1945. Under the direction of General Douglas MacArthur, the United States spearheaded the reconstruction effort and created a democratic framework. As political change occurred, the economy grew rapidly, and Japan overtook France and West Germany, soon ranking third in the world behind the United States and the Soviet Union.

So too did the Soviet Union rebuild. Reparations from West Germany and industrial extractions from Eastern Europe helped promote the reconstruction effort. The totalitarian structure of the Soviet state eliminated public debate about the allocation of resources, and the nation embarked upon a series of initiatives that led to the development of a Soviet atomic bomb and an increase in the size of collective farms.

The Corporate Impact on American Life

After 1945, the major corporations in the United States tightened their hold on the American economy. Government policy in World War II had produced tremendous industrial concentration, and that pattern continued after the war. Oligopoly—domination of a given industry by a few firms—became a feature of American capitalism. Several waves of mergers had taken place in the past, including one in the 1890s and another in the 1920s. Still another occurred in the 1950s. At the same time, the booming economy encouraged the development of conglomerates—firms with holdings in a variety of industries in order to protect themselves against instability in one particular area.

Expansion took other forms as well. Even as the major corporations grew, so did smaller franchise operations like McDonald's, Kentucky Fried Chicken, and Burger King. Ray Kroc, introduced at the start of this chapter, provided a widely imitated pattern.

While expanding at home, large corporations also moved increasingly into foreign markets, as they had in the 1890s. But at the same time, they began to build plants overseas, where labor costs were cheaper. In the decade after 1957, General Electric built 61 plants abroad, and numerous other firms did the same. Corporate planning, meanwhile, developed rapidly, as firms sought managers who could assess information, weigh marketing trends, and make rational decisions to maximize profit.

Changing Work Patterns

As corporations changed, so did the world of work. Reversing a 150-year trend after World War II, the United States became less a goods producer and more a service provider. Between 1947 and 1957, the number of factory workers fell by 4 percent, while the number of clerical workers increased 23 percent and the number of salaried, middle-class employees rose 61 percent. By 1956, a majority of American workers held white-collar jobs, and these new workers served as corporate managers, office workers, salespeople, and teachers.

Yet white-collar jobs came at a price. Work in the huge corporations became ever more impersonal and bureaucratic, and white-collar employees seemed to dress, think, and act the same (as depicted in a popular novel and film of the 1950s, *The Man in the Gray Flannel Suit*). Corporations, preaching that teamwork was all-important, indoctrinated employees with the appropriate standards of conduct. RCA issued company neckties. IBM had training programs to teach employees the company line. Social critic C. Wright Mills observed, "When white-collar people get jobs, they sell not only their time and energy but their personalities as well."

But not all Americans held white-collar jobs. Many were still blue-collar assembly line workers, who made the goods others enjoyed. They too dreamed of owning a suburban home and several cars and providing more for their children than they had enjoyed while growing up. Their lives were now more comfortable than ever before, as the union movement brought substantial gains These were the more fortunate members of the working class. Millions of others, perhaps totaling 40 percent of the workforce, held less appealing and less well-paying positions as taxi drivers, farm laborers, or dime-store sales clerks. For them, jobs were less stable, less secure, and less interesting.

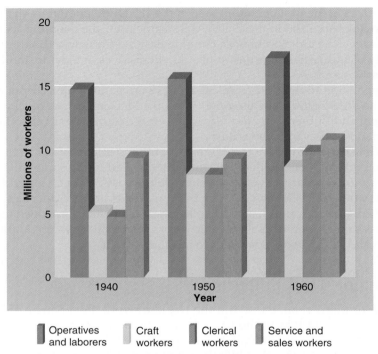

Occupational Distribution, 1940–1960 In the postwar years, the size of the workforce increased considerably. In this graph, observe how all categories grew, and indicate which expanded most extensively. How was the workforce different in 1960 than it had been in 1940? How did shifting patterns affect the attitudes of working men and women? *(Sources: U.S. Department of Labor and Historical Statistics of the United States)*

The Union Movement at High Tide

The union movement had come of age during the New Deal, and the end of World War II found it even stronger. There were more union members—14.5 million—than ever before. Ten million belonged to the American Federation of Labor (AFL); the other 4.5 million belonged to the Congress of Industrial Organizations (CIO). Having taken a wartime no-strike pledge and given their full support to the war effort, they now looked forward to better pay and a greater voice in workplace management.

The immediate postwar period was difficult. Cancellation of defense orders laid off war workers and prompted fears of a depression like the one that had followed World War I. Even workers who held their jobs lost the overtime pay they had enjoyed during the war. Many responded by striking. In 1946 alone, 4.6 million workers went out on strike—more than ever before in U.S. history. These disruptions alienated middle-class Americans and outraged conservative Republicans who felt that unionization had gone too far.

In the late 1940s, a new equilibrium emerged. In many industries, big business at last recognized the basic rights of industrial workers, and union leaders and members in turn acknowledged the prerogatives of management and accepted the principle of fair profit. Corporations in the same industry agreed to cooperate rather than compete with one another over labor costs. This meant that once a leading firm reached agreement with the union, the other firms in that area adopted similar terms.

At the same time, companies made material concessions to workers—for example, adjusting their pay to protect them against inflation. In 1948, General Motors offered the United Automobile Workers a contract that included a cost-of-living adjustment (COLA) and a 2 percent "annual improvement factor" wage increase intended to share GM's productivity gains with workers. In 1955, automobile workers won a guaranteed annual wage. The merger of the AFL and CIO into the **AFL-CIO** that same year ratified the changes that had occurred in the labor movement, as the new organization, led by building trade unionist George Meany, represented more than 90 percent of the country's now larger group of 17.5 million union members. By the end of the 1950s, the COLA principle was built into most union contracts.

Union gains, like middle-class affluence, came at a price. Co-opted by the materialistic benefits big business provided, workers fell increasingly under the control of middle-level managers and watched anxiously as companies automated at home or expanded abroad, where labor was cheaper. The anti-Communist crusade also undermined union radicalism. And throughout the period, in unions, as in other institutions, women and blacks faced continued discrimination.

Agricultural Workers in Trouble

The agricultural world changed even more than the industrial world in the postwar United States. On the eve of World War II, agriculture had supported one of every five Americans. Now, in one generation, mechanization and consolidation forced that figure down to one of every twenty. Altogether, some 15 million rural jobs disappeared.

New technology revolutionized farming. Improved planting and harvesting machines and better fertilizers and pesticides brought massive gains in productivity. Increasing profitability led to agricultural consolidation. In the 25 years after 1945, average farm size almost doubled and farming became a big business—often called "agribusiness." Family farms found it difficult to compete, and small farmers watched their share of the market fall.

In response, farmers left the land in increasing numbers. Some were midwestern whites who generally found jobs in offices and factories. In the South, many of the uprooted agricultural workers were African Americans, who became part of the huge migration north that had been going on since World War I. Millions of them gravitated to cities, where they faced problems of poverty and discrimination in housing and employment. The agricultural life, as it had been known for decades, even centuries, was over.

Demographic and Technological Shifts

The postwar economic boom was intertwined with a series of demographic changes. The population grew dramatically and continued to move west, while at the same time, millions of white Americans left the cities for the suburbs that began to grow exponentially in the postwar years. New patterns, revolving around television, air conditioning, and other gadgets provided by the advances of technology, came to characterize the consumer culture that dominated suburban life.

Population Growth

In post–World War II America, a growing population testified to prosperity's return. The birthrate soared as millions of Americans began families. The "baby boom" peaked in 1957, with a rate of more than 25 births per 1,000. In that year, 4.3 million babies were born—one every seven seconds—while in that entire decade, population growth increased by 29 million.

The rising birthrate was the dominant factor affecting population growth, but the death rate was also declining. Miracle drugs such as penicillin and streptomycin helped cure bacterial infections and more serious illnesses such as tuberculosis. A polio vaccine introduced a decade after the war virtually eliminated that dreaded disease. Life expectancy rose: midway through the 1950s, the average was 70 years for whites and 64 for blacks, compared with 55 for whites and 45 for blacks in 1920.

Movement West

Wartime mobility encouraged the development of the West. Although the scarcity of water in the western states required massive water projects to support population growth, war workers and their families streamed to western cities where shipyards, airplane factories, and other industrial plants were located. After the war, this migration pattern persisted. The Sun Belt—the region stretching along the southern tier of the United States from Florida to California—attracted millions from the working class and middle class alike. Cities like Houston, Albuquerque, Tucson, and Phoenix expanded phenomenally, and Los Angeles pulled ahead of Philadelphia as the third-largest city in the United States. By 1963, in a dramatic illustration of the importance of the West, California passed New York as the nation's most populous state.

The migration west resulted from a number of reasons. Servicemen who had been stationed in the West liked the scenery, climate, and pace of life. Many returned with their families after the war. Also, much of the Cold War military expansion occurred in the West. By 1962, the Pacific Coast as a whole held almost half of all Defense Department research and development contracts.

The West also benefited from the boom in the service economy. The percentage of workers in service jobs was higher in virtually all western states than in eastern counterparts. Denver became a major regional center of the federal bureaucracy in the postwar years. Albuquerque likewise gained numerous federal offices and became known as "little Washington." The old West of cowboys, farmers, and miners was turning into a new West of bureaucrats, lawyers, and clerks.

The New Suburbs

As the population shifted westward after World War II, another form of movement was taking place. Millions of white Americans fled the inner city, intensifying a movement that had begun before the war. Fourteen of the nation's largest cities, including New York and Chicago, actually lost population in the 1950s.

⊙ See the **Map**
Population Shifts, 1940–1950
at **www.myhistorylab.com**

As the cities declined, new suburbs blossomed. If the decade after World War I had witnessed a rural-to-urban shift, the decades after World War II saw a reverse shift to the regions outside the central cities, usually accessible only by car. By the end of the 1950s, one-third of all Americans resided in suburbs that promised the American dream of a home of one's own and seemed insulated from the troubles of the world outside.

The pioneer of the postwar suburbanization movement was William J. Levitt, a builder eager to gamble and reap the rewards of a growing demand.

Levittown Step-by-step mass production, with units completed in assembly-line fashion, was the key to William Levitt's approach to housing. But the suburban developments he and others created were marked by street after street of houses that all looked the same. The Levittown in this picture was built on 1,200 acres of potato fields on Long Island in New York. How did the pattern you see here reflect the overall culture of the 1950s?

Levitt had recognized the advantages of mass production during World War II, when his firm constructed housing for war workers. Aware that the GI Bill made mortgage money readily available, he saw the possibilities of suburban development. But to cash in, Levitt had to use new construction methods.

Individually designed houses were a thing of the past, he believed. "The reason we have it so good in this country," he said, "is that we can produce lots of things at low prices through mass production." Houses were among them. Working on a careful schedule, Levitt's team brought precut and preassembled materials to each site, put them together, and then moved on to the next location.

((•─ Hear the **Audio**

Little Boxes

at **www.myhistorylab.com**

Levitt proved that his system worked. Construction costs at Levittown, New York, a new community of 17,000 homes built in the late 1940s, were only $10 per square foot, compared with the $12 to $15 common elsewhere. Other Levittowns appeared in Pennsylvania and New Jersey. Levitt's success provided a model for other developers.

Levitt argued that his homes helped underscore American values. "No man who owns his own house and lot can be a Communist," he once said. "He has too much to do." Levitt also helped perpetuate segregation by refusing to sell homes to blacks. "We can solve a housing problem, or we can try to solve a racial problem but we cannot combine the two," he declared in the early 1950s.

Suburbanization transformed the American landscape. Huge tracts of former fields, pastures, and forests were now divided into tiny standardized squares, each bearing a small house with a two-car garage and a manicured lawn. Stands of trees disappeared, for it was cheaper to cut them down than to work around them.

As suburbs flourished, businesses followed their customers out of the cities. Shopping centers led the way. In a single three-month period in 1957, 17 new centers opened; by 1960, there were 3,840 in the United States. Shopping centers catered to the suburban clientele and transformed consumer patterns. They allowed shoppers to avoid the cities entirely and further eroded urban health.

The Environmental Impact

Suburbanization had environmental consequences. Rapid expansion often took place without extensive planning and encroached on some of the nation's most attractive rural areas. Before long, virtually every American city was ringed by an ugly highway sporting garish neon signs. Billboard advertisements filled whatever space was not yet developed.

Despite occasional protests, there was little real consciousness of environmental issues in the early post–World War II years. The term *environment* itself was hardly used prior to the war. Yet the very prosperity that created the dismal highway strips in the late 1940s and 1950s was leading more and more Americans to appreciate natural environments as treasured parts of their rising standard of living. The shorter workweek provided more free time, and many Americans now had the means for longer vacations. They began to explore mountains and rivers and ocean shores and to ponder how to protect them. In 1958, Congress established the National Outdoor Recreation Review Commission, a first step toward consideration of environmental issues that became far more common in the next decade. Americans also began to recognize the need for open space in their communities in order to compensate for urban overdevelopment.

Technology Supreme

A technological revolution transformed postwar America. Some developments—the use of atomic energy, for example—flowed directly from war research. Federal support for scientific activity increased dramatically, as the pattern of wartime collaboration continued. The government established the National Institutes of Health in 1948 to coordinate medical research and the National Science Foundation in 1950 to fund basic scientific research.

The advent of the Cold War led to ever-greater government involvement. The Atomic Energy Commission, created in 1946, and the Department of Defense, established in 1949, provided rapidly increasing funding for research and development. Scientists engaged in both basic and applied research and helped design nuclear weapons, jet planes, satellites, and consumer goods that were often the side products of military research.

Computers both reflected and assisted the process of technological development. Prior to World War II, Vannevar Bush, an electrical engineer at the Massachusetts Institute of Technology, had built a machine filled with gears and shafts, along with electronic tubes in place of some mechanical parts, to solve differential equations. Even more complicated was the Electronic Numerical Integrator and Calculator, called ENIAC, built in 1946 at the University of Pennsylvania. It was large, containing 18,000 electronic tubes and requiring tremendous amounts of electricity and special cooling procedures. It also needed to be "debugged" to remove insects attracted to the heat and light, giving rise to the term still used today by computer scientists for fixing software glitches. ENIAC performed impressively for the time but at a snail's pace by modern standards.

A key breakthrough in making computers faster and more reliable was the development of the transistor in 1948. Computers transformed American society as surely as industrial machines had changed it a century before, and computer programmers and operators were in increasing demand as computers contributed dramatically to the centralization and interdependence of American life.

Computers were essential for space exploration, which in the postwar years became increasingly sophisticated. Rocketry had developed during World War II but came of age after the war. Rockets could deliver nuclear weapons but could also launch satellites and provide the means to venture millions of miles into outer space.

An ominous technological trend related to computerization was the advent of automation. Mechanization was not new, but now it became far more widespread, threatening both skilled and unskilled workers. The implications of falling purchasing power as machines replaced workers were serious for an economy dependent on consumer demand.

The Consumer Culture

Americans were excited by everything they could buy. Television, developed in the 1930s, became a major influence on American life after World War II. In 1946, there were fewer than 17,000 television sets, but by 1960, three-quarters of all American families owned at least one set, and in 1955, the average American family tuned in four to five hours each day. Young Americans grew up to the melodies of "The Mickey Mouse Club," while older viewers watched situation comedies like *I Love Lucy* and *Father Knows Best* and live dramas such as *Playhouse 90*.

● View the Image
Cover Illustration for "The Desi-Lucy Love Story" (1956)
at **www.myhistorylab.com**

Consumption, increasingly a pillar of the American economy, required a vast expansion of consumer credit. Installment plans facilitated buying a new car, while credit cards encouraged the purchase of smaller items such as television sets and household appliances. The first of the consumer credit cards—the Diner's Club card—appeared in 1950, followed at the end of the decade by the American Express card and the BankAmericard (later renamed VISA). By the end of the 1960s, there were about 50 million credit cards of all kinds in use in the United States. Consumer credit—total private indebtedness—increased from $8.4 billion in 1946 to nearly $45 billion in 1958.

For consumers momentarily unsure about new purchases, a revitalized advertising industry was ready to convince them to go ahead and buy. Advertising had come of age in the 1920s, as businesses persuaded customers that buying new products brought status and satisfaction. It had faltered when the economy collapsed in the 1930s but began to revive during the war as firms kept the public aware of consumer goods, even those in short supply. With the postwar boom, advertisers again began to hawk their wares, this time even more aggressively than before.

Having weathered the poverty and unemployment of the 1930s and made sacrifices during a long war, Americans now regarded abundance and leisure as their due, sometimes neglecting to look beyond the immediate objects of their desire. As journalist William Shannon wrote, the decade was one of "self-satisfaction and gross materialism. . . . The loudest sound in the land has been the oink and grunt of private hoggishness. . . . It has been the age of the slob."

Consensus and Conformity

As the economy expanded, an increasing sense of sameness pervaded American society. Third- and fourth-generation ethnic Americans became much more alike. As immigration slowed to a trickle after 1924, ties to

Europe weakened, assimilation sped up, and interethnic marriage skyrocketed. Television gave young and old a shared, visually seductive experience. Escaping the homogenizing tendencies was difficult.

Contours of Religious Life

Postwar Americans discovered a shared religious sense and returned to their churches in record numbers. By the end of the 1950s, fully 95 percent of all Americans identified with some religious denomination.

Ecumenical activities—worldwide efforts on the part of different Christian churches—promoted greater religious involvement. Within the United States, evangelical revivalism, led by Southern Baptist **Billy Graham** and others, became increasingly popular. Catholicism also sought to broaden its appeal when Pope John XXIII convened the Vatican Ecumenical Council in 1962 to make the Catholic church's traditions and practices more accessible. Judaism likewise broadened its appeal. Jews relied on the GI Bill to move to the suburbs, where they bought new homes and built new synagogues, most of which followed the more casual patterns of Reform or Conservative, rather than Orthodox, Judaism. Across all faiths, religious revivals reinforced the importance of family life, for, according to one slogan, "The family that prays together stays together."

President Dwight D. Eisenhower reflected the national mood when he observed that "our government makes no sense unless it is founded in a deeply felt religious faith—and I don't care what it is." In 1954, Congress added the words "under God" to the pledge to the flag and the next year voted to require the phrase "In God We Trust" on all U.S. currency. Yet the revival sometimes seemed to rest on a shallow base of religious knowledge. In one public opinion poll, 80 percent of the respondents indicated that the Bible was God's revealed word, but only 35 percent were able to name the four Gospels, and over half were unable to name even one.

Traditional Roles for Men and Women

World War II had interrupted traditional patterns of behavior for both men and women. As servicemen went overseas, women left their homes to work. After 1945, women faced tremendous pressure to leave their jobs and conform to accepted prewar gender patterns, even though, paradoxically, more women entered the workforce than ever before.

Men and women had different postwar expectations. Most men expected to go to school and then find jobs to support their families as the primary breadwinners. For women, the situation was more complex. While they wanted to resume patterns of family life that had been disrupted by the war, many had enjoyed working in the military plants and were reluctant to retreat to the home, despite pressure to do so.

By the 1950s, middle-class doubts and questions had largely receded. The baby boom increased average family size and made the decision to remain home easier. The flight to the suburbs gave women more to do, and they settled into the routines of redecorating their homes and gardens and transporting children to and from activities and schools.

Marriage and home became the most important priorities. Many women went to college to find husbands—and dropped out if they succeeded. Almost two-thirds of the women in college, but less than half the men, left before completing a degree. Women were expected to marry young, have children early, and encourage their husbands' careers. An article in *Esquire* magazine in 1954 called working wives a "menace."

In 1946, pediatrician Benjamin Spock published *Baby and Child Care*, the book most responsible for the child-rearing patterns of the postwar generation. In it, he advised mothers to stay at home if they wanted to raise stable and secure youngsters. Working outside the home might jeopardize their children's mental and emotional health.

Popular culture highlighted the stereotype of the woman concerned only about marriage and family. Author Betty Friedan described these patterns in her explosive 1963 critique *The Feminine Mystique*. "It was unquestioned gospel," she wrote, "that women could identify with nothing beyond the home—not politics, not art, not science, not events large or small, war or peace, in the United States or the world, unless it could be approached through female experience as a wife or mother or translated into domestic detail."

The family was all-important in this scenario. Fewer than 10 percent of all Americans felt that an unmarried person could be happy. In a pattern endlessly reiterated by popular television programs, the family was meant to provide all satisfaction and contentment. The single-story ranch house that became so popular in this period reflected the focus on the family as the source of recreation and fun. Now houses, with far more shared and open space, stressed livability and family comfort.

Sexuality was a troublesome if compelling postwar concern. In 1948, zoologist Alfred C. Kinsey published the first of his "**Kinsey Reports.**" *Sexual Behavior in the Human Male* was based on his research on the sexual lives of 5,300 white males. He shocked the country with his statistics on premarital, extramarital, and otherwise illicit sexual acts. Among males who went to college, he concluded, 67 percent had engaged in sexual intercourse before marriage as had 84 percent of those who went to high school but not beyond. Thirty-seven percent of the total male population had experienced some kind of overt homosexual activity. Five years later, Kinsey published a companion volume, *Sexual Behavior in the Human Female*, which detailed many of the same sexual patterns. Although critics denounced Kinsey for what they considered his unscientific methodology and challenged his results, both books sold widely, for they opened the door to a subject previously considered taboo.

Interest in sexuality was reflected in the fascination with sex goddesses like Marilyn Monroe. The images of such film stars corresponded to male fantasies of women, visible in *Playboy* magazine, which first appeared in 1953 and soon achieved a huge readership. As for men's wives, they were expected to manage their suburban homes and to be cheerful and willing objects of their husbands' desire.

Despite reaffirming the old ideology that a woman's place was in the home, the 1950s were years of unnoticed but important change. Because the supply of single women workers fell as a result of the low birthrate of the Depression years and increased schooling and early marriage, older married women continued the pattern begun during the war and entered the labor force in larger numbers than before. In 1940, only 15 percent of American wives had jobs. By 1950, 21 percent were employed, and 10 years later, the figure had risen to 30 percent. Still, the conviction that women's main role was homemaking justified low wages and the denial of promotions. Comparatively few women entered professions where they would have challenged traditional notions of a woman's place.

African American women worked as always but often lost the jobs they had held during the war. In the 1950s, however, the employment picture improved somewhat. African American women succeeded both in moving into white-collar positions and in increasing their income. By 1960, more than one-third of all black women held clerical, sales, service, or professional jobs. The income gap between white women and black women holding similar jobs dropped from about 50 percent in 1940 to about 30 percent in 1960.

Cultural Rebels

Not all Americans fit the 1950s stereotypes. Some were alienated from the culture and rebelled against its values. Many were intrigued by Holden Caulfield, the main figure in J. D. Salinger's popular novel *The Catcher in the Rye* (1951), who rebelled against the "phonies" around him threatening his individuality and independence.

Writers of the "Beat Generation" espoused unconventional values in their stories and poems as they challenged the apathy and conformity of the period. The "**Beats**" deliberately outraged respectability by sneering at materialism, flaunting unconventional sex lives, and smoking marijuana.

Their literary work reflected their approach to life. Jack Kerouac dispensed with conventional punctuation and paragraphing as he typed his best-selling novel *On the Road* (1957) on a 250-foot roll of paper. Poet Allen Ginsberg, who, like Kerouac, was a Columbia University dropout, became equally well known for his poem "Howl," a scathing critique of modern, mechanized culture that began with the line "I saw the best minds of my generation destroyed by madness, starving hysterical naked." He and the other "Beats" furnished a model for rebellion in the 1960s.

The signs of cultural rebellion also appeared in popular music. Parents recoiled as their children flocked to hear a young Tennessee singer named Elvis Presley, whose sexy voice, gyrating hips, and other techniques borrowed from black singers made him the undisputed "king of rock and roll."

His black leather jacket and ducktail haircut became standard dress for rebellious male teenagers.

American painters, shucking off European influences that had shaped American artists for two centuries, also became a part of the cultural rebellion. Led by Jackson Pollock and the "New York school," some artists discarded the easel, laid gigantic canvases on the floor, and then used trowels, putty knives, and sticks to apply paint, glass shards, sand, and other materials in wild explosions of color. Abstract expressionism reflected the artist's alienation from a world filled with nuclear threats, computerization, and materialism.

Origins of the Welfare State

The modern American welfare state originated in the New Deal. Franklin D. Roosevelt's efforts to deal with the ravages of the Great Depression and protect Americans from the problems stemming from industrial capitalism provided the basis for subsequent efforts to commit the government to help those who could not help themselves, even in prosperous times. The **Fair Deal** of Harry Truman, who became president on FDR's death in the spring of 1945, built squarely on Roosevelt's New Deal. Truman's Republican successor, Dwight Eisenhower, sought to scale down spending but made no effort to roll back the most important initiatives of the welfare state.

Truman's Struggles with a Conservative Congress

Truman took the same feisty approach to public policy that characterized his conduct of foreign affairs. Believing in plain speaking, he attacked his political enemies vigorously when they resisted his initiatives and often took his case directly to the American people. He was, in many ways, an old-style Democratic politician, who hoped to use his authority to benefit the middle-class and working-class Americans who made up his political base.

Like Roosevelt, Harry Truman believed that the federal government had the responsibility for ensuring the social welfare of all Americans. Truman wanted his administration to embrace and act upon a series of carefully defined social and economic goals to extend New Deal initiatives even further.

Less than a week after the end of World War II, Truman called on Congress to pass a 21-point program providing for housing assistance, a higher minimum wage, more unemployment compensation, and a national commitment to maintaining full employment. Truman also sent blueprints of further proposals to Congress, including health insurance and atomic energy legislation. But this liberal program soon ran into fierce political opposition.

The debate surrounding the Employment Act of 1946 hinted at the fate of Truman's proposals. This measure was a deliberate effort to apply the theory of English economist John Maynard Keynes, who argued that aggressive spending could head off another depression and maintain economic equilibrium. While liberals and labor leaders hailed the measure, business groups claimed that government intervention would undermine free enterprise and promote socialism. Congress cut the proposal to bits. As finally passed, the act created a Council of Economic Advisers to make recommendations to the president, but it stopped short of committing the government to using fiscal tools to maintain full employment when economic indicators turned downward.

As the midterm elections of 1946 approached, Truman knew he was vulnerable. With more and more people questioning his competence as president, his support dropped from 87 percent of those polled after he assumed the office to 32 percent in November 1946. Gleeful Republicans asked the voters, "Had enough?" They had. Republicans won majorities in both houses of Congress for the first time since the 1928 elections and gained a majority of the governorships as well.

After the 1946 elections, Truman faced an unsympathetic 80th Congress, which planned to reverse the liberal policies of the Roosevelt years and reestablish congressional authority. When the new Congress met, it slashed federal spending and taxes. In 1947, Congress twice passed tax-cut measures, which Truman vetoed. In 1948, another election year, Congress overrode the veto.

Angry at the gains won by labor in the 1930s and 1940s, Republicans counterattacked. They wanted to check unions and to circumscribe their right to engage in the kind of disruptive strikes that had occurred immediately after the war. In 1947, the Republicans passed the **Taft-Hartley Act**, which sought to limit the power of unions by restricting the weapons they could employ. It spelled out unfair labor practices (such as preventing non-union workers from working if they wished) and outlawed the closed shop, whereby an employee had to join a union before getting a job. The law likewise allowed states to prohibit the union shop, which forced workers to join the union after they had been hired. It gave the president the right to call for an 80-day cooling-off period in strikes affecting national security and required union officials to sign non-Communist oaths.

Union leaders and members were furious. Vetoing the measure, Truman claimed that it was unworkable and unfair and went on nationwide radio to seek public approval. This regained him some of the support he had lost earlier when he had sought to force strikers to go back to work immediately after the war. Congress, however, passed the Taft-Hartley measure over Truman's veto.

The Fair Deal and Its Fate

In 1948, Truman wanted a chance to consolidate a liberal program and decided to seek the presidency in his own right. Aware that he was an accidental occupant of the White House, he won what most people thought was a worthless nomination. Not only was his own popularity waning, but the Democratic party itself seemed to be falling apart.

The civil rights issue split the Democrats. When liberals defeated a moderate platform proposal and pressed for a stronger commitment to African American rights, angry delegates from Mississippi and Alabama stormed out of the convention. They later formed the States' Rights, or Dixiecrat, party. At their own convention, delegates from 13 states nominated Governor J. Strom Thurmond of South Carolina and affirmed their support for continued racial segregation. Meanwhile, Henry A. Wallace, a longtime member of the government until Truman fired him for advocating a more moderate approach to the Soviet Union, mounted his own challenge, becoming the presidential candidate of the Progressive party.

In that fragmented state, the Democrats took on the Republicans, who coveted the White House after 16 years out of power. Once again, the GOP nominated New York Governor Thomas E. Dewey, the unsuccessful candidate in 1944. Even though he was stiff and egocentric, the polls uniformly picked the Republicans to win. Truman, meanwhile, conducted a two-fisted campaign. He appealed to ordinary Americans as an unpretentious man engaged in an uphill fight. Believing that everyone was against him but the people, he called the Republicans a "bunch of old mossbacks" out to destroy the New Deal as he attacked the "do nothing" 80th Congress. Speaking informally in his choppy, aggressive style, he appealed to crowds who yelled, "Give 'em hell, Harry!" He did.

The pollsters predicting a Republican victory were wrong. On election day, disproving the bold headline "Dewey Defeats Truman" in the *Chicago Daily Tribune*, the incumbent president scored one of the most unexpected political upsets in American history, winning 303–189 in the Electoral College. Democrats also swept both houses of Congress.

Truman won primarily because he was able to hold on to the labor, farm, and black votes that Franklin Roosevelt had won more than a decade before. Working men and women who were worried about Wallace backed Truman.

With the election behind him, Truman pursued his liberal program. In his 1949 State of the Union message, he declared, "Every segment of our population and every individual has a right to expect from our Government a fair deal." While parts of Truman's Fair Deal worked, others did not. Lawmakers raised the minimum wage and expanded social security programs. A housing program brought modest gains but did not really meet housing needs. A farm program, aimed at providing income support to farmers if prices fell, never made it through Congress. Although he desegregated the military, other parts of his civil rights program failed to win congressional support. The American Medical Association undermined the effort to provide national health insurance, and Congress rejected a measure to provide federal aid to education.

The mixed record was not entirely Truman's fault. Conservative legislators were largely responsible for sabotaging his efforts. At the same time, critics charged correctly that Truman was often unpragmatic and shrill in his struggles with an unsympathetic Congress. They argued that he sometimes

Harry Truman Celebrating His Unexpected Victory In one of the nation's most extraordinary political upsets, Harry Truman beat Thomas E. Dewey in 1948. Here an exuberant Truman holds a newspaper headline printed while he slept, before the vote turned his way. Why is Truman so gleeful?

seemed to provoke the confrontations that became a hallmark of his presidency. They also claimed that he was most concerned with foreign policy as he strove to secure bipartisan support for Cold War initiatives and allowed his domestic program to suffer.

Still, Truman kept the liberal vision alive. The Fair Deal ratified many of the initiatives begun during the New Deal and led Americans to take programs like social security for granted. Truman had not achieved everything he wanted—he had not even come close—but the nation had taken another step toward endorsing liberal goals.

The Election of Ike

Acceptance of the liberal state continued in the 1950s, even as the Republicans took control. By 1952, Truman's approval rating had plummeted to 23 percent of the American people, and all indicators pointed to a political shift. The Democrats nominated

Watch the Video
"Ike for President": Eisenhower Campaign Ad (1952)
at **www.myhistorylab.com**

Adlai Stevenson, governor of Illinois. The Republicans turned to Dwight Eisenhower, the World War II hero known as Ike.

While Stevenson approached political issues in intellectual terms, the Republicans focused on communism, corruption, and Korea as major priorities. They called the Democrats "soft on communism," condemned scandals in the administration, and promised to end the unpopular Korean War.

Eisenhower proved to be a highly effective campaigner. He had a natural talent for taking his case to the American people, speaking in simple, reassuring terms they could understand. He struck a grandfatherly pose, unified the various wings of his party, and went on to victory at the polls. He received 55 percent of the vote and carried 41 states. The new president took office with a Republican Congress as well and had little difficulty gaining a second term.

Eisenhower stood in stark contrast to Truman. The war hero's easy manner and warm smile made him widely popular. Despite his lack of formal political background, he had a real ability to get people to compromise and work together. But his limited experience with everyday politics conditioned his sense of the presidential role. Whereas Truman loved political infighting and wanted to take charge, Eisenhower was more restrained. The presidency for him was no "bully pulpit," as it had been for Theodore Roosevelt and even FDR. "I am not one of those desk-pounding types that likes to stick out his jaw and look like he is bossing the show," he declared.

A Popular and Personable President Dwight Eisenhower provided a reassuring presence in the White House in the 1950s. His very presence conveyed the impression that everything was going to be all right. How did his wide smile, pictured here, make Americans feel good about themselves and their country?

"Modern Republicanism"

Eisenhower wanted to limit the presidential role. He was uncomfortable with the growth of the executive office over the past 20 years. Like the Republicans in Congress with whom Truman had tangled, he wanted to restore the balance between the branches of government and to reduce the authority of the national government. He recognized, however, that it was impossible to scale back federal power to the limited levels of the 1920s, and he wanted to preserve social gains that even Republicans now accepted. Eisenhower sometimes termed his approach "dynamic conservatism" or "**modern Republicanism**," which, he explained, meant "conservative when it comes to money, liberal when it comes to human beings."

Economic concerns dominated the Eisenhower years. The president and his chief aides wanted desperately to preserve the value of the dollar, pare down levels of funding, cut taxes, and balance the budget after years of deficit spending. Eisenhower's administration also supported business interests. This orientation became obvious when Defense Secretary Charles E. Wilson, former president of General Motors, declared at his confirmation hearing, "What is good for our country is good for General Motors, and vice versa."

Eisenhower fulfilled his promise to reduce government's economic role. The administration sought to circumscribe federal activity in the electric power field. Eisenhower opposed a TVA proposal for expansion to provide power to the Atomic Energy Commission and instead authorized a private group to build a plant for that purpose. Later, when charges of scandal arose, the administration canceled the agreement, but the basic preference for private development remained.

The administration sometimes saw its program backfire. As a result of its reluctance to stimulate the economy too much, the annual rate of economic growth declined from 4.3 percent between 1947 and 1952 to 2.5 percent between 1953 and 1960. The economy was still growing, but more slowly than before. The country also suffered three recessions—in 1953–1954, 1957–1958, and 1960–1961—in Eisenhower's eight years. During the slumps, tax revenues fell and the deficits that Eisenhower so wanted to avoid increased.

Eisenhower's understated approach led to a legislative stalemate, particularly when the Democrats regained control of Congress in 1954. Opponents gibed at Ike's restrained stance and joked about what they called nonexistent White House leadership. Yet Eisenhower understood just what he was doing and had a better grasp of public policy than his critics realized.

Even more important was his role in ratifying the welfare state. By 1960, the government had become a major factor in ordinary people's lives. It had grown enormously, employing close to 2.5 million people throughout the

1950s. Federal expenditures, which had stood at $3.5 billion in 1927, rose to $97 billion in 1960. The White House now took the lead in initiating legislation and in steering bills through Congress. Individuals had come to expect old-age pensions, unemployment payments, and a minimum wage. By accepting the fundamental features of the national state that the Democrats had created, Eisenhower ensured its survival.

•••—Read the Document

Dwight D. Eisenhower, Farewell
to the Nation (January 17, 1961)
at **www.myhistorylab.com**

Eisenhower accomplished most of his goals, and he was one of the few presidents to leave office as highly regarded by the people as when he entered it. He was the kind of leader Americans wanted in prosperous times.

The Other America

Not all Americans shared postwar middle-class affluence. African Americans, torn from rural roots and transplanted into urban slums, were among the hardest hit. But members of other minority groups, as well as less fortunate whites, suffered similar dislocations unknown to the middle class.

Poverty amid Affluence

Many people in the "affluent society" lived in poverty. Although the popular "trickle-down" theory argued that economic expansion benefited all classes, little wealth, in fact, reached the citizens at the bottom. In 1960, the Federal Bureau of Labor Statistics reported that 40 million people (almost one-quarter of the population) lived below what it defined as the poverty level, with nearly the same number only marginally above the line.

Michael Harrington, socialist author and critic, shocked the country with his 1962 study *The Other America*. The poor, Harrington showed, were everywhere. He described New York City's "economic underworld," where "Puerto Ricans and Negroes, alcoholics, drifters, and disturbed people" haunted employment agencies for temporary positions as "dishwashers and day workers, the fly-by-night jobs." Despite the prosperity that surrounded them, the mountain folk of Appalachia, the tenant farmers of Mississippi, and the migrant farmers of Florida, Texas, and California were all caught in poverty's relentless cycle.

Hard Times for African Americans

African Americans were among the postwar nation's least prosperous citizens. In the South, agricultural workers continued to fall victim to foreign competition, mechanization, and eviction as white farmers turned to less labor-intensive crops like soybeans and peanuts. The southern agricultural population declined dramatically, as millions of blacks moved to southern cities, where they found better jobs, better schooling, and freedom from landlords. Some achieved middle-class status; many more did not. They remained poor, with even less of a support system than they had known before.

Millions of African Americans also headed for northern cities after 1940. In the 1950s, Detroit's black population increased from 16 percent to 29 percent, and at one point in this decade, Chicago's black population rose by more than 2,200 people each week. The new arrivals congregated in urban slums, where the growth of social services failed to keep pace with population growth.

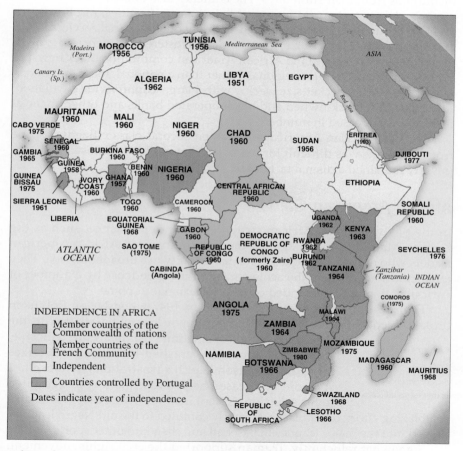

Independence in Africa In the 1950s and 1960s, most African nations threw off their colonial rulers and achieved independence. During which decade did more nations become free? How did attaining independence change social and economic patterns in the African nations? What effect did it have on the patterns of the Cold War? What effect did it have on the civil rights struggle in the United States?

The experiences of African Americans in the cities often proved different from what they had expected. As author Claude Brown recalled, blacks were told that in the North, "Negroes lived in houses with bathrooms, electricity, running water, and indoor toilets. To them, this was the 'promised land' that Mammy had been singing about in the cotton fields for many years." But no one had told them "about one of the most important aspects of the promised land: it was a slum ghetto." Poor conditions, and the constant slights that accompanied segregation in both the North and the South, took a heavy toll.

Still, the black community remained intact. The black church played an especially important role in sustaining African American life. Blacks moving into the cities retained churchgoing habits and a commitment to religious institutions from their rural days. The churches also offered more than religious sustenance alone. Many provided day-care facilities, ran Boy Scout and Girl Scout troops, and sponsored a variety of other social services.

The growth of the black urban population fostered the increased growth of businesses catering to the African American community. Black newspapers now provided a more regional, rather than a national, focus, but magazines such as *Jet*, a pocket-size weekly with a large, countrywide circulation, filled the void. Black-owned and black-operated banks and other financial institutions increased in number.

Yet most African Americans remained second-class citizens. Escape from the slums was difficult for many and impossible for most. Persistent poverty remained a dismal fact of life.

African American Gains

In the postwar years, African struggles for independence, such as the Kenyan Mau Mau revolt against the British, inspired African American leaders who now saw the quest for black equality in a broader context. They took enormous pride in the achievement of independence by a number of African nations and demanded comparable change at home.

The racial question was dramatized in 1947 when Jackie Robinson broke the color line and began playing major league baseball with the Brooklyn Dodgers. Sometimes teammates were hostile, sometimes opponents crashed into him with spikes high, but Robinson kept his frustrations to himself. A splendid first season helped ease the way and resulted in his selection as Rookie of the Year. After Robinson's trailblazing effort, other blacks, formerly confined to the old Negro leagues, moved into the major leagues in baseball and then into other sports.

Watch the Video
Jackie Robinson and the Integration of Baseball
at **www.myhistorylab.com**

Somewhat reluctantly, Truman supported the civil rights movement. In 1946, he appointed a Committee on Civil Rights to investigate the problem of lynching and other brutalities against blacks and recommend remedies. The committee's report, released in October 1947, showed that black Americans remained second-class citizens in every area of American

Baseball Superstar Jackie Robinson Jackie Robinson's electrifying play as the first African American in the major leagues led to acceptance of the integration of baseball. A spectacular rookie season in 1947 opened the way for other African Americans who had earlier been limited to the Negro leagues. In this photo, taken at Ebbets Field in Brooklyn during the 1957 World Series, Robinson is about to steal home. What impression do you have of Robinson here?

life and called for change. In February 1948, Truman sent a 10-point civil rights program to Congress, the first presidential civil rights plan since Reconstruction. Then he moved forward even more aggressively, first issuing an executive order barring discrimination in the federal establishment. Finally, he ordered equality of treatment in the military services. Manpower needs in the Korean War broke down the last restrictions, particularly when the army found that integrated units performed well.

As the civil rights struggle gained momentum during the 1950s, the judicial system played a crucial role. The National Association for the Advancement of Colored People (NAACP) was determined to overturn the 1896 Supreme Court decision *Plessy* v. *Ferguson*, in which the Court had declared that segregation of the black and white races was constitutional if the facilities used by each were "separate but equal." The decree had been used for generations to sanction rigid segregation, primarily in the South, even though separate facilities were seldom, if ever, equal.

Then in 1951, Oliver Brown, the father of eight-year-old Linda Brown, sued the school board of Topeka, Kansas, to allow his daughter to attend a school for white children that she passed as she walked to the bus that carried her to a black school farther away. The case reached the Supreme Court, which grouped several school segregation cases together.

On May 17, 1954, the Supreme Court released its bombshell ruling in *Brown* **v.** *Board of Education*. For more than a decade, Supreme Court decisions had gradually expanded black civil rights. Now the Court unanimously decreed that "separate facilities are inherently unequal" and concluded that the "separate but equal" doctrine had no place in public education. A year later, the Court turned to the question of implementation and declared that local school boards, acting with the guidance of lower courts, should move "with all deliberate speed" to desegregate their facilities.

*●◆●─*Read the Document

Brown *v.* Board of Education
of Topeka, Kansas *(1954)*
at **www.myhistorylab.com**

President Eisenhower had the ultimate responsibility for executing the law. While he thought privately that the *Brown* ruling was wrong, he knew that it was his constitutional duty to see that the decision was carried out. He acted immediately to desegregate the Washington, D.C., schools as a model for the rest of the country. He also ordered desegregation in navy yards and veterans' hospitals.

The South resisted. The crucial confrontation came in Little Rock, Arkansas, in 1957. Just before the school year began, Governor Orval Faubus declared on television that it would not be possible to maintain order if integration took place. In the face of hostile mobs, National Guardsmen mobilized by the governor turned away nine black students as they tried to enter Central High School.

*◆◎─*Watch the Video

*How Did the Civil Rights
Movement Change
American Schools?*
at **www.myhistorylab.com**

With the lines drawn, Ike knew that such resistance could not be tolerated, and he finally took the one action he had earlier called unthinkable. For the first time since the end of Reconstruction, an American president called out federal troops to protect the rights of black citizens. Eisenhower ordered paratroopers to Little Rock and placed National Guardsmen under federal command. The black children entered the school and attended classes with the military protecting their rights. Thus desegregation began.

Meanwhile, African Americans, encouraged by their churches, began organizing themselves to take direct action, and their efforts significantly advanced the civil rights movement. All were horrified by the brutal murder of Emmett Till, a 14-year-old boy from Chicago visiting Mississippi, who offended a white woman at a country store. Pictures of his mangled body in an open casket helped energize the effort to promote racial equality.

The catalyzing event occurred in Montgomery, Alabama, in December 1955. Rosa Parks, a 42-year-old black seamstress who was also secretary of her local NAACP branch, sat down in the front of a bus in a section reserved by custom for whites. When ordered to move back, the longtime activist refused to budge. The bus driver called the police at the next stop, and

Parks was arrested. The state NAACP president told Parks, "This is the case we've been looking for. We can break this situation on the bus with your case."

Martin Luther King, Jr., the 27-year-old minister of the Baptist church where a meeting to consider a boycott was held, soon emerged as the preeminent spokesman of the protest. King was an impressive figure and an inspiring speaker. "There comes a time when people get tired . . . of being kicked about by the brutal feet of oppression," he declared. It was time to be more assertive, to cease being "patient with anything less than freedom and justice."

For almost a year, 50,000 African Americans avoided the transit system, and their actions cut gross revenue on city buses by 65 percent. Ultimately, the Supreme Court ruled that bus segregation, like school segregation, violated the Constitution, and the boycott ended. But the mood it fostered continued, as ordinary black men and women challenged the racial status quo and forced both white and black leaders to respond.

Meanwhile, a concerted effort developed to guarantee black voting rights. Largely because of the legislative genius of Senate majority leader Lyndon B. Johnson of Texas, the Civil Rights Act of 1957 created a Civil Rights Commission and empowered the Justice Department to go to court in cases where blacks were denied the right to vote. The bill was a compromise measure, yet it was the first effort to protect civil rights in 82 years. Again led by Johnson, Congress passed the Civil Rights Act of 1960. This measure set stiffer penalties for people who interfered with the right to vote but once more stopped short of authorizing federal registrars to register blacks to vote and so, like its predecessor, was generally ineffective.

Latinos on the Fringe

Latinos, like other groups, had similar difficulties in the postwar United States. Latino immigrants from Cuba, Puerto Rico, Mexico, and Central America, often unskilled and illiterate, followed other less fortunate Americans to the cities. The conditions they encountered there were similar to those faced by blacks.

Chicanos, or Mexican Americans, were the most numerous of the newcomers and faced peculiar difficulties. During World War II, as the country experienced a labor shortage at home, American farmers sought Mexican *braceros* (helping hands) to harvest their crops, and seasonal immigration continued after the war when the government signed a Migratory Labor Agreement with Mexico. Between 1948 and 1964, some 4.5 million Mexicans were brought to the United States for temporary work. *Braceros* were expected to return to Mexico at the end of their labor contract, but often they stayed. Joining them were millions more who entered the country illegally.

RECOVERING *the* PAST

Clothing

Clothing can be an important source of information about the past. The clothes people wear often announce their age, gender, and class and frequently transmit some sense of their origin, occupation, and even their politics. The vocabulary of dress includes more than garments alone: hairstyles, jewelry, and makeup all contribute to the way people choose to present themselves. Clothing can signal strong emotions; a torn, unbuttoned shirt, for example, can indicate that a person who seldom dresses that way is really upset. Bright colors can demonstrate a sense of daring and a willingness to make a strong statement. By examining clothing styles in a number of different decades, we can begin to understand something of the changing patterns of people's lives.

In the 1920s, flappers and other women often dressed like children, with loose dresses usually in pastel colors ending just below the knee. Large trimmings, such as huge artificial flowers, accentuated the effect. A "boyish" figure was considered most attractive. The clothes conveyed a feeling of playfulness and a willingness to embrace the freedom of the young. Men's suits in the same period were now made out of lighter materials and looked less padded than before. As the tall, stiff collar of an earlier age disappeared and trousers became more high-waisted, men too had a more youthful look.

The Great Depression of the 1930s brought a change in style. Flappers now looked silly, especially as millions of people were starving. Advertisements and films promoted a new maturity and sophistication more appropriate to hard times. Men's suits became heavier and darker, as if symbolically to provide protection in a breadline. Trousers were wider, and jackets were frequently double-breasted. Overcoats became longer. Women's clothes were likewise made out of heavier fabrics and used darker colors. Skirts fell almost to the ankles on occasion and were covered by longer coats. Clothes indicated that there was no place for the playfulness of the decade before.

As conditions improved during and after World War II, styles changed once more. In the 1940s, teenage girls frequently wore bobby socks rolled down to their ankles. Working women wore overalls, but with their own adornments to maintain their femininity. "Rosie the Riveter," drawn by noted artist Norman Rockwell, wore her overalls proudly as she sat with a riveting gun in her lap and an attractive scarf around her hair. In the postwar years, the "Man in the Gray Flannel Suit" looked serious, sober, and well tailored, ready to go work for corporate America. His female partner wanted to look equally worldly and sophisticated and wore carefully tailored adult clothing, with the waist drawn in (often by a girdle) and heels as tall as three inches, when going out. The fashion industry helped define the decorative role women were supposed to play in supporting men as they advanced their business careers.

Then came the 1960s and an entirely new look. Casual clothing became a kind of uniform. The counterculture was a movement of the young, and clothing took on an increasingly youthful look. Skirts rose above the knee in 1963 and a few years later climbed to mid-thigh. Women began to wear pants and trouser suits. Men and women both favored jeans and informal shirts and let their hair grow longer. Men broke away from the gray suits of the preceding decade and indulged themselves in bright colors in what has been called the "peacock revolution."

REFLECTING ON THE PAST **Look carefully at the pictures on these pages. They show fashions from different periods and can tell us a good deal about how these people defined themselves. Examine first the photo of the three black women from the 1920s. What kinds of adornments do you notice? What impression do these women convey?**

Look at the photograph of Frances Perkins, secretary of labor in the 1930s. What kind of dress is she wearing? How do her clothes differ from those of the women in the 1920s? In the picture, she is talking to a number of working men. What do their clothes tell you about the kind of work they might be doing?

Harlem women in the 1920s.

Frances Perkins with laborers in the 1930s.

World War II women at work.

Two women in the 1950s.

Countercultural dress in the 1960s.

In the picture of two drill press operators during World War II, the women are dressed to handle the heavy machinery. Are their clothes different from those of the laborers in the preceding picture? How have the women accommodated themselves to their work, while still maintaining their individuality?

Now look at the picture of two women in the 1950s. What kind of work might they do? What kind of flexibility do these clothes give them? What do the stylistic touches convey? Finally, examine the photograph of the man and woman at an outdoor music festival in the 1960s. What does their clothing remind you of? Where might it come from? What impression are these people trying to create by their dress?

Conditions were harsh for the *braceros* in the best of times, but in periods of economic difficulty, troubles worsened. During a serious recession in 1953–1954, the government mounted Operation Wetback to deport illegal entrants and *braceros* who had remained in the country illegally and expelled 1.1 million. As immigration officials searched out illegal workers, all Chicanos found themselves vulnerable. Still, the demand for cheap labor attracted hundreds of thousands of newcomers.

Puerto Ricans were numerous in other parts of the country. As the island's sugarcane economy became more mechanized, nearly 40 percent of the inhabitants left their homes. By the end of the 1960s, New York City had more Puerto Ricans than San Juan, the island's capital. El Barrio, in East Harlem, became the center of Puerto Rican activity, the home of salsa music and small *bodegas*, grocery stores that served the neighborhood. Puerto Ricans, like many other immigrants, hoped to earn money in America and then return home. Some did; others stayed. Most failed to enjoy the promise of the American dream.

Like African Americans, Latinos fought for their own rights. The Community Service Organization mobilized Chicanos against discrimination, as did the more radical Asociación Nacional México-Americana. And the League of United Latin American Citizens continued reform efforts. Chicano activism in the 1950s, however, was fragmented. Some Mexican Americans considered their situation hopeless. More effective mobilization had to await another day.

The Native American Struggle

Native Americans likewise remained outsiders in the postwar years. As power lines reached their reservations and they partook of the consumer culture, old patterns inevitably changed. Reservation life lost its cohesiveness, and alcohol became a major problem. With good jobs unavailable on the reservations, more and more Indians gravitated to the cities. But they often had difficulty adjusting to urban life and frequently faced hostility from white Americans.

Native Americans, like Latinos, began their own struggle for equality. They achieved an important victory just after the end of World War II when Congress established the Indian Claims Commission, but in the 1950s, federal Indian policy shifted course. As part of its effort to limit the role of the national government, the Eisenhower administration turned away from the New Deal policy of government support for tribal autonomy. In 1953, instead of trying to encourage Native American self-government, the administration adopted a new approach, known as "termination." The government proposed settling all outstanding claims and eliminating reservations as legitimate political entities. To encourage their assimilation into mainstream society, the government offered small subsidies to families leaving the reservations and moving to cities.

The new policy infuriated American Indians. Earl Old Person, a Black-foot elder, declared: "It is important to note that in our Indian language the only translation for termination is to 'wipe out' or 'kill off' . . . How can we plan our future when the Indian Bureau threatens to wipe us out as a race?" Though promising more freedom, the new policy caused great disruption as the government terminated tribes like the Klamath in Oregon and bands of Paiute in Utah.

The policy increased Indian activism. It also sparked a dawning aware-ness among whites of the Indians' right to maintain their heritage. In 1958, the Eisenhower administration changed the policy of termination so that it required a tribe's consent. The policy continued to have the force of law, but implementation ceased.

Asian American Advances

For Asian Americans, conditions improved somewhat in the aftermath of World War II. The war against Nazism eroded the racism that proclaimed a commitment to white superiority. In 1952, the Immigration and Nationality Act, also known as the McCarran-Walter Act, eased immigration quotas. Although the basic framework of the National Origins Act of 1924 remained intact, it removed the longstanding ban on Japanese immigration and made first-generation Japanese immigrants eligible for citizenship. It also estab-lished a quota of 100 immigrants a year from each Asian country. While that number was tiny compared to those admitted annually from northern and western Europe, the measure was a first step in ending the discriminatory exclusion of the past.

By the 1950s, many second- and third-generation Chinese, Japanese, and Koreans had moved into white-collar work. Promoting education for their children, they became part of the growing middle class, hoping like others to enjoy the benefits of the American dream.

Conclusion
Qualms amid Affluence

In general, the United States during the decade and a half after World War II was stable and prosperous. Recessions occurred periodically, but the econ-omy righted itself after short downturns. For the most part, business boomed. The standard of living for many of the nation's citizens reached new heights, especially compared with standards in other parts of the world. Millions of middle-class Americans joined the ranks of suburban property owners, enjoying the benefits of shopping centers, fast-food establishments, and other material manifestations of what they considered the good life. Workers found themselves savoring the materialistic advantages of the era.

Some Americans did not share in the prosperity, but they were not visible in the affluent suburbs. Many African Americans and members of other minority groups were seriously disadvantaged, although they still believed they could share in the American dream and remained confident that deeply rooted patterns of discrimination could be changed.

Beneath the calm surface, though, there were signs of discontent. The seeds for the protest movements of the 1960s had already been sown. Disquieting signs were likewise evident on other fronts. The divorce rate increased, as one-third of all marriages in the 1950s broke apart. Americans increasingly used newly developed tranquilizers in an effort to cope with problems in their lives. Some Americans began to criticize the materialism that seemed to undermine American efforts in the Cold War. Such criticisms in turn legitimized challenges by other groups in the continuing struggle to make the realities of American life match the nation's ideals.

Criticisms and anxieties notwithstanding, the United States—for most whites and some people of color—continued to develop according to Ray Kroc's dreams as he first envisioned McDonald's establishments across the land. Healthy and comfortable, upper- and middle-class Americans expected prosperity and growth to continue without an inkling of the turbulence that lay ahead.

TIME*line*

1947 Jackie Robinson breaks the color line in major league baseball

1948 Truman defeats Dewey

1952 Dwight D. Eisenhower elected president

1954 *Brown* v. *Board of Education*

1955 Montgomery, Alabama, bus boycott begins

1956 Eisenhower reelected

1957 Little Rock, Arkansas, school integration crisis

Civil Rights Act

1960 Civil Rights Act

1963 Betty Friedan, *The Feminine Mystique*

✓•⎯Study and Review at **www.myhistorylab.com**

Questions for Review and Reflection

1. What were the sources of American prosperity?
2. Who prospered most in postwar America?
3. Who was left out?

4. Why did conformity become the norm in the postwar United States?
5. How would you characterize the broad social and economic changes that took place in America in the years after World War II?

Key Terms

AFL-CIO 817

Baby boom 810

Beats 825

Billy Graham 823

Brown v. *Board of Education* 836

Fair Deal 826

Kinsey Reports 824

Modern Republicanism 831

Taft-Hartley Act 827

The Other America 832

26

Reform and Rebellion in the Turbulent Sixties, 1960–1969

American Stories

A Young Liberal Questions the Welfare State

Paul Cowan was an idealist in the 1960s. Like many students who came of age in these years, he believed in the possibility of social change and plunged into the struggle for liberal reform. He shared the hopes and dreams of other members of his generation, who felt that their government could make a difference in people's lives.

Cowan's commitment had developed slowly. He was a child of the 1950s, when most Americans were caught up in the consumer culture and paid little attention to the problems of people less fortunate than themselves. His grandfather had sold used cement bags in Chicago, but his father had become an executive at CBS television, and Cowan grew up in comfortable surroundings. He graduated from the Choate School (where John Kennedy had gone) in 1958, and then from Harvard University (where Kennedy had also been a student) in 1963.

When he entered college, Cowan was interested in politically conscious writers such as John Dos Passos, John Steinbeck, and James Agee and folk singers such as Pete Seeger and Woody Guthrie. They offered him entrance, he later recalled, into a "nation that seemed to be filled with energy and decency," one that lurked "beneath the dull, conformist facade of the Eisenhower years." While at Harvard, he was excited by antinuclear campaigns in New England and civil rights demonstrations in the South.

After college, he made good on his commitment to civil rights by going to Mississippi to work in the Freedom Summer Project of 1964. He was inspired by the example of John Kennedy, the liberal president whose administration promised "a new kind of politics" that could make the nation, and the world, a better

Chapter Outline

John F. Kennedy: The Camelot Years

Lyndon B. Johnson and the Great Society

Continuing Confrontations with Communists

War in Vietnam and Turmoil at Home

Conclusion: Political and Social Upheaval

place. During that summer, he wrote, "it was possible to believe that by changing ourselves we could change, and redeem, our America."

The Peace Corps came next. Cowan and his wife, Rachel, were convinced that this organization, the idea of the young president, "really was a unique government agency, permanently protected by the lingering magic of John F. Kennedy's name." They were assigned to the city of Guayaquil, in Ecuador, in South America. Their task was to serve as mediators between administrators of the city hall and residents of the slums. They wanted to try to raise the standard of living by encouraging local governments to provide basic services such as garbage disposal and clean water.

But the work proved more frustrating than they had imagined. They bristled at the restrictions imposed by the Peace Corps bureaucracy. They despaired at the inadequate resources local government officials had to accomplish their aims. They wondered if they were simply new imperialists, trying to impose their values on others who had priorities of their own. "From the day we moved into the barrio," Cowan later recalled, "the question we were most frequently asked by the people we were supposed to be organizing was whether we would leave them our clothes when we returned to the States."

Cowan came home disillusioned. "I saw that even the liberals I had wanted to emulate, men who seemed to be devoting their lives to fighting injustice, were unable to accept people from alien cultures on any terms but their own." He called his account of his own odyssey *The Making of an Un-American.*

Paul Cowan's passage through the 1960s mirrored the passage of American society as a whole. Millions of Americans shared his views of the possibilities of democracy as the period began. Mostly comfortable and confident, they supported the liberal agenda advanced by the Democratic party of John Kennedy and Lyndon Johnson. They endorsed the proposition that the government had responsibility for the welfare of all its citizens and accepted the need for a more active government role to help those who were unable to help themselves. That commitment lay behind the legislative achievements of the "**Great Society**," the last wave of twentieth-century reform that built upon the gains of the Progressive era and the New Deal years before.

Then political reaction set in as the nation was torn apart by the ravages of the Vietnam War. The escalation of the war, which led to charges that the United States was engaging in an imperialistic crusade like those of other nations in the past, sent more than half a million American soldiers to fight in a far-off land and provoked a protest movement that ripped society apart. Young Americans, espousing different values and a different version of the American dream, challenged the priorities of their parents. At the same time, they paraded their sexuality more openly, experimented with different forms of mystical religious faith, and enjoyed readily available drugs. In the end, their challenges helped reverse the course of the war. But in the process, liberal assumptions eroded as conservatives argued that an activist approach was responsible for the social and political chaos that consumed the country.

This chapter describes both the climax of twentieth-century liberalism and the forces that led to its decline. It examines such questions as: How did the government draw on the example of the New Deal to help those caught short by the advances of industrial capitalism? How did turmoil then undermine the possibility of aid to the less fortunate members of American society? What efforts did Democratic administrations make to address the major structural changes in the post–World War II economy described in Chapter 25? And how did the Cold War assumptions outlined in Chapter 24 lead to the rifts that ripped the nation apart?

John F. Kennedy: The Camelot Years

The commitment to an American welfare state reached its high-water point in the 1960s. As the left-wing Labour Party in Great Britain played a more and more influential role and occasionally assumed power, and social democratic coalitions were equally active in other European nations, Americans took note. Democrats wanted to follow their example and broaden the role of government even further than Franklin D. Roosevelt and Harry S Truman had done in the 1930s and 1940s, in an effort to address the problems of poverty, unemployment, and racism. John F. Kennedy, a senator from Massachusetts, demanded that the United States move in the direction of what he called a **"New Frontier."**

The Election of 1960

In the 1960 presidential campaign, Kennedy ran against Vice President Richard Nixon, who clearly had more executive experience. Kennedy argued that the government in general, and the president in particular, had to play an even more active role than they had in the Eisenhower years. He charged that the country had become lazy as it reveled in the prosperity of the 1950s. There were, in fact, serious problems that needed to be solved.

Seventy million Americans tuned in to watch the two candidates square off against one another in the first televised presidential debate. Kennedy appeared tanned and rested. Nixon, who had recently been

An Energetic Young Leader John Kennedy's energy and enthusiasm captured the imagination of Americans and people around the world, though few were aware of the physical ailments that affected him. He was fond of using this rocking chair in the White House, which he found comfortable for his ailing back. How did Kennedy's appearance contribute to his popularity and appeal?

hospitalized with an infection, looked tired and gaunt. Even worse, the makeup he applied to hide his heavy beard growth only accentuated it and gave him a swarthy complexion on screen. The debates made a major difference in the campaign (see the "Recovering the Past" section of this chapter). Kennedy himself admitted, "It was TV more than anything else that turned the tide."

Watch the Video
Kennedy-Nixon Debate
at **www.myhistorylab.com**

Kennedy overcame seemingly insuperable odds to become the first Catholic in the White House. Yet his victory was razor-thin. The electoral margin of 303 to 219 concealed the close popular tally, in which he triumphed by fewer than 120,000 of 68 million votes cast. While Kennedy had Democratic majorities in Congress, many members of his party came from the South and were less sympathetic to liberal causes.

JFK

John Kennedy served as a symbol of the early 1960s. He was far younger than his predecessor; at the age of 43, he was the youngest man ever elected to the presidency. He came from an Irish Catholic family from

Massachusetts that saw politics as a means of acceptance in Protestant America. Raised in comfort, he graduated from Harvard University and went on to serve heroically in the navy during World War II. He was elected first to the House of Representatives in 1946, then to the Senate in 1952, and was reelected six years later by the largest majority in the history of the state.

•●•⎡Read the **Document**

John F. Kennedy,
Inaugural Address (1961)
at **www.myhistorylab.com**

The new president had a charismatic public presence. He was able to voice his aims in eloquent yet understandable language that motivated his followers. During the campaign, he pointed to challenges at home and abroad, observing that "the New Frontier is here whether we seek it or not." He made the same point even more movingly in his inaugural address when he declared that "the torch has been passed to a new generation of Americans" and inspired listeners by his ringing call to action: "And so, my fellow Americans: Ask not what your country can do for you—ask what you can do for your country."

For Kennedy, strong leadership was all-important. Viewing himself as "tough-minded" and "hard-nosed," he was determined to provide firm direction, just as Franklin Roosevelt had done. To do so, he surrounded himself with talented assistants. On his staff were 15 Rhodes scholars and several famous authors. The secretary of state was Dean Rusk, a former member of the State Department who had then served as president of the Rockefeller Foundation. The secretary of defense was Robert S. McNamara, the highly successful president of the Ford Motor Company.

Further contributing to Kennedy's attractive image were his glamorous wife, Jacqueline, and the Nobel Prize winners, musicians, and artists they invited to the White House. Energy, exuberance, and excitement filled the air. To many, the administration seemed like the Camelot of King Arthur's day, popularized in a Broadway musical in 1960.

The New Frontier in Action

In office, Kennedy sought to bolster the economy and to enlarge social welfare programs. On the economic front, he tried to end the lingering recession that began in Eisenhower's last year by working with the business community while controlling price inflation.

These two goals conflicted when, in the spring of 1962, the large steel companies decided on a major price increase after steel unions had accepted a modest wage package. The angry president termed the price increases unjustifiable and demanded action to force the steel companies to back down. The large companies capitulated, but they disliked Kennedy's heavy-handed approach and decided that this Democratic administration, like all others, was hostile to business. Six weeks after the steel crisis, the stock market plunged in the greatest drop since the Great Crash of 1929.

It now seemed doubly urgent to end the recession. Earlier a proponent of a balanced budget, Kennedy began to listen to his liberal advisers who proposed a Keynesian approach to economic growth. Budget deficits had promoted prosperity during the Second World War and might work in the same way in peacetime, too. A tax cut could put money in people's pockets, and their spending could stimulate the economy. In early 1963, the president called for a $13.5 billion cut in corporate taxes over the next three years. While that cut would cause a large deficit, it would also provide business capital to revive the economy and ultimately increase tax revenues.

Opposition mounted. Conservatives refused to accept the basic premise that deficits would stimulate economic growth and argued, in Eisenhower's words, that "no family, no business, no nation can spend itself into prosperity." Some liberals claimed that it would be better to stimulate the economy by spending money to improve society rather than by cutting taxes and letting people have the money. Congress pigeonholed the proposal in committee, and there it remained.

On other issues on the liberal agenda, Kennedy met similar resistance. Though he proposed legislation increasing the minimum wage and providing for federal aid for education, medical care for the elderly, housing subsidies, and urban renewal, the results were meager. His new minimum-wage measure passed Congress in pared-down form, but Kennedy did not have the votes in Congress to achieve most of his legislative program.

His inability to win necessary congressional support was most evident in the struggle to aid public education. Soon after taking office, Kennedy proposed a $2.3 billion program of education grants to the states. Immediately, a series of prickly questions emerged: Was it appropriate to spend large sums of money for social goals? Would federal aid bring federal control of school policies and curriculum? Should assistance go to segregated schools? Should it go to parochial schools? In the end, compromise on these issues proved impossible, and the school aid measure died in committee.

Kennedy was more successful in securing funding for the exploration of space. The space program was caught up in the competition of the Cold War, and with the Soviet launching of *Sputnik* and then the first manned space flights, the USSR clearly had the lead. In response, Kennedy proposed that the United States commit itself to landing a man on the moon and returning him to earth before the end of the decade. Congress assented and increased funding of the National Aeronautics and Space Administration (NASA).

View the **Image**
"Buzz" Aldrin on the Moon
at **www.myhistorylab.com**

Kennedy also established the Peace Corps, which sent young men and women overseas to assist developing countries by working with people at a grassroots level. Paul Cowan, introduced at the start of this

RECOVERING *the* PAST

Television

In the past 50 years, television has played an increasingly important part in American life, providing historians with another source of evidence about American culture and society in the recent past.

Television's popularity by the 1950s was the result of decades of experimentation dating back to the nineteenth century. In the 1930s, NBC installed a television station in the new Empire State Building in New York. Wearing green makeup and purple lipstick to provide better visual contrast, actors began to perform before live cameras in studios. At the end of the decade, *Amos 'n' Andy*, a popular radio show, was telecast, and as the 1940s began, Franklin D. Roosevelt became the first president to appear on the new medium. World War II interrupted the development of television, and Americans relied on radio to bring them news. After the war, however, the commercial development of television quickly resumed. Assembly lines that had made electronic implements of war were now converted to consumer production, and thousands of new sets appeared on the market. The opening of Congress could be seen live in 1947; baseball coverage improved that same year owing to the zoom lens; children's shows including *Howdy Doody* made their debut; and *Meet the Press*, a radio interview program, made the transition to television.

Although sports programs, variety shows hosted by Ed Sullivan and Milton Berle, TV dramas, and episodic series (*I Love Lucy* and *Gunsmoke*, for example) dominated TV broadcasting in the 1950s, television soon became entwined with politics and public affairs. Americans saw Senator Joseph McCarthy for themselves in the televised Army–McCarthy hearings in 1954; his heavy-handed behavior on camera contributed to his downfall. The 1948 presidential nominating conventions were the first to be televised, but the use of TV to enhance the public image of politicians was most thoroughly developed by the fatherly Dwight D. Eisenhower and the charismatic John F. Kennedy.

In November 1963, people throughout the United States shared the tragedy of John Kennedy's assassination, sitting stunned before their sets trying to understand the events of his fateful Texas trip. The shock and sorrow of the American people was repeated in the spring of 1968 as they gazed in disbelief at the funerals of Martin Luther King, Jr., and Robert F. Kennedy. A year later, a quarter of the world's population watched as Neil Armstrong became the first man to set foot on the moon. In that same era, television played an important part in shaping impressions of the war in Vietnam. More and more Americans began to understand the nature and impact of the conflict from what they saw on TV.

This combination of visual entertainment and enlightenment made owning a television set virtually a necessity. By 1970, fully 95 percent of American households owned a TV set, a staggering increase from the 9 percent only 20 years earlier. In fact, fewer families owned refrigerators or indoor toilets.

REFLECTING ON THE PAST The implications of the impact of television on American society are of obvious interest to historians. How has television affected other communications and entertainment industries, such as radio, newspapers, and movies? What does the content of TV programming tell us about the values, interests, and tastes of the American people?

Perhaps most significant, what impact has TV had on the course of historical events such as presidential campaigns, human relations, and wars? The pictures shown here are from the Kennedy–Nixon debates in the presidential campaign of 1960. The first picture shows the two candidates in the studio. The second picture shows a relaxed and energetic Kennedy staring directly into the TV camera. The third picture shows a taut and tense Nixon challenging the points made by his opponent. Which candidate seems to be speaking

directly to the American people? Which candidate makes the better impression? Why? Polls of radio listeners taken after the first debate showed Nixon the winner; surveys of television viewers placed Kennedy in front. How do you account for this discrepancy?

John Kennedy (left) and Richard Nixon (right).

The candidates squaring off in their debate.

chapter, was one of thousands of volunteers who hoped to share their liberal dreams.

If Kennedy's successes were modest, he had at least made commitments that could be broadened later. He had reaffirmed the importance of executive leadership in the effort to extend the boundaries of the welfare state. And he had committed himself to using modern economics to maintain fiscal stability. The nation was poised to achieve liberal goals.

Civil Rights and Kennedy's Response

So it was with civil rights. The pressures that had mounted after World War II had brought significant change in eliminating segregation in American society. As the effort continued, a spectrum of organizations carried the fight forward. The NAACP, founded in 1910, remained committed to overturning the legal bases for segregation in the aftermath of its victory in the *Brown* v. *Board of Education* case of 1954 (see Chapter 25). The Congress of Racial Equality (CORE), an interracial group established in 1942, promoted change through peaceful confrontation. In 1957, after their victory in the bus boycott in Montgomery, Alabama, Martin Luther King, Jr., and others formed the Southern Christian Leadership Conference (SCLC), an organization of southern black clergy. Far more militant was the Student Nonviolent Coordinating Committee (SNCC, pronounced "snick"), which began to operate in 1960 and recruited young Americans not previously involved.

Confrontations continued in the 1960s. On January 31, 1960, four black college students in Greensboro, North Carolina, frustrated that they were permitted to shop but not to eat at Woolworth's, a popular department store chain, sat down at the lunch counter and refused to leave. The next day more students showed up, and the following day still more. The sit-ins, which spread to other cities, captured media attention and eventually included as many as 70,000 participants. Those protesting often met with a brutal response.

The following year, sit-ins gave rise to freedom rides, aimed at testing southern transportation facilities that recently had been desegregated by a Supreme Court decision. Organized initially by CORE and aided by SNCC, the program sent groups of blacks and whites together on buses heading south. The riders, peaceful themselves, anticipated confrontations that would publicize their cause and generate political support, and they frequently ended up in jail.

The civil rights movement became the most powerful moral campaign since the abolitionist crusade before the Civil War. Anne Moody, who grew up in a small town in Mississippi, personified the awakening of black consciousness. As a child, she had watched the murder of friends and acquaintances who had somehow transgressed the limits set for blacks. Overcoming the hardships of growing up poor and black in the rural South, Moody became the first member of her family to go to college and later joined the NAACP and became involved in the activities of SNCC and CORE. Participating in sit-ins, where she was thrashed and jailed for her activities, she remained deeply involved in the movement.

Many whites also joined the struggle in the South. Mimi Feingold, a white student at Swarthmore College in Pennsylvania, helped picket the Woolworth's there. After her sophomore year, she headed south to join the freedom rides sponsored by CORE. Like many others, Feingold found herself in the midst of often violent confrontations and went to jail as an act of conscience.

In 1962, the civil rights movement accelerated. James Meredith, a black air force veteran, applied to the all-white University of Mississippi, only to be rejected on racial grounds. Although the Supreme Court affirmed his right to attend, Governor Ross Barnett, an adamant racist, announced defiantly that Meredith would not be admitted and on one occasion personally blocked the way. A major riot followed; tear gas covered the university grounds; and by the riot's end, two men lay dead and hundreds were hurt.

Other governors were equally aggressive. In his 1963 inaugural address, George C. Wallace of Alabama declared boldly, "Segregation now! Segregation tomorrow! Segregation forever!" as he voiced his opposition to integration.

Alabama became a national focus that year as a violent confrontation unfolded in Birmingham. Though the demonstrations against segregation were nonviolent, the responses were not. City officials declared that protest marches violated city regulations against parading without a license, and, over a five-week period, they arrested 2,200 blacks, some of them school-children. Police Commissioner Eugene "Bull" Connor used high-pressure fire hoses, electric cattle prods, and

◉ Watch the Video
Photographing the Civil Rights Movement: Birmingham, 1963
at **www.myhistorylab.com**

trained police dogs to force the protesters back. As the media recorded the events, Americans watching television and reading newspapers were horrified.

Kennedy claimed to be sickened by the pictures from Birmingham but insisted that he could do nothing, even though he had sought and won black support in 1960. The narrowness of his electoral victory made him reluctant to press white southerners on civil rights when he needed their votes on other issues. Events finally forced Kennedy to act more boldly. In the James Meredith confrontation, the president, like his predecessor in the Little Rock crisis, had to send federal troops to restore control and to guarantee Meredith's right to attend the university. The administration also forced the desegregation of the University of Alabama and helped arrange a compromise that eased discrimination in Birmingham's municipal facilities and hiring practices. And when white bombings aimed at eliminating black leaders in Birmingham caused thousands of blacks to abandon nonviolence and rampage through the streets, Kennedy readied federal troops to intervene.

He also spoke out more forcefully than before. In a nationally televised address, he called the quest for equal rights a "moral issue" and asked, "Are we to say to the world, and, much more importantly, to each other, that this is a land of the free except for the Negroes?" Just hours after the president spoke, assassins killed Medgar Evers, a black NAACP official, in his own driveway in Jackson, Mississippi.

Kennedy sent Congress a new and stronger civil rights bill, outlawing segregation in public places, banning discrimination wherever federal money was involved, and advancing the process of school integration. Polls showed that 63 percent of the nation supported his stand.

*•◦—*Read the Document

John Lewis, Address at the
March on Washington (1963)
at **www.myhistorylab.com**

To lobby for passage of this measure, civil rights leaders, pressed from below by black activists, arranged a massive **March on Washington** in August 1963. More than 200,000 people—black and white, common folk and celebrities—gathered from across the country.

The high point of the day was the address by Martin Luther King, Jr., who by now was the nation's preeminent spokesman for civil rights and

Sitting In In violation of southern law, black college students refused to leave a lunch counter, launching a new campaign in the struggle for civil rights. Here the students wait patiently for service, or forcible eviction, as a way of dramatizing their determination to end segregation. What did the students hope to achieve by their actions?

proponent of nonviolent protest. King proclaimed his faith in the decency of his fellow citizens and in their ability to extend the promises of the Constitution and the Declaration of Independence to every American. With all the power of a southern preacher, he implored his audience to share his faith.

"I have a dream," King declared, "that one day this nation will rise up and live out the true meaning of its creed: 'We hold these truths to be self-evident, that all men are created equal.' I have a dream that one day on the red hills of Georgia, the sons of former slaves and the sons of former slaveowners will be able to sit together at the table of brotherhood." Each time King used the refrain "I have a dream," thousands of blacks and whites roared together. King concluded by quoting from an old hymn: "Free at last! Free at last! Thank God almighty, we are free at last!"

Not all were moved. Despite large Democratic majorities, strong white southern resistance to the cause of civil rights continued in Congress, and the bill was bottled up in committee.

Lyndon B. Johnson and the Great Society

Kennedy knew he faced a difficult reelection battle in 1964. He wanted not only to win the presidency for a second term but also to increase liberal Democratic strength in Congress. Instead, an assassin's attack took his life and brought a new leader to the helm.

Change of Command

In November 1963, Kennedy traveled to Texas, where he hoped to unite the state's Democratic party for the upcoming election. Dallas, one of the stops on the trip, was reputed to be hostile to the administration. Entering the city in an open car, the president encountered friendly crowds. Suddenly shots rang out, and Kennedy slumped forward as bullets ripped through his head and throat. Mortally wounded, he died a short time later at a Dallas hospital. Lee Harvey Oswald, the accused assassin, was shot and killed a few days later by a minor underworld figure as he was being moved within the jail.

Americans were stunned. For days, people stayed at home and watched endless television replays of the assassination and its aftermath. The images of the handsome president felled by bullets, the funeral cortege, and the president's young son saluting his father's casket as it rolled by on the way to final burial at Arlington National Cemetery were all imprinted on people's minds.

Vice President Lyndon Johnson succeeded Kennedy as president. Though less polished, Johnson was a more effective political leader than Kennedy and brought his own special skills and vision to the presidency.

LBJ

Johnson had taken a different road to the White House and came from a far more humble background than Kennedy. He had begun his public career as a legislative assistant in the House of Representatives in Washington, D.C., then served as a New Deal official in Texas. He won election first to the House in 1937 and then to the Senate in 1948. Eager to be president, he accepted the vice presidential nomination when it became clear in 1960 that Kennedy was going to win the nomination for president.

Johnson was a man of elemental force. Always manipulative, he was often difficult to like. There was a streak of vulgarity that contributed to his earthy appeal but was offensive to many. Those qualities notwithstanding, he was successful in the passion of his life—politics—and was the most able legislator of the postwar years. As Senate majority leader, he became famous for knowing the strengths and weaknesses of everyone he faced and for his ability to get things done. He could flatter and cajole in what came to be called the "Johnson treatment." According to columnists Rowland Evans, Jr., and Robert Novak, he zeroed in, "his face a scant millimeter from his target, his eyes widening and narrowing, his eyebrows rising and falling." He grabbed people by the lapels, made them listen, and usually got his way.

As vice president, Johnson went into a state of eclipse. He felt useless and stifled in his new role without his power base in the Senate and felt uncomfortable with the Kennedy crowd.

Despite his own ambivalence about Kennedy, Johnson sensed the profound shock that gripped the United States after the assassination and was determined to utilize Kennedy's memory to achieve legislative success. Even more than Kennedy, he was willing to wield presidential power aggressively and to use the media to shape public opinion in pursuit of his vision of a society in which the comforts of life would be more widely shared and poverty would be eliminated.

The Great Society in Action

Lyndon Johnson had an expansive vision of the possibilities of reform. Using his considerable political skills, he succeeded in pushing through Congress the most extensive reform program in American history.

Johnson began to develop the support he needed the day he took office. In his first public address, delivered to Congress and televised nationwide, he sought to dispel the image of impostor as he embraced Kennedy's liberal

Lyndon Johnson in Action Lyndon Johnson kept tight control of the Senate in the 1950s and was known for his ability to get his way. Here he is shown giving the famous "Johnson treatment" to Senator Theodore Francis Green in 1957. Note the way Green is bending backward in an unsuccessful effort to keep his distance from LBJ. Why do you think LBJ usually got his way?

program. He began, in a measured tone, with the words, "All I have, I would have given gladly not to be standing here today." He asked members of Congress to work with him, and he underscored the theme "Let us continue."

As a first step, Johnson resolved to secure the measures Kennedy had been unable to extract from Congress. Bills to reduce taxes and ensure civil rights were his first and most pressing priorities, but he was interested too in aiding public education, providing medical care for the aged, and eliminating poverty. By the spring of 1964, he began to use the phrase "Great Society" to describe his expansive reform program.

Johnson's landslide victory over conservative Republican challenger Barry Goldwater in the election of 1964 validated his approach. This was the first time in recent history that a conservative had gained the Republican nomination. Goldwater, however, frightened even members of his own party by proclaiming that "extremism in the defense of liberty is no vice," and by speaking out against such popular programs as social security. LBJ received 61 percent of the popular vote and an electoral tally of 486 to 52 and gained Democratic majorities in both the Senate and the House. Goldwater's candidacy drove moderate Republicans to vote for the Democratic party and gave Johnson a far more impressive mandate than Kennedy had ever enjoyed.

Civil rights reform was LBJ's first legislative priority and an integral part of the Great Society program, but other measures were equally important. Following Kennedy's lead, Johnson pressed for a tax cut. He accepted the Keynesian theory that deficits, properly managed, could promote prosperity. If people had more money to spend, then their purchases could stimulate the economy. Soon the tax bill passed.

With the tax cut in hand, the president pressed for the antipoverty program that Kennedy had begun to plan. Such an effort was bold and unprecedented in the United States, even though social democracy had a long history in European nations and other countries around the world. During the Progressive era and the New Deal, programs had sought to assist those Americans who could not help themselves. Now Johnson took a step that no president had taken before; in his 1964 State of the Union message, he declared an "unconditional war on poverty in America."

The centerpiece of this utopian effort to eradicate poverty was the **Economic Opportunity Act** of 1964. It created an Office of Economic Opportunity (OEO) to provide education and training through programs such as the Job Corps for unskilled young people trapped in the poverty cycle. VISTA (Volunteers in Service to America), patterned after the Peace Corps, offered assistance to the poor at home, while Head Start tried to give disadvantaged children a chance to succeed in school. Assorted community action programs gave the poor a voice in improving housing, health, and education. Two agencies responded to Native American pressure by allowing Indians to devise programs and budgets and administer the programs.

Aware of the escalating costs of medical care, Johnson also proposed a medical assistance plan. Both Truman and Kennedy had supported such an initiative but had failed to win congressional approval. Johnson succeeded. To head off conservative attacks, the administration limited the **Medicare**

Roots of Selected Great Society Programs

Progressive Period	New Deal	Great Society
Settlement house activity of Jane Addams and others	Relief efforts to ease unemployment (FERA, WPA)	Poverty programs (OEO)
Efforts to clean up slums (tenement house laws)	Housing program	Rehabilitation of slums through Model Cities program
Progressive party platform calling for federal accident, old-age, and unemployment insurance	Social security system providing unemployment compensation and old-age pensions	Medical care for the aged through social security (Medicare)
Activity to break up monopolies and regulate business	Regulation of utility companies	Regulation of highway safety and transportation
Efforts to regulate working conditions and benefits	Establishment of standards for working conditions and minimum wage	Raising of minimum wage
Efforts to increase literacy and spread education at all levels	Efforts to keep college students in school through National Youth Administration	Assistance to elementary, secondary, and higher education
Theodore Roosevelt's efforts at wilderness preservation	Conservation efforts (CCC, TVA planning)	Safeguarding of wilderness lands
Establishment of federal income tax	Tax reform to close loopholes and increase taxes for the wealthy	Tax cut to stimulate business activity
Theodore Roosevelt's overtures to Booker T. Washington	Discussion (but not passage) of antilynching legislation	Civil rights measures to ban discrimination in public accommodations and to guarantee right to vote

measure to the elderly. The complementary Medicaid program met the needs of those on welfare and certain other groups who could not afford private insurance. The Medicare–Medicaid initiative was the most important extension of federally directed social benefits since the Social Security Act of 1935.

Johnson was similarly successful in his effort to provide aid for elementary and secondary schools. His legislation allocated education money to the states based on the number of children from low-income families. Those funds would then be distributed to assist deprived children in public as well as private schools.

In LBJ's expansive vision, the federal government would ensure that everyone shared in the promise of American life. Under his prodding, Congress passed a new housing act to give rent supplements to the poor and created a Cabinet Department of Housing and Urban Development. The federal government provided new forms of aid, such as legal assistance for the poor, and provided additional funds for higher education. Congress also provided artists and scholars with assistance through the National Endowments for the Arts and Humanities, created in 1965.

At the same time, Johnson's administration provided much-needed immigration reform. The Immigration Act of 1965 replaced the restrictive policy in place since 1924 with a measure that vastly increased the ceiling on immigration and opened the door to immigrants and refugees from Asia and Latin America. By the late 1960s, some 350,000 immigrants were entering the United States annually, compared to the average of 47,000 per year between 1931 and 1945. This new stream of immigration created a population more diverse than it had been since the early decades of the twentieth century.

The Great Society also reflected the stirring of the environmental movement. In 1962, naturalist Rachel Carson alerted the public to the dangers of pesticide poisoning and environmental pollution in her book *Silent Spring*. She took aim at chemical pesticides, especially DDT, which had increased crop yields but had brought disastrous side effects.

Johnson was determined to address such problems and to provide protection for wildlife. The National Wilderness Preservation Act of 1964 set aside 9.1 million acres of wilderness, and Congress passed other measures to limit air and water pollution. In addition, Lady Bird Johnson, the president's wife, led a beautification campaign to eliminate unsightly billboards and junkyards along the nation's highways.

Achievements and Challenges in Civil Rights

Lyndon Johnson was enormously successful in advancing the cause of civil rights. Seizing the opportunity provided by Kennedy's assassination,

Watch the Video

Civil Rights Movement

at **www.myhistorylab.com**

Johnson pushed new civil rights bills through Congress as a memorial to Kennedy. The Civil Rights Act of 1964 outlawed racial discrimination in all public accommodations and authorized the Justice Department to act with greater authority in school and voting matters. In addition, an equal-opportunity provision prohibited discriminatory hiring on grounds of race, gender, religion, or national origin in firms with more than 25 employees.

Although the law was one of the great achievements of the 1960s, widespread discrimination still existed in American society, and African Americans in large areas of the South still found it difficult to vote. Freedom Summer, sponsored by SNCC and other civil rights groups in 1964, focused attention on the problem by sending black and white students to

Mississippi to work for black rights. Early in the summer, two whites, Michael Schwerner and Andrew Goodman, and one black, James Chaney, were murdered. By the end of the summer, 80 workers had been beaten, 1,000 arrests had been made, and 37 churches had been bombed. In the face of such resistance, Johnson asked Congress for a voting bill that would close the loopholes of the previous two acts.

The Voting Rights Act of 1965, perhaps the most important law of the decade, singled out the South for its restrictive practices and authorized the U.S. attorney general to appoint federal examiners to register voters where local officials were obstructing the registration of blacks. In the year after passage of the act, 400,000 blacks registered to vote in the Deep South; by 1968, the number reached 1 million.

👁 See the **Map**
Impact of the Voting Rights Act of 1965
at **www.myhistorylab.com**

Despite passage of the Civil Rights Act of 1964 and the Voting Rights Act of 1965, racial discrimination remained throughout the country. Still-segregated schools, wretched housing, and inadequate job opportunities were continuing problems. As the struggle for civil rights moved north, dramatic divisions within the movement emerged.

Read the **Document**
Voting Literacy Test (1965)
at **www.myhistorylab.com**

Initially, the civil rights campaign had been integrated and nonviolent. Its acknowledged leader was Martin Luther King, Jr. But now tensions between blacks and whites flared within organizations, and younger black leaders began to challenge King's nonviolent approach. They were tired of beatings, jailings, church bombings, and the slow pace of change when dependent on white liberal support and government action.

One episode that contributed to many blacks' suspicion of white liberals occurred at the Democratic national convention of 1964 in Atlantic City. SNCC, active in the Freedom Summer project in Mississippi, had founded the Freedom Democratic party as an alternative to the all-white delegation that was to represent the state. Testifying before the credentials committee, black activist Fannie Lou Hamer reported that she had been beaten, jailed, and denied the right to vote. Yet the committee's final compromise, pressed by President Johnson, who worried about losing southern support in the coming election, was that the white delegation would still be seated, with two members of the protest organization offered seats at large. That response hardly satisfied those who had risked their lives and families to try to vote in Mississippi. SNCC, once a religious, integrated organization, began to change into an all-black cadre that could mobilize poor blacks for militant action.

Malcolm X was perhaps the leader most responsible for channeling black frustration into a new set of goals and tactics. Born Malcolm Little and reared in northern ghettos, he hustled gambling numbers and prostitutes in the big cities before becoming a convert to the Nation of Islam. Malcolm was impatient with the moderate civil rights movement.

Watch the **Video**
Malcolm X
at **www.myhistorylab.com**

Malcolm X at the Lectern
"The day of nonviolence is over," Malcolm X proclaimed, as many African Americans listened enthusiastically. A compelling speaker, Malcolm made a powerful case for a more aggressive campaign for black rights. What image does Malcolm X convey in this photograph?

He grew tired of hearing "all of this nonviolent, begging-the-white-man kind of dying . . . all of this sitting-in, sliding-in, wading-in, eating-in, diving-in, and all the rest." Espousing black separatism and black nationalism for most of his public career, he preached an international perspective embracing African peoples in diaspora, and appealed to blacks to fight racism "by any means necessary." Though Malcolm was assassinated by black antagonists in 1965, his African-centered, uncompromising perspective helped shape the struggle against racism.

One man influenced by Malcolm's message was Stokely Carmichael. Born in Trinidad, Carmichael came to the United States at the age of 11, where he grew up with an interest in political affairs and black protest. Frustrated with the strategy of civil disobedience as he became active in SNCC, he urged fieldworkers to carry weapons for self-defense. It was time for blacks to cease depending on whites, he argued, and to make SNCC into a black organization. His election as head of the student group reflected SNCC's growing radicalism.

The split in the black movement was dramatized in June 1966 when Carmichael's followers challenged those of Martin Luther King, Jr., during a march in Mississippi. King still adhered to nonviolence and interracial cooperation. Just out of jail after being arrested for his protest activities, Carmichael jumped onto a flatbed truck to address the group. "This is the twenty-seventh time I have been arrested—and I ain't going to jail no more!" he shouted. "The only way we gonna stop them white men from whippin' us is to take over. We been saying freedom for six years and we ain't got nothing. What we gonna start saying now is Black Power!" Carmichael had the audience in his hand as he repeated, and the crowd shouted back, "We . . . want . . . Black . . . Power!"

Black Power was a call to build independent institutions in the African American community, and it fostered a powerful sense of black pride. The movement included a wide variety of different figures ranging from cultural nationalists to revolutionaries to advocates of black capitalism. Its most enduring legacy was political and cultural mobilization at the grassroots level, even if it only partially realized its goals.

Black Power led to demands for more drastic action. The Black Panthers, radical activists who organized first in Oakland, California, and then in other cities, formed a militant organization that vowed to eradicate not only racial discrimination but capitalism as well. H. Rap Brown, who succeeded Carmichael as head of SNCC, became known for his statement that "violence is as American as cherry pie."

Violence accompanied the more militant calls for reform and showed that racial injustice was not a southern problem but an American one. Riots erupted in New York City and several other eastern cities in 1964. In 1965, in the Watts neighborhood of Los Angeles, a massive uprising lasting five days left 34 dead, more than 1,000 injured, and hundreds of structures burned to the ground. Violence broke out again in other cities in 1966, 1967, and 1968.

A Sympathetic Supreme Court

With the addition of liberal justices appointed by Kennedy and Johnson, the Supreme Court supported the liberal agenda. Under the leadership of Chief Justice Earl Warren, the Court followed the lead it had taken in *Brown* v. *Board of Education*, outlawing school segregation by moving against Jim Crow practices in other public establishments.

The Court also supported civil liberties by beginning to protect the rights of individuals with radical political views. Similarly, the Court sought to protect accused suspects from police harassment and to provide poor defendants with free legal counsel. In *Escobedo* v. *Illinois* (1964), it ruled that a suspect had to be given access to an attorney during questioning. In *Miranda* v. *Arizona* (1966), it argued that offenders had to be warned that statements extracted by the police could be used against them and that they could remain silent.

Other decisions similarly broke new ground. *Baker* v. *Carr* (1962) opened the way to reapportionment of state legislative bodies according to the standard, defined a year later in Justice William O. Douglas's words, of "one person, one vote." This crucial ruling helped break the political control of lightly populated rural districts in many state assemblies and similarly made the U.S. House of Representatives much more responsive to urban and suburban issues. Meanwhile, the Court outraged conservatives by ruling that prayer could not be required in the public schools and that obscenity laws could no longer restrict allegedly pornographic material that might have some "redeeming social value."

The Great Society Under Attack

Supported by healthy economic growth, the Great Society worked for a few years as Johnson had hoped. The tax cut proved effective, and the consumer and business spending that it promoted led to a steady increase in gross national product. As the economy improved, the budget deficit dropped just as predicted. Unemployment fell, and inflation remained under control. Medical programs provided basic security for the old and the poor. Education flourished as schools were built, and teachers' salaries increased as a result of federal aid.

Yet Johnson's dream of the Great Society proved illusory. Some programs promised too much; others were simply ill-conceived or were underfunded. Factionalism was also a problem. Lyndon Johnson had reconstituted the old Democratic coalition in his triumph in 1964, with urban Catholics and southern whites joining organized labor, the black electorate, and the middle class. But conservative white southerners and blue-collar white northerners felt threatened by the government's support of civil rights. Local urban bosses, long the backbone of the Democratic party, objected to grassroots participation of the urban poor, which threatened their own political control.

Criticisms of the Great Society and its liberal underpinnings came from across the political spectrum. Conservatives disliked the centralization of authority and the government's increased role in defining the

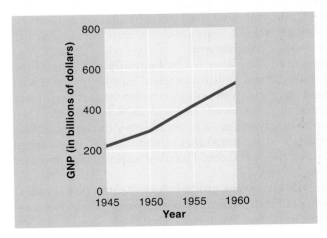

Increase in GNP, 1945–1960 The gross national product (GNP) rose steadily in the decade and a half after World War II as the United States enjoyed an unprecedented period of prosperity. *(National Income and Product Accounts, 1929–1994)*

national welfare. Even middle-class Americans, generally supportive of liberal goals, sometimes grumbled that the government was paying too much attention to the underprivileged and neglecting their own needs. Radicals, meanwhile, attacked the Great Society for not going far enough. With its assumption that the American system was basically sound, they argued, the Great Society made no real effort to redistribute income and thereby transform American life.

The Vietnam War (discussed later in this chapter) dealt the Great Society a fatal blow. LBJ wanted to maintain both the war and his treasured domestic reform programs, but his effort to pursue these goals simultaneously produced serious inflation. The economy was already booming as a result of the tax cut and the spending for reform. As military expenditures increased, the productive system of the country could not keep up with demand. When, in an effort to hide the costs of the war, Johnson refused to raise taxes, inflation spiraled out of control. Congress finally slashed Great Society programs, deciding it could no longer afford such extensive social reform.

Continuing Confrontations with Communists

The Cold War continued throughout the 1960s. Presidents Kennedy and Johnson were both aggressive cold warriors who subscribed to the policies of their predecessors. Their commitment to stopping the spread of communism kept the nation locked in the same bitter conflict that had dominated foreign policy in the 1950s and led to continuing global confrontations that sometimes threatened the stability of the entire world.

The Bay of Pigs Fiasco and Its Consequences

Kennedy was intensely interested in foreign affairs. In his ringing inaugural address, he eloquently described the dangers and challenges the United States faced in the Cold War. "In the long history of the world," he cried out, "only a few generations have been granted the role of defending freedom in its hour of maximum danger." The United States would "pay any price, bear any burden, meet any hardship, support any friend, oppose any foe, to assure the survival and success of liberty."

Kennedy perceived direct challenges from the Soviet Union almost from the beginning of his presidency. The first came at the **Bay of Pigs** in Cuba in the spring of 1961. Cuban–American relations had been strained since Fidel Castro's revolutionary army had seized power in 1959. A radical regime in Cuba, leaning toward the Soviet Union, could provide a model for upheaval elsewhere in Latin America and threaten the venerable Monroe Doctrine. One initiative to counter the Communist threat was the

Alliance for Progress, which provided social and economic assistance to the less-developed nations of the hemisphere. But other, more aggressive, responses seemed necessary as well.

Just before Kennedy assumed office, the United States broke diplomatic relations with Cuba. The CIA, meanwhile, was covertly training anti-Castro exiles to storm the Cuban coast at the Bay of Pigs. The American planners assumed the invasion would lead to an uprising of the Cuban people against Castro. While some top officials resisted the scheme, Kennedy approved the plan.

The invasion, which took place on April 17, 1961, was an unmitigated disaster. When an early air strike failed to destroy Cuban air power, Castro was able to hold off the troops coming ashore. Urged to use American planes for air cover, Kennedy refused, for by that time failure was clear. The United States stood exposed to the world in its attempt to overthrow a sovereign government. It had broken agreements not to interfere in the internal affairs of hemispheric neighbors and had intervened clumsily and unsuccessfully.

Although chastened by the debacle at the Bay of Pigs, Kennedy was determined to counter the perceived Communist threat. Germany became the next battleground. For more than a decade, the nation had been divided (see Chapter 24). The Western powers had promoted the industrial development of West Germany, which was prospering and which stood in stark contrast to the drab, Soviet-controlled East Germany. Berlin, likewise divided, remained an irritant to the Russians, particularly since some 2.6 million East Germans had fled to West Germany, often through the city. Following a hostile meeting with Soviet leader Nikita Khrushchev in Vienna in June 1961, Kennedy reacted aggressively. He asked Congress for $3 billion more in defense appropriations, as well as for funds for a civil defense fallout-shelter program, explicitly warning of the threat of nuclear war. The USSR responded in August by erecting a wall in Berlin to seal off its section entirely. The concrete structure, topped by barbed wire, was 96 miles long and an average of 11.8 feet high. Menacing machine-gun emplacements made escape difficult. People who were caught scaling the wall were shot. The wall became a dramatic symbol of the division between East and West.

The Cuban Missile Face-Off

The next year, a new crisis arose. American aerial photographs taken in October 1962 revealed that the USSR had begun to place what Kennedy considered offensive missiles on Cuban soil, although Cuba insisted they were defensive. This time Kennedy was determined to win a confrontation with the Soviet Union.

Top administration officials examined various alternatives. Some members of the Executive Committee of the National Security Council wanted

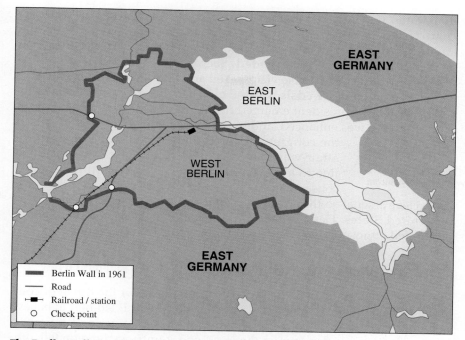

▬▬	Berlin Wall in 1961
───	Road
▬■▬	Railroad / station
○	Check point

The Berlin Wall The Berlin Wall effectively sealed West Berlin off both from the eastern sector of the city and from East Germany itself. Now people could only enter and exit West Berlin through a number of carefully monitored checkpoints. Why was it so important for East Germany to prevent people from going into West Berlin? Why would people in West Berlin have wanted to go into East Berlin? How effective do you think such a wall might be in keeping people in or out?

an air strike to knock out the sites; others, including Attorney General Robert F. Kennedy, the president's brother, opposed such a move. Still, the United States moved to a state of full alert. Bombers and missiles were armed with nuclear weapons and readied to go. The fleet prepared to move toward Cuba, and troops geared up to invade the island.

Kennedy went on nationwide television to tell the American people about the missiles and to demand their removal. He declared that the United States would not shrink from the risk of nuclear war and announced he had decided to impose a naval "quarantine"—not a blockade, which would have been an act of war—around Cuba to prevent Soviet ships from bringing in additional missiles.

As Soviet ships steamed toward the blockade, the nations stood "eyeball to eyeball" at the brink. Before they reached the quarantine line, Khrushchev called the Soviet ships back. He then sent a long letter by teletype, pledging to remove the missiles if the United States lifted the quarantine and promised to stay out of Cuba altogether. A second letter demanded that America remove its missiles from Turkey as well. The United States agreed to the first letter, ignored the second, and said nothing about its intention, already voiced, of removing its own missiles from Turkey. With that, the crisis ended. Secretary of State Rusk observed, "We have won a considerable victory. You and I are still alive."

The **Cuban missile crisis** was the most terrifying confrontation of the Cold War. Yet the president emerged from it as a hero who had stood firm. His reputation was enhanced, and his party benefited a few weeks later in the congressional elections. One consequence of the affair was the installation of a Soviet–American hot-line to avoid similar episodes in the future. Another consequence was the USSR's determination to increase its nuclear arsenal so that it would never again be exposed as inferior to the United States. Despite the Limited Test Ban Treaty of 1963, which prohibited atmospheric testing, the nuclear arms race continued.

Read the Document

Test Ban Treaty
at **www.myhistorylab.com**

Confrontation and Containment Under Johnson

Johnson shared many of Kennedy's assumptions about the threat of communism. His understanding of the onset of World War II led him to believe that aggressors had to be stopped cold. Like Eisenhower and Kennedy, Johnson believed in the domino theory: if one country in a region fell, others were bound to follow. He assumed he could treat foreign adversaries just as he treated political opponents in the United States, and in 1965, he dispatched over 20,000 troops to the Dominican Republic to counter "Castro-type elements" that were actually engaged in a democratic revolution. Johnson's credibility suffered badly from the episode.

In the Middle East, the United States sought to use its influence to temper the violence that erupted in the area. In 1967, Israeli forces defeated the Egyptian army in the Six-Day War and seized the West Bank and Jerusalem, the Golan Heights, and the Sinai Peninsula. Americans pressed for a quick end to the fighting to maintain regional equilibrium and uninterrupted supplies of oil.

War in Vietnam and Turmoil at Home

The commitment to stopping the spread of communism led to the massive U.S. involvement in Vietnam. The roots of the conflict, described in Chapter 24, extended back to the early post–World War II years, but American participation remained relatively limited until Kennedy took office. Then the United States became increasingly engaged in a major effort to resist a Communist takeover. That struggle wrought enormous damage in Southeast Asia, tore the United States apart, and finally forced a full-fledged reevaluation of America's Cold War policies.

Escalation in Vietnam

President Kennedy's commitment to Cold War victory led him to expand the American role in Vietnam. During the Kennedy administration, the number of advisers rose from 675 to more than 16,000, and American soldiers began to lose their lives.

Despite American backing, South Vietnamese leader Ngo Dinh Diem, a Catholic, was rapidly losing support in his own country. Buddhist priests burned themselves alive in the capital of Saigon to protest the corruption and rigidity of Diem's regime. With American approval, South Vietnamese military leaders assassinated Diem and seized the government. While Kennedy understood the importance of popular support for the South Vietnamese government, he was reluctant to withdraw and let the Vietnamese solve their own problems.

Lyndon Johnson shared the same reservations. Soon after assuming the presidency, he made a fundamental decision that guided policy for the next four years. Guerrillas, known as Viet Cong, challenged the regime, sometimes covertly and sometimes through the National Liberation Front, their political arm. Aided by Ho Chi Minh and the North Vietnamese, the insurgent Viet Cong slowly gained ground. Johnson chose to stand firm. "I am not going to lose Vietnam," he said. "I am not going to be the president who saw Southeast Asia go the way China went."

In the election campaign of 1964, Johnson posed as a man of peace. "We don't want our American boys to do the fighting for Asian boys," he declared. But secretly he was planning to escalate the American role.

In August 1964, Johnson charged that North Vietnamese torpedo boats had made unprovoked attacks on American destroyers in the international waters of the Gulf of Tonkin, 30 miles from North Vietnam. While there had been initial conflict, in fact the attacks Johnson highlighted never occurred. But before the real nature of the engagement became clear, LBJ used the episode to obtain from Congress a resolution giving him authority to "take all necessary measures to repel any armed attack against the forces of the United States and to prevent further aggression." The **Gulf of Tonkin Resolution** provided all the leverage he sought.

●●●―Read the Document

Lyndon Johnson, The Tonkin Gulf Resolution Message (1964)

at **www.myhistorylab.com**

Military escalation began in earnest in February 1965, after Johnson's landslide electoral victory. When Viet Cong forces killed seven Americans in an attack on an American base, Johnson responded by authorizing retaliatory bombing of North Vietnam to cut off the flow of supplies and to ease pressure on South Vietnam. A few months later, he sent American ground troops into action. This marked the crucial turning point in the Americanization of the Vietnam War. Only 25,000 American soldiers were in Vietnam at the start of 1965; by the end of the year, there were 184,000. The number swelled to 385,000 in 1966, to 485,000 in 1967, and to 543,000 in 1968.

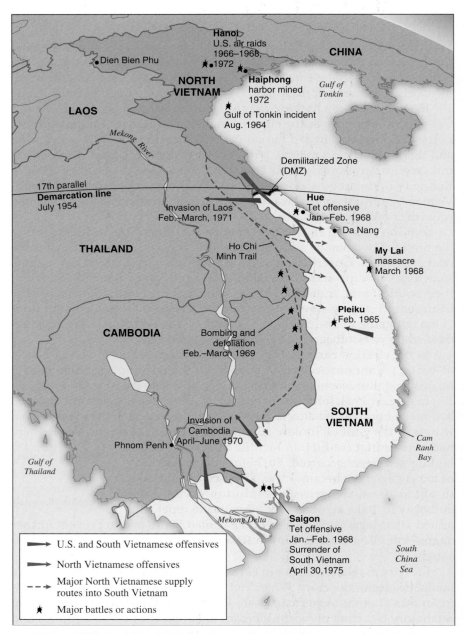

The Vietnam War This map shows the major campaigns of the Vietnam War. The North Vietnamese Tet offensive of early 1968, pictured with red arrows, turned the tide against U.S. participation in the war and led to peace talks. The U.S. invasion of Cambodia in 1970, pictured with blue arrows, provoked serious opposition. What role did North Vietnam play in the war? How far did American air power penetrate? Why did the United States and South Vietnam attack neighboring nations, such as Cambodia?

As escalation occurred, Johnson recognized his dilemma. He understood that the war was probably unwinnable, but he feared the loss of both American power and personal prestige if he pulled out.

View the Image
President Lyndon Johnson in Vietnam (1966)
at **www.myhistorylab.com**

And so American forces became direct participants in the fight to prop up a dictatorial regime in faraway South Vietnam. Although a somewhat more effective government headed by Nguyen Van Thieu and Nguyen Cao Ky was finally established, the level of violence increased. Saturation bombing of North Vietnam continued. Fragmentation bombs, killing and maiming countless civilians, and napalm, which seared off human flesh, were used extensively. Similar destruction wracked South Vietnam. And still, despite the repeatedly expressed contention of military commander William Westmoreland that there was "light at the end of the tunnel," the violence continued without pause.

Student Activism and Antiwar Protest

Americans began to protest U.S. involvement in the war. Members of the baby boom generation who came of age in the 1960s were in the forefront of the struggle. By the end of the 1960s, college enrollment was more than four times what it had been in the 1940s. College provided necessary training but also gave students time to experiment and grow before they had to make a living. Some students joined the struggle for civil rights. Hopeful at first, they gradually became discouraged by the gap between Kennedy's New Frontier rhetoric and the government's actual commitment.

Out of that disillusionment arose the radical spirit of the New Left. Civil rights activists were among those who in 1960 organized Students for a Democratic Society (SDS). In 1962, SDS issued a manifesto, the Port Huron Statement, written largely by Tom Hayden of the University of Michigan, which outlined both complaints and goals for a participatory democracy. "We are people of this generation, bred in at least modest comfort, housed now in universities, looking uncomfortably at the world we inherit," it began. It went on to deplore the vast social and economic distances separating people from each other and to condemn the estrangement of modern life.

The first blow of the growing student rebellion came at the University of California at Berkeley in 1964. There, civil rights activists became involved in a confrontation soon known as the Free Speech Movement. When the university refused to allow students, many of them civil rights activists, to distribute protest material outside the main campus gate, they surrounded a police car and kept it from moving all night. The university regents brought charges against the student leaders, and when the regents refused to drop the charges, the students occupied the administration building. Police stormed in and arrested the students. A strike, with faculty aid, mobilized wider support for the right to free speech.

The Free Speech Movement at Berkeley was basically a plea for traditional liberal reform. Students sought only the reaffirmation of the long-standing right to express themselves as they chose. Later, in other institutions, the attack broadened. Students wanted greater involvement in university affairs, argued for curricular reform, and demanded admission of more minority students.

The mounting protest against the escalation of the Vietnam War fueled and refocused the youth movement. The first antiwar teach-in took place in March 1965 at the University of Michigan. Others soon followed. Initially, both supporters and opponents of the war appeared at the teach-ins, but quickly the sessions became more like antiwar rallies than instructional affairs. Boxer Muhammad Ali legitimated draft resistance when he declared, "I ain't got no quarrel with them Viet Cong" and refused military induction on religious grounds. Working through SDS and other organizations, radical activists campaigned against the draft, attacked ROTC units on campus, and sought to discredit firms that produced the destructive tools of war. "Make love, not war," students proclaimed. As the antiwar movement expanded, students became even more shrill. "Hey, hey, LBJ. How many kids did you kill today?" they chanted as they marched in protest.

Working-class and middle-class Americans began to sour on the war at the time of the **Tet offensive**, celebrating the lunar new year, in early 1968. The North Vietnamese mounted massive attacks across South Vietnam. In Saigon, they struck the American embassy, Tan Son Nhut air base, and the presidential palace. Though beaten back, they won a psychological victory. American audiences saw images of burning huts and wounded soldiers each evening on television as they ate dinner. Gazing at such graphic representations of death and destruction, many Americans wondered about their nation's purposes and actions.

Protest became a way of life. Between January 1 and June 15, 1968, hundreds of thousands of students staged 221 major demonstrations at more than 100 educational institutions. One of the most dramatic episodes came in April 1968 at Columbia University, where the issues of civil rights and war were tightly intertwined. A strong SDS chapter urged the university to break ties with the Institute of Defense Analysis, which specialized in military research. The Students' Afro-American Society tried to stop the building of a new gymnasium, which it claimed encroached on the Harlem community and disrupted life there. Whites occupied one building, blacks another. Finally, the president of the university called in the police. Hundreds of students were arrested; many were hurt. A student sympathy strike followed, and Columbia closed for the summer several weeks early.

The student protests in the United States were part of a worldwide wave of student activism. French students demonstrated in the streets of Paris. In Germany, young radicals were equally vocal in challenging conventional norms. In Japan, students waged armed battles with police.

The Counterculture

Cultural change accompanied political upheaval. Many Americans—some politically active, some not—found new ways to assert their individuality and independence and, as in the political sphere, the young led the way in seeking new means of self-gratification and self-expression.

Surface appearances were most visible and, to older Americans, most troubling. The "hippies" of the 1960s carried themselves in different ways. Men let their hair grow and sprouted beards; men and women both donned jeans, muslin shirts, and other simple garments. Stressing spontaneity above all else, some rejected traditional marital customs and gravitated to communal living groups.

Sexual norms underwent a revolution as more people separated sex from its traditional ties to family life. A generation of young women came of age with access to "the pill"—an oral contraceptive that was effortless to use and freed sexual experimentation from the threat of pregnancy. In 1960, the Food and Drug Administration approved Enovid, the first oral contraceptive available on the market. Within three years of its introduction, more than 2 million women were on the pill, and as the cost dropped, millions more began to use it.

Americans of all social classes became more open to exploring, and enjoying, their sexuality. Author and editor Nora Ephron summed up the sexual changes in the 1960s as she reflected on her own experiences. Initially she had "a hangover from the whole Fifties virgin thing," she recalled. "The first man I went to bed with, I was in love with and wanted to marry.

Death of a Viet Cong Suspect In this picture, General Nguyen Ngoc Loan, the chief of the South Vietnamese National Police, looks at a Viet Cong prisoner, lifts his gun, and calmly blows out the captive's brains. This prizewinning photograph captured the horror of the war for many Americans. What impressions do you think this picture conveyed to people who saw it?

The second one I was in love with, but I didn't have to marry him. With the third one, I thought I might fall in love."

The arts reflected the sexual revolution. Federal courts ruled that books such as D. H. Lawrence's *Lady Chatterley's Lover* and other suppressed works could not be banned. Nudity became more common on stage and screen.

Paintings reflected both the mood of dissent and the urge to innovate, apparent in the larger society. "Op" artists painted sharply defined geometric figures in clear, vibrant colors, starkly different from the flowing, chaotic work of the abstract expressionists. "Pop" artists such as Andy Warhol, Roy Lichtenstein, and Jasper Johns made ironic comments on American materialism and taste with their representations of everyday objects including soup cans, comic strips, and pictures of Marilyn Monroe.

Hallucinogenic drugs also became a part of the counterculture. One prophet of the drug scene was Timothy Leary, a scientific researcher experimenting with LSD at Harvard University. He aggressively asserted that drugs were necessary to free the mind and urged followers to "Tune in, turn on, drop out." Another apostle of life with drugs was Ken Kesey, author of *One Flew Over the Cuckoo's Nest*, who established a commune of "Merry Pranksters." In 1964, the group headed east in a converted school bus painted in psychedelic Day-Glo colors and stocked with enough orange juice and "acid" (LSD) to sustain the Pranksters across the continent.

Drug use was no longer confined to urban subcultures. Soldiers brought experience with drugs back from Vietnam. Taking a "tab" of LSD became part of the coming-of-age ritual for many middle-class college students. Marijuana became phenomenally popular in the 1960s. "Joints" of "grass" were passed around at high school, neighborhood, and college parties as readily as cans of beer had been in the previous generation.

Music became intimately connected with these cultural changes. The rock and roll of the 1950s and the gentle strains of folk music gave way to a new kind of rock that swept the country—and the world.

Rock festivals became popular throughout the 1960s. On an August weekend in 1969, some 400,000 people gathered in a large pasture in upstate New York for the Woodstock rock festival, which featured around-the-clock entertainment and endlessly available marijuana and went off without a hitch. Another festival four months later at Altamont in California was less fortunate. Four people died when audience members clashed with members of Hell's Angels, a motorcycle gang hired to provide security for the Rolling Stones.

The underside of the counterculture was most visible in the Haight-Ashbury section of San Francisco, where runaway "flower children" mingled with "burned-out" drug users and radical activists. For all the spontaneity and exuberance, the counterculture had a darker side.

An Age of Assassination

In 1968, American society seemed to be tearing apart. The so-called "generation gap" caused major rifts between parents and children. Political protest grew increasingly violent. And yet there was still a basic confidence that the democratic process could bring meaningful change. John Kennedy had fallen to an assassin's bullet five years before and the nation had survived that trauma. Then two more killings of highly prominent figures undermined any sense of hope.

Martin Luther King, Jr., was the most visible spokesman for African Americans in the years after 1955. By the mid-1960s, he had broadened his crusade to attack poverty and economic injustice and had also begun to speak out against the war in Vietnam.

King knew he was a target. On April 3, 1968, he referred to threats on his life. "We've got some difficult days ahead," he said. "But it doesn't matter with me now, because I've been to the mountain top . . . and I've seen the promised land." The next day, as King stood on the balcony of his motel in Memphis, Tennessee, a bullet from a high-powered rifle ripped through his jaw and killed him.

King's assassination sparked a wave of violence throughout the United States. In a spontaneous outburst of rage, African Americans in 124 cities rioted, setting fires and looting stores. For all Americans, King's death eroded faith in the possibility of nonviolent change.

Several months later, Robert Kennedy likewise lost his life. Bobby had won election to the Senate from New York after his brother's death and was running for the Democratic presidential nomination. In June, he won an important victory in the California primary. That evening, after his victory speech, he too was shot by an assassin. Kennedy's death, like King's, shattered hopes for reconciliation or reform.

The Chaotic Election of 1968

The turbulent Democratic convention undermined any hopes the party had for victory. Chicago Mayor Richard Daley was outraged that radicals and hippies were coming to his city to protest and ordered police to clear out demonstrators. They did, in front of television cameras as the country watched. Hubert Humphrey, Johnson's vice president, running for the Democratic nomination after Johnson declined to seek reelection, won a tainted victory.

Humphrey faced former Vice President Richard Nixon. Nixon had failed in his first bid in 1960 and later lost a race for governor of California. Written off by most politicians, he staged a comeback after the Goldwater disaster of 1964, and by 1968, he seemed to have a good shot at the presidency.

Governor George C. Wallace of Alabama, a third-party candidate, exploited social and racial tensions in his campaign. Appealing to northern working-class voters as well as southern whites, Wallace hoped to ride into office on blue-collar resentment of social disorder and liberal aims.

Nixon addressed the same constituency, calling it the "silent majority." Capitalizing on the dismay these Americans felt over campus disruptions and inner-city riots and appealing to latent racism, he promised law and order if elected. He also called the Great Society a costly mistake. Nixon received 43 percent of the popular vote, not quite 1 percent more than Humphrey, with Wallace capturing the rest. But it was enough to give the Republicans a majority in the Electoral College and Nixon the presidency at last.

Continuing Protest

Meanwhile, protests continued. The next year, in October 1969, the Weathermen, a militant fringe group of SDS that took its name from a line in a Bob Dylan song—"You don't need a weatherman to know which way the wind blows"—descended on Chicago and rampaged through the streets for four days in an armed battle with police.

Why had the Weathermen launched their attack? "The status quo meant to us war, poverty, inequality, ignorance, famine and disease in most of the world," Bo Burlingham, a participant from Ohio, reflected. "To accept it was to condone and help perpetuate it." The rationale of the Chicago "national action" may have been clear to the participants, but it infuriated citizens around the country.

Conclusion
Political and Social Upheaval

The 1960s were turbulent years. In the first part of the decade, the United States was relatively calm. Liberal Democrats went even further than Franklin Roosevelt and Harry Truman as they pressed for large-scale government intervention to meet the problems that accompanied the modern industrial age. They were inspired by John Kennedy's rhetoric and saw the triumph of their approach in Lyndon Johnson's Great Society, as the nation strengthened its commitment to a capitalist welfare state. Then the Democratic party became impaled on the Vietnam War, and opposition to the conflict created more turbulence than the nation had known since the Civil War.

American society was in a state of upheaval. Young radicals challenged basic assumptions about how the government worked. They railed against social injustice at home, and they protested a foreign policy that they regarded as wrong. Their efforts faltered at first but then succeeded when they seized on the war in Vietnam as a primary focus and began to attack the Cold War policy that led to massive American military involvement. Student leaders soon found hundreds of thousands of followers, and together they finally forced the nation to reconsider its aims. Meanwhile, members of the counterculture promoted their own more fluid values, challenged the patterns of conformity so important in the 1950s, and led millions of other Americans to dress and act differently. The two strands of political activism and countercultural action were independent but intertwined, and they left the nation at the end of the decade very different than it had been before.

Most Americans, like Paul Cowan (introduced at the start of this chapter), embraced the message of John Kennedy and the New Frontier in the early 1960s and endorsed the liberal approach. But over time, as the 1960s gave way to the 1970s, they began to question the tenets of liberalism they had once taken for granted. They worried about the faltering economy as hard economic choices had to be made, and the turbulence created by an unwinnable war in Vietnam. Conservatives deplored the chaos, while disillusioned liberals like Paul Cowan wondered if their approach could ever succeed.

TIME*line*

✓•─Study and Review at **www.myhistorylab.com**

Questions for Review and Reflection

1. How did John F. Kennedy represent the hopes and ideals of Americans in the early 1960s?

2. How successful was Lyndon Johnson's Great Society?

3. What impact did the war in Vietnam have on protest at home?

4. What were the most important changes experienced by the United States in the late 1960s?

5. What was the lasting impact of the protest that rocked America in the 1960s?

Key Terms

Bay of Pigs 865

Black Power 863

Cuban missile crisis 868

Economic Opportunity Act 858

Great Society 845

Gulf of Tonkin Resolution 869

March on Washington 854

Medicare 858

New Frontier 846

Tet offensive 872

27

Disorder and Discontent, 1969–1980

American Stories

An Older Woman Returns to School

Ann Clarke—as she chooses to call herself now—always wanted to go to college. But girls from Italian families rarely did when she was growing up. Her mother, a Sicilian immigrant and widow, asked her brother for advice: "Should Antonina go to college?" What's the point?" he replied. "She's just going to get married."

Life had not been easy for Antonina Rose Rumore. As a child in the 1920s, her Italian-speaking grandmother cared for her while her mother worked to support the family, first in the sweatshops, then as a seamstress. Even as she dreamed about the future, she accommodated her culture's demands for dutiful daughters. Responsive to family needs, Ann finished the high school commercial course in three years. She struggled with ethnic prejudice as a legal secretary on Wall Street but still believed in the American dream and the Puritan work ethic. She was proud of her ability to bring money home to her family.

When World War II began, Ann wanted to join the WACS. "Better you should be a prostitute," her mother said. She went off to California instead, where she worked at a number of resorts. When she left California, she vowed to return to that land of freedom and opportunity.

After the war, Ann married Gerard Clarke, a college man with an English background. Her children would grow up accepted with Anglo-Saxon names. Over the next 15 years, she devoted herself to her family. She was a mother first and foremost, and that took all her time. But she still waited for her own chance. "I had this hunger to learn, this curiosity," she later recalled. By the early 1960s, her three children were all in school. Promising her husband to have dinner on the table every night at six, she enrolled at Pasadena City College. It was not easy, for family still came first, but Ann proved creative in finding time to study. When doing dishes or cleaning house, she memorized lists of dates, historical events, and other material for school. Holidays, however, complicated her efforts to complete assignments. Ann occasionally felt compelled to give everything up "to make Christmas." Forgetting about a whole semester's work two weeks before finals one year, she sewed night-gowns instead of writing her art history paper.

Her conflict over her studies was intensified by her position as one of the first older women to go back to college. "Sometimes I felt like I wanted to hide in the woodwork," she admitted. Often her teachers were younger than she was. It took four years to complete the two-year program. But she was not yet done, for she really wanted a bachelor's degree. Back she went, this time to California State College at Los Angeles.

As the years passed and the credits piled up, Ann became an honors student. Her children, now in college themselves, were proud and supportive; dinners became arguments over Faulkner and foreign policy. Even so, Ann still felt caught between her world at home and the world outside. Since she was at the top of her class, graduation should have been a special occasion. But she was only embarrassed when a letter from the school invited her parents to attend the final ceremonies. Ann could not bring herself to go.

With a college degree in hand, Ann returned to school for a teaching credential. Receiving her certificate at age 50, she faced the irony of social change. Once denied opportunities, Italians had assimilated into American society. Now she was just another Anglo in Los Angeles, caught in a changing immigration wave; now the city sought Latinos and other minorities to teach in the schools. Jobs in education were scarce, and she was close to retirement age, so she became a substitute teacher in Mexican American areas for the next 10 years, specializing in bilingual education.

Meanwhile, Ann was troubled by the Vietnam War. "For every boy that died, one of us should lie down," she told fellow workers. She was not an activist, but rather one of the millions of quieter Americans who ultimately helped bring about change. The social adjustments caused by the war affected her. Her son grew long hair and a beard and attended protest rallies. She worried that he would antagonize the ladies in Pasadena. Her daughter came home from college in boots and a leather miniskirt designed to shock. Clarke accepted her children's changes as relatively superficial, confident in their fundamental values; "they were good kids," she knew. She trusted them, even as she worried about them.

Ann Clarke's experience paralleled that of millions of women in the post–World War II years. Caught up in traditional patterns of family life, these women began to recognize their need for something more against a backdrop of continuing political turbulence that sometimes seemed to undermine the nation's stability. They worried about both the global and the domestic consequences of the war in Vietnam and the constitutional issues in the **Watergate** scandal that threatened the American democratic system and eventually brought President Richard Nixon down. Meanwhile, American women, like blacks, Latinos and Latinas, Native Americans, and members of other groups, struggled to transform the conditions of their lives and the rights they enjoyed within American society. Building on the successes of the past several decades, these diverse groups demanded their own right to equality and equitable treatment in fulfillment of their own American dreams. In the course of their struggle, they changed the nation itself.

This chapter describes the continuing upheaval that shook American society in the 1970s. It examines such questions as: What was the ongoing impact of global events as the Nixon administration struggled to find a way of ending the devastating struggle in Vietnam? What effect did widening the war into other parts of Southeast Asia have on the domestic front? How did the most serious political scandal in American history affect the national stability? How did the growing agitation of environmental and consumer activists influence public policy? And how did the ongoing effort to provide liberty and equality in racial, gender, and social relations change the nature of American society?

The Decline of Liberalism

After eight years of Democratic rule, many Americans were frustrated with the liberal approach. They questioned the liberal agenda and the government's ability to solve social problems. As the war in Vietnam polarized the country, critics argued that the government was trying to do too much. Capitalizing on the alienation sparked by the war, the Republican administration of Richard Nixon resolved to scale down the commitment to social change. Like Dwight Eisenhower a decade and a half before, Nixon accepted some social programs as necessary but still wanted to trim the federal bureaucracy. Furthermore, he and his political colleagues were determined to pay more attention to the needs of white, middle-class Americans who disliked the social disorder they saw as a consequence of rapid social change and resented the government's perceived favoritism toward the poor and dispossessed.

Richard Nixon and His Team

In and out of office, Nixon was a complex, remote man who carefully concealed his private self. Born poor, he was determined to be successful and accomplished that aim in the political sphere. Yet there was, one of his aides noted, "a mean side to his nature" that he sought to keep from public view. Physically awkward and humorless, he was most comfortable alone or with a few wealthy friends. Even at work he insulated himself, preferring written contacts to personal ones.

Nixon was keenly aware of the psychology of politics in the electronic age. He believed that "in the modern presidency, concern for image must rank with concern for substance." Thus, he posed in public as the defender of American morality, though in private he was frequently coarse and profane. Earlier in his career he had been labeled "Tricky Dick" for his apparent willingness to do anything to advance his career. In subsequent years, he had tried to create the appearance of a "new Nixon," but to many he still appeared to be a mechanical man, always calculating his next step. As author and columnist Garry Wills pointed out, "He is the least 'authentic' man alive, . . . A survivor. There is one Nixon only, though there seem to be new ones all the time—he will try to be what people want."

Philosophically, Nixon disagreed with the liberal faith in federal planning and wanted to decentralize social policy. But he agreed with his liberal predecessors that the presidency ought to be the engine of the political system. Faced with a Congress dominated by Democrats and their allocations of money for programs he opposed, he simply impounded (refused to spend) funds authorized by Congress. Later commentators saw the Nixon years as the height of what they came to call the "imperial presidency."

Nixon's cabinet appointees were white, male Republicans. For the most part, however, the president worked around his cabinet, relying on other White House staff members. In domestic affairs, Arthur Burns, a former chairman of the Council of Economic Advisers, and Daniel Patrick Moynihan,

The Intense Richard Nixon Speaking to the "silent majority," Nixon promised to reinstitute traditional values and restore law and order. A private man, Nixon tried to insulate himself from the public and present a carefully crafted image through the national media. What impression does Nixon convey in this photograph? How does his body language communicate his intentions?

a Harvard professor of government (and a Democrat), were the most important. In foreign affairs, the talented and ambitious Henry A. Kissinger, another Harvard government professor, directed the National Security Council staff and later became secretary of state.

Another tier of White House officials—none with public policy experience but all intensely loyal—insulated the president from the outside world and carried out his commands. Advertising executive H. R. Haldeman, a tireless Nixon campaigner, became chief of staff. Working with Haldeman was lawyer John Ehrlichman. Starting as a legal counselor, he rose to the post of chief domestic adviser. Haldeman and Ehrlichman came to be called the "Berlin Wall" for the way they guarded the president's privacy. John Mitchell was known as "El Supremo" by the staff, as the "Big Enchilada" by Ehrlichman. A tough, successful lawyer, Mitchell became a fast friend and managed Nixon's 1968 campaign. In the new administration, he became attorney general and gave the president daily advice.

The Republican Agenda at Home

Although Nixon had come to political maturity in Republican circles, he understood that it was impossible to roll back the government's expanded role altogether. He sought instead to systematize and scale back the programs of the welfare state, "to reverse the flow of power and resources" away from the federal government and channel them to state and local governments, where he believed they belonged.

Despite initial reservations, Nixon proved willing to use economic tools to maintain stability. The economy was faltering when he assumed office. As inflation rose, largely as a result of the Vietnam War, Nixon reduced government spending and pressed the Federal Reserve Board to raise interest rates. Although parts of the conservative plan worked, a mild recession occurred in 1969–1970, and inflation continued to rise. Realizing the political dangers of pursuing this policy, Nixon shifted course, imposed wage and price controls to stop inflation, and used monetary and fiscal policies to stimulate the economy. After his reelection in 1972, he lifted wage and price controls, and inflation resumed.

A number of factors besides the Vietnam War contributed to the troubling price spiral. Eager to court the farm vote, the administration made a large wheat sale to Russia in 1972. With insufficient wheat left for the American market, grain prices shot up. Between 1971 and 1974, farm prices rose 66 percent as agricultural inflation accompanied industrial inflation.

The most critical factor in disrupting the economy, though, was the Arab oil embargo. American economic expansion had rested on cheap energy, just as American patterns of life had depended on inexpensive gasoline. Turbulence in the Middle East intruded on the economic stability of the Western world.

The Six Day War in 1967 made it clear that the Middle East was still a battleground. Anticipating an attack and launching a preemptive strike, Israeli forces defeated the Egyptian army and seized the West Bank and the Golan Heights, as well as the Arab sector of Jerusalem, which was now reunited with the Israeli part of the city for the first time since 1948.

In the aftermath of the Six Day War, the Organization of Petroleum Exporting Countries (OPEC) slowly raised oil prices in the early 1970s. Another Arab-Israeli war in 1973—the Yom Kippur War—came as Jews

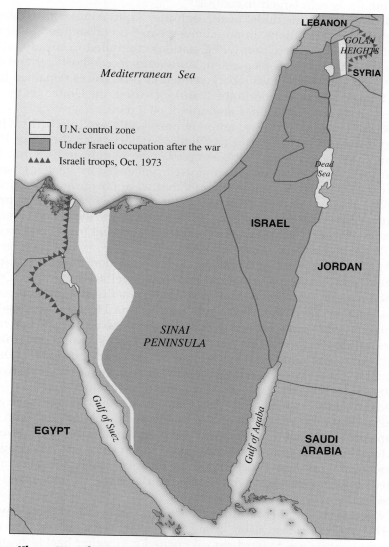

The Yom Kippur War of 1973 The Arab attack during the Yom Kippur holiday took Israel by surprise. Initially, Egypt and Syria regained some of their lost territory, but then the Israeli counterattack cut back many of the gains. In the end, United Nations troops were stationed on borders of the Sinai Peninsula and Golan Heights to help stabilize those regions. How has the map of the Middle East changed in the years after the establishment of the state of Israel in 1948? Who was the victor in the 1973 Yom Kippur War? Why could United Nations forces help maintain stability?

celebrated their holiest holiday—the Day of Atonement—and took the Arabs by surprise. The war pitted Israel against Egypt, Syria, Iraq, and Jordan. Initially Egypt, in the Sinai peninsula, and Syria, in the Golan Heights, were successful, but then the Israelis fought back. In the end, after several weeks of fighting, cease-fires went into effect, leaving Egypt and Syria with modest gains but the Israelis largely in control.

Meanwhile, in the midst of the fighting, Saudi Arabia, an economic leader of the Arab nations, imposed an embargo on oil shipped to Israel's ally, the United States. Other OPEC nations continued to supply oil but quadrupled their prices. Dependent Americans faced shortages and sky-rocketing prices. When the embargo ended in 1974, prices remained high. Even though oil prices around the world increased, the United States was hardest hit because of the huge amounts of oil it used.

Manufacturers, farmers, homeowners—all were touched by high energy prices. A loaf of bread that had cost 28 cents in the early 1970s jumped to 89 cents, and automobiles cost 72 percent more in 1978 than they had in 1973. The auto industry found itself challenged by smaller Japanese imports such as Hondas and Toyotas that were far more fuel-efficient. In 1974, inflation reached 11 percent. But then, as higher energy prices encouraged consumers to cut back on their purchases, the nation entered a recession as well. Unemployment climbed to 9 percent for several months in 1975, the highest level since the 1930s.

As economic growth and stability eluded the nation, Nixon also tried to reorganize rapidly expanding and expensive welfare programs. Critics claimed that welfare was inefficient and that benefits discouraged people from seeking work. Nixon faced a political dilemma. He recognized the conservative tide growing in the Sun Belt regions of the country, where many voters wanted cutbacks in what they viewed as excessive government programs. At the same time, he wanted to win over traditionally Democratic blue-collar workers with reassurances that the Republicans would not dismantle the parts of the welfare state on which they relied.

Nixon endorsed the Family Assistance Plan, which would have guaranteed a minimum yearly stipend of $1,600 to a family of four, with food stamps providing about $800 more. The program, aiming to cut "welfare cheaters" who took unfair advantage of the system and to encourage recipients to work, was attacked both by liberals, who believed it was too limited, and conservatives, who claimed it tried to do too much, and died in the Senate.

Nixon irritated liberals still further in his effort to restore "law and order." Political protest, rising crime rates, increased drug use, and more permissive attitudes toward sex all created a growing backlash among working-class and many middle-class Americans. Nixon decided to use government power to silence dissent and thereby strengthen his conservative political constituency.

Part of the administration's campaign involved denouncing disruptive elements. Nixon lashed out at demonstrators, but more and more he relied on his vice president to play the part of hatchet man. Spiro Agnew branded opposition elements, students in particular, as "ideological eunuchs" who made up an "effete corps of impudent snobs." At the same time, Nixon and Agnew attacked the communications industry, especially the news media, which Nixon believed voiced the views of the hostile "Eastern establishment."

The strongest part of Nixon's plan to circumscribe the liberal approach was Attorney General Mitchell's campaign against crime, sometimes waged at the expense of individuals' constitutional rights. Mitchell's plan included reshaping the Supreme Court, which had rendered increasingly liberal decisions in the past decade and a half. During his first term, Nixon had the opportunity to name four judges to the Court, and he nominated men who shared his views. His first choice was moderate Warren E. Burger as chief justice, who was confirmed quickly. Other appointments, however, were more partisan and reflected Nixon's aggressively conservative approach. Intent on appealing to white southerners, he first selected Clement Haynesworth of South Carolina, then G. Harold Carswell of Florida.

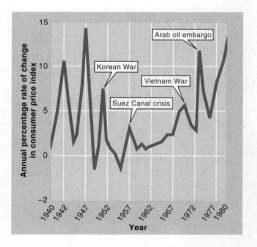

Rate of Inflation, 1940–1980 Inflation often accompanied military spending in the postwar years. In the early 1970s, the Arab oil embargo contributed to an even higher rate. Why have international crises often led to inflation? *(Source: U.S. Bureau of the Census)*

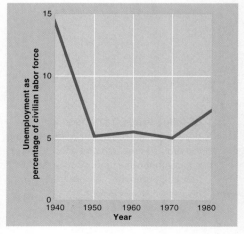

Unemployment Rate, 1940–1980 The unemployment rate fell dramatically during World War II, remained relatively constant from 1950 to 1969, and rose as inflation increased in the 1970s. How were unemployment and inflation related? *(Source: U.S. Bureau of Labor Statistics)*

Both men on examination showed such racial biases or limitations that the Senate refused to confirm them. Nixon then appointed Harry Blackmun, Lewis F. Powell, Jr., and William Rehnquist, all able and qualified, and all inclined to tilt the Court in a more conservative direction.

Not surprisingly, the Court gradually shifted to the right. It narrowed defendants' rights in an attempt to ease the burden of the prosecution in its cases and slowed the liberalizing of pornography laws. It supported Nixon's assault on the media by ruling that journalists did not have the right to refuse to answer questions for a grand jury, even if they had promised sources confidentiality. On other questions, however, the Court did not always act as the president had hoped. In the controversial 1973 *Roe* v. *Wade* decision, the Court legalized abortion, stating that women's rights included the right to control their own bodies.

•••—Read the Document
Roe *v.* Wade *(January 22, 1973)*
at **www.myhistorylab.com**

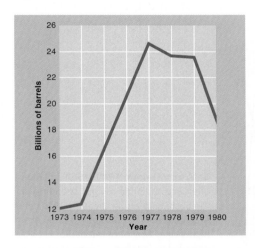

Oil Imports, 1973–1980 American reliance on foreign oil increased in the mid-1970s, until the United States tried to respond to price increases by reducing reliance on imports. Why did the United States seek to cut back on the use of oil? *(Source: U.S. Energy Information Administration)*

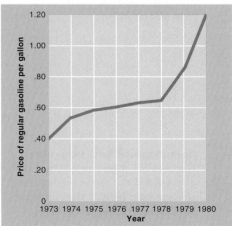

Gasoline Prices, 1973–1980 Gasoline prices rose steadily in the years following the Arab oil embargo and affected the entire American economy. Why did gasoline prices rise? *(Source: U.S. Energy Information Administration)*

Continuing Confrontations in Civil Rights

Nixon was less sympathetic to the cause of civil rights than his predecessors. In 1968, the Republicans won only 12 percent of the black vote, leading Nixon to employ the "southern strategy," which concluded that any effort to woo the black electorate would endanger his attempt to obtain white southern support.

From the start, the Nixon administration sought to scale back the federal commitment to civil rights. It first moved to reduce appropriations for fair-housing enforcement, and then tried to block an extension of the Voting Rights Act of 1965. Although Congress approved the extension, the administration's position on racial issues was clear. When South Carolina Senator Strom Thurmond and others tried to suspend federal school desegregation guidelines, the Justice Department lent support by urging a delay in meeting desegregation deadlines in 33 of Mississippi's school districts. While a unanimous Supreme Court rebuffed the effort, the president disagreed publicly with the decision.

Nixon also faced the growing controversy over **busing** as a means of desegregation, a highly charged issue in the 1970s. Transporting students from one area to another to attend school was nothing new. By 1970, over 18 million students, almost 40 percent of those in the United States, rode buses to school. Yet when busing became tangled with the question of integration, it inflamed passions.

In the South, before the Supreme Court endorsed integration, busing had long been used to maintain segregated schools. Now, however, busing was a means of breaking down racial barriers. In 1971, the Supreme Court ruled that district courts had broad authority to order the desegregation of school systems—by busing, if necessary.

In response, Nixon proposed a moratorium or even a restriction on busing and went on television to denounce it. Although Congress did not accede to his request, southerners knew where the president stood. So did northerners, for the issue became a national one. Many of the nation's largest northern cities had school segregation as rigid as in the South, largely because of residential patterns. This segregation was called *de facto* to differentiate it from the *de jure*, or legal, segregation that had existed in the South. Court decisions now ordered many northern cities to end such *de facto* segregation and to desegregate their schools.

For many younger students, attendance at different elementary schools went smoothly. Reassigned high school students were less fortunate. A white boycott at South Boston High in Massachusetts cut attendance from the anticipated 1,500 to fewer than 100 on the first day. Buses bringing in black students were stoned, and some children were injured. White, working-class South Bostonians felt that they were being asked to carry the burden of middle-class liberals' racial views. Some white families either enrolled their children in private schools or fled the city.

The Republicans managed to slow down the school desegregation movement. Nixon openly catered to his conservative constituents and demonstrated he was on their side. His successor, Gerald Ford, never came out squarely against civil rights, but his lukewarm approach to desegregation demonstrated a further weakening of the federal commitment.

Integration at the postsecondary level came easier. Federal affirmative action guidelines seeking to provide opportunities for groups discriminated against in the past brought more blacks into colleges and universities. Black enrollment in colleges reached 9.3 percent of the college population in 1976.

As blacks struggled on the educational and occupational fronts, some whites protested that gains came at their expense and amounted to "reverse discrimination." In 1973 and 1974, for example, Allan Bakke, a white, applied to the medical school at the University of California at Davis. Twice rejected, he sued on the grounds that a racial quota reserving 16 of 100 places for minority-group applicants was a form of reverse discrimination that violated the Civil Rights Act of 1964. In 1978, the Supreme Court ordered Bakke's admission to the medical school while allowing "consideration" of race in admissions policies, though not quotas.

The civil rights movement underscored the democratic values on which the nation was based, but the gap between rhetoric and reality remained. In an era when industrial and farming employment shrank and rents rose at a highly inflationary rate, most black families remained poor. After early optimism in the years when the movement made its greatest strides, black Americans and sympathetic whites were troubled by the wavering national commitment to reform in the 1970s.

The Ongoing Effort in Vietnam

The war in Vietnam continued into the 1970s. When Nixon assumed office in 1969, he understood the need to heal the rifts that the struggle created in American society. During the campaign, he had spoken about a plan to end involvement in the war without specifying details. Once in office, he embarked on an effort to bring American troops home as a way of defusing opposition to the struggle. Unfortunately, his decision to try to avoid losing the war led to even further chaos at home.

Watch the Video
The Vietnam War
at **www.myhistorylab.com**

Vietnamization—Bringing the Soldiers Home

Nixon gave top priority to extricating the United States from Vietnam while still seeking a way to win the war. To that end, he announced the **Nixon Doctrine**, which asserted that the United States would aid friends and allies but would not undertake the full burden of troop defense. The policy of **Vietnamization** entailed removing American forces and replacing them with Vietnamese troops. Between 1968 and 1972, American troop strength dropped from 543,000 to 39,000. Yet as the transition occurred, the South Vietnamese steadily lost ground to the Viet Cong.

At the same time, Americans launched ferocious air attacks on North Vietnam. Nixon used the bombing campaign to portray himself to the North Vietnamese as a madman with his hand on the nuclear trigger, thinking that fear of annihilation would bring the enemy to the peace table.

War protests multiplied in 1969 and 1970. In November 1969, as a massive protest demonstration took place in Washington, D.C., stories surfaced about a horrifying massacre of civilians in My Lai, a small village in South Vietnam, the year before. An American infantry company was helicoptered in to clear out the Viet Cong. Instead of troops, it found women, children, and old men. Perhaps concerned with the sometimes fuzzy distinction between combatants and civilians in a guerrilla war, the American forces lost control and mowed down hundreds of civilians in cold blood. Stories of the massacre at My Lai underscored the senseless violence associated with the war and increased pressure for the United States to get out.

Widening the War

As much as Nixon wanted to defuse opposition to the war, he was determined not to lose the struggle either. Realizing that the Vietnamese relied on supplies funneled through Cambodia, Nixon announced in mid-1970 that American and Vietnamese troops were invading that country to clear out Communist enclaves. Renewed demonstrations on college campuses had tragic results. Two days after the president announced his move, students at **Kent State** University in Ohio protested by setting the ROTC building on fire and watched it burn to the ground.

Governor James Rhodes of Ohio ordered the National Guard to the university. Tension grew, and finally the situation exploded as the Guardsmen fired without provocation on the students. When the shooting stopped, four students lay dead, nine wounded. Two of the dead had been demonstrators, who were more than 250 feet away when shot. The other two were innocent bystanders, almost 400 feet from the troops.

View the Image
Kent State Demonstrations
at **www.myhistorylab.com**

Students around the country, as well as other Americans, were outraged by the attack. Many were equally disturbed about a similar attack at Jackson State University in Mississippi, where a few students taunted police and National Guardsmen. Two people were killed, more wounded. The dead, however, were black students at a black institution, and white America paid less attention to this attack.

In 1971, the Vietnam War made major headlines once more when the *New York Times* began publishing the Pentagon Papers, a secret Department of Defense account of American involvement that gave Americans a firsthand look at the fabrications and faulty assumptions that had guided the war. Even though the study stopped with the Johnson years, the Nixon administration tried, without success, to block publication.

The End of the War and Détente

Vietnam remained a political football as Nixon ran for reelection in 1972, and the bombing continued even as peace negotiations got under way. Although a cease-fire was finally achieved in 1973, the conflict lingered on into the spring of 1975. When at last the North Vietnamese consolidated their control over the entire country, Gerald Ford, Nixon's successor as president, called for another $1 billion in aid, but Congress refused.

The long conflict had enormous consequences. Disillusionment with the war undermined assumptions about America's role in world affairs. In the longest war in its history, the United States lost almost 58,000 men, with far more wounded or maimed. Blacks and Latinos suffered more than whites, since they were disproportionately represented in combat units. In 1965, 24 percent of all soldiers killed in Vietnam were African American—a figure far higher than their percentage of the population as a whole. Financially, the nation spent over $150 billion on the unsuccessful war. Domestic reform slowed, then stopped. Cynicism about the government increased, and American society was deeply divided.

If the Republicans' Vietnam policy was a questionable success, accomplishments were impressive in other areas. Nixon, the consummate Red-baiter of the past, dealt imaginatively and successfully with the major Communist powers, reversing the direction of American policy since World War II.

Nixon's most dramatic step was establishing better relations with the People's Republic of China. In the two decades since Mao Zedong's victory in the Chinese revolution in 1949, the United States had refused to recognize the Communist government on the mainland, insisting that Jiang Jieshi's regime on Taiwan was the rightful government. In 1971, with an eye on the upcoming elections, Nixon began softening his administration's rigid stance by announcing that he intended to visit China the following year. He suspected that he could use Chinese friendship as a bargaining chip when he dealt with the Soviet Union. He acknowledged what most nations already knew: Communism was not monolithic. He also recognized that the press and television coverage of a dramatic trip could boost his image.

Nixon went to China in February 1972. He met with Chinese leaders Mao Zedong and Zhou Enlai (Chou En-lai), talked about international problems, exchanged toasts, and saw the Great Wall and other major sights. Wherever he went, American television cameras followed, helping introduce to the American public a nation about which it knew little. Though formal diplomatic relations were not yet restored, détente between the two countries had begun.

Seeking to play one Communist state against the other, Nixon also visited Russia, where he was likewise warmly welcomed. At a cordial summit meeting, the president and Soviet premier Leonid Brezhnev signed the first Strategic Arms Limitation Treaty (SALT I), which included a five-year agreement setting ceilings on intercontinental and other ballistic missiles, and an antiballistic missile treaty restricting the number of systems each nation could develop and deploy. At the same time, the two nations agreed to cooperate in space and to ease long-standing restrictions on trade. Business applauded the new approach, and most Americans approved of détente.

Nixon also recognized the need to promote peace in the Middle East. Secretary of State Henry Kissinger engaged in shuttle diplomacy—moving from one nation to another—in an effort that helped arrange a cease-fire in the Yom Kippur War. In the aftermath of the struggle, recognizing the need for oil, Nixon and Kissinger worked to establish better relations with the Arab nations, even if they intruded on American support of Israel.

When Gerald Ford assumed office, he followed the policies begun under Nixon. He continued the strategic arms limitation talks that provided hope for eventual nuclear disarmament and culminated in the even more comprehensive SALT II agreement, signed but never ratified during Jimmy Carter's presidency.

Constitutional Conflict and Its Consequences

As he dealt with chaos at home and abroad, Nixon worried about maintaining his political base. In his quest for reelection, he went too far and embroiled himself in a devastating political scandal that undermined his administration.

The Watergate Affair

Faced with a solidly Democratic Congress, the Nixon administration found many of its legislative initiatives blocked. Nixon was determined to end the stalemate by winning a second term and sweeping Republican majorities into both houses of Congress in 1972.

Nixon's reelection campaign was even better organized than the effort four years earlier. His fiercely loyal aides were prepared to do anything to win. Special counsel Charles W. Colson described himself as a "flag-waving, kick-'em-in-the-nuts, anti-press, anti-liberal Nixon fanatic." White House counsel John Dean defined his task as finding a way to "use the available federal machinery to screw our political enemies." One way was by authorizing tax audits of political opponents. Active in carrying out commands were E. Howard Hunt, a former CIA agent and a specialist in "dirty tricks," and G. Gordon Liddy, a onetime member of the FBI, with a flamboyant streak.

The Committee to Re-elect the President (**CREEP**), headed by John Mitchell, who resigned as attorney general and launched a massive fund-raising drive, aimed at collecting as much money as it could before a new campaign-finance law took effect. That money could be used for any purpose, including payments for the performance of dirty tricks designed to disrupt the opposition's campaign. Other funds financed an intelligence branch within CREEP.

Early in 1972, Liddy and his lieutenants proposed an elaborate scheme to wiretap the phones of various Democrats and to disrupt their nominating convention. Twice Mitchell refused to go along, arguing that the proposal was too risky and expensive. Finally, he approved a modified version of the illegal plan to tap the phones of the Democratic National Committee at its headquarters in the Watergate apartment complex in Washington, D.C.

The wiretapping attempt took place on the evening of June 16, 1972, and ended with the arrest of those involved. Nixon's aides played down the matter and used federal resources to head off any investigation. When the FBI traced the money carried by the burglars to CREEP, the president authorized the CIA to call off the FBI on the grounds that national security was at stake. Though not involved in the planning of the break-in, the president was now party to the cover-up. In the succeeding months, he authorized payment of hush money to silence the burglars. Members of the administration, including Mitchell, perjured themselves in court to shield the top officials who were involved.

Nixon trounced Democrat George McGovern in the election of 1972, receiving 61 percent of the popular vote. In a clear indication of the collapse of the Democratic coalition, 70 percent of southern voters cast their ballots for Nixon. The president, however, failed to gain the congressional majorities he sought.

The Watergate burglars pleaded guilty and were sentenced to jail, but the case refused to die. The evidence indicated that others had played a part, and the investigation of two zealous reporters, Bob Woodward and Carl Bernstein of the *Washington Post*, uncovered many of those involved.

The Senate Select Committee on Presidential Campaign Activities undertook its own investigation, and one of the convicted burglars testified that the White House had been involved in the episode. Newspaper stories generated further leads, and the Senate hearings in turn provided new material for the press. Faced with rumors that the White House was actively involved, Nixon decided to release Haldeman and Ehrlichman to save his own neck, claiming on nationwide television, "There can be no whitewash at the White House."

Watch the Video
Richard Nixon, "I am not a crook"
at **www.myhistorylab.com**

In May 1973, the Senate committee began televised public hearings, reminiscent of the McCarthy hearings of the 1950s. As millions of Americans watched, the drama built. John Dean, seeking to save himself, testified that Nixon knew about the cover-up, and other staffers revealed a host of illegal activities undertaken at the White House: money had been paid to the burglars to silence them; State Department documents had been forged to smear a previous administration; wiretaps had been used to prevent top-level leaks. The most electrifying moment was the disclosure that the president had installed a secret taping system in his office that recorded all conversations. Tapes could verify or disprove the growing rumors that Nixon was involved in the cover-up.

DOONESBURY

by **Garry Trudeau**

A Cartoonist Comments on Watergate Although Nixon steadfastly denied his complicity in the Watergate affair, his tape recordings of White House conversations told a different story. In this classic *Doonesbury* cartoon from September 17, 1973, Garry Trudeau notes Nixon's efforts to head off the investigation. What do you think the cartoonist is trying to say here?

To show his own honesty, Nixon appointed Harvard law professor Archibald Cox as a special prosecutor in the Department of Justice. But when Cox tried to gain access to the tapes, Nixon resisted and finally fired him. Nixon's own popularity plummeted, and even the appointment of another special prosecutor, Leon Jaworski, did not help. More and more Americans now believed that the president had played at least some part in the cover-up and should take responsibility for his acts. *Time* magazine ran an editorial headlined "The President Should Resign," and Congress considered impeachment.

●●●─[**Read** the **Document**
House Judiciary Committee's Conclusion on Impeachment (1972)
at **www.myhistorylab.com**

The first steps, in accordance with constitutional mandate, took place in the House of Representatives. The House Judiciary Committee, made up of 21 Democrats and 17 Republicans, began to debate the impeachment case in late July 1974. By sizable tallies, it voted to impeach the president on the grounds of obstruction of justice, abuse of power, and refusal to obey a congressional subpoena to turn over his tapes. The full House of Representatives still had to vote, and the Senate would have to preside over a trial before removal could take place. But for Nixon, the handwriting was on the wall.

After a brief delay, on August 5, Nixon obeyed a Supreme Court ruling and released the tapes. Despite a suspicious 18½-minute silence, they contained the "smoking gun"—clear evidence of his complicity in the cover-up. His ultimate resignation became but a matter of time. Four days later, on August 9, 1974, Nixon became the first American president ever to resign.

●─[**View** the **Image**
Nixon Releases Transcripts of Oval Office Tapes
at **www.myhistorylab.com**

The Watergate affair seemed disturbing evidence that the appropriate balance of power in the federal government had disappeared. Many began to question the centralization of authority in the American political system. Others simply lost faith in the presidency altogether. A 1974 survey showed that trust in the presidency had declined by 50 percent in a two-year period. Coming on the heels of Lyndon Johnson's lying to the American people about involvement in Vietnam, the Watergate affair contributed to the cumulative disillusionment with politics in Washington and to the steady decrease in political participation. Barely half of those eligible to vote bothered to go to the polls in the presidential elections of 1976, 1980, and 1984.

Gerald Ford: Caretaker President

Gerald Ford succeeded Nixon as president. An unpretentious, middle-American Republican who believed in traditional values, Ford had been appointed vice president in 1973 when Spiro Agnew resigned in disgrace for accepting bribes. Although he was an able congressman, there was significant doubt that Ford was qualified to be chief executive. The new president acknowledged his own limitations, declaring, "I am a Ford, not a Lincoln."

⟨View the Image⟩
Gerald Ford Presidential Campaign Ad: Feeling Good About America at **www.myhistorylab.com**

More important than his limitations were his views about public policy. In the House of Representatives, Ford had opposed federal aid to education, the poverty program, and mass transit. He had voted for civil rights measures only when weaker substitutes he had favored had gone down to defeat. Like his predecessor, he was determined to stop the liberal advances promoted by the Democrats in the 1960s.

A President by Appointment Gerald Ford, a genial man, sought to re-establish confidence in the government after succeeding Nixon as president. Far different from his predecessor, he served just over two years, as his bid for election to the presidency in 1976 ended in defeat. What impression does this photograph convey?

Ford faced a daunting task. After Watergate, Americans wondered whether any politician could be trusted to guide public affairs. Ford worked quickly to restore that trust in the presidency. He emphasized conciliation and compromise, and he promised to cooperate both with Congress and with American citizens. The nation responded gratefully. *Time* magazine pointed to a "mood of good feeling and even exhilaration in Washington that the city had not experienced for many years."

The new feeling did not last long. Ford weakened his base of support by pardoning Richard Nixon barely a month after his resignation. Ford's decidedly conservative bent in domestic policy often threw him into confrontation with a Democratic Congress. Economic problems proved most pressing in 1974, as inflation, fueled by oil price increases, hit 11 percent, unemployment reached 6.6 percent at the end of the year, and GNP declined. Nixon, preoccupied with the Watergate crisis, had been unable to curb these problems. Not since Franklin Roosevelt took office in the depths of the Great Depression had a new president faced economic difficulties so severe.

Like Herbert Hoover 45 years before, the conservative Ford hoped to restore confidence and persuade the public that conditions would improve with patience and goodwill. But his campaign to cajole Americans to "Whip Inflation Now" voluntarily failed dismally. At last convinced of the need for strong government action, the administration introduced a tight-money policy as a means of curbing inflation. It led to the most severe recession since the Great Depression, with unemployment peaking at 9 percent in early 1975. In response, Congress pushed for an antirecession spending program. Recognizing political reality, Ford endorsed a multibillion-dollar tax cut coupled with higher unemployment benefits. The economy made a modest recovery, although inflation and unemployment remained high and federal budget deficits soared.

The Carter Interlude

In the election of 1976, the nation's bicentennial year, Ford faced Jimmy Carter, former governor of Georgia. Carter, appealing to voters distrustful of political leadership, portrayed himself as an outsider. Assisted by public relations experts, he effectively utilized the media, especially television, which allowed him to bypass party machines and establish a direct electronic relationship with voters.

In the election, most elements of the old Democratic coalition came together once again as the Democrats profited from the fallout of the Watergate affair. Carter won a 50 to 48 percent majority of the popular vote and a 297 to 240 tally in the Electoral College. He did well with members of the working class, African Americans, and Catholics. He won most of the South, heartening to the Democrats after Nixon's gains there. Racial voting differences continued, however, as Carter attracted less than half of all white voters but an overwhelming majority of black voters.

Carter stood in stark contrast to his recent predecessors. Rooted in the rural South, he was a peanut farmer who shared the values of the region. He was also a graduate of the Naval Academy, trained as a manager and an engineer. A modest man, he was uncomfortable with the pomp and incessant political activity in Washington. He hoped to take a more restrained approach to the presidency and thereby defuse its imperial stamp.

Initially, voters saw Carter as a reform Democrat committed to his party's goals, but he was hardly the old-line liberal some had expected. Though he called himself a populist, his political philosophy and priorities were never clear. Critics charged that he had no legislative strategy. Rather, they said with some truth, he responded to problems in a haphazard way and failed to provide firm direction. His status as an outsider led him to ignore traditional political channels. He also seemed to become mired in detail and to lose sight of larger issues.

In economic affairs, Carter gave liberals some hope at first as he accepted deficit spending. But when record deficits brought inflation to about 10 percent a year, Carter slowed down the economy by reducing spending and cutting the deficit slightly. These budget cuts fell largely on social programs and distanced Carter from reform-minded Democrats who had supported him before. Yet even that effort to arrest growing deficits was not enough. When the budget released in early 1980 still showed high spending levels, the financial community reacted strongly. Bond prices fell, and interest rates rose dramatically.

Similarly, Carter disappointed liberals by failing to construct an effective energy policy. OPEC's increase of oil prices led many Americans to resent their dependence on foreign oil and to clamor for energy self-sufficiency. Carter responded in April 1977 with a comprehensive energy program, but critics ridiculed the plan. Never an effective leader in working with the legislative branch, Carter watched his proposals bog down in Congress for 26 months. Eventually, the program committed the nation to move from oil dependence to reliance on coal, possibly even on sun and wind, and established a new synthetic-fuel corporation. Nuclear power, another alternative, seemed less attractive as costs rose and accidents occurred.

Carter further upset liberals by beginning deregulation—the removal of government controls in economic life. Arguing that certain restrictions established over the past century stifled competition and increased consumer costs, he supported decontrol of oil and natural gas prices to spur production. He also deregulated the railroad, trucking, and airline industries.

One of the high points in Carter's administration came with his involvement in the ever-turbulent Middle East. In the aftermath of the Yom Kippur War, Egyptian leader Anwar al-Sadat was disappointed in the ultimate failure of the struggle and flew to Israel in a gesture of peace. At that point, Carter intervened and invited Sadat and Israeli leader Menachem Begin to come to the United States to work out an accord in September 1978 that led to a formal peace treaty the next March. Egypt recognized Israel—and the Israeli right to exist—for the first time, and the Israelis gave up part of the occupied Sinai Peninsula. The United States promised substantial military aid to both parties, which led to a closer relationship with Egypt that has continued ever since. As the United States superseded the Soviet Union as an ally of Egypt, the Russians countered by arming the radical Palestine Liberation Organization (PLO) and helped encourage leader Yasir Arafat in the ongoing guerrilla war.

Carter puzzled people overseas by his passionate commitment to human rights. It became a hallmark of his administration, especially when he ordered the United States to pull out of the Olympics in Moscow in 1980 in protest of a Soviet invasion of neighboring Afghanistan. Some Americans wondered how this commitment squared with the long-standing American approach of supporting dictators and overlooking human rights abuses in countries whose support the United States wanted in the Cold War.

Liberals were disappointed as the 1970s ended. Their hopes for a stronger commitment to a welfare state had been dashed, and conservatives had the upper hand. Despite a tenuous Democratic hold on the presidency at the end of the decade, liberalism was in trouble. And the turbulence that had marked the beginning of the decade had not disappeared.

Celebrating a Triumph at Camp David One of Jimmy Carter's greatest achievements was taking the first steps toward peace in the Middle East. Here he celebrates the Camp David Agreement of September 1978, in which Anwar al-Sadat of Egypt, on the left, and Menachem Begin, on the right, shook hands and agreed to work together. What do the faces of these three leaders convey about the moment captured in this photograph?

The Continuing Quest for Social Reform

A struggle for social reform was one more factor contributing to the turbulence of the 1970s. The black struggle for equality in the 1950s and 1960s helped spark a women's movement that soon developed a life of its own. This struggle, like the struggles of Latinos and Native Americans, employed the confrontational approach and the insistent vocabulary of the civil rights movement to create pressure for change. In time, other groups appropriated the same strategies and kept reform efforts alive. While these movements had preexisting roots and usually began in the 1960s, they came of age in the 1970s, and in these years achieved their greatest gains.

Attacking the Feminine Mystique

Although the civil rights movement helped spark the women's movement, broad social changes provided the preconditions. During the 1950s and 1960s, increasing numbers of married women entered the labor force (see Chapter 26). Equally important, many more young women were attending college. By 1970, women earned 41 percent of all B.A. degrees awarded, in comparison with only 25 percent in 1950. These educated young women held high hopes for themselves, even if they still earned substantially less than men and were often treated as second-class citizens.

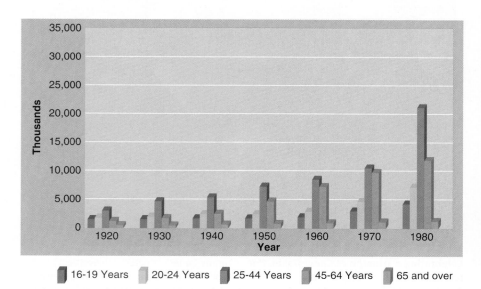

Women in the Workforce, 1920–1980 This graph shows the dramatic increase in the number of women in the workforce over the years. Which age cohort showed the largest gain in the 1970s? Why? *(Source: U.S. Bureau of the Census)*

The women's movement depended on reform legislation. Title VII of the 1964 Civil Rights bill, as originally drafted, prohibited discrimination on the grounds of race. During legislative debate, conservatives opposed to black civil rights seized on an amendment to include discrimination on the basis of gender, in the hope of defeating the entire bill. The amendment passed, and then the full measure was approved, giving women a legal tool for attacking discrimination.

Women's organizations played an important role in bringing about change in the 1970s. In 1966, a group of 28 professional women, including author Betty Friedan, established the National Organization for Women (**NOW**) to work toward not only fair pay and equal opportunity but a new, more egalitarian form of marriage. By 1967, some 1,000 women had joined the organization, and four years later, its membership reached 15,000.

To radical feminists who had come up through the civil rights movement, NOW's agenda failed to confront adequately the problem of gender discrimination. Jo Freeman, a radical activist, observed, "Women's liberation does not mean equality with men . . . [because] equality in an unjust society is meaningless." These feminists tried, through the technique of consciousness raising, to help women understand the extent of their oppression and to analyze their experience as a political phenomenon. They wanted to demonstrate, in their phrase, that the personal was political.

The radicals gained mass media attention at the Miss America pageant in Atlantic City, New Jersey, in September 1968. On the boardwalk, a hundred women nominated a sheep as their candidate for Miss America. They also set up a "freedom trash can" and placed in it "instruments of torture": bras, high heels, and copies of *Playboy* and *Cosmopolitan* magazines. In the pageant hall, they chanted "Freedom for Women" and unfurled banners reading "Women's Liberation."

In 1971, singer-songwriter Helen Reddy expressed the energy of the movement in a song called "I Am Woman" that reflected a new militancy and sense of self-confidence among women:

I am woman, hear me roar
In numbers too big to ignore
And I know too much to go back and pretend
'Cause I've heard it all before
And I've been down there on the floor
No one's ever gonna keep me down again.*

Real changes were under way. A 1970 survey of first-year college students showed that men interested in such fields as business, medicine, engineering, and law outnumbered women eight to one; by 1975, the ratio had dropped to three to one. Women gained access to the military academies and entered senior officer ranks, although they were still restricted from combat command ranks. According to the Census Bureau, 45 percent of mothers with preschool children held jobs outside the home in 1980. That figure was four times greater than it had been 30 years before.

*Reprinted with permission of the Hal Leonard Corporation.

Legal changes brought women more benefits and opportunities. Title IX of the Education Amendments of 1972 barred gender bias in federally assisted educational activities and programs, made easier the admission of women to colleges, and required schools to fund intercollegiate sports teams for women as well as men. By 1980, fully 30 percent of the participants in intercollegiate sports were women, compared with 15 percent before Title IX became law.

A flurry of publications spread the principles of the women's movement. In 1972, journalist Gloria Steinem and several other women founded a new magazine, *Ms.*, which attracted 200,000 subscribers by the next year. *Our Bodies, Ourselves*, a handbook published by a women's health collective, encouraged women to understand and control their bodies; it sold 850,000 copies between 1971 and 1976. Unlike older women's magazines, these publications dealt with such issues as abortion, employment, and discrimination.

●●─Read the Document

Shirley Chisholm, Equal Rights for Women (May 21, 1969)

at **www.myhistorylab.com**

Women both in and out of NOW worked for congressional passage, then ratification, of the Equal Rights Amendment (**ERA**) to the Constitution. Passed by Congress in 1972, with ratification seemingly assured, it stated simply, "Equality of rights under the law shall not be denied or abridged by the United States or by any State on account of sex."

Feminism was not monolithic. More radical feminists insisted that traditional gender and family roles would have to be discarded to end social exploitation. Socialist feminists claimed that capitalist society itself was responsible for women's plight. Only through revolution could women be free. Black women frequently viewed the women's movement with ambivalence. Some became feminists, but others felt that the struggle for racial equality took precedence, and they were reluctant to divert energy and attention from it. Members of NOW and similar organizations, they claimed, "suffered little more than dishpan hands" and were hardly confronting the most important issues when they burned their bras and insisted on using the title Ms. rather than Mrs. or Miss.

Not all women were feminists. Many felt the women's movement was contemptuous of women who stayed at home to perform traditional tasks. Marabel Morgan was one who insisted that the woman still had a place at home by her husband's side. In her book *The Total Woman* (1973), she counseled others to follow the "4A approach": accept, admire, adapt, appreciate. As of 1975, some 500,000 copies of the hardcover volume had been sold.

In politics, Phyllis Schlafly headed a nationwide campaign to block ratification of the ERA. The amendment, she predicted, would lead to the establishment of coed bathrooms, the elimination of alimony, and the legalization of homosexual marriage.

Schlafly and her allies had their way. Within a few years after passage of the ERA, 35 states had agreed to the measure, but then the momentum disappeared. Even with an extension in the deadline granted in 1979, the amendment could not win support of the necessary 38 states. By mid-1982, the ERA was dead.

Despite the counterattacks, the women's movement flourished in the late 1960s and 1970s. In the tenth anniversary issue of *Ms.* magazine in 1982, Gloria Steinem noted the differences a decade had made. "Ten years ago," she said, "we were trained to marry a doctor, not be one."

Latino Mobilization

Latinos, like women, profited from the example of blacks in their struggle for equality that came of age in the 1970s. Long denied equal access to the American dream, they became more vocal and confrontational as their numbers increased dramatically in the postwar years. In 1970, some 9 million residents of the United States declared they were of Spanish origin; in 1980, the figure was 14.6 million. But median household income remained less than three-fourths that of Anglos, and inferior education and political weakness reinforced social and cultural separation. Latinos included Puerto Ricans in the Northeast, Cubans in Florida, and Chicanos—Mexican Americans—in the West and Southwest. Though "Hispanic" still remained an acceptable term, "Latino" was now more commonly used. Chicanos took the lead in the protest struggle, though all groups developed a heightened sense of solidarity as they began to assert their own rights.

An Advocate for Migrant Workers César Chávez organized the United Farm Workers to give migrant Mexican workers representation in their struggle for better wages and working conditions. Here he works with laborers in his tireless campaign for their support. What kind of a leader do you think Chávez was on the basis of his appearance in this picture? *(Bob Finch/Stock Photo)*

RECOVERING *the* PAST

Popular Music

One way to recover the past is through music. Popular songs not only provide insight into attitudes and beliefs but also quickly convey the mood and feelings of an era. Through their lyrics, songwriters express the hopes and fears of a people and the emotional tone of an age. The decline of pop music and the rise of rock and roll in the 1950s tell historians a great deal about the mood of that period. Similarly, the popularity of both folk music and rock in the 1960s provides another way of following social change in that turbulent decade.

The music of the 1960s and 1970s moved beyond the syrupy ballads of the early 1950s and the rock and roll movement that Elvis Presley helped launch in the middle of the decade. As the United States confronted the challenges of the counterculture and the crosscurrents of political and social reform, new kinds of music began to be played.

Folk music took off at the start of the period. Building on a tradition launched by Woody Guthrie, Pete Seeger, and the Weavers, Joan Baez was one of the first folk singers to become popular. Accompanying herself on a guitar, she soon enthralled audiences with her crystal-clear voice. She sang ballads, laments, and spirituals such as "We Shall Overcome" and became caught up in the protest activities of the period.

Equally active was Bob Dylan, who grew up playing rock and roll in high school, then folk music in college at the University of Minnesota. Disheveled and gravelly voiced, he wrote remarkable songs including "Blowin' in the Wind" that were soon sung by other artists such as Peter, Paul, and Mary as well. His song "The Times They Are A-Changin'" captured the inexorable force of the student protest movement best of all.

But these years were marked by far more than folk music alone. In the early part of the decade, an English group from Liverpool began to build a following in Great Britain. At the start of 1964, the Beatles released "I Want to Hold Your Hand" in the United States and appeared on the popular Ed Sullivan television show. Within weeks, Beatles songs held the first, second, third, fourth, and fifth positions on the *Billboard* singles chart, and *Meet the Beatles* became the best-selling LP record to date. With the release of *Sergeant Pepper's Lonely Hearts Club Band* a few years later, the Beatles branched out in new musical directions and reflected the influence of the counterculture with songs such as "Lucy in the Sky with Diamonds" (which some people said referred to the hallucinogenic drug LSD).

Mick Jagger and the Rolling Stones followed at the end of the 1960s. Another English group that changed the nature of American music, the Stones played a blues-based rock music that proclaimed a commitment to drugs, sex, and a decadent life of social upheaval. Other artists, such as Jim Morrison of the Doors and Janis Joplin, reflected the same intensity of the new rock world, and both died from drug overdoses. This music, too, continued into the 1970s.

Meanwhile, other groups were setting off in different directions. On the pop scene, Motown Records in Detroit popularized a new kind of black rhythm and blues. By 1960, the gospel-pop-soul fusion was gaining followers. By the late 1960s, Motown Records was one of the largest black-owned companies in America and one of the most successful independent recording ventures in the business. Stevie Wonder, the Temptations, and the Supremes were among the groups who became enormously popular. The Supremes, led by Diana Ross, epitomized the Motown sound with such hits as "Where Did Our Love Go."

REFLECTING ON THE PAST **What songs come to your mind when you think of the 1960s and 1970s? How is the music different from that of the 1950s? What do the lyrics tell you about the period? What other songs can you think of that give you a similar handle on these turbulent years?**

Joan Baez

Bob Dylan

The Supremes

The Beatles

In the 1960s and 1970s, Mexican Americans became more active politically, winning several seats in Congress. More important than political representation was direct action, which triumphed in the 1970s. César Chávez, founder of the United Farm Workers, showed the way by organizing the migrant farmworkers of the West, among the most exploited and ignored laboring people in the country. Chávez concentrated on migrant Mexican field hands, who worked long hours for meager pay. By 1965, his organization had recruited 1,700 people and attracted volunteer help.

Latina women played an important part in the organizing effort. Dolores Huerta, a third-generation Mexican American who became vice president of the United Farm Workers, observed how entire families were involved:

> Excluding women, protecting them, keeping women at home, that's the middle-class way. Poor people's movements have always had whole families on the line, ready to move at a moment's notice, with more courage because that's all we had. It's a class not an ethnic thing.

Chávez first took on the grape growers of California. Calling the grape workers out on strike, the union demanded better pay and working conditions as well as recognition of the union. When the growers resisted, Chávez launched a nationwide consumer boycott of their products that was ultimately successful. Similar boycotts of lettuce and other products harvested by exploited labor also ended in success. In 1975, Chávez's long struggle for farmworkers won passage in California of a measure that required growers to bargain collectively with the elected representatives of the workers. Farmworkers now had achieved the legal basis for representation that could help bring higher wages and improved working conditions. And Chávez had become a national figure.

Meanwhile, Mexican Americans pressed for reform in other areas. In the West and Southwest, Mexican American studies programs flourished. Colleges and universities offered degrees, gave Chicanos access to their own past, and provided a network linking students together and mobilizing them for political action.

Beginning in 1968, Mexican American students began to protest conditions in secondary schools. They pointed to overcrowded and run-down institutions and to the 50 percent dropout rate that came from expulsion, transfer, or failure because students had never been taught to read. School walkouts took place in Colorado, Texas, and California and led to successful demands for Latino teachers, counselors, and courses as well as better facilities.

Other Latinos followed a more political path. In Texas, José Angel Gutiérrez formed a citizens' organization that developed into the La Raza Unida political party and successfully promoted Mexican American candidates for political offices. Throughout the 1970s, it gained strength in the West and Southwest.

Among the new Chicano leaders was the charismatic Reies López Tijerina, or "El Tigre." A preacher, he argued that the U.S. government had fraudulently deprived Chicanos of village lands. He formed an organization, La Alianza Federal de Mercedes (the Federal Alliance of Land Grants), which marched on the New Mexico state capital and occupied a number of national forests. Arrested, he stood trial and eventually served time in prison, where he became a symbol of political repression.

Rodolfo "Corky" Gonzáles was another such leader. He founded the Crusade for Justice to advance the Chicano cause through community organization. Like Tijerina, he was arrested for his part in a demonstration but was subsequently acquitted.

Latinos made a particular point of protesting the Vietnam War. Because the draft drew most heavily from the poorer segments of society, the Latino casualty rate was far higher than that of the population at large. In 1969, the National Chicano Moratorium Committee demonstrated against what it argued was a racial war, with black and brown Americans being used against their third world compatriots.

Aware of the growing numbers and growing demands of Latinos, the Nixon administration sought to defuse their anger and win their support. Cuban American refugees, strongly opposed to communism, shifted toward the Republican party, which they assumed was more likely eventually to intervene against Fidel Castro. Meanwhile, Nixon courted Chicanos by dangling political positions, government jobs, and promises of better programs for Mexican Americans. The effort paid off, as Nixon received 31 percent of the Latino vote in 1972.

Despite occasional gains in the 1970s, Latinos from all groups faced continuing problems. Discrimination persisted in housing, education, and employment. Activists had laid the groundwork for a campaign for equal rights, but the struggle had just begun.

Native American Protest

Like Latinos, Native Americans continued to suffer second-class status in the 1960s and 1970s. But, partly inspired by the confrontational tactics of other groups, they became more aggressive in their efforts to claim their rights and improve their living and working conditions. Their soaring numbers—the census put them at 550,000 in 1960 and 1,480,000 in 1980—gave them greater visibility and political clout.

American Indians learned from the examples of protest they saw around them in the rising nationalism of the developing world and, even more important, in the civil rights revolution. They too came to understand the place of interest-group politics in a diverse society. Finally, they were chastened by the excesses of the Vietnam War. They recognized a pattern of killing people of color that connected Indian–white relations to the excesses in the Philippines at the turn of the century and to atrocities in Korea and Vietnam.

Indians in the late 1960s and 1970s successfully promoted their own values and designs. Native American fashions became more common, museums and galleries displayed Indian art, and Indian jewelry found a new market. In 1968, N. Scott Momaday won the Pulitzer Prize for his book *House Made of Dawn*. Vine Deloria, Jr.'s *Custer Died for Your Sins* (1969) had even wider readership. Meanwhile, popular films such as *Little Big Man* (1970) provided sympathetic portrayals of Indian history. Indian studies programs were developed in colleges and universities. Organizations such as the American Indian Historical Society protested traditional textbook treatment of Indians and demanded more honest portrayals.

At the same time, Native Americans became more confrontational. Like other groups, they worked through the courts when they could but also challenged authority more aggressively when necessary.

Led by a new generation of leaders, American Indians tried to protect what was left of their tribal lands. For generations, federal and state governments had steadily encroached on Native American territory. That intrusion had to cease. The protest spirit was apparent on the Seneca Nation's Allegany reservation in New York State. When state authorities tried to condemn a section of Seneca land to build a superhighway through the Allegany reservation, the Indians went to court. In 1981, the state finally agreed to an exchange: state land elsewhere in addition to a cash settlement in return for an easement through the reservation. That decision encouraged tribal efforts in Montana, Wyoming, Utah, New Mexico, and Arizona to resist similar incursions on reservation lands.

Native American leaders found that lawsuits charging violations of treaty rights gave them powerful leverage. In 1967, in the first of many subsequent decisions upholding the Indian side, the U.S. Court of Claims ruled that the government in 1823 had forced the Seminole in Florida to cede their land for an unreasonably low price. The court directed the government to pay additional funds 144 years later. American Indians also vigorously and successfully protested new assaults on their long-abused water and fishing rights.

Urban Indian activism became highly visible in 1968 when George Mitchell and Dennis Banks, Chippewa living in Minneapolis, founded the activist American Indian Movement (AIM). AIM got Office of Economic Opportunity funds channeled to Indian-controlled organizations. It also established patrols to protect drunken Indians from harassment by the police. Soon chapters formed in other cities.

An incident in November 1969 dramatized Native American militancy. A landing party of 78 Indians seized Alcatraz Island in San Francisco Bay in an effort to protest symbolically the inability of the Bureau of Indian Affairs to "deal practically" with questions of Indian welfare. The Indians converted the island, with its defunct federal prison, into a cultural and educational center. In 1971, federal officials removed the Indians from Alcatraz.

Similar protests followed. In 1973, AIM took over the South Dakota village of Wounded Knee, where in 1890 the U.S. 7th Cavalry had massacred the Sioux. The reservation surrounding the town was mired in poverty. The occupation was meant to dramatize difficult conditions and to draw

The Occupation at Wounded Knee The Native American movement's armed occupation of Wounded Knee, South Dakota, the site of a late-nineteenth-century massacre of the Sioux, resulted in bloodshed that dramatized unfair government treatment of Native Americans. What elements of this scene convey the determination behind this episode?

attention to the 371 treaties AIM leaders claimed the government had broken. Federal officials responded by encircling the area and, when AIM tried to bring in supplies, killed one Indian and wounded another. The confrontation ended with a government agreement to reexamine the treaty rights of the Indians, although little changed.

Meanwhile, Native Americans devoted increasing attention to providing education and developing legal skills. Because roughly half of the Indian population continued to live on reservations, many tribal communities founded their own colleges. In 1971, the Oglala Sioux established Oglala Lakota College on the Pine Ridge Reservation in South Dakota. Nearby Sinte Gleska College was the first to offer accredited four-year and graduate programs. The number of Indians in college increased from a few hundred in the early 1960s to tens of thousands by 1980.

Indian protest brought results. The outcry against termination in the 1950s (see Chapter 26) had led the Kennedy and Johnson administrations in the 1960s to steer a middle course, neither endorsing nor disavowing the policy. Instead, they tried to bolster reservation economies and raise standards of living by persuading private industries to locate on reservations and by promoting the leasing of reservation lands to energy and development corporations. Many tribes confronted the hated policy head-on, and often gained the cancellation of such leases and the restoration of reservation status.

Legislation likewise disavowed the termination policy. In 1975, Congress passed an Indian Self-Determination Act. An Education Assistance Act that same year involved subcontracting federal services to tribal groups. Both laws reflected the government's decision to respond to Indian pressure and created a framework for federal policy.

Gay and Lesbian Rights

Closely tied to the revolution in sexual norms that affected sexual relations, marriage, and family life was a fast-growing and increasingly militant gay liberation movement. Because American society as a whole was unsympathetic, many homosexuals kept their preferences to themselves. The climate of the 1970s encouraged gays to "come out of the closet." A nightlong riot in

○ View the Image

Sign at a Gay Pride March at **www.myhistorylab.com**

1969, in response to a police raid on the Stonewall Inn, a homosexual bar in Greenwich Village in New York, helped spark a new consciousness and a movement for gay rights. Throughout the 1970s, homosexuals ended the most blatant forms of discrimination against them. In 1973, the American Psychiatric Association ruled that homosexuality should no longer be classified as a mental illness, and that decision was overwhelmingly supported in a vote by the membership the next year. In 1975, the U.S. Civil Service Commission lifted its ban on employment of homosexuals.

In this new climate of acceptance, many gay men who had hidden or suppressed their sexuality revealed their secret. Women, too, became more open about their sexual preferences as a lesbian movement developed. But many Americans and some churches remained unsympathetic—occasionally vehemently so—to anyone who challenged traditional sexual norms.

Environmental and Consumer Agitation

Although many of the social movements of the 1960s and 1970s were defined by race, gender, and sexual preference, the environmental movement cut across all boundaries. After World War II, many Americans began to recognize that clear air, unpolluted waters, and unspoiled wilderness were indispensable to a decent existence. They worried about threats to their natural surroundings, particularly after naturalist Rachel Carson published her brilliant book *Silent Spring* in 1962 (see Chapter 26). By 1970, 53 percent of the population considered air and water pollution to be one of the major national problems.

Public concern focused on a variety of targets. In 1969, Americans learned that thermal pollution from nuclear power plants was killing fish in both eastern and western rivers. A massive oil spill off the coast of southern California turned white beaches black and wiped out much of the marine life in the immediate area. In 1978, the public became alarmed about the lethal effects of toxic chemicals dumped in the Love Canal neighborhood of Niagara Falls, New York. A few years later, attention focused on the deadly substance dioxin.

Equally worrisome was the potential environmental damage from a nuclear accident. Such a calamity occurred in 1979 at Three Mile Island near Harrisburg, Pennsylvania. Human error compounded a mechanical problem, and part of the nuclear core began to disintegrate. An explosion releasing radioactivity into the atmosphere appeared possible, and thousands of area residents fled. The scenario of nuclear disaster depicted in the film *The China Syndrome* (1979) seemed frighteningly real. The plant remained shut down, filled with radioactive debris, a monument to a form of energy Americans feared.

The threat of a nuclear catastrophe underscored the arguments of grassroots environmental activists. Groups such as the Clamshell Alliance in New Hampshire and the Abalone Alliance in northern California campaigned aggressively against licensing new nuclear plants at Seabrook, New Hampshire, and Diablo Canyon, California, and no new plants were authorized after 1978 in the United States, though other countries around the world continued to rely on nuclear power.

Western environmentalists were particularly worried about excessive use of water. Massive irrigation systems had boosted the nation's use of water from 40 billion gallons a day in 1900 to 393 billion gallons by 1975, though the population had only tripled. Americans used three times as much water per capita as the world's average.

California was particularly vulnerable. Because the state was naturally dry, its prosperity rested on massive irrigation projects, and in the late 1970s, it had 1,251 major reservoirs. Virtually every large river had at least one dam. Almost as much water was pumped from the ground, with little natural replenishment and even less regulation. Pointing to the destruction of the nation's rivers and streams and the severe lowering of the water table in many areas, environmentalists argued that something needed to be done. Critic Marc Reisner later noted, "Forty years ago, only a handful of heretics, howling at wilderness, challenged the notion that the West needed hundreds of new dams. Today they are almost vindicated."

Environmental agitation produced legislative results in the 1960s and 1970s. Lyndon Johnson's Great Society brought basic legislation to halt the depletion of the country's natural resources. In the next few years, environmentalists went further, pressuring legislative and administrative bodies to regulate polluters. During Richard Nixon's presidency, Congress passed the Clean Air Act, the Water Quality Improvement Act, and the Resource Recovery Act and mandated a new Environmental Protection Agency (EPA) to spearhead the effort to control abuses.

One environmental effort developed into an extraordinarily bitter economic and ecological debate. The Endangered Species Act of 1973 prohibited the federal government from supporting any projects that might jeopardize species threatened with extinction. It ran into direct conflict with commercial imperatives in the Pacific Northwest. Loggers in the Olympic Peninsula had long exploited the land by clear-cutting (cutting down all trees in a region, without leaving any standing). Environmentalists claimed that the forests they cut provided the last refuge for the spotted owl. Scientists and members of the U.S. Forest Service pushed to set aside timberland so that the owl could survive. Loggers protested that this action jeopardized their livelihood. As the issue wound its way through the courts, logging fell off drastically.

Related to the environmental movement was a consumer movement. As Americans bought fashionable clothes, house furnishings, and electrical and electronic gadgets, they began to worry about unscrupulous sellers, just as they had earlier in the twentieth century during the Progressive era. Over the years, Congress had established a variety of regulatory efforts as it started to safeguard citizens from marketplace abuse. In the 1970s, a stronger consumer movement developed, aimed at protecting the interests of the purchasing public and making business more responsible to consumers.

Ralph Nader, a onetime Department of Labor consultant, led the movement. His book *Unsafe at Any Speed: The Designed-in Dangers of the American Automobile* (1965) argued that many cars were coffins on wheels. Head-on collisions, even at low speeds, could easily kill, for cosmetic bumpers could not withstand modest shocks. His efforts paved the way for the National Traffic and Motor Vehicle Safety Act of 1966, which set minimum safety standards for vehicles on public highways, provided for inspection to ensure compliance, and created a National Motor Vehicle Safety Advisory Council.

The consumer movement developed into a full-fledged campaign in the 1970s. Nader's efforts attracted scores of volunteers, called "Nader's Raiders." They turned out critiques and reports and, more important, inspired consumers to become more vocal in defending their rights.

Conclusion
Sorting Out the Pieces

The late 1960s and 1970s were turbulent years. The chaos that seemed to reach a peak in 1968 continued, even as American participation in the war in Vietnam wound down. Richard Nixon recognized that he could contain the protest movement by bringing American soldiers home. He understood, too, the growing frustration with liberal reform and the wish of some Americans to dispense with the excesses they attributed to the young. For a time, he managed to mute protest and to promote a measure of harmony by his policy of Vietnamization, which cut back on the number of Americans dying in battle. But his desire to avoid losing the war led him to expand the conflict into neighboring parts of Indochina, and that move sparked even greater opposition than before.

Meanwhile, Nixon's own overarching ambition and need for electoral support led to the worst political scandal in American history. At just the time that the nation was trying to pick up the pieces from the unpopular war, he found himself embroiled in the Watergate affair, which threatened the United States with a real constitutional crisis that ended only when the president resigned.

During this entire time, disadvantaged groups demanded that the nation expand the meaning of equality. Building on the accomplishments of the civil rights movement in the 1950s and 1960s, women like Ann Clarke, introduced at the start of the chapter, returned to school in ever-increasing numbers and found jobs and sometimes independence after years of being told that their place was at home. Native Americans and Latinos mobilized, too, and could see the stirrings of change. Gay rights activists made their voices heard. Environmentalists created a new awareness of the global dangers the nation and the world faced. Slowly, reformers succeeded in pressuring the government to help the nation fulfill its promise and ensure the realization of the ideals of American life.

But the course of change was ragged. Reform efforts suffered from the disillusionment with liberalism. Some movements were circumscribed by the changing political climate; others simply ran out of steam. Still, the various efforts left a legacy of ferment that could help spark further change, even as the nation became profoundly more conservative in the next decade.

TIME*line*

1968	Richard Nixon elected president
1969	La Raza Unida founded
1970	Shootings at Kent State and Jackson State Universities
1972	Nixon reelected
1973	Vietnam cease-fire agreement
	Watergate hearings in Congress
1974	Nixon resigns; Gerald Ford becomes president
1975	South Vietnam falls to the Communists
1976	Jimmy Carter elected president
1978	*Bakke* v. *Regents of the University of California*

Questions for Review and Reflection

1. What were Richard Nixon's social and political priorities in his presidency?
2. How did Nixon propose to end the war in Vietnam?
3. What impact did the Watergate crisis have on American political life?
4. What advances did the women's movement make in the 1970s?
5. How successful was the quest for social reform in the 1970s?

Key Terms

Busing 887

CREEP 891

ERA 900

Kent State 889

Nixon Doctrine 888

NOW 899

Vietnamization 888

Watergate 879

28

Conservatism and a Shift in Course, 1980–2010

American Stories

An Immigrant Family Struggles

In 1997, Marlene Garrett bundled up her three sleepy children—ages 4, 3, and 1—and took them to the babysitter's home every morning at 5 A.M. "Mama has to go to work so she can buy you shoes," she told them as she left for a job behind the counter at a bagel café in Fort Lauderdale, Florida, that began at 6 A.M. This was a new position and she did not want to be late.

Marlene had come to the United States from Jamaica eight years earlier. She and her husband, Rod, had high hopes for a better life in the United States, and they were fortunate enough to be employed at a time when the economy was on the upswing. But both of them held entry-level jobs and had to struggle to make ends meet. Rod worked in a factory making hospital curtains and brought home about $250 a week. Marlene had just left a $5.25-an-hour job selling sneakers for her $6-an-hour job at the bagel café. With the $200 she earned weekly she could pay the monthly rent of $400 and buy groceries. With luck, they could repair or replace the car, which had recently died, and perhaps begin to pay off their $5,000 debt from medical bills. They had no health insurance and could only hope that no one got sick.

Marlene was not happy about her babysitting arrangements. Her real preference was to stay at home. "Who's a better caretaker than mom?" she asked. But remaining at home was out of the question. Welfare might have been a possibility in the past, but the United States was in the process of cutting back drastically on its welfare rolls, and, in any event, Marlene was not comfortable with that alternative. "I don't want to plant that seed in my children," she said. "I want to work."

Marlene had few day-care options. She would have liked to have taken Scherrod, Angelique, and Hasia to the Holy Temple Christian Academy—her church's day-care center and preschool—but it cost $180 a week for three children and was beyond reach. Several months before, when she had been earning $8 an hour as a home health aide for the elderly, she had thought she could afford the church center and had even put money down for school uniforms for the kids. Then her car gave out and made it impossible to continue that job.

Instead of the Holy Temple Christian Academy, Marlene took the children to the home of Vivienne, a woman from the Bahamas who worked nights at the self-service laundry where Marlene did her wash. Vivienne's apartment was simple and clean but had no toys or books anywhere in sight. Most days, the children watched television during the 10 hours that Marlene was away.

The Garretts knew how important it was to stimulate their children. Reflecting longingly on the church center and what it offered, Marlene said, "The children play games. They go on field trips. They teach them, they train them. My children are bright. You would be amazed at what they would acquire in a year." But instead of a stimulating center, the Garretts had to settle for a place that was simply safe.

Marlene refused to give up hope. Her children were on a waiting list for help from the state that might make the Holy Temple Christian Academy accessible. Meanwhile, she took a second job working nights at the local Marriott Hotel. She had to pay Vivienne more money for the extra hours, and she worried even more about the additional time away from the children, but felt she had no choice. "It is temporary," she said. "I am doing what I have to do."

Marlene and Rod Garrett were like millions of poor Americans who found themselves at loose ends in the last 30 years. They suffered hard times in the early 1980s, then found themselves left out of the prosperity that returned in the 1990s in the longest period of economic growth in American history. And when, toward the end of the first decade of the twenty-first century, the economy crashed in the worst economic crisis since the Great Depression of the 1930s, they found themselves worse off than ever before.

Meanwhile, the global scene shifted abruptly. The cataclysmic events in Europe that ended nearly a half century of Cold War required the United States to redefine its international role. Then, as the new decade began, the United States confronted the menace of terrorism on a scale never known before. The attacks that destroyed the World Trade Center towers in New York City and left a gaping hole in the Pentagon in Washington, D.C., led to a war on terrorism and a fundamental reconfiguration of American foreign policy.

This chapter describes the enormous changes that occurred in the years after 1980. It examines such questions as: How did the growth of a conservative movement change the configurations of American politics? How did economic and technological shifts affect the daily lives of millions of Americans, bringing unprecedented prosperity to people at the top of the economic pyramid but leaving millions of less fortunate Americans behind?

How did different administrations seek to redefine the government's role in the economy, and how did those efforts influence the lives of ordinary Americans? And finally, how did foreign policy shift dramatically as the Cold War came to an end?

New Politics in a Conservative Age

Conservatism gained respect in the 1980s and remained a major force in the twenty-first century. It became powerful in Great Britain, where problems with both inflation and unemployment brought the Conservative party of Margaret Thatcher to power. In Eastern and Central Europe, as communism began to crumble, moderately conservative Christian Democratic movements became increasingly popular.

The New Politics

In the United States, conservatives seized on Thomas Jefferson's maxim: "That government is best which governs least." The dramatic economic growth of the 1960s and 1970s, they believed, left a legacy of rising inflation, falling productivity, enormous waste, and out-of-control **entitlements**. The liberal solution of "throwing money at social problems" no longer worked, conservatives argued. Therefore, they sought to downsize government, reduce taxes, and roll back regulations that they claimed hampered business competition, while restoring what they regarded as old-time moral values.

A new conservative coalition included economists who promoted the free play of market forces and a sharp restriction of governmental control, social activists opposed to pornography, whites irritated at what they viewed as the excesses of affirmative action, and religious fundamentalists who advocated a literal interpretation of Scriptures and often operated through an organization they called the Moral Majority.

Conservatives from all camps capitalized on changing political techniques more successfully than their liberal opponents. They understood the value of polling to assess and polish a candidate's image and the importance of television in providing instant access to the American public. They also relied on new electronic systems such as e-mail, fax machines, and the Internet to mobilize their followers and developed direct-mail appeals that assisted conservative candidates around the country.

Conservative Leadership

More than any other Republican, Ronald Reagan was responsible for the success of the conservative cause. An actor turned politician, he had been a radio broadcaster in his native Midwest, then gravitated to California, where he began a movie career. His success on the silver screen affected his

The Rugged Ronald Reagan Ronald Reagan was fond of projecting an old-fashioned cowboy image. This picture captured the sense of rugged individualism he valued and appeared on the covers of both *Time* and *Newsweek* magazines when he died in 2004. What qualities seem to come across in this photograph? Why did this image have such a powerful appeal? *(Courtesy Ronald Reagan Library)*

political inclinations, and he changed his affiliation from Democrat to Republican in the early 1960s. He went to work as a public spokesman for General Electric, where his visibility and ability to articulate corporate values attracted the attention of conservatives who recognized his political potential and helped him win election as governor of California in 1966. He failed in his first bid for the presidency in 1976 but consolidated his strength over the next four years. By 1980, he had the firm support of the growing Right, which applauded his promise to reduce the size of the federal government but bolster military might.

Running against incumbent Jimmy Carter in 1980, Reagan scored a landslide victory, gaining a popular vote of 51 to 41 percent and a 489 to 49 Electoral College advantage. He also led the Republican party to control of the Senate for the first time since 1955. In 1984, he was reelected by an even larger margin. He received 59 percent of the popular vote and swamped Democratic candidate Walter Mondale in the Electoral College 525 to 13, losing only Minnesota, Mondale's home state, and the District of Columbia, though the Democrats still controlled Congress.

⦿ Watch the Video

Ronald Reagan Presidential Campaign Ad: A Bear in the Woods at **www.myhistorylab.com**

Reagan had a pleasing manner and a special skill as a media communicator. Relying on his acting experience, he used television as Franklin D. Roosevelt had used radio in the 1930s. He spoke of the United States as "the last best hope of man on earth." Echoing John Winthrop's sermon to Puritans coming to the New World in 1630, he referred to America as a "shining city on a hill." In response to those who spoke of a "national malaise," he retorted, "I find nothing wrong with the American people."

•••⌐Read the Document

Ronald Reagan, Address to the National Association of Evangelicals (1983)

at **www.myhistorylab.com**

Throughout his eight years in office, Reagan enjoyed enormous popularity. People talked about a **"Teflon" presidency**, making a comparison with nonstick frying pans, for even serious criticisms failed to stick and disagreements over policy never diminished his personal-approval ratings. When he left the White House, an overwhelming 68 percent of the American public approved of his performance.

But Reagan had a number of liabilities that surfaced over time. As the oldest president the nation had ever had, his attention often drifted, and he occasionally fell asleep during meetings, including one with the pope. While he could speak eloquently with a script in front of him, he was frequently unsure about what was being asked in press conferences. Uninterested in governing, he delegated a great deal of authority, even if that left him unclear about policy decisions. Worst of all, he suffered from charges of "sleaze" in his administration, with several aides and even his attorney general forced from office for improprieties ranging from perjury to influence peddling.

In 1988, Republican George H. W. Bush, who served eight years as Reagan's vice president, ran for the presidency. Though a New Englander, he had prospered in the Texas oil industry, then served in Congress, as top envoy to China, and as head of the CIA. Termed a preppy wimp by the press, he became a pit bull who ran a mudslinging campaign against his Democratic opponent, Governor Michael Dukakis of Massachusetts. On election day, Bush swamped Dukakis, winning a 54–46 percent popular-vote majority and carrying 40 states, though Democrats controlled both houses of Congress.

Bush quickly put his own imprint on the presidency. Despite his upper-crust background, he was an unpretentious man who made a point of trying to appear down-to-earth. More than a year and a half into his term, he was still on his political honeymoon, with a personal-approval rating of 67 percent. Support grew even stronger as he presided over the Persian Gulf War in 1991. Then, as the economy faltered and the results of the war seemed suspect, approval levels began to drop, and he failed in his bid for reelection in 1992.

•••⌐Read the Document

George H.W. Bush, Gulf War Address (1990)

at **www.myhistorylab.com**

⌐Watch the Video

George H.W. Bush's Early Response in the Persian Gulf War

at **www.myhistorylab.com**

Republican Policies at Home

Republicans in the 1980s and early 1990s aimed to reverse the economic stagnation of the Carter years and to provide new opportunities for business

George H. W. Bush on the Stump George H. W. Bush capitalized on his position as vice president under Ronald Reagan and won a resounding victory in the election of 1988. Even so, he did not have the solid conservative mandate that Reagan enjoyed. How does the flag contribute to the impression Bush hoped to convey?

to prosper. To that end, Reagan proposed and implemented an economic recovery program that rested on the theory of **supply-side economics**. According to this much-criticized theory, reduction of taxes would encourage business expansion, which in turn would lead to a larger supply of goods to help stimulate the system as a whole. A 5 percent cut in the tax rate was enacted to go into effect on October 1, 1981, followed by 10 percent cuts in 1982 and 1983. Although all taxpayers received some tax relief, the rich gained far more than middle- and lower-income Americans. Poverty-level Americans did not benefit at all. Tax cuts and enormous defense expenditures increased the budget deficit. From $74 billion in 1980, it jumped to $290 billion in 1992. Such massive deficits drove the gross federal debt—the total national indebtedness—upward from $909 billion in 1980 to $4.4 trillion in 1992. When Reagan assumed office, the per capita national debt was $4,035; 10 years later, in 1990, it was about $12,400.

Faced with the need to raise more money and rectify an increasingly skewed tax code, in 1986 Congress passed and Reagan signed the most sweeping tax reform since the federal income tax began in 1913. It lowered rates, consolidated brackets, and closed loopholes. While all Americans benefited, most of the benefits went to the richest 5 percent of Americans.

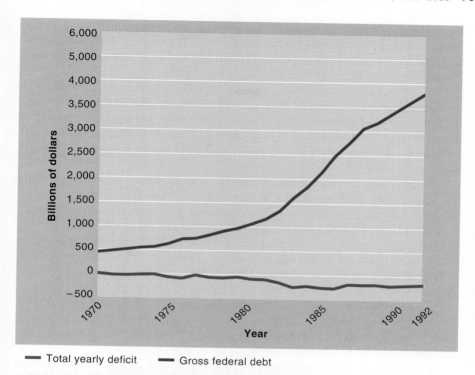

- Total yearly deficit   - Gross federal debt

Federal Budget Deficits and the National Debt, 1970–1992 In the 1970s, 1980s, and early 1990s, the yearly federal budget deficit grew steadily larger, and the gross federal debt skyrocketed. In this economy, deficits and debt affected spending priorities. When did the yearly deficit begin to grow? What changes in the yearly deficit occurred in the 1980s? When did the gross federal debt grow most quickly? *(Source: Data from Statistical Abstract of the United States)*

At the same time, Reagan followed Carter in a major deregulation effort that included agencies such as the Environmental Protection Agency (EPA), the Consumer Product Safety Commission, and the Occupational Safety and Health Administration (OSHA). The Republican administration argued that regulations pertaining to the consumer, the workplace, and the environment were inefficient, paternalistic, excessively expensive, and impeded business growth.

Meanwhile, Reagan challenged the New Deal consensus that the federal government should monitor the economy and assist the least fortunate citizens. He had played by the rules of the system and had succeeded. Others could do the same. He charged that government intruded too deeply into American life. It was time to eliminate "waste, fraud, and abuse" by cutting unnecessary programs.

Reagan needed to curtail social programs both because of sizable tax cuts and because of enormous military expenditures. Committed to a massive arms buildup, over a five-year period the administration sought an unprecedented military budget of $1.5 trillion. By 1985, the United States was spending half a million dollars a minute on defense and four times as much as at the height of the Vietnam War.

Ironically, despite the huge cuts, overall federal spending for social welfare rose from $313 billion in 1980 to $533 billion in 1988. The increase came about because of growth in the payments of entitlement programs such as social security and Medicare, which provided benefits automatically to citizens in need. Even the most aggressive efforts of the Republicans could not wholly dismantle the welfare state.

Reagan took a conservative approach to social issues as well. Accepting the support of the New Right, he strongly endorsed conservative social goals. To avoid compromising his economic program, however, he provided only symbolic support at first. He spoke out for public prayer in the schools without expending political capital in Congress to support the issue. In the same way, he showed his opposition to abortion by making sure that the first nongovernmental group to receive an audience at the White House was an antiabortion March for Life contingent.

George Bush faithfully adhered to Reagan's general economic policy. Running for president in 1988, he promised "no new taxes," although he later backed down from that pledge to join a bipartisan effort to bring the budget deficit under control.

Like Reagan, Bush wanted deep cuts in social programs. Tireless in his criticism of the Democratic majorities in the Senate and House of Representatives, he vetoed measure after measure to assist those caught in the ravages of a troubling recession that sent unemployment rates up to 8 percent and left one of every four urban children living in poverty. He was also more outspoken than Reagan in his support of conservative social goals.

The Republican philosophy under Reagan and Bush dramatically reversed the nation's domestic agenda. Liberalism in the 1960s had reached a high-water mark in a time of steady growth, but in the 1980s decisions about social programs became more difficult, and millions of Americans came to believe that most of the Great Society programs had failed to conquer poverty and in fact had created lifelong welfare dependency. Conservatism offered a more attractive answer, particularly to Americans in the middle and upper classes who were already comfortable.

Republican policy widened the gap between rich and poor. According to one study, the share of national wealth of the richest 1 percent of the nation rose from about 18 percent in 1976 to 36 percent in 1989.

Meanwhile, less fortunate Americans suffered more than they had since the Great Depression. In 1987, one out of every five American children lived in poverty, up 24 percent since 1979. And millions of people, ranging from foreclosed farmers to laid-off industrial workers, were struggling to make ends meet.

Democratic Revival

The 1990s saw a Democratic revival in politics. In 1992, Democrats mounted an aggressive challenge to Republican rule. After a fierce primary campaign, Governor Bill Clinton of Arkansas triumphed over a crowded field of candidates. Overcoming allegations of marital instability, marijuana use, and draft evasion, he argued that it was time for a new generation to take command. Forty-six years old, he had reached maturity in the 1960s and stood in stark contrast to President George H. W. Bush, now running for reelection, who had come of age during World War II. The third candidate in what became a three-way race was H. Ross Perot, a billionaire businessman from Texas who had made a fortune in the computer data-processing field.

On election day, Clinton won 43 percent of the popular vote to 38 percent for Bush and 19 percent for Perot. The electoral vote margin was even larger: 357 for Clinton, 168 for Bush, 0 for Perot. The Democrats retained control of both houses of Congress, with more women and minority members than ever before.

Clinton soon found his hands full at home. Although the economy finally began to improve, the public gave the president little credit for the upturn. He gained Senate ratification of the North American Free Trade Agreement (NAFTA)—aimed at promoting free trade between Canada, Mexico, and the United States—in November 1993 after a bitter battle in which opponents argued that American workers would lose their jobs to less well-paid Mexicans. He secured passage of a crime bill banning the manufacture, sale, or possession of assault weapons. But he failed to win approval of his major legislative initiative: health-care reform.

Republican Resurgence

Irritated voters demonstrated their dissatisfaction in the midterm elections of 1994. Republicans argued that government regulations were hampering business and costing too much. They challenged the notion that the federal government was primarily responsible for health care and other such services. Republicans swept control of both the Senate and the House of Representatives for the first time in more than 40 years. At the state level, Republicans picked up 12 governorships and took control in seven of the eight largest states.

The election marked the end of the commitment to the welfare state. The 104th Congress moved aggressively to make good on its promises—outlined during the campaign in the Republicans' **Contract with America**—to scale back the role of the federal government, eliminate environmental regulations, cut funding for educational programs such as Head Start, reduce taxes, and balance the budget. Under the leadership of Newt Gingrich, the new speaker of the House of Representatives, Congress launched a frontal attack on the budget, proposing massive cuts in virtually all social services. For all of the rhetoric, few of the proposals became law.

A Second Term for Clinton

In 1996, Clinton won a resounding victory over Republican Robert Dole, Senate minority leader. He received 49 percent of the popular vote to 41 percent for Dole and 8 percent for H. Ross Perot, who ran again, though this time less successfully. In the electoral tally, Clinton received 379 votes to 159 for Dole. Yet the Republicans kept control of Congress.

Partisan Politics and Impeachment

Republicans remained in control in the midterm elections of 1998, though Democrats made small gains. But that failed to help them as Clinton was accused by an independent prosecutor, appointed by the Justice Department, of having engaged in an improper sexual relationship with Monica Lewinsky, a White House intern. While Clinton denied the relationship at

The "Hip" Candidate Bill Clinton was an exuberant campaigner who used his musical talent to attract support when he ran for president in 1992. Here he plays his saxophone on nationwide television on *The Arsenio Hall Show* in Los Angeles. What kind of image was Clinton trying to convey in this photograph?

first, the lengthy report presented to Congress left little doubt that such a connection existed, and Clinton finally admitted to the relationship in a nationally televised address. Impeached but not convicted, he clung to his office until the end of his term.

Clinton was an enormously successful politician. Not only had he escaped conviction in the highly visible—and embarrassing—impeachment case, but he also managed to co-opt Republican issues and seize the political center. He quietly advanced liberal goals, with incremental appropriations, even when he was unable to push major programs through Congress.

The Election of 2000

The election of 2000 promised to be close. The strong economy gave Vice President Al Gore, the Democratic nominee, an initial advantage. Yet the Republicans, led by Texas governor George W. Bush, insisted the country needed a change. On election night, as the returns trickled in, neither Bush nor Gore had captured the 270 electoral votes necessary to win the presidency. In December, more than five weeks after the election, after suits and countersuits by both sides, the case reached the Supreme Court. In *Bush* v. *Gore,* the justices ruled, by a 5–4 vote, with the most conservative justices voting in a bloc, that a recount should be curtailed, leaving Bush the winner. Although Gore won the popular vote by about 450,000 votes, Bush triumphed in the Electoral College by a 271–266 majority.

George W. Bush

The new president had been a businessman, gravitating into the Texas oil business and then gaining part ownership of a professional baseball team before running successfully for governor of Texas. As president, Bush had the interests of corporate America at heart. During the campaign, he talked about a tax cut, and this became his first priority. By mid-2001, the tax cut became law. It lowered tax rates for everyone, allowed more tax-free saving for education, and reduced estate taxes. The measure promised to save every taxpayer at least several hundred dollars a year, though it was heavily skewed in favor of the wealthy.

Bush also wanted to reduce the size of government and squelch its intrusions into private affairs, but at the same time, he sought to bolster the military. His first budget, for example, proposed deep cuts in health programs for people without access to health insurance. He sought to weaken environmental regulation. But his proposals for defense called for far greater spending.

A Second Term for Bush

The election of 2004 was bitter and contentious. Running for reelection, Bush faced Massachusetts senator John Kerry, a Vietnam War hero who attacked Republican efforts in the foreign policy sphere, questioned the

Looking for a Place in History? George Bush paid close attention to the image conveyed to the American people, and photographers constantly captured him in ways that underscored his importance. Here he stands in front of Mt. Rushmore, with its famous rock sculptures of several of America's best-known presidents. What impression does the juxtaposition in this photograph convey to you?

administration's ability to protect the nation from terrorist attacks, and charged that tax cuts had done little to revive a still sluggish economy. In a race that remained close to the end, Bush prevailed with 51 percent of the popular vote and a modest Electoral College majority. Republicans added to their majorities in both the Senate and the House of Representatives, as voters in the heartland of American agreed with the Republican party's conservative moral values.

By the time of the 2006 midterm Congressional elections, many Americans were disturbed by military violence, frustrated by a series of scandals on Capitol Hill, and irritated by the insensitive response of the administration to the devastation caused by Hurricane Katrina in New Orleans in September 2005. Voter discontent shifted control of Congress. Democrats won a substantial majority in the House of Representatives and a narrow margin in the Senate. During his last two lame duck years in the White House, Bush faced more serious problems than ever before. Public support eroded, leaving him with a dismal 30 percent approval rating.

Barack Obama

◉ Watch the Video

The Historical Significance of the 2008 Presidential Election at **www.myhistorylab.com**

In 2008, the nation acted on its disaffection. In a spirited campaign, first-term Senator Barack Obama, an African American, beat Hillary Clinton for the Democratic nomination. Obama, hardly in the picture a year before, stayed on his message of change and hope in the general election to triumph by a vote of 365 to 173 over John McCain, the Republican candidate, a hero from the war in Vietnam now in the Senate. Obama's victory helped the Democrats to sizable majorities in the House and Senate. With the first African American President in its history, the United States seemed poised for a new era.

◉⸗[Watch the Video

The Connection Between Obama and Lincoln

at **www.myhistorylab.com**

An End to Social Reform

The Republican attack on the welfare state included an effort to limit the commitment to social reform. Enough had been done already, conservatives argued, and gains for less fortunate Americans came at the expense of the middle class. It was time to end federal "intrusion" in this area.

Slowdown in the Struggle for Civil Rights

Republican policies slowed the civil rights movement. Reagan opposed busing to achieve racial balance, and his attorney general worked to dismantle affirmative action programs. Initially reluctant to support extension of the enormously successful Voting Rights Act of 1965, Reagan relented only after severe bipartisan criticism. He also launched an assault on the Civil Rights Commission and hampered its effectiveness by appointing members who did not support its main goals. The courts similarly weakened commitments to equal rights. As a result of judicial appointments, federal courts stopped pushing for school integration.

Yet African Americans kept the struggle alive. The Reverend Jesse Jackson, a longtime civil rights activist, established what he called the Rainbow Coalition in 1984 and ran for the presidency. Though he lost his bid for the Democratic nomination, he had the support of nearly 400 delegates, and in a nationally televised speech at the convention, he vowed not to forget his constituency of "the desperate, the damned, the disinherited, the disrespected, and the despised." Four years later, in 1988, he sought the Democratic nomination again, this time with the support of 1,200 delegates at the convention, before falling short of his goal once more.

Despite significant victories in mayoral elections in major cities and other electoral gains, black–white relations remained tense. A riot in Los Angeles in 1992 revealed the continuing racial polarization. The year before, Americans had watched a videotaped, savage beating of black motorist Rodney King by white police officers, the most dramatic of a long string of incidents involving police brutality. When a California jury that did not include any African Americans acquitted the policemen, many people throughout the country became convinced that people of color could not obtain equal justice under the law. In Los Angeles, thousands reacted with uncontrolled fury, targeting supermarkets, drug stores, Korean businesses, restaurants, and mini-malls. It was the worst riot in decades and served notice that racial injustice, social inequality, and poverty could no longer be ignored.

Affirmative action, which had successfully brought blacks into the mainstream, led to a backlash. Energized by their political victories in 1994, conservatives launched a powerful attack on the policy of giving preferential treatment to groups that had suffered discrimination in the past. They pushed ballot initiatives and pressured public agencies to bring the practice to an end. Proposition 209 in California in 1996 prohibited the use of gender or race in awarding state government contracts or admitting students to state colleges and universities. In late 2003, the Supreme Court ruled in two cases involving the University of Michigan that affirmative action was acceptable, even as it rejected a point system the university used in carrying out the policy in undergraduate admissions.

Then, in 2007, an even more conservative Supreme Court, bolstered by two Bush appointees, ruled that public schools could not promote integration through measures taking account of a student's race. After more than 50 years, it appeared that *Brown v. Board of Education* had run its course.

Obstacles to Women's Rights

Women made significant electoral gains at the local, state, and national levels. In 1981, President Reagan named Sandra Day O'Connor as the first woman Supreme Court justice, and in 1984 Democrat Geraldine Ferraro became the first major-party female vice presidential nominee. The women's movement also became racially inclusive.

Yet women still faced problems that were compounded by conservative social policies. Access to new positions did not change their concentration in lower-paying jobs. In 1985, most working women were still secretaries, cashiers, bookkeepers, registered nurses, and waitresses—the same jobs most frequently held 10 years before. Even when women moved into positions traditionally held by men, their progress often stopped at the lower and middle levels, at what came to be called a "glass ceiling," and wage disparities continued to exist. In 1985, full-time working women still earned only 59 cents for every dollar earned by men.

In the new century there was continuing resistance to inclusion at the top. Women started to become the heads of major firms as the glass ceiling began to crack in the 1990s, yet most leaders were still men. In 2005, only about 17 percent of the partners at major law firms were women. Still, Hillary Clinton came close to winning the Democratic nomination for president in 2008.

Conservatives also waged a dedicated campaign against the right to legal abortion. Despite the 1973 Supreme Court decision legalizing the procedure, the issue remained very much alive. The number of abortions increased dramatically in the decade after the decision. In response, "pro-life" forces mobilized. Opponents lobbied to cut off federal funds that allowed the poor to obtain the abortions that the better-off could pay for themselves; they insisted that abortions should be performed in hospitals and not in less expensive clinics; and they worked to reverse the original decision itself.

Though the Supreme Court underscored its judgment in 1983, the pro-life movement was not deterred. A solidifying conservative majority on the Court ruled that while women's right to abortion remained intact, state legislatures could impose limitations if they chose, and many did. Such rulings and laws made an abortion harder to obtain, particularly for poor women and young women.

Abortion became increasingly controversial in the early twenty-first century. A number of physicians performing abortions lost their lives. Abortion opponents also took aim at a seldom-used, late-term procedure they called "partial birth abortion." Congress passed a measure banning the procedure, but President Clinton vetoed it twice. Then in 2003 President Bush signed a new version of the measure, which the Supreme Court upheld in 2007.

For all the progress, serious problems remained. The 2000 census revealed that the number of families headed by single mothers had risen to 7.5 million, an increase of 25 percent since 1990. A report based on census figures noted that in 2005, only 51 percent of all American women were living with a spouse. At the same time, the gender pay gap closed somewhat. In 2005, women earned about 75 cents for every dollar paid to men.

The Limited Commitment to Latino Rights

Latinos likewise faced continuing concerns in the 1980s and early 1990s as the commitment to reform eroded. The Latino population increased substantially as a result of immigration reform during the Great Society of the 1960s. Many other immigrants arrived illegally.

Many of the new arrivals were skilled workers or professionals, who still had to retool after arriving in the United States. But even more prevalent were laborers, service sector workers, and semiskilled employees, who needed the benefit of social services at just the time they were being cut back.

Like other groups, Latinos slowly extended their political gains. In the 1980s, Henry Cisneros became mayor of San Antonio and Federico Peña was elected mayor of Denver. Both later served in the Clinton Cabinet. In New Mexico, Governor Toney Anaya called himself the nation's highest-elected Hispanic. Lauro Cavazos became the first Latino Cabinet official when he was appointed secretary of education in 1988. In the George W. Bush administration, White House counsel Alberto Gonzales played a major role in advising the president during the first term and became attorney general in the second.

The Latino population increased dramatically in the new century. In 2003, Latinos edged past African Americans and became the nation's largest minority group, and experts predicted that by 2100, one in three Americans would be Latino.

As the economy faltered in the early part of the new century, median Latino household income fell, and unemployment increased. Some Mexican immigrants feared that they would become members of a permanent under-class. Latinos nevertheless had a growing impact on American culture. Merengue music could often be heard in music stores or on the radio. Argentine steakhouses could be found in many cities. Use of the Spanish language became more and more common around the country. President George W. Bush himself used Spanish in appealing to this important electoral bloc.

Continuing Problems for Native Americans

Native Americans likewise experienced the waning commitment to reform, but they made gains as a result of their own efforts. Some Indian groups adapted to the capitalist ethos. The Choctaw in Mississippi were among the most successful. By the middle of the 1980s, Choctaw owned all or part of three businesses on the reservation, employed 1,000 people, generated $30 million in work annually, and cut the unemployment rate in half. After Congress approved Native American gambling in 1988, an increasing number of tribes became involved in this industry. Despite entrepreneurial gains, Indians still remained (as the 1990 census showed) the nation's poorest group. As Ben Nighthorse Campbell, Republican senator from Colorado, noted in 1995, average Indian household income fell by 5 percent in the 1980s, while it rose for all other ethnic and racial groups.

Indians continued their legal efforts to regain lost land. In 1999, the federal government joined the Oneida Indians in a lawsuit demanding restitution for the 270,000 acres of land in central New York that they claimed state and local governments had illegally acquired from them in the late eighteenth and early nineteenth centuries. In early 2000, the federal government returned 84,000 acres in northern Utah that it had taken from the Ute in 1916 when it sought to secure the rights to valuable reserves of oil shale. In 2009, the federal government agreed to pay $3.4 billion to settle claims dating back to the nineteenth century.

Native American women became increasingly active in the larger reform effort. Ada Deer, who had successfully fought the government's termination policy in the 1970s, served as assistant secretary of the interior in the 1990s. Winona LaDuke, an environmental activist, directed the Honor the Earth Fund and the White Earth Land Recovery Project, fought needless hydroelectric development, and was singled out by *Time* magazine as one of the nation's 50 most promising leaders under age 40.

In the last months of the Clinton administration, the Bureau of Indian Affairs reversed the pattern that had been so predominant in the past in apologizing for the nation's repressive treatment of Native Americans. But many Indians still felt a sense of dislocation, captured by novelist Sherman Alexie in 1993. In one of the stories in *The Lone Ranger and Tonto Fistfight in Heaven*, he wrote: "Sometimes I still feel like half of me is lost in the city, with its foot wedged into a steam grate or something. Stuck in one of those revolving doors, going round and round while all the white people are laughing."

Asian American Gains

Asian Americans climbed the social and economic ladder one rung at a time. The Asian American population increased dramatically with the influx of refugees at the end of the Vietnam War, with more than half a million arriving after 1975. In the 1980s, 37 percent of all immigrants to the United States came from Asia. In Los Angeles and other cities, Samoans, Taiwanese, Koreans, Vietnamese, Filipinos, and Cambodians competed for jobs and apartments with Mexicans, African Americans, and Anglos, just as newcomers had contended with one another in New York City a century earlier.

Sometimes the media highlighted the successes of Asian immigrants, particularly in contrast to the problems encountered by other groups. In 1986, *U.S. News & World Report* noted Asian American advances in a cover story, while *Newsweek* ran a lead article on "Asian Americans: A 'Model Minority,'" and *Fortune* called them "America's Super Minority." Asian Americans were proud of the exposure but pointed out that many members of the working class still struggled for a foothold. In the Chinatowns of San Francisco and Los Angeles, 40 to 50 percent of the workers were employed in the low-paid service sector or garment industry; in New York's Chinatown, the figure was close to 70 percent. Chinese immigrant women, in particular, often had little choice but to work as seamstresses.

Asian Americans enjoyed real success in the 1990s. With about 11 million people—approximately 4 percent of the national population—of Asian descent in the United States in 2000, there was now a critical mass. Norman Y. Mineta became the first Asian American to hold a cabinet position in 2000.

Yet Asian Americans in the 1990s found themselves in an ambiguous position. While they had higher median incomes than whites, due in part to a dedicated work ethic, newcomers faced continuing economic problems. Older assumptions also persisted. A report in 2000 observed that many Americans still saw Asian Americans in stereotypical terms as secretive and "inscrutable."

Gays

The struggle for gay rights also continued, and slowly gays began to achieve their demands. In a major change in 2000, the Big Three automakers— General Motors, Ford, and Chrysler—announced health-care benefits for partners of gay employees, in a move that covered 465,000 workers. That same year, Vermont recognized same-sex relationships through civil unions, though stopped short of permitting gay marriages. In 2002, the American Academy of Pediatricians announced its support of the right of gay men and women to adopt the children of their partners. Gay activism helped broaden the definition of family. As the gay rights movement celebrated its 30-year anniversary in a parade commemorating the 1969 Stonewall Riot that had sparked gay resistance, proponents noted that the event had changed from a protest to a party. As the *New York Times* observed, "that in itself is a sign of success."

But resistance persisted. As a number of states legalized gay marriage, a backlash helped mobilize conservatives around the country, and in 2004, voters in a number of states approved constitutional bans on gay marriage. The issue remained ambiguous as the decade came to an end.

Pressures on the Environmental Movement

Environmentalists, too, were discouraged by the direction of public policy in the 1980s and early 1990s. Activists found that they faced fierce opposition in the Republican years. Reagan systematically restrained the EPA in his avowed effort to promote economic growth. The Department of the Interior opened forest lands, wilderness areas, and coastal waters to economic development, with no concern for preserving the natural environment. The first Bush initially proved more sympathetic to environmental causes and delighted environmentalists by signing new clean-air legislation. Later, as the economy faltered, he was less willing to support environmental action that he claimed might slow economic growth. In 1992, he accommodated business by easing clean-air restrictions. That same year, at a United Nations–sponsored Earth Summit in Rio de Janeiro, Brazil, with 100 other heads of state, Bush stood alone in his refusal to sign a biological diversity treaty framed to conserve plant and animal species.

Several years later, the United States signed but did not ratify the Kyoto accord, negotiated in 1997 to combat global warming by cutting down on greenhouse gases. In 2009, Barack Obama pushed through an agreement of larger nations at a similar meeting in Copenhagen, though it failed to gain the support of all 193 nations at the conference.

Economic and Demographic Change

Republicans sought to reorganize the government against the backdrop of an economy that was changing dramatically. Technology brought some changes. Demographic shifts brought others. Meanwhile the business cycle alternated between boom and bust.

The Shift to a Service Economy

In a trend that had been underway for more than half a century, the United States continued its shift from an industrial base, in which most workers actually produced things, to a service base, in which most provided expertise or service to others in the workforce. By the mid-1980s, three-fourths of the 113 million employees in the country toiled in the service sector as fast-food workers, clerks, computer programmers, doctors, lawyers, bankers, teachers, and bureaucrats. That shift, in turn, had its roots in the decline of the country's industrial sector. The United States had been the world's industrial leader since the late nineteenth century. By the 1980s and early 1990s, productivity had slowed in virtually all American industries. The most important factor in this decline was a widespread failure on the part of the United States to invest sufficiently in its basic productive capacity.

While American industry became less productive, other industrial nations moved forward. German and Japanese industries, rebuilt after World War II with U.S. aid and aggressively modernized thereafter, reached new heights of efficiency. As a result, the United States began to lose its share of the world market for industrial goods. In 1946, the country had provided 60 percent of the world's iron and steel; in 1978, it provided a mere 16 percent. By 1980, Japanese car manufacturers had captured nearly one-quarter of the American automobile market. The auto industry, which had been a mainstay of economic growth for much of the twentieth century, suffered plant shutdowns and massive layoffs. In 1991, its worst year ever, Ford lost a staggering $2.3 billion.

Workers in Transition

In the 1980s and early 1990s, American labor struggled to hold on to the gains realized by the post–World War II generation of blue-collar workers. The shift to a service economy, while providing new jobs, was difficult for many American workers. Millions of men and women who lost positions as a result of mergers, plant closings, and permanent economic contractions now found themselves in low-paying jobs with few opportunities for advancement.

Meanwhile, the trade union movement faltered as the economy moved from an industrial to a service base. Unions had been most successful in organizing the nation's industrial workers in the years since the 1930s, and the United States emerged from World War II with unions strong. In the years that followed, the percentage of workers belonging to unions dropped, from just over 25 percent in 1980 to barely over 16 percent a decade later. As the total number of wage and salary workers rose substantially between 1983 and 1993, the overall number of union members dropped from 17.7 million to 16.6 million.

Farmers also had to adjust as the larger workforce changed. Continuing a trend that began in the early twentieth century, the number of farms and farmers declined steadily. When Franklin Roosevelt took office in 1933, some 6.7 million farms covered the American landscape. Fifty years later, there were only 2.4 million, and the trend continued. As family farms disappeared, farming income became more concentrated in the hands of the largest operators. The top 1 percent of the growers in the United States had average annual incomes of $572,000, but the small and medium-sized farmers who were being forced off the land frequently had incomes below the official government poverty line.

Social Crises

Poverty was a relentless problem for urban as well as rural Americans. The Census Bureau reported in 1997 that 35.6 million people in the United States—the richest country in the world—still lived below what was defined as the poverty line of about $16,000 a year for a family of four. The percentage—13.3 percent—had fallen slightly in each of the previous few years, but it was still sizable, especially considering that it included one out of every three *working* Americans. Worse still was the fact that in 1998, there were 900,000 more Americans living below the poverty line than in 1990. Nor did the situation improve in the new century. In 2004, the Department of Agriculture reported that more than 12 million American families struggled—sometimes without success—to feed themselves. Meanwhile, record levels of Americans lacked health insurance. A Census Bureau report in 2004 showed a figure of 45 million in 2003, which increased to 47 million— or 16 percent of the population—two years later.

Just as the United States rediscovered its poor in the 1960s, so it rediscovered its homeless in the 1980s and 1990s. Even as unemployment dropped in the 1980s, the number of homeless quadrupled. Numbers were hard to ascertain, for the homeless had no fixed addresses, but one estimate

Homeless in America The homeless became far more visible in the 1990s. Here a man lies sleeping under a thin sheet of plastic, serving as his blanket, right in front of the White House in Washington, D.C. What impression does the proximity to the White House convey?

in 1990 calculated that 6 million to 7 million people had been homeless at some point in the past five years. In 2009, estimates noted about 3.5 million Americans, or one percent of the population, were homeless.

Illnesses affected rich and poor but were particularly corrosive for the less fortunate. The discovery of AIDS (acquired immune deficiency syndrome) in 1981 marked the start of one of the most serious diseases in the history of the United States—and the world. Some nations found themselves decimated by AIDS. In China, for example, entire villages were infected with HIV (the human immunodeficiency virus that causes AIDS). Africa was hit even harder.

While health conditions in the United States were better than those in many parts of the world, AIDS still had a devastating effect. The sexual revolution of the 1960s had brought a major change in sexual patterns, particularly among the young, but now sexual experimentation was threatened by this deadly new disease. Although it seemed to strike intravenous drug users and homosexuals with numerous partners more than other groups at first, it soon spread to the heterosexual population as well. AIDS became the leading cause of death in Americans between ages 25 and 44. The growing number of deaths—approximately 550,000 in 2005—was horrifying, even as more and more people learned how to survive with the disease. New drugs, taken in combination, extended the life span of those with the HIV virus and reduced the death rate in the 1990s, but AIDS remained a lethal, and ultimately fatal, disease.

Population Shifts

As the American people dealt with the swings of the economy, demographic patterns changed significantly. The nation's population increased from 228 million to approximately 308 million between 1980 and 2010. At the same time, the complexion of the country changed. The country's nonwhite population—African Americans, Latinos, Asians, and Native Americans—stood at an all-time high of 25 percent, the result of increased immigration and of minority birthrates significantly above the white birthrate.

The population shifted geographically as well. American cities increasingly filled with members of the nation's minorities. White families continued to leave for the steadily growing suburbs. In many of the nation's largest cities—New York, Chicago, and Houston among them—minorities made up at least half the population. Minority representation varied by urban region. In Detroit, Washington, New Orleans, and Chicago, African Americans were the largest minority; in Phoenix, El Paso, San Antonio, and Los Angeles, Latinos held that position; in San Francisco, Asians outnumbered other groups. The cities also grew steadily poorer. As had been the case since World War II, commuters from the suburbs took the better-paying jobs, while people living in the cities held lower-paying positions.

At the same time, the population was moving west. California was the nation's fastest-growing state, its population increasing in the 1980s by nearly 26 percent. Responding to a question about California's impact on the rest of the country, writer Wallace Stegner replied, "We *are* the national culture, at its most energetic end." Los Angeles became the most dynamic example of American vitality and creativity. The motion picture industry exerted a worldwide impact. The city became a capital of consumption and served as a symbol of a dynamic national life.

The New Pilgrims

Immigration changed the face of America in the years after 1980. The number of immigrants to the United States in the 20-year period from 1981 to 2000 was approximately 17.5 million, making it the most voluminous period of immigration in American history. In the decade of the 1990s, close to 10 million immigrants were counted, just less than the 10.1 million immigrants recorded in the 10 years from 1905 to 1914, which stands as the all-time record for that span of time. The increase continued in the first five years of the twenty-first century, and in 2005, immigrants made up 12.4 percent of America's population, compared to 11.2 percent in 2000.

Patterns of immigrant settlement changed. Whereas most immigrants around the turn of the preceding century remained near the East Coast or in contiguous states, in 2000, 39.9 percent of the foreign born settled in western states, with only 22.6 percent of them living in the Northeast. The shift was a result of larger demographic changes in the United States. As the twentieth century began, the Northeast still dominated the economic and cultural life of the nation. A hundred years later, the West was increasingly dominant. California had surpassed New York as the most populous state, and Los Angeles International Airport, known as LAX, had replaced Ellis Island as the port of entry for many immigrants.

The sources of recent immigration were similar to those of the 1970s and 1980s. In 2000, just over one-third of all immigrants—legal and illegal—came from Central America, and just over one-quarter came from Asia. Over the next six years, the total Latino population increased by 24 percent, while the Asian population grew by almost 28 percent. Immigrants everywhere, often living on the fringe, looked toward the United States, just as they had done in the past.

Illegal immigration remained a problem. Of the 33.5 million foreigners that the Census Bureau estimated lived in America in 2004, about a third, perhaps even more, were illegal entrants. After 2000, about 850,000 unauthorized immigrants arrived each year. People talked about the nation's "broken borders" as record numbers of immigrants lost their lives in the desert while trying to cross into the United States from Mexico.

Legislation contributed to increased immigration. In 1986, Congress passed the Immigration Reform and Control Act, aimed at curbing illegal immigration while offering amnesty to aliens living in the United States. The Immigration Act of 1990 opened the doors wider, raising immigration quotas while cutting back on restrictions that had limited entry in the past.

It also provided for swift deportation of aliens who committed crimes. Two other measures in 1992 expanded eligibility slightly. In 2001, the United States and Mexico began to talk about how to ease the plight of Mexican immigrants and permit illegal arrivals to stay.

Opposition to illegal immigration led to powerful resistance. Congress passed a measure to prevent illegal aliens from obtaining state drivers' licenses. Volunteers patrolled the border between Mexico and Arizona to keep people away. The federal government tried—and failed—in 2006 to enact legislation to tighten border security while making it easier for illegal immigrants to gain citizenship.

The Roller-Coaster Economy

The economy shifted back and forth in the years after 1980. The recession of 1980 to 1982 began during the Carter administration but worsened during Reagan's first year, the job situation deteriorated further, and by the end of 1982, the unemployment rate climbed to 10.8 percent (and over 20 percent among African Americans). Nearly one-third of the nation's industrial capacity lay idle, and 12 million Americans were out of work.

Economic conditions improved in late 1983 and early 1984, particularly for Americans in the middle- and upper-income ranges. The federal tax cut Reagan pushed through encouraged consumer spending, and huge defense expenditures had a stimulating effect. The Republican effort to reduce restrictions and cut waste sparked business confidence. The stock market climbed as it reflected the optimistic buying spree.

But the economic upswing masked a number of problems. Millions of Americans remained poor. Many families continued to earn a middle-class income, but only by having two full-time income earners. They also went deeply into debt. To buy homes, young people accepted vastly higher mortgage interest rates than their parents had. Stiff credit card debts, often at 20 percent interest, were common. Under such circumstances, some young families struggled to remain in the middle class. Blue-collar workers had to accept lower standards of living. Single mothers were hit hardest of all.

The huge and growing budget deficits reflected the fundamental economic instability. Those deficits provoked doubts that resulted in a stock market crash in 1987. The market revived, but the crash foreshadowed further problems.

Those problems surfaced in the early 1990s as the country experienced another recession. The huge increase in the national debt eroded business confidence, and this time the effects were felt not simply in the stock market but in the economy as a whole. American firms suffered a serious decline, and to cope with shrinking profits and decreased consumer demand, companies scaled back dramatically. Around the nation, state governments found it impossible to balance their budgets without resorting to massive spending cuts. Most had constitutional prohibitions against running deficits, and so they had to slash spending for social services and education.

RECOVERING *the* PAST

Autobiography

As we reach our own time, the historical past perhaps most worth recovering is our own. Our own story is as valid a part of the story of American history as the tale of Revolutionary War soldiers, frontier women, reform politicians, and immigrant grandparents. In this computerized age, the person we need to recover is ourself, a self that has been formed, at least in part, by the entire American experience we have been studying.

Autobiography is the form of writing in which people tell their own life history. Although written autobiographies are at least as old as the literature of the early Christians (for example, *The Confessions of St. Augustine*), the word *autobiography* dates from the late eighteenth century, around the time of the French and American revolutions. That is no accident. These momentous events represented the triumph of individual liberty and the sovereignty of the self. *The Autobiography of Benjamin Franklin*, written between 1771 and Franklin's death in 1790 (and excerpted here), is a classic celebration of the American success story. Franklin's work set the standard for one autobiographical form, the memoir of one's public achievements and success. The other brief autobiographical memoir, from the reminiscences of Elizabeth Cady Stanton, also reflects the tone and range of this tradition.

Not all autobiographies are written late in life to celebrate one's accomplishments. The confessional autobiography, unlike most memoirs, explores the author's interior life, acknowledging flaws and failures as well as successes; it may be written at any age. The purpose of this type of autobiography is not just to reconstruct one's past to preserve it for posterity, but to find from one's past an identity in order to know better how to live one's future. The story of religious confessions and conversions is an obvious example. This form also includes secular self-examinations such as those by Maxine Hong Kingston in *The Woman Warrior* (1976), Piri Thomas in *Down These Mean Streets* (1967), or Maya Angelou in a series of five autobiographical sketches beginning with *I Know Why the Caged Bird Sings* (1969). The two confessional excerpts presented here, those of Native American Black Elk and black activist Malcolm X, are among the finest examples of confessional autobiography and suggest its variety.

These examples hardly convey the full range of the autobiographical form or how available to all people is the opportunity to tell the story of one's life. In 1909, William Dean Howells called autobiography the "most democratic province in the republic of letters." A recent critic agrees, pointing out:

> To this genre have been drawn public and private figures: poets, philosophers, prizefighters; actresses, artists, political activists; statesmen and penitentiary prisoners; financiers and football players; Quakers and Black Muslims; immigrants and Indians. The range of personality, experience, and profession reflected in the forms of American autobiography is as varied as American life itself.

Your story, too, is a legitimate part of American history. But writing an autobiography, while open to all, is deceptively difficult. Like historians, autobiographers face problems of sources, selection, interpretation, and style. As in the writing of any history, the account of one's past must be objective, not only in the verifiable accuracy of details but also in the honest selection of representative events to be described. Moreover, in fiction as well as history, the autobiographer must provide a structured form, an organizing principle, literary merit, and thematic coherence to the story. Many other challenges face the would-be autobiographer, such as finding a balance between one's public life and the private self and handling problems of memory, ego—should one, for example, use the first or third person?—and death.

REFLECTING ON THE PAST To get an idea of the difficulties of writing an autobiography, try writing your own. Limit yourself to 1,000 words. Good luck.

Autobiographical Memoirs

BENJAMIN FRANKLIN

Dear son,

I have ever had a pleasure in obtaining any little anecdotes of my ancestors. . . . Imagining it may be equally agreeable to you to know the circumstances of my life—many of which you are yet unacquainted with—and expecting a week's uninterrupted leisure in my present country retirement, I sit down to write them for you. Besides, there are some other inducements that excite me to this undertaking. From the poverty and obscurity in which I was born and in which I passed my earliest years, I have raised myself to a state of affluence and some degree of celebrity in the world. As constant good fortune has accompanied me even to an advanced period of life, my posterity will perhaps be desirous of learning the means, which I employed, and which, thanks to Providence, so well succeeded with me. They may also deem them fit to be imitated, should any of them find themselves in similar circumstances.

Source: *The Autobiography of Benjamin Franklin* (1771).

ELIZABETH CADY STANTON

It was 'mid such exhilarating scenes that Miss Anthony and I wrote addresses for temperance, anti-slavery, educational and woman's rights conventions. Here we forged resolutions, protests, appeals, petitions, agricultural reports, and constitutional arguments; for we made it a matter of conscience to accept every invitation to speak on every question, in order to maintain woman's right to do so. . . .

It is often said, by those who know Miss Anthony best, that she has been my good angel, always pushing and goading me to work, and that but for her pertinacity I should never have accomplished the little I have. On the other hand it has been said that I forged the thunderbolts and she fired them. Perhaps all this is, in a measure, true. With the cares of a large family I might, in time, like too many women, have become wholly absorbed in a narrow family selfishness, had not my friend been continually exploring new fields for missionary labors.

Source: Elizabeth Cady Stanton, *Eighty Years and More: Reminiscences, 1815–1897* (1898).

Confessional Autobiographies

BLACK ELK

And so it was all over.

I did not know then how much was ended. When I look back now from this high hill of my old age, I can still see the butchered women and children lying heaped and scattered all along the crooked gulch as plain as when I saw them with eyes still young. And I can see that something else died there in the bloody mud, and was buried in the blizzard. A people's dream died there. It was a beautiful dream.

And I, to whom so great a vision was given in my youth,—you see me now a pitiful old man who has done nothing, for the nation's hoop is broken and scattered. There is no center any longer, and the sacred tree is dead.

Source: *Black Elk Speaks*, as told through John G. Neihardt (1932). Reprinted with permission from State University of New York Press, copyright 2008.

MALCOLM X

I want to say before I go on that I have never previously told anyone my sordid past in detail. I haven't done it now to sound as though I might be proud of how bad, how evil, I was.

But people are always speculating—why am I as I am? To understand that of any person, his whole life, from birth, must be reviewed. All of our experiences fuse into our personality. Everything that ever happened to us is an ingredient.

Today, when everything that I do has an urgency, I would not spend one hour in the preparation of a book which has the ambition to perhaps titillate some readers. But I am spending many hours because the full story is the best way that I know to have it seen, and understood, that I had sunk to the very bottom of the American white man's society when—soon now, in prison—I found Allah and the religion of Islam and it completely transformed my life.

Source: From *The Autobiography of Malcolmn X* by Malcolm X and Alex Haley, copyright 1964 by Alex Haley and Malcolm X. Copyright 1965 by Alex Haley and Betty Shabazz. Used by permission of Random House, Inc.

After a number of false starts, the economy began to recover in mid-1992. The unemployment rate dropped, the productivity index rose, and a concerted effort began to bring the federal deficit down. The lowering of interest rates by the Federal Reserve Board revived confidence and promoted consumer spending. Productivity rose steadily throughout the decade, and the national economic growth rate began to rise again. Growth, like productivity, was not as dramatic as it had sometimes been in the golden years of industrial development, but it was sustained in what became the longest expansion in American history. Inflation fell to a 30-year low. The unemployment rate also declined, dropping from 7.8 percent in 1992 to 4.6 percent in 1997.

One reflection of the return of prosperity was the soaring stock market. The market moved relentlessly ahead, with the Dow Jones average topping the once-unimaginable 10,000 barrier in 1999 and quickly moving past the 11,000 mark. An even more important sign of economic health was the dramatic reduction in the budget deficit. A Democratic effort to preempt a Republican issue and hold down spending paid off, particularly as low interest rates encouraged economic expansion. In 1998, the United States finished with a budget surplus for the first time in 29 years.

Then, all too quickly, the economy faltered. In 2000, the stock market began to slide, as investors realized that many of the financial gains did not reflect commensurate gains in productivity. By early 2001, it was clear that the economy was slumping, and it became increasingly fragile in the next few years. In 2007, the national debt—the sum of all yearly deficits—reached $9 trillion for the first time. As the housing market collapsed that year, with risky mortgages leading to foreclosure, ordinary working Americans saw the erosion of their dreams of becoming part of the middle class.

Everything fell apart in 2008. In the midst of the housing boom, banks, freed from regulation, gave mortgages to people who could not afford the houses they bought. When those banks failed, they started a downward spiral that soon brought down a number of the nation's major financial corporations, and the stock market plummeted. As the crisis worsened, companies across the country began to lay off workers, and unemployment reached 10 percent in 2009. Only quick action by the federal government averted a total collapse like the Great Depression of the 1930s.

Foreign Policy and the End of the Cold War

In the early 1990s, the United States emerged triumphant in the Cold War that had dominated international politics since the end of World War II. In one of the most momentous turns in modern world history, communism collapsed in Eastern Europe and in the Soviet Union, and the various republics in the Soviet orbit moved toward capitalism and democracy. Other regions—the Middle East and Africa—experienced equally breathtaking change.

Reagan, Bush, and the Soviet Union

The Cold War was very much alive when Ronald Reagan assumed power in 1981. Like most of his compatriots, Reagan believed in large defense budgets and a militant approach toward the Soviet Union. He wanted to cripple the USSR economically by forcing it to spend more than it could afford on defense.

Viewing the Soviet Union as an **"evil empire"** in his first term, Reagan promoted a larger atomic arsenal by arguing that a nuclear war could be fought and won. The administration dropped efforts to obtain Senate ratification of SALT II, the arms reduction plan negotiated under Carter, although it observed the pact's restrictions. Then Reagan proposed the enormously expensive and bitterly criticized Strategic Defense Initiative, popularly known as "Star Wars" after the 1977 movie, to intercept Soviet missiles in outer space.

In his second term, Reagan softened his belligerence. Mikhail Gorbachev, the new Soviet leader, watching his own economy collapse under the pressure of the superheated arms race, realized the need for greater accommodation with the West. He understood that the only way the Soviet Union could survive was through arms negotiations with the United States. He therefore proposed a policy of *perestroika* (restructuring the economy) and *glasnost* (political openness to encourage personal initiative). His overtures opened the way to better relations with the United States.

Concerned with his own place in history, Reagan met with Gorbachev, and the two developed a close working relationship. Summit meetings led to an Intermediate-Range Nuclear Forces Treaty in 1987 that provided for the withdrawal and destruction of 2,500 Soviet and American nuclear missiles in Europe.

George Bush maintained Reagan's comfortable relationship with Gorbachev. At several summit meetings in 1989 and 1990, the two leaders signed agreements reducing the number of long-range nuclear weapons, ending the manufacture of chemical weapons, and easing trade restrictions. The Strategic Arms Reduction Treaty (START) signed in 1991 dramatically cut stockpiles of long-range weapons.

The End of the Cold War

The Cold War ended with astonishing speed. Gorbachev's efforts to restructure Soviet society and to work with the United States brought him acclaim around the world but led to trouble at home. In mid-1991, he faced an old-guard Communist coup, led by those who opposed *glasnost* and *perestroika*. He survived this right-wing challenge, but he could not resist those who wanted to go even further to establish democracy and capitalism. The forces he had unleashed finally destroyed the Soviet system and tore the USSR apart. Boris Yeltsin, president of Russia, the strongest and largest of the Soviet republics, emerged as the dominant leader, but even he could not contain the forces of disintegration. Movements in the tiny Baltic republics of Latvia, Lithuania, and Estonia, culminating with independence in 1991, began the dismantling of the Soviet Union. The once-powerful superpower was now a collection of separate states. Although the republics coalesced loosely in a **Commonwealth of Independent States** led by Russia, they retained their autonomy—and independent leadership—in domestic and foreign affairs. The United States continued to try to promote both democracy and free-market capitalism, working closely with Yeltsin and then with his successor,

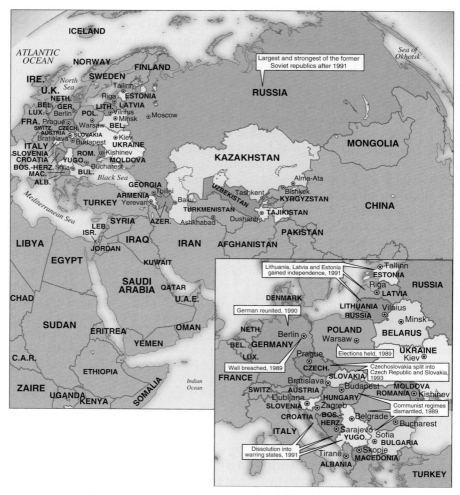

The Fall of Communism In the late 1980s and early 1990s, the Soviet Union fragmented and lost control of its satellites in Eastern Europe. As many countries shown here declared their independence, Czechoslovakia broke into two nations, while Yugoslavia ruptured into a group of feuding states. How widespread was the turbulence that led to the fall of communism? How quickly did the process take place? How did events in one country influence events in another country?

Vladimir Putin, who assumed power on the last day of the twentieth century and was then elected president in his own right in 2001. But Russia remained unstable, and relations remained chilly.

As the Soviet Union disintegrated, Communist regimes throughout Europe collapsed. The most dramatic chapter in this story unfolded in Germany in November 1989. Responding to Gorbachev's softening stance toward the West, East Germany's Communist party boss announced unexpectedly that citizens of his country would be free to leave East Germany. Within hours, thousands of people gathered on both sides of the 28-mile Berlin Wall—the symbol of the Cold War that divided Berlin into East and West sectors. As the border guards stepped aside, East Germans flooded into West Berlin amid dancing, shouting, and fireworks. Within days, sledgehammer-wielding Germans pulverized the Berlin Wall, and soon the Communist government itself came tumbling down. By October 1990, the two Germanys were reunited.

◉—[View the Image

Reagan in Front of the Berlin Wall (1987)

at **www.myhistorylab.com**

The fall of the Berlin Wall reverberated all over Eastern Europe. In Poland, the 10-year-old Solidarity movement led by Lech Walesa triumphed in its long struggle against Soviet domination and found itself in power in December 1990, with Walesa as president. In Czechoslovakia, two decades after Soviet tanks had rolled into the streets of Prague to suppress a policy of liberalization, the forces of freedom were likewise victorious.

The Balkan Crisis

Yugoslavia, held together by a Communist dictatorship since 1945, proved to be the extreme case of ethnic hostility resurging amid collapsing central authority. In 1991, Yugoslavia splintered into its ethnic components. In Bosnia, the decision of the Muslim and Croatian majority to secede from Serbian-dominated Yugoslavia led Bosnian Serbs, backed by the Serbian republic, to embark on a brutal siege of the city of Sarajevo and an even more ruthless campaign to liquidate opponents. The United States remained out of the conflict, unsure about what to do.

Ethnic and religious violence worsened in the mid-1990s. The world watched the Bosnian Serbs exterminate opponents in a process that came to be called "ethnic cleansing" during the siege of the city of Sarajevo. Finally, in mid-1995, a NATO bombing campaign forced the Bosnian Serbs into negotiations, and a peace conference held in Dayton, Ohio, led to the commitment of American troops, along with soldiers from other countries, to stabilize the region.

In 1999, a smoldering conflict in Kosovo, another of the provinces of the former Yugoslavia, led to war. In an effort to stop Slobodan Milosevic, the Serbian leader responsible for the devastation of Bosnia, from squelching a movement for autonomy in Kosovo, NATO launched an American-led bombing campaign. Milosevic responded with an even more violent ethnic cleansing campaign until he was finally arrested and brought to justice.

Dismantling the Berlin Wall The destruction of the Berlin Wall in November 1989 was a symbolic blow to the entire Cold War structure that had solidified in Europe in the postwar years. People grabbed hammers and joined together in tearing down the hated wall. Joyous celebrations marked the reunification of a city that had been divided for decades. How does this dramatic picture convey the exuberant mood of the time?

Latin America

In Latin America, the United States intervened frequently as it had in the past, hoping to impose order on the volatile region. Viewing Central America as a Cold War battlefield early in his presidency, Reagan openly opposed left-wing guerrillas in El Salvador who fought to overthrow a repressive right-wing regime.

Nicaragua became an even bloodier battleground. In 1979, revolutionaries calling themselves Sandinistas (after César Sandino, who fought in the 1920s against U.S. occupation troops) overthrew the repressive Somoza family, which had ruled for three decades. Republicans in their 1980 platform pledged to replace the Sandinistas with a "free and independent" government. Once in office, Reagan circumvented congressional opposition to his efforts to defeat the revolutionary reformers and signed a National Security directive in November 1981 authorizing the CIA to arm and train counterrevolutionaries known as *contras* as Nicaragua became enmeshed in a bitter civil war. Upon discovering the secret CIA missions, Congress cut off military aid to the *contras*. Peaceful elections in early 1990 finally drove the Sandinistas out and brought the fighting to an end. Though the country's economy remained in desperate straits, the new regime seemed to offer the best hope of healing the wounds of the bloody conflict.

Then, in what became known as the **Iran-*contra* affair** in 1987, Congress learned that the National Security Council had launched an effort to free American hostages in the Middle East by selling arms to Iran and then using the funds to aid the *contras*, in direct violation of both the law and congressional will. While top officials were involved, lower-ranking members of the administration took the blame.

Africa

In South Africa, the United States supported the long and ultimately successful struggle against **apartheid**. This policy, whereby the white minority (only 15 percent of the population) segregated, suppressed, and denied basic human rights to the black majority, was part of South African law. A resistance movement, spearheaded by the African National Congress (ANC) sought to end apartheid. While the United States had long expressed its dislike of this ruthless system of segregation, economic and political ties to South Africa kept the United States from taking steps to weaken it. Then, in 1986, bowing to increased domestic pressure, Congress imposed sanctions, including a rule prohibiting new American investments. The economic pressure damaged the South African economy and persuaded more than half of the 300 American firms doing business there to leave.

The final blow to apartheid came from the efforts of Nelson Mandela. The black ANC activist, who had become a symbol of the militant resistance movement during his 27 years in prison, steered his nation through a stunning transformation. In 1990, during Bush's presidency, South African prime minister Frederik W. de Klerk succumbed to pressure from the United States and the rest of the world and freed Mandela. Talks between the white government and the ANC produced a smooth transition to a biracial democracy and led to peaceful elections in 1994, in which blacks voted for the first time. The African National Congress assumed power, and Mandela himself became president. American aid provided support in transitional times.

Africa, ravaged by the AIDS epidemic, frequently received little attention from the rest of the world. The United States, like other countries, was baffled by a crisis in Rwanda, in central Africa. There a fragile balance of power between two ethnic groups—the Tutsis and the Hutus—broke down and hard-line Hutus embarked on a massive genocidal campaign that resulted in the slaughter of hundreds of thousands of innocent Tutsis and moderate Hutus. While outside nations, including the United States, debated the possibility of intervention on humanitarian grounds, they did nothing. Eventually the killing stopped, although the friction between the rival groups remained.

George W. Bush was much less interested in Africa than his predecessor. He chose not to attend a conference on sustainable development held in South Africa in the summer of 2002, which gave a clear signal that the United States was more interested in its own business interests than in the economic problems of the less developed world. In 2003, he visited five African nations, but it was a whirlwind trip aimed at supporting areas sympathetic to the United States.

The Middle East

The Middle East remained a trouble spot as Arabs and Israelis continued to feud with each other. A dramatic crisis occurred in 1990 when Saddam Hussein, the dictator of Iraq, invaded and annexed oil-rich neighboring Kuwait. President Bush reacted vigorously. Working through the UN, as Harry Truman had done in Korea, the United States persuaded the Security Council to vote unanimously to condemn the attack and impose an embargo on Iraq. After Hussein refused to relinquish Kuwait, in mid-January 1991, a 28-nation coalition struck at Iraq with an American-led multinational army of nearly half a million troops. In **Operation Desert Storm**, the coalition forces' sophisticated missiles, aircraft, and tanks swiftly overwhelmed the Iraqis. Americans were initially jubilant. Then the euphoria faded as Saddam turned his remaining military power against minorities in Iraq. Bush's unwillingness to become bogged down in an Iraqi civil war and his eagerness to return U.S. troops home left the conflict unfinished. A year after his defeat, Hussein was as strongly entrenched as ever.

Meanwhile, the United States was involved in a larger, and ultimately more important, effort to bring peace to the Middle East. In the early 1990s, Secretary of State James Baker finally secured agreement from the major parties in the region to speak to one another face to face. A victory in the Israeli parliamentary elections in mid-1992 for Yitzhak Rabin, a soldier who recognized the need for peace and was ready to compromise, offered further hope for the talks.

When Bill Clinton became President, he tried to play the part of peacemaker, just as Jimmy Carter had done 15 years before. On September 13, 1993, in a dramatic ceremony on the White House lawn, Palestine Liberation Organization leader Yasir Arafat and Israeli Prime Minister Yitzhak Rabin took the first public step toward ending years of conflict as they shook hands and signed a peace agreement that led to Palestinian self-rule in the Gaza strip. In 1995, Israel and the PLO signed a further agreement, and the Israelis handed over control of the West Bank of the Jordan River to the Palestinians. A treaty between Jordan and Israel brought peace on still another border. While extremists tried to destroy the peace process by assassinating Rabin, the effort to heal old animosities continued. As Clinton prepared to leave office, he sought to seal a final agreement

A Historic Handshake President Bill Clinton helped orchestrate this famous handshake between Israeli prime minister Yitzhak Rabin and Palestine Liberation Organization chairman Yasir Arafat in 1993. Though the two men had long been adversaries, they now began to work together to settle the bitter conflicts in the Middle East. How do Clinton's actions in the picture give a sense of his role? How do the two longtime adversaries appear to react to one another?

between the Israelis and the Palestinians, but this time he was not successful, as the Palestinians rejected a generous settlement offer, and the smoldering Middle Eastern tensions burst once more into flames that threatened to engulf the entire region.

The level of Mideast violence in the early twenty-first century was worse than it had ever been before. The shortsighted Israeli policy of building settlements in occupied Arab land, and the Palestinian unwillingness to compromise at the negotiating table, culminated in a horrifying escalation of suicide bombings and other bloody attacks following an Israeli visit to a holy Palestinian religious site in Jerusalem, a city claimed by both sides. Meanwhile, many European nations felt that only the United States could bring peace to the region.

At the end of 2007, at the urging of Secretary of State Condoleezza Rice, Bush became more engaged. Perhaps recognizing that only with American assistance might a peace settlement emerge, he convened a conference of Israeli and Palestinian participants to see if they might get back on track for what all agreed would be a long and extended process. As the situation deteriorated, Barack Obama sought to play such a role, but faced an uphill battle.

Terror on September 11

On September 11, 2001, three hijacked airplanes slammed into the World Trade Center towers in New York City and the Pentagon in Washington, D.C. The fires in New York from exploding jet fuel caused the towers to crumble, altering the skyline forever. Altogether about 3,000 people died in the terrorist attacks. A fourth plane, probably headed for either the White House or the Capitol, crashed in Pennsylvania when passengers fought back against the attackers.

The hijackers were Muslim extremists, most from Saudi Arabia, trained at flight schools in the United States, who belonged to the al Qaeda network headed by Saudi exile Osama bin Laden. Bin Laden and his organization

An Indelible Image of September 11, 2001
The World Trade Center towers in New York City once dominated the skyline on the Hudson River. As two hijacked commercial airplanes crashed into the tall structures on September 11, 2001, both towers burst into flames and later collapsed, killing most of the people who were still inside. What impression does this photograph of the burning towers convey?

were headquartered in Afghanistan, where the extremely conservative Muslim Taliban group had imposed the law of the Qur'an, the Muslim holy book, on civil society. Bin Laden and his associates hated the United States for its Middle Eastern policy of support for Israel, and they also hated its affluent and materialistic values that often conflicted with their religious values.

The terrorist attacks shattered America's sense of security within its own borders. Furious at the unprovoked strikes, President Bush vowed to find and punish the terrorists. Like his father in the Gulf War a decade earlier, he put together a worldwide coalition to assist the United States, and he quickly launched a bombing campaign to smoke out Osama bin Laden and his network. Although the bombing, followed by attacks by ground troops in Afghanistan, defeated the Taliban and drove its members from power, the campaign failed to find Osama bin Laden, who remained at large. As Bush's approval ratings soared to over 90 percent, he vowed a lengthy campaign to root out terrorism wherever it surfaced in the world. He embarked on a massive governmental reorganization to create a new Department of Homeland Security to help prevent future attacks. In the Patriot Act, he invoked terrorism as a reason to allow the government to encroach on individual liberties—in the interest of security—more extensively than in the past. Ironically, a president dedicated to smaller government now found himself in the forefront of an effort to give government a much larger role.

American Muslims were often the victims. Some faced attacks by Americans angry at the terrorist strikes. Others were taken into custody, often without being charged with a crime, on the suspicion that they were somehow involved, as the government instituted new security measures.

The antiterrorism campaign escalated. In early 2002, Bush spoke out forcefully against what he called an "axis of evil," as he referred to Iraq, Iran, and North Korea. He was particularly intent on driving Iraqi leader Saddam Hussein from power. Hussein had launched the attack on Kuwait that had led to the Gulf War during the administration of Bush's father. Now, 11 years later, Bush argued that Hussein was creating weapons of mass destruction and vowed to bring about a regime change. Within the Bush administration, Secretary of State Colin Powell, inclined to a more restrained foreign policy, fought against Secretary of Defense Donald Rumsfeld and Vice President Dick Cheney, who enthusiastically supported an attack. Bush's argument that he could invade Iraq even without the support of Congress aroused a firestorm of protest both in the United States and around the world.

The war in Iraq, fought with British but not United Nations support, began in March 2003. American forces were successful, and just a month and a half later, Bush declared that the major phase of combat operations was over. In December, U.S. soldiers captured Saddam Hussein hiding in a hole in the ground. But even the capture of the Iraqi dictator could not quell increasing opposition to the American occupation, which led to fierce fighting in the months that followed. As the deadline for handing sovereignty over to Iraq in mid-2004 approached, Sunnis, Shiites, and Kurds fought with each other for a share of power but were united in their opposition to the continuing American presence. Insurgent attacks against American troops and Iraqis in new official positions continued as Iraq descended into civil war. Photographs of American abuse of prisoners in the notorious Abu Ghraib prison aroused resentment in the Middle East and among people around the world. By early 2008, the American death toll in Iraq passed 4,000 and significantly exceeded the number killed in the terrorist attacks of 9/11, with another 30,000 Americans wounded. As the Iraqi government demonstrated its inability to maintain order in the face of mounting sectarian conflict, more and more Americans demanded an end to involvement in what they perceived as serious, and perhaps intractable, problems.

Conclusion

The Recent Past in Perspective

In the 1980s and early 1990s, the United States witnessed the resurgence of conservatism. For part of that time, the United States prospered in a period of economic growth longer than any in its history. After weathering recession in the 1980s, the economy began to boom, and the boom continued for the next 10 years. Most middle- and upper-class Americans prospered. The budget deficit disappeared, and the government ran a sizable surplus. Yet not all Americans shared in the prosperity. Despite the drop in the unemployment level, many of the available jobs paid little more than the minimum wage, and people like Marlene and Rod Garrett, met at the start of the chapter, had trouble making ends meet. Members of minority groups, whose numbers grew throughout the decade, had the toughest time of all. And matters got even worse toward the end of the first decade of the twenty-first century as the country suffered the worst economic decline since the Great Depression of the 1930s.

Meanwhile, Americans worried about their role in the outside world. As they enjoyed their newfound prosperity, which came with the end of the Cold War, some were reluctant to spend money in an activist role abroad. They debated what to do about the defense establishment, which had begun to deteriorate, and were hesitant to become deeply involved in foreign conflicts where they had trouble ascertaining American interests. Then, in 2001, the brutal terrorist attacks on New York City and Washington, D.C., mobilized the nation. Recognizing at long last that terrorism threatened the entire globe, including the United States, they prepared themselves for an extended effort to try to bring it under control and to make the world a safer place. As they had in years past, in both World War I and World War II, the United States again sought to protect the democratic way of life for the American people and for people elsewhere as well.

TIME*line*

1980	Ronald Reagan elected president
1981–1983	Tax cuts; deficit spending increases
1984	Reagan reelected
1986	Tax reform measure passed
1988	George H. W. Bush elected president
1989	Fall of the Berlin Wall
1990	Nelson Mandela freed in South Africa
1991	Persian Gulf War
	Disintegration of the Soviet Union
1992	Bill Clinton elected president
1993	Palestine Liberation Organization and Israel sign peace treaty
1994	Nelson Mandela elected president of South Africa
1996	Bill Clinton reelected
1998	Bill Clinton impeached by the House of Representatives
1999	Bill Clinton acquitted by the Senate
2000	George W. Bush elected president
2001	Tax cut passed
	Terrorists strike New York City and Washington, D.C.
2003	War in Iraq begins
2004	George W. Bush reelected
2008	Barack Obama elected

✓•⎯Study and Review at **www.myhistorylab.com**

Questions for Review and Reflection

1. How successful was Ronald Reagan in implementing his conservative program?
2. What was the fate of social reform movements in the 1980s?
3. What demographic changes did the United States experience in the years after 1980?
4. How did the economy fare in the years from 1980 to 2010?
5. What was the effect of the end of the Cold War?

Key Terms

APPENDIX

The Declaration of Independence in Congress, July 4, 1776

The Unanimous Declaration of the Thirteen United States of America

When, in the course of human events, it becomes necessary for one people to dissolve the political bonds which have connected them with another, and to assume, among the powers of the earth, the separate and equal station to which the laws of nature and of nature's God entitle them, a decent respect to the opinions of mankind requires that they should declare the causes which impel them to the separation.

We hold these truths to be self-evident: That all men are created equal; that they are endowed by their Creator with certain unalienable rights; that among these are life, liberty, and the pursuit of happiness; that, to secure these rights, governments are instituted among men, deriving their just powers from the consent of the governed; that whenever any form of government becomes destructive of these ends, it is the right of the people to alter or to abolish it, and to institute new government, laying its foundation on such principles, and organizing its powers in such form, as to them shall seem most likely to effect their safety and happiness. Prudence, indeed, will dictate that governments long established should not be changed for light and transient causes; and accordingly all experience hath shown that mankind are more disposed to suffer, while evils are sufferable, than to right themselves by abolishing the forms to which they are accustomed. But when a long train of abuses and usurpations, pursuing invariably the same object, evinces a design to reduce them under absolute despotism, it is their right, it is their duty, to throw off such government, and to provide new guards for their future security. Such has been the patient sufferance of these colonies; and such is now the necessity which constrains them to alter their former systems of government. The history of the present King of Great Britain is a history of repeated injuries and usurpations, all having in direct object the establishment of an absolute tyranny over these states. To prove this, let facts be submitted to a candid world.

He has refused his assent to laws, the most wholesome and necessary for the public good.

He has forbidden his governors to pass laws of immediate and pressing importance, unless suspended in their operation till his assent should be obtained; and, when so suspended, he has utterly neglected to attend to them.

He has refused to pass other laws for the accommodation of large districts of people, unless those people would relinquish the right of representation in the legislature, a right inestimable to them, and formidable to tyrants only.

He has called together legislative bodies at places unusual, uncomfortable, and distant from the depository of their public records, for the sole purpose of fatiguing them into compliance with his measures.

He has dissolved representative houses repeatedly, for opposing, with manly firmness, his invasions on the rights of the people.

He has refused for a long time, after such dissolutions, to cause others to be elected; whereby the legislative powers, incapable of annihilation, have returned to the people at large for their exercise; the state remaining, in the mean time, exposed to all the dangers of invasions from without and convulsions within.

He has endeavored to prevent the population of these states; for that purpose obstructing the laws for naturalization of foreigners; refusing to pass others to encourage their migration hither, and raising the conditions of new appropriations of lands.

He has obstructed the administration of justice, by refusing his assent to laws for establishing judiciary powers.

He has made judges dependent on his will alone, for the tenure of their offices, and the amount and payment of their salaries.

He has erected a multitude of new offices, and sent hither swarms of officers to harass our people and eat out their substance.

He has kept among us, in times of peace, standing armies, without the consent of our legislatures.

He has affected to render the military independent of, and superior to, the civil power.

He has combined with others to subject us to a jurisdiction foreign to our constitution, and unacknowledged by our laws, giving his assent to their acts of pretended legislation:

For quartering large bodies of armed troops among us;

For protecting them, by a mock trial, from punishment for any murder which they should commit on the inhabitants of these states;

For cutting off our trade with all parts of the world;

For imposing taxes on us without our consent;

For depriving us, in many cases, of the benefits of trial by jury;

For transporting us beyond seas, to be tried for pretended offenses;

For abolishing the free system of English laws in a neighboring province, establishing therein an arbitrary government, and enlarging its boundaries, so as to render it at once an example and fit instrument for introducing the same absolute rule into these colonies;

For taking away our charters, abolishing our most valuable laws, and altering fundamentally the forms of our governments;

For suspending our own legislatures, and declaring themselves invested with power to legislate for us in all cases whatsoever.

He has abdicated government here, by declaring us out of his protection and waging war against us.

He has plundered our seas, ravaged our coasts, burned our towns, and destroyed the lives of our people.

He is at this time transporting large armies of foreign mercenaries to complete the works of death, desolation, and tyranny already begun with circumstances of cruelty and perfidy scarcely paralleled in the most barbarous ages, and totally unworthy the head of a civilized nation.

He has constrained our fellow-citizens, taken captive on the high seas, to bear arms against their country, to become the executioners of their friends and brethren, or to fall themselves by their hands.

He has excited domestic insurrection among us, and has endeavored to bring on the inhabitants of our frontiers the merciless Indian savages, whose known rule of warfare is an undistinguished destruction of all ages, sexes, and conditions.

In every stage of these oppressions we have petitioned for redress in the most humble terms; our repeated petitions have been answered only by repeated injury. A prince, whose character is thus marked by every act which may define a tyrant, is unfit to be the ruler of a free people.

Nor have we been wanting in our attentions to our British brethren. We have warned them, from time to time, of attempts by their legislature to extend an unwarrantable jurisdiction over us. We have reminded them of the circumstances of our emigration and settlement here. We have appealed to their native justice and magnanimity; and we have conjured them, by the ties of our common kindred, to disavow these usurpations, which would inevitably interrupt our connections and correspondence. They, too, have been deaf to the voice of justice and of consanguinity. We must, therefore, acquiesce in the necessity which denounces our separation, and hold them, as we hold the rest of mankind, enemies in war, in peace friends.

We, therefore, the representatives of the United States of America, in General Congress assembled, appealing to the Supreme Judge of the world for the rectitude of our intentions, do, in the name and by the authority of the good people of these colonies, solemnly publish and declare, that these United Colonies are, and of right, ought to be, FREE AND INDEPENDENT STATES; that they are absolved from all allegiance to the British crown, and that all political connection between them and the state of Great Britain is, and ought to be, totally dissolved; and that, as free and independent states, they have full power to levy war, conclude peace, contract alliances, establish commerce, and do all other acts and things which independent states may of right do. And for the support of this declaration, with a firm reliance on the protection of Devine Providence, we mutually pledge to each other our lives, our fortunes, and our sacred honor.

John Hancock

Button Gwennett	*Francis Lightfoot Lee*	*Jno. Witherspoon*
Lyman Hall	*Carter Braxton*	*Fras. Hopkinson*
Geo. Walton	*Robt. Morris*	*John Hart*
Wm. Hooper	*Benjamin Rush*	*Abra. Clark*
Joseph Hewes	*Benja. Franklin*	*Josiah Bartlett*
John Penn	*John Morton*	*Wm. Whipple*
Edward Rutledge	*Geo. Clymer*	*Saml. Adams*
Thos. Heyward, Junr.	*Jas. Smith*	*John Adams*
Thomas Lynch, Junr.	*Geo. Taylor*	*Robt. Treat Paine*
Arthur Middleton	*James Wilson*	*Elbridge Gerry*
Samuel Chase	*Geo. Ross*	*Step. Hopkins*
Wm. Paca	*Caesar Rodney*	*William Ellery*
Thos. Stone	*Geo. Read*	*Roger Sherman*
Charles Carroll of Carrollton	*Tho. Mikean*	*Samiel. Huntington*
George Wythe	*Wm. Floyd*	*Wm. Williams*
Richard Henry Lee	*Phil. Livingston*	*Oliver Wolcott*
Th. Jefferson	*Frans. Lewis*	*Mathew Thornton*
Benja. Harrison	*Lewis Morris*	
Ths. Nelson, Jr.	*Richd. Stockton*	

The Constitution of the United States of America

Preamble

We the People of the United States, in Order to form a more perfect Union, establish Justice, insure domestic Tranquility, provide for the common defence, promote the general Welfare, and secure the Blessings of Liberty to ourselves and our Posterity, do ordain and establish this Constitution for the United States of America.

Article I.

Section 1 All legislative Powers herein granted shall be vested in a Congress of the United States, which shall consist of a Senate and House of Representatives.

Section 2 The House of Representatives shall be composed of Members chosen every second Year by the People of the several States, and the Electors in each State shall have the Qualifications requisite for Electors of the most numerous Branch of the State Legislature.

No Person shall be a Representative who shall not have attained to the Age of twenty five Years, and been seven Years a Citizen of the United States, and who shall not, when elected, be an Inhabitant of that State in which he shall be chosen.

Representatives and direct Taxes shall be apportioned among the several States which may be included within this Union, according to their respective Numbers, *which shall be determined by adding to the whole Number of free Persons, including those bound to Service for a Term of Years, and excluding Indians not taxed, three fifths of all other Persons.* The actual Enumeration shall be made within three Years after the first Meeting of the Congress of the United States, and within every subsequent Term of ten Years, in such Manner as they shall by Law direct. The Number of Representatives shall not exceed one for every thirty Thousand, but each State shall have at Least one Representative; *and until such enumeration shall be made, the State of New Hampshire shall be entitled to chuse three, Massachusetts eight, Rhode-Island and Providence Plantations one, Connecticut five, New-York six, New Jersey four, Pennsylvania eight, Delaware one, Maryland six, Virginia ten, North Carolina five, South Carolina five, and Georgia three.*

When vacancies happen in the Representation from any State, the Executive Authority thereof shall issue Writs of Election to fill such Vacancies.

The House of Representatives shall chuse their Speaker and other Officers; and shall have the sole Power of Impeachment.

Section 3 The Senate of the United States shall be composed of two Senators from each State, chosen by the Legislature thereof, for six Years; and each Senator shall have one Vote.

Immediately after they shall be assembled in Consequence of the first Election, they shall be divided as equally as may be into three Classes. The Seats of the Senators of the first Class shall be vacated at the Expiration of the second Year, of the second Class at the Expiration of the fourth Year, and of the third Class at the Expiration of the sixth Year, so that one third may be chosen every second Year; and if Vacancies happen by Resignation, or otherwise, during the Recess of the Legislature of any State, the Executive thereof may make temporary Appointments until the next Meeting of the Legislature, which shall then fill such Vacancies.

No Person shall be a Senator who shall not have attained to the Age of thirty Years, and been nine Years a Citizen of the United States, and who shall not, when elected, be an Inhabitant of that State for which he shall be chosen.

The Vice President of the United States shall be President of the Senate, but shall have no Vote, unless they be equally divided.

The Senate shall choose their other Officers, and also a President *pro tempore,* in the Absence of the Vice President, or when he shall exercise the Office of President of the United States.

The Senate shall have the sole Power to try all Impeachments. When sitting for that Purpose, they shall be on Oath or Affirmation. When the President of the United States is tried the Chief Justice shall preside: And no Person shall be convicted without the Concurrence of two thirds of the Members present.

Judgment in Cases of Impeachment shall not extend further than to removal from Office, and disqualification to hold and enjoy any Office of honor, Trust or Profit under the United States: but the Party convicted shall nevertheless be liable and subject to Indictment, Trial, Judgment and Punishment, according to Law.

Section 4 The Times, Places and Manner of holding Elections for Senators and Representatives, shall be prescribed in each State by the Legislature thereof; but the Congress may at any time by Law make or alter such Regulations, except as to the Places of chusing Senators.

The Congress shall assemble at least once in every Year, and such Meeting *shall be on the first Monday in December, unless they shall by Law appoint a different Day.*

Section 5   Each House shall be the Judge of the Elections, Returns and Qualifications of its own Members, and a Majority of each shall constitute a Quorum to do Business; but a smaller Number may adjourn from day to day, and may be authorized to compel the Attendance of absent Members, in such Manner, and under such Penalties as each House may provide.

Each House may determine the Rules of its Proceedings, punish its Members for disorderly Behaviour, and, with the Concurrence of two thirds, expel a Member.

Each House shall keep a Journal of its Proceedings, and from time to time publish the same, excepting such Parts as may in their Judgment require Secrecy; and the Yeas and Nays of the Members of either House on any question shall, at the Desire of one fifth of those Present, be entered on the Journal.

Neither House, during the Session of Congress, shall, without the Consent of the other, adjourn for more than three days, nor to any other Place than that in which the two Houses shall be sitting.

Section 6   The Senators and Representatives shall receive a Compensation for their Services, to be ascertained by Law, and paid out of the Treasury of the United States. They shall in all Cases, except Treason, Felony and Breach of the Peace, be privileged from Arrest during their Attendance at the Session of their respective Houses, and in going to and returning from the same; and for any Speech or Debate in either House, they shall not be questioned in any other Place.

No Senator or Representative shall, during the Time for which he was elected, be appointed to any civil Office under the Authority of the United States, which shall have been created, or the Emoluments whereof shall have been encreased during such time; and no Person holding any Office under the United States, shall be a Member of either House during his Continuance in Office.

Section 7   All Bills for raising Revenue shall originate in the House of Representatives; but the Senate may propose or concur with Amendments as on other Bills.

Every Bill which shall have passed the House of Representatives and the Senate, shall, before it become a Law, be presented to the President of the United States; If he approve he shall sign it, but if not he shall return it, with his Objections to that House in which it shall have originated, who shall enter the Objections at large on their Journal, and proceed to reconsider it. If after such Reconsideration two thirds of that House shall agree to pass the Bill, it shall be sent, together with the Objections, to the other House, by which it shall likewise be reconsidered, and if approved by two thirds of that House, it shall become a Law. But in all such Cases the Votes of both Houses shall be determined by yeas and Nays, and the Names of the Persons voting for and against the Bill shall be entered on the Journal of each House respectively. If any Bill shall not be returned by the President within ten Days (Sundays excepted) after it shall have been presented to him, the Same shall be a Law, in like Manner as if he had signed it, unless the Congress by their Adjournment prevent its Return, in which Case it shall not be a Law.

Every Order, Resolution, or Vote to which the Concurrence of the Senate and House of Representatives may be necessary (except on a question of Adjournment) shall be presented to the President of the United States; and before the Same shall take Effect, shall be approved by him, or being disapproved by him, shall be repassed by two thirds of the Senate and House of Representatives, according to the Rules and Limitations prescribed in the Case of a Bill.

Section 8   The Congress shall have Power:

To lay and collect Taxes, Duties, Imposts and Excises, to pay the Debts and provide for the common Defence and general Welfare of the United States; but all Duties, Imposts and Excises shall be uniform throughout the United States;

To borrow Money on the credit of the United States;

To regulate Commerce with foreign Nations, and among the several States, and with the Indian Tribes;

To establish an uniform Rule of Naturalization, and uniform Laws on the subject of Bankruptcies throughout the United States;

To coin Money, regulate the Value thereof, and of foreign Coin, and fix the Standard of Weights and Measures;

To provide for the Punishment of counterfeiting the Securities and current Coin of the United States;

To establish Post Offices and post Roads;

To promote the Progress of Science and useful Arts, by securing for limited Times to Authors and Inventors the exclusive Right to their respective Writings and Discoveries;

To constitute Tribunals inferior to the supreme Court;

To define and punish Piracies and Felonies committed on the high Seas, and Offences against the Law of Nations;

To declare War, grant Letters of Marque and Reprisal, and make Rules concerning Captures on Land and Water;

To raise and support Armies, but no Appropriation of Money to that Use shall be for a longer Term than two Years;

To provide and maintain a Navy;

To make Rules for the Government and Regulation of the land and naval Forces;

To provide for calling forth the Militia to execute the Laws of the Union, suppress Insurrections and repel Invasions;

To provide for organizing, arming, and disciplining, the Militia, and for governing such Part of them as may be employed in the Service of the United States, reserving to the States respectively, the Appointment of the Officers, and the Authority of training the Militia according to the discipline prescribed by Congress;

To exercise exclusive Legislation in all Cases whatsoever, over such District (not exceeding ten Miles square) as may, by Cession of particular States, and the Acceptance of Congress, become the Seat of the Government of the United States, and to exercise like Authority over all Places purchased by the Consent of the Legislature of the State in which the Same shall be, for the Erection of Forts, Magazines, Arsenals, dock-Yards, and other needful Buildings;

To make all Laws which shall be necessary and proper for carrying into Execution the foregoing Powers, and all other Powers vested by this Constitution in the Government of the United States, or in any Department or Officer thereof.

Section 9 *The Migration or Importation of such Persons as any of the States now existing shall think proper to admit, shall not be prohibited by the Congress prior to the Year one thousand eight hundred and eight, but a Tax or duty may be imposed on such Importation, not exceeding ten dollars for each Person.*

The Privilege of the Writ of Habeas Corpus shall not be suspended, unless when in Cases of Rebellion or Invasion the public Safety may require it.

No Bill of Attainder or ex post facto Law shall be passed.

No Capitation, or other direct, Tax shall be laid, unless in Proportion to the Census or Enumeration herein before directed to be taken.

No Tax or Duty shall be laid on Articles exported from any State.

No Preference shall be given by any Regulation of Commerce or Revenue to the Ports of one State over those of another: nor shall Vessels bound to, or from, one State, be obliged to enter, clear, or pay Duties in another.

No Money shall be drawn from the Treasury, but in Consequence of Appropriations made by Law; and a regular Statement and Account of the Receipts and Expenditures of all public Money shall be published from time to time.

No Title of Nobility shall be granted by the United States: And no Person holding any Office of Profit or Trust under them, shall, without the Consent of the Congress, accept of any present, Emolument, Office, or Title, of any kind whatever, from any King, Prince, or foreign State.

Section 10 No State shall enter into any Treaty, Alliance, or Confederation; grant Letters of Marque and Reprisal; coin Money; emit Bills of Credit; make any Thing but gold and silver

Coin a Tender in Payment of Debts; pass any Bill of Attainder, ex post facto Law, or Law impairing the Obligation of Contracts, or grant any Title of Nobility.

No State shall, without the Consent of the Congress, lay any Imposts or Duties on Imports or Exports, except what may be absolutely necessary for executing it's inspection Laws: and the net Produce of all Duties and Imposts, laid by any State on Imports or Exports, shall be for the Use of the Treasury of the United States; and all such Laws shall be subject to the Revision and Controul of the Congress.

No State shall, without the Consent of Congress, lay any Duty of Tonnage, keep Troops, or Ships of War in time of Peace, enter into any Agreement or Compact with another State, or with a foreign Power, or engage in War, unless actually invaded, or in such imminent Danger as will not admit of delay.

Article II.

Section 1 The executive Power shall be vested in a President of the United States of America. He shall hold his Office during the Term of four Years, and, together with the Vice President, chosen for the same Term, be elected, as follows

Each State shall appoint, in such Manner as the Legislature thereof may direct, a Number of Electors, equal to the whole Number of Senators and Representatives to which the State may be entitled in the Congress: but no Senator or Representative, or Person holding an Office of Trust or Profit under the United States, shall be appointed an Elector.

The Electors shall meet in their respective States, and vote by Ballot for two Persons, of whom one at least shall not be an Inhabitant of the same State with themselves. And they shall make a List of all the Persons voted for, and of the Number of Votes for each; which List they shall sign and certify, and transmit sealed to the Seat of Government of the United States, directed to the President of the Senate. The President of the Senate shall, in the Presence of the Senate and House of Representatives, open all the Certificates, and the Votes shall then be counted. The Person having the greatest Number of Votes shall be the President, if such Number be a Majority of the whole Number of Electors appointed; and if there be more than one who have such Majority, and have an equal Number of Votes, then the House of Representatives shall immediately chuse by Ballot one of them for President; and if no Person have a Majority, then from the five highest on the List the said House shall in like Manner chuse the President. But in chusing the President, the Votes shall be taken by States, the Representation from each State having one Vote; A quorum for this Purpose shall consist of a Member or Members from two thirds of the States, and a Majority of all the States shall be necessary to a Choice. In every Case, after the Choice of the President, the Person having the greatest Number of Votes of the Electors shall be the Vice President. But if there should remain two or more who have equal Votes, the Senate shall chuse from them by Ballot the Vice President.

The Congress may determine the Time of chusing the Electors, and the Day on which they shall give their Votes; which Day shall be the same throughout the United States.

No Person except a natural born Citizen, *or a Citizen of the United States, at the time of the Adoption of this Constitution*, shall be eligible to the Office of President; neither shall any Person be eligible to that Office who shall not have attained to the Age of thirty five Years, and been fourteen Years a Resident within the United States.

In Case of the Removal of the President from Office, or of his Death, Resignation, or Inability to discharge the Powers and Duties of the said Office, the Same shall devolve on the Vice President, and the Congress may by Law provide for the Case of Removal, Death, Resignation or Inability, both of the President and Vice President declaring what Officer shall then act as President, and such Officer shall act accordingly, until the Disability be removed, or a President shall be elected.

The President shall, at stated Times, receive for his Services, a Compensation, which shall neither be increased nor diminished during the Period for which he shall have been elected, and he shall not receive within that Period any other Emolument from the United States, or any of them.

Before he enter on the Execution of his Office, he shall take the following Oath or Affirmation: "I do solemnly swear (or affirm) that I will faithfully execute the Office of President of the United States, and will to the best of my Ability, preserve, protect and defend the Constitution of the United States."

Section 2 The President shall be Commander in Chief of the Army and Navy of the United States, and of the Militia of the several States, when called into the actual Service of the United States; he may require the Opinion, in writing, of the principal Officer in each of the executive Departments, upon any Subject relating to the Duties of their respective Offices, and he shall have Power to grant Reprieves and Pardons for Offences against the United States, except in Cases of Impeachment.

He shall have Power, by and with the Advice and Consent of the Senate, to make Treaties, provided two thirds of the Senators present concur; and he shall nominate, and by and with the Advice and Consent of the Senate, shall appoint Ambassadors, other public Ministers and Consuls, Judges of the supreme Court, and all other Officers of the United States, whose Appointments are not herein otherwise provided for, and which shall be established by Law: but the Congress may by Law vest the Appointment of such inferior Officers, as they think proper, in the President alone, in the Courts of Law, or in the Heads of Departments.

The President shall have Power to fill up all Vacancies that may happen during the Recess of the Senate, by granting Commissions which shall expire at the End of their next Session.

Section 3 He shall from time to time give to the Congress Information of the State of the Union, and recommend to their Consideration such Measures as he shall judge necessary and expedient; he may, on extraordinary Occasions, convene both Houses, or either of them, and in Case of Disagreement between them, with Respect to the Time of Adjournment, he may adjourn them to such Time as he shall think proper; he shall receive Ambassadors and other public Ministers; he shall take Care that the Laws be faithfully executed, and shall Commission all the Officers of the United States.

Section 4 The President, Vice President and all civil Officers of the United States, shall be removed from Office on Impeachment for, and Conviction of, Treason, Bribery, or other high Crimes and Misdemeanors.

Article III.

Section 1 The judicial Power of the United States, shall be vested in one supreme Court, and in such inferior Courts as the Congress may from time to time ordain and establish. The Judges, both of the supreme and inferior Courts, shall hold their Offices during good Behaviour, and shall, at stated Times, receive for their Services, a Compensation which shall not be diminished during their Continuance in Office.

Section 2 The judicial Power shall extend to all Cases, in Law and Equity, arising under this Constitution, the Laws of the United States, and Treaties made, or which shall be made, under their Authority;—to all Cases affecting Ambassadors, other public Ministers and Consuls;—to all Cases of admiralty and maritime Jurisdiction;—to Controversies to which the United States shall be a Party;—to Controversies between two or more States;—*between a State and Citizens of another State;*—between Citizens of different States;—between Citizens of the same State claiming Lands under Grants of different States, and between a State, or the Citizens thereof, and foreign States, Citizens or Subjects.

In all Cases affecting Ambassadors, other public Ministers and Consuls, and those in which a State shall be Party, the supreme Court shall have original Jurisdiction. In all the other Cases before mentioned, the supreme Court shall have appellate Jurisdiction, both as to Law and Fact, with such Exceptions, and under such Regulations as the Congress shall make.

The Trial of all Crimes, except in Cases of Impeachment, shall be by Jury; and such Trial shall be held in the State where the said Crimes shall have been committed; but when not committed within any State, the Trial shall be at such Place or Places as the Congress may by Law have directed.

Section 3 Treason against the United States, shall consist only in levying War against them, or in adhering to their Enemies, giving them Aid and Comfort. No Person shall be convicted of

Treason unless on the Testimony of two Witnesses to the same overt Act, or on Confession in open Court.

The Congress shall have Power to declare the Punishment of Treason, but no Attainder of Treason shall work Corruption of Blood, or Forfeiture except during the Life of the Person attainted.

Article IV.

Section 1 Full Faith and Credit shall be given in each State to the public Acts, Records, and judicial Proceedings of every other State. And the Congress may by general Laws prescribe the Manner in which such Acts, Records and Proceedings shall be proved, and the Effect thereof.

Section 2 The Citizens of each State shall be entitled to all Privileges and Immunities of Citizens in the several States.

A Person charged in any State with Treason, Felony, or other Crime, who shall flee from Justice, and be found in another State, shall on Demand of the executive Authority of the State from which he fled, be delivered up, to be removed to the State having Jurisdiction of the Crime.

No Person held to Service or Labour in one State, under the Laws thereof, escaping into another, shall, in Consequence of any Law or Regulation therein, be discharged from such Service or Labour, but shall be delivered up on Claim of the Party to whom such Service or Labour may be due.

Section 3 New States may be admitted by the Congress into this Union; but no new State shall be formed or erected within the Jurisdiction of any other State; nor any State be formed by the Junction of two or more States, or Parts of States, without the Consent of the Legislatures of the States concerned as well as of the Congress.

The Congress shall have Power to dispose of and make all needful Rules and Regulations respecting the Territory or other Property belonging to the United States; and nothing in this Constitution shall be so construed as to Prejudice any Claims of the United States, or of any particular State.

Section 4 The United States shall guarantee to every State in this Union a Republican Form of Government, and shall protect each of them against Invasion; and on Application of the Legislature, or of the Executive (when the Legislature cannot be convened) against domestic Violence.

Article V.

The Congress, whenever two thirds of both Houses shall deem it necessary, shall propose Amendments to this Constitution, or, on the Application of the Legislatures of two thirds of the several States, shall call a Convention for proposing Amendments, which, in either Case, shall be valid to all Intents and Purposes, as Part of this Constitution, when ratified by the Legislatures of three fourths of the several States, or by Conventions in three fourths thereof, as the one or the other Mode of Ratification may be proposed by the Congress; Provided that *no Amendment which may be made prior to the Year One thousand eight hundred and eight shall in any Manner affect the first and fourth Clauses in the Ninth Section of the first Article; and* that no State, without its Consent, shall be deprived of its equal Suffrage in the Senate.

Article VI.

All Debts contracted and Engagements entered into, before the Adoption of this Constitution, shall be as valid against the United States under this Constitution, as under the Confederation.

This Constitution, and the Laws of the United States which shall be made in Pursuance thereof; and all Treaties made or which shall be made, under the Authority of the United States, shall be the supreme Law of the Land; and the Judges in every State shall be bound thereby, any Thing in the Constitution or Laws of any State to the Contrary notwithstanding.

The Senators and Representatives before mentioned, and the Members of the several State Legislatures, and all executive and judicial Officers, both of the United States and of the several States, shall be bound by Oath or Affirmation, to support this Constitution; but no religious Test shall ever be required as a Qualification to any Office or public Trust under the United States.

Article VII.

The Ratification of the Conventions of nine States, shall be sufficient for the Establishment of this Constitution between the States so ratifying the Same.

Done in Convention by the Unanimous Consent of the States present the Seventeenth Day of September in the Year of our Lord one thousand seven hundred and Eighty seven and of the Independence of the United States of America the Twelfth. IN WITNESS whereof We have hereunto subscribed our Names,

George Washington,
President and Deputy from Virginia

North Carolina
William Blount
Richard Dobbs Spraight
Hu Williamson

Pennsylvania
Benjamin Franklin
Thomas Mifflin
Robert Morris
George Clymer
Thomas Fitzsimons
Jared Ingersoll
James Wilson
Gouverneur Morris

Delaware
George Read
Gunning Bedford, Jr.
John Dickinson
Richard Bassett
Jacob Broom

South Carolina
J. Rutledge
Charles C. Pinckney
Pierce Butler

Virginia
John Blair
James Madison, Jr.

New Jersey
William Livingston
David Brearley
William Paterson
Jonathan Dayton

Maryland
James Mchenry
Daniel of St. Thomas Jenifer
Daniel Carroll

Massachusetts
Nathaniel Gorham
Rufus King

Connecticut
William S. Johnson
Roger Sherman

New York
Alexander Hamilton

New Hampshire
John Langdon
Nicholas Gilman

Georgia
William Few
Abraham Baldwin

Amendments to the Constitution*

*The first ten amendments (the Bill of Rights) were adopted in 1791.

Amendment I

Congress shall make no law respecting an establishment of religion, or prohibiting the free exercise thereof; or abridging the freedom of speech, or of the press; or the right of the people peaceably to assemble, and to petition the Government for a redress of grievances.

Amendment II

A well regulated Militia, being necessary to the security of a free State, the right of the people to keep and bear Arms, shall not be infringed.

Amendment III

No Soldier shall, in time of peace be quartered in any house, without the consent of the Owner, nor in time of war, but in a manner to be prescribed by law.

Amendment IV

The right of the people to be secure in their persons, houses, papers, and effects, against unreasonable searches and seizures, shall not be violated, and no Warrants shall issue, but upon probable cause, supported by Oath or affirmation, and particularly describing the place to be searched, and the persons or things to be seized.

Amendment V

No person shall be held to answer for a capital, or otherwise infamous crime, unless on a presentment or indictment of a Grand Jury, except in cases arising in the land or naval forces, or in the Militia, when in actual service in time of War or public danger; nor shall any person be subject for the same offence to be twice put in jeopardy of life or limb; nor shall be compelled in any criminal case to be a witness against himself, nor be deprived of life, liberty, or property, without due process of law; nor shall private property be taken for public use, without just compensation.

Amendment VI

In all criminal prosecutions, the accused shall enjoy the right to a speedy and public trial, by an impartial jury of the State and district wherein the crime shall have been committed, which district shall have been previously ascertained by law, and to be informed of the nature and cause of the accusation; to be confronted with the witnesses against him; to have compulsory process for obtaining witnesses in his favor, and to have the Assistance of Counsel for his defence.

Amendment VII

In Suits at common law, where the value in controversy shall exceed twenty dollars, the right of trial by jury shall be preserved, and no fact tried by a jury, shall be otherwise re-examined in any Court of the United States, than according to the rules of the common law.

Amendment VIII

Excessive bail shall not be required, nor excessive fines imposed, nor cruel and unusual punishments inflicted.

Amendment IX

The enumeration in the Constitution, of certain rights, shall not be construed to deny or disparage others retained by the people.

Amendment X

The powers not delegated to the United States by the Constitution, nor prohibited by it to the States, are reserved to the States respectively, or to the people.

Amendment XI [Adopted 1798]

The Judicial power of the United States shall not be construed to extend to any suit in law or equity, commenced or prosecuted against one of the United States by Citizens of another State, or by Citizens or Subjects of any Foreign State.

Amendment XII [Adopted 1804]

The Electors shall meet in their respective states, and vote by ballot for President and Vice-President, one of whom, at least, shall not be an inhabitant of the same state with themselves; they shall name in their ballots the person voted for as President, and in distinct ballots the person voted for as Vice-President, and they shall make distinct lists of all persons voted for as President, and of all persons voted for as Vice-President, and of the number of votes for each, which list they shall sign and certify, and transmit sealed to the seat of the government of the United States, directed to the President of the Senate;—The President of the Senate shall, in the presence of the Senate and House of Representatives, open all the certificates and the votes shall then be counted;—The person having the greatest number of votes for President, shall be the President, if such number be a majority of the whole number of Electors appointed; and if no person have such majority, then from the persons having the highest numbers not exceeding three on the list of those voted for as President, the House of Representatives shall choose immediately, by ballot, the President. But in choosing the President, the votes shall be taken by states, the representation from each state having one vote; a quorum for this purpose shall consist of a member or members from two thirds of the states, and a majority of all the states shall be necessary to a choice. And if the House of Representatives shall not choose a President whenever the right of choice shall devolve upon them, before the *fourth day of March* next following, then the Vice-President shall act as President, as in the case of the death or other constitutional disability of the President.

The person having the greatest number of votes as Vice-President, shall be the Vice-President, if such number be a majority of the whole number of Electors appointed, and if no person have a majority, then from the two highest numbers on the list, the Senate shall choose the Vice-President; a quorum for the purpose shall consist of two thirds of the whole number of Senators, and a majority of the whole number shall be necessary to a choice. But no person constitutionally ineligible to the office of President shall be eligible to that of Vice-President of the United States.

Amendment XIII [Adopted 1865]

Section 1 Neither slavery nor involuntary servitude, except as a punishment for crime whereof the party shall have been duly convicted, shall exist within the United States, or any place subject to their jurisdiction.

Section 2 Congress shall have power to enforce this article by appropriate legislation.

Amendment XIV [Adopted 1868]

Section 1 All persons born or naturalized in the United States, and subject to the jurisdiction thereof, are citizens of the United States and of the State wherein they reside. No State shall make or enforce any law which shall abridge the privileges or immunities of citizens of the United States; nor shall any State deprive any person of life, liberty, or property, without due process of law; nor deny to any person within its jurisdiction the equal protection of the laws.

Section 2 Representatives shall be apportioned among the several States according to their respective numbers, counting the whole number of persons in each State, excluding Indians not taxed. But when the right to vote at any election for the choice of electors for President and Vice-President of the United States, Representatives in Congress, the Executive and Judicial officers of a State, or the members of the Legislature thereof, is denied to any of the male inhabitants of such State, being twenty-one years of age, and citizens of the United States, or in any way abridged, except for participation in rebellion, or other crime, the basis of representation therein shall be reduced in the proportion which the number of such male citizens shall bear to the whole number of male citizens twenty-one years of age in such State.

Section 3 No person shall be a Senator or Representative in Congress, or elector of President and Vice-President, or hold any office, civil or military, under the United States, or under any

State, who, having previously taken an oath, as a member of Congress, or as an officer of the United States, or as a member of any State legislature, or as an executive or judicial officer of any State, to support the Constitution of the United States, shall have engaged in insurrection or rebellion against the same, or given aid or comfort to the enemies thereof. But Congress may by a vote of two thirds of each House, remove such disability.

Section 4 The validity of the public debt of the United States, authorized by law, including debts incurred for payment of pensions and bounties for services in suppressing insurrection or rebellion, shall not be questioned. But neither the United States nor any State shall assume or pay any debt or obligation incurred in aid of insurrection or rebellion against the United States, or any claim for the loss or emancipation of any slave; but all such debts, obligations and claims shall be held illegal and void.

Section 5 The Congress shall have power to enforce, by appropriate legislation, the provisions of this article.

Amendment XV [Adopted 1870]

Section 1 The right of citizens of the United States to vote shall not be denied or abridged by the United States or by any State on account of race, color, or previous condition of servitude.

Section 2 The Congress shall have power to enforce this article by appropriate legislation.

Amendment XVI [Adopted 1913]

The Congress shall have power to lay and collect taxes on incomes, from whatever source derived, without apportionment among the several States, and without regard to any census or enumeration.

Amendment XVII [Adopted 1913]

The Senate of the United States shall be composed of two Senators from each State, elected by the people thereof, for six years; and each Senator shall have one vote. The electors in each State shall have the qualifications requisite for electors of the most numerous branch of the State legislatures.

When vacancies happen in the representation of any State in the Senate, the executive authority of such State shall issue writs of election to fill such vacancies: *Provided*, That the legislature of any State may empower the executive thereof to make temporary appointments until the people fill the vacancies by election as the legislature may direct.

This amendment shall not be so construed as to affect the election or term of any Senator chosen before it becomes valid as part of the Constitution.

Amendment XVIII [Adopted 1919; Repealed 1933]

Section 1 After one year from the ratification of this article the manufacture, sale, or transportation of intoxicating liquors within, the importation thereof into, or the exportation thereof from the United States and all territory subject to the jurisdiction thereof for beverage purposes is hereby prohibited.

Section 2 The Congress and the several States shall have concurrent power to enforce this article by appropriate legislation.

Section 3 This article shall be inoperative unless it shall have been ratified as an amendment to the Constitution by the legislatures of the several States, as provided in the Constitution, within seven years from the date of the submission hereof to the States by the Congress.

Amendment XIX [Adopted 1920]

Section 1 The right of citizens of the United States to vote shall not be denied or abridged by the United States or by any State on account of sex.

Section 2 Congress shall have power to enforce this article by appropriate legislation.

Amendment XX [Adopted 1933]

Section 1 The terms of the President and Vice-President shall end at noon on the 20th day of January, and the terms of Senators and Representatives at noon on the third day of January, of the years in which such terms would have ended if this article had not been ratified; and the terms of their successors shall then begin.

Section 2 The Congress shall assemble at least once in every year, and such meeting shall begin at noon on the third day of January, unless they shall by law appoint a different day.

Section 3 If, at the time fixed for the beginning of the term of the President, the President elect shall have died, the Vice-President elect shall become President. If a President shall not have been chosen before the time fixed for the beginning of his term, or if the President elect shall have failed to qualify, then the Vice-President elect shall act as President until a President shall have qualified; and the Congress may by law provide for the case wherein neither a President elect nor a Vice-President elect shall have qualified, declaring who shall then act as President, or the manner in which one who is to act shall be selected, and such person shall act accordingly until a President or Vice-President shall have qualified.

Section 4 The Congress may by law provide for the case of the death of any of the persons from whom the House of Representatives may choose a President whenever the right of choice shall have devolved upon them, and for the case of the death of any of the persons from whom the Senate may choose a Vice-President whenever the right of choice shall have devolved upon them.

Section 5 Sections 1 and 2 shall take effect on the 15th day of October following the ratification of this article.

Section 6 This article shall be inoperative unless it shall have been ratified as an amendment to the Constitution by the legislatures of three fourths of the several States within seven years from the date of its submission.

Amendment XXI [Adopted 1933]

Section 1 The eighteenth article of amendment to the Constitution of the United States is hereby repealed.

Section 2 The transportation or importation into any State, Territory, or possession of the United States for delivery or use therein of intoxicating liquors, in violation of the laws thereof, is hereby prohibited.

Section 3 This article shall be inoperative unless it shall have been ratified as an amendment to the Constitution by conventions in the several States, as provided in the Constitution, within seven years from the date of the submission hereof to the States by the Congress.

Amendment XXII [Adopted 1951]

Section 1 No person shall be elected to the office of the President more than twice, and no person who has held the office of President, or acted as President, for more than two years of a term to which some other person was elected President shall be elected to the office of the President more than once. But this Article shall not apply to any person holding the office of President when this Article was proposed by the Congress, and shall not prevent any person who may be holding the office of President, or acting as President, during the term within which this Article becomes operative from holding the office of President or acting as President during the remainder of such term.

Section 2 This article shall be inoperative unless it shall have been ratified as an amendment to the Constitution by the legislatures of three fourths of the several States within seven years from the date of its submission to the States by the Congress.

Amendment XXIII [Adopted 1961]

Section 1 The District constituting the seat of Government of the United States shall appoint in such manner as the Congress may direct:

A number of electors of President and Vice-President equal to the whole number of Senators and Representatives in Congress to which the District would be entitled if it were a State, but in no event more than the least populous State; they shall be in addition to those appointed by the States, but they shall be considered, for the purposes of the election of President and Vice-President, to be electors appointed by a State; and they shall meet in the District and perform such duties as provided by the twelfth article of amendment.

Section 2 The Congress shall have power to enforce this article by appropriate legislation.

Amendment XXIV [Adopted 1964]

Section 1 The right of citizens of the United States to vote in any primary or other election for President or Vice-President, for electors for President or Vice-President, or for Senator or Representative in Congress, shall not be denied or abridged by the United States or any State by reason of failure to pay any poll tax or other tax.

Section 2 The Congress shall have power to enforce this article by appropriate legislation.

Amendment XXV [Adopted 1967]

Section 1 In case of the removal of the President from office or his death or resignation, the Vice-President shall become President.

Section 2 Whenever there is a vacancy in the office of the Vice-President, the President shall nominate a Vice-President who shall take the office upon confirmation by a majority vote of both houses of Congress.

Section 3 Whenever the President transmits to the President pro tempore of the Senate and the Speaker of the House of Representatives his written declaration that he is unable to discharge the powers and duties of his office, and until he transmits to them a written declaration to the contrary, such powers and duties shall be discharged by the Vice-President as Acting President.

Section 4 Whenever the Vice-President and a majority of either the principal officers of the executive departments, or of such other body as Congress may by law provide, transmit to the President pro tempore of the Senate and the Speaker of the House of Representatives their written declaration that the President is unable to discharge the powers and duties of his office, the Vice-President shall immediately assume the powers and duties of the office as Acting President.

Thereafter, when the President transmits to the President pro tempore of the Senate and the Speaker of the House of Representatives his written declaration that no inability exists, he shall resume the powers and duties of his office unless the Vice-President and a majority of either the principal officers of the executive department, or of such other body as Congress may by law provide, transmit within four days to the President pro tempore of the Senate and the Speaker of the House of Representatives their written declaration that the President is unable to discharge the powers and duties of his office. Thereupon Congress shall decide the issue, assembling within 48 hours for that purpose if not in session. If the Congress, within 21 days after receipt of the latter written declaration, or, if Congress is not in session, within 21 days after Congress is required to assemble, determines by two-thirds vote of both houses that the President is unable to discharge the powers and duties of his office, the Vice-President shall continue to discharge the same as Acting President; otherwise, the President shall resume the powers and duties of his office.

Amendment XXVI [Adopted 1971]

Section 1 The right of citizens of the United States, who are eighteen years of age or older, to vote shall not be denied or abridged by the United States or any state on account of age.

Section 2 The Congress shall have power to enforce this article by appropriate legislation.

Amendment XXVII [Adopted 1992]

No law, varying the compensation for the services of Senators and Representatives, shall take effect until an election of Representatives have intervened.

Presidential Elections

Year	Candidates	Parties	Popular Vote	Electoral Vote	Voter Participation
1789	GEORGE WASHINGTON		*	69	
	John Adams			34	
	Others			35	
1792	GEORGE WASHINGTON		*	132	
	John Adams			77	
	George Clinton			50	
	Others			5	
1796	JOHN ADAMS	Federalist	*	71	
	Thomas Jefferson	Democratic-Republican		68	
	Thomas Pinckney	Federalist		59	
	Aaron Burr	Dem.-Rep.		30	
	Others			48	
1800	THOMAS JEFFERSON	Dem.-Rep.	*	73	
	Aaron Burr	Dem.-Rep.		73	
	C. C. Pinckney	Federalist		64	
	John Jay	Federalist		1	
1804	THOMAS JEFFERSON	Dem.-Rep.	*	122	
	C. C. Pinckney	Federalist		14	
1808	JAMES MADISON	Dem.-Rep.	*	122	
	C. C. Pinckney	Federalist		47	
	George Clinton	Dem.-Rep.		6	
1812	JAMES MADISON	Dem.-Rep.	*	128	
	De Witt Clinton	Federalist		89	
1816	JAMES MONROE	Dem.-Rep.	*	183	
	Rufus King	Federalist		34	
1820	JAMES MONROE	Dem.-Rep.	*	231	
	John Quincy Adams	Dem.-Rep.		1	
1824	JOHN Q. ADAMS	Dem.-Rep.	108,740 (10.5%)	84	26.9%
	Andrew Jackson	Dem.-Rep.	153,544 (43.1%)	99	
	William H. Crawford	Dem.-Rep.	46,618 (13.1%)	41	
	Henry Clay	Dem.-Rep.	47,136 (13.2%)	37	
1828	ANDREW JACKSON	Democratic	647,286 (56.0%)	178	57.6%
	John Quincy Adams	National Republican	508,064 (44.0%)	83	
1832	ANDREW JACKSON	Democratic	687,502 (55.0%)	219	55.4%
	Henry Clay	National Republican	530,189 (42.4%)	49	
	John Floyd	Independent		11	
	William Wirt	Anti-Mason	33,108 (2.6%)	7	
1836	MARTIN VAN BUREN	Democratic	765,483 (50.9%)	170	57.8%
	W. H. Harrison	Whig		73	
	Hugh L. White	Whig	739,795 (49.1%)	26	
	Daniel Webster	Whig		14	
	W. P. Magnum	Independent		11	

*Electors elected by state legislators.

Presidential Elections

Year	Candidates	Parties	Popular Vote	Electoral Vote	Voter Participation
1840	WILLIAM H. HARRISON	Whig	1,274,624 (53.1%)	234	80.2%
	Martin Van Buren	Democratic	1,127,781 (46.9%)	60	
	J. G. Birney	Liberty	7,069	—	
1844	JAMES K. POLK	Democratic	1,338,464 (49.6%)	170	78.9%
	Henry Clay	Whig	1,300,097 (48.1%)	105	
	J. G. Birney	Liberty	62,300 (2.3%)	—	
1848	ZACHARY TAYLOR	Whig	1,360,967 (47.4%)	163	72.7%
	Lewis Cass	Democratic	1,222,342 (42.5%)	127	
	Martin Van Buren	Free-Soil	291,263 (10.1%)	—	
1852	FRANKLIN PIERCE	Democratic	1,601,117 (50.9%)	254	69.6%
	Winfield Scott	Whig	1,385,453 (44.1%)	42	
	John P. Hale	Free-Soil	155,825 (5.0%)	—	
1856	JAMES BUCHANAN	Democratic	1,832,955 (45.3%)	174	78.9%
	John C. Fremont	Republican	1,339,932 (33.1%)	114	
	Millard Fillmore	American	871,731 (21.6%)	8	
1860	ABRAHAM LINCOLN	Republican	1,865,593 (39.8%)	180	81.2%
	Stephen A. Douglas	Democratic	1,382,713 (29.5%)	12	
	John C. Breckinridge	Democratic	848,356 (18.1%)	72	
	John Bell	Union	592,906 (12.6%)	39	
1864	ABRAHAM LINCOLN	Republican	2,213,655 (55.0%)	212	73.8%
	George B. McClellan	Democratic	1,805,237 (45.0%)	21	
1868	ULYSSES S. GRANT	Republican	3,012,833 (52.7%)	214	78.1%
	Horatio Seymour	Democratic	2,703,249 (47.3%)	80	
1872	ULYSSES S. GRANT	Republican	3,597,132 (55.6%)	286	71.3%
	Horace Greeley	Democratic; Liberal Republican	2,834,125 (43.9%)	66	
1876	RUTHERFORD B. HAYES	Republican	4,036,298 (48.0%)	185	81.8%
	Samuel J. Tilden	Democratic	4,300,590 (51.0%)	184	
1880	JAMES A. GARFIELD	Republican	4,454,416 (48.5%)	214	79.4%
	Winfield S. Hancock	Democratic	4,444,952 (48.1%)	155	
1884	GROVER CLEVELAND	Democratic	4,874,986 (48.5%)	219	77.5%
	James G. Blaine	Republican	4,851,981 (48.2%)	182	
1888	BENJAMIN HARRISON	Republican	5,439,853 (47.9%)	233	79.3%
	Grover Cleveland	Democratic	5,540,309 (48.6%)	168	
1892	GROVER CLEVELAND	Democratic	5,556,918 (46.1%)	277	74.7%
	Benjamin Harrison	Republican	5,176,108 (43.0%)	145	
	James B. Weaver	People's	1,041,028 (8.5%)	22	
1896	WILLIAM McKINLEY	Republican	7,104,779 (51.1%)	271	79.3%
	William J. Bryan	Democratic People's	6,502,925 (47.7%)	176	
1900	WILLIAM McKINLEY	Republican	7,207,923 (51.7%)	292	73.2%
	William J. Bryan	Dem.-Populist	6,358,133 (45.5%)	155	
1904	THEODORE ROOSEVELT	Republican	7,623,486 (57.9%)	336	65.2%
	Alton B. Parker	Democratic	5,077,911 (37.6%)	140	
	Eugene V. Debs	Socialist	402,283 (3.0%)	—	

Presidential Elections

Year	Candidates	Parties	Popular Vote	Electoral Vote	Voter Participation
1908	WILLIAM H. TAFT William J. Bryan Eugene V. Debs	Republican Democratic Socialist	7,678,908 (51.6%) 6,409,104 (43.1%) 420,793 (2.8%)	321 162 —	65.4%
1912	WOODROW WILSON Theodore Roosevelt William H. Taft Eugene V. Debs	Democratic Progressive Republican Socialist	6,293,454 (41.9%) 4,119,538 (27.4%) 3,484,980 (23.2%) 900,672 (6.0%)	435 88 8 —	58.8%
1916	WOODROW WILSON Charles E. Hughes A. L. Benson	Democratic Republican Socialist	9,129,606 (49.4%) 8,538,221 (46.2%) 585,113 (3.2%)	277 254 —	61.6%
1920	WARREN G. HARDING James M. Cox Eugene V. Debs	Republican Democratic Socialist	16,152,200 (60.4%) 9,147,353 (34.2%) 919,799 (3.4%)	404 127 —	49.2%
1924	CALVIN COOLIDGE John W. Davis Robert M. La Follette	Republican Democratic Progressive	15,725,016 (54.0%) 8,386,503 (28.8%) 4,822,856 (16.6%)	382 136 13	48.9%
1928	HERBERT HOOVER Alfred E. Smith Norman Thomas	Republican Democratic Socialist	21,391,381 (58.2%) 15,016,443 (40.9%) 267,835 (0.7%)	444 87 —	56.9%
1932	FRANKLIN D. ROOSEVELT Herbert Hoover Norman Thomas	Democratic Republican Socialist	22,821,857 (57.4%) 15,761,841 (39.7%) 881,951 (2.2%)	472 59 —	56.9%
1936	FRANKLIN D. ROOSEVELT Alfred M. Landon William Lemke	Democratic Republican Union	27,751,597 (60.8%) 16,679,583 (36.5%) 882,479 (1.9%)	523 8 —	61.0%
1940	FRANKLIN D. ROOSEVELT Wendell L. Willkie	Democratic Republican	27,244,160 (54.8%) 22,305,198 (44.8%)	449 82	62.5%
1944	FRANKLIN D. ROOSEVELT Thomas E. Dewey	Democrat Republican	25,602,504 (53.5%) 22,006,285 (46.0%)	432 99	55.9%
1948	HARRY S TRUMAN Thomas E. Dewey J. Strom Thurmond Henry A. Wallace	Democratic Republican State-Rights Democratic Progressive	24,105,695 (49.5%) 21,969,170 (45.1%) 1,169,021 (2.4%) 1,156,103 (2.4%)	304 189 38 —	53.0%
1952	DWIGHT D. EISENHOWER Adlai E. Stevenson	Republican Democratic	33,936,252 (55.1%) 27,314,992 (44.4%)	442 89	63.3%
1956	DWIGHT D. EISENHOWER Adlai E. Stevenson Other	Republican Democratic —	35,575,420 (57.6%) 26,033,066 (42.1%) —	457 73 1	60.5%
1960	JOHN F. KENNEDY Richard M. Nixon Other	Democratic Republican —	34,227,096 (49.9%) 34,108,546 (49.6%) —	303 219 15	62.8%

Presidential Elections

Year	Candidates	Parties	Popular Vote	Electoral Vote	Voter Participation
1964	LYNDON B. JOHNSON	Democratic	43,126,506 (61.1%)	486	61.7%
	Barry M. Goldwater	Republican	27,176,799 (38.5%)	52	
1968	RICHARD M. NIXON	Republican	31,770,237 (43.4%)	301	60.6%
	Hubert H. Humphrey	Democratic	31,270,633 (42.7%)	191	
	George Wallace	American Indep.	9,906,141 (13.5%)	46	
1972	RICHARD M. NIXON	Republican	47,169,911 (60.7%)	520	55.2%
	George S. McGovern	Democratic	29,170,383 (37.5%)	17	
	Other	—	—	1	
1976	JIMMY CARTER	Democratic	40,828,587 (50.0%)	297	53.5%
	Gerald R. Ford	Republican	39,147,613 (47.9%)	241	
	Other	—	1,575,459 (2.1%)	—	
1980	RONALD REAGAN	Republican	43,901,812 (50.7%)	489	52.6%
	Jimmy Carter	Democratic	35,483,820 (41.0%)	49	
	John B. Anderson	Independent	5,719,722 (6.6%)	—	
	Ed Clark	Libertarian	921,188 (1.1%)	—	
1984	RONALD REAGAN	Republican	54,455,075 (59.0%)	525	53.3%
	Walter Mondale	Democratic	37,577,185 (41.0%)	13	
1988	GEORGE H. W. BUSH	Republican	48,886,000 (45.6%)	426	57.4%
	Michael S. Dukakis	Democratic	41,809,000 (45.6%)	111	
1992	WILLIAM J. CLINTON	Democratic	43,728,375 (43%)	370	55.0%
	George H. W. Bush	Republican	38,167,416 (38%)	168	
	Ross Perot	—	19,237,247 (19%)	—	
1996	WILLIAM J. CLINTON	Democratic	45,590,703 (50%)	379	48.8%
	Robert Dole	Republican	37,816,307 (41%)	159	
	Ross Perot	Independent	7,866,284 (9%)		
2000	GEORGE W. BUSH	Republican	50,456,062 (47%)	271	51.0%
	Albert Gore	Democratic	50,996,582 (49%)	267	
	Ralph Nader	Independent	2,858,843 (3%)	—	
2004	GEORGE W. BUSH	Republican	60,934,251 (51%)	286	50.0%
	John F. Kerry	Democrat	57,765,291 (48%)	252	
	Ralph Nader	Independent	405,933 (0%)	—	
2008	BARACK H. OBAMA	Democratic	69,456,897 (52.9%)	365	61.7%
	John S. McCain	Republican	59,934,814 (45.7%)	173	

GLOSSARY

abolitionists Individuals who, while seriously divided amongst themselves, wanted an immediate and total end to slavery.

AFL-CIO New union organization formed in 1955 with the merger of two large, rival unions and headed by George Meany. For a time the AFL-CIO represented more than 90 percent of the nation's union members.

Agricultural Adjustment Act The New Deal's principal solution to the farm problem, which sought to control overproduction of basic commodities in an effort to raise prices.

agricultural revolution The process of domesticating (planting, cultivating, and harvesting) plant life for food that occurred worldwide from 7,000 to 9,000 years ago. It resulted in sedentary living, the division of labor, regional trading, and greater social and political complexity.

Allied Powers Great Britain, France, and Russia, the nations that fought with the United States against the Central Powers—Germany and Austria-Hungary—in World War I.

American Federation of Labor Federation of craft unions founded in 1886 and led by Samuel Gompers that organized skilled workers only and emphasized immediate, realizable "bread and butter" issues.

American Temperance Society Organization founded in 1826 that was dedicated to abstinence, that is, the total elimination of the consumption of alcohol. Its efforts significantly reduced the volume of alcoholic consumption in the United States.

amnesty Executive clemency for groups of people accused of violating federal law. Presidential Reconstruction policy offered amnesty to most former Confederates.

Antebellum South Term used to refer to the approximately three decades before 1860 when "king" cotton and slave labor dominated the economy of the southern states.

Antietam Battle in September 1862 following Lee's invasion of Maryland that proved the most costly day of the war in terms of soldiers killed and wounded. It also cleared the way for Lincoln's Emancipation Proclamation.

Anti-Federalists Those who opposed the Constitution of 1787 because they feared a strong centralized government and the absence of a bill of rights.

Anti-Imperialist League Organization opposed to the American acquisition of overseas territories, especially the annexation of the Philippines in 1900.

antinomianism Belief that stressed God's free gift of grace and discounted individual and societal efforts to gain salvation through good works. Followers of Anne Hutchinson were characterized as antinomians as part of the criticism aimed at them by a majority of the ministers and magistrates of Massachusetts Bay Colony.

apartheid The harshly racist segregationist policy in South Africa. Economic sanctions and world opinion finally brought the beginning of talks for ending the policy in the late 1980s.

Army-McCarthy hearings The televised congressional hearings in 1954 that discredited Senator Joseph McCarthy, leader of the second Red Scare, and led to his downfall.

artisan An individual who worked in handicraft industries, usually in small shops located in colonial towns and cities. As a group they formed an urban middle class.

Atlanta Compromise Speech delivered by Booker T. Washington at the Atlanta Exposition of 1895 in which he renounced black interest in the vote, civil rights, and social equality with whites while proclaiming black loyalty to the economic development of the South.

Axis powers The alliance between Germany, Italy, and Japan in World War II.

baby boom The popular name given population increase associated with the historically high birth rate between 1946 and 1957.

Bacon's Rebellion A combined civil war within Virginia and anti-Indian war on the frontier, this 1676 rebellion included an uprising against the royal governor. Sir William Berkeley's policies were unpopular in part because he sought to limit expansion into the interior, and land-hungry colonists objected.

Bank War The battle between Jackson and his supporters and Nicholas Biddle and his supporters over the recharter of the Second Bank of the United States. Jackson vetoed the recharter bill and effectively "killed" the bank.

Battle of Fallen Timbers Decisive battle in 1794 between Indians of the Old Northwest and whites led by General Anthony Wayne that opened that region to white control.

Battle of Horseshoe Bend Climactic battle of 1814 between Creek Red Sticks and whites led by Andrew Jackson that broke Indian resistance to white settlement in the Old Southwest.

Bay of Pigs The disastrous effort to overthrow Castro's regime in Cuba in 1961 that involved an invasion by CIA-trained Cuban exiles.

Beats A group of writers and artists who valued intuition and spirituality and rebelled against the conformity and materialism of the 1950s.

Black Belt The Lower South, stretching from South Carolina across the Gulf Coast states to eastern Texas, which was dependent on the growth of cotton as a cash crop and on slave labor.

Black Death A bubonic plague epidemic that swept Europe in the fourteenth century, killing at least a third of the population.

Black Power The slogan for the violent, direct-action phase of the civil rights movement after 1965.

Bleeding Kansas The civil war in Kansas that occurred in 1856 following the sack of Lawrence and the massacre at Pottawatomie Creek.

Board of Trade Agency established in 1696 by the British government to improve the management of the colonies.

bonanza farms Huge wheat farms on the northern plains, frequently owned by corporations, that depended on machinery, a hired work force, and efficient managers.

border states The states of the Upper South such as Kentucky, Tennessee, and Maryland, which lay between the Deep South and the free states. The eight border states divided their loyalties during the Civil War.

Brain Trust Roosevelt's informal cabinet of experts who advised him on early New Deal legislation.

Brown v. *Board of Education* Supreme Court decision in 1954 that overturned the "separate but equal" doctrine of *Plessy* v. *Ferguson*, saying separate is inherently unequal, and led to a 1955 order to desegregate public schools "with all deliberate speed."

Bull Run Battle fought on July 21, 1861, at Manassas, Virginia, where Union troops under General McDowell were routed by Confederate troops under P. G. T. Beauregard. It was a warning that the Civil War was going to be long and costly.

busing The court-ordered action in the 1970s as a means of integrating schools, which led to violence, white flight, and the demand for a return to "neighborhood" schools.

Calvinism A Protestant theology that centered on the doctrine of predestination. Developed by John Calvin, who emphasized self-discipline and social control.

cash crops Crops grown for sale on the national and international market such as wheat and cotton.

Central Powers Austria-Hungary and Germany, the nations that fought against the United States and the Allied Powers—Britain, France, and Russia—in World War I.

City Beautiful movement Effort to make cities more attractive and meaningful through the construction of museums, libraries, and other institutions.

Civilian Conservation Corps Popular New Deal program that put young unemployed men to work on projects designed to preserve the natural environment resources.

Cold War The nearly 50-year conflict following World War II between the United States and its allies and the Soviet Union and its allies fought by means other than direct military action.

Committees of Correspondence Communications network set up in 1772 to state the rights of colonists and to keep colonists informed of British activities.

Commonwealth of Independent States The loose confederation of former Soviet republics established following the collapse of communism and the disintegration of the Soviet empire after 1989.

concentration of wealth A situation in which the wealthy control an increasing amount of the resources of a society and the gap between the rich and the poor widens.

Confederation of New England Intercolonial political organization that established four New England colonies in 1643 to coordinate government and to provide greater defense against the French, Dutch, and Indians. The first American attempt at a federal system of government.

Congress of Industrial Organizations A group of industrial labor unions, born during the Depression, that sought to organize workers in industry-wide unions rather than separating them by skill or craft.

containment The American policy after World War II, first defined by George F. Kennan, that was designed to prevent the further expansion of the Soviet Union and the spread of communism.

contract labor Labor system established soon after the Civil War under which freedmen signed agreements with landowners to work for menial wages in gangs as field laborers on a year-by-year basis.

Contract with America The 104th Congress's attempt to scale back the role of the federal government, eliminate environmental regulations, cut funding for educational programs such as Head Start, reduce taxes, and balance the budget. Under the leadership of House speaker Newt Gingrich.

Copperheads Northern Peace Democrats, who claimed Lincoln had betrayed the Constitution, that working-class Americans bore the brunt of his policy of conscription, and that the Civil War should be ended immediately.

cotton diplomacy The South's policy of using the Europeans' need for raw cotton in an attempt to force their recognition of the Confederacy and an end to the Union blockade. Because Europeans had surpluses and found alternative sources of cotton, this Confederate strategy did not work.

cotton kingdom Term used to refer to the antebellum South, which was largely dependent on one cash crop, cotton.

Creel Committee The Committee on Public Information appointed by Wilson to convince the American people that World War I was just and they should unite behind the war effort.

CREEP Acronym for Committee to Re-elect the President, named for the organization established to manage President Nixon's reelection campaign in 1972.

Cuban missile crisis The incident that developed when U.S. aerial photographs revealed Soviet missiles were being deployed in Cuba, which brought the world to the brink of nuclear war.

Dawes Severalty Act Legislation intended to destroy tribal bonds by allotting tribal reservations to individual members of tribes as private property. It also gave citizenship to those Indians accepting individual allotments.

debt peonage A perpetual indebtedness tying the debtor to the land, which resulted from tenant farmers and sharecroppers buying supplies on credit based on future crops.

deflation Condition resulting from a declining supply of money in relation to goods produced, which creates a fall in prices and an increase in the real value of money and debts. The national economy was deflationary in the late nineteenth century.

Dominion of New England A centralized government for the New England colonies, New York, and New Jersey established by James II in 1686 and designed to streamline and centralize colonial administration. It collapsed following the Glorious Revolution in England in 1688.

Dred Scott case Supreme Court decision of 1857 declaring that slaves were not citizens and that the Missouri Compromise was unconstitutional.

dust bowl The name given to a region of the western and southwestern Great Plains, particularly western Kansas and Oklahoma, in the late 1930s as a result of a severe drought.

Economic Opportunity Act The major piece of legislation under President Johnson designed to end poverty through helping the poor gain better education and improve their health and housing.

Electoral College Group elected to meet to choose the president.

Emancipation Proclamation The announcement by President Lincoln on New Year's Day, 1863, that slaves in states still in rebellion against the Union were forever free.

Enlightenment Intellectual movement in Europe that stressed the acquisition of knowledge by humankind as a means of assuring progress and perfecting society—a view embraced by many in America's colonial elite.

entitlements Programs like Medicare, Medicaid, and Social Security that provide assistance to Americans on the basis of need. They are mandated by law and constitute a significant portion of the annual budget.

ERA Acronym for Equal Rights Amendment, the proposed constitutional amendment that stated "Equality of rights under the law shall not be denied or abridged by the United States or by any State on account of sex." The ERA failed ratification.

evil empire President Reagan's term for the Soviet Union in the early years of his administration, indicating his hostility toward that nation and his tendency to think of world issues in black and white terms.

excise taxes Indirect taxes levied on items produced in the United States. The tax on whiskey proposed by Secretary of the Treasury Hamilton provoked the Whiskey Rebellion in 1794.

faction Organized political interest group. The Revolutionary generation feared that factions would corrupt republican government and undermine public virtue.

Fair Deal President Truman's legislative program after 1948 that included expansion of New Deal programs plus a farm program, a civil rights program, national health insurance, and federal aid to education. Most of it went unenacted.

Fair Employment Practices Committee Agency established to carry out Executive Order 8802, which stated there would be no discrimination in war industries or government service on account of race, creed, color, or national origin.

Federal Reserve System Major banking reform measure passed during the Wilson administration that created a decentralized banking system under a centralized administration (Federal Reserve Board) and a flexible currency system.

Federal Trade Commission Federal agency established in 1914 to regulate corporations and act against those accused of restricting competition.

Federalist Papers Collection of essays written by Madison, Hamilton, and Jay in support of the Constitution of 1787 that described the political vision of those supporting the Constitution.

Federalist party The political party of Hamilton and Adams that advocated a strong central government to promote commerce and manufacturing in an effort to diversify the economy.

Federalists Those who supported a stronger national government and the replacement of the Articles of Confederation by the Constitution of 1787. Also taken as the name of one of the first political parties in America's two-party system.

Fifty-four forty or fight Polk's campaign slogan in 1844 asserting that the United States should annex all of the Oregon country.

Filipino-American War The war between the United States and the Philippines, 1899–1902, in which the Filipinos unsuccessfully attempted to gain independence from U.S. control.

First Continental Congress Meeting of representatives of 12 colonies that was held in Philadelphia in September 1774 to discuss the Coercive Acts.

First Hundred Days The first three months of Roosevelt's administration during which numerous bills to fight the Depression were proposed and passed.

flapper A young woman with a short skirt, bobbed hair, and a boyish figure who did the Charleston, smoked, drank, and was casual about sex and was the image of modern woman in the twenties. Few women were actually "flappers."

Force Acts Three acts passed in 1870 and 1871 that gave the president power to use federal supervisors to assure that citizens were not deprived of their right to vote. It also declared illegal secret organizations that used disguise and coercion to deprive others of equal protection of the laws.

Fort Laramie Council Meeting held in 1851 between the U.S. government and the northern Plains tribes at which the United States agreed to pay compensation to the Indians for destruction of their lands, but required the tribes to give up their rights of free movement and restricted them to greatly reduced lands.

Fort Sumter Federal installation in Charleston harbor that Lincoln attempted to resupply in 1861. When Confederates resisted that effort, the Civil War began.

four freedoms The points described by Roosevelt in a January 1941 speech before Congress as the rights of all men. They came to be viewed as U.S. war goals for World War II.

Fourteen Points President Wilson's peace plan announced in 1918 that called for freedom of the seas, equality of trade, self-determination of all peoples, open negotiation of treaties, and a League of Nations to preserve peace.

free silver Unlimited coinage of silver to inflate the currency and raise prices, which was demanded by the Populists and the Democrats in the 1896 election.

free soil Term representing the idea that the western territories should not be open to the expansion of slavery. Both the Free-Soil and Republican parties opposed the expansion of slavery into the territories.

Freedmen's Bureau Agency established by Congress to ease the transition from slavery to freedom for former ex-slaves by providing emergency supplies, education, help in relocating families, aid in finding land and jobs, and a variety of other services.

freehold tenure Individual ownership of land in the colonies, which allowed the colonists both economic independence and political rights such as the right to vote.

Fugitive Slave Act Federal measure designed to assure that runaway slaves were returned to their masters. Its enforcement outraged northerners who viewed it as a threat to individual liberties.

fugitive slave clause Part of the Constitution that sanctioned the capture and return of runaway slaves.

Gettysburg Battle in southern Pennsylvania in July 1863 in which Union forces under General Meade turned back an invading Confederate force under Lee, marking the turn of the military tide in the East.

Ghost Dance Movement centered in the revelations of Wovoka, a Paiute prophet, who predicted natural disasters would eliminate the white race, while dancing Indians would not only avoid destruction but would gain strength thanks to the return to life of their ancestors.

Gilded Age Mark Twain's phrase suggesting shallow glitter as characteristic of social and political life in the last quarter of the nineteenth century.

Glorious Revolution The replacement in 1688 of the Catholic King James II with the Protestant William and Mary, which its proponents saw as a victory for Protestantism, parliamentary power, and the limitation of kingly prerogatives.

Gospel of Wealth Andrew Carnegie's argument that the concentration of wealth in the hands of a few was beneficial but that the wealthy had an obligation to use their fortunes for the good of society.

Great Compromise Agreement at the Constitutional Convention whereby representation in the lower house was by population, representation in the upper house (Senate) was equal for all states, and three-fifths of the slave population was counted to determine representation in the House and to calculate states' taxes.

Great Society President Johnson's domestic program that sought to establish a society in which the comforts of life were more widely shared and poverty was eliminated.

greenbacks The nickname for paper money printed by the Union during the Civil War.

Gulf of Tonkin Resolution The congressional act that gave President Johnson the authority to conduct a war in Vietnam.

Half-Way Covenant Puritan compromise specifying that children of church members could join the church even if they could not demonstrate that they had undergone a conversion experience. However, they could not vote in church affairs or take communion.

Harlem Renaissance A flowering of black culture in the 1920s that emphasized black pride and grappled with the question of how to be black in America.

Hartford Convention Meeting of delegates from five New England states in 1814 that debated secession and urged constitutional amendments to reshape the Union more favorably to New England's interests.

Haymarket Riot When police arrived to break up a peaceful labor protest meeting at Haymarket Square in Chicago in 1886, a bomb exploded, seven policemen were killed, and newspapers branded the protesters as wild-eyed radicals.

horizontal integration Combining businesses in the same field in an effort to monopolize one stage of production in an industry. John D. Rockefeller horizontally integrated the oil refining business.

imperialism One nation gaining political or economic control or influence over other areas.

impressment The British policy of forcibly drafting British subjects employed on American vessels to serve in the British Navy. It sometimes resulted in the impressment of American seamen and was a cause of war between the United States and Britain in 1812.

Industrial Workers of the World Militant, radical labor organization that called for one big union of workers; admitted members regardless of sex, race, or skill; and had its greatest success in organizing lumbermen and migratory workers in the Northwest. Popularly called the IWW, or the "Wobblies."

internal improvements Roads, canals, and other similar projects that facilitate transportation and communication. In the early nineteenth century, the federal and state governments often provided loans, tax breaks, and bond guarantees to help finance internal improvements.

Interstate Commerce Commission Regulatory commission established by the Interstate Commerce Act of 1887 that had the power to investigate and prosecute railroad corporations charging unfair rates or engaging in illegal practices. It had little real enforcement authority.

Iran-*contra* affair The effort by the National Security Council to free Middle Eastern hostages by selling arms to Iran and then using the funds to aid the contras in Nicaragua in violation of the law and of the will of Congress. It became a major scandal of the Reagan presidency.

Iroquois Confederacy League of six tribes concentrated in upper New York State that the British sought as allies in the Seven Years' War. Instead, the Iroquois tried to serve their own best interests by playing British and French power off against each other. During the Revolutionary War, most Iroquois sided with the British; when the British lost, Iroquois dominance in the northeastern interior was broken.

Jacksonian Democrats Political party in the antebellum period that espoused personal liberty and local rule, emphasized the freedom of the individual to follow his own interests, and appealed primarily to the common man.

Jeffersonian Republicans The political party of Jefferson and Madison that advocated a weak central government, more power vested in the states, and a society and economy based on independent yeoman farmers.

Jim Crow laws Laws that segregated blacks from whites first in public facilities and ultimately in all aspects of life. These laws were passed in the South beginning in the 1890s.

John Brown's raid The attack on the federal arsenal at Harpers Ferry, Virginia, on October 16, 1859, which was intended to inspire a slave uprising but ended in the deaths of the attackers and increased tensions between North and South.

Kansas–Nebraska Act Measure introduced by Stephen Douglas and passed in 1854 that organized the lands west of Iowa and Missouri on the basis

of popular sovereignty, thus negating the Missouri Compromise.

Kent State The Ohio university that was the site of the 1970 killing of four students by National Guard troops who had been sent there to control antiwar protests.

King Philip's War Conflict in New England between Wampanoag Indians led by King Philip, or Metacomet, who were seeking to revitalize their culture, and land-hungry whites. The war occurred in 1675–1676 and ended in defeat for the Indians.

King William's War The war of 1689 to 1697, which was the first of the wars for empire fought between the English and the French in the 1600s and 1700s.

Kinsey reports The popular name for the books *Sexual Behavior in the Human Male* and *Sexual Behavior in the Human Female,* which shocked Americans in the 1950s with what was revealed about their sexual behavior.

kivas The religious shrines or temples of the Pueblos of New Mexico. The Pueblos gathered there to nurture and maintain their culture and traditions, and kept the existence of these places secret from Europeans.

League of Nations International organization proposed by President Wilson and established by the Treaty of Versailles to keep peace among nations. The Senate refused to ratify the treaty, and the United States never became a member of the League.

lend-lease Measure passed in 1941 under which the United States loaned to Britain and other nations materials to fight World War II, which would be paid back in kind after the war.

Lost Generation Writers, such as Ernest Hemingway and F. Scott Fitzgerald, whose works reflected their disillusionment with the materialism, conformity, and provincial prejudice that dominated American life in the 1920s.

Lusitania British passenger liner sunk off the coast of Ireland by a German submarine on May 7, 1915, with great loss of life, including 128 Americans.

Magna Carta Agreement forced on the English king by the aristocracy in 1215 that eventually led to the regular meeting of a parliament.

Manhattan Project The secret project organized by the U.S. government in 1941 to manufacture an atomic bomb before the Germans did.

March on Washington Massive protest demonstration in the District of Columbia in August 1963 organized to support passage of the Civil Rights Bill. It did not help much in that regard, but inspired much nationwide sympathy for the civil rights movement.

Marshall Plan The U.S. plan for economic reconstruction of western Europe after World War II, involving massive U.S. aid to help finance rebuilding. It was motivated by anticommunism and economic interest.

massive retaliation Secretary of State John Foster Dulles's policy in the 1950s that depended on atomic weapons for national defense and containment, and threatened an all-out nuclear response to any Soviet aggression.

matrilineal The determination of family membership and political and property rights through the female (mother's) line. Many pre-Columbian North American peoples were matrilineal cultures, as were many African tribal societies.

Medicare The national health plan passed under President Johnson to provide medical benefits for the elderly through the Social Security system.

mercantilism The state-regulated policy of economic nationalism, popular in Europe in the seventeenth century, which argued that colonies existed to serve the mother country by as acting as outlets for manufactured goods, providing raw materials and foodstuffs, stimulating trade, and contributing taxes (in the form of trade duties) to the nation's treasury.

Mexican War The war fought between 1846 and 1848 that resulted in U.S. acquisition of the Southwest from Texas to California.

middle-class values Such virtues as hard work, good character, diligence, punctuality, temperance, and thrift that are seen as upholding the status quo against unsettling changes.

Missouri Compromise Sectional agreement of 1820 under which Maine entered the Union as a free state, Missouri entered the Union as a slave state, and slavery was banned in the Louisiana Territory north of 36° 30′ latitude.

modern Republicanism President Eisenhower's political philosophy, also called "dynamic conservatism," which he said meant "conservative when it comes to money, liberal when it comes to human beings."

Mormons Members of the Church of Jesus Christ of Latter-day Saints. They escaped persecution in the United States by migrating to Utah in the 1840s and 1850s where they established successful communities based on communal agriculture and authoritarian leadership. Brigham Young led them.

moving assembly line System of assembly line production introduced by the Ford Motor Company in which the product is mechanically transported to the worker, who then has a limited time to finish his or her specific task.

muckrakers Writers who exposed corruption and scandal in American politics, society, and economy in articles published in new, widely circulated magazines such as *McClure's*.

Muslim A person believing in the religion of Islam, which began in the seventh century and spread throughout the Middle East and northern Africa and eventually to Asia and Europe. Muslims, or Moslems, were sometimes called Moors by Europeans.

NAACP Organization founded by white social justice progressives and blacks such as W. E. B. Du Bois that worked for equality and justice for African Americans.

Nat Turner revolt Slave uprising in Virginia in 1831 that was designed to spread terror among whites to protest slavery. It resulted in the death of 55 whites and at least as many blacks and revision of slave code laws throughout the South.

National Recovery Administration New Deal agency designed to help industry recover by setting fair competition codes and suspending antitrust laws in order to foster cooperation and planning rather than competition.

National Trades Union The first national labor organization in the United States, founded in 1834, which advocated shorter hours, better wages, and ways to ward off the competition of cheap labor.

NATO Collective security organization formed in 1949 by the United States and 11 other nations that vowed that an attack against one member would be considered an attack against all. Its original purpose was to prevent a Soviet invasion of western Europe.

Navigation Acts Parliamentary acts that regulated colonial trade in an attempt to make the colonies fit into a mercantile system. The system was designed to make England competitive with the Dutch, who dominated the Atlantic trade.

Nazi-Soviet Pact Agreement between Germany and the Soviet Union signed in August 1939 that freed Germany to invade Poland to begin World War II. Also known as the Nonaggression Pact.

Neutrality Acts Measures passed in the mid-1930s that banned arms shipments to belligerents, prohibited Americans from traveling on belligerent vessels, and made nonmilitary items available to belligerents only on a cash-and-carry basis, all in an effort to prevent U.S. involvement in another war.

New Freedom Woodrow Wilson's platform and philosophy in the 1912 presidential campaign that emphasized limited government with open competition.

New Frontier President Kennedy's program that included a number of social justice measures.

new immigrants Immigrants from southern and eastern Europe, primarily Jewish and Catholic in religion, who came to the United States in large numbers after 1880.

New Jersey Plan Plan introduced by William Paterson to counter the Virginia Plan and supported by smaller states at the Constitutional Convention. It urged retention of the Articles of Confederation, but with increased powers, a chief executive, and a supreme court.

New Nationalism Theodore Roosevelt's platform and philosophy in the 1912 presidential campaign arguing that a strong national government was necessary to regulate business and industry and to guarantee the rights of the people.

New Netherland Colony established by the Dutch in the Hudson River valley in 1624 as a center for the Dutch fur trade, which was ultimately taken over by the English and became New York.

New South The vision of a South that was modern, progressive, and self-sufficient by those, especially Henry Grady, who urged the South to abandon its dependence on cotton and industrialize and economically diversify.

Nixon Doctrine President Nixon's assertion that the United States would aid friends and allies but would not undertake the full burden of troop defense, which in practice led to the policy of Vietnamization in Vietnam.

Northwest Ordinance Legislation passed by the Confederation Congress in 1787 that provided for the political organization of the Old Northwest Territory and its ultimate incorporation into the Union as states on an equal footing with older states. The ordinance also prohibited the importation of new slaves into the territory.

NOW Acronym for the National Organization for Women, a political pressure organization established in 1966 to bring women into "full participation in the mainstream of American society."

Office of War Information World War II agency that was responsible for keeping Americans united behind the war effort by controlling war news and promoting patriotism.

Open Door policy U.S. China policy calling for equal trading rights for all nations and the territorial and administrative integrity of China.

Operation Desert Storm The name given the UN-sponsored military operation to liberate Kuwait from Iraq's control in early 1991.

Ordinance of Nullification Declaration by a South Carolina state convention that stated the tariffs of 1828 and 1832 were null and void (nullified) and would not be enforced in the state.

Oregon Trail The overland route west from Missouri and Iowa along the Platte River, through South Pass, and down the Snake and Columbia rivers to the Willamette valley.

outworkers Laborers, especially women, who did piecework in small shops or in their homes.

Palmer raids Raids conducted by the Justice Department in 1919–1920 to round up and deport alien radicals suspected of subversive activity that, in the process, resulted in widespread violation of civil liberties.

Pearl Harbor U.S. naval base in Hawaii that was hit by a surprise attack by the Japanese on December 7, 1941, resulting in American entry into World War II.

personal liberty laws State laws that prohibited the use of state officials and institutions in the recovery of fugitive slaves, passed in reaction to the Fugitive Slave Act.

Plessy v. Ferguson Supreme Court decision in 1896 that paved the way for legal segregation by declaring that "separate but equal" facilities did not violate the equal protection clause of the Fourteenth Amendment.

polygamy The practice of allowing one male to have several wives. It was one of the more controversial social customs of the Mormons.

poor whites Lowest class of southern whites who eked out a living from the poor soil of pine barrens, sand hills, and marshes, and who had a reputation of being lazy, shiftless, and illiterate.

popular sovereignty Lewis Cass's (later Stephen Douglas's) doctrine proposing that the decision of whether to permit slavery in a territory be left to the local territorial legislature. "Bleeding Kansas" exposed its shortcomings as a peaceful solution to the question of slavery in the territories.

Populists Reform political party that advocated legislation to benefit farmers and campaigned for the unlimited coinage of silver in the 1896 election.

power of the purse The authority to initiate money bills that specified how much money should be raised by taxes and how such money should be spent, which was used by assemblies to gain substantial control over colonial governments.

pre-Columbian The 2000-year epoch before the arrival of Europeans in the Americas that dates from the voyages of Christopher Columbus beginning in 1492.

Preemption acts Legislation passed in the 1830s and 1840s that gave "squatters" the right to settle public land and then purchase it at the minimum price once the government put it up for sale.

Presidential Reconstruction Lenient Reconstruction program followed by Lincoln and Johnson that was designed to regularize relations between the North and South as easily and rapidly as possible after the Civil War. The South was required to abolish slavery, void secession, repudiate Confederate debts, and then elect new officials.

price revolution The inflationary effect on the European economy during the 1500s that resulted from the enormous influx of silver from Spanish America. It stimulated commercial development, but also redistributed wealth and increased the number of Europeans living in poverty.

Prince Henry Dubbed "the Navigator" for his commitment to seafaring, this Portuguese prince encouraged improvements in navigation, mapmaking, and ship design, and financed voyages of exploration along the African coast and to China in the sixteenth century.

progressive movement Reform movement in the early twentieth century centered in the middle class that sought to resolve the problems of industrialization, immigration, and urbanization by using government to help the common people and by promoting order and efficiency.

protective tariff Tax on imported goods designed to protect American businessmen, wage earners, and farmers from the competition and products of foreign labor.

Protestant Reformation A sixteenth-century movement seeking to replace the Roman Catholic Church with alternative doctrines and church organization. This movement gave rise to many new Christian churches, splintering Western Europe.

Ptolemaic principles Navigational principles used by Portuguese explorers in the fifteenth century; they included the concept that the earth is round, that distances on its surfaces can be measured by degrees, and that navigators can "fix" their positions on a map by measuring the position of the stars. Named for the ancient Greek astronomer Ptolemy.

public virtue The willingness of the people to sacrifice their own self-interest for the good of the whole. The Revolutionary generation relied on this self-regulatory behavior to maintain public order in the absence of powerful government.

Pullman strike Strike against the Pullman company in 1894 that was broken by federal troops and a court injunction. It witnessed the emergence of Eugene V. Debs as a radical spokesman for organized labor.

Puritans Name given to religious reformers who wished to cleanse the Church of England of Catholic vestments and rituals. They established a number of colonies, including Massachusetts Bay Colony in New England, and tried to create a godly community devoted to realizing their faith.

Quakers Radical religious sect that discarded the ideas of original sin and predestination and, instead, preached that all believers could find grace through the "inward light," a spark of redemption that existed in every human being. They also believed in the spiritual equality of both sexes, and they renounced the use of force in human affairs.

Queen Anne's War The war of 1702 to 1713, which was the second of the wars for empire and ended with major gains for the English in the Peace of Utrecht.

radical Republicans A minority of northern Republicans who were dissatisfied with the leniency of presidential Reconstruction and instigated their own program to reconstruct the South with the Reconstruction Acts of 1867. They particularly insisted on the protection of blacks' rights and black male suffrage.

Reconstruction Acts Three acts passed by Congress in 1867 that divided the southern states into five military districts and required them to ratify the Fourteenth Amendment and write new constitutions guaranteeing black suffrage before being readmitted into the Union.

redemption Southern Democratic term for the end of Reconstruction and the return of white southern Democratic rule to the South.

Regulators Farmers from western North Carolina who, in the 1760s and 1770s, rebelled against the existing political and social power structure that was dominated by eastern planter interests.

Renaissance A cultural awakening that began in Italy and spread through Europe in the fifteenth and sixteenth centuries. Its emphasis on human abilities helped promote a spirit of discovery, exploration, and expansion.

Republican party The third party organized in 1854 that replaced the Whigs and was opposed to the expansion of slavery, anti-Catholic, reform oriented, and in favor of federal efforts to promote commerce and industry.

revolutionary republicanism Ideology that emphasized the dangers of government by arguing that only by controlling power and corruption could liberty be preserved. It was the ideology colonists used to justify their declaration of independence from Britain.

Roosevelt Corollary Theodore Roosevelt's reinterpretation of the Monroe Doctrine to justify U.S. intervention in Latin America.

Rosie the Riveter Name given to any woman who went to work in wartime factories as a patriotic duty, usually in jobs held before only by men.

Sacco–Vanzetti case Massachusetts court case in which two Italian anarchists were convicted and sentenced to death for robbery and murder on scant evidence primarily because of nativist sentiment.

scientific management Management system developed by Frederick Taylor that stressed efficiency through time and motion studies.

Scopes trial The case in which a Dayton, Tennessee, teacher was tried and convicted of violating a state law by teaching evolutionary theory to a high school biology class.

self-determination Belief in the right of all peoples to self-government; a basic tenet of American foreign policy in the twentieth century.

Seneca Falls Convention Meeting convened in 1848 in New York by Elizabeth Cady Stanton and Lucretia Mott to discuss problems confronting women. The convention issued the Declaration of Sentiments concerning the treatment of women and inaugurated the women's rights movement.

settlement house Movement led by educated, middle-class women such as Jane Addams to establish centers in urban lower-class neighborhoods to help immigrants adapt to American urban life.

Seven Years' War Fourth of the wars for empire between France and England, which lasted from 1756 to 1763 and resulted in the English gaining control of the eastern half of North America.

sharecropping Labor system whereby landowners provided land, equipment, and provisions for workers who then worked the land for a portion of the crop harvested. Freedmen who hated the contract labor system preferred this system.

Shays's Rebellion Uprising of farmers in western Massachusetts in 1786 that tried to prevent foreclosures on land. It posed a threat to social order and motivated some to call for a constitutional convention.

Social Darwinism Herbert Spencer's adaptation of Charles Darwin's biological concepts of natural selection and "survival of the fittest" to human society.

Social Gospel movement Movement to tie salvation to the improvement of society and to make Christianity relevant to industrial and urban problems.

Social Security Act New Deal measure passed in 1935 that provided old-age pensions, survivor insurance, unemployment compensation for industrial workers, and aid to dependent children and the handicapped.

Sons of Liberty Groups, composed mostly of artisans, shopkeepers, and ordinary citizens, who engaged in mob violence and crowd action to protest British policies.

Spanish Armada Spain dispatched its naval fleet (armada) in 1588 to invade England in an effort to stop the Protestant Queen Elizabeth from aiding Spain's Protestant opponents on the European Continent. The armada's defeat by the English opened the doors to English colonization in the New World.

Stamp Act Congress Convention of delegates from nine colonies held in October 1765 to protest British tax policies.

stratified society A society that maintains a system of social gradations of classes and subordinates lower classes to an upper class. Typical of Europe in the sixteenth century and favored by many members of the colonial elite (wealthy merchants and planters), who hoped to perpetuate a version of the traditional class structure.

streetcar suburbs Neighborhoods on the fringes of the city from which upper- and middle-class residents commuted to work in the inner city. Residents could afford the expense of commuting.

supply-side economics President Reagan's policy for restoring prosperity and ending inflation through a tax reduction that would encourage business expansion and lead to a larger supply of goods that would stimulate the whole economic system.

Taft-Hartley Act Measure passed in 1947 to limit the power of unions by restricting the weapons they could employ. It gave the president the right to call for an 80-day cooling-off period in strikes affecting national security, and required union officials to sign non-Communist oaths to use government procedures designed to protect their rights.

Tariff of Abominations High protective tariff passed in 1828 that was designed to win votes for Andrew Jackson's presidential campaign.

task system Type of organization of labor that gave each slave a specific assignment to complete daily. It had the potential for more leisure time for slaves, but involved greater scrutiny of the quality of their work.

"Teflon" presidency The term used to describe President Reagan's continued personal popularity despite criticisms and disagreements over his policies.

Tennessee Valley Authority Part of the New Deal, the TVA was an independent public corporation empowered to sell electricity and fertilizer and to promote flood control and reclamation in a seven-state area in the southeast.

Tet offensive The North Vietnamese offensive of 1968 showing U.S. reports of imminent victory were misleading.

The Other America Socialist Michael Harrington's book detailing the widespread existence of poverty amidst American affluence in the 1950s.

Trail of Tears The forced removal of the Cherokee west of the Mississippi River. The U.S. Army "escorted" the tribes from their ancestral lands. Many died on the way.

Treaty of Guadalupe-Hidalgo Treaty signed in 1848 that ended the Mexican War and resulted in U.S. acquisition of New Mexico and California.

Treaty of Tordesillas A 1494 treaty that moved the demarcation line, set by the pope in 1493 to divide Spanish and Portuguese spheres of exploration, 270 leagues to the west. Thus it included Brazil in the Portuguese sphere but left the remainder of the Western Hemisphere for Spanish exploration and colonization.

trench warfare The World War I strategy on the western front in northern France by which soldiers dug miles of ditches, strung barbed wire to protect them, and fought a costly defensive war of attrition over a few yards of territory.

Triangle Shirtwaist fire Fire that killed over 100 garment workers in New York City and inspired state legislation to mandate safer factory conditions.

Truman Doctrine The American policy, developed in 1947 in response to conditions in Greece and Turkey, that promised U.S. support to people resisting armed subjugation. It was the first implementation of the containment doctrine.

U.S.S. Maine U.S. battleship that exploded in Havana harbor in 1898, outraging the American public and pushing the United States and Spain toward war.

urbanization A development, such as began in the United States between 1820 and 1860, in which an increasing proportion of a society's population lives in cities.

vertical integration Method of expanding business by adding operations before or after the production process. Andrew Carnegie vertically integrated the steel business.

Vietnamization President Nixon's policy to withdraw U.S. troops from Vietnam and turn the responsibility for ground combat over to South Vietnam's armed forces.

Virginia and Kentucky Resolutions State resolutions that declared the Alien and Sedition Acts violated the Bill of Rights, and that the states could nullify unconstitutional laws.

Virginia Plan Plan of union designed by James Madison for a strong central government consisting of a bicameral congress, a president, a national judiciary, and a council of revision. It became the basis of the Constitution of 1787.

wage slavery The phrase used to describe workers' dependence on earning wages by working for others with little chance of becoming independent during the course of their lives.

walking city The type of city common before the Civil War, which was limited in size and shape by the necessity of walking to work and was not zoned, with businesses, residences, and classes mixed.

Watergate The apartment complex and location of the Democratic National Committee headquarters that was the site of a break-in financed by President Nixon's re-election committee. The name came to designate the crisis in government that led to Nixon's resignation.

welfare capitalism The introduction of pensions, profit-sharing plans, recreational facilities, cafeterias, and other amenities by employers to reduce worker discontent and discourage the growth of labor unions in the 1920s.

Whig ideology Political belief originating in England holding that concentrated power was the enemy of liberty, and the best defenses against concentrated power and political corruption were balanced government, elected legislatures, prohibition of standing armies, and eternal vigilance by the people.

Whigs Antebellum political party that endorsed Henry Clay's American System, advocated politics as a vehicle for the reform of society, and opposed Jackson and increases in the power of the executive branch of government.

Whiskey Rebellion Uprising of western Pennsylvania farmers to protest Hamilton's excise taxes. The 1794 rebellion posed no threat to the safety of the federal government, but offered the government an opportunity to show its determination to enforce its laws, even in remote western districts.

white man's burden Rudyard Kipling's phrase representing the idea that western civilizations have a duty and destiny to civilize supposed inferior peoples. The idea was popular with Theodore Roosevelt and other turn-of-the-century U.S. imperialists.

Wilmot Proviso An amendment to an army appropriations bill of 1846 that would have prohibited slavery in any territories acquired from Mexico resulting from the Mexican War.

Women's International League A group of prominent and successful women from around the world that met in Zurich, Switzerland, during the Versailles Conference, to promote lasting peace.

Works Progress Administration The major work relief program of the second New Deal, which employed about 3 million people a year on useful projects from capital construction to the arts.

World's Columbian Exposition Exhibition in Chicago in 1893 to celebrate the achievements of American enterprise. It gave rise to a "City Beautiful" movement.

XYZ affair Incident in which three French commissioners demanded a bribe in exchange for the opportunity to negotiate an accord between France and the United States. It provoked outcries for war in the United States.

CREDITS

INDEX

The World

ARCTIC OCEAN

80°N — 160°W — 140°W — 120°West Longitude

Arctic Circle

Alaska (U.S.)

60°N

CANADA

NORTH AMERICA

40°North Longitude

PACIFIC OCEAN

Midway Is. (U.S.)

UNITED STATES

See inset below

Bermuda (U.K.)

ATLANTIC OCEAN

Tropic of Cancer — Hawaii (U.S.)

20°N

MEXICO

CUBA

HAITI

DOMINICAN REPUBLIC

BELIZE

HONDURAS

GUATEMALA

EL SALVADOR

NICARAGUA

COSTA RICA

PANAMA

VENEZUELA

GUYANA

SURINAM

FR. GUIANA

Galápagos Islands (ECUADOR)

COLOMBIA

0° — Equator

KIRIBATI

ECUADOR

SOUTH AMERICA

WESTERN SAMOA

American Samoa (U.S.)

French Polynesia (FRANCE)

PERU

BRAZIL

TONGA

20°S

BOLIVIA

Tropic of Capricorn

Easter Island (CHILE)

PACIFIC OCEAN

PARAGUAY

CHILE

ARGENTINA

URUGUAY

40°S

Falkland Islands (U.K.)

South Georgia (Falk.)

60°S

Antarctic Circle

80°S — 160°W — 140°W — 120°W — 100°W — 80°W

ANTARCTICA

Central America and the Caribbean

30°N — 110°W — 100°W — 90°W — 80°W — 70°W — 60°W — 50°W

UNITED STATES

Gulf of Mexico

BAHAMAS

ATLANTIC OCEAN

NORTH AMERICA

MEXICO

CUBA

Cayman Is. (U.K.)

Turks and Caicos Is. (U.K.)

DOMINICAN REPUBLIC

Puerto Rico (U.S.)

Virgin Is. (U.S. – U.K.)

ANTIGUA-BARBUDA

Guadeloupe (Fr.)

DOMINICA

Martinique (Fr.)

ST. LUCIA

20°N

HAITI

JAMAICA

BELIZE

HONDURAS

GUATEMALA

EL SALVADOR

Central America

NICARAGUA

ST. KITTS AND NEVIS

West Indies

CARIBBEAN SEA

ST. VINCENT AND THE GRENADINES

BARBADOS

GRENADA

PACIFIC OCEAN

Panama Canal

TRINIDAD AND TOBAGO

10°N

COSTA RICA

VENEZUELA

PANAMA

COLOMBIA

SOUTH AMERICA

GUYANA

SURINAM

N
W — E
S

| 0 | 500 Miles |
| 0 | 500 Kilometers |

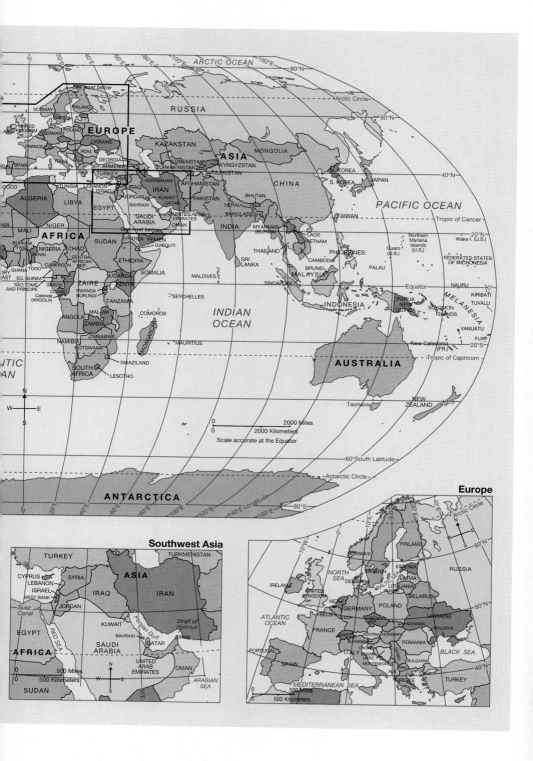